AMERICAN DECADES

PRIMARY SOURCES

1970-1979

AMERICAN DECADES
PRIMARY SOURCES
1970-1979

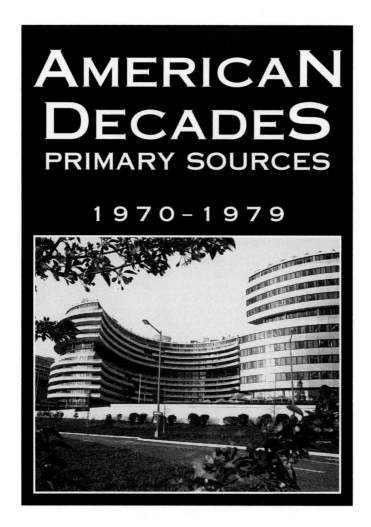

CYNTHIA ROSE, PROJECT EDITOR

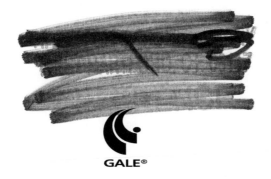

GALE®

THOMSON

GALE

Detroit • New York • San Diego • San Francisco • Cleveland • New Haven, Conn. • Waterville, Maine • London • Munich

THOMSON

GALE

American Decades Primary Sources, 1970–1979

Project Editor
Cynthia Rose

Editorial
Jason M. Everett, Rachel J. Kain, Pamela A. Dear, Andrew C. Claps, Thomas Carson, Kathleen Droste, Christy Justice, Lynn U. Koch, Michael D. Lesniak, Nancy Matuszak, John F. McCoy, Michael Reade, Rebecca Parks, Mark Mikula, Polly A. Rapp, Mark Springer

Data Capture
Civie A. Green, Beverly Jendrowski, Gwendolyn S. Tucker

Permissions
Margaret Abendroth, Margaret A. Chamberlain, Lori Hines, Jacqueline Key, Mari Masalin-Cooper, William Sampson, Shalice Shah-Caldwell, Kim Smilay, Sheila Spencer, Ann Taylor

Indexing Services
Lynne Maday, John Magee

Imaging and Multimedia
Randy Bassett, Dean Dauphinais, Leitha Etheridge-Sims, Mary K. Grimes, Lezlie Light, Daniel W. Newell, David G. Oblender, Christine O'Bryan, Kelly A. Quin, Luke A. Rademacher, Denay Wilding, Robyn V. Young

Product Design
Michelle DiMercurio

Composition and Electronic Prepress
Evi Seoud

Manufacturing
Rita Wimberley

For permission to use material from this product, submit your request via Web at http://gale-edit.com/permissions, or you may download our Permissions Request form and submit your request by fax or mail to:

Permissions Department
The Gale Group, Inc.
27500 Drake Rd.
Farmington Hills, MI 48331-3535
Permissions Hotline:
248-699-8006 or 800-877-4253, ext. 8006
Fax: 248-699-8074 or 800-762-4058

Cover photographs reproduced by permission of AP/Wide World Photos (Gloria Steinem, spine; National Guardsmen toss tear gas on the campus of Kent State University, center; Richard Nixon, right; Watergate complex, Washington, D.C., background), and National Archives and Records Administration (American soldier in My Lai, Vietnam, left).

Since this page cannot legibly accommodate all copyright notices, the acknowledgments constitute an extension of the copyright notice.

While every effort has been made to ensure the reliability of the information presented in this publication, The Gale Group, Inc. does not guarantee the accuracy of the data contained herein. The Gale Group, Inc. accepts no payment for listing; and inclusion in the publication of any organization, agency, institution, publication, service, or individual does not imply endorsement of the editors or publisher. Errors brought to the attention of the publisher and verified to the satisfaction of the publisher will be corrected in future editions.

LIBRARY OF CONGRESS CATALOGING-IN-PUBLICATION DATA

American decades primary sources / edited by Cynthia Rose.
   v. cm.
Includes bibliographical references and index.
Contents: [1] 1900-1909 — [2] 1910-1919 — [3] 1920-1929 — [4] 1930-1939 — [5] 1940-1949 — [6] 1950-1959 — [7] 1960-1969 — [8] 1970-1979 — [9] 1980-1989 — [10] 1990-1999.
   ISBN 0-7876-6587-8 (set : hardcover : alk. paper) — ISBN 0-7876-6588-6 (v. 1 : hardcover : alk. paper) — ISBN 0-7876-6589-4 (v. 2 : hardcover : alk. paper) — ISBN 0-7876-6590-8 (v. 3 : hardcover : alk. paper) — ISBN 0-7876-6591-6 (v. 4 : hardcover : alk. paper) — ISBN 0-7876-6592-4 (v. 5 : hardcover : alk. paper) — ISBN 0-7876-6593-2 (v. 6 : hardcover : alk. paper) — ISBN 0-7876-6594-0 (v. 7 : hardcover : alk. paper) — ISBN 0-7876-6595-9 (v. 8 : hardcover : alk. paper) — ISBN 0-7876-6596-7 (v. 9 : hardcover : alk. paper) — ISBN 0-7876-6597-5 (v. 10 : hardcover : alk. paper)
   1. United States—Civilization—20th century—Sources. I. Rose, Cynthia.
E169.1.A471977 2004
973.91—dc21

2002008155

CONTENTS

Entries are arranged in chronological order by date of primary source. For entries with one primary source, the entry title is the primary source title. Entries with more than one primary source have an overall entry title, followed by the titles of the primary sources.

Fashion and Design

Government and Politics

Law and Justice

Lifestyles and Social Trends

Religion

Science axnd Technology

Sports

ADVISORS AND CONTRIBUTORS

Advisors

CARL A. ANTONUCCI JR. has spent the past ten years as a reference librarian at various colleges and universities. Currently director of library services at Capital Community College, he holds two master's degrees and is a doctoral candidate at Providence College. He particularly enjoys researching Rhode Island political history during the 1960s and 1970s.

KATHY ARSENAULT is the dean of library at the University of South Florida, St. Petersburg's Poynter Library. She holds a master's degree in Library Science. She has written numerous book reviews for *Library Journal,* and has published articles in such publications as the *Journal of the Florida Medical Association* and *Collection Management.*

JAMES RETTIG holds two master's degrees. He has written numerous articles and has edited *Distinguished Classics of Reference Publishing* (1992). University librarian at the University of Richmond, he is the recipient of three American Library Association awards: the Isadore Gibert Mudge Citation (1988), the G.K. Hall Award for Library Literature (1993), and the Louis Shores-Oryx Press Award (1995).

HILDA K. WEISBURG is the head library media specialist at Morristown High School Library and specializes in building school library media programs. She has several publications to her credit, including *The*

School Librarians Workshop, Puzzles, Patterns, and Problem Solving: Creative Connections to Critical Thinking, and *Learning, Linking & Critical Thinking: Information Strategies for the K-12 Library Media Curriculum.*

Contributors

EUGENIA F. BELL is a freelance editor and publication manager who holds a bachelor's degree in Philosophy from Pennsylvania State University. She spent four years as an editor of architecture and design books for the Princeton Architectural Press before working for a year as a publications manager for the Walker Art Center in Minneapolis, Minnesota. She is the author of *The Chapel at Ronchamp* (1999).
Chapter: Fashion and Design.

SONIA G. BENSON is a self-employed writer and editor based in San Juan Capistrano, California. Prior to beginning her freelance career, she spent nine years at Gale Research in positions ranging from associate editor to managing editor. She is the author of the *Korean War Reference Library,* and has edited numerous books.
Chapter: Fashion and Design.

TIMOTHY G. BORDEN has contributed to such publications as *History Behind the Headlines, Michigan Historical Review, Polish American Studies,* and *Northwest Ohio Quarterly.* He also serves as reader/referee of Notre Dame University at Lebanon's *Palma Journal.*

Chapters: Government and Politics, Lifestyles and Social Trends.

PETER J. CAPRIOGLIO is professor emeritus at Middlesex Community College, where he taught social sciences for thirty years prior to his retirement. He has a master's degree in sociology, and he is currently at work on a book entitled *The Glory of God's Religions: A Beginner's Guide to Exploring the Beauty of the World's Faiths.*

Chapter: Religion.

PAUL G. CONNORS has a strong interest in Great Lakes maritime history, and has contributed the article "Beaver Island Ice Walkers" to *Michigan History.* He earned a doctorate in American history from Loyola University in Chicago. He has worked for the Michigan Legislative Service Bureau as a research analyst since 1996.

Essay: Using Primary Sources. *Chronologies:* Selected World Events Outside the United States; Government and Politics, Sports Chapters. *General Resources:* General, Government and Politics, Sports.

CHRISTOPHER CUMO is a staff writer for *The Adjunct Advocate Magazine.* Formerly an adjunct professor of history at Walsh University, he has written two books, *A History of the Ohio Agricultural Experiment Station, 1882–1997,* and *Seeds of Change,* and has contributed to numerous scholarly journals. He also holds a doctorate in History from the University of Akron.

Chapters: Medicine and Health, Science and Technology. *Chapter Chronologies, General Resources:* Business and the Economy, Education, Medicine and Health, Science and Technology.

JENNIFER HELLER holds bachelor's degrees in Religious Studies and English Education, as well as a master's in Curriculum and Instruction, all from the University of Kansas. She has been an adjunct associate professor at Johnson County Community College in Kansas since 1998. She is currently at work on a dissertation on contemporary women's religious literature.

Chapter Chronology, General Resources: Religion.

DAVID M. HOLFORD has worked as an adjunct instructor at Ohio University, Park College, and Columbus State Community College; education curator for the Ohio Historical Society; and held editorial positions at Glencoe/McGraw Hill, as well as Holt, Rinehard, and Winston. He also holds a doctorate degree in history from Ohio State University. A freelance writer/editor since 1996, he as published *Herbert*

Hoover (1999) and *Abraham Lincoln and the Emancipation Proclamation* (2002).

Chapter Chronologies, General Resources: Lifestyles and Social Trends, The Media.

MILLIE JACKSON is an associate librarian at Grand Valley State University in Allendale, Michigan. She has previously worked as an English teacher and as the special collections librarian at Oklahoma State University. Dr. Jackson's dissertation on ladies' library associations in Michigan won the American Library Association's Phyllis Dain Library History Dissertation Award in 2001.

Chapters: The Arts, Education.

JONATHAN KOLKEY is the author of *The New Right, 1960–1968,* and *Germany on the March: A Reinterpretation of War and Domestic Politics Over the Past Two Centuries.* He earned a doctorate in history from UCLA. Currently an instructor at West Los Angeles College, he is at work on *The Decision for War,* a comprehensive historical study of the politics and decision-making process behind war. Dr. Kolkey lives in Playa Del Rey, California.

Chapter: Business and the Economy.

SCOTT A. MERRIMAN currently works as a part-time instructor at the University of Kentucky and is finishing his doctoral dissertation on Espionage and Sedition Acts in the Sixth Court of Appeals. He has contributed to *The History Highway* and *History.edu,* among others. Scott is a resident of Lexington, Kentucky.

Chapter: Law and Justice.

WILLIAM L. PEPER is the president of WLP Enterprises in Warren, Michigan. An attorney since 1987, he has previously served as general counsel for Right to Life of Michigan and as director of Career Services for the Ave Maria School of Law. He has written articles for such journals as *Adoption Focus* and *Credo.*

Chapter: Business and the Economy.

JOSEPH R. PHELAN is a scholar in residence at Strayer University in Washington, D.C. Previously he served as director for the Office of the Bicentennial of the U.S. Constitution at the National Endowment for the Humanities and has taught at the University of Toronto, the Catholic University of America, and the Art Gallery of Ontario.

Chapter: The Media.

PATRICK D. REAGAN has taught history at Tennessee Technological University since 1982. He has written over forty book reviews and has contributed to such publications as *Designing a New America: The Origins of New Deal Planning, 1890–1943,* and *American*

Journey: World War I and the Jazz Age. He is also the author of *History and the Internet: A Guide.*

Chapter: Business and the Economy.

LORNA BIDDLE RINEAR is the editor and coauthor of *The Complete Idiot's Guide to Women's History.* A doctoral candidate at Rutger's University, she holds a bachelor's from Wellesley College and a master's degree from Boston College. She resides in Bellingham, Massachusetts.

Chapter Chronologies, General Resources: The Arts, Fashion and Design.

MARY HERTZ SCARBROUGH earned both her bachelor's in English and German and her J.D. from the University of South Dakota. Prior to becoming a freelance writer in 1996, she worked as a law clerk in the Federal District Court for the District of South Dakota and as legal counsel for the Immigration and Naturalization Service. She lives in Storm Lake, Iowa.

Chapter Chronology, General Resources: Law and Justice.

WILLIAM J. THOMPSON has been a history instructor at the Community College of Baltimore County, Catonsville, since 1996. He received both his bachelor's and master's degrees in History from the University of Maryland, Baltimore County. He has written for the *Encyclopedia of African American Civil Rights,* the *Washington Post,* and the *Baltimore Sun.*

Chapter: Sports.

ACKNOWLEDGMENTS

Following is a list of the copyright holders who have granted us permission to reproduce material in this volume of American Decades Primary Sources. *Every effort has been made to trace copyright, but if omissions have been made, please let us know.*

Copyrighted material in *American Decades Primary Sources, 1970–1979*, was reproduced from the following periodicals: *The American Federationist*, v. 77, May, 1970; v. 78, June 1971. Reproduced by permission. *—The American Scholar*, v. 44, Winter, 1974–75 for "Theater: The Stages of Joseph Papp" by Stanley Kauffmann. Copyright © 1974 by the United Chapters of the Phi Beta Kappa Society. Reproduced by permission of the author. *—Christian Century*, June 26, 1974; May 26, 1976; February 7–14, 1979; March 28, 1979. Reproduced by permission. *—*Clayton, Robert. From "Some Characteristics of the Historically Black Colleges," in ERIC Number ED176651, 1979. *—Columbia Journalism Review*, March/April, 1976 for "The New Regime at The New Republic: Or, Much Ado About Martin Peretz" by Robert Sherrill. © 1976 Graduate School of Journalism, Columbia University. Reprinted by permission of the publisher and the author. *—Dance Magazine*, October, 1978. Copyright 1978 by Danad Publishing Company, Inc. Reprinted with the permission of Dance Magazine, Inc. *—Esquire*, v. 83, April, 1975 for "The Doctrine of Multinational Sell" by Robert Scheer. Copyright © 1975, Esquire Associates. Reproduced by permission of Creators Syndicate on behalf of the author. *—Film Quarterly*, v. 29, Winter, 1975–76 for "Nashville" by Connie Byrne and William O Lopez. Copyright © 1975–76 by The Regents of the University of California. Reproduced by permission. *—Fortune*, v. 81, March, 1970. © 1958 Time Inc. All rights reserved. Reproduced by permission. *—Harvard Educational Review*, v. 41, August 1971. Copyright © 1971 by the President and Fellows of Harvard College. All rights reserved. Reproduced by permission. *—Harvard Educational Review*, v. 49, February 1979. Copyright © 1979 by the President and Fellows of Harvard College. All rights reserved. Reproduced by permission./ v. 49, November 1979. Harvard Educational Review, Copyright © by the President and Fellows of Harvard College. All rights reserved. Reproduced by permission of the author. *—Journal of Business Ethics*, v. 11, 1992. Reproduced by permission with kind permission from Kluwer Academic Publishers. *—Journal of Chronic Disease*, v. 26, 1973. Reproduced by permission. *—Journal of the American Medical Association*, v. 238, August 22, 1977. Reproduced by permission. *—Language Arts*, v. 56, November/December, 1979 for "The Frenetic Fantastic Phonic Backlash" by Maryann Eeds-Kniep. Copyright © 1979 by the National Council of Teachers of English. Reproduced by permission of the publisher. *—Life*, v. 170, March 19, 1971; September 1, 1972. © 1971, 1972 Time Inc. Reproduced by permission. *—Ms. Magazine*, v. 1, July 1, 1972. Reproduced by permission./ 1972 for "Sisterhood" by Gloria Steinem. © 1972 Ms. Magazine. Reproduced by permission of the author. *—The Nation (New York)*, January, 1979. © 1979 The Nation magazine/ The Nation Company, Inc. Reproduced by permission. *—National Geographic*, v. 150, December 1976. Reproduced by permission./ v. 154, December 1978 for "Smallpox—Epitaph for a Killer?" by Donald A. Henderson. Reproduced by permission of the author. *—New York Daily News*, May 28, 1970. Reproduced by permission.

lished by Oral History Project, 1995. Reprinted with permission. —Mirman, Carol, "Carol Mirman, Oral History." Online at: http://www.library.kent.edu/exhibits/4may95 /oralhist/ohmirman.html. Oral History Project, 1995. Reprinted with permission. —"President Gerald R. Ford's Address at a Tulane University Convocation, April 23, 1975." Online at: http://www.ford.utexas.edu /library/speeches/750208.htm. Published by Gerald R. Ford Library and Museum. Reprinted with permission. —"Remarks on Departure From the White House. August 9, 1974." Online at: http://www.nixonfoundation .org/Research_Center/1974_pdf_files/1974_0245.pdf. Published by The Richard Nixon Library & Birthplace.

Reprinted with permission. —Singer, Isaac Bashevis, "Isaac Bashevis Singer—Nobel Lecture: 8 December 1978." Online at: http://www.nobel.se/literature/laureates /1978/singer-lecture.html. Published by Nobel e-Museum. © The Nobel Foundation 1978. Reproduced by permission. —"U.S. Supreme Court SWANN v. BOARD OF EDUCATION, 402 U.S. 1 (1971)." Online at: http://laws .findlaw.com/us/402/1.html. Published by FindLaw.com. This column was originally published on FindLaw.com. Reproduced by permission. —Williams, Diane, "Diane Williams—Tape 1:A." Online at: http://library.kent .edu/exhibits/4may95/dwilliam.htm. Published by Oral History Project, 1995. Reprinted with permission.

ABOUT THE SET

American Decades Primary Sources is a ten-volume collection of more than two thousand primary sources on twentieth-century American history and culture. Each volume comprises about two hundred primary sources in 160–170 entries. Primary sources are enhanced by informative context, with illustrative images and sidebars—many of which are primary sources in their own right—adding perspective and a deeper understanding of both the primary sources and the milieu from which they originated.

Designed for students and teachers at the high school and undergraduate levels, as well as researchers and history buffs, *American Decades Primary Sources* meets the growing demand for primary source material.

Conceived as both a stand-alone reference and a companion to the popular *American Decades* set, *American Decades Primary Sources* is organized in the same subject-specific chapters for compatibility and ease of use.

Primary Sources

To provide fresh insights into the key events and figures of the century, thirty historians and four advisors selected unique primary sources far beyond the typical speeches, government documents, and literary works. Screenplays, scrapbooks, sports box scores, patent applications, college course outlines, military codes of conduct, environmental sculptures, and CD liner notes are but a sampling of the more than seventy-five types of primary sources included.

Diversity is shown not only in the wide range of primary source types, but in the range of subjects and opinions, and the frequent combination of primary sources in entries. Multiple perspectives in religious, political, artistic, and scientific thought demonstrate the commitment of *American Decades Primary Sources* to diversity, in addition to the inclusion of considerable content displaying ethnic, racial, and gender diversity. *American Decades Primary Sources* presents a variety of perspectives on issues and events, encouraging the reader to consider subjects more fully and critically.

American Decades Primary Sources' innovative approach often presents related primary sources in an entry. The primary sources act as contextual material for each other—creating a unique opportunity to understand each and its place in history, as well as their relation to one another. These may be point-counterpoint arguments, a variety of diverse opinions, or direct responses to another primary source. One example is President Franklin Delano Roosevelt's letter to clergy at the height of the Great Depression, with responses by a diverse group of religious leaders from across the country.

Multiple primary sources created by particularly significant individuals—Dr. Martin Luther King Jr., for example—reside in *American Decades Primary Sources*. Multiple primary sources on particularly significant subjects are often presented in more than one chapter of a volume, or in more than one decade, providing opportunities to see the significance and impact of an event or figure from many angles and historical perspectives. For example, seven primary sources on the controversial Scopes "monkey" trial are found in five chapters of the

1920s volume. Primary sources on evolutionary theory may be found in earlier and later volumes, allowing the reader to see and analyze the development of thought across time.

Entry Organization

Contextual material uses standardized rubrics that will soon become familiar to the reader, making the entries more accessible and allowing for easy comparison. Introduction and Significance essays—brief and focused—cover the historical background, contributing factors, importance, and impact of the primary source, encouraging the reader to think critically—not only about the primary source, but also about the way history is constructed. Key Facts and a Synopsis provide quick access and recognition of the primary sources, and the Further Resources are a stepping-stone to additional study.

Additional Features

Subject chronologies and thorough tables of contents (listing titles, authors, and dates) begin each chapter. The main table of contents assembles this information conveniently at the front of the book. An essay on using primary sources, a chronology of selected events outside the United States during the twentieth century, substantial general and subject resources, and primary source type and general indexes enrich *American Decades Primary Sources*.

The ten volumes of *American Decades Primary Sources* provide a vast array of primary sources integrated with supporting content and user-friendly features. This value-laden set gives the reader an unparalleled opportunity to travel into the past, to relive important events, to encounter key figures, and to gain a deep and full understanding of America in the twentieth century.

Acknowledgments

A number of people contributed to the successful completion of this project. The editor wishes to acknowledge them with thanks: Luann Brennan, Katrina Coach, Pamela S. Dear, Nikita L. Greene, Madeline Harris, Alesia James, Cynthia Jones, Pamela M. Kalte, Arlene Ann Kevonian, Frances L. Monroe, Charles B. Montney, Katherine H. Nemeh, James E. Person, Tyra Y. Phillips, Elizabeth Pilette, Noah Schusterbauer, Susan Strickland, Karissa Walker, Tracey Watson, and Jennifer M. York.

Contact Us

The editors of *American Decades Primary Sources* welcome your comments, suggestions, and questions. Please direct all correspondence to:

Editor, *American Decades Primary Sources*
The Gale Group, Inc.
27500 Drake Road
Farmington Hills, MI 48331-3535
(800) 877-4253

For email inquiries, please visit the Gale website at www.gale.com, and click on the Contact Us tab.

About the Volume

The 1970s continued the tumult of the previous decade with new political and social conflicts. While the country remained embroiled in the Vietnam War for the first half of the decade, the Nixon administration found itself sinking under the weight of the Watergate scandal. President Richard Nixon ultimately resigned before he could be impeached for his infractions, but not before he pulled U.S. troops out of Vietnam. The U.S. Supreme Court both pleased and appalled the public, depending on one's opinion of the matter, when it ruled that abortion was legal. A medical, social, and moral controversy surrounded the first test tube baby. By the decade's close, floppy disks were for sale, Microsoft was founded, and Americans had been taken hostage at the U.S. Embassy in Iran. The following documents are just a sampling of the offerings available in this volume.

Highlights of Primary Sources, 1970–1979

- "Born to Run," by Bruce Springsteen

- *Looking Out for Number One* by Robert J. Ringer

- *Now is the Time of the Furnaces . . . And the Light Will be Seen* Kent State SDS Flyer, and statements from witnesses to events that led to the deaths of four students

- Leisure suits—from the Sears, Roebuck Catalog

- *Yellow Ribbon,* the diary of Iran Hostage Crisis survivor Bruce Lanigen

- *U.S. v. Nixon,* the case against Richard M. Nixon

- Self-help books: *The Book of est* and *I'm OK, You're OK*

- "A Personal Report from Ms." an article about the creation of the magazine

- "A M*A*S*H Note for Docs," commencement speech given by Alan Alda

- Letter from the Catholic Bishops declaring racism a sin: *Brothers and Sisters To Us*

- Article from *Scientific American* about the Viking mission to Mars

- Norman Mailer's article on the first fight between Muhammad Ali and Joe Frasier, 1971

Volume Structure and Content

Front matter

- Table of Contents—lists primary sources, authors, and dates of origin, by chapter and chronologically within chapters.

- About the Set, About the Volume, About the Entry essays—guide the reader through the set and promote ease of use.

- Highlights of Primary Sources—a quick look at a dozen or so primary sources gives the reader a feel for the decade and the volume's contents.

- Using Primary Sources—provides a crash course in reading and interpreting primary sources.

- Chronology of Selected World Events Outside the United States—lends additional context in which to place the decade's primary sources.

Chapters:

- The Arts
- Business and the Economy
- Education
- Fashion and Design
- Government and Politics
- Law and Justice
- Lifestyles and Social Trends
- The Media
- Medicine and Health
- Religion
- Science and Technology
- Sports

Chapter structure

- Chapter table of contents—lists primary sources, authors, and dates of origin chronologically, showing each source's place in the decade.
- Chapter chronology—highlights the decade's important events in the chapter's subject.
- Primary sources—displays sources surrounded by contextual material.

Back matter

- General Resources—promotes further inquiry with books, periodicals, websites, and audio and visual media, all organized into general and subject-specific sections.
- General Index—provides comprehensive access to primary sources, people, events, and subjects, and cross-referencing to enhance comparison and analysis.
- Primary Source Type Index—locates primary sources by category, giving readers an opportunity to easily analyze sources across genres.

ABOUT THE ENTRY

The primary source is the centerpiece and main focus of each entry in *American Decades Primary Sources*. In keeping with the philosophy that much of the benefit from using primary sources derives from the reader's own process of inquiry, the contextual material surrounding each entry provides access and ease of use, as well as giving the reader a springboard for delving into the primary source. Rubrics identify each section and enable the reader to navigate entries with ease.

Entry structure

- Key Facts—essential information pertaining to the primary source, including full title, author, source type, source citation, and notes about the author.

- Introduction—historical background and contributing factors for the primary source.

- Significance—importance and impact of the primary source, at the time and since.

- Primary Source—in text, text facsimile, or image format; full or excerpted.

- Synopsis—encapsulated introduction to the primary source.

- Further Resources—books, periodicals, websites, and audio and visual material.

Navigating an Entry

Entry elements are numbered and reproduced here, with an explanation of the data contained in these elements explained immediately thereafter according to the corresponding numeral.

Primary Source/Entry Title, Primary Source Type

•1• **"Ego"**
•2• Magazine article

•1• **PRIMARY SOURCE/ENTRY TITLE** The entry title is the primary source title for entries with one primary source. Entry titles appear as catchwords at the top outer margin of each page.

•2• **PRIMARY SOURCE TYPE** The type of primary source is listed just below the title. When assigning source types, great weight was given to how the author of the primary source categorized it. If a primary source comprised more than one type—for example, an article about art in the United States that included paintings, or a scientific essay that included graphs and photographs—each primary source type included in the entry appears below the title.

Composite Entry Title

•3• Debate Over *The Birth of a Nation*

•1• **"Capitalizing Race Hatred"**
•2• Editorial

•1• **"Reply to the *New York Globe*"**

•2• Letter

•3• **COMPOSITE ENTRY TITLE** An overarching entry title is used for entries with more than one primary source, with the primary source titles and types below.

Key Facts

•4• **By:** Norman Mailer

•5• **Date:** March 19, 1971

•6• **Source:** Mailer, Norman. "Ego." *Life* 70, March 19, 1971, 30, 32–36.

•7• **About the Author:** Norman Mailer (1923–) was born in Long Branch, New Jersey. After graduating from Harvard and military service in World War II (1939–1945), Mailer began writing, publishing his first book, the best-selling novel *The Naked and the Dead,* in 1948. Mailer has written over thirty books, including novels, plays, political commentary, and essay collections, as well as numerous magazine articles. He won the Pulitzer Prize in 1969 and 1979. ∎

•4• **AUTHOR OR ORIGINATOR** The name of the author or originator of the primary source begins the Key Facts section.

•5• **DATE OF ORIGIN** The date of origin of the primary source appears in this field, and may differ from the date of publication in the source citation below it; for example, speeches are often given before they are published.

•6• **SOURCE CITATION** The source citation is a full bibliographic citation, giving original publication data as well as reprint and/or online availability (usually both the deep-link and home-page URLs).

•7• **ABOUT THE AUTHOR** A brief bio of the author or originator of the primary source gives birth and death dates and a quick overview of the person's life. This rubric has been customized in some cases. If the primary source is the autobiography of an artist, the term "author" appears; however, if the primary source is a work of art, the term "artist" is used, showing the person's direct relationship to the primary source. Terms like "inventor" and "designer" are used similarly. For primary sources created by a group, "organization" may have been used instead of "author." If an author is anonymous or unknown, a brief "About the Publication" sketch may appear.

Introduction and Significance Essays

•8• **Introduction**

. . . As images from the Vietnam War (1964–1975) flashed onto television screens across the United States in the late 1960s, however, some reporters took a more active role in questioning the pronouncements of public officials. The broad cul-

tural changes of the 1960s, including a sweeping suspicion of authority figures by younger people, also encouraged a more restive spirit in the reporting corps. By the end of the decade, the phrase "Gonzo Journalism" was coined to describe the new breed of reporter: young, rebellious, and unafraid to get personally involved in the story at hand. . . .

•8• **INTRODUCTION** The introduction is a brief essay on the contributing factors and historical context of the primary source. Intended to promote understanding and jump-start the reader's curiosity, this section may also describe an artist's approach, the nature of a scientific problem, or the struggles of a sports figure. If more than one primary source is included in the entry, the introduction and significance address each one, and often the relationship between them.

•9• **Significance**

Critics of the new style of journalism maintained that the emphasis on personalities and celebrity did not necessarily lead to better reporting. As political reporting seemed to focus more on personalities and images and less on substantive issues, some observers feared that the American public was ill-served by the new style of journalism. Others argued that the media had also encouraged political apathy among the public by superficial reporting. . . .

•9• **SIGNIFICANCE** The significance discusses the importance and impact of the primary source. This section may touch on how it was regarded at the time and since, its place in history, any awards given, related developments, and so on.

Primary Source Header, Synopsis, Primary Source

•10• **Primary Source**

The Boys on the Bus [excerpt]

•11• **SYNOPSIS:** A boisterous account of Senator George McGovern's ultimately unsuccessful 1972 presidential bid, Crouse's work popularized the term "pack journalism," describing the herd mentality that gripped reporters focusing endlessly on the same topic. In later years, political advisors would become more adept at "spinning" news stories to their candidates' advantage, but the essential dynamics of pack journalism remain in place.

•12• The feverish atmosphere was halfway between a high school bus trip to Washington and a gambler's jet junket to Las Vegas, where small-time Mafiosi were lured into betting away their restaurants. There was giddy camaraderie mixed with fear and low-grade hysteria. To file a story late, or to make one glaring factual error, was to chance losing everything—one's job, one's expense account, one's drinking buddies, one's mad-dash existence, and the methedrine buzz that comes from knowing stories that the public would not know for hours and secrets that the public would never know. Therefore reporters channeled their gambling instincts into late-night poker games and private bets on the outcome of the elections. When it came to writing a story, they were as cautious as diamond-cutters. . . .

•10• PRIMARY SOURCE HEADER The primary source header signals the beginning of the primary source, and "[excerpt]" is attached if the source does not appear in full.

•11• SYNOPSIS The synopsis gives a brief overview of the primary source.

•12• PRIMARY SOURCE The primary source may appear excerpted or in full, and may appear as text, text facsimile (photographic reproduction of the original text), image, or graphic display (such as a table, chart, or graph).

Text Primary Sources

The majority of primary sources are reproduced as plain text. The font and leading of the primary sources are distinct from that of the context—to provide a visual clue to the change, as well as to facilitate ease of reading. Often, the original formatting of the text was preserved in order to more accurately represent the original (screenplays, for example). In order to respect the integrity of the primary sources, content some readers may consider sensitive was retained where it was deemed to be integral to the source. Text facsimile formatting was used sparingly and where the original provided additional value (for example, Aaron Copland's typing and handwritten notes on "Notes for a Cowboy Ballet").

Narrative Break

•13• I told him I'd rest and then fix him something to eat when he got home. I could hear someone enter his office then, and Medgar laughed at something that was said. "I've got to go, honey. See you tonight. I love you." "All right," I said. "Take care." Those were our last words to each other.

■ ■ ■

Medgar had told me that President Kennedy was speaking on civil rights that night, and I made a mental note of the time. We ate alone, the children and I. It had become a habit now to set only four places for supper. Medgar's chair stared at us, and the children, who had heard

about the President's address to the nation, planned to watch it with me. There was something on later that they all wanted to see, and they begged to be allowed to wait up for Medgar to return home. School was out, and I knew that Van would fall asleep anyway, so I agreed.

•13• NARRATIVE BREAK A narrative break appears where there is a significant amount of elided material, beyond what ellipses would indicate (for example, excerpts from a nonfiction work's introduction and second chapter, or sections of dialogue from two acts of a play).

Image Primary Sources

Primary source images (whether photographs, text facsimiles, or graphic displays) are bordered with a distinctive double rule. The Primary Source header and Synopsis appear under the image, with the image reduced in size to accommodate the synopsis. For multipart images, the synopsis appears only under the first part of the image; subsequent parts have brief captions.

•14• "Art: U.S. Scene": *The Tornado* by John Steuart Curry (2 OF 4)

•14• PRIMARY SOURCE IMAGE HEADER The primary source image header assists the reader in tracking the images in a series. Also, the primary source header listed here indicates a primary source with both text and image components. The text of the *Time* magazine article "Art: U.S. Scene," appears with four of the paintings from the article. Under each painting, the title of the article appears first, followed by a colon, then the title of the painting. The header for the text component has a similar structure, with the term "magazine article" after the colon. Inclusion of images or graphic elements from primary sources, and their designation in the entry as main primary sources, is discretionary.

Further Resources

•15• Further Resources

BOOKS
Dixon, Phil. *The Negro Baseball Leagues, 1867–1955: A Photographic History*. Mattituck, N.Y.: Amereon House, 1992.

PERIODICALS
"Steven Spielberg: The Director Says It's Good-Bye to Spaceships and Hello to Relationships." *American Film* 13, no. 8, June 1988, 12–16.

WEBSITES
Architecture and Interior Design for 20th Century America, 1935–1955. American Memory digital primary source collection, Library of Congress. Available online at http://memory.loc.gov/ammem/gschtml/gotthome

.html; website home page: http://memory.loc.gov /ammem/ammemhome.html (accessed March 27, 2003).

AUDIO AND VISUAL MEDIA

E.T.: The Extra-Terrestrial. Original release, 1982, Universal. Directed by Steven Spielberg. Widescreen Collector's Edition DVD, 2002, Universal Studios.

•15• **FURTHER RESOURCES** A brief list of resources provides a stepping stone to further study. If it's known that a resource contains additional primary source material specifically related to the entry, a brief note in italics appears at the end of the citation. For websites, both the deep link and home page usually appear.

USING PRIMARY SOURCES

The philosopher R.G. Collingwood once said, "Every new generation must rewrite history in its own way." What Collingwood meant is that new events alter our perceptions of the past and necessitate that each generation interpret the past in a different light. For example, since September 11, 2001, and the "War on Terrorism," the collapse of the Soviet Union seemingly is no longer as historically important as the rise of Islamic fundamentalism, which was once only a minor concern. Seen from this viewpoint, history is not a rigid set of boring facts, but a fascinating, ever-changing field of study. Much of this fascination rests on the fact that historical interpretation is based on the reading of primary sources. To historians and students alike, primary sources are ambiguous objects because their underlying meanings are often not crystal clear. To learn a primary document's meaning(s), students must identify its main subject and recreate the historical context in which the document was created. In addition, students must compare the document with other primary sources from the same historical time and place. Further, students must cross-examine the primary source by asking of it a series of probing investigative questions.

To properly analyze a primary source, it is important that students become "active" rather than "casual" readers. As in reading a chemistry or algebra textbook, historical documents require students to analyze them carefully and extract specific information. In other words, history requires students to read "beyond the text" and focus on what the primary source tells us about the per-

son or group and the era in which they lived. Unlike chemistry and algebra, however, historical primary sources have the additional benefit of being part of a larger, interesting story full of drama, suspense, and hidden agendas. In order to detect and identify key historical themes, students need to keep in mind a set of questions. For example, Who created the primary source? Why did the person create it? What is the subject? What problem is being addressed? Who was the intended audience? How was the primary source received and how was it used? What are the most important characteristics of this person or group for understanding the primary source? For example, what were the authors' biases? What was their social class? Their race? Their gender? Their occupation? Once these questions have been answered reasonably, the primary source can be used as a piece of historical evidence to interpret history.

In each *American Decades Primary Sources* volume, students will study examples of the following categories of primary sources:

- Firsthand accounts of historic events by witnesses and participants. This category includes diary entries, letters, newspaper articles, oral-history interviews, memoirs, and legal testimony.

- Documents representing the official views of the nation's leaders or of their political opponents. These include court decisions, policy statements, political speeches, party platforms, petitions, legislative debates, press releases, and federal and state laws.

- Government statistics and reports on such topics as birth, employment, marriage, death, and taxation.

- Advertisers' images and jingles. Although designed to persuade consumers to purchase commodities or to adopt specific attitudes, advertisements can also be valuable sources of information about popular beliefs and concerns.

- Works of art, including paintings, symphonies, play scripts, photographs, murals, novels, and poems.

- The products of mass culture: cartoons, comic books, movies, radio scripts, and popular songs.

- Material artifacts. These are everyday objects that survived from the period in question. Examples include household appliances and furnishings, recipes, and clothing.

- Secondary sources. In some cases, secondary sources may be treated as primary sources. For example, from 1836 to 1920, public schools across America purchased 122 million copies of a series of textbooks called the McGuffey Reader. Although current textbooks have more instructional value, the Reader is an invaluable primary source. It provides important insights into the unifying morals and cultural values that shaped the worldview of several generations of Americans, who differed in ethnicity, race, class, and religion.

Each of the above-mentioned categories of primary sources reveals different types of historical information. A politician's diary, memoirs, or collection of letters, for example, often provide students with the politicians' unguarded, private thoughts and emotions concerning daily life and public events. Though these documents may be a truer reflection of the person's character and aspirations, students must keep in mind that when people write about themselves, they tend to put themselves at the center of the historical event or cast themselves in the best possible light. On the other hand, the politician's public speeches may be more cautious, less controversial, and limited to advancing his or her political party's goals or platform.

Like personal diaries, advertisements reveal other types of historical information. What information does the WAVES poster on this page reveal?

John Phillip Faller, a prolific commercial artist known for his *Saturday Evening Post* covers, designed this recruitment poster in 1944. It was one of over three hundred posters he produced for the U.S. Navy while enrolled in that service during World War II. The purpose of the poster was to encourage women to enlist in the WAVES (Women Accepted for Volunteer Emergency Service), a women's auxiliary to the Navy established in

1942. It depicts a schoolgirl gazing admiringly at a photograph of a proud, happy WAVE (perhaps an older sister), thus portraying the military service as an appropriate and admirable aspiration for women during wartime. However, what type of military service? Does the poster encourage women to enlist in military combat like World War II male recruitment posters? Does it reflect gender bias? What does this poster reveal about how the military and society in general feel about women in the military? Does the poster reflect current military and societal attitudes toward women in the military? How many women joined the WAVES? What type of duties did they perform?

Like personal diaries, photographs reveal other types of historical information. What information does the next photograph reveal?

Today, we take electricity for granted. However, in 1935, although 90 percent of city dwellers in America had electricity, only 10 percent of rural Americans did. Private utility companies refused to string electric lines

THE LIBRARY OF CONGRESS.

to isolated farms, arguing that the endeavor was too expensive and that most farmers were too poor to afford it anyway. As part of the Second New Deal, President Franklin Delano Roosevelt issued an executive order creating the Rural Electrification Administration (REA). The REA lent money at low interest rates to utility companies to bring electricity to rural America. By 1950, 90 percent of rural America had electricity. This photograph depicts a 1930s tenant farmer's house in Greene County, Georgia. Specifically, it shows a brand-new electric meter on the wall. The picture presents a host of questions: What was rural life like without electricity? How did electricity impact the lives of rural Americans, particularly rural Georgians? How many rural Georgians did not have electricity in the 1930s? Did Georgia have more electricity-connected farms than other Southern states? What was the poverty rate in rural Georgia, particularly among rural African Americans? Did rural electricity help lift farmers out of poverty?

Like personal diaries, official documents reveal other types of historical information. What information does the next document, a memo, reveal?

From the perspective of the early twenty-first century, in a democratic society, integration of the armed services seems to have been inevitable. For much of American history, however, African Americans were prevented from joining the military, and when they did enlist they were segregated into black units. In 1940, of the nearly 170,000-man Navy, only 4,007, or 2.3 percent, were African American personnel. The vast majority of these men worked in the mess halls as stewards—or, as labeled by the black press, "seagoing bellhops." In this official document, the chairman of the General Board refers to compliance with a directive that would enlist African Americans into positions of "unlimited general service." Who issued the directive? What was the motivation behind the new directive? Who were the members of the General Board? How much authority did they wield? Why did the Navy restrict African Americans to the "messman branch"? Notice the use of the term "colored race." Why was this term used and what did it imply? What did the board conclude? When did the Navy become integrated? Who was primarily responsible for integrating the Navy?

CONFIDENTIAL

DOD Dir. 5200.10, June 29, 1960
NND by *RB* date *Oct. 5, 1961*

DOWNGRADED AT 3 YEAR INTERVALS
DECLASSIFIED AFTER 12 YEARS
DOD DIR 5200.10 NARS-NT

G.B. No. 421
(Serial No. 201)
SECRET

Feb 3, 1942

From: Chairman General Board.
To: Secretary of the Navy.

Subject: Enlistment of men of colored race to other than
      Messman branch.

Ref: (a) SecNav let. (SC)P14-4/MM (03200A)/Gen of
      Jan 16, 1942.

   1. The General Board, complying with the directive
contained in reference (a), has given careful attention to the
problem of enlisting in the Navy, men of the colored race
in other than the messman branch.

   2. The General Board has endeavored to examine the
problem placed before it in a realistic manner.

A. Should negroes be enlisted for **unlimited general service?**

   (a) Enlistment for general service implies that the
individual may be sent anywhere, - to any ship or station where
he is needed. Men on board ship live in particularly close
association; in their messes, one man sits beside another; their
hammocks or bunks are close together; in their common tasks they
work side by side; and in particular tasks such as those of a
gun's crew, they form a closely knit, highly coordinated team.
How many white men would choose, of their own accord, that their
closest associates in sleeping quarters, at mess, and in a gun's
crew should be of another race? How many would accept such
conditions, if required to do so, without resentment and just
as a matter of course? The General Board believes that the
answer is "Few, if any," and further believes that if the issue were
forced, there would be a lowering of contentment, teamwork
and discipline in the service.

   (b) One of the tennets of the recruiting service
is that each recruit for general service is potentially a leading
petty officer. It is true that some men never do become petty
officers, and that when recruiting white men, it is not possible
to establish which will be found worthy of and secure promotion
and which will not. If negroes are recruited for general service,
it can be said at once that few will obtain advancement to petty
officers. With every desire to be fair, officers and leading
petty officers in general will not recommend negroes for promotion
to positions of authority over white men.

DOWNGRADED AND
DECLASSIFIED

- 1 -

CONFIDENTIAL

The General Board is convinced that the enlistment of negroes for unlimited general service is unadvisable.

B.   Should negroes be enlisted in general service but detailed in special ratings or for special ships or units?

(a) The ratings now in use in the naval service cover every phase of naval activity, and no new ratings are deemed necessary merely to promote the enlistment of negroes.

(b) At first thought, it might appear that assignment of negroes to certain vessels, and in particular to small vessels of the patrol type, would be feasible. In this connection, the following table is of interest:

Type of Ship	Total Crew	Men in Pay Grades 1 to 4	Men in Pay Grades 5 to 7 (Non-rated)
Battleship	1892	666	1226
Light Cruiser (10,000 ton)	988	365	623
Destroyer (1630 ton)	206	109	97
Submarine	54	47	7
Patrol Boat (180 foot)	55	36	19
Patrol Boat (110 foot)	20	15	5

NOTE: Pay grades 1 to 4 include Chief Petty Officers and Petty Officers, 1st, 2nd and 3rd Class; also Firemen, 1st Class and a few other ratings requiring length of service and experience equal to that required for qualification of Petty Officers, 3rd class. Pay grades 5 to 7 include all other non-rated men and recruits.

There are no negro officers and so few negro petty officers in the Navy at present that any vessels to which negroes might be assigned must have white officers and white petty officers. Examination of the table shows the small number of men in other than petty officer ratings that might be assigned to patrol vessels and indicates to the General Board that such assignments would not be happy ones. The assignment of negroes to the larger ships, where well over one-half of the crews are non-rated men, with mixture of whites and negroes, would inevitably lead to discontent on the part of one or the other, resulting in clashes and lowering of the efficiency of the vessels and of the Navy.

- 2 -

The material collected in these volumes of *American Decades Primary Sources* are significant because they will introduce students to a wide variety of historical sources that were created by those who participated in or witnessed the historical event. These primary sources not only vividly describe historical events, but also reveal the subjective perceptions and biases of their authors. Students should read these documents "actively," and with the contextual assistance of the introductory material, history will become relevant and entertaining.

—Paul G. Connors

Chronology of Selected World Events Outside the United States, 1970–1979

1970

- Soviet cosmonauts are in space seventeen days, a record to that date.

- In January, molecular biologist Hamilton O. Smith isolates the first enzyme that cuts a sequence of nucleotide bases from a strand of deoxyribonucleic acid (DNA).

- On January 12, the Biafran independence movement capitulates to the Nigerian government after a secessionist struggle of thirty-one months.

- On January 16, Colonel Muammar el-Gadhafi becomes premier of Libya in North Africa.

- On February 10, an Arab terrorist kills one person and wounds twenty-three in Munich, West Germany.

- On February 21, a Swissair jetliner explodes and crashes, killing forty-seven en route from Zürich to Tel Aviv, Israel.

- On March 1, Rhodesia declares independence from Britain.

- On March 4, the French submarine *Eurydice* disappears with fifty-seven sailors in the Mediterranean Sea.

- On March 15, Expo '70 opens in Osaka, Japan.

- On March 18, Gen. Lon Nol overthrows the Cambodian government of Prince Norodom Sihanouk.

- On April 8, gas explosions in Osaka, Japan, kill seventy-two and injure 282.

- On April 22, people in countries throughout the world celebrate the first Earth Day.

- On April 30, President Richard M. Nixon of the United States reports on television that he has ordered U.S. and South Vietnamese troops to invade Cambodia to attack North Vietnamese and Viet Cong sanctuaries.

- On May 5, West German chancellor Willy Brandt, following a policy of *Ostpolitik,* signs a nonaggression pact with the Soviet Union.

- On May 31, an earthquake in Peru kills seventy thousand people and leaves seven hundred thousand homeless.

- On June 7, Swiss voters reject a proposal to expel some three hundred thousand foreign workers.

- On June 19, in an electoral upset the British Conservative Party defeats the Labour Party, Great Britain.

- From June 24 to June 27, Israeli and Syrian troops clash on the Golan Heights in the heaviest fighting since the 1967 war.

- On June 29, the last U.S. and South Vietnamese troops leave Cambodia.

- On July 21, engineers complete the Aswan High Dam project in Egypt.

- On August 7, the United States negotiates a cease-fire between Israel and the Arab states.

- On September 6, Palestinian terrorists hijack four New York–bound airliners, carrying over six hundred people.

- On September 16, King Hussein of Jordan declares martial law.

- On September 24, the Soviet unmanned spacecraft *Luna 16* returns to Earth with a collection of Moon rocks.

- In October, the Swedish Royal Academy awards Russian novelist Alexander Solzhenitsyn the Nobel Prize in literature.

- On October 14, voters elect Anwar as-Sadat president of the United Arab Republic (Egypt).

- On October 24, voters elect Salvador Allende Gossens, leader of the Socialist Party, president of Chile.

- On November 13, cyclones and tidal waves kill two hundred thousand people and leave three million people homeless in East Pakistan.

- On November 25, Japanese novelist Yukio Mishima harangues one thousand Japanese troops on their defeat in World War II and challenges them to join him in a coup.

- On December 1, the Italian parliament approves Italy's first divorce law.

- On December 4, the Irish government assumes emergency powers to combat an outbreak of kidnapping and lawlessness.

- On December 11, U.S. agronomist Norman Borlaug becomes the first scientist to receive the Nobel Peace Prize.

- On December 11, the United States and the Soviet Union sign a treaty on fishing rights off the coast of the Middle Atlantic states.

- On December 16, fifty nations at The Hague, Netherlands, declare air hijacking an international crime.

1971

- A cholera epidemic sweeps Bangladesh (former East Pakistan).

- On January 1, the Shah of Iran celebrates the twenty-five-hundredth anniversary of the Persian empire with a gala, attended by over fifty heads of state, at Persepolis, the ancient Persian capital.

- On January 2, in Glasgow, Scotland, a crowd barrier at a soccer stadium collapses, killing sixty-six and wounding over one hundred.

- On January 25, General Idi Amin overthrows President Milton Obote of Uganda.

- On February 4, Rolls-Royce, the British automobile and airplane engine manufacturer, declares bankruptcy.

- On February 6, the British send six hundred troops to Northern Ireland to end renewed violence.

- On February 8, South Vietnamese troops, with American air support, invade Laos in an attempt to cut North Vietnamese supply lines.

- On February 9, the European Economic Community establishes a plan to unify member currencies over ten years.

- On February 14, twenty-three Western oil companies pay the Persian Gulf oil states $10 billion for the rights to sell Gulf oil for five years.

- On February 19, the Soviet newspaper *Pravda* warns Soviet Jews against espousing Zionism.

- On February 21, the 380-mile Karakoram highway links China to Pakistan.

- On February 28, male voters in Liechtenstein reject women's suffrage, leaving it the only Western nation denying women the right to vote.

- On March 11, Prime Minister Indira Gandhi of India wins a majority in national elections.

- On March 25, President Mohammad Yahya Khan of Pakistan sends troops to East Pakistan and declares martial law.

- In April, the British Parliament votes to join the European Common Market.

- On April 4, Salvador Allende Gossens's liberal coalition wins 49.7 percent of Chileans' votes in local elections.

- On April 27, Park Chung Hee wins a third term as South Korean president.

- On May 3, Erich Honecker replaces Walter Ulbricht as East German Communist Party leader.

- On May 19, the Soviet Union and Canada sign a friendship agreement.

- On May 20, in Leningrad nine Soviet Jews are sent to prison camp for "anti-Soviet activity."

- On June 21, the International Court of Justice at The Hague orders South Africa to end its administration of South-West Africa.

- On July 19, three Soviet cosmonauts are found dead in their returning spacecraft.

- On July 22, Sudanese leader Jaafar Mohammad Nimeiri crushes a three-day military coup.

- On July 30, a midair collision over Honshu, Japan, kills 162 people.

- On August 9, India and the Soviet Union sign a friendship treaty.

- On August 15, Bahrain declares independence from Britain.

- On August 19, Mount Etna produces its most spectacular eruption in forty-three years.

- On August 22, a military coup ousts General Juan José Torres of Bolivia as president.

- On September 18, Israel and Egypt exchange rocket fire over the Suez Canal.

- On September 21, Adam Malik of Indonesia is elected president of the twenty-sixth UN General Assembly.

- On September 24, Britain expels 105 Soviets suspected of espionage.

- On October 3, General Nguyen Van Thieu, the only candidate on the ballot, wins reelection as president of South Vietnam.

- From October 20 to October 21, West German chancellor Willy Brandt wins the Nobel Peace Prize and Chilean poet Pablo Neruda wins the Nobel Prize in literature.

- On October 25, the United Nations with U.S. support votes to admit the People's Republic of China and to expel Taiwan.

- On November 10, Cuban leader Fidel Castro begins a twenty-five-day visit to Chile.

- On November 19, one person dies and 1,785 are arrested during demonstrations in Tokyo, Japan, over the return of Okinawa to Japan.

- On December 2, President Salvador Allende Gossens of Chile decrees a state of emergency following demonstrations in Santiago over food shortages and the visit of Fidel Castro.

- On December 3, Pakistan attacks Indian airfields.

1972

- One hundred thousand die in fighting between the Tutsi and Hutu in Burundi.
- On January 22, Britain, Norway, Denmark, and Ireland seek admission to the European Economic Community.
- On January 24, the Soviet Union becomes the first major power to recognize Bangladesh.
- On January 30, thirteen die in riots in Northern Ireland.
- On February 13, the Soviet Union wins eight gold medals as the Winter Olympics end in Sapporo, Japan.
- On March 12, Indira Gandhi's Congress Party wins 70 percent of assembly seats in Indian national elections.
- On March 30, Northern Ireland's prime minister and his cabinet resign after the British Parliament establishes direct rule of Northern Ireland.
- On March 31, North Vietnam invades South Vietnam with tanks, artillery, and infantry.
- On April 10, seventy nations sign a treaty banning biological weapons.
- On May 15, the United States returns Okinawa to Japan.
- On May 17, the West German Parliament approves non-aggression treaties with the Soviet Union and Poland.
- On May 21, a Hungarian refugee damages part of Michelangelo's *Pieta* at Saint Peter's Basilica in Rome.
- On June 1, Iraq and Syria seize the assets of Iraq Petroleum Company, a consortium of Western firms.
- On June 13, Israeli and Egyptian fighter planes clash.
- On July 3, India and Pakistan sign a peace agreement.
- On July 18, Egypt expels Soviet military advisers and experts.
- On July 24, UN secretary-general Kurt Waldheim urges the United States to stop bombing North Vietnam.
- On August 3, Britain declares a state of emergency due to a dockworkers' strike.
- On August 16, King Hassan II of Morocco survives an assassination attempt.
- On August 26, seven thousand athletes from 120 nations open the twentieth Summer Olympics in Munich, West Germany.
- On September 1, American Bobby Fischer defeats Boris Spassky of the U.S.S.R. for the world chess championship in Reykjavík, Iceland.
- On September 5, Arab terrorists kill eleven Israeli Olympic athletes in Munich, West Germany.
- On September 17, Uganda reports that Tanzania has invaded it with one thousand troops.
- On September 23, President Ferdinand Marcos imposes martial law in the Philippines following terrorist attacks.
- On September 26, voters in Norway reject membership in the European Economic Community.
- On October 2, Danish voters approve membership in the European Economic Community.

- On October 13, an Aeroflot flight crashes in Moscow, killing 176 people.
- On October 24, opponents of President Allende Gossens stage a "day of silence" to protest his government in Chile.
- On October 29, Arab guerrillas win release of three Olympic terrorists after the hijacking of a German airline.
- On October 30, Prime Minister Pierre Trudeau loses his parliamentary majority in Canadian elections.
- On November 2, President Allende Gossens of Chile restructures his cabinet following three weeks of strikes.
- On November 4, the Bangladesh national assembly approves a new constitution.
- On November 17, former dictator Juan D. Perón returns to Argentina after seventeen years of exile.
- On November 21, Israel and Syria clash in the heaviest fighting in two years in the Golan Heights.
- On December 1, the Irish Parliament passes a bill to crack down on the Irish Republican Army.
- On December 23, an earthquake in Managua, Nicaragua, kills ten thousand people and destroys 80 percent of the city.

1973

- On January 17, President Ferdinand Marcos of the Philippines announces the indefinite continuation of martial law.
- On February 11, General Alfredo Stroessner wins a fifth term as president of Paraguay.
- On February 21, Israeli jets shoot down a Libyan airliner over the Sinai Peninsula, killing 106.
- On March 2, Palestinian terrorists kill one Belgian and two U.S. diplomats in Khartoum, Sudan.
- On March 12, China releases John T. Downey, a Central Intelligence Agency agent held since 1952.
- On March 17, President Lon Nol of Cambodia declares a state of emergency after a bomb attack on the presidential guard barracks.
- On April 21, the United Nations Security Council condemns Israel for attacks in Lebanon and for all violence against human life.
- On May 11, a new sixteen-member cabinet, headed by Premier Joop den Uyl, is sworn in, ending a 163-day political crisis in the Netherlands.
- On May 15, gold reaches $128.50 an ounce in Paris, a new high.
- On June 1, the Greek Council of Ministers abolishes the monarchy and proclaims a republic.
- From June 7 to June 11, West German chancellor Willy Brandt visits Israel.
- On June 8, Spanish dictator Francisco Franco appoints Admiral Luis Carrero Blanco premier of Spain, but Franco remains chief of state.
- On June 29, troops loyal to President Salvador Allende Gossens of Chile crush an attempted coup.

- On July 3, the thirty-five-nation Conference on Security and Cooperation in Europe convenes in Helsinki, Finland.

- On July 10, Britain grants the Bahamas independence.

- On July 17, the military overthrows King Mohammad Zahir Shah of Afghanistan.

- On July 21, France detonates a nuclear bomb in a test in the Pacific Ocean.

- On August 2, thirty-two members of the British Commonwealth begin a nine-day conference in Ottawa, Canada.

- On August 5, Arab terrorists attack the airport in Athens, Greece, killing three and injuring fifty-five.

- On August 19, George Papadopoulos is sworn in as the first president of Greece.

- On August 28, Indian officials agree to repatriate ninety thousand Pakistani prisoners from the 1971 Indian-Pakistani War.

- On September 1, Libya nationalizes 51 percent of all oil companies assets in Libya.

- On September 5, the fourth Conference of Nonaligned Nations meets in Algiers, Algeria.

- On September 18, the twenty-eighth meeting of the United Nations General Assembly votes to admit the Bahamas, East Germany, and West Germany as members.

- On September 23, voters elect Juan Perón president of Argentina.

- On September 29, the Austrian government announces it will no longer admit large numbers of Soviet Jews.

- In October, the Swedish Royal Academy awards the Nobel Peace Prize to Henry A. Kissinger of the United States and Le Duc Tho of North Vietnam for negotiating an end to the war between the United States and North Vietnam.

- On October 6, Israel and the combined forces of Egypt and Syria clash in the first battle of the Yom Kippur War.

- On October 16, the Organization of Petroleum Exporting Countries (OPEC), led by the Arab states, stops selling oil to the United States and Europe as punishment for their support of Israel.

- On October 22, Stanford University molecular biologist Stanley Cohen inserts a sequence of nucleotide bases into a bacterium, producing the world's first genetically-engineered organism.

- On October 24, Israel, Syria and Egypt cease fire in the Yom Kippur War.

- On October 27, the United Nations Security Council votes to send a peacekeeping force to the Middle East to diffuse tensions.

- In November, the Soviet Union agrees to abide by the Universal Copyright Convention and to cease publishing pirate editions of Western works.

- On November 7, the United States and Egypt reestablish diplomatic relations, suspended since 1967.

- On November 11, Israel and Egypt sign a cease-fire.

- On November 25, the military overthrows George Papadopoulos as president of Greece in a bloodless coup.

- On November 29, Egyptian-Israeli peace talks collapse.

- On December 12, Austrian zoologist Konrad Lorenz receives the Nobel Prize in physiology or medicine.

- On December 17, Arab terrorists attack a U.S. plane in Rome, killing thirty-one people.

- On December 20, assassins kill Spanish premier Luis Carrero Blanco in a car explosion in Madrid, Spain.

- On December 21, an Arab-Israeli peace conference begins in Geneva, Switzerland.

1974

- Russian novelist Aleksandr Solzhenitsyn's *The Gulag Archipelago* is published in English.

- On January 18, Israel and Egypt sign an accord on military disengagement.

- On January 19, China expels five Soviet citizens for espionage.

- On February 3, Communist Party chairman Mao Tse-tung launches a new cultural revolution in China.

- On February 13, the U.S.S.R. expels Nobel laureate and novelist Aleksandr Solzhenitsyn.

- On February 22, Pakistan recognizes Bangladesh, formerly East Pakistan.

- In March, Emperor Haile Selassie of Ethiopia attempts to placate a rebellious military by appointing Edalkachew Makonnen premier and increasing army wages.

- On March 2, archeologists unearth the first of six thousand life-size pottery figures of warriors and horses in China. Chinese Emperor Qin Shi Huangdi had them built and buried with him upon his death in 210 B.C.E.

- On March 3, a Turkish jumbo jet crashes outside Paris, killing 346 people, in the worst air disaster to date.

- On March 10, Premier Golda Meir and a new cabinet assume power in Israel.

- On April 9, India, Pakistan, and Bangladesh sign an agreement to repatriate all Pakistani prisoners of war.

- On April 12, Israel raids several villages in southern Lebanon after an Arab terrorist attack on Qiryat Shemona killed eighteen.

- On April 15, the military overthrows President Hamani Diori of Niger.

- On April 22, Israel's Labor Party nominates Yitzhak Rabin to replace Golda Meir, who resigned on April 10 as premier.

- On April 25, army officers in Portugal announce the end of forty years of authoritarian rule.

- On May 9, Prime Minister Pierre Trudeau of Canada loses a vote of confidence. The House of Commons schedules parliamentary elections for July 8.

- On May 18, India tests a nuclear weapon, raising fears of a nuclear arms race in southern and central Asia.

- On May 19, voters elect Finance Minister Valéry Giscard d'Estaing president of France.

- On May 28, Prime Minister Gough Whitlam and the Labour Party win the Australian parliamentary election.

- On May 29, a fifteen-day general strike ends after the coalition government of Northern Ireland resigns.

- On May 31, Israel and Syria sign a troop disengagement agreement.

- In June, President Richard Nixon of the United States conducts a whirlwind tour of the Middle East and the Soviet Union.

- On June 3, the Israeli parliament installs Yitzhak Rabin as head of a three-party coalition government.

- On June 16, the United States and Syria announce the resumption of diplomatic relations.

- On June 17, China and France conduct separate atmospheric nuclear tests.

- On June 24, Prime Minister Harold Wilson announces that Great Britain recently conducted underground nuclear tests.

- On June 27, France and Iran sign an agreement that includes the sale of nuclear reactors to Iran.

- On June 28, more than two hundred people die in a landslide ninety-five miles east of Bogota, Colombia.

- In July, civil war in Cyprus provokes a confrontation between Greece and Turkey.

- On July 1, Isabel Perón assumes the presidency of Argentina after the death of her husband, Juan D. Perón, seventy-eight.

- On July 7, West Germany wins the World Cup, defeating the Netherlands, 2-1.

- On July 8, Pierre Trudeau and the Liberal Party win a majority in Canada's parliamentary elections.

- On July 15, the military overthrows the government of Archbishop Makarios in Cyprus.

- On July 20, Turkish troops invade Cyprus by air and sea.

- From August to September, floods in India and Bangladesh kill fourteen hundred people.

- On August 14, Greece withdraws from the North Atlantic Treaty Organization (NATO).

- On September 4, the United States and East Germany establish diplomatic relations.

- On September 10, Portugal grants the Republic of Guinea-Bissau, formerly Portuguese Guinea, independence.

- On September 12, the military overthrows Emperor Haile Selassie of Ethiopia.

- On September 17, the United Nations elects Abdelaziz Bouteflika, foreign minister of Algeria, president of its twenty-ninth General Assembly.

- In October, the Vatican permits physicist Walter McCrone to examine the Shroud of Turin.

- On October 8, Eisaku Sato, former prime minister of Japan, and Sean MacBride of Ireland, United Nations commissioner for South-West Africa, share the 1974 Nobel Peace Prize.

- On October 10, Prime Minister Harold Wilson wins a three-seat majority for the Labour Party in Great Britain's second general election of 1974.

- On October 14, the United Nations General Assembly invites the Palestine Liberation Organization to participate in its deliberations.

- On October 20, Swiss voters reject a proposal to deport half its foreign population.

- On October 21, Mexico announces the discovery of oil in southeastern Mexico.

- On October 28, Arab heads of state meeting in Rabat, Morocco, call for the creation of an independent Palestinian state.

- On October 30, the United States, Britain, and France veto a Security Council resolution to expel South Africa from the United Nations.

- On November 12, the United Nations General Assembly suspends South Africa from participation in the remainder of the 1974 session as punishment for its oppression of blacks.

- On November 16, the United Nations creates the World Food Conference to distribute food to hungry people throughout the world.

- On November 18, Premier Konstantinos Karamanlis and his New Democracy Party win the first Greek parliamentary elections held in ten years.

- On November 22, the United Nations General Assembly grants observer status to the Palestine Liberation Organization (PLO).

- On November 24, Donald C. Johanson, then director of the Cleveland Museum of Natural History in Ohio, discovers in Ethiopia a 40 percent complete skeleton of an Australopithecine, an early man that lived between roughly 4 million and 1.5 million years ago.

- On November 26, Japanese prime minister Kakuei Tanaka resigns following a series of financial scandals. On December 9, Takeo Miki replaces him.

- On December 5, Premier Aldo Moro wins a vote of confidence from the Italian senate.

- On December 7, Archbishop Makarios returns to Cyprus to head the government.

- On December 8, Greek citizens vote in a national referendum to abolish the monarchy.

- On December 11, the white minority government of Rhodesia and black nationalists agree to a cease-fire in their civil war.

- On December 25, a cyclone destroys 90 percent of Darwin, Australia, and kills fifty people.

- On December 28, an earthquake in northern Pakistan kills fifty-two hundred people.

- On December 29, the government of Nicaragua agrees with leftist guerrillas to exchange political prisoners.

1975

- Portugal grants independence to Angola, Mozambique, the Cape Verde Islands, and lesser African possessions to end five hundred years of colonial rule.

- On January 2, the United Nations declares 1975 International Women's Year.

- On January 17, China adopts a new constitution.

- On February 11, Margaret Thatcher becomes the first woman to head a British political party when she is elected leader of the Conservatives.

- On February 12, a South Korean national referendum approves the government of Park Chung Hee.

- On February 13, Turkish Cypriots declare a separate state in the north of Cyprus.

- On February 25, the Greek government arrests twenty-five military officers for plotting a coup.

- On February 27, a Philippine national referendum supports President Ferdinand Marcos's declaration of martial law.

- On February 28, the European Economic Community signs a trade pact with forty-six nations in Africa, the Pacific, and the Caribbean.

- On March 2, Shah Mohammed Reza Pahlavi dissolves the political system in Iran and declares it a one-party state for the next two years.

- On March 4, Ethiopia's military government nationalizes all rural land.

- On March 11, Portugal's provisional government defeats a military coup.

- On April 13, a military coup kills President Ngarta Tombalbaye, who led Chad to independence in 1960.

- On April 14, voters in Sikkim approve referendums abolishing the monarchy and merging with India.

- On April 17, the capital of Cambodia, Phnom Penh, falls to the Communist army of the Khmer Rouge, ending five years of civil war.

- On April 22, a bloodless coup in Honduras ousts General Oswaldo López Arellano.

- On April 30, North Vietnamese troops capture Saigon, the capital of South Vietnam, ending the Vietnam War.

- On May 11, the European Economic Community and Israel sign a trade and cooperation pact.

- From May 13 to May 14, Cambodia seizes the U.S. merchant ship *Mayaguez,* releasing it following a rescue effort by the U.S. military.

- On May 15, Portugal declares martial law in Angola after weeks of violence.

- On May 28, officials of fifteen West African nations meeting in Lagos, Nigeria, agree to form the Economic Community of West African States.

- In June, the United States and the Soviet Union conduct a joint *Apollo-Soyuz* space mission—the first time manned spacecraft from different nations rendezvous in space.

- On June 5, Egypt reopens the Suez Canal, closed since the 1967 Arab-Israeli War.

- On June 7, UN discussions between Greek and Turkish Cypriot leaders end without an agreement on the future of the island.

- On June 9, Greece adopts a new constitution.

- On June 10, President Idi Amin of Uganda releases British citizen Denis Hills, whom Amin had condemned to death for his criticism of Amin.

- On June 13, Iraq and Iran sign a treaty of reconciliation, fixing the boundary between them and ending Iranian support of Iraq's Kurdish rebels.

- On June 17, the Italian Communist Party polls 33.4 percent of the vote in regional elections.

- On June 26, Prime Minister Indira Gandhi of India declares a state of emergency and imprisons her political foes after her conviction for manipulating election results.

- On June 29, the Organization of American States ends its ban on diplomatic and commercial relations with Cuba.

- On July 15, The United States and the Soviet Union launch the joint *Apollo-Soyuz* space station that will orbit Earth.

- On August 6, the Indian Parliament approves retroactive changes in the election law under which Prime Minister Gandhi was convicted of campaign violations.

- On August 15, a military coup kills Bangladesh president Sheik Mujibar Rahman.

- On August 18, China and Cambodia sign a trade agreement.

- On August 29, the military overthrows President Juan Velasco Alvarado of Peru.

- On September 1, Guillermo Rodriguez Lara, president of Ecuador, defeats a military coup.

- On September 2, Canada, with the world's fourth-largest foreign aid budget, announces grants to the world's forty poorest countries.

- On September 6, an earthquake in eastern Turkey kills 2,312 people.

- On September 9, Prince Norodom Sihanouk, deposed leader of Cambodia, returns home after five years of exile in China.

- On September 16, Britain grants Papua New Guinea independence and commonwealth status.

- On October 1, OPEC raises crude oil prices 10 percent, raising inflation and deepening a recession in the U.S.

- On October 16, Isabel Perón returns to the presidency of Argentina after a month's absence.

- On October 21, a nationwide postal strike begins in Canada.

- On November 7, India's supreme court, citing retroactive changes in the election code, reverses an earlier conviction of Prime Minister Indira Gandhi for election fraud.

- On November 10, the United Nations condemns Zionism as a form of racism by a 72-35 vote.

- On November 11, the governor-general of Australia, Sir John Kerr, removes the prime minister and dissolves parliament for the first time in history.

- On November 25, the Netherlands grants Suriname independence after three hundred years of colonial rule.

- On December 3, the Pathet Lao, a communist party, abolishes the monarchy and creates a coalition government in Laos.

- On December 5, Britain ends the detention of suspected terrorists from Northern Ireland without trial.

- On December 11, Russian physicist Andrei Sakharov receives the Nobel Peace Prize.

- On December 14, terrorists demanding the independence of South Moluccas from Indonesia release twenty-three hostages in Beilin, Holland.

1976

- On January 1, Venezuela nationalizes its oil industries.

- On January 7, Prime Minister Aldo Moro's Italian cabinet resigns.

- On February 10, Aldo Moro forms a one-party minority government in Italy.

- On February 26, with the agreement of Spain, Morocco and Mauritania annex the territory of the former Spanish Sahara.

- In March, hundreds of villagers die of a mysterious illness, with a 90 percent mortality in Zaire. Physicians isolate a new virus as the cause of the illness and name it Ebola, because the virus had first struck people near the Ebola River in Zaire.

- On March 5, Britain's secretary of state for Northern Ireland, Merlyn Rees, dismisses the seventy-eight-seat Northern Ireland Convention and announces that Britain will govern Northern Ireland.

- On March 24, the military overthrows President Isabel Perón of Argentina. Lt. General Jorge Videla assumes power.

- On April 25, socialists win a plurality of votes in Portugal's first free parliamentary elections in fifty years.

- On April 30, the Italian government of Aldo Moro collapses.

- On May 5, delegates from 153 nations meet in Nairobi, Kenya, for the fourth United Nations Conference on Trade and Development.

- From May 15 to May 19, Arab riots against Israeli rule of what was once Palestine leave three protesters dead.

- On May 17, Liechtensteiner women gain the right to vote in local elections.

- From May 20 to May 21, North Atlantic Treaty Organization foreign ministers meet in Oslo, Norway.

- In June, the French-English supersonic jet Concorde begins regular passenger service.

- From June 16 to June 19, blacks riot in South Africa against the use of the Afrikaans language, a variant of Dutch, in South African schools.

- On June 22, Italian Communists gain forty-nine seats in the chamber of deputies and twenty-three seats in the senate following national elections.

- On June 23, the United States vetoes the admission of Angola to the United Nations.

- On July 3, Israeli commandos raid Entebbe Airport in Uganda and free ninety-one passengers and twelve crew of an Air France jet that Palestinian terrorists had hijacked on June 27.

- On July 27, police arrest former prime minister Kakuei Tanaka for financial misconduct in Japan.

- On July 30, Italian prime minister Giulio Andreotti leads a new minority government.

- On August 7, Uganda and Kenya renew diplomatic relations.

- On August 11, Palestinian terrorists kill four and wound thirty in the airport in Istanbul, Turkey.

- On August 12, thirty-five to forty people die in a week of rioting in South Africa.

- On August 20, right-wing extremists murder forty-six people in Argentina in retaliation for the assassination of a retired army general.

- On September 21, the thirty-first session of the United Nations General Assembly elects H. S. Amerasinghe of Sri Lanka as president.

- In October, after Mao Tse-tung's death, India normalizes relations with China.

- On October 3, Chancellor Helmut Schmidt's Social Democratic Party wins a narrow majority in West German parliamentary elections.

- On October 10, Mairead Corrigan and Betty William, two peace activists from Northern Ireland, share the 1976 Nobel Peace Prize.

- On October 22, President Cearbhall O. Dalaigh of Ireland resigns. On November 9 Patrick J. Hillery replaces him.

- On November 1, the military overthrows President Michel Micombero of Burundi in a bloodless coup. Colonel Jean-Baptiste Bagaza assumes power.

- On November 13, the Donald A. Henderson, Johns Hopkins University physician and head of the World Health Organization (WHO) campaign against smallpox, reports Asia free of smallpox for the first time in history.

- On November 15, René Lévesque's separatist Parti Québécois wins a majority in Quebec's provincial elections.

- On November 26, Italy rescinds it recognition of Roman Catholicism as the state religion.

- In December, Donald Johanson discovers in Ethiopia the remains of thirteen Australopithecines. Johanson dubbed them the "First Family," because he suspected that all thirteen were part of the same clan and were thus related.

- On December 15, Prime Minister Michael Manley of Jamaica leads his People's National Party to victory in parliamentary elections.

- On December 17, OPEC announces a 5 percent increase in oil prices from Saudi Arabia and the United Arab Emirates and a 10 percent increase from the other eleven OPEC members.

- On December 20, Prime Minister Yitzhak Rabin of Israel dissolves parliament and calls for elections.

1977

- On January 6, 240 prominent intellectuals in Czechoslovakia sign Charter 77, demanding human rights as enumerated in the Helsinki accords of 1975.

- On January 18, Prime Minister Indira Gandhi of India announces parliamentary elections in March, the first since she had declared a state of emergency in 1975.
- On January 24, discussions between the white elite and blacks break down over whether to grant free election and thus black majority rule in Rhodesia.
- In February, the Soviet Union begins to seek alliances with African nations in hopes of bringing former European colonies within the Soviet sphere of influence.
- On February 9, Spain and the Soviet Union resume diplomatic relations, suspended since the Spanish Civil War.
- On February 23, President Idi Amin of Uganda forbids two hundred Americans from leaving Uganda in response to U.S. president Jimmy Carter's condemnation of Amin's brutality toward his own people.
- In March, a U.S. delegation visits Vietnam for the first time since the war.
- On March 7, Saudi Arabia announces $1 billion in assistance to black Africa at the opening of the fifty-nine nation Arab-African conference in Cairo, Egypt.
- On March 20, in a surprise defeat, Indira Gandhi and her Congress Party lose the Indian parliamentary election.
- On March 27, two jumbo jets collide in the Canary Islands, killing more than 570 people, the worst air disaster to date.
- On April 21, Prime Minister Zulfikar Ali Bhutto of Pakistan imposes martial law in three cities following weeks of political unrest.
- On April 22, Great Britain grants independence to the Solomon Islands.
- On April 30, an oil spill from a platform in the North Sea is capped after twenty thousand metric tons of crude oil had polluted the sea.
- In May, Guillermo Vilas becomes the first Argentine to win the French Open tennis championship. In September he will win the U.S. Open.
- From May 5 to May 9, leaders of five Western nations and Japan meet in London for economic discussions.
- On May 17, Menachem Begin's Likud Party defeats the Labour Party in Israeli parliamentary elections.
- On June 11, Dutch marines storm a hijacked train in northern Holland, where South Molluccan terrorists, seeking independence from Indonesia, held fifty-one hostages, some of them schoolchildren.
- In July, Mary Leakey, wife of the late British anthropologist Louis S.B. Leakey, discovers a set of Australopithecine footprints some 3.5 million years old. The tracks are of an adult and child and are in synchrony, suggesting that the two had held hands as they walked.
- In July, oceanographers discover deep-sea vents on the ocean floor near the Galapagos Islands.
- On July 5, the forty-eight member Organization of African Unity ends a four-day conference in Libreville, Gabon.
- On July 31, demonstrators riot during an antinuclear rally in Creys-Malville, France.
- On August 26, the province of Quebec passes Bill 101, making French the official—and principal—language of the province.

- On September 3, police arrest former Pakistani prime minister Zulfikar Ali Bhutto for conspiracy to murder his political opponents.
- On September 15, South African police arrest twelve hundred black students mourning the September 12 death of black nationalist leader Steven Biko in prison.
- On September 20, President Idi Amin of Uganda bans, as "security risks," twenty-seven religious organizations from his country.
- On September 26, Israeli-backed Christians and Palestinians cease fire after ten days of fighting on Lebanon's southern border.
- On September 28, Khmer Rouge leader Pol Pot arrives in Peking in hopes of gaining economic aid from China.
- On October 3, police arrest former Indian prime minister Indira Gandhi on two counts of corruption in office but later drop the charges.
- On October 10, Amnesty International, a human rights organization, wins the 1977 Nobel Peace Prize.
- On October 31, Western nations veto a UN resolution to impose economic sanctions against South Africa.
- On November 13, Somalia expels all Soviet advisers and breaks diplomatic relations with Cuba, charging both with favoring Ethiopia in its land dispute with Somalia.
- On November 20, President Anwar as-Sadat of Egypt journeys to Jerusalem to address the Israeli parliament in hopes of forging a peace agreement with Israel.
- On December 5, Arab states, meeting in Tripoli, Libya, denounce Egyptian president Sadat's peace overture to Israel.
- On December 26, President Sadat of Egypt and Prime Minister Menochem Begin of Israel continue peace talks in Egypt.
- On December 31, Cambodia and Vietnam break off diplomatic relations.

1978

- The cosmonauts of *Soyuz 27* spend a record ninety-six days in space.
- "Boat people" from Vietnam, Cambodia and Laos seek asylum in Malaysia, Thailand, and the United States.
- On January 4, General Augusto Pinochet of Chile confirms his dictatorship by plebiscite.
- On January 10, riots engulf Managua, Nicaragua, following the assassination of Pedro Joaquin Chamorro, publisher of the anti-government newspaper *La Prensa*.
- On January 20, President Suharto of Indonesia bans several newspapers and suppresses student dissent in an attempt to end criticism of his authoritarian rule.
- On January 24, fragments of a radioactive Soviet satellite crash into a remote area of Canada's Northwest Territories.
- On February 7, a nationwide general strike that began on January 23 ends in Managua, Nicaragua.
- In March, orchestras throughout the world sponsor Vivaldi festivals to commemorate the three hundredth anniversary of Italian composer Antonio Vivaldi's birth.

- On March 16, Red Brigades terrorists kidnap and kill former Italian premier Aldo Moro, leader of the Christian Democratic Party, in Rome.

- On March 17, the *Amoco Cadiz* runs aground near Brest, France, spilling oil along the Brittany coast in the worst spill to date.

- On March 18, Former Pakistani prime minister Zulfikar Ali Bhutto is sentenced to death for having ordered an assassination attempt on a political opponent.

- On March 24, Ethiopia declares it has reestablished control over the southeastern Ogaden region after an eight-month conflict with Somalia.

- On April 3, China and the European Economic Community sign a five-year trade agreement.

- On April 9, police charge antigovernment demonstrators with sedition in the Philippines following the first parliamentary elections since 1972.

- On April 21, thieves steal paintings valued at over $1 million, including Peter Paul Rubens's masterpiece *The Three Graces,* from the Uffizi Gallery in Florence, Italy.

- On April 30, the military overthrows the government in Kabul, Afghanistan. Nur Mohammad Taraki heads the new regime.

- On May 3, alternative energy advocates celebrate Sun Day to publicize the need for renewable sources of energy.

- On May 4, South African troops raid guerrilla bases of the South-West Africa People's Organization in Angola.

- On May 11, Muslim fundamentalists riot throughout Iran.

- On May 15, Peruvians angered at an austerity program riot.

- On May 18, Italy legalizes abortion.

- On May 22, Belgian troops rescue twenty-five hundred Europeans trapped in fighting between Zaire and the Congo.

- On June 23, an Italian court sentences twenty-nine members of the Red Brigades to prison in Turin, Italy, for murdering former Italian premier Aldo Moro.

- On June 25, Argentina defeats the Netherlands, 3-1, to win the World Cup soccer championship.

- On July 3, China ends economic assistance to Vietnam.

- On July 14, a Soviet court sentences dissident Anatoly B. Scharansky to thirteen years in prison for espionage.

- On July 19, Quebec modifies Bill 101—the 1977 law mandating the use of French in Quebec, now to include English, after many businesses relocate to English-speaking Ontario.

- On July 25, the first test-tube baby is born in England.

- On August 10, the ten provincial premiers of Canada reject Prime Minister Pierre Trudeau's plan for a new Canadian constitution.

- On August 12, Japan and China sign a ten-year peace treaty.

- On August 22, twenty-five Sandinista guerrillas seize the National Palace in Managua, Nicaragua, killing six guards and wounding dozens.

- In September, genetically-engineered bacteria begin to produce insulin, the first human hormone derived through recombinant DNA.

- On September 8, Shah Mohammad Reza Pahlavi declares martial law in Iran, following antigovernment demonstrations in twelve cities and hundreds of deaths in Tehran.

- On September 17, Prime Minister Menachem Begin of Israel, President Anwar as-Sadat of Egypt, and President Jimmy Carter of the Unites States conclude eleven days of peace negotiations at Camp David, Maryland.

- On September 20, an Italian court sentences Red Brigades leader Corrado Alunni to twelve years in prison for illegal possession of firearms.

- On September 26, China and Vietnam end diplomatic talks after China accuses Vietnam of amassing troops on its border.

- On September 28, Pieter Willem Botha succeeds B.J. Vorster as prime minister of South Africa.

- On October 12, Ugandan and Tanzanian troops clash over the Kagera Salient, land each nation claims its own.

- On October 31, forty thousand petroleum workers go on strike in Iran, halving Iranian oil exports.

- On November 2, two Soviet cosmonauts set a 139-day spaceflight record.

- On November 3, Vietnam and the Soviet Union sign a twenty-five-year peace treaty.

- On November 5, former prime minister Indira Gandhi wins election to India's lower house of parliament, demonstrating the loyalty of Indians to the Nehru-Gandhi legacy.

- On December 5, Afghanistan and the Soviet Union sign a twenty-year treaty of friendship.

- On December 10, President Anwar al-Sadat of Egypt and Prime Minister Menachem Begin of Israel share the Nobel Peace Prize for forging peace between their nations.

- From December 27 to December 30, the Shah of Iran attempts to placate fundamentalists by passing the government to Shahpur Bakhtiar, a government critic.

1979

- Peter Shaffer premieres the play *Amadeus,* which traces Wolfgang Amadeus Mozart's career from the lightweight pieces of his childhood to the dark, even violent, music of adulthood.

- On January 1, the United States and China establish diplomatic relations.

- On January 7, the Kampuchean United Front captures the Cambodian capital of Phnom Penh, ending the Khmer Rouge regime of Pol Pot.

- On January 16, Shah Mohammed Reza Pahlavi leaves Iran for a "vacation," presumed to be exile.

- On January 19, President Anastasio Somoza Debayle rejects a plebiscite, supervised by the Organization of American States, to end the civil war in Nicaragua.

- On February 1, the Ayatollah Ruhollah Khomeini returns to Iran to establish a fundamentalist Islamic state after fifteen years of exile in France.

- On February 17, several hundred thousand Chinese troops invade Vietnam following border clashes.

- On February 22, the United States cuts aid to Afghanistan following the assassination of U.S. ambassador Adolph Dubs.

- On February 24, troops clash along the border between North and South Yemen.

- On March 5, China announces the withdrawal of its troops from Vietnam after suffering thousands of casualties in less than a month of fighting.

- On March 13, Maurice Bishop, leader of the New Jewel Movement, ousts Prime Minister Eric Gairy in a bloodless coup on the Caribbean island of Grenada.

- On March 14, India and the Soviet Union sign treaties of economic and scientific cooperation.

- On March 18, Kurdish rebels in northern Iraq attack government troops.

- On March 26, Israel and Egypt sign a peace treaty in Washington, D.C., ending thirty-one years of war.

- On March 26, Prime Minister Pierre Elliott Trudeau of Canada dissolves Parliament and sets national elections for May 22.

- On March 27, the pro-Communist Revolutionary Council in Afghanistan names Hafizullah Amin prime minister.

- On March 28, the British House of Commons votes no confidence in the government of Prime Minister James Callaghan, who resigns.

- On March 29, North and South Yemen agree to end their border conflict and unite under one government.

- On March 31, the eighteen-nation Arab League denounces Egypt for its peace treaty with Israel.

- On April 4, Former prime minister Zulfikar Ali Bhutto of Pakistan is hanged on charges of conspiring to murder a political opponent.

- On April 11, Tanzanian troops capture the Ugandan capital of Kampala, deposing Ugandan president Idi Amin and installing a new government under Yusufu Lule.

- On April 12, five years of international negotiations conclude in Geneva, Switzerland, in the General Agreement on Tariffs and Trade (GATT), reducing world tariffs by 33 percent on average.

- On April 27, the United States exchanges two Soviet spies for five Soviet dissidents, including Aleksandr Ginzburg.

- On May 3, the Conservative Party defeats the Labour Party in British national elections, making Conservative leader Margaret Thatcher Britain's first woman prime minister.

- On May 8, police in El Salvador kill twenty-three and wound seventy during antigovernment demonstrations in San Salvador.

- On May 18, geologists discover 3.5-billion-year-old traces of bacteria and algae from Western Australia. The discovery is among the earliest evidence for life on Earth.

- On May 22, the Progressive Conservative Party wins a plurality of votes in Canadian national elections.

- On May 24, President Carlos Humberto Romero of El Salvador suspends the constitution and declares a thirty-day state of siege.

- From June 2 to June 10, Pope John Paul II visits his native Poland.

- On June 20, Godfrey Binaisa ousts President Yusufu Lule of Uganda in a bloodless coup.

- On July 11, the International Whaling Commission, meeting in London, bans hunting in the Red Sea, the Arabian Sea, and most of the Indian Ocean for ten years.

- On July 16, President Ahmad Hassan al-Bakr of Iraq resigns, citing poor health, and appoints Saddam Hussein, chairman of the Revolutionary Command Council and the armed forces, his successor.

- On July 17, President Anastasio Somoza Debayle of Nicaragua resigns and goes into exile.

- On July 23, Ayatollah Ruhollah Khomeini bans music broadcasting in Iran, saying it has corrupted Iranian youth.

- On August 13, China announces it will limit population growth by discouraging couples from having more than one child.

- On August 18, Muslim rebels in Afghanistan announce the formation of an insurgent government.

- On August 19, two Soviet cosmonauts set a 175-day spaceflight record.

- On August 27, the Irish Republican Army explodes a bomb on a fishing boat off the Irish coast, killing Earl Mountbatten of Burma, cousin to Queen Elizabeth II of Britain.

- On September 13, in Peking's Tiananmen Square nearly one thousand people protest Communist Party privileges.

- On September 21, Britain and France cancel the supersonic Concorde program declaring it too expensive.

- On October 12, President Fidel Castro of Cuba addresses the United Nations, denouncing the United States and calling for grants and loans for developing nations.

- On October 15, the military overthrows the government of General Carlos Humberto Romero in El Salvador.

- On October 24, the deposed Shah of Iran enters a New York hospital for a gallbladder operation and cancer treatments.

- On October 26, the head of the South Korean Central Intelligence Agency assassinates President Park Chung Hee of South Korea.

- On November 4, Iranian militants storm the U.S. embassy in Tehran, seizing ninety hostages and precipitating an international crisis.

- On November 20, several hundred Islamic extremists seize the Grand Mosque in Mecca, Saudi Arabia, a site sacred to Muslims.

- On November 21, Islamic extremists attack the U.S. embassy in Islamabad, Pakistan.

- On November 28, geologists discover amino acids in an Antarctic meteorite, believed to be uncontaminated by Earth, suggesting that life may have arisen elsewhere in our solar system.

- On December 3, Puerto Rican nationalists kill two American sailors outside the Sabana Seca naval communications center.

- On December 8, Greek poet Odysseus Elytis receives the Nobel Prize in literature.

- On December 11, Mother Teresa of Calcutta, India, receives the Nobel Peace Prize for her care of India's poor and homeless.

- On December 13, the Canadian Supreme Court strikes down the portions of Quebec's Bill 101 that had mandated the use of French language in Quebec.

- On December 15, the Shah of Iran leaves the United States to live in Panama.

- On December 27, the Soviet Union invades Afghanistan with tens of thousands of troops following a Soviet-sponsored coup that kills President Hafizullah Amin.

1

THE ARTS

MILLIE JACKSON

Entries are arranged in chronological order by date of primary source. For entries with one primary source, the entry title is the same as the primary source title. Entries with more than one primary source have an overall entry title, followed by the titles of the primary sources.

Important Events in the Arts, 1970–1979

1970

- An "information" exhibition, highlighting the fusion of art, text, sound, light, and video, is held in New York City at the Museum of Modern Art.

- "American Top 40," a weekly countdown of hits on the pop music charts hosted by Casey Kasem, debuts on nationwide radio.

- The recording industry introduces quadriphonic discs.

- The singing group Crosby, Stills, Nash and Young record "Ohio," protesting the killing of four students by the National Guard at Kent State University.

- The film and soundtrack album *Woodstock* are released.

- Guitarist Jimi Hendrix chokes to death after a heavy dose of drugs and alcohol; singer Janis Joplin dies less than three weeks later of a drug overdose.

- On February 5, *Who Cares?*, choreographed by George Balanchine and featuring the music of George Gershwin, is performed for the first time by the New York City Ballet.

- On February 25, two Vincent Van Gogh paintings are auctioned for a record $2.175 million in New York City.

- On March 10, the National Endowment for the Arts grants $706,000 to twelve symphony and opera companies.

- On July 11, the twentieth annual Marlboro Music Festival opens in Marlboro, Vermont.

- On September 29, Paul Mellon donates Paul Cézanne's *The Artist's Father*, valued at $1.5 million, to the National Gallery of Art, Washington, D.C.

- On November 30, in the first concert ever held in New York City's Saint Patrick's Cathedral, Leopold Stokowski conducts the Metropolitan Opera Orchestra.

MOVIES: *Airport,* directed by George Seaton and starring Burt Lancaster and Dean Martin; *Catch-22,* directed by Mike Nichols; *Diary of a Mad Housewife,* directed by Frank Perry and starring Carrie Snodgress and Richard Benjamin; *Five Easy Pieces,* directed by Bob Rafelson and starring Jack Nicholson and Karen Black; *Little Big Man,* directed by Arthur Penn and starring Dustin Hoffman and Faye Dunaway; *Love Story,* directed by Arthur Hiller and starring Ryan O'Neal and Ali McGraw, *M*A*S*H,* directed by Robert Altman and starring Donald Sutherland and Elliott Gould; *Patton,* directed by Franklin Schaffner and starring George C. Scott.

FICTION: Richard Bach, *Jonathan Livingston Seagull;* Saul Bellow, *Mr. Sammler's Planet;* Thomas Berger, *Vital Parts;* James Dickey, *Deliverance;* Joan Didion, *Play It as It Lays;* Lois Gould, *Such Good Friends;* Jerzy Kosinski, *Being There;* Toni Morrison, *The Bluest Eye;* William Saroyan, *Days of Life and Death;* Erich Segal, *Love Story;* Irwin Shaw, *Rich Man, Poor Man;* Leon Uris, *QBVII.*

POPULAR SONGS: The Beatles, "Let It Be" and "The Long and Winding Road"; the Carpenters, "Close to You"; the Guess Who, "American Woman"; the Jackson Five, "I Want You Back," "ABC," "I'll Be There," and "The Love You Save"; Led Zeppelin, "Whole Lotta Love"; Melanie, "Lay Down (Candles in the Rain)"; Joni Mitchell, "Big Yellow Taxi"; the Partridge Family, "I Think I Love You"; Diana Ross, "Ain't No Mountain High Enough"; Carly Simon, "That's the Way I Always Heard It Should Be"; Simon and Garfunkel, "Bridge Over Troubled Water"; Sly and the Family Stone, "Thank You (Falettin' Me Be Mice Elf Agin)" and "Everybody Is a Star"; Smokey Robinson and the Miracles, "Tears of a Clown"; Edwin Starr, "War."

1971

- *The Exorcist,* by William Peter Blatty is a best-seller.

- Margaret Harris becomes the first African American woman to lead a major orchestra, conducting the Chicago Symphony.

- Alan Jay Lerner, Dorothy Fields, and Duke Ellington are among the first to be inducted into the Songwriter's Hall of Fame.

- Singer Diana Ross, formerly of the Supremes, begins a solo career.

- Beatle George Harrison organizes the Concert for Bangladesh, a benefit concert to aid victims of starvation in that region.

- On May 17, the rock musical *Godspell* opens on Broadway.

- In July, the first major microfiche collection of books—the Library of American Civilization—is delivered to subscribers.

- On July 3, Jim Morrison, lead singer of the Doors, dies of a suspected drug overdose.

- On July 11, thousands pay tribute to the late jazz trumpeter Louis Armstrong at a public funeral in New Orleans.

- On September 8, the Kennedy Center for the Performing Arts opens in Washington, D.C.

- On October 12, the rock musical *Jesus Christ Superstar,* written by Andrew Lloyd Webber and Tim Rice, produced by Robert Stigwood, and starring Yvonne Elliman and Ben Vereen, opens on Broadway.

MOVIES: *Billy Jack,* directed by and starring Tom Laughlin; *Carnal Knowledge,* directed by Mike Nichols and starring Jack Nicholson, Art Garfunkel, Ann-Margret, and Candace Bergen; *A Clockwork Orange,* directed by Stanley Kubrick; *Dirty Harry,* directed by Don Siegel and starring Clint Eastwood; *The French Connection,* directed by William Friedkin and starring Gene Hackman; *The Hospital,* directed by Arthur Hiller and starring George C. Scott; *Klute,* directed by Alan J. Pakula and starring Jane Fonda and Donald

Sutherland; *The Last Picture Show,* directed by Peter Bogdanovich and starring Jeff Bridges, Cybill Shepherd, and Cloris Leachman; *McCabe and Mrs. Miller,* directed by Robert Altman and starring Warren Beatty and Julie Christie; *Play Misty for Me,* directed by Clint Eastwood and starring Clint Eastwood; *Shaft,* directed by Gordon Parks and starring Richard Roundtree.

FICTION: William Peter Blatty, *The Exorcist;* E. L. Doctorow, *The Book of Daniel;* James P. Donleavy, *The Onion Eaters;* Ernest J. Gaines, *The Autobiography of Miss Jane Pittman;* Bernard Malamud, *The Tenants;* Mary McCarthy, *Birds of America;* Walker Percy, *Love in the Ruins;* Harold Robbins, *The Betsy;* John Updike, *Rabbit Redux.*

POPULAR SONGS: The Bee Gees, "How Can You Mend a Broken Heart?"; Cher, "Gypsies, Tramps and Thieves"; Alice Cooper, "Eighteen"; John Denver, "Take Me Home, Country Roads"; the Doors, "Riders on the Storm"; Marvin Gaye, "What's Goin' On"; Hamilton, Joe, Frank and Reynolds, "Don't Pull Your Love"; George Harrison, "My Sweet Lord"; Isaac Hayes, "Theme from Shaft"; Janis Joplin, "Me and Bobby McGee"; Carole King, "It's Too Late" and "I Feel the Earth Move"; Led Zeppelin, "Black Dog" and "Stairway to Heaven"; John Lennon, "Imagine"; Paul and Linda McCartney, "Uncle Albert/Admiral Halsey"; Melanie, "Brand New Key"; the Osmonds, "One Bad Apple"; the Rolling Stones, "Brown Sugar"; Sly and the Family Stone, "Family Affair"; Rod Stewart, "Maggie May" and "Reason to Believe"; the Temptations, "Just My Imagination"; Three Dog Night, "Joy to the World."

1972

• The rock musical *Hair* ends its Broadway run after 1,742 performances.

• New York City radio station WCBS-FM becomes the first to adopt an oldies format.

• In New York City the exhibition "Sharp-Focus Realism" is held at the Sidney Janis Gallery.

• Don McLean's "American Pie" becomes the longest song ever to hit number one, clocking in at eight minutes.

• Charlie Chaplin returns to the U.S. to receive a special Oscar from the Academy of Motion Picture Arts and Sciences.

• Marlon Brando wins an Oscar for his role as Don Corleone in *The Godfather* but refuses it.

• On February 14, the musical *Grease* opens on Broadway.

• On June 17, *Fiddler on the Roof* becomes the longest running show in Broadway history, with 3,225 performances.

• On August 22, American audiences are exposed for the first time to British comedy troupe Monty Python with the release of their film *And Now for Something Completely Different.*

• On October 16, Henry Lewis becomes the first African American to conduct the New York Metropolitan Opera House Orchestra.

• On October 23, *Pippin,* directed by Bob Fosse and starring Ben Vereen and Jill Clayburgh, opens on Broadway.

MOVIES: *Cabaret,* directed by Bob Fosse and starring Liza Minnelli, Michael York, and Joel Grey; *Deliverance,* directed by John Boorman and starring Jon Voight and Burt Reynolds; *The Godfather,* directed by Francis Ford Coppola and starring Marlon Brando, Al Pacino, James Caan, Robert Duvall, Diane Keaton, and Talia Shire; *Lady Sings the Blues,* directed by Sidney J. Furie and starring Diana Ross, Billy Dee Williams, and Richard Pryor; *The Poseidon Adventure,* directed by Irwin Allen and starring Gene Hackman; *Sounder,* directed by Martin Ritt and starring Cicely Tyson and Paul Winfield; *Superfly,* directed by Gordon Parks and starring Ron O'Neal.

FICTION: Louis Auchincloss, *I Come as a Thief;* James Baldwin, *No Name in the Street;* Michael Crichton, *The Terminal Man;* John W. Gardner, *The Sunlight Dialogues;* Ira Levin, *The Stepford Wives;* Arthur Mizener, *The Saddest Story;* Chaim Potok, *My Name Is Asher Lev;* Irving Wallace, *The Ward;* Eudora Welty, *The Optimist's Daughter;* Herman Wouk, *The Winds of War.*

POPULAR SONGS: America, "A Horse With No Name"; Chuck Berry, "My Ding-a-Ling"; the Chi-Lites, "Oh Girl"; Mac Davis, "Baby Don't Get Hooked on Me"; Sammy Davis, Jr., "The Candy Man"; Donna Fargo, "The Happiest Girl in the Whole USA"; Roberta Flack, "The First Time Ever I Saw Your Face"; Al Green, "Let's Stay Together"; Looking Glass, "Brandy (You're a Fine Girl)"; Curtis Mayfield, "Freddie's Dead"; Don McLean, "American Pie"; Johnny Nash, "I Can See Clearly Now"; Nilsson, "Without You"; the O'Jays, "Back Stabbers"; Gilbert O'Sullivan, "Alone Again Naturally"; Billy Paul, "Me and Mrs. Jones"; Elvis Presley, "Burnin' Love"; Helen Reddy, "I Am Woman"; the Spinners, "I'll Be Around"; the Staple Singers, "I'll Take You There"; the Temptations, "Papa Was a Rollin' Stone"; Bill Withers, "Lean on Me"; Neil Young, "Heart of Gold."

1973

• Jasper Johns's *Double White Map* is sold for $240,000, the highest price ever paid to a living American artist at that time.

• A new Friday night television concert series, *Midnight Special,* debuts with Helen Reddy as host.

• The International Dance Council is established under the auspices of UNESCO.

• *Enter the Dragon,* starring martial artist Bruce Lee, is released, sparking a nationwide kung fu craze.

• On February 6, *The New York Times* reports that the Soviet Union has agreed to loan forty-one paintings by European masters to show in U.S. galleries.

• On February 25, Stephen Sondheim's *A Little Night Music,* featuring the song "Send in the Clowns," opens on Broadway.

• In March, Pink Floyd releases their landmark album *The Dark Side of the Moon.* It remains on the *Billboard* Top 200 Albums chart for 741 weeks—14¼ years.

• On April 4, Elvis Presley's Hawaiian concert, taped earlier in the year, is televised to a huge audience.

• On May 2, forty-seven artworks from the Norton Simon Collection are sold in New York City for $6.7 million.

• On May 10, Harold Lawrence, manager of the London Symphony Orchestra, is named to succeed Helen Thompson as manager of the New York Philharmonic.

MOVIES: *American Graffiti,* directed by George Lucas and starring Richard Dreyfuss, Ron Howard, Cindy Williams, Harrison Ford, and Suzanne Somers; *Badlands,* directed by Terence Malick and starring Martin Sheen and Sissy Spacek; *The Exorcist,* directed by William Friedkin and starring Ellen Burstyn and Linda Blair; *The Harder They Come,* directed by Perry Henzell and starring Jimmy Cliff; *The Last Detail,* directed by Hal Ashby and starring Jack Nicholson; *Mean Streets,* directed by Martin Scorcese and starring Harvey Keitel and Robert De Niro; *Paper Moon,* directed by Peter Bogdanovich and starring Ryan O'Neal and Tatum O'Neal; *Serpico,* directed by Sidney Lumet and starring Al Pacino; *Sleeper,* directed by Woody Allen and starring Allen and Diane Keaton; *The Sting,* directed by George Roy Hill and starring Robert Redford, Paul Newman, and Robert Shaw; *The Way We Were,* directed by Sydney Pollack and starring Barbra Streisand and Robert Redford; *What's Up, Doc?,* directed by Peter Bogdanovich and starring Barbra Streisand and Ryan O'Neal.

FICTION: Thomas Berger, *Regiment of Women;* John Cheever, *The World of Apples;* Alice Childress, *A Hero Ain't Nothin' But a Sandwich;* Leon Forrest, *There Is a Tree More Ancient Than Eden;* Erica Jong, *Fear of Flying;* Jerzy Kosinski, *The Devil Tree;* Bernard Malamud, *Rembrandt's Hat;* Iris Murdoch, *The Black Prince;* Marge Piercy, *Small Changes;* Thomas Pynchon, *Gravity's Rainbow;* Paul Theroux, *Saint Jack;* Kurt Vonnegut, Jr., *Breakfast of Champions.*

POPULAR SONGS: The Carpenters, "Top of the World"; Cher, "Half Breed"; Jim Croce, "Bad Bad Leroy Brown" and "Time in a Bottle"; Roberta Flack, "Killing Me Softly"; Gladys Knight and the Pips, "Midnight Train to Georgia"; Grand Funk Railroad, "We're an American Band"; Elton John, "Crocodile Rock" and "Goodbye Yellow Brick Road"; Eddie Kendricks, "Keep on Truckin'"; Vicki Lawrence, "The Night the Lights Went Out in Georgia"; Curtis Mayfield, "Superfly"; Maureen McGovern, "The Morning After"; the O'Jays, "Love Train"; Paul McCartney and Wings, "My Love" and "Live and Let Die"; Billy Preston, "Will It Go Round in Circles"; Charlie Rich, "The Most Beautiful Girl in the World"; the Rolling Stones, "Angie"; Diana Ross, "Touch Me in the Morning"; Carly Simon, "You're So Vain"; Ringo Starr, "Photograph"; Stories, "Brother Louie"; Tony Orlando and Dawn, "Tie a Yellow Ribbon"; Barry White, "I'm Gonna Love You Just a Little More, Baby"; Stevie Wonder, "Superstition" and "You Are the Sunshine of My Life."

1974

• "Open Circuits," an international conference on video art, is held in New York City at the Museum of Modern Art.

• Stand-up comedian Richard Pryor releases his hit album "That Nigger's Crazy."

• *People,* an offshoot of *Time* focusing on celebrities and "real life" stories, begins publishing. Mia Farrow, star of *The Great Gatsby,* is pictured on the cover of the first issue.

• The Ramones, a band in the "garage" tradition whose fast, loud three-chord sound will usher in the American punk rock movement, begins playing at the New York City club CBGB.

• Disco, a beat-driven dance music already popular in the African American and gay communities, begins to find mainstream success with hits such as "Rock the Boat," "Rock Your Baby," and "Kung Fu Fighting."

• On February 12, the rock club The Bottom Line opens in New York City.

• On February 19, Dick Clark launches the American Music Awards.

• On March 6, the film rights to Bob Woodward and Carl Bernstein's best-selling investigation of Watergate, *All the President's Men,* are sold for $450,000.

• On April 18, Allen Ginsberg wins the National Book Award for Poetry.

• On May 16, Leonard Bernstein's *The Dybbuk,* choreographed by Jerome Robbins, is premiered by the New York City Ballet.

• On September 9, the Senate approves a copyright reform bill requiring jukebox operators to pay royalties to composers and music publishers.

MOVIES: *Airport 1975,* starring Charlton Heston, Karen Black, George Kennedy, and Helen Reddy; *Alice Doesn't Live Here Anymore,* directed by Martin Scorcese and starring Ellen Burstyn, Kris Kristofferson, and Jodie Foster, *Blazing Saddles,* directed by Mel Brooks and starring Cleavon Little and Gene Wilder, *Chinatown,* directed by Roman Polanski and starring Jack Nicholson and Faye Dunaway; *Claudine,* directed by John Berry and starring Diahann Carroll and James Earl Jones; *The Conversation,* directed by Francis Ford Coppola and starring Gene Hackman; *Death Wish,* dircted by Michael Winner and starring Charles Bronson; *Earthquake,* starring Charlton Heston and George Kennedy; *The Godfather Part II,* directed by Francis Ford Coppola and starring Al Pacino, Robert De Niro, Robert Duvall, Talia Shire, and Diane Keaton; *The Great Gatsby,* directed by Jack Clayton and starring Robert Redford, Mia Farrow, and Karen Black; *Lenny,* directed by Bob Fosse and starring Dustin Hoffman; *The Towering Inferno,* directed by Irwin Allen and starring Paul Newman and Steve McQueen; *Uptown Saturday Night,* directed by Sidney Poitier and starring Poitier, Bill Cosby, and Richard Pryor; *Young Frankenstein,* directed by Mel Brooks and starring Gene Wilder.

FICTION: James Baldwin, *If Beale Street Could Talk;* Donald Barthelme, *Guilty Pleasures;* Peter Benchley, *Jaws;* Joseph Heller, *Something Happened;* James Michener, *Centennial;* Albert Murray, *Train Whistle Guitar;* Cornelius Ryan, *A Bridge Too Far;* John Updike, *Buchanan Dying;* Irving Wallace, *The Fan Club.*

POPULAR SONGS: Paul Anka, "You're Havin' My Baby"; Bachman-Turner Overdrive, "You Ain't Seen Nothin' Yet" and "Takin' Care of Business"; Bo Donaldson and the Heywoods, "Billy, Don't Be a Hero"; Brownsville Station, "Smokin' in the Boys' Room"; Harry Chapin, "Cat's in the Cradle"; Cher, "Dark Lady"; Eric Clapton, "I Shot the

Sheriff"; Dionne Warwick and the Spinners, "Then Came You"; Carl Douglas, "Kung Fu Fighting"; Roberta Flack, "Feel Like Makin' Love"; Grand Funk Railroad, "The Loco-Motion"; Hues Corporation, "Rock the Boat"; Terry Jacks, "Seasons in the Sun"; Elton John, "Don't Let the Sun Go Down on Me" and "The Bitch Is Back"; Gordon Lightfoot, "Sundown"; George McCrae, "Rock Your Baby"; Olivia Newton-John, "I Honestly Love You"; Paper Lace, "The Night Chicago Died"; Paul McCartney and Wings, "Band on the Run"; Ray Stevens, "The Streak"; Barbra Streisand, "The Way We Were"; The Stylistics, "You Make Me Feel Brand New"; Barry White, "Can't Get Enough of Your Love, Babe."

1975

• Elton John's *Captain Fantastic and the Brown Dirt Cowboy* becomes the first album to debut at number one on the *Billboard* album chart. His follow-up release, *Rock of the Westies,* also debuts at number one.

• Bruce Springsteen becomes the first and only rock performer to appear on the covers of *Time* and *Newsweek* in the same week, amid the hype for his album *Born to Run.*

• *The Rocky Horror Picture Show,* an offbeat musical about a Transylvanian transvestite, is released and soon gains cult status.

• On January 5, the all-African-American musical *The Wiz* opens on Broadway, eventually tallying 1,672 performances.

• On April 17, President Gerald Ford becomes the first U.S. president since Abraham Lincoln to attend a performance at Washington's Ford Theater.

• On September 5, the United States and the Soviet Union agree to five major art exchanges over the next five years.

MOVIES: *Barry Lyndon,* directed by Stanley Kubrick and starring Ryan O'Neal; *Cooley High,* directed by Michael Schultz; *Dog Day Afternoon,* directed by Sydney Lumet and starring Al Pacino; *Jaws,* directed by Steven Spielberg and starring Robert Shaw, Roy Scheider, and Richard Dreyfuss; *Love and Death,* directed by Woody Allen and starring Allen and Diane Keaton; *Mahogany,* directed by Berry Gordy and Tony Richardson and starring Diana Ross and Billy Dee Williams; *Nashville,* directed by Robert Altman; *One Flew Over the Cuckoo's Nest,* directed by Milos Forman and starring Jack Nicholson and Louise Fletcher; *The Rocky Horror Picture Show,* directed by Jim Sharman and starring Tim Curry, Susan Sarandon, and Barry Bostwick; *Shampoo,* directed by Hal Ashby and starring Warren Beatty, Julie Christie, and Goldie Hawn; *Tommy,* directed by Ken Russell and starring Roger Daltrey and Ann-Margret.

FICTION: Saul Bellow, *Humboldt's Gift;* Thomas Berger, *Sneaky People;* E. L. Doctorow, *Ragtime;* Jerzy Kosinski, *Cockpit;* Larry McMurtry, *Terms of Endearment;* Toni Morrison, *Sula;* Vladimir Nabokov, *Tyrants Destroyed;* Reynolds Price, *The Surface of Earth;* Judith Rossner, *Looking for Mr. Goodbar;* John Updike, *A Month of Sundays;* Joseph Wambaugh, *The Choirboys.*

POPULAR SONGS: America, "Sister Golden Hair"; the Bee Gees, "Jive Talkin'"; David Bowie, "Fame"; Glen Camp-

bell, "Rhinestone Cowboy"; the Captain and Tennille, "Love Will Keep Us Together"; John Denver, "Thank God I'm a Country Boy"; the Doobie Brothers, "Black Water"; the Eagles, "Best of My Love" and "One of These Nights"; Earth Wind & Fire, "Shining Star"; Fleetwood Mac, "Rhiannon"; Grand Funk Railroad, "Bad Time"; Elton John, "Island Girl" and "Philadelphia Freedom"; KC and the Sunshine Band, "Get Down Tonight" and "That's the Way (I Like It)"; Labelle, "Lady Marmalade"; Led Zeppelin, "Kashmir"; Barry Manilow, "Mandy"; Van McCoy, "The Hustle"; Michael Murphey, "Wildfire"; Olivia Newton-John, "Have You Never Been Mellow"; Ohio Players, "Fire"; Ozark Mountain Daredevils, "Jackie Blue"; Paul McCartney and Wings, "Listen to What the Man Said"; Pilot, "Magic"; Queen, "Killer Queen"; Minnie Ripperton, "Lovin' You"; Linda Ronstadt, "You're No Good"; Neil Sedaka, "Bad Blood" and "Laughter in the Rain"; Silver Connection, "Fly Robin Fly"; Donna Summer, "Love to Love You Baby"; Sweet, "Ballroom Blitz" and "Fox on the Run"; 10cc, "I'm Not in Love"; Tony Orlando and Dawn, "He Don't Love You (Like I Love You)"; Dwight Twilley Band, "I'm on Fire"

1976

• "Women Artists: 1550–1950," a retrospective exhibit, begins a national tour at the Los Angeles County Museum of Art.

• Conductor Arthur Fiedler, dancer/choreographer Martha Graham, and pianist Arthur Rubinstein are awarded the Medal of Freedom by President Gerald Ford. Rubinstein later retires from recitals due to blindness.

• Ragtime composer Scott Joplin, whose rags were popularized by the film *The Sting,* is awarded a posthumous Pulitzer Prize.

• Elton John performs an entire week of sold-out concerts in Madison Square Garden, breaking all attendance records for the venue.

• Peter Frampton's *Frampton Comes Alive!* becomes the biggest-selling live album ever released.

• The Recording Industry Association of America creates the Platinum Award for singles selling one million copies and albums selling two million copies. The first platinum single is "Disco Lady" by Johnnie Taylor; the first platinum album is *The Eagles/Their Greatest Hits 1971–1975.*

• Lasers are used in a rock show for the first time, by The Who.

• The exhibit "Two Centuries of Black American Art" opens at the Los Angeles County Museum of Art.

• Saul Bellow wins the Nobel Prize for Literature.

• On January 12, the National Endowment for the Arts awards grants totaling over $8 million to one hundred orchestras.

• On January 30, the first "Live from Lincoln Center" telecast features the New York Philharmonic with Andre Previn as conductor and Van Cliburn as pianist.

• On May 18, an all-star concert, the highlight of a $6.5 million fundraising drive to restore Carnegie Hall in New York

City, features Leonard Bernstein, Vladimir Horowitz, and Isaac Stern.

- On June 24, Joseph Papp's New York Shakespeare Festival opens, featuring *Henry V* with Paul Rudd and Meryl Streep.

- On June 30, *Swan Lake,* performed by the American Ballet Theater at Lincoln Center, becomes the first full-length ballet to be telecast live.

- On July 4, the works of ten U.S. sculptors are unveiled along a 455-mile stretch of interstate highway in Nebraska.

- On July 21, *Guys and Dolls* is revived on Broadway with an all-African-American cast.

- On August 4, Gian Carlo Menotti's *Symphony No. 1,* commissioned for the bicentennial, premieres in New York City.

- On October 6, Jackson Pollock's last privately owned painting, *Lavender Mist,* is sold to the National Gallery of Art for $2 million.

- On November 6, *Gone With the Wind* is broadcast on network television for the first time, setting a new Nielsen ratings record.

MOVIES: *All the President's Men,* directed by Alan J. Pakula and starring Robert Redford and Dustin Hoffman; *Carrie,* directed by Brian DePalma and starring Sissy Spacek and John Travolta; *Car Wash,* directed by Michael Schultz and starring Richard Pryor, *Family Plot,* directed by Alfred Hitchcock; *Logan's Run,* directed by Michael Anderson and starring Michael York and Farrah Fawcett; *Network,* directed by Sidney Lumet and starring Faye Dunaway, William Holden, Peter Finch, and Robert Duvall; *The Omen,* directed by Richard Donner and starring Gregory Peck and Lee Remick; *Rocky,* directed by John G. Avildsen and starring Sylvester Stallone and Talia Shire; *A Star Is Born,* directed by Frank Pierson and starring Barbra Streisand and Kris Kristofferson; *Taxi Driver,* directed by Martin Scorsese and starring Robert De Niro, Harvey Keitel, Cybill Shepherd, and Jodie Foster.

FICTION: John Gardner, *October Light;* Ira Levin, *The Boys from Brazil;* Marge Piercy, *Woman on the Edge of Time;* Paul Theroux, *The Family Arsenal;* Leon Uris, *Trinity;* Gore Vidal, *1876;* Kurt Vonnegut, *Slapstick;* Alice Walker, *Meridian;* Irving Wallace, *The R Document.*

POPULAR SONGS: Aerosmith, "Dream On"; Bay City Rollers, "Saturday Night"; The Bee Gees, "You Should Be Dancing"; Bellamy Brothers, "Let Your Love Flow"; Chicago, "If You Leave Me Now"; The Four Seasons, "December 1963 (Oh, What a Night)"; Elton John and Kiki Dee, "Don't Go Breakin' My Heart"; Gordon Lightfoot, "The Wreck of the Edmund Fitzgerald"; Barry Manilow, "I Write the Songs"; C.W. McCall, "Convoy"; Steve Miller Band, "Rock'n Me"; Paul McCartney and Wings, "Silly Love Songs"; Queen, "Bohemian Rhapsody"; Vickie Sue Robinson, "Turn the Beat Around"; Diana Ross, "Love Hangover" and "Theme from *Mahogany*"; Paul Simon, "50 Ways to Leave Your Lover"; Starland Vocal Band, "Afternoon Delight"; Rod Stewart, "Tonight's the Night"; Johnnie Taylor, "Disco Lady"; Andrea True Connection, "More More More"; Wild Cherry, "Play That Funky Music"

1977

- The national tour "Treasures of Tutankhamen," featuring Egyptian artifacts from King Tut's tomb, draws the largest attendance in history for an art show.

- Studio 54, the first celebrity disco, opens in New York City.

- Fleetwood Mac's album *Rumours* sells over eight million copies, holds the number one album slot on the *Billboard* chart for thirty-one weeks, and becomes the first album to produce four Top 10 singles. It remains on the chart for 3½ years.

- On February 20, Alex Haley's *Roots* is listed by *The New York Times* as the top-selling book in the country for twenty consecutive weeks.

- On April 21, the musical *Annie,* produced by Mike Nichols, opens on Broadway, eventually notching 2,377 performances.

- On May 26, *Beatlemania,* a mixed-media concert featuring Beatles songs performed by Beatles look-alikes, opens in New York City.

- On June 26, Elvis Presley makes his last concert appearance, in Indianapolis.

- On June 30, the Newport Jazz Festival announces a move to Saratoga Springs, New York, citing prohibitive costs.

- On August 19, Elvis Presley dies of heart failure at age forty-two.

- On October 15, the Metropolitan Opera performs *La Boheme,* marking its first live television broadcast. Renata Scotto and Luciano Pavarotti star.

- On November 22, the J. Paul Getty Museum in California reportedly pays between $3.5 and $5 million, a record price, for a fourth-century bronze sculpture.

MOVIES: *Annie Hall,* directed by Woody Allen and starring Allen and Diane Keaton; *Close Encounters of the Third Kind,* directed by Steven Spielberg and starring Richard Dreyfuss; *The Goodbye Girl,* directed by Herbert Ross and starring Richard Dreyfuss and Marsha Mason; *Julia,* directed by Fred Zinneman and starring Jane Fonda, Vanessa Redgrave, and Jason Robards; *New York, New York,* directed by Martin Scorsese and starring Robert De Niro and Liza Minnelli; *Saturday Night Fever,* directed by John Badham and starring John Travolta; *Smokey and the Bandit,* directed by Hal Needham and starring Burt Reynolds and Sally Field; *Star Wars,* directed by George Lucas and starring Mark Hamill, Harrison Ford, and Carrie Fisher; *The Turning Point,* directed by Herbert Ross and starring Anne Bancroft, Shirley MacLaine, and Mikhail Baryshnikov.

FICTION: Louis Auchincloss, *The Dark Lady;* John Cheever, *Falconer;* Richard Condon, *The Abandoned Woman;* Robert Coover, *The Public Burning;* Sarah Davidson, *Loose Change;* Joan Didion, *A Book of Common Prayer;* Leon Forrest, *The Bloodworth Orphans;* Marilyn French, *The Women's Room;* Jerzy Kosinski, *Blind Date;* James Alan McPherson, *Elbow Room;* Toni Morrison, *Song of Solomon;* Paul Theroux, *Consul's File.*

POPULAR SONGS: Abba, "Dancing Queen"; Debby Boone, "You Light Up My Life"; Bill Conti, "Gonna Fly Now

(Theme from *Rocky*)"; Steve Miller Band, "Fly Like an Eagle"; Eagles, "Hotel California"; Emotions, "Best of My Love"; Fleetwood Mac, "Dreams"; Andy Gibb, "I Just Want to Be Your Everything"; Hall and Oates, "Rich Girl"; Thelma Houston, "Don't Leave Me This Way"; Mary MacGregor, "Torn Between Two Lovers"; Meco, *Star Wars Theme*"; Rose Royce, "Car Wash"; Barbra Streisand, "Love Theme from *A Star Is Born* (Evergreen)"; Stevie Wonder, "Sir Duke."

1978

- The National Gallery of Art in Washington, D.C., opens the East Building, dedicated to modern art.

- Richard Rodgers and Arthur Rubinstein are honored at the Kennedy Center in New York City.

- Isaac Bashevis Singer wins the Nobel Prize for Literature, the second American writer to win in three years.

- Christina Crawford creates a stir with the best-seller *Mommie Dearest,* a scathing portrait of her late mother, actress Joan Crawford.

- In January, the English punk rock band the Sex Pistols breaks up in the middle of its first American tour when singer Johnny Rotten quits the band.

- On January 4, the top-selling paperback in the country, *Close Encounters of the Third Kind,* is a novelization of a film script.

- On April 13, an elaborate financial plan is announced to save Radio City Music Hall in New York City, known for its Rockettes dancers and Music Hall Symphony.

- On April 24, the Soviet press agency Tass reports that painter Andrew Wyeth has been elected honorary member of the Soviet Academy of Arts.

- On May 9, *Ain't Misbehavin',* an all-African-American musical featuring the music of Fats Waller, opens on Broadway, eventually racking up 1,604 performances.

- On July 20, John D. Rockefeller III bequeaths his American art collection to the Fine Arts Museum in San Francisco and to the Asia Society in New York City.

- On December 27, three paintings by Paul Cézanne, valued at between $2.5 and $3 million, are discovered to be missing from the Art Institute in Chicago.

MOVIES: *The Buddy Holly Story,* directed by Steve Rash and starring Gary Busey; *Coming Home,* directed by Hal Ashby and starring Jane Fonda and Jon Voight; *Days of Heaven,* directed by Terence Malick and starring Richard Gere; *The Deer Hunter,* directed by Michael Cimino and starring Robert De Niro, Meryl Streep, and Christopher Walken; *Grease,* directed by Randal Kleiser and starring John Travolta and Olivia Newton-John; *Heaven Can Wait,* directed by Warren Beatty and starring Beatty and Julie Christie; *Interiors,* directed by Woody Allen and starring Diane Keaton and Geraldine Page; *Midnight Express,* directed by Alan Parker and starring Brad Davis; *National Lampoon's Animal House,* directed by John Landis and starring John Belushi; *An Unmarried Woman,* directed by Paul Mazursky and starring Jill Clayburgh.

FICTION: Louis Auchincloss, *The Country Cousin;* John Cheever, *The Stories of John Cheever;* Ernest J. Gaines, *In My Father's House;* John Irving, *The World According to Garp;* Judith Krantz, *Scruples;* Herman Wouk, *War and Remembrance.*

POPULAR SONGS: The Bee Gees, "How Deep Is Your Love," "Night Fever," and "Stayin' Alive"; the Commodores, "Three Times a Lady"; Yvonne Elliman, "If I Can't Have You"; Exile, "Kiss You All Over"; Andy Gibb, "(Love Is) Thicker Than Water" and "Shadow Dancing"; Billy Joel, "Just the Way You Are"; Paul McCartney and Wings, "With a Little Luck"; Gerry Rafferty, "Baker Street"; the Rolling Stones, "Miss You"; Donna Summer, "Last Dance" and "MacArthur Park"; A Taste of Honey, "Boogie Oogie Oogie"; John Travolta and Olivia Newton-John, "You're the One That I Want"; Frankie Valli, "Grease"; Village People, "Macho Man" and "Y.M.C.A."

1979

- Aaron Copland is honored at the Kennedy Center in New York City.

- The first digitally recorded album—Ry Cooder's *Bop Till You Drop*—is released.

- Chuck Berry serves a four-month prison term for income-tax evasion.

- Eleven people are trampled to death at The Who concert in Cincinnati when fans rush to unassigned seating.

- On March 16, *The China Syndrome,* a film depicting the shutdown of an unsafe nuclear reactor, opens just twelve days before a malfunction of a reactor at Three Mile Island in Pennsylvania leads to a near meltdown.

- On September 15, Massachusetts adopts the nation's first lottery in support of the arts.

- On September 25, the musical *Evita,* written by Andrew Lloyd Webber and Tim Rice and produced by Robert Stigwood, opens on Broadway, eventually running 1,567 performances.

- On September 25, *Icebergs,* a long-lost painting by nineteenth-century landscape artist Frederick Edwin Church, is auctioned for a record $2.5 million.

MOVIES: *Alien,* directed by Ridley Scott and starring Sigourney Weaver; *All That Jazz,* directed by Bob Fosse and starring Roy Scheider and Jessica Lange; *Apocalypse Now,* directed by Francis Ford Coppola and starring Martin Sheen, Robert Duvall, and Marlon Brando; *The China Syndrome,* directed by James Bridges and starring Jane Fonda, Jack Lemmon, and Michael Douglas; *Kramer vs. Kramer,* directed by Robert Benton and starring Dustin Hoffman and Meryl Streep; *Manhattan,* directed by Woody Allen and starring Allen, Diane Keaton, and Meryl Streep; *Norma Rae,* directed by Martin Ritt and starring Sally Field; *Rock 'n' Roll High School,* starring the Ramones; *10,* directed by Blake Edwards and starring Dudley Moore, Bo Derek, and Julie Andrews.

FICTION: Jerzy Kosinski, *Passion Play;* Norman Mailer, *The Executioner's Song;* Bernard Malamud, *Dubin's Lives;* Philip Roth, *The Ghost Writer;* Isaac Bashevis Singer, *Old Love;* William Styron, *Sophie's Choice;* John Updike, *Too Far to Go;* Alice Walker, *Goodnight, Willie Lee, I'll See You in the Morning.*

POPULAR SONGS: Herb Alpert, "Rise"; the Bee Gees, "Tragedy"; Blondie, "Heart of Glass"; Chic, "Good Times" and "Le Freak"; the Doobie Brothers, "What a Fool Believes"; Gloria Gaynor, "I Will Survive"; Michael Jackson, "Don't Stop Til You Get Enough"; the Knack, "My Sharona"; M, "Pop Musik"; Peaches and Herb, "Reunited"; Sister Sledge, "We Are Family"; Rod Stewart, "Do Ya Think I'm Sexy"; Donna Summer, "Bad Girls," "Hot Stuff," and "No More Tears (Enough Is Enough)"; Anita Ward, "Ring My Bell."

The Bluest Eye
Novel

By: Toni Morrison

Date: 1970

Source: Morrison, Toni. *The Bluest Eye.* New York: Holt, Rinehart and Winston, Inc., 1970. Reprint, New York: Plume, 1994, 9–16.

About the Author: Toni Morrison (1931–) was born in Lorain, Ohio. She earned a B.A. in English and Classics from Howard University in Washington, D.C., in 1953 and an M.A. in English from Cornell in 1954. Morrison taught and worked as an editor at Random House before she began to publish. In 1993 Toni Morrison was the first African American woman awarded the Nobel Prize for Literature. She is currently the Robert F. Goheen Professor at Princeton University. ■

Introduction

Toni Morrison began writing *The Bluest Eye* as a story in 1962. It evolved into an idea for a novel in 1965, five years before it was published. Morrison frequently reflects on her writing practices in interviews and in articles. In the Afterward to the 1994 edition of *The Bluest Eye,* she writes about a child she knew in elementary school who wanted blue eyes, like Pecola Breedlove in the novel. She writes that "it was the first time I knew beautiful. Had imagined it for myself. Beauty was not simply something to behold; it was something one could *do*." The concept of the beautiful and the ugly are integral in her first novel. Cultural understanding and expectations for how one looks and acts influence the characters actions and self-respect. The cycle of poverty and abuse that the Breedlove family experiences adds to the rejection they feel in the community of Lorain. These are the themes that become common in Toni Morrison's work.

The Bluest Eye is set during 1940–1941. Claudia and Frieda McTeer befriend Pecola Breedlove when she is sent to stay with them after being "put outdoors." This, the reader quickly learns, is the worst thing that can happen because it means that there is nowhere to go. Through Claudia's narrative, Morrison weaves the story of lost innocence through the passing seasons. The girls, especially Pecola who is later raped by her father, are contrasted with the little white blonde girls who society honors for their outward beauty. Claudia and Frieda lose their innocence, but their souls and sense of character are preserved by their family home. Pecola is lost and goes mad because nothing can help her cure her unnatural life.

Significance

Toni Morrison depends upon the "ruse of memory" to evoke characters because "it ignites some process of invention" and because she "cannot trust the literature and sociology of other people to help me know the truth of my own cultural sources." Her memory provided the prayer for blue eyes heard from another child in her youth. This prayer became Pecola's prayer. The details of memory, setting, and language set Morrison apart from other novelists. She transports the reader to a distinct place and time while simultaneously remarking on the oppression of a people.

Ruby Dee, in McKay's collection of essays, wrote, "It's all I can do not to lie down and cry myself into some kind of relief from the life-pain of Pecola." She recognizes that Morrison has written a "series of painfully accurate impressions" about the lives of her characters. In *The New York Times,* John Leonard stated that Morrison exposed the negative images of reading primers in "prose so precise, so faithful to speech and so charged with pain and wonder that the novel becomes poetry." He goes on to praise her depiction of society at a certain moment in history.

Toni Morrison assesses the success and failure of Pecola Breedlove's story in the *Afterword* of the 1994 edition. She notes that even thirty years after she began this book, it is still difficult to translate the pain of a child like Pecola into language. Although *The Bluest Eye* was not an outstanding success at its publication, readers and critics gradually realized the power of her story and longings. *The Bluest Eye* is the first of a powerful collection of stories that Morrison has told about women and children who are too often forgotten or dismissed as crazy and worthless. She shows the reader the worth in every character's story and life.

Primary Source

The Bluest Eye [excerpt]

SYNOPSIS: The McTeer's home is cold and not in the best shape, but the people who live there care about one another. Conversation swirls over the children's heads in a "gently wicked dance." Through the language the good and the bad of the families in the novel are revealed.

Author Toni Morrison, 1977. **AP/WIDE WORLD PHOTOS.**
REPRODUCED BY PERMISSION.

Nuns go by as quiet as lust, and drunken men and sober eyes sing in the lobby of the Greek hotel. Rosemary Villanucci, our next-door friend who lives above her father's café, sits in a 1939 Buick eating bread and butter. She rolls down the window to tell my sister Frieda and me that we can't come in. We stare at her, wanting her bread, but more than that wanting to poke the arrogance out of her eyes and smash the pride of ownership that curls her chewing mouth. When she comes out of the car we will beat her up, make red marks on her white skin, and she will cry and ask us do we want her to pull her pants down. We will say no. We don't know what we should feel or do if she does, but whenever she asks us, we know she is offering us something precious and that our own pride must be asserted by refusing to accept.

School has started, and Frieda and I get new brown stockings and cod-liver oil. Grown-ups talk in tired, edgy voices about Zick's Coal Company and take us along in the evening to the railroad tracks where we fill burlap sacks with the tiny pieces of coal lying about. Later we walk home, glancing back to see the great carloads of slag being dumped, red hot and smoking, into the ravine that skirts the steel mill. The dying fire lights the sky with a dull orange glow. Frieda and I lag behind, staring at a patch of color surrounded by black. It is impossible not to feel a shiver when our feet leave the gravel path and sink into the dead grass in the field.

Our house is old, cold, and green. At night a kerosene lamp lights one large room. The others are braced in darkness, peopled by roaches and mice. Adults do not talk to us—they give us directions. They issue orders without providing information. When we trip and fall down they glance at us; if we cut or bruise ourselves, they ask us are we crazy. When we catch colds, they shake their heads in disgust at our lack of consideration. How, they ask us, do you expect anybody to get anything done if you all are sick? We cannot answer them. Our illness is treated with contempt, foul Black Draught, and castor oil that blunts our minds.

When, on a day after a trip to collect coal, I cough once, loudly, through bronchial tubes already packed tight with phlegm, my mother frowns. "Great Jesus. Get on in that bed. How many times do I have to tell you to wear something on your head? You must be the biggest fool in this town. Frieda? Get some rags and stuff that window."

Frieda restuffs the window. I trudge off to bed, full of guilt and self-pity. I lie down in my underwear, the metal in the black garters hurts my legs, but I do not take them off, for it is too cold to lie stockingless. It takes a long time for my body to heat its place in the bed. Once I have generated a silhouette of warmth, I dare not move, for there is a cold place one-half inch in any direction. No one speaks to me or asks how I feel. In an hour or two my mother comes. Her hands are large and rough, and when she rubs the Vicks salve on my chest, I am rigid with pain. She takes two fingers' full of it at a time, and massages my chest until I am faint. Just when I think I will tip over into a scream, she scoops out a little of the salve on her forefinger and puts it in my mouth, telling me to swallow. A hot flannel is wrapped about my neck and chest. I am covered up with heavy quilts and ordered to sweat, which I do—promptly.

Later I throw up, and my mother says, "What did you puke on the bed clothes for? Don't you have sense enough to hold your head out the bed? Now, look what you did. You think I got time for nothing but washing up your puke?"

The puke swaddles down the pillow onto the sheet—green-gray, with flecks of orange. It moves like the insides of an uncooked egg. Stubbornly clinging to its own mass, refusing to break up and be removed. How, I wonder, can it be so neat and nasty at the same time?

My mother's voice drones on. She is not talking to me. She is talking to the puke, but she is calling it my name: Claudia. She wipes it up as best she can and puts a scratchy towel over the large wet place. I lie down again. The rags have fallen from the window crack, and the air is cold. I dare not call her back and am reluctant to leave my warmth. My mother's anger humiliates me; her words chafe my cheeks, and I am crying. I do not know that she is not angry at me, but at my sickness. I believe she despises my weakness for letting the sickness "take holt." By and by I will not get sick; I will refuse to. But for now I am crying. I know I am making more snot, but I can't stop.

My sister comes in. Her eyes are full of sorrow. She sings to me: "When the deep purple falls over sleepy garden walls, someone thinks of me. . . ." I doze, thinking of plums, walls, and "someone."

But was it really like that? As painful as I remember? Only mildly. Or rather, it was a productive and fructifying pain. Love, thick and dark as Alaga syrup, eased up into that cracked window. I could smell it—taste it—sweet, musty, with an edge of wintergreen in its base—everywhere in that house. It stuck, along with my tongue, to the frosted windowpanes. It coated my chest, along with the salve, and when the flannel came undone in my sleep, the clear, sharp curves of air outlined its presence on my throat. And in the night, when my coughing was dry and tough, feet padded into the room, hands repinned the flannel, readjusted the quilt, and rested a moment on my forehead. So when I think of autumn, I think of somebody with hands who does not want me to die.

■ ■ ■

It was autumn too when Mr. Henry came. Our roomer. Our roomer. The words ballooned from the lips and hovered about our heads—silent, separate, and pleasantly mysterious. My mother was all ease and satisfaction in discussing his coming.

"You know him," she said to her friends. "Henry Washington. He's been living over there with Miss Della Jones on Thirteenth Street. But she's too addled now to keep up. So he's looking for another place."

"Oh, yes." Her friends do not hide their curiosity. "I been wondering how long he was going to stay up there with her. They say she's real bad off. Don't know who he is half the time, and nobody else."

"Well, that old crazy nigger she married up with didn't help her head none."

"Did you hear what he told folks when he left her?"

"Uh-uh. What?"

"Well, he run off with that trifling Peggy—from Elyria. You know."

"One of Old Slack Bessie's girls?"

"That's the one. Well, somebody asked him why he left a nice good church woman like Della for that heifer. You know Della always did keep a good house. And he said the honest-to-God real reason was he couldn't take no more of that violet water Della Jones used. Said he wanted a woman to smell like a woman. Said Della was just too clean for him."

"Old dog. Ain't that nasty!"

"You telling me. What kind of reasoning is that?"

"No kind. Some men just dogs."

"Is that what give her them strokes?"

"Must have helped. But you know, none of them girls wasn't too bright. Remember that grinning Hattie? She wasn't never right. And their Auntie Julia is still trotting up and down Sixteenth Street talking to herself."

"Didn't she get put away?"

"Naw. County wouldn't take her. Said she wasn't harming anybody."

"Well, she's harming me. You want something to scare the living shit out of you, you get up at five-thirty in the morning like I do and see that old hag floating by in that bonnet. Have mercy!"

They laugh.

Frieda and I are washing Mason jars. We do not hear their words, but with grown-ups we listen to and watch out for their voices.

"Well, I hope don't nobody let me roam around like that when I get senile. It's a shame."

"What they going to do about Della? Don't she have no people?"

"A sister's coming up from North Carolina to look after her. I expect she wants to get aholt of Della's house."

"Oh, come on. That's a evil thought, if ever I heard one."

"What you want to bet? Henry Washington said that sister ain't seen Della in fifteen years."

"I kind of thought Henry would marry her one of these days."

"That old woman?"

"Well, Henry ain't no chicken."

"No, but he ain't no buzzard, either."

"He ever been married to anybody?"

"No."

"How come? Somebody cut if off?"

"He's just picky."

"He ain't picky. You see anything around here you'd marry?"

"Well . . . no."

"He's just sensible. A steady worker with quiet ways. I hope it works out all right."

"It will. How much you charging?"

"Five dollars every two weeks."

"That'll be a big help to you."

"I'll say."

■ ■ ■

Their conversation is like a gently wicked dance: sound meets sound, curtsies, shimmies, and retires. Another sound enters but is upstaged by still another: the two circle each other and stop. Sometimes their words move in lofty spirals; other times they take strident leaps, and all of it is punctuated with warm-pulsed laughter—like the throb of a heart made of jelly. The edge, the curl, the thrust of their emotions is always clear to Frieda and me. We do not, cannot, know the meanings of all their words, for we are nine and ten years old. So we watch their faces, their hands, their feet, and listen for truth in timbre.

So when Mr. Henry arrived on a Saturday night, we smelled him. He smelled wonderful. Like trees and lemon vanishing cream, and Nu Nile Hair Oil and flecks of Sen-Sen.

He smiled a lot, showing small even teeth with a friendly gap in the middle. Frieda and I were not introduced to him—merely pointed out. Like, here is the bathroom; the clothes closet is here; and these are my kids, Frieda and Claudia; watch out for this window; it don't open all the way.

We looked sideways at him, saying nothing and expecting him to say nothing. Just to nod, as he had done at the clothes closet, acknowledging our existence. To our surprise, he spoke to us.

"Hello there. You must be Greta Garbo and you must be Ginger Rogers."

"We giggled. Even my father was startled into a smile."

"Want a penny?" He held out a shiny coin to us. Frieda lowered her head, too pleased to answer. I reached for it. He snapped his thumb and forefinger, and the penny disappeared. Our shock was laced with delight. We searched all over him, poking our fingers into his socks, looking up the inside back of his coat. If happiness is anticipation with certainty, we were happy. And while we waited for the coin to reappear, we knew we were amusing Mama and Daddy. Daddy was smiling, and Mama's eyes went soft as they followed our hands wandering over Mr. Henry's body.

We loved him. Even after what came later, there was no bitterness in our memory of him.

Further Resources

BOOKS

Bjork, Patrick Bryce. *The Novels of Toni Morrison: The Search for Self and Place Within the Community.* New York: Lang, 1992.

Carmean, Karen. *Toni Morrison's World of Fiction.* Troy, N.Y.: Whitston, 1993.

McKay, Nellie Y., ed. *Critical Essays on Toni Morrison.* Boston: G.K. Hall, 1988.

PERIODICALS

Leonard, John. "Three First Novels on Race." *The New York Times,* November 13, 1970, 35.

Morrison, Toni. "Memory, Creation, and Writing." *Thought* 59, no. 235, December 1984, 385–390.

WEBSITES

"Morrison, Toni." EducETH Teaching and Learning. Available online at http://www.educeth.ch/english/readinglist/morrisont /index.html; website home page: http://www.educeth.ch (accessed June 19, 2003).

Morrison, Toni. "*The Bluest Eye.*" Audio excerpts. Salon.com. Available online at http://www.salon.com/audio/fiction/2002 /01/07/morrison/; website home page: http://www.salon .com/ (accessed April 5, 2003).

AUDIO AND VISUAL MEDIA

Morrison, Toni. *The Bluest Eye.* Abridged. Original release, 1994. Random House AudioBooks, CD/Audiocassette.

"The Ladies Who Lunch"
Song

By: Stephen Sondheim

Date: 1970

Source: Sondheim, Stephen. "The Ladies Who Lunch." *Company: A Musical Comedy.* Winona, Minn.: Hal Leonard, 1970.

About the Artist: Stephen Sondheim (1930–) established his career as a lyricist with the musical *West Side Story*. He met Oscar Hammerstein, who became a mentor, when he was a child. Sondheim graduated from Williams College, where he studied music. He also studied with Milton Babbitt, an avant-garde composer. Sondheim's musicals include *A Funny Thing Happened on the Way to the Forum* (1962), *Sweeney Todd* (1979), and *Into the Woods* (1989). ■

Introduction

Through the 1960s, audiences generally expected musicals to present linear stories of young lovers who overcame difficulty and ended up happily ever after. *Company* changed that formula. Instead of a linear story, writer George Furth wrote a series of episodes that portrayed five couples and their single friend Robert talking about various situations. The couples struggle through the ups and downs of marriage and relationships, while Robert, often referred to as Bobby, leads the swinging single life. The couples alternately worry about his lack of a permanent relationship or are jealous of his freedom. The music is also not traditional show music. The lyrics for *Company* reflect the difficulties of the characters' relationships. One couple contemplates divorce while another gets married. Sondheim stated that the show was meant to be pro-marriage, even though most reviewers saw the musical as anti-marriage.

Rehearsals were difficult for everyone involved because of the new formula. As a result, staging and choreography for *Company* also took on non-traditional forms. Michael Bennett, who later choreographed *A Chorus Line,* worked with the cast of dancers and non-dancers. The characters were like real people: some could dance and sing, while others could not. Dancing and singing choruses were not part of the musical. The contemporary urban setting was another unusual feature. Boris Aronson, the set designer, created a set that depicted the complexity of New York City. Carol Ilson recounts his remark that New York was "becoming one enormous cubist painting," and the metal and glass set shows the cold, sterile world.

Company ran twenty months on Broadway and six months in London. The show never sold out, but Stephen Sondheim and Hal Prince felt that they had created a musical comedy that was uncompromising.

Significance

Company won the New York Drama Critics' Award for best musical of the season, along with six Tony awards. Despite the awards, the views of the New York critics may have been responsible for smaller audiences during the first run.

While *Company* broke ground in the musical comedy theater, the characters were generally unpleasant. As

Stephen Sondheim stands before a poster advertising one of his shows, 1976. © CORBIS. REPRODUCED BY PERMISSION.

The New York Times reviewer Clive Barnes wrote, the characters are "all the lovely, beautiful people you had spent the previous two hours avoiding" at a cocktail party. Many reviewers, including Barnes, recognized the outstanding score and lyrics by Stephen Sondheim. Barnes wrote that the lyrics have a "suppleness, sparse, elegant wit, and range from the virtuosity of a patter song to a kind of sweetly laconic cynicism in a modern love song." Walter Kerr stated that "Stephen Sondheim has never written a more sophisticated, more pertinent, or—this is the surprising thing in the circumstance—more melodious score." Carol Ilson concludes that *Company* "contained an innovative book and structure, extended the use of music, and broke down the old rules for dancing and singing choruses." Everything about *Company* defied the rules of musical comedy theater.

The 1995 revival of the show raised some questions about pertinence. Would the episodes from the 1970s hold up in 1995? The theme of the difficulty of relationships remained relevant twenty-five years later, perhaps even more so in the increased technological environment of the mid-1990s. Some of the scenes with sex, drugs, and rock and roll may be dated in the early 2000s, but questions about relationships are not. Audiences of the early twenty-first century are better able to understand the analysis of characters that Sondheim and Furth present in *Company* than was the case in 1970. The work remains a landmark in musical theater.

Primary Source

"The Ladies Who Lunch"

SYNOPSIS: Elaine Stritch played Joanne in the original cast of *Company*. Joanne, one of the "ladies who lunch," is a society matron who reveals her feeling about the empty life she leads in the satiric line "I'll drink to that."

Here's to the ladies who lunch—
Everybody laugh.
Lounging in their caftans and planning a brunch,
On their own behalf.
Off to the gym,
Then to a fitting,
Claiming they're fat,
And looking grim,
'Cause they've been sitting choosing a hat
Does anyone still wear a hat?
I'll drink to that.

Here's to the girls who stay smart.
Aren't they a gas?
Wishing it would pass.
Another long, exhausting day,
Another matinee:
A Pinter play,
Perhaps a piece of Mahler's.
I'll drink to that—
And one for Mahler.

Here's to the girls who play wife.
Aren't they too much?
Keeping house, but clutching a copy of Life
Just to keep in touch.
The ones who follow the rules
And meet themselves at the schools—
Too busy to know that they're fools.
Aren't they a gem?
I'll drink to them!
Let's all drink to them!

And Here's to the girls who just watch.
Aren't they the best?
When they get depressed, it's a bottle of scotch
Plus a little jest.
Another chance to disapprove.
Another brilliant zinger.
Another reason not to move
Another vodka stinger.
Aaah, I'll drink to that.

So Here's to the girls on the go,
Everybody tries.
Look into their eyes and you'll see what they know:
Everybody dies.
A toast to that invincible bunch,
The dinosaurs surviving the crunch,
Let's hear it for the ladies who lunch:

Everybody rise!
Rise!
Rise!
Rise!

Further Resources

BOOKS

Ilson, Carol. *Harold Prince: From "Pajama Game" to "Phantom of the Opera."* Ann Arbor, Mich.: UMI Research Press, 1989.

Olson, John. "Company—25 Years Later." In *Stephen Sondheim: A Casebook.* Joanne Gordon, ed. New York: Garland, 1997, 47–67.

Zadan, Craig. *Sondheim & Co.,* 2d ed. New York: Harper & Row, 1986.

PERIODICALS

Barnes, Clive. "Theater: 'Company' Offers a Guide to New York's Marital Jungle." *The New York Times,* April 27, 1970, 40.

Kerr, Walter. "'Company': Original and Uncompromising." *The New York Times,* May 3, 1970, sec. 2, 1, 9.

WEBSITES

Hutchins, Michael H., comp. "The Stephen Sondheim Reference Guide." Available online at http://www.geocities.com /sondheimguide (accessed March 20, 2003).

Sondheim.com. Available online at http://www.sondheim.com (accessed April 5, 2003).

AUDIO AND VISUAL MEDIA

Company: A Musical Comedy. Original release, 1971. Directed by D.A. Pennebaker. A&E Home Video. DVD, 2001, New Video Group; VHS, 2000.

Sondheim, Stephen. *Company: A Musical Comedy.* Original cast recording. Original release, 1970. Sony 65283, 1998, CD.

"Bridge Over Troubled Water"

Song

By: Paul Simon and Art Garfunkel

Date: 1970

Source: Simon, Paul, and Art Garfunkel. "Bridge Over Troubled Water." From the album *Bridge Over Trouble Water.* Original Release, 1970, Columbia KCS 9914, LP. Columbia CK9914, CD, 2001.

About the Artists: Paul Simon (1941–) and Art Garfunkel (1941–) met in the sixth grade. They began singing together when they were teenagers and released their first single, "Hey Schoolgirl," in 1957. They were a popular duo throughout the 1960s. Although they split to pursue solo careers in 1970, they occasionally reunite for a concert. ∎

Popular musicians Simon (right) and Garfunkel (left) give a performance. © CORBIS. REPRODUCED BY PERMISSION.

Introduction

Popular music in the 1960s and 1970s included rock and roll, folk music, and a blend of both. Lyrics reflected a time when young people felt the alienation of the society. Political messages often were part of rock or folk music. Artists like Bob Dylan emerged and the Beatles remained popular. Timothy Scheuer comments, "The music was geared to a young audience, now dominated by the burgeoning baby boom sector. Radio, both in the form of portable transistor types and in cars—the site where music and leisure most comfortably met for youth—allowed rock to be an ever-present force in the lives of kids."

Simon and Garfunkel formed their duo in the 1950s, went their separate ways, and then came back together in 1964. They recorded "Sounds of Silence" in 1966, which became a number one hit. "Mrs. Robinson," a single from the film, *The Graduate,* became a top song of 1968.

Simon's lyrics called out to a generation of college students looking for answers in a confused world. The

Rock and Roll Hall of Fame Inductees web page recalls their "dulcet harmonies" that made them a popular duo even after they split in 1970.

Bridge Over Troubled Water, released in 1970, was a top selling album and produced several hit singles. The songs included epic stories and cheerful tunes. The title track has a gospel feel and explores isolation and the promise of salvation through friendship. "The Boxer," which had already been a hit single, conveys the story of a down and out "poor boy" who suffers on the streets, while "Cecilia" is an upbeat, wacky and fun song of love lost and found. This would be the last album the duo recorded as a team. They reunited for a "Concert in Central Park" on September 19, 1981, which was recorded and subsequently released on videocassette and CD.

Significance

Despite their exhaustion from touring and knowing that they were close to ending their musical partnership,

Simon and Garfunkel produced what has been called the greatest album of 1970. *Bridge Over Troubled Water* rose to number one in March 1970 and remained there for ten weeks. Thirteen million copies of the album have been sold worldwide. The album was re-released in 2001 with extra tracks and continued to sell well.

The album produced hit singles in addition to the status as a hit album. "Bridge Over Troubled Water," "Cecelia," and "The Boxer" all made it to the top ten charts in America and Great Britain. At the 1971 Grammy Awards the duo won six awards for the album, including Record of the Year and Song of the Year.

The lyrics and performance are what are truly important, however. In his comparison of the album with Carole King's *Tapestry*, Robert Christgau called *Bridge Over Troubled Water* "funny and honest. It breathes life." On the other hand, Gregg Mitchell, writing for the *Rolling Stone,* thought "their music has gotten stale." Ellen Sanders, like Christgau, appreciated Simon and Garfunkel's 1970 release. She called it a "model of consistency and professionalism" and noted that the title song is "both sad and mighty, disturbing and comforting in one tonal exercise." Sanders also remarked on "So Long Frank Lloyd Wright," a song frequently overlooked on the album. She saw it as a "retrospective, almost amusing view of the artists as song stylists, growing, changing, marking off passage of time in tune."

No matter what the opinion of critics, audiences and record buyers liked the album enough to make it platinum. Simon and Garfunkel's popularity as a duo did not end with *Bridge Over Troubled Water.* It continues into the twenty-first century.

Primary Source

"Bridge Over Troubled Water"

SYNOPSIS: Paul Simon wrote the title song while living in a rented house on Bluejay Way in the Hollywood hills. He wanted a certain gospel feel for the song, which was accomplished with Garfunkel's tenor and the instrumentation used on the album.

When you're weary, feeling small,
When tears are in your eyes, I will dry them all;
I'm on your side. When times get rough
And friends just can't be found,
Like a bridge over troubled water
I will lay me down.
Like a bridge over troubled water
I will lay me down.

When you're down and out,
When you're on the street,
When evening falls so hard
I will comfort you.

I'll take your part.
When darkness comes
And pain is all around,
Like a bridge over troubled water
I will lay me down.
Like a bridge over troubled water
I will lay me down.

Sail on silvergirl,
Sail on by.
Your time has come to shine.
All your dreams are on their way.
See how they shine.
If you need a friend
I'm sailing right behind.

Like a bridge over troubled water
I will ease your mind.
Like a bridge over troubled water
I will ease your mind.

Further Resources

BOOKS

Christgau, Robert. *Any Old Way You Choose It: Rock and Other Pop Music, 1967–1973.* Baltimore: Penguin Books, 1973.

Kingston, Victoria. *Simon and Garfunkel: The Biography.* New York: Fromm International, 1998.

Scheurer, Timothy E. *Born in the U.S.A.: The Myth of America in Popular Music From Colonial Times to the Present.* Jackson: University Press of Mississippi, 1991.

PERIODICALS

Mitchell, Gregg. "Simon and Garfunkel: Bridge Over Troubled Water." *Rolling Stone* 58. Available online at http://www.rollingstone.com/reviews/cd/review.asp?aid=16926&cf=; webstie home page: http://www.rollingstone.com (accessed April 5, 2003).

Sander, Ellen. "Simon & Garfunkel: The Singers and the Songs." *Saturday Review,* February 28, 1970, 91, 98.

WEBSITES

"Bridge Over Troubled Water." Super Seventies Rocksite. Available online at http://www.superseventies.com/1970_1singles.html; website home page: http://www.superseventies.com/ (accessed April 5, 2003).

"Rock and Roll Hall of Fame and Museum: Hall of Fame: Inductees." Rock and Roll Hall of Fame and Museum Available online at http://www.rockhall.com/hof/inductee.asp?id=188; website home page: http://www.rockhall.com/ (accessed April 5, 2003).

AUDIO AND VISUAL MEDIA

Simon and Garfunkel–The Concert in Central Park (1982). Recorded September 19, 1981. Original release, 1982. Directed by Michael Lindsay-Hogg. VHS, 1994, Twentieth Century Fox. Warner Bros. 3654, 1990, CD.

Dirty Harry
Movie still

By: Don Siegel

Date: 1971

Source: *Dirty Harry.* Originally released, 1971, Warner Brothers. Directed by Don Siegel. DVD/VHS, 2001, Warner Studios.

About the Artist: Don Siegel (1912–1991) was born in Chicago. He began his career as an actor but switched to directing in 1945. Siegel was known as an action movie specialist, directing for the theater and for television. He won two Oscars in 1946: for *Star in the Night,* a short subject, and for *Hitler Lives?,* a documentary. ■

Introduction

Harry Callahan, the fictional vigilante San Francisco cop, first appeared in 1971. Don Siegel cast Clint East-wood in the role after Paul Newman it turned down. Siegel and Eastwood had worked together for years on other films.

The cop action film was a new genre in 1971, with the time period contributing to the story line of the film. Character is built through Harry's actions and through long silences when Harry observes what is going on around him and at crime scenes. The film opens scrolling through a list of the names of San Francisco policeman killed in the line of duty. The serial killer, Scorpio, is loosely based on the Zodiac Killer, who murdered several people in California in the late 1960s and was never captured. Portrayed as a young hippie, Scorpio is seen as a symbol of the counterculture. Callahan and his new partner, Chico, are assigned to find Scorpio. They have close calls on the streets and from the rooftops that Scorpio

Primary Source

Dirty Harry

SYNOPSIS: Actor Clint Eastwood, portraying the title character in the movie *Dirty Harry*, takes aim with his .44 Magnum handgun. The film remains a fascinating slice of American pop culture. THE KOBAL COLLECTION/WARNER BROS. REPRODUCED BY PERMISSION.

favors as spots to find victims, but never come quite close enough until Harry is chosen to deliver ransom demanded for the return of a teenage girl. Capturing the killer after a chase around the city, Harry fails to read him his rights, so the killer is released. Harry, now without Chico who was wounded in the chase, again stalks Scorpio, and again captures him after he hijacks a busload of children. By this time, Scorpio is far crazier than he was at the beginning of the story. The film ends at a quarry: Harry delivers his "Do I feel lucky?" speech for the second time and kills Scorpio. Harry has now given up on the system, and it seems that this is the end of his career. However, Dirty Harry would return for more movies and vigilantism.

Significance

Reviewers criticized the vigilantism of Harry Callahan and his anti-liberal actions. The reviewer in *Newsweek* asks "how long this new appetite for violence will endure." More than 30 years later, films depicting violent acts that reviewers and audiences could not imagine in 1971 were commonplace.

Although Harry Callahan takes the law into his own hands against a maniacal killer, he seeks to protect the innocent. The spareness of the plot has been recognized. Jay Cocks wrote in *Time* that Siegel's "films move with a closely calculated irresistible momentum." When the *Clint Eastwood Collection: The Dirty Harry Series* containing all the "Dirty Harry" films was released in 2002, Robert Cashill commented that "Dirty Harry films are comfort entertainment; politically, not terribly constructive nor very nourishing, but something to nosh on while considering more concrete solutions to the world's ills."

Pauline Kael's famous comment that the movie was "fascist" has been repeated in most articles about the film. But the movie was a piece of its time, commenting on a legal system that many felt gave more rights to criminals than to police officers. If the critics were skeptical, the audiences were not. The film brought in the tenth highest domestic revenue in 1972, and by 1988 had grossed more than $18 million in North America. Four more Dirty Harry films followed, and actors such as Arnold Schwarzenegger and Steven Segal have portrayed more violent vigilante characters than the first Dirty Harry. Paul Smith points out that those who view the film in the early twenty-first century must remember the context of the early 1970s. At that time the "police's lack of credibility and dubious reputation in those years was in part a result of thousands of incidents of police brutality against antiwar demonstrators." He, along with others, have pointed to the Miranda ruling in 1968 and the Escobedo ruling that gave suspects, as citizens, more rights under the law. Paul Smith quotes Clint Eastwood as remarking that "Harry is a fantasy character. Nobody does what Harry does. He cuts right down through the bull,

tells his boss to shove it, does all the things people would like to do in real life but can't."

Further Resources

BOOKS

Leitch, Thomas. *Crime Films.* Cambridge and New York: Cambridge University Press, 2002.

"Don Siegel." In *International Dictionary of Films and Filmmakers: Directors,* 3rd ed. Detroit: St. James Press, 1997, 921–922.

Smith, Paul. *Clint Eastwood: A Cultural Production.* Minneapolis: University of Minnesota Press, 1993.

PERIODICALS

Cashill, Robert. "The Dirty Harry Series." *Cineaste* 27, no. 3, Summer 2002, 38–40.

Cocks, Jay. "Outside Society." *Time,* January 3, 1972, 66–67.

"Cops, Creeps and Courts." *Newsweek,* January 10, 1972, 59.

Kael, Pauline. "Saint Cop." *The New Yorker,* January 15, 1972, 78–81.

WEBSITES

Eastwood: The World Wide Web Page. Available online at http://www.clinteastwood.net/ (accessed June 19, 2003).

AUDIO AND VISUAL MEDIA

The Clint Eastwood Collection: The Dirty Harry Series. DVD, 2002, Warner Home Studios.

"Nixon and McGovern: Statements on the Arts"

Letters

By: George McGovern; Leonard Garment

Date: 1972

Source: McGovern, George. Letter to Donald R. Wall; Garment, Leonard. Letter to Donald R. Wall. "Nixon and McGovern: Statements on the Arts." *Art in America* 60, no. 6, November-December 1972, 56–57.

About the Authors: George McGovern (1922–), born in Avon, South Dakota, was a professor of history and political science before entering politics. He served as both the Representative and Senator from South Dakota in the U.S. Congress. He was an unsuccessful Democratic candidate for president in 1972. He is known for his liberal views and opposition to the Vietnam War.

Leonard Garment (1924–), an attorney, was special counsel to President Richard M. Nixon (served 1969–1974) throughout Nixon's presidency. He met Nixon when they both worked for a Wall Street law firm. ∎

Introduction

Donald R. Wall, the publisher of *Art in America,* asked the presidential nominees of the 1972 campaign to provide statements about what they would do for the arts in their administration. The statements appeared in the November-December issue of the magazine, almost too late for the November general election.

Art in America is a magazine intended for artists in all mediums. An illustrated bimonthly publication, the magazine presents the work of new and established artists, and explores controversies related to the art world. It was a perfect forum for the candidates to present their views.

George McGovern signed his own letter, while Leonard Garment wrote on behalf of the president. Each set forth a plan for funding the arts. McGovern attacked the government's spending on the Vietnam War, a sensitive subject with voters in the early 1970s. He cited the differences in arts spending between European countries and the United States and proposes a $200 million budget for the arts in the 1974 fiscal year. Garment details what has been done and what is in progress. He notes that under the Nixon Administration arts funding has increased fivefold to $81 million per year. Garment makes no excuses for the Administration and does not mention other spending concerns.

Donald Wall raised two specific questions for the candidates: tax write-offs for gifts to museums and funding for art in federal buildings. McGovern addresses the questions, though he does allow himself the option of looking into the issues. Garment seems to evade the tax issue with a general vote of support for the arts. Arts funding is not generally a major issue in presidential campaigns, particularly not during a time the country is at war. These statements reflect the values each candidate held, whether the funding became available or not.

Significance

The National Foundation on the Arts and Humanities Act of 1965 provided a catalyst for federal funding of the arts in America. While the arts held an important place in cultural life of Americans, federal funding was not part of the mix. Private donors were still needed to match the governmental funding, and foundations such as the Ford Foundation in New York provided millions of dollars for artistic projects and programs. Stanley Katz traced the importance of the private and corporate funds in an interview with the *National Arts Stabilization Journal.* He contended that the real success of the National Endowment for the Arts (NEA) and National Endowment for the Humanities (NEH) funding was that it encouraged more private sector support for the arts. Federal arts funding went up and down throughout the 1970s and 1980s, hitting a high point in the early 1990s.

McGovern and Garment both point out important issues in the arts and the debates over funding. One such concern is that the arts should be for all people. Since individual artists do not earn high salaries, and arts programs are usually non-profit entities, subsidizing arts is vital. The idea that arts should be handled by regional or state and local councils is also important. Regions vary in their strength in the arts as do needs and interests. By placing control at a state or local level, the arts funding can be distributed in a way a state or community sees fit. A comment that both men make that should be noted is the importance of the government not interfering once a grant is awarded. Who receives money is often controversial, which was the case for the NEA during the 1990s, when the public viewed some artists' works as offensive.

Primary Source

"Nixon and McGovern: Statements on the Arts"

> **SYNOPSIS:** These two letters were written in response to a request from Donald Wall, the publisher of *Art in America,* that the two major candidates in the 1972 presidential election share their views on federal support for the arts. Democratic nominee George McGovern asserts that more public funding should be made available for artists, and contrasts that huge sums being spent on the Vietnam War with the vastly smaller amount that the Nixon Administration had spent on the arts. Writing on behalf of Republican candidate and incumbent president Richard Nixon, Leonard Garment stresses the support Nixon has already shown for the arts while in office.

Dear Mr. Wall:

I am pleased to be able to share my thoughts with you about the government's role in promoting the arts. I am especially pleased because I believe the arts to be an essential ingredient in American life and consequently I am concerned that the Nixon administration has been treating the arts with its familiar, and tragic, benign neglect.

Seven years have passed since Congress enacted legislation which established a National Foundation on the Arts and Humanities and provided Federal assistance for individuals, organizations and states. Although the initial organization was not large, it was a beginning. I had therefore hoped that the President and Congress would support a continually expanding program to cover a wide scope of artistic activity to improve on the limited and elitist program that exists today.

Yet the statistics show that the promise of seven years ago has not been fulfilled. In 1971 our government spent only 15¢ per person on promoting the arts, though Canada spent $1.40 per person, Germany spent $2.40, and Great Britain $1.23. To rectify this situation I have proposed legislation that would increase to $200 million the total funding for art and the humanities for fiscal 1974.

Those of us concerned with the arts realize that this is a modest start, but at least it will reverse government's shallow commitment to support of the arts. We have to realize that in the seven years since the initial grant for the National Foundation on the Arts and Humanities, our nation has been tied down by the morass of Vietnam. Where in 1964 we spent $51 billion on defense, we are now spending $76.5 billion a year on defense.

Two hundred million dollars is roughly equal to the cost of 12 F-14 fighter planes, or two B-1 bombers, or four C55 transport planes, or one quarter of an aircraft carrier. $200 million is near the cost of one week of fighting in Vietnam. The General Accounting Office reported in 1970 that Pentagon cost overruns cost $33.4 billion. That is $527 per family in a country that currently gives about 15¢ a person for culture.

We are a wealthy nation and a productive nation; and we are a creative nation. We must also be a wise nation which can balance our human needs with our military needs. The production of wealth is a technique America has mastered well. But the use of wealth is itself an art. Our wealth must be used to enrich the lives of our citizens, not to destroy the lives of helpless Asians. We must use our financial resources to uplift our human and artistic resources. To this end, I have three general suggestions on how the proposed additional funds should be allocated.

First, there must be a way of making direct grants to serious and talented artists in all our states. The creative individual is central to our nation's art and we must ensure that Federal funds are used to develop the individual artist's special talents, not to establish unwieldy bureaucratic programs. The massive unemployment and unconsciously low incomes of productive artists dampen their energy, their skills and their inspiration. It is in our power to help artists and I believe we have an obligation to help them achieve a measure of economic security and dignity.

Secondly, I believe we must use Federal funds to encourage every American who wishes to become involved in the cultural life of his or her community. I think that coequal with the government's obligation to support our great symphonies, theaters and mu-

seums is its responsibility to use Federal funds to make these facilities open to the broadest possible spectrum of Americans. Good music and fine art should not be the exclusive domain of a wealthy or intellectual ethic. One of the most positive actions the Federal program could make would be to subsidize the performing arts so that they could be brought within the reach of all who love culture.

By relying almost entirely on private and commercial support for the arts it has been harder to develop a rich indigenous culture which results from the involvement of all Americans in every region of the country. An advantage to the government's playing a larger role in support for the arts is its ability to bring exhibits and displays to areas now without major museums or established theaters.

As part of my plan for increased funding for the arts, I have recommended the creation of regional and community centers where artists can work, where people can see and hear national companies and their own local artists, and where there will be the best equipment and space for artists to use and for students to learn. These community centers will allow for and encourage innovations in the arts.

My third major point in any discussion of the government and the arts is that there must be a minimum of governmental control. Too many government programs set out to assist but end up directing. Nothing can destroy the effectiveness of a national program more than that. This spring, theatergoers in Washington were shocked to learn that the scripts of plays performed at Ford's Theater—which is owned by the U.S. Department of the Interior—were being censored. President Nixon made no effort to prevent this interference. Only after considerable outcry did this censorship stop. I believe emphatically that our government should stop treating the arts as though they were a frill to be casually removed from the budget; but I believe just as strongly that the government must supply money only—not esthetic control or judgement.

In conclusion, I have been asked to comment on two points raised by the *Art in America* staff— the new tax laws covering gifts to museums and the question of reserving one percent of all Federal building funds for art improvements.

As you well know, I do not approve of tax loopholes of any kind. Unfortunately in the past, these loopholes were open to some abuse, and contributions and art donated to museums were used to avoid taxation. To the extent that new tax laws rectify this situation, I am for them. Charity and education should not be made excuses for a tax dodge. However, I certainly do not want to discourage giving for *art's* sake, at an honest value, for public benefit. If elected, I will therefore take a hard look at this problem and recommend improvements.

I fully support the retention of some small percentage of Federal building funds to be used for works of art. I am not certain that a fixed flat figure is the most workable suggestion. But I have long been concerned with the lack of artistic taste and excellence exhibited in many of our Federal buildings, and as President I will use the lever of Federal contracting to make improvements on both these counts.

A measure of any society is the quality of its art. Let us reflect the high aspirations of America in the splendor and freshness of its creative endeavor.

Senator George McGovern

Dear Mr. Wall:

The role of the arts is expanding in the United States. At the same time, artists and arts institutions are threatened by rising costs and their future is uncertain. *Art in America,* a year ago, devoted an entire issue to the troubled state of our museums. In his introduction to the issue, the Editor held that " . . . the museum is in a state of physical, financial, esthetic and spiritual disarray. Its survival as a viable institution . . . is in doubt. . . ."

On my desk, as I write, is an invitation from the American Museum of National History in New York. "Venga y traiga a sus amigos y familia," says the invitation. "Come and bring your friends and family" to celebrate West Side Day in the Museum. Eighty-seven organizations are participating in the festival. They range from the New York City Fire Department and the American Red Cross, to the Council for the Aging and Zero Population Growth. Those who attend the festival are invited to weave in the manner of the Plains Indians, to make jewelry in the manner of the Masai. They are invited to the museum as participants in the process of artistic creation, and not simply as passive recipients of "culture" to look at art objects, or at the performances staged by others.

I remembered, as I read this invitation, the warning of André Malraux that the sacred obligation of the museum is to compile and to keep intact the record of human freedom and creativeness, and that this obligation must not be adulterated in the name of popular appeal. I find nothing in the festival that

adulterates the role of the Museum of Natural History. On the contrary, the festival enables the museum to advance its central role of making its collections available and meaningful to all our citizens. It testifies to the vitality of a long-established institution in a major city, and it points to one means by which institutions such as the Museum of Natural History will survive.

Occasions such as the West Side Day were taking place throughout the nation this summer. Summerthing in Boston, the mini-festivals presented by the Cincinnati Symphony in the river towns of Ohio, the concerts, the dance performances, the plays presented in most of our city parks and streets, all testify to the growing demand of our citizens for the arts, and the growing desire of our artists to respond to that demand. It is a matter of deep satisfaction to President Nixon and those of us who work in his Administration that these activities are carried on with the support of a Federal agency, the National Endowment for the Arts.

President Nixon believes that " . . . the Federal Government has a vital role as catalyst, innovator, and supporter of the public and private efforts for cultural development. . . ." He has supported an extension of the National Foundation on the Arts and the Humanities, increased the funding of its two Endowments almost fivefold, and augmented Federal support to State Arts Councils in all states and jurisdictions.

That National Endowment for the Arts was, of course, created in 1965, when Congress passed the National Foundation on the Arts and the Humanities Act. The foresight of the leaders in both parties, who wrote the act and who secured its passage, has been amply demonstrated over the past seven years. Since there are some who look with impatience on our progress, and who point to the European patterns of patronage as preferable to our own, let me cite four aspects of the present act which in the President's view have proved their worth:

First, the act is designed to discourage political interference by the Congress or the Executive Branch with the operations of the Endowment. The Endowment is an independent agency vested with broad discretionary powers which, in turn, is guided by a twenty-six member National Council of private citizens representing diverse interests and constituencies in the arts.

Second, the Endowment is itself prohibited by the act from interfering in the operations of its grantees. Thus the threat of government domination if the arts is countered, and the freedom of the artist is protected.

Third, the Endowment grants to organizations are, as a general rule limited to no more than fifty percent of the costs of the projects that are supported. Thus, the role of the Federal Government is defined: It is to reinforce private and local initiative and patronage, rather than to create an official arts establishment.

Fourth, the act encourages, by direct funding, the activities of the State Arts Councils. By this means public patronage is strengthened and diversified, and the dangers of a centralized bureaucracy dominating the national art scene are effectively set aside.

The Endowment, in its early years, had little to build on in the way of traditions of public patronage, save for the pioneering contributions of the New York State Council of the Arts. It moved boldly in support of the professional core of artists, under the guidance of leaders such as David Smith and René d'Harnoncourt, who served on the Endowment's advisory body, the National Council on the Arts. A principal handicap, in the earliest years of the Endowment, was the low level at which it was funded. Its appropriations were stabilized at a level less than $8 million a year. At this level, it was impossible for the Endowment to undertake more than a few pilot projects in central and critical areas of art patronage: our symphony orchestras and museums.

The breakthrough for the Endowment came, in my opinion, when, on December 10, 1969, President Nixon sent to the Congress his Special Message on the Arts and Humanities. "Need and opportunity combine . . ." he told the Congress, "to present the Federal government with an obligation to help broaden the base of our cultural legacy—not to make it fit some common denominator of official sanction, but rather to make its diversity and insight more readily accessible to millions of people everywhere." The President then called on the Congress to extend the life of the National Foundation on the Arts and the Humanities, and to double its existing level of funding to $40 million in new funds for the Foundation in Fiscal 1971.

The Congress responded to the President's message. At his initiative, and with the support of both parties, appropriations have been raised close to the authorized ceilings set by Congress in each of the past three years, so that, in this year, more than $81 million was appropriated for programs and administration of the two divisions of the Foundation, the Arts and the Humanities Endowments—five times more than the level of spending when the President took office.

At this level of funding, both Endowments are able to give meaningful support to the cultural activities of the nation as they set out to survive by meeting the challenges of our time. In the museum field, to return to an area of particular interest to the readers of *Art in America,* the Humanities Endowment is undertaking to provide substantial assistance to museums for the training of personnel, for the mounting of interpretive exhibitions, and for the expansion of services related to education.

The Arts Endowment is offering fellowships and training programs for museum professionals and matching grants for utilization of permanent collections and for special exhibitions. It has moved to support our museums in the urgent and neglected tasks of conservation of works of art and of renovation of museums for preservation purposes. It has encouraged institutions to reach broader audiences and it has enabled almost one hundred museums to extend their collections by providing matching grants for the purchase of works by living American artists.

In addition, the Arts Endowment has supported individual artists through its commissioning and its fellowship programs. Large works by Calder, Noguchi and Rosati have been placed in Grand Rapids, Seattle and Wichita under a program in which experts appointed by the Endowment and local patrons and authorities work closely together. And over $1 million has been awarded in individual fellowships to 184 artists. By the letters that these artists have written, I have been convinced that the fellowships and commissions were indispensable aids in advancing their work and their careers.

The programs of the Arts Endowment and the Humanities Endowment are one means by which the President and the Congress are undertaking to advance the arts in the United States. Another means, given great emphasis by the President, is the upgrading of government standards in architecture and design. The Federal Government is the largest client in the nation, commissioning $6 billion worth of new construction each year. It has, over many years, neglected its responsibility for setting standards of excellence for the nation to follow.

In May, 1971, President Nixon called on the heads of all Federal executive agencies to determine ways by which their agencies could more vigorously assist the arts, and, in turn, how the arts might be used to enhance their programs. This year, in response to the first set of recommendations he received, the President initiated actions that will lead to an annual Design Assembly for Federal administrators and artists, a review of the established principles that guide Federal architecture, and an upgrading of all of the graphics work of the executive agencies. These actions reflected his expressed conviction that "the Federal Government has a critical role to play in encouraging better design."

It was in furtherance of the President's conviction that the General Services Administration reinstated a regulation permitting one-half of one percent of the cost of buildings constructed by the G.S.A. to be set aside for art works to be integrated in each building's design.

President Nixon has insisted at all times that Federal support for the arts be divorced from political considerations. He is proud of the bipartisan support which the Arts Endowment and the Humanities Endowment have enjoyed over the past four years. The arts are too sensitive, too subtle an area to be subjected to the rancor and the rhetoric of our traditional political campaigns.

Nonetheless, since public patronage is important to our artists and their audiences, and since it will be increasingly important from now on, the readers of *Art in America* are entitled to ask some precise and searching questions of the candidates. Will they strongly support the reauthorization of the Arts and Humanities Endowments, whose enabling legislation expires in June, 1973? Will they strongly support adequate appropriations for these endowments? Will they offer meaningful incentives to individuals, to foundations, to corporations and to state and local governments to provide increased support for the arts? And, will they be able to advance their commitments from promises written out on pages such as this, to programs whose impact is felt in the classrooms, the prison cells, the music halls, the theatres, the city streets, such as those that surround the Museum of Natural History?

Knowing President Nixon as I do, I can say yes with full conviction that for him, the answer to these questions is *yes*.

Leonard Garment
Special Consultant to the President

Further Resources

BOOKS

Benedict, Stephen, ed. *Public Money and the Muse: Essays on Government Funding for the Arts.* New York: Norton, 1991.

Biddle, Livingston. *Our Government and the Arts: A Perspective from the Inside.* New York: American Council for the Arts, 1988.

Netzer, Dick. *The Subsidized Muse: Public Support for the Arts in the United States.* Cambridge and New York: Cambridge University Press, 1978.

PERIODICALS

"A Conversation with Stanley N. Katz, Woodrow Wilson School, Center for Arts and Cultural Policy Studies, Princeton University." *National Arts Stabilization* 2, no. 3, Summer 1999. Available online at http://www.princeton.edu /~artspol/nasjartl.html; website home page: http://www .princeton.edu/ (accessed April 5, 2003).

Hart, P. "Some Observations on Government Funding." *High Fidelity* 24, November 1974, MA18–19.

WEBSITES

"Learn about the NEA." National Endowment for the Arts. Available online at http://arts.endow.gov/learn/Legislation .html; website home page: http://arts.endow.gov/ (accessed March 24, 2003).

A Legacy of Leadership: Investing in America's Cultural Heritage Since 1965. National Endowment for the Arts. Available online at http://www.arts.gov/pub/Legacy.pdf; website home page: http://arts.endow.gov/ (accessed March 24, 2003).

Valley Curtain
Environmental sculpture

By: Christo and Jeanne-Claude

Date: 1972

Source: Christo and Jeanne-Claude. *The Valley Curtain.* Available online at http://christojeanneclaude.net/vc.html; website home page: http://christojeanneclaude.net (accessed March 18, 2003).

About the Artists: Christo Javacheff (1935–) was born in Bulgaria and moved to the United States in 1964. Christo trained at the Fine Arts Academy in Sofia, Bulgaria, and the Vienna Fine Arts Academy in Austria.

Jeanne-Claude de Guillebon (1935–) studied Latin and Philosophy at the University of Tunis. They work as a team to create works of art. They have one son, Cyril, who is a poet. ∎

Introduction

Christo and Jeanne-Claude are primarily known for the temporary art installments they construct. Beginning in the early 1960s, they conceived and created art that made political and social statements. In 1962, a "Wall of Oil Drums" was constructed in Paris, a work that resembled the iron curtain. In 1969, "Wrapped Coast" in

Primary Source

Valley Curtain

SYNOPSIS: Construction of *The Valley Curtain* took 28 months. Ecological factors are always important in Christo and Jeanne-Claude's projects. The sites for the art work are returned to their natural state when the work is removed. "VALLEY CURTAIN, RIFLE, COLORADO, 1970–72," BY CHRISTO AND JEANNE-CLAUDE, PHOTOGRAPH BY HARRY SHUNK. © CHRISTO 1972. REPRODUCED BY PERMISSION OF CHRISTO AND JEANNE-CLAUDE.

Little Bay, Australia, was completed. The project was one and a half miles long and remained in place for ten weeks. Not harming the environment is always an important factor in planning and constructing the projects. Christo also creates smaller works of fine art which reside in museums and private collections.

Christo and Jeanne-Claude envision art in the real world. Their works are large pieces of sculpture, part art, part architecture and part urban planning, depending on the location. Years of planning and negotiation take place before the pieces are erected. Although Christo and Jeanne-Claude are responsible for creating the artistic visions, engineers collaborate with them to make them a reality.

Valley Curtain was first discussed in June 1970. A fabric wall would create "an energy that is the essence of the culture's physicality" (Chernow 200). In August and September of 1970, Christo and Jeanne-Claude searched for a valley near Aspen, Colorado, for the curtain that would be 1,200-feet wide. They chose Rifle Gap, between Grand Junction and Glenwood Spring, Colorado, and began negotiations with property owners and the State Highway Department. The project involved frustrations and continued negotiations. *Valley Curtain* required two attempts before the curtain hung across the gap. On August 10, 1972, at 8:15 A.M. the curtain was complete. Twenty-eight hours later winds of 60 mph tore the curtain and caused its removal.

Significance

Two factors made this a significant project for Christo and Jeanne-Claude. The first is the establishment of a corporation. The second is the perseverance that the project took to complete.

Christo and Jeanne-Claude incorporated as The Valley Curtain Corporation in November 1970. This allows them to act on their own, selling to museums, collectors, dealers and galleries. The money from Christo's original works of art funds the larger installations. No profit is retained, not even money back from the installations. The kind of artwork that Christo and Jeanne-Claude engage in can be dangerous for the workers or for the environment if something goes wrong. "Through that structure, we achieved the ultimate, which was limited liability for the artist. The Valley Curtain Corporation executed all the contracts" (Chernow 202).

The project was scheduled for the summer of 1971. Engineering errors and miscalculations prevented the progress on the project and ultimately it was not completed. The project pushed into the fall, with the weekend of October 8th set for completion. On October 9th the curtain "started to come loose and billow out, in agonizing slow motion, two hundred feet below the east-slope anchor" (Chernow 214). In an unbelievable sight, the curtain tore apart as orange sections flew through the valley. Financially and artistically, the first attempt was a loss.

The next spring, Christo and Jeanne-Claude and a new team returned to the site. This time the project began in June with the curtain arriving at the end of July and being raised by August 4. The fabric used for the *Valley Curtain* was an orange woven nylon. "By suspending the *Valley Curtain,* at a width of 381 meters (1,250 feet) and a height curving from 111 meters (365 feet) at each end to 55.5 meters (182 feet) at the center, the *Curtain* remained clear of the slopes and the Valley bottom. A 3-meter (10 foot) skirt attached to the lower part of the *Curtain* visually completed the area between the thimbles and the ground" (Christo & Jeanne-Claude *Valley Curtain*). On August 10, 1972, *The Valley Cur-*

Christo and Jeanne-Claude, 1978. © **MORTIN BEEBE/CORBIS. REPRODUCED BY PERMISSION.**

tain spread across the Rifle Gap. It would not remain in place for long, tearing apart after only 28 hours. It lasted long enough to amaze viewers and to be filmed by the Maysles brothers.

Further Resources

BOOKS

Chernow, Burt. *Christo and Jeanne-Claude: A Biography.* New York: St. Martin's Press, 2002.

Christo. *Christo: Valley Curtain, Rifle, Colorado, 1970–72.* New York: Harry N. Abrams, 1973.

LaPorte, Dominique G. *Christo.* New York: Pantheon Books, 1986.

Vaizey, Marino. *Christo.* New York: Rizzoli, 1990.

PERIODICALS

Van Der Marck, Jan. "The Valley Curtain." *Art in America* 60, no. 3, May-June 1972, 54–67.

———. "The Valley Curtain is Up! But . . ." *Art in America* 61, no. 1, January-February, 1973, 75–77.

WEBSITES

"Christo and Jeanne-Claude." Available online at http://www .christojeanneclaude.net/ (accessed March 18, 2003).

Christo and Jeanne-Claude: Valley Curtain, Rifle, Colorado, 1970–72. Available online at http://christojeanneclaude .net/vc.html; website home page: http://christojeanneclaude .net (accessed April 17, 2003).

AUDIO AND VISUAL MEDIA

Christo's Valley Curtain. 1973. New York: Maysles Films. Directed by Albert Maysles, David Maysles, Ellen Giffard. VHS.

The Godfather
Movie stills

By: Francis Ford Coppola and Mario Puzo

Date: 1972

Source: *The Godfather.* Original release 1972, Paramount. Directed by Francis Ford Coppola. VHS, 2002, Paramount Studio; Godfather DVD Collection [includes parts I, II, and III], 2001, Paramount Home Video.

About the Artist: Francis Ford Coppola (1939–), director and writer, was born in Detroit, Michigan, but grew up near New York City in a large Italian American family. His father was a concert flautist, and his mother was an actress. After attending Hofstra College in Hempstead, New York, Coppola earned a film degree from the University of California Los Angeles. His Zoetrope Studios produces large and small films, his Niebaum-Coppola Estate produces and markets wine, and the Café Niebaum-Coppola is a combination wine bar, café, and retail store with locations in San Francisco and Palo Alto, California. Coppola won an Academy Award in 1972 for Best Director of *The Godfather.*

Mario Puzo (1920–1999) was a novelist and screenwriter. Born in New York, he attended the New School for Social Research and then Columbia University. He served in the U.S. Army Air Force during World War II. Puzo wrote his best-selling novel *The Godfather* in 1969. Puzo received an Academy Award for his screenplay for *The Godfather* in 1972 and *The Godfather, Part 2* in 1974. ■

Primary Source

The Godfather

SYNOPSIS: Francis Ford Coppola insisted on lesser known actors for the sons. Al Pacino, (left) who was unknown in films at the time, played Michael. James Caan (second right) portrayed Sonny and Robert Duvall (not pictured) the role of Tom Hagan, Don Vito Corleone's adopted son. John Cazale (right) played the Godfather's second son Fredo. © BETTMANN/CORBIS. REPRODUCED BY PERMISSION.

Primary Source

The Godfather

In a scene from the movie version of Mario Puzo's novel *The Godfather,* mafia Don Vito Corleone gestures as he speaks.
© CORBIS. REPRODUCED BY PERMISSION.

Introduction

Mario Puzo's novel, *The Godfather,* sold 500,000 hardcover copies and more than ten million paperback copies before the movie was released. Paramount Films purchased the rights to the film prior to the phenomenal success of the book. The film was controversial before production began because portrayals of the mafia and Italian Americans in the novel disturbed the Italian American Civil Rights League. When Francis Ford Coppola was hired as director, he agreed to eliminate the ethnically charged terms "mafia" and "cosa nostra" from the film to address the concerns.

Puzo and Coppola collaborated on the screenplay, as they would on the two sequels. Coppola objected to some of what he called the "sleazy" parts of the novel and insisted that they be removed. Puzo agreed, though according to Thomas Letich he "maintained that *The God-*

father was essentially a film about a family that happened to be in crime rather than a crime film whose criminal organization happened to be that of a family."

The Godfather told the story of the Corleone family between 1945 and 1952. Don Vito Corleone, the patriarch of a large multigenerational family, struggles with the underworld bosses for power and in transferring the family values to his sons. The novel explores themes of crime, love, and family as well as the Old World values of the family. Three sons wait to inherit their father's position, but only one is truly considered worthy. Michael, the youngest son and a war hero, becomes a more treacherous leader than his father ever imagined.

Significance

The Godfather premiered March 12, 1972. It was an immediate success with audiences and critics. Coppola

Francis Ford Coppola, director of *The Godfather*, 1972. **THE KOBAL COLLECTION/PARAMOUNT. REPRODUCED BY PERMISSION.**

Coppola took great pains to obtain the correct milieu. He had not been the first choice for director and had to fight for what he thought the movie needed, including filming on location in Sicily and props and settings from the 1940s. His insistence on detail made this a special film.

Further Resources

BOOKS
Browne, Nick, ed. *Francis Ford Coppola's Godfather Trilogy.* Cambridge and New York: Cambridge University Press, 2000.

Cowie, Peter. *Coppola: A Biography.* New York: Da Capo, 1994.

Leitch, Thomas M. *Crime Films.* Cambridge and New York: Cambridge University Press, 2002.

PERIODICALS
Canby, Victor. "Bravo, Brando's 'Godfather.'" *The New York Times,* March 12, 1972, sec. II, 1, 25.

"The Making of *The Godfather.*" *Time,* March 13, 1972, 57–58, 61.

WEBSITES
Malta, J. Geoff. "Mario Puzo's The Godfather." Available online at http://www.jgeoff.com/puzo/godfather/godfather.html; website home page: http://www.jgeoff.com/ (accessed April 6, 2003).

Virtanen, Panu S. "Francis Ford Coppola." Available online at http://film.tierranet.com/films/a.now/coppola.html; website home page: http://film.tierranet.com (accessed April 6, 2003).

"Zoetrope Studios." Available online at http://www.zoetrope.com/ (accessed April 6, 2003).

had succeeded in transforming a standard genre, the crime film, into an epic event. Nick Browne wrote that "The distinctiveness of Coppola's and Puzo's adaptation of Puzo's novel lies in its reinterpretation of the generic conventions of the crime film in the direction of the family melodrama and epic. It is this transformation of subject matter that gives the films their popular appeal." Writing, acting, and cinematography contributed to the success of the film with audiences, and the later sequels.

Coppola chose actor Marlon Brando for the lead. The reviewer in *Time* wrote, "Brando's stunning performance seemed to spur the entire cast. Coppola, working from the emotional inside of his subject, was able to succeed as few American film makers have in evoking the texture and variety of an ethnic subculture." In *The New York Times,* Victor Canby reflected that the "film has a life that completely eluded me in the novel." Further, he noted that the film "has about it, in fact, the quality of a romantic fable whose principal characters are in some ways charmed . . . ." William Petcher, in *Commentary,* as quoted by Nick Browne, recognized the "special excitement and authority available to a film which is both a work of artistic seriousness and one of truly popular appeal, a mass entertainment made without pandering or condescension."

"The Stages of Joseph Papp"
Journal article

By: Stanley Kauffmann

Date: 1974

Source: Kauffmann, Stanley. "The Stages of Joseph Papp." *The American Scholar* 44, no.1, Winter 1974–75, 110, 116–121.

About the Author: Stanley Kauffmann (1916–) is a film and theater critic for *The New Republic.* He received a Bachelor of Fine Arts degree in 1935 from New York University. His work also appears in *Saturday Review, The American Scholar,* and *Salmagundi.* Kauffmann has taught classes in film and theater and written several books on the subjects. He was awarded the George Jean Nathan Award in 1972–73 for dramatic criticism, and the Guggenheim Fellowship in 1979–80. ■

Introduction

Stanley Kauffmann called theatrical producer Joseph Papp (1921–1991) the most important figure in American theater in the 1970s. Papp, born to immigrant parents, served in the U.S. Navy and then returned to New York City. His love of theater and especially for Shakespeare was evident long before the 1970s.

Like the mission of the National Endowment for the Arts (NEA) programs funded by the federal government, Joseph Papp had a vision to include all people in theater. Papp noted the changing demographics of New York City and realized the need to reach new audiences. His productions included casts from different ethnic backgrounds and he produced plays from various cultures. By the 1970s, his reputation in the theater allowed him to draw on private and public sources for funding.

Papp did not shy away from controversy. Kauffmann outlines Papp's decisions, made when he took over Lincoln Center, to relegate the Beaumont Theater to new works and the Newhouse Theater to Shakespeare. The move was typical of Papp. While some of the new plays were heralded as successful, others were not. The plan was modified in the next seasons to include a mix of old and new plays.

Reviews that were critical of his work brought aggressive responses from Papp. Kauffmann had been critical of Papp's productions in the past and relates his personal experience with Papp's attitude. Despite this, Kauffmann recognizes Papp's talent and successes.

Significance

Joseph Papp had a long career in the theater. Beginning in the 1950s and ending with his death in 1991, Papp influenced what was performed in several on and off Broadway venues. His successes on Broadway, such as the 1975 *Chorus Line,* funded the lesser-known plays off Broadway. Grants and private funding also provided opportunities for plays to be staged and audiences to attend them who otherwise might not have had the opportunity.

An important aspect of Papp's career was his attitude toward access. Plays were seen as a necessary part of the cultural landscape. He recognized the difficulty of being a new playwright and trying to break into an established world. Papp provided opportunities for new playwrights and continued to showcase their work even when some plays were not successful. His longtime passion for Shakespeare is also important. Although Kauffmann is critical of some of the productions that had been repeated, Papp took chances on staging Shakespeare in new ways to attract audiences. His production in 1971 of *Two Gentleman of Verona* featured a rock score, a Puerto Rican as Proteus, and an African American as Silva. Kaufmann remarked, "The whole tone of the production

was: "See? Shakespeare can be fun. Forget all about the poetry and all that Elizabethan stuff. We can make it *now.* Watch. Listen." The mixture of ethnic groups in casts also encouraged a wider audience to attend plays.

Perhaps most important was Papp's attitude toward the audience. Since he commanded several stages in New York, he could provide plays to a range of audiences who had a range of financial abilities. The Central Park Shakespeare Festival was free, while the Public Theater featured low-cost tickets. The Public Theater was renamed in his honor in 1992 and continues to strive to remain an affordable theater.

Primary Source

"The Stages of Joseph Papp" [excerpt]

> **SYNOPSIS:** The pun on "stages" is obvious as one reads Kauffmann's article. Not only had Papp developed as a director and producer in two decades, but he had also directed on many stages in New York. Papp's socially conscious ideas about theater changed attitudes toward productions and attendance at plays.

Everyone who publishes theater criticism in New York has a Joseph Papp story. Here is mine. In October 1970 the late Jack MacGowran appeared in a Broadway play that flopped. Papp evidently knew that MacGowran had done a program of Beckett readings six months earlier in Paris with Beckett's approval; and Papp promptly whisked MacGowran downtown to do the Beckett readings in one of his theaters. I saw the program, enjoyed it greatly, and reviewed it favorably in the *New Republic.* Because I had recently written adverse comments on several Papp productions, I thought it only fair to note in my review that MacGowran was being presented on one of the stages of the Public Theater, "whose producer, Joseph Papp, whatever his defects, is certainly not short on energy and enterprise."

At 9:00 A.M. on the day that the review appeared, Papp telephoned me and said angrily, "What do you mean, my defects?"

Well, this article is what I mean, but it is also what I mean about his virtues. Whatever one's opinion of this or the other of his many productions, Papp demands serious discussion because he is an insistent cultural phenomenon. He is now unquestionably the most prominent person in the American theater. He operates in New York, which, unfortunately, is still the theater capital of the United States and thus the capital of theater publicity. He operates in almost every field of the contemporary theater. He

Broadway producer Joseph Papp. AP/WIDE WORLD PHOTOS.
REPRODUCED BY PERMISSION.

began and still works on Off Broadway. He has produced on Broadway. He is busy in the workshop-experimental sector called Off Off Broadway. He runs a summer Shakespeare festival in Central Park and some mobile theaters that tour greater New York. And, cutting across all these categories, he has long been active as a producer of black theater, presenting plays written, directed, and performed by blacks.

All his activities have been intertwined with a policy of free admissions, where possible, and low-priced tickets where it isn't, and with theater committed to social relevance and community service. Papp contrasts vividly with the previous most prominent individual in the American theater, David Merrick, who was in the spotlight during the 1960s. Merrick was the quintessential smooth, clever, ruthless, big-business operator, a rapist of success, a producer whose shows were sometimes mammoth hits *(Hello, Dolly)* but were uninteresting in any serious way even when they were hits. He made enough money to establish a tax-loss foundation that occasionally produced a valuable play that had been proved elsewhere *(Marat/Sade)*, but neither in this foundation work nor in his original productions did

he show any distinct taste or policy, and his career has had no effect whatever except on his and other bank accounts. Papp is a very different Number One figure. I think it is fair to say that Papp is more interested in his policy and his goals than he is in any one production. The productions implement the policy—something for which there is no analogy in Merrick. To investigate the Papp policy, how it grew and where it led, we must begin at the beginning. . . .

These two problems, one obvious and one subtle, cannot be solved by any manager of the Lincoln Center theaters; nevertheless, they face him, obviously and subtly, if he wants to establish a theater comparable with the famous ones of the world, which had ostensibly been the original aim. Those problems, added to the various personal deficiencies of the different managers, had ground down the administrations before Papp arrived. So grievously had the theater suffered in reputation that it was in terrible financial straits. Like the New York Philharmonic and the Metropolitan Opera, which are also at the Lincoln Center, the theater runs at a loss; unlike the Philharmonic and the Metropolitan, the theater attracted relatively little in donations and subsidies because no one had much faith in it or got much réclame from supporting it. That, quite clearly, was one of the reasons Papp was chosen. He could attract money.

From that point of view he was unquestionably the best choice. He was hot. He was rising. He seemed, in the public's eye and in the eyes of most of the eager New York critical corps, to be incapable of doing much wrong. He was fast becoming a municipal hero. Little could have pleased Papp more than the *New Yorker* cartoon that appeared shortly after his Lincoln Center appointment. It showed the Manhattan skyline and, arching over it like a rainbow, the legend "A Joseph Papp Production." The cartoon was striking because it made one think that this was what Papp had had in mind all along, particularly since he didn't give up anything to take on Lincoln Center. He just added those two theaters to his string.

One of the first announcements that he made in relation to his new post was about money. In March 1973 he said, "Before we put one foot in the door, we must have in hand or in assurances $5 million." He set a deadline for May. By May he had put some feet in the door without that sum, but he had done astonishingly well. Mrs. Mitzi E. Newhouse had given him a million—the downstairs Forum was renamed in her honor—and there were healthy assurances and prospects from various foundations and government agencies.

A second simultaneous announcement was radically more important. Papp exactly reversed previous Lincoln Center theater policy. The larger theater upstairs, the Beaumont, which had lamely been trying to become our leading "standard" theater, would be devoted to new plays, responsive to our era and problems. The smaller theater below it, now the Newhouse, which had formerly been used for new plays, would present Shakespeare. Part of the reason for this change may have been that Papp sensed the impossibility of licking the twofold Beaumont artistic problem outlined above. Part of it certainly was that he had his lines out to new writers and didn't want to subordinate work. Certainly, too, part of the reason was that he wanted, on his arrival, to set off a bombshell. The new policy meant that Papp could strengthen his affinities with working writers, could avoid imitation-European booby traps, and could run a Shakespeare Festival year round. It was, as theory, ingenious. The policy spelled death, or at least deep discouragement, for any major attempt at a "living museum" of dramatic heritage in New York, but it was congenial to Papp's temperament and it provided the new-broom impact that he wanted.

Prices at Lincoln Center had to be higher than at the Public Theater, where they are still low and where workshop productions are free. Summer Shakespeare in the Park is, of course, still free. And it is possible for anyone under twenty-five or over sixty-five or a full-time student of any age to buy a pass that gets him into plays at Lincoln Center for $3 each. Regular subscription prices go as high as $10 per, not much by Broadway levels but I'm sure discomfiting to Papp.

He began his productions at Lincoln Center in the fall of 1973, as the master of six theaters in New York as well as of various halls and mobile units. The official statement by his press representative said: "Since 1956, the Festival [still the collective name for Papp enterprises] has presented 77 admission-free shows; since 1967 at the Public Theater complex, 59. The first year's budget was $750; the coming five-year projection is $35,848,000." In Papp's own words about himself, he is "in a commanding position to exert an influence on the course of American theater."

His first Lincoln Center production, therefore, was in the eye of the spotlight and the storm. The play was *Boom Boom Room* by David Rabe. Papp had previously produced three Rabe plays at the Pub-

lic Theater, all of which, as it happens, I had disliked in varying degrees. The first two, *The Basic Training of Pavlo Hummel* and *Sticks and Bones,* were "undergraduate" antiwar plays, with gimmicks, although the second was occasionally somewhat better than that. They were cheered and garlanded, and Papp made extravagant remarks about the young author. The third play, *The Orphan,* was a complicated antiwar allegory that to me simply revealed more nakedly the sophomoric mind that had been there all along; and this time the press demurred— though, naturally, Papp was unshaken. More as if to prove his point about Rabe rather than out of a continuum of faith, Papp chose this new Rabe play to launch the new Lincoln Center. After the premiere there were published reports that Rabe himself thought the play was not ready for production—Rabe said he wasn't sure he had let the play "gestate" long enough—which lends credence to the belief that the production was more a willed act of personal vindication and suzerainty for Papp than of conviction about the readiness and worth of the play.

In the event *Boom Boom Room* turned out to be one more sophomoric exercise, this time about the sexual victimization of a Philadelphia go-go girl who ends up as a topless dancer in New York. Rabe had no more to say on the much-mooted matter of sexism than he had to say about Vietnam. Again, he had thought of one melodramatic central image— this time it was go-go girls hanging in cages above the stage throughout the play—and had filled in the interstices, which happened to be the play itself, with adolescent insights and cliché characters. Moreover, it was clumsily directed by Papp himself, who had stepped in to save the show from the first director, an Off Off Broadway amateur named Julie Bovasso.

Some of the critical response was what Papp must have wanted, but among other reviews (including mine) the most influential notice, by Clive Barnes in the *New York Times,* was heavily adverse. When he learned of Barnes's review, Papp went into the most extreme spasm of outrage in his career. As my opening anecdote shows, he has always been eager to contend with critics; he has always felt free to counterattack. This is neither new with Papp nor unwelcome; why shouldn't the subject of a criticism have the right to respond? But Papp's responses had usually had about them a sublimation of ego injury in a glow of civic outrage. The implicit air had been that to attack his plays meant attacking his policy—theater for the people—and was thus a sort of civic treason. Now, on this particularly tender occasion, when people were watching to see (a) whether he had overextended himself and (b) whether he could beat the Beaumont jinx, the Barnes notice provoked responses, too trivial to detail here, that indicated a change in Papp—a metamorphosis from dauntless guardian of public policy to towering egotist, outraged by dissent. Suffice it to say that, as a result of the brouhaha, a few months later at another Papp opening, there was a reported near-bout of fisticuffs between Papp and another critic, with Barnes figuring in it.

The revved-up aggression—again without long-distance psychoanalysis—is inescapably revealing. It kept revving up: soon after the Rabe opening Papp made a trip to Minneapolis and delivered a speech in which he berated the Guthrie Theater there for its lack of attention to new plays dealing with our lives. Then he came home and, for his next Beaumont production, did *The Au Pair Man,* a feeble allegory about the decline of the British Empire by an Irish writer, Hugh Leonard. This controversion of his own angry pronunciamento is, in its way, a confirmation of afflatus—putting himself above the requirements of his own stated policy, to which he wants to hold others.

As for the following three plays in Papp's first Beaumont season, each of them shows something significant about him. His next was *What the Wine-Sellers Buy* by Ron Milner, a black play by a black playwright; and it contained the first bit of deliberate whoring that I have seen in a Papp theater. The entire movement of the play, which was about ghetto life in Detroit, inexorably predicted a grim ending; in the last few minutes, either with Papp's permission or prescription, a happy ending was contrived. This was another facet of a new Papp, with concern for a kind of success he had never wooed before. Presumably he was acting on the Broadway and old-Hollywood line that ninety percent truth is better than none. He had never before rationalized or compromised in this way, to my knowledge. It didn't work now. Barnes of the *Times,* possibly chastened by the rough time Papp had given him on the Rabe play, was only one of the critics who blinked indulgently at the cop-out ending, but the play fizzled.

Next came a revival of Strindberg's *Dance of Death,* played for laughs under A. J. Antoon's direction and wasteful of Robert Shaw's power in the role of the Captain. Aside from questions about the performance itself, Papp's third production, after all the manifestos about new plays, after the excoriation of the Guthrie, was a revival. True, he had said in his

proclamation in the Beaumont program: "In some instances a 'great' old play may take the slot of a 'good' new play, but I suspect that this will be the exception, not the rule." The exception turned up pretty early, and again Papp controverted his own dicta with perfect coolness.

The season's last Beaumont production was *Short Eyes,* a new play by Miguel Piñero about a New York house of detention. I thought that, though well directed by Marvin Felix Camillo, it lolled about in what a friend of mine called "the pornography of bad conditions." But what was most interesting about it in terms of Papp's career was the play's provenance. He had produced it first on his main stage downtown at the Public Theater where it had made a hit. So he had moved it uptown to Lincoln Center. This indicated, first, that there was a vacancy in that last "slot," which contradicts his repeated statements in interviews that he has a wealth of new plays on hand that deserve to be produced even if they are not successes. And, second, it underscored the idea of hierarchy, of comparative rank between downtown and the Big Time. Before he had an uptown station, Papp moved some hit shows to Broadway from downtown or from Central Park so that they might pump money into his Off Broadway operations. Now, established uptown, he gave grounds for the suspicion that the emphasis had been reversed. By this move of *Short Eyes* and by hints he dropped later, it seemed that he was beginning to think of his other theaters, either by design or duress, as tryout stops for Lincoln Center.

His three Shakespeare productions at the Newhouse in 1973–74 were *Troilus and Cressida, The Tempest,* and *Macbeth.* The last of these was never officially opened: that is, it played for some weeks to subscribers and other ticket-buyers, but the press was never invited to review it. I saw some of *Macbeth* and thought it not notably worse than the first two; but the important point is that all three of these productions also showed something new in Papp. With the single exception of a *Hamlet* that Papp himself directed in 1967 in apparent imitation of the absurdist Shakespeare that Peter Brook and Charles Marowitz had done in London, his Shakespeare in the previous decade had been populist in intent. All three of these new productions were mannered and elitist, the work of directors whose ambitions were aesthetically pitiful but sheerly aesthetic. Again, an overall sense of "uptown" ambition.

Papp's concurrent season down at the Public Theater was skimpier than in previous years because, one can deduce, of his new uptown activities. The only success was *Short Eyes,* which turned into a lifesaving stopgap for the Beaumont. Nevertheless my two most interesting experiences of the Papp year took place downtown.

During the winter of 1973 he presented a musical down there called *More Than You Deserve.* It wanted to be a kind of black-humor inversion of *South Pacific* set in Vietnam and was only partially effective; but evidently it was sharp enough to irritate some patriotic folk because there was a bomb scare during the performance I attended. The theater was cleared while the police investigated. Within minutes Papp appeared, summoned from home, tieless and disheveled. He consulted with the police, then mixed with the audience waiting outside, chatting and explaining. When we were permitted to return to the auditorium, Papp spoke briefly, explaining and apologizing and joking, in the role of Your Friendly Neighborhood Theater Manager, and the audience loved it. They knew him, he knew them, and they had all just been through a common experience. I felt I was seeing the best, purely societal side of the man. It was the quintessential Pappian hour, the fruit of twenty years' public service, and I'm glad I was there.

And also at the Public Theater I saw an unsatisfactory production that was, for me, the most rewarding Papp venture of the year, uptown or down: a dramatization of Norman Mailer's second novel, *Barbary Shore.* It was adapted and directed by Jack Gelber, who wrote *The Connection* and has since directed frequently, but I had the feeling that it had been done unconventionally—that it had not begun with a neatly typed script which had then been memorized by actors but that it was a work of exploration. I had the feeling that Gelber had asked Papp for a place and some funds in order to work on a theater version of the novel. Much of the result was valuable. Two of the actors were Estelle Parsons, who could have done the slatternly wife in her sleep but was very wide-awake, and Rip Torn as the Irish radical. Torn's Irish accent was pathetic, but he increased my respect for him as a successful actor trying to grow, to extend his imagination, to make demands on himself that our theater generally neither encourages nor permits. (James Earl Jones, who has grown in good measure through Papp productions, is another example.) I had just been greatly impressed by Torn's performance as an egomaniacal country-music singer in a neglected film called *Payday,* and here again I was impressed with the

Stanley Kauffmann often reviewed Joseph Papp's work for *The New Republic.* **KAUFFMANN, STANLEY, PHOTOGRAPH. REPRODUCED BY PERMISSION.**

range that Torn was claiming and in good measure justifying, with Gelber's help. I left feeling happy that there was a theater locus where such work could be done by people already well along in their professional lives.

Any comment on Papp is obviously an interim report. This is underscored by three announcements made while I have been writing this article (early summer 1974), all of them sharply pertinent to it. First, Papp announced that he had gone to Olso to conclude deals with Liv Ullmann and Ingmar Bergman. Ullman will play at the Beaumont in the 1974–75 season in *A Doll's House.* The following year Bergman will direct *Rosmersholm* there. Second, Papp announced that within seven months or so he will direct a film version of Rabe's *Boom Boom Room.* Third, he announced that Al Pacino will play in a workshop production, downtown, of Brecht's *Resistible Rise of Arturo Ui.* "We will evaluate it and then groom it for the Vivian Beaumont," said Papp.

The first item forecasts the trajectory of Papp's future. His new subscription mailer has already told us that his exception-and-rule pronouncement about old and new plays has been discarded, that in the 1974–75 season three new plays and one revival will be presented. (This not only fixes the mixture, it reduces the total by one.) Patently Papp's resolute reliance on new works is modified; patently too he has seized the chance given by his new post to soar out into international wheeling and dealing. I'll be grateful for the chance to see Ullmann's and Bergman's theater work: that's not what is at issue. The point is the change in Papp, as against his past and his predictions, and what it means for his theater. The Ullman-Bergman arrangement is a managerial coup, not an act of creative imagination.

The film venture, in the light of the Rabe play's history, could be called kinetic camouflage: Papp, by persisting with the script, can show he is undaunted and can "vindicate" his questionable judgement about it, he apparently believes. Will he also make films of *The Au Pair Man* and *What the Wine-Sellers Buy?* Will the failure of any Beaumont script mean automatically that Papp will try to redeem it with a show of unshaken faith in another medium?

Also, of course, the announcement highlights something that used to be naturally true of Papp, and that is now almost a conscious performance: his protean business.

The Pacino announcement is less startling as a coup because Pacino has already played at Lincoln Center (wretchedly, in Williams's *Camino Real*) and, after his *Godfather* success, played Shakespeare with a small company in Boston. But Papp's comment on the matter confirms the hierarchical feeling prompted by the *Short Eyes* switch. Some of his theaters are now more important than others. His heart is in the highlands.

The summer Shakespeare Festival in Central Park was reduced to two plays in 1973 and remains at two in 1974. A faint air of enforced attention, like that of a somewhat bored but faithful husband, begins to hang over the event.

Further Resources

BOOKS

Epstein, Helen. *Joe Papp: An American Life.* Boston: Little, Brown, 1994.

Little, Stuart W. *Enter Joseph Papp: In Search of a New American Theater.* New York: Coward, McCann & Geoghegan, 1974.

PERIODICALS

Interview with Joseph Papp. *America* 136, January 15, 1977, 35–36.

Papp's Universal Theater. *Newsweek,* July 3, 1972, 52–56.

WEBSITES

The Public Theater Online. Available online at http://www.publictheater.org/ (accessed April 6, 2003).

Young Frankenstein
Movie stills

By: Mel Brooks

Date: 1974

Source: *Young Frankenstein.* Original release, 1974, Twentieth Century Fox. Directed by Mel Brooks. Special Edition, DVD/VHS, 2001, Twentieth Century Fox Home Entertainment.

About the Artist: Mel Brooks (1926–) is a comedian, writer, actor, film director, and producer. Born Melvin Kaminsky in New York, he is the son of a process server and a garment worker. He worked as a stand-up comic. As a teen, Brooks learned to play drums from Buddy Rich. He wrote television scripts for Sid Caesar's *Your Show of Shows* during the 1950s. Along with Buck Henry, Brooks created the 1965 TV

Comedian Mel Brooks. **AP/WIDE WORLD PHOTOS. REPRODUCED BY PERMISSION.**

Primary Source

Young Frankenstein

SYNOPSIS: Marty Feldman plays the character Igor in the Mel Brooks directed *Young Frankenstein*. Mel Brooks employs many of the same cast members from film to film. Gene Wilder and Madeline Kahn were also in Brooks's *Blazing Saddles*. Feldman, an Englishman, was new and added an extra wackiness to the part of Igor. THE KOBAL COLLECTION. REPRODUCED BY PERMISSION.

comedy, *Get Smart.* He won the Academy Award for best short subject in 1963 for *The Critic.* He also won the Nebula Award for dramatic writing and the Writers Guild Award in 1976, both for *Young Frankenstein.* Brooks was honored with the American Comedy Awards Lifetime Achievement Award in 1987. ∎

Introduction

Mary Shelley's 1818 gothic horror story *Franken-stein, or The Modern Prometheus* has inspired many film versions, both serious and satiric. James Whale directed the definitive version starring Boris Karloff as the monster in the 1931. In the 1935 *Bride of Franken-stein,* a classic sequel, Whale cast Elsa Lancaster as both Mary Shelley and the bride built for the monster. *Ab-bott and Castello Meet Frankenstein* (1948) is a spoof

of the story. But it was Mel Brooks who tackled Shelley's story, Whale's films, and the genre of horror films to create a parody that continues to make audiences laugh.

In Shelley's novel, the idealistic Frankenstein creates a monster that is so awful that it frightens everyone who sees it. Eventually the monster murders several people. Frankenstein follows the monster to the Arctic, but dies before he can destroy the monster. In the end the monster retreats to destroy itself. Brooks follows the story as far as the creation of the monster and its desire for female companionship. He twists the macabre ending, however, to create a lovable monster. Brooks and Gene Wilder's Frankenstein (played by Wilder in the film) is a neurosurgeon who learns that he has inherited the

Primary Source

Young Frankenstein

Gene Wilder and Peter Boyle play out a scene from the 1974 movie *Young Frankenstein*. THE KOBAL COLLECTION/20TH CENTURY FOX. REPRODUCED BY PERMISSION.

family castle in Transylvania. He denies his lineage, insisting that his name is "Fronk-enstein" instead of the original pronunciation. In Transylvania he discovers that his great grandfather's theories were not crackpot notions and he, too, creates life. This version is serious and satiric. Brooks inserts the need for love into the film, which creates humorous scenes between Frankenstein, the monster (Peter Boyle), and the housekeeper, Frau Blucher (Cloris Leachman). Igor, played by Marty Feldman, finds a brain from A.B. Normal. In the end, the monster and the doctor are married to their loves, and they both get what they need in a switch.

Significance

Comedy writing, themes, and technical style all make the movie *Young Frankenstein* important in Brooks's oeuvre of films. The comedy is sometimes physical and sometimes verbal. Brooks and Wilder remained true to Shelley's text for some lines in the film but also parodied both the novel and the previous Frankenstein movies. In *Young Frankenstein,* the novel is titled *How I Did It* and is Frederick Frankenstein's guidebook to his great grandfather's experiment. Igor, or "Eye-gor" as Feldman's character changes his name to, has a moveable hump that unnerves the doctor, and Wilder becomes more hysterical as the film progresses, depicting the madness of the good doctor. Brooks told Paul Zimmerman that he wanted "the truth behind horror conventions, the way real people—crazy, but real—would behave in that castle. And I wanted to do it with the greatest affection for those great old films."

The theme of love and the tension between modern science and the Frankenstein myth play important roles in making this film a great comedy. Love calms the monster. Music reaches his soul, and Wilder's character telling him that he is a "good boy" is what temporarily brings him to peace. The first scene in Frankenstein's classroom and the reactions of the townspeople when they hear another Frankenstein inhabits the castle exhibit the tensions and fears of myth versus reality. In the end, the monster receives part of Frankenstein's brain to make him more human, and Frankenstein receives part of the monster's physical body to make him more of a man.

Finally, the technical style of the film is perfect for the story. Shot in black and white, the film recalls the look and feel of the films of the thirties. Trick candle effects, electrical discharges, and low hanging fog add to the atmosphere. The greatest discovery may have been Ken Strickfaden, who worked with James Whale, and who, in his garage, still had part of the original laboratory from the 1931 film, which was able to be used for Brooks's movie. Make-up artists had to be creative to produce the desired effects of light and dark, as did the cameramen.

More than a quarter century after its release, the movie remains a classic spoof on horror films and a tribute to the talent of Brooks and his crew and cast.

Further Resources

BOOKS

Desser, David, and Lester D. Friedman. *American–Jewish Filmmakers: Traditions and Trends.* Urbana: University of Illinois Press, 1993.

Tropp, Martin. *Mary Shelley's Monster: The Story of Frankenstein.* Boston: Houghton Mifflin, 1976.

PERIODICALS

Albert, Hollis. "Comedy: The New King." *Saturday Review: World* 2, November 2, 1974, 52–53.

Hirschfeld, Gerald. "The Story Behind the Filming of Young Frankenstein." *American Cinematographer* 55, no. 7, July 1974, 802–805, 840–842.

Zimmerman, Paul D. "The Mad Mad Mel Brooks." *Newsweek,* February 17, 1975, 54–63.

WEBSITES

Dirks, Tim. "Young Frankenstein." Available online at http://www.filmsite.org/youn.html; website home page: http://www.filmsite.org/ (accessed April 7, 2003).

"Young Frankenstein." Twentieth Century Fox Home Entertainment. Available online at http://www.foxhome.com/youngfrankenstein/index_frames.html; website home page: http://www.foxhome.com/ (accessed April 7, 2003).

AUDIO AND VISUAL MEDIA

Shelley, Mary. *Frankenstein.* Originally released 1931, Universal Studios. Directed by James Whale. DVD/VHS, 2001, Universal Home Video.

Carrie
Novel

By: Stephen King

Date: 1974

Source: King, Stephen. *Carrie: A Novel of a Girl with a Frightening Power.* New York: Doubleday, 1974.

About the Author: Stephen King (1947–) was born in Portland, Maine. At the age of twelve he and his brother bought a mimeograph machine and published a small newspaper for which they charged five cents per copy. King earned a Bachelor of Science degree in 1970 from the University of Maine at Orono. Before becoming a well-known author, King worked at a laundry service and as a gas station attendant, and taught high school. He has also written several novels under the pseudonym "Richard Bachman." ■

Introduction

Stephen King does not remember a time when he did not write. Prior to publishing his first novel, *Carrie,* King had published seven short horror stories. He also had four novels rejected. He was close to giving up on his dream of writing when the idea for *Carrie* came to him. It began as a short story partially on a dare to write a believable female character. His wife helped him realize the potential for a novel.

King often relies on the everyday experiences in life to create his gothic worlds. For *Carrie,* he used the world of high school, one that he knew from experience and from teaching English for two years at Hampden Academy in Hampden, Maine.

George Beahm outlines King's fictional signature in *The Stephen King Companion.* King includes a "main character with a 'wild talent'; a fundamental honesty in the prose, the kind of writing that makes you trust the writer; colloquial English that mirrors the way real people talk; a real world intruded upon by an unreal element (telekinesis, in this case); the rite of passage (Carrie growing from adolescence to adulthood); and a downbeat ending (typical of American naturalist writers, whom King admires)." All of these elements appear in *Carrie.*

High school cruelty is at its peak in the novel. The girls in the locker room taunt Carrie White while her mother, a zealous religious fanatic, prays for her evil daughter's soul. A schoolmate, Sue, befriends Carrie. In an attempt to be kind, she "gives" her boyfriend, Tommy, to Carrie as a date for the prom. She also arranges for the pair to be crowned king and queen of the prom. When other students discover this, they arrange for pig's blood to be dumped on Carrie during the coronation. Tommy dies in the act and Carrie finds herself before her class-

Novelist Stephen King, 1970s. © CORBIS. REPRODUCED BY
PERMISSION.

mates, humiliated. As she rushes from the school, she realizes she can use her powers to teach the town a lesson.
Carrie's mother greets her with a butcher knife as she enters the house and kills her, thereby ending the nightmare
of Carrie's life.

Significance

Carrie began King's career as a best-selling horror
writer. He sold the book to Doubleday in 1973 for a
$2,500 advance. It was quickly purchased by New Amer-
ican Library for $400,000. These facts alone make the
story of *Carrie* incredible. However, in this novel are the
seeds of what would become King's successful literary
technique. King realized with *Carrie* and the four novels
he wrote in the six months following the purchase, that
he liked writing horror. In *Carrie* King experimented with
form and narrative. He included newspaper clippings,
hospital reports, interview transcripts, and other kinds of
texts to tell the story and aftermath of Carrie's life. These
forms of telling join together to present a modern or postmodern horror story. Lant and Thompson note that "King
demystifies print, making readers read the words on the
page not as some natural, transparent reflection of the
truth, but as a personally and politically motivated re-
fraction of reality."

The novel was particularly popular with younger
readers. Carrie is, like many of King's later characters,
an alienated teenager. Her mother, a "religious psy-
chopath," mirrors the evil stepmother of fairy tales.
Whether King was conscious of it or not, he used the
basic structure of Cinderella to turn the tale of Carrie's
life into a twisted fairy tale. Another of King's trademarks is the "wild talent" that his main characters possess. For Carrie, this was telekinesis, or being able to
make objects move.

The relationship between film and novel versions
was important for King's success. Sales continued when
the film version, starring Sissy Spacek, Piper Laurie,
John Travolta, and Amy Irving, was released. The film
Carrie was directed by Brian De Palma. This, along
with the release of *Salem's Lot,* provided King with the
audience attention needed to assure his future as a
writer.

Primary Source

Carrie [excerpt]

SYNOPSIS: Stephen King threw out the opening
scene for *Carrie,* but his wife Tabitha rescued the
crumpled pages from a wastepaper basket and encouraged him to continue writing. This is the scene
that identifies Carrie White as the outcast who will
eventually wreak havoc on her classmates and town.

News item from the Westover (Me.) weekly *Enterprise,* August 19, 1966:

RAIN OF STONES REPORTED

It was reliably reported by several persons
that a rain of stones fell from a clear blue sky
on Carlin Street in the town of Chamberlain on
August 17th. The stones fell principally on the
home of Mrs. Margaret White, damaging the
roof extensively and ruining two gutters and a
downspout valued at approximately $25. Mrs.
White, a widow, lives with her three-year-old
daughter, Carietta.

Mrs. White could not be reached for comment.

Nobody was really surprised when it happened,
not really, not at the subconscious level where savage things grow. On the surface, all the girls in the
shower room were shocked, thrilled, ashamed, or
simply glad that the White bitch had taken it in the
mouth again. Some of them might also have claimed
surprise, but of course their claim was untrue. Carrie had been going to school with some of them
since the first grade, and this had been building
since that time, building slowly and immutably, in

accordance with all the steadiness of a chain reaction approaching critical mass.

What none of them knew, of course, was that Carrie White was telekinetic.

Graffiti scratched on a desk of the Barket Street Grammar School in Chamberlain:

Carrie White eats shit.

The locker room was filled with shouts, echoes, and the subterranean sound of showers splashing on tile. The girls had been playing volleyball in Period One, and their morning sweat was light and eager.

Girls stretched and writhed under the hot water, squalling, flicking water, squirting white bars of soap from hand to hand. Carrie stood among them stolidly; a frog among swans. She was a chunky girl with pimples on her neck and back and buttocks, her wet hair completely without color. It rested against her face with dispirited sogginess and she simply stood, head slightly bent, letting the water splat against her flesh and roll off. She looked the part of the sacrificial goat, the constant butt, believer in left-handed monkey wrenches, perpetual foul-up, and she was. She wished forlornly and constantly that Ewen High had individual—and thus private—showers, like the high schools at Westover or Lewiston. They stared. They always *stared.*

Showers turning off one by one, girls stepping out, removing pastel bathing caps, toweling, spraying deodorant, checking the clock over the door. Bras were hooked, underpants stepped into. Steam hung in the air; the place might have been an Egyptian bathhouse except for the constant rumble of the Jacuzzi whirpool in the corner. Calls and catcalls rebounded with all the snap and flicker of billiard balls after a hard break.

"—so Tommy said he *hated* it on me and I—"

"—I'm going with my sister and her husband. He picks his nose but so does she, so they're very—"

"—shower after school and—"

"—too cheap to spend a goddam penny so Cindi and I—"

Miss Desjardin, their slim, nonbreasted gym teacher, stepped in, craned her neck around briefly, and slapped her hands together once, smartly. "What are you waiting for, Carrie? Doom? Bell in five minutes." Her shorts were blinding white, her legs not too curved but striking in their unobtrusive muscularity. A silver whistle, won in college archery competition, hung around her neck.

Sissy Spacek stars as Carrie in a movie adaptation of Stephen King's book by the same name, 1976. GETTY IMAGES. REPRODUCED BY PERMISSION.

The girls giggled and Carrie looked up, her eyes slow and dazed from the heat and the steady, pounding roar of the water. "Ohuh?"

It was a strangely froggy sound, grotesquely apt, and the girls giggled again. Sue Snell had whipped a towel from her hair with the speed of a magician embarking on a wondrous feat and began to comb rapidly. Miss Desjardin made an irritated cranking gesture at Carrie and stepped out.

Carrie turned off the shower. It died in a drip and a gurgle.

It wasn't until she stepped out that they all saw the blood running down her leg.

From *The Shadow Exploded: Documented Facts and Specific Conclusions Derived from the Case of Carietta White,* by David R. Congress (Tulane University Press: 1981), p.34:

It can hardly be disputed that failure to note specific instances of telekinesis during the White girl's earlier years must be attributed to the conclusion offered by White and Stearns in their paper *Telekinesis: A Wild Talent Revisited*—that the ability to move objects by effort of the will alone comes to the fore only in moments of extreme personal stress. The talent is well hidden indeed; how else could it have remained submerged for centuries with only the tip of the iceberg showing above a sea of quackery?

We have only skimpy hearsay evidence upon which to lay our foundation in this case, but even this is enough to indicate that a "TK" potential of immense magnitude existed within Carrie White. The great tragedy is that we are now all Monday-morning quarterbacks . . .

"Per-iod!"

The catcall came first from Chris Hargensen. It struck the tiled walls, rebounded, and struck again. Sue Snell gasped laughter from her nose and felt an odd, vexing mixture of hate, revulsion, exasperation, and pity. She just looked so *dumb,* standing there, not knowing what was going on. God, you'd think she never—

"PER-iod!"

It was becoming a chant, an incantation. Someone in the background (perhaps Hargensen again, Sue couldn't tell in the jungle of echoes) was yelling, *"Plug it up!"* with hoarse, uninhibited abandon.

"PER-iod, PER-iod, PER-iod!"

Carrie stood dumbly in the center of a forming circle, water rolling from her skin in beads. She stood like a patient ox, aware that the joke was on her (as always), dumbly embarrassed but unsurprised.

Sue felt welling disgust as the first dark drops of menstrual blood struck the tile in dime-sized drops. "For God's sake, Carrie, you got your period!" she cried. "Clean yourself up!"

"Ohuh?"

She looked around bovinely. Her hair stuck to her cheeks in a curving helmet shape. There was a cluster of acne on one shoulder. At sixteen, the elusive stamp of hurt was already clearly marked in her eyes.

"She thinks they're for lipstick!" Ruth Gogan suddenly shouted with cryptic glee, and then burst into a shriek of laughter. Sue remembered the comment later and fitted it into a general picture, but now it was only another senseless sound in the confusion. *Sixteen?* She was thinking. *She must know what's happening, she—*

More droplets of blood. Carrie still blinked around at her classmates in slow bewilderment.

Helen Shyres turned around and made mock throwing-up gestures.

"You're *bleeding!*" Sue yelled suddenly, furiously. "You're *bleeding,* you big dumb pudding!"

Carrie looked down at herself.

She shrieked.

The sound was very loud in the humid locker room.

A tampon suddenly struck her in the chest and fell with plop at her feet. A red flower stained the absorbent cotton and spread.

Then the laugher, disgusted, contemptuous, horrified, seemed to rise and bloom into something jagged and ugly, and the girls were bombarding her with tampons and sanitary napkins, some from purses, some from the broken dispenser on the wall. They flew like snow and the chant became: "Plug it *up,* plug it *up,* plug it *up,* plug it—"

Sue was throwing them too, throwing and chanting with the rest, not really sure what she was doing—a charm had occurred to her mind and glowed there like neon: *There's no harm in it really no harm in it really no harm—* It was still flashing and glowing, reassuringly, when Carrie suddenly began to howl and back away, flailing her arms and grunting and gobbling.

The girls stopped, realizing that fission and explosion had finally been reached. It was at this point, when looking back, that some of them would claim surprise. Yet there had been all these years, all these years of let's short-sheet Carrie's bed at Christian Youth Camp and I found this love letter from Carrie to Flash Bobby Pickett let's copy it and pass it around and hide her underpants somewhere and put this snake in her shoe and duck her *again,* duck her *again;* Carrie tagging along stubbornly on biking trips, known one year as pudd'n and the next year as truck-face, always smelling sweaty, not able to catch up; catching poison ivy from urinating in the bushes and everyone finding out (hey, scratch-ass, your bum itch?); Billy Preston putting peanut butter in her hair that time she fell asleep in study hall; the pinches, the legs outstretched in school aisles to trip her up, the books knocked from her desk, the obscene postcard tucked into her purse; Carrie on the church picnic and kneeling down clumsily to pray and the seam of her old madras skirt splitting along the zipper like the sound of a huge wind-breakage; Carrie always missing the ball, even in kickball, falling on her face in Modern Dance during their sophomore year and chipping a tooth; running into the net during volleyball; wearing stockings that were always run, running, or about to run, always showing sweat stains under the arms of her blouses; even the time Chris Hargensen called up after school from

Kelley Fruit Company downtown and asked her if she knew that *pig poop* was spelled C-A-R-R-I-E; Suddenly all this and the critical mass was reached. The ultimate shit-on, gross-out, put-down, long searched for, was found. Fission.

She backed away, howling in the new silence, fat forearms crossing her face, a tampon stuck in the middle of her pubic hair.

The girls watched her, their eyes shining solemnly.

Carrie backed into the side of one of the four large shower compartments and slowly collapsed into a sitting position. Slow, helpless groans jerked out of her. Her eyes rolled with wet whiteness, like the eyes of a hog in the slaughtering pen.

Sue said, slowly, hesitantly, "I think this must be the first time she ever—"

That was when the door pumped open with a flat and hurried bang and Miss Desjardin burst in to see what the matter was.

From *The Shadow Exploded* (p. 41):

Both medical and psychological writers on the subject are in agreement that Carrie White's exceptionally late and traumatic commencement of the menstrual cycle might well have provided the trigger for her latent talent.

It seems incredible that, as late as 1979, Carrie knew nothing of the mature woman's monthly cycle. It was nearly as incredible to believe that the girl's mother would permit her daughter to reach the age of nearly seventeen without consulting a gynecologist concerning the daugher's failure to menstruate.

Yet the facts are incontrovertible. When Carrie White realized she was bleeding from the vaginal opening, she had no idea of what was taking place. She was innocent of the entire concept of menstruation.

One of her surviving classmates, Ruth Gogan, tells of entering the girls' locker room at Ewen High School the year before the events we are concerned with and seeing Carrie using a tampon to blot her lipstick with. At that time, Miss Gogan said, "What the hell are you up to?" Miss White replied, "Isn't this right?" Miss Gogan replied, "Sure. Sure it is." Ruth Gogan let a number of her girl friends in on this (she later told this interviewer she thought it was "sorta cute"), and if anyone tried in the future to inform Carrie of the true purpose of what she was using to make up with, she apparently dismissed the explanation as an attempt to pull her leg. This was a facet of her life that she had become exceedingly wary of. . . .

Further Resources

BOOKS

Beahm, George, ed. *The Stephen King Companion.* Kansas City, Mo.: Andrews and McMeel, 1989.

Lant, Kathleen Margaret, and Theresa Thompson. *Imagining the Worst: Stephen King and the Representation of Women.* Westport, Conn.: Greenwood Publishing Group, 1998.

Reino, Joseph. *Stephen King: The First Decade, "Carrie" to "Pet Sematary."* Boston: Twayne, 1988.

PERIODICALS

Grant, Charles L. "Stephen King: 'I Like to go for the Jugular.'" *Twilight Zone* 1, no. 1, April 1981, 18–22.

Matusa, Paula. "Corruption and Catastrophe: De Palma's Carrie." *Film Quarterly* 31, no. 1, Fall 1997, 32–38.

WEBSITES

The Official Stephen King Web Presence. Available online at http://www.stephenking.com/ (accessed April 8, 2003).

AUDIO AND VISUAL MEDIA

Carrie. Original release, 1976, United Artists. Directed by Brian DePalma. VHS, 1988, MGM/United Artists. Special Edition DVD, 2001, MGM Home Entertainment.

"Born to Run"
Song

By: Bruce Springsteen

Date: 1975

Source: Springsteen, Bruce. "Born to Run." Available online at http://brucespringsteen.net/songs/BornToRun.html; website home page: http://brucespringsteen.net/ (accessed April 7, 2003).

About the Artist: Bruce Springsteen (1949–), musician and songwriter, was born in Freehold, New Jersey. He is the son of a bus driver and of a secretary. He attended Ocean City College. The Grammy winning artist formed his first band in 1965. The Bruce Springsteen Band, later called the E Street Band, released its debut album in 1973. He won a Gold Record from the Recording Institute Association of America in 1975 for "Born to Run." Springsteen was inducted into the Rock and Roll Hall of Fame in 1999. ■

Introduction

Bruce Springsteen's working class roots infused his songs, along with an eclectic mix of musical influences. The rock and roll of 1950s icons such as Elvis Presley and Chuck Berry blended with the poetic lyrics of Bob Dylan and Van Morrison to provide a basis for the music of Bruce Springsteen. Ed Ward writes that "he dared to be uneven" in an industry that was "releasing uniformly smooth, accommodating product." Being compared to Dylan did not initially prove to be an asset to Springsteen, however. The reviewer in *Time* magazine

Bruce Springsteen's third album, *Born to Run,* was the turning point of the musician's career. © CORBIS. REPRODUCED BY PERMISSION.

notes that the first albums had ecstatic reviews but slim sales, partially because of the Dylan comparison.

The name of the band changed to the E Street Band to honor the street on which the mother of David Sancious, the keyboardist, lived. The band's three-hour concerts quickly became legendary as the band began to tour the East Coast. Springsteen went from "a handful of loyal fans from the scuzzy Jersey shore" in the early 1960s to sold out concerts in major venues by the early 1970s. Following the release of the album *Born to Run,* Springsteen set off for his first West Coast tour.

Springsteen had unfortunately signed with Mike Appel, a manager who proved difficult to work with and with whom he found himself in a lawsuit after the release of *Born to Run.* Springsteen did not agree with Appel's judgment about his career and had used another producer for the *Born to Run* album. Springsteen sued Appel and then Appel brought an injunction against Springsteen, preventing him from recording for nearly three years.

"Born to Run" presents the American myth of escaping a small town for something better and speaks of open highways and love. Marcus wrote in *Rolling Stone* that, "We know the story: one thousand and one American nights, one long night of fear and love." The Rock and Roll Hall of Fame induction characterized the song

and the album as full of songs with an "epic sweep." The song has been recorded in a full rock version and in an acoustic version.

Significance

Born to Run was Bruce Springsteen's third album. Released in August 1975, the album produced a "million dollar gold album in six weeks," according to Newsweek. For a band that had produced two low-selling records, this was fantastic. Now Columbia was ready to back the singer and his band from the Jersey shore. The album had taken a year to record. Phil Spector produced the album and Jon Landau, a former editor from *Rolling Stone,* coproduced it. The combination of the Spector sound and Landau's ability to get the band into better recording studios helped make the album a success. This was the turning point for Springsteen's career.

Ward writes of the album, "Judged strictly as music that has by now withstood the test of a little time, *Born to Run* does indeed sound like one of the finest, most eloquent and hard-edged statements in all of rock music." The album "managed to compress [Springsteen's] lyrical ideas into useful, memorable turns of phrase." Marcus adds that "Springsteen's singing, his words and the band's music have turned the dreams and failures two generations have dropped along the road into an epic— an epic that began when that car went over the cliff in *Rebel Without a Cause.*" *Time* describes the music as "primal, directly in touch with all the impulses of wild humor and glancing melancholy, street tragedy and punk anarchy, that have made rock the distinctive voice of a generation." Jim Cullen compares Bruce Springsteen to a twentieth-century Walt Whitman, writing the songs for the open road of the working classes in America.

Feature articles in both *Time* and *Newsweek* quote Bruce Springsteen as wondering "What phenomenon?" and wondering why there was so much hype. He had always made music, had wanted to sing, and he was doing it. This was Bruce Springsteen's way of life, as it remains in the early 2000s.

Primary Source

"Born to Run"

> **SYNOPSIS:** The 1975 album and song hit the charts quickly after it was released. Both the album and the single rose steadily in popularity. In October 1975, Springsteen appeared on the covers of *Time* and *Newsweek.*

In the day we sweat it out in the streets of a runaway American dream
At night we ride through mansions of glory in suicide machines

Sprung from cages out on Highway 9,
Chrome wheeled, fuel injected
and steppin' out over the line
Baby this town rips the bones from your back
It's a death trap, it's a suicide rap
We gotta get out while we're young
'Cause tramps like us, baby we were born to run

Wendy let me in I wanna be your friend
I want to guard your dreams and visions
Just wrap your legs 'round these velvet rims
and strap your hands across my engines
Together we could break this trap
We'll run till we drop, baby we'll never go back
Will you walk with me out on the wire
'Cause baby I'm just a scared and lonely rider
But I gotta find out how it feels
I want to know if love is wild
girl I want to know if love is real

Beyond the Palace hemi-powered drones scream
    down the boulevard
The girls comb their hair in rearview mirrors
And the boys try to look so hard
The amusement park rises bold and stark
Kids are huddled on the beach in a mist
I wanna die with you Wendy on the streets tonight
In an everlasting kiss

The highway's jammed with broken heroes on a last
    chance power drive
Everybody's out on the run tonight
but there's no place left to hide
Together Wendy we'll live with the sadness
I'll love you with all the madness in my soul
Someday girl I don't know when
we're gonna get to that place
Where we really want to go
and we'll walk in the sun
But till then tramps like us
baby we were born to run

Further Resources

BOOKS

Cullen, Jim. *Born in the U.S.A.: Bruce Springsteen and the American Tradition.* New York: HarperCollins, 1997.

Marsh, Dave. *Born to Run: The Bruce Springsteen Story.* Garden City: Dolphin Books, 1979.

Ward, Ed, Geoffrey Stokes, and Ken Tucker. *Rock of Ages: The Rolling Stone History of Rock & Roll.* New York: Rolling Stone Press, 1986.

PERIODICALS

"Making of a Rock Star." *Newsweek,* October 27, 1975, 57–63.

Marcus, Greil. "Born to Run." *Rolling Stone* 197, October 9, 1975. Available online at http://www.rollingstone.com /reviews/cd/review.asp?aid=16693&cf=; website home page; http://www.rollingstone.com (accessed April 7, 2003).

"The Backstreet Phantom of Rock." *Time,* October 27, 1975, 48–58.

WEBSITES

"Rock and Roll Hall of Fame, Inductee: Bruce Springsteen." Rock and Roll Hall of Fame and Museum. Available online

at http://www.rockhall.com/hof/inductee.asp?id=194; website home page: http://www.rockhall.com/ (accessed April 7, 2003).

AUDIO AND VISUAL MEDIA

Bruce Springsteen: The Complete Video Anthology, 1978–2000. Directed by Brian De Palma and John Sayles. DVD/VHS, 2001, Sony/Columbia.

Springsteen, Bruce. *Born to Run.* Original release, 1975, Columbia PC-33795, LP. 1983, CD, Columbia CK 33795.

"Nashville"
Interview

By: Robert Altman

Date: 1976

Source: Altman, Robert. "Nashville." Interview by Connie Byrne and William O. Lopez. *Film Quarterly* 29, no. 2, Winter 1975–76, 14–17.

About the Artist: Robert Altman (1925–) was born in Kansas City, Missouri. Following a brief career in the U.S. Air Force, he was employed by the Calvin Company to create employee training films as well as industrial and sports documentaries. In the late 1950s Altman directed episodes of the television series *Alfred Hitchcock Presents,* and in the 1960s he directed episodes of *The Millionaire, Bonanza,* and *Kraft Suspense Theater.* Some of his notable feature films are *Countdown* (1968), *A Perfect Couple* (1979), *Popeye* (1980), *Short Cuts* (1993), and *Gosford Park* (2001). ■

Introduction

Robert Altman may be one of the best and most individual film directors in the country. Helene Keysser wrote that he "recognizes that we enjoy our despair in who we are." The director of the 1975 film *Nashville,* Altman has been described as one who makes films that viewers remember long after they have exited the theater.

Although he had been directing films since the 1940s, Altman's breakthrough film came in 1970 with *M*A*S*H.* The film about the Korean War was a commercial success and allowed Altman to pursue the offbeat, experimental projects that he wanted to do in collaboration with major studios. Altman tried a variety of genres and was willing to take chances on unknown actors. The studios were not happy when Altman did not deliver another commercial success like *M*A*S*H* as quickly as they wanted. In 1975 he directed *Nashville,* which became both a critical and commercial success, but not a huge money maker.

Daniel O'Brien outlines several of Altman's techniques that make him a unique director. Altman works with a collaborative team, and follows a "fixed pattern of production: medium budgets, location shooting, off-beat casting and a relaxed atmosphere." His collaborations include the actors. Altman encourages them to "contribute ideas for their characters and improvise dialogue." He also allows them to view the daily "rushes," or day's filming. All of these techniques were used in the filming of *Nashville.*

Joan Tewksbury's screenplay involves twenty-four characters who are interrelated through family and business. The performers present the good and the evil side of country western music. The political ambitions of Hal Philip Walker, the presidential candidate for the Replacement Party, are pushed by his public relations assistant John Triplette.

Significance

Nashville is a quasi-documentary. According to O'Brien, the film is a "darkly satirical look at contemporary American society." The story takes place in Nashville, Tennessee, over a long weekend where country-western stars arrive for a recording session and an appearance at the Grand Ole Opry. Woven into the storyline are political commentaries reflecting on the Watergate scandal and comments about life in America in the early 1970s.

Altman provided a considerable amount of freedom for the actors in interpreting their characters, according to Gerard Plecki. He allowed them to write songs and improvise dialogue as they saw fit. One of Altman's trademarks is that he does not film several takes of one scene. Instead he filmed at least twice the amount of film needed and cut the final version from that.

Sound and lighting were also experimental techniques. Plecki recalls that the eight-track sound system "recorded or 'mixed' multiple-sourced live sound from separate microphones within and outside the frame." Altman did not need to use mike booms and umbilical microphones with this system. Chemtone, the lighting system employed, increases a film stock's sensitivity to color. Together, Plecki notes, these new technical systems allowed Altman to "create an impressionistic and spontaneous feeling in the film."

One of the most controversial aspects of Robert Altman's *Nashville* was allowing a group of film critics to view the film as it was being cut. Pauline Kael of the *New Yorker* probably saw at least six hours of film before it was finally edited to 159 minutes. Critics not allowed to see the pre-edited versions complained. The debates between critics created more publicity for the film than if Altman had waited to release the final cut. The release of the DVD coincided with the twenty-fifth anniversary of the film, with the original length still being mentioned.

Primary Source

"Nashville" [excerpt]

SYNOPSIS: Robert Altman was not afraid to change the standards in filmmaking. Altman allowed his collaborators freedom that most directors did not to create a story that audiences would have to watch to fully understand.

Are there any particular things about Nashville *that you would like to start out talking about?*

I don't like the ads. And I can't criticize Paramount for them because they really like the picture and I think they just tried too hard. You can go through the grosses and look at the city and say Gee, I wonder why it isn't doing well there. . . . And you'll find that they are running the thing where you can't hear the sound, or the speakers are out, or they get reels mixed up. I mean the projection you just can't control. But those are just general industry complaints because unfortunately it is an industry.

Did Paramount send someone around to check out the sound?

They did it at all the key places we opened, but you know you can't suddenly do that to 10,000 places. And again, it's a unionization of the way those projectionists are and many of them . . . I mean you'll find a guy who cares and you'll find a guy who just really doesn't give a rat's fuck one way or the other.

What was wrong with the advertising?

What ad did they run where you are?

They had a bunch of critics' blurbs on them.

Then they were good. They like to settle in on one thing, and they just haven't been able to find it 'cause you can't find it in the picture. Commercially the biggest problem with the film is that it doesn't have a shark. So nobody really knows except by word of mouth, and somebody says You ought to see it, it's really good. And you say What's it about? And, well, you can't answer that. So that's the problem every time you do a film that doesn't have an absolute, *one* focal point. That's what we run into. . . . You know I'm up here in Calgary and we can't get anybody into a theater to see this picture with dynamite. I've gone on radio and television here and they don't seem to care that we are up here making a movie. I mean it's weird. . . .

Do you feel misunderstood by the public? Don't you feel somewhat gratified by the critical response to the film?

Robert Altman directs the 1978 film *A Wedding.* **THE KOBAL COLLECTION. REPRODUCED BY PERMISSION.**

Oh I'm thrilled, I'm thrilled with the whole thing *and* the public. I mean this picture is going to be the first picture in a long time that's going to go into profits for me. But what I really am probably trying to say is that isn't a reflection of what the whole movie industry considers itself. We run in those two theaters in New York forever. In San Francisco we're doing terrific, and in every metropolitan city other than Los Angeles, and they don't know what films are about at all. . . . We are in the process of changing what movies are, I think. It isn't just buying a bag of popcorn and walking in at the middle, and if you like it you sit through to the part where you came in.

What about the process of getting down to the final cut? Was anyone pressuring you to cut it down to a particular length?

Well, there were a lot of people biting their tongues. Nobody really said anything. They were nervous that the film came out as long as it did.

How long was the first version?

Well, uh, we always knew it would end up three hours or under. When I cut a film I start showing it daily. I start responding myself to anybody's reaction to the film. I don't pay much attention to what they say, but you can tell by their reaction.

The film that Pauline Kael saw is virtually the same film you saw. Your reaction to it, I dare say, would not be changed by the changes we made in it at all. Other than the fact that the sound track is mixed now and it wasn't before, and it was much rougher. We only cut it down by about ten minutes from that time and that was just removing a couple of songs.

What kind of material was removed from the longer versions?

Well, a lot of filler. A lot of just detailing the characters. It began and ended the same way. In fact, we are now starting to edit it back for eventual television release where it will be like four two-hour shows. It will begin and end the same way, it will just be fuller. And it will be specifically edited for television so that the commercial breaks will be at the end of each of the four episodes. That is three or four years away.

How long was the shooting schedule in Nashville?

Seven weeks.

Could you describe how you divide your energies during the principal photography amongst the various directorial demands such as organization, technical, rehearsing, etc.?

A lot of people made that picture. We used a lot of people. Actually, in *Nashville* more than any other film, what we did was sort of set up events and then just press the button and photograph them, pretty much like you would a documentary. In other words we didn't use the normal techniques of setting up a scene and then rehearsing it, and then saying, "OK, now let's set up a master shot," and getting what we wanted there, and then getting over-the-shoulders and close-ups. That's not to say we did it on the first take every time, but we basically shot each segment of the film as it was. We were covered because we knew we could cut from anything at anytime, we weren't stuck with the length, we didn't have to worry about that. The best example I think is Barbara Baxley when she's doing her Kennedy speech to Geraldine Chaplin. Barbara wrote that, and I didn't know, I didn't even bother to listen to her material before we shot it. And she had rehearsed it and learned it. And we turned the camera on her till we ran out of film, and then we loaded it up again and ran another roll, so that it literally took twenty minutes. It was done once and that was it. Because I knew that I could pull out the pieces of it that I wanted, and I could get away from it at any time. I had a song going on and I had all those other characters that I had to deal with.

It is said that you like to keep the whole company around and have everybody watch everything. . . .

I try to shoot in sequence and try to have all the actors available for the shoot, mainly so that we have the freedom to change our minds about what we are going to shoot.

You shot the film basically in sequence?

As much in sequence as you are going to find. I mean the opening scene was the first time we shot and the ending was the last scene we shot.

Could you talk about how your method of working with actors might differ from the methods of other directors?

I never have really watched anybody else direct a film, so I can just surmise what they do. I have no idea. I find more and more that the less I do the better the work comes out. So now my function is really to try and stay out of the way, and make the conditions and circumstances as *conducive* as I can for the actors to do what they do. . . . It really starts in the casting. You try to get it so that they don't have to manufacture very much—then they can draw on all their own particular things. And then after we cast, we try to get them to switch the character around closer to the actor. Originally, Susan Anspach

was hired for the part of Barbara Jean. She dropped out and we put Ronee Blakley in and Ronee Blakley happened to have some rather severe burns on her body, from when she was a little girl and her dress caught on fire from a sparkler at some sort of Fourth of July thing. And she has gone through a series of skin grafts and those scars on her chest still show. And so we just put that element into the character.

Was Joan Tewksbury down on the shoot?

Sure, all the time.

You worked on the script throughout the shooting?

Yes.

Did you work out sketches or plans with the cinematographer the night before?

No, never. Half the time one assistant will be working with the background people, and I don't know what he's telling them or what they'll be doing. He is making his own movie back there. Remember the scene when the soldier gets off the elevator and sneaks down into Barbara Jean's room, and the guard is standing there talking to the nurse about his gun and how he never had to kill anybody with it? Well I never heard that until we got into editing because we hadn't pulled that track out. In editing I said Gee that's teriffic. Well that's just something Alan set up with the guard. These aren't professional actors, and even if they were we like them to be dealing with something that belongs to them rather than something that they don't understand or that't totally foreign to them.

Is there any time when you were shooting that you would just turn on the camera and people wouldn't know they were actually being photographed? Was it that loose?

No.

What about the sound?

We used an 8-track system and it's really unmixing rather than mixing sound. We'd just put microphones on all the principals and hang them out the window and stick them in the clock and under the doorbell and wherever we want a live sound. And they all go down on different tracks, pretty much the way music is done today. And in our musical sequences we had an additional 16 tracks. We didn't have to come back later and put in dead sound effects.

For instance, when Elliot Gould drives up and we hear him talking in the back seat of the car before it stops and before he gets out. . . .

The microphone is on him inside the car. They are all hidden, they are really built into the wardrobe.

There's a psychological reality that you captured that could never be achieved with dubbed sound. . . .

No way. And the thing that people in our industry don't understand is that once you free one area, once you don't have the mike boom hanging overhead, and you don't have to worry about shadows and lights and all that, it gives you such freedom with your camera. You can put it wherever you want, you can get back as far as you want, it just compounds its qualities.

At the beginning of the Parthenon rally sequence when Michael Murphy comes out of the car and walks up to Beatty: were they radio miked?

Yes.

You could hear the transmission and the mike rubbing up against their clothes.

Yes, that what it is.

What about the sound truck and the crowd noises and other effects?

We added those later, but they were done down there. Thomas Hal Phillips went down to a recording studio and made his speech. . . .

I read that the public down there didn't actually know that the Phillips campaign was unreal. Is that true?

A lot of people didn't.

And people called up to volunteer their services to the Replacement Party?

I don't know if that specifically happened. But I know people would stop and ask about it. We had those bumper stickers on our own cars. My wife would wear a button around town. People would ask her, "Who is this guy?"

So you would drive the sound truck around without any sound actually blaring?

Yeah. There was no sound. Well, sometimes there was sound coming out of the truck when we were shooting it silent. We were equipped, we could play the speech or music or whatever we wanted to through those horns. And sometimes we'd do that just to get crowd reactions.

Speaking of crowd reactions, was there a unified reaction from the people of Nashville about your film? I read that the Nashville Banner *ran a big front-page headline saying "Altman's* Nashville Down on Nashville."

What happened was that the *Banner* sent a reporter up to New York and sneaked him into one of our initial screenings, which they didn't have to do, but they did. Then he went back and gave us the headline. The editor of the other paper, *The Tennesseean,* came up and we showed it to him. He

went back and gave us a headline saying it was the best picture he had seen and absolutely authentic. So for about four days in a row we had a nice argument going on the front pages of the two Nashville papers. And we took the film down there and showed it to the people—it hasn't opened in Nashville yet, but we had a screening before we opened in New York for the people in Nashville who contributed to the film. They had a lot of press down there, but it didn't amount to very much. The musicians like it. Some people thought it was too long. Some people thought that the music was not authentic, and some thought it was. It was kind of a bore.

You were quoted in an AP article as saying that the "people at Opryland aren't interested in the truth, they are interested in their corporate image." Did you actually say that?

Probably. They run that place like a church. Those people come in, they aren't there to be entertained nor *are* they entertained. That audience you saw in the film is the audience that's in the Grand Ole Opry. That was a legitimate audience. I mean we put up signs and advertised and those people came in. The only thing was that they didn't have to pay for it.

They came in to see "Connie White"?

They came in to see Lily Tomlin and Henry Gibson and to see a movie being made. And they brought their Instamatic cameras and they took pictures. At one point when Henry Gibson was on he said, "Now, Barbara Jean, she's in Vanderbilt Hospital," and he gave that address. In the film you'll see a woman take out a piece of paper and write it down.

What did the musicians who appeared in the film think of the music?

Some of them liked it, some didn't. But all of the musicians we used—except for Baskin and one bass player we brought in to play with the trio—were Nashville sidemen. So when they came in to work it was like a regular session. So they've played better music than that and worse.

Baskin commented that the people down there were pissed off because these Californians came in and knocked off a lot of good music and made a big movie and had a lots of fun and then just split, and they were still stuck in Nashville.

That's true.

Do you think that you've turned off whole segments of the population in the South with this film?

No, no. I think the people who feel that way haven't seen the picture. I mean anybody who would read Rex Reed and believe him. . . . It's just those kind of people who will respond in that manner.

Which were the most sensitive articles about your film?

It's hard to say . . . I like the good ones and don't like the bad ones. But people look at it in different ways. I just got a review sent to me from the *Kansas City Star* that I think is probably the best review of the film. Because I think the critic did what a critic is supposed to do. In the body of the review he said Don't go in expecting *this,* but if you look at it in *this* manner you will have one hell of a time. So he's helping to lead the audience toward really enjoying the film. Whereas somebody like Rex Reed is just absolutely infuriated because the other critics have liked it. He got on the *Merv Griffin Show* and said, "Well, all I can tell you is it's false advertising and false publicity and everybody is lying because people are staying away from that picture by the millions." That's true because nobody in China or India has seen the film. But Rex Reed has a personal problem with me. I had a hotel room next to him in Cannes in 1970. And he left his door open . . . I don't want to go into it, but anyway he's gone after me on every picture.

Further Resources

BOOKS

Keyssar, Helene. *Robert Altman's America.* New York: Oxford University Press, 1991.

O'Brien, Daniel. *Robert Altman: Hollywood Survivor.* New York: Continuum, 1995.

Plecki, Gerard. *Robert Altman.* Boston: Twayne, 1985.

PERIODICALS

Allen, Kimberly. "DVD Release of Altman's 'Nashville' to Coincide with Tribute to the Director." *Video Store* 22, no. 23, June 4–June 10, 2000, 10.

Kael, Pauline. "Coming: Nashville." *New Yorker* 51, March 3, 1975, 79–83.

WEBSITES

"Interview with Robert Altman." British Film Institute. Available online at http://www.bfi.org.uk/showing/nft/interviews /altman/1.html; website home page: http://www.bfi.org.uk/ (accessed April 8, 2003).

AUDIO AND VISUAL MEDIA

Nashville. Original release, 1975, Paramount. Directed by Robert Altman. VHS, 2002, Paramount Studio. Widescreen DVD, 2003, Paramount Home Video.

"Isaac Bashevis Singer—Nobel Lecture"

Lecture

By: Isaac Bashevis Singer

Date: December 8, 1978

Source: Singer, Isaac Bashevis. "Isaac Bashevis Singer—Nobel Lecture." Available online at http://www.nobel.se /literature/laureates/1978/singer-lecture.html; website home page: http://www.nobel.se/ (accessed April 9, 2003).

About the Author: Isaac Bashevis Singer (1904–1991) was born in Radzymin, Poland, the son of a rabbi. He taught Hebrew as a teenager, and in the 1920s translated novels and nonfiction works by authors such as Thomas Mann and Knut Hamsun into Yiddish. He attended the Tachkemoni Rabbinical Seminary, in Warsaw, Poland, from 1920–23. In 1935 he immigrated to the United States, becoming a citizen in 1943 and settling in New York. Singer was a writer of novels, short stories, and children's books as well as a translator. He won awards for writing in every category, including receiving the National Endowment for the Arts grant, 1967; Newbery Honor Book Award, 1968, for *The Fearsome Inn*; National Book Award for Children's Literature, 1970, for *A Day of Pleasure*; and the Children's Book Showcase Award, Children's Book Council, 1972, for *Alone in the Wild Forest.* Singer won the Nobel Prize in Literature in 1978. ■

Introduction

Isaac Bashevis Singer's first novel, published in Poland in 1932, was *Der Sotn in Goray* (Satan in Gray). The story takes place in seventeenth-century Poland and appeared as the Nazis were becoming a threat to Europeans. In the face of increasing anti-Semitism, Singer, a Jew, emigrated to America. Singer's long career as a writer draws on his heritage and the emotions of people.

Throughout his career Singer wrote in his native language, Yiddish. It was only after the words were written in his native tongue that he could translate them into English. In the 1978 Nobel Prize presentation, it was said that Yiddish "is Singer's language. And it is a storehouse which has gathered fairytales and anecdotes, wisdom, superstitions and memories for hundreds of years past through a history that seems to have left nothing untried in the way of adventures and afflictions." Although each culture and people have their own stories, common threads of passion, insanity, fear, and hope run through all tales.

In his Nobel lecture, Singer relates his values as an author. Literature should entertain; it should be full of the spirit of humanness and relate the morality, passion, good, and evil of life. The struggles of life cannot escape the writer's attention. Singer witnessed poverty in his childhood Poland, and the beginning of the Nazi terror and its result after he fled to America. He acknowledges that the "pessimism of the creative person is not decadence but a mighty passion for the redemption of man." The irony between pessimism and passion is ever present in the writer who observes the world—past, present and future—and who seeks to record the events of the people who struggle through life. Singer did this throughout his career, and it was fitting that he was recognized as a Nobel Laureate.

Significance

The significance of Singer's work is in the stories he told. He had a gift for the narrative art of spinning a tale. He was said to have been the only Yiddish writer who gained so much popularity with American audiences.

Recognizing not only Singer but also his language is a vital, but bittersweet, part of the Nobel honor. Yiddish, Singer said, is "a language of exile, without a land, without frontiers, not supported by any government, a language which possesses no words for weapons, ammunition, military exercises, war tactics. . . ." It is a language that is considered to be dead because of these reasons and because few people speak or write in it. Yet Singer's language allowed him to create characters who are almost mythical at times, but who lived in the real world. His short stories, of which "Gimpel the Fool" was an early success, are perhaps best known to many. By the 1970s, Singer was an internationally known author, with a broad command of genres ranging from novels to essays to children's books. Singer's works for children were recognized as among the best books of the genre by the American Library Association and *Horn Book*.

Singer focuses on the problems of humankind, regardless of whether the work is set in the seventeenth century or the present. The Nobel Prize for Literature is acknowledged throughout the world as the highest honor a writer can receive. The commonality of experiences draws readers to the books, which remain in print in Yiddish and English.

Primary Source

"Isaac Bashevis Singer—Nobel Lecture"

> **SYNOPSIS:** Like many other great writers, Singer drew upon his past, his heritage, and his language for the stories that meant something to him and, in turn, would have meaning to generations of readers. In this address, he particularly singles out the special meaning that the Yiddish language has had throughout his life.

The storyteller and poet of our time, as in any other time, must be an entertainer of the spirit in the full sense of the word, not just a preacher of social or political ideals. There is no paradise for bored

Singer Isaac Bashevis holds a copy of his book *A Day of Pleasure*, 1970. © CORBIS. REPRODUCED BY PERMISSION.

readers and no excuse for tedious literature that does not intrigue the reader, uplift him, give him the joy and the escape that true art always grants. Nevertheless, it is also true that the serious writer of our time must be deeply concerned about the problems of his generation. He cannot but see that the power of religion, especially belief in revelation, is weaker today than it was in any other epoch in human history. More and more children grow up without faith in God, without belief in reward and punishment, in the immortality of the soul and even in the validity of ethics. The genuine writer cannot ignore the fact that the family is losing its spiritual foundation. All the dismal prophecies of Oswald Spengler have become realities since the Second World War. No technological achievements can mitigate the disappointment of modern man, his loneliness, his feeling of inferiority, and his fear of war, revolution and terror. Not only has our generation lost faith in Providence but also in man himself, in his institutions and often in those who are nearest to him.

In their despair a number of those who no longer have confidence in the leadership of our society look up to the writer, the master of words. They hope against hope that the man of talent and sensitivity can perhaps rescue civilization. Maybe there is a spark of the prophet in the artist after all.

As the son of a people who received the worst blows that human madness can inflict, I must brood about the forthcoming dangers. I have many times resigned myself to never finding a true way out. But a new hope always emerges telling me that it is not yet too late for all of us to take stock and make a decision. I was brought up to believe in free will. Although I came to doubt all revelation, I can never accept the idea that the Universe is a physical or chemical accident, a result of blind evolution. Even though I learned to recognize the lies, the clichés and the idolatries of the human mind, I still cling to some truths which I think all of us might accept some day. There must be a way for man to attain all possible pleasures, all the powers and knowledge that nature can grant him, and still serve God—a God who speaks in deeds, not in words, and whose vocabulary is the Cosmos.

I am not ashamed to admit that I belong to those who fantasize that literature is capable of bringing new horizons and new perspectives—philosophical, religious, aesthetical and even social. In the history of old Jewish literature there was never any basic difference between the poet and the prophet. Our ancient poetry often became law and a way of life.

Some of my cronies in the cafeteria near the Jewish Daily Forward in New York call me a pessimist and a decadent, but there is always a background of faith behind resignation. I found comfort in such pessimists and decadents as Baudelaire, Verlaine, Edgar Allan Poe, and Strindberg. My interest in psychic research made me find solace in such mystics as your Swedenborg and in our own Rabbi Nachman Bratzlaver, as well as in a great poet of my time, my friend Aaron Zeitlin who died a few years ago and left a literary inheritance of high quality, most of it in Yiddish.

The pessimism of the creative person is not decadence but a mighty passion for the redemption of man. While the poet entertains he continues to search for eternal truths, for the essence of being. In his own fashion he tries to solve the riddle of time and change, to find an answer to suffering, to reveal love in the very abyss of cruelty and injustice. Strange as these words may sound I often play with the idea that when all the social theories collapse and wars and revolutions leave humanity in utter gloom, the poet—whom Plato banned from his Republic—may rise up to save us all.

The high honor bestowed upon me by the Swedish Academy is also a recognition of the Yiddish language—a language of exile, without a land, without frontiers, not supported by any government, a language which possesses no words for weapons, ammunition, military exercises, war tactics; a language that was despised by both gentiles and emancipated Jews. The truth is that what the great religions preached, the Yiddish-speaking people of the ghettos practiced day in and day out. They were the people of The Book in the truest sense of the word. They knew of no greater joy than the study of man and human relations, which they called Torah, Talmud, Mussar, Cabala. The ghetto was not only a place of refuge for a persecuted minority but a great experiment in peace, in self-discipline and in humanism. As such it still exists and refuses to give up in spite of all the brutality that surrounds it. I was brought up among those people. My father's home on Krochmalna Street in Warsaw was a study house, a court of justice, a house of prayer, of storytelling, as well as a place for weddings and Chassidic banquets. As a child I had heard from my older brother and master, I. J. Singer, who later wrote *The Brothers Ashkenazi,* all the arguments that the rationalists from Spinoza to Max Nordau brought out against religion. I have heard from my father and mother all the answers that faith in God could offer to those who doubt and search for the truth. In our home and in many other homes the eternal questions were more actual than the latest news in the Yiddish newspaper. In spite of all the disenchantments and all my skepticism I believe that the nations can learn much from those Jews, their way of thinking, their way of bringing up children, their finding happiness where others see nothing but misery and humiliation. To me the Yiddish language and the conduct of those who spoke it are identical. One can find in the Yiddish tongue and in the Yiddish spirit expressions of pious joy, lust for life, longing for the Messiah, patience and deep appreciation of human individuality. There is a quiet humor in Yiddish and a gratitude for every day of life, every crumb of success, each encounter of love. The Yiddish mentality is not haughty. It does not take victory for granted. It does not demand and command but it muddles through, sneaks by, smuggles itself amidst the powers of destruction, knowing somewhere that God's plan for Creation is still at the very beginning.

There are some who call Yiddish a dead language, but so was Hebrew called for two thousand years. It has been revived in our time in a most remarkable, almost miraculous way. Aramaic was certainly a dead language for centuries but then it brought to light the Zohar, a work of mysticism of sublime value. It is a fact that the classics of Yiddish literature are also the classics of the modern Hebrew literature. Yiddish has not yet said its last word. It contains treasures that have not been revealed to the eyes of the world. It was the tongue of martyrs and saints, of dreamers and Cabalists— rich in humor and in memories that mankind may never forget. In a figurative way, Yiddish is the wise and humble language of us all, the idiom of frightened and hopeful Humanity.

Further Resources

BOOKS

Farrell Lee, Grace. *From Exile to Redemption: The Fiction of Isaac Bashevis Singer.* Carbondale: Southern Illinois University Press, 1987.

Siegel, Ben. *Isaac Bashevis Singer.* Minneapolis, Minn.: University of Minneapolis Press, 1969.

Singer, Isaac Bashevis, and Richard Burgin. *Conversations with Isaac Bashevis Singer.* Garden City, N.Y.: Doubleday, 1985.

PERIODICALS

Burgin, Richard. "A Conversation with Isaac Bashevis Singer." *Michigan Quarterly Review* 17, 1978, 119–132.

Lee, Grace Farrell. "Seeing and Blindness: A Conversation with Isaac Bashevis Singer." *Novel: A Forum on Fiction* 9, 1976, 151–164.

WEBSITES

"The Nobel Prize in Literature 1978." Nobel e-Museum. Available online at http://www.nobel.se/literature/laureates/1978/; website home page: http://www.nobel.se/ (accessed April 9, 2003).

"The Salon Interview—Isaac Bashevis Singer." Salon Media Group. Available online at http://dir.salon.com/books/int /1998/04/cov_si_28int.html; website home page: http://dir .salon.com/ (accessed April 9, 2003).

"The Alvin Ailey American Dance Theater: Twenty Years Later"

Magazine article

By: Richard Philp

Date: 1978

Source: Philp, Richard. "The Alvin Ailey American Dance Theater: Twenty Years Later." *Dance Magazine* 52, October 1978, 63–77.

About the Author: Richard N. Philp (1943–) was educated at the University of North Carolina (1965) and Yale University (1968), and has been an editor at *Dance Magazine* since 1970, including more than eleven years as its editor-in-chief. A member of the founding board of directors of the World Dance Alliance, Philp has authored, co-authored, and edited several books in the field of dance, including *Dansuer: The Male in Ballet* (1977), *To Move, To Learn* (1978), and *Memoirs of a Dancer: Shadows of the Past, Dreams That Came True, Memories of Yesterdays (1979).* He has also served on the faculty of the summer dance festivals at the University of Wyoming. Philp received an award from the Society of Publication Designers, 1974, in recognition of his work at *Dance Magazine.* ∎

Introduction

Alvin Ailey (1931–1989) began life as a poor boy in Texas. He moved around with his mother, finally settling in California, where he discovered he had a love and gift for dance. Like Arthur Mitchell, his contemporary, Ailey started his career during a time when African American dancers were not seen on stage. In 1958 he founded the Alvin Ailey American Dance Theater. The organization has grown from a few dancers who gathered specifically to practice for a performance to an internationally known company and training program.

Ailey envisioned a multi-racial company. In the beginning most of its dancers were African American, but eventually dancers from other ethnic groups began to join the troupe. Ailey was a persistent exponent of American dance. He chose to choreograph ballets that reflected on American experiences, and he selected other American choreographers to work with him and his dancers. The company's repertoire expanded to include educational programs as well as performance programs.

The twentieth anniversary season was one of revivals. The dancers resurrected their best and most loved programs. Ailey's *Blue Suite* (1958) included scenes from his Texas childhood and characters based on people he knew. The choreography reflected a time period in American history when, as Jennifer Dunning notes, African Americans experienced "the pain of being told that there were suddenly no rooms when you walked in a hotel lobby in all your black glory after a thirteen-hour overnight bus trip on tour." Older dancers in the company taught the younger members not only the dances, but also told the stories of racism and oppression. *Revelations,* about religious experiences of southern African Americans, and *Cry,* written for dancer Judith Jamison, reflect pride and survival of a people and of the company. The choreography and influence of Ailey continues to be important in American dance.

Significance

In the article in *Dance Magazine,* Alvin Ailey tells Richard Philps, "You can teach people a lot if you teach with love; not be screaming at them, or threatening them, but by showing them what you want with patience and

Alvin Ailey founded his Alvin Ailey American Dance Theater in 1958. The organization has grown into an internationally known company and training program. © BETTMANN/CORBIS. REPRODUCED BY PERMISSION.

love, the way Lester taught." Lester was Lester Horton, Ailey's first dance teacher. He also acknowledged the legacy of Katherine Dunham, another African American dancer, in the article. She was a dance teacher and had established one of the first integrated dance companies in the nation.

The Alvin Ailey American Dance Theater began with dancers who worked other jobs and would stay up through the night to rehearse. By 1978, it comprised three companies—the well-known first company plus two others—along with an educational center that prepared dancers for the first company. The success of these companies and programs was in large part due to the vision of Ailey. They became well known for the celebrations of successes of the company, whether those were anniversary reunions or gala benefits. Former members of the troupe returned to dance alongside newer members.

Ailey was accused of being too commercial by some dance critics. Anne Kisselgoff wrote an essay, quoted by Jennifer Dunning, that placed "his work solidly within the framework of the larger dance scene in which it rightfully belonged but from which it was often implicitly excluded." Ailey's company, however, provided opportunities for dancers who would not have had an

opportunity in some of the more traditional, mainly white dance companies. Though Ailey died in 1989, the Alvin Ailey American Dance Theater continues to be viable and internationally acclaimed in the early 2000s.

Primary Source

"The Alvin Ailey American Dance Theater: Twenty Years Later" [excerpt]

SYNOPSIS: Celebrations have always been a part of the Alvin Ailey American Dance Theater. On the twentieth anniversary, Ailey reflects on the struggles and successes of his troupe.

Twenty years ago, on March 30, 1958, a group of twelve African American dancers gave a concert at New York's 92nd Street YM-YWHA; among them was a young actor-dancer named Alvin Ailey, and on the bill that evening was the premiere of a new work called *Blues Suite*—not Ailey's first ballet, but an extremely popular work which was to become a mainstay of the company known today as the Alvin Alley American Dance Theater. Although the company was one of those on-again, off-again sorts of things for a number of years, with dancers gathering together to rehearse and give one or two performances and then disbanding again, Ailey's company has succeeded where others failed. Part of this success is due to the persistence of the man himself. He attributes his success to his choice of repertoire from among American choreographers and to the strong performances for which his dancers are so well-known. For several generations of dancegoers, the Ailey company represents a revelation and a rich source of American-style dancing.

Anniversaries in the dance world are often celebrations of tenacity. In Ailey's case, the twelve-member performing group was the inauspicious beginning of what has become, in 1978, a complex of dance-related organizations: three companies (the world-famous first company, and two others connected with the school), and an educational center which teaches the diverse techniques which a dancer needs to know in order to qualify for the first company. There is an impressive scholarship program for talented students. Although there are always financial problems—a fact of life in any venture so deeply involved in the art of dance—various foundations and sources of funding have recognized the value of Ailey's organizations and *do* come through, often at the critical eleventh hour.

When the Alvin Ailey American Dance Theater turns twenty officially at a Gala at City Center on No-

Members of the Alvin Ailey Dance Company perform a scene from "The Mooch," 1977. © BEATRIZ SCHILLER 1997. REPRODUCED BY PERMISSION.

vember 29, Ailey will have on stage as many dancers as possible who have performed with his company in the past. For the season following the Gala, Ailey has scheduled revivals of several ballets which have slipped out of the company's rep—his own ballets and works by other choreographers.

"How long is a generation gap?" Ailey quizzes in a manner so theatrically exaggerated that he softens with humor what for him is a deadly serious issue these days—the lightning-quick passage of time.

Three years?

At the suggestion of an entire generation squeezed into such a ridiculously narrow straightjacket, even in this age of compression and condensation, Ailey explodes in spasms of laughter, *fits,* the kind of nervously energetic response which has probably made it possible for him to meet head-on all the absurdities and setbacks involved in trying to run his own company and to survive as a black man in the primarily white world of ballet and modern dance. Survive and *succeed,* not only in America, but on tour as far afield as Australia, Asia, Europe, Africa, and South America.

In his own distinctive way, Ailey is what we used to call a *mighty doer;* and he plans, he says, to *do* something about a problem often nagging him: the ignorance—*innocent* ignorance, a result of city life's fast pace—among his young dancers who are separated by a "generation gap" from their dance heritage, separated from the people who preceded Ailey, separated even from the forty-seven-year-old Ailey himself. Ailey points out that many of the young dancers in his school and companies weren't even born when he began. Saying this, he is thoughtful for a moment, then breaks the silence with a chuckle. Offering serious subjects up to humor's fire can be the most devastating kind of examination.

Further Resources

BOOKS

Defrantz, Thomas. "The Black Male Body in Concert Dance." In *Moving History/Dancing Cultures: A Dance History Reader.* Ann Dils and Ann Cooper Albright, eds. Middleton, Conn.: Wesleyan University Press, 2001, 342–349.

Dunning, Jennifer. *Alvin Ailey: A Life in Dance.* Reading, Mass.: Addison-Wesley Publishing Co., 1996.

Thorpe, Edward. *Black Dance.* Woodstock, N.Y.: Overlook Press, 1990.

PERIODICALS

Hering, Doris. "Alvin Ailey and Company." *Dance Magazine*, May 1958, 65–66.

Mazo, Joseph H. "Ailey & Company." *Horizon* 27, July–August 1984, 18–24.

WEBSITES

Alvin Ailey American Dance Theater Web Site. Available online at http://www.alvinailey.org/ (accessed April 9, 2003).

AUDIO AND VISUAL MEDIA

A Tribute to Alvin Ailey. Original Release, 1992, N.J. Kultur. VHS, 1997; DVD, 2000, Kultur Video.

Divining Revelations: An Evening with the Alvin Ailey American Dance Theater. Original release, 1986. DVD, 2001, Image Entertainment.

"A Woman Speaks"

Poem

By: Audre Lorde

Date: 1978

Source: Lorde, Audre. "A Woman Speaks." In *The Black Unicorn: Poems by Audre Lorde*. New York: Norton, 1978, 4–5.

About the Author: Audre Lorde (1934–1992) was frequently quoted as identifying herself as a "black, lesbian, mother, warrior, poet." A graduate of Columbia University and Hunter College, Lorde was a speaker and activist for women's voices being heard. Her struggles with cancer are documented in the 1980 volume, *The Cancer Journals*. New York governor Mario Cuomo appointed Lorde State Poet in 1991. She died of liver cancer the following year. ■

Introduction

Audre Lorde was the child of immigrants. During her childhood she had to attempt to merge the worlds of her parents, who were from Grenada, with the life around her in New York City. In Mari Evans's study of African American women writers, Audre Lorde wrote that her works spoke for "those women who do not speak, who do not have verbalization because they, we, are so terrified, because we are taught to respect fear more than ourselves. We've been taught to respect our fears, but we *must* learn to respect ourselves and our needs." She also acknowledged the care that needed to be taken not to make the African American woman, or any woman, just a victim in pain.

Sagri Dhairyam reports that Adrienne Rich, a fellow poet, tells the reader to "value [Lorde's] poetry precisely for the competing discourses of race, gender, and sexual persuasions." Lorde attempts to recover the Other, not only through being a "black, lesbian, feminist" but also through exploring the African culture and including the allusions to the myths and stories of ancient times. The

collection presents poems about the sorrow of war that contrast with the strength of personal identity. It is a collection about mothers, daughters, and sisters. The poem's narrator will "speak whatever language is needed," and will endure. "A Woman Speaks" provides a voice for women formerly silenced. Lorde recovers her West African heritage through symbolism and imagery. There are trickster figures in the poems and there is sadness and celebration. Lorde meant her poetry for a wide audience. She follows her own good advice in this volume. "Survive and teach; that's what we've got to do and to do it with joy" (Tate 116).

Significance

R. B. Stepto writes that *The Black Unicorn* contains new poems that reconfirm Lorde's talent while reseeding gardens and fields traversed before. Lorde's volume is "an event in contemporary letters" because of her immersion in West African religion, culture, and art. The poet could have attempted to write this volume without true knowledge of the culture, but it would not have been wise. Lorde, however, does have the knowledge and displays it in a volume that recreates voice, history, and geography of culture most American readers do not know. Lorde revises the myths. The daughter finds the language that Eshu had possessed, "whatever language is needed" to express thoughts and ideas.

Language is intertwined with Eshu, the trickster in the poems. Kara Provost notes that "Lorde borrows selectively from the trickster tradition, focusing on aspects she finds most relevant, including choosing to identify with a lesser-known, overtly female manifestation of the trickster, Afrekete, as a supplement to the phallic Eshu." A trickster can act as a translator. The characteristics include irony, magic, ambiguity, and sexuality. Tricksters disrupt the expected for the unexpected action. In *The Black Unicorn*, according to Povost, the trickster "must help translate among the other gods and between the gods and human beings." This is a metaphor for Lorde's attempts to communicate in a number of different communities in her world. It is not only Lorde who struggles with this problem of communication, many of her readers would as well.

The themes and subjects of Lorde's poetry included love, childhood, prisoners, and a quest for a voice in the literary world. Stepto concludes that *The Black Unicorn* offers contemporary poetry of a high order, and in doing so may be a "smoldering renaissance and revolution unto itself." Lorde's is a voice that needs to be remembered and read by current generations. This volume and others by Lorde remind readers that all people have a voice that should be heard.

Primary Source

"A Woman Speaks"

SYNOPSIS: Audre Lorde revises the mythical world of Africa and the definitions of womanhood in "A Woman Speaks." Woman becomes transparent when "the seas turn back." She is also hidden behind her "smile" and "treacherous with old magic." Lorde asserts the power of the female in the final stanza, drawing on her African cultural background for strength.

Moon marked and touched by sun
my magic is unwritten
but when the sea turns back
it will leave my shape behind.
I seek no favor
untouched by blood
unrelenting as the curse of love
permanet as my errors
or my pride
I do not mix
love with pity
nor hate with scorn
and if you would know me
look into the entrails of Uranus
where the restless oceans pound.

I do not dwell
within my birth nor my divinities
who am ageless and half-grown
and still seeking
my sisters
witches in Dahomey
wear me inside their coiled cloths
as our mother did
mourning.

I have been woman
for a long time
beware my smile
I am treacherous with old magic
and the noon's new fury
with all your wide futures
promised
I am
woman
and not white.

Further Resources

BOOKS

Evans, Mari, ed. *Black Women Writers (1950–1980): A Critical Evaluation.* New York: Anchor/Doubleday, 1984.

Tate, Claudia, ed. *Black Women Writers at Work.* New York: Continuum, 1983.

PERIODICALS

Dhairyam, Sagri. "'Artifacts for Survival': Remapping the Contours of Poetry with Audre Lorde." *Feminist Studies* 18, no. 2, Summer 1992, 229–256.

Provost, Kara. "Becoming Afrekete: The Trickster in the Work of Audre Lorde." *MELUS* 20, no.4, Winter 1995, 45–59.

Stepto, R.B. "The Phenomenal Woman and the Severed Daughter." *Parnassus: Poetry in Review* 8, no. 1, Fall/Winter 1979, 312–320.

Poet Audre Lorde published some of her work in *The Black Unicorn.*
THE LIBRARY OF CONGRESS.

WEBSITES

"Audre Lorde." Academy of American Poets. Available online at http://www.poets.org/poets/poets.cfm?prmID=314; website home page: http://www.poets.org/ (accessed April 10, 2003).

"Modern American Poetry: Audre Lorde (1934–1992)." University of Illinois at Urbana-Champaign. Available online at http://www.english.uiuc.edu/maps/poets/g_l/lorde/lorde .htm; website home page: http://www.english.uiuc.edu /maps/ (accessed April 10, 2003).

Judy Chicago's *The Dinner Party*

The Dinner Party: A Symbol of Our Heritage

Nonfiction work

By: Judy Chicago

Date: 1979

Source: Chicago, Judy. *The Dinner Party: A Symbol of Our Heritage* New York.: Doubleday, 1979.

The Dinner Party

Work of art

By: Judy Chicago

Date: 1974–1979

Source: Chicago, Judy. *The Dinner Party: The Brooklyn Museum, October 18, 1980–January 18, 1981.* Brooklyn, N.Y.: The Brooklyn Museum, 1980.

About the Artist: Judy Chicago (1939–), writer and artist, was born Judy Cohen in Chicago, Illinois. While attending the University of California-Los Angeles, where she earned a B.A. in 1962 and an M.F.A. in 1964, she studied traditional art and sculpture. However, Chicago is best known for her feminist art. At the California Institute of Arts in 1971 she helped to establish the Feminist Art Program at that school. She was named Outstanding Woman of the Year in Art by *Mademoiselle* magazine in 1973, and received grants from the National Endowment for the Arts in 1976 and 1977. ∎

Introduction

Judy Chicago developed the idea for *The Dinner Party* when she was looking for visual images depicting women's contributions to history. In her autobiography, she wrote, "most of all I was contemplating how to teach a society unversed in women's history something of the reality of our rich heritage." She decided on a table setting to transform the male oriented Last Supper into the female version, a dinner party. The idea was controversial from the beginning.

The Dinner Party took five years to research, construct, and finally install at the San Francisco Museum of Art, where it opened March 14, 1979. The exhibition is shaped as a triangle with thirty-nine place settings and 999 women's names on what was titled *The Heritage Floor*. The place settings and names represent women from the prehistory of Western civilization through contemporary America. Chicago has been criticized for including mostly white Anglo or European women in the work of art. She identifies herself as a Jewish feminist. Even when women of color or other ethnic groups are included, they are not identified as such or are represented in a different way than the white women. The place settings present the sexual images of women's bodies, primarily images of the vagina, which were seen as vulgar by conservative reviewers. Feminist critics and reviewers who were not professional art critics tended to react positively to the show. Despite the controversies, the exhibition drew large crowds. In San Francisco, "one hundred thousand people saw the exhibition, and twenty thousand hardcover copies of *The Dinner Party: A Symbol of Our Heritage* were sold in the first weeks of its release," according to Amelia Jones.

The exhibit did travel in the United States and throughout the world. Because of the size, cost, and time to install the exhibition it was stored for several years. The Elizabeth A. Sackler Foundation provided funding to permanently install Judy Chicago's *The Dinner Party* at the Brooklyn Museum of Art in 2004.

Significance

Judy Chicago did not create *The Dinner Party* by herself. It was a collective effort by several women, who worked twenty to thirty at a time, and a few men who collaborated in a studio. Those who assisted on the project were acknowledged in the exhibition and its accompanying publication; however, the fact that it is identified with Chicago is problematic for some artists. Chicago states in her autobiography that there was "continuous reinforcement for the feminist perspective and feminist values" in the studio. Without this assistance, the project would not have been possible.

The main table consists of three sides. Jones reports that Chicago identifies the thirteen place settings per side as "seats occupied by Christ and his disciples in The Last Supper. And the thirteen spots in its heathen opposite, the witches' coven." Embroidered runners are meant to represent altar cloths. Chicago had not included runners in her original design, but she was convinced that a table cloth would be too large. The runners provided a way to incorporate needlework, traditionally a female occupation, into the design of *The Dinner Party*.

Selecting and researching the 1,038 women who comprised the final exhibition took tremendous time and record keeping. There were three criteria for selection. First, said Chicago in her autobiography, the woman's "contributions or circumstances had to render her representative of a particular historical epoch. Second, her life needed to embody some type of significant achievement. Also she had to have in some way worked toward the betterment of conditions for women." The most difficult aspect for some women was finding a motif or image that could be used to depict the criteria in art work. Until it was installed at the San Francisco Museum of Art, no one had seen the entire exhibition put together. The work remains of interest because of the vision Judy Chicago had when she began it—to provide images and voices for unknown women.

Primary Source

The Dinner Party: A Symbol of Our Heritage

> **SYNOPSIS:** China painting, embroidery, and ceramics are incorporated into *The Dinner Party*. The work depicting female sexuality continued Chicago's early feminist artwork. Some names are familiar—Emily Dickinson, Virginia Woolf, Natalie Barney—while others included in *The Heritage Floor*, which accompanies the *Dinner Table*, were unknown.

The Dinner Party Project

I began working on *The Dinner Party* in 1974, and the concept for the piece gradually evolved dur-

Primary Source

The Dinner Party

SYNOPSIS: Judy Chicago utilized a triangle-shaped table as she put together "The Dinner Party Project." PAINTING BY JUDY CHICAGO, PHOTOGRAPH © BY DONALD WOODMAN. THROUGH THE FLOWER. REPRODUCED BY PERMISSION.

ing the first two years of my work in it. My research into women's history—begun in the 1960's as a result of my need for role models and resonance for my own esthetic impluses—had taught me that there was an enormous wealth of information on women's achievements, women's ideas, and women's art. I wanted to introduce that information into society and also express my rage at being deprived of my heritage. As an artist, I had been struggling for over a decade to build an art language to a large audience. One of my primary goals is to expand the role of art, and I saw *The Dinner Party* as way of doing that.

My original idea of representing the history of women in Western civilization took on the additional meaning of a reinterpretation of The Last Supper. I thought, "men had a last supper, but women have

had dinner parties." (Moreover, it was probably women who cooked the food for that famous Last Supper). The religious metaphor provided a way of dealing with the larger metaphysical issue of "feminine values" and the way in which they have been denigrated by modern society. The use of china painting and needlework—examples of women's traditional arts—suggests that in our cultural myopia about "women's work," we have deprived ourselves of the rich products, not only of women's culture, but also of women's minds and energies.

The Dinner Party and Heritage Floor

Thirteen place settings are on each forty-eight foot side of the triangular table. Each of the thirty-nine women is symbolized by a specially designed

Judy Chicago. AP/WIDE WORLD PHOTOS. REPRODUCED BY
PERMISSION.

and painted porcelain plate which is placed on a decorated fabric runner representing that woman's cultural and historic period. A porcelain knife, fork,
spoon and chalice complete the setting.

The tiled floor on which the table sits bears the
names of 999 women to honor the heritage of
women in history.

It required over two years and a team of more
than twenty researchers to compile the information
about the women represented on the Heritage
Floor. We chose the 999 women based on three
criteria: (1) Did the woman make a significant contribution to society? (2) Did she attempt to improve
conditions for women? (3) Did her life illuminate an
aspect of women's experience or provide a model
for the future? We selected women who, we believed, represented a range of nationalities, experiences, and contributions. All the women represented
on the floor are grouped around the women included at the table. These groupings are based on
common experiences, achievements, historic periods, or places of origin. Streaming out from each
of the place settings, the names inscribed on
the floor form a foundation for *The Dinner Party*
table.

Further Resources

BOOKS

Chicago, Judy. *Beyond the Flower: The Autobiography of a
Feminist Artist.* New York: Viking, 1996.

———. *The Dinner Party.* New York: Penguin, 1996.

Jones, Amelia, ed. *Sexual Politics: Judy Chicago's Dinner
Party in Feminist Art History.* Berkeley: University of California Press, 1996.

Lucie-Smith, Edward. *Judy Chicago: An American Vision.* New
York: Watson-Guptill, 2000.

PERIODICALS

"Judy Chicago–Elizabeth A. Sackler Foundation Donates 'Dinner Party' to Brooklyn Museum of Art in New York." *Ce-
ramics Monthly* 51, no. 1, January 2003, 22–23.

Lippard, Lucy R. "Judy Chicago's 'Dinner Party.'" *Art in America* 68, no. 4, April 1980, 115–127.

WEBSITES

Judy Chicago and Through the Flower Homepage. Available
online at http://www.judychicago.com/ (accessed April 6,
2003).

AUDIO AND VISUAL MEDIA

Chicago, Judy. *Judy Chicago's The Dinner Party: A Tour of
the Exhibition.* Directed by Donald Woodman. VHS, 1990,
Through the Flower Corporation.

*Right Out of History: The Making of Judy Chicago's "Dinner
Party."* Original release, 1980, Phoenix Films. Directed by
Johanna Demetrakas. VHS, 1999, Phoenix/BFA Films &
Video, Inc.

Einstein on the Beach
Liner notes

By: Tim Page

Date: 1993

Source: Page, Tim. "Einstein on the Beach." Commentary in
booklet accompanying *Einstein on the Beach,* composed by
Philip Glass and Robert Wilson. Performed by the Philip
Glass Ensemble. CD, 1993.

About the Author: Tim Page (1954–) is the author of sev-
eral books related to classical music, including *The Glenn
Gould Reader* (1990), *Music From the Road* (1992), *William
Kappell: A Documentary Life History of the American Pianist*
(1992), and *Tim Page on Music: Views and Reviews* (2002).
He has also provided informative notes in booklets accompa-
nying many recordings of classical music, most notably in
Sony's "Bernstein Century" series, and has contributed to
The New Grove Dictionary of Opera. Page won the Pulitzer
Prize for distinguished music criticism in 1997. ■

Introduction

Music critics adopted the art history term "minimal-
ist" to describe the music that composers such as La
Monte Young, Terry Riley, Steve Reich, and Philip Glass
began writing in the 1960s. Like artists, composers turned
away from traditional forms to experiment and create
something unique. This group of composers studied and
was influenced by non-western music, including music
from India and Africa.

Philip Glass (1937–), the most prominent of these composers, began writing music with repeated bars. Later he added layers, chordal progressions, and changing tempos. Glass restricted performance of his music to his Philip Glass Ensemble.

In 1973 Philip Glass met Robert Wilson (1941–), with whom he formed a partnership. The two began working on a four–act opera, *Einstein on the Beach.* Wilson's artistic abilities complimented Glass's musical talent. According to Keith Potter, Glass was attracted to Wilson, who had written and staged long operas, as a "rapidly emerging . . . formidable theater [talent]." Wilson, for his part, contributed sketches that provided the visual themes. Glass wrote a score for a sixteen-voice chamber choir plus the musicians of the Philip Glass Ensemble, and a solo violinist who represented Albert Einstein. The opera relies on visual imagery to tell the story of Einstein's life; there really is no plot in the traditional sense. The Einstein character sits in the orchestra pit, playing the violin. Images of trains, representing work on the theory of relativity; a trial; and a spaceship communicate Einstein's work and its implications. The opera ends with a space ship that releases tension built up by means of the sparse sets and the repetitions in the music. More dreamlike than dramatic, the work provided a new definition of "opera" in America. The four-hour, 40-minute composition is played without intermission—the audience is invited to come and go as they please throughout the performance.

Significance

Potter notes that *Einstein on the Beach* deals with "all the concerns of drama, as well as music, [and] is crucially 'on the edge' aesthetically and technically." The opera is controlled by the visual and the musical, rather than text, which exists as a combination of numbers and solfege syllables ("do–re–me" syllables). Short texts by Christopher Knowles, an autistic man who knew Wilson, are woven into the opera. The score evolved from *Music in Twelve Parts,* a composition Glass had just completed, and *Another Look at Harmony,* which he worked on simultaneously. Robert Wilson created "kneeplays," or interludes, which allowed sets to be easily changed.

After a successful European tour, *Einstein on the Beach* premiered at the Metropolitan Opera in New York on November 21, 1976. The opera was an addition to the Met's season. Two sold-out performances of 4,000 people attended the opera. Mel Gussow, a theater critic for *The New York Times,* notes that "gradually, as we are taken hostage by the sway of movement, stasis and repetition, we catch motifs, for example, geometric shapes." He accepts moments of boredom, while pointing out that the images and exceptional cast sustain the opera for the audience. Gussow concludes that it is "an

Musician Philip Glass. AP/WIDE WORLD PHOTOS. REPRODUCED BY PERMISSION.

organism with its own pulsating beat." Jack Kroll, *Newsweek*'s reviewer, writes that Wilson "has created an extraordinary universe" and that "Glass's score is exciting to listen to, providing much of the emotional kick and color of the work." Not everyone loved it: *Harper's* F. Joseph Spieler concluded that the experience was like being invited to dinner only to discover "you were to have brought your own food."

Einstein on the Beach brought Philip Glass fame and recognition. The opera also changed the direction of his career. Glass wrote two more operas, but also began writing for film, theater, and dance.

Primary Source

Einstein on the Beach [excerpt]

> **SYNOPSIS:** Philip Glass and Robert Wilson changed the sound and staging of opera. Their work forced audiences to listen and watch opera in new ways, becoming attentive to subtle clues that would provide meaning. Glass and Wilson continued to collaborate on operas over the next several years.

Einstein on the Beach (1976) is a pivotal work in the oeuvre of Philip Glass. It is the first, longest, and most famous of the composer's operas, yet it

Robert Wilson, 1978. © CORBIS. REPRODUCED BY PERMISSION.

is in almost every way unrepresentative of them. *Einstein* was, by design, a glorious "one-shot"—a work that invented its context, form and language, and then explored them so exhaustively that further development would have been redundant. But, by its own radical example, *Einstein* prepared the way—it *gave permission*—for much of what has happened in music theater since its premiere.

Einstein broke all the rules of opera. It was in four interconnected acts and five hours long, with no intermissions (the audience was invited to wander in and out at liberty during performances). The acts were intersticed by what Glass and Wilson called "knee plays"—brief interludes that also provided time for scenery changes. The text consisted of numbers, solfege syllables and some cryptic poems by Christopher Knowles, a young, neurologically impaired man with whom Wilson had worked as an instructor of disturbed children for the New York public schools. To this were added short texts by choreographer Lucinda Childs and Samuel M. Johnson, an actor who played the Judge in the "Trial" scenes and the bus driver in the finale. There were references to the trial of Patricia Hearst (which was underway during the creation of the opera); to the mid-'70s radio lineup on New York's WABC; to the popular song "Mr.

Bojangles"; to the Beatles and to teen idol David Cassidy. *Einstein* sometimes seemed a study in sensory overload, meaning everything and nothing.

A recording cannot capture the spectacular visual imagery that Robert Wilson devised for *Einstein on the Beach* but it should be said immediately that this was much more than the usual uneven collaboration between a librettist and composer. From its beginnings, worked out between Glass and Wilson over a series of luncheons at a restaurant on New York's Sullivan Street almost 20 years ago, this was truly a team effort.

At this time, Glass was writing long concert pieces for the Philip Glass Ensemble—most recently *Music in Twelve Parts (1974)* which might be considered Glass's "Art of the Repetition"—while working as a plumber and driving a taxi. "Foundation support was out of the question, of course," he recalled. "And most of my colleagues thought I'd gone completely off the wall." Still, by the mid-70s, the Ensemble had build a cult following in the lofts and galleries of Manhattan's nascent Soho district, and Glass had begun amassing credits as a theater composer by providing scores for the experimental Mabou Mines Company (of which his first wife, JoAnne Akalaitis, was a founding member).

Glass became aware of Wilson's stage work during an overnight performance of the twelve-hour *Life and Times of Josef Stalin,* presented at the Brooklyn Academy of Music in 1973. He was attracted to what he called Wilson's sense of "theatrical time, space and movement." The two men promptly determined to collaborate on a theatrical opus based on the life of a historic figure. Wilson proposed Chaplin, then Hitler; Glass countered with Gandhi. Finally, Glass and Wilson agreed upon Albert Einstein, and the name of the as-yet-unwritten work became "Einstein on the Beach on Wall Street." The title was later shortened; neither creator now remembers when or why.

"As a child, Einstein had been one of my heroes," the composer reflected in his book, *Music By Philip Glass* (Harper and Row, 1987). "Growing up just after World War II, as I had, it was impossible not to know who he was. The emphatic, if catastrophic, beginnings of the nuclear age had made atomic energy the most widely discussed issue of the day."

"Philip and I immediately agreed on the overall length of time we wanted to fill—four to five hours," Robert Wilson said in a recent interview. "We decided that each scene would be about 20 minutes

Philip Glass—American Minimalist

One of the most famous living American composers, Philip Glass describes himself as a "theatre composer who is tonal in orientation." By "theatre composer," Glass clarifies that the source of inspiration for his work is largely non-musical—"the image, movement, story." Although Glass's principal body of work consists of music for film, dance, and opera, he has also written in traditional forms, including symphonies, etudes for piano, and a violin concerto.

Although he skeptically questions the meaning of the term, Philip Glass is widely known as one of the founders of American Minimalism in classical music, along with Steve Reich, Terry Rilley, and John Adams. Glass describes his own works as "music with repetitive structures," producing "soundscapes" more akin to pictures than to more traditional melodic-oriented pieces with clear linear progression.

This interview, conducted by composer Alex Christaki, was recorded at the Royal Lancaster Hotel in London, England, on July 2, 1994. Christaki approached the interview as a fellow composer and musical admirer of Glass. Accordingly, his questions focused on certain issues reflecting his own personal experiences.

"An Interview with Philip Glass" [excerpt]

AC: I have found that your style has not really changed since around the 70's. Pinpointing North Star *and* Koyaanisqatsi, *how different are they?*

PG: Compared to *Einstein on the Beach*? Between 1966–76 that body of work more or less has an identifiable style, changes can appear normal. . . .

AC: The piece I am concentrating on is Powaqqatsi. *How did you go about writing it?*

PG: I started by looking at the pictures. The film was not completed and we had about twenty hours of film grouped in large categories. The opening "Serra Pelada," the "Gold Mine" was originally thirty minutes but was eventually ten. Working with the subject I generally wrote music which would work well with it, to support and suggest something either public or subtle. The distance or duration of the relationship may have a large range with each section having a large volume of images suggested by the music. The editor used my music to cut the film therefore creating a closeness between image and music. . . .

AC: . . . What were your influences?

PG: Probably Western classical music, the non-Western music for example the Indian music with Ravi Shankar in the 1960's. My time in Africa with Claude Sousot was useful. It helps to explode our own musical hobbies, those you come to naturally without thinking. To confront them with an exotic culture can shake them up. . . .

SOURCE: Glass, Philip, and Alex Christaki. "An Interview with Philip Glass." July 2, 1994. Available online at http://www.glasspages.org/interview.html; website home page: http://www.glasspages.org (accessed July 6, 2003).

long and that we would connect the scenes together with what I call 'knee plays'—the knee is a joint that links two similar elements, hence 'knee plays'. I did a series of drawings and Philip set them to music."

Wilson stresses that this marked a complete break with traditional theater. "In the past, theater has always been bound by literature. *Einstein on the Beach* is not. There is no plot—although there are many references to Einstein—and the visual book can stand on its own. We put together the opera the way an architect would build a building. The structure of the music was completely interwoven with the stage action and with the lighting. Everything was all of a piece."

The Glass-Wilson opera was intended as a metaphorical look at Einstein: scientist, humanist, amateur musician—and the man whose theories, for better and for worse, led to the splitting of the atom. Although it is difficult to discern a "plot" in *Einstein*, the climactic scene clearly depicted nuclear holocaust: with its renaissance-pure vocal lines, the blast of amplified instruments, a steady eighth-note pulse and the hysterical chorus chanting numerals as quickly and frantically as possible, it seemed to many a musical reflection of the anxious, *fin-de-siècle* late '70s.

Einstein on the Beach brought the composer fame—and notoriety. It was presented throughout Europe in the summer of 1976, then brought to the Metropolitan Opera House for two sold-out performances in November 1976. Then, as later, the audience response was mixed: Glass's works were presented to boos and bravos.

Further Resources

BOOKS

Duckworth, William. *Talking Music: Conversations with John Cage, Philip Glass, Laurie Anderson, and Five Generations of American Experimental Composers.* New York: Schirmer, 1995.

Griffiths, Paul. *Modern Music and After.* New York: Oxford University Press, 1995.

Page, Tim. "Einstein on the Beach." In *The New Grove Dictionary of Opera.* Stanley Sadie, ed. New York: Grove's Dictionaries of Music, 1992, 27–28.

Potter, Keith. *Four Musical Minimalists: La Monte Young, Terry Riley, Steve Reich, Philip Glass.* Cambridge, England, and New York: Cambridge University Press, 2000.

PERIODICALS

Gussow, Mel. "'Einstein' is a Science-Fiction Opera-Play." *The New York Times,* November 28, 1976, sect. 2, 3, 9.

Kroll, Jack. "Mind-Bender." *Newsweek,* December 6, 1976, 101.

Spieler, F. Joseph. "Adrift Among Images." *Harper's* 254, March 1977, 107, 110,112.

WEBSITES

Philip Glass—Official Web Site. Available online at http://www.philipglass.com/ (accessed April 9, 2003).

Sceaux, Nicolas. "Einstein on the Beach." Available online at http://nicolas.sceaux.free.fr/einstein/index.html; website home page: http://nicolas.sceaux.free.fr/ (accessed on April 9, 2003).

AUDIO AND VISUAL MEDIA

Einstein on the Beach: The Changing Image of Opera. Directed by Chrisann Verges and Mark Obenhaus. Direct Cinema, Ltd., 1985, VHS.

2

BUSINESS AND THE ECONOMY

JONATHAN KOLKEY, WILLIAM L. PEPER, PATRICK D. REAGAN

Entries are arranged in chronological order by date of primary source. For entries with one primary source, the entry title is the same as the primary source title. Entries with more than one primary source have an overall entry title, followed by the titles of the primary sources.

Important Events in Business and the Economy, 1970–1979

1970

- U.S. businesses spend $5.7 billion on computers.
- Advertisers spent $3.6 billion on television commercials.
- On January 1, U.S. consumer debt is $127 billion.
- On January 1, Americans own 89 million cars.
- On January 14, the U.S. Department of Justice indicts seven firms for polluting the New York harbor.
- On January 19, inflation reaches 6.1 percent, the highest since the Korean War (1950–1953).
- On January 28, Ford, Nissan, and Tokyo Kogyo form a joint venture to manufacture auto transmissions.
- On February 28, the January economic indicators fall by 1.8 percent, the worst monthly decline since the 1957 recession.
- On March 1, Westinghouse and four unions reach a contract raising wages 15 percent.
- On March 25, the first postal workers' strike in U.S. history ends after seven days.
- On April 1, Congress bans cigarette advertising on radio and television, beginning January 1, 1971.
- On April 15, Congress raises federal employees' wages 6 percent.
- On April 21, Congress allocates $4.6 billion for highway construction.
- On April 28, the Dow-Jones average falls to 724.33, the lowest since the November 1963 assassination of President John F. Kennedy.
- On May 5, a New Orleans grand jury indicts the Chevron Oil Company for violating pollution limits on ninety Gulf of Mexico oil rigs.
- On May 9, Walter Reuther, head of the United Auto Workers (UAW), dies, beginning a struggle among his successors for control of the union.
- On June 1, the U.S. Supreme Court rules 5-2 that federal judges can ban strikes that break no-strike contract clauses.
- On June 21, the Penn Central Railroad, which had been bankrupt, begins reorganization.
- On July 2, the U.S. Labor Department announces a drop in unemployment between May and June.
- On July 31, the House of Representatives authorizes President Richard Nixon to control wages, prices, and rents.

- On August 4, U.S. Steel announces an 11.8 percent increase on tin mill products.
- From September 15 to November 11, four hundred thousand UAW members strike General Motors.
- On September 17, Cesar Chavez, leader of the United Farm Workers (UFW), announces a national boycott against California's lettuce growers.
- On October 16, Paul Samuelson of the Massachusetts Institute of Technology becomes the first American to win the Nobel Prize in economics.
- On October 26, Congress mandates the use of unleaded gasoline in federal vehicles.
- On November 30, President Richard Nixon signs legislation creating the National Railroad Passenger Corporation, a private and public venture, to carry passengers between large cities.
- On December 4, the U.S. Labor Department reports that unemployment has risen to 5.8 percent.
- On December 11, following a five-month strike, Northwest Airlines increases wages 37.5 percent.
- On December 23, Congress empowers the secretary of labor to set safety regulations for factories, farms, and other enterprises.

1971

- The Department of the Post Office is reorganized as the semi-independent U.S. Postal Service.
- On January 7, the Nixon administration appeals a court order prohibiting the use of DDT for fear that crop yields may decline without the insecticide.
- On January 15, the Federal Trade Commission (FTC) charges seven soft-drink companies with price-fixing.
- On January 18, U.S. Steel accepts a court order to stop dumping waste into Lake Michigan.
- On January 22, General Motors recalls ten thousand school buses and forty-four thousand light trucks because of faulty clutches.
- On February 6, *Time* magazine reaches agreement on job discrimination with 140 women employees.
- On March 2, a grand jury indicts W. A. "Tony" Boyle, the president of the United Mine Workers, for using union funds to make illegal political contributions.
- On March 3, the three largest detergent makers cancel television ads that claim their products remove all stains following the FTC's "truth in advertising" campaign.
- On March 8, the U.S. Supreme Court prohibits employers from using job tests that discriminate against African Americans.
- On March 29, Ford recalls 220,000 Pintos because their engines may be susceptible to fire.
- On May 5, the U.S. Labor Department imposes racial hiring quotas at federally funded construction sites in three cities.
- On May 12, the Civil Service Commission bans men-only and women-only designations for most federal jobs.

- On May 17, the U.S. Justice Department sues the Wheeling-Pittsburgh Steel Corporation for polluting the Ohio and Monongahela rivers.

- On June 10, President Richard Nixon ends a twenty-year trade embargo against Communist China.

- On July 1, the International Longshoremen's and Warehousemen's Union strikes twenty-four ports on the West Coast.

- On July 8, Frank Fitzsimmons becomes president of the International Brotherhood of Teamsters, Chauffeurs, Warehousemen, and Helpers of America (Teamsters Union).

- On July 20, a strike by 532,000 American Telephone & Telegraph (AT&T) workers ends.

- On July 25, thirty-five thousand workers end their twenty-six-day strike at Kennecott Copper Corporation.

- On August 2, Congress authorizes a $250-million bailout of the Lockheed Aircraft Corporation.

- On August 15, President Richard Nixon announces his New Economic Policy, freezing wages, prices, and rents for ninety days and initiating other broad economic controls.

- On September 1, a precedent-setting U.S. Justice Department suit requires Florida Power and Light to build a $30-million system to clean the water it pumps into Biscayne Bay.

- On September 15, the U.S. Department of the Interior refuses to grant two oil-drilling permits in California's Santa Barbara Channel.

- On October 1, East and Gulf Coast longshoremen, as well as eighty thousand coal miners, go on strike.

- On October 15, Simon Kuznets of Harvard University wins the Nobel Prize in economics.

- On November 13, Anaconda Wire and Cable is fined two hundred thousand dollars for polluting the Hudson River.

- On November 24, Herbert Stein replaces Paul McCracken as chairman of the Council of Economic Advisers.

- On December 4, General Motors recalls 6.68 million defective Chevrolet cars and trucks.

- On December 10, President Richard Nixon signs a $25-billion tax cut.

- On December 14, Congress extends the Nixon administration's price controls until April 1973.

1972

- On February 18, a seven-month strike against the New York Telephone Company ends.

- On February 21, a new contract ends the 134-day West Coast longshoremen's strike.

- On March 9, the House of Representatives votes to end the killing of whales and other sea mammals in U.S. waters. On July 26, the Senate passes a fifteen-year ban on the killing of ocean mammals.

- On March 29, the U.S. Justice Department sues twenty aircraft manufacturers for stifling competition in research.

- On May 6, Japanese and European steel producers promise to limit exports to the United States for the next two years.

- On May 8, General Motors recalls 350,000 defective 1971 and 1972 Chevrolets.

- On May 16, George Shultz replaces John Connally as Treasury Secretary.

- In June, the Dow-Jones average hits 1,000 for the first time in history.

- On June 14, the EPA bans DDT.

- On June 29, Ford recalls over four million 1970 and 1971 cars and trucks.

- On July 8, Congress authorizes the sale of $750 million in grain to the Soviet Union, giving farmers a market for export.

- On August 2, the U.S. Department of Agriculture bans the use of the steroid DES in cattle feed, effective January 1, 1973, angering cattleman who had used the steroid to grow livestock to market weight in a shorter time than is possible without the steroid.

- On August 15, a federal court lifts an April 1970 injunction banning the construction of the Trans-Alaska Pipeline.

- On September 14, Congress authorizes the sale of eighteen million bushels of wheat to Communist China, again giving farmers a market for export.

- On October 2, the U.S. Atomic Energy Commission orders Consolidated Edison to clean pollution at its Indian Point plant on the Hudson River.

- On October 25, Kenneth J. Arrow of Harvard University shares the Nobel Prize in economics with John R. Hicks of Great Britain.

- On October 27, the U.S. Department of Labor reports that prices increased 40 percent more than wages under the Nixon administration's New Economic Policy.

- On November 1, Standard Oil of New Jersey is renamed Exxon.

- On November 16, Pepsico announces a deal to sell its products in the Soviet Union.

- On December 12, the U.S. Justice Department accuses Xerox of hindering competition.

1973

- On January 4, the Federal Communications Commission allows Western Union to build a domestic communications satellite system.

- On January 11, the Nixon administration ends wages and price controls, except in the food, construction, and health-care industries.

- On January 18, American Telephone and Telegraph (AT&T) pays fifteen thousand women and minority employees a total of fifteen million dollars as compensation for discriminatory practices.

- On February 13, a federal court fines the Ford Motor Company seven million dollars for improperly servicing 1973-model cars.

- On April 12, Occidental Petroleum Company reaches a multibillion-dollar agreement to build a fertilizer plant in the Soviet Union.

- On May 2, the Nixon administration tightens price controls on some six hundred large companies.
- On May 3, a court orders Delta Air Lines to open more positions to women and African Americans.
- On May 8, the United Rubber Workers union strikes B.F. Goodrich Company.
- On May 31, a four-month strike against the Shell Oil Company ends.
- On June 6, the House of Representatives votes to raise the minimum wage from $1.60 to $2.20. On July 19, the Senate votes to increase it to $2.00.
- On June 13, President Richard Nixon freezes consumer prices for sixty days, except for rent and unprocessed farm goods.
- On July 2, national banks raise their prime lending rates to 8 percent.
- On July 17, the Senate, following House approval, authorizes the construction of the 789-mile Trans-Alaska Pipeline.
- On September 3, George Meany, head of the American Federation of Labor and Congress of Industrial Organizations (AFL-CIO), denounces President Richard Nixon's economic policy.
- On September 17, Chrysler and the autoworkers' union reach a three-year contract, raising wages 5 percent the first year.
- On October 2, a federal court orders Detroit Edison to pay $4 million to African Americans who suffered employment discrimination.
- On October 18, Wassily Leontief of Harvard University wins the Nobel Prize in economics.
- From October 19 to October 21, some members of the Organization of Petroleum Exporting Countries (OPEC) stop selling oil to the United States and other Western nations for their support of Israel in the Yom Kippur War.
- On October 30, the U.S. Justice Department accuses 541 trucking companies of discriminating against women and minority employees.
- On November 16, President Richard Nixon signs a bill authorizing construction of the Trans-Alaska Pipeline.
- On November 30, Ford lays off twenty-five hundred workers following a decline in car sales. On December 28, General Motors will lay off eighty-six thousand workers.
- On December 4, Chrysler recalls sixty-four thousand defective 1973 and 1974 cars.
- From December 4 to December 7, oil shortages cause airlines to cancel flights. Truckers block highways to protest high fuel costs.
- On December 22, Congress orders states to reduce interstate speed limits to 55 MPH to conserve gasoline.

1974

- David Rockefeller forms the Trilateral Commission to promote international trade.
- On January 1, welfare payments account for 27 percent of state and federal expenditures.

- On January 31, a court orders Georgia Power and Light to pay $2.1 million in retroactive wages and benefits to African American employees denied equal job opportunities.
- On March 12, the U.S. fines Volkswagen $120,000 for violating auto-emission controls.
- On March 18, OPEC, with the exception of Libya and Syria, resumes selling oil to the U.S.
- On April 1, wage and price controls end in 165 industries; on April 15, they will end on food retailers and wholesalers.
- On April 2, the Soviet airline Aeroflot has access to Washington's Dulles Airport.
- On April 8, President Richard Nixon extends the minimum wage to eight million additional workers and signs an increase in it to $2.30 per hour.
- On April 17, William Simon replaces George Shultz as treasury secretary.
- On April 30, President Richard Nixon's authority to impose wage and price controls ends with the expiration of the 1970 Economic Wage Stabilization Act.
- On June 1, a seven-day strike begins between the Amalgamated Clothing Workers and the men's clothing industry—the first strike between the two parties since 1927.
- On June 28, the Occidental Petroleum Corporation signs four twenty-year contacts with the Soviet Union.
- On July 15, the machinists' union strikes Trans World Airways.
- On September 9, a 177-day strike between Dow Chemical and the United Steelworkers' union ends.
- On October 8, President Gerald Ford announces his program to control inflation, Whip Inflation Now (WIN).
- On October 29, Congress bans discrimination based on gender or marital status.
- From November to December, Sears Roebuck, Celanese, Ford, Chrysler, General Motors, American Motors, Bethlehem Steel, Motorola, Singer Sewing Machines, Weyerhauser Lumber, and Xerox all lay off workers as the economy contracts following the OPEC embargo.

1975

- Bankruptcies set a new record of 254,484.
- Exxon Corporation replaces General Motors as the wealthiest U.S. company.
- On January 1, U.S. Steel closes ten open-hearth furnaces in Gary, Indiana, following fines for pollution.
- On January 10, Matsushita Electric Industrial Company recalls three hundred thousand color televisions.
- On January 29, the U.S. Atomic Energy Commission, fearing defects, closes twenty-three nuclear reactors for inspection.
- On February 7, the U.S. Labor Department reports January unemployment at 8.2 percent, the highest since 1941.
- On February 18, General Motors recalls 220,000 defective cars.

- On March 17, the Chicago, Rock Island & Pacific Railroad declares bankruptcy.
- On March 29, President Gerald Ford signs a $22.8-billion tax bill.
- On May 14, President Ford rejects New York City's request for a federal loan to avoid bankruptcy.
- On June 22, Alan Greenspan of the Council of Economic Advisers announces an end to the recession.
- On June 26, the U.S. Labor Department announces that economic indicators rose in May, the fourth consecutive increase, evidence that Alan Greenspan had been right to declare an end to the recession.
- On July 18, railroads avert a strike by agreeing to increase pay 41 percent over three years.
- On August 1, Lockheed Aircraft admits to paying $22 million in bribes to obtain foreign contracts.
- On September 3, some 530,000 teachers in twelve states go on strike.
- On November 7, the U.S. Supreme Court overturns a Utah law denying unemployment benefits to women in the third trimester of pregnancy.
- On November 27, the Ford administration announces a five-year U.S.-Polish grain deal, opening Poland to U.S. food exports.
- On December 1, in Connecticut a 154-day strike ends at General Dynamics.

1976

- The last Cadillac Eldorado rolls off the assembly line, signaling an end to U.S. production of convertibles due to declining sales.
- Nissan beats Volkswagen as the leading foreign car importer in the United States.
- American farmers number 8.9 million, only 4.2 percent of total population.
- On January 2, President Gerald Ford vetoes a bill that would have broadened picketing rights by strikers at construction sites.
- On January 5, California fines American Motors $4.2 million and bans the sale of three models of AMC cars for violating state pollution laws.
- On February 4, Congress authorizes limited U.S. landings by the supersonic Anglo-French Concorde aircraft.
- On March 26, the U.S. Justice Deparment accuses the Encyclopaedia Britannica Company of deceptive selling practices.
- On April 1, Conrail, a federally funded consolidation of six bankrupt northeastern railroads, begins operation.
- On April 14, fourth-quarter indexes suggest economic recovery.
- On April 21, the United Rubber Workers strike four tire and rubber companies.
- From June 2 to June 21, the newspaper guild strikes *Time* magazine.

- On June 6, the Teamsters end a fourteen-week strike against Anheuser-Busch.
- On July 1, the U.S. Supreme Court orders mining operators to compensate miners for black-lung disease.
- On August 25, General Motors raises its car prices an average of $344; the base sticker price for its autos is now $6,000.
- On September 15, American Bank and Trust Company fails, the fourth largest banking default ever.
- On October 12, 165,000 workers return to Ford after a twenty-eight day strike.
- On October 14, University of Chicago economist Milton Friedman wins the Nobel Prize in economics.
- On December 10, Chrysler recalls 208,000 cars.

1977

- A five-month drought threatens farmers and ranchers in the Texas panhandle.
- Foreign auto sales increase 73 percent since 1976.
- Bethlehem Steel posts the worst quarterly losses in its history.
- The United States posts the highest trade deficit in its history, $31.1 billion.
- Personal income in the United States rises 11.1 percent, the largest increase since 1973.
- Many consumers respond to high coffee prices by switching to tea.
- On January 12, Atlantic Richfield, the eighth largest oil company, buys the Anaconda Company, the third largest copper-mining corporation in the United States.
- On March 10, the Teamsters and the United Farm Workers settle their dispute over organizing farm workers.
- On April 30, police arrest demonstrators trying to block the Seabrook, New Hampshire, nuclear-power plant construction site.
- On June 14, Arnold Miller is reelected president of the United Mine Workers.
- On June 20, oil begins to flow through the 789-mile Trans-Alaska Pipeline.
- From July 13 to July 14, an electrical blackout strikes New York City.
- On August 1, strikes in the iron ranges of Minnesota and Michigan halt most iron ore production.
- On August 4, Congress creates the Department of Energy. James Schlesinger becomes its first secretary.
- On September 21, Bert Lance, director of the Office of Management and Budget and a close friend of President Jimmy Carter, resigns following criticism of his activities with a Georgia bank.
- On September 26, Freddie Laker begins his no-frills New York-to-London Skytrain air service.
- On October 1, Longshoremen strike thirty ports from Maine to Texas. The strike will last nearly one month.

- On October 3, three hundred American Airlines stewardesses who were fired for pregnancy between 1965 and 1970 receive a $2.7 million civil rights settlement.

- On October 11, the U.S. Justice Department orders Leeway Motor Freight to pay forty-six African American employees $1.8 million to compensate for discrimination.

- On November 1, President Jimmy Carter signs a law raising the minimum wage to $3.35 per hour by 1981.

- On December 28, G. William Miller replaces Arthur Burns as chairman of the Federal Reserve Board.

1978

- Dean Witter and Reynolds Securities International merge to form Dean Witter Reynolds International.

- U.S. automakers recall a record twelve million vehicles.

- Due to inflation, goods costing $100.00 in 1967 now cost $200.90.

- The salaries and bonuses of corporate executives rise 16.7 percent.

- General Motors regains its position as the wealthiest U.S. corporation. Exxon Corporation is second.

- On January 2, the machinists' union ends a twelve-week strike against two Lockheed plants in California.

- On January 31, the United Farm Workers end their boycott on lettuce, table grapes, and Gallo wines.

- On February 1, the U.S. Justice Department sues the Teamsters and their president, Frank Fitzsimmons, for dubious pension-fund loans.

- On February 24, President Jimmy Carter announces a tentative settlement in the eighty-one-day coal strike. An agreement is signed 14 March.

- On March 2, the government fines Texaco $228,770 for safety lapses that killed eight workers in a Port Arthur, Texas, fire.

- On March 4, the *Chicago Daily News* ends publication after losing subscribers and advertisers.

- On March 25, a 110-day coal miners' strike, the longest in U.S. history, ends with the signing of a new three-year contract.

- On April 17, investors trade a record 63.5 million shares on the New York Stock Exchange.

- On May 3, alternative energy advocates declare Sun Day in order to publicize alternative energy sources.

- On June 15, the U.S. Supreme Court orders an indefinite halt to a $100-million project to build the Tellico Dam in

Tennessee because it threatens the habitat of the snail darter, an endangered species of perch.

- On October 16, Herbert A. Simon of Carnegie-Mellon University wins the Nobel Prize in economics.

- In November, California voters approve Proposition 13, which forbids state and local government from raising property taxes without voter consent.

- On December 15, McDonnell-Douglas admits that it distributed $18 million in bribes to gain foreign contracts.

1979

- On January 1, 26 million Americans are below the poverty line.

- In February, Iran stops exporting oil to the U.S., causing shortages and raising prices.

- On May 6, in Washington, D.C., sixty-five thousand demonstrate against nuclear power.

- On May 9, California begins gasoline rationing to cope with Iran's oil embargo.

- On June 7, truckers strike to protest rising fuel prices and lower speed limits.

- On June 16, Congress deregulates long-distance phone service.

- On July 31, the Chrysler Corporation, the third largest automaker in the United States, requests a $1-billion federal loan to prevent bankruptcy.

- In August, the Federal Reserve Board pushes interest rates near 20 percent, the highest since the Civil War, to contract the money supply and thereby end inflation caused by an increase in gasoline prices.

- On September 20, Lee Iacocca becomes the chief executive officer of Chrysler Corporation.

- On October 17, Theodore Schultz of the University of Chicago and Arthur Lewis of Princeton University share the Nobel Prize in economics.

- On October 22, the U.S. Justice Department charges Sears Roebuck and Company with job discrimination.

- On November 19, Lane Kirkland succeeds George Meany as AFL-CIO president.

- On November 27, U.S. Steel closes thirteen plants, laying off thirteen thousand workers.

- In December, Michigan, Illinois, and Pennsylvania report double-digit unemployment.

- On December 19, the U.S. Department of Energy accuses seven oil companies of $1 billion in overcharges from 1973 to 1976.

"Franchising's Troubled Dream World"

Magazine article

By: Charles G. Burck

Date: March 1970

Source: Burck, Charles G. "Franchising's Troubled Dream World." *Fortune,* March 1970, 116, 118, 121, 148, 152.

About the Author: Charles G. Burck is a successful writer and editor. He has written for *Fortune* and serves on the magazine's Board of Editors. ■

Introduction

Americans have always held both small business and the small-business owner in the highest regard. While citizens of the United States often display a healthy distrust of government and of big corporations that seem to dwarf the individual, small business appears to be the ideal societal counterweight for redressing the balance of power in favor of ordinary people. The small-scale entrepreneur (whether merchant, manufacturer, or service provider) frequently functions as the veritable backbone of the community. Not beholden to any distant authority, the small businessman or woman with deeply embedded roots in the community often exhibits a longstanding loyalty to the area. As the old saying goes, "the little guy," who often sponsors local charities, joins service clubs, or runs for city council, "is one of us." As such, that business owner can be more easily trusted than a larger and geographically remote enterprise. In addition, small business has always provided one of the most effective means for ambitious individuals to advance from worker to owner—and to make a potentially significant jump across class lines.

However, by 1960, a number of social forces combined to spell doom for many small businessmen who had struck out on their own in search of the "American Dream." The proliferation of national chains crowded out independents in communities across the country. Meanwhile, statutes that were once enacted to help small businessmen fend off cutthroat competition (for example, "fair trade" laws) were gradually repealed or were meet-

ing with lax enforcement. The public, increasingly squeezed by inflation, began to seek refuge at discount "super stores" that offered lower prices. Worse yet, from the small-business perspective, the flood of cheap foreign imports after 1960 helped condition consumers to rock-bottom pricing. Additionally, a new system of credit whereby large impersonal corporations provided credit cards came increasingly to replace the familiar and more informal practice of local merchants offering credit to individual customers in need. This change dramatically altered America's system of consumer financing.

After 1960, the American small business often took the form of an owner-operated franchise of a large, often national firm. Franchises became available for a bewildering array of products and services—including fast food, dry cleaning, home repairs, and printing. By 1970, the franchise had become a universally accepted institution in American life.

Significance

The new corporate franchises superficially resembled the old independent small businesses. After all, a hamburger, French fries, and a Coke still make the same meal, even under a different marketing arrangement. The chain outlet, however, was part of a larger network. No longer strictly neighborhood-oriented, the franchise outlet had access to national advertising and product selection.

In addition to well-recognized outlets such as McDonald's Hamburgers and Kentucky Fried Chicken, another type of franchise made its appearance during the 1970s—the home-based business, of which Amway may be considered the prototype. Unlike the better-known chains that required considerable capital to purchase a franchise and to set up operations, Amway-style businesses involved virtually no start-up investment. Moreover, unlike a fast-food outlet, the home-based business could be built up gradually on a part-time basis. Hence, the commitment of time and funds was less rigorous. Furthermore, even the casual home-based businessperson could take advantage of various tax breaks designed to foster entrepreneurship. Many Amway distributors, for instance, saw themselves as neighborhood guerrillas waging a battle to allow the proverbial "little guy" to obtain a larger piece of the pie in the troubled 1970s United States economy.

Problems arose in these new ventures owing to the inflated expectations of many enterprising individuals—especially those who attended franchisee recruitment seminars that were conducted with the fervor of a tent revival. As in any multilevel marketing scheme, those perched at the apex of the pyramid often reaped abundant riches. Those near the bottom, however, rarely prospered even if they managed to add a few dollars to the family budget every month. Then too, con artists and swindlers operated near the margins of these multilevel marketing organizations, preying relentlessly upon the naïve.

Primary Source

"Franchising's Troubled Dream World" [excerpt]

SYNOPSIS: Although traditional independent small business seemed doomed during the 1960s, this longstanding American entrepreneurial impulse found another outlet—the corporate franchise. By the 1970s, franchises were a powerful force in the U.S. economy, but not without their problems.

"Franchising has become the updated version of the American dream," exulted Ray Kroc, chairman of McDonald's Corp., at a symposium at Boston College two years ago. Kroc should know. Fifteen years ago he was a paper-cup salesman; today he is the chairman of a nationwide company with 1,300 outlets and annual sales of $450 million. He owns three million shares of McDonald's stock, and his net worth is well over $100 million.

Kroc's story is not unique. He is one of a number of people who have become wealthy by sensing that franchising is a profitable idea whose time has come. He capitalized on a form of business organization that seems to solve two irreconcilable conditions. While men dream of financial success and security against failure, they also cherish independence and freedom. At a time when more and more people are dissatisfied with the bureaucratic forms of business and demand more individual recognition, franchising updates the success dream by promising liberation as well. The holder of a franchise has access to sophisticated management techniques, yet he is not only a store manager but an investor in his own outlet and a seemingly independent businessman. The company—the franchisor—gets a highly motivated salesman and a source of capital. The concept has irresistible appeal to anyone with an entrepreneurial instinct.

Yet not all is sweetness and light in franchising. The institution is now in a state of turbulence, racked with disputes, clouded with legal problems, and—its boosters to the contrary—uncertain about its future. Leaders in the business are often hard put to find agreement on how to handle these problems, and some hold viewpoints that call into question the whole future of the system.

Though franchising seems like a new discovery, it has been around for more than half a century, used by automobile manufacturers, brewers, oil compa-

nies, and others for both wholesale and retail distribution. What *is* new is the phenomenal recent growth of franchised enterprises—not only in fast foods but also in a bewildering array of fields ranging from carpet shops and rent-a-car outlets to income-tax advisory services, business colleges, "community greeting" organizations, and high-rise combined one-stop mausoleum-funeral homes. About 90 percent of the franchise companies now in operation have started since 1954.

Being "new" and full of promise, the system is, above all, promotable. Virtually anything can be sold by franchise; and, it seems, virtually anything that is called a franchise can be sold to someone or other. Some of the hoopla is reminiscent of Florida land-boom days, or perhaps a carnival midway. Franchise shows—there are some forty a year across the country—are organized to attract prospects, who sign up often without knowing quite what they've got into. At one time Wall Street was every bit as much infatuated with franchising as it had been with conglomerates. (Lately it seems to have sobered up somewhat about franchising.)

The best estimates—though they tend to reflect the boosterism of franchising promoters—hold that there are more than 1,200 franchise companies and between 400,000 and 600,000 franchise outlets. Their sales total somewhere between $80 billion and $110 billion; if the generally accepted figure of $90 billion is realistic, the industry accounts for about 10 percent of the gross national product and 26 percent of all retail sales.

Many of the newer companies are in areas whose growth potential has only been scratched—e.g., convenience grocery stores, employment agencies, financial services, and tool and equipment rental shops. But in fast foods, which constitute only 2 percent of franchise sales, a shake-out appears imminent. Fast foods are the most nearly ubiquitous franchise operations, peppering the landscape with free-standing and often gaudy stores, to some of which celebrities like Joe Namath and Johnny Carson have lent their names (for a piece of the action). The ease of entry makes saturation likely, and the profusion of small, untested companies makes failures inevitable. If all the fried-chicken stores projected for the next three years survive (Kentucky Fried Chicken says it will have 4,000), it seems improbable that all the hamburger stands or fish and chip stores—to say nothing of pizza, roast beef, and manifold varied-menu restaurants—will have enough hungry customers to go around. . . .

A 1970s advertisement for McDonald's shows an employee presenting "The Big Meal," consisting of a Big Mac, fries, and a soft drink. **THE ADVERTISING ARCHIVE, LTD. REPRODUCED BY PERMISSION.**

Moreover, the franchising stampede has been joined by some really big corporations with plenty of staying power: General Foods and Pillsbury are in fast foods with their Burger Chef and Burger King chains. United Fruit Co. owns A & W root beer and Baskin-Robbins, which sells ice cream. RCA has acquired Arnold Palmer Enterprises, which includes driving ranges and dry-cleaning shops. The former International Milling Co. is now called International Multifoods Corp., and is building a franchise division based on a number of fast-food operations. City Investing has tried to build up a franchise-brokering division, while Consolidated Foods has its Chicken Delight operation. . . .

Buying them back

Franchising faces still bigger threats to its growth than stock-market evaluation and accounting reforms. One troublesome new development is the policy some franchisors have of buying back outlets and running them as company-owned stores. The implication of this policy is that franchising is useful only as a short-run, transitory stage for an expanding company. John Y. Brown Jr., head of Kentucky Fried Chicken, is one exponent of the buy-back. Brown told a security analysts' meeting last year: "We'll make more profit from 300 company-owned stores than we will from 2,100 franchise outlets." Brown would like to go to all company-owned units in the end. Other franchisors have said much the same thing, adding that the company store also gives them more control over prices, quality, and personnel, and more flexibility in meeting changing business conditions.

But it is not quite as easy as Brown makes it appear. McDonald's, for instance, is as capable a firm as can be found in fast-food management. That company has been gradually increasing its company-owned stores, mainly through new openings and also through repurchases of groups. At the end of 1968, about 15 percent of McDonald's outlets were company stores, and President Fred Turner would like to increase the amount to 20 percent.

The company likes to buy back groups of operators who have well-developed management and a single TV marketing area. It likes to maintain company stores because they provide leverage and leadership for changes the company wants to make throughout the chain. And the revenues *are* greater; even that slight 5 percent shift, says Turner, "would have a significant impact on corporate earnings." But, Turner goes on to say, "anything larger than 20 percent would create management problems . . . If we went to 40 percent, we'd come apart at the seams."

The reason is a distinction that many franchisors seem unable or unwilling to understand. As Lawrence Singer, onetime head of the Royal Castle system of company-owned stores, has explained, "Franchising is a business itself. The consumer is the franchisee and the product is the consulting service offered to him." With a majority of company-owned stores, the former franchisor is suddenly in the restaurant business himself, needing more managers with different skills. Brown insists that Kentucky Fried Chicken can retain its franchise operators after they have been acquired. Indeed he is now forecasting that his company will repeat the cycle by selling fish and chips franchises and then buying back the stores later at a low price-earnings multiple. If he can accomplish this, it will be one of the neatest examples of financial leverage in business.

Weeding out the fly-by-nights

The ambitious plans of the large companies are not always in the best interests of their franchise holders. Within and without the business, there are enough disenchanted men to have inspired a boomlet of self-protection organizations and crusading critics. Harold Brown, a caustic Boston attorney, has made a specialty of analyzing the legal rights of franchise holders, and has come to the conclusion that, "The franchise agreement presently in use by most franchisors is an instrument of repression."

Rhetoric aside, there are grounds for the anguished complaints of small businessmen who feel that they have been wronged. In most cases a franchisor can arbitrarily terminate a contract for the infringement of any one of hundreds of rules detailed in an operations manual. A Federal Trade Commission report concludes that, in many instances, termination clauses are frequently utilized "directly or subtly, to enforce restrictive or otherwise unlawful provisions of franchise agreements."

What makes the threat of termination especially vivid is that most contracts don't make any provision for good will when the franchisee sells—or is forced to sell—his business. The franchisor assumes that good will is the result of his own advertising and systems. Thus a terminated gas-station operator is left with only the inventory he has in stock; his initial investment and all of the work he put into building up a reputation and steady patronage are down the drain. A fast-food operator, similarly, is left with his inventory and equipment at book value, which in the case of restaurant equipment is usually far less than its actual value as functioning machinery. Senator Philip Hart, chairman of the Senate Antitrust and Monopoly Committee, has introduced a bill that would put the burden on the franchisor to show "good cause" in terminations—i.e., to prove that the franchisee failed to "substantially" carry out requirements that were "both essential and reasonable."

Any fast-growing unregulated industry attracts its share of fly-by-night operators, and franchising is no exception. The more responsible companies would like to see full-disclosure legislation that would force prospective franchisors to state their assets, experience, and the basis for their profit projections. The attorney general of California has gone a step further. He has ruled that all franchise offerings must be registered as securities. . . .

Franchisors and their trade organizations insist that things aren't all that bad in the business. They regard the critics as overzealous, often misinformed, and sometimes dated in their understanding of current franchise practices. "A good many things you hear are perfectly valid early versions of early franchise agreements," says Philip Zeidman, Washington lawyer for the International Franchise Association. "But contracts today bear no relation to those of a few years ago." Then, too, the aggrieved franchisee may not be suffering as much in reality as he imagines. As Harry Rudnick, general counsel to the L.F.A., points out, "One of the very human things that happens to a man down the road a few years is that he begins to attribute his success to himself—not to the franchisor—and asks himself: 'Why should I continue to pay royalties?'"

Despite the problems and abuses, most people in the industry see a boundless future for franchising. The future is there, to be sure, if the system can cope successfully with some thorny problems. Honest accounting practices are sorely needed. Antifraud laws need to be strengthened to prevent the promotion of paper franchises. And the industry should abandon the myth that a franchise holder is an independent small businessman. When companies reach the point of dealing candidly and openly with the issue of independence, they may still have dissatisfied franchisees. But they will avoid that special bitterness that comes from having been led down the garden path by a mirage-like American dream.

Further Resources

BOOKS

Dicke, Thomas S. *Franchising in America: The Development of a Business Method, 1840-1980.* Chapel Hill: University of North Carolina Press, 1992.

Xardel, Dominique. *The Direct Selling Revolution: Understanding the Growth of the Amway Corporation.* Cambridge, Mass.: Blackwell, 1993.

Conn, Charles Paul. *The Possible Dream: A Candid Look at Amway* Old Tappan, New Jersey: Revell, 1977.

"World Trade in the 1970s"
Journal article

By: AFL-CIO Economic Policy Committee
Date: May 1970
Source: AFL-CIO Economic Policy Committee. "World Trade in the 1970s." *American Federationist,* May 1970, 9, 10, 11–12, 13, 15.
About the Organization: The AFL-CIO (American Federation of Labor-Congress of Industrial Organizations) Economic Policy Committee was charged by the national AFL-CIO to prepare a report on the impact of the growing, global, free-trade movement on American organized labor. This report was published in May 1970. ∎

Introduction

Tariffs and import/export taxes—second only to slavery—were the most divisive political issues in American politics during the nineteenth and early twentieth centuries. The United States has used tariffs as a tool of economic policy throughout its history, both in order to raise money for the government and to encourage the sale and purchase of American products. Other countries have similar tariffs, and U.S. foreign trade policy has tried to strike a balance between properly protecting and overprotecting U.S. industries—weighing the effects of free-market competition with its impact on the U.S. economy and jobs. Deciding what industries will receive special protection and what tariff rate will apply to each has historically been a very difficult political issue, as have negotiations with other countries over trade issues.

Prior to World War II (1939–1945), U.S. tariff decisions generally had less impact than they did later both because the economy was much smaller and because, between 1894 and the start of World War II, the United States sold more goods abroad than it imported. After World War II, however, economic production in the U.S. and the level of foreign trade both increased dramatically, closing the gap between U.S. exports and imports. Technological advances and the growing economies of other countries provided stiff competition to some U.S. industries. Since foreign workers were often paid less than American workers, some foreign manufacturers realized substantial savings and produced the same products for less than American companies could do. In particular, the U.S. automotive, textile, and steel manufacturing industries found themselves losing market share and jobs to foreign manufacturers in the 1970s. Major American corporations, including automobile manufacturer Chrysler, faced the real possibility of bankruptcy because of the strong foreign competition. American consumers, on the other hand, benefited from the increased competition through the lower prices they paid and the higher quality of products they purchased.

Many AFL-CIO members lost their jobs during the layoffs in the affected industries—and as an increasing number of American corporations moved their operations abroad in order to compete better in the manufacturing process. The AFL-CIO Economic Policy Committee addressed this issue by focussing on the effect of the trade policy on American organized labor while also raising important public policy questions. The Committee's report called on American leaders to establish a trade policy that allowed orderly expansion into foreign markets—while keeping the best interests of the American worker in mind. In practice, however, trade policy necessarily favors some and hurts others in every situation. For that reason, it will continue to be a divisive issue.

Significance

Congress has responded in two distinct ways to the challenge of establishing a U.S. trade policy. First, Congress passed the 1974 Trade and Tariff Act to ensure that American products would given reasonable access to foreign markets. The Act gave the president great discretion in retaliating against countries that used unjustifiable restrictions to keep out American goods. The act also permitted retaliation against countries that "dumped" goods into the U.S. market and sold them for far less than fair market value. While this law has enabled the president to protect certain U.S. interests and to take action against unfair competition, other countries have responded by increasing their own tariffs. In addition, the use of these measures has hurt the process of negotiating international trade agreements. Of the 150 international trade agreements in effect in the early twenty-first century, the United States was a party to only three.

The 1994 passage of the North America Free Trade Agreement (NAFTA)—an agreement between the United States, Canada, and Mexico gradually to eliminate all tariffs and quotas and to establish free trade between the countries—represented a very different approach to the challenge of establishing U.S. trade policy. Congress also provided the president with trade promotion authority in

August 2002 by giving that office much broader authority to negotiate international trade agreements. Both of these actions—bitterly opposed by organized labor—demonstrate that ensuring access to foreign markets—ninety-six percent of the world's population lives outside the United States—and expanding free trade will continue to be a central consideration in negotiating American trade policy.

The AFL-CIO Economic Policy Committee focused on the real impact of trade policy on American workers, particularly those in organized labor. The trend at the beginning of the twenty-first century in American trade policy is toward expansion of free-market access and forging of international agreements that limit tariffs and quotas. This policy will significantly impact many American workers, some benefiting and others being disadvantaged. Trade policies and tariff issues are likely to continue to create controversy within American society.

Primary Source

"World Trade in the 1970s"

> **SYNOPSIS:** The impact of the burgeoning world-wide free-trade movement of the 1970s is analyzed in the following excerpt from a report prepared by the AFL-CIO Economic Policy Committee and published in their monthly magazine, *American Federationist*. Many of the economic problems devastating the American worker by century's end were already in evidence three decades earlier when this report was written.

The United States position in world trade deteriorated in the 1960s, with an adverse impact on American workers, communities and industries. A thorough revision of U.S. government posture and policy is required to meet present realities in world markets.

In every year since 1894, the United States has sold more to foreign nations than it has bought. But by 1968 and 1969, this surplus of merchandise exports over imports almost disappeared—despite the fact that the reported volume of merchandise exports includes shipments financed under AID and Food for Peace. . . .

The adverse impact of the deteriorating U.S. trade position is particularly harsh on affected workers and their communities. Shutdowns of plants or departments usually result in the loss to workers of seniority and seniority-related benefits and, sometimes, the jobloss means that special work skills developed in a specific plant cannot be applied elsewhere. Moreover, workers and their families cannot move from one town to another without considerable

Japanese-made Toyota automobiles are unloaded at a shipping terminal in Boston, Massachusetts, August 17, 1971. President Richard Nixon had recently announced a 10 percent surcharge to be placed on imported automobiles. © BETTMANN/CORBIS. REPRODUCED BY PERMISSION.

expense as well as the loss of friends, schools, church and social relationships developed over many years. An affected community, particularly a small town, can experience a shrinking tax base, losses for merchants and professionals and the waste of public facilities. In contrast, invested money in a business can be moved around and equipment can be sold and shipped.

Major causes of the deterioration of the U.S. position in world trade have been new developments in the post-World War II period that accelerated in the 1960s. Among these developments have been the spread of managed national economies, with direct and indirect government barriers to imports and aid to exports; the internationalization of technology; the skyrocketing rise of investments by U.S. companies in foreign subsidiaries and the spread of U.S.-based multinational corporations.

Such changes have made old concepts of "free trade" and "protectionism" outdated and increasingly irrelevant. Yet, U.S. government policy has failed, for the most part, to face up to these new developments, leaving a policy that is more applicable to the world of the late 1940s and 1950s than the 1970s.

A substantial change in U.S. trade policy is needed—for the orderly expansion of world trade on a reciprocal basis and for the improvement of the U.S. trade position in the interest of the American people. . . .

The rapid expansion of manufactured imports in the 1960s was particularly great in several products for which the United States had previously been a world leader—steel, autos, machinery and electrical products (including TV, radios and telecommunications apparatus). In the 1960s these products joined others that had previously posed import problems—such as shoes, textiles, clothing, glass and leather goods. These industries are mostly labor-intensive—with sizable numbers of production and maintenance workers per dollar of output. . . .

Every industrial country gives preference to domestic producers when governments buy products. In the United States, limited "Buy American" laws affect many government purchases in varying degrees. But in most other countries, more stringent results are achieved by national administrative policies rather than by openly declared legislation. . . .

In Japan, national policy involves both written and unwritten rules that discriminate against imports and spur exports. In general, Japan maintains import quota controls on more commodities than any other developed country in the free world. But the "administrative guidance" of the Japanese government is the most important barrier to imports and spur to exports.

Developing countries also have extensive trade practices, for a variety of reasons. Many such countries, like Mexico, tell firms they may not sell a variety of U.S.-made products in their countries, but must produce the goods within their borders. The policy of "import substitution" in such countries means that all imports are licensed and imports are allowed only when the country itself does not produce the product.

The combination of these practices means that imports, which are frequently subsidized or otherwise encouraged by governments, surge into the huge U.S. market, with its high living standards—probably the most open market to imports of all major countries. At the same time, U.S. exports are often retarded by barriers and other practices of foreign governments. . . .

The internationalization of technology has been reducing or eliminating the former U.S. productivity-lead in many industries. Thus, in many industries and products the lead in technology and productivity, which enabled high-wage U.S. industries to compete successfully in world markets, even against low-wage competition, has been reduced or eliminated. The world-wide, growing emphasis on science and technology has been only one factor in the internationalization of technology. . . .

These developments have resulted in the export of American jobs as well as technology. Moreover, the outflows of U.S. private capital that have financed part of these soaring investments have been a major factor in U.S. balance-of-payments problems. . . .

Foreign subsidiaries of U.S. firms and foreign companies using U.S. licenses, patents and the like from U.S. technology can take maximum advantage of lower wage and fringe benefit costs and produce goods at lower unit costs and at productivity levels similar to those in the United States. . . .

The deterioration of the U.S. foreign trade position has significant impact on jobs, the collective bargaining strength of unions and on wages and labor standards in adversely affected industries.

Precise information on the job-loss of imports is not available and estimates of the job-impact of exports are only rough guesses that are clouded by the increasing complexity of trade patterns. Unfortunately, foreign trade experts usually show little interest and even less knowledge about the impact which developments in foreign trade have on employment. . . .

Yet the fact of job losses is clear. And recent changes in the composition of imports have been a special burden on semi-skilled and unskilled production workers in an increasing number of industries and product-lines—with the surge of imports of such relatively labor-intensive products as shoes, textiles, clothing, steel, autos, ceramic tile, radios, TV, leather goods and others. The loss of such job opportunities has occurred at a time when jobs for the unskilled and semiskilled in production are urgently needed in the U.S. labor force, which is growing about 1.5 million each year. These jobs are particularly needed for Negroes and members of other minority groups who are seeking to enter the economy's mainstream.

Further Resources

BOOKS

Halberstam, David. *The Reckoning.* New York: Morrow, 1986.

Plaff, William. *Barbarian Sentiments How the American Century Ends.* New York: Hill and Wang, 1989.

Thompson, William R. *The Emergence of the Global Political Economy.* New York: Routledge, 2000.

WEBSITES

Bovard, James. "The Myth of Free Trade." Cato Policy Analysis No. 164, Cato Institute. Available online at http://www.cato.org/cgi-bin/scripts/printtech.cgi/pubs/pas/pa-164.html; website home page: http://www.cato.org (accessed June 18, 2003).

Fitzgerald, Sarah J. "The Effects of NAFTA on Exports, Jobs, and the Environment: Myths vs. Reality." *The Heritage Foundation Backgrounder."* Available online at http://www.heritage.org/Research/TradeandForeignAid/BG1462.cfm; website home page: http://www.heritage.org (accessed June 18, 2003).

———. "Needed: A New Vision for U.S. Trade Policy." *The Heritage Foundation.* Available online at http://www.heritage.org/Research/TradeandForeignAid/BG1543.cfm; website home page: http://www.heritage.org (accessed June 18, 2003).

"More Companies Hire Workers They Once Spurned—The Elderly"

Newspaper article

By: Bill Paul

Date: November 2, 1970

Source: Paul, Bill. "More Companies Hire Workers They Once Spurned—The Elderly." *Wall Street Journal,* November 2, 1970, 1, 18.

About the Author: Bill Paul wrote for the *Wall Street Journal,* which is published by Dow Jones & Company. The *Wall Street Journal* first began publication in the United States in 1889, and has since gone on to become a successful newspaper with a wide readership and several global editions. Dow Jones & Company also publishes *Barron's* and the *Far Eastern Economic Review.* ∎

Introduction

Both life expectancy and perceptions about retirement have changed dramatically in the United States since 1900. Americans are living twenty-nine years longer on average, and the transition to a "knowledge economy"—no longer requiring as much hard physical labor as in the past—has enabled post-retirement age employees to remain active participants in the workforce. The 1970s saw the beginning of this trend in employment, as the cultural assumption that one stops working at sixty-five came to be challenged.

During the 1970s, major corporations needed employees for two distinct types of jobs: first, difficult-to-fill positions that required extensive knowledge and skill; and second, low-paying—or "dead-end,"—jobs that were essential to continued operations. Workers entering the workforce often either lacked the skills and experience necessary for the available positions, or they had better long-term alternatives than to take employment without any prospect of career advancement. Retirees, who faced substantial reductions in Social Security benefits if they earned too much, were ideally suited to fill these needs—often as consultants or part-time employees. Many retirees who were already receiving pensions and benefits were happy to work on a contract basis or for a relatively low salary in order to supplement their incomes.

This arrangement worked out exceptionally well for the corporations. Rather than investing time and energy in training employees, they capitalized on the expertise of these experienced workers, often without having to supply employee benefits. While the transition required a change in the structures of many businesses to incorporate part-time workers, the rewards were great. Studies have shown that, compared to younger workers, seniors have lower absenteeism, a stronger work ethic, higher productivity, and better judgment and people skills, and that they are more willing to listen and learn on the job. Older workers can also serve as effective role models and mentors to younger employees.

Significance

The availability of meaningful employment opportunities has changed the perceptions about retirement for many older workers. Instead of using retirement for rest and relaxation, many seniors now plan to continue contributing their expertise in the work place, and to take advantage of the opportunity both to keep physically and mentally active and to supplement their retirement income.

Corporations have had to change their historic assumptions about older workers. Mandatory retirement ages, nearly universal in 1970, have been repealed at most companies. Innovative companies that recognize the value of integrating part-time employees—the older people and many of the women who enter the workforce—have realized a significant competitive advantage. Traditional concepts of lifetime employment and the bias against elderly consultants and part-time employees have given way to the realization that elderly workers can play an active, productive role in the modern economy. Companies have started actively recruiting retirees in light of these benefits, and employment agencies that specialize in the placement of retired consultants and temporary workers are flourishing.

Demographic data reveal that the trend toward employment of elderly workers will continue to increase as the United States' largest age-group, the Baby Boomers, approaches retirement age. Those over sixty-five, comprising 12.4 percent of the U.S. population in 2000, will exceed twenty percent of the population by 2030 according to Census 2000 estimates. Ninety-five percent of all American adults are planning to work at least part-time after age sixty-five.

Primary Source

"More Companies Hire Workers They Once Spurned—The Elderly"

SYNOPSIS: Bill Paul of *The Wall Street Journal* describes the efforts of major corporations to attract elderly employees, a new trend in 1970s.

They're More Reliable, Less Choosy and Work for Less Pay Than Younger Workers

Social Security Stops Some

Note to personnel men:

Go find Harry Glitz and hire him back.

An older person sells tickets in a Boston, Massachusetts, movie theater box office in 1972. © JEFF ALBERTSON/CORBIS. REPRODUCED BY PERMISSION.

You remember Harry. You tossed him out the door 10 years ago when he reached the mandatory retirement age. Today Harry is 75 years old and probably a bit frail.

Nonetheless, Harry will not only do better on the job than the youngster who replaced him, but he will also complain less, show up more regularly and gladly work for less money and no fringe benefits at all.

That, at least, is the story told by a growing number of companies across the country. Corporate personnel chiefs are finding that oldsters form a ready and willing labor pool for a wide variety of part-time, temporary or hard-to-fill jobs—jobs that even in a time of high unemployment still exceed the number of workers willing or qualified to accept them. And retirees, many of them feeling the pinch of inflation and many others just plain sick of sitting at home staring at the walls, are responding to the new demand with alacrity.

A Happy Pairing

Retirees are seldom sought out to fill skilled blue-collar jobs or high-level white-collar positions. More typical is the sort of work that recently lured

John Rossi and Bob Weaiat, both 67, and Ruby Bates, whose age is her own secret, back from retirement. Miss Bates was called in by General Motors' New York office to file paperwork. Mr. Rossi sorts mail for Texaco executives in Manhattan. And Mr. Weaiat was hired by IBM to edit and update sales and engineering manuals.

Almost without exception, both the workers and the companies are delighted. Mr. Rossi, for example, worked 32 years for the Post Office . . . retired last year and discovered he could neither make ends meet nor pass the time of day. "There's never going to be any retirement for this man," he now declares. "You've always got to keep your mind occupied." Besides that, he adds, "How can a man live on a $80-a-week pension?"

A spokesman for GM's New York office says the company recently became "disappointed with the young temporaries we'd hired." So in the first half of this year GM took on 11 retirees as temporary clerical workers, Ruby Bates included. Somewhat to its surprise, "we found that the seniors did as good a job, and in some instances better, than our young contemporaries," says the spokesman.

No one knows the full extent of the trend. The Bureau of Labor Statistics says about two million of the 20 million Americans over 65 hold jobs, but it believes most are self-employed or do volunteer work or work for small mom-and-pop operations unburdened by retirement rules or pension plans. Not until recently has big industry begun to drop the bars against old folks.

Last August, for example, Bankers Trust Co., New York, launched a citywide recruiting effort to find more than 100 old people for temporary and part-time work as tellers, accountants and security men. United Fruit Co. has been hiring retirees in the Boston area since last January as mail room and communications employees, and Manpower Inc., a leading personnel agency, has a two-year-old employment program for oldsters that, according to a spokesman, "has really caught on with employers."

Welcome Up to 90

Although the recent rise in unemployment has made it easier to fill vacant job slots, some companies still go out of their way to seek out oldsters. "The older worker may go at a slower pace, but over a year's time you get more out of him because he's more steady, conscientious and always shows up for work," says Jack Heeran, chairman of Circuit Systems Corp., of Villa Park, Ill. As a rule, says Mr.

Heeran, who is 47 himself, he prefers employees over 40, and he will happily take on a worker as old as 80 or 85. Once they pass their 90th birthday, Mr. Heeran is less interested.

Mr. Heeran feels old folks get an unfair shake at most companies. He is a self-made millionaire who retired at age 40 to play golf in California. He got bored with that in short order, but when he tried to get a job with former business associates, they all told him he was too old. That angered Mr. Heeran, who started his own company, which is doing quite well, he says, with a good number of old folks on the payroll.

Few executives are as committed as Mr. Heeran to hiring the elderly, but clearly the practice is catching on. Colonial Penn Group, a diversified Philadelphia concern, has set up employment agencies that specialize in retirees in more than 25 cities, and it says business is booming.

That's not to say there aren't obstacles for the company that decides to hire people over 65. "I could use older people," says one personnel director, "but our pension and insurance plans are geared to mandatory retirement at 65, no exceptions allowed. Even if I decided to change that, the union would say no."

There is a way around that problem, however. Many companies—Texaco among them—simply hire their over-65 help through a personnel agency, which keeps the workers on its own books as employees of the agency. Texaco pays the salaries, but it avoids having to shell out the sick pay, pensions, and other fringe benefits that its own internal rules call for it to grant to employees.

That might seem like a raw deal for the oldsters, but most of them are so happy to work that they don't complain. Such eagerness may help explain why senior workers perform some jobs better than younger men or women. These include jobs in which the accumulated expertise of an oldster is needed on a limited basis—as is the case with Mr. Weaiat at IBM—and so-called dead-end jobs that young people shun or purposely do poorly at. One major Eastern manufacturer turned to retirees after finding most of its young mail room staff was smoking marijuana and taking drugs on the job.

One reason retirees may enjoy and therefore perform well at unglamorous jobs is that they usually work part-time. Woodward & Lothrop, a department store chain, based in Washington, D.C., employs 200 to 400 over-65 workers a year as part-time sales personnel to spell regular employes during lunch hours or to increase the work force during the Christmas shopping season. Though the work is strenuous, the oldsters generally work only a few hours a day. "These people do a superb job," says Fred Thompson, the concern's personnel director. He is convinced that many companies are "missing the boat" by not hiring the elderly.

An Eager Labor Pool

The store's personnel men began appealing to senior citizens' groups in Washington a few years ago after a sizable radio, newspaper and direct mail employment campaign failed to turn up enough qualified younger people to fill the firm's temporary vacancies. They found hundreds of qualified elderly persons eager to put in a few hours a day.

Social Security laws inhibit many oldsters from working full-time. Currently, if a retired person between the ages 65 and 72 earns more than $1,680 but less than $2,880 annually, he loses half his annual benefits. If he earns over $2,880 he gets no Social Security payments at all. Consequently, retirees prefer part-time work and, if they do work full-time, many of them do so for low salaries so as to retain their Social Security benefits.

Some employers have that reason in mind when they hire the elderly. Butcher & Sherrerd, a Philadelphia brokerage house, figures it saves about $25,000 a year by employing four over-65 men as runners.

Legislation pending in the Senate would increase the cut-off point on earnings that disqualify a person for Social Security to $3,000, but many critics feel that will be hardly any help at all for the elderly person who wants to work but can't afford to give up his Social Security. Students of the problems of the aged point out that Social Security laws were passed before many companies instituted mandatory early retirement and before many medical advances that have lengthened life spans and improved the health of the elderly.

Skeptics Abound

So far, the Federal Government has done little more about the problem than to hire a handful of oldsters itself. Two months ago, the Federal National Mortgage Association began using 15 retirees to take bids over the phone twice a month during its open market operations. Previously the bids were mailed—a method that proved increasingly unreliable.

Most Federal agencies, though, do no more than private industry to encourage employes to stay on after their 65th birthdays. And it's clear that many a skeptical personnel man has yet to be convinced that hiring the old is wise. Typical is the East Coast executive who says: "Sure, some old people are still able to turn out a good day's work, but we have a mandatory retirement age for a reason. By and large, older folks can't cut the mustard anymore."

Most labor unions, which have fought long and hard for early retirement rules, also frown on the elderly taking up slots in the work force, although for a different reason. "People should retire by 65 on a decent pension," says a spokesman for the International Electrical, Radio & Machine Workers. "Otherwise, it blocks opportunities for younger guys down the road."

Despite such obstacles, the hiring of oldsters is picking up as more and more companies spread the word that the elderly do well on the job. "There is no substitute for experience," says Jim Berg, a personnel man at Perkin-Elmer Corp., a Norwalk, Conn., maker of optical equipment. Perkin-Elmer employs several engineers and scientists over 65, some of whom came on board after being retired by other companies. "They think just as young as the young ones," says Mr. Berg, "and often they hold up better."

Further Resources

BOOKS

Levine, Martin. *Age Discrimination and the Mandatory Retirement Controversy* Baltimore: Johns Hopkins University Press, 1989.

Myles, John, and Jill Quadagno. *States, Labor Markets, and the Future of Old Age Policy* Philadelphia: Temple University Press, 1991.

WEBSITES

notretiredyet.com Available online at http://www.notretiredyet .com (accessed June 18, 2003). *Contains numerous resources for seniors seeking positions, as well as employment of the elderly.*

"Update on Older Workers: 2000." AARP. Available online at http://research.aarp.org/econ/dd62_worker.html; website home page: http://research.aarp.org (accessed June 18, 2003). *Contains comprehensive statistical data on elderly in the workplace.*

"The Surge of Public Employee Unionism"

Journal article

By: David L. Perlman

Date: June 1971

Source: Perlman, David L. "The Surge of Public Employee Unionism." *American Federationist,* June 1971, 1, 2, 3–4, 5.

About the Publication: The *American Federationist* is a pro-labor journal published by the American Federation of Labor and the Congress of Industrial Organizations (AFL-CIO). The AFL-CIO is a voluntary federation of over 60 international labor organizations that work to advance, promote, and protect the interests of workers in the economy. ∎

Introduction

When the American Federation of Labor (AFL) and the Congress of Industrial Organizations (CIO) merged to form the AFL-CIO in 1955, the American labor movement achieved its highest point in membership in U.S. history: Roughly thirty-five percent of the non-agricultural work force were union members. In subsequent years, the nature of U.S. labor changed in two significant ways: By the middle of the 1950s, the majority of the American labor force was already migrating from blue-collar to white-collar employment. At the same time, union membership was beginning to shift from private firms to the public sector

During the postwar years, industrial blue-collar jobs shrank in number, while service and white-collar jobs grew. When union organizers faced growing anti-union efforts by private employers in the 1960s and 1970s, they turned to organizing the growing numbers of government employees in federal, state, and local government agencies and offices. During those two decades, organizing drives by unions of postal workers; the American Federation of State, County, and Municipal Employees (AF-SCME); the Transport Workers Union of America (TWUA); the National Education Association (NEA); the American Federation of Teachers (AFT) for public school teachers; the Service Employees International Union (SEIU); and local fire-fighter unions brought thousands of public-sector, white-collar workers into the labor movement. The surge in union membership in these sectors was in part a response to the civil rights movement, the war on poverty, and the revival of the women's rights movement.

Historically, public-sector employees had resisted unionization efforts, while politicians and tax-paying citizens were reluctant to allow unions into the realm of government under the collective-bargaining system created in the 1930s and 1940s. Yet public-employee union membership grew from 400,000 in 1955 to more than

Two thousand school teachers and other union supporters protest outside a Philadelphia prison February 11, 1973, where Federation of Teachers president Frank Sullivan and chief negotiator John Ryan are being held for refusing to order striking Philadelphia teachers back to work. © BETTMANN/CORBIS. REPRODUCED BY PERMISSION.

four million by the early 1970s. By then, AFSCME membership growth made that union one of the largest in the entire AFL-CIO. NEA membership reached over one million, while even the smaller AFT claimed over 250,000 members. Total government employment, which in 1947 had been 5.5 million, reached 11.6 million by 1967, about 85 percent in state and local governments. By 1970, government workers made up 18 percent of the country's labor force.

Significance

During the 1970s, Americans began to acknowledge a long-term trend in the workforce that had actually begun in the 1950s. More employees in both the private and the public sectors were engaging in white-collar work for private corporations and small businesses in the financial, retail, and service industries and in government, especially at the state and local levels. In the wake of the turbulent social protests of the 1960s, middle-class taxpayers saw the surge in public-sector unionism at the national level as tied to expanding federal spending and the creation of a range of social-welfare agencies.

Most Americans remained unaware of this major change in the composition of the workforce until the postal strike in the summer of 1970. That year, 180,000

postal workers and letter carriers across the nation went on strike to win better pay and benefits. As the economy softened and the unemployment rate went up, many Americans grew to resent public employees and their unions for accepting lower pay than workers in the private sector were earning in exchange for job security. As economic stagnation reduced the number and the pay of available jobs, American attitudes toward unionization in both the private and public sectors grew more negative exactly when public-sector union membership grew in numbers and strength. Union membership, and with it political influence, entered a period of long-term decline in the mid 1970s that would continue until a revival of union organizing activity and membership in the 1990s.

Primary Source

"The Surge of Public Employee Unionism" [excerpt]

SYNOPSIS: The surprising surge in public employee union membership during the 1970s—despite an overall downward trend for every other segment of the American labor movement—is the subject of this piece by David L. Perlman that originally appeared in the *American Federationist*, the monthly magazine of the national AFL-CIO. Perlman lauds this new spurt of union-organizing activity, perhaps unmindful of the strength of the sharp reaction by opponents that would coalesce later in the decade.

Not since the surge of unionism in the 1930s has the labor movement experienced anything comparable to the current trade union breakthrough among public employees.

In less than a decade, union membership has at least tripled among employees of federal, state and local governments.

Today, thousands of collective bargaining agreements cover millions of workers. Ten years ago, the proud claim was that several hundred written agreements covered tens of thousands of public employees.

Most dramatically on the picket line, but in other ways as well, public employees have demonstrated their growing militancy.

A mere chronology of this phenomenal growth of union organization in the public sector would make an impressive chapter in any labor history. But it is too soon for the book to go to press; we are only midway through the chapter.

Ground rules for public employee collective bargaining are still evolving. Some state and local laws prohibiting public workers from organizing have been struck down as unconstitutional. Legislatures that once debated whether to allow government administrators to "meet and confer" with employee organizations are now considering how best to deal with impasses in collective bargaining. Experience has shown them that such impasses cannot be overcome by punitive anti-strike laws.

In the absence of any legal mandate, some public jurisdictions have applied common sense procedures to achieve a good bargaining relationship with unions. But in a rural Maryland county, 130 determined road workers struck for 227 days during 1970 before winning recognition of their union. And there, significantly, it took an election turnover of the county commissioners to bring an end to the longest public employee strike in the nation's history.

Last year's genuinely spontaneous walkout by 200,000 postal workers made front-page, banner headlines in every newspaper. But the labor historian will surely consider at least equally important the manner in which the dispute was resolved—direct, top-level labor-management negotiations. In those negotiations, the executive assistant to the president of the AFL-CIO served as chief negotiator

for the postal union team, the deputy postmaster general led the management negotiators and Assistant Secretary of Labor W. J. Usery Jr., who enjoyed the confidence of both sides, had an important mediation role.

The agreement provided for a big two-step pay raise that Congress subsequently approved, but it also did much more.

It created a whole new structure of collective bargaining covering almost all aspects of employment for 600,000 workers as part of a semi-autonomous U.S. Postal Service.

"Quite candidly," AFL-CIO President George Meany told newsmen at the time, "we in the AFL-CIO see these negotiations as setting the stage for the future." Similar collective bargaining procedures, he stressed, "can and should be extended to all workers of the federal government." . . .

Postal union officials are outspoken in their disappointment that the management of the new U.S. Postal Service put no money offer on the table and offered no meaningful concessions in the first set of negotiations under the new law.

The impasse-settling procedures of the law were invoked, starting with fact-finding. But from the union standpoint, the "last resort" stage is being reached without meaningful, face-to-face bargaining.

One indirect result has been overwhelming rank-and-file support for worker unity. When five postal unions merged recently to form a new 300,000-strong American Postal Union, the unity agreement was ratified by 96 percent of the membership voting in a mail referendum. The merger included the entry into an AFL-CIO union of the largest unaffiliated organization of postal workers.

Other difficulties will certainly arise as the evolution of collective bargaining in the public sector continues. But the pace of change in the past decade has been rapid enough to convince the doubters. . . .

While the federal civil service has its own peculiarities in terms of labor-management relations, it at least has a common set of ground rules. This can't be said for the even bigger field of state and local employment.

Pennsylvania and Hawaii have comprehensive bargaining laws and dispute-settling mechanisms for public employees, including the right to strike except where the public health and safety clearly prohibits it. South Dakota law requires local officials to "meet and confer" with unions of public employees. But any agreement has to be implemented by resolution.

Massachusetts permits agency shop agreements—but only in Boston and in Suffolk County. Minnesota, following a practice common in Europe but illegal in this country in private industry covered by the National Labor Relations Act, provides for proportional representation of teacher organizations on bargaining committees representing teachers in a community.

Vermont allows teachers to strike if their actions do not represent a clear and present danger to a sound educational program. How would you like to interpret that law?

And hundreds of smaller jurisdictions—cities and counties—have their own ordinances. Or, as noted before, they have no legal guidelines at all.

The overwhelming majority of the nation's fire fighters, nevertheless, are effectively represented by a strong union. In nearly every city of any size, either the AFL-CIO American Federation of Teachers or an independent union engages in negotiations—even if a euphemism is sometimes used as a substitute for collective bargaining.

The State, County and Municipal Employees represent and bargain for thousands of units, ranging from zoo keepers to social workers, from highway workers to prison guards, from tax collectors to hospital attendants and to scores of other occupations.

Over 100,000 members of the Service Employees are public workers, about one-fourth of SEIU's total. The Laborers are rapidly becoming a major union in the public employee field, with 80,000 members, or about 12 percent of their total. Transit unions, of course, increasingly deal with public employers—often under the same ground rules set by collective bargaining in private industry. A recent survey by the Transit Union showed that over 41,000, or 57 percent, of its members are on the public payroll and the Transport Workers estimate that 40 percent of its members work for government-owned systems. . . .

Governors, mayors and county officials are increasingly coming to accept the premise contained in a booklet on "State-Local Employee Labor Relations" published last year by the Council of State Governments.

"Unions are here to stay," it declares. "We have seen that unionism is on the rise, that it tends to be more militant than in the past and that there is no legal way, nor few practical ways, to stop it."

Further Resources

BOOKS

Billings, Richard N., and John Greenya. *Power to the Public Worker.* Washington: R.B. Luce, 1974.

Dubofsky, Melvyn. *The State and Labor in Modern America.* Chapel Hill: University of North Carolina Press, 1994.

Dubofsky, Melvyn and Foster Rhea Dulles. *Labor in America,* sixth edition. Wheeling, IL: Harlan Davidson, 1999.

Murphy, Marjorie. *Blackboard Unions: The AFT and the NEA, 1900–1980.* Ithaca, N.Y.: Cornell University Press, 1990.

Zieger, Robert H. and Gilbert J. Gall. *American Workers, American Unions,* third edition. Baltimore: Johns Hopkins University Press, 2002.

"The Post Freeze-Economic Stabilization Program"

Press conference

By: John B. Connally

Date: October 8, 1971

Source: Connally, John B. "The Post Freeze-Economic Stabilization Program." Transcript of Press Conference, October 8, 1971, Washington, D.C., 2–4, 4–5, 5–6, 6–7, 8–9, 11, 12–13, 15–16, 19–20, 22–24, 26–27.

About the Author: John Bowden Connally, Jr. (1917–1993), legendary Texas governor, served from 1963 to 1969. He is perhaps best known for being wounded during Lee Harvey Oswald's assassination of President John F. Kennedy (served 1961–1963) in 1963. Connally survived his wounds to become President Richard M. Nixon's (served 1969–1974) secretary of the treasury. In a highly publicized political maneuver, Connally switched parties from the Democratic to the Republican Party in 1973. ■

Introduction

Wars demand sacrifice—not just from the soldier in the field who places his life and limb in jeopardy—but also from the citizens back home. They are called upon to do without in many ways, including rationing scarce items deemed necessary for the war effort, managing with shortages of many normally available peacetime goods, and being faced with higher consumer prices, higher taxes, and the pressure to invest savings in government war bonds. All in all, these domestic sacrifices (or perhaps inconveniences) may not lead directly to tangible military advantages, but they serve, at the very least, as a symbol of a nation's support for its troops.

The United States' most successful wartime home front undoubtedly developed during World War II (1939–1945)—seen as the "Good War," in the words of author Studs Terkel—when the contrast between good and evil seemed unambiguous. Accordingly, a huge patriotic wave inundated the United States and motivated ordinary citizens to make sacrifices for their nation at war. President Franklin D. Roosevelt (served 1933–1945), for example, instituted an effective wage-and-price freeze in 1942. This kind of control (especially on prices) had previously created a "black market," which flourished because normal luxury items— and even necessities—came in short supply. All told, government controls during World War II engendered some public discontent, although the availability of goods and services in wartime America was probably better than most nations enjoy even in peacetime.

The home front attitude during the Korean War (1950–1953) was decidedly more ambivalent. The goals of President Harry S. Truman (served 1945–1953) and his administration were not clearly defined, and the limited war strategy prompted severe criticism. Hence Korean War wage-and-price controls barely worked. Home-front sacrifices were not deemed as necessary as during World War II, and they were met with more public resistance.

The next conflict—the Vietnam War (1964–1975)—was an altogether different story. The unpopular military action in Vietnam divided the nation as the conflict was prolonged and American losses mounted. Protest against the war went beyond discontent with wage-and-price controls on economic goods to find expression in mass demonstrations and even violence. So controversial was the war in Vietnam—and the growing suspicion of the government's motivations—that many people felt no need to sacrifice for a war they did not support. Wage-and-price controls were not applied during the Vietnam War in the 1960s, despite the fact that inflation soared after 1965. In August 1971, however, as American participation in the war was clearly winding down, the American economy was mired in recession, and a presidential election was looming, President Nixon took action.

Significance

On August 15, 1971, President Nixon shocked the country when he announced a "New Economic Program" in a nationally televised address. The plan included an immediate ninety-day wage-and-price freeze. Nixon, an allegedly conservative Republican, was widely thought to be opposed to such controls. Indeed, he had more than once expressed his belief—one formed from early personal experience—that they did not work. Nixon's first experience with wage-and-price controls had occurred prior to the U.S. entry into World War II, when, as a young California attorney, he worked briefly for the Roosevelt administration's Office of Price Management, where he had a very negative experience with this economic strategy.

Critics jumped on Nixon and his 1971 decision. The following year witnessed then-record corporate profits, fueled in part by modest wage hikes. Nonetheless, though the remedy was drastic enough, Nixon's partial controls lacked the high-profile, wartime-inspired bureaucracy that was needed to enforce them. Much of Nixon's program was "voluntary." It also remained unclear what measures would follow the initial ninety-day wage-and-price freeze. Vague talk of an ill-defined economic "stabilization," was widespread.

On October 7, 1971, Nixon once again spoke directly to the American people. This time he unveiled his "Post-Freeze Economic Stabilization Program." The details were hazy; much would be improvised in the weeks and months ahead. In the end the program floundered. For example, cattlemen who anticipated beef prices too low to cover costs slaughtered calves rather than to take the trouble and expense of fattening them up for later sale. The result by spring 1973 was a government-induced beef shortage. In the final analysis, the United States' last attempt at wartime wage-and-price controls dissolved into a mass of recriminations. These furnished a stark public lesson in the actual workings of the free-enterprise system that helped persuade the American people to accept a revival of strict market economics by the mid-1970s.

Primary Source

"The Post Freeze-Economic Stability Program" [excerpt]

> **SYNOPSIS:** Treasury Secretary John Connally held a press conference on October 8, 1971, as a follow-up to President Nixon's major economic address to the country on the previous evening. At that press conference, Connally answered reporters' questions about the federal government's future economic regulations now that a short, ninety-day wage-and-price freeze was set to expire.

Secretary Connally: Good afternoon. Thank you for being here. If I may, I will take a few minutes to briefly outline the details of the President's speech last night, and the actions he has taken with respect to the Stabilization Program that will begin on November 14, at the expiration of the Wage/Price Freeze.

As many of you know, the President is committed in his fight against inflation in this Country. He is determined to continue that fight to bring down the rate of inflation; and a goal of 2% to 3% on the rate of inflation has been established as a goal to be achieved by the end of 1972.

Now, with that in mind, he has created several Boards and Commissions:

First, the Pay Board:

The Pay Board will be composed of 15 people—five from Labor; five from Business; and five Public Members, one of whom will serve as Chairman. All fifteen will be appointed by the President.

They will have the jurisdiction, the authority, and the responsibility for setting the standards and criteria relating to pay in this Country: Wages, Salary, Fringe Benefits. They will make the decisions.

They will grant the exemptions, if any.

They will determine what action is necessary to cure and alleviate inequities that, unquestionably existed—and do exist—during the Freeze period.

He has also created a Price Commission, which is composed of seven public members. The Chairman will be a full time Member, as will the Chairman of the Pay Board.

The Chairman of the Price Commission will also be named by the President, as will all of the Members.

The Price Commission will have jurisdiction over prices in this Country.

They will have jurisdiction over rents.

They will have jurisdiction over windfall profits and, in addition, they will set their own standards and criteria by which they will, also, attempt to achieve the goals which the President has set in his fight against inflation.

They will make the decisions, case by case.

They will grant the exemptions.

They will permit the increases as their own standards and criteria justify.

Their decisions will be final, as will the decisions of the Pay Board. They are not to be appealed to the Cost of Living Council.

In addition, the President has created a Committee on Interest and Dividends, which will be chaired by Dr. Arthur Burns, Chairman of the Board of Governors of the Federal Reserve System. All of the Members that will serve on that particular Committee will also be Public Members; all Government Members.

These are the essential actions which he took. . . .

I think I should make clear to you at the outset, and stress at the outset, that the Freeze will continue through November 13 of this year. Beginning on the next day, November 14, the Freeze will still be in effect—subject to whatever standards and criteria the two principal Boards set, in the meantime. That is to say, the Pay Board has now 37 days, as does the Price Commission—it has 37 days in which to establish standards and criteria by which they in-

tend to operate, and under which they intend to operate, in the period following the expiration of the Freeze on November 13. . . .

I again want to point out that, with respect to the 15 Members of the Pay Board and the 7 Members of the Price Commission, that they each should understand that it is going to be their responsibility, and they will have the authority, to set their own standards; their own criteria for balancing the equities; alleviating inequities; alleviating hardships; granting exceptions, or exemptions. That will be their decision. And they should understand that from the very outset, because the Cost of Living Council does not anticipate, nor want, nor expect, nor will we accept them passing the buck up to the Cost of Living Council. Their decisions in the Pay field, and in the Price field, are going to be final. They will not be appealed to the Cost of Living Council. . . .

Member of the Press: Mr. Secretary, as you probably know, Organized Labor has withheld its formal announcement of support of this plan because of misgivings about the authority and jurisdiction of the Pay Board. Some of that, I think you may have cleared up, but the question remains, as a result of the briefings in the White House last night: Will the Cost of Living Council have any authority to review, to modify, or possibly to veto the standards set by the Pay Board?

Secretary Connally: The Cost of Living Council is not going to veto actions of the Pay Board, or the Price Commission. Now, the Cost of Living Council is an arm of the President and it will, for the President, continue to function as it is now constituted. It will have an overall responsibility in the field; for the President. . . .

We need their help. We want their help, obviously; Labor organized, and unorganized—particularly Union Labor—is a very strong force in this American economy, and we would hope that they would cooperate. We would hope that they will serve on this Commission, because, without them it is going to be extremely difficult. There is no point in that. We all have the same objective. They want to hold down the cost-of-living increases. They want to stop the rate of inflation.

The working people—Union and non-Union—throughout this Country, made it abundantly clear over the past several weeks that they are in support of the President's program. We have tried to structure a system here that will work fairly and equitably, and permit various elements to participate—not just participate, but make the decisions under which they are going to have to live. . . .

Treasury Secretary John Connally, 1973. AP/WIDE WORLD PHOTOS. REPRODUCED BY PERMISSION.

Member of the Press: Mr. Secretary, what if the Pay Board adopts standards that the Cost of Living Council does not like. Would it override it? Would it request the resignation of the Members of the Pay Board? That is the key issue, it seems.

Secretary Connally: I don't think it is a key issue at all, if you permit me to disagree with you for a moment.

We approach it from a completely different standpoint. We approach it from the standpoint that, first, the interest of the working people of this Country is best served by holding down inflation so that, whatever increases they get as a result of their labors and their productivity increases will, in effect, be real increases, and paid in real value.

So that there is no divergence in objective; there is no difference in our approach.

Obviously, the people that are going to serve on this Pay Board are going to be reasonable people; intelligent people who have a sense of responsibility for making a system like this work. So I don't anticipate we are going to run into this. I don't think it is going to arise. . . .

Member of the Press: Mr. Secretary, you set a goal for the rate of inflation, but not for unemployment.

Why not? What do you expect the rate of unemployment to be by the end of 1972?

Secretary Connally: Well, we certainly expect it to be lower than it is today. We have not set a goal for it, although, as you know, the goal of this Administration has been two-fold for months; in simplified form:

No. 1: To stop the rate of inflation.

No. 2: To bring down the rate of unemployment.

It has dropped a little bit last month, to 6%. It has dropped one-tenth of one percent. That is nothing, frankly, to crow about. It is still too high, but with the on-going Stabilization Program which the President announced last night; with the tax measures that we have pending in the Congress, on which I testified yesterday before the Senate Finance Committee; with other actions in the Government, we have every reason to hope—every reason, really, to believe—that we are going to provide the economic expansion, the vitality, the growth, that will create the jobs. We estimate that this overall package will create between 500,000 and a million jobs.

So that we think it is reasonable to assume that the rate of unemployment will decline during 1972. . . .

Member of the Press: Sir, who is screening these appointees that are coming up before these Boards? Are they being screened on conflict of interest, or philosophy on inflation, and security reasons?

Secretary Connally: I must say a lot of us are screening them. A great many people are in on the discussions. Obviously, you try to find people who have a background and knowledge of the respective fields in which they are going to operate. We try to get the most competent people we can; people we think have a capacity both for understanding the problem, and having the courage to face up to it; having the basic objectivity to be fair in their deliberations.

The conflict of interest matter is a matter of concern and, as a consequence, any full-time employee of the Federal Government immediately subjects himself to the conflict of interest question. So that the only full-time members of the Pay Board and the Price Commission will be the Chairmen. So that the conflict of interest question is not raised.

If you attempted to make all of the members full time members, and subject them to conflict of interest, you would indeed have difficulty getting Labor leaders, and Business leaders, very frankly, to serve on these Boards.

So this question does not arise in the light of the structure of the Boards themselves. . . .

Member of the Press: Mr. Secretary, you said that the goal is to get inflation down to 2% to 3% by the end of '72. What will have to be accomplished before the program will be terminated?

Secretary Connally: I think there will have to be a basic agreement and feeling throughout the Country that the inflationary psychology has been halted and has been broken, and that there is in this Country a commitment to stability; to price stability; to wage stability; so that we can know what to expect in terms of the future. We have been going several years with inflation, and the anticipation of inflation, as an integral part of economic activities in this Country. It has reached the point where we cannot abide it any more. We have to stop it.

Now, I can't tell you what month and what day we will reach the point where we have, indeed, erased from the minds of people that they are living in a Society where there is going to be nothing but continuing inflation.

We want to reach the point—we have to reach the point—where the people understand that they can experience, and that they can hope to expect, stability in this economic system. . . .

Member of the Press: Mr. Secretary, from your experience in Government, what makes you think that a structure as complicated as this, will work?

Secretary Connally: Well, everything is relative. I think this is fairly simple. There is no great Bureaucracy. We anticipate that this whole program will be run by approximately 3,000 people.

All you have here involved is a Pay Board that is going to make decisions with respect to wages, salaries, and fringe benefits. Fifteen people are going to make this decision. They are going to have a relatively small staff; probably 100 people.

You are going to have a Price Commission of seven people; all Public Members. They are going to make the basic decision with respect to prices.

You are going to have a Public Board dealing with interest and dividends. They are going to make those decisions. I don't think it is complicated. I think it is all very simple.

Member of the Press: Are you not going to have thousands of contested decisions that some Solomon is going to have to eventually decide?

Secretary Connally: You obviously are going to have questions.

You obviously are going to have requests for exemptions. There is no question about that. But,

again, part of these problems can be resolved by the establishment of the standards and criteria to begin with; so that everyone knows what the rules are.

This is why the President has given these two Boards 37 days. This is why he made his announcement as early as he possibly could, in order to get these Boards constituted; get them on board; get them functioning; get their standards and criteria developed before they become effective on November 14.

Sure, there are going to be requests for exemptions. I don't know any way around that, but I think if the people basically understand what the objectives are, that our experience during the Freeze period has indicated that it is going to amaze you how few complaints, and how few difficulties, you really have. . . .

Member of the Press: To avoid a wage/price spiral, Mr. Secretary: let's suppose one Union wins a fairly large increase. The Company then comes in and asks for a price increase to justify that. How would you manage to sit on that?

Secretary Connally: I don't want to get into specific cases about what is going to happen, but I assume that neither will be operating in a vacuum. Both will be informed about what is happening in the other. They are two very small groups. They are all going to know each other. Part of their responsibility, obviously, is going to be working in tandem, even though they work in different fields, to achieve the desired objectives.

Member of the Press: What do you plan to do about the other side of inflation? That is, the reduction of quality in goods and services.

Secretary Connally: Well, I would hope that the American workmen and the American businessman would not think that it was in their long term interest to try to cheat on the quality of the products that they produce. I cannot imagine that there are going to be many people in this Country that take that type of an attitude.

The answer is: I don't know of anything we are going to do; except that the Price Commission, again, has the responsibility and the authority to determine prices and, obviously, they can do so in terms of the quality of the commodity, or the product.

Further Resources

BOOKS

Connally, John Bowen, with Mickey Herskowitz. *In History's Shadow: An American Odyssey.* New York: Hyperion, 1993.

Reston, James. *The Lone Star: The Life of John Connally.* New York: Harper & Harper Row, 1989.

Silk, Leonard Solomon. *Nixonomics: How the Dismal Science of Free Enterprise Became the Black Art of Controls.* New York: Praeger, 1972.

"H. Ross Perot: America's First Welfare Billionaire"

Magazine article

By: Robert Fitch

Date: November 1971

Source: Fitch, Robert. "H. Ross Perot: America's First Welfare Billionaire." *Ramparts,* November 1971, 43–44, 44–45, 53.

About the Author: Robert Fitch (1938–), a veteran journalist, lecturer, and faculty member at New York University, specializes in the problems of urban America. Fitch authored the well-known 1993 exposé, *The Assassination of New York,* chronicling in agonizing detail the half-century-long economic, social, political, and cultural decline of the United States' largest city. ■

Introduction

Private businessmen have often made money over the centuries by furnishing goods and services or by lending money to governments—sometimes for purposes of waging war. Historians note, for instance, that private contractors with inside political and family connections sold supplies to the Roman Imperial armies. In more modern times, financiers like the legendary Rothschilds often bankrolled imperialistic kings, princes, and an occasional prime minister. In the contemporary world, the arms industries make their profits by servicing the peace-keeping, war-making state. Indeed, these defense contractors have been dubbed the "Merchants of Death," and, as such, have come under intense fire from critics.

Industrious entrepreneurs throughout history have seized opportunities for lucrative business in providing goods and services the government needs. In many modern municipalities, contractors are frequently criticized for overcharging for shoddy goods and substandard service. Perhaps the most conspicuous example of this trend comes from the American aerospace industry, where stories surface about five-hundred-dollar hammers and thousand-dollar toilet seats.

In addition to waging war, twentieth-century governments throughout the world have created the "welfare state" for the benefit of their citizens. The advent of the welfare state has created additional money-making opportunities for a host of interests and occupations, in-cluding public school teachers, social workers, health care professionals, and health and safety inspectors, among others. Nonetheless, it is perhaps difficult to envision anyone acquiring truly great wealth by furnishing domestically oriented, welfare-state goods and services to the government—that is, until the emergence of H. (Henry) Ross Perot. The November 1971 edition of *Ramparts* dubbed Perot, a computer entrepreneur, "America's First Welfare Billionaire."

Significance

Decades before Ross Perot captured the nation's attention with his spectacular 1992 and 1996 independent presidential campaigns (running on the newly-created Reform Party), the former United States Navy officer founded Electronic Data Systems (EDS). At first, like many entrepreneurs, Perot had trouble jump-starting his company. The spectacular rise of EDS started when Perot received early seed money from the federal government—in particular, from the Office of Economic Opportunity (OEO), that was established in 1964 to begin the Johnson Administration's vaunted "War on Poverty." EDS eventually received government contracts to manage data for state and federal welfare programs, including what turned out to be the plum prize with the creation of Medicare in 1965 under the auspices of the Social Security System.

Hence, in many ways Perot's sizable fortune could be attributed in large part to the sudden expansion of government—primarily its demand for adequate data processing. The irony of the situation is that, while helping governments ferret out waste and fraud, EDS stood accused by critics of overcharging for its services and reaping huge profits at taxpayer expense. This turnabout is not unheard of with government contractors. Even when government services that are intended to benefit the public meet with uncertain success, the contractors providing the services for the government make a profit, bringing rise to the question: For whose primary benefit do social programs such as welfare exist? Fitch's article in *Ramparts* offers one possible answer.

Primary Source

"H. Ross Perot: America's First Welfare Billionaire" [excerpt]

> **SYNOPSIS:** H. Ross Perot, who later ran twice for U.S. president, is the subject of this 1971 *Ramparts* article by journalist Robert Fitch. Described in the article as "America's First Welfare Billionaire," Perot made his fortune offering data processing to governments at various levels who were busily engaged in administering social programs—many of them newly established during the spectacular mid-1960s expansion of the American welfare system.

Your ordinary, ham-handed, shirt-sleeved Dallas billionaire rose out of the interminable vastness of the Texas steppes on a wild-cat gusher of crude oil or a gigantic blast of natural gas. His private *Weltanschauung,* somewhat to the right of Charlemagne, emerged out of the confrontation between his native cracker barrel and the Internal Revenue Code. And with his generous benefactions he has kept the political stage crowded with such Texas bravos as former Governor Allan Shivers, General Edwin L. Walker, John Connally and LBJ.

Dallas' most recent addition to its financial Pantheon, 41-year-old H. Ross Perot, tries not to fit the image too precisely. The founder of the fabulously successful computer software company, Electronic Data Systems (EDS), is a small man with big ears. He wears suits, white shirts, wing-tip shoes and a 1950s style crew cut. With his earnest smile and operations research vocabulary, Perot could easily be mistaken for the supervisor of a computer division in some medium-sized company—which is exactly what he was only five years ago. It's hard to realize that Perot—whose physiognomy and manner suggest busy Rabbit in Winnie-the-Pooh, more than H. L. Hunt—has compiled a personal fortune estimated as high as $1 billion.

The staggering fortune, greater than Henry Ford's or David Rockefeller's, his sense of humor (everyone likes a billionaire who can laugh), his recent Wall Street coup against the DuPonts and efforts to bring home U.S. POWs from Hanoi, have all earned him extensive press coverage. *Fortune* has featured him twice—"The Fastest Richest Texan Ever" and "Ross Perot Moves on Wall Street—" and *The New York Times Magazine* carried a moving tribute ("H. Ross Perot Pays His Dues") to an unaffected billionaire who wears off-the-rack suits and eats cheeseburgers; the kind of man whose sincerity inspires women to say things like "I'd love that man if he didn't have a penny"; a philanthropist who helps poor black folks in Dallas; "a surprisingly modest man" who has no political ambitions and who even fights against politics arising in his own company. But what *Fortune* and *The New York Times* left out of the stories is more interesting than what they put in. Because somehow they neglected to ask the central question: where does Perot's money come from? Or, how did he make a billion dollars in five years?

The answer, drawn from interviews with Perot's former employees and from outraged lower-echelon employees of the Social Security Administration (SSA), is that the prime sources of Perot's revenues are state and federal welfare funds and the Medicare program. Through a special relationship with Blue Cross and Blue Shield plans, Perot has won subcontracts to administer Medicare and Medicaid in 11 states, including 4 out of 5 of the biggest revenue producers. Perot's charges just for electronic data processing now represent the second largest item on the Medicare administrative (Part B) budget. So lucrative are these contracts that in the last two years EDS' profit has averaged nearly 40 percent!

Fortune's kindly benefactor of the Dallas ghetto is simultaneously responsible for the racist purge of black employees in his company's largest operations division. And *The New York Times'* "surprisingly modest man" operates as an absolute dictator and petty marinet, enforcing company dress and behavior regulations so rigidly that in the San Francisco Bay Area, EDS executives are frequently called the "Southern fascists." But it's the methods he's used to crack open the welfare fund barrel together with the way he's been able to penetrate the multibillion dollar Medicare Golconda that constitute the real story of Ross Perot. While the national pogrom against "welfare abuse" is reaching an hysterical pitch, Perot's company has been profiteering remorselessly. Both California welfare officials and Blue Shield executives involved with his firm appear to have been guilty of serious conflicts of interest. Investigations of Perot's activities are now underway in both the California Assembly and in secret executive session of the House Intergovernmental Relations Subcommittee. These undisclosed chapters in the Ross Perot story, one of the financial epics of our time, give us a more complete measure of the man than the public relations jobs done thus far, and an insight into the appalling state of federal and state welfare and health care programs in America today.

The pre-history of the Ross Perot saga spans the five years before he landed his first Medicare gusher in 1966. Prior to that contract, Perot was just a 36-year-old wildcat software salesman running around Dallas buying spare computer time on corporate IBM machines and selling it to other companies that needed computer software work done for them. He'd quit IBM in 1961 to found his own company, and cushioned the income jolt by running the Texas Blue Shield computer department on a part-time basis. (Perot first got acquainted with Texas Blue Shield officials as a salesman, servicing the account for IBM.)

For his fledgling Electronic Data Systems it was just one dry hole after another during those first five years. Perot got a dribble in the form of an initial $250,000 contract with the Office of Economic Opportunity (OEO). But nothing further developed and the contract was scrapped. So by 1965, EDS was still basically a moonlight operation for a small group of former Dallas IBMers—an observation that has to be modified by Vice President Tom Marquez' recollection that "we had to have two full years' salary in the bank to work for Ross," at the time. Still, the entire company's sales amounted to less than half a million dollars. Profits were only about three percent of the scrawny revenues.

Then came the enactment of Medicare and Medicaid in 1965. The Social Security Administration gave Texas Blue Shield a contract to develop a computerized system for paying the Medicare bills. Perot's exact relationship with Texas Blue Shield at that time is still a point of current controversy. Perot himself says he was working part-time for Texas Blue Shield and part-time for EDS, and that he quit Blue Shield when that organization gave him a subcontract to take over their data processing on the new Medicare program, using of course the system just developed at government expense. What's clear is that the $250,000 seed money provided by the Social Security Administration must be one of the worst investments it has made in its entire bureaucratic history. Because not only did Perot appropriate what was essentially a government system developed at government expense; he's been selling it back to the government at fantastic rates ever since. . . .

In the last five years, EDS has grown to the point where the company has Medicare or Medicaid contracts all over the country and is doing business at the rate of 100 million dollars a year. . . .

So company officials simply refuse to identify EDS' main source of revenues. Nor will they divulge the name of any of the company's corporate clients. "If we gave that kind of information out," said company Vice President Tom Marquez, "our clients would have a bunch of security analysts bothering them all the time asking about us." Looking at EDS' annual reports or the company's filing with the Securities and Exchange Commission is no more revealing. We find out only that:

"During the year ended June 30, 1970 EDS derived substantially all of its revenues through contracts with 1) health care institutions, 2) insurance companies, 3) banking and other financial institutions and 4) consumer product companies."

This is highly misleading. It gives the impression that EDS sells its computer software services pri-

marily to private profit-making corporations. This is what most people suppose, even in the financial community. The truth is, even though EDS denies it, that almost all the company's revenue is funneled through Blue Cross and Blue Shield either on their standard business or on a subcontract basis with the government.

These highly decentralized, non-profit, tax-exempt "service" organizations, "The Blues," are an EDS subcontractor's dream, enrolling 90 million customers in their private health insurance business. And as the main contractors on the Medicare and Medicaid programs, they deal with another 30 million Americans. All this creates forests of paper work; mountains of data to be moved electronically and ground up into "information" and stored; millions upon millions of claims to be processed; dozens of complex systems to be designed; hundreds of programs to be written.

As the prime Medicare and Medicaid contractors, "The Blues" wield tremendous power over the American health care system—power that's delegated to them by the Social Security Administration. Practically speaking it's The Blues that wind up deciding how much doctors, hospitals, pharmacists and nursing home operators can charge for their services to the poor and aged. As "fiscal intermediaries" for the SSA, The Blues process the hospitals' and doctors' claims for payment and mail out their checks using federal and state welfare funds. They're also supposed to monitor the quality of care dealt out by health care providers, supposedly seeing to it that poor patients get "mainstream" care.

But more and more, The Blues—especially Blue Shield—delegate to private profit-making companies like EDS many of their functions. And nothing promotes profit-making more than the very Medicare provisions designed to exclude it. For while the law forbids the intermediaries—prime contractors like Blue Shield—from making profits (all The Blues' government business is supposed to be done on a no-profit-no loss basis) it's ambiguous on the subject of *sub*-contractors. . . .

[N]o matter how much companies like EDS charge them, they know they'll be reimbursed by state welfare departments or by the Social Security Administration. So in The Blues, old country boy Perot, the son of a skilled horsetrader, has found a model customer: the big dumb city kid with a rich uncle who always stands ready to bail him out of his financial problems.

In Baltimore, at uncle's SSA headquarters, top Medicare officials are concerned with larger matters than how many millions in profits companies like EDS make from contracts with the government's prime contractors, The Blues. As a spokesman said recently, "We're not interested in profits. Just costs." And in Washington, at the Social and Rehabilitation Service, where responsibility for Medicaid rests, there's no one keeping track of federal matching money that winds up in EDS' profit column. "It's impossible to break those figures out," they say.

Questions of legality and propriety aside, this attitude has helped Ross Perot build a billion-dollar fortune. It gives him the incentive and the leeway he needs to write contract after contract with the Blue Shield and Blue Cross plans around the country. In eleven states, including four out of the states with the largest Medicare "business," EDS has established itself—California, New York, Pennsylvania and Texas. EDS' Medicaid business in California, Texas and Indiana make it America's largest poverty subcontractor. The rest of the software companies have been left scrambling for bits and pieces in the smaller, less profitable states.

Perot signed his biggest contract of all in California, with California Blue Shield in September 1969. Nearly a third of all EDS revenues now result from this deal. It turned over to EDS the data processing for Medicare and Medicaid as well as Blue Shield's standard business. It's also in California where the company's standard operating procedure—numbing conformity, obsessive racism and high level conflicts of interest—has created the biggest scandal. Taking advantage of Blue Shield's paper-work crisis, Perot stepped in with an offer to take over complete facilities management. The price was staggering but Blue Shield didn't have to pay all of it. The state of California was picking up the tab. . . .

Under a system whose outstanding professors have no students, whose greatest statesmen betray their allies and whose most respected peacemakers counsel bombing of cities, it is logical that the man responsible for administering more of the nation's welfare medical programs than anyone else is a hard-core, free-enterprise freak ("Profit is a fantastic thing!" Perot says) who earned a billion-dollar fortune in the process. He's a man who can say without irony that the trouble with the Johnson poverty program was that too little money actually reached the poor people themselves.

Ross Perot speaks at a press conference, December 15, 1969.
© BETTMANN/CORBIS. REPRODUCED BY PERMISSION.

In order to see where the American health care system is headed, it's important to realize that Perot and EDS are simply the logical expressions of the greatest triumph of American domestic liberalism of the 1960s—the passage of Medicare and Medicaid. The liberals knew in 1965 that capitalism in medicine stinks. They also knew that the status quo—represented by The Blues and the AMA—was very powerful. It had stopped reform efforts for thirty years. So congressional liberals decided to be practical. Their prescription was: make capitalism in medicine stink less. Give health care away free or nearly free to those who can't afford it—the aged and the indigent. Meanwhile keep organized medicine happy by letting it administer the new federal programs. It wasn't long, of course, before the health care market broke apart after a storm of profit-taking by organized medicine. So the next step liberals took was to demand more controls over the program. The Blues had to be monitored more closely by the federal government; they had to be subject to audits. Computers had to be used to keep doctors and insurance companies from further profiteering. But liberals still knew that the health care status quo was very powerful, so they let a Blue Cross executive be the chief federal monitor and they let The Blues choose the companies they wanted to have run the computer checks and perform the audits on themselves. In this atmosphere of politically flatulent and unfocused concern with health care costs, Ross Perot rose like a bag of helium. And just as it took a complete outsider, the former Trotskyist social worker Bernie Cornfield, to exploit the potential of the mutual fund racket to its furthest limits, it took a right-wing anti-communist to exploit the medical welfare program to its furthest limits. H. Ross Perot is a true child of his times and ward of the welfare state.

Further Resources

BOOKS

Gross, Ken. *Ross Perot: The Man Behind the Myth.* New York: Random House, 1992

Posner, Gerald L. *Citizen Perot: His Life and Times.* New York: Random House, 1996.

"The Doctrine of Multinational Sell"

Magazine article

By: Robert Scheer

Date: April 1975

Source: Scheer, Robert. "The Doctrine of Multinational Sell." *Esquire,* April 1975, 124, 126, 127, 160, 162.

About the Author: Robert Scheer (1936–) is one of the nation's outstanding progressive journalists. Born in New York City, Scheer attended City College, Syracuse, and the University of California-Berkeley. During the 1960s, he served as editor of the highly regarded literary/current affairs magazine, *Ramparts.* Along the way, Scheer has been a foreign correspondent and authored several books on American foreign policy. He writes a syndicated newspaper column and appears as a regular commentator on various radio talk shows. ■

Introduction

The term "Cola Wars" refers to the fierce competition over the past century between cola manufacturers Coca-Cola and Pepsi. Dr. John Pemberton created Coca-Cola in 1886, and Caleb Bradham created Pepsi in 1898. Coca-Cola (or Coke) became instantly popular, and the company was the leading soda pop manufacturer throughout the twentieth century. Pepsi survived two early bankruptcies only to achieve wide success during the Great Depression by offering twice as much soda for a reduced price. The growth of these two companies provides insight into the rapid development of American capitalism over the past one hundred years.

Thanks to effective marketing, soft drinks have become an indispensable part of American life. Coke and Pepsi have saturated the American public with constant advertisements, creating some of the strongest brand loyalties in consumer marketing. Pepsi's first radio jingle in 1939 became a hit song that played on jukeboxes across the country. Coca-Cola merchandise became instant collectibles. Celebrities appearing on ads for the companies have included Connie Francis, Tom Jones, The Supremes, Michael Jackson, Michael Jordan, Elton John, Bill Cosby, and Ray Charles. According to statistics from the Beverage Marketing Industry, the average American consumed 22.4 gallons of soda per year in 1970. In 1998, the average American's yearly consumption reached 56.1 gallons—with twenty-five percent of teenage boys drinking more than two cans of soda a day, and five percent drinking six or more cans daily.

By the 1970s, Coke and Pepsi both needed to expand their markets and took the "Cola Wars" international. Both companies became involved with foreign trade issues and political issues. Pepsi's experiences are discussed in the excerpt from the article "The Doctrine of the Multinational Sell." By 1970, the companies had grown into multibillion-dollar international conglomerates. No longer just concerned with selling soda, the companies took over their bottling and distribution processes, as well as many other unrelated businesses. The phenomenal growth of these companies mirrors the development of the American economy during that period.

Significance

The efforts of Pepsi to break into the Soviet Union's market at the height of the Cold War demonstrates the tremendous focus of cola rivals Pepsi and Coca-Cola during the twentieth century. Both companies identified their goals and aggressively and effectively brought their visions into realities. They took chances—sometimes successful (Diet Coke) and sometimes disastrous (New Coke)—never resting on their previous successes.

The excerpted article highlights the growth in the soft drink industry in foreign markets in the early 1970s. Operating effectively in international markets required the companies also to become involved in U.S. trade policy efforts and politics. Accepting that reality, both companies explored and took every opportunity to establish market share across the globe. The modern economy requires expertise in brand marketing, mergers and acquisitions, international marketing, trade policy expertise, and political connections.

Recent events demonstrate that the "Cola Wars" are far from over. The latest battle lines include exclusive contracts with public school districts—together with ample scholarship and equipment funding—and marketing soda to the Muslim world. Both companies have invested heavily in NASA space projects, taking the battle even into space.

Primary Source

"The Doctrine of Multinational Sell"

SYNOPSIS: U.S. soft drink company PepsiCo uses strong measures in its battle with competitor Coca-Cola for world domination of the soft-drink market.

Don Kendall does love to talk about PepsiCo's conglomerate acquisitions, ranging from Wilson Sporting Goods to Frito-Lay snack foods, with North American Van Lines and Monsieur Henri Wines (Yago Sant'Gria) thrown in for good measure. Beyond that, the current favorites include "free trade" (particularly with the Soviet Union), moving ahead with Jerry Ford, corporate responsibility ("What Boy Scouting means to the corporations of America"), and the general virtues of multinational corporations.

Kendall has emerged as one of the more visible and articulate corporate spokesmen, is a friend of Presidents and even knows David Rockefeller, who picked him to be chairman of the Emergency Committee for American Trade. E.C.A.T. lists the heads of the top sixty-two corporations as members, and is the chief lobbyist for multinational companies. Kendall also serves as U.S. chairman of the U.S.-U.S.S.R. Trade and Economic Council. . . .

In 1963, Kendall got the company president to move upstairs to become chairman of the board and give Kendall his day. In ten years' time Don Kendall was to kick, pull and mash a bumbling, relatively small, one-product company into a modern multinational conglomerate giant. One of his first acts was to begin plans for the new world headquarters in Purchase, New York, ten minutes from his Greenwich, Connecticut, home. Another was to move to acquire the giant Frito-Lay Company, the nation's largest snack-food business, thereby increasing Pepsi's sales and establishing the company as a major conglomerate. He named the new conglomerate PepsiCo, and it has come out of things on top, or at least number ninety-three on the *Fortune* Five Hundred ratings. It's finally breathing hard on "the competitor" (number sixty-nine). . . .

Kendall's responsibility is to open markets—for Pepsi in Russia, for Frito-Lay in Japan—to initiate mergers or conquests of other companies, and to gain the acquiescence of various governments for whatever business is at hand. . . .

PepsiCo's growth is dependent on acquisitions and expanding markets that require political intervention or at least acquiescence at virtually every level, from the S.E.C. to foreign governments. And

it's those strings that Kendall knows how to play. As Pearson notes, in giving Kendall his due, "You couldn't *be* as political as Don." Pearson went to Russia with the Pepsi board and never met Brezhnev, while Kendall and the Soviet leader have had several four-hour private sessions. Kendall has been at ease with Johnson and Nixon and he knows Gerald Ford. Pearson, who comes from Southern California, met then Senator Nixon (by accident) at Santa Barbara's San Ysidro ranch but Pearson did not see him once during his years in office. Kendall was popping down to the Nixon White House regularly, and that pattern continues with the new President. "I've never met Ford—I'd say that Don is, by design [political]—he likes to do that and he does it superbly. I don't covet that side of things and I'm very proud and impressed with the job he does, and I think it does have some of the benefits that you have cited for us."

The benefits which I cited ranged from Kendall's establishment of important domestic business and political contacts to opening up the potentially lucrative Soviet market to Pepsi. . . .

Pearson was quick to assure me that Kendall's impact has been quite the opposite. He brushed aside the effect of a boycott of Pepsi on the issue of Soviet Jewish emigration. He noted that Pepsi sales were up in New York City and that a Soviet trade deal had gotten Pepsi a lot of favorable publicity, particularly in the business press, as well as a huge potential market.

But it would be an error to think of Kendall as small-minded or exclusively preoccupied with the trade deals of his company. Along the way, while selling both Chiang Kai-shek and Khrushchev a Pepsi, he has picked up a broader perspective of what's good for America. And there's no reason to deny the sincerity of his espousal of a host of causes, from free trade to the corporate conscience, for they are consistent with the perspective and the needs of a multinational corporation, which, by the nature of its far-flung operations, is given to a certain cosmopolitanism. You get used to hiring dark people who speak funny languages (although the only black vice-president at PepsiCo is V. P. for community affairs), and you get passionate about wanting to bring down tariffs. You also have few qualms about interfering in other people's (or nations') affairs; you need assistants who can act discreetly. . . .

Kendall was one of the business internationalists whose obsession with sales in the world market

A truckload of Coca-Cola cases is unloaded in Hong Kong onto a train bound for Canton, China, January 1979. This was part of the first shipment of Coca-Cola to China, and China's first cola beverage imports since the Communists came to power in 1949. © **BETTMANN/CORBIS. REPRODUCED BY PERMISSION.**

helped Richard Nixon transcend the hysterical anti-communism of his earlier years. Nixon's serious apprenticeship for the Presidency began (after the 1962 defeat) when he joined the Wall Street law firm of Mudge, Rose, bringing in PepsiCo as his main client. When Kendall first gave the PepsiCo business over to Nixon he was not simply extending a personal favor. Nixon possessed the sort of international connections that were useful to PepsiCo and vice versa.

One of the people who traveled with Nixon in those days was Herman A. Schaefer, the PepsiCo vice-president for finance. He recalls, "Nixon was an unofficial guest of Nasser, and I arranged to be there then to resolve some problems we were having. I spent three days with him." Schaefer's recollection of his first session with Nixon on that trip provides a nice footnote on the past President's work habits: "When we first went into some room at the Nile Hilton he [Nixon] said, 'Now let's get off in a corner someplace and make sure we're not bugged because we're gonna talk about what you want me to do tomorrow when I see such and such and what I'm supposed to tell him.'" Schaefer now thinks that

Nixon always had an obsession with tapes that was part of a pattern of self-destructiveness. When I interviewed him the day of Nixon's resignation he was chortling somewhat happily, but, perhaps out of deference to Kendall's sensibilities, he made me turn off the tape recorder first. He did *not* ask me to turn off the tape recorder when he recounted the purposes of his and Nixon's trip to Egypt: "At that time Coke had been blacklisted, boycotted [in the Arab countries], and we wanted to be able to really move that market—take it over."

Aside from the pragmatic business usefulness of his Soviet contacts, there is no doubt that Don Kendall has a genuine respect and indeed enthusiasm for the Soviet leadership dating back to Khrushchev's Pepsi-quaffing day. (Nikita's drinking Pepsi before the cameras of the world supposedly saved Kendall's job because, as head of the International Division, he had put money into an exhibit in Moscow after Coke had turned it down, and some guys at the home office had their knives out for him.)

For the then president of Pepsi-Cola International it was the beginning of a gripping awareness that the Soviet leadership was made up of human beings. It is a perception that has been confirmed on his subsequent trips to the Soviet Union: "General Secretary Brezhnev is a very warm, very outgoing person, he's an extrovert, not an introvert. I've got some pictures taken in June and you can see it [emphatically]. He's a *warm* person. He's very outspoken. When you talk to General Secretary Brezhnev and he says something, you don't have to wonder what he meant by that, which I like because I'm a direct outspoken person myself. I don't want to think 'what did he really mean?'" . . .

Don Kendall does not want to tell the Russians how to treat their minority groups (Jews, Czechs, poets, etc.)—that's their internal affair—and he doesn't want them telling our companies what to do in Chile—that's our internal affair. We (meaning Kissinger, Nixon, Ford) do not intervene when the Russians throw their weight around in Eastern Europe and they pay similar respects to our prerogatives in Latin America and, as Kendall frequently points out, once you've got that understanding down, it will be kept, because it's in the interests of both sides. . . .

The Soviets want or need trade, consumer goods and a lower military budget, and they therefore need a Don Kendall more than an Allende. And the Kendalls, or rather the multinational corporations that Kendall speaks for, now need trade and normalization of relations with the Soviets more than the anti-communism (and defense contracts) of the Cold War. For the Soviets, the Pepsi connection is a very good deal and it certainly has less to do with the desire for that magical syrup than with the formation of certain alliances within the United States.

Kendall may have dreams of a vast market with a "Boss" Pepsi bottle replacing vodka and kvass in every Russian home, and the Russians do seem interested in getting their people off alcohol (certainly our experience shows that people work harder when they're guzzling Pepsi rather than booze). As Kendall told the sales execs, "We're gonna sober them up with Pepsi and bring their vodka over here and get the Americans drunk." But it's this second part—increasing Soviet exports to the U.S. to earn hard currency as a basis for importing more sophisticated industrial equipment—that is at the heart of the trade deals. In the process the Soviets are rewarding and further enlisting the support of Kendall who has been useful as a friend of Presidents and perhaps the most vociferous business lobbyist.

Further Resources

BOOKS

Louis, J.C., and Harvey Yazijian. *The Cola Wars.* New York: Everett House, 1980.

Pendergrast, Mark. *For God, Country, and Cola-Cola: The Definitive History of the Great American Soft Drink and the Company that Makes It.* New York: Basic Books, 2000.

Stoddard, Bob. *Pepsi:100 Years.* Los Angeles: General Publishing Group, 1997.

PERIODICALS

Kaufman, Marc. "Fighting the Cola Wars in Schools." *The Washington Post,* March 23, 1999, Z12. Available online at http://www.washingtonpost.com/wp-srv/national/colawars032399.htm; website home page: http://www.washingtonpost.com (accessed June 18, 2003).

McLean, Bethany. "Coke & Pepsi: Guess Who's Winning the Cola Wars." *Fortune,* March 21, 2001. Available online at http://www.fortune.com/fortune/investing/articles/0,15114,373729,00.html; website home page: http://www.fortune.com (accessed June 18, 2003).

WEBSITES

Johnson, Robin. "The Cola Wars: Over a Century of Cola Slogans, Commercials, Blunders, and Coups." Available online at http://www.geocities.com/colacentury/; website home page: http://www.geocities.com (accessed June 18, 2003). *Contains extensive information on the advertisements of Coke and Pepsi, together with links to audio files.*

"When Cities Turn to Private Firms for Help"
Magazine article

By: *U.S. News & World Report*

Date: August 16, 1976

Source: "When Cities Turn to Private Firms for Help," *U.S. News & World Report,* August 16, 1976, 35–37.

About the Publication: *U.S. News & World Report* began as the 1948 merger of two weekly magazines, *United States News* and *World Report.* The magazine is read by 11.2 million American adult readers every week. *U.S. News & World Report* is headquartered in New York City. ■

Introduction

Efforts to privatize government services—saving taxpayer money by contracting out services to private business rather than relying on government workers—has a long history in the United States. The practice allows governments to hire private contractors to perform specific public services, almost invariably at a reduced cost. Another advantage is that instead of carrying workers on a permanent public payroll, the government can use contract labor on an "as-needed" basis. In addition, private companies usually have more flexibility than the government enjoys to employ whomever they choose and to select employees on merit rather than on criteria unrelated to the demands of the job.

Privatization offers a real potential for abuse. One example from U.S. history is the Southern convict-lease system that was put in place after the Civil War (1861–1865) when Southern leaders felt the need to repress both freed blacks and poor whites during the post-war turmoil. Private planters, miners, loggers, and road builders (operating the legendary "chain gangs") could "rent" workers from the prisons and sometimes mistreated them. Many Southern prisons—while not technically under "private control"—nevertheless became an adjunct of the Southern corporate regimen. For a society that had been based on slave labor until a few years earlier, this practice seemed perfectly acceptable. Yet it undermined the value of labor throughout the region, since competition from convicts necessarily drove down free market wages. Meanwhile, since the state made money off its prisoners, there was an unhealthy incentive to "manufacture" criminals.

Though less exploitative in more modern times, the use of outside contractors has always given government a handy means for disciplining its own workers. The practice serves as a constant reminder to public employees that if they are too demanding, they can easily be replaced or, at the very least, reduced in numbers. From the state's perspective, this point became increasingly relevant during the late 1960s and early 1970s, as vigorous public-employee unions made their appearance. Privatization was the almost inevitable reaction to the challenge posed by this latest development in the American labor movement.

Significance

The United States experienced a spate of labor-union organizing activity among public employees during the late 1960s and 1970s. These unions seemed particularly aggressive in recruiting members and, once ensconced, in using their power. The two most prominent leaders of this movement were Jerry Wurf, president of the American Federation of State, County and Municipal Employees (AFSCME)—the militant unionist described by author Joseph C. Goulden as "Labor's last angry man,"—and Albert Shanker, president of the American Federation of Teachers (AFT), who came to national attention during the 1968-1969 New York City teachers strike. Workers in these public-employee unions, who were reasonably well paid and enjoyed a fair measure of job security, were very active through the 1960s, while private-industry union members, facing the alarming prospect of losing their jobs to public-sector competition, largely acquiesced in their own decline.

The public-employee unions of the 1970s focused not only on economic issues affecting their members, even though the rate of inflation after 1965 threatened to lower every American's standard of living. Rather these unions—more so than with virtually any other segment of organized labor—engaged extensively in political and social activism in an effort to engage with the larger community. Their militancy appears, at least partially, to have been a reflection of the social and political ferment of the period.

The predictable reaction to the surge in public-employee unionization was privatization. The practice simultaneously reduced labor costs and circumvented what were often antagonistic and difficult negotiations with public-employee unions.

Primary Source

"When Cities Turn to Private Firms for Help" [excerpt]

SYNOPSIS: The government's privatization movement, a large-scale effort to employ contractors to provide various government services, represented a deliberate response to the rise of aggressive public-employee unions throughout the United States through the 1960s. The privatization thrust is the subject of the following article, that appeared in an August 1976 edition of *U.S. News & World Report*.

A new weapon has emerged in the struggle to hold down the costs of State and local governments. It's called private enterprise.

In one place after another, profit-minded firms are being called on to furnish a wide range of services that traditionally have been provided by public employes, from landscaping to protecting communities against fires.

What public officials have discovered is that, in many cases, private contractors can do the jobs more efficiently, sometimes more cheaply, than government can do them. And it helps keep a lid on public payrolls.

Private businesses have long furnished some city services, such as garbage collection. Now contracts are being issued for all sorts of other things.

Private firms are plowing snow, operating land fills, tending parking meters, collecting tax bills, trimming trees and feeding prisoners.

In San Francisco, some park and recreational facilities are being run by private operators—at a profit rather than an expense to the city, officials say.

High-school cafeteria service in Benton, Ark., is provided by the McDonald's fast-food chain. Serving the usual McDonald's fare, the firm apparently has turned a financial loser into a profit-maker.

Computer Sciences Corporation has taken over data processing for Orange County, Calif., under a seven-year, 26-million-dollar contract. The county expects to save 11 million dollars by not doing the job itself. Says a county official: "The contract has done everything we had hoped and has brought some benefits we hadn't anticipated."

Undercover narcotics investigations in such places as Barnesville, Ohio, are handled by the private firm of NET, Inc., which claims a 100 per cent conviction rate in the 21 States in which it operates under contracts with small local governments.

Private security guards protect the city hall and municipal-courts buildings in Houston, Tex., even though police headquarters is just a half block away. Officials figure they are saving money by hiring the guards, whose pay is lower than that of fully trained policemen.

Although experiments with private-service contractors have not all been successful, checks by staff members of *U.S. News & World Report* indicate that in many cases taxpayers may be getting a bargain.

"It's not necessarily for the sake of efficiency or saving money, though," observes Arthur Spindler, a social-welfare consultant, of Bethesda, Md. "In many cases, it's a way of getting more services performed without adding to government work rolls."

William Bouchara, president of Bustop Shelters, Inc., which furnishes shelters for bus patrons in New York City, asks: "Why should a city spend its own money on needed services when a business can do it?"

Bustop Shelters has built 254 shelters in Manhattan and the Bronx. It pays the city a franchise fee of $54 per shelter, plus 5 per cent of the revenue it derives from selling advertising space on the shelters.

By contracting with private companies, municipalities and States can avoid "the large initial costs of facilities and personnel, the 'trial and error' costs and the long-term financial commitments that are associated with service delivery," says William C. Schilling, associate director of Public Service Options in Minneapolis.

Public Service Options is a privately funded organization that seeks, among other things, to act as a matchmaker between local governments and private contractors.

Some Drawbacks

Opposition from organized civil-service workers, together with the politicians' fear of voter retaliation if the firm fails to meet its promises, has helped keep private-service contracting from spreading faster.

And not all companies are rushing to get into it, either. Some are hesitant because of the risks of failure, limited opportunity for profits and inevitable red tape that accompanies doing business with government at any level.

Still a study of private contracting by the Urban Institute, an independent Washington-based research organization, concludes: "A large, untouched market for business exists in the local-government sector."

There seem to be few government-provided services where private contracting has not been tried, sometimes with surprising success.

For instance, in Scottsdale, Ariz., a privately owned company for years has furnished fire protection and, according to enthusiastic city officials, has done a better job of it than most municipally managed fire departments.

"In all measurements of productivity or achievement, this fire department is comparable with any fire department I've ever seen, but they do it for half price," says Scottsdale City Manager Frank Aleshire.

With a nonunion force of 150 full-time and 250 part-time employes, Rural-Metro Fire Department, Inc., serves some 80,000 Scottsdale residents at a cost of $11 per capita—less than half the national average for fire protection, Mr. Aleshire says. When they are not fighting fires, employees also take on extra jobs for the city, including patrolling city property and fixing broken water mains.

Rural-Metro's president and fire chief, Louis Witzeman, believes private ownership gives the company incentive to seek cost-cutting innovations and to use "a smaller number of men to do the work of a larger number."

Arlington Heights, Ill., contracts with a local firm for landscaping and maintenance of public property.

In Downey, Calif., upkeep costs of the public golf course have dropped 20 per cent since the city gave the job to a private firm.

Milwaukee officials decided in 1971 that it was too expensive for the city to repair and improve incinerators to meet pollution-control standards. That is when they contracted with a company to collect city waste and deposit it in a sanitary land fill.

American Can Company, which has Milwaukee's waste-hauling contract, this year is opening a complete waste-recovery plant to extract reusable materials from the refuse it hauls. Eventually the city will have an opportunity to buy into the system and share the profits.

Milwaukee already is offsetting some of its costs by manufacturing fertilizer from sewage wastes. About 70,000 tons of the turf-green fertilizer, called Milorganite, is now being produced and sold annually.

A number of cities, New Orleans, La., and Portland, Oreg., among them, are getting out of the garbage-disposal business and turning that job over to private operators.

When new public buildings went up in Des Moines, Ia., and Fort Lauderdale, Fla., officials hired outside companies to clean the windows regularly rather than buy special equipment and put window washers on the cities' payrolls. Says the Des Moines city manager: "Contracting is cheaper."

Offbeat Classes

In Grand Rapids, Mich., school officials concluded it is less costly to send some vocational-high-school students to private institutions than to offer regular classes in such narrow-interest subjects as cosmetology and electronics.

And in Dade County, Fla., officials are contracting for child day-care services rather than operating more county facilities. Charge per child at the private centers is less than half that for equivalent service in a county-run center, county officials claim.

A danger in private contracting is that profits don't always materialize, causing firms to lose interest or go bankrupt. Government bodies occasionally have had to step back in, sometimes on short notice, when their private contractor failed to perform as promised.

Such a possibility has been raised in North Carolina, where a private firm, Health Application Systems, a subsidiary of Bergen Brunswig Corporation, agreed to administer the State's medicaid program for a fixed fee.

The unique arrangement, watched nationwide by officials seeking to improve the efficiency and reduce the costs of medicaid and similar health programs, provided that the firm would meet all expenses, including all claims, from its contractual fee.

Distress Signals

After about a year of operation, the plan has faltered. State officials were informed recently that the company was short of money and could not cover some 3 million dollars in medicaid payments due in May. Claim checks are being mailed out on time since the State advanced the company its June payment.

What went wrong, the company maintains, was that the economic recession caused more people to sign up for medicaid than had been projected. Also the company was called on to pay more than it had budgeted for claims that were incurred before it took over management of the program.

How it will all turn out is not yet clear. The company is currently negotiating with the State for more money.

Despite the occasional failures, the prospect of cutting costs, improving efficiency and curbing public employment is likely to tempt more grass-roots governments to let private enterprise take over public-service jobs.

Further Resources

BOOKS

Goulden, Joseph C. *Jerry Wurf, Labor's Last Angry Man.* New York: Atheneum, 1982.

Levitt, Martin Jay, with Terry Conrow. *Confessions of a Union Buster.* New York: Crown Publishers, 1993.

Murphy, Marjorie. *Blackboard Unions: The AFT and the NEA, 1900-1980.* Ithaca, New York: Cornell University Press, 1990.

Looking Out for Number One

Handbook

By: Robert J. Ringer

Date: 1977

Source: Ringer, Robert J. *Looking Out for Number One.* Beverly Hills, Calif.: Los Angeles Book Corporation, 1977, ix, x, 1–2, 2, 5–6, 7, 9–11, 79, 117, 205, 207–208, 209, 216–217.

About the Author: Robert J. Ringer was an executive in the record and film industries. In 1973, Ringer found himself deep in debt. He self-published two best-selling books, *Winning Through Intimidation* (1974) and *Looking Out for Number One* (1977). After publishing his third book, *Restoring the American Dream* (1980), Ringer started a newsletter and a book publishing company. ∎

Introduction

When Robert Ringer could not find a publisher for his 1974 self-help book, *Winning Through Intimidation,* he self-published the work and it became a national bestseller. *Winning Through Intimidation* describes the techniques Ringer used to negotiate deals in the advertising and entertainment industries. Ringer's anecdotes feature his "take-no-prisoners" approach to negotiations, emphasizing that business deals require participants to protect their own interests vigorously.

The tremendous success of *Winning Through Intimidation* led Ringer to publish *Looking Out For Number One.* This book applied the underlying philosophy of *Winning Through Intimidation* to several areas of daily life, including love, friendship, and personal finance. While Ringer's philosophy of rational self-interest had long been a part of economic theories, freely applying these principles outside the business context was novel. Ringer advocated that people should do what brought them the most pleasure, as long it did not forcibly interfere with the rights of others. Ringer rejected an absolute morality that created social customs, mores, and guilt. Following these conventions blindly was irrational according to Ringer. Rather than to base one's decisions on tradition, the opinion of others, or chance, Ringer argued that it was rational decisions that led to personal happiness.

Ringer's ideas reflected an emerging philosophy that resonated during the 1970s, a period which writer Tom Wolfe dubbed the "Me Decade." The cynical generation that came of age during the 1970s—fueled by the United States' continued turmoil over Vietnam and Watergate—distrusted authority and rejected traditional mores and conventions of American life as never before.

Significance

Ringer's philosophy of rational self-interest reflected the economic policy that was largely favored at the end the 1970s. The new attitude marked the end of an era during which the federal government created national economic plans to address specific issues. In the past, U.S. economic policies had featured national programs such as the New Deal to end the Great Depression, the Great Society to alleviate poverty in the United States, and the national wage and price controls that were put in place to counteract inflation. By the end of the 1970s, Americans recognized that big government programs had not achieved the results promised by generations of government officials. The 1970s were a decade of inflation, a stagnant economy, record high interest rates, and high unemployment—all of which were compiled into a "misery index" to reflect the combined impact of these economic factors on typical American families. In reaction, political pressure mounted at the end of the 1970s for economic policies that would help the "middle class" rather than focusing on the most disadvantaged in the economy.

This new political philosophy also contributed to the property tax revolution—highlighted by the 1975 passage of California's Proposition 13—that significantly reduced the tax burden on American taxpayers at the expense of expanding or maintaining ambitious government services. The "Me Decade" ended with a growing call for smaller government, lower taxes, and an economic policy that would help the average American to prosper.

Ronald Reagan's (served 1981–1989) 1980 presidential campaign reflected the emerging "Looking Out for Number One" philosophy, as Reagan denounced government as "part of the problem, not the solution." His campaign promised much less government intrusion and lower taxes for all Americans, allowing them to keep more of what they earned. The libertarian aspects of the Reagan tax policy appealed to large numbers of voters. In 1981, Reagan signed into law the largest tax cut in American history, one that dramatically reduced the income taxes paid by Americans. The prosperity that followed these tax cuts led to Reagan's landslide 1984 victory over Democrat Walter Mondale. With few exceptions—including President Bill Clinton's (served 1993–2001) ill-fated National Health Care initiative—U.S. policy has avoided collective solutions to economic challenges since the end of the 1970s.

Primary Source

Looking Out for Number One [excerpt]

> **SYNOPSIS:** In the following excerpt from his best-selling 1977 book, *Looking Out For Number One,*

Robert Ringer introduces his doctrine of rational self-interest and urges the reader to take advantage of his counsels for greater happiness and satisfaction.

Anyone who is familiar with my philosophy would be disappointed if I didn't say that my sole reason for writing this book was to make as much money as possible.

Perhaps without realizing it, you have, by purchasing this book, entered into a value-for-value relationship with me. I'm exchanging my ideas—ideas which I believe can make your life more pleasurable—for your money. This value-for-value approach enables you to dispense with the notion that I'm doing you some kind of favor by sharing these ideas; I'm not. That's your safety valve in this transaction—the security of knowing that I'm interested in making money by selling you more books in the years ahead and that I recognize that I'm likely to retain you as a customer only if this book is worth its price to you.

There are no ulterior motives involved. I'm not out to convert you to a cause, to enlist your aid in destroying an "evil," or to gain your support for or against anything. If you understand that the means to my end is to provide you with a valuable product, then you're already in the proper frame of mind for the realities which lie ahead. . . .

Clear your mind, then. Forget foundationless traditions, forget the "moral" standards others may have tried to cram down your throat, forget the beliefs people may have tried to intimidate you into accepting as "right." Allow your intellect to take control as you read, and, most important, think of yourself—Number One—as a unique individual.

It is not my intention to give you legal advice, to act as a marriage counselor, or to prompt you to take radical action based on the assumption that what I have to say should be construed as some sort of guarantee. Should you fail, I have no desire to bear any guilt; by the same token, I don't expect to share in your "profits" should you succeed—whether your success be in love, finance, or any other area discussed in these pages. You and you alone will be responsible for your success or failure. . . .

Looking out for Number One is the conscious, rational effort to spend as much time as possible doing those things which bring you the greatest amount of pleasure and less time on those which cause pain. Everyone automatically makes the effort to be happy, so the key word is "rational."

To act rationally, and thus to experience pleasure and avoid pain on a consistent basis, you have to be aware of what you're doing and why you're doing it. If you are not aware, you're not living life; you're merely passing through. Because people always do that which they *think* will bring them the greatest pleasure, selfishness is not the issue. Therefore, when people engage in what appear to be altruistic acts, they are not being selfless, as they might like to believe (and might like to have you believe). What they are doing is acting with a lack of awareness. Either they are not completely aware of what they're doing, or they are not aware of why they're doing it, or both. In any case, they are acting selfishly—but not rationally. . . .

Why is it important to act out of choice? What's in it for you? You already know: more pleasure and less pain—a better life for Number One.

In everyday terms, it means feeling refreshed instead of tired. It means making enough money to be able comfortably to afford the material things you want out of life instead of being bitter about not having them. It means enjoying love relationships instead of longing for them. It means experiencing warm friendships instead of concentrating your thoughts on people for whom you harbor negative feelings. It means feeling healthy instead of lousy. It means having a relatively clear mind instead of one that is cluttered and confused. It means more free time instead of never enough time.

Looking out for Number One is important because it leads to a simple, uncomplicated life in which you spend more time doing those things which give you the greatest amount of pleasure. It's the discovery of where it's all at—the realization that life is worth living and that it can and should be a joy rather than a dread. The natural offspring of this realization are feelings of self-control and self-esteem, which in turn perpetuate still more joy in your life. . . .

It's that old inescapable cosmic reality again: no such thing as something for nothing. The greater the happiness you wish to achieve, the greater the price you must pay to achieve it. It's up to you to decide how great a price you're willing to pay, and it's to your advantage to decide on that price *before* you take action. . . .

Most important, remember that happiness is not what someone else deems it to be. Happiness is that which makes *you* feel good. . . .

Is looking out for Number One "right?" As a preface, I find it necessary to describe an old nemesis of mine—a creature who's been running around loose on Planet Earth over the millennia, steadily increasing in number. He is the Absolute Moralist. His mission in life is to whip you and me into line. Like Satan, he disguises himself in various human forms. He may appear as a politician on one occasion, next as a minister, and still later as your mother-in-law.

Whatever his disguise, he is relentless. He'll stalk you to your grave if you let him. If he senses that you're one of his prey—that you do not base your actions on rational self-choice—he'll punish you unmercifully. He will make guilt your bedfellow until you're convinced you're a bad guy.

The Absolute Moralist is the creature—looking deceptively like any ordinary human being—who spends his life deciding what is right for *you.* If he gives to charity, he'll try to shame you into "understanding" that it's your moral duty to give to charity too (usually the charity of his choice). If he believes in Christ, he's certain that it's his moral duty to help you "see the light." (In the most extreme cases, he may even feel morally obliged to kill you in order to "save" you from your disbelief.) If he doesn't smoke or drink, it takes little effort for him "logically" to conclude that smoking and drinking are wrong for you. In essence, all he wants is to run your life. There is only one thing which can frustrate him into leaving you alone, and that is your firm decision never to allow him to impose his beliefs on you.

In deciding whether it's right to look out for Number One, I suggest that the first thing you do is eliminate from consideration all unsolicited moral opinions of others. Morality—the quality of character—is a very personal and private matter. No other living person has the right to decide what is moral (right or wrong) for you. I further suggest that you make a prompt and thorough effort to eliminate from your life all individuals who claim—by words or actions, directly or by inference—to possess such a right. You should concern yourself only with whether looking out for Number One is moral from your own rational, aware viewpoint.

Looking out for Number One means spending more time doing those things which give you pleasure. It does not, however, give you carte blanche to do whatever you please. It is not hedonistic in concept, because the looking-out-for-Number-One philosophy does not end with the hedonistic assertion that man's primary moral duty lies in the pursuit of pleasure.

Looking out for Number One adds a rational, civilized tag: man's primary moral duty lies in the pursuit of pleasure *so long as he does not forcibly interfere with the rights of others.* If you picked up this book in the hope that it might explain how to get ahead in life by trampling on the rights of your fellow man, I'm afraid you've made a bad choice. I suggest instead that you read *Life and Death of Adolf Hitler, The Communist Manifesto,* or the U.S. Internal Revenue Code.

There is a rational reason why forcible interference with others has no place in the philosophy of looking out for Number One. It's simply not in your best interest. In the long run it will bring you more pain than pleasure—the exact opposite of what you wish to accomplish. It's possible that you may, on occasion, experience short-term pleasure by violating the rights of others, but I assure you that the long-term losses (i.e., pain) from such actions will more than offset any short-term enjoyment. . . .

You have but one life to live. Is there anything unreasonable about watching over that life carefully and doing everything within your power to make it a pleasant and fulfilling one? Is it wrong to be aware of what you're doing and why you're doing it? Is it evil to act out of free choice rather than out of the choice of others or out of blind chance? . . .

Governments, of course, are the masters of intimidation through slogan, simply because they have the money, the manpower and, if needed, the guns to back them up. My candidate for the most intimidating government slogan ever tossed at the American public was John F. Kennedy's emotion-grabber: "And so, my fellow Americans, ask not what your country can do for you; ask what you can do for your country." The face was handsome, the personality pleasing, the smile captivating, but the words terrified me. . . .

Charity is fine, so long as you can afford the time and/or money to engage in it. I must again emphasize, however, that the best way to help the poor is by not becoming one of them. If your own situation is cool, by all means work on charity if it brings you happiness. It's no one else's business how you derive selfish pleasure, and if you've come to the conclusion that working on charitable causes is rational, don't be dissuaded. . . .

Never deceive yourself by refusing to face the reality that the government is your chief adversary when it comes to making money. All your competitors combined are not a force formidabe enough to compare to the government, if for no other reason than because the government won't allow them to use guns. The plain truth is that Big Government is the most ominous obstacle in the path of the person seeking to look out for Number One. . . .

The question is, if what the government has to offer is so great for the individual—if everyone really wants it—why must the Washington Gang use force? The obvious answer to that question is that what the government offers is not great; it is restraint of freedom. The practical consequences of government are that it uses the threat of violence either to

1. Force you to stop doing something you want to do,

2. Force you to do something you don't want to do, or

3. Force you to give up something that's rightfully yours.

Who needs the government for this? You can walk through Central Park at night and accomplish the same things. . . .

All the government really does is: steal a large portion of your personal income; close the doors to your business if you don't fork over a specified percentage of your profits; make the money you do retain worth less every day by illegally printing new currency that has no value behind it; charge you for the privilege of living in your own home ("property taxes"); tell you what minimum you have to pay your employees and whom you must hire; dictate what you can charge for your products or services . . . ; pass judgment on what products you can sell (through the FDA); and . . . make it illegal for you to compete against its own poorly run monopolies (such as the Postal Service).

My God, even a walk through Central Park can't accomplish that! . . .

It's perverted nonsense to believe that your success causes others to suffer (unless they're neurotic, which is something you can't control). Be proud of your achievements, not ashamed. If you're lucky enough to obtain material wealth, don't allow anyone to cheat you out of enjoying it.

It's irrational to think you should repent because there are people who live in poverty. Unless someone is poor because you robbed him, no downtrodden individual is your responsibility and shouldn't be a mental blockade to your happiness. On the con-

trary, you're not being a burden to the rest of the world if *you* aren't living in poverty.

Further Resources

BOOKS

Browne, Harry. *How I Found Freedom in an Unfree World.* New York: Macmillan Publishing, 1973.

———. *Why Government Doesn't Work.* New York: St. Martin's Press, 1995.

Murray, Charles A. *What it Meant to be a Libertarian: A Personal Interpretation* New York: Broadway Books, 1997.

Rand, Ayn. *The Virtue of Selfishness.* New York: Signet Books, 1964.

Tilman, Rick. *Ideology and Utopia in the Social Philosophy of the Libertarian Economists.* Westport, Conn.: Greenwood Press, 2001.

WEBSITES

Seligman, Martin. "Authentic Happiness: Using the New Positive Psychology to Realize Your Potential For Lasting Fulfillment." Available online at http://www.authentichappiness.com (accessed June 22, 2003). *This site contains several tests and links to developments in modern psychology relating to personal happiness and fulfillment.*

A Time for Truth

Memoir

By: William E. Simon

Date: 1978

Source: Simon, William E. *A Time for Truth.* New York: Reader's Digest Press, 1978, 126–131, 165–166.

About the Author: William E. Simon (1922–2000), a New Jersey native and longtime successful municipal bond broker, was appointed U.S. secretary of the treasury in May 1974, during the final days of President Richard Nixon's (served 1969–1974) administration. Simon also served as President Gerald R. Ford's (served 1974–1977) secretary of the treasury and remained in office during the 1975 New York City Bankruptcy Crisis. Simon was the Ford administration's principle liaison with both Congress and New York City during the acrimonious debate over a potential federal government bailout of the troubled metropolis. ■

Introduction

Settled by Dutch, Jews, French Huguenots, and Germans, and home to the largest black population outside the South, as well as to significant Hispanic and Asian communities, New York has always boasted an ethnically mixed population full of enterprising citizens who are active in all areas of the economy. At the start of the Civil War (1861–1865), New Yorkers, who largely sympathized with the slaveholding South, toyed with the idea of leaving the Union and establishing themselves as a third force—an independent city-state that could trade with either side in the event of war.

Since the 1790s, the Democratic Party (formerly known as the "Republicans" until the 1820s) has controlled New York City. The infamous Tammany Hall political machine, that controlled the city (with a few interruptions) between 1855 and the early 1930s, established the mode for how government and business worked (and colluded) in the world's biggest city. What developed under this system of corruption and administrative abuse came to represent everything that is objectionable about big-city life in America—great disparities of wealth and power between rich and poor, fresh waves of newcomers washing ashore daily, violent crime, easy toleration of vices among its populace, and rampant municipal corruption.

Significance

After decades of gross financial mismanagement, New York City was teetering on the brink of fiscal insolvency by 1975. Americans became aware of the impending crisis very abruptly, although few people who understood the city were surprised by the news. After all, when dealing with the nation's largest metropolis, many believed that almost any level of incompetence or corruption was possible.

Bankers and others who made money off the city were naturally loath to go public and burst the bubble. When this conspiracy of silence was finally pierced, the whole unseemly mess erupted into full view. As the truth unfolded, it became apparent that New York's elected officials and bureaucrats had been engaging in a giant financial shell game that, had it occurred in the private sector, would have landed many people in prison for fraud.

Throughout the rest of the United States scant sympathy existed for New York. The city's ills were viewed as the result of a combination of greedy public employees, a bloated bureaucracy, and a corrupt municipal service featuring payoffs to organized crime. Now New Yorkers expected the American taxpayer to rescue the city from its folly, but those outside New York strenuously opposed any bailout since they were unwilling to assist a city that might never reform its ways. Indeed, some compared giving help to New York to buying an alcoholic another drink.

When the federal government under President Gerald Ford balked at providing direct financial assistance to the troubled city, those who favored a bailout demonized the bankers who had loaned the city money and then expected repayment. American municipalities that operated in a style similar to that of New York lobbied the federal government to help the city, seeking to establish a precedent for when other cities encountered their own days of reckoning.

The Ford administration itself finally came under intense fire for being "heartless." In surely one of the twentieth century's most memorable headlines, the New York *Daily News* blared: "Ford to City, Drop Dead." In the end, a political compromise was reached: The federal government provided limited, short-term financial assistance to ease a cash-crunch in return for New York's pledge to tighten its belt and restore some semblance of fiscal sanity. The city survived.

Primary Source

A Time for Truth [excerpt]

> **SYNOPSIS:** Ford administration treasury secretary, William E. Simon, reveals the backstage maneuvering that transpired during the high-level 1975 negotiations for assisting New York City during its bankruptcy crisis. The following excerpt from Simon's candid 1978 memoir, *A Time For Truth*, describes the troubles Simon encountered when sorting through the mass of disinformation designed to exculpate New York leaders from their own fiscal folly.

In 1975 New York City collapsed financially. The catastrophe was not a result of the recession. Nor was it a result of the energy crisis. However severe the economic difficulties of the period, no other great American city collapsed. It was a problem unique to New York—but unique in only one sense. The philosophy that has ruled our nation for forty years had emerged in large measure from that very city which was America's intellectual headquarters, and inevitably, it was carried to its fullest expression in that city. In the collapse of New York those who chose to understand it could see a terrifying dress rehearsal of the fate that lies ahead for this country if it continues to be guided by the same philosophy of government.

The most understandable description of the more technical aspects of New York's financial trauma was provided by Martin Mayer, author of *The Bankers*. I quote it because Mayer is splendidly uninhibited by the requirements of political diplomacy that limited my own discourse throughout the New York crisis. He writes:

> On the simplest level, the story of New York's financial collapse is the tale of Ponzi game in municipal paper—the regular and inevitably increasing issuance of notes to be paid off not by the future taxes or revenue cer-

Treasury Secretary William E. Simon speaks before the Senate Finance Committee, 1974. **ARCHIVE PHOTOS. REPRODUCED BY PERMISSION.**

tified to be available for that purpose, but by the sale of future notes. Like all chain-letter swindles, Ponzi games self-destruct when the seller runs out of suckers, as New York did in spring 1975.

It was a tawdry way for one of the greatest cities in the world to fulfill its philosophical destiny, but it was inevitable.

As a specialist in municipal bonds I had known for years that New York was borrowing heavily to finance the promises of its politicians to the New York electorate. The New York *Times* had observed: "No one ever won any election by proposing to give the people less." In New York people won elections exclusively by using the word "more": more public services of all kinds for the working and middle classes; ever greater salaries and pensions for the hundreds of thousands who worked for the New York City government; more extensive social programs for the less fortunate. All these had been considered political absolutes, and notes and bonds were sold to finance them. By the end of 1974 the city was seeking to sell about $600 million of bonds every month to finance delivery on the campaign promises.

Until 1974 the system worked. But in that year the borrowing pace stepped up ominously. New York's need for funds suddenly seemed to be insatiable; the city went to the market for funds eighteen times in that year alone. Warning signs began to appear in the market. Suspicious buyers, signaling an awareness of risk, were demanding more return for their investments in city notes. On November 4 tax-free city notes were going at a record rate of 8.34 percent. On top of this was the fact that the bonds offered for sale the month before had not sold well; there was a large balance for which there had been no takers. Thus, on December 2, $600 million in new notes were offered for sale at a record 9.48 percent. And on December 18 the city announced plans to persuade the trustees of the municipal pension funds to use those funds to purchase $250 million in city obligations. The city's frantic search for funds in an increasingly suspicious market had reached some kind of dead end; it was now attempting to feed on the trust funds of its employees.

At about this time I heard from a distraught Mayor Abraham Beame. He told me that New York was suffering what he perceived to be a great injustice: The city was being forced to sell its notes at the highest rate in the country. He asked the U.S. Treasury to buy the notes. I told him I had no authority to do such a thing and could not recommend it. "If we did that," I said, "the taxpayers would end up financing the campaign promises of every profligate local politician in the country." It was an unsatisfactory answer for Mayor Beame. I asked the city, however, to send us the New York balance sheets immediately so we could determine what might be done to assist the city. The Treasury did not receive those records. I did not realize, then, that the last thing on earth any New York politician desired to confront was the city's bookkeeping.

Then, in February 1975, after a young lawyer representing Bankers Trust discovered, apparently by accident, that the city did not have the tax receipts required by law to secure a $260 million note sale, both Bankers Trust and Chase Manhattan refused to go through with the underwriting. At approximately the same time New York State's Urban Development Corporation defaulted on $104.5 million worth of bond-anticipation notes. A lawsuit was started to enjoin as unconstitutional the sale of more than $500 million of ten-year bonds, for New York City was constitutionally and legally mandated to balance its budget. Fully aware that New York might not be able to honor its debts, investors were not inclined to await the outcome of the lawsuit. By the tens of thousands they simply refused to buy any more New York paper.

There were charges that this decision was made secretly by a small group of men in a smoke-filled room. It was not. It was made in the clear light of day, visible to all, by that omniscient judge: the market. On March 13 and 20 the city, through its underwriters, offered for sale $912 million of short-term notes at tax-exempt interest rates of up to 8 percent. Even for investors of relatively moderate means, this looked on the surface like a very good opportunity. For such investors the effective yield, on a tax equivalent basis, was three times greater than that available at a savings bank. Yet weeks after the offering, despite vigorous marketing, more than half the notes remained unsold.

The market had spoken. Investors had recognized that purchase of the notes would make them just another vulnerable layer in the borrowing pyramid and that they could be repaid only by the creation of still more layers of debt in the months ahead. They simply shied away, choosing instead from a variety of competing investment opportunities. Although the returns did not match what New York was offering, the risks as perceived by the market were much lower. For New York the market had closed. The Ponzi game had "self-destructed."

The shock of New York's financial collapse was explosive—in New York, in the rest of the country, and throughout the world. How could it have happened so suddenly? everyone wondered. In fact, it had not happened suddenly. For a decade the public had been aware that New York City was spending heavily. But in the Great Society of the sixties that was not perceived as a serious threat. The illusion was that we had found the political formula for permanent wealth: promise-borrow-spend, promise-borrow-spend. Thus, the liberal economists assured us, could we eternally "stimulate" our economy. To question the efficacy of that formula was to question the very premise of the welfare state, of government intervention into the economy, and of the redistributionist philosophy that had swept the country. It was to question liberalism itself. And to question liberalism was to be a reactionary blackguard.

No one—whether the New York politicians or the unions or the most prominent bankers of New York or the New York press—has ever given a coherent explanation of why a collapse that had been building for a decade had not been anticipated. I cannot point the finger in this respect, for I hadn't expected it either. It was particularly ironic in my case, for in the late sixties and early seventies, when I worked at Salomon Brothers, I had been a member of the Technical Debt Advisory Committee set up by Abraham Beame when he was Comptroller of New York. We supplied the city market advice on its financial transactions, but at no point during any of these sessions did any one of us seriously question the underlying fiscal condition of New York. We all worked with the numbers given to us by the city itself, just as do the advisory committees to the federal government. It never occurred to us to disbelieve those figures, which always indicated that New York would be able to repay its debt.

From today's perspective this was a naive faith in the fiscal stability and honesty of governments. But before New York collapsed, that faith did exist. No one questioned the assumptions that the city's budget would be balanced, that city officials could and would raise taxes, if needed, to honor debts, and that the city's government was fundamentally sound. I shared these assumptions, and so did all the "hardheaded" bankers of New York. . . .

There was, finally, the forum in which this drama played itself out: Congress. For the most part, Congressmen were not eager to bail out New York. The responsible men were as aware as I of the constitutional pitfalls of such a bailout, and the less responsible discovered that their constituencies would not tolerate it. They were willing, as I was, to assist New York if a mode of assistance could be discovered which would not set a destructive precedent for other cities and if New York City showed authentic signs of self-correction. Within this shared context, however, the liberal leadership—Senators Hubert Humphrey, Abraham Ribicoff, Henry Jackson, *et al.*—differentiated itself by a ritual keening over New York's crucifixion on behalf of the "poor" and by ritual denunciations of those of us in the administration who named the problem in other, more realistic terms.

Above all, the liberal Congressmen enjoyed denouncing me as "flinty," "callous," and "inhumane." The degree to which much of this was sheer rhetoric was startling even to me. The outstanding example of this playacting at moral outrage was Hubert Humphrey. Privately Hubert and I were good friends, and he knew quite well that I was no more "inhumane" than he. He got a prankish pleasure, however, out of denouncing me publicly during the New York crisis. On one occasion, when I was testifying before the Joint Economic Committee on the possible financial impact of default, Hubert put on a remarkable show. As the cameras rolled, he peered down at me grimly and ranted away about my "inhumanity"—and then, as the cameras swung away from him to capture my reaction, Hubert *winked!*

Further Resources

BOOKS

Auletta, Ken. *Hard Feelings: Reporting on Pols, the Press, People, and the City.* New York: Random House, 1980.

Fitch, Robert. *The Assassination of New York.* New York: Verso, 1993.

Meyer, Martin. *The Bankers.* New York: Weybright and Talley, 1974.

"Labor Law Reform and Its Enemies"

Magazine article

By: Thomas Ferguson and Joel Rogers

Date: January 6–13, 1979

Source: Ferguson, Thomas, and Joel Rogers. "Labor Law Reform and Its Enemies." *The Nation,* January 6-13, 1979, 1, 17–18, 19, 20.

About the Authors: Thomas Ferguson (1949–), a political scientist at the University of Massachusetts, Boston, is one of the nation's leading experts on the role of organized labor in American electoral politics.

Joel Rogers (1952–)is a professor of law, political science, and sociology at the University of Wisconsin, Madison, who has written extensively on the future of the American working class. ∎

Introduction

In 1935, passage of the Wagner Act (formally called the National Labor Relations Act) changed the relations between managers and employees, business and government, and business and organized labor in the United States. The act, enforced by the newly created National Labor Relations Board, recognized the rights of American workers to organize into labor unions, to use those unions in collective bargaining for legally binding contracts with their employers, and to have access to government agencies for mediation of disputes.

For most of the post-World War II period, the new system of collective bargaining appeared to promote cooperation between business and labor, with government as a mediator. Yet, from the 1950s through the end of the

century, the membership, political influence, and bargaining power of organized labor all went into a decline.

From the middle of World War II (1939–1945), conservatives in Congress formed alliances with well-organized elements of the corporate and small-business communities to change national labor law. In the Taft-Hartley Act of 1947 and the Landrum-Griffin Act of 1959, they succeeded in reversing some of the gains for labor encompassed within the 1935 Wagner Act. In the strongly anti-union atmosphere of the 1950s and 1960s, these political actors made further inroads on union privilege, power, and influence. Union-busting organizations emerged to advise businesses on ways to block or reverse union elections and on how to gain the advantage in collective bargaining contracts. This article from *The Nation* describes the complex interaction among the Carter administration, organized labor, the Business Roundtable, and the National Right to Work Committee in struggling to shape "reform" of national labor law in an era of increasingly conservative politics.

Significance

Since the New Deal in the 1930s, many Americans had come to assume that the federal government usually sided with organized labor in the area of labor-management relations. Yet even though the Wagner Act of 1935 granted American workers the right to organize unions and to undertake colletive bargaining, that legal right had to be backed by real worker and union action. By the end of the 1970s, the social composition of the American labor force had begun to change, comprising more African Americans, women, immigrants, and young people. Structural changes in the national economy meant that industrial jobs, which had dominated the labor market for two generations, were being replaced by white-collar and unskilled work in non-union work places. Since the core of organized labor was in the older industrial sector, the political influence of labor waned during the decade. It didn't help labor that the National Labor Relations Board simultaneously came under the control of representatives of strongly anti-union interests.

The postwar system of collective bargaining, that had given millions of Americans higher wages, good benefits, shorter hours, and better working conditions, began to break down. Economic stagnation, lower productivity, and price inflation meant that both small and big businesses could play a much more powerful role in "reforming" labor law. As the political alliance that was forged in the New Deal between organized labor and the Democratic Party began to falter, Democrats in the White House and Congress often chose to desert the cause of labor in the midst of labor-law fights. In 1979, facing an imminent and bitter re-election battle and fearing that he would lose the support of both business and the public if he sided with labor, President Carter refused to back labor in an effort to resist changes that would hurt workers and unions. In 1980, Reagan Democrats abandoned the party of FDR to join the conservative Republican coalition that would dominate American politics in the 1980s.

Primary Source

"Labor Law Reform and Its Enemies"

> **SYNOPSIS:** Two of the most astute authorities on the worsening condition of the country's working class, Professors Thomas Ferguson and Joel Rogers, lament the diminishing political influence wielded by organized labor and its abject failure during the crucial Carter years to convince Congress to arrest organized labor's decline. In the end, as this piece in *The Nation* relates, labor unions in the United States suffered blows from which they have yet to recover.

The defeat last June of the proposed Labor Law Reform Bill (L.L.R.B.) at the hands of an unprecedentedly broad coalition of business groups was a catastrophe for American labor.

By shattering the consensus on goals that has long guided much of industry and most of labor, the bill's demise heralds an end to the epoch of industrial relations that began in the later stages of the New Deal. By setting in motion powerful tides of interest and sentiment, it virtually insures a long period of turmoil in American society and politics. And by highlighting the inability of trade union leaders either to bargain successfully with a presumptively friendly Democratic Congress, or to exact major support from an Administration they helped place in power, the wreck of labor law reform forces the United States labor movement to face the fact of its own decline, and compels it, however unwillingly, to begin the protracted and painful process of measuring its aspirations against its capabilities.

Any number of statistics testify to the gravity of the situation. The percentage of the work force organized into trade unions has dropped steadily since the mid 1950s, standing now at a postwar low of 20.1 percent. Organizing drives mounted by unions are increasingly ineffective. While as late as the mid-1960s unions won 60 percent of representation elections, by last year their percentage of victories had plunged to 46 percent. Both because of membership discontent with union leadership and employers' increasingly sophisticated union-busting

tactics, the number of proposed contract agreements rejected by rank and file has in recent years risen sharply, and unions now lose close to 80 percent of the growing number of decertification elections (which challenge the union's status as bargaining representative) and de-authorization polls (which challenge "union shop" agreements) conducted by the National Labor Relations Board. Right-to-work laws, already on the books in some twenty states, are being lavishly promoted by opponents of labor in at least six others, though a campaign in Missouri was defeated in the November elections.

No less unfavorable for unions has been the trend of public opinion. Various polls conducted while Congress considered the L.L.R.B. showed labor lagging far behind business in both public confidence and belief in its representative character. In addition, a majority of those polled felt that leaders of the larger unions wielded excessive power.

But aggregate indices such as these veil a more subtle aspect of labor's decline: the decay of its position inside the American party system. Although the unions' power within the Roosevelt New Deal coalition was probably less than most contemporary observers recognized, shared as it was with large numbers of investment and commercial bankers, representatives of a variety of high technology industries, and too many oil men to count conveniently, from 1935 onward they did exercise significant influence within Democratic circles.

But by the late 1950s labor's position within the Democratic Party had already begun to deteriorate. A year before the pivotal Presidential election of 1960, a Congress top-heavy with Democrats in wake of the recession-induced landslide of 1958 passed the sharply anti-labor Landrum-Griffin Act. Simultaneously the Republican business coalition of the 1950s began to splinter over the issue of free trade, which threatened major industries such as steel, textiles and shoe manufacturing, but was ardently promoted by the G.O.P.'s "Eastern Establishment" of bankers and multinationally oriented business firms.

When the right wing of the party, supported strongly by such protectionist and nationalistically inclined figures as National Steel's George Humphrey, textile magnate Roger Milliken, and independent oil men John Pew and Henry Salvatori, seized control of the G.O.P. in the early 1960s, a mass exit commenced of multinational (and, commonly, high technology) businesses from the Republicans to the Democrats. Their impact on the Democratic Party's foreign economic policy was immediately evident.

With the Trade Expansion Act of 1962 and the Kennedy Round of substantial tariff reductions, the party reaffirmed its New Deal commitment to a liberally structured world economic order, providing for the free multilateral flow of goods and capital.

This was a disaster for labor, which was best organized in those older industrial sectors most threatened by international competition, and which experienced the flood of imports from Western European, Japanese and American-owned corporations abroad as a loss of union jobs. Nor was labor able to stem the flow of shops from the North to right-to-work states in the South. In 1965 the most heavily Democratic Congress since Roosevelt's second term declined to amend the right-to-work provision of the Taft-Hartley Act, and other Democratic Congresses of the period, despite routine election-year promises to labor, contrived to avoid the issue altogether.

With the return of a Democratic Administration in 1977, labor attempted once again to improve its organizing position by legislation. The A.F.L.-C.I.O. proposed a series of amendments to existing labor law whose general thrust was to speed up representation elections, increase penalties for the skyrocketing number of unfair labor practices committed by employers, afford unions access to employer promises to combat "captive audience" employer union-busting tactics, and grant the N.L.R.B. additional power in "refusal to bargain" cases, while increasing the size of the N.L.R.B. and streamlining the review process for regional Administrative Law Judge findings.

But the realignment of party elites that took such dramatic shape in 1964 had crystallized by the middle of the 1970s. The hegemonic element in President Carter's victorious coalition of 1976 was the free-trade oriented Trilateral Commission, not the ever more protectionist A.F.L.-C.I.O. And the defeat of the common situs picketing bill foreshadowed what was vividly illustrated by the fate of the Labor Law Reform Bill: When forced to choose between his big business and labor supporters, Carter would throw his weight behind the former.

This was apparent from the start of last fall's Congressional session, when Carter and Senate Majority Leader Robert Byrd set their legislative agenda. They decided to shelve the L.L.R.B. until after the Senate approved the controversial Panama Canal treaties, an item of first importance to a phalanx of big banks and multinationals who feared the impact a rejection of the treaties might have on their Latin American investments. As Carter and Byrd well knew,

voting twice for positions publicly identified (however outlandishly) as "liberal" would be too much to expect of some Senators who faced re-election campaigns. Whichever bill came up first would therefore enjoy the better chance. In addition, Carter's and Byrd's decision gave the growing ranks of anti-union lobbyists (far more professional than their opponents) more time to mobilize support. By the time the L.L.R.B. finally came up in Congress, an army of new actors had been recruited for the struggle. . . .

But what lifted the L.L.R.B. battle to historic significance was the struggle that took place on the heights of the American economy where, for the first time in decades, the largest American corporations allied with the small business community and committed major resources for a blitz against labor.

The center of deliberations leading up to this step was the Policy Committee of the Business Roundtable. The Roundtable, originally organized out of much less publicized groups such as the Construction Users League, and the so-called "March Group" (and with a Policy Committee that heavily overlaps the much more discreet Business Council), has grown since it was founded in the early days of the 1970's recession into corporate America's major high-profile public lobbying and consensus center. Unlike the American contingent on the Trilateral Commission, which is exclusively oriented toward multinationalism and free trade, the Roundtable membership represents both sides of the controversy over American foreign economic policy.

All belligerents in the great labor war of 1978 recognized the critical role the Roundtable would necessarily play, and pressure on the organization to commit itself was intense. A bloc of big firms on the Policy Committee pressed for a quick decision to join N.A.M. and the Chamber in opposition to the bill. Prominent among these were firms relying on unskilled labor, like Sears Roebuck, as well as firms in mass production industries, such as Firestone and Goodyear, that are under pressure in the current world recession. Most of the chemical companies urged a strong position against the bill, in part out of anxiety about their own work force, but also because they depend on industries like textiles which use large quantities of chemicals and are threatened by unionization. And of course the steel companies favored a strong stand against the bill, with Bethlehem donating the full-time services of industrial relations vice president J.J. O'Connell to the National Action Committee's own policy committee.

Nevertheless, another important segment of the Roundtable was initially skeptical about a major attack on the bill, and favored neutrality. Firms like I.B.M. and A.T.&T. that operate with ultra-high technology (and hence comparatively low direct labor costs), saw no pronounced gain for them in defeating the L.L.R.B. With the probable exception of Shell, oil companies, although certainly worried about an extension of union activity in their industry, seem to have opposed a harsh public position. Although busily engaged in the flight south from the unions (recently slowed somewhat by agreements to turn over some of the new plants to the U.A.W.), heavily unionized firms like General Motors did not wish to spark a class war, and so temporized at the start. And other firms, notably General Electric and Du Pont, frankly argued that the benefits of big business-big labor collaboration outweighed the costs, even during a world recession.

Organized labor made some attempt to exploit this division within the Roundtable. Its spokesmen repeatedly held out the carrot of cooperative labor relations. Unions inveigled the steel industry, for example, with a provision in the bill banning "stranger picketing" of the type rampant earlier this year in the coal fields—a measure that would, incidentally, subordinate union rank and file to headquarters.

Labor also brandished the stick. Earlier this year, some unions threatened to remove their pension funds from banks whose personnel sat on the boards of corporations renowned for their hard line toward union organizing. Reportedly, representatives of labor reminded the major banks on the Roundtable Policy Committee of this episode early in the Roundtable deliberations. And though diffusion of electronic processing equipment has deskilled a significant proportion of bank work and thus made it more vulnerable to unionization, the big banks maintained a low profile throughout the struggle. (By contrast, the American Banking Association, dominated by small banks, lobbied against the L.L.R.B. from the beginning.) Finally, labor seems to have brought special pressure on Ralph Lazarus, chairman of Federated Department Stores and a Policy Committee member, who also chose to stay on the sidelines.

In August 1977, reportedly amid threats by some of the small business organizations to boycott big businesses that wavered, and complaints from the lower ranks of the firms that favored neutrality, the Policy Committee voted 19 to 11 to move actively against the bill rather than stay neutral. On the los-

Poster sponsored by the AFL-CIO Task Force on Labor Law Reform. THE LIBRARY OF CONGRESS.

ing side were General Electric, Du Pont, Federated Department Stores and, in all probability, I.B.M., A.T.&T., Citibank, Chase, General Motors, Mobil and most of the other oil companies (save Shell).

The Roundtable then closed ranks with N.A.M. and the Chamber on the National Action Committee. In the end, even G.E., which had been perhaps the most vigorous defender of neutrality, sent plant managers to lobby against the bill at the height of the debate. Fraser Associates handled publicity for the Roundtable on the bill, and McGuiness and Williams, whose Labor Policy Association had previously acted for Roundtable members on labor affairs, were retained as counsel.

As the bill moved toward a vote on the Senate floor, lobbying and bargaining were intense. Planeloads of businessmen flooded Washington, business launched a nationwide press campaign of canned editorials and advertising, and much grass-roots organizing was attempted by both sides.

Although President Carter had been involved in the bill's formative stages—during which he had insisted on removing a projected 14(b) repeal provision that labor wished to use later as a bargaining chip—he for the most part kept out of the campaign to enact the L.L.R.B. Responsibility for White House lobbying was delegated to Vice President Mondale and Labor Secretary Ray Marshall, men whose strongly pro-labor backgrounds deprived them of much leverage with anti-labor Senators. Carter, so adept earlier at mobilizing Senate support for the Canal treaties, quietly allowed his newly acquired reputation as a skilled negotiator to dissipate.

By the time of the June filibuster, all the interest groups were aligned, but the bill was in tatters. Several important provisions had disappeared, including the heavy compensation clause for employees found victim of unfair labor practices (of special significance to small businesses unprepared to pay such fees), and many features of the procedure to accelerate representation elections. As bargaining over specific parts of the bill extended debate for a period longer than that afforded any other major piece of labor legislation in the nation's history, the crucial question became whether the filibuster led by Senators Hatch, Helms, Lugar and others could be broken.

The forces opposing the bill retained a remarkable cohesion, which was only in part an achievement of ideology. When Sen. Howard Baker, a leading unannounced candidate for the 1980 G.O.P. Presidential nomination (and who would like to run as a free trade advocate), flirted with the idea of casting his vote for cloture, Senator Hatch applied strong pressure. Working closely with the National Right to Work Committee, Hatch coolly dispatched a letter, on Senate stationery, outlining the current status of the bill to every 1976 G.O.P. contributor. This move, along with earlier criticism he had received from the Citizens for the Republic (legatee of the residual $1 million war chest of Citizens for Reagan), kept Baker in line. The National Right to Work Committee alone mailed its constituents more than fifty million preprinted postcards attacking the bill. Reportedly, six million of them were mailed back to the Senate Office Building, and by the end of the spring, nearly every postcard maker in the East had been bought out.

As the filibuster continued, Carter, under tremendous pressure from labor, was finally forced to move. . . .

As swing Senators held out for amendment of one or another of the bill's provisions, labor lobbyists consistently overestimated the number of cloture votes they really had in hand. Byrd's own more pessimistic tallies proved to be correct on this score, for after six separate votes the bill was eventually

scuttled, amid promises from Long to attempt a compromise in the next session, albeit for a drastically enfeebled bill.

This ended the first disastrous act of a performance that labor had envisioned as calling back its old appreciative audience.

Further Resources

BOOKS

Dubofsky, Melvyn. *The State and Labor in Modern America.* Chapel Hill: University of North Carolina Press, 1994.

Ferguson, Thomas, and Joel Rogers, eds. *Right Turn: The Decline of the Democrats and the Future of American Politics.* New York: Hill and Wang, 1986.

Gall, Gilbert J. *The Politics of Right to Work: The Labor Federations as Special Interests, 1943-1979.* Westport, CT: Greenwood Press, 1988.

Lichtenstein, Nelson. *State of the Union: A Century of American Labor.* Princeton: Princeton University Press, 2002.

McQuaid, Kim. *Big Business and Presidential Power: From FDR to Reagan.* New York: Morrow, 1982.

———. *Uneasy Partners: Big Business in American Politics, 1945-1990.* Baltimore: Johns Hopkins University Press, 1994.

Moody, Kim. *An Injury to All: The Decline of American Unionism.* London and New York: Verso, 1988.

Zieger, Robert H. and Gilbert J. Gall. *American Workers, American Unions,* third edition. Baltimore: Johns Hopkins University Press, 2002.

"Low Pay, Bossy Bosses Kill Kids' Enthusiasm for Food-Service Jobs"

Newspaper article

By: Jim Montgomery

Date: March 15, 1979

Source: Jim Montgomery. "Low Pay, Bossy Bosses Kill Kids' Enthusiasm for Food-Service Jobs." *Wall Street Journal,* March 15, 1979, 1, 11, 33.

About the Author: Jim Montgomery wrote for the *Wall Street Journal*, which is published by Dow Jones & Company. The *Wall Street Journal* first began publication in the United States in 1889, and has since gone on to become a successful newspaper with a wide readership and several global editions. Dow Jones & Company also publishes *Barron's* and the *Far Eastern Economic Review.* ■

Introduction

American postwar consumer culture often centered on the ubiquitous fast-food restaurant. Emerging from the suburban retail culture of California in the 1950s, the McDonald's hamburger and french fries franchise expanded throughout the country in the 1960s and 1970s. Relying on the franchise model of local entrepreneurs putting up cash to sell recognizable brand-name products, fast-food chains such as Shoney's, Kentucky Fried Chicken, Denny's, Wendy's, Burger King, Steak 'n Shake, and others created not just a long-running retail phenomenon but an entire segment of consumer culture. These restaurants served as gathering places for young people and families and popular stopping places for travelers, largely because customers could count on knowing ahead of time just what they would get and how much their food would cost.

These retail establishments looked very different in the eyes of young, unskilled workers in these establishments, who often labored in hot, dangerous environments at what could become a frenzied pace during lunch and dinner times. Since the profit margin of these stores, as elsewhere in the food industry, was razor thin, managers often cut corners by paying employees minimum wages and keeping hours worked per week to a minimum so as to avoid having to provide benefits or overtime pay. By the end of the decade, many people referred to such low-paying, unskilled, entry-level jobs as "McJobs." This 1979 article from the *Wall Street Journal* gives a detailed look at the work world of young Americans in the 1970s who became part of what author Eric Schlosser would later call the "fast-food nation."

Significance

The postwar United States created the first mass youth culture in U.S. history. By the 1970s, millions of American teenagers got their first experience of paid employment at a local franchise of one of the nation's fast food restaurants. It would be several decades before careful observers of the labor market recognized that this work experience represented more than a simple morality tale of American children coming of age. Increasingly, the U.S. labor market moved toward a two-tiered system of work. The top tier consisted of relatively well-paying jobs that offered hourly pay above the minimum wage, along with generous benefits such as health insurance, a pension plan, a set number of sick days, paid holidays and vacation, and chances for higher pay and advancement. The second tier, represented by the kind of jobs discussed in this investigative article, rarely paid above minimum wage, restricted the work week to less than forty hours to avoid payment of overtime, and provided few, if any, benefits. As the American economy began

to face more competition from abroad, conditions in these "McJobs" became worse as employers sought to reduce labor costs even further in order to keep the prices low for customers while maintaining good profit margins that would appeal to investors.

Many business leaders and economists in the 1970s argued that entry-level jobs were not intended as permanent employment. Rather, by hiring young, inexperienced workers, employers were giving the next generation valuable experience in building an industrious work ethic, earning their own pay, learning how to manage time and money, and preparing for lifetime employment. Only later, as the structure of the national labor market came to reflect more and more of these kinds of jobs, did scholars and analysts realize that the postwar American social contract between business and labor was being undermined. No single manager, corporation, or industry brought about such changes, yet the social consequences of the emergence of this second-tier labor market created tensions and challenges for millions of Americans. Already caught up in the stagnant economy of the 1970s, facing rapid increases in prices that brought high levels of inflation, and concerned about becoming trapped in dead-end jobs, many Americans found that the experience of young workers provided a discouraging preview of things to come in the next decade and beyond.

Primary Source

"Low Pay, Bossy Bosses Kill Kids' Enthusiasm for Food-Service Jobs" [excerpt]

SYNOPSIS: The world of fast-food restaurants, manned by a horde of fresh-faced teenagers working for minimum wage, is the topic of this *Wall Street Journal* investigation by staff reporter Jim Montgomery. This piece shines the spotlight on Burger King, but it could have applied equally well to McDonald's.

Average Teen-Age Worker Quits After Four Months, Fast-Food Survey Shows

Learning to Steal in Texas

Wendy Hamburger no longer makes Wendy's Old-Fashioned Hamburgers. After working three months at a Wendy's fast-food shop in suburban Chicago, she got fed up and quit.

Miss Hamburger, a winsome 17-year-old, was a press agent's dream come true when she applied for a job last summer at a Wendy's outlet near her Barrington, Ill., home. She hoped to earn some money toward entering art school after she graduates from high school this year.

What she earned mostly was a lot of free publicity for Wendy's hamburger chain in Chicago-area newspapers. And a little attention from R. David Thomas founder and chairman of Wendy's International Inc., who mailed her an autographed photograph of himself. Until she walked out on a manager who threatened to fire her if she refused to work an extra turn on a holiday, she earned about $40 for 15 hours' work a week. "It seemed," she recalls, "like the job cost me more than I made."

Frequent Turnover

Low pay, distasteful working conditions and autocratic bosses are hardly a new story to the millions of teen-agers that the fast food industry depends upon to peddle the billions of hamburgers, fries and shakes it sells every year. But, like Wendy J. Hamburger, few youngsters realize when they apply for a fast-food job that they will be doing better than average if they don't get disgusted and quit within four months.

Some critics, in fact, contend that the fast-food chains, by and large, actually count on frequent turnover. Just about every job in these restaurants changes hands three or four times a year. In most businesses such turnover would be catastrophic. In the fast-food business it means almost everyone is paid the minimum wage and almost no one ever gets a merit raise or joins a union.

"The whole system is designed to have turnover," thus averting pay increases and frustrating organizing efforts, asserts Robert Harbrant, secretary treasurer of the AFL-CIO Food and Beverage Trades Department in Washington, D.C.

To be sure, a fast-food job is the first work experience for many youngsters, and some of them have a hard time adjusting to the discipline of getting to work on time or even showing up every day. "You have about an 80% reliability factor," says one restaurant executive whose chief complaint about his teen-age work force is that "about the time you get them trained they take off."

Cause . . . or Effect?

However, Harlow F. White, president of Systems for Human Resources Inc., Mill Valley, Calif., a management-consulting firm that recently did a national survey of food-service-employee attitudes, questions whether the 300% annual turnover of fast-food employees is a cause or an effect of the way the industry operates. In any event, he says, "the industry has managed to manufacture a self-fulfilling prophecy: 'We're going to have turnover. And, by God, we do.'"

A sudden, sharp decline in employment turnover, Mr. White adds, would plunge the industry into turmoil, a development neither he nor anyone else sees as an imminent possibility. In fact, the survey found that more than one-third of management employees and four-fifths of hourly employees in the food-service industry plan to get out of it.

Operators of fast-food chains acknowledge that teen-age part-timers working for the minimum wage are the backbone of their business. But the operators deny that they purposely encourage turnover or do anything worse than to provide youngsters a chance to earn some spending money.

"Turnover costs us money," says a spokesman for the Burger King unit of Pillsbury Co., even though "it only takes a day or two" to train a new employee to a level of reasonable proficiency. Also, he says, there's "nothing we can do about a lot of the turnover" because employees are students who only want the jobs for the summer or for a school term or two.

Undercurrent of Discontent

Despite such declarations of good intentions by executives at fast-food home offices, it is quickly evident that out in the field, at the restaurants themselves, there is a strong undercurrent of discontent and a feeling of being exploited among the unsophisticated young workers.

At an Atlanta Steak n Shake, for instance, a black teen-age waitress complains that she has been scheduled to work a two-hour day although it takes her more than two hours of riding time on city buses to get there and back home. (A company official concedes this reflects "mismanagement at that store." He says that if a worker is called in at all, "we have a written policy to pay them for a minimum of three hours.")

In New York's Washington Square, Burger King keeps a 17-year-old applicant waiting expectantly for weeks before telling him it won't have an opening after all, costing him a month of job hunting and $200 in forgone pay. (A Burger King spokesman says, "Unfortunately, things like that do happen." He adds that the chain has installed a "new scheduling technique" that will allow better estimates of their future manpower needs.)

A suburban New York McDonald's orders teen-age part-timers to arrive up to an hour ahead of work

A student at Burger King University learns how to fill a soft drink cup. © BETTMANN/CORBIS. REPRODUCED BY PERMISSION.

time and then "wait in the back room and punch in later when they need you. . . .

Teen-agers usually don't know that the law requires that they be paid for such waiting time and that they be paid for even a few minutes of work that many of them do voluntarily before or after their work turn.

Store managers should know better but often don't. Richard Gilbert, a compliance official in the U.S. Labor Department's wage and hour division, faults the store-manager training programs run by the home offices of franchise chains. He says, "We find in many cases that these 20-year-old managers are sales-oriented and cleanliness-oriented. But they aren't taught much about employee relations. And the Wage-Hour Law is just another three pages in the operating manual."

There's a lot of agreement on that score from insiders and outsiders alike. "I went through three

managers in the short time I was at Wendy's," recalls Miss Hamburger, "They needed managers so badly they hired anyone. They get a lot of young guys in there who think they're Mr. Macho and want to exercise their power. They don't know anything."

"They Call You Stupid"

"I quit because I didn't like the way managers treated us," says a 17-year-old who was cashier at an Atlanta McDonald's last summer. The managers, she says, "are real snotty. They yell at the workers in front of customers and call you stupid. At the end of August, 15 of us quit because of one manager. Otherwise, most of us would have kept working after school."

The industry deserves much of the criticism, says the Burger King spokesman, for "putting young men or women in their early 20s in charge of a $1 million restaurant with 40 employees under age 18 and expecting them (the managers) to function" like professionals. As a practical matter, he says, "you can train someone to fix a piece of equipment a lot easier than you can to deal with people." To remedy this situation, he says the company is "formalizing people skills" as part of 10 day training courses for managers at its new $1.6 million Burger King University in Miami. . . .

The industry still has a lot to learn, if one believes the anonymous remarks scribbled on Mr. White's firm's survey questionnaires, which were filled out by thousands of fast-food employees last summer and fall. A worker in Arizona griped that "management seems very reluctant to employ enough people. We seem to be constantly asked to work a double turn or nights off." An Alabama worker wrote: "We have too many schedule changes. You never know when you will have to work, so it is hard to plan anything else."

Low pay is a constant irritant. A 16-year-old who quit an Atlanta Wendy's last fall says he was "doing more work than I was getting paid for" at $2.65 an hour. "Sometimes I'd have to work 12 hours a day. Other times there weren't enough of us for lunch-time crowds. One month we went through five assistant managers. When I get another job it won't be in fast foods."

James Badger, another 16-year-old, says in an interview that he learned more than he wanted to know about the fast-food business while working nights as a part-time head cook for a Long John Silver's outlet in Atlanta at $2.60 an hour. One week, he says, "I could have sworn I earned $85. I worked about 32 hours. But I only got a check for $47." Also, he says, "we were supposed to be paid on Fridays, but often we didn't get our checks until Monday or Tuesday."

Another young Southerner said his only gripe was pay: "I receive $2.06 an hour. I would like at least the minimum wage." The national minimum wage was $2.65 in 1978; it increased to $2.90 on Jan. 1.

Numerous Violations

While some small fast-food operations are exempt from the minimum-wage and overtime pay provisions of federal law, most chains are covered and are subject to enforcement actions for failure to comply. Thus, in 1977, Kentucky Fried Chicken of Middlesboro, Ky., had to make up $2,086 in overtime pay to 35 employees. Last summer a Florida operator of Lum's and Ranch House restaurants was or-

dered by federal court in Miami to reimburse $100,000 to 1,290 employees who weren't paid required minimum and overtime wages. And, in New Jersey, the Department of Labor last December charged 18 Burger King restaurants in that state with systematically underpaying their employees and failing to keep adequate wage reports. Similar cases dot court records in all parts of the country.

To be sure, the survey found a number of fast-food employees who felt well-treated. "I like working here," says an Alabama fast-food worker. "It gives me a chance to meet new people." Another teenager, who makes $2.65 an hour as a Burger King food handler, says, "It's a lot of fun. The managers are nice to work for. I work pretty much the time I want to." And a young man working the counter in a Florida store says, "All the hard work is rewarding in the long run because the manager is a friend, parent, counselor, adviser, teacher and boss."

More numerous, however, were comments such as the one from a counter employee in Texas who complained: "Management puts tremendous mental strain on the employees. We have all learned how to successfully steal enough money . . . to make working here with all the bull and pressure worthwhile.

Working Round the Clock

The manager's job is no bed of roses either. One young woman, who is paid $12,000 a year to run a McDonald's franchise store that grosses more than $750,000 a year, declares, "They don't pay managers enough. I'm on my feet from 6 a.m. to 6 p.m. Often I don't have time to eat all day. On days off I come in a couple of hours or call in to check on my assistant managers. And I have to take work home, like the weekly scheduling."

McDonald's officials say they can't control everything a licensee does but that managers of company-owned stores are better trained and paid. Stanley Stein, McDonald's assistant vice president of employee relations, says that "we try to establish mutual respect" with employees. The company must be succeeding, he adds, because "we haven't had a union organizing attempt in four or five years, and we've cut our turnover to maybe a little more than 100% from between 200% and 300% several years back."

Mr. White, the management consultant, says the industry has only itself to blame for employee ill-will. "Most (store) managers are "insensitive rather than malicious in most cases." In his report on the survey, he observed that "the industry doesn't do the kind of manpower planning a labor-intensive environment demands," and that this is resulting in "higher labor costs."

Nation's Restaurant News, which sponsored the survey, echoes his warnings. "Unless food-service executives move quickly to develop an effective working relationship between top management and all unit employees—from general manager to dishwasher," the trade publication declared recently, "the industry will soon face a labor-management debacle of crisis proportions."

Further Resources

BOOKS

Dicke, Thomas S. *Franchising in America: The Development of a Business Method, 1840-1980.* Chapel Hill: University of North Carolina Press, 1992.

Dubofsky, Melvyn and Foster Rhea Dulles. *Labor in America,* sixth edition. Wheeling, Ill.: Harlan Davidson, 1999.

Fishwick, Marshall W., ed. *Ronald Revisited: The World of Ronald McDonald.* Bowling Green, Ohio: Bowling Green University Popular Press, 1983.

Kincheloe, Joe L. *The Sign of the Burger: McDonald's and the Culture of Power.* Philadelphia: Temple University Press, 2002.

Love, John F. *McDonald's: Behind the Arches.* New York: Bantam Books, 1986.

McCraw, Thomas K. *American Business, 1920-2000: How It Worked.* Wheeling, IL: Harlan Davidson, 2000.

Ritzer, George. *The McDonaldization of Society: An Investigation Into the Changing Character of Contemporary Social Life.* Newbury Park, Calif.: Pine Forge Press, 1993.

———. *The McDonaldization Thesis: Explorations and Extensions.* London: Sage, 1998.

Schlosser, Eric. *Fast Food Nation: The Dark Side of the All-American Meal.* Boston: Houghton Mifflin, 2001.

An American Renaissance: A Strategy for the 1980s

Nonfiction work

By: Jack F. Kemp

Date: 1979

Source: Kemp, Jack F. *An American Renaissance: A Strategy for the 1980s.* New York: Harper & Row, 1979, 1–3, 5–7, 7–8, 9, 10, 10–11.

About the Author: Jack French Kemp (1935–), a California native, played professional football as a quarterback for the San Diego Chargers and the Buffalo Bills before entering

politics. Kemp was elected to the U.S. House of Representatives in 1970 as a Republican from Buffalo, New York. An unsuccessful aspirant for the 1988 G.O.P. presidential nomination, he was appointed by President George H.W. Bush (served 1989–1993) as his secretary of Housing and Urban Development. In 1996, Kemp ran on the unsuccessful Republican national ticket as Robert Dole's vice presidential running mate. ∎

Introduction

Between 1947 to 1973, U.S. annual productivity and growth rates rose to historically high levels but then began to fall. Since the end of World War II (1939–1945), economists had assumed that price inflation and unemployment were like two ends of a seesaw: If the economy grew too quickly, prices would rise to a point where the cost of inflation led employers to cut jobs. If employment rose too far too fast, price inflation would be the result. Yet by the mid-1970s, the U.S. economy faced slow growth, rising unemployment, and rapid price inflation. Economists, business leaders, and politicians did not know how to address this new phenomenon, which was dubbed "stagflation." Americans were equally baffled by the problem of how to restore the economic growth that had been the foundation of the postwar economy and the consumer culture.

In the last half of the 1970s, a new, younger generation of conservatives emerged with fresh ideas. One of their leaders was Representative Jack Kemp (R-NY), a former professional football quarterback turned politician. Along with fellow conservative Senator William Roth (R-Del.), Kemp advocated a modified version of the famous 1964 federal tax cut as the way to revive U.S. economic growth. In this excerpt from his 1979 work, *An American Renaissance,* Kemp presented the ideological rationale for his tax-cut plan. He hoped for a revival of traditional Republican economic policy based on hard work, individualism, competition, rewarding innovation with incentives, and restoration of "the American dream" in the coming decade of the 1980s. In 1980, Republican presidential candidate Ronald W. Reagan (served 1981–1989) endorsed the economic policy of supply-side economics using the Kemp-Roth idea of a dramatic three-year tax cut as the centerpiece of Republican-led economic revival from the stagnant growth and double-digit inflation of the 1970s.

Significance

During the administrations of presidents John F. Kennedy (served 1961–1963) and Lyndon B. Johnson (served 1963–1969), there was a call for a New Economics of growth advocating that government reduce taxes and raise expenditures, thus allowing the resulting federal budget deficit to fuel growth. Yet, in failing to

Jack Kemp, Republican congressman from New York, c. 1975. **THE LIBRARY OF CONGRESS.**

increase federal taxes soon enough at the end of the 1960s to pay the costs of the Vietnam War (1964–1975), President Johnson sparked a period of price inflation that carried over into the next decade. By the early 1970s, liberalism had lost power, while conservatives under the leadership of President Richard M. Nixon (served (1969–1974) experimented with a variety of economic policies to little avail. Middle-class Americans, angered over continuing price inflation, responded favorably to the younger generation of political activists such as Jack Kemp. Former New Deal Democrats, later called "Reagan Democrats," supported new ideas in the hope that they would help revive an economy suffering from stagflation.

After presenting his argument in his 1979 book for tax cuts as a way to create sustained growth for the 1980s, Kemp joined Senator Roth in proposing the Kemp-Roth tax bill in the early months of the new administration of Republican president Ronald Reagan. While the original bill called for a one-third cut in federal taxes over a three-year period, the final version of the Reagan administration tax bill of 1981 changed that to a twenty-five percent tax cut over the same period. Adoption of this supply-side economics promised much on the basis of little evidence from the postwar period, but, at first, millions of Americans hoped for the best, having lived with stagnant rates

of growth through most of the 1970s. Ironically, this call for "new" economic policy ideas led to a revival of ideas that had been used by earlier administrations for much of the nineteenth century and part of the twentieth century. Large increases in national defense expenditures, along with the 1981 tax cuts, lead to massive spending for most of the 1980s that would fail to deliver on the high expectations and lofty promises of the Kemp-Roth plan.

Primary Source

An American Renaissance: A Strategy for the 1980s

> **SYNOPSIS:** New York Representative Jack F. Kemp sets forth his philosophy for the 1980s in his 1979 book, *An American Renaissance: A Strategy for the 1980s.* To jump-start an American economy bedeviled with inflation and stagnation, Kemp proposes massive tax cuts to stimulate the economy, coupled with a swift return to free-market principles. The whys and wherefores of his ambitious program are outlined in the book.

Unlike most dreams, the American Dream was not mere fancy. Wherever people were invigorated with its message, good things happened. It was a dream that brought results—and still can. Not long ago, every American, almost without exception, could trace for you his or her family's history of ascent. That is to say, their personal histories of dreaming and achieving.

Here in America was the one place on earth where you could climb as far as your abilities could take you, unimpeded by your lack of noble birth or laws of entail and privilege that separated the people of other countries from their God-given right to pursue the good things in life and claim a portion of them for themselves. If you were a first-rate carpenter or mezzo soprano or football quarterback, and you gave it your best—here, if anywhere, you'd make it. And if you didn't make it to the very top, perhaps because you didn't try hard enough or the natural talent just wasn't there, at least you were better off for the attempt. A lot better off than that vast majority of mankind that never had a chance to do their best—or even to do what they wanted to do—with their own lives.

Opportunity, the chance to make it and to improve your life, that's what the American Dream was and is all about. What poisons that dream is when government stands in the way, throwing up roadblocks that are really unnecessary. More and more people sense along the way that they're not going to fulfill their potential, not because of a deficiency in their ambition or ability, but because of a deficiency in the political structure. Their honest ambitions are frustrated. They believe, often rightly, that somehow the flaws of government have held them back or cut them down.

What really gripes is that we also know it is not a case of an individual sacrifice for the good of all. That we could understand and appreciate when it is necessary. But more and more there is the feeling that the system is so fouled up that neither the individual good nor the collective good is being served. Instead of government serving to create a climate of opportunity, acting as the impartial referee dispensing justice, we now sense that government has become the competition. Our government is the other team—and it's winning!

Now, I happen to be a Republican. In fact, I happen to believe that our American renaissance requires for its fulfillment the revival of the Republican Party as a first-rate political force. But that requires that we Republicans face up to the truth of our part in shaping our current national predicament. The hardest, most important step for Republicans to take is to recognize that we can't go on blaming the Democratic Party.

There was a time when I thought Democrats and their policies were the root of our problems, but I don't any more. Rather, I realize that Democrats have been running the show *because they have been beating Republicans.* And when Democrats beat Republicans it is for the same reason that the Yankees beat the Dodgers or the Steelers beat the Cowboys: *They were better at what they did.* Why? Because for many years Republicans rejected competition as the test of value in the political market-place. That's when the GOP got in real trouble. You still hear from some Republicans that Democrats win because the poor ignorant voters just don't know what's good for them, or that democracy won't work because the voters don't want to elect the good guys. Nonsense. Badmouthing democracy is the occupational disease of political losers. . . .

Think about a wagon. It is a simple but forceful way of visualizing an important aspect of government. The wagon is loaded here. It's unloaded over there. The folks who are loading it are Republicans. The folks who are unloading it are Democrats. You need both groups, both parties. The Democrats are the party of redistribution. The Republicans must be the party of growth. It is useless to argue, as some libertarians do, that we do not need redistribution at all. The people, as a people, rightly insist that the whole look after the weakest of its parts. This is a primary function of collective action, of government.

The system works best when each party does its job. But instead of loading the wagon, some Republicans have jumped aside to complain about how fast an unloading job the Democrats have been doing. Other Republicans have argued that it's more fun to unload, and the trouble with the GOP is that it spends too much time complaining about the unloaders when it should be helping unload.

Obviously you can't unload a wagon faster than you load it. Sooner or later it's empty, and while you're then living from hand to mouth, the unloaders will complain. They will persuade the populace that since the loaders have failed, what you need is a new system of loading, one that rewards collective effort instead of individual effort. The next step suggests itself: Nationalize the wagons.

It is not enough that the Republican Party somehow survives. It is not enough that it enjoys a mild success, that it only wins enough elections to hang on as a minority political party. What is really necessary to the system is that the GOP become the *dominant* party in America during the 1980s. I don't mean this as a partisan, but as an American. And I mean it only in the sense that the GOP must be the party of growth, and growth must dominate redistribution in the decade ahead. The emptying wagon must soon enjoy a period of bountiful years.

When we discuss growth, *real* growth—not inflated, "paper" growth—we are talking about the American Dream. The Democrats, the unloaders, do not really understand the mechanisms that lead to real growth. (To be fair, the Republican sensitivity about social programs has been similarly unimpressive.) But because Democrats have dominated the system for generations, their idea of growth has become the conventional one. They picture an America, already gobbling a third of the earth's mineral resources, gobbling more. *Growth is seen as the exact opposite of redistribution instead of its prerequisite.* Growth must be fought and prevented, according to the new Malthusians, otherwise the planet will be stripped clean to provide the handful of humanity that resides in North America with three-car garages. . . .

When the American Dream is alive, this application of human ingenuity is operating near its potential. A thousand people can grow up to produce opera, Broadway musicals, or a *Wizard of Oz.* A few generations later, with government in the way, a thousand people are born to create; but of the fraction of these who survive the system, many end up making porno. Instead of several thousand restaurants worthy of three stars in the New York *Times,* we get ten thousand plastic restaurants. In so many ways, the failure of Republicanism over the last few generations has resulted in a collapse of quality and a substitution of quantity. . . .

These are some of the ideas behind the tax-rate-reduction bill I sponsored in the 95th Congress with Senator Bill Roth of Delaware, and which I have revised in the current Congress. The legislation—a one-third cut in federal income tax rates over three years and reductions in business tax rates—is not intended as a measure to simply "stimulate" the economy. It is not meant as a one-shot boost of consumption so people will buy more autos or TV sets. It is rather the beginning of the process of restoring incentives in our political economy by a transfusion of fresh economic thinking. The Kemp-Roth proposal aims at removing a barrier between effort and reward, and thereby increasing the willingness of individuals to supply the marketplace. The resulting competition will boost the quality as well as quantity of goods and services. . . .

Unhappily, the idea had also infected my party, which is why Republicans have so often advocated austerity (unemployment) as the only way to combat inflation. That dismal period in the Republican Party is ending, however. The GOP is in the process of rediscovering growth, and with the rediscovery is coming a political success it will not soon forget. The cornerstone of that growth is this crucial insight: Instead of high tax rates with low production, government can raise the same amount of revenue through low tax rates applied to the high production base that will result from lessening taxes and increasing incentives. The party is beginning to be rewarded at the polls, and will continue to be rewarded, by an electorate that has been patiently waiting for us to remember that oppressive tax rates are economically destructive and politically unpopular. . . .

Does anyone doubt that the American people would respond to the incentives that such reasonable tax rates would provide? Does anyone doubt that there would be an explosion of *real* economic activity? The entrepreneurial talent, the managerial talent, the creative talent of men and women that

is now boxed into mediocrity would be unleashed and would flourish. Real prosperity would help rebuild and renew America's cities through private initiatives; and government revenues would become available for a host of needed public projects in our cities and across our states. It would help reduce inflation. The wagon would load up with quality goods, and instead of widespread fears about the deficits of the Social Security system, there will be solvency, with funds for expansion of public and private retirement benefits. For a nation's elderly can never be secure unless that nation's young are realizing their potential in a way that provides resources across age and class lines.

Is this only a pollyannish dream? Not at all. It is a vision built not on a wish but on hardheaded logic. If we only stop what we have been doing to destroy ourselves by destroying incentives, we can once again thrive. *We are the most free and most educated, creative, talented, energetic, and healthy people on earth—and we are now operating at less than half our potential, perhaps less than a third our potential!* There's no telling what we can accomplish if only the government would get out of the way and let us load the wagon. The American Dream is not a sniveling, envious hope that everyone be leveled with everyone else. It is the freedom and encouragement to climb as high up the ladder of opportunity as possible, and obtain a just reward based upon our efforts and abilities.

Further Resources

BOOKS

Biven, W. Carl *Jimmy Carter's Economy: Policy in an Age of Limits.* Chapel Hill: University of North Carolina Press, 2002.

Campagna, Anthony S. *Economic Policy in the Carter Administration.* Westport, CT: Greenwood Press, 1995.

Matusow, Allen S. *Nixon's Economy: Booms, Busts, Dollars, and Votes.* Lawrence: University Press of Kansas, 1998.

Schulman, Bruce J. *The Seventies: The Great Shift in American Culture, Society, and Politics.* New York: Free Press, 2001.

Simon, William E. *A Time for Truth.* New York: Reader's Digest Press, 1978.

Wanniski, Jude. *The Way the World Works: How Economies Fail—and Succeed.* New York: Basic Books, 1978.

3 EDUCATION

MILLIE JACKSON

Entries are arranged in chronological order by date of primary source. For entries with one primary source, the entry title is the same as the primary source title. Entries with more than one primary source have an overall entry title, followed by the titles of the primary sources.

Important Events in Education, 1970–1979

1970

- English, French, and social studies teachers are in surplus throughout the U.S.

- The Saint Louis School District adopts a twelve-month schedule for elementary school and junior high; students attend nine weeks, then take three weeks off.

- On February 8, Alabama Governor and 1968 presidential candidate of the American Independent Party, George Wallace urges southern governors to defy integration orders at a Birmingham rally; he vows to run for president again in 1972 if President Richard Nixon "doesn't do something about the mess our schools are in."

- On April 22, the first Earth Day celebration calls attention to the environmental dangers of pollutants. Two thousand college campuses host events and over ten thousand elementary and high-school students take part.

- On May 4, the Ohio National Guard kills four students and wounds eight at a Kent State University student rally protesting President Richard M. Nixon's decision to invade Cambodia, a country neighboring North and South Vietnam, through which runs the Ho Chi Minh Trail.

- On May 14, police fire into a student dorm at Jackson State College in Mississippi, killing a student and a local high-school senior, both of whom are African American.

- On May 25, Secretary of the Interior Walter J. Hickel sends a letter to President Richard M. Nixon warning that the administration's hard-line approach to student dissent is contributing to anarchy among U.S. students. Hickel recommends that Nixon stop Vice-President Spiro Agnew from attacking campus leaders in his speeches.

- From May to June, some colleges close and others call off graduation ceremonies in favor of antiwar demonstrations and in honor of students killed at Kent State and Jackson State.

- In July, Pennsylvania becomes the second state to legalize teacher strikes. Hawaii had been the first.

- In September, only 300 of 892 teacher graduates from the June commencement at Sacramento State College have found employment.

- In September, the sixteenth annual fall survey of public elementary and secondary-school enrollments by the U.S. Office of Education (USOE) shows yearly growth of only 1.5 percent, the smallest increase since the late 1940s.

- In December, the White House Conference on Children is named one of ten major educational events of the year.

1971

- Sidney Marland, commissioner of the U.S. Office of Education, recommends an end to the "general track" in high schools, calling it an "abomination."

- African Americans, who are 11 percent of the U.S. population, are only 7 percent of the college population.

- Applications to Ivy League colleges decline 6.7 percent. Private colleges nationwide experience declines, a consequence of the recession.

- Census data show that the proportion of Americans with high-school diplomas has risen from 38 percent in the 1940s to 75 percent.

- Thousands of schoolchildren take Ritalin as an "aid to general treatment of minimal brain dysfunction," which is thought to be the cause of hyperactivity.

- More than one million men and women receive college degrees during the calendar year, the first time that the U.S. Office of Education has reported degree recipients in excess of one million over twelve months.

- On January 1, only seven women are school superintendents in the United States.

- On April 20, the U.S. Supreme Court unanimously rules that busing to achieve racial balance is constitutional wherever schools have not integrated.

- In May, federal authorities order Austin, Texas, schools to integrate through busing.

- In June, the first Native American school opens on a Navajo reservation in northeastern Arizona.

- On August 3, President Richard M. Nixon repudiates the federally imposed busing plan in Texas and orders that busing be limited to the "minimum required by law."

- In September, Philadelphia's Parkway School gets a Ford Foundation grant of $290,000; this unusual school has no building so students attend tutorials or pursue self-directed study in businesses or other cooperating institutions in the city.

- On October 28, the New York legislature passes a bill permitting a brief period of silent prayer or reflection in school.

- In December, schools in Chicago close twelve days early for the Christmas holidays to reduce expenses amid a $26 million budget deficit.

1972

- The average age of public-school teachers declines from forty to thirty-five during the past ten years.

- On January 18, sixteen African American protesters interrupt a Stanford University semiconductor course exam taught by Nobel Laureate William Shockley to protest his belief that African Americans are less intelligent than whites.

- In March, the California State Board of Education requires public schools to teach creationism alongside evolution in biology classes.

- On March 18, twenty-nine men and women draw lots and begin living together in a University of Michigan housing unit to "break down some of the barriers between the sexes."

- On March 19, the U.S. Supreme Court rules 6-3 that state colleges and universities cannot expel a student for distributing material on campus that administrators find offensive.

- On March 21, the U.S. Supreme Court rules in *Rodriguez v. Board of Education* that states can finance schools through local property taxes even when funding varies from district to district.

- In June, the National Institute for Education (NIE) is formed to "muster the power of research to solve problems."

- In June, the College Placement Council announces that the job market is the worst for B.A. recipients in two decades.

- From June 12 to June 17, Campus Crusade for Christ stages Expo '72 in the Cotton Bowl in Dallas, hosting about seventy-five thousand students.

- On June 28, the U.S. Supreme Court in *Wisconsin v. Yoder* affirms the right of the Amish to withdraw their children from school after grade 8.

- In September, the teachers' union in New York City negotiates a public-school teaching contract that wins most qualified teachers salaries above twenty thousand dollars.

- On October 22, the American Association for the Advancement of Science (AAAS) issues a resolution condemning the decision of the California Board of Education to mandate the teaching of creationism in public-school biology classes.

1973

- On April 4, the U.S. District Court in Atlanta orders a compromise school integration plan.

- On April 5, a three-judge panel in New Jersey bans state aid to private and parochial schools.

- On August 3, Massachusetts Governor Francis Sargent vetoes a bill that would have allowed silent prayer in schools.

- On August 10, the U.S. Justice Department files suit against an Omaha, Nebraska school district to force desegregation.

- On September 8, a Gallup poll reports that only 5 percent of U.S. adults support court-ordered busing to integrate schools.

- On September 9, the U.S. Office of Education reports that about sixty thousand college and trade-school students have defaulted on $55.2 million in federally guaranteed loans.

- On September 11, teacher strikes throughout the U.S. keep eight hundred thousand students home.

- On October 9, the Carnegie Commission on Higher Education issues the final report of a six-year study concluding that the nation's colleges and universities face the greatest trauma and self-doubt in history.

- On November 13, the Department of Health, Education and Welfare (HEW) rejects college desegregation plans in Arkansas, Florida, Georgia, Louisiana, Mississippi, North Carolina, Oklahoma, Pennsylvania, and Virginia for doing too little to integrate public colleges and universities.

- On December 14, the New York Board of Regents orders colleges to disallow minorities to segregate themselves in on-campus housing.

1974

- On January 9, the U.S. Office of Education reports higher education enrollment is up 3.9 percent from 1972–1973.

- On January 17, the U.S. Department of Health, Education and Welfare says racial discrimination still exists in Topeka, Kansas schools, the site of the *Brown v. Board of Education* suit in 1954.

- On January 21, the U.S. Supreme Court rules unanimously that a San Francisco school district must provide English-language instruction for Chinese students.

- On March 21, the U.S. Department of Health, Education and Welfare finds the New York City school system guilty of misusing $28 million in federal funds from 1965 to 1972.

- On April 8, a federal judge orders integration of Denver's seventy-thousand-student school system.

- On April 23, the U.S. Supreme Court refuses to rule on the constitutionality of law-school admissions policies giving preference to minority applicants.

- In June, Federal Judge Arthur Garrity rules that the Boston School Committee has deliberately segregated schools by race; he orders the exchange of students between white South Boston and African American Roxbury schools.

- On September 14, white mobs in Boston greet buses carrying African Americans to their schools by shouting, "Nigger, go home!"

- On October 9, Massachusetts Governor Francis Sargent orders the Massachusetts National Guard to restore calm in South Boston, the site of protests against school integration.

- On December 27, a court holds three members of the Boston School Committee in contempt for their defiance of court-ordered busing.

1975

- On January 5, the Educational Testing Service reports that women with doctorates lag behind men in salary and promotion in higher education, charging discrimination against women on these grounds.

- On January 20, the U.S. Justice Department charges that students and faculty of Mississippi's twenty-five state schools remain segregated in violation of federal law.

- On February 22, Congress passes the Metric Conversion Act, prompting schools to teach the metric system in mathematics classes with the goal of producing citizens literate in metric units.

- On February 25, the U.S. Supreme Court rules that school-board members are liable for damages if students prove their rights were denied.

- On March 31, the College Board predicts the cost of higher education will rise 6 to 8 percent by fall 1975.

- On August 1, a court orders Indianapolis city schools to transfer 6,533 African American students to eight suburban districts.

- On September 26, the U.S. Senate approves $36.2 billion in appropriations for the Department of Health, Education and Welfare with the proviso it not order school busing.

- On October 7, Congress passes a $1.2 billion school lunch bill and other child nutrition laws over President Gerald Ford's veto.

1976

- On January 26, court-ordered busing in Detroit begins without incident.

- On February 24, Judge Arthur Garrity orders the Boston school system to appoint African Americans to 20 percent of administrative posts.

- In April, a California Circuit Court of Appeals bars a high school graduate from suing the public school he attended for malpractice because he could read at only a fifth-grade level.

- On October 13, President Gerald Ford signs a medical-education bill aimed at increasing the proportion of doctors and health professionals in deprived areas.

1977

- On January 17, a Boston Schools Department report asserts that the quality of public education has deteriorated since the start of busing.

- On April 11, Ernest Boyer, Commissioner of Education, announces a reorganization of the Department of Health, Education and Welfare's Office of Education.

- On April 19, the U.S. Supreme Court rules 5-4 that school officials can spank students without violating their constitutional rights.

- In May, a Florida court prohibits the Gideon Society from distributing Bibles to students during the school day.

- On May 11, the National Association of the Advancement of Colored People (NAACP) Legal Defense Fund files suit in federal court against the Department of Health, Education and Welfare, charging abandonment of integration in vocational education and programs for the handicapped in the South.

- On May 12, the discovery of a stick of dynamite at South Boston High, the site of tensions over busing, creates a furor which results in the arrest of seven and injuries to seven others.

- On June 5, Joseph Califano, Commissioner of the Department of Health, Education and Welfare, tells the graduating class at City College in New York that the government will rely on numerical goals, not quotas, in measuring minority access to higher education.

- On September 24, SAT scores of entering freshmen are the lowest in the test's fifty-one-year existence.

- On November 23, the Cleveland, Ohio, school system fails to meet its payroll.

- On December 15, the Carnegie Foundation urges colleges and universities to strengthen general-education core courses and eliminate electives.

1978

- On February 2, the Department of Health, Education and Welfare rejects higher-education desegregation plans in Virginia and Georgia for doing too little to integrate public colleges and universities.

- On February 21, the U.S. Supreme Court affirms a U.S. Circuit Court of Appeals decision that the University of Missouri must recognize Gay Liberation, a student homosexual group, as an official campus organization.

- On March 21, the U.S. Supreme Court rules 8-0 that public-school students suspended without hearings cannot collect more than one dollar in damages.

- On April 7, New York City drops its 1977 plan of assigning teachers on the basis of race.

- On June 1, the U.S. House of Representatives approves, 237-158, a bill to grant tuition tax credits to middle-income parents of college students.

- On June 23, the New York State Supreme Court rules illegal the state's method of financing public schools through property tax.

- On June 28, the U.S. Supreme Court in *Regents of the University of California v. Bakke* orders the University of California at Davis Medical School to end the setting aside of seats for minorities.

- On September 16, the Educational Testing Service announces that the latest SAT verbal scores hold steady at 429; math scores drop from 470 to 468.

1979

- On February 8, President Jimmy Carter sends Congress his proposal for a cabinet-level Department of Education.

- On April 23, the U.S. Supreme Court affirms a ruling that denies an Italian-American man the right to sue a law school for rejecting his application to a special-admissions program.

- On June 11, the U.S. Supreme Court rules unanimously that federally funded colleges need not admit all handicapped applicants or make extensive modifications to accommodate them.

- On July 2, the U.S. Supreme Court upholds desegregation orders for two large school systems in Dayton and Columbus, Ohio.

- On August 15, the Ann Arbor, Michigan school board approves a program to teach "Black English" to all twenty-eight teachers at Martin Luther King Elementary.

- On September 10, Cleveland, Ohio, schools desegregate, ending a six-year court battle.

- On December 21, the Chicago school board fails to meet its payroll.

"Now is the Time of the Furnaces, And Only Light Should be Seen"

Flyers

By: Kent State Students for a Democratic Society

Date: April 1969

Source: Kent State Students for a Democratic Society. "Now is the Time of the Furnaces, And Only Light Should be Seen." Michigan State Special Collections, Students for Democratic Society ARVF.

About the Organization: The Kent State Students for a Democratic Society (SDS) was part of the larger SDS, a radical student movement across the United States. Mark Rudd, the president of the Columbia University SDS, visited the Kent State University campus in 1968. Soon after Rudd's visit, the chapter joined with other militant groups on campus to stage protests. Kent State's SDS became more violent than many chapters due to the affiliation with leaders who later became part of the Weathermen. ■

Introduction

Students for a Democratic Society reorganized in 1962 when leaders met in Port Huron, Michigan. They developed the Port Huron Statement, which provided a manifesto for chapters across the country. Kent State University, located in northeast Ohio, was a large regional college. Irwin Unger writes that Kent State "was no more implicated in capitalist misdeeds of Vietnam than five hundred other college campuses." Still, the student radicals at KSU became more militant than on many campuses across the county. In 1968, members of SDS joined African American militants on campus to protest campus recruitment by the Oakland, California police department. Students took over the placement office for five hours. Following the confrontation with campus police, SDS encouraged student radicals through pamphlets and speeches.

After the protest, six participants were arrested, including four students who were later suspended. On April 20, 1969, SDS held a rally to present four demands to the campus administration. They implored the Uni-

versity to abolish ROTC, the law enforcement school, and the crime lab, and to end the grant called Project Themis for the Liquid Crystals Institute. SDS leaders capitalized on the campus administration's fears about further violence.

In June of 1969 Kent State University SDS was one of many groups investigated by the United States House of Representatives. The transcript of the investigation includes photographs of the leaders and documents that detail protests and demands. SDS was banned from campus in 1969, but there were enough student radicals to continue the protests. President Nixon announcement on April 30, 1970 that he was sending troops into Cambodia, led to four days of student riots on the campus and the deaths of four students.

Significance

The organization and mobilization of student radicals on campuses across the country led to more violent confrontations with police as the Vietnam War dragged on. Student groups at Kent State had already clashed with campus police on several occasions and were experienced in taking over buildings and leading marches against the war and related efforts. The leaders of the radical movement pitted the "ruling class" against the oppressed students. They particularly targeted the treatment of blacks as a way to enrage protestors. In the pamphlets and flyers the writers invoked the memory of Jose Marti, a nineteenth century Cuban freedom fighter. Marti fought for individual rights and freedoms, just as the SDS leaders proposed that they were doing.

The protests that involved ending ROTC on campus continued in the spring of 1970, beginning on May 1 with a demonstration. The next day one thousand people gathered at the Army ROTC barracks and set them on fire. The National Guard was called in and the campus cleared. On Sunday evening demonstrators gathered again at the Victory Bell and then later at East Main and Lincoln. Both times the crowds were cleared with tear gas and the Ohio Riot Act was read. On Monday, May 4, 1970, two thousand people gathered on the commons at Kent State. A riot broke out and National Guardsmen fired shots. Allison Krause, Jeffrey Miller, William Schroeder, and Sandra Scheuer were killed. Nine other students were wounded. The disorder that had begun in 1968 ended with an injunction to close the campus. Classes did not resume until summer. The events at Kent State University shocked the nation and caused ongoing questions about what happened that day. This was an outrageous act that resulted in investigations over the next year. Memories of May 4 continue each year. The victims and actions are remembered not only on the campus at Kent State University, but across the country.

NOW IS THE TIME OF THE FURNACES . . .

AND THE LIGHT WILL BE SEEN!

M A R C H   ***   7 PM. Sunday, April 20

          Assemble in front of the Union

R A L L Y   ***   After March in front of the AdministrationBldg.
          Attended by three Mothers of the Kent 6

SUPPORT THE FOUR DEMANDS:

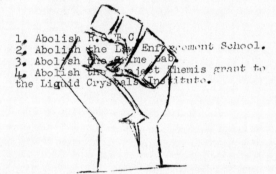

1. Abolish R.O.T.C
2. Abolish the Law Enforcement School.
3. Abolish the Crime Lab.
4. Abolish the Project Themis grant to
the Liquid Crystals Institute.

Dig it : It's because of these demands that the

Kent 6 are sitting in the jug. The political

repression brought down on them cannot be separate

from the non-negotiable demands. It's through

rationalizations to political repression that the

thugs who run this country and Kent State hope to fool

the people.

         BE THERE.

                      KENT sds

Dare to Struggle, Dare to Win !

Primary Source

Now is the Time of the Furnaces . . . And the Light Will be Seen: Flyer

SYNOPSIS: An SDS flyer announces a march and rally to be held on April 20, 1969. Although the group was later banned from campus, members of the group continued to gather and protest. COURTESY OF MICHIGAN STATE UNIVERSITY LIBRARIES, SPECIAL COLLECTIONS.

Primary Source

"Now is the Time of the Furnaces, And Only Light Should be Seen"

SYNOPSIS: Students rallied to protest the ROTC and other military activities on campus at Kent State University. They also gathered to support the students and other protestors who had been arrested as a result of their demands. SDS members viewed the campus administration's actions as political repression which they also saw throughout the country.

Introduction

Before SDS offensive began last week, Kent State University reflected only one side of the worldwide war against U.S. imperialism: Ruling class exploitation and oppression. We watched ROTC guys training to give tactical leadership to the genocide of the Vietnamese; we heard smart liberal professors training smart liberal students to be the administrators of the white occupation army in the black colony (police); we sat forever in boring classrooms geared to the needs of a future employer.

Then we witnessed the entrance to the war in the anti-imperialist, anti-racist assault, and the University's repressive reaction; SDS tussling with KSU police after the doors to the administration building were closed to us; constant discussion and conflict among students about the SDS demands and action; arrests, suspensions, and court injunctions barring SDS and 5 SDS members from campus; tactical police on campus; growing resentment against the imperialism, racism, and repression of KSU.

The Board of Trustees and the administration are scared. First, they are scared of SDS. They know that we are willing to act on our demands. Secondly, *they are scared of you.* They know that students see ROTC, for example, as exploitative to the Vietnamese people and to ROTC guys themselves. They know that students can see the justice of our demands.

However, they need to keep large numbers of people from acting. So they say the reason for their repressive reaction is that SDS broke certain university rules seemingly divorced from the anti-racists, anti-imperialist content of our demands. Through repression against a few they hope to scare many. By devising rationalizations to political repression they hope to fool the people.

But all they can accomplish is proving once again that their liberalism is a facade. The people can only grow in strength and determination.

Support the Four Demands

1. Abolish ROTC

Today, reliance upon colleges and universities for officers is greater than ever. For example, the 1968 graduating classes contained over 11,000 newly commissioned officers, who, as they enter the ranks of the active army, will fill 85% of the required annual input needed to provide the junior leaders for today's troop units. The armed forces simply cannot function without an officer corps largely of college graduates.

—U.S. Army Instructor's Group, ROTC, Harvard University

We have learned from our experience in anti-war struggles over the past 5 years that if we want to aid the Vietnamese people, we must be able to strike a real blow against the American military. The junior leaders of that military are trained on American university campuses—as members of the Reserve Officer Training Corps.

We are opposed to ROTC for 3 reasons:

1. It provides the leadership for an army engaged in imperialist aggression against popular movements at home and abroad. The caretakers of imperialism must be stopped.

2. ROTC is a privilege—available only to those segments of the working class who can go to college. Particularly, ideologically it strengthens the view that ordinary working people in America are unworthy to guide the nation's destiny. (In the NLF soldiers elect their officers.) " . . . Who is prepared to trust their sons—let alone the nation's destiny—to the leadership of high school boys and college drop-outs?"—U. S. Army Instructors' Group.

3. But when you get down to it, that privilege is really a delusion, and ROTC people are themselves oppressed. ROTC can only be seen as an alternative to an even worse reality—the draft; and still, second lieutenants are being killed at an incredibly high rate in Vietnam. Just as many college kids are being channelled into managerial slots in civilian life (teachers, social workers, etc.)—and turning off to those slots with great rapidity—so ROTC is the army's middle man, serving the generals and fucking the privates.

One of the major arguments people will undoubtedly pursue for maintaining ROTC is the "basic civil liberties" of the students to join any organization they choose. This is a real and serious distortion of the is-

A student hurls a tear gas canister back towards National Guardsmen at Kent State University during a May 4, 1970, antiwar demonstration that turned violent. © BETTMANN/CORBIS. REPRODUCED BY PERMISSION.

sue. We are talking about what ROTC does—not its right to "free speech." Any society, set of lows or morality takes it upon itself to prohibit certain actions. This society prohibits people from joining many groups—the Mafia, for example. Any yet it is this same society that "allows" other people to join in the oppression, exploitation and murder of people in the Third World. The only "right" that ROTC and the Army have is the right to conquest. And that is no right at all.

Put in another way it becomes a simple question of taking sides. To support ROTC's right to exist or people's right to join it is to deny the Vietnamese right to rebel—and in so doing to deny the oppression that they face daily. "It is the right of conquest, not freedom of speech; what ROTC does, not what individual officers say, which will be suppressed by driving ROTC off the campus."

(For more, see Alan Gilbert's "ROTC—SDS Challenges the Liberal Position, New Left Notes, Feb. 5, 1969).

2. End Project Themis Grant to the Liquid Crystals Institute

There are only two institutes in the U. S. developed solely to study liquid crystals—Kent State has one of them. This year the Liquid Crystals Institute received a research grant from Project Themis to develop "liquid crystal detectors." ("Army Research and Development Magazine"—July/August 1968 issue). In the last year Project Themis has funded 43 new counter-insurgency research programs in 24 states. "The Project's objective is twofold—to create new centers of scientific excellence responsive to Department of Defense solutions to problems in the future; and to achieve a wider geographical distribution of Defense research funds, giving preference to institutions that receive little or no D.O.D. support of science."

Kent State is part of Project Themis' spidery web of institutions which are currently developing sophisticated weaponry to be used against people's struggles for their freedon. Liquid crystals are extremely sensitive to heat, and are used in devices to detect campfires in jungle areas and in some cases to detect body heat at long range. (The "sniffer" is currently used in Vietnam and a similar device was used in Bolivia to find and kill Che Guevara. The tremendous importance of "liquid crystal detectors" can be seen by the fact that in every country in Latin America, Southeast Asia and many in

Witness Statements Related to the ROTC Building Arson [excerpts]

August 6, 1970

Eugene L. Jewell, Chief
State Arson Bureau
31 N. Grant Ave.
Columbus, Ohio 43215

Dear Sir:

On May 2, 1970 between 8:00 and 9:00 P.M. at the Kent State University campus, Kent, Portage County, Ohio members of a large crowd attacked the R.O.T.C. Building and burned it. The following is a summary of witnesses' statements concerning the events that took place prior, during, and after the burning.

Nicholaus M. Haskakis
Home: 103 Second Ave.
Yorkville, Ohio
Kent: 309 Jackson Hall

Statement taken by Det. Thomas Kelley, Kent State University Police Department.

At about 8:20 P.M. on Saturday, May 2, 1970, he left his dorm with a camera to take pictures of the campus demonstration. While in the area of the R.O.T.C. Building he saw some students throwing rocks at the building and he saw one person take an American flag out and start to burn it. It seemed like the most appropriate act to capture on film so he took a picture of it. He was then attacked by members of the crowd and forced to give up his film. . . .

Louis Szari
3185 W. 117 St.
Cleveland, Ohio 252–5371

Statement taken by Investigators Brininger and McLaughlin, State Arson Bureau

Szari stated that he heard there was going to be a rally on the Commons. After visiting the Commons he left and got a white arm band and returned to the Commons as a student deputy. He followed the group over to Tri-Towers, down to the parking lot where whey were doing damage in general. Then on to the practice football field where they regrouped and headed back to the Commons. He witnessed people pick up stones and putting them in their pockets. He witnessed people throwing stones through the windows of the R.O.T.C. Building. He witnessed two individuals, one wearing a white t-shirt with a red fist on the front and back, go behind some cars, light a Molotov cocktail and throw it at the building. It did not do any damage to the building, however. He saw two men, one he can positively identify, take a white rag and go to a motorcycle that was parked nearby, dip the rag in the gasoline tank and then both ran to the building, light the rag and throw it in. They both ran back into the crowd. He followed one of the individuals, the one he identified as Peter Bliek. . . .

Roger Berry
3595 St. Rt. 95
Ravenna, Ohio 297–1201
He is employed as a food service manager at the Student Union at K.S.U.
Statement taken by Investigator Brininger, State Arson Bureau

Saturday evening, May 2, 1970, he was at work in the Student Union and noticed a group was forming on the Commons. Then the group left and went up the hill between Johnson and Taylor Halls. The group returned 15 or 20 minutes later and came to the R.O.T.C. Building. He observed different individuals throwing stones and fusees at the building. He saw an individual attempt to throw a trash can through a window and there were others breaking windows with sticks. He observed a group jump the firemen and take the fire hose. He also observed them chopping the hose up. He could not identify any of these people because it was dark. . . .

William Robert Maxwell
4543 Stow Rd.
Stow, Ohio 688–7980
Statement taken by Sgt. Sumrok, Ohio State Patrol and reinterviewed by Brininger, Ohio State Arson Bureau

Friday night, May 1, 1970, Maxwell witnessed a large group of people walking south on North Water Street in the city of Kent shouting and breaking windows. The City Riot Squad then moved the crowd eastward back to the Main entrance of the campus. The police stopped and the crowd began shouting at them.

Saturday night, May 2, 1970, Maxwell stated he arrived on campus at approximately 7:50 P.M., he caught up with the crowd of approximately 1500 on the practice football field. Members of the crowd were armed with rocks and clubs. The crowd moved to the Commons and then on to the R.O.T.C. Building. The leaders yelled at the crowd to throw rocks at the building. He saw Jerry Rupe throw one of the first rocks, then another of the leaders, a fellow with blonde hair, charged the building with clubs and rocks. By this time many people were throwing rocks. The blonde-haired leader spotted a person with a camera. The man with the camera was then attacked by the crowd. He witnessed Jerry Rupe beat and kick the photographer along with two or three others. The blonde-haired leader along with an individual later identified as Larry A. Shub plus two or three others charged the building and started a fire inside the east window. After the Kent City Fire Department arrived, he witnessed the leaders and others attack the firemen and take their hose. He identified Jerry Rupe as one of these individuals and also the blonde haired leader whom he could not identify from photographs. After the police arrived, he followed the crowd across the Commons to the archery shed. Part of the crowd tore down the fence around the area while the leaders broke into and set fire to the shed. The group then headed towards President White's house and went on to State Route 59 headed west towards town. Before reaching town the group was met by the National Guard and pushed back to the campus.

SOURCE: Kent State University. Available online at http://www.library.kent .edu/exhibits/4may95/box107/107f24pl.html; website home page: http://www .library.kent.edu (accessed March 24, 2003).

Africa, guerilla warfare is being waged by people's movements struggling against U.S. imperialism. That struggle will continue on Kent's campus—the development of Liquid Crystals for Project Themis must be stopped.

3. Abolish the Law Enforcement School

4. Abolish the Northeast Ohio Crime Lab

The members of the ruling class are the only real criminals in this society. Corporate financiers reap tremendous profits at the expense of the poverty-stricken unemployed, the tax-ridden worker, and the mortgaged "middle-class." The ruling class should be jailed not the people.

Law enforcement defends the American status quo, and therefore protects the interests of the ruling class. Black people, the most oppressed, witness overt police violence daily.

Blacks are colonized. They are oppressed not only as part of the working class but as a people. Huey Newton, jailed Minister of Defense for the Black Panther Party, describes the role of police as an occupying military force in the black colony. He says, "The pig can't be in the colony to protect our property, because we own no property." Pig violence in the black colony does not result only from the sadism of individual policemen. Just as in Vietnam military violence in the black colony is intended to protect the business interests of ruling class imperialism.

The Law Enforcement School and the Northeast Ohio Crime Lab serve two different functions in protecting ruling class imperialism and racism against the black colony. The *Law Enforcement School* trains students for police careers. It was the Law Enforcement School which invited the racist Oakland pigs to recruit at Kent this past fall. The Northeast Ohio Crimes Lab serves all of the police forces in northeast Ohio with identification and lab processing techniques. So doing they play an important role in evidence gathering procedures.

We can't emphasize enough that the major task of the whole police network in this society—to protect the interests of the ruling class particularly at the expense of black people—must be fought.

THE NEED FOR THE AMERICAN RULING CLASS TO MAKE PROFIT AND TO PROTECT ITS PROFIT-MAKING VENTURES CAN ONLY BE MET THROUGH IMPERIALISM AND RACISM. THESE NEEDS ARE IN IRRECONCILABLE CONFLICT WITH THE PEOPLE'S NEED FOR HUMAN FREEDOM.

THE SDS DEMANDS ARE NON-NEGOTIABLE BECAUSE THE FREEDOM AND SELF-DETERMINATION OF THE WORLD'S PEOPLE IS NON-NEGOTIABLE.

DARE TO STRUGGLE—DARE TO WIN!

Further Resources

BOOKS

Michener, James A. *Kent State: What Happened and Why*. New York: Random House, 1971.

Unger, Irwin. *The Movement: A History of the American New Left, 1959–1972*. New York: Dodd, Mead & Co., 1974.

United States. Congress. House. Committee on Internal Security. *Investigation of Students for a Democratic Society. Hearings, Ninety-first Congress, first session.* vol. 2. Washington, D.C.: U.S. Govt. Print. Off., 1969.

PERIODICALS

Corelis, Joe. "Kent State Reconsidered As A Nightmare." *Journal of Psychohistory* 8, no. 2, 1980, 137–147.

"Kent State One Year Later: on the Long Road Back." *U.S. News & World Report* 70, no. 24, June 14, 1970, 17–20.

WEBSITES

FBI–Freedom of Information Act: Kent State University. Available online at http://foia.fbi.gov/kentstat.htm; website home page: http://flia.fbi.gov (accessed May 28, 2003).

Kent State University, May 4: Inquire, Learn, Reflect. Available online at http://www.library.kent.edu/exhibits/4may95/index.html; website home page: http://www.library.kent.edu (accessed May 28, 2003).

May Fourth Task Force. Available online at http://dept.kent.edu/may4/index.html; website home page: http://dept.kent.edu (accessed May 28, 2003).

AUDIO AND VISUAL MEDIA

Kent State: The Day the War Came Home. Directed by Chris Triffo. Falls Church, VA.: Landmark Media, Inc., 2001. Videocassette.

The Legacy of Kent State. Produced by CBS News. New York: History Channel, 1996. Videocassette.

Pedagogy of the Oppressed
Nonfiction work

By: Paulo Freire

Date: 1970

Source: Freire, Paulo. *Pedagogy of the Oppressed*. New York: Continuum, 1992, 57–64.

About the Author: Paulo Freire (1921–1997), born in Brazil, was an educator who developed literacy programs throughout the world. His work concentrated on freedom and democracy for all people. Following his exile from Brazil in 1964, he worked in Chile. Later he taught at Harvard University in the Center for Studies in Education and Development. ∎

Introduction

In 1962 Freire taught 300 rural farm workers in Brazil to read and write in 45 days. He taught them the meanings of words that impacted daily living. The people were able to change their lives politically and socially as their reading and writing skills developed; no longer would they live in what Freire called a "culture of silence." This began Freire's approach to literacy training not only for peasants, but for all people who could not read or write. Freire was jailed, and later exiled from Brazil, for these efforts to teach people to read.

Paulo Freire first visited the United States in 1969–1970. Educators were attracted to his methods of teaching literacy, particularly to adult learners. There were divisions in thought, however, because Freire's methods also involved political philosophies. Freire's works cannot be broken down as easily as some theories of education. His Latin American and Catholic background, as well as his knowledge of Marxism, can make it difficult for a student in America to decipher the contradictions that appear in Freire's work.

An important aspect of Freire's work in *Pedagogy of the Oppressed* is the definition of two groups: the oppressed and the oppressors. The poor generally fall into the oppressed category in the United States. In any country the poor must fight their own battles for human rights and education. In this book, Freire expands on his basic assumption that man's work is "to be a Subject who acts upon and transforms his world, and in so doing moves towards ever new possibilities of fuller and richer life individually and collectively."

Significance

Paulo Freire's works were published in the United States several years after they had been published elsewhere. *Pedagogy of the Oppressed* was originally published in 1967 but was not translated for publication in the United States until 1970. American societal struggles during the 1970s may have helped give the book greater prominence.

Ann E. Berthoff points out a strength in Freire's pedagogy for literacy workers. "At the heart of Paulo Freire's pedagogy of knowing is the idea that naming the world become a model for changing the world." The juxtaposition of *reading the word* and *reading the world* provide acts of meaning for teaching literacy. The benefits of these concepts can be applied across disciplines, including composition, English as a Second Language (ESL), and adult learning.

Reviewers who sought "how to" methods for education did not appreciate Freire's philosophies. However, those who looked at how the theory could be applied to practice did see the benefits. J.W. Evans noted that the text did not present the usual American education jargon. "The reader will sense a reality and optimism emerging not from an imaginative reconstruction of human past but rather a determination to shape a human future." Like David Harman, several reviewers found points to praise but also found gaps in the methods. Harman recognizes the lack of a post-literacy program in Freire's book; however, he realizes that much of the information in the book is "universally applicable.."

When Freire joined educator Ira Shor to publish *Freire for the Classroom: A Sourcebook for Liberatory Teaching,* his work took on greater importance in the United States. In a collection of essays, practical and theoretical methods are explained with an emphasis on applications for American classrooms. The work also remains important because of the role of social justice embedded in Freire's methods.

Primary Source

Pedagogy of the Oppressed [excerpt]

SYNOPSIS: In chapter two, Freire presents the flaws of the "banking method" of teaching, which involves memorization and mechanical learning. This is not productive regardless of the student's age because people are not merely containers for information.

A careful analysis of the teacher-student relationship at any level, inside or outside the school, reveals its fundamentally *narrative* character. This relationship involves a narrating Subject (the teacher) and patient, listening objects (the students). The contents, whether values or empirical dimensions of reality, tend in the process of being narrated to become lifeless and petrified. Education is suffering from narration sickness.

The teacher talks about reality as if it were motionless, static, compartmentalized, and predictable. Or else he expounds on a topic completely alien to the existential experience of the students. His task is to "fill" the students with the contents of his narration—contents which are detached from reality, disconnected from the totality that engendered them and could give them significance. Words are emptied of their concreteness and become a hollow, alienated, and alienating verbosity.

The outstanding characteristic of this narrative education, then, is the sonority of words, not their transforming power. "Four times four is sixteen; the capital of Pará is Belém." The student records, memorizes, and repeats these phrases without perceiving what four times four really means, or realizing the true significance of "capital" in the affirmation "the capital of Pará is Belém," that is, what Belém means for Pará and what Pará means for Brazil.

Narration (with the teacher as narrator) leads the students to memorize mechanically the narrated content. Worse yet, it turns them into "containers," into "receptacles" to be "filled" by the teacher. The more completely he fills the receptacles, the better a teacher he is. The more meekly the receptacles permit themselves to be filled, the better students they are.

Education thus becomes an act of depositing, in which the students are the depositories and the teacher is the depositor. Instead of communicating, the teacher issues communiqués and makes deposits which the students patiently receive, memorize, and repeat. This is the "banking" concept of education, in which the scope of action allowed to the students extends only as far as receiving, filing, and storing the deposits. They do, it is true, have the opportunity to become collectors or cataloguers of the things they store. But in the last analysis, it is men themselves who are filed away through the lack of creativity, transformation, and knowledge in this (at best) misguided system. For apart from inquiry, apart from the praxis, men cannot be truly human. Knowledge emerges only through invention and re-invention, through the restless, impatient, continuing, hopeful inquiry men pursue in the world, with the world, and with each other.

In the banking concept of education, knowledge is a gift bestowed by those who consider themselves knowledgeable upon those whom they consider to know nothing. Projecting an absolute ignorance onto others, a characteristic of the ideology of oppression, negates education and knowledge as processes of inquiry. The teacher presents himself to his students as their necessary opposite; by considering their ignorance absolute, he justifies his own existence. The students, alienated like the slave in the Hegelian dialectic, accept their ignorance as justifying the teacher's existence—but, unlike the slave, they never discover that they educate the teacher.

The *raison d'être* of libertarian education, on the other hand, lies in its drive towards reconciliation. Education must begin with the solution of the teacher-student contradiction, by reconciling the poles of the contradiction so that both are simultaneously teachers *and* students.

This solution is not (nor can it be) found in the banking concept. On the contrary, banking education maintains and even stimulates the contradiction through the following attitudes and practices, which mirror oppressive society as a whole:

a. the teacher teaches and the students are taught;

b. the teacher knows everything and the students know nothing;

c. the teacher thinks and the students are thought about;

d. the teacher talks and the students listen—meekly;

e. the teacher disciplines and the students are disciplined;

f. the teacher chooses and enforces his choice, and the students comply;

g. the teacher acts and the students have the illusion of acting through the action of the teacher;

h. the teacher chooses the program content, and the students (who were not consulted) adapt to it;

i. the teacher confuses the authority of knowledge with his own professional authority, which he sets in opposition to the freedom of the students;

j. the teacher is the Subject of the learning process, while the pupils are mere objects.

It is not surprising that the banking concept of education regards men as adaptable, manageable beings. The more students work at storing the deposits entrusted to them, the less they develop the critical consciousness which would result from their intervention in the world as transformers of that world. The more completely they accept the passive role imposed on them, the more they tend simply to adapt to the world as it is and to the fragmented view of reality deposited in them.

The capability of banking education to minimize or annul the students' creative power and to stimulate their credulity serves the interests of the oppressors, who care neither to have the world revealed nor to see it transformed. The oppressors use their "humanitarianism" to preserve a profitable situation. Thus they react almost instinctively against any experiment in education which stimulates the critical faculties and is not content with a partial view of reality but always seeks out the ties which link one point to another and one problem to another.

Indeed, the interests of the oppressors lie in "changing the consciousness of the oppressed, not the situation which oppresses them"; for the more the oppressed can be led to adapt to that situation, the more easily they can be dominated. To achieve this end, the oppressors use the banking concept of education in conjunction with a paternalistic social action apparatus, within which the oppressed receive the euphemistic title of "welfare recipients." They are treated as individual cases, as marginal men who deviate from the general configuration of a "good, organized, and just" society. The oppressed are regarded as the pathology of the healthy society, which must therefore adjust these "incompetent and lazy" folk to its own patterns by changing their mentality. These marginals need to be "integrated," "incorporated" into the healthy society that they have "forsaken."

The truth is, however, that the oppressed are not "marginals," are not men living "outside" society. They have always been "inside"—inside the structure which made them "beings for others." The solution is not to "integrate" them into the structure of oppression, but to transform that structure so that they can become "beings for themselves." Such transformation, of course, would undermine the oppressors' purposes; hence their utilization of the banking concept of education to avoid the threat of student *conscientização.*

The banking approach to adult education, for example, will never propose to students that they critically consider reality. It will deal instead with such vital questions as whether Roger gave green grass to the goat, and insist upon the importance of learning that, on the contrary, Roger gave green grass to the *r* abbit. The "humanism" of the banking approach masks the effort to turn men into automatons—the very negation of their ontological vocation to be more fully human.

Those who use the banking approach, knowingly or unknowingly (for there are innumerable well-intentioned bank-clerk teachers who do not realize that they are serving only to dehumanize), fail to perceive that the deposits themselves contain contradictions about reality. But, sooner or later, these contradictions may lead formerly passive students to turn against their domestication and the attempt to domesticate reality. They may discover through existential experience that their present way of life is irreconcilable with their vocation to become fully human. They may perceive through their relations with reality that reality is really a *process,* undergoing constant transformation. If men are searchers and their ontological vocation is humanization, sooner or later they may perceive the contradiction in which banking education seeks to maintain them, and then engage themselves in the struggle for their liberation.

But the humanist, revolutionary educator cannot wait for this possibility to materialize. From the outset, his efforts must coincide with those of the students to engage in critical thinking and the quest for mutual humanization. His efforts must be imbued with a profound trust in men and their creative power. To achieve this, he must be a partner of the students in his relations with them.

The banking concept does not admit to such partnership—and necessarily so. To resolve the teacher-student contradiction, to exchange the role of depositor, prescriber, domesticator, for the role of student among students would be to undermine the power of oppression and serve the cause of liberation.

Implicit in the banking concept is the assumption of a dichotomy between man and the world: man is merely *in* the world, not *with* the world or with others; man is spectator, not re-creator. In this view, man is not a conscious being *(corpo consciente)*; he is rather the possessor of *a* consciousness: an empty "mind" passively open to the reception of deposits of reality from the world outside. For example, my desk, my books, my coffee cup, all the objects before me—as bits of the world which surrounds me—would be "inside" me, exactly as I am inside my study right now. This view makes no distinction between being accessible to consciousness and entering consciousness. The distinction, however, is essential: the objects which surround me are simply accessible to my consciousness, not located within it. I am aware of them, but they are not inside me.

It follows logically from the banking notion of consciousness that the educator's role is to regulate the way the world "enters into" the students. His task is to organize a process which already occurs spontaneously, to "fill" the students by making deposits of information which he considers to constitute true knowledge. And since men "receive" the world as passive entities, education should make them more passive still, and adapt them to the world. The educated man is the adapted man, because he is better "fit" for the world. Translated into practice, this concept is well suited to the purposes of the oppressors, whose tranquility rests on how well men fit the world the oppressors have created, and how little they question it.

The more completely the majority adapt to the purposes which the dominant minority prescribe for them (thereby depriving them of the right to their own purposes), the more easily the minority can continue to prescribe. The theory and practice of banking education serve this end quite efficiently. Verbalistic lessons, reading requirements, the methods for evaluating "knowledge," the distance between the teacher and the taught, the criteria for promotion: everything in this ready-to-wear approach serves to obviate thinking.

The bank-clerk educator does not realize that there is no true security in his hypertrophied role, that one must seek to live *with* others in solidarity. One cannot impose oneself, nor even merely co-exist with one's students. Solidarity requires true communication, and the concept by which such an educator is guided fears and proscribes communication.

Yet only through communication can human life hold meaning. The teacher's thinking is authenticated only by the authenticity of the students' thinking. The teacher cannot think for his students, nor can he impose his thought on them. Authentic thinking, thinking that is concerned about *reality,* does not take place in ivory tower isolation, but only in communication. If it is true that thought has meaning only when generated by action upon the world, the subordination of students to teachers becomes impossible.

Further Resources

BOOKS

Berthoff, Ann E. "Reading the World . . . Reading the Word": Paulo Freire's Pedagogy of Knowing." In *Only Connect: Uniting Reading and Writing.* Upper Montclair, N.J.: Boynton/Cook Publishers, Inc., 1986.

McLaren, Peter. *Che Guevara, Paulo Freire, and the Pedagogy of Revolution.* Lanham, Md.: Rowman & Littlefield Publishers, Inc., 2000.

Shor, Ira, ed. *Freire for the Classroom: A Sourcebook for Liberatory Teaching.* Portsmouth, N.H.: Boynton/Cook Publishers, Inc., 1987.

PERIODICALS

Evans, J.W. "Pedagogy of the Oppressed." *America* 124, March 13, 1971, 272.

Harman, David. "Methodology for Revolution." *Saturday Review* 54, June 19, 1971, 54–55.

WEBSITES

Instituto Paulo Freire. Available online at http://www.paulofreire.org/ (accessed May 28, 2003).

Adult Educators you should know: Paulo Freire. Available online at http://nlu.nl.edu/ace/ (accessed May 28, 2003).

"Rethinking Black History"

Journal article

By: Orlando Patterson

Date: 1971

Source: Patterson, Orlando. "Rethinking Black History." *Harvard Educational Review* 41, no. 3, 1971, 299–304.

About the Author: Orlando Patterson (1940–) is the John Cowles Professor of Sociology at Harvard University. Patterson was born in Jamaica and moved to the United States in 1970. He has made important scholarly contributions to the study of slavery and ethnicity. Patterson also wrote three novels and several short stories. ∎

Introduction

Beginning in the 1950s, there was an interest for black history to be written and included in the curriculum. The Civil Rights era in the 1960s increased the quest for knowledge of the past—people needed to define themselves and their historical struggles. Students demanded courses in black history. Early attempts to comply with this request followed the "great man tradition," much like white history. That is, great male figures from black history were presented, written about, and discussed. This has changed. Now historians place more emphasis on primary documents such as oral histories, diaries, and letters and other first-hand accounts of the past.

Orlando Patterson describes five ways that academics have discussed and written about the history of blacks. These are the radical and conservative catastrophism, radical and conservative survivalism, and contributionism. These are unsatisfying in his view, because Patterson believes that relying on methods concerning civilization and African culture are inadequate. In this essay, he states that he is looking at "the sociology of Black historical knowledge." Those whom he calls "catastrophists" see life over three hundred years as a long series of disasters. For these historians, "Blacks experienced every conceivable form of exploitation, humiliation, and anguish at the hands of their white oppressors." Survivalists, on the other hand, do not deny slavery or other catastrophes, but they "see the Black man as having triumphed in maintaining his African roots in spite of the destructive and hostile environments." The two views can be seen radically or conservatively. The fifth view, contributionism, examines the black man's contributions to civilization. Patterson feels that more would be gained if historians actually examined blacks' continuities and noncontinuities within their own society, rather than trying to make the race fit a mold of scholarship that does not suit its history.

Significance

Patterson exposes a way of looking at history that differs from using the traditional methods of looking for great figures. Rather than a few people, many of whom were known because of their connections to white society, Patterson asks historians to explore the connections in the black community. Looking for stability and instability in the black community in the United States and in Africa will bring to light true experiences of daily life for the black community. He also calls for historians to look at different geographical areas of Africa than have been examined previously. Patterson's methods signal a new era in examining roots of a culture and the importance of people's everyday lives. In examining the oral and the non-literary sources, the historian discovers how people communicated with one another and how they left traces of their lives for the generations beyond their own. How did they survive the struggles that had already been documented in the history of black slavery? How were rituals and customs passed along? Since many slaves did not read or write, these stories had to be passed on orally. This is often a difficult history to trace. However, historians in the past three decades have proven it possible.

The kind of historical and sociological examination that Patterson called for in 1971 has become more commonplace in the late twentieth and early twenty-first centuries. Slave narratives, oral histories, and other documents that survive are all taken into consideration as writers try to recover the history of the black community. It is not to say that the great men are unimportant, but that the ordinary people who lived their lives within communities are also important—they also made lasting contributions to the history of a culture and of a race.

Primary Source

"Rethinking Black History" [excerpt]

SYNOPSIS: Patterson calls on scholars to move beyond traditional methods of history with an open mind. He believes that only a small part of African history impacts African American history and that the question of those connections should be tackled.

Catastrophe vs. Survival

New World Blacks show a basic division in current interpretations of their past. This division hinges on the view taken of the critical period of slavery: more specifically, on whether or not the past three centuries of experience in the New World was essentially destructive in its impact on the social and cultural development of the race. On the one hand, there is what may be called the catastrophic interpretation of the New World Black past and, on the other hand, the survivalist view. For catastrophists, Black history in the New World is simply one long disaster, a chronicle of horrors in which Blacks ex-

Orlando Patterson. Orlando Patterson has made important contributions to the study of slavery and ethnicity. AP/WIDE WORLD PHOTOS. REPRODUCED BY PERMISSION.

perienced every conceivable form of exploitation, humiliation, and anguish at the hands of their white oppressors. According to this view, the Black man was culturally and spiritually deracinated and, having lost his African roots, was "brain-washed" or, to use the more polite academic term, forced to acculturate the way of life and mode of thinking—including that part which was racially offensive—of his white oppressor. Until recently, the catastrophic view was the most popular among Black intellectuals and activists, its adherents ranging from E. Franklin Frazier to Malcolm X. Typical of this position is Nathan Hare's statement that the Negro in America "has been everlastingly misled, tricked, and brainwashed by the ruling race of whites." Comparing Black Americans with Africans, he writes that: "This was accomplished even more successfully in the case of American Blacks, compared to Africans, because of the fact that brainwashing is 'best implemented by removing the subject from his normal setting' . . . Communication is then restricted—in the case of the Negro slave it was virtually destroyed—and the 'stripping process,' the process of self-mortification (the destruction of identity and self-esteem) is then almost a matter of course."

Those who hold the survivalist view tend to underplay or wholly deny the destructive impact of slavery on the Black man's culture. The survivalists do not in any way seek to deny the horrors of slavery or the white man's iniquity. They see the Black man as having triumphed in maintaining his African roots in spite of the destructive and hostile environment. Slavery was a kind of cosmic test of the Black man's strength and of the resilience of his cultural heritage and he passed that test heroically. Ironically, the most distinguished exponent of the survivalist view in the United States, especially during the heyday of catastrophism, was the white American anthropologist, Melville Herskovits. Within recent years, however, the survivalist view has come strongly in vogue among Blacks and it forms the intellectual core of almost all Black nationalists who have bothered to think through their position.

Each of these positions may be formulated in ways that are either radical or conservative in their implications, creating four basic categories: radical and conservative catastrophism, and radical and conservative survivalism. Let us briefly examine these four categories before going on to a fifth and more pervasive interpretation of the Black past.

It is not difficult to see how the catastrophic view of the Black man's past can be employed as an intellectual tool in radical polemics. Drawing attention to the horrors of the Black past, seeing it as a great loss and as a long process of psychological maiming does two things. First, it clearly defines the enemy—the white man. It emphasizes the enormity of his crime and stimulates the need for racial vengeance. There is an elemental, almost Biblical attraction in this position which has the added merit of exploiting the fundamentalist religious imagery and sentiments of most Black Americans: vengeance is mine, saith the historian.

Secondly, this view of Black history offers possibly the best point of departure for Black leaders and intellectuals who are acutely conscious of the psychological problems of their race and, accepting their role as at least partly therapeutic, seek to emancipate their people from their lowly self-image and their imitation of white values. It is always a delicate matter getting an individual or group of people to admit that they are in some way maimed or warped in their outlook or conception of themselves, especially when such individuals are educationally deprived and not given to uncomfortable self-examination. Using the facts of history to blame the white man for the damage sufficiently compensates psychologically by

providing a hate object, a devil, to allay the pain of recognition and admission of the damage done. Again, the use of catastrophism has the advantage of striking a familiar religious chord in the Black American, this time his highly developed sense of sin and defilement. Radical catastrophism is, indeed, a secularized form of Black fundamentalism. For once the defilement is admitted, a veritable exorcism takes place. All the psychic wounds, the sins heaped upon one, can be released, for now it is understood clearly that these wounds are the works of the devil who after three hundred years of mystery, stands revealed as the white man. No Black leader better understood this process than Malcolm X. His intuitive grasp of its mechanisms is seen quite clearly in the recorded texts of his historically-oriented speeches, and, more importantly, in the revivalist fervor of the audience's participation whenever he spoke.

Finally, radical catastrophism offers the further advantage of redemption. If what history informs us is true, then the white man has a great deal to answer for, not only ultimately in the projected vengeance, but, until the right moment arrives, in reparation. One has the right to demand anything from any quarter, without apology, since it is one's just due. And if the state will not pay up, then the white churches, who are most vulnerable on this ground, must be made to.

Catastrophism does have its conservative side. For many Blacks, Africa is an embarrassment and slavery a shameful experience to be quietly forgotten. The problem of the race becomes one of "catching up" with the whites and any interpretation of the Black past which might suggest that there is anything "special" about Blacks is seen as a threat to the claim of full and immediate participation in the white majority society and culture. Perhaps the most sophisticated apologist for this view of the Black past is James Baldwin. In his essay, "Stranger in the Village," Baldwin claims that the American Negro slave "is unique among the Black men of the world in that his past was taken from him, almost literally, at one blow." Baldwin uses his confrontation with the inhabitants of a remote Swiss village as a means of exploring this theme. There is, of course, the usual Baldwinesque prevarication about the white American conscience as well as the pleading yet self-indulgent exhibitionism, but, through it all, the final message is clear enough. To Baldwin, and those conservative catastrophists who think like him, these remote Swiss villagers, who "have never seen America" or much of Europe beyond their village, nonetheless "move with an authority which I shall never have; and they regard me, quite rightly, not only as a stranger in their village but as a suspect late comer, bearing no credentials, to everything they have—however unconsciously—inherited." Unlike Dubois, LeRoi Jones and other sophisticated catastrophists, Baldwin is clearly more concerned with being a latecomer to European culture and with what the inheritors of this tradition think of him than with courageously coming to terms with the implications of his view of his own past or with present African cultures. And in this regard, it is perhaps significant that although Baldwin now lives in Europe and has travelled widely in that continent, he has never once visited Africa.

A less whimpering and altogether more palatable version of conservative catastrophism is found in the works of Black scholars such as E. Franklin Frazier and Margaret Just Butcher. Butcher, whose work was based largely on materials left by the late literateur, Alain Locke, states that there was a "nearly complete loss of his [the Black man's] aboriginal culture and the resultant vacuumlike emptiness undoubtedly speeded up the absorption" of white American culture. And Frazier states categorically in his major work that:

> Probably never before in history has a people been so completely stripped of its social heritage as the Negroes who were brought to America.

Both authors agree that, as Frazier puts it,

> . . . The Negro, stripped of the relatively simple pre-literate culture in which he was nurtured, has created a folk culture and has gradually taken over the more sophisticated American culture.

Radical survivalism had its origins not in the United States, but the Caribbean, especially among the artists, writers, and intellectuals of Haiti and the French West Indies who founded the now familiar school of Afro-Caribbean literature known as Negritude. Apart from a few isolated Black scholars, such as the American linguist Lorenzo Turner and the Haitian ethnographer Price-Mars, not many Black scholars of distinction have supported the survivalist thesis.

Whatever the academic situation, however, there is no doubt that the belief in African cultural continuity forms an important part of radical Black ideology. Belief and pride in this continuity are often basic prerequisites for the rejection of white American culture and the emergence of a separate Black identity, and, in extreme cases, a separate Black state. Several militant Black movements have been directly linked to the Zionist goal of returning to Africa. Indeed, the activist phase of the civil rights movement, insofar as it had mass support, may be said to date back to the Marcus Garvey movement. Garvey's extremely influential teachings assumed African cultural continuity and saw in a return to Africa the only path to salvation.

But survivalism has its conservative side. Too often survivalism becomes an excuse for sheer fantasy or a devious means of copping out of the problem of Black existence in America. Even more conservative, if also more constructive, than those Black intellectual chauvinists attempting to set up some bizarre "Republic of New Africa" in the United States are the Black Muslims. This group of blacks are remarkably middle-class in their attitudes and trace their ancestry back to Allah and what they call "Arabian-Egyptian civilization." Their publications, especially the newspaper Muhammad Speaks, reveal no great love for the Negro peoples of sub-Saharan Africa. E. U. Essien-Udom, in his study of the group, writes that: "The quest for respectability within and without the Negro community is a primary goal . . . The effort to strengthen the Moslem's sense of pride is apparent in Muhammad's emphasis on the 'glorious' past which is, of course, 'Arabian-Egyptian civilization.'"

One unfortunate aspect of survivalism is that, so often, it so easily degenerates into a vulgar exoticism in which there is not only an obsessive glorification of one's "soul" but all sorts of inverted racist claims of superior sexual potency and greater zest and passion for life, a crass wallowing in none too "noble savagery," and, worse, a cheap, sensational form of modern minstrelsy aimed at a winking white audience who, in their intellectual slumming, are only too willing to tap their toes to the "boom boom of the tom-tom." Claude McKay, perhaps the most successful novelist of the so-called "Harlem Renaissance" of the twenties, was, at times, prone to this sort of nativistic vulgarity.

What is particularly sad about many activists and lay intellectuals of survivalist persuasion is their frequent ignorance of Africa, its land, and cultures. In a recent issue of a newspaper published by the Student Organization for Black Unity, the editorial opens with the following paragraph: "The latest fad sweeping the movement is Africa fever. It seems like everybody and his momma suddenly had to go to Africa, has to see Tanzania, must visit Zambia, got to go to Ghana, need to observe in Guyana." Ironically, the same issue of SOBU carried a front-page feature on Guyana.

Nothing I have said above is intended to undermine the great importance of the study of African cultural continuities in the New World. I merely question the lack of serious thinking that has gone into the subject and the extent to which unproven and confused conceptions of Afro-American history has been used in socially sterile and politically conservative ways.

Further Resources

BOOKS

Glover, Denise M. *Voices of the Spirit: Sources for Interpreting the African American Experience.* Chicago: American Library Association, 1995.

Hall, Perry A. *In the Vineyard: Working in African American Studies.* Knoxville: University of Tennessee Press, 1999.

PERIODICALS

Harding, Vincent. "Power from Our People: The Sources of the Modern Revival of Black History." *The Black Scholar* 18, no. 1, January/February 1987, 40–51.

Horton, James Oliver. "New Directions for Research in Black History." *The Black Scholar* 7, no. 6, March 1976, 36–39.

Patterson, Orlando. "Toward a Study of Black America: Notes on the Culture of Racism." *Dissent,* Fall 1989, 476–486.

WEBSITES

"Orlando Patterson." Sociology Department. Harvard University. Available online at http://www.wjh.harvard.edu/soc/faculty/patterson; website home page: http://www.wjh.harvard.edu (accessed May 28, 2003).

Schomburg Center for Research in Black Culture. The New York Public Library. Available online at http://www.nypl.org/research/sc/sc.html; website home page: http://www.nypl.org (accessed May 28, 2003).

"The Joy of Learning—In the Open Corridor"

Magazine article

By: Walter Schneir and Miriam Schneir

Date: 1971

Source: Schneir, Walter, and Miriam Schneir. "The Joy of Learning—In the Open Corridor." *The New York Times Magazine,* April 4, 1971, 30–31, 72–80, 92–97. Reprinted in Silberman, Charles E., ed. *The Open Classroom Reader.* New York: Vintage Books, 1973, 39–42.

About the Authors: Miriam and Walter Schneir are journalists who write about history and education. In 1965 they coauthored the book, *Invitation to an Inquest: A New Look at the Rosenberg-Sobell Case.* ■

Introduction

The Open Classroom Reader, edited by Charles Silberman, offers a collection of essays on the theories and practices of the open classroom in America. Grounded in an English tradition, the open classroom was one of the experimental programs of the 1970s and 1980s.

Silberman is a critic of the traditional classroom with straight rows and the teacher in the front of the class. He calls this a joyless place to learn. His previous work, *Crisis in the Classroom,* challenged failures he saw in American education. As a reformer, Silberman prefers the informal classroom, referred to as "open education" or the "open classroom." The open classroom is arranged in areas where children work on different subjects at the same time. Instead of formal lessons taught at the same time each day, children go from area to area learning at their own pace. Teachers and aides monitor and assist the children in their studies. For the person accustomed to teaching in a traditional classroom, this method of education looks like chaos. Children are at different tables or areas. Some may be in the hallways. The method was used more at the elementary level than at higher levels. He writes that "open educators share a conception of childhood as something to be cherished" and that they see the classroom "not merely as preparation for later schooling or later life."

The selection by Miriam and Walter Schneir paints a picture of one school located in New York. The article describes how the children move from place to place, and talks about the supervision they receive from teachers and other assistants. The children seem to be intent on what they are doing, but are not inhibited in the classroom. A boy breaks out in song when he feels like it. He does not have to be noticed, but he is not punished for his outburst that would be unacceptable in a traditional classroom. In the open classroom, teachers monitor students's progress through notations they make as they observe activities and answer children's questions.

Significance

Chaos seems to be the watchword in the classroom that the Schneirs observe. However, after describing the various activities, they point out the subtle organization of the activity in which the children are involved. Children are free to learn at their own pace and may ask a teacher a question or talk to her as the need arises. Not all children may be ready for this kind of experience, but the ones in this school seem to be content and learning. The article, which originally appeared in *The New York Times Magazine,* points out the benefits of this kind of classroom. It is important to note that the article's audience is the general public. The Schneirs did not use the jargon of educational theory to explain what they saw; rather they wrote in a language for parents and other readers.

The open classroom that the Schneirs observe is not limited to a small room. The corridors are full of activity, including tumbling, reading, and talking. The chil-

An open classroom at an elementary school in Lawrence Township, New Jersey. Children in the foreground are learning math while those in the rear of the room conduct a reading group. AP/WIDE WORLD PHOTOS. REPRODUCED BY PERMISSION.

dren seem to have access to a wider variety of activities than they might in a traditional school. The Schneirs notice that a group of girls speak in Spanish to one another but address the teacher in English. The allowance for bilingualism is important to note. Students are clearly learning English but are also allowed to use their native language as they read and work together.

Adaptation is key to open education. The Schneirs note that there is a "things to do" sign in a first grade room, and that the "teacher seems alert to the nuances of all the activity" around her. One of the important aspects of education discussed in the article is that children can teach one another. Adults are not always able to explain concepts in the language of children. In their own language and at their own pace, a child may be able to break down a difficult math or science concept for another child so that he or she can learn. The teacher obviously remains necessary, but the child's natural abilities are not discounted in the open classroom.

When first proposed, educational theorists opposed open classrooms for obvious reasons. There is the appearance that nothing truly productive is going on. However, the articles in Silberman's collection show the positive aspects of the open classroom experiment.

Primary Source

"The Joy of Learning—In the Open Corridor" [excerpt]

> **SYNOPSIS:** In the open classroom, each child selects what interests him or her for a period of time. The Schneirs's article does not address any formal timing within the open classroom. If it is present, or if requirements are placed on the children to meet certain objectives, we do not see them here.

Portraits of American Open Classrooms

The "open corridor" came into being at P.S. 123 in the spring of 1968. Before that first semester was over, a group of parents and teachers from P.S. 84, an elementary school in a racially mixed neighborhood of low-income to high-income families, came to observe the program in action. They were sufficiently impressed to invite Professor Weber to introduce the open corridor the following year in P.S. 84. The following selection describes the operation of the program two years later. (Walter and Miriam Schneir, free-lance writers and journalists, have been active in encouraging the creation of open classrooms in Westchester County, New York, where they live.)

■ ■ ■

The underlying assumption of "informal" schools, both British and American, is that in an enriched and carefully planned environment that supports *the natural drive toward learning* children are able to learn mostly by themselves, from each other and from books. They learn in encounters with the things and people around them, and they do so at their own irregular and individual pace. They learn most intensely when they are interested and see the pertinence of what they are doing. The role of the teacher is important, but quite untraditional: there are few, if any, whole-class lessons, no standardized tests, no meticulously detailed and rigidly enforced curriculum.

Informal methods are being tried in New York City and in the Westchester communities of New Rochelle, Greenburgh and Irvington, and across the country in such cities as Washington, Detroit, New Haven, Newark and Berkeley, as well as such states as North Dakota, Vermont, Maine and Arizona.

One of the most interesting experiments singled out for mention by the Carnegie report is taking place at P.S. 84, a school in a racially and economically varied neighborhood along Manhattan's Upper West Side. The school, with 900 children in pre-kindergarten through sixth grade, has an enrollment that is about one-third black, one-third white and one-third Spanish-American.

Today at P.S. 84, the visitor can see in operation the most dramatic physical innovation of the British primary schools: the use of hallways as extensions of the classroom. The British were forced to adopt this plan because of overcrowded schools. But necessity proved to be a virtue when classroom doors were thrown open and the children were allowed free access to the corridors. The arrangement made possible a sense of community among students and staff, a spirit of mutual help and learning. The educator who has promoted this particular

approach in New York, Mrs. Lillian Weber, describes it as the "open corridor" program.

The sight of a small boy sliding down a bannister greets the two visitors to P.S. 84, situated at 92d Street between Columbus Avenue and Central Park West. The sliding boy and a companion, who is taking the more conventional route down a short flight of stairs from a first floor landing, are conversing animatedly.

Walking up a half dozen steps, we come upon a first floor corridor that is the connecting passage between four primary classrooms that open off it. At 10 A.M. in the corridor, four kindergarten girls, seated cross-legged on some cushions with a pile of magazines, a paste pot and a very large sheet of brown paper, are cutting and pasting. Nearby, a third grader is reading a story to a younger child; both are giggling at the antics of "Curious George." Two girls sitting side by side on the corridor floor are each absorbed in a book, as is a boy leaning against the opposite wall. Several youngsters are writing in notebooks or on loose sheets of paper. A large, bright yellow wooden tub on wheels, with two children and an oversized stuffed dog crowded into it, is being pushed along the corridor by a highly energetic boy.

The children who are working do not look up as the cart rolls by. No adult is present in the corridor aside from the visitors. From time to time, a child gets up and goes into one of the classrooms to ask some available adult a question; occasionally, a child turns to us for help. One asks, "How do you spell Morison?," the name of the school's principal to whom she is writing a letter. Presently, a teacher comes out of a classroom and offers the four kindergarten girls a few more illustrated magazines. The girls speak English to their teacher, and converse quietly in Spanish together.

The institutional tile walls of the corridor are covered with a variety of art work and posters. Any child who wants to can tape up his work. It is not long past Halloween and a group of highly individualistic jack-o'-lanterns leer down. A poster, one of many, provides the following information: "We guessed how much our pumpkin would weigh. Risa thought it weighed 21 pounds. She weighed it and it weighed 20 pounds. After we took out the seeds and pulp, it weighed 16 pounds." In the corridor we are nearly surrounded by words, words of songs, poems, stories, announcements, news items—all placed at a convenient height for children to read.

A third-grade classroom opens off the corridor. At first our eyes are assailed by the apparent chaos of the scene—a profusion of movement, sounds, colors, shapes. Gradually, however, the organization of the class reveals itself. The room is perhaps a little smaller than is standard and has a class register of 30 children, a few of whom are in the corridor or visiting other classes. What is most striking is that there are no desks for pupils or teachers. Instead, the room is arranged as a workshop.

Carelessly draped over the seat, arm and back of a big old easy chair are three children, each reading to himself. Several other children nearby sprawl comfortably on a covered mattress on the floor, rehearsing a song they have written and copied neatly into a song folio.

One grouping of tables is a science area with equipment ranging from magnets, mirrors, a prism, magnifying glasses, a microscope, a kaleidoscope, batteries, wires, an electric bell, to various natural objects (shells, seeds, feathers, bones and a bird's nest). Also on nearby shelves are a cage with gerbils, a turtle tank and plants grown by the children. Several other tables placed together and surrounded by chairs hold a great variety of math materials such as shaped blocks known as "geo blocks," combination locks and Cuisenaire rods, rulers and graph paper. A separate balance table contains four scales.

The teacher sits down at a small, round table for a few minutes with two boys, and they work together on vocabulary with word cards; her paraprofessional assistant is at the blackboard with several children who are writing. A student teacher (available in the mornings only) praises a drawing a girl has brought over to show her; other children display their work to the visitors with obvious pride.

Children move in and out of the classroom constantly. The teacher seems alert to the nuances of all the activity. To a boy trying to explain to a classmate how to construct a rather complex paper fan, she suggests, "As a game, see if you can describe it to her with your hands behind your back." To a child who has produced a collection of ink-blot pictures, she casually introduces the idea of "symmetry." She keeps a record book handy in which she jots notations on each of the children. Seeing a child filling and emptying different sized plastic containers at the sink, she stops for a moment and talks about pints and quarts. Weighing, measuring and graph-making appear to be favorite activities.

In spite of all that is happening—the constant conversation, the singing—the noise level is quite subdued. The children look engaged, bright-eyed, happy. A little boy breaks into an impromptu rock 'n'

roll dance; nobody takes any particular notice. Apparently satisfied, he returns to the math area.

In the corridor on the second floor of P.S. 84, a tumbling mat is taken out for the first time this year. Children from classrooms off this hallway line up and take turns: handstands, cartwheels, but mostly somersaults. They are good. One boy does a headstand and holds the pose. After a few moments, the "corridor teacher" begins to count and the children chime in. They get up to 47 before the child stands again and proudly struts to the end of the line.

In a first-grade classroom a prominent sign suggests: "Things to Do. Play at the math table. Paint a picture. Make a book. Play with sand. Use the typewriter. Use the chalk board. Play a reading game. Listen to a record. Read a book. Play checkers." Most of these activities are being sampled. The level of noise and movement, though noticeably higher than in the older third grade, is not overpowering. As in the other class visited, the teacher has a record book in which she makes notes about individual children, such as: "Speaks in monosyllables," "Counts to 15, recognizes number symbols to 8," "Built huge bridge out of blocks—I promised to bring book on bridges."

A box labeled "story starters" contains pictures that are employed to suggest narrative. On a wall is a collection of such stories dictated by the children and copied down by an adult. A Chagall print adorns one wall and beneath it is a story by a child named Rachel:

> This bird is playing in the water. The flying horse is watching it play. The bird is having fun playing in the water. Now the bird is chasing its tail while the flying horse is shaking the weeds. The flying horse is getting closer to the river while the bird is getting dizzier and dizzier. The flying horse is getting closer and closer to the bird near the river. Then the bird sees the flying horse and then the bird paddles away.

Further Resources

BOOKS

Barth, Roland S. *Open Education and the American School.* New York: Agathon Press, 1972.

Devaney, Kathleen. *Developing Open Education in America: A Review of Theory and Practice in the Public Schools.* Washington: National Association for the Education of Young Children, 1974.

Dropkin, Ruth, and Arthur Tobier, eds. *Roots of Open Education in America: Reminiscences and Reflections.* New York: City College Workshop Center for Open Education, 1976.

PERIODICALS

Galbraith, Ronald E. "Open Space: Two Different Examples. An Educator's Perspective." *Social Education* 43, no. 1, January 1979, 81–83.

Elias, Susan F., and Jeffrey H. Elias. "Open Education and Teacher Attitudes Toward Openness: The Impact on Students." *Education* 99, no. 2, Winter 1978, 208–214.

AUDIO AND VISUAL MEDIA

To Make a Difference: An Open Classroom in the 80's. Directed by Tom Valens. Forest Knolls, Calif.: Tamalpais Productions. 1985, VHS.

"Busing—The Supreme Court Goes North"

Magazine article

By: Christopher Jencks

Date: 1972

Source: Jencks, Christopher. "Busing—The Supreme Court Goes North." *The New York Times Magazine,* November 19, 1972, 41, 118.

About the Author: Christopher "Sandy" Jencks (1936–) is the Malcolm Wiener Professor of Social Policy at Harvard University. He was educated at Harvard and the London School of Economics and Political Science. Jencks's research deals with the inequality in the standard of living over the past generation. ∎

Introduction

Numerous cases regarding desegregation of schools made their way to the Supreme Court in addition to the 1954 decision in *Brown v. The Board of Education of Topeka.* That decision, sometimes referred to as *Brown I,* stated that state-imposed segregated schools were unequal and illegal. The *Brown I* decision set the path for integration in the schools in the southern United States, but not without much turmoil and controversy. *Brown II,* in 1955, tried to define how and when the schools would be desegregated across the country. The court did not take a strong stand on a time line, however. The *Civil Rights Act of 1964* furthered the movement of eliminating inequality, not only in the schools, but in work, housing, and every way of life. Laws and court decisions were not always enough to end decades of unfair treatment.

The case that preceded the *Keyes* case, which Jencks writes about, was *Swann v. Charlotte-Mecklenburg Board of Education.* This decision stipulated that the school board could not use residential patterns as an excuse for the district being segregated. This was still a case that was in a southern state, however. The case of *Keyes v. School District #1* was the first case to challenge a northern and western city regarding segregation. The plaintiffs stated that the reasons were not just residential patterns in Denver, but were also due to the School Board purposely building schools in African American and His-

panic neighborhoods to keep the children segregated from white children. They also charged that the district had changed school boundaries purposely to keep the district's schools segregated. Prior to the case being filed in court, the School Board had agreed to remedy some of the problems the *Keyes* case noted. However, an election changed the composition of the board and the battle began again. The case proceeded to the Supreme Court where School District #1 in Denver was found to be in violation of the law and ordered to integrate the schools.

Significance

The *Keyes* case is most significant because of the location of the district. Northern school districts had not fought challenges on segregation that went all the way to the Supreme Court. There were districts beginning to face the problems of schools that were largely or entirely African American or Hispanic, but these districts had not found solutions. The school district in Denver had manipulated boundaries and had built schools in African American and Hispanic neighborhoods throughout the 1960s to keep the other schools in the district white. There was a small population of minority students in Denver at the time. Other northern cities, like Detroit and Boston, with more significant minority populations would face a decade or more of battles over how to draw district lines.

The case does not just involve where schools are placed. Busing became a major issue in the court decisions of the 1970s. Forced busing brought on problems of its own, sometimes accompanied by violence. It also caused costs to increase and children to be taken away from neighborhood schools. If both white and minority students were bused, the decision was accepted more easily than if only African American or Hispanic children were bused.

Jencks notes that there are still larger problems based on racial inequality in jobs, housing, and opportunities in general. If the society as a whole does not address the issue of racism, then sending a child to a different school will not matter much.

Cases continued being heard by the Supreme Court over racial injustices in schools. A conservation Court backed away from some decisions, stating that they could do nothing about inner city housing problems. This effectively reversed the progress that had started toward integration of schools and providing equal and fair access to education for all.

Primary Source

"Busing—The Supreme Court Goes North"
[excerpt]

SYNOPSIS: Questions of busing for desegregation had been primarily limited to the South. Racial inequality in Northern schools had started to be ad-

Police escort school buses down a Boston street in 1974, enforcing court ordered busing to integrate the city's schools. **AP/WIDE WORLD PHOTOS. REPRODUCED BY PERMISSION.**

dressed by the time the Keyes case reached the Supreme Court, but no implementation for desegregation had taken place.

Sometime in the next few months the Supreme Court will decide the case of *Keyes v. School District No. 1*. School District No. 1 is in Denver, Colo., and the *Keyes* case deals with racial segregation in the Denver schools. The Court may decide the case on narrow grounds that have no clear implications for other Northern cities, but this seems unlikely. In all probability the *Keyes* decision will tell us whether the Court intends to launch a major attack on school segregation in the North.

Unlike some Northern school systems, Denver still has a white majority. About 15 per cent of Denver's students are black and another 20 per cent are Hispano (the local term for those with Latin-American roots). Most of the blacks live in central or northwestern Denver. The Hispanos are also concentrated in a few areas. Since Denver has traditionally assigned students to neighborhood schools, the blacks and Hispanos generally end up in different schools from the whites. Yet school segregation has not always been unavoidable in Denver, or even unintentional. A school board can draw neighborhood boundaries in any way it finds politically convenient. The Denver School Board, like many others in America, has often used ethnic criteria to define neighborhoods. As the black population grew, the board deliberately redrew some neighborhood boundaries and built at least one new school in such a way as to keep blacks and whites in separate buildings. As a result, Denver's schools were even more segregated than they would have been under a color-blind neighborhood assignment system.

In 1969, the board briefly adopted a new policy, aimed at desegregating a number of schools in northeastern Denver. This plan involved busing some whites to schools in black neighborhoods and some blacks to white neighborhoods. Before this policy could be implemented, however, a school board election was held. Two board members who had supported desegregation were defeated, and the new board rescinded the plan. Advocates of desegregation therefore turned to the courts.

Both the Federal District Court and the conservative United States Court of Appeals for the 10th Circuit found that Denver's use of racial criteria to define neighborhood attendance zones violated the

14th Amendment's "equal protection" clause. It seems reasonably certain that the Supreme Court will uphold this judgment. The real question posed by this part of the *Keyes* case is not whether the Denver board acted illegally in the past, but rather what remedy it is now required to provide. The N.A.A.C.P. Legal Defense Fund, which represented the plaintiffs, has argued that the board engaged in *de jure* segregation of essentially the same kind as employed by Southern school boards. The Fund has therefore asked the Supreme Court to order the same kind of remedial efforts in Denver that it has ordered in Southern districts. If the Court agrees, Denver will have to redraw almost all its attendance zones, not just those it had previously gerrymandered. Furthermore, if Southern precedents are followed, it will not now suffice to redraw attendance zones on a color-blind basis. Instead, Denver will have to redraw its zones in such a way as to offset the effects of neighborhood segregation and produce racially mixed schools. This will mean busing some blacks to schools in white neighborhoods and some whites to schools in black neighborhoods.

A decision of this kind would have repercussions throughout the North. Virtually every Northern school board has done something at one time or another to keep blacks and whites in separate schools. If Northern school boards must now not only eliminate the direct consequences of their past discrimination but also neutralize the effects of residential segregation, almost every major city will eventually have to desegregate all its schools. In most big cities this will require two-way busing.

Desegregation would not occur overnight, because integrationists would have to assemble evidence that each Northern district had contributed in some deliberate way to segregating its schools. Such cases have, however, already been brought in a number of Northern cities, and Federal district judges have usually found them convincing. Last year in San Francisco, for example, Judge Stanley Weigel ordered complete desegregation of all San Francisco schools, on such grounds. Similarly, this year in Detroit, Judge Stephen Roth found a pattern of officially maintained segregation, and ordered desegregation of the entire metropolitan area. (This order has been stayed, pending a review by the Court of Appeals.) Ironically, many Southern segregationists are hoping that the Supreme Court will require a similar remedy in Denver. They believe that if the Supreme Court applies this principle to all Northern cities, they will be able to win Northern support for an antibusing constitutional amendment.

Mindful of this possibility, the Court could decide to reject N.A.A.C.P.'s contention that Denver is essentially similar to the South. The Court might hold that racial segregation was never official policy in Denver, that it was never anything like total and that it was therefore qualitatively different from segregation in the South. Thus the Court might simply require Denver to redraw attendance zones on a color-blind basis. Or, the Court might order the board to desegregate the specific schools where the plaintiffs have proved deliberate segregation but might allow other attendance zones to remain as they are.

Whether the Burger Court will start down a road leading to large-scale desegregation in the North depends on how much the Justices are influenced by public opinion, how much by social science and how much by the logic of past Supreme Court decisions. If the Court is guided primarily by public opinion, it will draw a clear distinction between Northern and Southern style *de jure* segregation and will only require school boards to eliminate segregation in those specific schools where the board originally caused the problem. If it is guided by social science, which is unlikely, the Court will have to render some sort of ambiguous verdict. If it is guided primarily by the logic of its own past decisions, it will treat cities like Denver just as it has treated their Southern counterparts and will order large-scale, two-way busing where this is necessary to achieve desegregation.

The politics of desegregation depends to a significant extent on the methods used to achieve it. The most popular and least effective method has been what Northerners call "open enrollment" and Southerners call "freedom of choice." Ideally, open enrollment ought to allow any child to attend any school in his district and provide him with free transportation. In practice, open enrollment programs usually give students who live near a school the right to attend it, and admit "outsiders" only if there are still vacancies. Some open enrollment programs also require parents to pay the transportation costs. In its ideal form, open enrollment could neutralize the effects of residential segregation by allowing black parents to send their children to schools in white neighborhoods. In practice, however, only 5 to 15 per cent of black parents usually exercise this right, even when transportation is free and places are available. (This estimate is very rough. While many cities have tried open enrollment, few have collected statistics that showed how many of the eligible blacks used it to move to a desegregated school.)

Open enrollment seldom arouses as much white opposition as other approaches to desegregation, since it allows white children to attend their neighborhood schools, and these schools remain predominantly white. Indeed, whites sometimes use open enrollment more than blacks, since whites in racially mixed neighborhoods may be more anxious to transfer their children to predominantly white schools than blacks are. (Some open enrollment programs do not allow white transfers that increase the level of segregation.) Integrationists object to open enrollment because it does not eliminate all-black schools. Whites almost never move to schools in black areas, whereas blacks usually remain in them. For those whose primary concern is with the rights of individual black parents, this outcome may not seem particularly disturbing, since it is more or less voluntary. But for those who believe that black schools are educationally inferior, or that every school needs a substantial cadre of middle-class students, or that segregated schools breed racist alumni, a solution that leaves most schools segregated is unsatisfactory.

A second common approach to desegregation in the North has been to redraw neighborhood boundaries so as to achieve racial balance. In small cities, where most blacks live within walking distance of a white neighborhood, this often eliminates all-black schools or at least sharply reduces their number. In big cities, where many blacks live miles from the nearest white neighborhood, this approach is impossible. Regardless of city size, redrawing neighborhood boundaries is very unpopular with whites when it results in white children having to attend schools with large numbers of blacks or their having to walk though black areas to get to school. Indeed, white parents whose children get assigned to such schools often become-strong supporters of city-wide busing, because they want the whole city to share the burden of desegregation. In Seattle, for example, where blacks are still a small minority, some central-city whites see citywide busing as a device for maintaining a substantial white majority in every school. Redrawing neighborhood boundaries may also be unpopular with blacks as it may under open enroll-if they end up doing most of the walking or if they think it will cost them control over schools in black neighborhoods.

The third and least popular approach to desegregation is busing. Only a handful of American cities (for example, Berkeley and Riverside, Calif., and Evanston, Ill.) have voluntarily established two-way busing programs aimed at achieving racial balance in every school. Most two-way busing programs have been the result of court orders or strong state pressure. This is no accident. Most white parents are deeply fearful of sending their children to schools in black areas, whether by bus, by foot or by any other means. Many fear for their children's physical safety. White parents' anxieties on this score are not entirely groundless, any more than Southern black parents' fears were groundless when their children entered traditionally white schools. In addition, many white parents belive that predominantly black schools have low academic standards. Educational researchers have almost never found that white students' test scores actually fell as a result of being in desegregated schools. Nonetheless, both blacks and many whites have been proclaiming the inferiority of schools in black neighborhoods for a generation, so it is not surprising that many white parents believe the difference important.

Black attitudes toward mandatory busing seem to be mixed. Opinion polls show overwhelming black support for desegregated schooling, but experience with open enrollment suggests that only a small minority of blacks send their children to desegregated schools when this requires individual action and a long bus ride. Black parents' attitudes seem to depend, however, on how the choice is presented. In Hartford, for example, Project Concern picks random classrooms from black neighborhood schools and offers the parents a chance to send the children to schools in white suburbs. Almost all black parents accept this offer. The evidence suggests, then, that when busing is initiated by the school Establishment and parents expect their children to be welcome in the new school, most black parents like the idea. But when busing requires individual initiative and may lead to an indifferent or hostile reception, as it may under open enrollment, relatively few black parents make the move.

Further Resources

BOOKS

Lomotey, Kofi, and Charles Teddlie, eds. *Forty Years After the Brown Decision: Implications of School Desegregation for U.S. Education.* New York: AMS Press, 1996.

Orfield, Gary, Susan E. Eaton, and The Harvard Project on School Desegregation. *Dismantling Desegregation: The Quiet Reversal of "Brown v. Board of Education".* New York: The New Press, 1996.

PERIODICALS

Hyde, Alison A. "School Desegregation: The Role of the Courts and Means of Achievement." *NASSP Bulletin* 78, no. 565, November 1994, 29–37.

Richardson, Joanna. "Voluntary Busing Plan is Unveiled in Denver." *Education Week* 15, January 24, 1996, 6.

Schmidt, Peter. "Judge Declares Denver Schools Desegregated. *Keyes v. School District No. 1.*" *Education Week* 15, September 20, 1995, 3.

WEBSITES

The Civil Rights Project: Harvard University. Available online at http://www.civilrightsproject.harvard.edu (accessed May 28, 2003).

Keyes v. School District No. 1. Supreme Court of the United States. 413 U.S. 189; 93 S.Ct. 2686; 37 L. Ed. 2d 548 (1973). Available online at http://www.law.duke.edu/curriculum /courseHomepages/Fall2002/329_01/syllabusReadings /Class12-Keyes.pdf; website home page: http://www.law.duke .edu (accessed May 28, 2003).

Landmark Cases: Supreme Court. *Brown v. Board of Education* (1954). Available online at http://www.landmarkcases .org/brown/ifyouwere.html; website home page: http://www .landmarkcases.org (accessed May 28, 2003).

Writing Without Teachers
Manual

By: Peter Elbow

Date: 1973

Source: Elbow, Peter. "Freewriting Exercises." In *Writing Without Teachers.* New York: Oxford University Press, 1973, 3–7.

About the Author: Peter Elbow (1935–) is an Emeritus Professor of English at the University of Massachusetts, Amherst. He directed the writing program there between 1996 and 2000. *Everyone Can Write: Essays toward a Hopeful Theory of Writing* won the James Britton Award in 2002. In 2001 the National Council Teachers of English awarded Peter Elbow the James Squire Award for his transforming influence on the profession. ■

Introduction

During the late 1960s and 1970s, a method of teaching writing labeled expressivism developed. This kind of writing provided power to the student or writer, rather than just to the teacher. Expressivism opposed the traditional methods of teaching writing, which emphasized academic forms, five-paragraph themes, and standard forms of "correct" grammar. Donald Murray, Ken Macrorie, and Peter Elbow were all part of this movement.

Donald Murray's *A Writer Teaches Writing* (1968), Ken Macrorie's *Telling Writing* (1970), and Peter Elbow's *Writing Without Teachers* (1973) were cornerstones for the process of teaching students to write reflectively. Murray's emphasis on conferences and drafts, Macrorie's instruction in "telling" the details of a story, and Elbow's practices of freewriting combined to create what some saw as a radical pedagogy. All three stressed a student-centered classroom.

Expressivism highlighted practice, rather than theory. They approached writing by teaching, providing anecdotes about teaching practices and rationalizing why these processes worked when the traditional methods failed. Model workshops, practicing journaling and freewriting, conferencing, and revising were part of instructing future teachers in this method. Expressivism was not without a theoretical background, however. James Britton's theories on the expressive functions of language and James Kinneavy's theories on expressive discourse provided the groundwork for this new method of teaching.

Peter Elbow "values the act of writing as a means for both making meaning and creating identity." After discussing the steps of the writing process, Elbow provides instructions for a teacherless classroom. The classes should be seven to twelve people who write and meet weekly. Being part of the group involves commitment to the process, to writing, and to one another. Though the class does not teach grammar in a traditional way, grammar is not ignored.

Significance

Peter Elbow's *Writing Without Teachers* was published in 1973 as an alternative text for learning how to write. Elbow is most passionate about freewriting. In a later essay, he wrote, "I learn most from it. I get my best ideas and writing from it. I get my best group and community work done that way."

Some teachers loved freewriting, while others hated it. Geraldine Pittman Rubenstein, reviewing for the *Harvard Educational Review,* points out the strengths of Elbow's arguments. Although freewriting allows students to explore subjects, it does not discount discipline in the process. Students must sit down and write and share that writing with others. Only then will a writer get to a point of editing and producing a work that is more than initial thoughts. Rubenstein realizes that the students in her classroom often do not even have basic language skills, a common criticism of the freewriting method. Richard Larson's review in *College Composition and Communication* praises Elbow's book. Larson points out Elbow's concern for "what goes on in the writer's life—in his mind—as he writes." This alone makes Elbow's work different from most other textbooks available. Larson notes that the teacher's commitment, especially the ability to let go of the fear of failure, is necessary to use Elbow's method. He concludes that more books need to let go of the traditional views and propose Elbow's kind of methods.

In the 1990s, David Bartholomae, who believes in training students in traditional academic discourse, became involved in an ongoing debate with Elbow about the value of personal writing. Elbow remained a believer in his own methods.

Several generations of writing instructors have acknowledged Elbow's influence on their writing and teaching. The freewriting method has evolved over the last three decades and continues to be debated in the pages of the professional journals.

Primary Source

Writing Without Teachers [excerpt]

SYNOPSIS: Elbow says that just as physical exercise is important, so is it important to practice writing. Elbow "prescribes" freewriting at least three times per week for ten to fifteen minutes. These sessions allow the writer to become free in expressing thoughts on paper without editing.

Freewriting Exercises

The most effective way I know to improve your writing is to do freewriting exercises regularly. At least three times a week. They are sometimes called "automatic writing," "babbling," or "jabbering" exercises. The idea is simply to write for ten minutes (later on, perhaps fifteen or twenty). Don't stop for anything. Go quickly without rushing. Never stop to look back, to cross something out, to wonder how to spell something, to wonder what word or thought to use, or to think about what you are doing. If you can't think of a word or a spelling, just use a squiggle or else write, "I can't think of it." Just put down something. The easiest thing is just to put down whatever is in your mind. If you get stuck it's fine to write "I can't think what to say, I can't think what to say" as many times as you want; or repeat the last word you wrote over and over again; or anything else. The only requirement is that you *never* stop.

What happens to a freewriting exercise is important. It must be a piece of writing which, even if someone reads it, doesn't send any ripples back to you. It is like writing something and putting it in a bottle in the sea. The teacherless class helps your writing by providing maximum feedback. Freewritings help you by providing no feedback at all. When I assign one, I invite the writer to let me read it. But also tell him to keep it if he prefers. I read it quickly and make no comments at all and I do not speak with him about it. The main thing is that a freewriting must never be evaluated in any way; in fact there must be no discussion or comment at all.

Here is an example of a fairly coherent exercise (sometimes they are very incoherent, which is fine):

I think I'll write what's on my mind, but the only thing on my mind right now is what to write for ten minutes. I've never done this be-

The cover of Peter Elbow's *Writing Without Teachers*. ELBOW, PETER. COVER OF *WRITING WITHOUT TEACHERS*. OXFORD UNIVERSITY PRESS, INC. 1973. REPRODUCED BY PERMISSION.

fore and I'm not prepared in any way—the sky is cloudy today, how's that? now I'm afraid I won't be able to think of what to write when I get to the end of the sentence—well, here I am at the end of the sentence—here I am again, again, again, again, at least I'm still writing—Now I ask is there some reason to be happy that I'm still writing—ah yes! Here comes the question again—What am I getting out of this? What point is there in it? It's almost obscene to always ask it but I seem to question everything that way and I was gonna say something else pertaining to that but I got so busy writing down the first part that I forgot what I was leading into. This is kind of fun oh don't stop writing—cars and trucks speeding by somewhere out the window, pens clittering across peoples' papers. The sky is still cloudy—is it symbolic that I should be mentioning it? Huh? I dunno. Maybe I should try colors, blue, red, dirty words—wait a minute—no can't do that, orange, yellow, arm tired, green pink violet magenta lavender red brown black green—now that I can't think of any more colors—just about done—relief? maybe.

How Freewriting Exercises Help

Freewriting may seem crazy but actually it makes simple sense. Think of the difference between speaking and writing. Writing has the advantage of permitting more editing. But that's its downfall too. Almost everybody interposes a massive and complicated series of editings between the time words start to be born into consciousness and when they finally come off the end of the pencil or typewriter onto the page. This is partly because schooling makes us obsessed with the "mistakes" we make in writing. Many people are constantly thinking about spelling and grammar as they try to write. I am always thinking about the awkwardness, wordiness, and general mushiness of my natural verbal product as I try to write down words.

But it's not just "mistakes" or "bad writing" we edit as we write. We also edit unacceptable thoughts and feelings, as we do in speaking. In writing there is more time to do it so the editing is heavier: when speaking, there's someone right there waiting for a reply and he'll get bored or think we're crazy if we don't come out with *something.* Most of the time in speaking, we settle for the catch-as-catch-can way in which the words tumble out. In writing, however, there's a chance to try to get them right. But the opportunity to get them right is a terrible burden: you can work for two hours trying to get a paragraph "right" and discover it's not right at all. And then give up.

Editing, *in itself,* is not the problem. Editing is usually necessary if we want to end up with something satisfactory. The problem is that editing goes on *at the same time* as producing. The editor is, as it were, constantly looking over the shoulder of the producer and constantly fiddling with what he's doing while he's in the middle of trying to do it. No wonder the producer gets nervous, jumpy, inhibited, and finally can't be coherent. It's an unnecessary burden to try to think of words and also worry at the same time whether they're the right words.

The main thing about freewriting is that it is *nonediting.* It is an exercise in bringing together the process of producing words and putting them down on the page. Practiced regularly, it undoes the ingrained habit of editing at the same time you are trying to produce. It will make writing less blocked because words will come more easily. You will use up more paper, but chew up fewer pencils.

Next time you write, notice how often you stop yourself from writing down something you were going to write down. Or else cross it out after it's written. "Naturally," you say, "it wasn't any good." But think for a moment about the occasions when you spoke well. Seldom was it because you first got the beginning just right. Usually it was a matter of a halt-ing or even garbled beginning, but you kept going and your speech finally became coherent and even powerful. There is a lesson here for writing: trying to get the beginning just right is a formula for failure— and probably a secret tactic to make yourself give up writing. Make some words, whatever they are, and then grab hold of that line and reel in as hard as you can. Afterwards you can throw away lousy beginnings and make new ones. This is the quickest way to get into good writing.

The habit of compulsive, premature editing doesn't just make writing hard. It also makes writing dead. Your voice is damped out by all the interruptions, changes, and hesitations between the consciousness and the page. In your natural way of producing words there is a sound, a texture, a rhythm—a voice—which is the main source of power in your writing. I don't know how it works, but this voice is the force that will make a reader listen to you, the energy that drives the meanings through his thick skull. Maybe you don't *like* your voice; maybe people have made fun of it. But it's the only voice you've got. It's your only source of power. You better get back into it, no matter what you think of it. If you keep writing in it, it may change into something you like better. But if you abandon it, you'll likely never have a voice and never be heard.

Freewritings are vacuums. Gradually you will begin to carry over into your regular writing some of the voice, force, and connectedness that creep into those vacuums.

Further Resources

BOOKS

Belanoff, Pat, Marcia Dickson, Sheryl I. Fontaine, Charles Moran, ed. *Writing with Elbow.* Logan: Utah State University Press, 2002.

Belanoff, Pat, Peter Elbow, and Sheryl I. Fontaine, eds. "Toward a Phenomenology of Freewriting." In *Nothing begins with N: New Investigations of Freewriting.* Carbondale, Ill.: Southern Illinois University Press, 1991. 189–213.

Burnham, Christopher C. "Expressivism." In *Theorizing Composition: A Critical Sourcebook of Theory and Scholarship in Contemporary Composition Studies.* Westport, Conn.: Greenwood Press, 1998. 107–116.

PERIODICALS

Larson, Richard L. "Of Books on Composition and Rhetoric." *College Composition and Communication* 25, no. 1, February 1974, 66–70.

Rubenstein, Geraldine Pittman. "Writing Without Teachers." *Harvard Educational Review* 44, no. 3, 1974, 468–471.

WEBSITES

Peter Elbow. Available online at http://www.umass.edu/english /eng/facProfiles/Elbow.html; website home page: http://www .umass.edu (accessed May 29, 2003).

AUDIO AND VISUAL MEDIA
Peter Elbow on Writing. Director Sut Jhally. Northampton, MA: Media Education Foundation, 2002. DVD.

College Opportunity Act of 1978

Report, Table

By: U.S. Senate Committee on Human Resources

Date: 1978

Source: Congress of the U.S. Washington D.C. Senate Committee on Human Resources. *College Opportunity Act of 1978.* Report, with Additional Views. 95th Congress, 2nd Session. Washington, D.C.: Government Printing Office, 1978. Available online at http://newfirstsearch.oclc.org. (accessed October 3, 2002).

About the Organization: The Senate Committee on Human Resources was a committee in the 95th Congress. Bills are reported to the Senate via a committee chair and placed on a calendar. Reported bills and written reports are numbered, and the actions of the committee are in the copy of the bill. ■

Introduction

The *Higher Education Act of 1965* (Public Law 89-329) provided insured student loans for eligible college students. The act also provided grants to colleges and universities and provided for a number of training programs. Amendments between 1968 and 1978 added programs, grants, and loans for disadvantaged students. All of these acts and amendments contributed to the necessity for the *College Opportunity Act of 1978.*

In the 1960s, grant and scholarship money mainly went to the very poor or the very rich. Students who were financially disadvantaged were singled out for grant programs by the federal government. Opportunities for higher education were viewed as vital for a group of the population that had been overlooked for decades. These programs focused particularly on African Americans, Hispanics, and other minority groups. Basic Opportunity Education Grants were authorized in 1972. These were renamed Pell Grants in 1980. Wealthy students had always been able to afford college and, therefore, were not included in the governmental programs. They could still count on scholarship money from private and public institutions.

Now the disenfranchised group was the middle class. Since financial need depended in part on the parents' discretionary income, students in the middle income brackets often did not qualify for grants from the federal government. The *College Opportunity Act of 1978* sought to change the percentage of parental discretionary income that must be counted toward financial aid. Prior to this Act, the figure was 20 percent of the first $5,000 and 30 percent of the excess. Now the percentage would be no higher than 10.5 percent of the discretionary income, and more grant money would be available. The Act also increased funding for college work study programs: part time jobs for which the government provided 80% of the funding to colleges and universities. The Act brought college within reach of thousands of students who could not afford the cost to attend prior to 1978.

Significance

The *College Opportunity Act of 1978* gave middle class students more opportunities to afford a college education. Previously, these students "were unable to find any form of assistance except, possibly, loans, to enable them to meet the staggering costs of college." The Act views students as consumers—customers who are looking for the best education for the most affordable price. Opportunity for aid increased the population of middle class students on college campuses across the country.

Along with increasingly available funds, the act sought to streamline the required paperwork to apply for financial aid. Financial aid forms would be sent to a central address and processed by a computer. A form would be returned telling the student how much and what kind of aid they were eligible for, and to return the form to the college of their choice. The goal was to reduce confusion for students and parents. The forms, called the FAFSA (Free Application for Federal Student Aid), can now be processed on the Internet.

Federal financial aid for college students continues to be a hot button issue in Congress. The Act sought to balance the campus population between the poor, middle class, and affluent student. Findings in Thomas Mortenson's 1990 report for the American College Testing Program show that while middle class and affluent students were receiving more gift aid, or grants and scholarships, the poorest students were often receiving more loans. In order to reduce the need for loans, students must work more hours, and so do not get the most from their college education. The Congressional debate reauthorizing allocations for federal financial aid goes on each year. As costs continue to rise and the college-age population grows, the debate about who will pay for college will continue as well.

Primary Source

College Opportunity Act of 1978 [excerpt]: Report

> **SYNOPSIS:** In this excerpt and the accompanying table, Senator Claiborne Pell of Rhode Island reports that the Senate Committee on Human Resources

favors adopting the proposed amendments to the Higher Education Act of 1965. He then explains what the College Opportunity Act of 1978 is expected to accomplish.

Need for the Legislation

In the past decade, the costs of sending a child to college have sky-rocketed. Between 1967 and 1976, the cost of sending a child to an average college has increased by 77 percent.

The average cost of tuition, room, and board at a nonpublic institution today is more than $4,800 per year, a staggering $19,200 for the 4 years necessary to obtain a bachelor's degree. The number of colleges which cost between $6,000 and $7,000 for a single year is increasing. And the costs of public institutions, whose charges are already partially subsidized by the taxpayers, are also rising sharply. At many public universities today, a student can be expected to pay more than $2,500 a year to cover education-related expenses.

Although Federal assistance, in the form of grants, loans, and work-study opportunities, has been steadily rising during the past decade, it has not been able to keep pace with the more rapidly rising demand for aid. Given limited Federal dollars, more and more emphasis has been given to aiding those with greatest financial need. Middle-income families, who do the work of our society, pay the bills, and bear the brunt of the tax burden, found themselves increasingly unable to get aid for their children's higher education. Colleges found themselves increasingly facing student bodies made up of the able poor, who could get Federal aid, and the able rich, who could afford to pay their own way.

It was the able children of middle-income families who were unable to find any form of assistance except, possibly, loans, to enable them to meet the staggering costs of college. Many promising careers undoubtedly were abandoned because of inability to seek further education, whether at an institution of higher education or in a trade or technical school. The Nation is the loser.

The bill proposed by the committee is designed to meet this overwhelming need to increase student assistance so that it meets the needs of middle-income families. S. 2539 builds upon the basic building blocks of student aid—basic educational opportunity grants, supplemental educational opportunity grants, college work-study, State student incentive grants, and guaranteed student loans—already familiar to schools and colleges across the country,

as well as to millions of parents and students in postsecondary education.

In framing S. 2539, the committee has attempted to make as few changes in the provisions of the programs as possible, to reduce confusion and to assure that the greatest number of eligible students benefit from the programs. Another major goal of the committee bill is the reduction of paperwork already accompanying Federal aid program, such as the needs test in the guaranteed loan program. A third is the avoidance of the creation of any new bureaucracy to monitor or administer any of the programs contained in the bill. By building on existing structures, the committee is confident that no new bureaucracies will grow up.

Provisions of the Committee Bill

Basic educational opportunity grant programs

The basic educational opportunity grant program, commonly known as basic grants, was originally enacted in 1972. In the past 5 years, it has grown from a mere idea to a program which aids more than 2.1 million students a year in pursuing their postsecondary education.

Prior to the enactment of basic grants. Federal student assistance programs administered by the Department of Health, Education, and Welfare, with the exception of the guaranteed loan program, were administered through participating colleges and schools. Appropriated funds were divided pursuant to statutory State-level formulas. Distribution within-State to schools and colleges was initially determined by a regional panel of student aid experts, based on their judgments of institutional requests for funds. The Commissioner of Education retained final authority over all institutional allotments.

However, the essential element in this process was that it was the institution, not the student, which was the focus of attention and decisionmaking. In too many cases, a student was forced to choose his college because funds were available, whereas a preferred institution was unable to offer assistance. Even the amount of aid was, within statutory limits, totally dependent on institutional decisions. Selection of a student to receive assistance, from a pool of equally qualified candidates, was equally totally within the discretion of institutional officials.

Basic grants were developed to provide a counterforce to these pressures. Under the basic grant program the student is the consumer. He takes his grant eligibility to the institution of his choice, re-

Basic Educational Opportunity Grants, Program Comparisons

Existing Program

Income	Recipients Number (thousands)	Percent	Funds Amount (millions)	Percent	Average award
0 to $5,300	464	21.1	$483	23.5	$1,041
$5,301 to $9,900	733	33.3	811	39.5	1,106
$9,901 to $15,900	745	33.8	624	30.4	838
$15,901 to $19,900	227	10.3	124	6.0	546
$19,901 to $26,500	35	1.6	12	.6	343
$26,501-plus	0	0	0	0	0
Total	2,204	100.0	2,054	100.0	934

Program Proposed by S. 2539

Income	Recipients Number (thousands)	Percent	Funds Amount (millions)	Percent	Average award
0 to $5,300	464	12.6	$483	14.9	$1,041
$5,301 to $9,900	735	20.0	837	25.8	1,139
$9,901 to $15,900	881	23.9	897	27.7	1,018
$15,901 to $19,900	627	17.0	505	15.6	805
$19,901 to $26,500	698	19.0	412	12.7	590
$26,501-plus	276	7.5	106	3.3	384
Total	3,680	100.0	3,240	100.0	880

Estimated Grant Awards, Average Family of Four

Income	S.2539	President's proposal
$6,000	$1,800	$1,800
$8,000	1,630	1,600
$10,000	1,450	1,270
$12,000	1,280	940
$15,000	1,020	250
$19,000	700	250
$21,000	540	250
$23,000	390	250
$24,000	310	250
$25,000	250	250
Total cost (billions)	1.2	1

SOURCE: Tables from U.S. Congress. Senate. Committee on Human Resources. *College Opportunity Act of 1978.* 95th Cong., 2d sess., 1978. S. Report 95-643, 5.

Primary Source

College Opportunity Act of 1978 [excerpt]: Table

SYNOPSIS: Three tables from the *College Opportunity Act of 1978* report. The top table describes the existing student grant program. The middle table describes the program proposed in the 1978 act. The last table compares the Senate's plan with the plan proposed by President Jimmy Carter (served 1977–81).

gardless of the institution's other financial aid resources. Any equally situated students are treated in exactly the same manner by basic grants.

The mechanism is relatively simple. The statute sets the grant ceiling—$1,400 for the first several years, $1,800 under the education amendments of 1976 (although appropriations for fiscal year 1977 were sufficient only to increase the maximum grant to $1,600). A student and his family fill out a form setting forth income and assets for the preceding calendar year, a form not unlike the one generations of students have been filling out for their colleges in order to establish eligibility for student aid. This form is mailed to a central address for a calculation, free of charge, of possible eligibility for a basic grant.

The calculation is purely mechanical, made by a computer. Information provided by the student or his parents is programmed to arrive at a single fig-

Rhode Island Senator Claiborne Pell sponsored the legislation that established the Basic Educational Opportunity Grant Program.
© BETTMANN/CORBIS. REPRODUCED BY PERMISSION.

ure representing parental discretionary income—that income to which a student might look for some assistance with his education. To arrive at this figure, certain subtractions are made from net income—tax liability, a family size offset (that amount necessary for the family to meet daily living expenses such as rent and food), any unusual expenses such as high medical bills. additional costs for siblings in college or in private elementary and secondary schools, and any special circumstances or disasters which might have affected the family's ability to pay during the year. After all of these deductions have been made, the figure that remains, if any, is labeled "parental discretionary income." Under current practice, a family is expected to contribute 20 percent of the first $5,000 of this figure, and 30 percent of any excess, toward their child's education.

This contribution is deducted from the grant ceiling; the remainder is the size of the student's basic grant.

Of course, a student and his family are not required to make these calculations themselves, although detailed explanations are available. The student receives a single sheet of paper indicating

the size of the grant for which he or she is eligible. or the reasons for ineligibility. This Student Eligibility Report is taken by the student to the school of his choice and submitted to the student financial aid officer for payment or credit toward the student's bills. No individual checks are required to be issued, as the institutions operate under a letter of credit system with the Department of Health, Education, and Welfare, and certify to the Department as payments are made to students as they enroll.

The amendment made by the committee bill would effect a simple change in the computer's calculations of families' ability to pay. Where the computer is now programed to assess discretionary income at 20 percent and 30 percent, the committee bill would require a flat assessment rate of 10.5 percent.

This would cost approximately $1.2 billion over the current level of $2.054 billion, but would add approximately 1.5 million new students as eligible basic grant recipients. . . .

The amendment to the basic educational opportunity grant program proposed by President Carter would have expanded the program to aid middle-income families by guaranteeing a flat grant of $250 to students from families with incomes between $15,000 and $25,000. The committee rejected this approach, as it did not believe it to be a fair reflection of the relative abilities of families within that income range to finance their children's education. While a family at the $25,000 range of the scale might be conceived to have a liquidity problem as propounded by Secretary Califano in the joint hearing, it appeared to the committee that a family at the $15,000 end of the scale had actual need for grant assistance, and assistance above the level of $250.

Therefore, the committee bill provides for a graduated program of grants, based on families' actual income and ability to afford the spiraling costs of postsecondary education. . . .

One of the major concerns of the committee in proposing this legislation is that it not lead to the creation of massive new bureaucracies to administer it. S. 2539 avoids this pitfall. By building on an existing program, and by making a change in a computer program rather than in any other element of the legislation, the bill assures that no new bureaucracy will be needed. The form a student and his parents must fill out will remain unchanged. No new data items will be required by the committee bill, so no additional burden of data collection and reporting will be placed on students and parents. If anything, the committee would urge the Department of Health, Education, and Welfare, as it has consistently done in the past, to simplify the existing form as much as possible, so that it serves as no conceivable deterrent to any individual's applying for the grant to which he is entitled. The committee pledges to continue to work with the Department in seeking ways to simplify the legislation, if that is necessary to simplify the basic grants form.

One area of change in the basic grant program which the President proposed, on which the committee did not act, relates to the treatment of the assets of a single independent student who has dependents. Under current regulations, assets of independent students are considered to be available for such students' education up to 33 percent per year of their total value. While this may make some sense in the case of an independent student in his early twenties who has a small bank account, such treatment can work substantial inequities upon the widow who must return for further postsecondary education in order to support her family. Witnesses before the committee last September urged the Department to reconsider their treatment of the single independent student with dependents and to change the current regulations. While the committee does not at this time propose to amend the law to change HEW's regulations on this point, it would add its voice to that of the higher education community in urging the Department of Health, Education, and Welfare to take administrative steps currently well within its authority to remedy this inequity of treatment.

Further Resources

BOOKS

Finn, Chester E. *Scholars, Dollars, and Bureaucrats.* Washington, D.C.: Brookings Institution, 1978.

McPherson, Michael S. and Morton Owen Schapiro. *Keeping College Affordable: Government and Educational Opportunity.* Washington, D.C.: Brookings Institution, 1991.

Mortenson, Thomas G. *The Reallocation of Financial Aid from Poor to Middle Income and Affluent Students, 1978 to 1990. ACT Student Financial Aid Research Report Series 90–92.* Iowa City, Iowa: American College Testing Program, 1990. ED319312.

PERIODICALS

Chase, Alston. "Financing a College Education." *Atlantic Monthly* 245, no. 4, April 1980, 92–98.

Mohrman, Kathryn. "Unintended Consequences of Federal Student Aid Policies." *The Brookings Review* 5, no. 4, Fall 1987, 24–31.

WEBSITES

Financial Aid–U.S. Department of Education. Available online at http://www.ed.gov/topics/topics.jsp?.⊤=Financial+Aid; website home page: http://www.ed.gov(accessed May 29, 2003).

"Open Admissions and Equal Access: A Study of Ethnic Groups in the City University of New York"

Journal article

By: David E. Lavin, et al.

Date: February 1979

Source: Lavin, David E. et al." Open Admissions and Equal Access: A Study of Ethnic Groups in the City University of New York." *Harvard Educational Review* 49, no. 1, February 1979, 53–57.

About the Author: David Lavin is a professor of Sociology at the Graduate School of the City University of New York. He has studied sociology of education and issues involving social inequality in education. Lavin has written a number of articles and books on the open admissions policies at CUNY. ∎

Introduction

Colleges and universities adopted open admissions policies in the 1970s to increase minority enrollment. The policy of the seventeen-campus City University of New York (CUNY) system has been studied since it began in 1970. Criticized by many for opening the doors of the university to unqualified students, the system had to justify why they were doing this and how it was working. The policy was implemented after student protests in 1969 demanding admission of more minority students. Until the 1970s, the CUNY system was primarily composed of white students. The protest focused on City College in particular because of its location in Harlem.

David Lavin has spent his career studying open admissions policies at CUNY. The 1979 study presented here follows the first three classes admitted under the policy. This study documents the history of CUNY's success for children of immigrants as well as the growing concern in education during the late 1960s about students' preparation for college. The open admission policy guaranteed admission to one of the city's colleges for all students who had graduated from a New York City high school. As the decade progressed, other programs were instituted to track or stratify the system once again. Students were placed in community colleges or vocational programs. Remediation was necessary for students who were not prepared for college courses. Critics stated that open admissions did not signify equality in education.

This study analyzes the first three classes of students, particularly African American and Hispanic students. As Lavin and his colleagues note, there is no way on many of the test instruments to determine other ethnic or minority groups. The authors examined five different kinds of documents to reach their conclusions. Problems with how to account for the other programs at CUNY which admitted minority and senior students arose as the results were tabulated. The study found positive outcomes as of 1979.

Significance

The Lavin study provides much data for supporters and critics of the open admissions policies at CUNY. Admissions to the freshman class rose dramatically, as would be expected. The class of 1970 was "75 percent larger than it had been in the previous year and the increase was almost entirely attributable to the new policy." These new students were mainly African American and Hispanic. The percentage of minority students more than doubled between 1969 and 1975 at most of the CUNY institutions. While percentages show one number, raw numbers indicate a different picture. Open admission students who were Catholic or Jewish outnumbered those who were African American or Hispanic. Lavin's numbers are important when tackling the arguments made by the critics. The critics of the system thought that standards would be lowered for the open admission minority candidates.

Other important factor that this study notes is that students admitted under open admissions compare favorably to their national counterparts. A difference that is significant is that the students in the CUNY system were staying in school longer, even to finish a two-year degree. This shows that the students valued the opportunity they received and remained in school at least part time until they did finish.

The policies had already begun to change by the time this Lavin study was published. Further changes have taken place in the ensuing decades. Educational policy and decisions are ultimately political in nature. The policy at CUNY began after protests by student groups. In the 1990s the policy ended due to protests by politicians. By the late 1990s the system had grown to encompass a diverse system that included six community colleges, seven four-year colleges, and four colleges that offered both an associate and bachelor's degree. Debates about the system appeared in the popular and academic press. Mayor Giuliani formed a task force to study the open admissions policy and the role of city funding. Open admissions and remedial education were phased out at CUNY in 1999.

Primary Source

"Open Admissions and Equal Access: A Study of Ethnic Groups in the City University of New York" [excerpt]

SYNOPSIS: Open Admissions could be described as another one of the grand educational experiments of the 1970s. As early as 1975 the CUNY Board of Higher Education was trying to dismantle the structure that allowed opportunities for students who may not have had the opportunity to attend college.

In 1970 the City University of New York (CUNY) adopted a policy which guaranteed admission to every graduate of the city's high schools. Designed to increase the proportion of minority students in the university and to slow the reproduction of social inequality, CUNY's open-admissions policy has been criticized as a threat to academic standards and as an unnecessary expense during periods of economic scarcity. In this article, David Lavin, Richard Alba, and Richard Silberstein argue instead that there has been no definitive evidence of a decline in standards and that the policy has been successful in reducing educational inequality. Basing their conclusions on a detailed study of the first three classes admitted under this policy, the authors examine its effects on the university's ethnic composition and integration at various levels, and on the academic performance of different ethnic groups.

In the spring of 1969 a series of angry and ominous confrontations broke out on the campus of the City College of New York, the oldest and most famous of the fifteen colleges then comprising the City University of New York (CUNY). The confrontations focused on a list of demands issued by groups favoring increased access to City College for minority students, especially Blacks and Hispanics.

The demands had a forceful logic given the history of the City University. The University, and particularly City College, had played a unique role in the lives of the children and grandchildren of European immigrants, especially for Jews coming from eastern Europe at the end of the nineteenth and the beginning of the twentieth centuries. And it was largely as a result of these students that, by the 1920s and the 1930s, City College students were regarded as among the most able in the nation, and the college was often referred to as the "proletarian Harvard." The list of its graduates' accomplishments—in academia, in business, and in public life—contributed to faith in City University as an open door to the middle class.

Although the University had done much for earlier groups coming from Europe, it failed to do the same for new arrivals from the American South and the Caribbean. In the post-World War II period the major clients of the University continued to be the descendants of European immigrants, even though the ethnic demography of New York was changing rapidly as a result of newer migrations. Southern Blacks and Puerto Ricans had settled in New York in large numbers but were virtually excluded from the University's four-year colleges, primarily because they could not pass the increasingly stringent entrance requirements. While City College was an open-access institution in the nineteenth century—any high-school graduate could attend free of charge—by the 1960s it required a high-school average in the mid-to upper-eighties for admission. Although a special admissions program for minority students was initiated in 1966 with city and state funding, Blacks and Hispanics continued to be underrepresented.

Although the problem existed throughout the city system, the situation was especially dramatic in the case of City College. Sitting high on a hill in Harlem, it appeared insulated from the hopes and dreams of the people below. It was not surprising then that, in the spring of 1969, a group of minority students along with some activist whites occupied campus buildings and issued a set of demands, including one for a drastic increase in minority enrollment. After lengthy and complex negotiations between the dissidents and various segments of the City College faculty and administration, and after hearings held by the Board of Higher Education, a decision was made to guarantee to all graduates of New York City high schools places at the campuses of the University, beginning in the fall of 1970.

Paradoxically, the open-admissions policy began at CUNY at the same time that doubts were growing about the ability of educational systems to remedy inequality. The Coleman Report, published in 1966, had begun a decade of debate over the role of education in American society. The immediate doubts created by that report and other works—most notably Christopher Jenck's *Inequality*—concerned the effects of schooling. The Coleman Report concluded that the characteristics of the schools students attended and, presumably, the quality of the education they received in them, seemed remarkably ineffective in accounting for academic success. In particular, differences between races in test results could not be explained by the characteristics

San Francisco State College students on strike demand open admission.
© TED STRESHINSKY/CORBIS. REPRODUCED BY PERMISSION.

of schools. The analysis of Jencks and his coworkers not only supported these conclusions, but also indicated that school characteristics and amount of education explain little of the subsequent inequalities of occupational status or income.

Responding in part to the findings of Coleman and Jencks, a number of social theorists began to examine the functions of the educational system from a critical perspective. Perhaps the most prominent of these critics were Samuel Bowles and Herbert Gintis, whose *Schooling in Capitalist America* emphasized education's functions in reinforcing the existing system of social stratification. In their view, education is closely harnessed to American capitalism and serves the needs of its hierarchical division of labor.

In this critical interpretation, open access to higher education does not guarantee social mobility, especially for the poor, because such access is offset by increases in the internal stratification of the system. Higher educational systems are divided into tracks distinguished by the curricula they provide and the occupations for which they destine students. Students are assigned to tracks by apparently meritocratic criteria, such as scores on standardized tests. Since lower-class Black and Hispanic students tend to score lower on these measures, they are confined largely to community colleges or vocational schools that train them for clerical and technical jobs near the bottom of the white-collar world. Middle-class white students on the other hand are more apt to be placed into four-year colleges with liberal arts curricula that may lead to professional careers. This interpretation concludes that, rather than alleviating inequality, open admissions may strengthen it by providing the illusion of equal opportunity to those destined for the lowest level white-collar jobs.

Thus, there is ample room to doubt the impact of the CUNY open-admissions policy and need for a detailed analysis of its results. In this article we will examine the academic fate of students from different ethnic groups under open admissions at CUNY. The program was aimed at minority students, primarily lower-class Blacks and Hispanics, but, to a degree not generally recognized, it also benefited working- and middle-class whites. In particular, it attracted a substantial number of Jewish and Catholic students, the former predominantly of eastern European background, the latter frequently of Irish or Italian descent.

After an introductory discussion of open admissions and an explanation of our data, we will first consider how the overall ethnic composition of the University was affected by open admissions. Secondly, we will examine the degree to which the various levels of the University became ethnically integrated. Finally, we will explore how well the members of the various groups did, using measures of academic failure or success (such as dropout and graduation rates) to determine whether open admissions led to a reduction of inequality in the attainment of those educational credentials required for middle-class occupational careers.

Structure of the CUNY Open-Access Model

Open-access education is hardly new in the United States. Its roots go back to the mid-nineteenth century when the land grant colleges were first established under the Morrill Act of 1862. These colleges, most of them located in the Midwest, offered admission to all high-school graduates. More recently, the California public higher education system received wide notice after World War II, when its "differential access" version of open admissions developed rapidly.

In light of these precedents, it seems curious that the new CUNY admissions policy received such widespread attention, though a closer look reveals features in the CUNY system not duplicated in the others. One of these was the actual admission criteria. In 1970, CUNY consisted of eight four-year senior colleges and seven two-year community colleges; by the following year, another four-year and another two-year college had been opened. Admission to the University was guaranteed by the new policy. Entrance to a senior college was generally assured if the student had attained a high-school average of at least 80 in academic, college preparatory courses or had graduated in the top half of the high-school class. All other high school graduates could enroll in a community college.

At face value, this system was much less stratified than the three-tier California system, where the university level accepts only the top 12.5 percent of high-school graduates; the state colleges accept the top third; and the two-year junior colleges accept all the others. CUNY's system formally distinguished only two- and four-year colleges, thus constituting a two-tier system. Its use of either high-school average or rank to admit a student to the upper tier was designed to increase minority enrollment in senior colleges, since students with low averages in predominantly minority high schools could still qualify on the rank criterion. Increased opportunity was also the apparent goal of a second major feature of the policy, which guaranteed a place in one of the senior colleges for any graduate of a two-year community college. At least on paper, then, the community colleges were not designed as "dead-end" institutions whose primary function was to provide terminal vocational education.

A third aspect of the CUNY plan was the attempt to provide equality of educational opportunity encompassing not only access but also outcome. Other open-enrollment systems had been characterized by early and high dropout rates. As Christopher Jencks and David Riesman have pointed out, in colleges with unselective admissions criteria, the faculty tends to be skeptical toward freshmen, viewing them as inept until they prove themselves able. There is usually an exodus of "misfits" by the end of their first year. The CUNY plan attempted to stop, or at least slow, this revolving door by introducing remedial programs, counseling, and other services on a large scale. The University also decreed that no student could be dismissed for academic failure during the "grace period" of the freshman year. Since other open-access programs ordinarily end their obligation with admission, the responsibility for academic success belongs to the student. Those who drop out reflect no discredit to the institution. At CUNY, the failure of the student was to be considered a failure of the institution as well.

The uniqueness of the CUNY program can only be understood in terms of the political context in which it arose. While open-enrollment programs in other universities were begun largely on the initiative of a policy-making establishment, the CUNY program was the result, both in structure and timing, of the demands of those minority constituencies who were its intended beneficiaries. A comparison of this open-admissions policy with an earlier version proposed by the University in its master plan of 1968 shows this clearly. In the original plan, any high school graduate would have been admitted to the University, but access was to be expanded primarily in the community colleges and noncollegiate "skills centers." The administration's plan, which was to be put into effect in the fall of 1975, was thus more stratified and vocational in its intent. The City College confrontation succeeded in changing both the conception and the starting date of open admissions. The policy was, therefore, as much a political response designed to restore order in the university and the city as it was an educational policy.

Further Resources

BOOKS

Jencks, Christopher, et al. *Who Gets Ahead? The Determinants of Economic Success in America.* New York: Basic Books, 1979.

Lavin, David E. and David Hyllegard. *Changing the Odds: Open Admissions and the Life Chances of the Disadvantaged.* New Haven, Conn.: Yale University Press, 1996.

McGrath, Dennis and Martin B. Spear. *The Academic Crisis of the Community College.* Albany, N.Y.: State University of New York Press, 1991.

PERIODICALS

Harrington, M. "Keep Open Admissions Open." *The New York Times Magazine,* November 2, 1975, 16–17.

O'Malley, Susan Gushee. "Schmidt Report Restructures City University of New York." *Radical Teacher* 56, 1999, 36–38.

Reitano, Joanne. "CUNY's Community Colleges: Democratic Education on Trial." *New Directions for Community Colleges* 107, Fall 1999, 23–40.

WEBSITES

Open Admissions and Remedial Education at the City University of New York. Available online at http://www.nyc.gov /html/cuny/html/admissions.html; website home page: http:// www.nyc.gov (accessed May 29, 2003).

"Introduction: The First Decade of Women's Studies"
Journal article

By: Florence Howe

Date: 1979

Source: Howe, Florence. "Introduction: The First Decade of Women's Studies." *Harvard Educational Review* 49, no. 4, November 1979, 413–421.

About the Author: Florence Howe (1929–) has been an advocate for women's voices and for educational and social reform. She served as the President of the Modern Language Association in 1973. In 1970, Howe founded the Feminist Press, a non-profit publisher and the oldest press dedicated to works by and about women. ∎

Introduction

Following a decade of the Civil Rights Movement and the Women's Movement, women's studies programs and courses began appearing in colleges across the country. This demand for courses in women's studies matched the demand for courses in other specialty areas. The 1970s was an era of progress for curricular change and development in women's studies. "Lost" women writers began being discovered and published, allowing women and men to read the works of women along with the canonical works of men.

Organizations and journals were founded to support the women's studies movement. The Feminist Press began in 1970 in New York City. Devoted to publishing women's work, the press was a leader as an independent voice. The National Women's Studies Association (NWSA) was founded in 1977 to further the development of educational opportunities for women. The *NWSA Journal* and the *Women's Studies Quarterly* address scholarly issues. These contributed to the growth of programs that Florence Howe summarizes.

Equity and politics were motives for the beginning of women's studies programs, according to Florence Howe. Hiring practices were unfair to females, especially in academic departments. There were not enough leadership roles for women in education and in business. Images of women that appeared in the press and in textbooks showed domestic scenes without acknowledging women's contributions in other arenas. All of these factors led to the desire and need for a voice in higher education. Great progress was made throughout the 1970s, but many goals remained unattained. While Title IX was fairly new and women's history was being recovered, not all women had been heard. Howe notes the lack of attention to lesbian issues and to reviews of women's studies programs. These were areas for future attention.

Significance

Florence Howe has been at the forefront of the women's studies movement since it started. She points out progress and goals in this essay. The progress since 1979 is also significant and should be reviewed.

Two methodologies are vital to women's studies research. These are the comparative approach and the documentary approach. The comparative approach is natural—many areas of academic inquiry compare one discipline or group to another. This is important in providing statistics for inequities that exist as well as for comparing accomplishments of women to men. The documentary approach reintroduces and locates women whose voices have been silenced. Documentation provides portraits of the lives of ordinary and well-known women. It looks at individuals and groups and provides a way to introduce these women to the history of a changing society. Women, like other minority groups, were absent from history texts and from reading lists before women began looking for them. Both methods mentioned above can be used to provide a more complete picture of life in America and throughout the world.

Since the end of the 1970s, women's studies programs have continued to grow on college campuses. In 1979, Howe noted 112 programs that had been established. As of March 2003, over 200 institutional members are listed on the NWSA home page. The number of tenure-track jobs for faculty has increased since the 1970s. Gender equity became a major issue in the 1980s and 1990s, both in academics and in the larger workplace. Women made strides in all areas. Textbooks have been revised to depict women doing more than baking cookies or fixing dinner. Girls and boys have positive, diverse images presented to them in the classroom. Even though much has been done, there is always more to accomplish.

Primary Source

"Introduction: The First Decade of Women's Studies"

> **SYNOPSIS:** This special issue of the *Harvard Educational Review* includes several articles outlining the history of women's studies in the United States. Howe introduces both the history and the issue in her opening essay.

The scholarship in this special double issue, *Women and Education*, illuminates the vitality of women's studies a decade after its beginnings. We could not have had this issue until quite recently, at least in part because schools of education have been among the most resistant to the impact of the women's movement, which first touched the campus a decade ago. As the academic arm of the women's movement, women's studies has developed an area of research and curriculum focused on women as a distinguishable group to be studied *from their own perspective* and on gender as a significant issue in a democratic society founded and administered as a patriarchy. Like most educational movements of the past, this one has a political goal: to establish equity for women, which, as John Stuart Mill said more than a hundred years ago, would be as healthy for men as it was essential for women. Unlike most educational movements, this one has moved very rapidly, at least in higher education, to develop a body of knowledge and many of the elements of academic consequence, including degree-granting programs, professional associations, research institutes, journals, and special issues of journals like this one.

The Impact of the Decade on Education

Ten years ago, women's studies pioneers lived on the daily excitement of discoveries razor-sharp and double-edged. The subordination of women in history and in the present suddenly loomed visible to those who would see; and within the gloomy frame, are dim outlines of a lost cultural heritage that might, if restored, disperse the gloom and help women to envision a future more equitable than the past. But at first the news was almost all bad, whether it came from Kate Millett's *Sexual Politics* (1970) or from a revival of interest in Simone de Beauvoir's *The Second Sex* (1949), or from the hundreds of studies, both of status and of curriculum and textbooks that began to pour out of new underground women's networks and spill over even into such journals as *Science.*

As early as 1968, women were studying their own status in academe. They were reviewing the presence (and absence) of women from the rosters of professional associations; the sharp pyramids that represented women's profiles in the ranks of each profession; and the downward trends in the statistics of hiring and tenuring women on each campus across the country. While these reports were dismal, forecasts of change were gloomier still. The Carnegie Commission on Higher Education projected in 1973 that even by the year 2000 some of the most prestigious campuses in the country—allegedly coeducational—would not have managed to bring their faculties to the national norm of 20 percent women, spread unequally of course through the ranks.

We are not more sanguine in 1979 about the hiring of women, but we now know clearly what we guessed in 1969—that there is more than discrimination at issue in academe. Then, the statistics not only suggested that women were not hired or tenured when available and qualified; they also revealed the disappearance of "qualified" women from the ranks of graduate students, as well as the absence of vast numbers who declined to apply in the first place, or who opted for the "women's professions." The studies showed that large numbers of women, with bachelor's degrees as good as or better than those of the men who had sat beside them in classes, took part-time clerical jobs to add to families' budgets. Then, we *guessed* that discrimination was only the tip of the cultural iceberg that had kept women, educated or not, in a place different from and unequal to that of men. Now we *know* that the problems are deeper and wider, that they involve our entire culture and the massive educational system we have constructed to keep that male-centered culture going.

A decade ago, in a private enclave near Princeton University, a group of feminists (some of whom were faculty wives) who called themselves Women on Words and Images began to study the portraits of girls and boys, women and men in more than 130 readers used in elementary schools across the country. Their report, *Dick and Jane as Victims,* was probably the single most important scholarly instrument for galvanizing feminist researchers to study and evaluate the entire curriculum with regard to its treatment of women—when they were present at all. In elementary school texts, mommies were present, of course, aproned and, in the main, stupid. Daddies went to work each day, and when they returned at night still had to solve major family problems—like removing a balloon that had lodged in a tree in the ubiquitous suburban yard. Little girls fared no better than mommies in these readers, and, as Lenore Weitzman's research on a variety of elementary texts has shown, the pattern is deep and persistent; and as insidious as it is on gender, so much more is it when gender intersects with race and age.

Studies of the traditional curriculum and texts in secondary and postsecondary education amplified the patterns evident in basic readers. Unless the scene was domestic, women were absent from the curriculum. Present, their portraits demeaned the complexity of human nature, or suggested that women were less than human. In literature, for example, where women characters might at least occasionally appear, they were either patient Griseldas or whoring bitches, saints or sinners—or simply dumb mommies. Women were absent from history and philosophy; as painters, sculptors, or composers, they were absent from art and music. With the exception of psychology, where they were viewed as "deviants," or as neurotic or defective, "incomplete" versions of males, women were ignored in the social sciences.

Where *were* the women? What had *women* been doing through the ages? Why didn't the curriculum reflect the reality of women's lives in 1969? And what might the effect be of creating a curriculum to compensate for the silences, the vast ignorance about women, and the lies and the perversions in circulation?

As dramatic as the volume of research responding to such questions has been the river of women's studies courses. In elementary and secondary education, where the pace has been slower than in higher education, no one has yet surveyed the field, but through the decade more than 5,000 teachers have written to The Feminist Press for information about teaching women's studies in their classrooms. In 1974, with a small grant from the Ford Foundation. The Feminist Press produced *Who's Who and Where in Women's Studies,* a listing of 4,990 women's studies courses, taught by 2,225 faculty members, at 995 institutions of higher education. At that time, on 112 campuses, women's studies programs had been established. While no institution has continued to count women's studies courses, The Feminist Press has continued to publish an annual update of women's studies programs in the *Women's Studies Newsletter.* Between 1974 and 1979, these had tripled in number, and some large programs that had once offered 20 or 25 courses were offering 75 to 100 annually.

To summarize the content of these courses and the research on which they are built is to illustrate one impact of women's studies on the traditional male-centered curriculum and body of knowledge that, until our own time, have gone unquestioned as "true" and "objective." The list that follows names both the areas in which women's studies has developed groups or "streams" of courses (both disciplinary and interdisciplinary); and, at the same time, classifies the areas of scholarship emerging from women's studies and illuminated by this special issue of the *Harvard Educational Review.*

- an understanding of patriarchy in historical perspective: philosophically and sociologically; its relationship to the religions of the world, and to ideas of knowledge and power—hence, an understanding of what it means to be born "permanently" into a subordinate or dominant status; a knowledge of feminist theory.

- an understanding of the complex, confusing, and still chaotic area of biological/psychological sex differences; the importance of null findings.

- an understanding of socialization and sex roles, as well as of sex-role stereotyping; the relationships among gender, race, and class—all from a cross-cultural perspective.

- an understanding of women in history, not only in the United States, but throughout the world; recognizing that such study includes legal as well as medical history—the history of birth control, for example, is essential to the study of women, even to the study of fiction about women.

- an understanding of women as represented in the arts they have produced, some of which have been buried or ignored as arts—quilt-making, for example, or the pottery of North American Indian women; and as represented in the significant literature by women of all races and nationalities that never was included in the literary curriculum; as well as an awareness that the images of women portrayed by the male-created arts have helped to control the dominant conceptions of women—hence, the importance of studying images of women on TV, in the film and the theatre, and in advertising.

- an understanding of the ways in which post-Freudian psychology has attempted to control women's destiny; an awareness that other male-centered psychological constructs like those of Erikson and Kohlberg are potentially damaging to women; an understanding of new woman-centered theories of female development.

- an understanding of female sexuality, including perspectives on both heterosexuality and lesbianism; special issues involved in birth control and reproduction.

- an understanding of the history and function of education as support and codifier of sex-segregation and of limited opportunities for women; some perspectives on education as an agent for change in the past and present.

- an understanding of the history and function of the family in the United States and cross-culturally; of the current variety of family structures, and of the conflict between beliefs and research findings with reference especially to issues surrounding childcare.

- an understanding of women in the workforce through history, in the present, and cross-culturally; the economy in relation to women; the relationship between money and power in personal interactions, in the family, and in society.

- an understanding of the relationship between laws affecting women and social change; the history of women and social movements.

It should be clear that the items above are meant to include women of all social classes, races, nationalities, and ethnic, religious, and sexual identities. This approach distinguishes women's studies from the "men's curriculum" that has tended to be the study of very few men at the top—the lawmakers, leaders, warmakers, and those few cultural heroes, like Hemingway or Fitzgerald, who have emulated or allegedly critiqued them.

Throughout the items above, two methodological issues are taken for granted. First, the comparative approach. Since most if not all learning occurs through comparisons, it would be strange indeed if the study of women did not also illuminate the study of men. On the other hand, it is possible to study cohorts of half the human race in their own contexts and on their own terms, without reference to the other half—which is, of course, what male-centered social science has done for almost a century. Obviously, we need both the comparative data and the data for each sex separately, but it may take a couple of generations before we have sufficient data about women to move on to some of the comparative questions. In the meantime, of course, there are also scholars attempting to look at the male data anew.

Second, the documentary base. Though we could see the outlines only dimly in 1969, a decade later we have many full portraits of the lives of women both famous and obscure, public and private, singly and in groups, and we understand that we have only touched the surface of the material still to be collected, studied, sifted, made available. For several hundred years women have been recorders, letter-writers, diary-keepers, secretaries of clubs and other women's groups, as well as professional writers. There are also many more painters and composers than we had even been able to dream of. Beyond those documents still coming to light in attics, county museums, and private libraries, women speak mutely in statistics of births, marriages, employment, deaths. In addition, there are the millions who await the social scientist: subjects of research for the next century at least, to compensate for their absence, and to improve by their presence the body of knowledge on which public policy is based.

Her's Special Issues on Women and Education

Given the women's studies agenda developed in the 1970s, it is not surprising that this end-of-the-decade collection should spill over into two issues; it is also not surprising that it should be incomplete. Lesbian women are almost absent even from mention; research on the intersections of gender with race, class, and sexual preference is not a central concern of the issue. Absent entirely are reviews of women's studies programs either on campuses or in school systems, as well as studies of their impact as intervention strategies on the lives and learning of students and faculty or on the curriculum itself. Such studies are being planned, carried out, and reported, and one would expect that another search for articles for a special issue even one year hence might feature them.

The contents of *Women and Education* are not easily categorized. The variety and breadth both of the dozen feature articles and the more than two dozen book reviews may seem bewildering to those unaccustomed to the notion that women are half the human race and that, therefore, all aspects of teaching and learning affect their lives. The concept of women's "education" is as inclusive as the concept of women's "history." In one sense, therefore, the editors have attempted to introduce their readers to the "field." In another sense, they are measuring, at least in a few areas of that field, the well-worn paths and the new avenues recently constructed.

Four articles are concerned with status: the interview on Title IX, the two autobiographical essays by Linda Nielsen and Sophie Freud Loewenstein, and the review of women in educational administration by Kathleen Lyman and Jeanne Speizer. In one sense, these are introductory: the Title IX interview, for example, summarizes legal and political information about the most important Federal instrument we have not yet learned to use. The essay on women in administration measures the decade's failure to change the virtual exclusion of women from administrative positions, and reviews the theories that have accounted for the failure, as well as strategies designed to effect change. In another sense, these articles move us forward to the questions we will

have to answer in the 1980s: How can we make Title IX work for women, as it was meant to do? Will compensatory programs for women administrators move them onto and up career ladders? And, as we read the two autobiographical essays, the questions grow more complex still: Which patterns of women's lives lead them to "success"?

Both autobiographical essays attempt to provide not only testimony, but analysis documented extensively by citations to the decade's work in social science, mainly of the feminist variety. Nielsen's especially candid and painful story exposes the multiple ironies evident as an educational psychologist comes to acknowledge the double standard academe holds for women—and her inability to communicate rationally to male peers in that world. Is it entirely an accident that the "success" story reported by Sophie Freud Loewenstein comes from a woman who put family and marriage first, and that the "failure" comes from a woman who has tried to compete with men in the full-time professional world of academe? Or is it a sign of the backlash that may be finding new ways to keep women inside traditional sex-segregated occupations and family-centered patterns?

A second group of articles reviews research on educational outcomes, and asks: If you educate a woman, what happens to her? What does she learn? How does she think? On what are her anxieties focused? How does she behave in relation to her family and her ethnicity? Only in this last instance are women not measured against men: while their husbands' lives may be affected by Chicanas' education and employment, Maxine Baca Zinn does not focus on Chicanos' education, family responsibilities, and ethnicity. In four other articles, however, the questions asked about women's education pose male norms against which women are measured—and not always found wanting. Indeed, at least two of these articles—Georgia Sassen's and Carol Gilligan's—sharply critique both the male models and such research as Matina Horner's that has measured women against male norms.

A decade ago Horner's "fear of success" was the best-known feminist construct for the psychology of achieving and nonachieving females. Supported by Gilligan's new research, Sassen postulates a "constructivist" approach to data derived from young women on the subject of high educational achievement. The key concept is what Gilligan calls a "contextual" structure in which women learn to make moral and social judgments, as distinct from the "competitive" structures in which men are evidently more at home. Sassen, Gilligan, and others, like Nancy Chodorow, whose work is reviewed in the volume, refuse to acknowledge that something is wrong with women who do not behave like men. Rather, they propose several rational alternatives to that model of behavior and research design. For example, something may be "wrong" with the idea of "success" or even with the idea of competitive achievement, perhaps for men as well as for women; or there may be empirically located a strikingly different pattern of female values, thought, attitudes, judgment, and behavior—not surprisingly based on women's markedly distinct socialization, even on their distinct experience of male-centered education. And these judgments may not be "defective" versions of male constructs, but valuable on their own terms.

As Jean Baker Miller pointed out earlier in the 1970s in an effort to explain why it was that women were "Doing Good and Feeling Bad," the values women hold and use to nurture families and rear children are those without which no society can long exist. Love and caring, sharing and cooperation, especially in a world of depleted and vanishing resources, may be essential to human survival. "To think like a man" may not be a compliment once the flat stereotypes of "male" and "female" and their associated values are fleshed out by the researchers of the coming decades.

But what about the schooling of girls and boys, women and men, in the meantime? What are we teaching at the end of this decade of development? Will such interventions as "math anxiety" clinics and workshops alter the pattern of women's education and employment in the decades to come? Is co-education good for women? Should women be learning exactly what is taught to men, and in the same manner? What difference would the elimination of sex bias make? Is it possible to eliminate sex bias? Some of these questions, including the last, are discussed in the book reviews. Others are at least touched on in three essays on aspects of the curriculum and texts, as well as in the long review of "Sex Differences in Educational Attainment" by Jeremy Finn, Loretta Dulberg, and Janet Reis. The latter is chillingly repetitive in its findings, whether one considers the pattern of sex-segregated educational facilities and limited access for women, as in India and other Third World countries, or the more equitable pattern of access and allegedly coeducational facilities to be found in many communist countries

and in the United States. Indeed, as Finn, Dulberg, and Reis finally suggest, the ultimate problem may not be *access* at all, but rather *equity.* Though they do not manage to conceptualize the problem aggressively, the authors come close to suggesting that girls and boys who do sit side by side in schools hear different messages from the same lesson. "Given present educational and socioeconomic practices," the authors conclude, "equal educational results for males and females, and equal effects of education on life changes may not be possible"—anywhere in the world.

That dismal news is hardly assuaged by two of the three articles on aspects of the curriculum and texts. Myra and David Sadker's review of teacher-education textbooks reminds us of critiques a decade ago of elementary-school readers and the pervasive sex-role stereotyping (not to mention the ignorance) of such sources of information, especially on the family and employment. Mary Roth Walsh's "Rediscovery of the Need for a Feminist Medical Education" is one of the few places, in addition to Patricia Palmieri's essay review, in which we catch a glimpse of the history of women's education and of the value of women-run and women-centered institutions. The loss of women's medical colleges (there were seventeen by the last decade of the nineteenth century), as Walsh recalls, was in no sense replaceable for women students and faculty in an educational universe that called itself coeducational but was really male-centered and controlled.

Both Walsh and the Sadkers, however, offer the hope of remediation through women's studies: Walsh notes that "Women and Medicine" courses (like their counterparts, "Women and the Law") offer students the consciousness of their lost history and the harsh news of their current status, and the Sadkers announce that they are at work on a nonsexist teacher education curriculum and supplementary textbooks. This hope makes sense as a direction for the future when placed beside Marcia Westkott's "Feminist Criticism of the Social Sciences." This is an essay one would not expect to find in a collection called *Women and Education.* Perhaps one might say the same of half the book reviews, as authors comment on topics as diverse as sexism in biology and the status of women in China, or the difference between radical feminism and Marxist feminism, or the history of black women in Africa and the United States, or the *Silences* of writers. The inclusion of the smorgasbord attests to the richness of the "field." Westkott and other reviewers supply the ideological frame for the educational movement that would improve the lot of at least half the human race. Westkott's essay attempts to explicate both the goal and the process through which equity may be achieved. She provides a critique of patriarchal ideology, especially of the idea of "objectivity" and the male subterfuge of "universality," as well as an extensive justification for feminist research methodology. She takes for granted the whole development of women's studies through the decade and builds on it. Especially those engaged in educational research, in teaching social science, or who believe in its findings should read this essay.

And with regard to the volume as a whole, readers seeking access to women and education broadly understood as a "field" of women's studies will not be disappointed. Many of the essays point toward the 1980s, even as their comprehensive footnotes chart the last decade's accomplishments. As important, perhaps, is the possibility that the volume will perform its educative function so well that, a decade hence, it will appear as the first step toward the *Harvard Educational Review's* systematic and continuous coverage of feminist educational research and institutional change.

Further Resources

BOOKS

Boxer, Marilyn Jacoby. *When Women Ask the Questions: Creating Women's Studies in America.* Baltimore, Md.: The Johns Hopkins University Press, 1998.

Howe, Florence and Paul Lauter. *The Impact of Women's Studies on the Campus and the Disciplines.* Washington, D.C.: U.S. Department of Health, Education, and Welfare, 1980.

Luebke, Barbara F. and Mary Ellen Reilly. *Women's Studies Graduates: The First Generation.* New York: Teachers College Press, 1995.

PERIODICALS

McDermott, Patrice. "The Risks and Responsibilities of Feminist Academic Journals." *NWSA Journal* 6, no. 3, Fall 1994, 373–383.

Winkler, Karen J. "Women's Studies After Two Decades: Debates Over Politics, New Directions for Research." *Chronicle of Higher Education* 35, no. 5, September 28, 1988, A4–7.

WEBSITES

Feminist Press. Available online at http://www.feministpress.org (accessed May 29, 2003).

National Women Studies Association. Available online at http://www.nwsa.org/ (accessed May 29, 2003).

"An Interview on Title IX with Shirley Chisholm, Holly Knox, Leslie R. Wolfe, Cynthia G. Brown, and Mary Kaaren Jolly"

Interview

By: Editors of *Harvard Educational Review*
Date: November 1979
Source: "An Interview on Title IX with Shirley Chisholm, Holly Knox, Leslie R. Wolfe, Cynthia G. Brown, and Mary Kaaren Jolly." *Harvard Educational Review* 49, no.4, November 1979, 504–508, 519.
About the Publication: The *Harvard Educational Review* is a leading journal in the field of education. Its mission is to provide an interdisciplinary forum for discussion and debate about education's most vital issues. A quarterly publication, the HER presents opinions and research articles. ■

Introduction

Equity for women as well as for African Americans was a goal during the Civil Rights era. Title IX, instituted by the Federal Government in 1972, is part of an affirmative action program. It prohibits discrimination based on sex in elementary and secondary schools and on college and university campuses. Although it is commonly associated with equality in sports, Title IX is about much more than athletics. It "guarantees equal access for women in the academic world and in athletics."

The editors of the *Harvard Educational Review* interviewed five women who were important in women's issues and in the implementation of Title IX: Shirley Chisholm, a Democratic Congresswoman from New York; Mary Jolly, Staff Director and Counsel to the Senate Subcommittee on the Constitution; Leslie Wolfe, Director of the Women's Educational Equity Act; Cindy Brown, Principal Deputy Director for the Office for Civil Rights; and Holly Knox, Director of PEER (Project on Equal Education Rights). The women did not necessarily agree on each point that was discussed; however, they realized the role of Title IX in women's and girls' lives.

Implementation of the Title IX statute was not easy in the 1970s and still was not easy in the early twenty-first century. Implementation guidelines took three more years to write, and the five-woman panel disagree on how this process slowed down. They also discuss the role of athletics in the law and the problems that have arisen over states' rights for enforcing it. The women also discuss what lies ahead and the difficulties that remain as long as men are making the decisions for educational institutions and organizations. Monitoring, funding, and settling

Democratic Congresswoman Shirley Chisholm. **AP/WIDE WORLD PHOTOS. REPRODUCED BY PERMISSION.**

complaints are all issues that are recognized as needing attention for Title IX to be successful.

Significance

This interview is part of a special issue on Women's Studies and the progress of women's issues during the 1970s. Title IX was a major step forward for women's equity, not only on the playing field but in the classroom. The panelists point out important steps that need to be addressed before Title IX is labeled successful.

Shirley Chisholm represents a unique voice on the panel. As one of the few women in Congress, she represents her constituents and women throughout the country. Chisholm mentions the role of society in enacting and in carrying out the tasks laid out in Title IX. Without acceptance by society in general, Title IX will fail. She notes that the policy has already been "misinterpreted" as detrimental to college sports. This is an important factor in the controversy that still exists over Title IX. Most people associate it with sports, rather than with a broader base of opportunities.

Equally as important is the discussion of what was left out of Title IX. "Textbook discrimination was one of the main issues women's groups had been looking at before Title IX passed," according to Holly Knox. Textbooks

were left out of Title IX, however. HEW cited that textbooks could not be included because that would violate the first amendment. This is an issue that involves politics and censorship. Those who made the decision did not want to regulate publishers of textbooks under Title IX.

The women also discuss how final decisions were made on Title IX. While women did most of the background work for the regulation, a group of men met and made the decisions about implementation and what would be included in the final regulation. This not only violates the spirit of Title IX, but it seems to violate the very heart of the reason for it in the first place. Title IX remains controversial over 30 years later.

Primary Source

"An Interview on Title IX with Shirley Chisholm, Holly Knox, Leslie R. Wolfe, Cynthia G. Brown, and Mary Kaaren Jolly" [excerpt]

SYNOPSIS: Five leading women and the editors of the *Harvard Educational Review* discuss enforcement of Title IX and the real meaning of its regulations. Issues about scholarships for men and women and the number of teams that a school or college can field remain the most contentious.

Title IX of the Education Amendments of 1972 specifically prohibits discrimination on the basis of sex in elementary and secondary schools, colleges, and universities. It states: "No person in the United States shall, on the basis of sex, be excluded from participation in, be denied the benefits of, or be subjected to discrimination under any education program or activity receiving federal financial assistance. . . ." Conflict over the formulation and interpretation of the regulation erupted immediately after the passage of Title IX, and its statutory limits continue to be tested, increasingly in the courts, across the country. This interview explores the effects of Title IX and the controversy surrounding its implementation. Five women, each uniquely involved with the short but volatile history of Title IX, discuss its implications and potential for ensuring a more equitable educational system. The interview participants include The Honorable Shirley Chisholm, Democratic Congresswoman from New York; Mary Jolly, Staff Director and Counsel to the Senate Subcommittee on the Constitution chaired by Senator Birch Bayh; Leslie Wolfe, Director of the Women's Educational Equity Act Program, and formerly Special Assistant to the Assistant Secretary for Education, who earlier had been Deputy Director of the Women's Rights Program of the Commission on Civil Rights; Cindy Brown, Principal

Deputy Director of the Office for Civil Rights in HEW; and Holly Knox, Director of PEER, the Project on Equal Education Rights of the NOW Legal Defense and Education Fund, and former Legislative Specialist in the United States Office of Education.

Shirley Chisholm: First let's give a definition of what Title IX is all about. The purpose of Title IX is to guarantee equal access for women in the academic world and in athletics. In reality, it is part of an affirmative action program. Women have always occupied a secondary status in the United States. And in the same way that it was necessary for Blacks to get recognition by virtue of the Voting Rights Act and the Civil Rights Act—Title IX is of the same import to women. I think that while racial discrimination has been looked at as one of the social blights in our society, many of our citizens still do not believe that sexism is a problem. Consequently, the necessity for having on the record, once and for all, the fact that women must not be discriminated against on the basis of their sex, and particularly where federal funds are involved, is one of the main reasons why we felt that Title IX would be so important.

Unfortunately, there have been many misinterpretations of Title IX. This, of course, is to be expected, primarily from white men, specifically the college presidents and college coaches who descended on Washington to let everybody know what a deleterious effect the Title IX sports policy would have if it were implemented. But we have to understand that these particular persons in our society have been the beneficiaries of the status quo, and anything that poses a threat, or anything that seems to be a little disconcerting to them— propels them to get into the act and try to block progress. However, I'd like to say that it was very unfortunate that back in 1972, when the legislation was enacted, President Nixon did not enforce many pieces of progressive legislation. The regulations finally came out three years later, and here we are, still attempting to see whether or not we can get them implemented.

I personally feel that a great deal of education has to be done so that those persons in our universities and colleges who oversee our athletics programs understand the importance of Title IX. For me, the question of women's equal access to sports is especially interest-ing because of its importance to black women. The woman who happens to be black faces a double barrier and the entire sports policy, especially with respect to scholarships, is most important. As a black woman, the potential access to college education for black and other minority women is of priority value.

[Interviewer:] What would you say are now the urgent issues affecting the implementation of Title IX?

Chisholm: I think one of the major issues, of course, is the role of society. Women have been given prescribed roles from the moment of their birth; now they are moving in another direction. The tradition women were supposed to follow in that particular scheme of things runs contrary to what Title IX is all about. We talk of a dynamic, changing, moving society, and quite often it's very difficult to get people to accept change, because change is very frightening. Change is somewhat threatening.

I also think there are a great many confusions about Title IX outside of Washington. The very fact that so many college presidents and football coaches came to Washington because they perceived that something was going to be detrimental to their specific interests is a clear indication that they misinterpreted the policy. The policy really attempts to develop some type of equity. It is not a literal policy in terms of dollar for dollar; there are so many other factors that enter into the picture.

[Interviewer:] Mrs. Chisholm, what do you see as the role of the legislature now with respect to Title IX?

Chisholm: I think the role of the legislature is to monitor the implementation of Title IX. But I personally cannot see the legislative bodies implementing, enforcing, or monitoring Title IX until there is a clearcut understanding of the legislation by those who are in positions of authority and have the power to see that the policies are carried out.

Holly Knox: Shirley, as you mentioned, there's a major assault on Title IX's coverage of athletics, backed by the male college establishment. We've had some very damaging amendments introduced recently, which have been aimed at Title IX, and I'm sure there will be more. To whom in Congress can we look to lead the fight to defend women's rights under Title IX?

Chisholm: To be very truthful, we have to look to the women on the House side. I don't know to whom we look in the Senate. I think there are many senators who, on the basis of their past patterns of political behavior, have indicated a clear interest and concern with issues pertaining to women. We have to look to Senators Bayh and Kennedy—those gentlemen who have always indicated by their behavior and by their actions that they have a commitment to women's rights.

An unfortunate thing happened recently on the Hill. A few months ago many college coaches from all over the country came down and got the gentlemen's ears—they got the "old-boy" network going. It is very hard to get around that sort of thing. The women on the House side will have to be very persuasive and will have to find techniques to convice the gentlemen that this is an issue that deals with human rights and equal rights. I have found that unless we are able to convince them in two specific ways—that economically something is going to happen and that constitutionally this is a basic right—other tactics don't usually work.

We, as seventeen women in the House, find it difficult to go up against all these men especially when men have been the lobbyists, have been the male presidents, and have been the male coaches. It becomes very difficult. But we have handled the ball in the House, and although few in number, we have succeeded. It's not easy, but we accept the challenge.

[Interviewer:] What exactly is Congress's role in appropriating funds for Title IX?

Chisholm: I foresee the role of Congress as appropriating the necessary funds to carry out the intent of the Title IX regulation. Of course, we have to remember that again the Appropriations Committee and the subcommittees are headed by gentlemen—gentlemen who may or may not be sympathetic or have any empathy for women's issues. We also have a great deal of lobbying to do with the appropriate committees.

Leslie Wolfe: I feel I should interject something here as the new Director of the Women's Educational Equity Act Program. As you all know, there is a new mandate to that program, a new authorization. Any appropriation over $15 million is automatically targeted primarily to local school districts and local groups, and to institutions of higher education, to fund projects that they develop themselves to implement Title IX. If the Congress were able to appropriate more than $15 million in 1981, we could begin the process of awarding grants for local Title IX activities. That would be a kind of appropriation for Title IX that is not earmarked for Title IX enforcement. Instead, it really focuses on the need to involve the local school districts in caring about Title IX implementation. It means they will have to begin thinking about the kinds of projects they need to develop for themselves and planning specific activities related to Title IX compliance. Then we will hold out the promise of a few dollars to help them. We hope that it will be an effective mechanism for ensuring compliance with Title IX, going beyond compliance with the "letter" of the law to compliance with the "spirit" of the law.

Chisholm: I know that Secretary Califano put together a team out of the Office for Civil Rights—I have to call it a "road show" for want of a better term—to visit different campuses to talk with the presidents and coaches, to get a feeling about what was happening. This had to be done as a result of the furor that developed around Title IX, and I was wondering whether a report is ready.

Cindy Brown: I was the one whom Secretary Califano charged with leading that series of visits to a number of universities to look at how their athletic programs worked. Particularly, we looked at what steps they've taken to develop their women's athletic programs and how the proposed athletic policy, which we published in December, would actually work in practice at a number of diverse institutions. We also talked with college officials about possible revisions in that proposal.

Mary Jolly: Cindy, can we have on record the eight universities you visited?

Brown: They were Duke University, University of California at Los Angeles, Stanford University, Ohio State University, University of Richmond, Lincoln University in Missouri, Villanova University, and the University of Maryland. I don't know how familiar you are with the range of universities this list represents, but they're very different. Some are private, some are public. They offer different kinds of academic programs. They vary in size, in the nature of their athletic programs, and in how those athletic programs are funded.

Every university we visited has taken major steps in upgrading their women's athletic programs. Some have done more than others. The schools that have big, successful programs for men tend to be the ones that are making the greatest efforts in developing programs for women. And they seem committed to developing their women's programs to the same level of competition and excellence as their men's. That's not to say that, even at those schools that are doing a lot, there aren't some problems that need to be dealt with. There are problems with coaches' salaries; the basic notion of equal pay for equal work has not been universally followed in athletic programs at our universities. There are also problems in recruiting. While women's programs have been developed quickly, I'd say that the effort to recruit highly skilled women athletes has lagged behind. At some of the schools I visited there are serious problems in scholarship equity. As Mrs. Chisholm said, direct benefits to students, like scholarship aid, affect their whole educational and economic futures as well as their abilities to excel in athletics.

Chisholm: I think college presidents and a few coaches became quite perturbed over Title IX because they saw it primarily in terms of the fact that women were going to be invading their territory. They didn't even take it a step further, which is what I did with them. I said, "All right, if it's a possibility that you feel women are going to be invading your territory, you haven't even thought about black women, who also should be able to benefit from some of these scholarships. They're at the very bottom of everything, and here's an opportunity for them not only to get an education, but also to become involved in the sports program of a particular university." Many of them smiled rather sheepishly. I persuaded some of them. I don't know how effective that persuasion was, nor how long it's going to last.

Brown: I think one of the indications of discrimination in athletics is that so many women who have been able to excel have done it through their parents' help. The middle-income kids

have been able to find the resources outside the high schools and the colleges to develop their skills, whereas low-income women, often minority women, have not received that kind of assistance because their families don't have the economic means to go outside the public institutions. You can see that minority women are not present in large numbers in intercollegiate athletic programs, and that's another indication that there is discrimination in intercollegiate athletics. . . .

[Interviewer:] We've talked a lot about past problems with enforcement, now we'd like you to comment on whether things have changed. Are the obstacles still the same? Is it still bad will on the part of people in power? Or do you think different forces are operating now?

Wolfe: I think a lot of the same things are still operating and will continue to operate. I think Holly and Cindy are right that to promote the possibility of real enforcement, fund termination is the only effective sanction. There's still a great fear of change, especially in times of possible recession and inflation. As unemployment gets higher, there will be a desire to keep women somewhat limited, very similar to what happened in the fifties—you know, back to the hearth and out of the factory—because there were too many returning veterans who needed jobs. That policy was supported by a tremendous ideological and media blitz, and similar things may happen again. I think we've gone too far to stop, though. But the obstacles in terms of attitudes and consciousness will continue to exist; the economic situation makes it even more difficult. For example, we have limited slots in vocational education, and we are asking for them to be open to women, to minorities, and to handicapped persons— people who have traditionally been excluded. There's a good deal of resistance to this based on economic realities as well as on simple sexism and racism.

Brown: Technical assistance, like the Women's Educational Equity Act Program, is important to help institutions comply, but I agree with Leslie that it has to go with a strong enforcement program. WEEA is an important source of HEW funds that can help in Title IX enforcement.

Knox: As long as decisions are made at the federal level, the state level, and the local level predominantly by men, we are going to have to struggle to win equal rights for women. It will be interesting to see the effect of having a woman, a black woman, as Secretary of HEW, and whether she will be a more sympathetic ear to the cries for equal rights for women under Title IX and other issues. The last Secretary of HEW, despite his push to show better results from the Office for Civil Rights from a management point of view, has been notoriously unsympathetic to equal rights for women and has personally been, to my mind, the main obstacle at HEW for the last two-and-one-half years. ∎

Further Resources

BOOKS

Gavora, Jessica. *Tilting the Playing Field: Schools, Sports, Sex, and Title IX*. San Francisco: Encounter Books, 2002.

McCune, Shirley D. and Martha Matthews. *Complying with Title IX: The First Twelve Months*. Washington, D.C.: Dept. of Health, Education, and Welfare, 1976.

United States Commission on Civil Rights. *Enforcing Title IX: A Report of the U.S. Commission on Civil Rights*. Washington, D.C.: The Commission, 1980.

PERIODICALS

Lewis, Anne C. "Taking Women Seriously." *Phi Delta Kappan* 73, December 1991, 268–269.

Suggs, Welch. "Title IX at 30." *Chronicle of Higher Education* 48, no. 41, June 21, 2002, A38–42.

WEBSITES

Sex Discrimination. Available online at http://www.ed.gov/offices /OCR/sex.html; website home page: http://www.ed.gov (accessed May 29, 2003).

Title IX: 25 Years of Progress. Available online at http://www .ed.gov/pubs/TitleIX/; website home page: http://www.ed.gov (accessed May 29, 2003).

"The Frenetic Fanatic Phonic Backlash"

Journal article

By: Maryann Eeds-Kniep

Date: November/December 1979

Source: Eeds-Kniep, Maryann. "The Frenetic Fanatic Phonic Backlash." *Language Arts* 56, no. 8, November/December 1979, 909–911. ∎

Introduction

The debate about how to teach reading has been long and hard-fought. On one side are those who believe that teaching phonics should be the basic method for teaching young children to read. On the other side are those who believe in "whole language" teaching, or in using books to teach rather than breaking language into small bits. Maryann Eeds-Kniep finds value in both methods, depending on the situation and the student.

Eeds-Kniep's article addresses the question of how children learn language. Do they learn sounds and then words? Or do they learn whole words and recognize them as distinct units? This has been the focus of the "reading wars," as they are often called. Eeds-Kniep also mentions that it can be difficult to know what the child knows when he comes to school. What kind of training or knowledge does a child already possess? Is the child ready to learn to read, or is he already reading?

Kniep writes that "no matter what reading program we use, and sometimes in spite of them, a good majority of our children seem to be able to learn to read with little difficulty." Children rise up to meet the educational theory of the day. While publishers were adding skills lists to the basal reading series to satisfy the phonics camp, children were still reading stories. Eeds-Kniep asks whether children will read when they finally learn to read? And she asks whether instead they will become turned off to reading due to a jumble of methods that do not meet their needs.

Significance

Political discourse and educational rhetoric surround the debate about how to teach reading. The phonics supporters tend to be more conservative than the whole language proponents. At times these political associations stand in the way of how a child is taught to read.

The publishers of reading programs are invested in what is current. They conduct research and marketing analysis into what the educational community wants and will purchase. Sometimes this has nothing to do with education at all. If teachers are allowed to teach what they understand to be the best method for the students in their classrooms, then more students may learn to read. Eeds-Kniep thinks it should be the "right" of "teachers to supplement, substitute or discard a published program based on their knowledge of the children they are teaching." The power of the classroom teacher to understand the needs in their classroom is often discarded based on current educational theory. Eeds–Kniep points out the good in both teaching methods. Children should automatically recognize words that will appear over and over in reading. This basic sight word list is a necessary part of more efficient reading. Children also need to learn components or how to decode sounds and letters and then blend them into new words.

How to teach a child to read is still a controversial issue in education. Phonics instruction has once again become popular, and this concept has support both within the educational community and outside it. Worries about if and whether children read appear in the popular press and in professional publications on a regular basis. Eeds–Kniep's final thoughts about children's reading habits may be the clue to the whole problem. She writes that a reason children seem to avoid reading "may be the incredible kinds of things we have been asking children to do in the name of reading instruction."

Primary Source

"The Frenetic Fanatic Phonic Backlash" [excerpt]

> **SYNOPSIS:** Children who come to school with developed language skills are ready to read or learn to read, no matter what method is used. What happens to those children who do not have the same kind of language skills? Do they suffer if a whole language rather than a phonics method is used or vice versa? By the time the research is complete, it is too late.

Despite the almost certain disengagement of attention whenever the word *phonics* is mentioned around reading people, the great debate is far from over. Instead of calling it the "phonics versus whole word" controversy, we now have new terminology, but the division remains and appears to be widening. Even though phonics programs have become quite unfashionable among many influential reading theorists, proponents of these programs still vociferously claim that they are talking about the basic basic. Several groups still flourish around the country, touting phonics instruction as the answer to all our educational ills (and even to some of our social ones) in a simplistic fashion that often dismays and embarrasses those of us who think of ourselves as rational, reasonable reading folk. Even though we might agree with a part of what they say, the association of phonics instruction and conservatism suppresses our saying so. In some circles, mentioning that you think a code-breaking approach to beginning reading might be appropriate for some children is tantamount to supporting John Birch, corporal punishment in first grade, or the research efforts of Arthur Jensen.

We seem to be experiencing a phonics backlash, with the very same kind of simplistic and wild-eyed claims and accusations made by phonics proponents now being matched by the "whole-language" people. Each side seems to have retrenched and taken all or nothing stances—each accusing the other of deliberately trying to keep little children from learning to read. Instruction in word analysis is now being dismissed, whole word instruction in context is advocated for any and all situations, and discussion is closed off with accusations that presenting words or parts of words in isolation will surely produce students who will only "bark at words," eventually resulting in that most dreaded of all outcomes—the wordcaller. A common answer to the presentation of evidence that children who have been exposed to decoding programs can often indeed decode is "Well, sure, they can pronounce the words all right, but are they comprehending?" Somehow there's an implication that it's better not to have accomplished what for some children is a very difficult task—being able to pronounce the words.

I realize that it may be very difficult not to grow emotionally attached to a particular method of teaching or defining reading. (Some reading educators would unfortunately face financial disaster if they ever did change their minds on a major issue.) But the espousal of one way of thinking to the exclusion of all others seems particularly disturbing among those who claim that intellectual inquiry and open-minded examination of objective data is their primary reason for functioning.

Let us look at the phonics versus whole word, code-breaking versus meaning, decoding versus organization controversy one more time. In a recent publication from the Center for Applied Linguistics, Dieterich, Freeman and Griffin (1978) used the latter term to describe their perceptions of the division occurring among reading educators. According to these authors, those who espouse a decoding philosophy of reading (with decoding defined as being able to pronounce text with facility, not necessarily to extract meaning) believe that reading problems are primarily decoding problems. If a reader does not comprehend text because of difficulty in semantic and syntactic processing, these same difficulties will be evident when the same material is presented orally. If there is no difficulty in the aural processing of the material, then any reading problem must necessarily stem from interference from the decoding task. Reading instruction congruent with this view would focus on decoding skills and oral language development.

Conversely, those who support the organization view of reading (according to Dieterich, et al.) would argue that written language is not the same as oral language and that it is very possible that comprehension difficulties may arise from processing structures in text which would not arise when the same structures are presented orally. In fact, they say, many written structures may never occur in oral language. Therefore, reading instruction must include instruction in the author's organization of text.

I think this definition of the controversy focuses on a peripheral issue. Certainly it does not seem to account for the anger and vehemence expressed against each other by those who advocate phonics instruction and those who advocate instruction only in context. The issue may be better defined by examining the differing views of the decoding (or recoding) step in learning to become a proficient reader and by the way each group approaches the teaching of reading in general.

The organizational view of reading holds that proficient reading is a process of systematically predicting meaning in text and then confirming and revising predictions. These predictions are based much more on what the reader brings to the reading task in background of experience, ability to infer, and facility with processing text semantically and syntactically than on recognizing words in print. Proponents of this view have deemphasized the decoding component on the grounds that it would be impossible for a proficient reader to use letter-by-letter processing because of the speed at which such facile reading occurs. Instead, the proficient reader must sample the print just enough to test his or her predictions. Although this view seems intuitively acceptable, some rather successful challenges of its basic premises have been made. Wanat (1977) reviews Gough's (1976) argument that even for a fluent reader, reading can be a letter-by-letter process. Citing Rayner's (1975) research which indicated that the actual identification of word meanings seems to occur only for words beginning no farther than four to six letter spaces to the right of the fixation point, Gough reasoned that if the mature reader can pick up as many letter spaces to the left, then s/he should be able to pick up meaning identification information from eight-twelve (say an average of ten) letter spaces per fixation. Since the mature reader averages about four fixations per second (Geyer and Kilers 1974), the reader can pick up word meanings from forty letter spaces per second. In a minute then, the reader can pick up sixty times this number or 2400 letter spaces. If a word is estimated to contain seven letter spaces, a reading speed of approximately 340 words per minute can be arrived at by dividing seven letter spaces per word into the 2400 available letter spaces. According to Sticht and Beck (1976), the optimal rate for comprehending text has been found to be about 250 to 300 words per minute. Since 340 words per minute is a very respectable reading rate, the argument can be made that a fluent reader can and does (but probably not always) process text letter-by-letter.

On the basis of this evidence, claims that the sound-letter system is only sampled can be questioned—perhaps it *is* taken in wholly by proficient readers. Other evidence, however, such as the reality of the responses of children reported by Y. Goodman and others (see Goodman and Greene 1977) and the confirmation of our daily readings with children provide much support for the view that children do make predictions in their reading in a highly interactive kind of process—and that they often go back and correct themselves when what they have predicted doesn't make sense. K. Smith (1977) has reported that minimal cues are needed for children to be able to recognize words in context. He found that when every seventh word was omitted from passages of first through eighth grade difficulty, readers could predict the missing word seventy-four to ninety-six percent of the time when supplied with only the beginning consonant of the missing word. He cited this evidence as support for the use of combined strategies for reading text rather than depending on a decoding strategy alone, suggesting that children be taught that reading is indeed, in Smith's words, "a guessing game with corroborative data" (p. 57).

Further Resources

BOOKS

Adams, Marilyn Jager. *Beginning to Read: Thinking and Learning about Print.* Cambridge, Mass.: The MIT Press, 1994.

Chall, Jeanne S. *Learning to Read: The Great Debate; An Inquiry into the Science, Art, and Ideology of Old and New Methods of Teaching Children to Read, 1910–1965.* New York: McGraw Hill, 1967.

PERIODICALS

Schaffer, Gary L., Patricia Campbell, and Sondra Rakes. "Investigating the Status and Perceived Importance of Explicit Phonic Instruction in Elementary Classrooms." *Reading Improvement* 37, no. 3, Fall 2000, 110–118.

Krashen, Stephen D. "Whole Language and the Great Plummet of 1987–92: An Urban Legend from California." *Phi Delta Kappan* 83, no. 10, June 2002, 748–753.

WEBSITES

Teach a Child to Read: Phonics vs. Whole Language. Available online at http://www.succeedtoread.com/phonics.html (accessed May 29, 2003).

The National Right to Read Foundation. Available online at http://www.nrrf.org/index.html (accessed May 29, 2003).

"Some Characteristics of the Historically Black Colleges"

Essay

By: Robert Clayton

Date: 1979

Source: Clayton, Robert. "Some Characteristics of the Historically Black Colleges." No publisher. Available online at http://newfirstsearch.oclc.org. ERIC ED 176651. 1979. (accessed October 3, 2002).*The Educational Resource Information Center (ERIC) is a clearinghouse of papers and research on topics of interest to educators, including both published and previously unpublished material.* ∎

Introduction

Historically Black Colleges and Universities (HB-CUs) have over a 150-year history in the United States. The first colleges were opened before the Civil War by abolitionists. As the century progressed, and particularly after the Civil War, more HBCUs were founded. Many of these were affiliated with religious groups that saw the need for institutions of higher education for African Americans. When legislation calling for desegregation became law in the 1950s and 1960s, some feared that HBCUs would close. They did not. In fact, they were strengthened in the ensuing decades by support of students who selected the colleges and by the federal government programs. In 2003 there are approximately 106 Historically Black Colleges and Universities across the United States.

Robert Clayton's study provides data that proves the positive impact of HBCUs. His study outlines the differences and similarities between test scores, geographic areas, majors, and financial aid. One factor that Clayton points out is where these schools are located. A disproportionately high number are in the South because of the history of segregation. Also, many are in small towns, which can be a factor for recruiting and growth. While some students will attend a smaller college or a school near home, others may want to be in a city larger than the place where they grew up. Clayton notes several other statistics that show HBCUs are competitive with predominately white schools. HBCUs do provide opportunities for students who may not otherwise attend college because of admissions policies. They have high retention and graduation rates.

Significance

Robert Clayton and others argue that historically black colleges are still necessary. Research studies demonstrate that the colleges, though smaller, offer positive experiences for students who attend them. Clayton's study shows that the students have the same desires and

In May 1970, police fired into the women's dormitory at Jackson State College, an historically black college in Mississippi. Two students were killed and fifteen were injured. © **BETTMANN/CORBIS. REPRODUCED BY PERMISSION.**

the same needs as those at other small colleges or large public colleges and universities. He points out that the historically black college often offers an opportunity for a student who might not otherwise go to college because of admissions policies. He also provides research to show that students who attend black colleges have similar achievements and choices of majors as those students who attend other schools.

Later studies support Clayton's findings. Bohl and others found that African American students attending HBCUs and those attending predominately white insti-

Two men study in a classroom at the separatist Clark College in Atlanta, Georgia. © HULTON-DEUTSCH COLLECTION/CORBIS. REPRODUCED BY PERMISSION.

tutions were at similar levels of achievement at the end of their freshman year of college. Freeman and Thomas cite that students chose their schools for similar reasons: academic reputations. Also, all of these studies document the positive social and cultural experiences African American students have at a predominately black campus. Students of other races do select HBCUs, but not for the reasons that are typically assigned—not because they cannot go to other schools. They attend the schools because the environment is supportive or because of financial aid packages. Clayton's study was a beginning point to prove the worth and necessity of HBCUs. Other scholars, such as Charles V. Willie and Ronald R. Edmonds, were also conducting research during the 1970s and formulating studies to show the public the importance of these historical institutions. The work of these researchers and others like them has been worthwhile for the success and continuation of the schools.

Primary Source

"Some Characteristics of the Historically Black Colleges" [excerpt]

SYNOPSIS: Research shows that the achievement of students at historically black colleges does not dif-

fer significantly from those students at other institutions. Clayton provides statistics on retention, college majors, and other factors that educators debate and document.

Summary of Findings

By and large, the historically Black Colleges compare favorably with All Colleges in most facets associated with American Higher Education. Some key areas of difference and concern provide opportunities for expanding educational offerings during the coming years. These are:

1. The populations under 100,000.

2. The strange apparently opposite picture of many of these colleges being located within these towns and cities as vital economic factors and civic factors in the lives of these towns and cities.

3. The small number of Black Colleges involved in continuing education toward the terminal degree.

4. The historical life blood in education provided by Black churches from a time when their memberships were non-college trained to a present day of slightly more college trained members.

5. All of the Black Colleges identified in this study are either accredited or recognized candidates for accreditation by their regional accrediting agency.

6. These colleges do serve students who are basically Afro-American/Black.

7. The historically Black Colleges have been and still are liberal and open regarding admissions policies.

8. Tests are desired or required at the majority of Black Colleges.

9. The majority of entrants do complete their baccalaureate degree at the historically Black Colleges.

10. While Black Colleges are liberal and open in admissions policies, they tend to be conservative in relations to credit by exam, advanced placement, foreign study, and independent study opportunities.

11. Black Colleges have more ROTC programs on their campuses than other colleges.

12. Most Black Colleges have either Early Semester or Traditional Semester academic calendar.

13. Education, Business, and Social Science are the families of programs and majors for nearly

6 out of 10 students enrolled at historically Black Colleges.

Since financial aid is so important to the future of both student and institutions, it is important to observe that:

1. The average cost for tuition as well as room and board at Black Colleges is not that much different from other colleges and

2. Awarding of financial aid to accepted freshmen with judged need at Black Colleges is similar to that at other colleges.

This is a beginning in an identification of Black Colleges. For over a hundred years, most have provided an education for young people who would not have been educated. Both Black church members and Black taxpayers shared in the financial support needed by these institutions. A generation of Blacks whose educational levels were far below what they are today created the Black Colleges and forged the dream that has enabled most of today's Black leadership to be realized. A very frightening spectre hovers over the future of these colleges. Could it be that the most educated generation of Blacks will give up the legacy of an education at a Black College and prevent future generations from having that definite alternative in the pursuit of higher education in America today? Shall Black Colleges be placed on the list of endangered species? Or shall this generation rise up and provided philosophical as well as statistically relevant support for insuring that an education is available to Black students and all other students interested in pursuing an education in a multiethnic/racial context with designs to promote development from the view of the common man's hope and belief in America. With philosophical and statistical support for that ideal, Black Colleges can continue to justify their existence as key components in the vast socio-communications network which spans the technological universe ahead. They can, as only they can, provide the laboratory for developing nations and for the masses of people whose life styles are more like the environments of students at Black Colleges. This must be done. To do less is to fail. To do less is to curse unborn generations yet to have their "day in the sun." Only the future will be able to document "For when the bell tolls."

Further Resources

BOOKS

Roebuck, Julian B. And Komanduri S. Murty. *Historically Black Colleges and Universities: Their Place in American Higher Education.* Westport, Conn.: Praeger, 1993.

Willie, Charles V. and Ronald R. Edmonds, ed. *Black Colleges in America: Challenge, Development, Survival.* New York: Teachers College Press, 1978.

PERIODICALS

Bohr, Louise. "Do Black Students Learn More at Historically Black or Predominantly White Colleges?" *Journal of College Student Development* 36, no. 1, January/February 1995, 75–85.

Freeman, Kassie and Gail E. Thomas. "Black Colleges and College Choice: Characteristics of Students Who Choose HBCUs." *The Review of Higher Education* 25, no. 3, Spring 2002, 349–358.

WEBSITES

Historically Black Colleges and Universities. Available online at http://www.omhrc.gov/omh/historically%20black/index .htm; website home page: http://www.omhrc.gov (accessed May 29, 2003).

The HBCU Network. Available online at http://www.hbcunetwork .com/ (accessed May 29, 2003).

Martin Luther King Junior Elementary School Children, et al., Plaintiffs, v. Ann Arbor School District Board

Legal decision

By: District Court, Detroit, MI. Eastern District of Michigan Southern District

Date: 1979

Source: District Court, Detroit, MI. Eastern District of Michigan Southern District. *Martin Luther King Junior Elementary School Children, et. al., Plaintiffs, v. Ann Arbor School District Board,* Defendant; Memorandum Opinion and Order. Civil Action No. 7–71861. ERIC 183684.

About the Organization: Eastern District of Michigan Southern District is part of the United States Court System. District Courts are trial courts and rule on nearly all categories of federal civil and criminal cases. ■

Introduction

The case regarding teaching children who spoke black English was filed in U.S. District Court against the Ann Arbor School District in 1977. The plaintiffs in the suit were "fifteen black preschool or elementary school children residing at the Green Road Housing Project in Ann Arbor, Michigan, who previously attended, are currently attending, or will be eligible to attend the Martin Luther King, Jr., Elementary School." The lawsuit was filed by mothers and by the Student Advocacy Center, a non-profit organization in Michigan. The basic argument was that the fifteen children were being denied rights to special education, which they were entitled to because of their language barriers.

The plaintiffs contested that they and their children were being denied their rights under the law and specifically cited Title 20 of the United States Code in one section of the case. Based on Title 20, they said the children were being denied rights because of their race and economic status. There were not enough children in the school who were low income to have the programs that the children needed to learn to read and write.

The Memorandum Opinion and Order outlines what the school district must provide for the children in the lawsuit, as well as all children who speak with different dialects. The court says it is determined to stay out of the educational theory and curriculum planning process. This will be left to the experts in the district and those whom they consult. The court does make it clear that there must be a plan for the education of the teachers and of the children. The parents also must be involved in monitoring the progress of their children in learning.

Significance

The case regarding the Martin Luther King Jr. Elementary School Children was significant because the courts recognized that black English was a distinct dialect and that the Ann Arbor School District had to make accommodations for the teaching of children who spoke it. The Court's memorandum included an order for inservice training for the teachers who taught the children. This plan included helping the professional staff "appreciate and understand the features, characteristics, and background of black English dialect." It also included consulting with an expert in the field to remain up to date on the changes involved in providing reading instruction to students who spoke in dialect. In addition, the involvement of the parents who filed the suit is an important factor in the court's decision.

This case involved several factors: equal opportunity to education, stigmatization because of the language barrier, and the rights to programs that were provided at other schools. The court attempted to provide a fair settlement for the children and for the school district. The issue that could not be addressed was that of attitudes of the teachers or of those in the district responsible for curriculum. The plan that was presented in the memorandum only outlined what kind of training was to be done for the professional staff of the school. It did not mention curricular reform in the school or in the district as a whole. This is important to note when reading the decision. Experts in black English, such as Geneva Smitherman, who served as an expert witness in the trial, point out that black English has its own syntax, grammar, and history. The teachers had to recognize not only this fact, but also

the fact that the children spoke this language in their homes. The question of teaching black English appeared again in the 1990s when the Ebonics question was raised in California. As in the case in Ann Arbor, the solution involved the way educators and society view and think about language and culture.

Primary Source

Martin Luther King Junior Elementary School Children, et. al., Plaintiffs, v. Ann Arbor School District Board [excerpt]

SYNOPSIS: The plan follows the court's decision on the case filed in 1977. The case applied to one school in the Ann Arbor, Michigan Public School District.

Memorandum Opinion and Order

This court has directed the defendant School District Board to submit a proposed plan defining the exact steps to be taken, (1) to help the teachers of the plaintiff children at King School to identify children speaking "black English" and the language spoken as a home or community language, and (2) to use that knowledge in teaching such children how to read standard English.

This ruling was a result of findings that the School District Board was in violation of Title 20, United States Code, § 1703(f), which reads as follows:

> No State shall deny equal educational opportunity to an individual on account of his or her race, color, sex, or national origin, by—
>
> (f) the failure by an educational agency to take appropriate action to overcome language barriers that impede equal participation by its students in its instructional programs.

The court found:

1. That a language barrier existed between the plaintiff children and the teachers in the Martin Luther King Junior Elementary School because of the failure of the teachers to take into account the home language or dialect of the children in trying to teach them to read standard English. This was caused by the failure on the part of the defendant School Board to develop a program to assist the teachers in this respect.

2. That the dialect spoken by the children is a version of English called "black English" and is related to race.

3. That the barrier was one of the causes of the children's reading problems which they all ex-

perienced and which impeded the children's equal participation in the school's educational program.

4. That the statute enacted in 1974 by Congress directs the school system to take appropriate action to overcome the language barrier.

As a result of these findings, the School Board was directed to file a plan of "appropriate action."

The court, in its earlier opinion, was careful to point out that it was dealing only with the statutory mandate as evidenced by the law passed by Congress and was not dealing with educational policy. It said: "It is not the intention of this court to tell educators how to educate, but only to see that this defendant carries out an obligation imposed by law to help the teachers use existing knowledge as this may bear on appropriate action to overcome language barriers." (P. 41). It indicated that: "It is the intention of this court that the method of using the students' home language in teaching reading of standard English meet the test of reasonableness and rationality in light of knowledge on the subject." (P. 41). And it said: "It does not, however, seem to the court that the judicial forum is the appropriate place to make determinations of this sort [decision as to how to teach reading]. What is 'appropriate' is not what this court believes should be done in light of evidence presented in this case. The courts are not the place to test the validity of educational programs and pedagogical methods. It is not for the courts to harmonize conflicting objectives by making judgments involving issues of pedagogy." (P. 38).

Further Resources

BOOKS

Dillard, J.L. *Black English: Its History and Usage in the United States.* New York: Random House, 1972.

Martin Luther King Junior Elementary School Children v. Michigan Bd. of Ed., 463 F.Supp. 1027, 1029 (E.D.Mich. Dec 29, 1978) (NO. CIV. 7-71861)

Smitherman, Geneva. *Talkin and Testifyin: The Language of Black America.* Boston: Houghton Mifflin, 1977.

PERIODICALS

"Black English gets its Day in Court." *U.S. News & World Report* 87, July 9, 1979, 42.

Hollie, Sharroky. "Acknowledging the Language of African American Students: Instructional Strategies." *English Journal,* March 2001, 51–59.

Kossack, S. "District Court's Ruling on Nonstandard Dialects Needs Cautious Interpretation." *Phi Delta Kappan* 61, May 1980, 617–619.

WEBSITES

Martin Luther King Jr. Elementary School. Available online at http://king.aaps.k12.mi.us/ (accessed May 29, 2003).

The Read-Aloud Handbook
Handbook

By: Jim Trelease

Date: 1985

Source: Trelease, Jim. *The Read-Aloud Handbook.* New York: Penguin, 1985, 14–17.

About the Author: Jim Trelease (1941–) has written and lectured widely about the importance of reading. He was educated at the University of Massachusetts-Amherst (1963) and spent several years working as a journalist. Trelease began Reading Tree Productions in 1983. The International Reading Association honored Trelease in 1989 as one of the people who had made the biggest difference in reading in the 1980s. ∎

Introduction

Jim Trelease began his journey to discover and write about the importance of reading aloud to children as a parent of small children. Parents like Trelease have known the value of reading aloud to small children for generations. His concern grew for those children who did not have this opportunity and who had not learned how to read. As a result, he wrote and self published the first edition of *The Read-Aloud Handbook* in 1979. The first edition, published by Penguin, spent four months on the *New York Times* bestseller list.

The connections between reading aloud and reading readiness have been explored in research for the past four decades by researchers such as Jeanne Chall and Frank Smith. The increasing exposure to television, computers, and other electronic media has caused children to become a generation of passive viewers, rather than active participants. This passivity has caused children's language to develop in different ways than when we were primarily a print culture. Programs like *Sesame Street* and other educational programs help children with alphabets and learning, but they do not replace reading aloud to a child.

In his book and in his lectures, Jim Trelease points out that reading aloud is not a secret skill. There are some guidelines for reading aloud, but they involve common sense. The person reading the book must be enthusiastic about the book and the child must be interested. Some children will react differently than others. Some will listen while others will become actively involved with the text and the pictures. The child who does not react may be learning at a different pace. The important element is not to push a child to learn to read on his own before he is ready. The child will come to it naturally, especially if he is surrounded by books that are loved.

Significance

Jim Trelease writes that "when you read aloud to children you are fulfilling one of the noblest duties of cultured man." One person, whether it is a parent, teacher, or other adult, can influence a child's lifelong passion for reading. Reading aloud does not have to be complicated—it does not require expensive materials or machines. A storybook, a chair, and a child are all that are required.

Reading aloud has been the focus of many academic research studies. This research documents what Jim Trelease, a former journalist, knows. Reading aloud "works better than reading drills, expensive pre-school programs or instruction to help a child learn to read." In addition, researcher Lawrence Sipe points out that children "translate, as it were, the visual illustrations and written language to expressive spoken language." Children become engaged with the reading and internalize the story in a number of ways, including acting out scenes and becoming a character in their own version. Trelease spelled out similar ideas in his book long before some of the academic research took place.

Mem Fox, an author and teacher, advocates methods similar to Trelease. Her daughter learned to read because she had been read to and talked to from birth. Fox cites brain research that supports both authors' theories. Seventy-five percent of the child's brain is developed from being held, talked to, cuddled, and cared for. This includes reading. The more children hear language and are engaged in conversation, reading and writing, the more their language skills and brains will develop. Trelease's book is for parents, grandparents, and other adults who have contact with small children. It is not full of educational jargon. It is practical advice to help a child learn to enjoy the world of reading. The added benefits of spending time together with children are a bonus. Reading to a child is a necessity, not an option.

Primary Source

The Read-Aloud Handbook [excerpt]

> **SYNOPSIS:** At what age should a parent or grandparent start reading to a child? Jim Trelease thinks it's never too early and that it's probably never too late. Children will accept stories in their own way and at their own time. Some may squirm and wiggle, while others will sit quietly and listen. But you never know what might sink in and take hold to make a child a reader.

Children who are not spoken to by live and responsive adults will not learn to speak properly. Children who are not answered will stop asking questions. They will become incurious. And children who are not told stories and who are not read to will have few reasons for wanting to learn to read.

—Gail E. Haley, 1971 Caldecott Medal acceptance speech

"How old must the child be before you start reading to him?" That is the question I am most often asked by parents. The next most often asked question is: "When is the child too old to be read to?"

In answer to the first question, let me share an anecdote involving a junior high school English teacher who happened to be a proud new father and was assuring me that as soon as his daughter was a year old, he and his wife would start reading to her every day. "That's wonderful, Bill," I said. "But why not read to her now?"

"What?" he asked incredulously. "At six months she won't understand the words I'm reading to her." Conceding there was some truth in that, I asked him if he *talked* to his daughter. Taken aback momentarily, he said proudly, "Of course, we *talk* to her."

"Why are you talking to her?" I asked. "At six months she doesn't understand the words you're saying." He sheepishly conceded the irony in the situation: if the child is old enough to talk to, she is old enough to read to; after all, it's the same English language. Obviously, from infancy until six months of age we are concerned less with "understanding" than with "conditioning" the child to your voice and to the sight of books.

Dr. T. Berry Brazelton, chief of the child development unit of Boston Children's Hospital Medical Center, says that new parents' most critical task during these early stages is learning how to calm the child, how to bring it under control, so he or she can begin to look around and listen when you pass on information. Much the same task confronts the classroom teacher as she faces a new class each September.

The human voice is one of the most powerful tools a parent has for calming the child. At the earliest stages—there is even some evidence to suggest as early as the sixth or seventh month in the womb—a child is capable of discerning tone of voice: positive or negative, soothing or disturbing. A child's sense of hearing is so acute that when a male and female speak simultaneously to an infant only a few hours old, he will always turn toward the woman's voice. The evidence seems to point to his months of listening to the female voice while *in utero*. Thus it is easy for him to start associating certain tones of voice with comfort and security. The baby is being conditioned—his first class in learning.

In exactly the same way that the child is conditioned by a soothing tone of voice to expect calmness and security, so, too, can the child be conditioned to the sound of the reading voice. Over a period of months the child will recognize it as an unthreatening sound, one that is associated with warmth, attention, and pretty pictures, and he will gravitate naturally to that sound.

Dorothy Butler demonstrates this thesis in *Cushla and Her Books,* where the parents began reading aloud to Cushla Yeoman at 4 months of age. By 9 months the child was able to respond to the sight of certain books and convey to her parents that these were her favorites. By age 5 she had taught herself to read.

What makes Cushla's story so dramatic is the fact that she was born with chromosome damage which caused deformities of the spleen, kidney, and mouth cavity. It also produced muscle spasms—which prevented her from sleeping for more than two hours a night or holding anything in her hand until she was 3 years old—and hazy vision beyond her fingertips.

Until she was 3, the doctors diagnosed Cushla as "mentally and physically retarded" and recommended that she be institutionalized. Her parents, after seeing her early responses to books, refused; instead, they put her on a dose of fourteen read-aloud books a day. By age 5 the psychologists found her to be well above average in intelligence and a socially well-adjusted child.

If such attention and reading aloud could accomplish so much with Cushla, think how much can be achieved with children who have none or few of Cushla's handicaps.

Historical research offers the evidence of Puritan New England, where in 1765 John Adams noted that "a native American who cannot read or write is as rare an appearance as . . . a comet or an earthquake." Such verbal competence in our forefathers is attributed to the fact that the colonial child was exposed from infancy to the family's daily oral reading of the Bible.

The crucial timing of such exposure has been discovered only in recent years, most powerfully by Professor Benjamin Bloom's famous study of 1,000 children's development profiles. His findings demonstrated that 50 percent of the intelligence a child

Two children read aloud from a book. © **BUDDY MAYS/CORBIS. REPRODUCED BY PERMISSION.**

will have at maturity is already formed by age 4—at least a year before the child enters kindergarten.

The key is to *gently* match the skill with the developing interest. It is commonplace for the children of diplomats to learn easily both their parents' language and that of the country in which they are stationed—providing both tongues are introduced while the child has this voracious appetite for words. Back in the 1930s, Myrtle McGraw, a psychologist doing a study of twins, routinely taught an 11-month-old boy to roller skate as he was also learning to walk. His twin, who did not receive skates until almost a year later, experienced considerably more difficulty in learning to skate. The same concept can be applied to an early introduction of rich vocabulary and the concept of books.

Much of a child's intense mental growth during these early years can be attributed to the fact that he is at the height of his imitative powers during this period. Not only will they imitate the sounds of their home and family (and television set), but they will imitate also the actions of their parents, grandparents, and siblings. They are their first role models, their "superheroes." If the child sees these heroes reading and involved with books, experience shows us that it is very likely that he will wish to do the same.

Martin Deutsch's study "The Disadvantaged Child and the Learning Process" demonstrates what happens when the role models do not stimulate the child. In homes where conversation, questions, and reading are not encouraged, the child eventually enters school markedly short of the basic tools he will need to accomplish his tasks. He will ask fewer questions, use shorter sentences, and have both a smaller vocabulary and a shorter attention span than his more advantaged classmates.

In studying methods to reverse such verbal shortcomings among children, Harvard psychologist Jerome Kagan found intensified one-to-one attention to be especially effective. His studies indicated the advantages of reading to children and of listening attentively to their responses to the reading, but they also point to the desirability of reading to your children separately, if possible. I recognize this approach poses a problem for working mothers and fathers with more than one child. But somewhere in that seven-day week there must be time for your child to discover the specialness of you, one-on-one—even if it is only once or twice a week.

This is a good time to ask ourselves exactly why we are reading to children. Living as we do in a society that is so success-oriented, it is a common mistake for parents to associate books only with skills. "If I read to my child," reasons the parent, "he will be that much smarter and he'll eventually be way ahead of the others in school." On and on drones the achievement syndrome. The objective in reading to children is not to build "superbabies" or children who are hurried into adulthood. But just as a child's body is fed, so, too, should be his mind. When the child can name the people and things in his environment, he can begin to ask questions and express his needs and fears. The sooner the child can put his feelings into words, the more human and civilized he becomes.

Further Resources

BOOKS

Fox, Mem. *Reading Magic: Why Reading Aloud to Our Children Will Change Their Lives Forever.* New York: Harcourt, 2001.

Schulman, Janet. *The 20th Century Children's Book Treasury: Celebrated Picture Books and Stories to Read Aloud.* New York: Knopf, 1998.

PERIODICALS

Hurst, Carol Otis. "Reading With Your Child at Home." *Teaching Pre K–8* 26, no. 5, February 1996, 52.

Sipe, Lawrence R. "Talking back and taking over: Young Children's Expressive Engagement during Storybook Read-Alouds." *The Reading Teacher* 55, no. 5, February 2002, 476–483.

WEBSITES

Jim Trelease Home Page. Available online at http://www.trelease-on-reading.com/default.html (accessed May 29, 2003).

Literacy Connections: Promoting Literacy and a Love of Reading. Available online at http://www.literacyconnections.com/index.html (accessed May 29, 2003).

AUDIO AND VISUAL MEDIA

Trelease, James J. *Jim Trelease on Reading Aloud.* Springfield, Mass.: Reading Tree Productions, Revised edition. VHS, 1999.

Trelease, Jim. *Jim Trelease on Reading Aloud.* Springfield, Mass: Reading Tree Productions. 2 cassettes, 1989.

4

FASHION AND DESIGN

EUGENIA F. BELL, SONIA G. BENSON

Entries are arranged in chronological order by date of primary source. For entries with one primary source, the entry title is the same as the primary source title. Entries with more than one primary source have an overall entry title, followed by the titles of the primary sources.

Important Events in Fashion and Design, 1970–1979

1970

- According to Rosemary McMurty, vice-president of McCall Patterns, denim blue jeans are "the youth status symbol of the world."

- Young fashion is found in Army Navy surplus stores and thrift shops.

- The miniskirt continues to grow in popularity.

- The unisex T-shirt-and-jeans look becomes the uniform of choice for the college and high-school set.

- The shag haircut is the ultimate unisex hairstyle.

- The weekly haircut for men ends. Barbers complain that they are losing business as more men keep their hair long or go to salons for stylized haircuts.

- New words are: hassle, rip-off, preppie, fast-food, put down.

- American automobile producers suffer a 10 percent decline in car sales during the 1970 model year due to new fuel-efficient foreign imports.

1971

- Hot pants, very brief shorts for women, become a fashion sensation.

- Ralph Lauren premieres his first design for women: a women's version of the classic men's cotton Oxford shirt.

- All U.S. automobile producers adjust their 1971 engines to use new low-lead or leadless gasolines in an effort to reduce pollutants from new cars.

- Chinese influence is apparent in American fashion as China rejoins the international community.

- "Hair stylist" is the new term for a barber.

- Architects Robert Venturi and Denise Scott Brown publish *Learning From Las Vegas.*

- The National Organization of Minority Architects (NOMA) is founded in Detroit, Michigan by twelve African American architects.

- Trendy new vocabulary words are: gross out, right on, workaholic, think tank, and demo.

1972

- Clogs, platform sandals, and high boots are the hot new trends in women's footware.

- Men are wearing flared bell-bottom pants.

- "Glitter rock," cross-dressing, and androgyny sweep major urban areas.

- Body tattoos become popular among young women after celebrities such as Cher, Joan Baez, and Grace Slick make them hip.

- American Motors introduces a new sports car, the Levi Gremlin, that has its bucket seats covered with the popular denim fabric.

- A Japanese department-store chain woos U.S. designer Bill Blass to export his menswear. Blass is quoted as saying "It's now necessary to move [fashion] towards an international basis."

- Designed by architect Louis Kahn, the Kimbell Art Museum in Fort Worth, Texas, is completed with five long parallel galleries of exposed concrete with skylights providing a rhythmic, linear sequence and natural light to the interior.

- The "New York Five"—architects Michael Graves, Peter Eisenman, Richard Meier, John Hejduk, and Charles Gwathmey—publish a book of their innovative designs called *Five Architects.*

1973

- In the spirit of antifashion, the sleeveless tank top is a runaway hit in both men's and women's apparel.

- The fads of 1973 include: backgammon, CB radios, pet rocks, and martial arts.

- Rejecting the unisex look, Yves St. Laurent makes a decidedly feminine pantsuit high fashion for women.

- "Not being dressed to the teeth," as American designer Anne Klein puts it, becomes the first rule of fashion.

- Riding the popularity of hand-decorated jeans, Levi Strauss and Company sponsors a denim design contest that draws over ten thousand entries.

- Pioneering architectural firm Johnson and Burgee completes its first postmodern high-rise office building, the IDS Center in Minneapolis, Minnesota.

- Ralph Lauren designs the costumes for Robert Redford in the film *The Great Gatsby.*

- Interior fabrics of American cars are required by the government to meet new federal flammability standards.

- Popular 1973 automobile models bring U.S. auto manufacturers within 1 percent of realizing the "10-million-car-year."

- The American architectural firm Skidmore, Owings and Merrill completes the world's tallest building, the Sears Tower in Chicago.

- Movie hits *The Sting, The Great Gatsby,* and *Paper Moon* fuel a popular Depression-era clothing craze.

- On October 16, the Arab-dominated Organization of Petroleum Exporting Countries (OPEC) cuts the flow of oil to the United States, triggering gasoline shortages across the country.

1974

- Men turn the muscle shirt into a unique fashion statement, emphasizing the body differences between men and women.
- The bulky fisherman sweater tied with a belt becomes fall high fashion.
- The return of the curl harkens the end of the long, straight hair look for women.
- The new string bikini bathing suit becomes popular.
- In the summer the cotton espadrille sandal with rope wedge sole moves off the beach and onto city streets.
- *Architectural Forum,* one of the more avant-garde publications in the field, ceases publication with its March issue.
- In November, the Mormon Tabernacle opens in Kensington, Maryland. It is a "superb blend of church and futuristic fantasy," comments *The New York Times* critic Paul Goldberg.

1975

- Polyester and mixed-blend fabrics become popular in both men's and women's wear.
- Men's platform shoes become popular.
- Fads in 1975 include: mood rings, skateboards, and dance marathons.
- Discotheques are the hottest new dance clubs, triggering a new form-fitting, more explicitly sexy look for men and women.
- Levi Strauss, with sales of more than $1 billion in 1975, claims to be the world's largest apparel maker.

1976

- The architectural firm Johnson and Burgee completes Pennzoil Place in Houston, Texas, a project designed to prove that good architecture is economically profitable for developers.
- Designer Yves St. Laurent launches his rich-peasant look for women. With its long full skirts, drawstring blouses, and vests worn with boots, this look harkens back to America's cowboy days, with a new ethnic twist.
- Figure skater and Olympian gold medalist Dorothy Hamill is the model for a popular new hairstyle for women.
- The newest look in women's fashion is the tabard, a sandwich-board styled garment that ties under the arms and at the waist, and is worn over pants or skirts.
- Cowl neck sweaters are popular.
- In London, punk rock arrives, oriented around bands such as the Sex Pistols and the Clash; in New York City clubs such as CBGB and Max's Kansas City host the Ramones and Blondie.

1977

- Architects at I.M. Pei and Associates complete plans for Dallas City Hall in Dallas, Texas.

- The feminine look returns to women's fashion, with longer graceful skirts, printed shawls, sundresses, and more elegant evening wear making fashion headlines.
- Top fashion model Cheryl Tiegs earns one thousand dollars a day.
- Fur coats become fashionable after a seven-year absence.
- Fads in 1977 include: bottled water, mopeds, health foods, and Farah Fawcett posters.
- The need for fuel efficiency drives the auto industry to downsize its biggest cars.
- Studio 54 opens in New York City.
- Legwarmers in patterned knits and wool become popular.
- Diane Keaton, in her starring role in the film *Annie Hall,* catapults Ralph Lauren's rumpled men's look for women to high fashion.
- The film *Saturday Night Fever,* starring John Travolta, sweeps the country and leaves a new disco look in its wake.

1978

- The new Federal Energy Act requires all automobiles to attain a mileage-per-gallon average of 18 (28.8 km), leading U.S. producers to downsize their 1978 models.
- Chrysler introduces the first domestic fifth-door hatchback on the Horizon and Omni sedans to compete against Japan's Honda Civic and Germany's Volkswagen Rabbit.
- Architects Philip Johnson and John Burgee unveil their designs for the American Telephone and Telegraph (AT&T) Building in New York City and launch postmodern architecture.
- Lead singer Johnny Rotten and the punk rock group the Sex Pistols open their first and only American tour in Atlanta.
- On June 1, in Washington, D.C., President Jimmy Carter officially opens the new East Wing of the National Gallery of Art, designed by architect I.M. Pei.
- On November 29, blue jeans manufactured by Levi Strauss and Company go on sale in East Berlin. It is the first time the denim pants are available to ordinary East German consumers using East German currency.

1979

- Architects at I.M. Pei and Associates complete the John F. Kennedy Library in Boston, Massachusetts.
- In the spring, architect Michael Graves exhibits his drawings, murals, sketches, models, and photographs at the Max Protech Gallery in New York City.
- Roller disco becomes popular, and so do the satin stretch bodysuits in neon colors worn by the dancers.
- A second oil crisis grips the nation as Iranian oil is cut off by an Islamic revolution and OPEC hikes its oil prices.

Corporate Logos by Paul Rand

UPS Logo; IBM Logo

Logos

By: Paul Rand

Date: 1961, 1972

Source: Rand, Paul. UPS Logo and IBM Logo. Reproduced in *Paul Rand: A Designer's Art.* New Haven, Conn.: Yale University Press, 1985.

About the Designer: Paul Rand (1914–1996) was one of the most influential figures in American graphic design. He developed a unique American graphic style characterized by simplicity, humor, and taste. Educated at New York's Pratt Institute, the Parsons School of Design, and the Art Students League, Rand started his career as art director of *Esquire* and *Apparel Arts* (later known as *GQ*). Going on to a successful career in advertising design, Rand eventually focused solely on his highly effective identity systems for major corporations such as IBM and Westinghouse. ■

Introduction

Paul Rand is a seminal figure in the fields of advertising and graphic design. His role in creating a prestigious school of graphic design in the United States was based on his deep understanding and appreciation of European modernism. His biographer Stephen Heller summarizes that Rand "was the channel through which European modern art and design—Russian Constructivism, Dutch De Stijl and the German Bauhaus—was introduced to American commercial art."

From 1937 to 1941 Rand's professional life was devoted to media promotion and cover design for magazines. While working at *Esquire*, he designed other magazine covers in his spare time, many without pay. He felt he could be more honest in his art without the compensation factor. Rand left magazine editorial design to work as an advertising designer for the Henry Weintraub Agency. He is credited with accomplishing a raise in the level of advertising above mediocrity. Near the end of the 1940s, he published his book *Thoughts on Design* to

great acclaim, winning a global reputation as a designer. Discussing tastelessness in advertising, he observed: "Even if it is true that commonplace advertising and exhibitions of bad taste are indicative of the mental capacity of the man in the street, the opposing argument is equally valid. Bromodic advertising catering to that bad taste merely perpetuates that mediocrity and denies him one of the most easily accessible means of aesthetic development."

In 1954 Rand moved into the field for which he is best remembered—designing corporate identities and logos. Working out of his studio, he began designing trademarks, but by 1955 he had moved into the corporate identity business. In this work, he distilled the essences of modernity and simplicity for his patrons. For Rand, "commercial art" was not a practice catering to the lowest common denominator of taste, but rather a fine art. He exercised great skill in merging art with business and achieving at the top level of both fields. Among the numerous clients for which he became a consultant and/or designer were the American Broadcasting Company, IBM Corporation, United Parcel Service, and Westinghouse Electric Corporation.

In his book *A Designer's Art,* Rand wrote:

In this, the speed generation, practically any corporation, large or small, can have its "image" made to order. A vast army of image makers have made a business out of art large enough almost to rival the businesses they help to portray. Much has been touted about the virtues of corporate identity programs. Because the corporate image so often conveys the impression that it is all-encompassing, it leaves little doubt in the mind of the onlooker that the image he sees represents a company which is really in the swim; that it's the best, the first, and the most.

Rand was, no doubt, speaking with some of his most recognizable work in mind.

Significance

Paul Rand has been called the father of modern branding. His professional philosophy was that "the trademark should embody in the simplest form the essential characteristics of the product or institution being advertised." With his thoroughly modern conception of corporate identity, Rand revised the way brands are marketed and perceived, while at the same time revising the public perception of commercial arts. Many of Rand's logos are still in use, decades after he created them.

Many of Rand's commercial designs have become classics. He introduced his eight-bar IBM striped logo in 1972, using horizontal stripes to suggest "speed and dynamism." The basic design remained constant over the

Primary Source

UPS Logo

SYNOPSIS: Paul Rand's designs for the United Parcel Service and International Business Machines corporate identities are by far his most recognizable work. The logos have evolved over time without losing their original visual power. COURTESY OF UNITED PARCEL SERVICE. REPRODUCED BY PERMISSION.

Primary Source

IBM Logo
Designer Paul Rand updated his previous incarnation of the IBM logo by superimposing stripes over the three letters. The letters had been in the same typeface but were solid rather than striped. IBM IS A REGISTERED TRADEMARK OF INTERNATIONAL BUSINESS MACHINES CORPORATION.

next twenty-five years and is still one of the most recognized logotypes in the world. In 1961 Rand designed a package logo for United Parcel Service. The logo was in use for forty years before being replaced in 2003.

Further Resources

BOOKS

Heller, Steven. *Paul Rand.* London: Phaidon, 1999.

Rand, Paul. *Thoughts on Design.* New York: Van Nostrand Reinhold, 1970.

PERIODICALS

Abrams, Janet. "Paul Rand." *ID (New York, N.Y.),* September–October 1993, 44–51.

Heller, Steven. "Paul Rand" (obituary). *The New York Times,* November 28, 1996, D19.

AUDIO AND VISUAL MEDIA

Conversations with Paul Rand. PM Films. VHS. 1997.

1971 AMC Gremlin
Photograph

By: American Motors Corporation

Date: 1971

Source: AP/Wide World Photos.

About the Organization: The American Motors Corporation (AMC) was an independent car manufacturer formed by the merger of Hudson Motors and Nash-Kelvinator in 1954. The merger, with a price tag of $197,793,366, was the largest corporate merger in history at that time. AMC was in business for thirty-four years and produced a wide variety of makes and models of automobiles. It went out of business in 1987. ■

Introduction

On April 1, 1970, the first American subcompact car, the Gremlin, was introduced by AMC. The car's designer, Richard Teague, is said to have come up with his idea for the Gremlin while on a plane trip, sketching it out on the back of an airsick bag. In his design, Teague combined many of the rear-end styling features from other models. Much of the body was similar to the Hornet, but

Primary Source

1971 AMC Gremlin

SYNOPSIS: The Gremlin was produced by AMC for eight years and became one of its most successful compact cars. Popular despite its front-heavy, bulbous design, Gremlins are now collectors items. AP/WIDE WORLD PHOTOS. REPRODUCED BY PERMISSION.

the back was cut off and replaced with a sloping hatch-back, called the "kamm-back." The wheelbase was a tiny 96 inches long. The design was quite popular, although the "kamm-back" tail treatment was criticized by some. In 1970, AMC introduced two basic Gremlin models: a two-seater offered at $1,879, and a four-passenger version with a flip-up rear window, similar to the later hatchback, priced at $1,959. The notorious back seat of the four-passenger Gremlin had almost no legroom for any unlucky passengers.

Significance

AMC built about 75,000 Gremlins that first year, aiming at the market of young drivers. In 1973, AMC partnered with Levi's to add a modicum of style to the car. The partnership produced the "Levi's trim package," adorning the cars with denim/spun-nylon seat coverings, door inserts, and map storage pockets on the door panels. The Levi's touch was added with the use of orange stitching and copper rivets. A "Levi's" trademark emblem was placed on the front fenders of those cars equipped with the Levi package. In a more practical re-

vision, AMC eventually redesigned the Gremlin's tiny rear seat to allow more legroom. It remained a very small car at a low price with few extras.

In 1977, the Gremlin received its first major restyling. The front end of the car was shortened by four inches. The rear received a larger glass hatch and enlarged taillights. In its final production year, 1978, the outside of the Gremlin stayed as it had been in 1977, but the interior was given some new style features, including a simulated wood dashboard that it shared with the new AMC Concord, which had replaced the AMC Hornet that year.

According to the *Standard Catalog of American Cars,* 671,475 Gremlins were produced from 1970 through 1978, with the car's best year in 1974, when 171,128 were produced. Like many AMC models, Gremlins had a tendency to rust, especially their front fenders. With the front end heavier than the back, the handling of the Gremlin was not always smooth. Despite these drawbacks and its slightly odd shape, the little Gremlin served the needs of quite a few drivers and was a successful model for AMC.

Further Resources

BOOKS

Conde, John A. *The American Motors Family Album.* Detroit: Public Relations Dept., American Motors, 1976.

The Nike "Swoosh"

Logo

By: Caroline Davidson

Date: 1971

Source: The Nike "Swoosh." The Advertising Archive. Image no. 30521234.

About the Designer: Caroline Davidson (1952–) was a student at Portland State University in 1971 when she developed the Nike logo. She ran an independent design firm for nearly thirty years in Portand before retiring. ■

Introduction

Nike, perhaps the best known athletic shoe company in the world, was founded by Phil Knight in 1971. Before founding Nike, Knight had spent years after college and military service distributing athletic shoes to college track and field teams. Knight had run track at the University of Oregon at the end of the 1950s, and he and his coach had searched for appropriate running shoes. His interest in developing a lightweight shoe for the University of Oregon's team, along with his search for a career that would allow him to stay close to athletics, led to a trip to Japan, a contract with "Tiger" shoes there, and his subsequent founding of Nike. Knight quickly had a million-dollar business, but it didn't skyrocket until he found his logo.

The "Swoosh" logo, as it has come to be called, is a design created by Caroline Davidson in 1971. Davidson was at that time a student at Portland State University with an interest in advertising. She met Phil Knight when he was teaching accounting classes and began to work as a freelancer for Nike. Knight asked Caroline to design a logo that could be placed on the side of a new line of shoes. When she gave him the logo that will forever be associated with Nike, Knight famously paid her a mere $35 for her work.

Primary Source

The Nike "Swoosh"

SYNOPSIS: The Nike "Swoosh," as seen in this ad, was developed in 1971 and first appeared on a Nike shoe in 1972. The designer, then a college student, was initially paid only $35 for designing what became one of the most famous corporate logos in the world. THE ADVERTISING ARCHIVE LTD./NIKE. REPRODUCED BY PERMISSION.

Significance

The logo was designed to embody the spirit of Nike, the winged Greek goddess of victory. In Greek mythology, Nike presided over battlefields and was credited by warriors for their victories. Nike is represented in a simple shape, certainly not recognizable as the goddess without prior knowledge. When the "Swoosh" is inverted and placed next to an image of the wing of Nike, one can see the correlation. Without reference to Greek mythology, the shape of the icon suggests flight and motion.

The first shoe with the Nike "Swoosh" was introduced in 1972. Nike shoes became so popular that by the end of the 1970s, Phil Knight's company jumped from $10 million to $270 million in sales. The Nike "Swoosh," now applied to Nike apparel as well as shoes, is among the most recognizable corporate logos of our time, so effective that it more often than not appears without the company's name.

Further Resources

BOOKS

Andrews, David, ed. *Michael Jordan, Inc.: Corporate Sport, Media Culture, and Late Modern America.* Albany: State University of New York Press, 2001.

Goldman, Robert. *Nike Culture: The Sign of the Swoosh.* Thousand Oaks, Calif.: Sage, 1998.

PERIODICALS

Schuchardt, Read Mercer. "Swoosh!" *Utne Reader*, September–October 1998, 76–77.

Learning from Las Vegas
Nonfiction work

By: Robert Venturi, Denise Scott Brown, and Steven Izenour

Date: 1972

Source: Venturi, Robert, Denise Scott Brown, and Steven Izenour. *Learning from Las Vegas: The Forgotten Symbolism of Architectural Form.* Cambridge, Mass.: MIT Press, 1972, xi–xiii.

About the Author: Robert Venturi (1925–) has been credited with many things—notably of being one of the founders of postmodern architecture, restoring credence to both historical perspective and the pop world, and saving the world from being bored to death by modernist architectural design. He authored, or coauthored, books on the theory of architecture and he won the coveted Pritzker Prize in 1991.

Denise Scott Brown (1931–) Venturi's wife and partner in their Philadelphia architectural firm, is an architect, planner, author, and educator. Together, Scott Brown and Venturi won the National Building Museum's Vincent Scully Prize for 2002.

Steven Izenour (1941–2001), a partner in the Venturi, Scott Brown architectural firm, was also a writer and an architectural educator. ∎

Introduction

Robert Venturi was known as something of a cynic in the 1960s and 1970s. He did not follow the International style of Mies van der Rohe, nor was he particularly interested in the "organic" architecture of Frank Lloyd Wright. He is known for quipping "Less is a bore" (a parody of van der Rohe's statement "Less is more.") Early in his career, Venturi established himself as a controversial and influential writer on architecture when he took on the purism of modernists and described alternative possibilities. Relying on knowledge of past architectural styles and traditions, Venturi wrote about a new, self-critical architecture grounded in social considerations and thoughtful urban planning.

Venturi wrote *Complexity and Contradiction in Architecture* in 1966. In this book, he advocated what he called the "messy vitality" of architectural design in communities. He wrote, "We were calling for an architecture that promotes richness and ambiguity over unity and clarity, contradiction and redundancy over harmony and simplicity." Rather than one pure form of architecture, he wanted to draw from all the architectural forms available from history. He pointed to Rome, with its great mix of historic styles.

Venturi and Denise Scott Brown have been married and partners in their architecture firm since 1967. A student of Venturi and Scott Brown, Steve Izenour joined them soon after they formed their partnership, to work with the firm until his death in 2001. In 1968, Venturi, Scott Brown, and Izenour took thirteen Yale University students to Las Vegas to learn about architecture in the nation's capital of commercial culture. The resulting book project, *Learning from Las Vegas*, became one of the seminal texts in the postmodern debate.

With Las Vegas (and along with it suburbs and urban sprawl) as a learning ground for understanding the meaning of American icons, the authors explored design in America, looking particularly at the symbolism in architecture and the iconography of urban sprawl. They argued that the modernist movement, by ignoring decoration, no matter how ugly and ordinary, had missed the important symbols of modern life, washing the cultural diversity and humanity from their designs in their quest for purity.

Significance

Learning from Las Vegas uses a multitude of maps and pictures to analyze the city's teeming, man-made landscape. Accepting the city's imagery as something to

Neon signs light the Las Vegas Strip at night. © NIK WHEELER/CORBIS. REPRODUCED BY PERMISSION.

learn from, they lauded the bold, creative spirit behind the tacky commercial strips and glaring neon signs. They believed that to read and interpret the city of Las Vegas was to make an attempt to understand the culture, their fellow human beings, and American tastes. And to follow the designs of history and the tastes of the common person in architectural design was to contextualize architecture within the world, and not in theory or art, which directly conflicted with the precepts of modernism.

Primary Source

Learning from Las Vegas [excerpt]

SYNOPSIS: In this excerpt from the preface to their book, the authors summarize their goals in leading a study of Las Vegas architecture and offer a brief critique of Modernist architecture.

Passing through Las Vegas is Route 91, the archetype of the commercial strip, the phenomenon at its purest and most intense. We believe a careful documentation and analysis of its physical form is as important to architects and urbanists today as were the studies of medieval Europe and ancient Rome and Greece to earlier generations. Such a study will help to define a new type of urban form emerging in America and Europe, radically dif-

ferent from that we have known; one that we have been ill-equipped to deal with and that, from ignorance, we define today as urban sprawl. An aim of this studio will be, through open-minded and nonjudgmental investigation, to come to understand this new form and to begin to evolve techniques for its handling.

■ ■ ■

Our ideas too were met with polite skepticism, and we gathered that the Beautification Committee would continue to recommend turning the Strip into a western Champs Elysées, obscuring the signs with trees and raising the humidity level with giant fountains, and that the local planning and zoning agencies would continue to try to persuade the gasoline stations to imitate the architecture of the casinos, in the interest of architectural unity. . . .

Because we have criticized Modern architecture, it is proper here to state our intense admiration of its early period when its founders, sensitive to their own times, proclaimed the right revolution. Our argument lies mainly with the irrelevant and distorted prolongation of that old revolution today. Similarly we have no argument with the many architects today who, having discovered in practice through economic pressure that the rhetoric of architectural revolution would not work, have jettisoned it and are building straightforward buildings in line with the needs of the client and the times. Nor is this a criticism of those architects and academics who are developing new approaches to architecture through research in allied fields and in scientific methods. These too are in part a reaction to the same architecture we have criticized. We think the more directions that architecture takes at this point, the better. Ours does not exclude theirs and vice versa.

Further Resources

BOOKS

Brownlee, David B., David G. DeLong, and Kathryn B. Hiesinger. *Out of the Ordinary: Robert Venturi, Denise Scott Brown and Associates: Architecture, Urbanism, Design.* New Haven, Conn.: Yale University Press, 2001.

Venturi, Robert. *Complexity and Contradiction in Architecture,* 2nd ed. New York: Museum of Modern Art, 1977.

PERIODICALS

Sischy, Ingrid. "Venturi Scott Brown." *Interview* 31, no. 7, July 2001, 84–91.

"Venturi, Scott Brown." *Architectural Digest,* August 15, 1991, 238.

Minoru Yamasaki, designer of the World Trade Center buildings. **AP/WIDE WORLD PHOTOS. REPRODUCED BY PERMISSION.**

World Trade Center

Architectural Design

By: Minoru Yamasaki

Date: 1973

Source: Rotkin, Charles. "Aerial View of World Trade Center." 1973. Corbis. Image no. RT003704. Available online at http://pro.corbis.com (accessed July 1, 2003).

About the Architect: Minoru Yamasaki (1912–1986) was an American architect born in Seattle and educated at the University of Washington. In the late 1950s he became known for his architectural designs combining aesthetic appeal and functional efficiency. Included in his portfolio of designs in the 1950s and 1960s were the St. Louis Airport and public housing in St. Louis, the Dhahran Air Terminal in Saudi Arabia, and Century Plaza Hotel in Los Angeles. In many of these projects, he departed from the clean, angular look of traditional, modernist corporate building design, with its concrete and brick, preferring a softer and more refined, some even say sensual, look using woods and polished steel. Yamasaki will always be remembered for changing the skyline of New York City with his design of the World Trade Center. ■

Introduction

Since September 11, 2001, reference to the towers of the World Trade Center brings to everyone's mind

their terrible destruction by terrorists. The shocking and devastating destruction followed a history of massive proportions in design and construction. The towers had, in their time, been an architectural and urban planning feat—in architect Minoru Yamasaki's words, the planning of them in the 1960s was the "greatest architectural challenge of the twentieth century."

In 1966 Yamasaki was working in the architecture firm of Emery Roth and Sons when he was chosen to design the massive building. The project was immense. The World Trade Center was established by the Port of Authority of New York and the Rockefeller banking family to house international traders of every kind, bringing increased global trade to New York. Twelve million square feet of office space was to be created on a 16-acre site for less than $500 million. To make room, an entire neighborhood was demolished—164 buildings were razed and five streets were rerouted.

Yamasaki decided on two towers of 110 floors each. At 1,353 feet tall, the towers would be the highest in the world when they opened in 1973, but by 1974 they had been outdone—the completed Sears Tower in Chicago was taller. At the base of the twin towers of the World Trade Center there was to be an open plaza area, with shops and a hotel. Critics of the project were widespread

Primary Source

World Trade Center

SYNOPSIS: Though remembered now for having been destroyed in a terrorist attack, the World Trade Center's twin towers became universal symbols of New York City. They were significant not just for architectural and engineering advances but for their dominance of the New York City skyline. © CHARLES E. ROTKIN/CORBIS. REPRODUCED BY PERMISSION.

and vocal, protesting that the Trade Center project would ruin New York's skyline and change the character of Manhattan. Still, the project was approved.

Everything about the project was massive. As construction began, more than 1.2 million cubic yards of earth were excavated from the site. As many as 3,500 people worked at the building site at one time. A total of 10,000 people worked on the towers; 60 died during its construction. The World Trade Center faced major financial problems and high vacancy rates when it opened. The space was vast: the upper floors of the center had as many as 40,000 square feet of office space per floor. Some of the space was opened in 1973, before the completion of the towers in 1976.

The World Trade Center soared above the New York skyline. In time, 50,000 would people work there daily and as many as another 70,000 would visit the Center each day. The new World Trade Center was loved by some and hated by others. It was a tremendous feat of modern technology that such a building could be created at all, and some of the engineering advances that made it possible have come under close scrutiny as possibly contributing to the tragedy on September 11.

Significance

Yamasaki used the hull-core structure in the World Trade Center's design, similar to the structural system that had been used for the IBM Building in Seattle. The outer structure, a 208-foot-wide façade, was rectilinear and made of prefabricated steel lattice. Outer columns on 39-inch centers served as braces to resist wind and other forces. Thus the greatest support was on the outside of the building while the central core bore only the building's gravity loads. This was made possible by keeping the structure very light, with the wind braces in the most efficient places. There were no interior columns in the office space within the building. The building's floor was made of 33-inch-deep prefabricated steel spanning to the building's core, which braced the outer wall against some of the wind's force.

Yamasaki reflected about the project as a symbol of world peace, a poignant statement when viewed in light of the events of September 11, 2001:

I feel this way about it. World trade means world peace and consequently the World Trade Center buildings in New York . . . had a bigger purpose than just to provide room for tenants. The World Trade Center is a living symbol of man's dedication to world peace . . . beyond the compelling need to make this a monument to world peace, the World Trade Center should, because of its importance, become a representation of man's belief in humanity, his need for individual dignity, his be-

liefs in the cooperation of men, and through cooperation, his ability to find greatness.

(From Heyer, Paul. *Architects on Architecture.* New York: Walker, 1966.)

Further Resources

BOOKS

Darton, Eric. *Divided We Stand: A Biography of the World Trade Center.* New York: Basic Books, 1999.

Vergara, Camilo J. *Twin Towers Remembered.* New York: Princeton Architectural Press, 2001.

Yamasaki, Minoru. *A Life in Architecture.* New York: Weatherhill, 1979.

WEBSITES

"World Trade Center—History." Available online at http://www.GreatBuildings.com/buildings/World_Trade_Center_History.html; website home page: http://www.GreatBuildings.com/gbc.html (accessed April 14, 2003).

High Platform Shoes
Clothing style

Date: 1974

Source: High Platform Shoes. 1972. Corbis. Image no. HU015673. Available online at http://pro.corbis.com (accessed July 1, 2003). ∎

Introduction

The platform shoe probably originated in China, where it was used to keep a woman's feet out of water and mud. It was introduced to Europe around the fourteenth century, when it was called a *chopine,* which was, in effect, an overshoe that fit over a slipper, protecting it from dirt. As the fifteenth century rolled around the *chopine*'s function was less to protect than to look good, and at that time it came to look like the modern platform shoe, usually constructed with a cork- or wood-stacked sole covered by velvet. In Venice, the platform shoe signified wealth and social stature. After the 1600s, the shoe disappeared for centuries.

During the late 1930s, the platform shoe reappeared. Though shoes of the 1930s had generally been practical and modest, shoe designers of the day were becoming more adventurous. The platform shoe designed in the 1930s generally had a cork-wedged heel that was basically an elevated sole, tilting the foot like any high heel. Platforms became wildly popular in the 1930s. They were used as sandals, and cork-bottomed platforms were frequently seen at the beach.

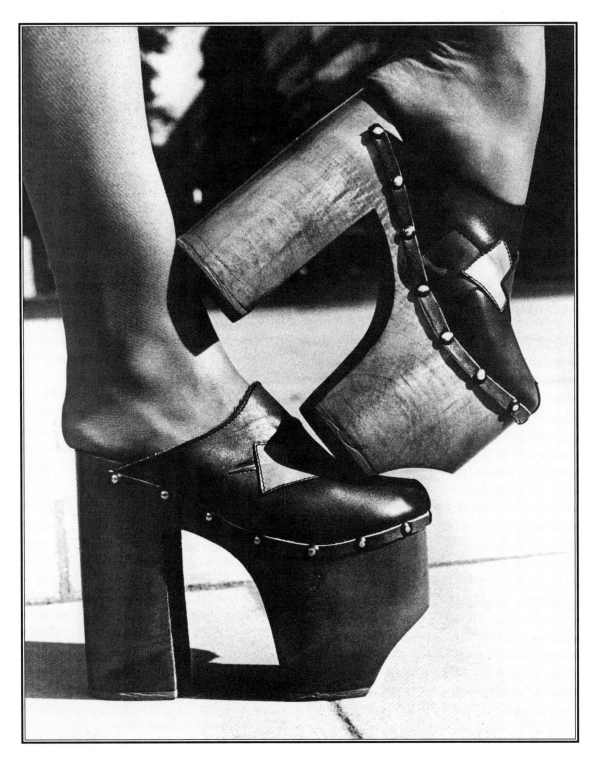

Primary Source

High Platform Shoes

SYNOPSIS: The flamboyant platform shoe has a history dating back to at least the fourteenth century, but this pair was regarded as very "hip" in 1972. Popular on men and women, it wasn't uncommon to see two- to three-inch soles and five-inch heels on the dance floor. © BETTMANN/CORBIS. REPRODUCED BY PERMISSION.

Significance

After disappearing from the fashion scene for some years, platform shoes reemerged in the 1960s. They reached the height of their popularity in the mid-1970s, and in this incarnation they were fashionable for men as well as women. The shoes were big and clunky. Most pairs had at least two-inch soles and five-inch heels. They were a vital part of the 1970s fashion trend, emphasizing the extreme, the outrageous, and the flashy. The shockingly high footwear went with an entire "look" that was perpetuated by such performers as Elton John and KISS, with their flamboyant colors, appliqués, makeup, and otherwise eye-catching costumes.

Along with the fashion statement, however, came danger. From the staggering elevations of platform shoes, it was not uncommon to fall off one's shoes. Doctors warned that the spines of the fashionable could be severely damaged by wearing platforms. Even so, platforms did not disappear from the fashion scene after the 1970s. Most shoe stores today have a good mix of rational and irrational shoes in stock, and platforms themselves come in both tame and outrageous styles in the early 2000s.

Further Resources

BOOKS

Baclawski, Karen. *The Guide to Historic Costume*. New York: Drama Book Publishers, 1995.

Jones, Mablen. *Getting It On: The Clothing of Rock n' Roll*. New York: Abbeville, 1987.

McDowell, Colin. *Shoes: Fashion and Fantasy*. New York: Rizzoli International, 1989.

"What Makes Me Tick"

Lecture

By: Philip Johnson

Date: 1975

Source: Johnson, Philip. *Philip Cortelyou Johnson: Writings*. New York: Oxford University Press, 1979, 261–265.

About the Author: Philip Johnson (1906–) was born in Cleveland, Ohio. After graduating from Harvard, he met the modernist architect Ludwig Mies van der Rohe, who profoundly influenced him. He would go on to set down the principles of modern art, along with architectural historian Henry-Russell Hitchcock, in the book *The International Style: Architecture Since 1922*. In 1941 Johnson designed a house for himself in New Canaan, Connecticut, now known simply as the Glass House; it is considered one of the finest examples of modernist architecture. In later years Johnson worked in postmodern as well as modernist approaches. ■

Two 36-story towers make up Pennzoil Place in Houston. An atrium sits between the two main buildings. © G.E. KIDDER SMITH/CORBIS. REPRODUCED BY PERMISSION.

Introduction

Johnson's early works, such as the Glass House, the Four Seasons Restaurant in the Seagram's Building, and the State Theater at Lincoln Center in New York are done in pure modernist form. In keeping with the ideals of modernism, he found that he liked working in glass office buildings. As time went on, though, he lost interest in modernism and the International style, especially when he saw many poor imitations. By the mid-1960s, Johnson had become critical of the movement he had promoted and codified.

By the time of his turning away from modernism, Johnson had become known for building huge corporate headquarters. He continued with his work, but began to combine concepts. In 1967, Johnson entered into partnership with John Burgee and began experimenting with postmodernism and even post-postmodernism. One of the most acclaimed buildings born from the partnership was the AT&T Corporate Headquarters in New York, designed in 1978. When Johnson combined classic elements

Architect Philip Johnson studies plans. © BETTMANN/CORBIS. REPRODUCED BY PERMISSION.

with modern design in this building, he pushed corporate architecture into the postmodern era. At the age of 90, he was still creating corporate buildings, including an office complex at Check Point Charlie in Berlin.

Significance

Johnson was outspoken and critical, a member of the radical right wing in politics. He was often accused of having Nazi and fascist sympathies, although he has denied this. During the 1960s and 1970s, his opinions made him unwelcome on most American campuses, but he spoke on architecture when and where he was given the floor. Johnson delivered a lecture at Columbia University in New York in 1975 that marked his return to the lecture circuit, after the political turmoil of the 1960s and the protest of American participation had ended. He uncharacteristically prepared this lecture in advance, critiquing some of his own work.

Primary Source

"What Makes Me Tick" [excerpt]

SYNOPSIS: Philip Johnson, in this 1975 lecture to Columbia University students, "What Makes Me Tick," discusses three aspects of approaching a large architectural project—the footprint, the cave, and the sculpture—illustrating these aspects in the

context of Pennzoil Place corporate headquarters in Houston, Texas, one of his great legacies.

Maybe what makes me tick is unique I don't and, but it may be of interest to know how different my tick is from ours and yours.

Whenever I start a building design, three aspects—as I might call them—act as a sort of measure, aim, discipline, hope for my work.

First, the Aspect of the Footprint—that is, how space unfolds from the moment I catch a glimpse of a building until with my feet I have approached, entered, and arrived at my goal. In a church, the aspect of the footprint is simple; the hieratic procession to the altar itself. In a home, from the automobile the footprints may lead to a seat by the fire; in an office building, from the street to the elevator door. . . . The processional for most buildings, including homes, is complex, and in different eras is differently complex. At Ur in Mesopotamia five thousand years ago, the processional was also the architecture. Three enormous staircases that ascended eighty feet without landings, from three different directions, but all visible from the approaching visitor's path. . . .

The medieval approach was a small diagonal street leading to a small square, where, facing nothing at all, usually off center in the piazza, stood the church. The bursting into the Piazza San Marco in Venice is a huge example.

The Baroque processional was symmetrical, straight, and grand; Versailles or St. Peter's, the grandest of all.

In modern times, at Taliesin West, Frank Lloyd Wright made the most intriguingly complex series of turns, twists, low tunnels, surprise views, framed landscapes, that human imagination could achieve.

In urban street and plaza design, we find the same differences of processional in different periods: the Greek, the interrupted gridiron street system, the medieval diagonal, the Baroque *allée*. . . .

Second, the Aspect of the Cave. All architecture is shelter; all great architecture is the design of space that contains, cuddles, exalts, or stimulates the persons in that space. It is the design of the cave part of a building that overrides all other design questions. Like Lao-tse's cup, it is the emptiness within that is of the essence.

There are lots of "insidenesses" to be studied besides the obvious interiors like Chartres Cathedral or the Grand Central Terminal. Nowicki once said all architecture is interior architecture—the Piazza San Marco in Venice, even the Acropolis in Athens, since walls that descend around you can hold you as securely as walls rising around you.

A plain box can hardly be an exciting cave; visit your local auto factory building. Nor does size alone count; once more visit your local auto factory. The modulation of interior space must have complexity: the side chapels of Brunelleschi's Santo Spirito, Michelangelo's transepts in St. Peter's, the spiral walks in the Guggenheim, the aisles of a hall church in the thirteenth century, the polychrome columns of Le Corbusier's High Court in Chandigarh, the scale-shifting boulders floating in the Ryōanji Garden of Kyoto, are all tricks of molding caves to excite and thrill the observer. Spaces go in and our, up and down. They overlap, they cheat or suggest, all the time enriching the architectural experience. With all these noble paradigms in mind, I still like to try my hand at caves.

The third aspect, the most difficult, is the Building as a Work of Sculpture. Architecture is usually thought of as different from sculpture and indeed not much great architecture is sculpture, Pyramids, yes; Taliesin West, no. Stonehenge, perhaps; Ver-

sailles, no; the Guggenheim Museum, maybe. The Parthenon, certainly not. (Columns and entablatures see to that.) Frank Lloyd Wright roofs, arcades, colonnades, all speak architecture, not sculpture.

In the last few years, however, it seems to me sculptural forms, not necessarily geometric, have become a mark of architecture. As we have become impoverished in our external architecture by the lack of decorative motifs our forerunners could use— steeples, pointed and unpointed arches, and the like—we have turned to other modes of expression. Since there are no structural limitations today like the lintels of Stonehenge or the Parthenon, we can warp or carve or tilt our buildings the way we will. A wonderful example comes to mind: the fantastic gouges and the slithering angles of I. M. Pei's National Gallery addition—majestic, playful, abstract sculptures. Or take Kevin Roche's nine stelae at Indianapolis (only three have been built): desert megaliths serving as an insurance company's headquarters. . . .

Let us now talk of the third aspect—Sculpture. On the outside the building has the shape of a southern Spanish white barn gone awry. The ridge beam is set diagonally to the main rectangle, suggesting many 45° and 135° angles jarringly juxtaposed.

The most successful sculpture that John Burgee and I have built is Pennzoil Place in Houston. Two trapezoidal buildings each composed, it you can imagine it, of a square plus a right triangle, that almost meet at a point in their corners, each roof sloping 45° toward each other. In plan, each building of course has a 45° point at the triangle. The ridges of the buildings, however, are also broken to slope away to a corner, giving the rather absurd impression of a twisted parrot's beak. At the base there are two courts, again with roofs that pitch 45° up a hundred feet high, tapering in plan to ten feet wide.

The work of sculpture sounds more complex than it is. Straight walls or 45° slanted walls; no roof at all. The plan is orthogonal, with occasional 45° elements. All is play of simple angular volumes. But these simple volumes meet at the all-important ten-foot slot which is the key of the design—a non-volume which makes the sculpture. The gap is visible, but only sometimes; the rest of the time it is a mystery known about, but unseen. Parenthetically, it must be admitted that the processional element of Pennzoil is really automobilistic. The parrot's beaks, the surprising lot, are best seen from the freeways that surround the city.

Further Resources

BOOKS

Fox, Stephen. *The Architecture of Philip Johnson.* Boston: Bulfinch Press, 2002.

Welch, Frank. *Philip Johnson and Texas.* Austin: University of Texas Press, 2000.

PERIODICALS

Andersen, Kurt. "Philip the Great." *Vanity Fair,* June 1993, 130–139.

Pearson, Clifford A. "Still the Bad Boy, Philip Johnson Looks Ahead at Age 95." *Architectural Record,* July 2001, 59–61.

WEBSITES

American Masters series. "Philip Johnson." Available online at http://www.pbs.org/wnet/americanmasters/database /johnson_p.html; website home page: http://www.pbs.org/ (accessed April 14, 2003).

Hunter-Gault, Charlayne. "Portrait of an Artist." Available online at http://www.pbs.org/newshour/bb/environment/john son_7-9a.html; website home page: http://www.pbs.org/ (accessed April 14, 2003).

"Everything I Know"

Lecture

By: Buckminster Fuller

Date: 1975

Source: Fuller, Buckminster. "Everything I Know." Session 4. 1975. Buckminster Fuller Institute. Available online at http://www.bfi.org (accessed April 15, 2003).

About the Author: Buckminster Fuller (1895–1982) was born in Milton, Massachusetts, and educated at Harvard University, before being expelled from the institution. During his long career, the architect, engineer, mathematician, writer, philosopher, and educator contributed an astonishing range of ideas, designs, and inventions. He is particularly remembered for his work in the areas of practical, inexpensive shelter and transportation. His international career took off after the success of his geodesic domes in the 1950s. Fuller circled the globe repeatedly, lecturing internationally until his death. ■

Introduction

To many people, Buckminster Fuller was a genius and a visionary, although his unconventional ideas and methods led others to consider him a crackpot—though a brilliant one. Among his many achievements, Fuller was awarded 25 U.S. patents; he authored 28 books; he received 47 honorary doctorates; and among the dozens of major architectural and design awards, he won the Gold Medal of the American Institute of Architects and the Gold Medal of the Royal Institute of British Architects. He is probably best known as the person who popularized the geodesic dome, a very cost efficient

structure. Fuller's Dymaxion map was the first flat map that didn't distort the size and shape of the world. Using the map, he created World Game(r), in which players strategize about the world's resources. Fuller also invented a new system of mathematics known as "synergetics." Indeed, Fuller's lifelong pursuit was to view the world as a whole and to fix its problems with every resource available to humans, particularly the rapidly advancing technology of the 1960s and 1970s. He coined the term "Comprehensive Anticipatory Design Science" to explain his attempt to anticipate and solve humanity's major problems through technology, by providing "more and more life support for everybody, with less and less resources." One of his beliefs was that hunger could be quickly eliminated from the entire world by modern know-how.

Fuller credits his lifetime of achievements to a single event when he was a young man. By the time he had reached the age of 32 he had experienced being thrown out of Harvard and many business failures. Then one of his two children died. Without money or job and terribly depressed, he was considering suicide. In a moment of revelation, he decided that his life should be devoted to helping—or perhaps "fixing"—the universe. In his words, he chose to embark on "an experiment to discover what the little, penniless, unknown individual might be able to do effectively on behalf of all humanity." His life and work became that experiment; his most controversial ideas generally proved to be workable and beneficial.

Significance

Buckminster Fuller wrote, lectured, and spread his word in the same effusive way he conducted his life. In January 1975, at the age of nearly 80, Fuller delivered a series of lectures in Philadelphia. The lecture series, which together span 42 hours, encompassed his own biography as well as the history of science and industrialization. Most of his inventions and discoveries are discussed in detail in the "Everything I Know" lectures, from the stories behind the 1927 Dymaxion car to the popularizing of the geodesic dome. The greatest thrust of the lecture series was to further explain his "Comprehensive Anticipatory Design Science" and its integration of science with social planning, further developed by his system of synergetic geometry. He promoted technology as the means to humane solutions and he urged the universal adoption of a holistic, global method of thinking. It is interesting to note that at the time of these lectures Fuller had won the most prestigious architectural awards and was highly distinguished in design, but he had not yet received a license to practice architecture. He finally received that license the year of this speech, at the age of 79.

Buckminster Fuller stands with a geodesic dome. © BETTMANN/CORBIS. REPRODUCED BY PERMISSION.

Primary Source

"Everything I Know" [excerpt]

SYNOPSIS: In 1975, when Buckminster Fuller decided to record "everything he knew" in a lecture series. It lasted 42 hours. The remarkable lecture series has only recently been transcribed. The following excerpt is from Session 4 of the series.

I think it is very, very possible to really use advanced technology only going into the war and the weaponry for the housing . . . I saw that nobody ever looked at the buildings, and they keep staying in that fortress kind of phenomena . . . this is what brought me then around to the individual homes, to the geodesic, the Dymaxion House, and later on geodesic domes and so forth. That brought me in then to the structuring, and you can understand then how I feel about getting into tensegrity how much you can do with how little. Because I really now know that it is highly feasible, I can enclose an environment, because tensegrity you remember tension has no limit length. This is very different from compressional structures, very limited in length. So all of our buildings are on a compression basis. And all of the engineering is that way, and they will not accredit tension. Yet, I found what makes my geodesic

Key Terms

GEODESIC DOME: The geodesic dome has become Fuller's trademark (even though he didn't really invent it but patented and popularized it) and his only financial success in life. The domes have proven significant and effective in two ways: Technically, they offer maximum efficiency in volume-to-weight ratio; and culturally, the domes signified a societal dream of life freed from the constraints of Western architecture.

TENSEGRITY AND LIVINGRY: Fuller invented these two terms. Tensegrity may be considered as an approach to construction that implies a reversal of perception: What appears to be solid is just a passing or transient phenomenon. Fuller noticed this reversal in the qualities of the wire wheel and then applied it to his revolutionary constructions. Livingry is often referred to as the opposite of weaponry.

domes stand up IS the tension, so I can make any span you want we can go right around the earth if we wanted to we can have a complete sphere that goes right around the earth a tensegrity sphere. If there is enough material on earth, we can make another environment control for the whole earth as far as that goes. But the point, in pure principle, is that I saw I could get into very large, beautiful, environment controls, and I can really tell you now, that I now know the technology, I know exactly the ways of environment controlling to take care of snow loads, hurricane loads, incidentally, these structures, it's incredible as far as earthquakes go they are just like bell buoys, nothing happens to them at all they're a ship, they are finite, they come back to themselves. And the buildings we build which open up, they're squares and everything, just rack apart. Nothing happens to it (the tensegrity) in a earthquake it maybe just tips over like that just like any bell buoy, any boat. So that the, I know, that it is possible to give you 300 buildings for one for given hurricane, earthquake loading, or any of the things that buildings have to do I can give you 300 buildings for one against the best known engineering strategy, with the tensegrity, spherical structures. Spheroidal, they can be caterpillars and so forth they don't have to be a pure symmetry, but the point is, I know I can give you 300 to 1. And when I do get into that, I now know that it is, not only compounding what I gave you about the energy studies we did here, I now know it is highly feasible to take care of

all humanity! The area has never really been looked into, and nobody has looked into it because they've said there is no use in really looking into it the building LIVINGRY. So it's not a matter then of the customs of yesterday at all, it's really a matter of if man is really going to survive we're going to have to use the technology we see really coming up. And if we do get somewhere now, if we get to any kind of disarmament, then what's been high priority to build the whole air-space technology is going to be released for the home front.

Further Resources

BOOKS

Sieden, Lawrence. *Buckminster Fuller's Universe: His Life and Work.* New York: Perseus, 2000.

Zung, Thomas, T.K. *Anthology for a New Millennium.* New York: St. Martin's Press, 2001.

Sears, Roebuck Ad for Polyester Pant Suit

Clothing style

By: Sears, Roebuck

Date: 1976

Source: Sears, Roebuck and Company Catalog. Fall/Winter 1976. Reproduced in Skinner, Tina. *Fashionable Clothing from the Sears Catalog: The 1970s.* Atglen, Pa.: Schiffer Publishing, 1998.

About the Organization: Sears, Roebuck and Company was established in the 1880s, when R.W. Sears, a railroad agent in Minnesota, mistakenly received a shipment of watches he did not order. He bought the watches and resold them, thereby forming the R.W. Sears Watch Company in 1886. A year later, Sears entered into a partnership with Alvah Roebuck and moved the business to Chicago. In 1893, Sears, Roebuck was formed. At that time, most Americans lived in rural areas, where shopping areas were few and far between. For decades, Sears, Roebuck sold most of its general merchandise through its famous catalogs. In the twentieth century, it began to branch out with retail stores throughout the nation, though it retained a large catalog business. The company became one of the leading retailers in the United States. In 1973, work was completed on the Sears Tower in Chicago, then the world's tallest building. ∎

Introduction

In the 1970s, Sears, Roebuck and Company was America's largest retailer. The company had begun its business through catalog-only sales, but had opened retail outlets beginning in 1925. Although its stores did a brisk business, Sears catalog sales held strong into the

Primary Source

Sears, Roebuck Ad for Polyester Pant Suit

SYNOPSIS: Sears, Roebuck offered tens of different styles of leisure suits to fill the needs of its customer base and, significantly, keep prices low. Designs suitable for the office, those that could transition to more formal evening wear, and flamboyantly designed suits are featured in this 1976 Sears catalog. LEISURE SUIT ADVERTISEMENT FROM THE SEARS CATALOG, FALL/WINTER 1976, PHOTOGRAPH, SEARS.

1970s. Some of the best catalog business was in the company's reasonably priced, popular clothing for men, women, and children. In fact, Sears, though not usually thought of as a frontrunner in fashion design, did have an important influence on what average people wore on a daily basis. Items such as leisure suits for men sold strongly through the catalog in the 1970s.

The leisure suit was developed in 1970 by designer Jerry Rosengarten. His first polyester double-knit leisure suit was a reversible navy blue/houndstooth two-piece outfit in double-knit polyester. The leisure suit soared in popularity in the mid-1970s. When actor John Travolta strutted out onto the dance floor in the film *Saturday Night Fever* (1977), clad in his clinging, but not constraining, leisure suit, the double-knit suit became a necessary part of many men's wardrobes.

Significance

The 1960s brought about a revolution in men's fashion. Until that time, most professional men were limited to conservative business suits and sport coats in varying shades of gray and dark blue for work attire. In the 1960s, men ventured into a new world of style: bold and colorful paisley shirts, flared pants, turtlenecks, jewelry, and new lines and colors previously unavailable to them. The 1970s followed up on the styles of the 1960s with some new twists, like the leisure suit.

Today, the polyester leisure suit is much maligned as one of the tacky fashions of the disco years. At the time, it no doubt filled a need for many men. It was an easy-to-care-for suit, as appropriate in one social or professional environment as it was in another. For many it had become a staple outfit by the mid-1970s. There were some variations of the leisure suit. It often consisted of a two-piece jacket and pant set, but sometimes leisure suits came in wild colors, or with wide lapels or flared-leg pants.

The technology in the fabric industry of the 1960s increased mass-produced clothing, including the leisure suit of the 1970s. This kept the prices fairly low. And the relaxed look and feel of the slightly stretchy, no-belt suit, fit 1970s lifestyles, particularly with the new dress-down Fridays at work. Above all, while this suit was appropriate for work, it transitioned easily into the evening, disco-dancing hours.

Further Resources

BOOKS

Emmet, Boris. *Catalogues and Counters: A History of Sears, Roebuck and Company.* Chicago: University of Chicago Press, 1950.

Sears, Roebuck. *The Story of Sears, Roebuck and Co.* New York: Fairchild Publications, 1961.

PERIODICALS

Read, Nat B. "Look Who's One Hundred Years Old in 1986!" *Good Housekeeping,* July 1986, 54.

Sears Tower
Architectural Design

By: Skidmore, Owings and Merrill

Date: 1976

Source: Sailors, David. "Sears Tower in Chicago." 2002. Corbis. Image no. NT2168436. Available online at http://pro.corbis.com (accessed July 1, 2003).

About the Organization: Skidmore, Owings and Merrill (SOM), an architectural design firm, was founded in Chicago in 1936. By the early 1970s, it was one of the largest architectural firms in the United States and a leader in designing skyscrapers and corporate centers. With offices in New York and Chicago, SOM was responsible for many massive projects in both cities. ■

Introduction

In the late 1960s, Sears, Roebuck and Company had become the world's largest retailer, with nearly $9 billion in sales and 13,000 employees. When the company decided to move its administrative operations to downtown Chicago, it clearly needed a very large headquarters building. The company determined that it would need at least 3 million square feet of office space. Real estate developers who had become involved in the project encouraged Sears to create a landmark presence in Chicago with a tall tower that included upper floors to be rented out to other tenants as office space.

SOM architect Bruce Graham and architectural engineer Fazlur Kahn were the designated architects of the Sears Tower. Kahn had recently designed the structure of the John Hancock Center in Chicago, and would use the same frame-tube system to structure the Sears Tower that had been used in the Hancock. The plans that soon developed were for a 4.5-million-square-foot, 110-story structure. The "bundled tube" structure was to be sheathed in anodized aluminum. With the frame-tube system, the building would gain most of its structural support from a network of beams and columns in the outer walls; this is considered one of the most efficient systems to brace against wind while allowing for height. In the Sears Tower there are nine independent tube systems worked together in one building, with fewer and fewer tubes at higher levels. This reduces the wind forces on the building and also gives it a unique shape.

Primary Source

Sears Tower

SYNOPSIS: The Sears Tower in Chicago, though no longer the world's tallest building, still contains the highest occupied floor of a building. Its innovative "tube" structural design was developed by engineer Fazlur Kahn and is still a significant element in building design today. © BETTMANN/ CORBIS. REPRODUCED BY PERMISSION.

Significance

In 1974, the Sears Tower in Chicago became the world's tallest building, surpassing the World Trade Center, which was still under construction. The Sears Tower remained the world's tallest building until 1998, when the Cesar Pelli–designed Petronas Towers in Malaysia surpassed the Sears Tower's height by a mere 33 feet. The efficient structural design of the Sears Tower set a new standard for skyscrapers. It had used about one-third less structural steel than previous skyscrapers. Aesthetically, too, its structure led to new design possibilities, since the taller towers could depart from the box form. Tube units could take on a variety of forms and shapes and still provide spacious and open floors.

Further Resources

BOOKS

Doherty, Craig A. *The Sears Tower.* Woodbridge, Conn.: Blackbirch Press, 1995.

Willis, Carol. *Form Follows Finance: Skyscrapers and Skylines in New York and Chicago.* New York: Princeton Architectural Press, 1996.

PERIODICALS

"Chicago." *Architectural Forum,* January–February 1974.

Green, Lee. "Beneath Their Skin Skyscrapers Fight Wind." *Popular Mechanics,* July 1986, 146.

Schwarz, Frederic D. "The Tallest Building." *American Heritage,* May–June 1998, 111.

Still from *Annie Hall*

Movie still

By: Woody Allen

Date: 1977

Source: "Woody Allen and Diane Keaton." 1978. Corbis. Image no. U1926151. Available online at http://pro.corbis.com (accessed July 1, 2003).

About the Artist: Woody Allen (1935–) was born Allen Konigsberg in Brooklyn, New York. When he was sixteen, he failed a college course in filmmaking, so he wrote for radio and television, eventually getting a staff position with Sid Caesar's cast. He also tried standup comedy. His film career began in 1964 when he wrote and acted in *What's New, Pussycat?* He made his directorial debut in 1969 with *Take the Money and Run.* His breakthrough film was the Academy Award–winning *Annie Hall* (1977). ■

Introduction

In Woody Allen's 1977 film *Annie Hall,* Annie, played by Diane Keaton, is a budding Midwestern singer, and Alvy, played by Allen, is a Brooklyn comic. They meet in Manhattan and begin a romantic relationship. Annie matures because of Alvy's attentions, and, by the end of the film, chooses southern California over New York. *Annie Hall* won four Oscars, including one for Keaton's Annie. Keaton's look in the film became a fashion sensation. Her clothes had a thrown-together look with oddly matched, but very fun and quirky

Primary Source

Still from *Annie Hall*

SYNOPSIS: Annie Hall's thrown-together androgynous look inspired a whole new attitude toward women's fashion, one that placed more importance on how a woman interpreted her personality through her clothes and less on the importance of the clothes' designer. © BETTMANN/CORBIS. REPRODUCED BY PERMISSION.

combinations: men's suit coats and ties, baggy trousers with suspenders, and fedora hats. Women wanted to look like Annie Hall. A chain of "Annie Look" boutiques sprouted up in Britain, but the Annie Hall Look had more to do with artfully collecting accessories and clothing at thrift stores than paying for a particular style. It was the quirkiness, an expression of individual tastes, that caught people's attention. The Annie Hall look perfectly suited America's relaxed attitude toward fashion in the 1970s.

Significance

Diane Keaton's wardrobe as Annie Hall—her wide ties, masculine shirts, wide-leg pants, vests, and hats— convinced many women that wearing menswear could be glamourous. The androgynous look had taken other forms in the earlier part of the decade; *Annie Hall* brought it more to the mainstream.

In the 1970s, fashion in New York City was going in many directions. In keeping with the film *Annie Hall*, designers there were creating clothes with the high style yet low-key urban look that dominated the New York streets in the decade. Well-selected and coordinated thrift store clothing could make as strong a fashion statement as designer clothes, and women in the city did not want to have style dictated to them. In the film, Annie Hall loses the look after she moves to California, where she wears fluffy peasant skirts. The look belonged to the East Coast and to the city.

Further Resources

BOOKS

Benaim, Laurence. *Trousers.* London: Vilo Publishing, 2001.

Milbank, Caroline Rennolds. *New York Fashion.* New York: Abrams, 1989.

PERIODICALS

Allen, Woody. "Annie Hall." *Newsweek,* June 28, 1999, 65.

Collins, Nancy. "Annie Hall Doesn't Live Here Anymore." *Vanity Fair,* November 1995, 92.

Evening Ensemble
Clothing style

By: Norma Kamali

Date: 1977

Source: *Evening Ensemble.* The Costume Institute, The Metropolitan Museum of Art. Available online at http://www.metmuseum.org/collections/ (July 1, 2003).

About the Designer: Designer Norma Kamali (1945–), a native of New York, was educated at the Fashion Institute of Technology, graduating with a bachelor of fine arts degree in 1964. She opened her first boutique on East 53rd Street in New York in 1968. In a long and ongoing career, she has designed inventive clothing as well as accessories and fragrances, winning numerous awards for her achievements. In 2002, she was inducted to the Fashion Walk of Fame in New York. ■

Primary Source

Evening Ensemble

SYNOPSIS: This Norma Kamali dress is in the permanent collection of the Metropolitan Museum of Art's Costume Institute. It is known as a parachute dress, as it was made from silk manufactured for parachutes. Experimentation with fabrics and shapes is a hallmark of Kamali's designs. THE METROPOLITAN MUSEUM OF ART, GIFT OF EDDIE KAMALI, 1978. (1978.163.1AB-.2AB) PHOTOGRAPH © 1995 THE METROPOLITAN MUSEUM OF ART.

Introduction

Norma Kamali had received minor notoriety with her boutique on East 53rd prior to introducing her line of parachute clothing in 1974, but the new line of clothing put her into the forefront of the fashion scene. The dresses were made from silk Kamali had purchased from parachute manufacturers. With its unique finish, the parachute silk challenged her to create elegant and inventive designs. Kamali championed material informality while challenging notions of stylistic acceptability. Many of her parachute dresses for evening wear were based on eighteenth- and nineteenth-century shapes.

Significance

Kamali designed her famous sleeping bag coat in 1975 (still in production over 25 years later) and her "pull bikini" in 1977. She enjoyed numerous successes with her unusual designs, which had a profound effect on women's fashion of the 1970s. In 1977, influential fashion editor Diana Vreeland included Kamali's designs in an exhibit at the Metropolitan Museum of Art. Kamali has become increasingly popular and accepted in the world of high fashion through the years. She has introduced a wide variety of new products and opened stores worldwide. Kamali's influence in using unorthodox materials can be seen in the work of the many designers who have imitated her.

Further Resources

BOOKS

Milbank, Caroline. *New York Fashion: The Evolution of American Fashion.* New York: Abrams, 1989.

Mulvagh, Jane. *Vogue History of Twentieth Century Fashion.* New York: Viking, 1988.

PERIODICALS

Donovan, Carrie. "The Americans Who Lead." *New York Times Magazine,* June 28, 1987, 48–53.

Soorikian, Anne. "Kamali: Fashion's Freshest Face." *McCall's,* January 1983, 66.

Sony Walkman Advertisement

Advertisement

By: Sony Corporation

Date: 1978

Source: Sony Walkman Advertisement. The Advertising Archive Image no. 30506755.

About the Organization: In 1946 a group of engineers formed the Tokyo Telecommunications Engineering Corporation. The group had worked in Japan during World War II developing military equipment. The company would be re-named Sony and over the next half century, it would become a world leader in the development of electronic equipment, including such household items as transistor radios, tape recorders, televisions, and computers. ∎

Introduction

In 1978, legend has it that Sony president Akio Morita decided he would like to listen to his own selections of music while flying on airplanes. He brought the idea to the company, and soon, the simple, hand-sized cassette player with lightweight headphones was out on the market. Another story credits the tape recorder division with the invention. Faced with the dreaded corporate reorganization if they didn't find a new product, the tape recorder division came up with the small cassette player capable of stereo playback by tweaking some of their existing products. Morita learned of their invention and supported it.

Whatever its origins, Sony put together a strong marketing campaign for their new product, beginning with its name. Stereo Walky, Sound About, and Stow Away were considered before the Walkman name was decided. Sony decided to target the younger market with this product. It began sending its product to movie and rock stars, so that young people would see that the product was hip.

The Walkman took off almost instantly. Released from the burden of heavy boom boxes and the static of transistor radios, people flocked to the portable cassette player. It became commonplace to see people listening to music while they walked, worked out, and traveled. Personal electronics had become an industry. The first Walkman was expensive, retailing at nearly $200. It was by today's standards quite primitive, offering as controls only play, stop, rewind, and volume. People still wanted to buy it, first in Japan, and then around the world.

Significance

By the 1980s, there was a huge $1.3 billion market for personal tape players. Although other audio companies had introduced their own personal stereos, Sony retained its dominance in the market, with 30 percent of worldwide sales. The company continued on its inventive marketing campaign, making more than a hundred Walkman models to suit almost every taste and budget. When compact disc sales rose, Sony quickly made models for CD use. The product name, Walkman, is generally the word people use when they refer to personal stereos of any kind, and the word can now be found in most dictionaries, signifying the dominance of the Sony brand and its impact on the culture.

Further Resources

BOOKS

Du Gay, Paul. *Doing Cultural Studies: The Story of the Sony Walkman.* London: Sage, 1997.

Primary Source

Sony Walkman Advertisement

SYNOPSIS: When first introduced in Great Britain the Sony Walkman was known as the Stowaway, as seen in this advertisement. Introduced in 1978, the Walkman had an enormous impact on the way music was consumed. It gave people the ability to listen to a personal stereo in public for the first time, and greatly boosted the popularity of cassette tapes. THE ADVERTISING ARCHIVE LTD./SONY. REPRODUCED BY PERMISSION.

5

GOVERNMENT AND POLITICS

TIMOTHY G. BORDEN

Entries are arranged in chronological order by date of primary source. For entries with one primary source, the entry title is the same as the primary source title. Entries with more than one primary source have an overall entry title, followed by the titles of the primary sources.

Important Events in Government and Politics, 1970–1979

1970

- On January 19, Federal Judge G. Harrold Carswell is nominated to the Supreme Court. Citing his weak civil rights record, the Senate will reject the nomination.

- On February 18, the antiwar radicals known as the Chicago Seven are acquitted of conspiracy to incite riots during the 1968 Democratic National Convention.

- On May 4, members of the National Guard kill four students during an antiwar protest at Kent State University in Ohio.

- On June 15, in *Welsh v. United States* the Supreme Court rules that the claim of conscientious-objector status can be argued on the basis of moral objection to war, rather than long-standing religious belief alone.

- On September 22, President Nixon signs a bill authorizing a nonvoting congressional representative to the House of Representatives for the District of Columbia. No District of Columbia representative had sat in the House since 1875.

- On October 15, promising "total war against organized crime," President Nixon signs the Organized Crime Control Act.

- On December 2, the Environmental Protection Agency (EPA) begins operations. William D. Ruckelshaus is the first director.

- On December 29, President Nixon signs the Occupational Safety and Health Administration act giving the Secretary of Labor the power to establish safety standards for factories, farms, and construction sites.

1971

- On January 2, House Speaker John McCormack retires after forty-two years in office.

- On March 1, a radical activist group, the Weathermen, explode a bomb in a restroom of the U.S. Capitol. No one is injured, but the bomb causes three hundred thousand dollars in damages.

- On March 29, First Lt. William Calley is found guilty of murder in the 1968 massacre of Vietnamese civilians at My Lai.

- On April 7, Chicago Mayor Richard Daley wins his re-election to his fifth term in office.

- On April 24, two hundred thousand antiwar demonstrators march from the White House to the Capitol urging Congress to end American military intervention in Indochina.

- On June 10, President Nixon ends the trade embargo with China by allowing limited exports.

- On June 13, *The New York Times* begins publication of the secret Defense Department study of the Vietnam War known as the Pentagon Papers.

- On June 30, the United States Supreme Court sustains the right of *The New York Times* to publish the Pentagon Papers.

- Ratified by thirty-eight states, the Twenty-sixth Amendment to the Constitution, lowering the voting age from twenty-one to eighteen, goes into effect.

- On July 17, the White House organizes the infamous "plumbers unit," which investigates Daniel Ellsberg, the former Defense Department official who made the Pentagon Papers public. Over Labor Day weekend they illegally break into the office of Ellsberg's psychiatrist in an attempt to find information with which to ruin Ellsberg's reputation. They find none.

- On August 15, President Nixon implements wage-and-price freezes and takes American currency off the gold standard.

- On December 18, President Nixon signs into law the second largest military appropriation bill, $70.5 billion, in the country's history.

1972

- On January 5, President Nixon announces a six-year, $5.5 billion spaceshuttle program.

- On February 14, President Nixon announces that he will take steps to limit the scope of court-ordered busing.

- On February 15, United States Attorney General John Mitchell resigns from office in order to take over President Nixon's reelection campaign.

- On March 22, the Twenty-seventh Amendment to the United States Constitution, prohibiting discrimination on the basis of gender, is passed by Congress and sent to the states for ratification. By the end of 1972, twenty-two of the necessary thirty-eight states have ratified the amendment, also known as the Equal Rights Amendment.

- On March 22, the National Commission on Marijuana and Drug Abuse recommends that private possession and use of marijuana not be penalized.

- On April 7, the Federal Election Campaign Act goes into effect. The law sets limits and requires disclosures on personal contributions to political candidates.

- On May 15, Democratic presidential candidate George C. Wallace, governor of Alabama, is shot while campaigning in Laurel, Maryland. Wallace survives the assassination attempt but is left paralyzed from the waist down.

- On June 17, five men are arrested for breaking into the Democratic National Committee headquarters at the Watergate office complex in Washington, D.C.

- On June 19, the FBI announces that it will investigate the Watergate break-in.

- On June 19, the United States Supreme Court rules that the Justice Department's claim of inherent power to wiretap without warrant is not a reasonable extension of the president's national-security authority.

- On June 23, President Nixon signs the higher education-desegregation act providing federal money to universities and federal assistance to students.

- On July 1, John Mitchell, chairman of the Committee to Reelect the President, resigns, citing family problems.

- On July 12, the Democratic National Convention nominates Senator George McGovern of South Dakota for President. Two days later, Senator Thomas F. Eagleton of Missouri is nominated for Vice president.

- On July 31, following revelations that he had been hospitalized for depression, Senator Eagleton quits the Democratic ticket. He is replaced by former Peace Corps head Sergeant Shriver.

- On August 4, the ultra-conservative American Party nominates John Schmitz of California for President.

- On August 22, the Republican National Convention renominates President Nixon on a vote of 1,347-1 and Spiro Agnew for Vice president. The sole opposing vote is tallied for NBC Television analyst David Brinkley.

- On August 29, President Nixon announces that no administration officials were involved in the Watergate burglary.

- On September 15, a federal grand jury indicts former White House aides G. Gordon Liddy and E. Howard Hunt, along with the five original burglars, in the Watergate break-in case.

- On September 29, the Washington Post reveals that former Attorney General John Mitchell controls a secret Republican slush fund to finance dirty tricks against Democrats.

- On October 10, the Washington Post reports that the Watergate break-in was part of a larger espionage plan by the Nixon reelection committee to sabotage Democrats.

- On October 18, Congress overrides President Nixon's veto of a $25 billion water-pollution control measure.

- On October 25, the Washington Post reports that President Nixon's Chief-of-Staff H.R. Haldeman approved of payments from the slush fund used to politically discredit Democrats.

- On November 7, Richard Nixon defeats Senator McGovern for the presidency by 17,409,550 votes. McGovern wins electoral-college victories only in ultra-liberal Massachusetts and the District of Columbia. The Democrats nonetheless retain their majorities in both houses of Congress.

- From November 27 to November 30, President Nixon restructures his cabinet. Elliot Richardson replaces Melvin Laird as secretary of defense; Caspar Weinberger replaces Richardson as secretary of health, education, and welfare (HEW); James T. Lynn replaces George Romney as secretary of housing and urban development (HUD); and Peter J. Brennan is nominated to be secretary of labor.

- On December 12, Ronald Ziegler, President Nixon's Press Secretary, confirms the existence of the White House operation known as the plumbers, but denies that E. Howard Hunt was part of the operation.

- On December 26, former President Harry S. Truman, age eighty-eight, dies in Kansas City, Missouri.

1973

- On January 2, the Democratic Caucus of the House of Representatives votes 154-75 to cut off funds for the Vietnam War. Two days later, the Senate Democratic Caucus votes 36-12 to cut off funds for the war.

- On January 11, the Senate Democratic Caucus votes unanimously to establish a special committee to investigate the Watergate affair; Senator Sam Ervin (D-NC) chairs the committee.

- On January 11, the Justice Department charges President Nixon's reelection committee with eight criminal violations of the election-financing law enacted on April 7, 1972.

- On January 22, former President Lyndon B. Johnson dies of a heart attack at his ranch in Johnson City, Texas.

- On January 22, the United States Supreme Court, in *Roe v. Wade*, rules that a woman's right to an abortion falls within her right to privacy.

- On January 23, President Nixon announces that a peace settlement has been reached on Vietnam. The settlement leaves the North Vietnamese military in place in South Vietnam; retains the non-Communist government of Nguyen Van Thieu in the south; requires the United States to withdraw all forces and dismantle all installations within sixty days; demands the North Vietnamese release all American prisoners of war (POWs) within sixty days; and establishes a framework for the peaceful reunification of North and South Vietnam.

- On January 30, former Nixon campaign members James W. McCord and G. Gordon Liddy are convicted of breaking into and illegally wiretapping the Democratic party headquarters at the Watergate office complex.

- On February 28, about two hundred members of the American Indian Movement (AIM) exchange gunfire with federal agents in Wounded Knee, South Dakota. A confrontation between AIM and the government continues until May 8.

- On March 30, White House Press Secretary Ziegler states that no one in the administration had prior knowledge of the Watergate break-in and promises that the White House will not cover up or withhold any information on the matter.

- On April 30, in the wake of the Watergate scandal H. R. Haldeman, White House chief of staff; John Ehrlichman, domestic policy assistant; John Dean, presidential counsel; and Richard Kleindienst, attorney general, all resign their offices. In a televised address President Nixon denies any involvement in the Watergate break-in or cover-up. Secretary of Defense Richardson becomes attorney general. James Schlesinger becomes secretary of defense. William E. Colby succeeds Schlesinger as director of the CIA.

- On May 17, the Senate Select Committee on Presidential Campaign Activities, led by Senator Ervin, convenes public hearings to investigate the Watergate affair and other illegal activities conducted by the Committee to Reelect the President.

- On May 25, Harvard Law School professor Archibald Cox is sworn in as Watergate special prosecutor.

- On May 29, Los Angeles elects its first African American mayor, fifty-five-year-old City Councilman Thomas Bradley.

- On June 13, President Nixon orders a sixty-day freeze on consumer prices to check inflation.

- From June 25 to June 29, former White House counsel Dean testifies before the Ervin committee, implicating himself, Haldeman, Ehrlichman, Mitchell, President Nixon, and others in the Watergate cover-up. Dean also reveals the existence of the so-called enemies list—a roster of prominent Americans and celebrities considered by the White House as administration opponents and targeted for possible harassment.

- On July 13, during congressional testimony former White House aide Alexander Butterfield reveals the existence of taped conversations secretly recorded at the White House.

- On July 22, since January 1973, President Nixon's public support has plummeted from 60 percent to 40 percent.

- On July 26, after the Ervin committee, Federal Judge John J. Sirica, and Special Prosecutor Cox subpoena these tapes, the Nixon administration refuses to release them, throwing the issue to the courts.

- On July 31, Rep. Robert F. Drinan (D-Mass.) introduces a resolution calling for Nixon's impeachment on four grounds: the bombing of Cambodia; the taping of conversations; the refusal to spend impounded funds; and the establishment of a "supersecret security force within the White House."

- On August 6, Vice President Spiro Agnew reveals that he is under investigation for receiving kickbacks while serving as Baltimore County executive and governor of Maryland. He denies the charges as "false and scurrilous and malicious."

- On October 10, Vice President Agnew resigns from office pleads nolo contendere (no contest) to income-tax evasion in return for the dropping of other criminal charges. He receives a three-year suspended sentence and a ten-thousand-dollar fine.

- On October 12, President Nixon nominates United States House of Representative Gerald Ford (R-Mich.) for Vice president.

- On October 20, after Special Prosecutor Cox reproves the White House for noncompliance in the Watergate investigation, Nixon orders him fired. When both Attorney General Richardson and Deputy Attorney General Ruckelshaus refuse, Nixon dismisses them. Solicitor General Robert Bork finally fires Cox and dismisses Cox's staff of sixty attorneys, who had been investigating Watergate for over five months. Over 250,000 telegrams denounce what comes to be known as the "Saturday Night Massacre."

- On October 23, eight resolutions sponsored by thirty-one Democrats to impeach Nixon are introduced in the House of Representatives even as Nixon begins to comply with subpoenas and turns over some of the Watergate tapes to federal Judge Sirica.

- On October 26, President Nixon blames the media of grossly distorting the facts of the Watergate controversy.

- On October 31, the White House announces that two of the nine subpoenaed Watergate tapes are missing.

- On November 1, Leon A. Jaworski replaces Cox as Watergate special prosecutor. William Saxbe replaces Richardson as attorney general.

- On November 7, over Nixon's veto Congress passes the War Powers Act, requiring congressional approval for any commitment of U.S. forces abroad longer than sixty days.

- On November 16, President Nixon signs an act authorizing the Alaska pipeline.

- On November 21, the White House reveals the existence of a mysterious 18.5-minute gap in a key Watergate tape.

- On November 21, Nixon's personal secretary, Rose Mary Woods, testifies that she accidentally caused five minutes of the erasure; a panel of experts later concludes that the gap was deliberately created.

- On December 6, Gerald Ford is sworn in as vice president.

- On December 8, responding to charges of financial improprieties, President Nixon releases his income-tax returns and agrees to an Internal Revenue Service audit. The audit reveals that Nixon owes $432,787.13 in back taxes.

1974

- On January 2, President Nixon signs into law a bill that requires states to lower speed limits to 55 mph in order to receive federal highway funds. The bill is designed to help conserve energy.

- On February 6, the House of Representatives on a vote of 410-4 grants authority to the House Judiciary Committee to investigate the Watergate affair.

- On March 29, eight former members of the Ohio National Guard are indicted by a federal grand jury for violating the civil rights of students they shot and wounded during an antiwar protest at Kent State University on May 4, 1970. Although they are acquitted, in 1979 the state of Ohio will settle a civil suit with survivors of the shooting, giving them a total of $675,000.

- On April 29, in a nationally televised address, President Nixon announces that he will release summary transcripts of the Watergate tapes on the following morning.

- On July 24, the Supreme Court rules, in *United States v. Richard M. Nixon,* that the White House has no claim to "executive privilege" in withholding the Watergate tapes from Special Prosecutor Jaworski. President Nixon turns over the tapes on July 30 and August 5.

- On July 24, the House Judiciary Committee commences formal impeachment hearings against President Nixon.

- On July 30, the House Judiciary Committee recommends that the House of Representatives impeach the president for three offenses: obstruction of justice, abuse of power, and contempt of Congress. Two other articles of impeachment, for secretly bombing Cambodia and for filing false tax returns, are rejected.

- On July 31, former White House official John Ehrlichman is sentenced to five years in prison for conspiracy related to his involvement in the burglary at the office of the psychiatrist of Daniel Ellsberg, who published the Pentagon Papers.

- On August 2, former White House counsel John Dean is sentenced to one to four years in prison for conspiracy to cover up the Watergate affair.

- On August 5, newly released Watergate tapes demonstrate that on June 23, 1972 President Nixon ordered a cover-up of the Watergate break-in.

- On August 8, in a televised address Richard Nixon announces his resignation from the presidency, effective at noon on August 9. He becomes the first president to resign in American history.

- On August 9, Gerald R. Ford is inaugurated as the thirty-eighth President of the United States.

- On August 19, President Ford offers "earned reentry" amnesty for Vietnam War resisters.

- On August 20, President Ford nominates former New York Governor Nelson A. Rockefeller for vice president. He is confirmed in December.

- On August 22, the House Judiciary Committee releases its final report on the Watergate affair, detailing "clear and convincing evidence" that Richard Nixon had obstructed justice thirty-six times. The House approves the report 412-3.

- On September 4, George H. Bush is named head of the U.S. liaison to China.

- On September 8, President Ford grants Nixon "a full, free, and absolute pardon" for any crimes he might have committed while in office. In opinion polls Ford's popularity drops from 71 percent to 49 percent.

- On October 8, President Ford unveils his program Whip Inflation Now (WIN) to Congress.

- On October 10, Congress passes legislation providing for public funding of presidential primaries and elections. President Ford signs the legislation on 14 October.

- On October 17, President Ford testifies before a House subcommittee that he had no prior arrangement with Nixon to grant the former president a pardon.

- On November 5, in the wake of the Watergate scandal, Democrats win in congressional elections, gaining a 61-37 majority in the Senate (with two seats held by independents) and a 291-144 majority in the House. Democrat Ella Grasso of Connecticut becomes the first woman elected governor of a U.S. state without having been preceded in office by her husband.

- On November 21, over President Ford's veto Congress passes the Freedom of Information Act, increasing public access to government files.

- On December 3, over President Ford's veto Congress passes a bill increasing educational benefits for veterans by almost 23 percent.

- On December 7, the United States Department of Labor releases figures showing that the unemployment rate reached 6.5 percent in November—the highest monthly rate since 1961.

1975

- On January 1, former White House officials Haldeman, Ehrlichman, and Mitchell are all found guilty of conspiracy and obstructing justice in the Watergate affair.

- On January 8, three former Nixon aides, John Dean, Herbert W. Kalmbach, and Jeb Stuart Magruder, are released from prison.

- On January 24, a terrorist group seeking Puerto Rican independence bombs the Revolutionary War landmark Fraunces Tavern in New York City, killing four and injuring fifty-three.

- On January 25, the Washington Post reveals that in 1964 President Johnson ordered the FBI to bug civil rights leaders during the Democratic National Convention in Atlantic City, New Jersey.

- On February 7, the United States Department of Labor announces that the January unemployment rate is 8.2 percent—the highest rate in thirty-four years.

- On February 21, former White House officials Haldeman, Ehrlichman, and Mitchell are each sentenced to three years in prison for their involvement in the Watergate scandal.

- On February 27, the United States Department of Justice announces that former FBI director J. Edgar Hoover kept secret files on the private lives of presidents, congressmen, and other prominent public figures.

- On March 4, President Ford agrees to a sixty-day delay in increasing oil tariffs by three dollars a barrel but also vetoes a congressional effort to suspend his power to increase tariffs.

- On March 12, former Nixon cabinet member and chief fund-raiser Maurice Stans pleads guilty to one of five counts of violating federal campaign-finance laws.

- On March 29, President Ford signs a $22.8 billion tax cut.

- On March 31, after only 22,500 of the possible 124,400 eligible participate, the clemency program for Vietnam War draft resisters and evaders ends.

- On May 29, President Ford vetoes a $5.3 billion job bill because would be ineffective. On the same day, the Labor Department reports that a record 127 major cities have substantial levels of unemployment.

- On May 31, former California Governor Ronald Reagan charges that democratic countries throughout the world desperately need leadership against Communist domination and America is not providing it.

- On June 10, the Rockefeller commission on CIA domestic activities reports that the CIA had undertaken unlawful surveillance of three hundred thousand American citizens and organizations and had supplied former president Nixon with information on his political opponents.

- On June 30, the federal government extends unemployment assistance to sixty-five weeks.

- On July 14, FBI Director Clarence B. Kelly confirms that the agency conducts burglaries and break-ins in national security cases. On July 16, the *Washington Post* reports that the FBI also uses break-ins during criminal investigations.

- On August 6, President Ford approves a seven-year extension of the Voting Rights Act.

- On August 27, the eight former members of the Ohio National Guard are acquitted of the federal grand jury charges that they violated the civil rights of students they shot during a May 4, 1970, antiwar protest at Kent State University.

- On August 31, the House Select Committee on Intelligence Activities reveals that the National Security Agency monitors almost all overseas calls to and from the United States.

- On October 17, New York City, on the verge of bankruptcy, is saved from default by the New York City Teachers Union's purchase of $150 million in municipal bonds.

- On November 3, President Ford shuffles members of his administration. Secretary of State Kissinger resigns as head of the National Security Council and is replaced by Brent Scowcroft; Secretary of Defense James Schlesinger is replaced by Donald Rumsfeld; CIA Director William Colby is replaced by George Bush; Secretary of Commerce Rogers Morton is replaced by Eliott Richardson. Vice President Nelson Rockefeller announces he will not be a candidate for vice president in 1976.

- On November 12, United States Supreme Court Justice William O. Douglas, seventy-seven, suffering from a stroke, announces his retirement. He had sat on the bench for thirty-six years, earning a reputation as a civil libertarian. He will be replaced by Judge John Paul Stevens.

- On November 20, the bipartisan Senate investigation of FBI and CIA activities concludes. The Senate committee, led by Frank Church (D-Idaho), reports that both agencies illegally spied on American citizens. It further charges the CIA with plotting the assassination of foreign leaders and with maintaining stocks of illegal poisons.

1976

- From April 26 to April 28, the Senate Select Committee on Intelligence issues a heavily censored report on covert intelligence operations. It urges closer congressional oversight of intelligence operations and better safeguards against violations of civil liberties.

- On July 2, the United States Supreme Court, in a landmark decision, holds that the death penalty for murder convictions is constitutional.

- From July 3 to July 4, the nation celebrates its two hundredth anniversary.

- On July 14, the Democratic National Convention nominates former Georgia Governor James Earl ("Jimmy") Carter, Jr. for President. Walter Mondale, senator from Minnesota, is nominated for vice president.

- On August 19, the Republican National Convention narrowly nominates President Gerald Ford for President over California Governor Ronald Reagan. Kansas Senator Robert Dole is nominated for vice president.

- On September 27, Ford and Carter conduct the first of three presidential debates on national television. The vice presidential candidates debate on 15 October.

- On November 2, Jimmy Carter defeats Gerald Ford for President. The Democrats retain majorities in both houses of Congress.

- On December 6, the ninetieth Congress elects Thomas P. ("Tip") O'Neill, Jr. (D-Massachusetts), as Speaker of the House.

1977

- On January 20, Jimmy Carter is inaugurated thirty-ninth President of the United States. Walter Mondale takes the oath as vice president.

- On January 21, President Carter signs an unconditional pardon for almost all Vietnam-era draft evaders.

- On April 12, President Carter grants Watergate conspirator G. Gordon Liddy a commutation, making him available for parole in July.

- On April 20, President Carter unveils a national energy policy designed to reduce oil dependence and increase dependence on coal.

- On May 4, former President Nixon begins a series of paid televised interviews with David Frost.

- On July 9, Alice Paul, age ninety-two, the founder of the National Woman's Party in 1913 and a prominent leader in the women's suffrage movement dies.

- On August 4, the Department of Energy is created. James Schlesinger is nominated as secretary.

- On August 20, only 20 percent of American voters favor the Republican Party, the lowest level in forty years.

- On October 4, Judge John J. Sirica reduces the prison sentences of Watergate conspirators Mitchell, Haldeman, and Ehrlichman.

- On November 1, President Carter signs legislation raising the minimum wage to $2.30 an hour.

1978

- On January 11, the United States Department of Labor announces that the unemployment rate for December 1977 was 6.4 percent—the lowest in three years.

- On January 13, Senator Hubert Humphrey dies of cancer in Minnesota.

- On March 16, the United States Senate on a vote of 68-32 ratifies the Panama Canal Treaty, turning the canal over to Panama in 2000.

- On May 30, the United States Department of Agriculture reports that food prices are expected to rise between 8 and 10 percent in 1978.

- On June 6, California voters approve Proposition 13, a state constitutional amendment reducing property taxes 57 percent.

- On June 17, Senator George McGovern claims that California's Proposition 13 is racist because it reflects a desire by voters to reduce social services to minorities.

- On June 28, the Supreme Court rules that Allan P. Bakke, a thirty-eight-year-old white engineer, be admitted to the University of California Medical School. Claiming reverse discrimination, Bakke argued that affirmative-action programs had prevented him from being admitted. While not affirming racial quotas, the Court did uphold the constitutionality of affirmative action.

• On August 8, President Carter signs a bill giving New York City $1.65 billion in federal long-term loan guarantees.

• On August 21, President Carter's popularity with the American people has stabilized at 39 percent.

• On August 12, the United States Census Bureau reports that, in 1977, 11.6 percent of Americans lived below the poverty level.

• On October 6, the United States Senate votes to extend the deadline for ratification of the Equal Rights Amendment to June 30, 1982. Thirty-five states have already approved the amendment, three short of the necessary thirty-eight.

• On November 7, in midterm elections, despite solid gains by the Republicans, Democrats retain hold of both houses of Congress.

• On December 30, the House Select Committee on Assassinations ends its two-year inquiry by concluding that the murders of President John F. Kennedy and Dr. Martin Luther King, Jr., were possibly the result of conspiracies.

1979

• On January 12, President Carter dismisses Bella Abzug from her post as cochair of the National Advisory Committee on Women. Twenty-one of the forty committee members resign in protest of the firing.

• On February 5, three thousand farmers protest federal price supports hold a rally in Washington, D.C.

• On February 26, President Carter asks Congress for the power to authorize gasoline rationing and weekend gas station closures.

• On March 28, a major accident at the Three Mile Island nuclear generating plant near Harrisburg, Pennsylvania, results in the evacuation of thousands. The plant manages to avoid a catastrophic core meltdown, and by April 9, the accident is fully contained.

• On April 3, Jane M. Byrne is elected the first woman mayor of Chicago with a record 82.5 percent of the vote.

• On April 5, President Carter announces a program to remove oil price controls and asks Congress for a windfall-profits tax on oil companies.

• On April 20, while on a fishing trip, President Carter is attacked by a rabbit, which he fends off with a canoe paddle.

• On April 27, President Carter announces that he favors limiting a president to one six-year term.

• On May 26, since the first of the year, retail gasoline prices have risen in the United States an average of fifteen cents a gallon.

• On June 4, President Carter's job approval rate falls to 29 percent, slightly above the level of former President Nixon prior to his resignation from office in 1974.

• On July 15, President Carter announces a new energy program designed to lessen the American "crisis of confidence" and dependence on foreign oil. He also radically alters the composition of his cabinet.

• On July 31, the Chrysler Corporation, facing a record $207 million loss in the second quarter of 1979, seeks a $1 billion loan from the federal government in order to prevent bankruptcy. The third largest automaker employs 250,000 workers. In November, the Carter administration proposes loaning the company $1.5 billion.

• On November 4, in Tehran several hundred Iranian militants storm the U.S. embassy and seize the diplomatic personnel. The militants announce they will release the hostages when the United States returns the shah, who is recovering from medical treatments in a New York hospital, to Iran to stand trial. President Carter declares he will not extradite the shah; Iranian prime minister Mehdi Barzargan resigns when it becomes known that Ayatollah Ruholla Mussaui Khomeini and the Revolutionary Council had sanctioned the hostage-taking, a violation of international law.

• On November 13, former California Governor Ronald Reagan announces his candidacy for the 1980 Republican presidential nomination. He calls for a spiritual revival and a renewal of confidence in the United States.

The End of the Vietnam War

"Vietnamization"

Speech

By: Richard M. Nixon

Date: November 3, 1969

Source: Richard M. Nixon, "Vietnamization." November 3, 1969, delivered in Washington, D.C. Public Papers of President Richard M. Nixon, courtesy of Richard M. Nixon Library & Birthplace.

About the Author: Richard M. Nixon (1913–1994) was the nation's thirty-seventh president (served 1969–1974). Elected in 1968, in part on his promise to end U.S. involvement in the Vietnam War (1964–1975), Nixon enacted a policy of Vietnamization that indeed curtailed the American presence there.

"President Gerald R. Ford's Address at a Tulane University Convocation"

Speech

By: Gerald R. Ford

Date: April 23, 1975

Source: Gerald R. Ford, Presidential Speech on "Looking Past Vietnam," April 23, 1975, delivered at Tulane University. Public Papers of President Gerald R. Ford, courtesy of Gerald R. Ford Library and Museum.

About the Author: Gerald R. Ford (1913–) assumed the presidency (served 1974–1977) in 1974 after Nixon resigned over the Watergate scandal. In office when the South Vietnamese government fell to the North Vietnamese in 1975, Ford tried to reassure the public that the defeat did not dim the United States' reputation abroad. ■

Introduction

The Vietnam War arguably was the most divisive issue of the 1960s. As American casualties mounted and the public watched gruesome, televised images of frontline battles, popular sentiment gradually turned toward opposing the nation's continued military presence in the southeastern Asian country. Although most elected offi-

cials voiced support for the war effort through 1968, the shift in public opinion led some to openly question U.S. efforts in the region. While no politician wanted to appear soft on containing communism—the primary reason why the United States became so involved in Vietnam—they could not ignore the antiwar protests that had gathered momentum by the end of the 1960s.

As one of the shrewdest politicians of his age, Richard Nixon carefully constructed his statements on Vietnam during his successful presidential campaign of 1968, in which he defeated Democrat Hubert Humphrey. In a compromise measure, Nixon proposed gradually de-escalating U.S. presence in Vietnam. Although military and financial support to South Vietnam would continue in its fight against the communist-controlled North, the number of American military forces would diminish. Under this policy of "Vietnamization," announced to the public in a televised speech in November 1969, American troops would leave Vietnam without having to declare surrender. This last, face-saving factor was crucial in Nixon's arguments for Vietnamization, as the United States had never been defeated in a war in the past.

Although American military fatalities declined as the troops were pulled out of Vietnam, protests continued over the Nixon administration's controversial decisions to invade Cambodia in May 1970 and its air support of the South Vietnamese invasion of Laos in February 1971. A new wave of protests erupted over the incidents, which many viewed as proof that Nixon reneged on his promise to end U.S. involvement in the war.

Significance

The Vietnamization of the war had been completed before Nixon's resignation in August 1974, a fact confirmed by the Paris Peace Accords of January 1973—declaring a cease-fire in the country. North Vietnam quickly resumed its invasion of the South, however, and thousands of American military advisors and other officials remained there until the final days before South Vietnam surrendered in April 1975. As Saigon, the capital of South Vietnam, fell to the communists, dramatic television images of frantic, last-minute evacuations of American personnel from the U.S. Embassy seemed to bring Nixon's worst fear to life: the United States had been ousted by the North Vietnamese. Between 1961 and 1973, about 57,000 Americans had died in Vietnam, and another 300,000 were wounded.

On the heels of the fall of Saigon, President Gerald R. Ford urged Americans to put the episode behind them and emerge from the experience with their optimism intact. The president's rhetoric, however, was taken by some as a call to forget the war and its losses—little

President Nixon was determined to extract the United States from the war in Vietnam. As part of his plans for withdrawal, he promoted the policy of "Vietnamization," in which the South Vietnamese would take over the war operations that were being handled by the United States. It was considered to be an ineffective policy. **THE LIBRARY OF CONGRESS.**

comfort for those who had lost a loved one or been wounded in combat. Future presidents would have an equally difficult time coming to terms with the lessons of Vietnam. Although the United States' basic anti-communist outlook remained central to its foreign policy, some Americans no longer believed that their leaders were infallible—or even trustworthy—when it came to fighting the Cold War.

Military and intelligence leaders also struggled to learn from the U.S. experience in Vietnam. Outmaneuvered by the guerilla tactics of the North Vietnamese, not even a vastly superior technological edge and air power could assure an American victory. With the American public also hesitant to support another large-scale American combat force after Vietnam, it would not be until the Persian Gulf War of 1991 that American troops again fought abroad in significant numbers.

Primary Source

"Vietnamization" [excerpt]

SYNOPSIS: With popular sentiment turning decidedly against U.S. involvement in the Vietnam War, Richard Nixon campaigned for the presidency in 1968 on a promise to end the war. Several months after taking office in 1969, he delivered this speech to declare the new policy of "Vietnamization," designed to allow the gradual withdrawal of American troops from Vietnam.

Good evening, my fellow Americans:

Tonight I want to talk to you on a subject of deep concern to all Americans and to many people in all parts of the world—the war in Vietnam.

I believe that one of the reasons for the deep division about Vietnam is that many Americans have lost confidence in what their Government has told them about our policy. The American people cannot and should not be asked to support a policy which involves the overriding issues of war and peace unless they know the truth about that policy.

Tonight, therefore, I would like to answer some of the questions that I know are on the minds of many of you listening to me.

How and why did America get involved in Vietnam in the first place?

How has this administration changed the policy of the previous administration?

What has really happened in the negotiations in Paris and on the battlefront in Vietnam?

What choices do we have if we are to end the war?

What are the prospects for peace?

Now, let me begin by describing the situation I found when I was inaugurated on January 20.

• The war had been going on for 4 years.

• 31,000 Americans had been killed in action.

• The training program for the South Vietnamese was behind schedule.

• 540,000 Americans were in Vietnam with no plans to reduce the number.

• No progress had been made at the negotiations in Paris and the United States had not put forth a comprehensive peace proposal.

• The war was causing deep division at home and criticism from many of our friends as well as our enemies abroad.

In view of these circumstances there were some who urged that I end the war at once by ordering the immediate withdrawal of all American forces.

From a political standpoint this would have been a popular and easy course to follow. After all, we became involved in the war while my predecessor was in office.

I could blame the defeat which would be the result of my action on him and come out as the peacemaker. Some put it to me quite bluntly: This was the only way to avoid allowing Johnson's war to become Nixon's war.

But I had a greater obligation than to think only of the years of my administration and of the next election. I had to think of the effect of my decision on the next generation and on the future of peace and freedom in America and in the world.

Let us all understand that the question before us is not whether some Americans are for peace and some Americans are against peace. The question at issue is not whether Johnson's war becomes Nixon's war. . . .

For the United States, this first defeat in our Nation's history would result in a collapse of confidence in American leadership, not only in Asia but throughout the world.

Primary Source

"President Gerald R. Ford's Address at a Tulane University Convocation" [excerpt]

SYNOPSIS: After the withdrawal of most American forces from South Vietnam, the country quickly fell to the North Vietnamese. Following the fall of Saigon in April 1975, President Ford tried to reassure the public that the defeat did not signal a loss of American power and prestige in the international community. In this speech, Ford also urges the country move forward in the spirit of reconciliation and optimism—serious challenges to a nation that had been deeply divided on the war for so long.

On January 8, 1815, a monumental American victory was achieved here—the Battle of New Orleans.

Louisiana had been a State for less than 3 years, but outnumbered Americans innovated, outnumbered Americans used the tactics of the frontier to defeat a veteran British force trained in the strategy of the Napoleonic wars.

We as a nation had suffered humiliation and a measure of defeat in the War of 1812. Our National Capital in Washington had been captured and burned. So, the illustrious victory in the Battle of New Orleans was a powerful restorative to our national pride.

Yet, the victory at New Orleans actually took place 2 weeks after the signing of the armistice in Europe. Thousands died although a peace had been negotiated. The combatants had not gotten the word. Yet, the epic struggle nevertheless restored America's pride.

Today, America can regain the sense of pride that existed before Vietnam. But it cannot be achieved by refighting a war that is finished as far as America is concerned. As I see it, the time has come to look forward to an agenda for the future, to unify, to bind up the Nation's wounds, and to restore its health and its optimistic self-confidence.

With the fall of Saigon to the north imminent, many South Vietnamese sought to escape in U.S. evacuation helicopters, mobbing the U.S. Embassy in their desperation. **AP/WIDE WORLD PHOTOS. REPRODUCED BY PERMISSION.**

In New Orleans, a great battle was fought after a war was over. In New Orleans tonight, we can begin a great national reconciliation. The first engagement must be with the problems of today, but just as importantly, the problems of the future. That is why I think it is so appropriate that I find myself tonight at a university which addresses itself to preparing young people for the challenge of tomorrow.

I ask that we stop refighting the battles and the recriminations of the past. I ask that we look now at what is right with America, at our possibilities and our potentialities for change and growth and achievement and sharing. I ask that we accept the responsibilities of leadership as a good neighbor to all peoples and the enemy of none. I ask that we strive to become, in the finest American tradition, something more tomorrow than we are today.

Instead of my addressing the image of America, I prefer to consider the reality of America. It is true that we have launched our Bicentennial celebration without having achieved human perfection, but we have attained a very remarkable self-governed society that possesses the flexibility and the dynamism to grow and undertake an entirely new agenda, an agenda for America's third century.

So, I ask you to join me in helping to write that agenda. I am as determined as a President can be to seek national rediscovery of the belief in ourselves that characterized the most creative periods in our Nation's history. The greatest challenge of creativity, as I see it, lies ahead.

We, of course, are saddened indeed by the events in Indochina. But these events, tragic as they are, portend neither the end of the world nor of America's leadership in the world.

Further Resources

BOOKS

Appy, Christian G. *Working-Class War: American Combat Soldiers and Vietnam.* Chapel Hill: University of North Carolina Press, 1993.

Davidson, Philip B. *Vietnam at War: The History, 1946–1975.* New York: Oxford University Press, 1988.

Franklin, H. Bruce. *M.I.A., or Mythmaking in America.* New Brunswick, N.J.: Rutgers University Press, 1993.

Kimball, Jeffrey. *Nixon's Vietnam War.* Lawrence: The University of Kansas Press, 1998.

Reeves, Richard. *A Ford, Not a Lincoln.* New York: Harcourt Brace Jovanovich, 1975.

Shawcross, William. *Sideshow: Kissinger, Nixon, and the Destruction of Cambodia.* New York: Simon and Schuster, 1979.

Summers, Anthony, with Robbyn Swan. *The Arrogance of Power: The Secret World of Richard Nixon.* New York: Viking, 2000.

Law and Order

"U.S. to Tighten Surveillance of Radicals"

Newspaper article

By: James M. Naughton

Date: April 12, 1970

Source: Naughton, James M., "U.S. to Tighten Surveillance of Radicals." *The New York Times,* April 12, 1970, 1, 69.

About the Author: James M. Naughton (1938–) began his career as a reporter and photographer while still in high school. After completing his bachelor's degree at the University of Notre Dame, he worked for the Cleveland *Plain Dealer* for seven years, before joining the staff of *The New York Times* in 1969. He remained at *The New York Times* as a political reporter until 1977, when he became an editor of the Philadelphia *Inquirer.* In 1996, Naughton was named president of the Poynter Institute, one of the country's leading centers for the study of journalism.

"Listen to Youths, Hickel Writes Nixon"

Magazine article

By: Walter J. Hickel

Date: May 18, 1970

Source: "Listen to Youths, Hickel Writes Nixon." *U.S. News & World Report,* May 18, 1970, 84.

About the Author: Walter J. Hickel (1919–) served as Alaska's second governor in 1966. In 1969, he was named Secretary of the Interior by President Richard M. Nixon (served 1969–1974) and served one year in the post. In the 1970s and 1980s, Hickel resumed his business career in the energy sector, and he won a second term as governor of Alaska in 1990. *U.S. News & World Report* began as the 1948 merger of two weekly magazines, *United States News* and *World Report.* The magazine is read by 11.2 million American adult readers every week. ■

Introduction

The social movements of the 1960s fundamentally transformed the United States in many ways, but produced deep divisions as well. Although many Americans supported and participated in the antiwar protests and civil rights marches that were a regular feature of the decade, a more angry and defiant tone gripped some of the movements in the last years of the sixties. Student-based protest groups produced radical, and sometimes violent, offshoots such as the Weathermen. When civil rights organizations splintered over calls for separatism, some Americans came to fear that chaos had taken over.

Richard M. Nixon, who staged an impressive political comeback to win the Republican presidential nomi-

nation in 1968, brilliantly manipulated the public's fears over disorder and crime in his campaign. Referring to the urban riots that marred the landscape of several American cities and the antiwar protests that swept the streets and college campuses of the country, Nixon promised a return to "law and order" that resonated with the public.

After winning the presidency Nixon did not soften his rhetoric against what he perceived to be an organized and extremist radical effort to create disorder in the country. Although violent protests remained rare and an overwhelming majority of protesters did not endorse violence or terrorism, Nixon and his advisors nevertheless insisted that the threat to the nation's existence was real. Calling for increased surveillance of suspected radicals, the administration also argued that the maintenance of the nation's civil liberties could only be guaranteed by taking the seemingly paradoxical step of stepping up secret domestic-security efforts. As one top Nixon aide warned in a front-page *The New York Times* article on April 12, 1970, "We are facing the most severe internal security threat this country has seen since the Depression."

Significance

The tough, law-and-order stance articulated by the Nixon administration soon had tragic consequences on the campus of Kent State University in Ohio. After Nixon announced an invasion of Cambodia in support of South Vietnamese troops on April 30, 1970, a renewed wave of protests was staged against the military action. At KSU, antiwar protests the next day attracted as many as five hundred supporters on the campus, a number that swelled to as many as 2,000 protesters over the weekend of May 2–3. During a march on the KSU ROTC building that Saturday, the building was set on fire and the crowd was pushed back with tear gas and bayonets. Ohio Governor James Rhodes sent in the National Guard to quell the violence and to enforce a curfew. On Monday, May 4, organizers announced a noon antiwar rally that would also protest the violence that had occurred.

The May 4 rally attracted about 1,500 students and supporters who gathered to listen to antiwar speeches and show their disagreement with the Governor's actions. After ordering the protesters to disperse, the National Guard then sent tear gas into the crowd, which began dispersing from the campus commons. After a brief standoff with a smaller group of protesters, the National Guard commander ordered the troops to withdraw and regroup. Instead, while the other Guardsmen marched off, some of the members of Troop G turned around and fired into the crowd. Four KSU students were killed, and nine others had been shot.

The Kent State tragedy was followed ten days later by similarly lethal incident at Jackson State in Mississippi. The two events, combined with the Nixon administration's callous reaction to the events, underscored the generational and social divide that the Vietnam War (1964–1975) had produced in American society. Although Rhodes, Nixon, and other law-and-order politicians were roundly condemned in some quarters for their words and actions, others praised them for taking an uncompromising stand, despite the horrific outcomes.

Primary Source

"U.S. to Tighten Surveillance of Radicals"

SYNOPSIS: In this front-page *The New York Times* article, the Nixon administration clearly outlines its uncompromising stance against potentially dangerous protesters. As a reaction to the sometimes-violent urban riots and campus protests that shocked many Americans, Nixon had campaigned for office on a law-and-order platform. As the remarks of his advisors show, the president was not about to abandon that position in office.

The Nixon Administration, alarmed by what it regards as a rising tide of radical extremism, is planning to step up surveillance of militant left-wing groups and individuals.

The objective, according to White House officials, is to find out who the potential bomb planters and snipers may be before they endanger others.

Preparations for expanding and improving the domestic intelligence apparatus—informers, undercover agents, wiretaps—were disclosed in a series of interviews with key officials, who requested anonymity.

According to these officials, President Nixon is disturbed by the rash of bombings and bomb scares, courtroom disruptions and reports of small but growing numbers of young people who feel alienated from the American system.

Parallels Are Drawn

On March 12, the same day that bombs exploded in three Manhattan office buildings, Mr. Nixon met over dinner in the White House with Irving Kristol, professor of urban values at New York University.

One aide who attended the dinner said the discussion included attempts to draw parallels between young, middle-class, white Americans who are resorting to violence and the Narodniki—children of the mid-19th century Russian aristocracy who murdered Czar Alexander II, and between militant black nationalists here and Algerian revolutionaries.

Mr. Kristol told the President it was not unrealistic to expect the Latin American resort to political kidnappings to spread soon to Washington. Mr. Kristol confirmed the dinner meeting and commented, "Some of these kids don't know what country this is. They think it's Bolivia."

Some, but not all, of Mr. Nixon's domestic advisers are convinced that the situation is critical. One of the more conservative aides contended, "We are facing the most severe internal security threat this country has seen since the Depression."

The officials have concluded that attempts to bring militants back into society's mainstream are as futile, as one stated it, "as turning off the radio in the middle of a ball game to try to change the score."

The official view is that extreme radicals cannot be won over with welfare, electoral or draft reforms or by White House appeals. "It wouldn't make a bit of difference if the war and racism ended overnight," said a highly placed Nixon assistant. "We're dealing with the criminal mind, with people who have snapped for some reason. Accordingly, the Administration sees its prime responsibility as protecting the innocent from "revolutionary terrorism." The President said last month, when he asked Congress for broader Federal jurisdiction and stiffer penalties in bombing cases, that they were the work of "young criminals posturing as romantic revolutionaries."

Tougher Problem Today

To keep tabs on individuals referred to by the President as "potential murderers" will require updating an intelligence system geared to monitoring the Communists three decades ago, the aides said.

They said it was easy to keep track of the Communists because they had a highly organized system that undercover agents could penetrate easily. But today's alleged anarchists are disorganized, operating in groups of three or four, and difficult to detect.

We know there are people training themselves in certain forms of guerrilla warfare and the use of explosives," said one official, "but it's extremely difficult to answer the who, when and how."

A Nixon aide who is aware of the Justice Department's intelligence operations said there was no advance warning of the arson that destroyed a Bank of America branch in Santa Barbara, Calif., last month. He said that "We knew of the New York bomb factory" in a Greenwich Village townhouse, but only just before it exploded on March 6, killing three young people.

White House officials wonder aloud why one of the victims, Diana Oughton, 28 years old, once active in legitimate reform efforts, became a member of a militant faction of the Students for a Democratic Society.

"If we had a (phone) tap on Diana Oughton," a Presidential assistant said, "we might have arrested her before the bombs went off and nobody would have died."

Survivor Is Traced

The official said that Federal agents had traced a survivor of the Greenwich Village blast, Cathlyn Platt Wilkerson, to Canada, but he expressed distress that the intelligence system was not capable of pinpointing her activities before she became a fugitive.

Administration sources would not disclose details of the changes they are preparing in the intelligence mechanism, although they said a good deal of interdepartmental discussion about them was under way.

One suggestion was said to be the possibility of the Justice Department providing grants through the Law Enforcement Assistance Administration to local police departments for training in domestic intelligence gathering.

Only New York City and District of Columbia policemen have adequate intelligence systems, one official said, adding: "We need better trained people in metropolitan police departments so they can distinguish between a guy with a beard and a subversive."

The White House is aware of the political sensitivity of domestic intelligence gathering, which one aide described as "hangups in the question of snooping." He contended, however, that the Government was less interested in prosecuting individuals than in gathering information to "prevent the perpetration of an act of violence."

Liberties Gain Seen

It would help to have "broader public awareness" of the need for improved surveillance techniques, he said, "One of the greatest disservices Senator [Joseph] McCarthy did to this country was to swing the pendulum so far that people no longer want to think about internal security," the official said.

He argued that it would, in fact, increase safeguards of the civil liberties of individuals to have a greater awareness of which members of society posed a threat.

"My concern is that sooner or later this is going to kill innocent people," the official said. "There will be tremendous public outrage and not enough time for restrained, measured response. People will demand that their police start cracking heads.

"The greatest safeguard for rights of individuals is to have good information on what the [radical fringes] are doing. Stop them before the bombings. Bomb legislation [with heavier penalties] is after the fact."

Mr. Nixon, who prefers to decide on Administration policy after receiving a set of clearly defined options, apparently has little choice but to adopt the recommendations of his more conservative staff members for increased surveillance. Liberal advisers have not provided him with alternatives.

Indeed, the liberals do not appear to have any answers to the problem of American radicalism. As one White House liberal put it: "What does Richard Nixon do for these people, short of resigning the Presidency?"

Primary Source

"Listen to Youths, Hickel Writes Nixon"

SYNOPSIS: In the days after the Kent State University shootings, many elected officials came under criticism for allowing lethal violence to be unleashed on innocent bystanders. The seemingly callous reaction of Vice President Spiro Agnew, who referred to the administration's critics as "choleric young intellectuals and tired, embittered elders," typified the administration's stance. The Kent State tragedy remained one of the most symbolic and divisive moments of the 1970s.

If we read history, it clearly shows that youth in its protest must be heard.

This advice to President Nixon—disclosed during a week of riotous protest by U. S. youths—came not from a demonstrator but from a Cabinet member: Interior Secretary Walter J. Hickel.

Mr. Hickel said the Administration seems "to lack appropriate concern" for youthful complaints and added:

I believe the Vice President initially has answered a deep-seated mood of America in his public statements. However, a continued attack on the young—not on their attitudes so much as their motives—can serve little purpose other than to further cement . . . attitudes to a solidity impossible to penetrate with reason.

As Interior Secretary Walter Hickel encouraged the Nixon administration to listen more to the country's youth on their beliefs about war and other matters, the government implemented a broader mandate for surveillance on anti-war radicals, and arrests continued. © **BETTMANN/CORBIS. REPRODUCED BY PERMISSION.**

The views were expressed in a letter to Mr. Nixon that became public on May 6—although Mr. Hickel said it was intended to be private.

On May 1, President Nixon had made an off-hand remark about "these bums" who are "blowing up the campuses" and "burning up the books." In remarks to Defense Department employees, he contrasted them with "kids who are just doing their duty" in Vietnam.

Secretary Hickel, in his letter to the President, also said:

- "I believe we are in error if we set out consciously to alienate those who could be our friends."

- "Today, our young people—or at least a vast segment of them—believe they have no opportunity to communicate with Government, regardless of Administration, other than through violent confrontation."

Mr. Hickel noted his own suggestion that Earth Day, last April 22, be declared a national holiday. This was not done. He said he and many Interior employees took part in Earth Day activities and that

this "showed that it was possible to communicate with youth."

The letter also asked that Mr. Nixon meet with college presidents to discuss campus problems. It was not clear whether this was why Mr. Nixon called in eight university presidents for conferences May 7. He acted in the wake of four deaths at Kent State University and eruptions on many campuses in protests over Cambodia.

After the meeting, one of the educators said Mr. Nixon had assured the group that hostile comments by Administration officials about college students would cease.

Agnew Comment

Of the Kent State killings, Vice President Agnew said on May 7 there apparently was "overreaction in the heat of anger" by Guardsmen. In taping a TV show, he was asked whether the deaths might not be "murder" if it were established that no shots were fired at the troops. "Yes," replied Mr. Agnew, "but not first-degree murder—there was no premeditation."

In a speech prepared for delivery on May 8 at Boise, Ida., Mr. Agnew had sharp words for "choleric young intellectuals and tired, embittered elders." Singled out for attack: Senator J. W. Fulbright (Dem.), of Arkansas, chairman of the Senate Foreign Relations Committee, for "the baldest and most reactionary pleas for isolationism."

Seeing the President

Concerning the Hickel letter, some felt it might have reflected complaints heard from officials that they are finding it difficult to have personal talks with Mr. Nixon.

Mr. Hickel asked the President to "consider meeting, on an individual and conversational basis, with members of your Cabinet" in order to "gain greater insight" into youth problems.

Mr. Hickel is reported to feel that he is already able to communicate with youth to a degree. One of the reasons: He is the father of six sons ranging in age from 8 to 30. Two are in college and two still live at home.

Further Resources

BOOKS

Bills, Scott L. *May Fourth: Echoes Through a Decade.* Kent, Ohio: Kent State University Press, 1982.

Edsall, Thomas Byrne and Mary Edsall. *Chain Reaction: The Impact of Race, Rights, and Taxes on the American Electorate.* New York: W.W. Norton & Company, 1991.

Farber, David. *The Age of Great Dreams: America in the 1960s.* New York: Hill & Wang, 1994.

Hayden, Tom. *Reunion: A Memoir.* New York: Random House, 1988.

Hickel, Walter J. *Who Owns America?* Englewood Cliffs, N.J.: Prentice-Hall, 1971.

Summers, Anthony and Robbyn Swan. *The Arrogance of Power: The Secret World of Richard Nixon.* New York: Viking, 2000.

WEBSITES

"Kent State University: Freedom of Information Act Files." Available online at http://foia.fbi.gov/kentstat.htm; website home page http://foia.fbi.gov (accessed May 25, 2003).

"Presidential Speech Announcing Acceptance of an Invitation to Visit the People's Republic of China"

Speech

By: Richard M. Nixon

Date: July 15, 1971

Source: Nixon, Richard M. "Presidential Speech Announcing Acceptance of an Invitation to Visit the People's Republic of China," July 15, 1971, delivered in Los Angeles, California. Public Papers of President Richard M. Nixon, courtesy of Richard M. Nixon Library & Birthplace.

About the Author: Richard M. Nixon (1913–1994) became the thirty-seventh president of the United States (served 1969–1974) in 1968, and he won re-election in 1972. Among his most important accomplishments was opening of diplomatic relations with the People's Republic of China, severed since the communist takeover in 1949. Nixon was forced to resign from office in 1974 during the Watergate scandal, however, before full diplomatic relations could be restored. Although his reputation never recovered, Nixon regained a measure of respect as an elder statesman in his final years, particularly for his continued willingness to broker ties with China. ■

Introduction

One of the longest stalemates of the Cold War took place between the United States—the world's wealthiest and most powerful country—and the People's Republic of China, its most populous. The United States severed ties with mainland China after its takeover by the Chinese Communist Party under Mao Zedong in 1949, after a bitter civil war. When the defeated, pro-western faction under Chiang Kai-shek set up rule on the neighboring island of Taiwan, the United States recognized it as the legitimate Chinese government. The refusal of the United States to recognize the legitimacy of the People's Republic of China under the communists intensified during the Korean War (1950–1953). After China aided North Korean forces invading South Korea, United Nations forces, with a predominantly American presence, pushed them back. The war dragged on for three years, with the United Nation forces stopping just short of entering Chinese soil, before it ended with a ceasefire.

Southeast Asia witnessed another major Cold War conflict between communist and western forces during the Vietnam War (1964–1975), which escalated throughout the 1960s. Once again, the two nations seemed to be locked in a military stalemate as diplomatic negotiations floundered. In contrast to the Korean conflict, however, the American public gradually turned away from supporting the United States' involvement in Vietnam. As an-

U.S. President Richard Nixon and Chinese Premier Zhou Enlai share a toast in Beijing, February 25, 1972. Nixon was the first U.S. president to make an official visit to the People's Republic of China. AP/WIDE WORLD PHOTOS. REPRODUCED BY PERMISSION.

tiwar protests swept college campuses in the late 1960s, polls showed that a growing majority of Americans favored a resolution to the war, even if it meant withdrawing from the region. Carefully reading public opinion on the war, presidential candidate Richard M. Nixon announced that he would end U.S. involvement in Vietnam if elected in 1968. In Nixon's view, however, it would first be necessary to reestablish official ties with the People's Republic of China, then the dominant power in Asia.

Significance

After the Nixon administration took office in 1969, it began a lengthy, and often secretive, series of diplomatic efforts to establish relations with the People's Republic of China. As anti-communism remained the cornerstone of U.S. foreign policy, Nixon did not want to appear soft on the issue. Nor did he want to abandon the United States' alliance with Taiwan, where U.S. forces remained as a deterrent to a possible invasion from the Chinese mainland. Against this backdrop, administration officials laid the groundwork for diplomatic talks beginning in January 1970. Within months, however, the talks broke down after the Chinese government protested the U.S. invasion of Cambodia as part of its strategy to bring the Vietnam War to a conclusion. While President

Nixon publicly expressed his desire to continue negotiations, they resumed in secret in October 1970. The second round of talks also foundered after the United States supported the South Vietnamese invasion of Laos in February 1971.

As the Nixon administration worked to reopen negotiations, the Chinese government offered a surprising invitation to the U.S. Ping-Pong team to play at a tournament in China in April 1971. It was the first official visit of any American delegation to the People's Republic of China since 1949. Seizing on the momentum generated by the "ping-pong diplomacy" offered by the Chinese, Nixon delivered a televised speech on July 15, 1971, announcing his acceptance of an invitation to visit China. During the delegation's eight-day visit in February 1972, President and Mrs. Nixon made headlines by appearing at some of the country's most famous attractions, including the Great Wall and the Great Hall of the People. During this period, the Nixon administration also eased many of the trade and travel restrictions that had been enforced against China and dropped U.S. opposition to granting China a place on the United Nations Security Council.

Ironically, although the resumption of diplomatic relations with China stood as perhaps Nixon's greatest foreign policy triumph, he was forced to resign in 1974, before full diplomatic ties were restored between the two countries. That event took place on January 1, 1979, under the administration of President Jimmy Carter (served 1977–1981).

Primary Source

"Presidential Speech Announcing Acceptance of an Invitation to Visit the People's Republic of China"

SYNOPSIS: As Nixon notes in this brief speech, one of his priorities in office was to resume diplomatic relations with the People's Republic of China. Not only was China the most populous nation on earth, it also played a key role in the regional security of East Asia, including the countries of North and South Korea and Vietnam, then also divided between North and South.

Good evening:

I have requested this television time tonight to announce a major development in our efforts to build a lasting peace in the world.

As I have pointed out on a number of occasions over the past 3 years, there can be no stable and enduring peace without the participation of the People's Republic of China and its 750 million people. That is why I have undertaken initiatives in several areas to open the door for more normal relations between our two countries.

In pursuance of that goal, I sent Dr. Kissinger, my Assistant for National Security Affairs, to Peking during his recent world tour for the purpose of having talks with Premier Chou En-lai.

The announcement I shall now read is being issued simultaneously in Peking and in the United States:

Premier Chou En-lai and Dr. Henry Kissinger, President Nixon's Assistant for National Security Affairs, held talks in Peking from July 9 to 11, 1971. Knowing of President Nixon's expressed desire to visit the People's Republic of China, Premier Chou En-lai, on behalf of the Government of the People's Republic of China, has extended an invitation to President Nixon to visit China at an appropriate date before May 1972. President Nixon has accepted the invitation with pleasure.

The meeting between the leaders of China and the United States is to seek the normalization of relations between the two countries and also to exchange views on questions of concern to the two sides.

In anticipation of the inevitable speculation which will follow this announcement, I want to put our policy in the clearest possible context.

Our action in seeking a new relationship with the People's Republic of China will not be at the expense of our old friends. It is not directed against any other nation. We seek friendly relations with all nations. Any nation can be our friend without being any other nation's enemy.

I have taken this action because of my profound conviction that all nations will gain from a reduction of tensions and a better relationship between the United States and the People's Republic of China.

It is in this spirit that I will undertake what I deeply hope will become a journey for peace, peace not just for our generation but for future generations on this earth we share together.

Thank you and good night.

Further Resources

BOOKS

Chang, Gordon H. *Friends and Enemies: The United States, China, and the Soviet Union, 1948–1972.* Stanford: Stanford University Press, 1990.

Foot, Rosemary. *The Practice of Power: U.S. Relations with China since 1949.* New York: Oxford University Press, 1995.

Mann, James. *About Face: A History of America's Curious Relationship with China, from Nixon to Clinton.* New York: Alfred A. Knopf, 1999.

McCormick, Thomas J. *America's Half-Century: United States Foreign Policy in the Cold War and After.* 2nd edition: Baltimore: Johns Hopkins University Press, 1995.

Nixon, Richard. *In the Arena: A Memoir of Victory, Defeat, and Renewal.* New York: Simon & Schuster, 1990.

Reeves, Richard. *President Nixon: Alone in the White House.* New York: Simon & Schuster, 2001.

Summers, Anthony, with Robbyn Swan. *The Arrogance of Power: The Secret World of Richard Nixon.* New York: Viking, 2000.

WEBSITES

"Nixon's China Game." *The American Experience.* Available online at http://www.pbs.org/wgbh/amex/china/; website home page: http://www.pbs.org (accessed May 25, 2003).

"Richard Nixon Library and Birthplace." Available online at http://www.nixonfoundation.org (accessed May 25, 2003).

A Thaw in the Cold War

"Convention on the Prohibition of the Development, Production and Stockpiling of Bacteriological (Biological) and Toxin Weapons and on Their Destruction"

Treaty

By: United Nations General Assembly and the Conference of the Committee on Disarmament

Date: April 10, 1972

Source: "Convention on the Prohibition of the Development, Production and Stockpiling of Bacteriological (Biological) and Toxin Weapons and on Their Destruction." April 10, 1972, signed in Washington, D.C., London, and Moscow. Available online at http://www.state.gov/www/global/arms /treaties/bwc1.html; website home page http://www.state.gov (accessed May 25, 2003).

Notes About the Organization: The United Nations (UN) tackled the issue of chemical and biological weapons disarmament in 1969 through its Conference of the Committee on Disarmament, encompassing twenty-six member nations. The committee gained momentum for its mission after President Nixon (served 1969–1974) announced that the United States unilaterally renounced the use of chemical, biological, or other toxic weapons in two separate declarations in late 1969 and early 1970. The following year, the Soviet Union agreed to undertake negotiations through the UN committee on the matter, who produced a draft resolution endorsed by the UN General Assembly in December 1971. On April 10, 1972, the Biological Weapons Convention, as it was commonly known, was signed by the governments of seventy-nine nations.

"Interim Agreement Between the United States of America and the Union of Soviet Socialist Republics on Certain Measures with Respect to the Limitation of Strategic Offensive Arms"

Treaty

By: The governments of the United States of America and the Union of Soviet Socialist Republics

Date: May 26, 1972

Source: "Interim Agreement Between the United States of America and the Union of Soviet Socialist Republics on Certain Measures with Respect to the Limitation of Strategic Offensive Arms." May 26, 1972, signed in Moscow. Available online at http://www.atomicarchive.com/Treaties /Treaty8fulltext.shtml; website home page: http:// www.atomicarchive.com (accessed May 25, 2003).

Notes About the Authors: The "Interim Agreement Between the United States of America and the Union of Soviet Socialist Republics on Certain Measures with Respect to the Limitation of Strategic Offensive Arms," commonly known as the SALT I Treaty, resulted from two-and-a-half years of negotiations between the two countries. Viewed as an important step in slowing down the nuclear arms race, the agreement opened the door to future arms-reduction talks between the two world superpowers.

President Richard Nixon's Second Inaugural Address, January 20, 1973

Speech

By: Richard M. Nixon

Date: January 20, 1973

Source: Nixon, Richard M. "President Nixon's Second Inaugural Address." January 20, 1973. Available online at http://www.watergate.info/nixon/inaugural-speech-second .shtml; website home page: http://www.watergate.info/ (accessed May 25, 2003).

Notes About the Author: Richard M. Nixon (1913–1994) served as the nation's thirty-seventh President at the time the Biological Weapons Convention and SALT I Treaty were negotiated. Nixon highlighted these accomplishments as he spoke at his second inauguration in January 1973, yet he would be forced to resign from office in August 1974 as a result of the Watergate affair. ■

Introduction

For generations after the end of World War II (1939–1945), Americans lived under the threat of nuclear war. "Duck-and-cover" safety drills to prepare for a nuclear attack became a routine part of the grade-school curriculum across the country, and some families even built bomb shelters in their backyards in case of a nuclear attack. Despite these fears, a direct, nuclear confrontation between the capitalist West and communist Eastern Bloc never occurred. Although "proxy wars" between the two camps broke out in Korea (1950–1953), Vietnam (1964–1975), and a host of other countries, the Cold War mostly lived up to its name.

As tensions between the United States and the Soviet Union gradually eased in the 1960s, a spirit of *détente* replaced the nervous anxiety and outright suspicion that had characterized their past relationship. Although the Vietnam War still raged as President Nixon took office in 1969, he surprised the international community later that year by offering a unilateral ban on the use of biological weapons, and he pledged that the United States would never offensively use chemical weapons. Nixon's announcement revitalized the United Nations's attempts to negotiate such a treaty for its member states, and a subsequent convention banning biological, chemical, and other toxic weapons was signed by seventy-nine nations on April 10, 1972.

On the heels of the biological weapons convention, Nixon traveled in May 1972 to Moscow for a summit meeting with Soviet general secretary Leonid Brezhnev. At the meeting's conclusion, the two leaders signed the Strategic Arms Limitation Treaty (SALT I), the result of negotiations over the previous two-and-a-half years. Although the SALT agreement did not ban the manufacture or possession of nuclear weapons by the two countries, it was a major step in easing their proliferation by the superpowers. SALT also promised to create a bilateral system of observation over the agreement, another step in linking the two countries together and easing Cold War tensions.

Significance

President Nixon used the momentum generated by the weapons agreements in his 1972 reelection campaign and went on to win a decisive victory. Together with the large-scale withdrawal of American troops from Vietnam, it appeared that the country was indeed putting the more lethal confrontations of the Cold War behind it. Nixon's international achievements, however, could not prevent the gradual corrosion of his presidency by the ongoing Watergate scandal, and he left office in disgrace in August 1974.

Of the two 1972 agreements, the SALT I treaty proved to be a more lasting contribution to world peace, as it opened up a permanent dialogue between the United States and the Soviet Union on arms control. Assuming that the United States would not abide by the convention on biological and chemical weapons, however, the Soviet Union made little attempt to destroy its existing stockpiles of the weapons. It continued to operate the largest chemical and biological weapons programs in the world through the eventual dissolution of the country in 1991. In contrast to the policies of the Soviet Union, the United States actually did live up to the convention and immediately destroyed its biological and chemical weapons in accordance with the agreement. It was only after the break up of the Soviet Union that the rest of the world learned how flagrantly the country had violated the international accord.

Although President Ronald Reagan (served 1981–1989) jumpstarted the arms race after taking office in 1981, the United States maintained its arms negotiations with the Soviet Union, even as it dramatically increased its own defense spending. As proxy wars between East and West flared up in Central America, central Asia, and Africa, the fact that two superpowers had remained committed to direct arms negotiations helped the conflicts from developing into regional, or even world, wars.

Primary Source

"Convention on the Prohibition of the Development, Production and Stockpiling of Bacteriological (Biological) and Toxin Weapons and on Their Destruction" [excerpt]

SYNOPSIS: International agreements to limit biological and chemical weapons dated back to the nineteenth century, yet by 1972 no comprehensive ban on the weapons had been enacted in the post-World War II era. In addition to banning the use of biological and chemical weapons, this Convention orders all such existing stocks to be destroyed and empowers the United Nations Security Council to supervise the maintenance of the agreement.

Signed at Washington, London, and Moscow
April 10, 1972
Ratification advised by U.S. Senate
December 16, 1974
Ratified by U.S. President January 22, 1975
U.S. ratification deposited at Washington, London, and Moscow March 26, 1975
Proclaimed by U.S. President March 26, 1975
Entered into force March 26, 1975

The States Parties to this Convention,

Determined to act with a view to achieving effective progress towards general and complete disarmament, including the prohibition and elimination of all types of weapons of mass destruction, and convinced that the prohibition of the development, production and stockpiling of chemical and bacteriological (biological) weapons and their elimination, through effective measures, will facilitate the achievement of general and complete disarmament under strict and effective international control,

Recognizing the important significance of the Protocol for the Prohibition of the Use in War of Asphyxiating, Poisonous or Other Gases, and of Bacteriological Methods of Warfare, signed at Geneva on June 17, 1925, and conscious also of the contribution which the said Protocol has already made, and continues to make, to mitigating the horrors of war,

Reaffirming their adherence to the principles and objectives of that Protocol and calling upon all States to comply strictly with them,

Recalling that the General Assembly of the United Nations has repeatedly condemned all actions contrary to the principles and objectives of the Geneva Protocol of June 17, 1925,

Desiring to contribute to the strengthening of confidence between peoples and the general improvement of the international atmosphere,

Desiring also to contribute to the realization of the purposes and principles of the Charter of the United Nations,

Convinced of the importance and urgency of eliminating from the arsenals of States, through effective measures, such dangerous weapons of mass destruction as those using chemical or bacteriological (biological) agents,

Recognizing that an agreement on the prohibition of bacteriological (biological) and toxin weapons represents a first possible step towards the achievement of agreement on effective measures also for the prohibition of the development, production and stockpiling of chemical weapons, and determined to continue negotiations to that end,

Determined, for the sake of all mankind, to exclude completely the possibility of bacteriological (biological) agents and toxins being used as weapons,

Convinced that such use would be repugnant to the conscience of mankind and that no effort should be spared to minimize this risk,

Have agreed as follows:

Article I

Each State Party to this Convention undertakes never in any circumstances to develop, produce, stockpile or otherwise acquire or retain:

1. Microbial or other biological agents, or toxins whatever their origin or method of production, of types and in quantities that have no justification for prophylactic, protective or other peaceful purposes;

2. Weapons, equipment or means of delivery designed to use such agents or toxins for hostile purposes or in armed conflict.

Article II

Each State Party to this Convention undertakes to destroy, or to divert to peaceful purposes, as soon as possible but not later than nine months after the entry into force of the Convention, all agents, toxins, weapons, equipment and means of delivery specified in article I of the Convention, which are in its possession or under its jurisdiction or control. In implementing the provisions of this article all necessary safety precautions shall be observed to protect populations and the environment.

Article III

Each State Party to this Convention undertakes not to transfer to any recipient whatsoever, directly or indirectly, and not in any way to assist, encourage, or induce any State, group of States or international organizations to manufacture or otherwise acquire any of the agents, toxins, weapons, equipment or means of delivery specified in article I of the Convention.

Article IV

Each State Party to this Convention shall, in accordance with its constitutional processes, take any necessary measures to prohibit and prevent the development, production, stockpiling, acquisition, or retention of the agents, toxins, weapons, equipment and means of delivery specified in article I of the Convention, within the territory of such State, under its jurisdiction or under its control anywhere.

Article V

The States Parties to this Convention undertake to consult one another and to cooperate in solving any problems which may arise in relation to the objective of, or in the application of the provisions of, the Convention. Consultation and cooperation pursuant to this article may also be undertaken through appropriate international procedures within the framework of the United Nations and in accordance with its Charter. . . .

IN WITNESS WHEREOF the undersigned, duly authorized, have signed this Convention.

DONE in triplicate, at the cities of Washington, London and Moscow, this tenth day of April, one thousand nine hundred and seventy-two.

Primary Source

"Interim Agreement Between the United States of America and the Union of Soviet Socialist Republics on Certain Measures with Respect to the Limitation of Strategic Offensive Arms" [excerpt]

SYNOPSIS: Although the nuclear arms race was not limited to the United States and the Soviet Union, the two superpowers possessed the overwhelming majority of such weapons. This agreement, commonly known as the Strategic Arms Limitation Treaty (SALT), was the first significant arms-reduction treaty between the two countries and led to future negotiations between them. Another treaty, SALT II, resulted from later negotiations but was not ratified by the U.S. Senate.

Signed at Moscow May 26, 1972
Approval authorized by U.S. Congress September 30, 1972

U.S. President Jimmy Carter, left center, and Soviet President Leonid Brezhnev, right center, shake hands after signing the SALT II Treaty on June 8, 1979. **AP/WIDE WORLD PHOTOS. REPRODUCED BY PERMISSION.**

Approved by U.S. President September 30, 1972
Notices of acceptance exchanged October 3, 1972
Entered into force October 3, 1972

The United States of America and the Union of Soviet Socialist Republics, hereinafter referred to as the Parties,

Convinced that the Treaty on the Limitation of Anti-Ballistic Missile Systems and this Interim Agreement on Certain Measures with Respect to the Limitation of Strategic Offensive Arms will contribute to the creation of more favorable conditions for active negotiations on limiting strategic arms as well as to the relaxation of international tension and the strengthening of trust between States,

Taking into account the relationship between strategic offensive and defensive arms,

Mindful of their obligations under Article VI of the Treaty on the Non-Proliferation of Nuclear Weapons,

Have agreed as follows:

Article I

The Parties undertake not to start construction of additional fixed land-based intercontinental ballistic missile (ICBM) launchers after July 1, 1972.

Article II

The Parties undertake not to convert land-based launchers for light ICBMs, or for ICBMs of older types deployed prior to 1964, into land-based launchers for heavy ICBMs of types deployed after that time.

Article III

The Parties undertake to limit submarine-launched ballistic missile (SLBM) launchers and modern ballistic missile submarines to the numbers operational and under construction on the date of signature of this Interim Agreement, and in addition to launchers and submarines constructed under procedures established by the Parties as replacements for an equal number of ICBM launchers of older types deployed prior to 1964 or for launchers on older submarines.

Article IV

Subject to the provisions of this Interim Agreement, modernization and replacement of strategic offensive ballistic missiles and launchers covered by this Interim Agreement may be undertaken.

Article V

1. For the purpose of providing assurance of compliance with the provisions of this Interim Agreement, each Party shall use national technical means of verification at its disposal in a manner consistent with generally recognized principles of international law.

2. Each Party undertakes not to interfere with the national technical means of verification of the other Party operating in accordance with paragraph 1 of this Article.

3. Each Party undertakes not to use deliberate concealment measures which impede verification by national technical means of compliance with the provisions of this Interim Agreement. This obligation shall not require changes in current construction, assembly, conversion, or overhaul practices.

Article VI

To promote the objectives and implementation of the provisions of this Interim Agreement, the Parties shall use the Standing Consultative Commission established under Article XIII of the Treaty on the Limitation of Anti-Ballistic Missile Systems in accordance with the provisions of that Article.

Article VII

The Parties undertake to continue active negotiations for limitations on strategic offensive arms. The obligations provided for in this Interim Agreement shall not prejudice the scope or terms of the limitations on strategic offensive arms which may be worked out in the course of further negotiations.

Article VIII

1. This Interim Agreement shall enter into force upon exchange of written notices of acceptance by each Party, which exchange shall take place simultaneously with the exchange of instruments of ratification of the Treaty on the Limitation of Anti-Ballistic Missile Systems.

2. This Interim Agreement shall remain in force for a period of five years unless replaced earlier by an agreement on more complete measures limiting strategic offensive arms. It is the objective of the Parties to conduct active follow-on negotiations with the aim of concluding such an agreement as soon as possible.

3. Each Party shall, in exercising its national sovereignty, have the right to withdraw from this Interim Agreement if it decides that extraordinary events re-lated to the subject matter of this Interim Agreement have jeopardized its supreme interests. It shall give notice of its decision to the other Party six months prior to withdrawal from this Interim Agreement. Such notice shall include a statement of the extraordinary events the notifying Party regards as having jeopardized its supreme interests.

DONE at Moscow on May 26, 1972, in two copies, each in the English and Russian languages, both texts being equally authentic.

FOR THE UNITED STATES OF AMERICA:
RICHARD NIXON
President of the United States of America

FOR THE UNION OF SOVIET SOCIALIST REPUBLICS:
L.I. BREZHNEV
General Secretary of the Central Committee of the CPSU

Primary Source

President Richard Nixon's Second Inaugural Address, January 20, 1973 [excerpt]

SYNOPSIS: Nixon prided himself on his foreign relations experience and frequently noted his success in normalizing relations with the Soviet Union and the People's Republic of China during his reelection effort in 1972. After winning the election, Nixon returned to these themes in his inaugural address, challenging Americans to "build a structure of peace in the world in which the weak are as safe as the strong . . . in which those who would influence others will do so by the strength of their ideas, and not by the force of their arms."

Mr. Vice President, Mr. Speaker, Mr. Chief Justice, Senator Cook, Mrs. Eisenhower, and my fellow citizens of this great and good country we share together:

When we met here four years ago, America was bleak in spirit, depressed by the prospect of seemingly endless war abroad and of destructive conflict at home.

As we meet here today, we stand on the threshold of a new era of peace in the world.

The central question before us is: How shall we use that peace? Let us resolve that this era we are about to enter will not be what other postwar periods have so often been: a time of retreat and isolation that leads to stagnation at home and invites new danger abroad.

Let us resolve that this will be what it can become: a time of great responsibilities greatly borne, in which we renew the spirit and the promise of America as we enter our third century as a nation.

This past year saw far-reaching results from our new policies for peace. By continuing to revitalize our traditional friendships, and by our missions to Peking and to Moscow, we were able to establish the base for a new and more durable pattern of relationships among the nations of the world. Because of America's bold initiatives, 1972 will be long remembered as the year of the greatest progress since the end of World War II toward a lasting peace in the world.

The peace we seek in the world is not the flimsy peace which is merely an interlude between wars, but a peace which can endure for generations to come.

It is important that we understand both the necessity and the limitations of America's role in maintaining that peace.

Unless we in America work to preserve the peace, there will be no peace.

Unless we in America work to preserve freedom, there will be no freedom.

But let us clearly understand the new nature of America's role, as a result of the new policies we have adopted over these past four years.

We shall respect our treaty commitments.

We shall support vigorously the principle that no country has the right to impose its will or rule on another by force.

We shall continue, in this era of negotiation, to work for the limitation of nuclear arms, and to reduce the danger of confrontation between the great powers.

We shall do our share in defending peace and freedom in the world. But we shall expect others to do their share.

The time has passed when America will make every other nation's conflict our own, or make every other nation's future our responsibility, or presume to tell the people of other nations how to manage their own affairs.

Just as we respect the right of each nation to determine its own future, we also recognize the responsibility of each nation to secure its own future.

Just as America's role is indispensable in preserving the world's peace, so is each nation's role indispensable in preserving its own peace.

Together with the rest of the world, let us resolve to move forward from the beginnings we have made. Let us continue to bring down the walls of hostility which have divided the world for too long, and to build in their place bridges of understanding—so that despite profound differences between systems of government, the people of the world can be friends.

Let us build a structure of peace in the world in which the weak are as safe as the strong—in which each respects the right of the other to live by a different system—in which those who would influence others will do so by the strength of their ideas, and not by the force of their arms. . . .

America's record in this century has been unparalleled in the world's history for its responsibility, for its generosity, for its creativity and for its progress.

Let us be proud that our system has produced and provided more freedom and more abundance, more widely shared, than any other system in the history of the world.

Let us be proud that in each of the four wars in which we have been engaged in this century, including the one we are now bringing to an end, we have fought not for our selfish advantage, but to help others resist aggression.

Let us be proud that by our bold, new initiatives, and by our steadfastness for peace with honor, we have made a break-through toward creating in the world what the world has not known before—a structure of peace that can last, not merely for our time, but for generations to come.

We are embarking here today on an era that presents challenges great as those any nation, or any generation, has ever faced.

We shall answer to God, to history, and to our conscience for the way in which we use these years.

As I stand in this place, so hallowed by history, I think of others who have stood here before me. I think of the dreams they had for America, and I think of how each recognized that he needed help far beyond himself in order to make those dreams come true.

Today, I ask your prayers that in the years ahead I may have God's help in making decisions that are right for America, and I pray for your help so that together we may be worthy of our challenge.

Let us pledge together to make these next four years the best four years in America's history, so that on its 200th birthday America will be as young and as vital as when it began, and as bright a beacon of hope for all the world.

Let us go forward from here confident in hope, strong in our faith in one another, sustained by our faith in God who created us, and striving always to serve His purpose.

Further Resources

BOOKS

Alibek, Ken, with Stephen Handelman. *Biohazard: The Chilling True Story of the Largest Covert Biological Weapons Program in the World.* New York: Random House, 1999.

Miller, Judith, et al. *Germs: Biological Weapons and America's Secret War.* New York: Simon and Schuster, 2001.

Payne Jr., Samuel B. *The Soviet Union and SALT.* Cambridge, Mass.: MIT University Press, 1980.

Sheehan, Michael J. *Arms Control: Theory and Practice.* New York: Basil Blackwell, 1988.

Smith, Gerard. *Doubletalk: The Story of the First Strategic Arms Limitation Talks.* Garden City, N.Y.: Doubleday, 1980.

Stern, Jessica. *Chemical and Biological Weapons in Our Times.* Cambridge, Mass.: Harvard University Press, 1999.

WEBSITES

"Treaty Between the United States of America and the Union of Soviet Socialist Republics on the Limitation of Strategic Offensive Arms (SALT I)" Available online at http://www.state.gov/t/ac/trt/5191pf.htm; website home page http://www.state.gov (accessed May 25, 2003).

Dark Days in the White House

"5 Held in Plot to Bug Democrats' Office Here"

Newspaper article

By: Alfred E. Lewis

Date: June 18, 1972

Source: Lewis, Alfred E. "5 Held in Plot to Bug Democrats' Office Here." *Washington Post,* June 18, 1972, 1, 22.

About the Author: Alfred E. Lewis, a veteran crime reporter who joined the staff of the *Washington Post* in the 1930s, delivered the first front-page article on the Watergate break-in on Sunday, July 18, 1972.

"Suspect Aided, Fought Castro"

Newspaper article

By: Carl Bernstein and Kirk Scharfenberg

Date: June 18, 1972

Source: Bernstein, Carl, and Kirk Scharfenberg. "Suspect Aided, Fought Castro." *Washington Post,* June 18, 1972.

About the Author: Carl Bernstein and Kirk Scharfenberg also contributed a story on the Watergate suspects in that day's *Washington Post.* Bernstein would later team with reporter Bob Woodward to write most of the paper's Watergate coverage over the next two years, culminating in President Nixon's (served 1969–1974) resignation in August 1974. ∎

Introduction

In the early morning of Saturday, July 17, 1972, five men were arrested after breaking into the offices of the Democrat National Committee headquarters, located in the Watergate building in Washington, D.C. Although it was at first suspected that they were there to plant a wiretap, the group actually had sought to replace a faulty wiretap that they had planted earlier. Reporters Bob Woodward and Carl Bernstein, who took the lead on investigating the Watergate story for the *Washington Post,* quickly learned that the leader of the Watergate suspects, James McCord, also worked as a security coordinator on the Committee to Re-elect the President (CREEP), devoted to delivering a second term to incumbent President Richard M. Nixon. Although the alleged ties to the White House made the Watergate story an important one, it was largely drowned out in the national media in favor of covering the presidential race itself. Although the *Post* reported in August 1972 that a $25,000 check designated for CREEP actually went to pay for the Watergate burglary, the direct ties between the White House and the break-in did little to stop the momentum of the Nixon campaign. While Nixon's advisors staged a cover-up of the Watergate scandal, the administration continued to deny any direct involvement in the break-in. On election day, Nixon trounced Democrat George McGovern with 60.7 percent of the popular vote and 520 electoral votes to McGovern's seventeen.

It was only as the Watergate defendants came to trial before Judge John Sirica in January 1973 that the Watergate story grabbed national attention. One month later, a Special Senate Committee to Investigate Watergate, led by North Carolina senator Sam Ervin, began an inquiry into Watergate as well. In April 1972, the first mass resignations and firings of top White House officials made headlines and signaled the beginning of the end of Nixon's second term.

Significance

On Monday, July 16, 1973, presidential aide Alexander P. Butterfield revealed in a nationally televised interview before the Senate Committee on Watergate that President Nixon had recorded all of his conversations in the Oval Office on a secret taping system. The revelation of the Watergate tapes—and the Nixon administration's futile attempts to keep from handing them over—transfixed the nation. As the biggest political scandal of the century—and perhaps in the entire history of American politics—the Watergate affair was rarely off the front pages during the remainder of Nixon's second term, culminating in his resignation on August 8, 1974. Still refusing to admit his guilt in the Watergate cover-up, Nixon left the White House the following day.

In revealing just how far the corruption and deceit reached into the White House, the Watergate scandal profoundly disillusioned many Americans. Not only had CREEP operated out of a secret campaign slush fund from illegal contributions, it had implemented a well-planned "dirty tricks" campaign to discredit and disrupt the candidacies of Nixon's Democratic rivals. In ordering a cover-up of CREEP's activities, Nixon had also authorized his staff to spin a series of lies to the media and independent investigators. The president even went so far as to fire Archibald Cox, the special prosecutor assigned to the Watergate Committee, in an attempt to derail the investigation.

While the country struggled to come to terms with the enormity of the Watergate scandal, some Americans took comfort in the ultimate integrity of the political system. Despite their pattern of illegal activities, deceit, and intimidation, twenty-five Nixon aides eventually served time in prison, and four cabinet-level officers, including Attorney General John Mitchell, were convicted in criminal prosecutions. The former president himself, however, was pardoned for his role in Watergate by his successor, Gerald R. Ford (served 1974–1977), just a month after his resignation.

Primary Source

"5 Held in Plot to Bug Democrats' Office Here"

SYNOPSIS: When Barry Sussman, the city editor of the *Washington Post,* received a phone call alerting him to a break-in at the Watergate building, he immediately assigned the paper's most respected crime reporter, Alfred E. Lewis, to the story. Lewis delivered an article that stuck to the facts of the break-in, as they were then known. It was only later that substantive ties to the White House were revealed.

Five men, one of whom said he is a former employee of the Central Intelligence Agency, were arrested at 2:30 a.m. yesterday in what authorities described as an elaborate plot to bug the offices of the Democratic National Committee here.

Three of the men were native-born Cubans and another was said to have trained Cuban exiles for guerrilla activity after the 1961 Bay of Pigs invasion.

They were surprised at gunpoint by three plainclothes officers of the metropolitan police depart-

Tape recordings President Nixon secretly made of his White House conversations ultimately proved his culpability in the Watergate scandal. **THE LIBRARY OF CONGRESS.**

ment in a sixth-floor office at the plush Watergate, 2600 Virginia Ave., NW. where the Democratic National Committee occupies the entire floor.

There was no immediate explanation as to why the five suspects would want to bug the Democratic National Committee offices or whether or not they were working for any other individuals or organizations.

A spokesman for the Democratic National Committee said records kept in those offices are "not of a sensitive variety" although there are "financial records and other such information."

Police said two ceiling panels in the office of Dorothy V. Bush, secretary of the Democratic Party, had been removed.

Her office is adjacent to the office of Democratic National Chairman Lawrence F. O'Brien. Presumably, it would have been possible to slide a bugging device through the panels in that office to a place above the ceiling panels in O'Brien's office.

All wearing rubber surgical gloves, the five suspects were captured inside a small office within the committee's headquarters suite.

Police said the men had with them at least two sophisticated devices capable of picking up and transmitting all talk, including telephone conversations. In addition, police found lock-picks and door jimmies, almost $2,300 in cash, most of it in $100 bills with the serial numbers in sequence.

The men also had with them one walkie-talkie, a short wave receiver that could pick up police calls, 40 rolls of unexposed film, two 35 millimeter cameras and three pen-sized tear gas guns.

Near where they were captured were two open file drawers, and one national committee source conjectured that the men were preparing to photograph the contents.

In Court yesterday, one suspect said the men were "anti-Communists" and the others nodded agreement. The operation was described in court by prosecutor Earl J. Silbert as "professional" and "clandestine." One of the Cuban natives, The Washington Post learned, is now a Miami locksmith.

Many of the burglary tools found at the Democratic National Committee offices appeared to be packaged in what police said were burglary kits.

The five men were identified as:

- Edward Martin, alias James W. McCord, of New York City and perhaps the Washington metropolitan area. Martin said in court yesterday that he retired from the CIA two years ago. He said he presently is employed as a "security consultant."

- Frank Sturgis of 2515 NW 122d St., Miami. Prosecutors said that an FBI check on Sturgis showed that he had served in the Cuban Military army intelligence in 1958, recently travelled to Honduras in Central America, and presently is the agent for a Havana salvage agency. He has a home and family in Miami. Sturgis also was once charged with a gun violation in Miami, according to FBI records.

- Eugenio R. Martinez of 4044 North Meridian Ave., Miami. Prosecutors said that Martinez violated the immigration laws in 1958 by flying in a private plane to Cuba. He is a licensed real estate agent and a notary public in Florida.

- Virgilio R. Gonzales of 930 NW 23d Ave. Miami. In Miami yesterday, his wife told a Washington Post reporter that her husband works as a locksmith at the Missing Link Key Shop. Harry Collot, the shop owner, said that Gonzales was scheduled to work yesterday but didn't show up. "He's done it before, but it's not a regular thing." Collot said. He said he thought Gonzales came to America about the time Fidel Castro became well-known, and began working for Missing Links sometime in 1959. He described Gonzales as "pro-American and anti-Castro . . . he doesn't rant or rave like some of them do."

- Bernard L. Barker of 5229 NW 4th St., Miami. Douglas Caddy, one of the attorneys for the five men told a reporter that shortly after 3 a.m. yesterday, he received a call from Barker's wife. "She said that her husband told her to call me if he hadn't called her by 3 a.m.: that it might mean he was in trouble."

All were charged with felonious burglary and with possession of implements of crime. All but Martin were ordered held in $50,000 bail. Martin, who has ties in the area, was held in $30,000 bail.

In court yesterday, prosecutors said Sturgis also used the alias Frank Fiorini—an assertion confirmed by Miami area police.

(In 1959, the Federal Aviation Agency identified Fiorini as the pilot of a plane that dropped anti-Castro leaflets over Havana. Described in newspaper clippings as a "soldier of fortune," Fiorini reportedly was head of the International anticommunist Brigade, after the Bay of Pigs invasion, that trained 23 Cuban exiles who in 1962 landed by boat in Cuba's Matanzas Province and set up guerrilla operations.

(Fiorini reportedly is a native of Norfolk, Va., who fought with the Marines in the Pacific during World War II. An early supporter of the Cuban revolution, he reportedly fought with Castro and was named by the premier to be overseer of gambling operations in Havana before the casinos were shut down by the premier.)

The early morning arrests occurred about 40 minutes after a security guard at the Watergate no-

The 1972 events at the Watergate, first perceived as a simple break-in, soon expanded into a much larger scandal that engulfed the Nixon administration and led to the president's resignation. AP/WIDE WORLD PHOTOS. REPRODUCED BY PERMISSION.

ticed that a door connecting a stairwell with the hotel's basement garage had been taped so it would not lock.

The guard, 24-year-old Frank Wills, removed the tape, but when he passed by about 10 minutes later a new piece had been put on. Wills then called police.

Three officers from the tactical squad responded and entered the stairwell.

From the basement to the sixth floor, they found every door leading from the stairwell to a hallway of the building had been taped to prevent them from locking. At the sixth floor, where the stairwell door leads directly into the Democratic National Committee offices, they found the door had been jimmied.

Led by Sgt. Paul Leper, the tactical force team, which also included Officers John Barret and Carl Shollfer, began searching the suite, which includes 29 offices and where approximately 70 persons work.

When the officers entered an office occupied by a secretary to Stanley Griegg, deputy party chairman, one of the suspects jumped up from behind a desk, put his hands in the air and cried "Don't shoot," police said.

According to police and a desk clerk at the Watergate, four of the suspects—all using fictitious names—rented two rooms, number 214 and 314 at the Watergate Hotel around noon on Friday. They were said to have dined together on lobster at the Watergate Restaurant on Friday night.

Yesterday afternoon, the U.S. Attorney's office obtained warrants to search the hotel rooms rented by the suspects. They found another $4,200 in $100 bills of the same serial number sequence as the money taken from the suspects, more burglary tools and electronic bugging equipment stashed in six suitcases.

One of the bugging devices found at the scene of the Democratic National Committee offices was described as being about the size of a silver dollar and capable of being hidden underneath a telephone or a desk.

According to police the break-in at the Democratic National Committee offices yesterday was the third incident there since May 28.

On that date, according to police, an attempt was made to unscrew a lock on the door between 11 p.m. and 8 a.m.

According to one police source, at least some of the suspects registered as guests at the Watergate Hotel on that date.

On June 7, police said, a safe at the Committee headquarters was reported broken into and $100 in cash and checks stolen. That break-in occurred about 9 p.m. but there was no door jimmied since the suite was unlocked and people were still working there.

Within hours after the arrests, the suite was sealed off and scores of metropolitan police officers directed by acting Chief Charles Wright, FBI agents and Secret Service men were assigned to the investigation.

Caddy, one of the attorneys for the five, said he met Barker a year ago over cocktails at the Army-Navy Club in Washington. "We had a sympathetic conversation—that's all I'll say." Caddy told a reporter.

Caddy said that he was probably the only attorney whom Barker knew in Washington.

Caddy, who says he is a corporate lawyer, attempted to stay in the background of yesterday's 4 p.m. court hearing. He did not argue before Superior Court Judge James A. Belson himself but brought another attorney, Joseph A. Rafferty Jr., who has experience in criminal law, to do the arguing.

In that 30-minute arraignment Assistant U.S. Attorney Earl Silbert, the No. 2 man in the chief prosecutor's office, unsuccessfully urged the court to order the five men held without bond.

Silbert argued that the men had no community ties and would be likely to leave the country to avoid trial. He said they gave false names to the police after they were arrested and refused to cooperate.

"They were caught red-handed," Silbert said. With such strong evidence against them, their apparent tendency to travel abroad and their access to large amounts of cash, the men should not be released, Silbert said.

Silbert called the men professionals with a "clandestine" purpose.

Rafferty said the five men didn't have firearms and didn't harm anyone, and should be released on bond.

In setting the bond at $50,000 for the Miami men and $30,000 for Martin, Judge Belson also placed restrictions on their movements.

He required the four Miami men to stay in the Washington area and check in daily with the court, if released. Martin would have to check in weekly if released, Belson ruled.

Griegg, deputy party chairman, called it "obviously important" that some of the suspects come from the area around Miami and Miami Beach, where the Democratic National Convention will be held next month.

Primary Source

"Suspect Aided, Fought Castro"

SYNOPSIS: At the time of the Watergate break-in, it appeared that the suspects might have had ties to anti-communist crusaders against Cuban leader Fidel Castro. Only later was it learned that the Watergate break-in was just part of a coordinated "dirty tricks" effort on the part of the Committee to Reelect the President (CREEP), with important ties to the Nixon administration.

The suspects in the apparent plot to bug the offices of the Democratic National Committee include a locksmith, a man who said he was a former CIA employee, an American soldier of fortune who fought with Fidel Castro in Cuba and later trained anti-Castro exiles, and another man linked by Cuban exiles to the CIA.

The best known of the suspects appears to be Frank Sturgis, a native of Norfolk, who joined Fidel Castro in the hills of Oriente Province in 1958.

According to newspaper reports and Cuban exile sources in Miami, Sturgis—also known as Frank Fiorini—was named by Castro to oversee the gambling casinos in Havana until they were closed shortly after the revolution in January, 1959.

Sturgis left Cuba in 1959 for Miami and later became head of the International Anti-Communist Brigade.

The Brigade trained Cuban exiles who in 1962—a year after the Bay of Pigs invasion—landed in Matanzas Province and set up anti-Castro guerrilla operations east of Havana.

Sturgis, who is 47, also was identified by federal authorities as the copilot of the plane that dropped anti-Castro leaflets over Havana in 1959.

A former manager of a tavern in Norfolk, Sturgis served in the Marine Corps in Korea, was wounded while fighting with Castro in Cuba and—according to exiles—has worked recently as a plate glass salesman in Miami.

The same exiles said yesterday that another of the suspects, Bernard L. Barker, 55, has worked off and on for the CIA since the Bay of Pigs invasion.

Barker's wife Clara said in a telephone interview from Miami yesterday that her husband, a native of Havana, has owned a real estate firm in Miami for about a year.

Mrs. Barker said her husband was imprisoned briefly by Castro in 1959 shortly before they moved to Miami. Exile sources said Barker is known in the Cuban community as "Macho"—meaning husky or beefy—and that he was closely associated with Frank Bender, the CIA operative who recruited many members Brigade 2506: the Bay of Pigs invasion force.

In court yesterday, another of the suspects—Edward Martin, alias James W. McCord—identified himself as a former CIA agent.

His purported employment by the agency came to light when the judge questioned a bail report that listed Martin as a "security consultant" retired from government service. The judge asked what "government service"? Martin conferred with his lawyer, then said "intelligence," the "CIA." His lawyer repeated, "CIA."

A CIA spokesman said that, based on the date of birth provided from yesterday's Washington police arrest record, Edward Martin "has never worked for the CIA."

The arrest record listed Martin's date of birth as Oct. 9, 1918. The CIA said there is no record of an Edward Martin's with that birthdate having worked for the agency. However, the spokesman said agency records contain a "drawerful" of Edward Martins with other dates of birth.

Later, the CIA was unable to confirm or deny that a James W. McCord had been employed there.

Martin, who police say has lived in New York City and possibly Washington, was the only suspect who is not known to have a Miami address.

The suspect identified as a locksmith. Virgilio R. Gonzales, was said by his wife to be an employee of the Missing Link Key Shop in Miami.

The fifth suspect, Eugenio R. Martinez, was said by prosecutors and exiles to have violated American immigration laws in 1958 when he flew a plane to his native Cuba to join Castro's insurrection against Fulgencio Batista. Martinez reportedly later turned against Castro.

Further Resources

BOOKS

Bernstein, Carl, and Bob Woodward. *All the President's Men.* New York: Simon and Schuster, 1974.

———. *The Final Days.* New York: Avon, 1976.

Dean, John W. *Blind Ambition: The White House Years.* New York: Simon and Schuster, 1976.

Schudson, Michael. *Watergate in American Memory: How We Remember, Forget, and Recontstruct the Past.* New York: BasicBooks, 1993.

Wicker, Tom. *One of Us: Richard Nixon and the American Dream.* New York: Random House, 1991.

AUDIO AND VISUAL MEDIA

All the President's Men. Directed by Alan J. Pakula. Warner Studios, Videocassette, 1976.

WEBSITES

"Case Study: Watergate." Available online at http://www.journalism.org/resources/education/case_studies/watergate.asp; website home page http://www.journalism.org (accessed May 25, 2003).

"The Richard Nixon Library & Birthplace." Available online at http://www.nixonfoundation.org (accessed May 25, 2003).

"Text of Address by McGovern Accepting the Democratic Presidential Nomination"

Speech

By: George S. McGovern

Date: July 14, 1972

Source: McGovern, George S. "Text of Address by McGovern Accepting the Democratic Presidential Nomination." *The New York Times,* July 14, 1972, 11.

About the Author: George S. McGovern (1922–) briefly pursued an academic career before winning a Congressional seat from South Dakota in 1956. The Democrat was elected to the U.S. Senate in 1962, and he remained in that body until his retirement from politics in 1980. In 1972, he won the Democratic nomination for the presidency, but was defeated by President Richard R. Nixon (served 1969–1974) in the election. McGovern remained a respected public figure in his retirement in the 1990s, serving as the U.S. ambassador to the United Nations Agencies on Food and Agriculture, where he was recognized as one of the world's leading experts on the issue of world hunger. ∎

Introduction

The Democrats had hoped to retain the White House in 1968 with the presidential candidacy of Robert F. Kennedy, who appealed to both traditional Democratic bases and younger voters. After Kennedy's assassination in June 1968, the party's nomination went to Hubert Humphrey, who lost the election by a half-million votes to Republican Richard M. Nixon. Nixon's appeal to the "silent majority" of voters shocked by antiwar protests and urban riots, as well as the third-party campaign of George C. Wallace, a Democrat from Alabama who gained fame as a segregationist, left Humphrey without enough support to win the White House.

In 1972, Humphrey once again hoped to win the Democratic nomination to challenge Nixon. This time, however, the party's left wing—dominated by antiwar sentiments and frustrated by the party's "old guard" that Humphrey represented—worked to deliver the nomination to South Dakota Senator, George McGovern. McGovern had served in Congress as a representative and senator since 1956, but he was hardly a nationally known name as he launched his presidential bid. Through a series of contested primaries, however, McGovern slowly built enough support to win his party's nomination. Crucial to his success was the support of his party's more liberal-minded members: feminists, Civil Rights activists, and young people, who were attracted to McGovern's candidacy for his unflagging opposition to the Vietnam War (1964–1975). McGovern's antiwar stance became the best-known plank in his platform, which otherwise mostly adhered to the traditional Democratic agenda.

Although reports of White House ties to a break in at the Democratic National Committee offices in the Watergate building surfaced in the final weeks of the 1972 presidential race, the media paid more attention to the problems of McGovern's running mate, Missouri Senator Thomas Eagleton. After it was reported that Eagleton had suffered from a nervous breakdown and received electroshock therapy several years earlier, McGovern replaced Eagleton with R. Sargent Shriver as his vice-presidential running mate. The move did little to enhance McGovern's reputation for leadership, as he at first insisted that Eagleton would remain on the ticket.

Significance

If McGovern's nomination to lead his party in the presidential race represented liberalism's triumph in the Democratic Party, his defeat in November showed the limits of liberal political candidates in the two-party system. McGovern carried only Massachusetts and the District of Columbia in the Electoral College, and he won just 37.5 percent of the popular vote. Nixon, campaigning on a platform of "Vietnamization" to end America's involvement in the war, combined with his renewed promise to restore law and order on the nation's streets, resulted in a victory for the Republican.

In the wake of McGovern's dismal showing at the polls, Democrats were put on notice that the liberal agenda of Civil Rights, women's rights, social welfare

programs, and stringent antiwar measures no longer had the broad base of support they had seemingly enjoyed in the 1960s. As the party's leaders struggled to retain their traditional bases of support while courting middle-of-the-road voters, a new generation of "moderate Democrats" came to the party's front ranks. Typified by Jimmy Carter (served 1977–1981) and later Michael Dukakis and Bill Clinton (served 1993–2001), these moderate Democrats tried to steer clear of controversial social issues, while promising to practice fiscal responsibility in office.

Nixon's astounding margin of victory in the 1972 election turned out to be a short-lived triumph. The president resigned in disgrace in 1974 after a dogged, two-year media and Senate inquiry into Watergate. McGovern continued his political career and retained his Senate seat until he retired from politics in 1980. Despite his historic election defeat, McGovern emerged as one of the country's most respected statesmen, particularly for his work to end world hunger as an ambassador to the United Nations Agencies on Food and Agriculture.

Primary Source

"Text of Address by McGovern Accepting the Democratic Presidential Nomination"

SYNOPSIS: McGovern's triumph in the Democratic primaries signaled the ascent of the liberal wing of the party over its more moderate and conservative elements, many of whom had defected to support the segregationist, third-party candidacy of former Alabama Governor, George C. Wallace. In his acceptance speech at the Democratic National Convention, McGovern highlighted the themes that resonated with his party's younger members, particularly ending the war in Vietnam. Although McGovern also tried to hold on to the support of his party's traditional supporters, his failure to do so dealt him a crushing loss on election day to Richard M. Nixon.

With a full heart, I accept your nomination.

And this afternoon, I crossed the wide Missouri to recommend a running mate of wide vision and deep compassion—Tom Eagleton.

My nomination is all the more precious in that it is the gift of the most open political process in our national history. It is the sweet harvest cultivated by tens of thousands of tireless volunteers—old and young—and funded by literally hundreds of thousands of small contributors. Those who lingered on the edge of despair a brief time ago had been brought into this campaign—heart, hand, head and soul.

I have been the beneficiary of the most remarkable political organization in American history—

an organization that gives dramatic proof to the power of love and to a faith that can move mountains.

As Yeats put it: "Count where man's glory most begins and ends, and say, my glory was I had such friends."

This is a nomination of the people and I hereby dedicate this campaign to the people.

And next January we will restore the government to the people. American politics will never be the same again.

We are entering a new period of important, hopeful change in America comparable to the political ferment released in the eras of Jefferson, Jackson and Roosevelt.

I treasure this nomination especially because it comes after vigorous competition with the ablest men and women our party can offer.

My old and treasured friend and neighbor, Hubert Humphrey; that gracious and good man from Maine, Ed Muskie; a tough fighter for his beliefs, Scoop Jackson; a brave and spirited woman, Shirley Chisholm; a wise and powerful lawmaker from Arkansas, Wilbur Mills; the man from North Carolina who opened new vistas in education and public excellence, Terry Sanford; the leader who in 1968 combined the travail and the hope of the American spirit, Gene McCarthy.

Help of Every Democrat

I was as moved as all of you by the appearance at this convention of the Governor of Alabama, George Wallace, whose votes in the primary showed the depths of discontent in this country, and whose courage in the face of pain and adversity is the mark of a man of boundless will. We all depise the senseless act that disrupted his campaign. Governor, we pray for your speedy and full recovery, so you can stand up and speak out forcefully for all of those who see you as their champion.

In the months ahead, I covet the help of every Democrat and every Republican and independent who wants America to be the great and good land it can be.

This is going to be a national campaign carried to every part of the nation—North, South, East and West. We are not conceding a single state to Richard Nixon. I want to say to my friend, Frank King, that Ohio may have passed a few times at this convention, but I'm not going to pass Ohio. Governor Gilligan, Ohio may be a little slow counting the votes,

Democratic candidate George McGovern lost his 1972 bid for the U.S. presidency. **THE LIBRARY OF CONGRESS.**

but when they come in this November, they are going to show a Democratic victory.

To anyone in this hall or beyond who doubts the ability of Democrats to join together in common cause, I say never underestimate the power of Richard Nixon to bring harmony to Democratic ranks. He is the unwitting unifier and the fundamental issue of this campaign. And all of us together are going to help him redeem the pledge he made 10 years ago. Next year you won't have Richard Nixon to kick around any more.

We have had our fury and our frustrations in these past months and at this convention.

Well, I frankly welcome the contrast with the smug, dull and empty event which will take place here in Miami next month. We chose this struggle. We reformed our party and let the people in.

A Million-Member Club

And we stand today not as a collection of backroom strategists, not as a tool of I.T.T. or any other special interest, but as a direct reflection of the public will.

So let our opponents stand on the status quo, while we seek to refresh the American spirit.

Let the opposition collect their $10 million in secret money from the privileged. And let us find one million ordinary Americans who will contribute $25 to this campaign—a McGovern "million-member club" with members who will expect not special favors for themselves but a better land for us all.

In Scripture and in the music of our children we are told: "To everything there is a season, and a time to every purpose under heaven."

And for America, the time has come at last.

This is the time for truth, not falsehood.

In a democratic nation, no one likes to say that his inspiration came from secret arrangements behind closed doors. But in a sense that is how my candidacy began. I am here as your candidate tonight in large part because during four administrations of both parties, a terrible war has been charted behind closed doors.

I want those doors opened, and I want that war closed. And I make these pledges above all others—the doors of government will be open, and that brutal war will be closed.

Truth is a habit of integrity, not a strategy of politics. And if we nurture the habit of candor in this campaign, we will continue to be candid once we are in the White House. Let us say to Americans, as Woodrow Wilson said in his first campaign, "Let me inside [the government] and I will tell you everything that is going on in there."

And this is a time not for death, but for life.

In 1968, Americans voted to bring our sons home from Vietnam in peace—and since then, 20,000 have come home in coffins.

I have no secret plan for peace. I have a public plan.

As one whose heart has ached for 10 years over the agony of Vietnam, I will halt the senseless bombing of Indochina on Inauguration Day.

There will be no more Asian children running ablaze from bombed-out schools.

There will be no more talk of bombing the dikes or the cities of the North.

Within 90 days of my inauguration, every American soldier and every American prisoner will be out of the jungle and out of their cells and back home in America where they belong.

Resolution on War

And then let us resolve that never again will we shed the precious young blood of this nation to perpetuate an unrepresentative client abroad.

Let us choose life, not death, this is the time.

This is also the time to turn away from excessive preoccupation overseas to rebuilding our own nation.

America must be restored to her proper role in the world. But we can do that only through the recovery of confidence in ourselves. The greatest contribution America can make to our fellow mortals is to heal our own great but deeply troubled land. We must respond to the ancient command: "Physician, heal thyself."

It is necessary in an age of nuclear power and hostile ideology that we be militarily strong. America must never become a second-rate nation. As one who has tasted the bitter fruits of our weakness before Pearl Harbor, 1941, I give you my sacred pledge that if I become President of the United States, America will keep its defenses alert and fully sufficient to meet any danger. We will do that not only for ourselves, but for those who deserve and need the shield of our strength—our old allies in Europe, and elsewhere, including the people of Israel, who will always have our help to hold their promised land.

Yet we know that for 30 years we have been so absorbed with fear and danger from abroad that we have permitted our own house to fall into disarray. We must now show that peace and prosperity can exist side by side—indeed, each now depends on the other.

National strength includes the credibility of our system in the eyes of our own people as well as the credibility of our deterrent in the eyes of others abroad.

National security includes schools for our children as well as silos for our missiles, the health of our families as much as the size of our bombs, the safety of our streets and the condition of our cities and not just the engines of war.

And if we some day choke on the pollution of our own air, there will be little consolation in leaving behind a dying continent ringed with steel.

Let us protect ourselves abroad and perfect ourselves at home.

This is the time.

And we must make this a time of justice and jobs for all.

For more than three years, we have tolerated stagnation and a rising level of joblessness, with more than five million of our best workers unemployed. Surely this is the most false and wasteful economics.

Our deep need is not for idleness but for new housing and hospitals, for facilities to combat pollution and take us home from work, for products better able to compete on vigorous work markets.

A Job Guarantee

The highest domestic priority of my Administration will be to ensure that every American able to work has a job to do. This job guarantee will and must depend upon a reinvigorated private economy, freed at last from the uncertainties and burdens of war.

But it is our commitment that whatever employment the private sector does not provide, the Federal Government will either stimulate, or provide itself. Whatever it takes, this country is going back to work.

America cannot exist with most of our people working and paying taxes to support too many others mired in the demeaning, bureaucratic welfare system. Therefore, we intend to begin by putting millions back to work; and after that is done, we will assure to those unable to work an income sufficient to assure a decent life.

Beyond this, a program to put America back to work demands that work be properly rewarded. That means the end of a system of economic controls in which labor is depressed, but prices and corporate profits are the highest in history. It means a system of national health insurance, so that a worker can afford decent health care for himself and his family. It means real enforcement of the laws so that the drug racketeers are put behind bars for good and our streets are once again safe for our families.

Above all, honest work must be rewarded by a fair and just tax system. The tax system today does not reward hard work—it penalizes it. Inherited or invested wealth frequently multiplies itself while paying no taxes at all. But wages earned on the assembly line, or laying bricks, or picking fruit— these hard earned dollars are taxed to the last penny. There is a depletion allowance for oil wells, but no allowance for the depletion of a man's body in years of toil.

The Administration tells us that we should not discuss tax reform in an election year. They would prefer to keep all discussion of the tax code in closed committee rooms, where the Administration, its powerful friends and their paid lobbysts can turn every effort at reform into a new loophole for the rich. But an election year is the people's year to speak—and this year, the people are going to ensure that the tax system is changed so that work is rewarded and so that those who derive the highest benefits will pay their fair share, rather than slipping through the loopholes at the expense of the rest of us.

So let us stand for justice and jobs, and against special privilege. This is the time.

We are not content with things as they are. We reject the view of those who say: "America—love it or leave it." We reply: "Let us change it so we can love it the more."

And this is the time. It is the time for this land to become again a witness to the world for what is noble and just in human affairs. It is the time to live more with faith and less with fear—with an abiding confidence that can sweep away the strongest barriers between us and teach us that we truly are brothers and sisters.

So join with me in this campaign, lend me your strength and your support, give me your voice—and together, we will call America home to the founding ideals that nourished us in the beginning.

From secrecy and deception in high places, come home, America.

From a conflict in Indochina which maims our ideals as well as our soldiers, come home, America.

From military spending so wasteful that it weakens our nation, come home, America.

From the entrenchment of special privilege and tax favoritism, come home, America.

From the waste of idle hands to the joy of useful labor, come home, America.

From the prejudice of race and sex, come home, America.

From the loneliness of the aging poor and the despair of the neglected sick, come home, America.

Come home to the affirmation that we have a dream.

Come home to the conviction that we can move our country forward.

Come home to the belief that we can seek a newer world.

For:

This land is your land,
This land is my land,

From California to the New York Island,
From the Redwood Forest
To the Gulfstream waters,
This land was made for you and me.

May God grant us the wisdom to cherish this good land to meet the great challenge that beckons us home.

Further Resources

BOOKS

Blum, John Morton. *Years of Discord: American Politics and Society, 1961–1974.* New York: W.W. Norton & Company, 1991.

McGovern, George. *Grassroots: The Autobiography of George McGovern.* New York: Random House, 1977.

———. *Terry: My Daughter's Life-and-Death Struggle with Alcoholism.* New York: Villard, 1976.

———. *The Third Freedom: Ending Hunger in Our Time.* New York: Simon and Schuster, 2001.

White, Theodore H. *The Making of the President, 1972.* New York: Atheneum, 1973.

Wicker, Tom. *One of Us: Richard Nixon and the American Dream.* New York: Random House, 1991.

From Victor to Vanquished

"How the President Sees His Second Term"

Magazine article

By: Daniel P. Moynihan

Date: September 1, 1972

Source: Moynihan, Daniel P. "How the President Sees His Second Term." *Life,* September 1, 1972, 26–29.

About the Author: Daniel P. Moynihan (1927–2003) pursued successful careers as a political advisor and urban studies professor in the 1960s. He gained fame as the author of several controversial studies of the American welfare system. He served as a special advisor to President Nixon (served 1969–1974) from 1971 to 1973, and was elected as a Democrat to the U.S. Senate from New York in 1976. Moynihan retired from politics in 2001.

Richard Nixon's Remarks on Leaving the White House, August 9, 1974

Speech

By: Richard M. Nixon

Date: August 9, 1974

Source: Nixon, Richard M. Remarks on Leaving the White House, August 9, 1974, delivered in Washington, D.C. Public Papers of President Richard M. Nixon, courtesy of Richard M. Nixon Library & Birthplace.

About the Author: Richard M. Nixon (1913–1994) served as the thirty-seventh president of the United States until 1974, when he resigned from office. Although his efforts to restore diplomatic ties with the People's Republic from China and end America's military involvement in Vietnam were generally applauded, his administration was largely helpless to protect the American economy from the devastating effects of the Organization of Petroleum Exporting Countries (OPEC) oil embargo of 1973–1974. ■

Introduction

Richard M. Nixon was perhaps the shrewdest American politician of the twentieth century. Indeed, few other elected officials managed to stage so many comebacks from seemingly total defeat. He came to power as a Republican congressman from California in 1946, riding a wave of anti-communist sentiment and quickly demonstrating his ability to form strategic alliances with conservative Republicans and moderate Democrats. In 1952, he was selected as the vice presidential nominee to join the presidential ticket led by General Dwight D. Eisenhower (served 1953–1961), but was almost forced to drop his candidacy when allegations of misused campaign funds tarnished his image. Nixon went on television to deliver a speech, claiming that his dog, "Checkers," was the only gift his family had ever accepted during his political career. The "Checkers Speech" generated enough public sympathy for Nixon that he remained on the ticket. He became vice president when the Republicans swept the White House and both houses of Congress.

Nixon tried to win the presidency himself in 1960 against Democrat John F. Kennedy (served 1961–1963) and was bitter over his narrow defeat. Two years later, Nixon lost the gubernatorial race in California, after which he bitterly told reporters, "You won't have Nixon to kick around anymore." After resuming his law career, Nixon reentered politics with a second presidential run in 1968. Running on a law-and-order platform that capitalized on many Americans' fears of urban riots and disorder, Nixon courted the moderate vote by pledging to end U.S. involvement in the Vietnam War (1964–1975). With the third-party ticket of segregationalist George C. Wallace splitting the traditional Democratic vote in the South, Nixon won his long-sought post as president over Hubert Humphrey. Demonstrating his interest in international relations, Nixon announced his policy of implementing a "Vietnamization" of the war during his first year in office, and his administration started pursuing diplomatic ties with the People's Republic of China.

Significance

Nixon's visit to the People's Republic of China in February 1972 marked the high point of his first term.

He proudly noted the restoration of relations with China as evidence that his leadership had restored the United States' reputation in the international community, widely viewed as diminished by the ongoing hostilities in Vietnam. To ensure his place in history, however, Nixon desperately wanted a second term; his Committee to Re-Elect the President (CREEP) engaged in numerous "dirty tricks"—including wiretapping the Democratic National Committee (DNC) headquarters in the Watergate building—to ensure a second term in 1972. After five burglars connected to CREEP were arrested in June 1972 for breaking into the DNC's offices to restore one of the wiretaps, the media started investigating the group's ties to the highest levels of Nixon's administration. It was not until after the presidential election of 1972, a Nixon landslide over George McGovern, that evidence of a cover-up of the Watergate affair by the White House forced several of Nixon's top aides to resign. Nixon himself resigned in August 1974, making him the only president ever to resign from office. The transition from his landslide victory to humiliating ousting was as dramatic as any of Nixon's previous political transformations.

The abrupt changes that marked Nixon's second term led some Americans to become profoundly disillusioned with the political system. It was difficult to comprehend how a leader who had accomplished so much and seemingly assured of re-election would willingly engage in a pattern of deceit that eventually triggered a constitutional crisis. Others took a more optimistic view of Nixon's fate; the government, after all, had not fallen into disarray, demonstrating that the system had worked to prevent the abuses of a small group of people from bringing the entire government down.

Primary Source

"How the President Sees His Second Term" [excerpt]

> **SYNOPSIS:** Nixon was particularly proud of his foreign policy initiatives, and he saw his role in shaping the United States' international relations as his chief priority. As it turned out, Nixon's greatest challenges came on the domestic front during his second term, particularly in dealing with the fallout from the century's greatest political scandal, Watergate.

Assuming he is reelected, how will Richard Nixon shape his second term? A defining characteristic of the administration so far has been the President's steadfastness of purpose. This may not be an admirable quality; in fact much of the criticism directed at him has really been directed at this trait, described less neutrally. But a well-conceived order of

priorities has guided his administration through four years, and will probably continue to do so through the next four.

His first priority (his second and third and fourth) is world peace. Few people have learned to see themselves with an immediate operational responsibility for the future of mankind, but an American President must. It is this perspective in which Richard Nixon has held and holds the war in Vietnam. He sees it as having been long, frustrating and difficult. Despite our strength, it has cost thousands of lives and billions of dollars. It distorted our economy, distorted our relations with other countries, and, in the President's view, has had a massive effect on the American spirit. Nevertheless, to Nixon the war is only an aspect of a far more dangerous condition. Every aware person, he believes, knows that the Vietnam war will soon be over. The urgency now lies in ensuring that there will be no more Vietnams and, far more important, no nuclear holocaust.

The President feels that his place in history will turn upon his success in this. The central achievement of his first term he believes to have been the two great initiatives first with China, then Russia. With them, he asserts, we have changed the world. By inference, he suggests that if Vietnam had come to an end without such movement, nothing surely would have been gained by it. Here, perhaps, the President's views are not widely known or widely shared. He will say that we have changed the world— and that we changed it at the last possible moment we could. The postwar world was breaking up fast: China, Europe and Japan rising in influence rapidly, the influence of the United States bound to recede. Meanwhile, the growing possibility of world destruction—if not the U.S. versus the U.S.S.R in the immediate future, then the U.S.S.R. and the People's Republic of China 15 years hence.

There may be nothing closer to Nixon's present sense of the presidency than the fact that what happened in respect to the first of his priorities was exactly what he planned and hoped would happen. By opening a dialogue with the People's Republic and negotiating a historic arms limitation agreement with the Soviet Union, in his judgment, the chances for a nuclear holocaust were reduced.

But though better than even odds of surviving are preferable to uneven ones, they are still not good enough, and this is the logic that will command his second term. He hopes to expand the initiatives with China and Russia. His plans are specific with respect to the Soviets. Following the already accomplished

Phase I in arms control, Phase II must be the development of a mutually beneficial limit on all offensive nuclear weapons, Phase III their reduction. Even with a nuclear arms agreement, nuclear arms are still being built, and too many are in existence for the safety of the human race.

There are other world issues. He feels that when he came to the presidency he was not aware of how pressing was the need for a new international economic structure that would adapt to the existence of the Common Market and Japan as major industrial and trading complexes, nor yet of the similar role he sees for China a quarter-century hence. A world order that will avoid military collision must also, he assumes, be one that will avoid disastrous economic warfare, and that can attend to the rightful demands of underderdeveloped countries.

Nor will peace in Vietnam mean peace everywhere. Maintaining the integrity of Israel and stability in the Middle East, for example, will in his opinion take very skillful diplomacy.

For the United States to play a proper role in world affairs, we must in the President's view not only be strong militarily but strong in spirit, strong in self-respect. We must be able to govern ourselves if we are to help govern the world. Here the President becomes animated. How could we live with a $30 billion cut in the defense budget? Here he is with six carriers in the Atlantic and only two on station. The United States does not maintain its strength in order to push other people around. It does so in order to play a role which only the United States can play. We have accepted arms parity with the Soviet Union. China will achieve parity in 25 years. If we drop out no one will succeed to our role. We must maintain the strength of our military establishment, and of our economy, and *we must show that we can govern ourselves.*

This in a way is a curious thing for an American President to have to say. Writing from Europe, Walter Laqueur reports in *Commentary,* "The image of America as far as the outside world is concerned is more and more that of a nation unwilling to exercise power, a nation beset by a mood of pervasive defeatism, and ridden with internal dissent." This is what worries the President, indeed obsesses him, and has done from his first day in office. It is in these terms that he cannot accept the proposition that it is time to turn the whole of our attention inward. He knows, or in any event feels, that the people are tired of world adventures. But to him it begs the question to pose as alternatives a vigorous role

in world affairs, or a vibrant concentration on domestic matters. To his thinking, you have to do both, or you have neither.

In truth his initiatives at home have not had anything like the success of his efforts abroad. He lists them: welfare reform, revenue-sharing, government reorganization, a new health program, and says he is disappointed. This is the predicament of Presidents. They can *do* things in foreign affairs and ask to be judged by their performance. In domestic matters they most often can only propose to do things, and thereafter the record becomes fuzzy. It is three years since, in a series of messages to Congress preceded by a nationwide television address, he set forth both his family assistance plan, a proposal to place a floor under the income of every family with children in the land, and to share federal revenue with state and local governments. But, he notes, in these three years the Congress has not rejected his proposals. It simply has not acted on them. The House, for example, has twice passed welfare reform by resounding majorities. The Senate is yet to vote on the measure. When proposed it was widely declared to be the most important piece of social legislation since the New Deal. Such failures suggest to him that we face a crisis in our ability to govern, that the machinery of government is obsolete. It is after all 18th-century machinery. Efforts to change it never succeed dramatically, but he feels the main thing is not to be satisfied with conditions as they are. He considers his record respectable in domestic matters—certainly the level of domestic peace is notably higher than it was four years ago—but that it is only a beginning.

Old issues continue with him. Welfare reform and revenue-sharing responded primarily to the problem of poverty and the fiscal crisis of the cities. But new issues arise. No one development disturbs him more than the rise of what some have called "quota democracy," the imposition of the proportionate representation of socially defined groups in a variety of private and public institutions. He becomes personal and specific on this issue, pointing as an instance to the number of Jews among his closest advisers. Henry A. Kissinger, assistant for national security affairs; Arthur F. Burns, chairman of the Federal Reserve Board and former counsellor; Herbert Stein, chairman of the Council of Economic Advisers; Edward E. David Jr., science adviser; Leonard Garment, his special consultant on the widest range of social and cultural issues; William L. Safire, a trusted speech-writer. If he had made appointments by quota, he asserts, he would have had to fire them all, all except Kissinger whom he would insist on keeping, but might have to settle for using on a quarter-time basis. Why does he have them? Not, he emphasizes, because of their religion, but because of their qualities.

With equal vehemence he insists that prejudice continues into our time against blacks, women, Mexican-Americans, Italian-Americans; a long and disturbing list. It is his view that persons from such groups should be given an edge in the selection process; that government and other institutions should look harder for excellence in such groups. But he insists that the idea of quotas will penalize our most able persons and undermine our most essential standards. He allows that such issues involve questions of morale and of style and of purpose; questions about which a President's influence is uncertain.

The President shares the view of commentators who hold that the coming election is likely to be crucial, historic. In his view it will be the first election since America assumed its present role in world affairs in which that role is genuinely under challenge. There are also basic differences about the general features of the American economic system. In the past the electorate has been asked to choose between different men; this time, he maintains, the choice is between different principles, between men who disagree on goals.

He does not, evidently, foresee any distinct Republican majority emerging from this confrontation, even assuming that he wins. The Gallup Poll shows that about one-quarter of the electorate regards itself as Republican. There is no way, in his view, that this can be made a majority. If anything, the trend is away from party identification. Already almost a third of the voters consider themselves independent. But in the 1972 election, he points out, someone is going to get a majority of the vote. Only two of the past five Presidents have been elected with a true majority. This time there is going to be a majority, and clearly he hopes it will be his. He does not see the campaign in terms of advancing Republican principles. The Republican party has its own differences—he speaks with resignation on the beating he has been getting from the Birchers and others on the far right. But he does feel that a new coalition is possible, built around the perception of a grand mosaic of concerns which he feels a majority of Americans share with regard to the future of the nation and the world. In part, as he sees it,

our trouble has been that American Presidents in the 20th century have not had a strong enough sense of the interconnection of things. Theodore Roosevelt, in his judgement, was about the last Chief Executive to measure up to this standard. Wilson tried, but it wasn't his dish of tea. His first term was excellent, but then he was dragged into foreign affairs. It was not his decision, and he could not in the end control events. In much the same way, the second Roosevelt was dragged into war; Truman, he feels, saw some of it: much of it. Eisenhower had a world view, but no political experience. Kennedy—always there is a pause when he mentions Kennedy—did not have enough time. But the record, he seems to say, is too random. We are now at a time when whoever is President must have such a world view, think in terms of the mosaic, think in terms of the next quarter-century, of the next four centuries. What is needed is to enunciate a coherent philosophy of what it is we hope for and how we propose to realize our hopes. . . .

In a phrase, he believes in the old values, including the value of change, but change that works. He is well enough aware that there are new values, and sees no reason there can be no dialogue between the two. He has journeyed to Peking; one assumes he can make it to Woodstock. But nothing will come of it without civility, without some quest for clarity as to what unites and what divides. . . . A quality of the presidency is that it focuses on the future. He has changed the world, he feels. He knows it has changed him.

Primary Source

Richard Nixon's Remarks on Leaving the White House, August 9, 1974

> **SYNOPSIS:** In his final remarks before leaving the White House, Nixon passed on his chance to issue a public apology for his role in the Watergate scandal. Although he worked diligently to restore his reputation by publishing numerous books after resigning from office, his stubborn refusal to accept full responsibility for Watergate marred his reputation until his death in 1994.

Members of the Cabinet, members of the White House Staff, all of our friends here:

I think the record should show that this is one of those spontaneous things that we always arrange whenever the President comes in to speak, and it will be so reported in the press, and we don't mind, because they have to call it as they see it.

Resigning president Richard Nixon gives a victorious salute to staff members as he leaves office. AP/WIDE WORLD PHOTOS. REPRODUCED BY PERMISSION.

But on our part, believe me, it is spontaneous.

You are here to say goodby to us, and we don't have a good word for it in English—the best is *au revoir*. We will see you again.

I just met with the members of the White House staff, you know, those who serve here in the White House day in and day out, and I asked them to do what I ask all of you to do to the extent that you can and, of course, are requested to do so: to serve our next President as you have served me and previous Presidents—because many of you have been here for many years—with devotion and dedication, because this office, great as it is, can only be as great as the men and women who work for and with the President.

This house, for example—I was thinking of it as we walked down this hall, and I was comparing it to some of the great houses of the world that I have been in. This isn't the biggest house. Many, and most, in even smaller countries, are much bigger. This isn't the finest house. Many in Europe, particularly, and in China, Asia, have paintings of great, great value, things that we just don't have here and, probably, will never have until we are 1,000 years old or older.

But this is the best house. It is the best house, because it has something far more important than numbers of people who serve, far more important than numbers of rooms or how big it is, far more important than numbers of magnificent pieces of art.

This house has a great heart, and that heart comes from those who serve. . . .

And so it is with you. I look around here, and I see so many on this staff that, you know, I should have been by your offices and shaken hands, and I would love to have talked to you and found out how to run the world—everybody wants to tell the President what to do, and boy, he needs to be told many times—but I just haven't had the time. But I want you to know that each and every one of you, I know, is indispensable to this Government.

I am proud of this Cabinet. I am proud of all the members who have served in our Cabinet. I am proud of our sub-Cabinet. I am proud of our White House Staff. As I pointed out last night, sure, we have done some things wrong in this Administration, and the top man always takes the responsibility, and I have never ducked it. But I want to say one thing: We can be proud of it . . .

Mistakes, yes. But for personal gain, never. You did what you believed in. Sometimes right, sometimes wrong. And I only wish that I were a wealthy man—at the present time, I have got to find a way to pay my taxes—[*laughter*]—and if I were, I would like to recompense you for the sacrifices that all of you have made to serve in government.

But you are getting something in government—and I want you to tell this to your children, and I hope the Nation's children will hear it, too—something in government service that is far more important than money. It is a cause bigger than yourself. It is the cause of making this the greatest nation in the world, the leader of the world, because without our leadership, the world will know nothing but war, possibly starvation or worse, in the years ahead. With our leadership it will know peace, it will know plenty.

We have been generous, and we will be more generous in the future as we are able to. But most important, we must be strong here, strong in our hearts, strong in our souls, strong in our belief, and strong in our willingness to sacrifice, as you have been willing to sacrifice, in a pecuniary way, to serve in government. . . .

Now, however, we look to the future. I had a little quote in the speech last night from T.R. As you know, I kind of like to read books. I am not educated, but I do read books—[*laughter*]—and the T.R. quote was a pretty good one.

Here is another one I found as I was reading, my last night in the White House, and this quote is about a young man. He was a young lawyer in New York. He had married a beautiful girl, and they had a lovely daughter, and then suddenly she died, and this is what he wrote. This was in his diary.

He said, "She was beautiful in face and form and lovelier still in spirit. As a flower she grew and as a fair young flower she died. Her life had been always in the sunshine. There had never come to her a single great sorrow. None ever knew her who did not love and revere her for her bright and sunny temper and her saintly unselfishness. Fair, pure and joyous as a maiden, loving, tender and happy as a young wife. When she had just become a mother, when her life seemed to be just begun and when the years seemed so bright before her, then by a strange and terrible fate death came to her. And when my heart's dearest died, the light went from my life forever."

That was T.R. in his twenties. He thought the light had gone from his life forever—but he went on. And he not only became President but, as an ex-President, he served his country, always in the arena, tempestuous, strong, sometimes wrong, sometimes right, but he was a man.

And as I leave, let me say, that is an example I think all of us should remember. We think sometimes when things happen that don't go the right way; we think that when you don't pass the bar exam the first time—I happened to, but I was just lucky; I mean, my writing was so poor the bar examiner said, "We have just got to let the guy through." We think that when someone dear to us dies, we think that when we lose an election, we think that when we suffer a defeat that all is ended. We think, as T.R. said, that the light had left his life forever.

Not true. It is only a beginning, always. The young must know it; the old must know it. It must always sustain us, because the greatness comes not when things go always good for you, but the greatness comes and you are really tested, when you take some knocks, some disappointments, when sadness comes, because only if you have been in the deepest valley can you ever know how magnificent it is to be on the highest mountain.

And so I say to you on this occasion, as we leave, we leave proud of the people who have stood by us and worked for us and served this country.

We want you to be proud of what you have done. We want you to continue to serve in government, if that is your wish. Always give your best, never get discouraged, never be petty; always remember, others may hate you, but those who hate you don't win unless you hate them, and then you destroy yourself.

And so, we leave with high hopes, in good spirit, and with deep humility, and with very much gratefulness in our hearts. I can only say to each and every one of you, we come from many faiths, we pray perhaps to different gods—but really the same God in a sense—but I want to say for each and every one of you, not only will we always remember you, not only will we always be grateful to you but always you will be in our hearts and you will be in our prayers.

Thank you very much.

Further Resources
BOOKS

Hodgson, Godfrey. *The Gentleman from New York: Daniel Patrick Moynihan: A Biography.* Boston: Houghton Mifflin, 2000.

Matusow, Allen J. *Nixon's Economy: Booms, Busts, Dollars, and Votes.* Lawrence: University Press of Kansas, 1998.

Moynihan, Daniel P. *Miles to Go: A Personal History of Social Policy.* Cambridge, Mass.: Harvard University Press, 1996.

Schudson, Michael. *Watergate in American Memory: How We Remember, Forget, and Recontstruct the Past.* New York: BasicBooks, 1993.

Summer, Anthony, with Robbyn Swan. *The Arrogance of Power: The Secret World of Richard Nixon.* New York: Viking, 2000.

White, Theodore H. *The Making of the President, 1972.* New York: Atheneum, 1973.

Wicker, Tom. *One of Us: Richard Nixon and the American Dream.* New York: Random House, 1991.

WEBSITES

"The Richard Nixon Library & Birthplace." Available online at http://www.nixonfoundation.org (accessed May 25, 2003).

The Boys on the Bus
Memoir

By: Timothy Crouse

Date: 1973

Source: Crouse, Timothy. *The Boys on the Bus.* New York: Random House, 1973, 3–8, 10–15.

About the Author: Timothy Crouse (1947–), New York City native, completed his bachelor's degree at Harvard University in 1968. After a tour in the Peace Corps, he wrote for the *Boston Herald,* before joining the staff of *Rolling Stone* as a contributing editor from 1971 to 1975. While at the magazine, he covered the presidential campaign of South Dakota senator George S. McGovern, the subject of his 1973 book *The Boys on the Bus.* ∎

Introduction

Through the 1970s, journalists adopted a mostly deferential tone when reporting on public figures. Pictures of President Franklin D. Roosevelt (served 1933–1945), who was confined to a wheelchair after a crippling bout of polio, were never publicized; nor did reports on the numerous indiscretions of President John F. Kennedy (served 1961–1963) become public until years after his assassination. Although political writers justified the news blackouts of potentially scandalous or disturbing reports that might offend public sensibilities, most reporters acquiesced to the limits in order to maintain their access to public figures or, in some cases, to appease their editors.

As images from the Vietnam War (1964–1975) flashed onto television screens across the United States in the late 1960s, however, some reporters took a more active role in questioning the pronouncements of public officials. The broad cultural changes of the 1960s, including a sweeping suspicion of authority figures by younger people, also encouraged a more restive spirit in the reporting corps. By the end of the decade, the phrase "Gonzo Journalism" was coined to describe the new breed of reporter: young, rebellious, and unafraid to get personally involved in the story at hand. Typified by *Rolling Stone* writer, Hunter S. Thompson, the gonzo journalist was also a macho figure who sometimes indulged in drugs and alcohol.

In 1972, Thompson was joined by his *Rolling Stone* colleague, Timothy Crouse, to cover that year's presidential campaign. Crouse spent his time with the pack of journalists covering Democratic candidate George S. McGovern, later publishing a biting memoir of his adventures, *The Boys on the Bus.* As Crouse recalled in a 2000 interview with the *PBS NewsHour,* "If your idea of a good time is flying around the country week after week, in the company of journalists and politicians freed of all the normal strictures of daily life, in an environment where nobody is going to raise an eyebrow if you want to have your first drink at 11:00 in the morning, this is the job for you." (February 17, 2000)

Significance

The emphasis on the personal narrative that made *The Boys on the Bus* and similar works so compelling transformed political reporting in the 1970s. Many journalists became celebrities in their own right, most notably the two reporters at the center of the Watergate story, Carl Bernstein and Bob Woodward. The *Washington Post* colleagues were later played by Dustin Hoffman and Robert Redford in the movie version of their investigation into President Richard Nixon (served 1969–1974) and his administration's corruption, *All the President's Men.* Hunter S. Thompson also became a media fixture in the 1970s, often for his colorful personal life rather than his writing. Thompson was later the subject of two movies about his career, *Where the Buffalo Roam* and *Fear and Loathing in Las Vegas.*

Critics of the new style of journalism maintained that the emphasis on personalities and celebrity did not necessarily lead to better reporting. As political reporting seemed to focus more on personalities and images and less on substantive issues, some observers feared that the American public was ill-served by the new style of journalism. Others argued that the media had also encouraged political apathy among the public by superficial reporting. Voter turnout for the 1972 presidential election between Richard M. Nixon and George S. McGovern stood at just over fifty-five percent, the lowest turnout since the 1920s.

Primary Source

The Boys on the Bus [excerpt]

> **SYNOPSIS:** A boisterous account of Senator George McGovern's ultimately unsuccessful 1972 presidential bid, Crouse's work popularized the term "pack journalism," describing the herd mentality that gripped reporters focusing endlessly on the same topic. In later years, political advisors would become more adept at "spinning" news stories to their candidates' advantage, but the essential dynamics of pack journalism remain in place.

June 1—five days before the California primary. A grey dawn was fighting its way through the orange curtains in the Wilshire Hyatt House Hotel in Los Angeles, where George McGovern was encamped with his wife, his staff, and the press assigned to cover his snowballing campaign.

While reporters still snored like Hessians in a hundred beds throughout the hotel, the McGovern munchkins were at work, plying the halls, slipping the long legal-sized handouts through the cracks under the door of each room. According to one of these handouts, the Baptist Ministers' Union of Oakland had decided after "prayerful and careful deliberation" to endorse Senator McGovern. And there was a detailed profile of Alameda County (" . . . agricultural products include sweet corn, cucumbers, and lettuce"), across which the press would be dragged today—or was it tomorrow? Finally, there was the mimeographed schedule, the orders of the day.

At 6:45 the phone on the bed table rang, and a sweet, chipper voice announced: "Good Morning, Mr. Crouse. It's six forty-five. The press bus leaves in forty-five minutes from the front of the hotel." She was up there in Room 819, the Press Suite, calling up the dozens of names on the press manifest, awaking the agents of every great newspaper, wire service and network not only of America but of the world. In response to her calls, she was getting a shocking series of startled grunts, snarls and obscenities.

The media heavies were rolling over, stumbling to the bathroom, and tripping over the handouts. Stooping to pick up the schedule, they read: *"8:00–8:15, Arrive Roger Young Center, Breakfast with Ministers."* Suddenly, desperately, they thought: "Maybe I can pick McGovern up in Burbank at nine fifty-five and sleep for another hour." Then, probably at almost the same instant, several score minds flashed the same guilty thought: "But maybe he will get shot at the ministers' breakfast," and then each mind branched off into its own private nightmare recollections of the correspondent who was taking a piss at Laurel when they shot Wallace, of the ABC cameraman who couldn't get his Bolex to start as Bremer emptied his revolver. A hundred hands groped for the toothbrush.

It was lonely on these early mornings and often excruciatingly painful to tear oneself away from a brief, sodden spell of sleep. More painful for some than others. The press was consuming two hundred dollars a night worth of free cheap booze up there in the Press Suite, and some were consuming the lion's share. Last night it had taken six reporters to subdue a prominent radio correspondent who kept upsetting the portable bar, knocking bottles and ice on the floor. The radioman had the resiliency of a Rasputin—each time he was put to bed, he would reappear to cause yet more bedlam.

And yet, at 7:15 Rasputin was there for the baggage call, milling in the hall outside the Press Suite with fifty-odd reporters. The first glance at all these fellow sufferers was deeply reassuring—they all felt the same pressures you felt, their problems were your problems. Together, they seemed to have the cohesiveness of an ant colony, but when you examined the scene more closely, each reporter appeared to be jitterbugging around in quest of the answer that would quell some private anxiety.

They were three deep at the main table in the Press Suite, badgering the McGovern people for a variety of assurances. "Will I have a room in San Francisco tonight?" "Are you sure I'm booked on the whistle-stop train?" "Have you seen my partner?"

The feverish atmosphere was halfway between a high school bus trip to Washington and a gambler's jet junket to Las Vegas, where small-time Mafiosi were lured into betting away their restaurants. There was giddy camaraderie mixed with fear and low-grade hysteria. To file a story late, or to make one glaring factual error, was to chance losing everything—one's job, one's expense account, one's drinking buddies, one's mad-dash existence, and the methedrine buzz that comes from knowing stories that the public would not know for hours and secrets that the public would never know. Therefore reporters channeled their gambling instincts into late-night poker games and private bets on the outcome of the elections. When it came to writing a story, they were as cautious as diamond-cutters.

It being Thursday, many reporters were knotting their stomachs over their Sunday pieces, which had to be filed that afternoon at the latest. They were inhaling their cigarettes with more of a vengeance, and patting themselves more distractedly to make sure they had their pens and notebooks. In the hall, a Secret Service agent was dispensing press tags for the baggage, along with string and scissors to attach them. From time to time, in the best Baden-Powell tradition, he courteously stepped forward to assist a drink-palsied journalist in the process of threading a tag.

The reporters often consulted their watches or asked for the time of departure. Among this crew, there was one great phobia—the fear of getting left behind. Fresh troops had arrived today from the Humphrey Bus, which was the Russian Front of the California primary, and they had come bearing tales of horror. The Humphrey Bus had left half the press corps at the Biltmore Hotel on Tuesday night; in Santa Barbara, the bus had deserted Richard Bergholz of the Los Angeles *Times,* and it had twice stranded George Shelton, the UPI man.

"Jesus, am I glad I'm off the Humphrey Bus," said one reporter, as he siphoned some coffee out of the McGovern samovar and helped himself to a McGovern sweet roll. "Shelton asked Humphrey's press officer, Hackel, if there was time to file. Hackel said, 'Sure, the candidate's gonna mingle and shake some hands.' Well, old Hubie couldn't find but six hands to shake, so they got in the bus and took off and left the poor bastard in a phone booth right in the middle of Watts."

To the men whom duty had called to slog along at the side of the Hump, the switch to the McGovern Bus brought miraculous relief. "You gotta go see the Hump's pressroom, just to see what disaster looks like," a reporter urged me. The Humphrey pressroom, a bunker-like affair in the bowels of the Beverly Hilton, contained three tables covered with white tablecloths, no typewriters, no chairs, no bar, no food, one phone (with outside lines available only to registered guests), and no reporters. The McGovern press suite, on the other hand, contained twelve typewriters, eight phones, a Xerox Telecopier, a free bar, free cigarettes, free munchies, and a skeleton crew of three staffers. It was not only Rumor Central, but also a miniature road version of Thomas Cook and Son. As the new arrivals to the McGovern Bus quickly found out, the McGovern staff ran the kind of guided tour that people pay great sums of money to get carted around on. They booked reservations on planes, trains and hotels; gave and received messages; and handled Secret Service accreditation with a fierce Teutonic efficiency. And handed out reams of free information. On any given day, the table in the middle of the Press Suite was laden with at least a dozen fat piles of handouts, and the door was papered with pool reports.

It was just these womblike conditions that gave rise to the notorious phenomenon called "pack journalism" (also known as "herd journalism" and "fuselage journalism"). A group of reporters were assigned to follow a single candidate for weeks or months at a time, like a pack of hounds sicked on a fox. Trapped on the same bus or plane, they ate, drank, gambled, and compared notes with the same bunch of colleagues week after week.

Actually, this group was as hierarchical as a chess set. The pack was divided into cliques—the national political reporters, who were constantly coming and going; the campaign reporters from the big, prestige papers and the ones from the small papers; the wire-service men; the network correspondents; and other configurations that formed according to age and old Washington friendships. The most experienced national political reporters, wire men, and big-paper reporters, who were at the top of the pecking order, often did not know the names of the men from the smaller papers, who were at the bottom. But they all fed off the same pool report, the same daily handout, the same speech by the candidate; the whole pack was isolated in the same mobile village. After a while, they began to believe the same rumors, subscribe to the same theories, and write the same stories.

Everybody denounces pack journalism, including the men who form the pack. Any self-respecting journalist would sooner endorse incest than come out in favor of pack journalism. It is the classic villain of every campaign year. Many reporters and journalism professors blame it for everything that is shallow, obvious, meretricious, misleading, or dull in American campaign coverage.

On a muggy afternoon during the California primary campaign, I went to consult with Karl Fleming, a former political reporter and Los Angeles bureau chief for *Newsweek,* who was rumored to be a formidable critic of pack journalism. Fleming was beginning a whole new gig as editor of a fledgling semi-underground paper called *LA;* I found him in dungarees and shirtsleeves, sitting behind a desk that was covered with the makings of *LA*'s pilot issue. He was a ruggedly built North Carolinian with the looks and accent to play Davy Crockett in a Disney remake. He was very busy putting his magazine together, taking phone calls, and giving instructions to one long-haired writer after another, but he seemed to enjoy letting off steam about political journalism. One of the reasons he quit *Newsweek* was that he got fed up riding around on campaign extravaganzas. . . .

Fleming said that in June, and as I followed the press through the next five months of the campaign, I discovered that some of his accusations checked out, but others did not. Almost everything he said held true for the White House press corps, but his charges did not always apply to the men who covered the Democratic candidates in 1972. It was true that some editors were still reluctant to run a story by their own man until the wire services had confirmed it. It was true that newsmagazine reporters and network correspondents occasionally leaked part of a hot story to *The New York Times* or *The Wall Street Journal;* after the story had gained respectability by appearing in one of these major establishment organs, the correspondent would write the whole story for his own organization. And it was impossible to tell how often the reporters censored themselves in anticipation of some imaginary showdown with a cautious editor, preferring to play it safe and go along with whatever the rest of the pack was writing.

But things had also begun to change since Fleming's campaign stories in 1968. The men on the bus had more authority and independence than ever before, and many of them were searching for new ways to report on the freakish, insular existence of the press bus, and for ways to break away from the pack. Very few of them filed any confidential memos to their superiors, or phoned in any inside information, except to suggest that such information might be worked up into a story.

Take, for example, the case of Curtis Wilkie, a young reporter for the Wilmington, Delaware *News-Journal* whom I met for the first time on the morning of June 1. I walked out of the lobby of the Wilshire Hyatt House, past all the black Nauga-hide furniture, and stepped into the first of the two silver buses that were waiting at the curb. It was the kind of bus to which most bus-fanciers would give three stars— the windows were tinted and there was a toilet in the rear, but the seats did not recline. The time was 7:30 A.M. and two-thirds of the seats were already filled with silent and bleary-eyed reporters who looked as cheerful as a Georgia chain gang on its way to a new roadbed. Most of them were sending out powerful "No Trespassing" vibes. My company was in no great demand, word having gotten around that I was researching an article on the press. Reporters snapped their notebooks shut when I drew near. The night before, Harry Kelly, a tall, hard-eyed Irishman from the Hearst papers, had looked at me over his shoulder and muttered, "Goddam gossip columnist."

I finally sat down next to a thirtyish dark-haired reporter wearing a Palm Beach suit and a drooping moustache, who looked too hungover to object to my presence. After a long silence, he spoke up in a twangy Southern accent and introduced himself as Curtis Wilkie. He was from Mississippi and had been a senior at Ole Miss in 1964 when General Walker led his famous charge on the administration building. After graduating, Wilkie had put in seven years as a reporter on the Clarksdale, Mississippi *Register* (circ. 7,000), and, as I later found out, had won a slew of journalism prizes. In 1968, he had gone to the Chicago Convention as a member of the "loyalist" Mississippi delegation and had cast his vote for Eugene McCarthy. Soon after that, he won a Congressional fellowship and worked for Walter Mondale in the Senate and John Brademas in the House. In 1971, the Wilmington paper hired him as its main political writer; they got their money's worth, for he wrote two separate 750-word articles every day, a "hard" news story for the morning *News* and a "soft" feature story for the afternoon *Journal*.

George McGovern shakes hands with supporters in San Mateo, California, four days before the California presidential primary.
© BETTMANN/CORBIS. REPRODUCED BY PERMISSION.

"Last night, I filed a story unconditionally predicting that the Hump's gonna get rubbed out in the primary," he said. Now he was worried that his editors might object to so firm a stand, or that Humphrey, through some terrible accident, might win. As if to reassure himself, Wilkie kept telling funny, mordant stories about the last-ditch hysterics of the Humphrey campaign.

Wilkie had experienced a few bad moments over a Humphrey story once before. During the Pennsylvania primary Humphrey unwisely decided to hold a student rally at the University of Pennsylvania. The students booed and heckled, calling Humphrey "America's Number 2 War Criminal," until Humphrey, close to tears, was forced to retreat from the stage. Wilkie filed a long story describing the incident and concluding that Humphrey was so unpopular with students that he could no longer speak on a college campus.

There were no TV cameramen at the rally, and of the fifteen reporters who covered the speech, only one beside Wilkie filed a detailed account of the heckling. The next day, when Wilkie went into the office, the managing editor was laughing about the story. "We've kind of started wondering," he teased Wilkie. "Several people have called and said that they didn't see anything about Humphrey on Channel Six, and they seem to think you made it up. And we're beginning to wonder ourselves, because none of the wire services mentioned it." Wilkie began to sweat; he nearly convinced himself that he had grossly exaggerated the incident. Late that afternoon, Wilkie came across a piece by Phil Potter, a veteran reporter for the Baltimore *Sun.* Potter's version of the incident agreed with Wilkie's. With great relief, Curt clipped the article and showed it to the managing editor.

For months afterward, Wilkie felt slightly qualmish whenever he thought about the Humphrey story. "They sort of put me on notice that somebody was carefully reading my stuff, that time," he said after the election. "It may have inhibited me, I don't know." But it didn't drive him back to the safety of the pack. He continued to trust his own judgment and write about whatever he himself thought was important. In October, when he was one of the few reporters to file a full account of an ugly Nixon rally where the President smiled at the sight of demonstrators being beaten up, the paper printed his articles without questioning them. "After a while," he said, "the guys on my desk began to have enough faith in me that they would accept anything I gave them regardless of what their wire services were telling them. They may have wondered a couple of times, but that didn't prevent them from running it."

What made this all the more remarkable was that the *News-Journal* was owned by the arch-conservative DuPont family, and had long been famous for resisting news stories that gave any comfort to liberals. Ben Bagdikian, in his book *The Effete Conspiracy,* had used the *News-Journal* as a case study in biased journalism. According to Bagdikian, one of the owners had once even "complained bitterly to the editors that the paper's reporter had written a conventional news account of a Democratic rally when he should have turned it into a pro-Republican essay." In the late sixties, however, stronger editors had taken over, and in the fall of 1972 they decided not to endorse either Nixon or McGovern, much to the displeasure of the DuPonts. The DuPonts' dissenting editorial, which exhorted readers to vote for every Republican on the ballot, was relegated to the letters column under the coy heading "A View from the Top." Wilkie was assigned to write a story about the rift. Interviewing the DuPonts, he asked whether a proposed merger pending before the SEC had any-

thing to do with their endorsement of Nixon. Only a few years before, such impertinence would have been unthinkable.

But one should not make too much of Curt Wilkie and the *News-Journal.* There were still lazy men on the bus, and men with large families to feed or powerful ambitions to nurture, who feared losing their jobs and thus played it safe by sticking with the pack. And there were still editors whose suspicions of any unusual story made pack journalism look cozy and inviting to their reporters. Campaign journalism is, by definition, pack journalism; to follow a candidate, you must join a pack of other reporters; even the most independent journalist cannot completely escape the pressures of the pack.

Further Resources

BOOKS

Blum, John Morton. *Years of Discord: American Politics and Society, 1961–1974.* New York: W.W. Norton & Company, 1991.

Dougherty, Richard. *Goodbye, Mr. Christian: A Personal Account of McGovern's Rise and Fall.* Garden City, N.Y.: Doubleday, 1973.

Hart, Gary. *Right from the Start: A Chronicle of the McGovern Campaign.* New York: Quadrangle, 1973.

Matusow, Allen J. *The Unraveling of America: A History of Liberalism in the 1960s.* New York: Harper & Row, 1984.

McGovern, George. *An American Journey: The Presidential Campaign Speeches of George McGovern.* New York: Random House, 1974.

————. *Grassroots: The Autobiography of George McGovern.* New York: Random House, 1977.

Thompson, Hunter S. *Fear and Loathing on the Campaign Trail '72.* New York: Popular Library, 1973.

WEBSITES

"Covering the Candidates." *PBS NewsHour,* February 17, 2000. Available online at http://www.pbs.org/newshour/bb/media/jan-june00/coverage_2-17.html; website home page http://www.pbs.org (accessed May 25, 2003).

Why Not the Best?
Memoir

By: Jimmy Carter

Date: November 3, 1975

Source: Carter, Jimmy. *Why Not the Best?* New York: Bantam Books, 1975, 158–166.

About the Author: Jimmy Carter (1924–) entered the 1976 presidential race as a relative underdog. During his campaign, Carter (served 1977–1981) emphasized his integrity and presented himself as a moderate Democrat who would practice fiscal responsibility, while maintaining his party's commitment to social welfare programs. Carter narrowly won the election over incumbent Gerald R. Ford (served 1974–1977), and he served one term as the nation's thirty-eighth president. After leaving the White House in 1981, Carter and his wife, Rosalynn, have devoted themselves to numerous philanthropic projects. Carter received the Nobel Peace Prize in 2002. ■

Introduction

In 1972, Richard Nixon (served 1969–1974) won a landslide victory over his Democratic challenger, George S. McGovern, for a second term in the White House. The margin of Nixon's victory seemed to confirm the trend away from sixties-style liberalism and toward law-and-order conservatism. Yet Nixon's triumph was short-lived, as his second term degenerated into disillusionment over the corruption and deceit of the Watergate scandal. With a majority of the public calling for his ousting, Nixon resigned from office in August 1974, rather than face impeachment.

The revelations of such deep-seated corruption in the Nixon administration dealt a major setback to the Republican Party. Congressional Democrats made gains in the 1974 elections, as voters showed their disapproval of Nixon's party. As the economy continued to bog down in inflation and recession, the hopes of Nixon's successor, Gerald R. Ford, to stay in the White House also seemed bleak. Although Ford was given high marks for moving the nation to reconciliation after Nixon's resignation, his occasional public gaffes became fodder for the popular television show, *Saturday Night Live,* where comedian Chevy Chase portrayed the president as a bumbling, out-of-touch figure. Some commentators also mocked Ford's "Whip Inflation Now" (WIN) program to hold down prices. Although thousands of "WIN" buttons were distributed to the public, the measure failed to inspire confidence in the administration's economic policies.

With high hopes of winning the White House for the first time since 1964, several Democratic candidates expressed an interest in entering the 1976 presidential race. Massachusetts senator Ted Kennedy, the perennial front-runner among the Democrats, faded from contention after it became obvious that questions about his character—especially a fatal car accident he was involved in several years earlier—were still a major liability to his national candidacy. In a wide-open field, the eventual nominee instead emerged from the unlikely small town of Plains, Georgia: James Earl Carter, Jr., better known by his nickname, Jimmy.

Significance

Carter, who had served as governor of Georgia between 1971 and 1975, announced his presidential aspi-

rations in 1974, and he began an aggressive speaking tour across the United States to gain national name recognition. Presenting himself as a moderate Democrat, Carter hoped to appeal to conservative voters who had identified themselves as members of Nixon's "silent majority," while retaining the support of traditional left-leaning groups, including labor union members and minority voters. A deeply spiritual man, Carter also highlighted his reputation for honesty and integrity by promising voters, "I'll never lie to you," a theme of his campaign that drew a direct comparison to the Watergate affair. Carter also pledged to practice fiscal prudence while in office, a tactic that helped him avoid getting stuck with the "tax-and-spend" label that Republicans had effectively used against past Democratic rivals.

Carter also scored a public relations coup with the publication of his 1975 memoir, *Why Not the Best?*, just as his campaign gained momentum. Part autobiography and part political philosophy, the book outlined Carter's platform and served as a road map of his campaign strategy. Well received by most critics, *Why Not the Best?* proved crucial in delivering the Democratic nomination to Carter, who went on to win the election over Gerald Ford with just over fifty percent of the vote.

The effectiveness of Carter's campaign served as a blueprint for later presidential candidates, particularly those who followed in his moderate Democrat footsteps. Carter created an image as a political outsider—despite his lengthy career as a politician. Carter's description of himself as a small-town peanut farmer resonated with voters disillusioned by the post-Watergate political environment. The emphasis on personal integrity also served Carter well, as the country came to terms with the deep divisions and mistrust that lingered after the Vietnam War (1964–1975).

Primary Source

Why Not the Best? [excerpt]

SYNOPSIS: In this excerpt, Carter outlines his initial strategy on entering the presidential race in 1976. Although he was perceived to be at a disadvantage for his lack of national name recognition and roots in the deep South, Carter successfully built upon his image as a small town farmer with integrity and humility. On election day, the candidate once referred to as "Jimmy Who?" won the presidency in a narrow victory over incumbent Gerald R. Ford.

Presidential Plans

I have always looked on the presidency of the United States with reverence and awe, and I still do. But recently I have begun to realize that the president is just a human being. I can almost remember

In his book *Why Not the Best?*, Jimmy Carter discusses his background and his decision to run for the presidency. **THE LIBRARY OF CONGRESS.**

when I began to change my mind and form this opinion.

Before becoming governor I had never met a president, although I once saw Harry Truman at a distance. He was present when we laid the keel of the first atomic submarine *Nautilus* in New London, Connecticut, in 1952. Great presidents like Washington, Jefferson, Lincoln, and Roosevelt have always been historical figures to me, and even the intimate biographical information published about them has never made them seem quite human.

Then during 1971 and 1972 I met Richard Nixon, Spiro Agnew, George McGovern, Henry Jackson, Hubert Humphrey, Ed Muskie, George Wallace, Ronald Reagan, Nelson Rockefeller, and other presidential hopefuls, and I lost my feeling of awe about presidents. This is not meant as a criticism of them, but it is merely a simple statement of fact.

After the 1972 convention I began with the help of those close to me to think seriously about a presidential campaign, and to assess my own strengths and weaknesses. In fact, the frank assessment of my shortcomings became one of the most enjoyable experiences for my staff, my friends, and my family,

and was a time-consuming process. We talked about politics, geography, character, education, experience, appearance, age, mannerisms, and lack of fame. In spite of these critical assessments, I decided to run.

Let me try to relate a brief list of the kinds of things we discussed.

1. I am a farmer. That seemed a disadvantage to some, but the other side was that this would not hurt the farm vote, a real factor. Moreover, over the period of a lifetime, being a farmer makes one willing to face apparently insuperable difficulties and still take a chance even though the future—the weather, the economy, and variables—may seem just one big gamble. Also, I can claim with credentials to be an engineer, a planner, a nuclear physicist, a businessman, and a professional naval officer. So, for those who might have an aversion to farmers, for whatever reason, there are some alternative ways of looking at what my candidacy has to offer.

2. I live in the Deep South, and no Southerner has been elected president in more than a hundred years. And yet I remember fifteen years ago when the political analysts said that Southerners would never vote for an Irish Catholic from Boston, but when the returns were counted in 1960 John Kennedy got a bigger margin of victory—not in Massachusetts but in Georgia! Also, in a predominantly white voter district in 1972 we elected a man who came into his first public visibility as the young field worker for Martin Luther King, Jr.—Congressman Andrew Young. In 1974, even as a freshman congressman, his opposition for a second term was hardly detectable. Sectional or geographical prejudice is becoming a minimal political factor.

More disadvantages:

1. My home is Plains, Georgia, population about 600. This gives me little urban base, but in microcosm, nonetheless, our people in Plains represent very well the people of the nation—and I know all of the Plains people. We live and work together in a spirit of friendship and harmony.

Our 250 white citizens and our 350 black citizens learn from one another, and always have. There may even be some political advantage with voters because rural people sometimes have the reputation (perhaps undeserved) of living close to the earth, close to God, close to poverty, and closer to their government. Anyhow, Plains has about the same population density as Atlanta: about 800 people to the square mile.

2. I would not be holding office while running for the White House in 1976; but this would give me full time to campaign, unlike members of Congress who at least in theory would be obliged to pay attention to their proper responsibilities in Washington.

3. The national news media are concentrated in Washington, a disadvantage for a former Georgia governor, age 50, politically unemployed. True again, as a disadvantage, but on the other hand there are 535 members of Congress reaching for every microphone and struggling for every headline.

In the meantime, I reasoned, I likely would be the only presidential candidate that day in Sioux City, or in St. Petersburg, or Phoenix, or Rochester. Furthermore, a lot of national news people stop over in Georgia and Atlanta on their way to Montgomery for their monthly interview with Alabama Governor George Wallace! Maybe, later, the word might drift back to Washington about me.

4. A fault; I don't know how to compromise on any principle I believe is right. Georgia Secretary of State Ben Fortson, probably the most respected, statewide-elected official in my home state, a white-haired patriarch who speaks as eloquently about American history as any man I have ever heard, once called me "as stubborn as a South Georgia turtle." Unthinking non-compromise is of course foolish; but maybe this is a time, on matters of principle, for an absence of compromise.

5. Others might have a head start on financing. True enough: three other candidates had already raised more than a million dollars before the new campaign finance law went into effect. Yet, with a small, effective staff, and the hope of a large group of politically attractive volunteers, plus plenty of personal effort by me and my family, and a total commitment to campaign full-time throughout the nation, it seemed likely that it would be possible to attract enough financial support to help win the nomination and the election.

How does one prepare for such an undertaking? Of course, the first step was to assess my own current and ongoing responsibilities which had to be fulfilled. As governor of Georgia I had completed the most critical and demanding portion of my term, but there were hundreds of administrative duties which I enjoyed and which I had to perform. My routine of arriving at the capitol office early and working a full day continued until I completed my final day in office. But I began to discern from the governor's job special experiences which would be similar to those of a president. The administration of federal pro-

grams involving welfare, health, education, transportation, environment, recreation, energy, housing, and urban renewal took on additional meanings. Long-range planning techniques, budgeting procedures, government organizations, tax measures, prison reform, criminal justice, foreign trade, and social problems became more challenging subjects as they were analyzed for comparative application to both state and federal government service delivery systems.

I had always read three or four books each week, and it was easy and natural to revise my reading lists to encompass subjects relating more toward foreign affairs, defense, and economics. I accumulated and read histories and biographies concerning our nation and the presidency, and, in order to avoid mistakes, even studied the campaign platforms of all the unsuccessful candidates for president since our electoral process began.

I read scientific journals about every conceivable source of energy, so I might understand the potential for meeting the world's needs during the decades ahead. Nuclear disarmament proposals and agreements were studied, along with budgets of the different services within the defense department. A special effort was made to meet the authors of these books and articles, so I might obtain more information about their subjects at first hand. Later several of them provided me with prepublication drafts of their writings. Service on the Trilateral Commission gave me an excellent opportunity to know national and international leaders in many fields of study concerning foreign affairs.

We continued to accumulate names of those who attended the numerous conventions in Atlanta. Since part of my job as governor was to give a welcoming talk or a more substantive speech, it was easy for us to ask for a list of the conventioneers and their home addresses. Foreign travel and my numerous meetings with visitors from other nations became more interesting to me, and I used each such opportunity as a means for studying the country involved.

As chairman of the National Democratic Party 1974 Campaign Committee it was my responsibility to learn as much as possible about all the states and congressional districts involved in the elections. We began to monitor the thirty-five gubernatorial campaigns, the thirty-four campaigns for U.S. Senator, and all of the 435 elections for Congress. During 1973 and 1974 I met frequently with leaders of groups who ordinarily support Democratic candidates. These leaders, from about twenty-five different organizations, represented labor unions, farmers, Spanish-Americans, teachers, environmentalists, women, local officials, retired persons, government workers, blacks, and the House and Senate campaign committees.

Four or five of the major opinion pollsters worked closely with me, and helped to delineate the most important issues among the American electorate as the elections approached. With the help of a volunteer staff, we recruited several experts in each of about thirty issue subjects to give me their opinions of what our nation should do about that particular question, and then we edited those disparate suggestions into one coherent issue paper on each subject. These were printed in a standard format and mailed out to more than 1,000 Democratic candidates for high political office, Later, after the primaries were over and nominees of our Party had been selected, I went out into more than sixty campaigns to work personally with the candidates and their staffs. Our staff members from the Democratic National Committee worked in dozens of other campaigns. All of this was also a good learning experience for me.

A major factor in any political campaign is always the identity and characteristics of potential opponents, and, of course, we discussed in some detail those who might run for president in 1976. There was never any hesitancy about our plans because of other prospective candidates.

Our strategy was simple: make a total effort all over the nation. After leaving office as governor, during the first months alone, I visited more than half the states, some of them several times. Each visit was carefully planned—by my small Atlanta staff and a local volunteer in each community—to be included during the week's trip. Our purposes during this early stage of the campaign were: to become known among those who have a continuing interest in politics and government; to recruit supporters and to raise campaign funds; and to obtain maximum news coverage for myself and my stand on the many local and national issues. The most important purpose of all was for me to learn this nation—what it is, and what it ought to be.

Our trips proved to be interesting and educational—and politically successful. One of the standard events which we scheduled was a meeting with the full editorial boards of the major newspapers and magazines of our country. There seemed to be a standard format. We would sit down to lunch promptly at

a scheduled time, in a private dining room within the office building of the publication. As the first course of salad or soup was served, the questions began. They continued in an uninterrupted stream until the session adjourned about two hours later. I could never find time to eat a bite, although dishes of delicious looking food were placed in front of me and the others, and then later removed after the editors had eaten theirs. Among the more competent groups, specialists among the editors and news reporters had carefully prepared their questions on issues of national and international interest. These meetings were invariably enjoyable to me, and greatly helped me to understand which issues were of most importance in that particular section of the nation or among the readers of that magazine or newspaper.

My staff learned to have a hamburger and a milkshake waiting after the luncheon so I could eat on the way to our next appointment.

I have thought about New Hampshire a lot, maybe for the obvious reason that it does have that tradition of the first state presidential primary in the nation, and I like the state. Our family lived in New England at three different times while we were in the Navy, so we naturally felt at home in that region. But there does seem something special about the people of New Hampshire and their attitude toward politics and the presidential primary. It is a major industry for them each four years, as candidates, staffs, volunteers, and news reporters traipse from one community to the other during our first primary contest. A few of the political "workers" in the state just want to be entertained by presidential aspirants, want to meet all of them to complete a check-off list, or want to see their own names in *The New York Times*. But these political dilettantes are rare.

It was amazing to me as I began campaigning how few of the people in New Hampshire have actually seen a candidate for president. Apparently most of the campaigning in the past has been superficial, and arranged mostly for the benefit of the news media. It has always been my custom to go directly to the people where they live or work. On my first two visits, I campaigned at prominent downtown bus stops and then went through the stores and government office buildings in Manchester and in Concord when the people arrived at work. Local workers in the state's largest city and many state workers in the capitol said to me they had never before been visited by a national candidate! A few of them had seen Pat Paulsen in 1972. In factories, in churches, in schools, and in shopping centers I found the people much more aware of the then-distant election than in other states, and much more interested in meeting me and in knowing about my campaign.

As my visits to the different states continued, I became more and more convinced of the inherent and unshakeable greatness of our country. For instance, my ancestors and I have always been farmers, and this is one subject which I have studied and practiced as a profession. But I have been thrilled again and again as I met those Americans who produce artichokes in California, syrup in Vermont, cheese in Wisconsin, wheat in Kansas, beef in Nebraska, sweet corn in Florida, rice in Louisiana, sugar in Minnesota, shadegrown tobacco in Connecticut and honey in Iowa.

Further Resources

BOOKS

Anderson, Patrick. *Electing Jimmy Carter: The Campaign of 1976*. Baton Rouge: Louisiana State University Press, 1994.

Bourne, Peter G. *Jimmy Carter: A Comprehensive Biography from Plains to Post-Presidency*. New York: Scribner, 1997.

Carter, Jimmy, with Robert Turner, ed. *"I'll Never Lie to You": Jimmy Carter in His Own Words*. New York: Ballantine, 1976.

Carter, Jimmy. *Keeping Faith: Memoirs of a President*. New York: Bantam Books, 1982.

Jordan, Hamilton. *Crisis: The Last Year of the Carter Presidency*. New York: G.P. Putnam's Sons, 1982.

Morris, Kenneth E. *Jimmy Cater, American Moralist*. Athens: University of Georgia Press, 1997.

WEBSITES

"The Carter Center." Available online at http://www.carter-center.org (accessed May 25, 2003).

"Jimmy Carter Library and Museum." Available online at http://carterlibrary.galileo.peachnet.edu (accessed May 25, 2003).

"Is America Turning Right?"

Magazine article

By: David Gelman, et al.

Date: November 7, 1977

Source: Gelman, David, et al. *Newsweek*. November 7, 1977, 34–36, 43–45.

About the Author: David Graham Gelman (1926–), born in New York City, studied at the City University of New York while working as a reporter for the *New York Post*. He joined the staff of the Peace Corps in 1962 as the director of special

projects. In 1966, Gelman became the associate editor for national affairs at *Newsweek*; three years later, he became the national editor of *Newsday*, before rejoining *Newsweek* as a general editor and senior writer in 1975. ∎

Introduction

After a decade dominated by liberalism, the political right hailed the election of Richard M. Nixon (served 1969–1974) to the presidency in 1968 as proof that the American public wanted a return to conservative values. Criticizing the urban riots, campus protests, and political upheavals of the era, Nixon came into office on a law-and-order platform that seemed to resonate with the "silent majority" of Americans appalled by the perceived excesses of the Woodstock generation. Yet, Nixon disappointed some of his supporters by withdrawing from the Vietnam War (1964–1975), a move that admitted the United States' failure in the region, and others by compromising with Democrats in Congress to get legislation passed. Even more disturbing was the fallout from the Watergate scandal that ended Nixon's presidency in 1974. Watergate doomed the Republicans in the next round of congressional elections. Not only did the Democrats gain seats in both legislative houses, they also recaptured the White House in 1976 when Jimmy Carter (served 1977–1981) edged out President Gerald R. Ford (served 1974–1977) in the election. Surveys showed that many voters resented Ford's presidential pardon of Nixon, and the issue may have been decisive in Ford's defeat.

Even as the political right hit rock bottom in the wake of Watergate, other trends fueled a resurgence of conservatism in the political arena. The perceived excesses of federal social programs frustrated some Americans in the 1960s, and they resisted further attempts to expand the government's welfare programs. Other voters, hurt by skyrocketing energy prices and recessions in the 1970s, also criticized the federal government for spending money on welfare programs at a time when middle class and working class Americans were feeling the economic pinch as well. By the end of the decade, the more ambitious social programs of the 1960s had been all but abandoned—as politicians struggled to adopt a more moderate, if not conservative, stance.

Significance

The backlash against sixties-style liberalism, combined with a lingering economic malaise, brought Ronald Reagan (served 1981–1989) to the White House in 1980. Although President Carter had attempted to portray himself as a fiscally conservative, "moderate" Democrat, Reagan's patriotic rhetoric and promises to roll back government programs resonated with voters. Reagan quickly set to work on a series of deregulation measures to decrease the government's watchdog role in the economy, and his administration slashed spending on social welfare programs while increasing defense spending. Reagan's popularity and ability to articulate a clear position on these issues helped to turn the political sentiment firmly to the right during his two terms in office. Even many of the Democrats who opposed Reagan began to adopt his rhetoric of patriotism, personal responsibility, and a decreased role of the government in U.S. society.

Outside of the political arena, the neoconservative movement had less success in implementing its agenda. Movements to ban or reduce abortions, restrict certain rights for gays and lesbians, and reverse affirmative action measures were major policy initiatives by conservatives, yet they were largely unsuccessful. Each remained intact, if not expanded, by the end of the decade. In the 1980s, these battles would be characterized as a "culture war" by neoconservatives to restore the country to supposedly more traditional values.

The rise of the neoconservative movement also confirmed the entrenchment of the political right within intellectual circles, which had formerly been dominated by liberals. Pundits such as Irving Kristol and Norman Podheretz, two leading figures of the neoconservative movement, were joined by a host of other right-leaning political thinkers including William Bennett, Lynne Cheney, and Allan Bloom. These influential, conservative figures aided the ascent of the political right in the 1980s on issues including economic deregulation, educational reform, and anti-communist foreign policy measures.

Primary Source

"Is America Turning Right? [excerpt]

SYNOPSIS: The Watergate scandal dealt a major blow to the conservative movement, and in 1976 the Democrats recaptured the White House. Yet Jimmy Carter's ascension to the presidency did not signal a full return to the liberalism of the 1960s, as this *Newsweek* article shows. Still reeling from the perceived excesses of the previous decade and dealing with economic uncertainties, most Americans advocated a more moderate, if not conservative, course for the country.

Nearly 45 years after Franklin D. Roosevelt first invoked the massive power of the Federal government for social action, Americans have grown increasingly ambivalent about the role of government in their lives. There has indisputably been a loss of faith—a feeling that Washington has tried for too long to do too much and, for the most part, has done it badly. Angered at everything from higher taxes and excessive regulation to reverse discrimination and moral permissiveness, more and more people are calling themselves conservatives. Even so, polls show that the majority of Americans favor more public spending on the environment, schooling, medical care, the elderly and the unemployed—staples of the liberal welfare state. Clearly, Americans want it both ways—lower taxes, but more services, less interference from Washington but more help with their problems. Out of the conflict, a new set of political views, what Rep. Richard Bolling of Missouri calls "a new synthesis," is struggling to emerge.

At first blush, the "new synthesis" has a decidedly conservative cast. It is not the conservatism of the traditional right, as represented by William F. Buckley Jr. or economist Milton Friedman. Nor is it an attempt to gut social security or medicare, or to return to an unregulated economy. Rather, it is an effort to draw the line on public spending, to apply a stringent cost-benefit analysis to social programs and in general to lower expectations. The new conservatism supports equality of opportunity for minorities and women, but balks at "coercive" measures such as affirmative-action quotas that seek to guarantee not just equal opportunity but equal results. And at times, the conservative mood explodes over such emotional issues as abortion, homosexual rights, the Equal Rights Amendment or the Panama Canal. . . .

In politics, Gov. Michael Dukakis of Massachussetts and California's Gov. Jerry Brown have become national symbols of the pragmatic new conservatism—tight-fisted political hybrids who seek to limit the further spread of government and place a balanced budget at the top of the public agenda. There is also a new breed in Congress—cost-conscious liberals like Democratic Sen. Gary Hart, who was George McGovern's campaign manager in 1972 but now tells his Colorado constituents that to "get the government off your back, get your hands out of the government's pockets." Or Democratic Rep. Elliott Levitas of Georgia, who sees his role as helping to "usher out the New Deal and move into a new era."

In intellectual circles, the social thinkers who were once the driving force of Democratic liberalism—men like Arthur Schlesinger Jr. and John Kenneth Galbraith—have been upstaged by a group of "neo-conservative" academics, many of them refugees from the liberal left, including Daniel Bell, Nathan Glazer, Irving Kristol, James Q. Wilson, Edward Banfield, Seymour Martin Lipset and Sen. Daniel P. Moynihan of New York. Their number is small but their energetic writings in such intellectual journals as The Public Interest, edited by Kristol and Glazer, and Commentary magazine, edited by Norman Podhoretz, have helped shape the outlines of a liberal-conservative synthesis. Some of them are doing their research at American Enterprise Institute, a so-called "Brookings of the right" that has begun to match the Brookings Institution brain-for-brain as the most influential think-tank in Washington.

Nationally, the conservative mood is producing backlash and belt-tightening. In California, the legislature recently restored the death penalty, overriding the governor's veto, and The Los Angeles Times slapped a ban on ads for X-rated movies. In Massachusetts, state senators waving American flags and singing "God Bless America" ordered teachers to lead their classes in a "group recitation of the pledge of allegiance"—against legal opinions that a mandatory pledge is unconstitutional. In Illinois, Phyllis Schlafly's formidable stop-ERA group again blocked approval of the Equal Rights Amendment in the legislature where, according to liberal State Rep. Aaron Jaffe, there is a wave of "conservative hysteria." And in Atlanta last spring, liberal black mayor Maynard Jackson fired sanitation workers who had struck for higher wages, then declared: "Before I take the city into a deficit financial position, elephants will roost in the trees."

Students, who are often a leading indicator of the national mood, also seem to reflect a return to traditional values. The campuses are quiet for the most part, and young people are again concerned with getting good grades and finding a job in a very tight labor market. Bread-and-butter courses are now more in demand—accounting is the most popular undergraduate subject—and the more fanciful elective courses are frequently dismissed as irrelevant. In general, there is a back-to-basics movement among educators and parents—a tightening of standards and a stress on core courses.

Yet, in the broad picture, what is happening in the country is far more complicated than a collective swing to the right or a return to tradition. Though polls show that the number of Americans calling themselves conservatives is half again the number who count themselves as liberals, the number who say they are Republicans stands at 20 per cent, down 8 points from 1972 and a 40-year low. And the most recent definitive Gallup poll on the subject, in 1976, confirmed the paradox in popular attitudes toward government. Despite the mounting mistrust of Washington since the late '60s, the survey showed majorities favoring at least some increase

Massachusetts governor Michael Dukakis (left) was a national symbol of a pragmatic new conservativism in the 1970s. AP/WIDE WORLD PHOTOS. REPRODUCED BY PERMISSION.

in spending on such Federal initiatives as helping the elderly, making college possible for young people, coping with drug addicts, supporting and improving public schools, and improving medical and health care.

But when it came to helping the poor with welfare programs or improving the situation of black Americans, substantial majorities in the Gallup cross section did not want to increase present funding. The split could represent racism. But some experts see a strong element of simple middle-class self-interest in current attitudes, a phenomenon that seems to rise with the cost of living. What looks like a trend toward conservatism might actually be a matter of selective social consciousness—the view that the government has given too much welfare to the minority poor, not enough to the middle class caught in an unaccustomed economic squeeze. "The middle-class is not feeling guilty anymore," says Willie Woods, coordinator of the Georgia Association of Black Elected Officials. "They're worried about their own survival."

Similarly, the life-style changes of the '70s scarcely suggest a return to traditional values. The divorce rate is higher than ever, premarital sex is prevalent, and the Senate Judiciary Committee has just voted to decriminalize possession of small amounts of marijuana. Although there has been some backlash on abortion and women's rights, the fact remains that abortions are now legal. A fight is raging in Congress over public funding of abortions—another confrontation over the limits of welfare—but an estimated 1 million American women availed themselves of the right to abortion in a single year.

To date, Carter Administration policies have only added to the confusion. Carter was elected as an anti-Washington outsider who tempered his populist plans for social action with talk of fiscal restraint, a balanced budget and a less intrusive government. A Gallup poll released last week showed 45 per cent of Americans consider him a conservative and 36 per cent see him as a liberal. But beneath its sometimes conservative rhetoric, his Administration is pushing ambitious Federal programs rivaling those of the New Deal and the Great Society. Pressured by urban and minority leaders, Carter has expanded his welfare-reform proposal by $2.8 billion, and the plan envisages the biggest public-jobs program since the New Deal and the equivalent of a guaranteed annual income. His Housing and Urban Development agency has revived the subsidized housing program virtually abandoned by the Nixon and Ford administrations. His energy policy is centered on an aggressively interventionist program that would heavily tax oil and gas consumption and thrust government into the daily decisions of every corporation and individual.

This confusing flux can be called neither liberal nor conservative. More than anything, the period is marked by shifting political alliances and a search for new political definitions. In Seattle, where voters recently rejected a number of highly qualified candidates for mayor and instead chose two relatively inexperienced outsiders, a local publisher labeled it "the politics of newness." Mayor Jackson of Atlanta calls his successful courtship of business "the politics of inclusion." And in Boston, Governor Dukakis's tough budget-slashing tactics have come under the nomenclature of "new pragmatism."

Dukakis, who is up for reelection next year, is now under attack by liberals like ex-aide Barney Frank, who charges Dukakis with balancing the budget "on the backs of the poor." Dukakis has cut off medical care for all welfare recipients and whittled cost-of-living increases for welfare families with dependent children. He also developed a mandatory "workfare" program under which unemployed fathers must work three days a week in government or non-profit agencies or forfeit their own benefits. This flinty approach to social spending—popular with many voters—prompted some people to label him "Jerry Brown East." Frank has come up with some wry tag lines of his own. "It's the new opportunism, the new electability," he says. "It's Calvin Coolidge with a smile."

Whatever the label, there is no question that some of the liberal orthodoxies of the past are under strenuous challenge for a variety of reasons. During the 1960s, the economic wisdom held that a growing economy free of inflation and fine-tuned by Keynesian managers would generate enough new tax revenues every year—the so-called fiscal dividend—to finance Kennedy's New Frontier and Johnson's Great Society. But the theory collapsed with the ill-fated "guns and butter" policy of the Vietnam war. A long inflationary spiral began, culminating in the unprecedented recession-cum-inflation that followed the Arab oil embargo of 1973. The end of the dream of unlimited growth and prosperity is the overarching fact of daily existence in the '70s. Says one-time radical leader Tom Hayden, who now heads a California-based Campaign for Economic Democracy: "During the 1960s, we fought the pigs. Now we fight the high price of bacon." Or, as columnist George Will puts it, "Inflation is a great conservatizing issue."

Today's conservatives look back on the 1960s as a time when things got out of hand. On the campuses, legitimate dissent boiled over into movements that disrupted and undermined academic life. In the ghettos, grievances exploded into brutal riots. On the left, reformists turned into revolutionaries who attacked middle-class values. To many blue-collar workers and academics alike, the breakdown of order was the end result of excessive moral permissiveness and lax law enforcement—liberalism gone beserk. Like Hamilton and Madison, they have embraced the notion of a little less populist democracy, a little more rule of law. . . .

One of the rankling symbols of misdirected government largesse is the notorious Pruitt-Igoe housing project in St. Louis. Opened as a model of social planning for the poor, the project ultimately turned into a welfare ghetto. Crime-infested buildings were vandalized, then abandoned by their tenants, and finally demolished. Subsidized housing is still suspect because of abuses and mismanagement in several cities. In Detroit, shoddy construction work and bribery of Housing and Urban Development agency officials resulted in over 200 convictions. Real-estate hustlers made quick killings in the program by buying up dilapidated buildings, getting inflated appraisals, then moving in poor families on federally insured mortgages. In the end, houses fell apart, tenants fled, and HUD was left with 9,000 repossessed houses and 5,000 vacant lots.

The neo-conservatives now want to rely more on market mechanisms and less on government agencies to solve social problems. They tend to favor giving housing vouchers to the poor instead of building government housing projects. They would rather establish pollution taxes than cumbersome environmental regulations. And they want a negative income tax for the poor instead of a welfare bureaucracy. Such market-oriented solutions, they contend, would get the job done more efficiently and allow poor people some measure of choice about how to spend their money or where to live. Liberals are not necessarily opposed to such ideas, but with little experience to go on, they question whether the market would work as well as the conservatives say.

Besides emphasizing market efficiency and the primacy of individual freedom, the neo-conservatives also seek something of a return to traditional social values. In an influential essay on "The Limits of Social Policy," Glazer argued that government welfare programs too often pre-empted the function of family, church, school and neighborhood organizations, and thus perpetuated the social dependency they sought to resolve. "I am increasingly convinced," he wrote, "that some important part of the solution to our social problems lies in traditional practices and traditional restraints." But it is unclear whether most Americans agree. As the government has assumed many of the functions once performed by family or church—caring for the elderly or infirm, for instance —individuals have more time and money to spend on themselves. In effect, the government has become an extended family—and many people like it that way.

Not all the neo-conservatives agree on principles or practices, and some doubt the efficiency of the market. Only Kristol seems fully comfortable with the neo-conservative label though he acknowledges that it describes "only a tendency, not a clearly defined 'movement'." But almost all his like-minded ideologues are genuinely alarmed that affirmative action will destroy a society based on merit. It "has become the central focus in the country—the growth of state power to shape the society in certain directions," asserts Podhoretz.

The neo-conservative argument has thus touched the heart of the national distemper: the recoil from the "excesses" of the '60s, the reaction against blundering bureaucracy, the indignation over the Bakke case as a new form of state-encouraged discrimination in pursuit of egalitarianism. It is the mood first tapped by George Wallace in his populist jihads against "pointy-headed bureaucrats" who steal the bread of working men to fill the stomachs of the shiftless. Now apparently, it has been absorbed into the American mainstream. "What we may be reaping is a harvest of fear and uncertainty, acting much more like a frightened country," says Carl Holman, head of the National Urban Coalition. "You can look at Bakke and say there is a turn to the right. But what's behind Bakke is a cold calculation of whose sons are going to get through those narrow doors into the professions."

To old-line liberals, all of this shows that the country is turning its back on historic commitments. "I think there's been a loss of social sympathy," says City University of New York Professor Irving Howe. "What the neo-conservatives don't acknowledge is that standing still can bring unforeseen consequences, too." . . .

The question now is how much neo-conservative thinking will come to bear on public policy. If the nation's mood is indeed shifting to the right, it is mostly for pragmatic reasons. "The bureaucracy is the enemy," says Carter pollster Pat Caddell. "The public is not rejecting the ideas, it is rejecting the execution." HUD Secretary Patricia Roberts Harris agrees. "People are now result oriented," she says. "I think they will pay for anything that works." . . .

Playing both liberal and conservative impulses in his first nine months in office, Carter has become emblematic of the country's own confusion. Much will depend on the Administration's ability to find a unified stance that will focus the country's goals. "People are not conservative, they're very uncomfortable, they're unsure," says Missouri's Congressman Bolling. "What's going on now is that we've finished up the World War II era, both in terms of the economy and the society, and we're not quite set on the next go-round. We're struggling to find the basic facts for us to come up with the new synthesis, so that we can go on in a society that's more complicated, more dependent on the world than it was . . . I don't think we know enough yet for the next set of answers."

The search for those answers will be going on for some time, and the lines between right and left in America may become even more blurred and eroded than they already are. Americans, by and large, have never been comfortable with ideologies of any political stripe; they are still pragmatists at heart. Today's new conservatives lie very much within this pragmatic tradition: they are drawing attention to solutions that often do not work. The continuing necessity for them, and for Americans as a whole, is to show they can take account of the mistakes of the past without being paralyzed by them.

Further Resources

BOOKS

Berman, William C. *America's Right Turn: From Nixon to Clinton*. 2nd edition. Baltimore: Johns Hopkins University Press, 1998.

Blum, John Morton. *Years of Discord: American Politics and Society, 1961-1974*. New York: W.W. Norton & Company, 1991.

Edsall, Thomas Byrne, and Mary Edsall. *Chain Reaction: The Impact of Race, Rights, and Taxes on American Politics*. New York: W.W. Norton & Company, 1991.

Rieder, Jonathan. *Canarsie: The Jews and Italians of Brooklyn Against Liberalism*. Cambridge, Mass.: Harvard University Press, 1985.

Steinfels, Peter. *The Neoconservatives: The Men Who Are Changing America's Politics*. New York: Simon & Schuster, 1979.

"Foreign Affairs: The Need for Leadership"
Speech

By: Ronald Reagan

Date: March 17, 1978

Source: Reagan, Ronald. "Foreign Affairs: The Need for Leadership." March 17, 1978, speech delivered to the Conservative Political Action Conference in Washington, D.C. Available online at http://www.reaganlegacy.org/speeches/reagan.americas.purpose.3.25.78.htm; website home page: http://www.reaganlegacy.org (accessed May 25, 2003).

About the Author: Ronald Reagan (1911–) was a successful movie and television actor from the 1930s through the 1950s. In his first bid for political office, he won the governorship of California in 1966 on a pro-business platform that took direct aim at the liberalism of the era. Despite an unsuccessful presidential run in 1976, Reagan remained in the national political spotlight and emerged as the Republican presidential nominee in 1980. Reagan (served 1981–1989) went on to win the election and served two terms as the nation's fortieth president. ■

Introduction

The isthmus of Panama's value as a transport point between the Atlantic and Pacific Oceans became crucially important during the nineteenth century, when international trade, spurred by the Industrial Revolution, greatly expanded. The United States had formally been involved in the region since the 1850s, when it entered into an agreement with Great Britain to share control of a proposed canal connecting the Atlantic and Pacific oceans. It was another half century, however, before work on the Panama Canal actually began. After the United States encouraged and supported a revolt to establish a separate nation of Panama, previously part of Colombia, the two countries signed the Hay-Bunau-Varilla Treaty in 1903. Under the terms of the treaty, the United States retained exclusive control through the end of 1999 of a ten-mile wide canal zone in Panama, for which it paid $10 million up front and $250,000 annually thereafter. The amount of the annual payment was regularly increased, and, by the 1970s, the United States paid Panama over $2.3 million each year for its continued rights to the Panama Canal Zone.

Although the canal and its related operations were a boon to their economy, the American presence irked many Panamanians, who routinely accused the United States of exercising undue influence on the nation's domestic affairs. Calls for the return of the Canal Zone to full Panamanian control picked up pace in the 1960s, and, in the 1970s, the threat of civil unrest in the country spurred the United States and Panama to enter into negotiations over the return of the Canal Zone to Panamanian sovereignty. Despite significant opposition to handing over the Canal Zone, President Carter (served 1977–1981) ushered two treaties through Congress in 1977, one to return the canal to Panama—known as the Panama Canal Treaty—and the other to guarantee the right of the United States to undertake military action, if necessary, to keep the canal open—known as the Neutrality Treaty.

Significance

Of the two agreements, the Panama Canal Treaty provoked a storm of criticism, particularly by conservatives who viewed the return of the canal as another sign of the United States' diminished reputation in international affairs. To these critics, it seemed that the United States had been bullied by a much smaller and weaker nation into handing over an extremely valuable asset for which it had the full rights to retain for more than another decade. Led by isolationist North Carolina senator Jesse Helms, the anti-Canal Treaty advocates almost succeeded in preventing the agreement from being ratified. It passed by just one more vote needed for a two-thirds majority, and it was duly ratified on April 18, 1978. Although the United States retained operational control of part of the Canal Zone until the end of 1999, Panama resumed its authority over the entire area after the treaties went into effect in 1979.

President Carter viewed his success in implementing the Panama Canal Treaty as one of his greatest foreign policy accomplishments. Not only did the agreement recognize Panama's sovereignty over its own lands, but arranged for a peaceful transfer of control that did not interrupt trade through the region. The treaties also reflected a new respect between the United States and its Latin American neighbors. In the past, the United States had sometimes acted unilaterally to achieve its goals in the region, generating mistrust and resentment among its southern neighbors. Carter and other supporters of the agreements hoped that the example set by the Panama Canal Treaty would go a long way towards fostering trust and goodwill throughout the western hemisphere.

Foreign policy conservatives, however, took a different view. For a country still reeling from the humiliations of the Vietnam War (1964–1975), it seemed that turning over the Panama Canal further tarnished the image of the United States in the eyes of the international community. It also appeared damaging to acknowledge a far smaller and weaker country as the equal of the United States, regardless of the goodwill it generated in the region. In the following decade, the conservative point of view would triumph as Ronald Reagan, one of the leading critics of the Panama Canal Treaty, swept into office in 1980.

Primary Source

"Foreign Affairs: The Need for Leadership [excerpt]

SYNOPSIS: In this speech excerpt, the central themes of soon-to-be presidential candidate Ronald Reagan's political outlook are evident: pride in the United States, confidence that the American people would prevail in a just cause, and faith that free market economics would improve the lives of people everywhere. Reagan returned time and again to these same themes, serving as the basis for his ideological battle against the Soviet Union in the Cold War. Here he addresses the U.S. position towards Latin America, particularly Panama.

As a part-time journalist faced with producing a syndicated daily radio broadcast and twice-a-week newspaper column, I find being on the mailing lists of an almost endless array of organizations most helpful. Now some of the flood of materials crosses my desk very swiftly. But not all of it. One thick handout I got late last year was especially fascinating, not only because of content but just because it was mailed to me at all.

It was from the White House Press Office. Under the title "Domestic and Foreign Policy Accomplishments" it told me, in 21 single-spaced pages, of the wonders of the Carter administration's first year.

Beginning with the modest statement that—quote—"The president tackled directly and comprehensively major domestic problems that had been almost completely ignored in previous years."—unquote—it then recited an impressive list of major accomplishments. True, the White House hadn't claimed to find a way to control the weather or to eliminate crab grass on the White House lawn, but it did think it had solved—or nearly solved—our energy problems, Social Security's $17-trillion deficit, the size of a big government (we added 52,000 new employees in the first 10 months of 1977), the welfare mess and a host of other problems that have been center stage in American life for quite some time.

Tonight, perhaps we should discuss some of those White House claims and see if they have stood the test of even the three months that have passed since they were made. I know that's a little cruel—like checking up on someone's New Year's resolutions. After all, the administration has scarcely gotten a single domestic program worth noting through Congress. I'll tell you what. Let us concentrate on the administration's handling of foreign affairs, national security and its sense of priorities. . . .

Few Americans accept the belief of some of those now in positions of importance in guiding our foreign policy that America's purpose in the world is to appease the might out of a sense of fear or to appease the weak out of a sense of guilt.

But a question remains. Is the faulty thinking that has led us to these particular treaties an isolated particle, or is it part of a much larger whole?

In reviewing the foreign policy of this administration, one can only come to the conclusion that the mistaken assumptions that led to its course on the Panama Canal treaties are being duplicated around the world.

Its policy is rooted in well-meaning intentions, but it shows a woeful uncertainty as to America's purpose in the world. . . .

First, let us end this cycle of American indifference, followed by frenzied activity in Latin America (as it has been elsewhere). It leaves our southern neighbors bewildered and cynical. Instead, I propose a steadier course in which Latin America's growing

Under the agreement the United States signed with Panama in 1977, control of the Panama Canal was set to transfer to Panama in December 1999.
© BETTMANN/CORBIS. REPRODUCED BY PERMISSION.

importance is recognized not as an act of charity, but in our own self-interest. Latin America, with all its resources and vitality, should be encouraged to join not the Third World, much less the Communists' Second World, but the First World—that community of stable, prosperous and free nations of Western Europe, North America and Japan.

Today, there is hope that much of Latin America might do so. First, many nations have learned the cost of Socialist experimentation: Argentina under the Perons, Chile under Allende, Peru under Velasco, Mexico under Echeverria. All suffered economic catastrophe. Their successors learned the bitter truth that defying the laws of economics benefits no one and, in fact, hurts most the poor whose cause those earlier leaders so demagogically espoused.

Today, as a result of those experiments which went so badly out of control, more and more of our neighbors are turning to the free market as a model of development. Their acceptance of economic rationality should be neither ignored nor penalized but actively encouraged.

At the same time, we must recognize that Latin America is once again leaving a period of strictly military rule and entering a more democratic phase. But in this case the United States is doing too much pushing, rather than too little.

Unhappily, the change from military to civilian rule is not an easy one. Nor can it be rushed. If it is, we will only succeed in creating weak and vulnerable democratic governments that will soon be swept out of power by just another generation of military strongmen even more convinced of the defects of democracy.

Above all, we want a free and prosperous Latin America. And, to obtain that, we cannot continue to reward our self-declared enemies and then turn around and punish our friends.

That leads me again to Panama. The treaties that have occupied so much of our attention in recent months represent both the good instincts and the bad impulses of American diplomacy.

The bad, for reasons I have repeated on many occasions: the feeling that we are guilty of some sin for which we must now atone and our inability to say "no," not out of truculence, but because it was the proper thing to say to secure our interests and to reaffirm our greater responsibility, which is leadership of all that remains of the free world.

Yes, the treaties represent the good instincts of American diplomacy, too—a spirit of generosity and willingness to change with times. A good foreign policy must have both elements: the need to say "no" and the willingness to change, in just the right proportions. Unfortunately, accepting change because it seems fashionable to do so, with little real regard for the consequences, seems to dominate our foreign policy today.

Too many in positions of importance believe that through generosity and self-effacement we can avoid trouble, whether it's with Panama and the canal or the Soviet Union and SALT.

But, like it or not, trouble will not be avoided. The American people and their elected leaders will continue to be faced with hard choices and difficult moments, for resolve is continually being tested by those who envy us our prosperity and begrudge us our freedom.

America will remain great and act responsibly so long as it exercises power—wisely, and not in the bullying sense—but exercises it, nonetheless.

Leadership is a great burden. We grow weary of it at times. And the Carter administration, despite its own cheerful propaganda about accomplishments, reflects that weariness.

But if we are not to shoulder the burdens of leadership in the free world, then who will?

The alternatives are neither pleasant nor acceptable. Great nations which fail to meet their responsibilities are consigned to the dust bin of history. We grew from that small, weak republic which had as its assets spirit, optimism, faith in God and an unshakeable belief that free men and women could govern themselves wisely. We became the leader of the free world, an example for all those who cherish freedom.

If we are to continue to be that example—if we are to preserve our own freedom—we must understand those who would dominate us and deal with them with determination.

We must shoulder our burden with our eyes fixed on the future, but recognizing the realities of today, not counting on mere hope or wishes. We must be willing to carry out our responsibility as the custodian of individual freedom. Then we will achieve our destiny to be as a shining city on a hill for all mankind to see.

Further Resources

BOOKS

Buckley, Kevin. *Panama: The Whole Story.* New York: Simon and Schuster, 1991.

Falcoff, Mark. *Panama's Canal: What Happens When the United States Gives a Small Country What It Wants?* Washington, D.C.: AEI Press, 1998.

Gold, Susan Dudley. *The Panama Canal Transfer: Controversy at the Crossroads.* Austin, Tex.: Raintree Steck-Vaughan, 1999.

Knapp, Herbert, and Mary Knapp. *Red, White, and Blue Paradise: The American Canal Zone in Panama.* San Diego: Harcourt Brace Jovanovich, 1984.

McCullough, David. *The Path Between the Seas: The Creation of the Panama Canal, 1870–1914.* New York: Simon and Schuster, 1977.

WEBSITES

"A Man, a Plan, a Canal, Panama!" Available online at http://memory.loc.gov/ammem/today/sep07.html; website home page http://memory.loc.gov (accessed May 25, 2003).

"Panama Canal Treaty Information." Available online at http://www.orbi.net/pancanal/public/organiza/treaty/treaty. htm; website home page http://www.orbi.net (accessed May 25, 2003).

Harvard Hates America: The Odyssey of a Born-Again American

Memoir

By: John LeBoutillier

Date: 1978

Source: LeBoutillier, John. *Harvard Hates America: The Odyssey of a Born-Again American.* South Bend, Ind.: Gateway Edition, 1978, 50–56.

About the Author: John LeBoutillier (1953–) graduated from Harvard University in 1976 with a bachelor's degree, and he later completed a master's degree in business administration. While attending Harvard, he became a high profile political fundraiser for conservative candidates. In 1976, he served as the New Jersey coordinator for the presidential campaign of Gerald Ford (served 1974–1977). In 1980, LeBoutillier was elected to the U.S. House of Representatives from the 6th District of New York. After serving one term, LeBoutillier resumed his career as a conservative commentator. ∎

Introduction

In the 1960s, many American college campuses were rocked by protests against the government, the Vietnam War (1964–1975), and social issues such as poverty, sexism, and racial discrimination. Many stu-

John LeBoutillier wrote about the change in political tendencies from liberalism to conservativism. LEBOUTILLIER, JOHN, PHOTOGRAPH BY D. DEBOUTILLIER. REPRODUCED BY PERMISSION.

dents also joined political groups such as the Students for a Democratic Society to express their demands for change. Although not every student was politically active during the era, those who were tended to follow the political left. The leaders of the two major political parties also seemed to reflect a generation gap, as the youthfulness and optimism of Democrats such as Robert F. Kennedy contrasted with the law-and-order image of Richard M. Nixon (served 1969–1974). As the 1960s drew to a close, it was far less fashionable to be a conservative Republican than a liberal Democrat.

In contrast to the political fervor of the 1960s, college campuses were decidedly more restrained in the 1970s. With the United States' involvement in the Vietnam War ending, students were less worried about being drafted and more concerned about their professional lives, particularly after the recessions of the decade dimmed their job prospects. Although college life was still high-spirited—as a brief fad for streaking in the early 1970s demonstrated—students were perceived as more conservative, self-interested, and career-minded than their 1960s counterparts.

Many young people also became disengaged from the political process as a result of the corruption revealed by the Watergate scandal, which led to President Nixon's

resignation in 1974. Whereas dissatisfaction with elected leaders in the 1960s had led to an increase in political participation in the 1960s, it produced apathy in the 1970s. As the new generation came of age in the 1970s, it gave the era the label "The Me Decade," a phrase that summed up its preoccupation with individual interests at the expense of civic pursuits.

Significance

In contrast to the general political disengagement that characterized the 1970s, a growing number of young people embraced conservative beliefs during the decade. For some, the turn to the political right represented another generational conflict: now that universities were seemingly ensconced in the liberal camp, it was almost inevitable that some young people would take the opposite political path. Others were simply turned off by what they perceived as the excesses of the previous generation, in which drug use, sexual activity, and defiant counterculture expressions became more commonplace. Still others were dismayed by the expansion of the federal social welfare programs of the 1960s in an effort to create a "Great Society" for all Americans. Those who viewed the ambitious federal programs as ineffective and wasteful turned toward conservatism and its call for individual responsibility and a reduced role of government in American life.

For students such as John LeBoutillier, who studied at Harvard in the 1970s, each of these trends culminated in a lasting commitment to conservative politics. In his 1978 book, *Harvard Hates America*, LeBoutillier described his political journey toward conservatism as a lonely one. Perceiving the university as an institution dominated by conceited and conformist liberals, LeBoutillier accused them of choosing their political beliefs based on expediency and guilt. "They had no commitment to anything, no real desire to make a sacrifice for any sort of constructive change," he wrote, "They were along for the ride on a 'crusade without a cause.'"

The swing in support of conservatism among young people translated in to a shift toward the Republican Party in the 1980s. Although Ronald Reagan (served 1981–1989) was hardly a youthful presidential candidate in 1980, his effective use of the themes of patriotism, individualism, and conservatism appealed to many Americans across the generational divide.

Primary Source

Harvard Hates America: The Odyssey of a Born-Again American [excerpt]

SYNOPSIS: In this passage, LeBoutillier describes the development of his conservative perspective and philosophy. He takes particular aim at his Harvard

University professors and his classmates, whom he derides as thoughtlessly conforming to liberalism. LeBoutillier even deems their criticism of the United States government as unpatriotic and dangerous.

About half-way through my undergraduate career at Harvard I decided where I stood politically. I was able to decide the merits and demerits of the arguments I encountered. I was able to examine a way of thinking; I was able to analyse and to draw conclusions about a basic ideological framework I call the Liberal Mind.

For one thing, I gradually realized that the Liberal Mind operates on an extremely high level of self-confidence. Basically, the Liberal thinks he can tell you how to live your life better than you can. For some reason, he feels he is better equipped to determine other people's futures than they are. The Harvard Liberal Mind belongs to an elite that says to the middle class American: "Look, we're better educated than you. We'll look after your interests. We'll tell you where to send your kids to school, how much money you should earn, what you can leave to your kids, what protection you should have in your house. We'll tell you how to live—and if we increase your taxes, well, trust us."

To the Liberal Mind the federal government is the tool to implement their plans. On every issue, from health care to gun control, from busing to economics, the Liberal Mind turns to government to "intervene in order to make things fair." I don't doubt the Liberals' good intentions; they *do* want to stop injustice, hunger, and suffering. They mean well. No, it is the *how* that is wrong. And it is the *how* that runs counter to what this country stands for. . . .

During my Harvard years I was basically reacting to the Liberal Mind. I observed it, understood it, and began thinking of ways to challenge it. I came to see that both my peers and my liberal teachers were not ideological soldiers engaged in a lifetime commitment to some ideal, but rather that they were insecure people desperately searching for some sort of identity. In almost every case, the loud and ranting voices calling for "radical changes" in America were not the voices of dedicated, sacrificing ideologues; no, they really were the voices of a generation searching for something to identify with, something that would provide an umbrella under which they could find security and legitimacy.

These students shouting "Fuck the Feds" were, and are, in most cases eighteen- or nineteen-year-olds who have no reason to villify their government.

They are students; they are extremely brilliant—after all, aren't they part of what everybody told us was the brightest generation ever? Yet, in most cases, they also are exceedingly ignorant.

And, what about the liberal teachers? To me, many of them are hypocrites, both intellectually and personally. They live the soft life, sheltered inside the all-encompassing institution called Harvard, which gives them legitimacy, security, and an identity which many of them could not have found outside in the real world. This unique form of protection does nothing but help these professors feed off of each other—the Liberal line is the accepted line. Thus, paradoxically, Harvard, supposedly the greatest of all universities, designed to promote independence of thought and mind, in fact promotes one type of thought almost exclusively. And this jaundiced view of America, in no way representative of the prevailing American values, does nothing but influence the students in a negative and cynical way.

I believe that many of these Liberals I am describing have never really stopped to think about what they are advocating. They have never really questioned the logic of their arguments. And they have never understood the motivations of their mentors. Why? Why do they simply parrot a few misguided spokesmen? In the case of my peers at Harvard, most joined in the demonstrations and advocated the Liberal rhetoric because it was a fad—the thing to do. It was the social thing to do. Join the crowd; blow some dope and attack America. It was definitely "in." The funny thing is, these people were all phonies. They had no commitment to anything, no real desire to make a sacrifice for any sort of constructive change. They were along for the ride on a "crusade without a cause."

At Harvard I detected another reason behind the mindless, unquestioned parroting of this twisted logic. Many of these teachers and students were so fueled by hatred that they could not stop to see what, in fact, they were actually saying. When advocating "sweeping changes in the redistribution of income" or "massive alterations in the social fabric of this country," they seemed to attack America—to hate America. Yet in reality it was themselves they hated, for they suffered from a massive case of guilt. On race, they felt guilty because their ancestors discriminated against blacks; economically, they felt guilty about living comfortably off large trust funds or inheritances; socially, they felt guilty about the fact that coming from where they do opens doors closed to the less fortunate.

And it was the Great Society programs, drafted and legislated by Liberals of the same breed I encountered at Harvard, that were the real-life manifestation of these guilt feelings. It would be hard to defend the Great Society based on results. It would be hard to say America is a better place to live because of those programs. You would have an even more difficult time defending busing if your premise is that we want our children to have better education. In general, you would have a tough time defending increased governmental participation in our everyday lives as a result of the big spending programs of the 1960s. Whether it be the home, or the school, or the church, the neighborhood, or local government, it is the Liberal thinking that has entered, dictated, and weakened. It has instilled an accepted premise in America that the role of government is to intervene more, not less; to administrate, not regulate; and to order, not guide.

These facts were in my mind as I began formulating my views. Also weighing heavily in my thoughts was a visceral reaction to those advocates of Liberal programs. The hypocrisy of a professor advocating a 100 percent inheritance tax while using his wife's inheritance was, and is, shocking. And so were other instances of students from affluent backgrounds attacking the very system which enabled them to live comfortably. I found it disgraceful for a professor living well, in a lavishly furnished house paid for by Harvard, with life-time tenure, to attack the corporations which in part finance private educational institutions.

And, so, as my career at Harvard drew to a conclusion, I had journeyed a long way. I had grown tremendously. I came to see that for all its grandeur and reputation, Harvard was really a myth—a home for an elite divorced from the real world. And, sadly, Harvard, the institution founded for the express purpose of producing leaders, did just the opposite: producing insecure followers, able only to regurgitate the nonsense put forth by the George McGoverns of the world.

I had also observed firsthand the very thought processes which in 1976, my graduation year, were resulting in widespread voter dissatisfaction in the presidential and Congressional elections. And, while seeing all of this, I had grown more confident in the ability of individual Americans, given an opportunity, to solve their own problems. At least, I was certain, they couldn't do a worse job than had the Liberal programs of the 1960s.

Most of all, I had begun formulating my beliefs into a new political philosophy. And, it seemed, the best home for this philosophy was the Republican party.

The tale of my political growth at Harvard would not be complete without describing my graduation, for even on that auspicious occasion we catch a glimpse of Liberal elitism attempting to impose its will.

Graduating from Harvard University should be, and is designed to be, one of a handful of cherished memories that one accumulates in life. Although it is a symbolic ceremony, the symbolism is important. The graduate has competed with, and learned from, the greatest academic minds in the world. Hopefully he or she has prospered from this and is now ready to move forward in life to use those lessons in a just and good cause.

Graduating from Harvard is also a great time for pride, not personal pride as much as family pride. For most families, seeing their son or daughter graduate from Harvard is the culmination of a dream, a realization that they had succeeded in providing well for their child. Most of all, it is a moment for all to share and cherish. It is special.

Our graduation was in June—a very, very hot June. The mercury hit 96 that Thursday morning. It was a sunny day, with little breeze to break up the sticky humidity. With all my classmates from Kirkland House, I lined up in the morning for the ceremonies which took place in front of Memorial Church. After some speeches and the awarding of nine honorary degrees, we walked back to our undergraduate houses for lunch, which was to be followed by the actual diploma presentation.

Lunch was a picnic in the rectangular, ivy-coated courtyard of Kirkland House, where I had lived for the past three years. Lunch was emotional because for the last time friends were eating together, and families who had journeyed from all over the world shared a meal with their children just minutes before the actual graduation.

Then the trays were cleared away, the seniors lined up, and one by one the names were read off. The graduate would walk to the platform, climb the two steps, and accept his diploma. He would then shake hands with the House master, kiss the House master's wife, shake some more hands, and then be an alumnus of one of the great universities in the world. Because I was graduating Magna Cum Laude, I was near the end of the line. By the time my turn came, I had memorized the entire setting.

The House master, Dr. Warren Wacker, was wearing the usual ceremonial robe and mortar board. A crimson tassle hung over his left ear.

As my turn came, I was escorted by two Ph.D.'s up to the platform. I climbed the steps. The diploma was handed to me. I was thinking of my family and how proud I knew they were. And I was so proud of them for all they had done to achieve this. Then, instead of congratulating me, Dr. Wacker simply said, "Now, John, if you'd only move a few steps to your left." It took me more than a moment to realize he was not talking about my physical location on the platform.

Further Resources

BOOKS

Brock, David. *Blinded by the Right: The Conscience of an Ex-Conservative.* New York: Crown Publishers, 2002.

Buchanan, Patrick. *Right from the Beginning.* Washington, D.C.: Regnery Publishing, 1990.

Kristol, Irving. *Neoconservatism: The Autobiography of an Idea.* New York: Free Press, 1995.

Murray, Charles. *Losing Ground: American Social Policy, 1950–1980.* New York: Basic Books, 1995.

Nash, George. *The Conservative Intellectual Movement in America since 1945.* Wilmington, Del.: Intercollegiate Studies Institute, 1996.

WEBSITES

"Biography of John LeBoutillier." Available online at http://www.newsmax.com/articles/print.shtml?a=2000/2/14/190256; website home page http://www.newsmax.com (accessed May 25, 2003).

A National Malaise

"The Crisis of Confidence"

Speech

By: Jimmy Carter

Date: July 15, 1979

Source: Carter, Jimmy. "The Crisis of Confidence," July 15, 1979, delivered in Washington, D.C. The Program in Presidential Rhetoric, Department of Communication, Texas A&M University. Available online at http://www.tamu.edu/scom/pres/speeches/jccrisis; website home page http://www.tamu.edu (accessed May 25, 2003).

Notes About the Author: Jimmy Carter (1924–) entered the 1976 presidential race as a relative underdog. During his campaign, Carter emphasized his integrity and presented himself as a moderate Democrat—who would practice fiscal responsibility, while maintaining his party's commitment to social welfare programs. Carter narrowly won the election over incumbent Gerald R. Ford (served 1974–1977) and served one term as the nation's thirty-eighth president. His term was beset by numerous problems and he was defeated in his reelection bid in 1980. Although his presidency was regarded as one of the less successful of the twentieth century, Carter's numerous philanthropic efforts after leaving office earned him the reputation as one of the country's great statesmen. Carter received the Nobel Peace Prize in 2002.

"Carter at the Crossroads"

Magazine article

By: Hugh Sidey

Date: July 23, 1979

Source: Sidey, Hugh. "Carter at the Crossroads." *Time,* July 23, 1979, 20, 23–24, 27.

Notes About the Author: Hugh Sidey (1927–) began working for *Time* in 1958, and in 1969 became the chief of the magazine's Washington bureau. With his unique political access, Sidey was a close associate of several presidents and other national political figures. The article "Carter at the Crossroads" was one of the most revealing portraits of President Carter (served 1977–1981) while in office. ■

Introduction

The election of Jimmy Carter to the presidency in 1976 capped the remarkable political rise of a man who described himself as a peanut farmer from Plains, Georgia. Obviously Carter was a shrewd politician, as he had already served as Georgia's governor from 1971 to 1974. Yet his humble demeanor and sincere references to his religious faith contrasted greatly with the image and rhetoric of most politicians. Impressed by his integrity and forthrightness, enough Americans voted for the man once known as "Jimmy Who?" that Carter won the election over incumbent president Gerald R. Ford, and he became the first Democrat to win the White House since Lyndon Johnson (served 1963–1969) in 1964.

Carter faced a number of challenges as he assumed the presidency in January 1977. The nation's economy had never fully adapted to the wild energy price swings that resulted from the Organization of Petroleum Exporting Countries (OPEC) cartel's 1973 oil embargo. As U.S. industries suffered, unemployment climbed and began to seem like a permanent feature of the U.S. economy. Inflation also was a major concern for consumers; although the biggest price hikes came from the energy sector, the effects of rising prices wiped out most workers' wage gains. Economists even coined a new term, "stagflation," to describe the twin impact of rising prices and a recession to describe the dismal prospects that the U.S. economy faced as Carter took office.

Carter was also hampered by the negative mood that gripped many Americans regarding the political system in the post-Watergate era. As the public learned the full

The energy crisis that hit the United States during the mid-1970s had significant impact on the nation's economy and the public's faith in its leadership. © OWEN FRANKEN/CORBIS. REPRODUCED BY PERMISSION.

range of the Nixon administration's illegal activities, some Americans became pessimistic about the integrity and honesty of elected officials in general. Combined with the lingering national divisions over the Vietnam War and conflicts over matters of race, gender, and sexual orientation, the American electorate was still deeply divided on the country's future.

Significance

As a man of deep and sincere religious faith who refused to separate his principles from his political career,

Carter seemed to be an ideal leader to help the nation reconcile in the post-Watergate era. Yet the president's character alone was not enough to bring the nation together. Perceived by some as indecisive and too detail-oriented, Carter struggled to articulate a broad mission for his presidency. On July 15, 1979, he delivered a televised speech that referred openly to the "crisis of confidence" that had taken hold in the nation. Instead of being inspired to renew their civic commitment, however, many Americans derided the speech as unnecessarily downbeat and critical. When Carter decried the materialism of American life, for example, he stood in direct contrast to the rampant consumerism that was the hallmark of the "Me Decade." Such observations might have been appropriate for a social critic, but for a president they came as a shock.

Carter also faced an endless round of political battles during his term in office. His hard work in the Democratic primaries had secured him the presidential nomination in 1976, but his success also deepened some divisions within the party. Massachusetts senator Ted Kennedy, one of the most powerful and liberal members of Congress, remained a bitter foe of Carter's and threatened to run against the president in the 1980 primaries. Republicans also painted Carter as a "tax-and-spend" Democrat who failed to mend the economy. Foreign policy conservatives were also disturbed over Carter's agreement to return the Panama Canal back to the Panamanian people, which they saw as a sign of the United States' diminishing reputation around the world.

By the end of his term, Carter's popularity had not recovered sufficiently to win him a second term in office. He lost the 1980 election to Ronald Reagan (served 1981–1989), whose relentlessly optimistic and far-ranging vision of the American nation stood in stark contrast to Carter's "crisis of confidence."

Primary Source

"The Crisis of Confidence"

SYNOPSIS: President Carter delivered this speech in the hope that he would reconnect with the American people and inspire them to shake off the feelings of pessimism that engulfed the country during a time of economic uncertainty and unsettled international relations. Some critics mocked Carter's humility in addressing the American people in such pessimistic terms, and, indeed, his tone contrasted greatly with the opponent he faced in his race for re-election, Ronald Reagan.

Ten days ago I had planned to speak to you again about a very important subject—energy. For the fifth time I would have described the urgency of the problem and laid out a series of legislative recommendations to the Congress. But as I was preparing to speak, I began to ask myself the same question that I now know has been troubling many of you. Why have we not been able to get together as a nation to resolve our serious energy problem?

It's clear that the true problems of our Nation are much deeper—deeper than gasoline lines or energy shortages, deeper even than inflation or recession. And I realize more than ever that as President I need your help. So, I decided to reach out and listen to the voices of America.

I invited to Camp David people from almost every segment of our society—business and labor, teachers and preachers, Governors, mayors, and private citizens. And then I left Camp David to listen to other Americans, men and women like you.

It has been an extraordinary 10 days, and I want to share with you what I've heard. First of all, I got a lot of personal advice. Let me quote a few of the typical comments that I wrote down. . . .

"Mr. President, we're in trouble. Talk to us about blood and sweat and tears." . . .

Many people talked about themselves and about the condition of our Nation. . . .

This kind of summarized a lot of other statements: "Mr. President, we are confronted with a moral and a spiritual crisis." . . .

I know, of course, being President, that government actions and legislation can be very important. That's why I've worked hard to put my campaign promises into law—and I have to admit, with just mixed success. But after listening to the American people I have been reminded again that all the legislation in the world can't fix what's wrong with America. So, I want to speak to you first tonight about a subject even more serious than energy or inflation. I want to talk to you right now about a fundamental threat to American democracy.

I do not mean our political and civil liberties. They will endure. And I do not refer to the outward strength of America, a nation that is at peace tonight everywhere in the world, with unmatched economic power and military might.

The threat is nearly invisible in ordinary ways. It is a crisis of confidence. It is a crisis that strikes at the very heart and soul and spirit of our national will. We can see this crisis in the growing doubt about the meaning of our own lives and in the loss of a unity of purpose for our Nation.

The erosion of our confidence in the future is threatening to destroy the social and the political fabric of America. . . .

The symptoms of this crisis of the American spirit are all around us. For the first time in the history of our country a majority of our people believe that the next 5 years will be worse than the past 5 years. Two-thirds of our people do not even vote. The productivity of American workers is actually dropping, and the willingness of Americans to save for the future has fallen below that of all other people in the Western world.

As you know, there is a growing disrespect for government and for churches and for schools, the news media, and other institutions. This is not a message of happiness or reassurance, but it is the truth and it is a warning. . . .

Energy will be the immediate test of our ability to unite this Nation, and it can also be the standard around which we rally. On the battlefield of energy we can win for our Nation a new confidence, and we can seize control again of our common destiny.

In little more than two decades we've gone from a position of energy independence to one in which almost half the oil we use comes from foreign countries, at prices that are going through the roof. Our excessive dependence on OPEC has already taken a tremendous toll on our economy and our people. This is the direct cause of the long lines which have made millions of you spend aggravating hours waiting for gasoline. It's a cause of the increased inflation and unemployment that we now face. This intolerable dependence on foreign oil threatens our economic independence and the very security of our Nation. The energy crisis is real. It is worldwide. It is a clear and present danger to our Nation. These are facts and we simply must face them.

Primary Source

"Carter at the Crossroads" [excerpt]

SYNOPSIS: Hugh Sidney wrote this article after spending time with President Carter at Camp David, the country retreat of U.S. presidents. The portrait emphasized Carter's fundamental decency and integrity, but did not shy away from outlining the challenges that confronted his presidency.

In the whole history of American politics, there had never been anything quite like it. As theater, it offered mystery, an aura of crisis, a high moral purpose and a dash of comedy. For six days an eclec-

President Carter signs his energy proposals in the White House in January 1977. AP/WIDE WORLD PHOTOS. REPRODUCED BY PERMISSION.

tic representation of the American Establishment— Governors, Cabinet members, bankers, insurance executives, professors of sociology, obscure local politicians and even a Greek Orthodox archbishop— gathered in groups in Washington. Marine helicopters ferried them to the mountaintop presidential retreat at Camp David. There Jimmy Carter, outfitted sometimes in blue jeans, at other times in snappy sport coats, pressed them for their ideas about energy, the economy, his own Administration, the national mood—and himself. Toward week's end, while aides were drafting the Sunday-night TV speech that he hoped would rally the nation, the President lent confusion to the proceedings by twice vanishing from his mountain by helicopter to confer with ordinary citizens. Thursday night he descended on the Carnegie, Pa., home of Machinist William Fisher and his wife Bette, and sipped lemonade with their friends on the back porch for 90 minutes. Friday morning he swooped into Martinsburg, W. Va., where

he called on Marvin Porterfield, a retired Marine major and disabled veteran of World War II, his wife Ginny and 17 friends and neighbors.

Carter's declared purpose was to renew his contact with the American people, to discover their anxieties and to reassure them of the concern of their chosen leaders. "There has been a lost sense of trust," he told aides, "a loss of confidence in the future." Part of that concern, he inevitably learned, involved the President himself. For some time past, but more sharply this summer, the U.S. has been slipping into a morass of interrelated problems. One is the energy crisis, marked by its gas lines and soaring prices. One is the painful combination of inflation and economic stagnation. One is the widespread perception that Jimmy Carter has seemed unable to make a strong attack on either of the first two.

While the President was at Camp David, his economic advisers made it official: the U.S. is in an inflationary recession. National output, they predicted, will shrink 0.5% this year; prices nonetheless will climb 10.6%, and the number of jobless may grow by 1.3 million, to around 7 million late next year. The inflation is being fanned and the recession worsened by large OPEC oil price boosts that underscore the debilitating U.S. dependence on imported petroleum. Carter was earnestly aware, if the people of the U.S. were not yet, that the nation must find some way to start breaking that dependence if it is to have any chance for long-term, noninflationary economic growth.

But to make headway against these problems, the President realized he also must start overcoming his chief political weakness, his reputation for hesitancy and indecision. Two weeks ago, returning from the Tokyo summit to a nation exasperated by a siege of gas lines, he compounded his difficulties by first scheduling a major policy speech on energy, then abruptly canceling it without a word of explanation. The Camp David summit, which began 48 hours later, represented above all an attempt to start rebuilding an image of purposeful leadership.

In one way it succeeded; many guests came away with new respect and sympathy for Carter. In another it probably would prove unsuccessful: it was unlikely that any Carter speech could live up to the expectations that surrounded his appearance on Sunday night. Ironically, on CBS-TV, the speech preempted a segment of *Moses—The Lawgiver,* a series that depicts Moses descending from Mount Sinai with the Ten Commandments.

Carter's Sunday-night goal was to appeal to the national sense of purpose and express confidence that the traditions of self-discipline and determination could solve even the most intractable problems.

Further Resources

BOOKS

Brinkley, Douglas. *The Unfinished Presidency: Jimmy Carter's Journey Beyond the White House.* New York: Viking, 1998.

Carter, Jimmy. *A Government as Good as Its People.* New York: Simon & Schuster, 1977.

———. *Keeping Faith: Memoirs of a President.* New York: Bantam Books, 1982.

Carter, Jimmy, with Rosalynn Carter. *Everything to Gain: Making the Most of the Rest of Your Life.* New York: Ballantine Books, 1987.

Drew, Elizabeth. *Portrait of an Election: The 1980 Presidential Election Campaign.* New York: Simon & Schuster, 1981.

Jordan, Hamilton. *Crisis: The Last Year of the Carter Presidency.* New York: G.P. Putnam's Sons, 1982.

WEBSITES

"Selected Speeches of Jimmy Carter." Available online at http://carterlibrary.galileo.peachnet.edu/documents/speeches/index.phtml; website home page http://carterlibrary.galileo.peachnet.edu (accessed May 25, 2003).

I'm Mad as Hell: The Exclusive Story of the Tax Revolt and Its Leader

Memoir

By: Howard Jarvis with Robert Pack

Date: 1979

Source: Jarvis, Howard, with Robert Pack. *I'm Mad as Hell: The Exclusive Story of the Tax Revolt and Its Leader.* New York: Times Books, 1979, 4–10, 12–13.

About the Author: Howard Jarvis (1902–1986) was a successful businessman with careers as the owner of a Utah-based newspaper chain and numerous manufacturing businesses in California. Always active in Republican Party affairs, Jarvis devoted himself full-time to politics in the last decades of his life, particularly on the issue of reducing corporate and personal taxes. After several tries to get a property-tax reduction initiative on the California ballot, Jarvis succeeded in putting Proposition 13 before the voters in June 1978. The effort made Jarvis a national spokesman on the issue of taxation. ∎

Introduction

In the 1960s, federal and state governments expanded social welfare programs, many the result of the Great Society vision articulated by President Lyndon Johnson (served 1963–1969). As the expenditures for the new programs collided with the faltering economy of the 1970s, however, governments were hard pressed to find enough revenue to continue funding the programs. Some Americans started to view the programs, enacted during the height of liberal euphoria, as wasteful and questioned whether the government should continue to maintain them. Some conservatives even claimed that the government was placing exorbitant taxes on the middle class to pay for the antipoverty measures; they called for nothing short of a tax revolt to free taxpayers from this burden.

The anti-tax movement generated the most headlines in California, that for generations had typified the American Dream of prosperity and opportunity. The state also had instituted some of the most comprehensive welfare measures in the country, and earned its reputation as one of the most liberal states in the union. Like the rest of the country in the depressed economy of the 1970s, however, the state resorted to tax increases to keep its many programs funded. Among the most controversial moves was the enactment of a series of steep property tax hikes.

Although grumbling about taxation was a perennial American pastime, one retired businessman in California, Howard Jarvis, devoted himself wholeheartedly to the cause of reducing corporate and personal taxes on property and income. Jarvis had been an anti-tax crusader since the New Deal of the 1930s; he viewed most government programs as unnecessary, wasteful, and downright unfair to the average taxpayer. Putting part of his multimillion-dollar fortune into an anti-tax lobbying organization, Jarvis attempted throughout the 1970s to place a property tax reduction measure on the California ballot. He finally succeeded in 1978, when Proposition 13 was put before the state's voters.

Significance

Proposition 13 required an immediate rollback of corporate and personal property taxes to their 1975–76 assessed values and limited future increases to two percent per year. Although most elected officials predicted an immediate drop of eight billion dollars in state and local tax revenues as a result of the initiative, voters nonetheless approved it by a 65–35 margin on June 8, 1978. Already a celebrity for his bombastic speeches and public appearances, Howard Jarvis immediately began to campaign for similar measures in other states.

Critics of Proposition 13 saw their fears of a budget crisis in California come true as state, county, and local governments experienced a 6.15 billion dollar drop in revenues. Los Angeles County alone was forced to trim one billion dollars out of its 3.5 billion dollar budget. School districts across the state were the most affected, as funding immediately shrank by one-third. Critics of the measure also noted that the biggest beneficiaries of Proposition 13 were not individual homeowners, as claimed by Jarvis, but rather corporations, such as Pacific Telephone & Telegraph, realizing a tax reduction of 130 million dollars. A state "rainy day" fund kept most schools and local governments from devastating cuts for a year or two after Proposition 13 was passed, but, by 1980, school and library districts across the state slashed their services and staffs.

As governments scrambled to increase other fees in other areas to make up for the property-tax reductions, it was also apparent that poorer Californians would now pay more of their incomes for basic public services, including recreational facilities, educational opportunities, and necessary services such as garbage collection. Supporters of Proposition 13, however, claimed that it was a populist revolt against an unresponsive, bloated government that had placed an unfair tax burden on the middle and working classes. As Jarvis constantly reminded voters, after all, demonstrating against unfair taxation was an American tradition that dated back to the Boston Tea Party.

Primary Source

I'm Mad as Hell: The Exclusive Story of the Tax Revolt and Its Leader [excerpt]

SYNOPSIS: Howard Jarvis's book mirrored his public rhetoric during his numerous anti-tax campaigns: fiery and confrontational, with a potent mixture of questionable anecdotes and debatable premises to back up his arguments. His most persuasive tactic was raising the fear that middle class homeowners would be thrown out on the streets because they could no longer afford to pay their property taxes. Although a self-styled populist, Jarvis retired as a multimillionaire before devoting himself full time to his political pursuits.

About 12 years ago, at the time I was becoming totally absorbed in the fight to reduce taxes, I saw a middle-aged woman drop dead at the Los Angeles County Hall of Administration in the very act of pleading about the prohibitive level of the property taxes on her home. She was a woman I had come to know during the tax movement. I had been over at her house in the San Fernando Valley to talk to her about her tax problems. By then I had been involved in the crusade against taxes for nearly five years, and I was already fired up. You can bet that seeing this lady die suddenly fired me up even more. That event was the inspiration for a slogan I used to sum up the situation for my audiences during the campaign for Proposition 13 in 1978: "Death and taxes may be inevitable, but being taxed to death is not!"

As many people are aware, "I'm mad as hell" was a phrase coined by the television anchorman played by Peter Finch in the movie *Network* several years ago. The character played by Finch was as angry with the problems he saw as those of us in the tax fight were with property taxes, and he urged his followers to yell, "I'm mad as hell, and I'm not going to take it anymore."

For me, the words "I'm mad as hell" are more than a national saying, more than the title of this book; they express exactly how I feel and exactly how I felt about the woman who died at the County building, as well as countless other victims of exorbitant taxes. I can tell you, there have been thousands of people who've had heart attacks—some fatal—or suffered severe emotional distress as they saw their lives drastically worsened by intolerable, unproductive, and unfair taxes made all the worse by inflation and an energy crisis that the politicians and bureaucrats have not been willing to face up to.

Since Proposition 13 passed on June 6, 1978, many people have told me that I must be a master of timing, that I had this tax-reduction thing ready just when people wanted it. I have to laugh at that. Actually, I started working on this campaign to reduce taxes in California in 1962. In fact, I've been a lifelong activist for lowering taxes. Way back in 1932, when I was a young newspaper publisher in Utah, where I originally came from, Governor George H. Dern, knowing of my concern about high taxes, appointed me as a member of the State Tax Commission and as a delegate to the tenth annual conference of the Western States Taxpayers' Association, which met in Colorado Springs. My basic feeling hasn't changed a bit over all those years: money is much better off in the hands of the average citizen than it is in the greedy hands of those who live off the public payroll. Dern knew how I felt because I ran many stories and editorials about the problems caused by excessive taxation in the chain of newspapers I owned. . . .

When I served as a delegate to the Western States Taxpayers' Association meeting in 1932, I exchanged ideas on cutting taxes with other delegates from about ten states. After that convention, each of us returned home with better ideas for lowering taxes in our own states. This experience may well have planted the seed that later grew into Proposition 13. Of course, I had no way of knowing then that nearly a half century later I would lead the campaign.

In 1935 I sold my newspapers in Utah and moved to California, where I was involved in a number of manufacturing firms until 1962. Meanwhile, starting in Utah in the mid-1920s and continuing after I relocated in Los Angeles, I was active in politics for almost forty years. In 1962, when I was nearly sixty, I decided to retire from both business and politics and enjoy what remaining years I had left.

It was at that point that I was invited to my first meeting on taxes. The meeting took place at a neighbor's home in Los Angeles, with about twenty ordinary people who were concerned about how fast property taxes were rising in California. Ever since World War II, land prices have been booming in California, particularly in the Los Angeles, Orange County and San Diego areas. The land boom had resulted in spiraling assessed valuations placed on land creating the monumental increases in property taxes, which the politicians were unwilling or unable to do anything about before Proposition 13.

Although I have been financially independent for half a century and I never had any problem paying my own taxes, I was deeply worried about the tens of thousands of people who were being forced out of their own homes because, through no fault of theirs, the taxes on their homes were rising to a point beyond their ability to pay them. Love for this country was instilled in me when I was growing up outside of Salt Lake City, and I have always believed that private ownership of property and the idea that a man's home was his castle made the United States the greatest and freest country the world has ever known. If you destroy the residential property base, you destroy the country—and that was exactly what I could see taking place.

Many people don't understand that property taxes have absolutely no relation to a property owner's ability to pay—unlike the two other major forms of taxation, income taxes and sales taxes. From that very first meeting back in 1962, those of us in the tax movement decided that our efforts must be directed toward bringing all taxes—but especially property taxes—down to a level where most people could pay them without undue hardship.

None of us who gathered around a living-room table in that modest California house seventeen years ago foresaw back then that one day there would be a proposition called 13 which would shake up the entire country. At that point, none of us even knew very much about the details of property taxes or other taxes, except that we were unified by the belief that they were too high and counterproductive.

Howard Jarvis, right, and Paul Gann celebrate the success of their co-authored California initiative Proposition 13, which offered tax relief to property owners. **AP/WIDE WORLD PHOTOS. REPRODUCED BY PERMISSION.**

We did know that the American dream of home ownership for everyone was being sabotaged by exploding property taxes. The entire basis of free government in America was being destroyed by virtually unlimited taxation, which can only lead first to bankruptcy and then to dictatorship. A French Controller General of Finance had expressed the way most politicians and bureaucrats think when he declared, around 1700, "The art of taxation consists of so plucking the goose as to obtain the largest amount of feathers with the least amount of hissing."

We made up our minds, back in 1962, that government officials might continue plucking our feathers, but that we were not going to allow them to do it without a lot of hissing on our part. Most of all, we determined that we were never going to quit until we won. Since Proposition 13 won, those of us who stuck it out all those years have received a lot of glory and a huge share of the limelight. But believe me: there wasn't any glory during those fifteen years when every time I walked across the street, someone shot me in the rear, when most people either ignored us or called us a bunch of kooks, just because we wanted to reduce taxes to a reasonable level.

A year or two after that first meeting, several dozen of us formed a California group called the United Organizations of Taxpayers, of which I was elected state chairman. As the years went by, we affiliated with hundreds of tax organizations and thousands of people all over the state. Volunteer organizations are hard to hold together, but we fought very hard and managed to sell the idea of loyalty and unity among ourselves. We told our tax fighters to hang tight because we knew that numbers gave us some political clout. We knew which side we were on and who our enemies were. We knew we were in a political war; one that was not fought with guns, clubs or bullets. Our weapons were fountain pens, and we had to prove again that the pen is mightier than the sword. We took a credo from former Secretary of State James E. Byrnes, who said, "I discovered at an early age that most of the difference between average people and great people can be explained in three words: 'And then some.'" The top people in our group did what was expected of them—and then some. They were considerate and thoughtful of others—and then some. They met their obligations and responsibilities fairly and squarely—and then some. They could be counted on in emergencies, of which there were many over the years—and then some. . . .

We experienced a number of defeats before we got the sweet taste of victory. During our fifteen-year struggle against property taxes, we were never even able to gather enough signatures to qualify our tax initiatives for the ballot, until the end of 1977, when we succeeded in collecting 1.5 million signatures of registered California voters—the most in the state's history. In thousands of appearances all over the state during the Proposition 13 campaign, Paul Gann, other people, and I hammered home the message: "You have a chance to vote for yourselves just this once. The people of California are the government. The people we elect are not the bosses; we are. The elected officials are just temporary employees, and this is your chance to tell them you're fed up with their record of 'Tax, tax, tax, spend, spend, spend, reelect, reelect, reelect.'" It was the truth; it was exciting; it triumphed.

Finally on D-day, June 6, 1978, we won an overwhelming victory, with 65% of California voters opting for 13. Proposition 13 cut California property taxes in half, but, in spite of politicians' dire predictions about the effect 13 would have, it seems to have been beneficial. For instance, a UCLA study that was widely cited during the campaign by Governor Jerry Brown and other opponents of 13 predicted that 451,000 employees of state and local governments would lose their jobs if 13 passed. Nearly a year after 13's victory, only 20,000 public workers had been laid off. Some 91,000 people had found jobs in the private sector as a result of 13, according to studies by the state Employment Development Department. In short, just as we had anticipated, 13 not only cut taxes, it stimulated the state's economy by giving the consumers more money to spend. Proposition 13 was intended to benefit the people, not the government, and that's the way it worked out. Isn't that the way it should be? Shouldn't government serve the people, instead of vice versa? Who lost on 13? Certainly not the people. . . .

Proposition 13 is not the end of the movement to lower taxes; it is just the beginning. In the months and years ahead you'll be hearing more from me. I'll probably be visiting your state, and possibly even meeting you, as I have met tens of thousands of other concerned citizens during and since the 13 campaign. In fact, since 13 passed, I have visited forty-eight of the fifty states—so far every one but North Dakota and Alaska. And every place I go, people say to me, "I want my taxes cut, and I don't care what else happens." These sentiments are borne out by polls which show that 13 is even more popular in California now than it was when we won by a margin of almost 2 to 1, and that the idea of 13-type reductions is very popular all across the land. In fact, in November 1978, five months after 13 passed in California, voters in Idaho and Nevada approved similar amendments. Voters in nine other states from coast to coast and from the Dakotas to Texas came out in favor of measures to reduce government taxes, spending, or both. . . .

In addition, I am trying to help angry taxpayers all over the country gain approval of tax-reduction measures, either through the ballot process, as we were able to do in California, or through action of their state legislatures. . . .

The message of Proposition 13 and its aftermath is clear: People *can* collectively effect change in the public interest, if only they get mad enough, and if their anger is rational and justified. People who want to do something don't have to wait for somebody else to lead them. I hope that's one message that will come loud and clear out of 13: Americans can do things for themselves. Everyone knows ten or twenty or thirty people who will work with them. You don't need a campaign manager to lead you; you can be your own campaign manager and lead yourself. If there is something about government you don't like, get together and do something about it. Get as many people as you know to put their names on a petition. Even if the petition has no legal effect, it will impress and scare the hell out of the elected officials. That's all you have to do to get action, whether you're trying to reach a member of the city council or the President of the United States. . . .

The last lines in our national anthem, "The Star Spangled Banner," are: "The land of the free and the home of the brave." These words mean that the people cannot be free if they are not brave. Our small group of taxpayers in California consisted of brave souls who eventually slew the giant. They had the will, the persistence, and the guts to fight and win against great political odds. They re-established the definition of what freedom is, what it is worth and what it takes to keep it. Proposition 13 proved beyond any reasonable doubt that the people can achieve the kind of government structure they want if they are willing to fight for it. In an important sense this realization is more significant than the actual victory of 13. . . .

You, too, can get mad as hell, along with us Californians. We won, and so can you. Get going now!

Further Resources

BOOKS

Becker, Robert. *Revolution, Reform, and the Politics of American Taxation.* Baton Rouge: Louisiana State University Press, 1980.

Edsall, Thomas Byrne, and Mary Edsall. *Chain Reaction: The Impact of Race, Rights, and Taxes on the American Electorate.* New York: W.W. Norton & Company, 1991.

Kemp, Roger. *Coping with Proposition 13.* Lexington, Mass.: D.C. Heath and Company, 1980.

Kuttner, Robert. *Revolt of the Haves: Tax Rebellions and Hard Times.* New York: Simon and Schuster, 1980.

Lo, Clarence. *Small Property, Big Government: The Property Tax Revolt.* Berkeley: University of California Press, 1990.

Smith, Daniel A. *Tax Crusaders and the Politics of Direct Democracy.* New York: Routledge, 1998.

WEBSITES

"The Howard Jarvis Tax Association." Available online at http://www.hjta.org/(accessed May 25, 2003).

Yellow Ribbon: The Secret Journal of Bruce Laingen

Diary

By: L. Bruce Laingen

Date: 1992

Source: Laingen, L. Bruce. *Yellow Ribbon: The Secret Journal of Bruce Laingen.* Washington: Brassey's, 1992, 11, 12–13, 45, 126–127, 266–267.

About the Author: Lowell Bruce Laingen (1922–) pursued a distinguished career as a diplomat that took him to Germany, Pakistan, and Afghanistan, among many other countries. After serving as the U.S. Ambassador to Malta from 1977–1979, Laingen became the *chargé d' affaires* of the U.S. Embassy in Tehran, Iran, where he was responsible for many of the day-to-day operations of the outpost. On November 4, 1979, Laingen became one of the fifty-two Americans held hostage by the revolutionary government of Iran that had just ousted longtime dictator Muhammad Reza Shah Pahlevi. After a 444-day captivity, Laingen returned to the United States and continued his public service career for another decade. ∎

Introduction

In January 1979, facing unprecedented domestic unrest, the longtime ruler of Iran, Muhammad Reza Shah Pahlevi—known simply as the Shah of Iran—fled the country. Although the United States had propped up the Shah in past crises, and, in fact, had reinstalled him as Iran's leader in 1953 after a power struggle, the opposition to the Shah's rule this time was too great to counter. In the wake of the Shah's departure, the Islamic fundamentalist leaders who had spurred their followers to riot against the regime now turned their growing power against the interim government of Prime Minister Shahpur Bakhtiar. By February 1979, the Bakhtiar government had also fallen to the revolutionaries, who looked to the Ayatollah Ruhollah Khomeini, a religious fundamentalist who had been living in exile in Iraq and France for fifteen years, as their new leader. After returning to the country in February 1979, Khomeini immediately began instituting fundamentalist laws and nationalized the country's economy. Among the new prohibitions were a slew of laws banning many forms of western culture, proclaimed to be perverse and corrupting influences.

As the anti-western sentiment crystallized under Khomeini, a group of revolutionaries took over the U.S. Embassy in the nation's capital, Tehran, with the tacit approval of the new government. Of the nearly one hundred Americans seized on November 4, 1979, fifty-two were held hostage for the next 444 days. Although some moderate allies of Khomeini protested the act, they were quickly ousted from the new regime that quickly became even more extreme. With Khomeini declared the country's political and religious leader under its new, Islamic constitution, moderates such as President Abolhassan Bani-Sadr were soon removed from power. After trying to negotiate the release of the hostages in the first weeks of their captivity, the United Nations implemented economic sanctions against Iran that only seemed to stiffen the extremism of the regime.

Significance

President Jimmy Carter (served 1977–1981) also attempted to start diplomatic negotiations to secure the release of the hostages, while also instituting economic sanctions against Iran—including the freezing of all of the country's assets in the United States. As thousands of Americans tied yellow ribbons around trees as a symbol of the hostages' plight, however, a sense of frustration and helplessness gripped many people. That pessimism deepened after a secret rescue mission failed on April 24, 1980. The attempted evacuation had to be aborted after three of the squadron's eight helicopters were damaged in a sandstorm; eight of the rescue team members died during the mission. In the aftermath of the failed rescue mission, the hostages were relocated throughout Iran, and their whereabouts were not divulged.

The failed rescue mission also frustrated the ongoing diplomatic efforts to free the hostages. It was only after neighboring Iraq invaded Iran, in September 1980, that the Iranian regime became more receptive to negotiating the release of the Americans. Shortly before the presidential elections in the United States in November, the Iranian parliament finally announced its terms for the release of the hostages, including the freeing of all Iranian assets in the United States as well as all of the assets of the deposed Shah, who had died by this time. After Ronald Reagan (served 1981–1989) won the 1980 election over Carter, the negotiations picked up pace, and the hostages were finally freed on January 20, 1981—the very day of Reagan's inauguration as president.

The Iranian hostage crisis greatly influenced the 1980 presidential election in the United States, where incumbent President Carter's efforts to free the hostages were largely deemed a failure. The episode also marked the beginning of an era in which the United States would have to deal with the rise of Islamic fundamentalism as a potent force in international relations.

Primary Source

Yellow Ribbon: The Secret Journal of Bruce Laingen [excerpt]

SYNOPSIS: As *chargé d'affaires* of the U.S. embassy in the Iranian capital of Tehran, L. Bruce Laingen was one of fifty-two Americans held for 444 days in the aftermath of the revolution against the regime of the Shah of Iran. In 1992, he published *Yellow Ribbon*, presenting about one-fourth of the diary entries he wrote while in captivity.

The Embassy Is Taken

On Sunday morning, November 4, we were a reasonably confident group at the embassy's 9:00 A.M. staff meeting, having relaxed over a holiday weekend in the aftermath of the large demonstrations around the compound walls three days earlier. We noted that more demonstrations had been announced in the press for that day, but these were targeted at the university grounds some miles away to commemorate the martyrdom of students who had died a year earlier in demonstrations there as well as to mark the anniversary of Khomeini's forced exile to Turkey in 1964. We sensed no imminent danger to us, though we agreed to remain on alert, and I decided to keep a long-scheduled morning appointment at the Foreign Ministry with its director general for political affairs.

At the Foreign Ministry our conversation was amicable, over traditional glasses of Iranian tea, but would also prove ironic on two counts. I took the opportunity to convey Washington's appreciation for the good cooperation we had had from the police in dealing with the demonstrations three days earlier. But even more ironic, the subject of my conversation with the director general that morning was the diplomatic immunity status of our six-man Defense Liaison Office, a new element in the embassy staff, intended to replace the cast of hundreds who during the Shah's rule had implemented an enormous arms sales program and advised on its use. An hour later, that new group would be seized and held hostage, in total contempt of the very concept of diplomatic immunity.

Meanwhile, our colleagues in the besieged chancery—in sporadic touch with us by radio and telephone—reported seeing among the milling mob below their windows only a few police at the motor pool gates, a lone Revolutionary Guard at one point, and allegedly a fire truck or two following reports of smoke from the other side of the barricaded entrance to the chancery's second floor. At one point we broached the idea that I would try to reach the compound to talk it out with the demonstrators, but poor communications left this idea stillborn—fortunately, perhaps, because in retrospect the result would have been my being held at the compound as well.

By this time my initial shock had turned into a deepening anger and an anguish over the safety of my staff, relieved only partially by the impressive calm and courage evident in the voices of Political Officer Ann Swift and others at the other end of our phone lines. Aware that hundreds of militants were in the compound, I declined to order the use of firearms by the marine guards, authorizing only the use of tear gas and that only in *extremis.* The Marines were there, as in any embassy, not to fight "Custer's last stand" operations but to buy time while the Bazargan government came to our assistance pursuant to its obligations under international law. Some two and a half hours after that first call of alarm to us on the limousine radio, it became clear that there would be no help from the regime's security forces. The embassy clearly had no alternative but to surrender, especially when word reached us that Golacinski, Political Officer John Limbert, and one or more of the Marines had been taken captive outside the barricaded second floor and were being threatened with death if that door was not opened. It was midafternoon when I gave my concurrence; my last words to a staff I would not see again for 444 days were that in surrendering they "do it in style" and only when they themselves judged that to concede control was their only alternative.

Day 50, December 23, 1979

The day has been uneventful for us. A wicker basket full of plastic boxes of various kinds of Iranian candy and decorated with a large pink bow arrived from the Spanish ambassador and his wife, two people who served twice in Washington and cannot tell you enough how warmly they feel toward the United States . . . I had my 30 minutes of stair walking in the ceremonial entrance to this building, an area where we are now admitted by special request only. Try walking stairs for 30 minutes sometime; it's boring, but it helps keep me in reasonable shape. That plus my calisthenics in the morning manages to keep me tolerably fit. . . .

Our friendly chief of protocol came by, as always, late in the day. Today I found it hard to carry on a conversation—we have exhausted almost every conceivable topic of conversation long since. So after he describes briefly what his day was like and kindly asks after ours, there isn't much left to say. Depending on my mood, I sometimes grouch a bit about what this government is doing to us, and to itself, and to the hostages, but there is little point to this— and I then quiet myself. . . .

Day 197, May 18, 1980

Today the local press continues what appears to be a sustained effort by President Bani-Sadr to

An American hostage is led to the front of the U.S. Embassy in Tehran, Iran, November 8, 1979. AP/WIDE WORLD PHOTOS. REPRODUCED BY PERMISSION.

enhance his revolutionary credentials by finding new and better charges against the United States and its "evil ways." Today we read that his newspaper has come out with the news that the United States has 20(!) secret airstrips in Iran, similar to that used at Tabas in the attempted rescue mission. Some of these have not yet been "traced," some had not even been asphalted! The implication is that yet further U.S. intrigues are planned, against which the Revolution must be on redoubled guard.

It is all wearisome. And yet I suppose one could say it is also normal. This Revolution is by no means complete, and until it is, or is replaced, we will have more of this kind of thing. There is also the political power struggle that is a part of the Revolution, a struggle that has seen Bani-Sadr in recent months constantly undermined and frustrated by the clerical forces, still in the ascendancy. The assumption is that these forces will be similarly strong in the Majlis, although it is also probable that a good number of those newly elected are malleable, politically, and will go with the highest bidder, in political and ideological terms. All of which will have a bearing on our fate in the decision the Majlis is to take to resolve the issue. In that respect, today's press also quotes our good friend, Dr. Yazdi, late of this ministry, as saying that the hostages, in the view of most members of the Majlis, must be tried . . . as a means of putting the United States on trial for its role in the restoration of the Shah in 1953, etc. For good measure, he throws in the idea that Iran should seek financial compensation for U.S. "interventions" in Iran, causing the loss of "basic rights" of 35 million Iranians.

Day 436, January 12, 1981

I think I have never felt quite the sense of isolation bordering on despair that I felt last night when the power was cut for some 10 or 15 minutes in this part of the city. The isolation was physical and mental. In the physical sense the darkness was total as can be imagined—inside a room whose walls are two feet thick, the only windows 10 to 12 feet up one side, with iron bars on the inside and out, two layers of steel mesh in addition to that, and dirty cracked or broken glass panes in between. When the power was cut, the guards—presumably responding to standing instructions in case of such situations—double-locked my steel doors, the clanking of steel on steel and the flash of flashlights adding to the sense of being totally isolated.

Mental isolation came in the sense I think I have never felt so totally cut off from the outside world, in a cell somewhere in this city but without a clue as to what is happening beyond these thick walls. And the sense of forced isolation was heightened in last night's power cut because it coincided with one of the Revolution's periodic exercises in bringing the faithful out on the rooftops and streets at a given hour (9:00 P.M.) to shout "Allah O'Akbar" for 15 minutes.

So in the total darkness, deep inside this prison, the only sounds were the clatter of steel chains and locks on our doors, the hurried moving about of the guards, and the distant shouting of the "Allah O'Akbars." The reason, I learned incidentally today, was to celebrate a "major victory" somewhere on the Iraqi front.

For those few minutes last night I felt totally drained emotionally, totally alone physically, and—more than ever in this crisis—a momentary sense of total defeat. I know better now what feelings my colleagues must often have had, especially those held in solitary confinement in those long months of captivity and especially those early months when street demonstrations were constant around the compound. I wondered, as I groped around this cell last night, what my two colleagues in their cells here were thinking. Presumably we feel the isolation even more, because of our having been together, reinforcing each other's spirits for all of the 14 months until now. And perhaps a special sense of defeat because of the assurances given us the other night when we left the ministry about the conditions in which we would be held here, assurances that proved totally worthless.

But the despair and defeat were and are temporary. I am confident we are close to settlement and that we will be free within the next few weeks. Our colleagues having weathered this treatment all these long months, we can the more easily do so now.

Further Resources

BOOKS

Drew, Elizabeth. *Portrait of an Election: The 1980 Presidential Election.* New York: Simon and Schuster, 1981.

Jordan, Hamilton. *Crisis: The Last Year of the Carter Presidency.* New York: G.P. Putnam's Sons, 1982.

Sick, Gary. *October Surprise: America's Hostages in Iran and the Election of Ronald Reagan.* New York: Times Books, 1991.

Wells, Tim. *444 Days: The Hostages Remember.* San Diego: Harcourt Brace Jovanovich, 1985.

Wright, Robin. *In the Name of God: The Khomeini Decade.* New York: Simon and Schuster, 1989.

———. *The Last Great Revolution: Turmoil and Transformation in Iran.* New York: Alfred A. Knopf, 2000.

6

LAW AND JUSTICE

SCOTT A. MERRIMAN

Entries are arranged in chronological order by date of primary source. For entries with one primary source, the entry title is the same as the primary source title. Entries with more than one primary source have an overall entry title, followed by the titles of the primary sources.

Important Events in Law and Justice, 1970–1979

1970

- On January 19, President Richard Nixon nominates G. Harrold Carswell for Supreme Court justice. On April 8, the Senate rejects Carswell because of his weak record on civil rights.

- On February 18, the trial of the Chicago Seven ends. All defendants are acquitted on charges that they conspired to cause a riot at the 1968 Democratic National Convention. Five defendants are eventually convicted of individually crossing state lines with intent to cause a riot. In 1972 these convictions are overturned because of prejudicial conduct by the trial judge.

- On March 23, the Supreme Court rules that people receiving Aid to Families with Dependent Children are entitled to a hearing before their benefits are cut off.

- On March 31, the Supreme Court rules in *In re Winship* that juvenile convictions that rest on "preponderance of the evidence" burden of proof violate the Fourteenth Amendment's Due Process Clause. Instead, juvenile convictions must be held to the stricter "beyond a reasonable doubt" threshold.

- On May 15, the Supreme Court decides that men who object to military service for moral reasons are entitled to draft exemptions as conscientious objectors.

- On June 9, Harry A. Blackmun was sworn in as an associate justice of the Supreme Court.

- On June 22, the Supreme Court rules in *Williams v. Florida* that a twelve-member jury is not constitutionally mandated.

- On August 7, African American radical Jonathan Jackson springs convicts James McClain and William Christmas from McClain's trial for stabbing a prison guard. The three take five hostages—the trial judge, the prosecutor, and three women jurors. When they are stopped at a roadblock, they shoot the judge and then are killed by police gunfire. African American activist and UCLA philosophy professor Angela Davis is charged with providing Jackson with the weapons. She is acquitted.

- On August 24, Vietnam protestors plant a bomb at the University of Wisconsin's Army Math Research Center in Madison, killing researcher Robert Fassnacht.

1971

- On February 24, the Supreme Court holds that the statement of a defendant can be used in court to contradict his testimony, even if the defendant had not been read his rights beforehand.

- On March 8, in *Griggs v. Duke Power Company,* the Supreme Court decides that a promotion practice that requires a high school education and the achievement of minimum scores on two separate aptitude tests violates Title VII of the 1964 Civil Rights Act, because the subtle purpose of the requirements was to give job preferences to white employees.

- On March 29, a military court finds Lieutenant William Calley guilty of the murder of at least twenty-two civilians and sentences him to life imprisonment at hard labor for his role in the My Lai Massacre. Calley's platoon killed over one hundred women, children, and old men in My Lai, even though there were no enemy soldiers present.

- On March 29, a Los Angeles jury recommends the death penalty for Charles Manson and three female accomplices for the murders of actress Sharon Tate, the La Biancas, and others. The sentences are later commuted.

- On April 20, the Supreme Court rules in *Swann v. Charlotte-Mecklenberg Board of Education* that courts have broad and flexible powers, including the authority to order busing, when overseeing remedies to combat state-imposed segregation.

- On May 24, trial judge Harold Mulvey declares a mistrial in the murder trial of two members of the Black Panther party, a radical black nationalist group. Bobby Seale and Erika Huggins are charged with ordering the torture and murder of a suspected informer, but the jury declares itself hopelessly deadlocked. On May 25 Mulvey dismisses all charges against Seale and Huggins because the massive pretrial publicity makes it impossible for them to receive a fair trial.

- On June 7, in *Cohen v. California,* the Supreme Court upholds a person's First Amendment right to wear a jacket with a vulgar antiwar message on it in a public place.

- On June 13, *The New York Times* begins to publish the Pentagon Papers, excerpts from a Department of Defense study of U.S. policy regarding Vietnam.

- On June 21, the Supreme Court decides that juveniles do not have a constitutional right to a jury trial.

- On June 30, the Supreme Court rules that the government cannot prohibit publication of the Pentagon Papers.

- On August 21, George Jackson, an inmate at San Quentin prison, is killed along with two other inmates and three prison guards in an apparent escape attempt. Jackson, a black activist, is one of the "Soledad Brothers" accused of killing a prison guard at Soledad prison. Jackson's family and attorneys accuse prison officials of murdering Jackson.

- On September 9, prisoners riot in the Attica prison in New York State. After four days Gov. Nelson Rockefeller orders the state police to retake the prison by force. Forty-three are killed.

- On September 17, Justice Hugo L. Black retires from the Supreme Court. He dies just eight days later.

- On September 23, Justice John Marshall Harlan retires from the Supreme Court. He dies on December 29, 1971.

- On November 22, the Supreme Court rules in *Reed v. Reed* that an Idaho probate law is unconstitutional based upon the Equal Protection Clause of the Fourteenth Amendement because it required that "males must be preferred to females" when appointing administrators of an estate.

- On November 24, hijacker D.B. Cooper parachutes from a 727 over Washington State, carrying two hundred thousand dollars in ransom. He has never been found.

- On December 6, Lewis Powell is confirmed by the Senate in his appointment to the Supreme Court.

- On December 10, William Rehnquist is confirmed in his appointment to the Supreme Court.

1972

- Oregon becomes the first state to decriminalize the possession of small amounts of marijuana.

- On January 7, Powell and Rehnquist are sworn is as associate justices to the Supreme Court.

- On May 15, in *Wisconsin v. Yoder,* the Supreme Court holds that a Wisconsin criminal statute is unconstitutional where it requires school attendance until age sixteen and punishes parents who refuse to send their children to school for religious reasons. The law had been challenged by Old Order Amish parents who refused to send their children to school after eighth grade.

- On May 15, George C. Wallace is shot and paralyzed while campaigning for the Democratic presidential nomination in Maryland.

- On May 22, in *Johnson v. Louisiana,* the Supreme Court upholds a criminal conviction where, according to state law, only nine of twelve jurors were needed to convict. The court reaches the same conclusion in *Apodaca v. Oregon.*

- On June 12, in *Moose Lodge No. 107 v. Irvis,* the Supreme Court holds that the Moose Lodge is "a private social club in a private building," and it did not violate the Equal Protection Clause when it adhered to its policy of refusing to serve a man because of his race.

- On June 12, in *Argersinger v. Hamlin,* the Supreme Court holds that a defendant is entitled to an attorney whenever a jail sentence is a possible penalty for the crime with which a defendant is accused.

- On June 17, Police arrest five men for breaking into the Democratic National Committee's headquarters at the Watergate Hotel. Three of the men have ties to President Nixon's reelection campaign.

- On June 29, the Supreme Court in *Furman v. Georgia* holds the death penalty unconstitutional unless administered equally and in specific circumstances that the state must list ahead of time. The decision sparks a massive reworking of the nation's death penalty laws.

- On June 29, the Supreme Court in *In re Pappas* holds that the First Amendment does not give reporters the right to withhold information during a government investigation, including testimony before a grand jury.

- On November 2, the Commission on Inquiry into the Black Panthers and Law Enforcement in Illinois issues a report condemning the Illinois state attorney's handling of a 1969 Chicago raid of the Black Panthers, calling the use of guns unnecessary.

- On November 20, in *Gottschalk v. Benson,* the Supreme Court rules that a computer program is not patentable. The decision results in the Patent Office no longer reviewing computer program inventions, and using instead trade secrets and copyrighting to protect computer programs. The Supreme Court revisits the issue in *Diamond v. Diehr* in 1982.

1973

- On January 22, the Supreme Court, in *Roe v. Wade* and *Doe v. Bolton,* holds by a vote of 6-3 that women's interest in privacy means that states cannot prohibit abortion in the first trimester of pregnancy.

- On February 1, the District of Columbia Court of Appeals tells the Environmental Protection Agency that it cannot give seventeen states a two-year extension to comply with the 1970 Clean Air Act.

- On February 27, American Indian Movement leaders occupy Wounded Knee, South Dakota, in a take-over that will last until May. Wounded Knee was the site of an 1890 government massacre of Sioux.

- On May 14, in *Frontiero v. Richardson,* the Supreme Court rules that a federal law which required different qualification criteria for male and female military spousal dependency discriminates against women in violation of Due Process Clause of the Fifth Amendment.

- On June 21, the Supreme Court decides that a roving border patrol cannot conduct searches of cars without a warrant or probable cause.

- On June 21, the Supreme Court rules in *Paris Adult Theatre v. Slaton* that Georgia has the authority to ban the showing of pornographic movies at an adult theater, and that the films in question did not acquire constitutional protection by the fact that they were shown to consenting adults only.

- On June 21, the Supreme Court announces a three-prong test for determining obscenity in *Miller v. California.*

- On October 20, in what is known as the "Saturday Night Massacre," Acting Attorney General Robert H. Bork fires the Watergate special prosecutor, Archibald Cox. Attorney General Elliot Richardson and Deputy Attorney General William Ruckelshaus resign rather than fire Cox.

- On October 23, President Nixon agrees to turn over White House tape recordings to federal judge John J. Sirica.

- On November 1, Leon Jaworski is appointed Watergate special prosecutor.

- On November 23, Charles E. Whittaker, associate justice of the Supreme Court from 1957 to 1962, dies.

- On November 26, Rose Mary Woods, personal secretary to President Nixon, testifies in federal court that she had inadvertently caused part of the 18½ minute gap on one of the Watergate tapes.

1974

- On February 5, Patricia Hearst is kidnapped from her Berkeley, California, home by the Symbionese Liberation Army (SLA). In April, she joins the SLA in their robbery of the Hibernia Bank in San Francisco.

- On March 29, eight Ohio National Guardsmen are indicted for the shooting deaths of four students at Kent State University. They are eventually acquitted.

- On June 24, in *Jenkins v. Georgia,*the Supreme Court overturned the obscenity conviction of a theater owner for showing the Jack Nicholson and Ann Margaret film, *Carnal Knowledge.*

- On July 9, Earl Warren, former chief justice of the Supreme Court, dies. Warren served on the Supreme Court from 1953 to 1969.

- On July 12, in a case stemming from the Pentagon Papers, former presidential aide John Ehrlichman and three others are convicted of conspiring to violate the civil rights of Daniel Ellsberg's former psychiatrist.

- On July 24, the Supreme Court unanimously rules in *U.S. v. Nixon* that President Nixon must turn over tapes requested by the special prosecutor. The Court holds that the president does not have unlimited "executive privilege" as he claims.

- On August 9, President Nixon resigns, and Vice President Gerald R. Ford becomes president.

- On September 8, Ford pardons former president Nixon.

- On November 13, Karen Silkwood, who claimed to have damaging evidence about serious lapses in quality control at the Kerr-McGee nuclear fuel plant, is killed in a car accident on her way to a meeting with a *New York Times* reporter. No evidence is found.

1975

- On January 22, in *Goss* and *Lopez,*the Supreme Court decides that before suspending students from school, officials must grant students informal hearings.

- On February 21, former Attorney General John N. Mitchell and former White House aides H.R. Haldeman and John D. Ehrlichman receive sentences from 2½ to 8 years for their roles in the Watergate cover-up.

- On June 26, a standoff between federal government officials and the American Indian Movement (AIM) at the Pine Ridge Sioux Indian Reservation in South Dakota erupts into a shoot-out. One AIM member and two FBI agents are killed.

- On September 18, the FBI capture Patricia Hearst.

- On October 20, the Supreme Court holds that school administrators may hit students to punish them, even if parents object.

- On November 12, Justice William O. Douglas retires from the Supreme Court after serving a record-setting thirty-six years and seven months.

- On November 18, Eldridge Cleaver, former minister of information for the Black Panther party, returns to the United States and is immediately arrested by the FBI. Cleaver fled the country in 1968 to avoid trial on attempted murder charges, stemming from a shoot-out between Oakland police and the Black Panthers. Cleaver does not stand trial. In December 1979 he pleads guilty to an assault charge and is sentenced to community service and probation.

- On December 17, the Senate unanimously confirms the appointment of John Paul Stevens to the Supreme Court to fill the vacancy left by Douglas. Stevens is sworn in on December 19.

- On December 17, Lynette "Squeaky Fromme" receives life in prison for attempting to assassinate President Gerald Ford in Sacramento on September 5, 1975.

- On December 29, a bomb explodes in New York's LaGuardia Airport, killing eleven.

1976

- On January 16, Sara Jane Moore receives life in prison for her assassination attempt on President Gerald Ford on September 22, 1975.

- On January 30, the Supreme Court rules on campaign funding and First Amendment issues in *Buckley v. Valeo.* The court rules that restrictions imposed by the Federal Election Campaign Act of 1971 on individual contributions to political campaigns and candidates did not violate the First Amendment. However, the court also finds that the First Amendment was violated by governmental restriction of independent expenditures, limitations on expenditures by candidates from their own personal or family resources, and the limitation on total campaign expenditures.

- On March 20, heiress Patricia Hearst is convicted of armed robbery for her participation in a San Francisco bank heist.

- On March 31, the New Jersey Supreme Court rules that comatose patient Karen Ann Quinlan may be removed from her respirator by her father Joseph Quinlan. Quinlan lives another nine years.

- On May 24, the Supreme Court rules in *Virginia Pharmacy Board v. Virginia Consumer Council* that a law banning licensed pharmacists from advertising prescription drug prices violates commercial speech guarantees of the First Amendment.

- On July 2, the Supreme Court, following up on the 1972 case of *Furman v. Georgia,* holds in *Gregg v. Georgia* that the death penalty does not inherently constitute "cruel and unusual punishment," nor does it necessarily violate the Eighth or Fourteenth amendments. On this same day, four other death penalty cases are decided as well.

- On July 15, Frank Edward Ray, a school bus driver, and twenty-six children on his school bus are kidnapped and held underground in Chowchilla, California, for sixteen hours. All escape unharmed.

- On December 7, the Supreme Court rules by a vote of six to three in *General Electric v. Gilbert* that it is not sex discrimination for companies to provide disability insurance that covers some men-only disabilities but not pregnancy.

- On December 20, the Supreme Court rules in *Craig v. Boren* that it is unconstitutional for a state to have different legal drinking ages for men and women.

- On December 22, boxer Rubin "Hurricane" Carter is convicted in a retrial on a murder charge. In 1985 the verdict of this trial is overturned because the reviewing judge finds that the prosecution case was based on racism.

- On December 31, the California Supreme Court decides that when people who are living together separate, a partner could be entitled to payment like alimony—"palimony."

1977

- On January 17, Gary Gilmore, convicted of murder in Utah, is the first person in ten years to be executed under the death penalty.

- On March 11, Hanafi Muslims free more than 130 hostages held for two days in Washington, D.C.

- On April 18, Leonard Peltier, an American Indian Movement activist, is convicted of the murder of two FBI agents at the Pine Ridge Reservation in June 1975.

- On April 19, the Supreme Court rules that corporal punishment of students is not "cruel and unusual punishment" and is therefore not prohibited by the Eighth Amendment.

- On April 20, in *Wooley v. Maynard,*the Supreme Court holds that a New Hampshire state law unconstitutionally interfered with First Amendment freedom of speech guarantees where it led to the conviction of a Jehovah's Witness who, for religious reasons, cut off part of the state's "Live Free or Die" motto from his automobile license plate.

- On April 26, in *Trimble v. Gordon,*the Supreme Court holds an Illinois law unconstitutional where it forbids an illegitimate child from inheriting from the father who dies without a will, but permits an illegitimate child to inherit where the mother dies without a will.

- On June 10, James Earl Ray, convicted assassin of Martin Luther King, Jr., escapes from prison in Tennessee. He is recaptured three days later.

- On June 13, retired Justice Tom C. Clark dies. Clark served on the high court from 1949 to 1967.

- On June 20, the Supreme Court upholds the authority of the states to refuse to pay for poor women's abortions unless a physician says that it is medically necessary.

- On June 29, the Supreme Court, by a vote of six to three, overturns a school desegregation order for the city of Omaha, saying that the lower courts have to look more closely at the effect of segregation on schoolchildren.

- On June 29, the Supreme Court rules in *Coker v. Georgia* that the death penalty for the crime of rape violates the Eighth Amendment.

- On August 10, David Berkowitz, better known as Son of Sam, is arrested in Yonkers, New York. He was responsible for six slayings and injuries to seven others.

- On September 21, Bert Lance resigns as the director of the Office of Management and Budget with "regret and sorrow" after accusations of financial misdealings.

- On December 3, the FBI issues a report calling wife battering the country's least reported crime. The women's movement calls for more public attention and more police effort in response to this crime.

1978

- On January 17, the Supreme Court rules in *Bordenkircher v. Hayes* that a defendant's due process rights are not violated by a state prosecutor who threatens during plea negotiations to re-indict the accused on more serious charges if the defendant does not plead guilty to the offense with which he was originally charged.

- On March 21, in *Ballew v. Georgia,* the Supreme Court rules that a state criminal trial decided by a jury of five persons deprives a defendant of Sixth and Fourteenth Amendment rights.

- On April 10, a federal grand jury indicts former FBI acting director L. Patrick Gray and two former high-ranking FBI officials, Edward Miller and Mark Felt. Unable to obtain search warrants, the FBI officials had ordered FBI agents to break into the homes of friends and relatives of fugitive members of the radical Weatherman group in 1972 and 1973.

- On April 24, the Supreme Court lets stand the lower court's conviction of Patricia Hearst for armed robbery.

- On May 31, the Supreme Court decides that newspapers can be searched and their reporting and photographs used in the investigation of a crime.

- On June 8, a Nevada jury finds that a will purportedly written by the eccentric deceased billionaire Howard Hughes is a fake.

- On June 28, the Supreme Court rules that the medical school at the University of California in Davis must admit Allan Bakke, a white man who charged he had been the victim of reverse discrimination.

- On July 3, the Supreme Court decides the case of *FCC v. Pacifica Foundation.* The case involved a radio monologue by comedian George Carlin, called "Filthy Words." The court concluded that the First Amendment did not prohibit sanctioning the radio station for broadcasting Carlin's monologue, reasoning that broadcasting is entitled to less First Amendment protection than any other communication.

- On July 3, the Supreme Court decides in *Lockett v. Ohio* that the death penalty may only be imposed if the sentencing jury is allowed to consider a wide range of mitigating factors.

- On July 3, the Supreme Court decides that universities may take race into account in admissions to try to diversify the student body but may not have strict numerical quotas.

- On October 26, President Carter signs an ethics-in-government law provoked largely by Watergate; it provides for the appointment of special prosecutors.

- On November 27, Mayor George Moscone and Supervisor Harvey Milk of San Francisco are murdered by Dan White in part for their support of rights for gay men. White is convicted of voluntary manslaughter on May 21, 1979.

1979

- On March 5, the Supreme Court decides that it is unconstitutional sex discrimination for state laws to require divorcing husbands to pay alimony.

- On March 5, the Supreme Court rules in *Scott v. Illinois* that a state is not obligated to provide an attorney where a defendant is convicted of a crime but not incarcerated, even though incarceration is permissible under the law.

- On April 17, the Supreme Court rules in *Burch v. Louisiana* that a guilty verdict obtained from a nonunanimous six-member jury in a state criminal trial for a nonpetty offense violates a defendant's right to a trial by jury under the Sixth and Fourteenth Amendments.

- On May 23, a federal grand jury charges Bert Lance, former director of the Office of Management and Budget under President Carter, with conspiracy to file false statements and mislead government regulatory agencies.

- On June 26, the Supreme Court rules in *Smith v. Daily Mail Publishing Company* that a law making it illegal for a newspaper to publish, without court approval, the name of any youth charged as a juvenile offender, violated the First Amendment.

- On June 27, the Supreme Court okays a voluntary affirmative action plan to increase the proportion of black employees holding skilled positions at an aluminum and chemical plant.

- On July 2, the Supreme Court rules that a state may require parental consent for a minor's abortion. However, the state must provide the option of having a judge decide if the minor does not want to tell her parents or cannot.

- On July 2, the Supreme Court holds by a vote of five to four that members of the public have no constitutional right to attend trials. A court can close trials if pretrial publicity would hurt a defendant's chances of a fair trial.

- On September 6, President Jimmy Carter, citing humane considerations, frees four Puerto Rican nationalists who committed acts of political terrorism in the 1950s. Carter commutes the sentence of Oscar Collazo, who tried to assassinate President Harry S. Truman in 1950. He also grants clemency to Lolita Lebron, Irving Flores Rodriguez, and Rafael Cancel-Miranda who shot and wounded five U.S. congressmen in 1954.

- On December 17, Arthur McDuffie, an African American businessman, is fatally beaten after a police chase in Miami. Four white police officers were later acquitted in charges related to his death.

"Prescription for a Planet"

Speech

By: Russell E. Train

Date: 1970

Source: Train, Russell E. "Prescription for a Planet." New York: American Public Health Association, 1970, 10–11, 14–17.

About the Author: Russell E. Train (1920–) was the first administrator of the Environmental Quality Council, many of whose responsibilities were transferred to the Environmental Protection Agency (EPA) in 1970. Even though he was trained as a tax lawyer, his interests led him to become involved in conservation. In 1961, he founded the African Wildlife Leadership Foundation. In 1965, Train became president of the Conservation Foundation. After leaving the Environmental Quality Council, he became the president of the World Wildlife Fund. ∎

Introduction

When the first European explorers arrived in North America, they were astonished by the wide open ranges and vast quantities of wildlife. They were convinced that the open ranges and plentiful wildlife would last indefinitely. By the mid-1800s, however, Americans had spanned the continent and were beginning to fill in the open prairies. By the end of the 1800s, some thoughts were beginning to turn toward the preservation of the environment.

Those concerned about nature were divided into two camps: conservationists and preservationists. The conservationists wanted to make the best use of America's natural resources, which required careful planning and planned use, rather than just headlong development. The preservationists wanted to preserve nature for future generations.

President Theodore Roosevelt (served 1901–1909) was the first president to have nature issues high on his agenda, as he was a hunter and very interested in nature himself. Under Roosevelt, the government added more acres to the national parks and forests than under all of the previous presidents combined.

Even though parts of nature had been preserved and conserved, there was not a widespread concern for the environment. There was a common belief that America would find technological solutions for its concerns. However, the development of new technologies in the first sixty years of the twentieth century merely caused more damage to the environment, and the 1960s brought a renewed concern for that environment. New sciences and research prompted a call for a government agency that would protect the environment. The EPA was established under President Richard Nixon (served 1969–1974), and Russell E. Train was one of its first administrators.

Significance

The EPA, combined with new legislation, greatly helped to clean up America. The Cuyahoga River, near Cleveland, was so dirty that it actually caught on fire. Today, however, it is clean enough for people to enjoy fishing and boating on it. The government also created new nationwide standards for clean air and water, and the EPA helped to enforce these.

These accomplishments were not without their setbacks, however. The United States, even with the help of the EPA, has yet to find a fuel source that does not depend on fossil fuels (coal, oil, and natural gas). Attempts to find workable widespread solar power have been to little avail, while discussion to build more nuclear power plants has brought about protests and failure. When high oil prices existed, people were interested in small cars and alternative fuels and the EPA announced higher fuel standards. When oil prices dropped, sports utility vehicles increased in popularity and the EPA was ordered to reduce fuel standards.

The environment and the EPA have also been political footballs. During the administration of President Ronald Reagan (served 1981–1989), the EPA was ordered to scrap many of the rules that it had promulgated and deregulation of industry reigned. President Bill Clinton (served 1992–2001) reimposed many of those regulations and ordered more, but was charged by conservatives with caring more about the spotted owl than people. Drilling in the Arctic National Forest remains a hot political issue. There is also the debate of whether or not the United States will sign and follow international agreements like the Kyoto Summit. Even though progress has been made and the EPA has produced success, the environment is far from being both saved and a noncontroversial issue.

Primary Source

"Prescription for a Planet" [excerpt]

SYNOPSIS: Train opens his speech, which was given in front of a medical convention, with a comment that humanity needs to clean up the planet. He then discusses many of the issues that were troubling the planet at the time, including the burning of fossil fuels, and he argues that humanity needs to change its ways.

As physicians, many of you must have mused on that timeworn advice: "Physician, heal thyself." As an attorney, I have heard counter counsel: "The lawyer who represents himself has a fool for a client." However, I am also an environmentalist—if there is such a "critter." And environmental health, which is my subject tonight, casts every man in the role of his own physician.

From the Delphic oracle to the first earthling ever to set foot on any other world but this, has come the admonition to man to "know" the universal laws, to "know" man's place in this scheme of universal jurisprudence, to apply this knowledge to "heal himself."

We have a challenging mix here: mankind cast in the dual role of lawyer and physician, and then, just for confusing kicks, a second duality of roles— that of client and patient, standing to win or lose forever our place in this particular sun.

It is my thesis tonight that the outcome depends upon how adroitly we can shift our attitudes and actions to where we regard ourselves as part of the total world environment. It is the only context in which man can be *either* wise counselor or wise client, let alone both; it is the only set of circumstances under which he can be either wise physician or wise patient, let alone both. The indications are overwhelming that he *must* be both.

The outlook is not without hope. We have been both the teachers and the taught in every new step we have taken down the evolutionary trail—from crawling out of the planetary soup onto the oozing estuarial flats to piloting a lunar module for a rocket-powered landing on the moon. No one taught us. We had to find the ways ourselves.

We have taken each step as we had to, as it became necessary or possible. Or perhaps *impossible.* It was the columnist, Russell Baker, the week following the moon landing, who suggested that the reason we reached the moon with such efficiency, alacrity, and elan was precisely because the odds were against it. The *possible* things, like cleaning up our air and water and slums, are not challenging enough. Mr. Baker suggested that such tasks bore us.

Nevertheless, today we are faced with a worsening health crisis of planetary proportions. Our air and water and soil and cities are sick, and the sick-ness is people. As Pogo put it, "We have met the enemy, and they is us." The task of reversing this planetary disease is rapidly approaching the condition which sometimes seems to be the flash point for human action—namely, impossibility. . . .

It is a thought that carries a seed of hope. Can man indeed become his own "Mission Impossible" hero? Will he accept the challenge to heal himself and his world while there is yet time? Or will he, instead, emulate the tape and self-destruct in whatever number of seconds are left to us?

Your own past president, Dr. John Hanlon, has spoken to you of the "incongruity of standing knee-deep in refuse, shooting rockets at the moon . . ."; of " . . . waters laced with nondegradable detergents and pesticides and lands littered with imperishable aluminum cans."

I think our technology is big enough to do both jobs. It can continue on the one hand to finger the outer limits of our cosmic cage; at the same time, it can liberate us from this moment of aluminum immortality. The packagers show earnest signs of searching for ways to introduce "death" to solid wastes—thus closing the energy cycle again, in the sense that personal death is necessary if life in general is to go on.

More than 2.7 billion years ago, photosynthesis developed on this planet, and saved the life in that dim, distant broth from eating its way to extinction by virtue of its exploitative economy. It was at that point, so far back in time, that "life acquired the potential for a balanced, nonexploitative economy— one not based on destruction of nonrenewable resources."

Man's dependence on fossil fuels today is one of the most significant features of the industrial world. It has been estimated that half of all the fuel ever burned by man has been burned in the last half century. These fuels are nonrenewable resources and represent the unused energy potential of about 8,400 years of plant production spread over all geological time and unutilized in at least two billion years of photosynthesis. This is the reckoning of Lamont Cole.

When the rate of fuel-burning matches the rate of photosynthesis on earth, the oxygen content of the atmosphere will start to decrease. This may already have occurred in the United States and some other industrial nations. It may be only the oceanic plankton meadows, the estuarial chlorophyl activities, the Amazonian rain forest, and similar areas that are keeping the balance in our favor. The developer and the polluter threaten all three. Clearly, the present exploitative economy of life cannot be allowed to continue indefinitely. Atomic energy will not halt completely the exploitation of nonrenewable resources, but it can slow us down enough to take us quite a long way into the future if, as Cole hopes, "man will use it responsibly."

Glenn Seaborg, chairman of the U.S. Atomic Energy Commission, assures us that this is precisely what we are doing. In a paper delivered to the National Academy of Sciences at Argonne National Laboratory in May, 1969, Dr. Seaborg described the exceeding care and safety measures exercised in the nuclear field—the cautious siting of plants, the promising new research made possible by radioactive tracers, the thoroughness with which so-called "side effects," such as the raising of water temperatures at plant sites, are being studied.

Rather than spew out its wastes in the heedless manner that has characterized the behavior of fossil fuel-users from the very beginning, atomic energy producers have taken elaborate precautions to leave no dangerous legacy for the future. Concentration and solidification techniques now allow reduction of 100 gallons of high activity reactor wastes to only one cubic foot of solid waste. These wastes can safely be stored in salt mines. And Dr. Seaborg maintains that all the solid waste produced by nuclear reactors in the year 2,000 would occupy less than one percent of the volume of salt now being mined each year from the 400,000 square miles of salt deposits that underlie the United States.

This is only part—albeit a major part—of the increasingly intricate interaction between modern technological man and everything else in and on the earth. It represents a new stage in planetary metabolism. Just when we seem to have set ourselves on another exploitative, dead-end course—one that threatens to exhaust our stored energies and choke us on our own wastes—we begin to see hopeful signs of an upward spiral toward new ways of extracting, entrapping, using, and reusing energy to run the life systems of the earth. If we can actually accomplish this, while we mark time to the slower consumption beat of nuclear energy, we will have wrought with our reason and our technology an achievement whose equal, in terms of the survival of life on this planet, has happened only once before—with the appearance of photosynthesis.

The times are calling for new responses from us all. Only yesterday, someone came up with the con-

President Nixon signs legislation designed to curb smog from auto exhaust, December 31, 1974. AP/WIDE WORLD PHOTOS. REPRODUCED BY PERMISSION.

cept of "spaceship earth" and we all bought it, eagerly and enthusiastically. It was a great leap forward from the old idea of earth as a kingdom in which man's primary objective was to "multiply and subdue."

But there is emerging today another concept—one that I think holds even more hope for survival. It is the idea of the whole earth as a living organism, of which man is simply a part, in exactly the same sense that the myriad organisms participating in a single man's physical life processes are a part. Just as some of those organisms can be synergistically involved in promoting and prolonging creative, energetic survival of both themselves and their "host," so can man be in relation to *his* host, the earth or, more precisely, the air and water and soil and sunlight that make up the tough and fragile and exceedingly precious envelope around it.

There are other organisms that occasionally invade the environment provided by our human selves—organisms that are destructive and that quickly reduce our energy to survival zero. The process here is parasitism and, eventually, if another host cannot be found and a transfer effected, even the parasites perish.

We can still hope that we have it in our power to choose—to be synergistic, creative, high-energy participants in a healthy world—a kind of benign, perhaps some day even a therapeutic agent, in an incredibly rich, varied, endlessly inviting and delighting planetary organism. If cancer cells could contemplate their own fate, they might prudently change their ways. It is not too much to hope that man, faced with many of the same alternatives, might do the same.

Further Resources

BOOKS

Braunstein, Peter, and Michael William Doyle. *Imagine Nation: The American Counterculture of the 1960s and '70s.* New York: Routledge, 2002.

Carroll, Peter N. *It Seemed Like Nothing Happened: The Tragedy and Promise of America in the 1970s.* New York: Holt, Rinehart and Winston, 1982.

Harris, Richard A., and Sidney M. Milkis. *The Politics of Regulatory Change: A Tale of Two Agencies.* New York: Oxford University Press, 1989.

Schulman, Bruce J. *The Seventies: The Great Shift in American Culture, Society, and Politics.* New York: The Free Press, 2001.

Train, Russell E. *A Memoir.* Washington, D.C.: R. E. Train, 2000.

U.S. Environmental Protection Agency. *EPA: The First Twenty Years.* Washington, D.C.: U.S. Environmental Protection Agency, 1990.

Williams, Dennis C. *The Guardian: EPA's Formative Years, 1970–1973.* Washington, D.C.: U.S. Environmental Protection Agency, 1993.

WEBSITES

"History of the U.S. Environmental Protection Agency." U.S. Environmental Protection Agency. Available online at http://www.epa.gov/history (accessed April 16, 2003).

AUDIO AND VISUAL MEDIA

Jennings, Peter. "Approaching the Apocalypse." Episode 12 of the ABC series *The Century: America's Time.* ABC Video, 1999, VHS.

Swann v. Board of Education

Supreme Court decision

By: Warren Burger

Date: April 20, 1971

Source: Burger, Warren. *Swann v. Board of Education.* 402 U.S. 1 (1971). Available online at http://laws.findlaw.com/us/402/1.html; website home page: http://www.findlaw.com (accessed April 16, 2003).

About the Author: Warren Burger (1907–1995) had a private practice for over twenty years before he became a U.S. assistant attorney general and then a judge in the U.S. Court of Appeals. He was appointed chief justice in 1969 and served until 1986. His judicial record reflected his belief in "strict constructionism," where the Constitution was construed narrowly, and that society's rights should outweigh the rights of the accused. ■

Introduction

Slavery legally ended in the United States in 1865, but it took many more decades before the last of its vestiges were finally removed. After the Thirteenth Amendment in 1865, which ended slavery across the United States, the North took steps to help former slaves and to rebuild the South. Part of that Reconstruction was the passage of the Fourteenth Amendment (1868), guaranteeing due process and equal protection to all citizens, and of the Fifteenth Amendment (1870), providing that the right to vote would not be denied on the basis of the color of one's skin.

The North soon tired of Reconstruction though and left the former slaves at the mercy of their former owners. The South quickly passed Jim Crow laws that segregated all aspects of southern life, including courtrooms, railroad cars, bathrooms, and schools. The Supreme Court gave this system its stamp of approval in *Plessy v. Ferguson* (1896), which held that a separate system was allowable as long as it was equal. Of course, with whites holding all the political power in the South, the system was separate, but hardly equal.

The National Association for the Advancement of Colored People (NAACP) challenged segregation throughout the South, especially segregation within educational institutions. Its first victory in education came in *Missouri ex rel. Gaines v. Canada* (1938), where Missouri was forced to provide the opportunity for a black man to go to law school. Most states responded to this by providing token schools for blacks in their states. After victories at the graduate school level attacked many parts of segregated education, the NAACP directly attacked segregated schools in *Brown v. Board of Education,* and in 1954 the Supreme Court held that segregated schools were illegal.

Significance

Segregation did not end to any meaningful extent until the 1960s when the 1964 Civil Rights Act was passed, allowing the federal government to sue schools to force integration. However, many states still allowed "freedom of choice" plans that permitted children to pick their own schools, thereby allowing the perseverance of segregation.

In the absence of any other successful plan, North Carolina's district court oversaw the busing of students to create integrated education. The Supreme Court upheld the use of busing in order to achieve this integration. Since *Swann v. Board of Education,* busing has generally been upheld within a single county as a way to achieve integration, and federal judges have kept an eye on the integration process, although less scrutiny has been given in recent years. The Supreme Court, however, struck down the imposition of a multicounty busing system in Detroit, Michigan, as a way to desegregate that school system, and many parents have moved their children to the suburbs or to private schools as a way to avoid integrated schools.

In the 1990s, many district judges terminated their oversight of educational systems since they found that the schools have done as much as possible to desegregate and the Supreme Court has generally upheld these cessations. Segregated education still exists in many areas, not due to official policy, but due to housing patterns. The United States still has not found a way, or the will, to deal with this issue.

Primary Source

Swann v. Board of Education [excerpt]

> **SYNOPSIS:** Chief Justice Warren Burger notes that *Brown* will be followed and that only when constitutional violations occur will the courts step in. He states that the use of quotas in desegregating the schools is acceptable, but it is only a starting point. He also comments that the pairing of schools and transportation from area to area are both acceptable tools if a court finds them necessary to assist the process of desegregation. The decision ends by upholding all parts of the lower court's ruling.

Mr. Chief Justice Burger delivered the opinion of the Court. . . .

Nearly 17 years ago this Court held, in explicit terms, that state-imposed segregation by race in public schools denies equal protection of the laws. At no time has the Court deviated in the slightest degree from that holding or its constitutional underpinnings. . . .

Over the 16 years since Brown II, many difficulties were encountered in implementation of the basic constitutional requirement that the State not discriminate between public school children on the basis of their race. Nothing in our national experience prior to 1955 prepared anyone for dealing with changes and adjustments of the magnitude and complexity encountered since then. Deliberate resistance of some to the Court's mandates has impeded the good-faith efforts of others to bring school systems into compliance. The detail and nature of these dilatory tactics have been noted frequently by this Court and other courts. . . .

The objective today remains to eliminate from the public schools all vestiges of state-imposed segregation. Segregation was the evil struck down by Brown I as contrary to the equal protection guarantees of the Constitution. That was the violation sought to be corrected by the remedial measures of Brown II. . . .

If school authorities fail in their affirmative obligations under these holdings, judicial authority may be invoked. Once a right and a violation have been shown, the scope of a district court's equitable powers to remedy past wrongs is broad, for breadth and flexibility are inherent in equitable remedies. . . .

. . . [I]t is important to remember that judicial powers may be exercised only on the basis of a constitutional violation. Remedial judicial authority does not put judges automatically in the shoes of school authorities whose powers are plenary. Judicial authority enters only when local authority defaults.

School authorities are traditionally charged with broad power to formulate and implement educational policy and might well conclude, for example, that in order to prepare students to live in a pluralistic society each school should have a prescribed ratio of Negro to white students reflecting the proportion for the district as a whole. To do this as an educational policy is within the broad discretionary powers of school authorities; absent a finding of a constitutional violation, however, that would not be within the authority of a federal court. As with any equity case, the nature of the violation determines the scope of the remedy. In default by the school authorities of their obligation to proffer acceptable remedies, a district court has broad power to fashion a remedy that will assure a unitary school system. . . .

. . . The basis of our decision must be the prohibition of the Fourteenth Amendment that no State shall "deny to any person within its jurisdiction the equal protection of the laws."

We turn now to the problem of defining with more particularity the responsibilities of school authorities in desegregating a state-enforced dual school system in light of the Equal Protection Clause. . . .

The central issue in this case is that of student assignment, and there are essentially four problem areas:

1. to what extent racial balance or racial quotas may be used as an implement in a remedial order to correct a previously segregated system;

2. whether every all-Negro and all-white school must be eliminated as an indispensable part of a remedial process of desegregation;

A National Guardsman meets a school bus as it arrives with African American students to be integrated into the Lamar School in South Carolina, March 23, 1970. Lamar residents resisted integration by acts such as turning over buses as they arrived at the school. © BETTMANN/CORBIS. REPRODUCED BY PERMISSION.

3. what the limits are, if any, on the rearrangement of school districts and attendance zones, as a remedial measure; and

4. what the limits are, if any, on the use of transportation facilities to correct state-enforced racial school segregation.

(1) Racial Balances or Racial Quotas

The constant theme and thrust of every holding from Brown I to date is that state-enforced separation of races in public schools is discrimination that violates the Equal Protection Clause. The remedy commanded was to dismantle dual school systems. . . .

Our objective in dealing with the issues presented by these cases is to see that school authorities exclude no pupil of a racial minority from any school, directly or indirectly, on account of race; it does not and cannot embrace all the problems of racial prejudice, even when those problems contribute to disproportionate racial concentrations in some schools. . . .

As the voluminous record in this case shows, the predicate for the District Court's use of the 71%-29% ratio was twofold: first, its express finding, approved by the Court of Appeals and not challenged here, that a dual school system had been maintained by the school authorities at least until 1969; second, its finding, also approved by the Court of Appeals, that the school board had totally defaulted in its acknowledged duty to come forward with an acceptable plan of its own, notwithstanding the patient efforts of the District Judge who, on at least three occasions, urged the board to submit plans. As the statement of facts shows, these findings are abundantly supported by the record. . . .

We see therefore that the use made of mathematical ratios was no more than a starting point in the process of shaping a remedy, rather than an inflexible requirement. From that starting point the District Court proceeded to frame a decree that was within its discretionary powers, as an equitable remedy for the particular circumstances. . . . Awareness of the racial composition of the whole school system is likely to be a useful starting point in shaping a remedy to correct past constitutional violations. In sum, the very limited use made of mathematical ratios was within the equitable remedial discretion of the District Court.

(2) One-race Schools

The record in this case reveals the familiar phenomenon that in metropolitan areas minority groups are often found concentrated in one part of the city. In some circumstances certain schools may remain all or largely of one race until new schools can be provided or neighborhood patterns change. Schools all or predominately of one race in a district of mixed population will require close scrutiny to determine that school assignments are not part of state-enforced segregation.

In light of the above, it should be clear that the existence of some small number of one-race, or virtually one-race, schools within a district is not in and of itself the mark of a system that still practices segregation by law. The district judge or school authorities should make every effort to achieve the greatest possible degree of actual desegregation and will thus necessarily be concerned with the elimination of one-race schools. No per se rule can adequately embrace all the difficulties of reconciling the competing interests involved; but in a system with a history of segregation the need for remedial criteria of sufficient specificity to assure a school authority's compliance with its constitutional duty warrants a presumption against schools that are substantially disproportionate in their racial composition. Where the school authority's proposed plan for conversion from a dual to a unitary system contemplates the continued existence of some schools that are all or predominately of one race, they have the burden of showing that such school assignments are genuinely nondiscriminatory. The court should scrutinize such schools, and the burden upon the school authorities will be to satisfy the court that their racial composition is not the result of present or past discriminatory action on their part. . . .

(3) Remedial Altering of Attendance Zones

The maps submitted in these cases graphically demonstrate that one of the principal tools employed by school planners and by courts to break up the dual school system has been a frank—and sometimes drastic—gerrymandering of school districts and attendance zones. An additional step was pairing, "clustering," or "grouping" of schools with attendance assignments made deliberately to accomplish the transfer of Negro students out of formerly segregated Negro schools and transfer of white students to formerly all-Negro schools. More often than not, these zones are neither compact nor contiguous; indeed they may be on opposite ends of the city. As an interim corrective measure, this cannot be said to be beyond the broad remedial powers of a court. . . .

We hold that the pairing and grouping of noncontiguous school zones is a permissible tool and such action is to be considered in light of the objectives sought. Judicial steps in shaping such zones going beyond combinations of contiguous areas should be examined in light of what is said in subdivisions (1), (2), and (3) of this opinion concerning the objectives to be sought. Maps do not tell the whole story since noncontiguous school zones may be more accessible to each other in terms of the critical travel time, because of traffic patterns and good highways, than schools geographically closer together. Conditions in different localities will vary so widely that no rigid rules can be laid down to govern all situations.

(4) Transportation of Students

The scope of permissible transportation of students as an implement of a remedial decree has never been defined by this Court and by the very nature of the problem it cannot be defined with precision. No rigid guidelines as to student transportation can be given for application to the infinite variety of problems presented in thousands of situations. Bus transportation has been an integral part of the public education system for years, and was perhaps the single most important factor in the transition from the one-room schoolhouse to the consolidated school. Eighteen million of the Nation's public school children, approximately 39%, were transported to their schools by bus in 1969–1970 in all parts of the country.

The importance of bus transportation as a normal and accepted tool of educational policy is readily discernible in this and the companion case. . . . The Charlotte school authorities did not purport to assign students on the basis of geographically drawn zones until 1965 and then they allowed almost unlimited transfer privileges. The District Court's conclusion that assignment of children to the school nearest their home serving their grade would not produce an effective dismantling of the dual system is supported by the record.

Thus the remedial techniques used in the District Court's order were within that court's power to provide equitable relief; implementation of the decree is well within the capacity of the school authority. . . .

. . . In these circumstances, we find no basis for holding that the local school authorities may not be required to employ bus transportation as one tool of school desegregation. Desegregation plans cannot be limited to the walk-in school.

An objection to transportation of students may have validity when the time or distance of travel is so great as to either risk the health of the children or significantly impinge on the educational process. District courts must weigh the soundness of any transportation plan in light of what is said in subdivisions (1), (2), and (3) above. It hardly needs stating that the limits on time of travel will vary with many factors, but probably with none more than the age of the students. The reconciliation of competing values in a desegregation case is, of course, a difficult task with many sensitive facets but fundamentally no more so than remedial measures courts of equity have traditionally employed.

. . . On the facts of this case, we are unable to conclude that the order of the District Court is not reasonable, feasible and workable. However, in seeking to define the scope of remedial power or the limits on remedial power of courts in an area as sensitive as we deal with here, words are poor instruments to convey the sense of basic fairness inherent in equity. Substance, not semantics, must govern, and we have sought to suggest the nature of limitations without frustrating the appropriate scope of equity.

At some point, these school authorities and others like them should have achieved full compliance with this Court's decision in Brown I. The systems would then be "unitary" in the sense required by our decisions in *Green* and *Alexander*.

It does not follow that the communities served by such systems will remain demographically stable, for in a growing, mobile society, few will do so. Neither school authorities nor district courts are constitutionally required to make year-by-year adjustments of the racial composition of student bodies once the affirmative duty to desegregate has been accomplished and racial discrimination through official action is eliminated from the system. This does not mean that federal courts are without power to deal with future problems; but in the absence of a showing that either the school authorities or some other agency of the State has deliberately attempted to fix or alter demographic patterns to affect the racial composition of the schools, further intervention by a district court should not be necessary.

Further Resources

BOOKS

Douglas, Davison M. *School Busing: Constitutional and Political Developments.* New York: Garland, 1994.

Galub, Arthur L. *The Burger Court, 1968–1984.* Danbury, Conn.: Grolier Educational Corporation, 1995.

Maltz, Earl M. *The Chief Justiceship of Warren Burger, 1969–1986.* Columbia: University of South Carolina Press, 2000.

Matney, Brian Keith. "Two Decades After *Swann*: A Qualitative Study of School Desegregation Efforts in Charlotte and Mecklenburg County, North Carolina." Ph.D. diss., University of North Carolina, Chapel Hill, 1992.

Schwartz, Bernard. *Swann's Way: The School Busing Case and the Supreme Court.* New York: Oxford University Press, 1986.

PERIODICALS

Detlefsen, Robert R. "Civil Rights, the Courts, and the Reagan Justice Department." *Journal of Contemporary Studies* 8, no. 2, Spring–Summer 1985, 91–115.

WEBSITES

"Education." Legal Program, NAACP Legal Defense Fund. Available online at http://www.naacpldf.org/legalprogram /education.html; website home page: http://www.naacpldf .org/legalprogram/ (accessed April 16, 2003).

AUDIO AND VISUAL MEDIA

"Busing: Complying With *Swann* in 1976." Part of the CBS series *Integration and Busing: The Earlier Years.* Films for the Humanities and Sciences, 1976, VHS.

New York Times Co. v. U.S.

Supreme Court decision

By: Hugo L. Black and Warren Burger

Date: June 30, 1971

Source: Black, Hugo L. and Warren Burger. *New York Times Co. v. United States.* 403 U.S. 713 (1971). Available online at http://laws.findlaw.com/us/403/713.html; website home page: http://www.findlaw.com (accessed April 16, 2003).

About the Authors: Hugo L. Black (1886–1971) graduated from the University of Alabama Law School in 1906. After serving two terms in the U.S. Senate, he was appointed to the U.S. Supreme Court in 1937. His term was distinguished by his support of civil rights.

Warren Burger (1907–1995) had a private practice for over twenty years before he became a U.S. assistant attorney general and then a judge in the U.S. Court of Appeals. In 1969, he was named by President Richard Nixon (served 1969–1974) as chief justice of the U.S. Supreme Court. ∎

Introduction

The First Amendment, which went into effect in 1791, enshrines freedom of the press into our Constitution, along with several other freedoms. However, the exact meaning of the freedom of the press was not tested in the courts for most of the next one hundred years. One reason for this is that the whole Bill of Rights, including the First Amendment, was held to apply only against the federal government. The federal government's main infringement on the freedom of the press was during the Civil War (1861–1865), but this censorship was never tested in the Supreme Court.

In the twentieth century, this all began to change. First, the First Amendment was held to apply against both the federal government and the states. Second, the press began to increase in importance and so came to be involved in more court cases. Third, the courts began to take a wider view of exactly what the First Amendment meant.

Some initially argued that the First Amendment's freedom of the press only meant a ban on prior restraints, but courts soon moved beyond this idea. In 1931, the Supreme Court struck down a state law that allowed the suppression of any scandalous newspaper, as the Court held that the law violated the First Amendment.

Freedom of the press continued to grow as the twentieth century progressed. In the 1960s, as part of the Cold War, the United States became involved in the Vietnam War (1964–1975). By the late 1960s, even though the U.S. government had been regularly announcing that it was winning the war, it was facing growing opposition to the conflict. In 1971, the *New York Times* wanted to publish the Pentagon Papers, a collection of classified documents that presented a history of the Vietnam War. The U.S. government's opposition to this resulted in *New York Times Co. v. U.S.*

Significance

The Supreme Court, in its main opinion, rejected the government's contention that the publication of the papers should be banned. The government had argued that irreparable injury would be caused and that the papers contained information that would help the enemy and harm the war effort. The Court stated that any government wanting a prior restraint to ban publication of an item had to meet a very heavy burden—the first time this standard was articulated. The Court concluded that this burden had not been met.

Justice Hugo L. Black, in his concurrence, stated that no prior restraints were allowable, but he did not carry the court. Chief Justice Warren Burger, in his dissent, argued that this decision (on whether or not publication is allowable) had been taken too quickly. He did not argue that publication should be banned, however. Six justices, in a variety of opinions, also argued that criminal sanc-

tions could be undertaken against the paper if the publication of these documents proved damaging to the nation's security, even though most of them did not think that a ban on publication was proven to be necessary.

Ultimately, the papers did not prove damaging to the nation's security, but only to the government's honor. What the Pentagon Papers showed was that many in the military believed, as early as 1965, the same year that the United States committed large numbers of ground troops, that the war was lost. The fact that the United States continued to fight and to claim that it was winning, lowered most people's faith in their government. The Pentagon Papers, along with Watergate in the early 1970s, combined to severely weaken the government's credibility. Since that time, prior restraints have not been used, but the government's credibility has not been fully returned either.

Primary Source

New York Times Co. v. U.S. [excerpt]

SYNOPSIS: Justice Black argues that that First Amendment creates absolute freedom of the press and that censorship is never justified. He contends that the revelations of the Pentagon Papers clearly prove that the press is doing its job. Justice Burger comments that there was an undue rush to judgment, that more time should have been taken, and that the First Amendment was not absolute. He also noted that those who possessed stolen government documents could be prosecuted.

Mr. Justice Black, with whom Mr. Justice Douglas joins, concurring.

. . . I believe that every moment's continuance of the injunctions against these newspapers amounts to a flagrant, indefensible, and continuing violation of the First Amendment. Furthermore, after oral argument, I agree completely that we must affirm the judgment of the Court of Appeals for the District of Columbia Circuit and reverse the judgment of the Court of Appeals for the Second Circuit. . . . In my view it is unfortunate that some of my Brethren are apparently willing to hold that the publication of news may sometimes be enjoined. Such a holding would make a shambles of the First Amendment.

Our Government was launched in 1789 with the adoption of the Constitution. The Bill of Rights, including the First Amendment, followed in 1791. Now, for the first time in the 182 years since the founding of the Republic, the federal courts are asked to hold that the First Amendment does not mean what it says, but rather means that the Government can halt the publication of current news of vital importance to the people of this country.

In seeking injunctions against these newspapers and in its presentation to the Court, the Executive Branch seems to have forgotten the essential purpose and history of the First Amendment. When the Constitution was adopted, many people strongly opposed it because the document contained no Bill of Rights to safeguard certain basic freedoms. They especially feared that the new powers granted to a central government might be interpreted to permit the government to curtail freedom of religion, press, assembly, and speech. In response to an overwhelming public clamor, James Madison offered a series of amendments to satisfy citizens that these great liberties would remain safe and beyond the power of government to abridge. Madison proposed what later became the First Amendment in three parts. . . . The amendments were offered to curtail and restrict the general powers granted to the Executive, Legislative, and Judicial Branches two years before in the original Constitution. The Bill of Rights changed the original Constitution into a new charter under which no branch of government could abridge the people's freedoms of press, speech, religion, and assembly. Yet the Solicitor General argues and some members of the Court appear to agree that the general powers of the Government adopted in the original Constitution should be interpreted to limit and restrict the specific and emphatic guarantees of the Bill of Rights adopted later. I can imagine no greater perversion of history. Madison and the other Framers of the First Amendment, able men that they were, wrote in language they earnestly believed could never be misunderstood: "Congress shall make no law . . . abridging the freedom . . . of the press. . . ." Both the history and language of the First Amendment support the view that the press must be left free to publish news, whatever the source, without censorship, injunctions, or prior restraints.

In the First Amendment the Founding Fathers gave the free press the protection it must have to fulfill its essential role in our democracy. The press was to serve the governed, not the governors. The Government's power to censor the press was abolished so that the press would remain forever free to censure the Government. The press was protected so that it could bare the secrets of government and inform the people. Only a free and unrestrained press can effectively expose deception in government. And paramount among the responsibilities of a free press is the duty to prevent any part of the government from deceiving the people and sending them off to distant lands to die of foreign fevers and foreign shot and shell. In my view, far from deserving condemnation for their courageous reporting, the New York Times, the Washington Post, and other newspapers should be commended for serving the purpose that the Founding Fathers saw so clearly. In revealing the workings of government that led to the Vietnam war, the newspapers nobly did precisely that which the Founders hoped and trusted they would do.

The Government's case here is based on premises entirely different from those that guided the Framers of the First Amendment. . . . [T]he Government argues in its brief that in spite of the First Amendment, "[t]he authority of the Executive Department to protect the nation against publication of information whose disclosure would endanger the national security stems from two interrelated sources: the constitutional power of the President over the conduct of foreign affairs and his authority as Commander-in-Chief."

In other words, we are asked to hold that despite the First Amendment's emphatic command, the Executive Branch, the Congress, and the Judiciary can make laws enjoining publication of current news and abridging freedom of the press in the name of "national security." The Government does not even attempt to rely on any act of Congress. Instead it makes the bold and dangerously far-reaching contention that the courts should take it upon themselves to "make" a law abridging freedom of the press in the name of equity, presidential power and national security, even when the representatives of the people in Congress have adhered to the command of the First Amendment and refused to make such a law. . . . To find that the President has "inherent power" to halt the publication of news by resort to the courts would wipe out the First Amendment and destroy the fundamental liberty and security of the very people the Government hopes to make "secure." No one can read the history of the adoption of the First Amendment without being convinced beyond any doubt that it was injunctions like those sought here that Madison and his collaborators intended to outlaw in this Nation for all time.

The word "security" is a broad, vague generality whose contours should not be invoked to abrogate the fundamental law embodied in the First Amendment. The guarding of military and diplomatic secrets at the expense of informed representative government provides no real security for our Republic. The Framers of the First Amendment, fully aware of both the need to defend a new nation and

William Frazee, the Chief of the Presses for the *Washington Post*, holds up a paper and makes the victory sign after the Supreme Court's decision to allow the resumption of newspaper publication of the top secret Pentagon Papers, June 30, 1971. © BETTMANN/CORBIS. REPRODUCED BY PERMISSION.

the abuses of the English and Colonial governments, sought to give this new society strength and security by providing that freedom of speech, press, religion, and assembly should not be abridged. . . .

Mr. Chief Justice Burger, dissenting.

. . . There is, therefore, little variation among the members of the Court in terms of resistance to prior restraints against publication. Adherence to this basic constitutional principle, however, does not make these cases simple. In these cases, the imperative of a free and unfettered press comes into collision with another imperative, the effective functioning of a complex modern government and specifically the effective exercise of certain constitutional powers of the Executive. Only those who view the First Amendment as an absolute in all circumstances—a view I respect, but reject—can find such cases as these to be simple or easy.

These cases are not simple for another and more immediate reason. We do not know the facts of the cases. No District Judge knew all the facts. No Court of Appeals judge knew all the facts. No member of this Court knows all the facts.

Why are we in this posture, in which only those judges to whom the First Amendment is absolute and permits of no restraint in any circumstances or for any reason, are really in a position to act?

I suggest we are in this posture because these cases have been conducted in unseemly haste. . . . The prompt setting of these cases reflects our universal abhorrence of prior restraint. But prompt judicial action does not mean unjudicial haste.

Here, moreover, the frenetic haste is due in large part to the manner in which the Times proceeded from the date it obtained the purloined documents. It seems reasonably clear now that the haste precluded reasonable and deliberate judicial treatment of these cases and was not warranted. The precipitate action of this Court aborting trials not yet completed is not the kind of judicial conduct that ought to attend the disposition of a great issue.

The newspapers make a derivative claim under the First Amendment; they denominate this right as the public "right to know"; by implication, the Times asserts a sole trusteeship of that right by virtue of its journalistic "scoop." The right is asserted as an absolute. Of course, the First Amendment right itself is not an absolute, as Justice Holmes so long ago pointed out in his aphorism concerning the right to shout "fire" in a crowded theater if there was no fire. . . . There are no doubt other exceptions no one has had occasion to describe or discuss. Conceivably such exceptions may be lurking in these cases and would have been flushed had they been properly considered in the trial courts, free from unwarranted deadlines and frenetic pressures. An issue of this importance should be tried and heard in a judicial atmosphere conducive to thoughtful, reflective deliberation, especially when haste, in terms of hours, is unwarranted in light of the long period the Times, by its own choice, deferred publication.

It is not disputed that the Times has had unauthorized possession of the documents for three to four months, during which it has had its expert analysts studying them, presumably digesting them and preparing the material for publication. During all of this time, the Times, presumably in its capacity as trustee of the public's "right to know," has held up publication for purposes it considered proper and thus public knowledge was delayed. No doubt this was for a good reason; the analysis of 7,000 pages of complex material drawn from a vastly greater volume of material would inevitably take time and the writing of good news stories takes time. But why should the United States Government, from whom this information was illegally acquired by someone, along with all the counsel, trial judges, and appellate judges be placed under needless pressure? After these months of deferral, the alleged "right to know" has somehow and suddenly become a right that must be vindicated instanter.

Would it have been unreasonable, since the newspaper could anticipate the Government's objections to release of secret material, to give the Government an opportunity to review the entire collection and determine whether agreement could be reached on publication? Stolen or not, if security was not in fact jeopardized, much of the material could no doubt have been declassified, since it spans a period ending in 1968. With such an approach—one that great newspapers have in the past practiced and stated editorially to be the duty of an honorable press—the newspapers and Government might well have narrowed the area of disagreement as to what was and was not publishable, leaving the remainder to be resolved in orderly litigation, if necessary. To me it is hardly believable that a newspaper long regarded as a great institution in American life would fail to perform one of the basic and simple duties of every citizen with respect to the discovery or possession of stolen property or secret government documents. That duty, I had thought—perhaps naively—was to report forthwith, to responsible public officers. This duty rests on taxi drivers, Justices, and the New York Times. The course followed by the Times, whether so calculated or not, removed any possibility of orderly litigation of the issues. If the action of the judges up to now has been correct, that result is sheer happenstance.

Our grant of the writ of certiorari before final judgment in the Times case aborted the trial in the District Court before it had made a complete record pursuant to the mandate of the Court of Appeals for the Second Circuit.

The consequence of all this melancholy series of events is that we literally do not know what we are acting on. As I see it, we have been forced to deal with litigation concerning rights of great magnitude without an adequate record, and surely without time for adequate treatment either in the prior proceedings or in this Court. It is interesting to note that counsel on both sides, in oral argument before this Court, were frequently unable to respond to questions on factual points. Not surprisingly they pointed out that they had been working literally "around the clock" and simply were unable to review the documents that give rise to these cases and were not familiar with them. This Court is in no better posture. . . .

I would affirm the Court of Appeals for the Second Circuit and allow the District Court to complete the trial aborted by our grant of certiorari, meanwhile preserving the status quo in the Post case. I would direct that the District Court on remand give priority to the Times case to the exclusion of all other business of that court but I would not set arbitrary deadlines.

I should add that I am in general agreement with much of what Mr. Justice White has expressed with respect to penal sanctions concerning communication or retention of documents or information relating to the national defense.

We all crave speedier judicial processes but when judges are pressured as in these cases the result is a parody of the judicial function.

Further Resources

BOOKS

Ellsberg, Daniel. *Secrets: A Memoir of Vietnam and the Pentagon Papers.* New York: Viking, 2002.

Herda, D. J. *"New York Times v. United States": National Security and Censorship.* Hillside, N.J.: Enslow, 1994.

Hockett, Jeffrey D. *New Deal Justice: The Constitutional Jurisprudence of Hugo L. Black, Felix Frankfurter, and Robert H. Jackson.* Lanham, Md.: Rowman and Littlefield Publishers, 1996.

Maltz, Earl M. *The Chief Justiceship of Warren Burger, 1969–1986.* Columbia: University of South Carolina Press, 2000.

Rudenstine, David. *The Day the Presses Stopped: A History of the Pentagon Papers Case.* Berkeley: University of California Press, 1996.

Schwartz, Bernard. *The Ascent of Pragmatism: The Burger Court in Action.* Reading, Mass.: Addison-Wesley, 1990.

Ungar, Sanford J. *The Papers and the Papers: An Account of the Legal and Political Battle Over the Pentagon Papers.* New York: Columbia University Press, 1989.

PERIODICALS

Schmuhl, Robert. "Government Accountability and External Watchdogs." *Issues of Democracy* 5, no. 2, August 2000. Available online at http://usinfo.state.gov/journals/itdhr/0800 /ijde/schmuhl.htm; website home page: http://usinfo.state .gov/journals/ (accessed April 16, 2003).

Lt. William Calley, right, leaves a military courtroom after pretrial hearings in his case, February 12, 1970. © BETTMANN/CORBIS. REPRODUCED BY PERMISSION.

Lieutenant Calley: His Own Story

Memoir

By: William Calley and John Sack

Date: 1971

Source: Calley, William, and John Sack. *Lieutenant Calley: His Own Story.* New York: Viking, 1971, 161–165, 168–169, 176–177.

About the Authors: William Calley (1943–) served a short time in prison for his role in the My Lai massacre. After the Vietnam War (1964–1975), he served as the manager of a jewelry store owned by his father-in-law.

John Sack (1930–) was educated at Harvard University. He served in the Korean War (1950–1953) and has been a writer for United Press, CBS, and *Esquire*. His other books include *Report From Practically Nowhere* (1959). ∎

Introduction

Early warfare in the United States was covered in newspapers, which were greatly limited by their capacity to report the news as quickly as technology allowed. Newspapers also tended to support the United States' side of the war. In the Civil War (1861–1865), southern newspapers reported on (and for) the South, and northern papers reported on (and for) the North. The Civil War was also one of the first wars to be recorded by photographers for posterity.

Besides having a variety of reporting and photographs, the Civil War was also one of the first wars where people were tried for what would later be called "war crimes." Several southern prison commanders were tried for the mismanagement of their institutions. In the Spanish American War (1898), the issue of war conduct was raised when several U.S. soldiers in the Philippines were tried for "looting, torture, and murder." Only seven of those tried were convicted, and none were imprisoned.

In the twentieth century, however, the concepts of a "just" way to fight a war and of fighting wars according to civilized principles were given several pushes. Those winning World War I (1914–1918) viewed the losers as immoral, and some suggested trying Kaiser Wilhelm II of Germany for war crimes. In 1925, the Geneva Convention on the treatment of prisoners of war was signed, which tried to make that element of warfare more humane.

After World War II (1939–1945), the United States participated in the Nuremberg and Tokyo Trials, where leaders of Germany and Japan were tried for their part in war crimes. The U.S. Army, though, stayed remarkably out of the limelight, both because it won the wars and winners are the ones who conduct the trials, and because the United States controlled access to what was printed about the war.

Significance

In the Vietnam War, however, the U.S. government could not control what the media presented to Americans on their living room television sets. This fact, combined with antiwar sentiment and the reporting of U.S. military-led massacres, called for punishment. The most well known massacre was that at My Lai, and Lieutenant William Calley was the one marked as being the most responsible.

Calley was convicted of murdering at least twenty-two civilians. He could, under army rules, have received the death penalty, but he was given life imprisonment instead. Calley was the only one convicted, as those below him were only following orders, and none above him, except for his captain, were tried. His captain was acquitted of the charges and other high-ranking officers, who tried to cover it up, were punished but not court-martialed.

Calley was unique in the Vietnam War era in that both pro- and antiwar advocates supported him. Those in favor of the war said that he was only doing his duty, while the antiwar protesters said that the war was to blame, not Calley. President Richard Nixon (served 1969–1974) ordered that Calley be moved from hard labor to house arrest, and Calley's sentence was reduced, first to twenty years and then to ten. Calley was finally paroled after serving less than four years.

Charges of "friendly fire" casualties, where the U.S. military accidentally kills allied soldiers, and of atrocities in the Persian Gulf War (1991) and other conflicts, reveal that many of the issues in Calley's case, including what standards of justice and conduct should be expected and applied in wartime, have not left us.

Primary Source

Lieutenant Calley: His Own Story [excerpt]

SYNOPSIS: John Sack opens with the testimony of a witness, who discusses the brutality of the attack and Calley's participation in the slaughter. Sack then relates how Calley invited witnesses over to his house, showing that he held no personal grudge. The book goes on to argue that the army needed to pin it on Calley in order to make the nation feel better, and Calley ends by stating that he believes the whole Vietnam War was wrong.

Meadlo was just bewildered about it. One hundred people. And fifteen clips. Or three hundred rounds. The next witness said it was twenty to thirty people and two ammunition clips.

"Your name."

"My name is Charles Sledge."

"And your address?"

"Sardis City." In Mississippi.

"And your occupation?"

"I work as a case sealer at Sardis Luggage Company."

"How old are you, Mr. Sledge?"

"I'm twenty-three years old."

"Are you married?"

"Yes sir."

"Would you raise your voice, please? Do you know the accused?"

"Yes."

"And would you point to him and repeat his name."

"Lieutenant William Calley."

"Did you know Lieutenant Calley in March, 1968?"

"Yes sir."

"How did you know Lieutenant Calley?"

"He was my platoon leader, and I was his RTO."

"For the record, what is an RTO?"

"A radio telephone operator."

Weber, the RTO and the GI closest to me, had been killed back in February, remember. In Mylai, Sledge had become the GI beside me. I knew, *He didn't dislike me. He wasn't emotional there. He wouldn't lie.* And yet, Sledge testified as Conti and Meadlo had. A third into Mylai, and thirty to forty people, and old men, women, and children, and I supposedly said to Meadlo, "Waste them." But for Sledge, I didn't fire at those people myself. I did at the irrigation ditch.

"And what did the people do?"

"They started falling. And screaming."

"How long did they fire?"

"Not very long."

"And then what?"

"A helicopter landed."

"And then what?"

"Lieutenant Calley went over. And started talking to the helicopter pilot."

"And then what?"

"Lieutenant Calley came back. And said something like, 'He don't like the way I'm running this show, but I'm the boss.'"

"How did he say it?"

"In anger."

"Then what did the helicopter do?"

"Took off."

"Then what did you do?"

"We started moving up the ditch, like. We came up onto a priest—"

"A what?"

"A priest."

"How did you know that he was a priest?"

"He was dressed like a priest. In white."

"What was he doing?"

"Just standing there."

"Where?"

"Up where the ditch made an L shape."

"What did you do?"

"Nothing, but Lieutenant Calley started interrogating. He started asking, '*Vietcong adai,*' but the priest would say, '*No bitt,*' and he would take—"

"Go ahead."

"And he would take his palms and would bow his head."

"Let the record reflect that the witness placed the palms of his hands together and he moved forward," the prosecutor said. "And so?"

"He was just saying, '*No bitt.*' And then, he hit him with the butt of his rifle."

"Where?"

"In the mouth."

"What did the priest do?"

"He sort of felled back, and he started doing this again. Sort of like pleading."

"How old was this individual?"

"He looked about forty or fifty."

"So then what?"

"Lieutenant Calley took his rifle and pulled the trigger."

"Where?"

"In the priest's face."

"What did the priest do?"

"He felled."

"And what happened to the priest's head?"

"It was blown off. It was blown away."

"What's the next thing you recall?"

"Someone hollered, 'There is a child!' You know, running back to the village. Lieutenant Calley ran back and he grabbed it."

"How far was this?"

"From where I was standing?"

"Yes."

"I guess twenty, maybe thirty, feet."

"What did you do?"

"Just stood there."

"Could you describe the child?"

"A little child. About one, maybe two, years old."

"How did he pick it up?"

"By the arms."

"And what did he do?"

"Swung it into the ditch."

"And what did he do?"

"Fired."

"And where did he fire?"

"Into the ditch."

"How many shots?"

"One."

"And how far away were you?"

"About twenty to thirty feet."

"I object," my attorney said. "We're getting repetitive testimony."

"Overruled."

And really, I seemed like a mad killer now. A monster: I loved killing men, women, children, babies, and Buddhist priests. Calley kills baby, I knew what those thirty reporters would say. All they wanted in Georgia were the bodies with the blood dripping off or the brains out of someone's head: the Monster stories. At times, I wanted to shake their hands and say, "I hope I'm not slimy today." Even *The New York Times:* the *Times* man didn't try to know me, didn't even talk to me. He just wrote, "As the details of the slaughter of Vietnamese were related, the Lieutenant broke into a grin that lasted for—" It sells papers, I suppose.

But Sledge. I just didn't understand it. He had nothing against me, Sledge: no reason to hurt me. It came out on cross-examination that he had been

An American soldier enters a grass hut with his weapon in hand, at My Lai, Vietnam. NATIONAL ARCHIVES AND RECORDS ADMINISTRATION.

imprisoned once: for a couple years as a Peeping Tom. I say that means nothing. A black man in Mississippi? Seen out in someone's alley? Hell, I say that's nothing but Sledge's race. I sat there, I listened, and I could only say, *He is wrong about me.* Or could it be, I was wrong instead? I just didn't know. . . .

I had asked most of the prosecution witnesses home. And they had come.

"All right."

"We better not go together, though. They," I said, and I meant the newspaper people, "will say, *It's conspiracy.*"

"All right."

We got together later. And talked together of GI friends: of old times together. My girl friend didn't understand it: Dursi and I coming home. She told me, "It seems incongruous. He crucifies you and you say, 'Come for a bourbon.'" She's right, I suppose, but I enjoyed it: a college reunion, sort of. Dursi had already told me, "No hard feelings," and I wanted to say something like it. But also, I wanted to see

what motivated him. To sit on the witness stand and to say those things.

"My attorney," I said. "I hope he wasn't too hard on you."

"No."

"That's his job. To try to demolish you."

"Yes." He sat there. He sipped from a very small shot of Jim Beam. "You know there's no hard feelings: I've nothing against you."

"I know."

"I had to say it. I got here, and I had to stick to that story—"

"I know."

"—so other people wouldn't be hurt."

"I respect you," I said. "I want to keep other people clean."

I understood it. Dursi wasn't the first one to say it, I knew. A sergeant told me, "I didn't want to testify against you. But others, I had to protect them." The others: I think that was Dursi's motive now. And Sledge's, and Meadlo's, and Conti's, and I think that was the Army's too. It had been headline news, the Mylai assault, and *Life* had those color photographs of it. A screaming woman. A crying child. A row of dead women, children, and babies halfway into Mylai. And the American government couldn't say, "Oh, that's how it is in Vietnam, everyone." It had to protect two million veterans and two hundred million citizens. It had to tell everyone, "A mad killer did it." . . .

Americans like to think that war is John Wayne. To get a grenade and a VC's throat, to shove the grenade right down it. Americans sit at television sets and say, "One hundred bodies. Boy!" And they think, *Great,* and they think that I'm the ugly one. I tell you, a hundred bodies still are a hundred people, and if they're dead their guts are just hanging out. And that's pretty horrible: I had once thought, *Oh, war is hell.* And then I saw war, and I could only sit and cry. And ask, *Why did I do it?* Why didn't I stand on a corner and say, "It's wrong." Why didn't I burn my draft card, and I wouldn't have had to go?

I didn't know. I was just an American who was put together with a philosophy: democracy's right. And there was no gray and white, no beige and white, no other colors: there was just black or white, and I was to kill someone if his philosophy's wrong. In school I had never thought about it, communism. I knew the Lord's Prayer, *Our father, etcetera,* and I knew, *Communism's bad.* I wasn't like the Miami girl who talked about it, Mary. Once, I was at a birthday party and I heard her say, "It's worth evaluating. The poverty there is ten percent less—" Or twenty percent less, I didn't listen. I thought, *I've better things to do.* Like dancing, drinking, and raising hell, and I asked another girl, "Let's dance." If communism wasn't bad, I didn't want to hear about it. Americans believe in ancestors too: if our mother, our father, and everyone say, "Niggers are bad," or "Communism's bad," we believe them. It's law. It's God. Or should be, except we were in Vietnam: in the midst of communism, and we saw nothing bad. And became afraid. And had to destroy it.

I'm different now. I said a long while ago, if Americans tell me, "Go massacre one thousand communists," I will massacre one thousand communists. No longer: today if Americans said, "Go to Mylai. Kill everyone there," I would refuse to. I'd really say, "It's illegal, and I can't be a part of it." Of course, to kill everyone in Mylai isn't the only illegal thing we do. To evacuate them is illegal too: is against the Geneva convention, I've learned. Is kidnapping them. To burn their houses is very illegal, and I don't know why the Judge didn't say, "A reasonable man would realize it: *One shouldn't burn a Vietnamese village.* It is against the Uniform Code of Military Justice, Article CIX." It doesn't carry death, but it does carry five years at Leavenworth. Hell, to just *be* in Mylai with an M-16 and some ammunition is illegal too. You may say, "It isn't a dumdum round." It tears like a dumdum, though. It takes out a VC's organs in a way that's against the Geneva convention. I now think, to go to Vietnam is illegal too.

To go to war anywhere. As for me, I went to Vietnam believing, *I will stop communism. And there will be no one ever to hurt us. And there will be No More War.* I think every man in Vietnam—in history thought, *I'll go and there will be No More War.* And thought this in World War II and World War I and Rome, I suppose.

Further Resources

BOOKS

Anderson, David L. *Facing My Lai: Moving Beyond the Massacre.* Lawrence: University Press of Kansas, 1998.

Angers, Trent. *The Forgotten Hero of My Lai: The Hugh Thompson Story.* Lafayette, La.: Acadian House, 1999.

Belknap, Michael R. *The Vietnam War on Trial: The My Lai Massacre and the Court-Martial of Lieutenant Calley.* Lawrence: University Press of Kansas, 2002.

Hersh, Seymour M. *My Lai 4: A Report on the Massacre and Its Aftermath.* New York: Random House, 1970.

Olson, James Stuart, and Randy Roberts. *My Lai: A Brief History with Documents.* Boston: Bedford, 1998.

Peers, William R., et al. *The My Lai Massacre and Its Cover-Up: Beyond the Reach of Law?—The Peers Commission Report.* New York: The Free Press, 1976.

WEBSITES

"Vietnam: A Television History." American Experience, Public Broadcasting Service. Available online at http://www.pbs.org/wgbh/amex/vietnam/intro.html; website home page: http://www.pbs.org/wgbh/amex/ (accessed April 16, 2003).

AUDIO AND VISUAL MEDIA

The Court-Martial of Lt. Calley. World Almanac Video, 2000, VHS.

"The Right to Be a Woman"

Journal article

By: Phyllis Schlafly

Date: November 1972

Source: Schlafly, Phyllis. "The Right to Be a Woman." *The Phyllis Schlafly Report* 6, no. 4, November 1972, 1, 3–4.

About the Author: Phyllis Schlafly (1924–) graduated from Harvard University with a master's in art in 1945 and from Washington University Law School in 1978. She is most known for her conservative opposition to the Equal Rights Amendment (ERA). She also has been a broadcaster for CBS and a television commentator, along with authoring over a dozen books. Self-described as a housewife and mother of six, she also ran for Congress three times and campaigned for Barry Goldwater and Joseph McCarthy. ■

Introduction

Discrimination on the basis of race, gender, and other factors has existed since the nation's founding. Considering the issue of gender, the few places that allowed women to vote in 1789 soon removed that right. In the nineteenth century, women, without being asked, were (theoretically) put on a pedestal and elevated to the "cult of domesticity," which said that women had a special role to run the home, to protect it, and to elevate the morals of the home and that women would be "contaminated" and destroyed if they operated outside the home.

In the early twentieth century, the barriers to women being involved outside the home began to be lowered. The Nineteenth Amendment (1920) provided that the right to vote would not be denied on the basis of sex. Women also served in the armed forces and worked in factories during World War I (1914–1918) and World War II (1939–1945).

The 1960s brought about the biggest changes on behalf of women's rights. Many of the crusaders for civil rights had been women, who applied the lessons learned in that struggle to the battle of equal rights for women. The 1964 Civil Rights Act outlawed discrimination on the basis of sex. As a result, law and medical schools, as well as most other educational institutions, became co-educational, accepting women on the same basis as men.

After these victories, women's rights advocates pushed for an equal rights amendment, which stated that equality could not be denied on the basis of sex. Some people opposed this legislation, saying that it would remove protective legislation that helped women, while supporters of the legislation stated that it was time for full equality to be reached. The ERA passed Congress in 1972 and went to the states, where it was opposed by a wide variety of groups and people, including Phyllis Schlafly.

Significance

In her 1972 article "The Right to Be a Woman," Schlafly was able to organize and articulate a wide variety of issues about the ERA. One concern she noted was that the ERA would destroy the institution of marriage. She also identified, by description, but not by name, gays and lesbians as being the main people behind the ERA. Her pamphlet seemingly asked if one wanted these groups to determine the future of America. Schlafly also argued that the ERA would lead to sexually integrated bathrooms and prison cells, even though such were not ever among the goals of any large segment of the equal rights movement.

Schlafly capably answered some of the arguments of the equal rights movement, suggesting that present laws cover some of the movement's concerns. In an interesting move, she argued that the equal rights movement would have enough power to ban marriage, but not enough to protect women who chose to be homemakers, thus many women would be forced to work against their will. Such arguments worked well enough, as only thirty-five states, three short of the needed thirty-eight, ever ratified the ERA.

After the defeat of the ERA, many equal rights advocates moved on to other causes, became less interested, or focused on state issues. One cause many focused their energy on was protecting a woman's right to choose, as *Roe v. Wade* (1973) came under increasing attack in the 1980s. The ERA, and ideas like it, also suffered in the 1980s and 1990s as an antigovernment backlash swept the nation. Even without the ERA, though, women continue to make strides, fight for equality, and control their own futures.

Primary Source

"The Right to Be a Woman" [excerpt]

SYNOPSIS: Schlafly's article argues that the ERA destroys a woman's right to be a woman and removes the requirement of men having to support their wives, if the wives choose not to take a job outside the home. She quotes Professor Paul A. Freund who stated that the ERA would end separate bathrooms, and notes that other professors were opposed. Schlafly agrees that women are exploited by men, but thinks that the ERA is not the answer.

Women's magazines, the women's pages of newspapers, and television and radio talk shows have been filled for months with a strident advocacy of the "rights" of women to be treated on an equal basis with men in all walks of life. But what about the rights of the woman who doesn't want to compete on an equal basis with men? Does she have the right to be treated as a woman—by her family, by society, and by the law? Surely the right to be a woman should be as sacred as the right to be treated like a man.

The laws of every one of our 50 states now guarantee the right to be a woman—protected and provided for in her career as a woman, wife and mother. The proposed Equal Rights Amendment will wipe out all our laws which—through rights, benefits and exemptions—guarantee this right to be a woman. ERA will replace these present laws with a doctrinaire equality under which women must be treated exactly the same as men. This Equal Rights Amendment has already been passed by the U.S. Congress and ratified by 21 states. If it is ratified by 38 states, it will become part of the United States Constitution. Is this what American women want? Is this what American men want?

The laws of every one of the 50 states now require the *husband* to support his wife and children—and to provide a home for them to live in. In other words, the law protects a woman's right to be a full-time wife and mother, her right *not* to take a job outside the home, her right to care for her own baby in her own home while being financially supported by her husband. The Equal Rights Amendment will remove this sole obligation from the husband, and make the wife *equally* responsible to provide a home for her family, and to provide 50 percent of the financial support of her family.

Some of the advocates of the Equal Rights Amendment have tried to deny that the Equal Rights Amendment will wipe out the husband's present obligation to support his wife and children and to provide them with a home. Therefore, it has become necessary to prove these truisms to the uneducated. When the courts adjudicate cases which will arise under the Equal Rights Amendment if it is passed, they will refer to standard law books and to the opinions of eminent constitutional lawyers. Let us look at what they say.

What Is The Present Law?

The most comprehensive modern text statement of American law is probably contained in the legal reference work entitled *American Jurisprudence, 2d.* Volume 41 of this authoritative series, under the heading "Husband and Wife," states clearly and emphatically: . . .

> Section 331: The husband's obligation of support requires him to provide his wife with a place of abode that will be deemed a suitable home when considered in the light of modern standards of civilization pertaining to the health, comfort, welfare, and normal living of persons, the particular estate, social rank, and condition of the husband and wife, and the means and earning power of the husband. . . . Assuming that the means and earning power of the husband permit, he must provide a home the control of which she [the wife] need not relinquish or share with others, but a home in which she is the mistress. . . .

> Section 332: The duty of a husband to support his wife and family, arising out of the marriage relationship, exists without reference to the wife's separate estate or independent means, and the husband has no right to resort to her separate estate or means, as a general rule, to support her or the family. A husband's duty to support his wife also exists without reference to what she can earn by her own labor, and he has no right to demand that she earn all that she can in order to contribute to her support. . . .

> Section 334: At common law, as between husband and wife, the duty of providing support for the household is on the husband. The wife is under no duty to support the husband and there is no ground on which he may require her to do so. The same view prevails generally in equity. Although the law does not prohibit a wife from using her separate means for the maintenance of the household, as a general rule the husband has no right to resort to her separate property in order to obtain support for her and their family. A wife is under no obligation to furnish her husband with a home, even if she has one and he does not . . .

Professor Freund then goes into detail in comparing the matter of sex discrimination with race discrimination. He shows that there is no logical or legal basis for the court deciding differently in the matter

Phyllis Schlafly speaks out against the Equal Rights Amendment, January 1977. Schlafly led a nationwide campaign to stop the amendment. **AP/WIDE WORLD PHOTOS. REPRODUCED BY PERMISSION.**

of sex from their decisions in the matter of race. Here are some of the examples he gives.

We find it repugnant to hold separate athletic competitions for whites and blacks. Are we now going to say that under ERA it is equally repugnant to hold separate athletic competitions for men and women?

Professor Freund also warns that "presumably the [ERA] Amendment would" reduce the present "higher Social Security retirement benefits for women." The present Social Security Act pays higher benefits to women because it "provides for the computation of a female wage earner's average monthly wage on the basis of three years less than that computation for a male. 42 U.S. Code 415(b)(3)(A) and (C). This eliminates years of lower earnings and increases the average monthly wage and the primary insurance amount for the female." Giving women "equal rights" under ERA means that they will lose the higher Social Security retirement benefits they now enjoy.

The courts have held that racial equality does not permit the individual to have the freedom of choice between all-white schools, all-black schools, and mixed schools. Are we now going to say that equality of the sexes does not permit us to have freedom of choice between boys' schools, girls' schools and coed schools?

Professor Freund points out that one of the prime targets of the equal-rights movement has been the color-segregated rest rooms. He indicates that we must assume that rest rooms segregated by sex would be prohibited by the courts just as the courts prohibit color-segregated rest rooms. In a very scholarly way, he demolishes the argument that we could maintain separate rest rooms on the principle of the "right of privacy."

He points out the effects the Equal Rights Amendment would have on separate physical education classes in public schools for girls and boys, and on separate prison cells for men and women, etc.

Professor Freund concludes that "the real issue is not the legal status of women. *The issue is the integrity and responsibility of the law-making process itself.*"

Professor Kurland's Statement

Another distinguished constitutional authority on the Equal Rights Amendment is Professor Philip B. Kurland of the University of Chicago Law School. He also wrote an article for the same issue of the *Harvard Civil Rights-Civil Liberties Law Review.*

In this article, Professor Kurland explains one of the most important aspects of the current ERA controversy. He showed that the Equal Rights Amendment originally had attached to it what was known as the "Hayden modification" (named after Senator Hayden) which stated:

> The provisions of this article shall not be construed to impair any rights, benefits or exemptions conferred by law upon persons of the female sex.

The women's libbers, however, successfully agitated until the Hayden modification was removed from the Equal Rights Amendment. It is *not* in the Equal Rights Amendment as passed by the Congress and, under our constitutional process, there is no way to put it back in.

This removal of the Hayden modification reveals the motivation of the proponents of the Equal Rights Amendment. It makes clear that they deliberately and purposefully want to eliminate the "rights, benefits and exemptions" conferred by law upon women. The removal of the Hayden modification shows that

the ERA was purposefully designed to wipe out the right to be a woman and replace it with the right to be treated like a man. As Professor Kurland stated forcefully:

> The refusal by some protagonists to accept the qualification was probably not, however, inadvertent; it was calculated. It represented a deliberate choice between two different objectives, either but not both of which the proposed Amendment might fully serve.

When the Equal Rights Amendment was being debated before the Illinois Legislature, on June 5, 1972 Professor Kurland sent a telegram reinforcing his position as expressed in his Law Review article. His telegram read: "Regret inability to appear before your Committee on so-called Equal Rights Amendment because I think that it is largely misrepresented as a women's rights amendment when in fact the primary beneficiary will be men. I am opposed to its approval."

Are Women Discriminated Against?

Are women discriminated against in employment? They certainly have been. When I started to work at the age of 18, I discovered within a few days that I was doing exactly the same work for $105 per month for which men were being paid $125 per month.

The reason the Equal Rights Amendment has gotten so far is that Americans have been led to believe that it means "equal pay for equal work." This is a good slogan, a desirable objective, and is supported by practically everyone. The trouble is that there is nothing the Equal Rights Amendment can "give" women which they do not already have, or have a way of getting.

"Equal pay for equal work" is guaranteed by the Civil Rights Act of 1964, Subchapter VI: Equal Employment Opportunities (42 U.S. Code 2000e-2) and by the Equal Employment Opportunity Act of 1972 (Public Law 92–261) which forbids discrimination in every aspect of employment, including hiring, pay and promotions. Even executive, professional and administrative positions are covered. (See *U.S. News & World Report,* August 14, 1972, page 69.) If any woman is discriminated against in employment, she can file a claim with the Equal Employment Opportunity Commission, and it will pay the costs of processing the claim and filing suit for back pay.

Complete protection against discrimination is provided by these two laws. There is absolutely nothing the Equal Rights Amendment can add in terms of fair employment practices for women.

Are Women Exploited by Men?

Are women exploited by men? Yes, some women are, and we should wipe out such exploitation. We should demand strong enforcement of the laws against procurers, the Mann Act, and the laws against statutory rape. These laws are some of the safeguards which are good and necessary to protect women, especially young girls, against exploitation by men. But these laws will be wiped out by the Equal Rights Amendment in the phony name of "equality."

The whole subject of pornography is an area of exploitation of women by men which should be eradicated from our society. When Marvin Miller paid $1,000 to a girl to pose for pictures for his obscene book called *Intercourse,* and then grossed $2,500,000 in sales in one year, he was certainly exploiting women in the basest way for his own financial gain. When the Earl Warren Supreme Court ruled in favor of the sadistic pornographers who produce the "bondage" books and magazines (materials which portray and describe the whipping, chaining and mistreatment of women in connection with sexual assault), it was opening the floodgates to a type of exploitation of women never before condoned in a civilized society.

Anyone who is truly interested in the liberation of women from male exploiters should go after the pornographers who have made fortunes out of the bodies of women. Pornography can be accurately defined as the degradation and exploitation of women.

Another group of men who exploit women is the Parisian male couturiers. For years, women's fashions have been practically dominated by unmarried men who do not understand or like women. Now that Coco Chanel has died and Schiaparelli has closed shop, women's clothes are completely dominated by these Parisian women-haters. Shortly before she died, Coco tried to alert women to the facts of life about women's clothes, saying: "High fashion is losing its influence because it is in the hands of men who do not like women and whose only aim is to make them look ridiculous." Others are less charitable in describing the morals and motives of the queer breed of men who dominate the designing of women's fashions.

So, there is plenty of work for those who want to eliminate the real exploitation of women, but they are 100 percent wrong when they blame husbands and the institution of marriage.

Who is Promoting ERA?

There are two very different types of women lobbying for the Equal Rights Amendment. One group is the women's liberationists. Their motive is totally radical. They hate men, marriage, and children. They are out to destroy morality and the family. They look upon husbands as the exploiters, children as an evil to be avoided (by abortion if necessary), and the family as an institution which keeps women in "second-class citizenship" or even "slavery."

Anyone who doubts the radical objectives and tactics of the women's liberationists should read their own literature, such as the magazine *Ms.* It is all rather plainly stated. A New York *Times* News Service article of September 26, 1972 frankly described the ultimate objectives of the women's liberation movement in these words:

> To give women full participation in society, they say, it is necessary to overthrow the structures on which the system is based. The first things to go would be the political institutions that perpetuate the system, such as institutional marriage, which they assert, enslaves women for economic reasons. . . . Probably the most important and most emotional issue that unites the reformers with the radicals is the proposed repeal of all abortion laws.

The most thorough analysis of the more than 400 books, hundreds of magazine articles and stacks of newsletters which make up the literature of the women's liberation movement was made by Midge Decter who is currently the literary editor of *World* Magazine, and formerly was executive editor of *Harper's* Magazine. In her recent book called *The New Chastity and Other Arguments Against Women's Liberation* she concludes that the women's lib literature is totally radical and nihilistic.

The women's liberationists have found some willing allies among certain male politicians who are quite cognizant of the radical changes they are promoting. For example, Senator Tunney put in the *Congressional Record* of September 7, 1972 a copy of his own speech in which he flatly rejects the role of the man as the protector of women. Urging that women be "subject to the draft on the same basis as men," he argued that "the fact that women have been excluded from the draft has contributed disproportionately to the perpetuation of the stereotype of the male as protector."

Stating his own position, Senator Tunney said: "As a male, I accept the responsibility of protecting those who need protection, but I shun any preconceived notion which would prevent women from sharing this responsibility."

This male rejection of marital responsibilities and chivalry toward women is, fortunately, not the view of the overwhelming majority of men and women. Women want and need protection. Any male who is a man—or a gentleman—will accept the responsibility of protecting women.

There is another type of woman supporting the Equal Rights Amendment from the most sincere motives. It is easy to see why the business and professional women are supporting the Equal Rights Amendment—many of them have felt the keen edge of discrimination in their employment. Many have been in a situation where the woman does most of the work, and some man gets the bigger salary and the credit.

To these business and professional women, we say:

1. We support you in your efforts to eliminate all injustices, and we believe this can be done through the Civil Rights Act and the Equal Employment Opportunity Act.

2. If the Hayden modification had remained in the Equal Rights Amendment, we would have supported it.

3. Without the Hayden modification, the Equal Rights Amendment won't give you anything—but it will *take away* fundamental rights and benefits from the rest of women. You have every right to lobby for the extension of *your* rights—but not at the expense of the rights of *other* women.

Please urge your State Legislators to vote NO on the Equal Rights Amendment. It will take away from young girls their exemption from the draft and their legal protection against predatory males. It will take away from wives and mothers their right to be provided with a home and financial support by their husbands. It will take away from senior women their extra social security benefits. It will take away a woman's present *freedom of choice* to take a job—or to be a full-time wife and mother. In short, it will take away the right to be a woman.

Further Resources

BOOKS

Boles, Janet K. *The Politics of the Equal Rights Amendment: Conflict and the Decision Process.* New York: Longman, 1979.

Evans, Sara M. *Tidal Wave: The Story of the Modern Women's Movement and How It Continues to Change America.* New York: The Free Press, 2003.

Feinberg, Renee. *The Equal Rights Amendment: An Annotated Bibliography of the Issues, 1976–1985.* London: Greenwood, 1987.

Hoff, Joan. *Rights of Passage: The Past and Future of the ERA.* Bloomington: Indiana University Press, 1986.

Mansbridge, Jane J. *Why We Lost the ERA.* Chicago: University of Chicago Press, 1986.

Schlafly, Phyllis. *Feminist Fantasies.* Dallas: Spence, 2003.

Steiner, Gilbert Yale. *Constitutional Inequality: The Political Fortunes of the Equal Rights Amendment.* Washington, D.C.: Brookings Institution, 1985.

WEBSITES

"Chronology of the Equal Rights Amendment, 1923–1996." National Organization of Women. Available online at http://www.now.org/issues/economic/cea/history.html; website home page: http://www.now.org (accessed April 16, 2003).

"Equal Rights Amendment." Missouri Right to Life. Available online at http://www.missourilife.org/legislation/era.htm; website home page: http://www.missourilife.org (accessed April 16, 2003).

Frontiero v. Richardson

Supreme Court decision

By: William Brennan Jr. and Lewis Powell

Date: May 14, 1973

Source: Brennan Jr., William and Lewis Powell. *Frontiero v. Richardson.* 411 U.S. 677 (1973). Available online at http://laws.findlaw.com/us/411/677.html; website home page: http://www.findlaw.com (accessed April 16, 2003).

About the Authors: William Brennan Jr. (1906–1997), the son of Irish immigrants, went to the University of Pennsylvania for his undergraduate degree and Harvard University for his law degree. In 1957, Brennan was appointed to the U.S. Supreme Court.

Lewis Powell (1907–1998) graduated from Harvard Law School. He was president of the American Bar Association in 1964, and championed legal services for the poor. He was nominated to the Supreme Court in 1971 and served until 1987. ∎

Introduction

Discrimination on the basis of sex has long been a part of American history. Women were allowed to vote in a few places, but soon after the nation's founding, most states removed that right from women. In the nineteenth century, women were expected to protect the home and to elevate the morals of the home.

However, in the early part of the twentieth century the barriers to women being involved outside the home began to be lowered. In 1920, the Nineteenth Amendment provided that the right to vote would not be denied on the basis of sex. And even though women served in the armed forces and auxiliary units in World War I (1914–1918) and World War II (1939–1945), they were generally not accepted as full military members in those conflicts.

The 1960s brought about many changes in women's rights. Many of the crusaders for civil rights applied the lessons that they had learned in that struggle to battle for equal rights for women. The Civil Rights Act (1964) outlawed discrimination on the basis of sex, and several educational institutions, such as law and medical schools, became coeducational. Many institutions still had discriminatory policies, including the armed forces, which automatically denied male spouses of female members of the armed services dependent benefits, unless they could prove they were dependent on their spouse for over half their support, while automatically granting female spouses benefits. After being denied benefits for her spouse, Sharron Frontiero, a female U.S. Air Force lieutenant, sued.

Significance

Frontiero won her case, since the only justification the armed forces had was that this classification was an administrative convenience. In the armed forces' way of thinking, most women would be dependent on their male spouses, unlike most men, which meant that this classification was the easiest way to do it.

The Court held that convenience was no excuse for discrimination. However, the Court split on the reasoning. Four of the members held that sex-based classifications should be viewed as "inherently suspect," similar to race-based classifications, and could only be justified by a compelling state interest that cannot be achieved any other way. One member held that the classification was discriminatory, and three others held that the classification was discriminatory but that sex-based classifications should not be "inherently suspect." The ninth member of the court, Justice William Rehnquist, upheld the classification.

Since *Frontiero,* sex-based classifications have sometimes been upheld and have been generally subjected to an intermediate level of review, where the government must prove that the classification used is substantially related to a governmental interest. In the military, women are now allowed to go to all of the service academies and to hold most jobs, except for those that are directly involved in combat. Sex still plays a role in the military though, as homosexuals are technically banned from participation and are sometimes discharged from the military. The level of witch-hunting for gays and lesbians, particularly since President Bill Clinton's (served 1992–2000) "don't ask, don't tell" policy, varies with whom one speaks.

In the civilian world, the Equal Rights Amendment (ERA) pushed by women in the 1960s and 1970s failed, but most colleges, including previously all-male schools such as the Virginia Military Institute, now admit women. Some progress has been made, but full equality still has not been reached.

Primary Source

Frontiero v. Richardson [excerpt]

SYNOPSIS: Justice William Brennan Jr. first notes the nature of the disagreement and the basis on which benefits were awarded. He then details the history of sex discrimination, arguing that it still exists, and concludes that sex-based classifications are inherently suspect. Justice Lewis Powell, although agreeing that the classification is unconstitutional, holds that sex-based classifications are not inherently suspect. Powell comments that the ERA may soon make the question moot.

Mr. Justice Brennan announced the judgment of the Court and an opinion in which Mr. Justice Douglas, Mr. Justice White, and Mr. Justice Marshall join.

The question before us concerns the right of a female member of the uniformed services to claim her spouse as a "dependent" for the purposes of obtaining increased quarters allowances and medical and dental benefits . . . on an equal footing with male members. Under these statutes, a serviceman may claim his wife as a "dependent" without regard to whether she is in fact dependent upon him for any part of her support. . . . A servicewoman, on the other hand, may not claim her husband as a "dependent" under these programs unless he is in fact dependent upon her for over one-half of his support. . . . Thus, the question for decision is whether this difference in treatment constitutes an unconstitutional discrimination against servicewomen in violation of the Due Process Clause of the Fifth Amendment. . . .

In an effort to attract career personnel through reenlistment, Congress established . . . a scheme for the provision of fringe benefits to members of the uniformed services on a competitive basis with business and industry. Thus . . . a member of the uniformed services with dependents is entitled to an

Air Force lieutenant Sharron Frontiero sits with her husband, whom she claimed as a dependent under U.S. statutes only to have the military deny her application. © BETTMANN/CORBIS. REPRODUCED BY PERMISSION.

increased "basic allowance for quarters" and . . . a member's dependents are provided comprehensive medical and dental care.

Appellant Sharron Frontiero, a lieutenant in the United States Air Force, sought increased quarters allowances, and housing and medical benefits for her husband, appellant Joseph Frontiero, on the ground that he was her "dependent." Although such benefits would automatically have been granted with respect to the wife of a male member of the uniformed services, appellant's application was denied because she failed to demonstrate that her husband was dependent on her for more than one-half of his support. Appellants then commenced this suit, contending that, by making this distinction, the statutes unreasonably discriminate on the basis of sex in violation of the Due Process Clause of the Fifth Amendment. In essence, appellants asserted that the discriminatory impact of the statutes is twofold: first, as a procedural matter, a female member is required to demonstrate her spouse's dependency, while no such burden is imposed upon male members; and, second, as a substantive matter, a male

member who does not provide more than one-half of his wife's support receives benefits, while a similarly situated female member is denied such benefits. Appellants therefore sought a permanent injunction against the continued enforcement of these statutes and an order directing the appellees to provide Lieutenant Frontiero with the same housing and medical benefits that a similarly situated male member would receive. . . .

At the outset, appellants contend that classifications based upon sex, like classifications based upon race, alienage, and national origin, are inherently suspect and must therefore be subjected to close judicial scrutiny. . . .

There can be no doubt that our Nation has had a long and unfortunate history of sex discrimination. Traditionally, such discrimination was rationalized by an attitude of "romantic paternalism" which, in practical effect, put women, not on a pedestal, but in a cage. . . .

As a result of notions such as these, our statute books gradually became laden with gross, stereotyped distinctions between the sexes and, indeed, throughout much of the 19th century the position of women in our society was, in many respects, comparable to that of blacks under the pre–Civil War slave codes. Neither slaves nor women could hold office, serve on juries, or bring suit in their own names, and married women traditionally were denied the legal capacity to hold or convey property or to serve as legal guardians of their own children. . . . And although blacks were guaranteed the right to vote in 1870, women were denied even that right—which is itself "preservative of other basic civil and political rights"—until adoption of the Nineteenth Amendment half a century later.

It is true, of course, that the position of women in America has improved markedly in recent decades. Nevertheless, it can hardly be doubted that, in part because of the high visibility of the sex characteristic, women still face pervasive, although at times more subtle, discrimination in our educational institutions, in the job market and, perhaps most conspicuously, in the political arena. . . .

Moreover, since sex, like race and national origin, is an immutable characteristic determined solely by the accident of birth, . . . statutory distinctions between the sexes often have the effect of invidiously relegating the entire class of females to inferior legal status without regard to the actual capabilities of its individual members.

We might also note that, over the past decade, Congress has itself manifested an increasing sensitivity to sex-based classifications. . . .

With these considerations in mind, we can only conclude that classifications based upon sex, like classifications based upon race, alienage, or national origin, are inherently suspect, and must therefore be subjected to strict judicial scrutiny. Applying the analysis mandated by that stricter standard of review, it is clear that the statutory scheme now before us is constitutionally invalid.

The sole basis of the classification established in the challenged statutes is the sex of the individuals involved. . . .

Moreover, the Government concedes that the differential treatment accorded men and women under these statutes serves no purpose other than mere "administrative convenience." In essence, the Government maintains that, as an empirical matter, wives in our society frequently are dependent upon their husbands, while husbands rarely are dependent upon their wives. Thus, the Government argues that Congress might reasonably have concluded that it would be both cheaper and easier simply conclusively to presume that wives of male members are financially dependent upon their husbands, while burdening female members with the task of establishing dependency in fact.

The Government offers no concrete evidence, however, tending to support its view that such differential treatment in fact saves the Government any money. In order to satisfy the demands of strict judicial scrutiny, the Government must demonstrate, for example, that it is actually cheaper to grant increased benefits with respect to all male members, than it is to determine which male members are in fact entitled to such benefits and to grant increased benefits only to those members whose wives actually meet the dependency requirement. Here, however, there is substantial evidence that, if put to the test, many of the wives of male members would fail to qualify for benefits. And in light of the fact that the dependency determination with respect to the husbands of female members is presently made solely on the basis of affidavits, rather than through the more costly hearing process, the Government's explanation of the statutory scheme is, to say the least, questionable.

In any case, our prior decisions make clear that, although efficacious administration of governmental programs is not without some importance, "the Con-stitution recognizes higher values than speed and efficiency." . . . And when we enter the realm of "strict judicial scrutiny," there can be no doubt that "administrative convenience" is not a shibboleth, the mere recitation of which dictates constitutionality. . . . On the contrary, any statutory scheme which draws a sharp line between the sexes, solely for the purpose of achieving administrative convenience, necessarily commands "dissimilar treatment for men and women who are . . . similarly situated," and therefore involves the "very kind of arbitrary legislative choice forbidden by the [Constitution]. . . ." . . . We therefore conclude that, by according differential treatment to male and female members of the uniformed services for the sole purpose of achieving administrative convenience, the challenged statutes violate the Due Process Clause of the Fifth Amendment insofar as they require a female member to prove the dependency of her husband.

Reversed. . . .

Mr. Justice Powell, with whom The Chief Justice and Mr. Justice Blackmun join, concurring in the judgment.

I agree that the challenged statutes constitute an unconstitutional discrimination against servicewomen in violation of the Due Process Clause of the Fifth Amendment, but I cannot join the opinion of Mr. Justice Brennan, which would hold that all classifications based upon sex, "like classifications based upon race, alienage, and national origin," are "inherently suspect and must therefore be subjected to close judicial scrutiny." . . . It is unnecessary for the Court in this case to characterize sex as a suspect classification, with all of the far-reaching implications of such a holding. *Reed v. Reed* . . . which abundantly supports our decision today, did not add sex to the narrowly limited group of classifications which are inherently suspect. In my view, we can and should decide this case on the authority of Reed and reserve for the future any expansion of its rationale.

There is another, and I find compelling, reason for deferring a general categorizing of sex classifications as invoking the strictest test of judicial scrutiny. The Equal Rights Amendment, which if adopted will resolve the substance of this precise question, has been approved by the Congress and submitted for ratification by the States. If this Amendment is duly adopted, it will represent the will of the people accomplished in the manner prescribed by the Constitution. By acting prematurely and unnecessarily, as I view it, the Court has assumed a decisional responsibility at the very time when state legislatures, functioning within the traditional democratic process, are debating the proposed Amendment. It seems to me that this reaching out to pre-empt by judicial action a major political decision which is currently in process of resolution does not reflect appropriate respect for duly prescribed legislative processes.

There are times when this Court, under our system, cannot avoid a constitutional decision on issues which normally should be resolved by the elected representatives of the people. But democratic institutions are weakened, and confidence in the restraint of the Court is impaired, when we appear unnecessarily to decide sensitive issues of broad social and political importance at the very time they are under consideration within the prescribed constitutional processes.

Further Resources

BOOKS

Evans, Sara M. *Tidal Wave: The Story of the Modern Women's Movement and How It Continues to Change America.* New York: The Free Press, 2003.

Feinberg, Joel, and Hyman Gross. *Justice: Selected Readings.* Encino, Calif.: Dickenson, 1977.

Francke, Linda Bird. *Ground Zero: The Gender Wars in the Military.* New York: Simon and Schuster, 1997.

Irons, Peter H. *Brennan vs. Rehnquist: The Battle for the Constitution.* New York: Knopf, 1994.

Jeffries, John Calvin. *Justice Lewis F. Powell, Jr.* New York: Scribner's, 1994.

McMillian, Willie. *Women in the Military: Sexual Harassment.* Carlisle Barracks, Penn.: U.S. Army War College, 1993.

Rosenkranz, E. Joshua, and Bernard Schwartz. *Reason and Passion: Justice Brennan's Enduring Influence.* New York: Norton, 1997.

WEBSITES

"Frontiero v. Richardson." Your Constitutional Rights, ACLU Montana. Available online at http://www.aclumontana.org/rights/frontiero.html; website home page: http://www.aclumontana.org/rights/ (accessed April 16, 2003).

U.S. v. Nixon

Supreme Court decision

By: Warren Burger

Date: July 24, 1974

Source: Burger, Warren. *United States v. Nixon.* 418 U.S. 683 (1974). Available online at http://laws.findlaw.com/us/418/683.html; website home page: http://www.findlaw.com (accessed April 16, 2003).

About the Author: Warren Burger (1907–1995) graduated from St. Paul College of Law. After having a private practice for over twenty years and serving as a U.S. assistant attorney general and then a judge in the U.S. Court of Appeals, he was appointed chief justice in 1969. Burger's judicial record reflected his belief in "strict constructionism," where the Constitution was construed narrowly, and that society's rights should outweigh the rights of the accused. ■

Introduction

One item about the British governmental system that irked the colonists before the American Revolution (1775–1783) was the supposedly unchecked power of the British monarch. To prevent a repeat of this, but to give a central figure enough power to govern, the United States created the U.S. Constitution. This system had a bailiwick of separation of powers and checks and balances, with three, supposedly equal branches of government: judicial, legislative, and executive.

In the twentieth century, however, the executive branch had been growing in power, especially with the creation of agencies to fight the Cold War, such as the Central Intelligence Agency (CIA). At the same time, the United States' involvement in the Vietnam War (1964–1975), along with a large number of American servicemen killed there, led to severe criticism of Presidents Lyndon Johnson (served 1963–1969) and Richard Nixon (served 1969–1974).

Nixon did not like criticism, so he created a secret team, drawing on people who had experience with the CIA and similar agencies, to stop leaks and eliminate criticism. He called this team his "plumbers" and funded it with assets diverted from his reelection campaign. The plumbers hired people to break into Democratic National Headquarters in the Watergate building, people who were caught and arrested. In spite of the Watergate incident, Nixon still managed to win the 1972 election.

For quite some time, the congressional committee that had been established to investigate the Watergate incident failed to make much progress. But then, at one point the committee asked a White House aide about the existence of a taping system, and this line of inquiry revealed that Nixon taped almost everything that went on in the Oval Office. A special prosecutor who was appointed to investigate the whole matter asked for the tapes; Nixon refused. Eventually, the matter of whether or not Nixon had to hand over the tapes came before the Supreme Court.

Significance

The Supreme Court unanimously held that Nixon had to hand over the tapes. The separation of powers had been upheld, at least in theory, as no branch of government was supposed to be above any other. The question then became whether or not Nixon would obey the Court's ruling.

Nixon finally did hand them over, even though there was a gap of eighteen and a half minutes on one of the tapes. Then, on August 9, 1974, four days after surrendering the tapes, he resigned from his office. Gerald Ford (served 1974–1977) became president and pardoned Nixon, so that, to paraphrase Ford, "the long national nightmare" would be over.

Even though the nation as a whole eventually recovered from this scandal, few have trusted the post-Watergate presidents as much as they trusted pre-Watergate presidents. Some argue that the system worked to check Nixon's abuse of power, but the nation paid a heavy price to be sure that the system worked. Others argue that previous presidents had done things just as scandalous as Nixon, but managed not to get caught. Regardless, the record indicates that Nixon's abuse and pursuit of his enemies outshadows any before him. While *U.S. v. Nixon*, and its result, is a victory for "law and order," the circumstances that brought it about are a dark shadow on that span of American history.

Primary Source

U.S. v. Nixon [excerpt]

SYNOPSIS: Chief Justice Warren Burger comments that the Court does have jurisdiction over the case and that there is a judicial issue to be adjudicated. He then notes that there is no absolute right to executive privilege and that while executive authority is given deference, it cannot be used to avoid the law. He closes his decision by indicating that the review of the material by the district court judge should prevent any improper materials from being released.

Mr. Chief Justice Burger delivered the opinion of the Court. . . .

In the District Court, the President's counsel argued that the court lacked jurisdiction to issue the subpoena because the matter was an intra-branch dispute between a subordinate and superior officer of the Executive Branch and hence not subject to judicial resolution. That argument has been renewed in this Court with emphasis on the contention that the dispute does not present a "case" or "controversy" which can be adjudicated in the federal courts. . . . The Special Prosecutor's demand for the items therefore presents, in the view of the President's counsel, a political question under *Baker v. Carr* . . . since it involves a "textually demonstrable" grant of power under Art. II.

Special Watergate Prosecutor Leon Jaworski speaks to reporters on May 16, 1974. AP/WIDE WORLD PHOTOS. REPRODUCED BY PERMISSION.

The mere assertion of a claim of an "intra-branch dispute," without more, has never operated to defeat federal jurisdiction; justiciability does not depend on such a surface inquiry. . . .

Our starting point is the nature of the proceeding for which the evidence is sought—here a pending criminal prosecution. It is a judicial proceeding in a federal court alleging violation of federal laws and is brought in the name of the United States as sovereign. . . . Under the authority of Art. II, 2, Congress has vested in the Attorney General the power to conduct the criminal litigation of the United States Government. . . . It has also vested in him the power to appoint subordinate officers to assist him in the discharge of his duties. . . . Acting pursuant to those statutes, the Attorney General has delegated the authority to represent the United States in these particular matters to a Special Prosecutor with unique authority and tenure. The regulation gives the Special Prosecutor explicit power to contest the invocation of executive privilege in the process of seeking evidence deemed relevant to the performance of these specially delegated duties. . . .

In light of the uniqueness of the setting in which the conflict arises, the fact that both parties are officers of the Executive Branch cannot be viewed as a barrier to justiciability. It would be inconsistent with the applicable law and regulation, and the unique facts of this case to conclude other than that the Special Prosecutor has standing to bring this action and that a justiciable controversy is presented for decision. . . .

Having determined that the requirements of Rule 17 (c) were satisfied, we turn to the claim that the subpoena should be quashed because it demands "confidential conversations between a President and his close advisors that it would be inconsistent with the public interest to produce." . . . The first contention is a broad claim that the separation of powers doctrine precludes judicial review of a President's claim of privilege. The second contention is that if he does not prevail on the claim of absolute privilege, the court should hold as a matter of constitutional law that the privilege prevails over the subpoena duces tecum.

In the performance of assigned constitutional duties each branch of the Government must initially interpret the Constitution, and the interpretation of its powers by any branch is due great respect from the others. The President's counsel, as we have noted, reads the Constitution as providing an absolute privilege of confidentiality for all Presidential communications. Many decisions of this Court, however, have unequivocally reaffirmed the holding of *Marbury v. Madison,* . . . that "[i]t is emphatically the province and duty of the judicial department to say what the law is." . . .

No holding of the Court has defined the scope of judicial power specifically relating to the enforcement of a subpoena for confidential Presidential communications for use in a criminal prosecution, but other exercises of power by the Executive Branch and the Legislative Branch have been found invalid as in conflict with the Constitution. . . . Since this Court has consistently exercised the power to construe and delineate claims arising under express powers, it must follow that the Court has authority to interpret claims with respect to powers alleged to derive from enumerated powers. . . .

. . . We therefore reaffirm that it is the province and duty of this Court "to say what the law is" with respect to the claim of privilege presented in this case. . . .

In support of his claim of absolute privilege, the President's counsel urges two grounds, one of which is common to all governments and one of which is peculiar to our system of separation of powers. The first ground is the valid need for protection of communications between high Government officials and those who advise and assist them in the performance of their manifold duties; the importance of this confidentiality is too plain to require further discussion. Human experience teaches that those who expect public dissemination of their remarks may well temper candor with a concern for appearances and for their own interests to the detriment of the decisionmaking process. Whatever the nature of the privilege of confidentiality of Presidential communications in the exercise of Art. II powers, the privilege can be said to derive from the supremacy of each branch within its own assigned area of constitutional duties. Certain powers and privileges flow from the nature of enumerated powers; the protection of the confidentiality of Presidential communications has similar constitutional underpinnings.

The second ground asserted by the President's counsel in support of the claim of absolute privilege rests on the doctrine of separation of powers. Here it is argued that the independence of the Executive Branch within its own sphere, . . . insulates a President from a judicial subpoena in an ongoing criminal prosecution, and thereby protects confidential Presidential communications.

However, neither the doctrine of separation of powers, nor the need for confidentiality of high-level communications, without more, can sustain an absolute, unqualified Presidential privilege of immunity from judicial process under all circumstances. The President's need for complete candor and objectivity from advisers calls for great deference from the courts. However, when the privilege depends solely on the broad, undifferentiated claim of public interest in the confidentiality of such conversations, a confrontation with other values arises. Absent a claim of need to protect military, diplomatic, or sensitive national security secrets, we find it difficult to accept the argument that even the very important interest in confidentiality of Presidential communications is significantly diminished by production of such material for in camera inspection with all the protection that a district court will be obliged to provide.

The impediment that an absolute, unqualified privilege would place in the way of the primary constitutional duty of the Judicial Branch to do justice

President Nixon, having resigned from office, waves the victory sign as he leaves the White House for the final time. U.S. V. NIXON (EX-PRESIDENT), PHOTOGRAPH.

in criminal prosecutions would plainly conflict with the function of the courts under Art. III. In designing the structure of our Government and dividing and al-

locating the sovereign power among three co-equal branches, the Framers of the Constitution sought to provide a comprehensive system, but the separate powers were not intended to operate with absolute independence. . . .

To read the Art. II powers of the President as providing an absolute privilege as against a subpoena essential to enforcement of criminal statutes on no more than a generalized claim of the public interest in confidentiality of nonmilitary and nondiplomatic discussions would upset the constitutional balance of "a workable government" and gravely impair the role of the courts under Art. III.

. . . Since we conclude that the legitimate needs of the judicial process may outweigh Presidential privilege, it is necessary to resolve those competing interests in a manner that preserves the essential functions of each branch. The right and indeed the duty to resolve that question does not free the Judiciary from according high respect to the representations made on behalf of the President. . . .

The expectation of a President to the confidentiality of his conversations and correspondence, like the claim of confidentiality of judicial deliberations, for example, has all the values to which we accord deference for the privacy of all citizens and, added to those values, is the necessity for protection of the public interest in candid, objective, and even blunt or harsh opinions in Presidential decision-making. A President and those who assist him must be free to explore alternatives in the process of shaping policies and making decisions and to do so in a way many would be unwilling to express except privately. These are the considerations justifying a presumptive privilege for Presidential communications. The privilege is fundamental to the operation of Government and inextricably rooted in the separation of powers under the Constitution. . . .

But this presumptive privilege must be considered in light of our historic commitment to the rule of law. This is nowhere more profoundly manifest than in our view that "the twofold aim [of criminal justice] is that guilt shall not escape or innocence suffer." . . . We have elected to employ an adversary system of criminal justice in which the parties contest all issues before a court of law. The need to develop all relevant facts in the adversary system is both fundamental and comprehensive. The ends of criminal justice would be defeated if judgments were to be founded on a partial or speculative presentation of the facts. The very integrity of the judicial system and public confidence in the system depend on full disclosure of all the facts, within the framework of the rules of evidence. To ensure that justice is done, it is imperative to the function of courts that compulsory process be available for the production of evidence needed either by the prosecution or by the defense. . . .

In this case the President challenges a subpoena served on him as a third party requiring the production of materials for use in a criminal prosecution; he does so on the claim that he has a privilege against disclosure of confidential communications. He does not place his claim of privilege on the ground they are military or diplomatic secrets. As to these areas of Art. II duties the courts have traditionally shown the utmost deference to Presidential responsibilities. . . .

No case of the Court, however, has extended this high degree of deference to a President's generalized interest in confidentiality. Nowhere in the Constitution, as we have noted earlier, is there any explicit reference to a privilege of confidentiality, yet to the extent this interest relates to the effective discharge of a President's powers, it is constitutionally based.

The right to the production of all evidence at a criminal trial similarly has constitutional dimensions. The Sixth Amendment explicitly confers upon every defendant in a criminal trial the right "to be confronted with the witnesses against him" and "to have compulsory process for obtaining witnesses in his favor." Moreover, the Fifth Amendment also guarantees that no person shall be deprived of liberty without due process of law. It is the manifest duty of the courts to vindicate those guarantees, and to accomplish that it is essential that all relevant and admissible evidence be produced.

In this case we must weigh the importance of the general privilege of confidentiality of Presidential communications in performance of the President's responsibilities against the inroads of such a privilege on the fair administration of criminal justice. The interest in preserving confidentiality is weighty indeed and entitled to great respect. However, we cannot conclude that advisers will be moved to temper the candor of their remarks by the infrequent occasions of disclosure because of the possibility that such conversations will be called for in the context of a criminal prosecution.

On the other hand, the allowance of the privilege to withhold evidence that is demonstrably relevant in a criminal trial would cut deeply into the guarantee of due process of law and gravely impair the basic function of the courts. A President's acknowledged need for confidentiality in the communications of his office is general in nature, whereas the constitutional need for production of relevant evidence in a criminal proceeding is specific and central to the fair adjudication of a particular criminal case in the administration of justice. Without access to specific facts a criminal prosecution may be totally frustrated. The President's broad interest in confidentiality of communications will not be vitiated by disclosure of a limited number of conversations preliminarily shown to have some bearing on the pending criminal cases.

We conclude that when the ground for asserting privilege as to subpoenaed materials sought for use in a criminal trial is based only on the generalized interest in confidentiality, it cannot prevail over the fundamental demands of due process of law in the fair administration of criminal justice. The generalized assertion of privilege must yield to the demonstrated, specific need for evidence in a pending criminal trial.

. . . It is elementary that in camera inspection of evidence is always a procedure calling for scrupulous protection against any release or publication of material not found by the court, at that stage, probably admissible in evidence and relevant to the issues of the trial for which it is sought. That being true of an ordinary situation, it is obvious that the District Court has a very heavy responsibility to see to it that Presidential conversations, which are either not relevant or not admissible, are accorded that high degree of respect due the President of the United States. . . .

Marshall's statement cannot be read to mean in any sense that a President is above the law, but relates to the singularly unique role under Art. II of a President's communications and activities, related to the performance of duties under that Article. Moreover, a President's communications and activities encompass a vastly wider range of sensitive material than would be true of any "ordinary individual." It is therefore necessary in the public interest to afford Presidential confidentiality the greatest protection consistent with the fair administration of justice. The need for confidentiality even as to idle conversations with associates in which casual reference might be made concerning political leaders within the country or foreign statesmen is too obvious to call for further treatment. We have no doubt that the District Judge will at all times accord to Presidential records that high degree of deference suggested in United States v. Burr . . . and will discharge his responsibility to see to it that until released to the

Special Prosecutor no in camera material is revealed to anyone. This burden applies with even greater force to excised material; once the decision is made to excise, the material is restored to its privileged status and should be returned under seal to its lawful custodian.

Further Resources

BOOKS

Bernstein, Carl, and Bob Woodward. *All the President's Men.* New York: Simon and Schuster, 1974.

Crowley, Monica. *Nixon in Winter: The Final Revelations.* London: Tauris, 1998.

Dudley, William. *Watergate.* San Diego: Greenhaven, 2002.

Jaworski, Leon. *The Right and the Power: The Prosecution of Watergate.* New York: Reader's Digest, 1976.

Kutler, Stanley I. *The Wars of Watergate: The Last Crisis of Richard Nixon.* New York: Knopf, 1990.

Maltz, Earl M. *The Chief Justiceship of Warren Burger, 1969–1986.* Columbia: University of South Carolina Press, 2000.

Schwartz, Bernard. *The Ascent of Pragmatism: The Burger Court in Action.* Reading, Mass.: Addison-Wesley, 1990.

PERIODICALS

Hager, L. Michael. "The Constitution, the Court, and the Coverup: Reflections on *United States v. Nixon.*" *Oklahoma Law Review* 29, no. 3, Summer 1976, 591–606.

WEBSITES

"Revisiting Watergate." Washingtonpost.com. Available online at http://www.washingtonpost.com/wp-srv/national/longterm /watergate/front.htm; website home page: http://www.wash ingtonpost.com (accessed April 16, 2003).

Buckley v. Valeo

Supreme Court decision

By: U.S. Supreme Court

Date: January 30, 1976

Source: U.S. Supreme Court. *Buckley v. Valeo.* 424 U.S. 1 (1976). Available online at http://laws.findlaw.com/us/424/1 .html; website home page: http://www.findlaw.com (accessed April 16, 2003).

About the Organization: The Burger Court was created largely by President Richard Nixon's (served 1969–1974) nominations, because he desired to severely limit the Warren Court's rulings. Nixon appointed Warren Burger to lead the Court in 1969 and appointed three more justices, but only William Rehnquist was predictably conservative. Nixon's other appointments, Harry Blackmun and Lewis Powell, were often more liberal than Nixon liked. The Burger Court did limit the Warren Court somewhat, but it was the Rehnquist Court that created a counterrevolution. ■

Introduction

Politics was originally thought of as a way for the best of society to serve the rest of society. Parties were not necessary, as the best people would stand for office, serve for a time, and then return to being average citizens. The rise of political parties changed this ideal, but the idea of the interest of the common man returned theoretically in the 1820s with Jacksonian reforms that greatly increased the electorate. With the rise of big business though in the late 1800s, politics seemed again to be the province of the rich, with politicians allegedly at the beck and call of companies. Companies worked to control local legislators by employing them, such as company attorneys, by giving them free things, like a train ticket if a railroad company was soliciting favors, and so on.

Populists complained about the lack of democracy, but little changed. Progressives, although arising from quite different groups than the populists, had many of the same concerns and pushed for democratic reforms. Many states passed referendums, initiatives, and recall laws, and the Seventeenth Amendment (1913) allowed for the direct election of senators. All of these reforms were aimed at giving power back to the people.

With the rise of television, however, the costs of elections skyrocketed, both in the primaries and the general elections. This required either wealthy people to run for office or have the backing of wealthy individuals. For a time, the cost of elections was not a front-page issue. However, President Nixon's misuse of campaign funds, which supported many of the escapades that became Watergate, along with a growing belief that political donors were buying influence and special considerations, sparked a move for campaign finance reform. In 1974, Congress amended an earlier campaign finance law that had never been truly enforced. These reforms were challenged in *Buckley v. Valeo* (1976).

Significance

The decision in *Buckley* allowed limitations on campaign contributions, but did not allow limitations on campaign expenditures. At best, the decision required a candidate to raise funds widely, as campaign costs continued to escalate. At worst, it did nothing, as people began to contribute through political action committees, their spouses and families, and other groups, giving $1,000 each time in order to get around the law. The decision also did little to deal with what came to be called "soft money," which was given to the party organizations, which in turn was used to promote a candidate or a candidate's fund-raising activities.

There has been a growth industry in "issue ads," which promote a certain view, such as being in favor of tax cuts, and are run in a district where the incumbent is against tax cuts. The ad ends with a message for the viewer to call the incumbent and tell him or her to cut taxes. The implied message, of course, is that tax cuts are good and one should promote them, and the best way to do that is to vote for a candidate who favors them. Such ads, though, had not been covered by campaign finance laws until the early 2000s.

Supreme Court cases since *Buckley* have generally followed *Buckley*'s trend of limiting contributions, but few other limits. In 2002, Congress passed the Bipartisan Campaign Reform Act, which aimed to eliminate soft money and control other ways in which individuals and corporations were getting around the current laws and controlling legislation. (Senators differ on what effect it will really have). This law had been suggested for years, but was widely opposed by those getting the most contributions.

Primary Source

Buckley v. Valeo [excerpt]

> **SYNOPSIS:** The opinion begins by noting the ideas behind the act. It then addresses the fact that the limits on contributions and expenditures reaches into an area protected by the freedom of speech and the freedom of association, both parts of the First Amendment. The Court then upholds the contribution limits and the disclosure requirements of the act, but strikes down the expenditure limits as impinging too much on the freedom of speech.

I. Contribution and Expenditure Limitations

The intricate statutory scheme adopted by Congress to regulate federal election campaigns includes restrictions on political contributions and expenditures that apply broadly to all phases of and all participants in the election process. The major contribution and expenditure limitations in the Act prohibit individuals from contributing more than $25,000 in a single year or more than $1,000 to any single candidate for an election campaign and from spending more than $1,000 a year "relative to a clearly identified candidate." Other provisions restrict a candidate's use of personal and family resources in his campaign and limit the overall amount that can be spent by a candidate in campaigning for federal office.

The constitutional power of Congress to regulate federal elections is well established and is not questioned by any of the parties in this case. Thus, the critical constitutional questions presented here go not to the basic power of Congress to legislate in this area, but to whether the specific legislation that

Congress has enacted interferes with First Amendment freedoms or invidiously discriminates against nonincumbent candidates and minor parties in contravention of the Fifth Amendment.

A. General Principles

The Act's contribution and expenditure limitations operate in an area of the most fundamental First Amendment activities. Discussion of public issues and debate on the qualifications of candidates are integral to the operation of the system of government established by our Constitution. The First Amendment affords the broadest protection to such political expression in order "to assure [the] unfettered interchange of ideas for the bringing about of political and social changes desired by the people." . . .

The First Amendment protects political association as well as political expression. The constitutional right of association explicated in *NAACP v. Alabama* . . . stemmed from the Court's recognition that "[e]ffective advocacy of both public and private points of view, particularly controversial ones, is undeniably enhanced by group association." . . .

The expenditure limitations contained in the Act represent substantial rather than merely theoretical restraints on the quantity and diversity of political speech. . . .

By contrast with a limitation upon expenditures for political expression, a limitation upon the amount that any one person or group may contribute to a candidate or political committee entails only a marginal restriction upon the contributor's ability to engage in free communication. . . . A limitation on the amount of money a person may give to a candidate or campaign organization thus involves little direct restraint on his political communication, for it permits the symbolic expression of support evidenced by a contribution but does not in any way infringe the contributor's freedom to discuss candidates and issues. . . .

The Act's contribution and expenditure limitations also impinge on protected associational freedoms. Making a contribution, like joining a political party, serves to affiliate a person with a candidate. In addition, it enables like-minded persons to pool their resources in furtherance of common political goals. The Act's contribution ceilings thus limit one important means of associating with a candidate or committee, but leave the contributor free to become a member of any political association and to assist personally in the association's efforts on behalf of candidates. And the Act's contribution limitations permit associations and candidates to aggregate large sums of money to promote effective advocacy. By contrast, the Act's $1,000 limitation on independent expenditures "relative to a clearly identified candidate" precludes most associations from effectively amplifying the voice of their adherents, the original basis for the recognition of First Amendment protection of the freedom of association. . . .

In sum, although the Act's contribution and expenditure limitations both implicate fundamental First Amendment interests, its expenditure ceilings impose significantly more severe restrictions on protected freedoms of political expression and association than do its limitations on financial contributions.

B. Contribution Limitations . . .

. . . Even a "'significant interference' with protected rights of political association" may be sustained if the State demonstrates a sufficiently important interest and employs means closely drawn to avoid unnecessary abridgment of associational freedoms. . . .

It is unnecessary to look beyond the Act's primary purpose—to limit the actuality and appearance of corruption resulting from large individual financial contributions—in order to find a constitutionally sufficient justification for the $1,000 contribution limitation. Under a system of private financing of elections, a candidate lacking immense personal or family wealth must depend on financial contributions from others to provide the resources necessary to conduct a successful campaign. The increasing importance of the communications media and sophisticated mass-mailing and polling operations to effective campaigning make the raising of large sums of money an ever more essential ingredient of an effective candidacy. To the extent that large contributions are given to secure a political quid pro quo from current and potential office holders, the integrity of our system of representative democracy is undermined. Although the scope of such pernicious practices can never be reliably ascertained, the deeply disturbing examples surfacing after the 1972 election demonstrate that the problem is not an illusory one.

Of almost equal concern as the danger of actual quid pro quo arrangements is the impact of the appearance of corruption stemming from public awareness of the opportunities for abuse inherent in a regime of large individual financial contributions. . . .

Appellants contend that the contribution limitations must be invalidated because bribery laws and

President Gerald Ford and the First Lady campaign for the presidential election, September 25, 1976, just months after the Supreme Court handed down its decision in *Buckley v. Valeo*. © WALLY MCNAMEE/ CORBIS. REPRODUCED BY PERMISSION.

narrowly drawn disclosure requirements constitute a less restrictive means of dealing with "proven and suspected quid pro quo arrangements." But laws making criminal the giving and taking of bribes deal with only the most blatant and specific attempts of those with money to influence governmental action. And while disclosure requirements serve the many salutary purposes discussed elsewhere in this opinion, Congress was surely entitled to conclude that disclosure was only a partial measure, and that contribution ceilings were a necessary legislative concomitant to deal with the reality or appearance of corruption inherent in a system permitting unlimited financial contributions, even when the identities of the contributors and the amounts of their contributions are fully disclosed. . . .

We find that, under the rigorous standard of review established by our prior decisions, the weighty interests served by restricting the size of financial contributions to political candidates are sufficient to justify the limited effect upon First Amendment freedoms caused by the $1,000 contribution ceiling. . . .

C. Expenditure Limitations

1. The $1,000 Limitation on Expenditures "Relative to a Clearly Identified Candidate"

. . . The plain effect of 608 (e) (1) is to prohibit all individuals, who are neither candidates nor owners of institutional press facilities, and all groups, except political parties and campaign organizations, from voicing their views "relative to a clearly identified candidate" through means that entail aggregate expenditures of more than $1,000 during a calendar year. The provision, for example, would make it a federal criminal offense for a person or association to place a single one-quarter page advertisement "relative to a clearly identified candidate" in a major metropolitan newspaper.

We find that the governmental interest in preventing corruption and the appearance of corruption is inadequate to justify 608 (e) (1)'s ceiling on independent expenditures. First, assuming, arguendo, that large independent expenditures pose the same dangers of actual or apparent quid pro quo arrangements as do large contributions, 608 (e) (1) does not provide an answer that sufficiently relates to the elimination of those dangers. Unlike the contribution limitations' total ban on the giving of large amounts of money to candidates, 608 (e) (1) prevents only some large expenditures. So long as persons and groups eschew expenditures that in express terms advocate the election or defeat of a clearly identified candidate, they are free to spend as much as they want to promote the candidate and his views. . . .

While the independent expenditure ceiling thus fails to serve any substantial governmental interest in stemming the reality or appearance of corruption in the electoral process, it heavily burdens core First Amendment expression. For the First Amendment right to "'speak one's mind . . . on all public institutions'" includes the right to engage in "'vigorous advocacy' no less than 'abstract discussion.'" . . . Advocacy of the election or defeat of candidates for federal office is no less entitled to protection under the First Amendment than the discussion of political policy generally or advocacy of the passage or defeat of legislation.

It is argued, however, that the ancillary governmental interest in equalizing the relative ability of individuals and groups to influence the outcome of elections serves to justify the limitation on express advocacy of the election or defeat of candidates imposed by 608 (e) (1)'s expenditure ceiling. But the concept that government may restrict the speech of some elements of our society in order to enhance the relative voice of others is wholly foreign to the First Amendment, which was designed "to secure 'the widest possible dissemination of information from diverse and antagonistic sources,'" and "'to assure unfettered interchange of ideas for the bringing about of political and social changes desired by the people.'" . . .

For the reasons stated, we conclude that 608 (e) (1)'s independent expenditure limitation is unconstitutional under the First Amendment.

2. Limitation on Expenditures by Candidates from Personal or Family Resources . . .

The ceiling on personal expenditures by candidates on their own behalf, like the limitations on independent expenditures contained in 608 (e) (1), imposes a substantial restraint on the ability of persons to engage in protected First Amendment expression. The candidate, no less than any other person, has a First Amendment right to engage in the discussion of public issues and vigorously and tirelessly to advocate his own election and the election of other candidates. Indeed, it is of particular importance that candidates have the unfettered opportunity to make their views known so that the electorate may intelligently evaluate the candidates' personal qualities and their positions on vital public issues before choosing among them on election day. . . .

The primary governmental interest served by the Act—the prevention of actual and apparent corruption of the political process—does not support the limitation on the candidate's expenditure of his own personal funds. . . . Indeed, the use of personal funds reduces the candidate's dependence on outside contributions and thereby counteracts the coercive pressures and attendant risks of abuse to which the Act's contribution limitations are directed.

The ancillary interest in equalizing the relative financial resources of candidates competing for elective office, therefore, provides the sole relevant rationale for 608 (a)'s expenditure ceiling. That interest is clearly not sufficient to justify the provision's infringement of fundamental First Amendment rights. First, the limitation may fail to promote financial equality among candidates. A candidate who spends less of his personal resources on his campaign may nonetheless outspend his rival as a result of more successful fundraising efforts. Indeed, a candidate's personal wealth may impede his efforts to persuade others that he needs their financial contributions or volunteer efforts to conduct an effective campaign. Second, and more fundamentally, the First Amendment simply cannot tolerate 608 (a)'s restriction upon the freedom of a candidate to speak without legislative limit on behalf of his own candidacy. We therefore hold that 608 (a)'s restriction on a candidate's personal expenditures is unconstitutional. . . .

In sum, the provisions of the Act that impose a $1,000 limitation on contributions to a single candidate, 608 (b) (1), a $5,000 limitation on contributions by a political committee to a single candidate, 608 (b) (2), and a $25,000 limitation on total contributions by an individual during any calendar year, 608 (b) (3), are constitutionally valid. . . . The contribution ceilings thus serve the basic governmental interest in safeguarding the integrity of the electoral process without directly impinging upon the rights of individual citizens and candidates to engage in political debate and discussion. By contrast, the First Amendment requires the invalidation of the Act's independent expenditure ceiling, 608 (e) (1), its limitation on a candidate's expenditures from his own personal funds, 608 (a), and its ceilings on overall campaign expenditures, 608 (c). These provisions place substantial and direct restrictions on the ability of candidates, citizens, and associations to engage in protected political expression, restrictions that the First Amendment cannot tolerate. . . .

II. Reporting and Disclosure Requirements

A. General Principles

Unlike the overall limitations on contributions and expenditures, the disclosure requirements impose no ceiling on campaign-related activities. But we have repeatedly found that compelled disclosure, in itself, can seriously infringe on privacy of association and belief guaranteed by the First Amendment. . . .

We long have recognized that significant encroachments on First Amendment rights of the sort that compelled disclosure imposes cannot be justified by a mere showing of some legitimate governmental interest. Since *NAACP v. Alabama* we have required that the subordinating interests of the State must survive exacting scrutiny. . . . This type of scrutiny is necessary even if any deterrent effect on the exercise of First Amendment rights arises, not through direct government action, but indirectly as an unintended but inevitable result of the government's conduct in requiring disclosure. . . .

The governmental interests sought to be vindicated by the disclosure requirements are of this magnitude. They fall into three categories. First, disclosure provides the electorate with information "as to where political campaign money comes from and how it is spent by the candidate" in order to aid the voters in evaluating those who seek federal office. It allows voters to place each candidate in the political spectrum more precisely than is often possible solely on the basis of party labels and campaign speeches. The sources of a candidate's financial support also alert the voter to the interests to which a candidate is most likely to be responsive and thus facilitate predictions of future performance in office.

Second, disclosure requirements deter actual corruption and avoid the appearance of corruption by exposing large contributions and expenditures to the light of publicity. . . .

Third, and not least significant, recordkeeping, reporting, and disclosure requirements are an essential means of gathering the data necessary to detect violations of the contribution limitations described above.

The disclosure requirements, as a general matter, directly serve substantial governmental interests. In determining whether these interests are sufficient to justify the requirements we must look to the extent of the burden that they place on individual rights.

It is undoubtedly true that public disclosure of contributions to candidates and political parties will deter some individuals who otherwise might contribute. In some instances, disclosure may even expose contributors to harassment or retaliation. These are not insignificant burdens on individual rights, and they must be weighed carefully against the interests which Congress has sought to promote by this legislation. In this process, we note and agree with appellants' concession that disclosure requirements—certainly in most applications—appear to be the least restrictive means of curbing the evils of campaign ignorance and corruption that Congress found to exist. . . .

In summary, we find no constitutional infirmities in the recordkeeping, reporting, and disclosure provisions of the Act.

Further Resources

BOOKS

Banks, Christopher P., and John Clifford Green. *Superintending Democracy: The Courts and the Political Process.* Akron, Ohio: University of Akron Press, 2001.

Campaign Finance Study Group. *An Analysis of the Impact of the Federal Election Campaign Act, 1972–1978, From the Institute of Politics, John F. Kennedy School of Government, Harvard University.* Washington, D.C.: U.S. Government Printing Office, 1979.

Carter, Jimmy. *To Assure Pride and Confidence in the Electoral Process.* Washington, D.C.: Brookings Institution, 2002.

Luna, Christopher. *Campaign Finance Reform.* New York: Wilson, 2001.

Utter, Glenn H., and Ruth Ann Strickland. *Campaign and Election Reform: A Reference Handbook.* Santa Barbara, Calif.: ABC-CLIO, 1997.

WEBSITES

"Campaign Finance Regulation and the First Amendment." Exploring Constitutional Conflicts, University of Missouri, Kansas City. Available online at http://www.law.umkc.edu /faculty/projects/ftrials/conlaw/campaign.htm; website home page: http://www.law.umkc.edu (accessed April 16, 2003).

AUDIO AND VISUAL MEDIA

Campaign Finance Reform. Public Affairs Video Archives, 1991, VHS.

So You Want to Buy a President? PBS Video, 1996, VHS.

Washington v. Davis
Supreme Court decision

By: Byron White and William Brennan Jr.

Date: June 7, 1976

Source: White, Byron and William Brennan Jr. *Washington v. Davis.* 426 U.S. 229 (1976). Available online at http://laws .findlaw.com/us/426/229.html; website home page: http://www .findlaw.com (accessed April 16, 2003).

About the Authors: Byron White (1917–2002) was a Rhodes Scholar and a talented athlete in college. He received his law degree from Yale University and served in World War II (1939–1945), winning two Bronze Stars. Appointed to the Supreme Court in 1962, he served until 1993.

William Brennan Jr. (1906–1997) went to Harvard University for his law degree. In 1952, he was appointed to the New Jersey Supreme Court. He served in the army during World War II, holding the rank of colonel. In 1956, he was nominated by President Dwight Eisenhower (served 1953–1961) for the U.S. Supreme Court. ■

Introduction

In the colonial and early national period, few tests were administered for college admission or for job placement. To get into college, there were two crucial factors: who one's parents were and who one knew. Jobs, especially at the state and federal levels, were given as political rewards, in what was called the "spoils system." People were rewarded for getting their friends, living, dead, fictional, or otherwise, out to vote. In the late 1800s, a merit-based civil service system was put into effect for much of the federal government, and one could not get dismissed except for "gross neglect of duty." One qualified for appointment, or at least for entering the appointment process, by taking a civil service exam, which asked supposedly general knowledge questions.

In the twentieth century, intelligence quotient tests and other exams abounded. One of the first was the Army General Knowledge Test, which was applied to recruits during World War I (1914–1918). Even though it was supposedly testing general knowledge, it was administered in English, despite the high number of nonnative English speakers, and was based on a classical education. Throughout the rest of the century, testing companies and a wide variety of tests were developed. These included the American College Test and the Scholastic Assessment Test for college-bound students, the Armed Services Vocational Aptitude Battery for those military-bound, and the Medical College Admission Test for those medical school–bound.

Many of the tests given in the 1950s and 1960s, however, were written by white men for white men, and discriminated, either intentionally or unintentionally, against women as well as against other races. In 1971, the Supreme Court ruled that a general education test with a discriminatory effect was invalid and required that tests must be job related. That same question of what types of tests could be required returned to the Court in *Washington v. Davis* (1976).

Significance

In this case, the Supreme Court held that a qualifying test is legal, even if it has a discriminatory impact, if it is racially neutral on its face and has a rational purpose. The Court also took into account the Washington, D.C., Police Department's efforts to recruit blacks. In doing so, it held that affirmative action programs, aimed to create diversity and perhaps remedy some of the discriminatory impact of these tests, are valid in some instances.

Quota programs, with a certain number of seats set aside for one race, have generally been held to be invalid, while the use of race as a factor in admissions has generally been upheld. Companies that discriminated in the past or that have racially unbalanced workforces and have voluntarily adopted affirmative action programs as a remedy are generally met with approval by the Court. However, affirmative action programs mandated by the state and federal governments, unless those programs are narrowly tailored to remedy past discrimination, have been struck down.

How the Supreme Court will rule on the question of affirmative action in education is unknown. Furthermore, President George W. Bush's administration has announced its opposition to affirmative action. Without affirmative action programs, tests will increase in importance, particularly in education. Some tests, it is argued, are more of a reflection of one's sex, race, or family income than one's chance of success in college or graduate school, never mind one's chances of success after college or graduate school, however that might be measured. These tests are more of an administrative convenience than a true predictor of success. How society will deal with the potentially discriminatory impact of these tests, if affirmative action is banned, remains to be seen.

Primary Source

Washington v. Davis [excerpt]

SYNOPSIS: Justice Byron White first points out that laws are not condemned simply because they have a discriminatory impact, provided they have a racially neutral purpose. He then points out that Congress did not intend that such laws be struck down. He also holds that the test in question is job related, which supports the test's validity. In dissent, Justice William Brennan Jr. suggests that the test had not yet been proven job related and that a high standard was imposed by Congress.

Mr. Justice White delivered the opinion of the Court.

This case involves the validity of a qualifying test administered to applicants for positions as police officers in the District of Columbia Metropolitan Police Department. The test was sustained by the District Court but invalidated by the Court of Appeals. We are in agreement with the District Court and hence reverse the judgment of the Court of Appeals. . . .

According to the findings and conclusions of the District Court, to be accepted by the Department and to enter an intensive 17-week training program, the police recruit was required to satisfy certain physical and character standards, to be a high school graduate or its equivalent, and to receive a grade of at least 40 out of 80 on "Test 21," which is "an examination that is used generally throughout the federal service," which "was developed by the Civil Service Commission, not the Police Department," and which was "designed to test verbal ability, vocabulary, reading and comprehension." . . .

The validity of Test 21 was the sole issue before the court on the motions for summary judgment. . . . The District Court ultimately concluded that "[t]he proof is wholly lacking that a police officer qualifies on the color of his skin rather than ability" and that the Department "should not be required on this showing to lower standards or to abandon efforts to achieve excellence." . . .

Having lost on both constitutional and statutory issues in the District Court, respondents brought the case to the Court of Appeals claiming that their summary judgment motion, which rested on purely constitutional grounds, should have been granted. The tendered constitutional issue was whether the use of Test 21 invidiously discriminated against Negroes and hence denied them due process of law contrary to the commands of the Fifth Amendment. . . .

Because the Court of Appeals erroneously applied the legal standards applicable to Title VII cases in resolving the constitutional issue before it, we reverse its judgment in respondents' favor. . . .

The central purpose of the Equal Protection Clause of the Fourteenth Amendment is the prevention of official conduct discriminating on the basis of race. It is also true that the Due Process Clause of the Fifth Amendment contains an equal protection component prohibiting the United States from invidiously discriminating between individuals or groups. . . . But our cases have not embraced the proposition that a law or other official act, without regard to whether it reflects a racially discriminatory purpose, is unconstitutional solely because it has a racially disproportionate impact. . . .

This is not to say that the necessary discriminatory racial purpose must be express or appear on the face of the statute, or that a law's disproportionate impact is irrelevant in cases involving Constitution-based claims of racial discrimination. A statute, otherwise neutral on its face, must not be applied so as invidiously to discriminate on the basis of race. . . . It is also clear from the cases dealing with racial discrimination in the selection of juries that the systematic exclusion of Negroes is itself such an "unequal application of the law . . . as to show intentional discrimination." . . . A prima facie case of discriminatory purpose may be proved as well by the absence of Negroes on a particular jury combined with the failure of the jury commissioners to be informed of eligible Negro jurors in a community. . . . With a prima facie case made out, "the burden of proof shifts to the State to rebut the presumption of unconstitutional action by showing that permissible racially neutral selection criteria and procedures have produced the monochromatic result." . . .

. . . Nevertheless, we have not held that a law, neutral on its face and serving ends otherwise within the power of government to pursue, is invalid under the Equal Protection Clause simply because it may affect a greater proportion of one race than of another. Disproportionate impact is not irrelevant, but it is not the sole touchstone of an invidious racial discrimination forbidden by the Constitution. Standing alone, it does not trigger the rule, . . . that racial classifications are to be subjected to the strictest scrutiny and are justifiable only by the weightiest of considerations. . . .

As an initial matter, we have difficulty understanding how a law establishing a racially neutral qualification for employment is nevertheless racially discriminatory and denies "any person . . . equal protection of the laws" simply because a greater proportion of Negroes fail to qualify than members of other racial or ethnic groups. Had respondents, along with all others who had failed Test 21, whether white or black, brought an action claiming that the test denied each of them equal protection of the laws as compared with those who had passed with high enough scores to qualify them as police recruits, it is most unlikely that their challenge would have been sustained. Test 21, which is administered generally to prospective Government employees, concededly seeks to ascertain whether those who take it have acquired a particular level of verbal skill; and it is untenable that the Constitution prevents the Government from seeking modestly to upgrade the communicative abilities of its employees rather than to be satisfied with some lower level of competence, particularly where the job requires special ability to communicate orally and in writing. Respondents, as Negroes, could no more successfully claim that the test denied them equal protection than could white applicants who also failed. The conclusion would not be different in the face of proof that more Negroes than whites had been disqualified by Test 21. That other Negroes also failed to score well would, alone, not demonstrate that respondents individually were being denied equal protection of the laws by the application of an otherwise valid qualifying test being administered to prospective police recruits.

Nor on the facts of the case before us would the disproportionate impact of Test 21 warrant the conclusion that it is a purposeful device to discriminate against Negroes and hence an infringement of the constitutional rights of respondents as well as other black applicants. As we have said, the test is neutral on its face and rationally may be said to serve a purpose the Government is constitutionally empowered to pursue. . . .

Under Title VII, Congress provided that when hiring and promotion practices disqualifying substantially disproportionate numbers of blacks are challenged, discriminatory purpose need not be proved, and that it is an insufficient response to demonstrate some rational basis for the challenged practices. It is necessary, in addition, that they be "validated" in terms of job performance in any one of several ways, perhaps by ascertaining the minimum skill, ability, or potential necessary for the position at issue and determining whether the qualifying tests are appropriate for the selection of qualified applicants for the job in question. However this process proceeds, it involves a more probing judicial review of, and less deference to, the seemingly reasonable acts of administrators and executives than is appropriate under the Constitution where special racial impact, without discriminatory purpose, is claimed. We are not disposed to adopt this more rigorous standard for the purposes of applying the Fifth and the Fourteenth Amendments in cases such as this.

A rule that a statute designed to serve neutral ends is nevertheless invalid, absent compelling justification, if in practice it benefits or burdens one race more than another would be far reaching and would raise serious questions about, and perhaps invalidate, a whole range of tax, welfare, public service, regulatory, and licensing statutes that may be more burdensome to the poor and to the average black than to the more affluent white. . . .

We also hold that the Court of Appeals should have affirmed the judgment of the District Court granting the motions for summary judgment filed by petitioners and the federal parties. Respondents were entitled to relief on neither constitutional nor statutory grounds. . . .

We agree with petitioners and the federal parties that this was error. The advisability of the police recruit training course informing the recruit about his upcoming job, acquainting him with its demands, and attempting to impart a modicum of required skills seems conceded. It is also apparent to us, as it was to the District Judge, that some minimum verbal and communicative skill would be very useful, if not essential, to satisfactory progress in the train-

ing regimen. Based on the evidence before him, the District Judge concluded that Test 21 was directly related to the requirements of the police training program and that a positive relationship between the test and training-course performance was sufficient to validate the former, wholly aside from its possible relationship to actual performance as a police officer. This conclusion of the District Judge that training-program validation may itself be sufficient is supported by regulations of the Civil Service Commission, by the opinion evidence placed before the District Judge, and by the current views of the Civil Service Commissioners who were parties to the case. . . .

The District Court's accompanying conclusion that Test 21 was in fact directly related to the requirements of the police training program was supported by a validation study, as well as by other evidence of record; and we are not convinced that this conclusion was erroneous. . . .

The judgment of the Court of Appeals accordingly is reversed.

So ordered. . . .

Mr. Justice Brennan with whom Mr. Justice Marshall joins, dissenting. . . .

Nevertheless, although it appears unnecessary to reach the statutory questions, I will accept the Court's conclusion that respondents were entitled to summary judgment if they were correct in their statutory arguments, and I would affirm the Court of Appeals because petitioners have failed to prove that Test 21 satisfies the applicable statutory standards. . . .

The EEOC regulations require that the validity of a job qualification test be proved by "empirical data demonstrating that the test is predictive of or significantly correlated with important elements of work behavior which comprise or are relevant to the job or jobs for which candidates are being evaluated." . . . This construction of Title VII was approved in *Albemarle,* where we quoted this provision and remarked that "[t]he message of these Guidelines is the same as that of the Griggs case." . . .

If we measure the validity of Test 21 by this standard, which I submit we are bound to do, petitioners' proof is deficient in a number of ways similar to those noted above. . . .

Accordingly, EEOC regulations that have previously been approved by the Court set forth a construction of Title VII that is distinctly opposed to today's statutory result. The Court also says that its conclusion is not foreclosed by *Griggs* and *Albemarle,* but today's result plainly conflicts with those cases. *Griggs* held that "[i]f an employment practice which operates to exclude Negroes cannot be shown to be related to job performance, the practice is prohibited." . . . Once a discriminatory impact is shown, the employer carries the burden of proving that the challenged practice "bear[s] a demonstrable relationship to successful performance of the jobs for which it was used." . . .

It may well be that in some circumstances, proof of a relationship between a discriminatory qualification test and training performance is an acceptable substitute for establishing a relationship to job performance. But this question is not settled, and it should not be resolved by the minimal analysis in the Court's opinion. Moreover, it is particularly inappropriate to decide the question on this record. . . . But no authority, whether professional, administrative, or judicial, has accepted the sufficiency of a correlation with training performance in the absence of such proof. For reasons that I have stated above, the record does not adequately establish either factor. As a result, the Court's conclusion cannot be squared with the focus on job performance in Griggs and Albemarle, even if this substitute showing is reconcilable with the holdings in those cases.

Today's reduced emphasis on a relationship to job performance is also inconsistent with clearly expressed congressional intent. . . .

Finally, it should be observed that every federal court, except the District Court in this case, presented with proof identical to that offered to validate Test 21 has reached a conclusion directly opposite to that of the Court today. Sound policy considerations support the view that, at a minimum, petitioners should have been required to prove that the police training examinations either measure job-related skills or predict job performance. Where employers try to validate written qualification tests by proving a correlation with written examinations in a training course, there is a substantial danger that people who have good verbal skills will achieve high scores on both tests due to verbal ability, rather than "job-specific ability." As a result, employers could validate any entrance examination that measures only verbal ability by giving another written test that measures verbal ability at the end of a training course. Any contention that the resulting correlation between examination scores would be evidence that the initial test is "job related" is plainly erroneous. It seems to me, however, that the Court's holding

in this case can be read as endorsing this dubious proposition. Today's result will prove particularly unfortunate if it is extended to govern Title VII cases.

Accordingly, accepting the Court's assertion that it is necessary to reach the statutory issue, I would hold that petitioners have not met their burden of proof and affirm the judgment of the Court of Appeals.

Further Resources

BOOKS

Hutchinson, Dennis J. *The Man Who Once Was Whizzer White: A Portrait of Justice Byron R. White.* New York: The Free Press, 1998.

Picott, J. Rupert. *Walter Washington, the District of Columbia's First Elected Mayor Since Reconstruction.* Washington, D.C.: Associated Publishers, 1975.

Schwartz, Bernard. *The Ascent of Pragmatism: The Burger Court in Action.* Reading, Mass.: Addison-Wesley, 1990.

U.S. Senate Committee on the District of Columbia. *Hearing on the Nomination of Walter E. Washington to be Mayor-Commissioner of the District of Columbia for a Term Expiring February 1, 1977 (reappointment) January 30, 1973,* 93rd Cong., 1st sess., 1973.

PERIODICALS

Miller, Christopher S. "The End Justifies the Means: Affirmative Action, Standards of Review, and Justice White." *University of Miami Law Review* 46, no. 5, May 1992, 1305–1324.

WEBSITES

The Affirmative Action and Diversity Project: A Web Page for Research. Available online at http://aad.english.ucsb.edu/ (accessed April 16, 2003).

Gregg v. Georgia

Supreme Court decision

By: Potter Stewart, William Brennan Jr., and Thurgood Marshall

Date: July 2, 1976

Source: Stewart, Potter, William Brennan Jr., and Thurgood Marshall. *Gregg v. Georgia.* 428 U.S. 153 (1976). Available online at http://laws.findlaw.com/us/428/153.html; website home page: http://www.findlaw.com (accessed April 16, 2003).

About the Authors: Potter Stewart (1915–1985) graduated from Yale Law School in 1941. He practiced law until he was nominated by President Dwight Eisenhower (served 1953–1961) for the U.S. Court of Appeals in 1954 and then for the Supreme Court in 1958. He retired in 1981.

William Brennan Jr. (1906–1997) graduated from Harvard Law School in 1931. After practicing law for nearly twenty years, he was appointed first to the New Jersey Superior

Court and then to the New Jersey Supreme Court, before being nominated for the U.S. Supreme Court in 1956 by President Eisenhower.

Thurgood Marshall (1908–1993) graduated from Howard University Law School in 1933. In 1967, he became the first African American to serve on the U.S. Supreme Court when he was nominated by President Lyndon Johnson (served 1963–1969). He retired from the Court in 1991. ■

Introduction

The Eighth Amendment to the U.S. Constitution reads "[e]xcessive bail shall not be required, nor excessive fines imposed, nor cruel and unusual punishments inflicted." There is no clear definition, however, of the term "cruel and unusual punishments."

When the Constitution was created, many jurisdictions borrowed from the English law, which allowed hundreds of crimes to be punished with the death penalty. It appeared that the Constitution would not ban the death penalty as being unusual. The English statute from which it was borrowed aimed at prohibiting penalties such as beheading, burning at the stake, and drawing and quartering. Furthermore, the Fifth Amendment states that no one shall "be deprived of life . . . without due process of law," which seems to recognize capital punishment.

The Supreme Court, however, was not quick to recognize the validity of capital punishment. In the late 1800s, the Court ruled that both the firing squad and the electric chair did not constitute cruel and unusual punishment, but passed on deciding the validity of the death penalty. Eventually, American society started limiting (if not abolishing) the list of crimes for which the death penalty was automatic.

By the late 1960s, critics of the death penalty questioned whether it deterred crime and produced studies indicating that it was applied capriciously. Furthermore, they noted that African Americans were much more likely to be sentenced to death than whites for the same crimes, and that the race of the victim played a role, as those who killed whites were more likely to die.

In *Furman v. Georgia* (1972), the Supreme Court struck down the death penalty as cruel and unusual. Following this ruling, many states began passing new death penalty laws that provided more guidance and mandating that certain "aggravating factors" had to be found for the death penalty to apply. Such a law was tested in *Gregg v. Georgia* (1976).

Significance

The Supreme Court upheld the death penalty as it was used in Georgia, holding that the safeguards imposed, the new requirements, and the Georgia Supreme Court's mandatory review did not violate the Eighth Amendment. Two justices did dissent though, arguing that it was excessive and unnecessary. Even the majority admitted that the Eighth Amendment and the Constitution as a whole was supposed to evolve. Since *Gregg,* the death penalty itself has always been upheld. However, the death penalty for certain crimes, such as rape or aiding and abetting a murder, has been struck down on some occasions.

The imposition of the death penalty in the United States is mostly carried out on the state level and the number of executions varies widely, with Texas having carried out hundreds and many other states having carried out none. The death penalty system is also maintained very unevenly. In some states, one is given enough assistance to receive a fair trial, while in other ones, lawyers fall asleep during trial and are paid paltry sums for their services. (One's lawyer falling asleep during the trial was not held to be "reversible error" and so the defendant, after conviction, did not get a new trial.)

In 2000, Illinois governor George Ryan ordered a moratorium on Illinois's death penalty. In 2003 Ryan pardoned four men sentenced to death and commuted the sentences of the other 156 death-row inmates to life imprisonment. Meanwhile, other states and the federal courts have moved to speed up executions. Clearly, the death penalty is not going to go away and it will still continue to provoke controversy.

Primary Source

Gregg v. Georgia [excerpt]

> **SYNOPSIS:** The opinion opens by noting the nature of the aggravating circumstances that must be found before the death penalty can be imposed. Justice Potter Stewart notes that legislative judgments must be presumed to be constitutional, holds that the death penalty is not per se unconstitutional, and upholds the method by which Georgia uses it. Justice William Brennan Jr. dissents, arguing that the death penalty cannot constitute justice. Justice Thurgood Marshall holds that the death penalty does not deter crime and is unconstitutional.

Judgment of the Court, and opinion of Mr. Justice Stewart, Mr. Justice Powell, and Mr. Justice Stevens, announced by Mr. Justice Stewart. . . .

. . . Before a convicted defendant may be sentenced to death, however, except in cases of treason or aircraft hijacking, the jury, or the trial judge in cases tried without a jury, must find beyond a reasonable doubt one of the 10 aggravating circumstances specified in the statute. The sentence of death may be imposed only if the jury (or judge) finds one of the statutory aggravating circumstances and then elects to impose that sentence. . . . If the verdict is death, the jury or judge must specify the aggravating circumstance(s) found. . . .

In addition to the conventional appellate process available in all criminal cases, provision is made for special expedited direct review by the Supreme Court of Georgia of the appropriateness of imposing the sentence of death in the particular case. . . .

If the court affirms a death sentence, it is required to include in its decision reference to similar cases that it has taken into consideration. . . .

. . . We now hold that the punishment of death does not invariably violate the Constitution. . . .

. . . The American draftsmen, who adopted the English phrasing in drafting the Eighth Amendment, were primarily concerned, however, with proscribing "tortures" and other "barbarous" methods of punishment." . . .

But the Court has not confined the prohibition embodied in the Eighth Amendment to "barbarous" methods that were generally outlawed in the 18th century. Instead, the Amendment has been interpreted in a flexible and dynamic manner. . . .

. . . Thus, an assessment of contemporary values concerning the infliction of a challenged sanction is relevant to the application of the Eighth Amendment. . . . [T]his assessment does not call for a subjective judgment. It requires, rather, that we look to objective indicia that reflect the public attitude toward a given sanction.

But our cases also make clear that public perceptions of standards of decency with respect to criminal sanctions are not conclusive. A penalty also must accord with "the dignity of man," which is the "basic concept underlying the Eighth Amendment." . . . This means, at least, that the punishment not be "excessive." When a form of punishment in the abstract (in this case, whether capital punishment may ever be imposed as a sanction for murder) rather than in the particular (the propriety of death as a penalty to be applied to a specific defendant for a specific crime) is under consideration, the inquiry into "excessiveness" has two aspects. First, the punishment must not involve the unnecessary and wanton infliction of pain. . . . Second, the punishment must not be grossly out of proportion to the severity of the crime. . . .

Therefore, in assessing a punishment selected by a democratically elected legislature against the constitutional measure, we presume its validity. We may not require the legislature to select the least severe penalty possible so long as the penalty se-

lected is not cruelly inhumane or disproportionate to the crime involved. And a heavy burden rests on those who would attack the judgment of the representatives of the people.

This is true in part because the constitutional test is intertwined with an assessment of contemporary standards and the legislative judgment weighs heavily in ascertaining such standards. . . . A decision that a given punishment is impermissible under the Eighth Amendment cannot be reversed short of a constitutional amendment. The ability of the people to express their preference through the normal democratic processes, as well as through ballot referenda, is shut off. Revisions cannot be made in the light of further experience. . . .

. . . We now consider specifically whether the sentence of death for the crime of murder is a per se violation of the Eighth and Fourteenth Amendments to the Constitution. We note first that history and precedent strongly support a negative answer to this question.

The imposition of the death penalty for the crime of murder has a long history of acceptance both in the United States and in England. . . .

It is apparent from the text of the Constitution itself that the existence of capital punishment was accepted by the Framers. At the time the Eighth Amendment was ratified, capital punishment was a common sanction in every State. Indeed, the First Congress of the United States enacted legislation providing death as the penalty for specified crimes. . . . The Fifth Amendment, adopted at the same time as the Eighth, contemplated the continued existence of the capital sanction by imposing certain limits on the prosecution of capital cases. . . .

And the Fourteenth Amendment, adopted over three-quarters of a century later, similarly contemplates the existence of the capital sanction in providing that no State shall deprive any person of "life, liberty, or property" without due process of law.

For nearly two centuries, this Court, repeatedly and often expressly, has recognized that capital punishment is not invalid per se. . . .

The most marked indication of society's endorsement of the death penalty for murder is the legislative response to Furman. The legislatures of at least 35 States have enacted new statutes that provide for the death penalty for at least some crimes that result in the death of another person. . . .

As we have seen, however, the Eighth Amendment demands more than that a challenged punishment be acceptable to contemporary society. The Court also must ask whether it comports with the basic concept of human dignity at the core of the Amendment. . . .

The death penalty is said to serve two principal social purposes: retribution and deterrence of capital crimes by prospective offenders.

In part, capital punishment is an expression of society's moral outrage at particularly offensive conduct. This function may be unappealing to many, but it is essential in an ordered society that asks its citizens to rely on legal processes rather than self-help to vindicate their wrongs. . . .

Statistical attempts to evaluate the worth of the death penalty as a deterrent to crimes by potential offenders have occasioned a great deal of debate. The results simply have been inconclusive. . . .

In sum, we cannot say that the judgment of the Georgia Legislature that capital punishment may be necessary in some cases is clearly wrong. Considerations of federalism, as well as respect for the ability of a legislature to evaluate, in terms of its particular State, the moral consensus concerning the death penalty and its social utility as a sanction, require us to conclude, in the absence of more convincing evidence, that the infliction of death as a punishment for murder is not without justification and thus is not unconstitutionally severe.

Finally, we must consider whether the punishment of death is disproportionate in relation to the crime for which it is imposed. There is no question that death as a punishment is unique in its severity and irrevocability. . . . When a defendant's life is at stake, the Court has been particularly sensitive to insure that every safeguard is observed. . . . But we are concerned here only with the imposition of capital punishment for the crime of murder, and when a life has been taken deliberately by the offender, we cannot say that the punishment is invariably disproportionate to the crime. It is an extreme sanction, suitable to the most extreme of crimes.

We hold that the death penalty is not a form of punishment that may never be imposed, regardless of the circumstances of the offense, regardless of the character of the offender, and regardless of the procedure followed in reaching the decision to impose it. . . .

We now turn to consideration of the constitutionality of Georgia's capital-sentencing procedures. . . .

Troy Leon Gregg challenged the death penalty sentence handed out to him by a Georgia court of law, but the U.S. Supreme Court upheld the ruling. © **THE BETTMANN ARCHIVE/CORBIS. REPRODUCED BY PERMISSION.**

. . . The new Georgia sentencing procedures, by contrast, focus the jury's attention on the particularized nature of the crime and the particularized characteristics of the individual defendant. While the jury is permitted to consider any aggravating or mitigating circumstances, it must find and identify at least one statutory aggravating factor before it may impose a penalty of death. In this way the jury's discretion is channeled. No longer can a jury wantonly and freakishly impose the death sentence; it is always circumscribed by the legislative guidelines. In addition, the review function of the Supreme Court of Georgia affords additional assurance that the concerns that prompted our decision in Furman are not present to any significant degree in the Georgia procedure applied here.

For the reasons expressed in this opinion, we hold that the statutory system under which Gregg was sentenced to death does not violate the Constitution. Accordingly, the judgment of the Georgia Supreme Court is affirmed.

It is so ordered. . . .

Mr. Justice Brennan, dissenting. . . .

This Court inescapably has the duty, as the ultimate arbiter of the meaning of our Constitution, to say whether, when individuals condemned to death stand before our Bar, "moral concepts" require us to hold that the law has progressed to the point where we should declare that the punishment of death, like punishments on the rack, the screw, and the wheel, is no longer morally tolerable in our civilized society. . . . I emphasize only that foremost among the "moral concepts" recognized in our cases and inherent in the Clause is the primary moral principle that the State, even as it punishes, must treat its citizens in a manner consistent with their intrinsic worth as human beings—a punishment must not be so severe as to be degrading to human dignity. A judicial determination whether the punishment of death comports with human dignity is therefore not only permitted but compelled by the Clause. . . .

. . . For three of my Brethren hold today that mandatory infliction of the death penalty constitutes the penalty cruel and unusual punishment. I perceive no principled basis for this limitation. Death for whatever crime and under all circumstances "is truly an awesome punishment. The calculated killing of a human being by the State involves, by its very nature, a denial of the executed person's humanity. . . . An executed person has indeed 'lost the right to have rights.'" . . . Death is not only an unusually severe punishment, unusual in its pain, in its finality, and in its enormity, but it serves no penal purpose more effectively than a less severe punishment; therefore the principle inherent in the Clause that prohibits pointless infliction of excessive punishment when less severe punishment can adequately achieve the same purposes invalidates the punishment. . . .

The fatal constitutional infirmity in the punishment of death is that it treats "members of the human race as nonhumans, as objects to be toyed with and discarded. [It is] thus inconsistent with the fundamental premise of the Clause that even the vilest criminal remains a human being possessed of common human dignity." . . . As such it is a penalty that "subjects the individual to a fate forbidden by the principle of civilized treatment guaranteed by the [Clause]." I therefore would hold, on that ground alone, that death is today a cruel and unusual punishment prohibited by the Clause. "Justice of this kind is obviously no less shocking than the crime itself, and the new 'official' murder, far from offering redress for the offense committed against society, adds instead a second defilement to the first." . . .

Mr. Justice Marshall, dissenting. . . .

In Furman I concluded that the death penalty is constitutionally invalid for two reasons. First, the death penalty is excessive. . . . And second, the American people, fully informed as to the purposes of the death penalty and its liabilities, would in my view reject it as morally unacceptable. . . .

. . . An excessive penalty is invalid under the Cruel and Unusual Punishments Clause "even though popular sentiment may favor" it. . . . The inquiry here, then, is simply whether the death penalty is necessary to accomplish the legitimate legislative purposes in punishment, or whether a less severe penalty—life imprisonment—would do as well. . . .

The two purposes that sustain the death penalty as nonexcessive in the Court's view are general deterrence and retribution. In Furman, I canvassed the relevant data on the deterrent effect of capital punishment. . . .

The available evidence, I concluded in Furman, was convincing that "capital punishment is not necessary as a deterrent to crime in our society." . . .

. . . The evidence I reviewed in Furman remains convincing, in my view, that "capital punishment is not necessary as a deterrent to crime in our society." . . . The justification for the death penalty must be found elsewhere.

The other principal purpose said to be served by the death penalty is retribution. . . . It is this notion that I find to be the most disturbing aspect of today's unfortunate decisions.

The concept of retribution is a multifaceted one, and any discussion of its role in the criminal law must be undertaken with caution. On one level, it can be said that the notion of retribution or reprobation is the basis of our insistence that only those who have broken the law be punished, and in this sense the notion is quite obviously central to a just system of criminal sanctions. But our recognition that retribution plays a crucial role in determining who may be punished by no means requires approval of retribution as a general justification for punishment. It is the question whether retribution can provide a moral justification for punishment—in particular, capital punishment—that we must consider. . . .

This statement is wholly inadequate to justify the death penalty. . . . It simply defies belief to suggest that the death penalty is necessary to prevent the American people from taking the law into their own hands. . . .

. . . But the implication of the statements appears to me to be quite different—namely, that society's judgment that the murderer "deserves" death must be respected not simply because the preservation of order requires it, but because it is appropriate that society make the judgment and carry it out. It is this latter notion, in particular, that I consider to be fundamentally at odds with the Eighth Amendment. . . . The mere fact that the community demands the murderer's life in return for the evil he has done cannot sustain the death penalty, for as Justices Stewart, Powell, and Stevens remind us, "the Eighth Amendment demands more than that a challenged punishment be acceptable to contemporary society." . . . To be sustained under the Eighth Amendment, the death penalty must "compor[t] with the basic concept of human dignity at the core of the Amendment" . . . ; the objective in imposing it must be "[consistent] with our respect for the dignity of [other] men." . . . Under these standards, the taking of life "because the wrongdoer deserves it" surely must fall, for such a punishment has as its very basis the total denial of the wrongdoer's dignity and worth.

The death penalty, unnecessary to promote the goal of deterrence or to further any legitimate notion of retribution, is an excessive penalty forbidden by the Eighth and Fourteenth Amendments.

Further Resources

BOOKS

Banner, Stuart. *The Death Penalty: An American History.* Cambridge, Mass.: Harvard University Press, 2002.

Bosco, Antoinette. *Choosing Mercy: A Mother of Murder Victims Pleads to End the Death Penalty.* Maryknoll, N.Y.: Orbis, 2001.

Jackson, Jesse, and Bruce Shapiro. *Legal Lynching: The Death Penalty and America's Future.* New York: The New Press, 2001.

Mello, Michael. *Against the Death Penalty: The Relentless Dissents of Justices Brennan and Marshall.* Boston: Northeastern University Press, 1996.

Sarat, Austin. *When the State Kills: Capital Punishment and the American Condition.* Princeton, N.J.: Princeton University Press, 2001.

Winters, Paul A. *The Death Penalty: Opposing Viewpoints,* 3rd ed. San Diego: Greenhaven, 1997.

PERIODICALS

Bailey, William C., and Ruth P. Lott. "Crime, Punishment and Personality: An Examination of the Deterrence Question." *Journal of Criminal Law and Criminology* 67, no. 1, 1976, 99–109.

WEBSITES

"The Death Penalty in America: Twenty-five Years After *Gregg v. Georgia.*" Death Penalty, Amnesty International. Available online at http://www.amnestyusa.org/abolish/greggvgeorgia/; website home page: http://www.amnestyusa.org/abolish/ (accessed April 16, 2003).

University of California Regents v. Bakke

Supreme Court decision

By: Lewis Powell, William Brennan Jr., and Thurgood Marshall

Date: June 28, 1978

Source: Powell, Lewis, William Brennan Jr., and Thurgood Marshall. *University of California Regents v. Bakke.* 438 U.S. 265 (1978). Available online at http://laws.findlaw.com/us/438/265.html; website home page: http://www.findlaw.com (accessed April 16, 2003).

About the Authors: Lewis Powell (1907–1998) graduated from Harvard Law School. He was president of the American Bar Association in 1964, and championed legal services for the poor. He was a Supreme Court justice from 1971 to 1987. William Brennan Jr. (1906–1997) went to Harvard Law School. To spend more time with his family, he served in the appellate division in New Jersey. He served on the Supreme Court from 1956 to 1990.

Thurgood Marshall (1908–1993) was the first African American to serve on the Supreme Court. He litigated many important cases for the National Association for the Advancement of Colored People (NAACP), including *Brown v. Board of Education* (1954). He served as a justice of the Supreme Court from 1967 to 1991. ∎

Introduction

The Declaration of Independence states "all men are created equal." However, during the first century of America's existence, all men were not treated equally, nor did most people believe that they were created equally. The Fourteenth Amendment in 1868 reaffirmed the whole idea of equality with its mandate requiring "equal protection of the laws" by the states. However, states almost immediately began denying people equal protection and equal opportunity. For example, most southern states enacted Jim Crow laws that segregated all aspects of southern life.

Finally, in *Brown v. Board of Education* (1954) the Supreme Court struck down segregation in education as being inherently unequal. Congress followed a few years later with the 1964 Civil Rights Act, the 1965 Voting Rights Act, and the 1968 Civil Rights Act.

In the area of education, many facilities, especially at the higher levels, were not models of equality either.

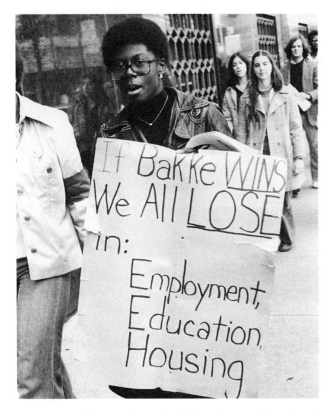

Protestors march in opposition to Allan Bakke, who, in a suit being heard by the U.S. Supreme Court, claims that he was denied admission to the University of California Medical School due to affirmative action, October 3, 1977. © BETTMANN/CORBIS. REPRODUCED BY PERMISSION.

Many schools, especially before the 1960s gave preference to the children of alumni and since these alumni were virtually all white, their children generally were too. African American children had grown up without seeing African American doctors or councilmen, for the most part, and so had few role models. African Americans also tended to go to schools that had suffered from decades of neglect and inadequate funding. All of this produced fewer African Americans than whites in undergraduate and graduate programs.

Some schools tried to produce classes mirroring America by setting aside places in their classes for minorities. The University of California, Davis (UC-Davis), Medical School had such a program; it reserved sixteen openings for minorities, who could also compete for the eighty-four "open" spots. Allan Bakke was denied admission twice at UC-Davis, even though he had higher grades and test scores than applicants admitted through the minority program. He responded by suing UC-Davis.

Significance

The *Bakke* decision has set the groundwork for affirmative action programs up to the present. Universities

and other institutions are not allowed, legally, to set aside a certain number of seats for people of one race, just as they are not permitted to admit only one race. Universities can, however, consider race as a factor in admissions. The idea behind this policy is that it allows a university to bring in a representative class and enables role models of all races, ethnicities, and sexes to be admitted to graduate and professional schools. Where a preference becomes a quota is a difficult call, one that has produced a myriad of legislation.

Affirmative action programs have been allowed elsewhere, but the Supreme Court has begun to require that, when these programs are required by government, they must be narrowly tailored to remedy past discrimination. In 2003, in two cases, the Supreme Court, in a 5-4 decision, upheld the use of affirmative action, as used in Michigan, in law school admissions, while striking it down, as used in Michigan, in undergraduate admissions. The binding criteria was that a school can individually consider candidates and use race as a factor in admissions, while a school cannot universally grant racial minorities an advantage in admissions. While that distinction might seem vague to some, it continues the criteria, for the most part, advanced in Bakke. Additionally, some states have passed public referendums and/or laws requiring that admissions be wholly color blind.

The issue has also become politicized, with Democrats favoring affirmative action as a needed remedy and Republicans opposing it as being unfair and "unAmerican." Justice Clarence Thomas himself opposes affirmative action, but one must wonder if he would have been nominated to the Court if he were white with the same qualifications. Clearly, the Supreme Court's decision on *Bakke* has hardly quenched the fire of this debate.

Primary Source

University of California Regents v. Bakke [excerpt]

> **SYNOPSIS:** Justice Lewis Powell announces the judgment of the Court, which is that the program of affirmative action in this case is unconstitutional, but that race can be considered as a factor in admission. Justice William Brennan Jr. notes that the law has not been color blind in the past, so quotas are allowable to remedy this. Justice Thurgood Marshall chronicles past discrimination and holds that the Fourteenth Amendment should not ban attempts to remedy past discrimination that that amendment had allowed.

Mr. Justice Powell announced the judgment of the Court. . . .

For the reasons stated in the following opinion, I believe that so much of the judgment of the California court as holds petitioner's special admissions program unlawful and directs that respondent be admitted to the Medical School must be affirmed. . . . Brothers The Chief Justice, Mr. Justice Stewart, Mr. Justice Rehnquist, and Mr. Justice Stevens concur in this judgment.

I also conclude for the reasons stated in the following opinion that the portion of the court's judgment enjoining petitioner from according any consideration to race in its admissions process must be reversed. . . . Brothers Mr. Justice Brennan, Mr. Justice White, Mr. Justice Marshall, and Mr. Justice Blackmun concur in this judgment.

Affirmed in part and reversed in part. . . .

. . . Racial and ethnic distinctions of any sort are inherently suspect and thus call for the most exacting judicial examination. . . .

Although many of the Framers of the Fourteenth Amendment conceived of its primary function as bridging the vast distance between members of the Negro race and the white "majority," . . . the Amendment itself was framed in universal terms, without reference to color, ethnic origin, or condition of prior servitude. . . .

Petitioner urges us to adopt for the first time a more restrictive view of the Equal Protection Clause and hold that discrimination against members of the white "majority" cannot be suspect if its purpose can be characterized as "benign." . . . The clock of our liberties, however, cannot be turned back to 1868. . . . It is far too late to argue that the guarantee of equal protection to all persons permits the recognition of special wards entitled to a degree of protection greater than that accorded others. . . .

Moreover, there are serious problems of justice connected with the idea of preference itself. . . . [T]here is a measure of inequity in forcing innocent persons in respondent's position to bear the burdens of redressing grievances not of their making. . . .

Hence, the purpose of helping certain groups whom the faculty of the Davis Medical School perceived as victims of "societal discrimination" does not justify a classification that imposes disadvantages upon persons like respondent, who bear no responsibility for whatever harm the beneficiaries of the special admissions program are thought to have suffered. To hold otherwise would be to convert a remedy heretofore reserved for violations of legal rights into a privilege that all institutions throughout the Nation could grant at their pleasure to whatever groups are perceived as victims of societal discrimination. That is a step we have never approved. . . .

Petitioner identifies, as another purpose of its program, improving the delivery of health-care services to communities currently underserved. . . .

Petitioner simply has not carried its burden of demonstrating that it must prefer members of particular ethnic groups over all other individuals in order to promote better health-care delivery to deprived citizens. Indeed, petitioner has not shown that its preferential classification is likely to have any significant effect on the problem.

The fourth goal asserted by petitioner is the attainment of a diverse student body. . . .

The atmosphere of "speculation, experiment and creation"—so essential to the quality of higher education—is widely believed to be promoted by a diverse student body. . . .

Ethnic diversity, however, is only one element in a range of factors a university properly may consider in attaining the goal of a heterogeneous student body. . . .

The experience of other university admissions programs, which take race into account in achieving the educational diversity valued by the First Amendment, demonstrates that the assignment of a fixed number of places to a minority group is not a necessary means toward that end. . . .

In such an admissions program, race or ethnic background may be deemed a "plus" in a particular applicant's file, yet it does not insulate the individual from comparison with all other candidates for the available seats. . . . In short, an admissions program operated in this way is flexible enough to consider all pertinent elements of diversity in light of the particular qualifications of each applicant, and to place them on the same footing for consideration, although not necessarily according them the same weight. Indeed, the weight attributed to a particular quality may vary from year to year depending upon the "mix" both of the student body and the applicants for the incoming class. . . .

It has been suggested that an admissions program which considers race only as one factor is simply a subtle and more sophisticated—but no less effective—means of according racial preference than the Davis program. A facial intent to discriminate, however, is evident in petitioner's preference program and not denied in this case. No such facial infirmity exists in an admissions program where race or ethnic background is simply one element—to be weighed fairly against other elements—in the selection process. . . . And a court would not assume that a university, professing to employ a facially nondiscriminatory admissions policy, would operate it as a cover for the functional equivalent of a quota system. . . .

The fatal flaw in petitioner's preferential program is its disregard of individual rights as guaranteed by the Fourteenth Amendment. . . . Such rights are not absolute. But when a State's distribution of benefits or imposition of burdens hinges on ancestry or the color of a person's skin, that individual is entitled to a demonstration that the challenged classification is necessary to promote a substantial state interest. Petitioner has failed to carry this burden. For this reason, that portion of the California court's judgment holding petitioner's special admissions program invalid under the Fourteenth Amendment must be affirmed.

In enjoining petitioner from ever considering the race of any applicant, however, the courts below failed to recognize that the State has a substantial interest that legitimately may be served by a properly devised admissions program involving the competitive consideration of race and ethnic origin. For this reason, so much of the California court's judgment as enjoins petitioner from any consideration of the race of any applicant must be reversed. . . .

Opinion of Mr. Justice Brennan, Mr. Justice White, Mr. Justice Marshall, and Mr. Justice Blackmun, concurring in the judgment in part and dissenting in part. . . .

Our Nation was founded on the principle that "all Men are created equal." Yet candor requires acknowledgment that the Framers of our Constitution, to forge the 13 Colonies into one Nation, openly compromised this principle of equality with its antithesis: slavery. The consequences of this compromise are well known and have aptly been called our promise are well known and have aptly been called our "American Dilemma." Still, it is well to recount how recent the time has been, if it has yet come, when the promise of our principles has flowered into the actuality of equal opportunity for all regardless of race or color.

The Fourteenth Amendment, the embodiment in the Constitution of our abiding belief in human equality, has been the law of our land for only slightly more than half its 200 years. And for half of that half, the Equal Protection Clause of the Amendment was largely moribund so that, as late as 1927, Mr. Justice Holmes could sum up the importance of that Clause by remarking that it was the "last resort of constitutional arguments." . . .

Against this background, claims that law must be "color-blind" or that the datum of race is no longer relevant to public policy must be seen as aspiration rather than as description of reality. This is not to denigrate aspiration; for reality rebukes us that race has too often been used by those who would stigmatize and oppress minorities. Yet we cannot . . . let color blindness become myopia which masks the reality that many "created equal" have been treated within our lifetimes as inferior both by the law and by their fellow citizens. . . .

Davis' articulated purpose of remedying the effects of past societal discrimination is, under our cases, sufficiently important to justify the use of race-conscious admissions programs where there is a sound basis for concluding that minority underrepresentation is substantial and chronic, and that the handicap of past discrimination is impeding access of minorities to the Medical School. . . .

Certainly, on the basis of the undisputed factual submissions before this Court, Davis had a sound basis for believing that the problem of under representation of minorities was substantial and chronic and that the problem was attributable to handicaps imposed on minority applicants by past and present racial discrimination. Until at least 1973, the practice of medicine in this country was, in fact, if not in law, largely the prerogative of whites. . . . The number of Negro admittees to predominantly white medical schools, moreover, had declined in absolute numbers during the years 1955 to 1964. . . .

The second prong of our test—whether the Davis program stigmatizes any discrete group or individual and whether race is reasonably used in light of the program's objectives—is clearly satisfied by the Davis program. . . .

. . . Unlike discrimination against racial minorities, the use of racial preferences for remedial purposes does not inflict a pervasive injury upon individual whites in the sense that wherever they go or whatever they do there is a significant likelihood that they will be treated as second-class citizens because of their color. This distinction does not mean that the exclusion of a white resulting from the preferential use of race is not sufficiently serious to require justification; but it does mean that the injury inflicted by such a policy is not distinguishable from disadvantages caused by a wide range of govern-

Allan Bakke is surrounded by media during his first day of classes at the Univeristy of California's Medical School at Davis, September 25, 1978.
AP/WIDE WORLD PHOTOS. REPRODUCED BY PERMISSION.

ment actions, none of which has ever been thought impermissible for that reason alone.

. . . The Davis program does not simply advance less qualified applicants; rather, it compensates applicants, who it is uncontested are fully qualified to study medicine, for educational disadvantages which it was reasonable to conclude were a product of state-fostered discrimination. . . . Since minority graduates cannot justifiably be regarded as less well qualified than nonminority graduates by virtue of the special admissions program, there is no reasonable basis to conclude that minority graduates at schools using such programs would be stigmatized as inferior by the existence of such programs. . . .

Finally, Davis' special admissions program cannot be said to violate the Constitution simply because it has set aside a predetermined number of places for qualified minority applicants rather than using minority status as a positive factor to be considered in evaluating the applications of disadvantaged minority applicants. For purposes of constitutional adjudication, there is no difference between the two approaches. In any admissions program which accords special consideration to disad-

vantaged racial minorities, a determination of the degree of preference to be given is unavoidable, and any given preference that results in the exclusion of a white candidate is no more or less constitutionally acceptable than a program such as that at Davis. Furthermore, the extent of the preference inevitably depends on how many minority applicants the particular school is seeking to admit in any particular year so long as the number of qualified minority applicants exceeds that number. There is no sensible, and certainly no constitutional, distinction between, for example, adding a set number of points to the admissions rating of disadvantaged minority applicants as an expression of the preference with the expectation that this will result in the admission of an approximately determined number of qualified minority applicants and setting a fixed number of places for such applicants as was done here. . . .

Accordingly, we would reverse the judgment of the Supreme Court of California holding the Medical School's special admissions program unconstitutional and directing respondent's admission, as well as that portion of the judgment enjoining the Medical School from according any consideration to race in the admissions process. . . .

Mr. Justice Marshall.

I agree with the judgment of the Court only insofar as it permits a university to consider the race of an applicant in making admissions decisions. I do not agree that petitioner's admissions program violates the Constitution. For it must be remembered that, during most of the past 200 years, the Constitution as interpreted by this Court did not prohibit the most ingenious and pervasive forms of discrimination against the Negro. Now, when a state acts to remedy the effects of that legacy of discrimination, I cannot believe that this same Constitution stands as a barrier. . . .

The position of the Negro today in America is the tragic but inevitable consequence of centuries of unequal treatment. Measured by any benchmark of comfort or achievement, meaningful equality remains a distant dream for the Negro.

A Negro child today has a life expectancy which is shorter by more than five years than that of a white child. The Negro child's mother is over three times more likely to die of complications in childbirth, and the infant mortality rate for Negroes is nearly twice that for whites. The median income of the Negro family is only 60% that of the median of a white family, and the percentage of Negroes who live in families with incomes below the poverty line is nearly four times greater than that of whites. . . .

In light of the sorry history of discrimination and its devastating impact on the lives of Negroes, bringing the Negro into the mainstream of American life should be a state interest of the highest order. To fail to do so is to ensure that America will forever remain a divided society.

I do not believe that the Fourteenth Amendment requires us to accept that fate. Neither its history nor our past cases lend any support to the conclusion that a university may not remedy the cumulative effects of society's discrimination by giving consideration to race in an effort to increase the number and percentage of Negro doctors. . . .

These differences in the experience of the Negro make it difficult for me to accept that Negroes cannot be afforded greater protection under the Fourteenth Amendment where it is necessary to remedy the effects of past discrimination.

Further Resources

BOOKS

Ball, Howard. *The "Bakke" Case: Race, Education, and Affirmative Action.* Lawrence: University Press of Kansas, 2000.

Jeffries, John Calvin. *Justice Lewis F. Powell, Jr.* New York: Scribner's, 1994.

McCormack, Wayne. *The "Bakke" Decision: Implications for Higher Education Admissions: A Report.* Washington, D.C.: American Council on Education, Association of American Law Schools, 1978.

Rosenkranz, E. Joshua, and Bernard Schwartz. *Reason and Passion: Justice Brennan's Enduring Influence.* New York: Norton, 1997.

Tushnet, Mark V. *Making Constitutional Law: Thurgood Marshall and the Supreme Court, 1961–1991.* New York: Oxford University Press, 1997.

Welch, Susan, and John Gruhl. *Affirmative Action and Minority Enrollments in Medical and Law Schools.* Ann Arbor: University of Michigan Press, 1998.

Williams, Juan. *Thurgood Marshall: American Revolutionary.* New York: Times Books, 1998.

WEBSITES

"Regents of the University of California v. Bakke (1978)." Civitas International. Available online at http://www.civnet.org /resources/teach/basic/part6/41.htm; website home page: http://www.civnet.org/ (accessed April 16, 2003).

"Pinto Fires and Personal Ethics: A Script Analysis of Missed Opportunities"

Memoir

By: Dennis A. Gioia

Date: 1994

Source: Gioia, Dennis A. "Pinto Fires and Personal Ethics: A Script Analysis of Missed Opportunities." *Journal of Business Ethics* 11, 1992, 379–389. Reprinted in Birsch, Douglas and John H. Fielder, eds. *The Ford Pinto Case: A Study in Applied Ethics, Business, and Technology.* Albany: State University of New York Press, 1994, 97–105.

About the Author: Dennis A. Gioia graduated from Florida State University with degrees in engineering science and management. He worked as an engineer for Boeing Aerospace and Ford Motor Company. For Ford, he was the corporate vehicle recall coordinator. He served as a project director for several management development programs for the state of Florida, and later became a professor in the College of Business at Pennsylvania State University. He is widely published on management and human relations issues. ∎

Introduction

The Ford Pinto was produced as the result of a determined effort by Ford Motor Company to put a small, cheap, and fuel efficient car on the market. Ford felt that a car like the Pinto was needed in order to compete with Japanese and European imports. In the late 1960s Americans were showing increasing interest in these foreign made cars, which were smaller and cheaper than American models.

The typical American car of the 1950s and 1960s was large and powerful, and Fords were no exception. Desiging a small car therefore presented new challenges to Ford's engineers, challenges that were made more difficult by the tight project requirements. Ford president Lee Iacocca insisted throughout the Pinto's development that the car weigh no more than two thousand pounds and cost no more than two thousand dollars. The Pinto was also developed and put into production much faster than was the norm, leaving little time to consider design changes. It was released to the public in 1970.

Crash tests done at Ford during the Pinto's development revealed that the Pinto's gas tank was prone to ruptures in relatively low-speed crashes. These ruptures often led to dangerous fires. Ford did not consider this problem to be especially serious, however. The automaker felt that smaller cars like the Pinto were inherently less safe than larger automobiles, and that even if fires were more likely than they had to be, they were not so common as to require design changes. Since there were no federal safety standards on this issue at the time it was up to Ford to decide what to do, and production of the Pinto went ahead on schedule.

It did not take long for the Pinto's problems to come to the public's attention. In 1972, a Pinto burst into flames after being rear ended, killing the driver and injuring and disfiguring passenger Richard Grimshaw. He sued Ford for damages, in a case that would take many years to resolve. Over the years, a number of other people also died or were injured in Pinto fires, some sued, and bad publicity about the car began to mount. However, Ford continued to assert that their car was not so unsafe that it required modifications.

This state of affairs continued for several years. In 1977, *Mother Jones* magazine published the article "Pinto Madness," by Mark Dowie. It described the problems with the Pinto in graphic detail. Dowie had gained access to Ford's private files on the car, and thus was able to tell the public how Ford had known about problems in the Pinto's fuel tank since 1970. He asserted that Ford had decided not to fix the problem because they were in such a rush to get the Pinto to market at low cost.

Dowie's next accusation cast Ford in an even worse light. To help determine if the Pinto's gas tank should be modified, Ford had conducted a cost-benefit analysis. According to federal guidelines in 1970, the death of a hu-

Ford Motor Company chairman Henry Ford II, right, speaks with Ford president Lee Iacocca about the state of the automotive industry, December 18, 1975. © BETTMANN/CORBIS. REPRODUCED BY PERMISSION.

man being "cost" society $200,000. Ford estimated that 180 people would die in fire-related Pinto accidents if the car was not modified, with a similar number of serious injuries. Based on these estimates they determined that the benefit of fixing the Pinto's gas tank would be $49.5 million. That is to say, that the value of the lives and health saved by fixing the car would be worth that amount. The cost of fixing the gas tank problem, estimated at $11 per vehicle, would be $137 million. Since the cost of the fix was greater than the benefit, this analysis indicated that Ford need not alter the Pinto.

Significance

The revelations about Ford's knowledge and acceptance of the Pinto's problems created an outrage. This anger was reflected by the jury in the *Grimshaw v. Ford* case. In 1978, they found in favor of Grimshaw and awarded him $125 million in punitive damages. The jury specifically chose $125 million because that amount was more than the profit that Ford had made on the Pinto line since its introduction in 1970 (the punitive damages were later reduced to $3.5 million).

The huge Grimshaw jury award, the largest in California history up to that point, drew even more attention to the Pinto. The National Highway Traffic Safety Administration had begun testing the Pinto in 1977, and in the summer of 1978 it concluded that the vehicle did not meet current safety standards (these standards had not been in place when the Pinto was introduced). Ford finally issued a recall of 1971–1976 model year Pintos in

September, 1978. (1977 and later Pintos had a new, safer, gas tank).

Even the recall did not end the Pinto, and Ford's problems. When an August, 1978, accident resulted in three teenagers dying in a Pinto-related fire, Ford was charged with reckless homicide. No corporation had ever faced criminal charges stemming from a defective product before. Ford won the case, but it nevertheless helped establish a precedent for holding corporations responsible for the safety of their products.

The Pinto was a major embarassment for Ford and for business in general. Ford's seemingly greedy attitude and lack of concern for human life angered many Americans and made them distrustful of big business. Thus the Pinto fires helped spur the growth of the consumer movement during the 1970s and 1980s. The fires also made safety and quality a much higher concern for American car buyers. By 1980 no auto executive could claim, as Iacocca had supposedly done, that "safety doesn't sell" and thus wasn't important in automobile design. The Pinto itself was discontinued in 1980.

Primary Source

"Pinto Fires and Personal Ethics: A Script Analysis of Missed Opportunities" [excerpt]

> **SYNOPSIS:** Dennis A. Gioia notes that he entered Ford in 1972 and was in charge of safety recalls. He then discusses the requirements given for the Ford Pinto. The safety issue was known at the time, as he details, and he gives the decision-making process behind not correcting the flaw. He also explains why he did not begin a safety recall on the Pinto. Gioia closes by noting what happened to the Pinto after he left Ford.

Pinto Fires and Personal Ethics: A Script Analysis of Missed Opportunities

In the summer of 1972 I made one of those important transitions in life, the significance of which becomes obvious only in retrospect. I left academe with a BS in Engineering Science and an MBA to enter the world of big business. I joined Ford Motor Company at World Headquarters in Dearborn, Michigan, fulfilling a long-standing dream to work in the heart of the auto industry. I felt confident that I was in the right place at the right time to make a difference. My initial job title was "Problem Analyst"—a catchall label that superficially described what I would be thinking about and doing in the coming years. On some deeper level, however, the title paradoxically came to connote the many critical things that I would *not* be thinking about and acting upon. . . .

Therefore, it struck quite a few of my friends in the MBA program as rather strange that I was in the program at all. ("If you are so disappointed in business, why study business?"). Subsequently, they were practically dumbstruck when I accepted the job offer from Ford, apparently one of the great purveyors of the very actions I reviled. I countered that it was an ideal strategy, arguing that I would have a greater chance of influencing social change in business if I worked behind the scenes on the inside, rather than as a strident voice on the outside. It was clear to me that somebody needed to prod these staid companies into socially responsible action. I certainly aimed to do my part. Besides, I liked cars.

Into the Fray: Setting the Personal Stage

Predictably enough, I found myself on the fast track at Ford, participating in a "tournament" type of socialization (Van Maanen, 1978), engaged in a competition for recognition with other MBA's who had recently joined the company. And I quickly became caught up in the game. The company itself was dynamic; the environment of business, especially the auto industry, was intriguing; the job was challenging and the pay was great. The psychic rewards of working and succeeding in a major corporation proved unexpectedly seductive. I really became involved in the job. . . .

By the summer of 1973 I was pitched into the thick of the battle. I became Ford's Field Recall Coordinator—not a position that was particularly high in the hierarchy, but one that wielded influence far beyond its level. I was in charge of the operational coordination of all of the recall campaigns currently underway and also in charge of tracking incoming information to identify developing problems. Therefore, I was in a position to make initial recommendations about possible future recalls. . . .

The Pinto Case: Setting the Corporate Stage

In 1970 Ford introduced the Pinto, a small car that was intended to compete with the then current challenge from European cars and the ominous presence on the horizon of Japanese manufacturers. The Pinto was brought from inception to production in the record time of approximately 25 months (compared to the industry average of 43 months), a time frame that suggested the necessity for doing things expediently. In addition to the time pressure, the engineering and development teams were required to adhere to the production "limits of 2000" for the diminutive car: it was not to exceed either $2000 in cost or 2000 pounds in weight. Any decisions that threatened these targets or the timing of the car's introduction were discouraged. Under normal conditions design, styling, product planning, engineering, etc., were completed prior to production tooling. Because of the foreshortened time frame, however, some of these usually sequential processes were executed in parallel.

As a consequence, tooling was already well under way (thus "freezing" the basic design) when routine crash testing revealed that the Pinto's fuel tank often ruptured when struck from the rear at a relatively low speed (31 mph in crash tests). Reports (revealed much later) showed that the fuel tank failures were the result of some rather marginal design features. The tank was positioned between the rear bumper and the rear axle (a standard industry practice for the time). During impact, however, several studs protruding from the rear of the axle housing would puncture holes in the tank; the fuel filler neck also was likely to rip away. Spilled gasoline then could be ignited by sparks. Ford had in fact crash-tested 11 vehicles; 8 of these cars suffered potentially catastrophic gas tank ruptures. The only 3 cars that survived intact had each been modified in some way to protect the tank.

These crash tests, however, were conducted under the guidelines of Federal Motor Vehicle Safety Standard 301 which had been proposed in 1968 and strenuously opposed by the auto industry. FMVSS 301 was not actually adopted until 1976; thus, at the time of the tests, Ford was not in violation of the law. There were several possibilities for fixing the problem, including the option of redesigning the tank integrity in a high-speed crash. That solution, however, was not only time consuming and expensive, but also usurped trunk space, which was seen as a critical competitive sales factor. One of the production modifications to the tank, however, would have cost only $11 to install, but given the tight margins and restrictions of the "limits of 2000," there was reluctance to make even this relatively minor change. There were other reasons for not approving the change, as well, including a widespread industry belief that all small cars were inherently unsafe solely because of their size and weight. Another more prominent reason was a corporate belief that "safety doesn't sell." This observation was attributed to Lee Iacocca and stemmed from Ford's earlier attempt to make safety a sales theme, an attempt that failed rather dismally in the marketplace.

Perhaps the most controversial reason for rejecting the production change to the gas tank, however, was Ford's use of cost-benefit analysis to justify the decision. The National Highway Traffic Safety Association (NHTSA, a federal agency) had approved the use of cost-benefit analysis as a appropriate means for establishing automotive safety design standards. The controversial aspect in making such calculations was that they required the assignment of some specific value for a human life. In 1970, that value was deemed to be approximately $200,000 as a "cost to society" for each fatality. Ford used NHTSA's figures in estimating the costs and benefits of altering the tank production design. An internal memo, later revealed in court, indicates the following tabulations concerning potential fires (Dowie, 1977):

Costs: $137,000,000

(Estimated as the costs of a production fix to all similarly designed cars and trucks with the gas tank aft of the axle (12,500,000 vehicles × $11/vehicle))

Benefits: $49,530,000

(Estimated as the savings from preventing (180 projected deaths × $200,000/death) + (180 projected burn injuries × $67,000/injury) + (2100 burned cars × $700/car))

The cost-benefit decision was then construed as straightforward: No production fix would be undertaken. The philosophical and ethical implications of assigning a financial value for human life or disfigurement do not seem to have been a major consideration in reaching this decision. . . .

Pintos and Personal Experience

One of these new files concerned reports of Pintos "lighting up" (in the words of a field representative) in rear-end accidents. There were actually very few reports, perhaps because component failure was not initially assumed. These cars simply were consumed by fire after apparently very low speed accidents. Was there a problem? Not as far as I was concerned. My cue for labeling a case as a problem either required high frequencies of occurrence or directly traceable causes. I had little time for speculative contemplation on potential problems that did not fit a pattern that suggested known courses of action leading to possible recall. I do, however, remember being disquieted by a field report accompanied by graphic, detailed photos of the remains of a burned-out Pinto in which several people had

The Ford Pinto became known as the "death car" after many vehicles' gas tanks exploded. **AP/WIDE WORLD PHOTOS. REPRODUCED BY PERMISSION.**

died. Although that report became part of my file, I did not flag it as any special case. . . .

It is also important to convey the muting of emotion involved in the Recall Coordinator's job. I remember contemplating the fact that my job literally involved life-and-death matters. I was sometimes responsible for finding and fixing cars NOW, because somebody's life might depend on it. I took it *very* seriously. Early in the job, I sometimes woke up at night wondering whether I had covered all the bases. Had I left some unknown person at risk because I had not thought of something? That soon faded, however, and of necessity the consideration of people's lives became a fairly removed, dispassionate process. To do the job "well" there was little room for emotion. Allowing it to surface was potentially paralyzing and prevented rational decisions about which cases to recommend for recall. On moral grounds I knew I could recommend most of the vehicles on my safety tracking list for recall (and risk earning the label of a "bleeding heart"). On practical grounds, I recognized that people implicitly accept risks in cars. We could not recall all cars with *potential* problems and stay in business. I learned

to be responsive to those cases that suggested an imminent, dangerous problem.

I should also note, that the country was in the midst of its first, and worst, oil crisis at this time. The effects of the crisis had cast a pall over Ford and the rest of the automobile industry. Ford's product line, with the perhaps notable exception of the Pinto and Maverick small cars, was not well-suited to dealing with the crisis. Layoffs were imminent for many people. Recalling the Pinto in this context would have damaged one of the few trump cards the company had (although, quite frankly, I do not remember overtly thinking about that issue). . . .

Later, the existence of the crash test data did become known within Ford, which suggested that the Pinto might actually have a recallable problem. This information led to a reconsideration of the case within our office. The data, however, prompted a comparison of the Pinto's survivability in a rear end accident with that of other competitor's small cars. These comparisons revealed that although many cars in this subcompact class suffered appalling deformation in relatively low speed collisions, the Pinto was merely the worst of a bad lot. Furthermore, the gap between the Pinto and the competition was not dramatic in terms of the speed at which fuel tank rupture was likely to occur. On that basis it would be difficult to justify the recall of cars that were comparable with others on the market. In the face of even more compelling evidence that people were probably going to die in this car, I again included myself in a group of decision makers who voted not to recommend recall to the higher levels of the organization.

Coda to the Corporate Case

Subsequent to my departure from Ford in 1975, reports of Pinto fires escalated, attracting increasing media attention, almost all of it critical of Ford. Anderson and Whitten (1976) revealed the internal memos concerning the gas tank problem and questioned how the few dollars saved per car could be justified when human lives were at stake. Shortly thereafter, a scathing article by Dowie (1977) attacked not only the Pinto's design, but also accused Ford of gross negligence, stonewalling, and unethical corporate conduct by alleging that Ford knowingly sold "firetraps" after willfully calculating the cost of lives against profits (see also Gatewood and Carroll, 1983). Dowie's provocative quote speculating on "how long the Ford Motor Company would continue to market lethal cars were Henry Ford II and Lee Iacocca serving 20 year terms in Leavenworth for consumer homicide" (1977, p. 32) was particularly effective in focusing attention on the case. Public sentiment edged toward labeling Ford as socially deviant because management was seen as knowing that the car was defective, choosing profit over lives, resisting demands to fix the car, and apparently showing no public remorse (Swigert and Farrell, 1980–81).

Shortly after Dowie's (1977) esposé, NHTSA initiated its own investigation. Then, early in 1978 a jury awarded a Pinto burn victim $125 million in punitive damages (later reduced to $6.6 million, a judgment upheld on an appeal that prompted the judge to assert that "Ford's institutional mentality was shown to be one of callous indifference to public safety" (quoted in Cullen *et. al.,* 1987, p. 164). A siege atmosphere emerged at Ford. Insiders characterized the mounting media campaign as "hysterical" and "a crusade against us" (personal communications). The crisis deepened. In the summer of 1978 NHTSA issued a formal determination that the Pinto was defective. Ford then launched a reluctant recall of all 1971–1976 cars (those built

for the 1977 model year were equipped with a production fix prompted by the adoption of the FMVSS 301 gas tank standard). Ford hoped that the issue would then recede, but worse was yet to come.

The culmination of the case and the demise of the Pinto itself began in Indiana on August 10, 1978, when three teenage girls died in a fire triggered after their 1973 Pinto was hit from behind by a van. A grand jury took the unheard of step of indicting Ford on charges of reckless homicide (Cullen *et al.,* 1987). Because of the precedent-setting possibilities for all manufacturing industries, Ford assembled a formidable legal team headed by Watergate prosecutor James Neal to defend itself at the trial. The trial was a media event; it was the first time that a corporation was tried for alleged *criminal* behavior. After a protracted, acrimonious courtroom battle that included vivid clashes among the opposing attorneys, surprise witnesses, etc., the jury ultimately found in favor of Ford. Ford had dodged a bullet in the form of a consequential legal precedent, but because of the negative publicity of the case and the charges of corporate crime and ethical deviance, the conduct of manufacturing businesses was altered, probably forever. As a relatively minor footnote to the case, Ford ceased production of the Pinto.

Further Resources

BOOKS

Banham, Russ. *The Ford Century: Ford Motor Company and the Innovations That Shaped the World.* New York: Artisan, 2002.

Bonsall, Thomas E. *Disaster in Dearborn: The Story of the Edsel.* Stanford, Calif.: Stanford General Books, 2002.

Cullen, Francis T., William J. Maakestad, and Gray Cavender. *Corporate Crime Under Attack: The Ford Pinto Case and Beyond.* Cincinnati, Ohio: Anderson, 1987.

Donaldson, Thomas. *Case Studies in Business Ethics.* Englewood Cliffs, N.J.: Prentice-Hall, 1984.

Newton, Lisa H., and Maureen M. Ford. *Taking Sides: Clashing Views on Controversial Issues in Business Ethics and Society,* 2nd ed. Guilford, Conn.: Dushkin, 1991.

Snider, Clare J., and Michael W. R. Davis. *The Ford Fleet, 1923–1989.* Cleveland, Ohio: Freshwater, 1994.

Strobel, Lee Patrick. *Reckless Homicide?: Ford's Pinto Trial.* South Bend, Ind.: And Books, 1980.

Warnock, C. Gayle. *Innocents, Incidents and Indiscretions.* Scottsdale, Ariz.: Pro West, 1996.

PERIODICALS

Dowie, Mark. "Pinto Madness." *Mother Jones,* September–October 1977. Available online at http://www.motherjones .com/mother_jones/SO77/dowie.html; website home page: http://www.motherjones.com (accessed April 16, 2003).

I Am Roe: My Life, "Roe v. Wade," and Freedom of Choice

Memoir

By: Norma McCorvey

Date: 1994

Source: McCorvey, Norma, with Andy Meisler. *I Am Roe: My Life, "Roe v. Wade," and Freedom of Choice.* New York: HarperCollins, 1994, 117–123.

About the Author: Norma McCorvey (1947–) was born into a broken home. By twenty-three, she was pregnant for the third time and wanted an abortion. This led her to becoming the plaintiff in *Roe v. Wade* (1973). McCorvey, though, was not directly involved in the suit, and it was not until the late 1980s that she publicly announced herself as "Jane Roe." ■

Introduction

Even though abortion was decried by some ancient medical texts, most midwives were knowledgeable about which herbs and roots generally promoted removal of what were euphemistically called "blockages." Common law put much emphasis on the idea of "quickening," which is when "viability" (capable of surviving outside the womb without artificial support, usually by the end of the seventh month) occurred.

In the nineteenth century, several states began to take more of an interest in the matter. A large part of this was due to the fact that abortion, when attempted through medical and not herbal methods, was very risky. During the first three-quarters of the twentieth century, however, abortion became a much safer procedure. Also during this time the legal system became much more interested in the individual. As early as 1928, Justice Louis Brandeis argued for the "right to be let alone" as part of a right to privacy. Years later, the Supreme Court built on this right to overturn a Connecticut ban on the use of contraceptives.

As women took more control of their own lives with the development of the birth control pill during the 1960s, they began arguing for changes in state laws against abortion. Women pushed for the Equal Rights Amendment, and some women, including Sarah Weddington, began to look for a test case to challenge the state abortion laws.

Norma McCorvey was not overly knowledgeable about sex, nor was she interested in changing the world. She was in and out of reform school as a youth and had two children from a bad relationship and a failed marriage. When she became pregnant for a third time, she decided that she wanted an abortion. Eventually, she was put in contact with Weddington by another lawyer.

Significance

Weddington carried McCorvey's case all the way to the Supreme Court as *Roe v. Wade.* The Supreme Court used this case to strike down Texas's abortion law and to declare a fundamental right to privacy in the area of abortion. Justice Harry Blackmun argued that the right to privacy outweighed the state interest up to the point of viability, and then after viability, abortions could be banned or restricted. Appropriate medical regulations to safeguard the health of the woman undertaking the abortion could, however, be instituted after the first trimester of pregnancy.

This decision came too late to help McCorvey. By the end of 1970, she had had her baby, and even though she had won at the state court level, Henry Wade, the Dallas district attorney who was defending the Texas law, appealed the case to the next highest level and would enforce the Texas law until all the levels of appeal had been heard. Thus, McCorvey had no chance for an abortion.

McCorvey put the child up for adoption and moved on with her life, eventually founding a cleaning company. She lost touch with Weddington and others who took her case to the Supreme Court, but did, for a time in the late 1980s, become active again in the pro-choice movement. In the 1990s, McCorvey announced herself as pro-life.

Roe v. Wade lead to attempts to get a constitutional amendment passed and pledges by conservative presidential candidates to appoint only Supreme Court justices who would overturn *Roe.* In two cases in the 1980s, *Roe* came close to being overturned. However, in *Planned Parenthood v. Casey* (1992), Justice Sandra Day O'Connor led a plurality of three justices in an opinion that directly upheld *Roe* and argued that stare decesis, the idea that a ruling of the Supreme Court should stand until there is a compelling reason to reexamine it, should apply here. As of 2003 *Roe* still stands.

Primary Source

I Am Roe: My Life, "Roe v. Wade," and Freedom of Choice [excerpt]

SYNOPSIS: McCorvey opens by describing her initial meeting with Weddington and Linda Coffee, who were her attorneys in *Roe v. Wade.* She then goes on to explain that Weddington and Coffee could not get her an abortion, and told her of the consequences of illegal abortions. The excerpt closes by noting how the case came to be titled "Roe."

In February 1970 I was Norma McCorvey, a pregnant street person. A twenty-one-year-old woman in big trouble. I became Jane Roe at a corner table at

Columbo's, an Italian restaurant at Mockingbird Lane and Greenville Avenue, in Dallas. I'd suggested to Linda Coffee that we meet there.

Columbo's is gone now, which is a shame. It was an inexpensive place, clean, and made very good pizza. The tables had red-and-white checked tablecloths—just like the one I'd bought for Woody back in California. Columbo's wasn't very big. When I walked into the place that evening, I didn't have any trouble figuring out who was waiting for me.

Linda Coffee and Sarah Weddington, sitting together, stood out in Columbo's. Both were older than me, and both were wearing two-piece business suits. Nice clothing, expensive looking. One of them was tall and dark and thin. Delicate. The other was short and blond and a little plump, her hair in a stiff-looking permanent. Her hairdo was old-fashioned, even for then.

I was wearing jeans, a button-down shirt tied at the waist, and sandals. I wore my bandanna tied around my left leg, above the knee. That meant I didn't have a girlfriend.

I walked over to their table. It was obvious to me even from across the room that these women hadn't talked to a person like me for a long time, if ever. For a second, I felt like turning around and running out the door, writing the whole meeting off and starting over again. But I didn't. Instead, I thought, Norma, they're just as scared of you as you are of them. Looking at the nervousness and doubt in their eyes, I almost believed it.

"Hi. I'm Norma McCorvey?" I said.

The shorter blond woman came to life.

"I'm Sarah Weddington," she said.

Sarah Weddington reached out and shook my hand. Linda introduced herself, too, but it was apparent right away that Sarah was the one who would speak for both of them. For most of that meeting—in fact, for most of all our meetings—it was Sarah who talked, and it was Sarah who listened to me with the most concentration.

"Thanks for showing up," I said.

I don't remember much else about the first few minutes. Small talk was awkward for us, considering how little we had in common. I talked about Henry and how much I liked him. Sarah agreed. She told me that she and Linda were lawyers, which I already knew. The conversation died down.

I went to order our pizza and beer at the counter. While I stood there, waiting, I worked up the courage

Anti-abortion demonstrators gather in front of the U.S. Capitol to protest the anniversary of the Supreme Court's 1973 decision in *Roe v. Wade*, January 22, 1976. © BETTMANN/CORBIS. REPRODUCED BY PERMISSION.

to ask these women the only question I was interested in getting an answer to.

I brought the beer back to the table.

"Do you know where I can get an abortion?" I said.

"No," said Sarah, "I don't."

. . . I sat up in my chair and got ready to leave. I didn't want to hear the adoption spiel again.

But surprisingly, Sarah didn't begin to give it to me. Instead—and this is what kept me from leaving—she went off in another direction entirely.

"Norma, do you really want an abortion?" she asked.

"Yes," I said.

"Why?"

"Because I don't want this baby. I don't even figure it's a baby. And I figure it's making my life pretty miserable, right now."

"Yes," said Sarah. "Go on."

I looked closely at her to see if what I'd said disgusted her. Or made her dislike me. But no, all

I could see was that she was interested in my story. And maybe, just maybe, interested in helping me somehow.

"See, Sarah," I said, "my being pregnant, I don't think I'll be able to find work. And if I can't get work I can't take care of myself. I don't want to be pregnant. I don't want this *thing* growing inside my body!"

By the end of my answer I was almost shouting. But Sarah didn't seem to mind.

"Norma," she said, "do you know what the abortion process is? Do you know what women have to go through when they get one?"

"Not really," I admitted. "But I kind of have a general idea."

Sarah told me, roughly, what a doctor did during a regular abortion. It sounded awful. But the truth was, it wasn't much different from what I had imagined all along.

Sarah leaned forward. "Norma. Don't you think women should have access to abortions? Safe, legal abortions?"

For the first time I realized that Sarah and Linda weren't just ordinary lawyers. For the first time I realized how interested she was in what *I* was interested in. Abortions. And in my getting one, too? Despite everything, my hopes rose a little.

"Sure," I said, "of course they should. But there aren't any legal ones around. So I guess I've got to find an illegal one, don't I?"

"No!" said Sarah and Linda, together.

"Why the hell not?" I said.

I felt a little flare of anger. First they were for abortions. Then they didn't want me to have one. What kind of mind games were these women playing with me?

"Because they're dangerous, Norma," said Sarah. "Illegal abortions are dangerous."

"Yeah, so?" I said.

Sarah shook her head. Then this woman in her nice suit, a woman I couldn't have imagined even going to a horror movie, began to tell me stories.

Terrible stories. Stories of women who'd had illegal abortions and lived to regret them. Or hadn't lived. Women who'd gone to gangsters, or shady doctors, and had their insides torn out. And who'd gone home and bled to death.

"These women were murdered," said Sarah. Then she told me about pregnant, unmarried women who had been so desperate to get rid of their babies that they'd tried to give themselves abortions with coat hangers. And killed themselves.

Then the worst story—one that made me shiver with fear. Sarah told me about a woman who didn't want anyone to know she had gotten the abortion—who was found, in a pool of blood, in a hotel room in New York City.

"They didn't find her for a couple of days," said Sarah. "And even when they did, she had no identification. So they didn't know who she was. They couldn't notify her family. All they could do was call her Jane Doe. And wait for someone to come forward and claim her body."

Jane Doe! That could be me.

An awful picture passed through my mind. Of me, alone—no friends, no lovers, not even a name—lying dead in that hotel room. Who would claim my body?

I began to cry, in front of strangers. Smart, rich strangers, who made me feel poor and ignorant. It was awful that they were seeing me cry. Embarrassing. Sarah handed me a Kleenex from her purse.

"Yes," she said, "it's really unfair and inhuman. And it shouldn't have to happen to any woman. Rich or poor. Anywhere." That's why, she said, she and Linda and some other people who thought just like them were working hard to overturn the Texas law against abortions. Their weapon was a legal project, a lawsuit, to challenge the law in the courts.

She wasn't sure if they would be successful, but if they could do it—and it would take a lot of hard work, plus a pregnant women like me, who wanted but wasn't able to get an abortion, to put her name on their lawsuit—then abortions would be legal in the state of Texas.

"Would that mean that somebody like me would be able to get an abortion?" I said.

"Yes," said Sarah, "it would."

It would? New hope began to flood through me, even though I'd been crying my eyes out a few seconds ago.

"That would be great," I said, excited despite myself.

"Yes!" said Sarah, just as excitedly.

In her excitement, Sarah began describing the road the lawsuit would take—through district courts and appeals courts, state courts and federal courts. Early on, I lost the thread of what she was saying.

But I kept nodding anyway. Sarah sounded so revved up, so intense, so passionate about her plans, that it was as if she were telling me her innermost personal secrets—instead of describing all sorts of complicated legal business, using words that I was certain only lawyers understood.

I thought, I don't really want to hear about courts. I've been in too many courts in my life. But I didn't want to interrupt her. This woman might be able to help me.

Finally, she stopped.

"That's great," I said, a little bit too late.

But I must not have fooled anybody, because there was an awkward silence. Then somebody, either Sarah or Linda, asked me to tell them all about myself.

Another silence. A longer one. All about myself? What would these woman think about me if I told them all about myself? I didn't know much—anything at all, really—about their lives, but I was pretty sure they hadn't gone to reform school or dealt drugs or been beaten by their husbands or spent their days and nights in gay bars.

They might be shocked—or worse, maybe disgusted—by my story. On the other hand, they seemed to like me, wanted to connect with me, in their own way.

Would they still want to help if me I told them that my private life was none of their damn business? I took a deep breath and made my decision.

Over that red checkered tablecloth. I told them everything. Or almost everything. Louisiana and Dallas and Woody McCorvey. The whole miserable story. Over pizza and a pitcher of beer. While the people at the next table laughed and whooped it up.

Sarah and Linda hung in and listened sympathetically for a while. Then I got to the part of telling them I was a lesbian. That I liked girls. That I lived with women, get it?

Sarah and Linda looked at each other. They frowned. I felt the flashes of fear and doubt and confusion passing between them. I realized what they were thinking: how could this woman who says she's a lesbian have gotten herself pregnant all these times? It doesn't make sense. Maybe nothing she's told us makes sense. But here's what does make sense: maybe she's lying to us. Or maybe there's something we don't understand about her. Something weird. Something dangerous. Something that will hurt our lawsuit. Hurt us.

Abortion activist Norma McCorvey. © BETTMANN/CORBIS. REPRODUCED BY PERMISSION.

No! Inside my head, I shouted back to them: You don't have to worry about my hurting you! I'm only dangerous to myself!

They didn't hear me. But how could I explain it all in words? I could sense them thinking about brushing me off and finding another pregnant woman. They were slipping away from me. And with them, my only chance for an abortion.

I panicked.

"You know," I said, "I was raped. That's how I became pregnant with this baby."

The horrible lie—this was the second time I'd used it—pulled at the insides of my stomach. But it got their attention. The two lawyers turned away from each other and quickly said they were sorry to hear this. That rape is a terrible thing. A crime.

"Was the rapist arrested?" asked Sarah.

"No," I said.

"Did the police look very hard for him?"

"No," I said, sinking deeper and deeper.

"Did you report the rape to the police?"

"No," I said, burning inside with shame.

Sarah stopped quizzing me. I tried to figure out whether she thought I was lying. This time, I couldn't read her.

She looked at Linda again. They seemed to come to some sort of conclusion.

"Well, Norma," she said, "it's awful that you were raped. But actually, the Texas abortion law doesn't make any exception for rape. So it doesn't matter in terms of our lawsuit."

"Oh, that's too bad," I said.

"Yes, it is," said Sarah.

A long pause.

"Well, anyway, we would like to have you as a plaintiff in our lawsuit. Would you like to help us?"

"Sure," I said, trying to be as cool as I could. A plaintiff. What was that? Well, I'd look it up in the dictionary later. At least I hadn't lost this chance.

We drank a beer toast to our lawsuit. Before she left, Sarah explained to me that they'd need me to sign some legal papers. With my own name, if I wanted to, but under a false name if I wanted to stay anonymous.

"Great," I said.

Sarah asked me if I had any questions. I said yes, I did.

"How much will I have to pay you two for being my lawyers?" I said.

Sarah smiled. "Nothing, Norma. We're doing this case *pro bono*." That meant, she said, that they were doing it for free.

"Then when can I get my abortion?" I asked.

"When the case is over, if we've won," said Sarah.

I was two and a half months pregnant. I didn't know how late you could get an abortion, but I did know that it was better to do it as soon as possible. How long could a lawsuit take? I remembered some of the trials I'd seen on television. The times I'd been in court myself. None of those occasions seemed to have taken much time at all.

"When will that be?" I said.

Sarah looked at me closely. I can see her sitting across from me, right now.

"It's really impossible to tell you that, Norma," she said. "We'll just have to let due process take its course."

Further Resources

BOOKS

Ball, Howard. *The Supreme Court in the Intimate Lives of Americans: Birth, Sex, Marriage, Childbearing, and Death.* New York: New York University Press, 2002.

Garrow, David J. *Liberty and Sexuality: The Right to Privacy and the Making of "Roe v. Wade."* New York: Macmillan, 1994.

Hull, N. E. H., and Peter Charles Hoffer. *"Roe v. Wade": The Abortion Rights Controversy in American History.* Lawrence: University Press of Kansas, 2001.

Reagan, Leslie J. *When Abortion Was a Crime: Women, Medicine, and Law in the United States, 1867–1973.* Berkeley: University of California Press, 1997.

Rubin, Eva R. *The Abortion Controversy: A Documentary History.* Westport, Conn.: Greenwood, 1994.

Solinger, Rickie. *Abortion Wars: A Half-Century of Struggle, 1950–2000.* Berkeley: University of California Press, 1998.

WEBSITES

"Roe v. Wade." Women's Rights on Trial, Gale Group. Available online at http://www.galegroup.com/free_resources/whm/trials/roe.htm; website home page: http://www.galegroup.com (accessed April 16, 2003).

My Life As a Radical Lawyer

Autobiography

By: William Kunstler

Date: 1994

Source: Kunstler, William M., with Shelia Isenberg. *My Life As a Radical Lawyer.* New York: Birch Lane, 1994, 214–216, 222–224.

About the Author: William Kunstler (1919–1995) graduated from Columbia Law School in 1948 and was one of the 1960s' and 1970s' most well known lawyers. He was either loved or hated. He defended, among others, Martin Luther King Jr., crime boss John Gotti, and the Chicago Seven. He took on other high-profile cases, such as the two American Indians indicted for the Attica riot. He also worked with those who took over Wounded Knee in protest of the 1890 Wounded Knee massacre. In the 1980s and 1990s, he defended Wayne Williams, a man convicted for murdering two Atlanta people, and El Sayyid Nassir, who was charged with murdering Rabbi Meir Kahane, head of the Jewish Defense League. Kunstler managed to remain in the news. ■

Introduction

The American prison system suffered from many problems in the early 1970s. The prisons themselves were often overcrowded and poorly maintained. Groups that were minorities in the U.S. population, especially

African Americans, made up the majority of prisoners, whereas most guards and administrators were white. This led to racism and bias on both sides. The treatment of prisoners was generally poor, in that their rights were restricted more than the law called for and they had little chance of getting their greivances addressed within the system.

Attica State Correctional Facility in New York, east of Buffalo, was a prime example of all of these issues. It housed over 2,500 prisoners, in a facility designed for 1,600. Roughly 85 percent of the inmates were African American or Hispanic, while all but one of the guards were white. Access to education was limited, some inmates faced restrictions of their religious freedoms, and the food available in the prison was poor.

In the summer of 1971, the already charged atmosphere in Attica was made worse by the death of George Jackson, a prominent African American activist and advocate for prison reform, at San Quentin prison in California. Inmates at Attica began to organize and demand improvements in the prison's conditions. They were rebuffed by prison officials. On September 9, 1971, roughly 1,200 prisoners rioted. They took control of part of the prison and seized fifty hostages.

Attica was qucikly surrounded by police and National Guardsmen. The prisoners released some of their hostages who had been badly hurt, but kept thirty-nine in their hands and issued a number of demands for better conditions at Attica. These included a minimum wage for prison labor, religious freedom, better medical treatment and diets, the replacement of the prison's superindent, and complete amnesty for those involved in the riot. They criticized the "racist administration" of the prison and decried the "disregard for the lives of prisoners here and throughout the United States." The prisoners also requested mediators, to facilitate communication between themselves and the police, including the famous attorney William Kunstler.

The police and prison authorities agreed to many of the prisoners demands. However, they would not grant unconditional amnesty to the rioters. While the negotiations were going on, one of the prison guards injured during the riot died. Faced with the prospect of murder chargers, the prisoners continued to insist on amnesty. The prisoners demanded that New York governor Nelson Rockefeller come to negotiate with them, but he refused. On September 13, 1971, the prisoners refused an ultimatum to accept the government's offer, and government officials decided to end the standoff by force. The inmates were tear gassed, and roughly 1,500 heavily armed policemen assaulted the Cell Block D compound held by the rioters.

Significance

As Kunstler describes in his 1994 book *My Life As a Radical Lawyer,* the result was a massacre. The police fired indiscriminately into the tear gassed compound, killing thirty-nine people. Ten of the dead were hostages, and although police initially denied it, it was later proven that all ten were killed by police gunfire during their intended rescue. Attica was now the bloodiest prison riot in U.S. history, and yet most of the deaths had been caused by the police. After the compound was retaken and the riotous inmates were once again under police control, many of them were beaten or otherwise absued by their angry captors.

There was nationwide outrage in the wake of the violent end of Attica's riot. An investigation by a citizen's committee concluded that the assault on the prison was ill conceived and unneccesary, laying the blame for the bloodshed on Governor Rockerfeller and other state officials. A subsequent investigation in the U.S. Congress concurred that the wrong tactics were used to end the riot, and condemned the poor treatment of prisoners after the police retook Attica. Many of the prisoners and their families sued New York State over their ill-treatment.

Attica became the most famous symbol of an overburdened prison system that many felt treated its inmates inhumanely. It gave added impetus to the prison reform movement and brought the issues surrounding prisons to greater public awareness. Many of the smaller changes requested by the Attica prisoners were adopted, at least for a time, but other problems have since cropped up. And many of the largest problems have never been successfully address. Kunstler mentions in his book that one of the problems facing Attica was overcrowding—40 percent over capacity. Many prisons in the early twenty-first century are 70 percent or more over capacity. Prisons also continued to be populated largely by minority groups, fostering racial tensions. Thus few would argue that prisons have improved much since the 1970s.

Primary Source

My Life As a Radical Lawyer [excerpt]

SYNOPSIS: Kunstler first notes how he came to be called to Attica and how he reacted to the demands of the inmates. He then details the days of the siege and how he felt betrayed by the officials on a variety of occasions. This excerpt closes with a discussion of the retaking of the yard. Kunstler argues that New York governor Nelson A. Rockefeller was personally responsible for the bloodshed.

Attica: The Worst of Deceptions

When I first saw the great, grim prison buildings of Attica, the trees were just starting their annual transformation from green to gold and red. The rising began in the early hours of September 9, 1971, a quiet, ordinary autumn morning. But moments later there was nothing normal any longer as scores of angry, frustrated men crashed through a flimsy barrier and took control of a prison yard. For the next four days the insurrection at the Attica Correctional Facility in upstate New York, thirty miles to the east of Buffalo, commanded the attention of the nation.

Then, on September 13, at 9:43 *A.M.,* without adequate warning, certainly without an acknowledgment that the men inside—inmates and guards alike—had any essential value or humanity the prison yard was attacked by the armies of the law. When the brief, bloody massacre was over, the body count was thirty-nine, and scores of people lay seriously injured.

The insurrection of 1,281 inmates at Attica was inspired by the prison system's inhumane treatment of those it housed. The inmates revolted for better medical care, translators for Hispanic inmates, more black and Latino guards, better educational programs, and better food, including special diets for Muslim inmates. They wanted the guards to accept them as human beings, even though they were imprisoned. They were also expressing their grief and anger over the August 21 killing of political revolutionary George Jackson, shot while supposedly trying to escape from California's San Quentin prison.

At the time of the rebellion, Attica held twenty-two hundred men, even though it was built to house only sixteen hundred. The inmates were 54 percent black and 9 percent Puerto Rican, with their keepers almost all young white males from nearby rural counties. Attica was a ticking bomb in September 1971, a bomb that exploded, causing fallout for more than two decades on the political and social landscape of New York State.

Thursday: Day One

When the Attica takeover occurred, I was in sunny, peaceful West Palm Beach. While arguing a motion for Ben Chaney, I was handed a telegram which informed me of the Attica rebellion and requested my presence. The inmates wanted me there right away. The judge on the Chaney case allowed me to leave. "You go. That's important," he said when he learned that fifty hostages had been taken.

I knew some of the Attica inmates from a similar uprising the year before at the Auburn Correctional Facility, also in upstate New York. There, inmates who had been denied permission to hold a Black Solidarity Day engaged in a sit-down protest after taking several guards as hostages. Although the prison's administrators assured the inmates that those who led the action would not be punished, they never kept their word. All of the Auburn leaders were beaten, then shipped to Attica and put in the hole—solitary confinement.

That prison officials had lied at Auburn played a key role in the Attica tragedy and caused the rebelling inmates to suspect a similar betrayal. Their distrust was compounded when, right after the Attica takeover, New York governor Nelson A. Rockefeller ignored requests that he personally assure inmates there would be no reprisals. These requests were made by inmates, hostages, prison officials, and a group of observers, including me. Rockefeller's silence understandably caused the inmates to fear repercussions, and that fear inevitably overshadowed any negotiation attempts.

Arthur O. Eve and Herman Schwartz were at Attica almost from the very beginning of the crisis. Eve, a New York State assemblyman, was a prison-reform advocate, and Schwartz was a law professor at the State University of New York in Buffalo and an appellate attorney for some of the inmates. They asked the state to call in the other observers the inmates wanted. The observers were to act as witnesses to what was happening as well as advocates and negotiators.

Initially, I thought I could be useful at Attica as an intermediary. The takeover also appealed to my sense of the dramatic. My reasons for becoming involved in any case or situation were all here: Attica was high stakes, in lives and in political importance, and it was high profile. . . .

Sunday, Day Four

On Sunday morning, a woman eating breakfast in a diner near the prison became hysterical at the sight of a black man sitting near her: It was Assemblyman Arthur Eve. This hysteria was a reflection of the level of anxiety in the entire community, not only inside the walls of Attica but among all the people who lived and worked nearby.

In the prison, the atmosphere continued to be terribly tense. None of the observers had left the prison for more than brief periods of time. Some

Inmates at Attica state prison in New York show their support for demands made during negotiations with state prisons commissioner Russel Oswald, September 10, 1971. **AP/WIDE WORLD PHOTOS. REPRODUCED BY PERMISSION.**

nights, we stayed there all night, and food was delivered to us by prison officials. I wore the same suit the whole time I was there and washed out socks and underwear when I could get back to my motel room, where Lotte was waiting. Each time we entered or left the building, we had to walk through a gauntlet of jeering troopers and corrections officers. State troopers were bivouacked at the prison, turning it into an armed camp.

During the entire four days, the prison was surrounded by the husbands, wives, children, and parents of the hostages, as well as the news media.

Inside the prison, I felt as if I were watching a huge bomb that could be set off by anything or anyone at any second. I hoped the observers could help defuse the situation peacefully, if that were humanly possible. We spent much of Sunday trying to convince Rockefeller to come to Attica and meet with the observers, then make a public address to the inmates regarding their demands. We failed miserably, for we never counted on the governor of New York State being the murderer he was.

Tom Wicker's wife called before we went in on Sunday to warn him not to go into the yard. "Don't

Attorney William Kunstler tells inmates at Attica prison that he will represent them in negotiations with prison officials, September 11, 1971. AP/WIDE WORLD PHOTOS. REPRODUCED BY PERMISSION.

go in there. You've been in three days already. You're a southerner, and it could be dangerous," she told him, but he ignored her warning, and we trooped in.

That morning, for the first time, we were asked to sign liability waivers saying the state was not responsible should anything happen to us. We should have smelled a rat then, because Russell Oswald, New York's commissioner of correctional services, showed us a letter that he wanted to send in to the inmates. One sentence stood out as if it had been neon lit: "Your committee agrees with me that you should surrender, and that we should talk later." We opposed the letter; we thought it would jeopardize our lives. We had not agreed to a surrender, and if the inmates believed we had, they would think we had deserted them. At this point, the state police were firing rubber pellets into the yard. (I was hit once, causing a trickle of blood that wasn't serious.) The shots were reminders that everyone in the yard was in range and vulnerable.

Finally, Oswald agreed not to send in that letter. Then we signed the waivers. By that time, we were down to a handful who were willing to go into D-yard: Wicker, myself, Jones, Eve, reporters Rudy Garcia and Dick Edwards, and a new arrival, Minister

Franklin Florence. Among those who turned tail and refused to enter D-yard was state senator John Dunne, who would later become a member of the attorney general's Civil Rights Division during the Bush administration.

Although we didn't know it, this would be our last trip into D-yard. Down a long tunnel, into an empty yard, through the connecting cross of Times Square, and finally, into D-yard.

We were outraged when we found out from the inmates who were escorting us that the commissioner had betrayed us and sent in the letter. One of the inmates said some of the prisoners wanted to kill us. I was standing right behind Tom Wicker and watched the back of his neck turn, very slowly, a deep beet red. As scared as I had ever been, I wanted to run as fast as I could back to the safety of the prison officials.

In my mind, I prepared to have my throat cut. I intellectualized that it wouldn't hurt much; it would be over quickly. But if I ran, I would always be remembered as a coward. I thought it was all going to end here, for me, in the Attica yard. And I understood why we had been made to sign the waivers.

Oswald wanted us to be killed, for then the authorities would have a perfect excuse for going in, guns blazing. If we were killed, with the state cleared of all liability, they could retake the yard. Why else make us sign releases at this point? But their plan didn't work.

I decided not to run and steeled myself against whatever was to come. They took us into D-yard two by two, with Wicker in the third group and me in the fourth. When I was taken through, I looked quickly to see whether there was any blood on the ground and was relieved to see none. I joined Wicker and the others at the command table. Big Black Smith told the men that the observers had not approved the letter and that Oswald had lied. The men applauded, and we each got a chance to speak, thus stopping any hotheads in the group from slitting our throats.

When I spoke—and I've gotten lots of flak on this—I told the inmates that I had been informed by members of the Black Panther party that they had been in touch with the embassy of an unnamed foreign country—North Vietnam—which had agreed to grant asylum to all prisoners who were released. Although I knew the state would never let them go, I thought it was good to give the men hope and even offered to take their names. Later on, the McKay Commission, which investigated the Attica massacre, Tom Wicker, and some others were critical of me for doing this, saying I had raised false hopes. I thought at the time that gaining confidence for the observers was the most important thing.

Wicker had been talking to some of the guards who had been held as hostages. "Governor, come in here or we're dead men," one said, sending a message to the governor. Another, Sgt. Edward Cunningham, who was killed in the final shootout, said that Rockefeller "must give [the inmates] clemency from criminal prosecution. . . . Anything else other than this is just as good as dropping dead."

Commissioner Oswald contacted Rockefeller that night and asked him to come to the prison to talk to the observers. He suggested that Rockefeller make an announcement to the inmates over the loudspeaker. The governor refused. We observers saw that time was fast running out. There was a doomed feeling hanging over the prison. I went back to the motel to sleep.

Bloody Monday, the Final Day

When I arrived back at Attica at about 9:00 A.M., I was not allowed inside. I heard the drone of helicopters and moments later smelled the pungent Mace-like gas. People began to cry. I heard very faint *pop-pop-pop* sounds, the sound of shooting, of double-O buckshot and dumdum bullets entering human flesh. Until that moment, I somehow had never believed that the rebellion would end in bloodshed. I felt it would be worked out, that the two sides would come to some agreement. As I heard the guns, I felt totally impotent. I couldn't do a damn thing.

In ten minutes, a prison official came out and said, "It's all over. We've retaken the yard." Nine corrections officers were dead, their throats slit, he said. The onslaught had been ordered because the inmates were cutting the throats of the hostages, he added.

Naively, I believed what he had said about the cut throats. He was in there; I was outside. I didn't know that what he said was all a lie. I was interviewed by reporters and said it should never have happened, that the governor should have made an appearance and spoken to the inmates—through a megaphone from the safety of the catwalk over the yard if he was unwilling to go into D-yard itself. I was crying.

There was no excuse for what happened that morning at Attica. The troops that retook the yard included state police, sheriff's deputies in bright orange raincoats, and corrections officers; they used rifles, shotguns, and sidearms. They blasted away, even at people lying on the ground, overcome by the gas. You can see this carnage on film, since some of the rifles were equipped with motion picture cameras. They shot indiscriminately at anyone who moved, and the bodies of those who were killed were simply torn apart by state-issued ammunition.

An eighteen-minute amateur videotape of the massacre shows hostages with prisoners holding knives to their throats. Then you can see tear gas everywhere and hear an amplified voice saying: "Surrender peacefully. You will not be harmed." Then you hear rifle shots and automatic gunfire, and you see the dead and dying on the catwalk over the prison yard.

When the assault began, the unlucky guards who thought they were being rescued stood up. And were shot down. They were dressed in prison garb, and they were simply mowed down by their own side. At the front gate, as the state forces charged the prison, the troopers and deputies were yelling, "Save me a nigger!" I heard it all over the place. They were out for blood.

Later that day, I was eager to leave this horrifying scene as fast as possible and asked Lotte to pick me up after she checked out of the motel. Carrying our luggage, we walked down the street in front of the prison. Suddenly, a car rushed toward us, trying to hit us. We managed to jump behind a tree. Years later, during an unrelated criminal trial, I met the state trooper who was driving that car. He said that he was sorry he had scared us, but his fury at me overtook him. He didn't think he would have gone through with it, but he wasn't certain. I wasn't, either.

Further Resources

BOOKS

Attica: The Official Report of the New York State Special Commission on Attica. New York: Bantam, 1972.

Bell, Malcolm. *The Turkey Shoot: Tracking the Attica Cover-Up.* New York: Grove, 1985.

Hudson, Daniel. *Managing Death-Sentenced Inmates: A Survey of Practices,* 2nd ed. Lanham, Md.: American Correctional Association, 2000.

Johnson, Robert. *Hard Time: Understanding and Reforming the Prison,* 3rd ed. Belmont, Calif.: Wadsworth, 2002.

May, John P., and Khalid R. Pitts. *Building Violence: How America's Rush to Incarcerate Creates More Violence.* Thousand Oaks, Calif.: Sage, 2000.

Wicker, Tom. *A Time to Die.* New York: Quadrangle/New York Times, 1975.

WEBSITES

"The Rockefellers: Attica Prison Riot." American Experience, Public Broadcasting Service. Available online at http://www.pbs.org/wgbh/amex/rockefellers/sfeature/sf_5.html; website home page: http://www.pbs.org/wgbh/amex/ (accessed April 16, 2003).

AUDIO AND VISUAL MEDIA

Attica. Embassy Home Entertainment, 1980, VHS.

Attica Riot: Chaos Behind Bars. A&E Home Video, 1984, VHS.

7

LIFESTYLES AND SOCIAL TRENDS

TIMOTHY G. BORDEN

Entries are arranged in chronological order by date of primary source. For entries with one primary source, the entry title is the same as the primary source title. Entries with more than one primary source have an overall entry title, followed by the titles of the primary sources.

Important Events in Lifestyles and Social Trends, 1970–1979

1970

• Ralph Nader's citizens' lobbying group, nicknamed "Nader's Raiders," petitions the government for consumer protection. Common Cause, a citizens' group lobbying for political reform, is formed.

• The Census Bureau puts the nation's population at just over 203 million. But the 13 percent growth since 1960 is the result of the lowest birth rate since the Great Depression of the 1930s. An increased divorce rate and a trend toward marrying at an older age are given as factors. California has passed New York to become the nation's most populous state.

• In two firsts, California adopts no-fault divorce and Massachusetts adopts no-fault auto insurance.

• For the first time in American history, a majority of Americans live in suburbs.

• Police touch off a riot in the barrio of East Los Angeles, resulting in the death of prominent Hispanic journalist Ruben Salazar and inspiring the growing Chicano consciousness movement.

• On January 14, more than 15 years after its first desegregation order, the Supreme Court sets a February 1 deadline for the integration of public schools in Alabama, Florida, Georgia, Louisiana, Mississippi, and Tennessee.

• In May, student strikes and other protests against the Vietnam War take place at 451 colleges and universities nationwide. War protest is also beginning to reach small-town America. A poll indicates that only 48 percent of Americans support the war.

• On May 4, the governor of Ohio calls out the National Guard to end a six-hour battle between student protesters and police on the campus of Kent State University. Four students are killed, thirteen injured, and six hundred arrested in the affair.

• On May 9, over one hundred thousand protestors rally against the war in Washington, D.C. Many other parts of the country experience similar demonstrations.

• On June 26, the American Medical Association votes to permit doctors to perform abortions for economic and social reasons.

• On July 1, a law takes effect in New York that allows abortions to be performed on demand, with no questions asked.

Sixteen states already allow abortions if a pregnancy puts a woman's health at risk. However, New York joins Alaska and Hawaii in having the nation's most liberal abortion laws. Over the next six months, an estimated sixty-nine thousand abortions are performed in New York.

• On August 26, a parade of ten thousand women in New York celebrates the fiftieth anniversary of the passage of the Nineteenth Amendment. The women demand abortion reform, day care, and equal opportunity.

1971

• The Twenty-sixth Amendment to the Constitution is ratified, lowering the voting age from twenty-one to eighteen.

• In *Reed v. Reed* the U.S. Supreme Court bans gender discrimination.

• The hot-pants fad begins in New York City boutiques.

• In Chicago the Reverend Jesse Jackson forms People United to Save Humanity (PUSH).

• A poll indicates that 34 percent of Americans believe marriage is obsolete, compared to 24 percent who held that opinion in 1960. A survey at a major eastern college reveals that only 18 percent of women students plan to stop working if they become mothers. This compares to 59 percent in 1943.

• Three-fourths of all moviegoers are under the age of thirty.

• On March 1, the U.S. Capitol is bombed by the Weather Underground, a radical guerrilla group, as a protest of the Vietnam War. The bomb explodes in a Senate restroom. No one is injured, but three hundred thousand dollars in damage is done.

• On May 3, thousands of antiwar demonstrators are arrested in Washington, D.C., for blocking traffic in an attempt to bring government to a halt in the city. The arrests conclude several weeks of antiwar activities in the capital.

• On October 1, Walt Disney World opens near Orlando, Florida.

1972

• Congress approves the Equal Right Amendment (ERA) and sends it to the states to be ratified.

• The number of women in the workplace increases to thirty-four million.

• Congress passes the Ethnic Heritage Studies Act "to legitimatize ethnicity and pluralism in America."

• Opposition to the war in Vietnam has grown to include every segment of American society, including veterans of the conflict itself.

• On June 17, police in Washington, D.C., arrest five burglars inside the headquarters of the Democratic Party. The arrests will mushroom into a scandal known as the Watergate Affair and will eventually lead to the resignation of President Nixon and to criminal indictments of his closest advisors and former members of his cabinet.

• On November 9, Georgia's Andrew Young is the first southern African American elected to Congress since reconstruction.

1973

• On December 15, the American Psychiatric Association announces that homosexuality is not a mental disorder, reversing its one-hundred-year-old position on the subject.

• Phyllis Schlafly organizes the Stop ERA lobby.

• Maynard Jackson is elected the first African American mayor of Atlanta; Thomas Bradley is elected the first African American mayor of Los Angeles; Coleman Young becomes the first African American mayor of Detroit.

• The Organization of Petroleum Exporting Countries' (OPEC) oil embargo leads Americans to lower their thermostats, cease Sunday drives, and cancel airline trips, all in an effort to save fuel.

• The Census Bureau reports that interracial marriages increased 63 percent during the 1960s.

• Little League Baseball teams in New Jersey accept the first female players in the league.

• Federal agencies accept *Ms.* in place of *Miss* or *Mrs.*

• Inspired by the Bruce Lee film *Enter the Dragon,* a martial arts craze sweeps U.S. urban centers.

• On January 22, in *Roe v. Wade,* the Supreme Court upholds a woman's right to choose to have an abortion.

• On January 27, with U.S. involvement in the Vietnam War at an end, the government ends the military draft.

• On January 29, the first female commercial pilot is hired.

• On March 1, the birthrate is reported to be at 1.98 children per couple, below the rate required to sustain the current population.

1974

• Maternity leave for teachers is approved by the U.S. Supreme Court.

• A fad known as "streaking," where people sprint naked through public thoroughfares and ceremonies, sweeps the country.

• On February 4, in Berkeley, California, nineteen-year-old newspaper heiress Patricia Hearst is kidnapped by the Symbionese Liberation Army.

• On February 22, the editor of the *Atlanta Constitution,* J. Reginald Murphy, is found unharmed after seven hundred thousand dollars is paid to his kidnappers, the self-proclaimed American Revolutionary Army.

• On May 4, Expo '74, a world's fair with an environmental theme, opens in Spokane, Washington.

• On September 12, three months of sometimes violent protests begin in Boston over the court-ordered busing of students to integrate the city's public schools.

• On November 13, the first official dog Frisbee competition is held in Fullerton, California.

1975

• The first personal computer for home use is introduced by retailers.

• The so-called "typical" family of a working father, stay-at-home mom, and two children represents only 7 percent of the nation's population. The average family unit consists of 3.4 members, compared to 4.1 members in 1920.

• Violent resistance to school bussing rocks Boston, Denver, Detroit, and Louisville.

• Some 130,000 refugees from Southeast Asia are resettled in the United States.

• General Motors recalls 220,000 defective cars.

• The disco-music fad emerges from the gay and Latino underground of many American cities.

• Twenty million mood rings—a type of jewelry that changes color with body temperature—are sold in the United States.

• The pet rock, an elaborately packaged stone, becomes a popular holiday gift.

• On January 12, layoffs in the auto industry reach a record 275,000, or nearly 40 percent of the workforce. To boost sales, U.S. automakers begin offering rebates to buyers of new cars.

• On February 4, Menominee Indian activists agree to end a takeover of a Roman Catholic novitiate in Gresham, Wisconsin, in return for the deed to what they argue is their property.

• On June 26, the Supreme Court rules that mentally ill persons cannot be involuntarily confined if they are able to care for themselves and present no danger to the community.

• On December 31, higher U.S. postal rates are imposed.

1976

• Punk fashions from London arrive in U.S. shops.

• The National Aeronautics and Space Administration (NASA) accepts its first female astronaut trainees.

• The Census Bureau reports that 15 percent of American adults are "functionally illiterate"—unable to read a newspaper or write a simple letter.

• Although average SAT scores have fallen nearly 10 percent since 1968, nearly one-third of high school graduates are going on to college.

• Dr. Benjamin Spock's revision of his classic how-to child-raising manual, *Baby and Child Care* reflects society's changing gender roles. Spock now writes that the father's responsibility in bringing up the children is as great as the mother's.

• On May 24, the first transatlantic flights of the supersonic Concorde aircraft begin.

• On July 4, the United States celebrates the two hundredth anniversary of the Declaration of Independence.

• On July 9, the National Institute on Drug Abuse reports that Valium is the nation's most prescribed drug.

• On August 27, transsexual Renee Richards, formerly Richard Raskind, an eye surgeon, is barred from competing in the women's tennis competition at the U.S. Open after she refuses a chromosome test.

• On September 16, the Episcopal Church approves the ordination of women as priests.

• On September 18, the Reverend Sun Myung Moon presides over a God Bless America rally in Washington, D.C. Fifty thousand followers of Moon attend.

• On September 30, California approves the nation's first right-to-die law. It gives adult patients the right to have their physician shut off life-support equipment when death is at hand.

1977

• The Apple II, the first personal computer with color graphics, is introduced for home use.

• The State Department urges an emergency admission of ten thousand Indochinese boat people.

• Congress bans fluorocarbon aerosol spray cans.

• Twenty-five million CB radios are in use by motorists.

• Nearly 20 percent of new cars on American roads are foreign imports. In some western states, foreign cars, mainly from Japan, account for 40 percent of sales

• The movie *Saturday Night Fever,* starring John Travolta and with a soundtrack by the Bee Gees and Donna Summer, launches a disco dance craze across the nation.

• On January 21, newly inaugurated President Jimmy Carter issues a blanket pardon to most Americans who resisted or evaded the draft during the Vietnam War.

• On April 27, a government task force reports that between six and eight million illegal immigrants are living in the United States.

• From April 30 to May 2, two thousand protestors occupy the site of a nuclear power plant at Seabrook, New Hampshire, in an attempt to block its construction. The event demonstrates the growing environmental concerns of some Americans about the use of nuclear energy to produce electricity.

• On June 6, Joseph Lason becomes the Roman Catholic bishop of Biloxi, Mississippi, making him the first African American bishop since the 1800s.

• On November 1, President Carter signs a law raising the federal minimum wage from $2.30 to $2.65 an hour, and to $3.35 an hour by 1981.

• From November 18 to 21, the first National Women's Conference is held in Houston, Texas. It is the largest such gathering since the Seneca Falls Convention of 1848. The delegates call for ratification of the Equal Rights Amendment and for the end of all discrimination against women.

1978

• In Washington, D.C., sixty-five thousand women march in support of the Equal Rights Amendment.

• An Ohio court rules that girls may play on Little League Baseball teams.

• Twice as many unmarried couples are living together—1.1 million couples—as in 1970. However, there has also been an increase in the number of people who live alone—some 23 percent of the population.

• Alex Haley's book and popular television miniseries *Roots* has inspired a growing public interest in genealogy.

• Construction of a nuclear-power plant in Seabrook, New Hampshire, is suspended due to public opposition.

• The first American-made "foreign" car—a Volkswagen—begins production in New Stanton, Pennsylvania.

• Rubber-soled shoes, generically called "tennis shoes" or "sneakers," account for 50 percent of all shoe sales in the United States.

• Following a traveling museum exhibit of Egyptian antiquities, a King Tut craze sweeps the nation.

• Morris, Nine-Lives cat food's spokescat, dies in Chicago at the age of 17.

• On February 1, the U.S. government issues its first postage stamp honoring an African American woman, when abolitionist Harriet Tubman is commemorated.

• On April 19, the first African American female pilot for a major U.S. airline is hired.

• On May 11, the first female general in the Marine Corps, Margaret A. Brewer, is appointed.

• On May 26, the first legal casino outside of Las Vegas opens in Atlantic City, New Jersey.

• On June 9, the Church of Jesus Christ of Latter Day Saints (Mormons) makes African American males eligible for admission to the priesthood.

• On June 28, the Supreme Court decision in the *Regents of the University of California v. Bakke* case limits the scope of affirmative action.

• On October 6, at the University of Chicago the first female president of a coed university, Hannah H. Gray, is inaugurated.

• On December 15, signaling a growing financial crisis in the nation's cities, Cleveland defaults on $15.5 million in debts. It is the first major city to fail to meet its financial obligations since the Great Depression of the 1930s.

1979

• Over 14.5 million Americans identify themselves as Hispanic.

• The divorce rate has risen by 69 percent since 1968. The average marriage now lasts just 6.6 years. This trend means that 40 percent of children born in the 1970s will be raised in single-parent homes.

• A sociological study reports that clothing and bumper stickers that contain mottoes and slogans express people's wish for connection with others.

• Jerry Falwell organizes the conservative Moral Majority lobby.

• The Sony Walkman portable personal radio is introduced.

• Health food sales total $1.6 billion, compared to $140 million in 1970.

- According to a *Washington Post* poll, 99 percent of homes own a TV set. But 54 percent of Americans watch less TV than they did five years ago. This may be because 41 percent of Americans feel that the quality of TV shows has declined over that period, compared to only 17 percent who said that shows were better.

- One hundred thousand march in Washington, D.C., in support of gay liberation.

- On February 13, a report by the U.S. Civil Rights Commission states that 46 percent of the nation's minority children are still attending segregated schools, twenty-five years after the Supreme Court declared them unconstitutional.

- On March 28, a disaster is narrowly averted when a reactor malfunctions at Three Mile Island power plant near Harrisburg, Pennsylvania. The event fans fears across the nation about the use of nuclear power.

- On April 3, Jane Byrne is elected Chicago's first female mayor. Her margin of victory is the largest since 1901.

- On May 5, the Supreme Court rules that laws which require only divorced husbands, but not divorced wives, to pay alimony to their exes are unconstitutional.

- On December 3, eleven young people are trampled to death as rock fans scramble to get the best seats at a concert by The Who in Cincinnati, Ohio.

The Me Decade

I'm OK—You're OK: A Practical Guide to Transactional Analysis

Nonfiction work

By: Thomas A. Harris

Date: 1967

Source: Harris, Thomas A. *I'm OK—You're OK.* New York: Harper & Row, 1967, 18, 43, 50–51.

About the Author: Psychiatrist Thomas A. Harris (1910–1995) completed his medical training at Temple University and served as the chief of the U.S. Navy's psychiatric branch in the 1940s. In his 1967 book *I'm OK—You're OK: A Practical Guide to Transactional Analysis,* he suggested that a person develops his or her identity based on social interactions. The volume was a consistent best-seller in the 1970s and led to a sequel, *Staying OK,* co-authored with his wife, Amy Bjork Harris, in 1985.

The Book of est

Nonfiction work

By: Luke Rhinehart

Date: 1976

Source: Rhinehart, Luke. *The Book of est.* New York: Holt, Rinehart and Winston, 1976, xi–xiii, 212–216.

About the Author: Luke Rhinehart (1932–), born George Powers Croft, based *The Book of est* (1976) on the self-help program designed and promoted by Werner Erhard, one of the most charismatic and mysterious figures of the 1970s. A student of several self-help programs in the late 1960s and early 1970s, Erhard formed his own program, the Erhard Seminars Training (est), in 1971. With several celebrity clients, the est craze reached a peak in 1976. ■

Introduction

In the 1960s, thousands of Americans mobilized in mass movements to change society, influence foreign policy, and protest against injustice. In contrast, the 1970s were characterized by more individualized quests for self-improvement, often in the form of designer clothing, the use of status-symbol drugs such as cocaine or Quaaludes, and participation in self-help programs. The obsession

with indulgence, status, and personal fulfillment was so pervasive that writer Tom Wolfe called the era "The Me Decade" in a 1976 *New York* article, and the label stuck. The idealism and activism of the 1960s seemed very far away indeed.

The theory of transactional analysis, popularized by psychiatrists Eric Berne and Thomas A. Harris, looked at human behavior as the result of human relationships—or transactions—that taught individuals the roles they would play in life. In his 1967 work *I'm OK—You're OK,* Harris defined these roles as the parent, who represented ingrained habits, even detrimental ones; the adult, or the voice of reason; and the child, who obeyed what others wanted without questioning. Using these archetypes to explain human relationships and individual behavior, Harris hoped that transactional analysis would help individuals reach the "I'm OK—You're OK" stage, in which they made better decisions in life with an increased awareness of their motivations and goals.

With no education beyond high school, former encyclopedia salesman Werner Erhard was one of many self-help gurus who capitalized on the self-improvement craze in America. Incorporating the strategies of Scientology, Mind Dynamics, and Dale Carnegie, Erhard formulated the Erhard Training Seminars, or est, in 1971 as an aggressive program to achieve emotional and intellectual awakenings in its pupils. Emphasizing total commitment to following Erhard's guidelines, est sessions took place over two weekends. Est trainers subjected participants to an authoritarian regimen that nonetheless promised to transform their lives and unlock their inner potential. With celebrity adherents like John Denver and Valerie Harper, est grossed over $82 million between 1975 and 1981.

Significance

Although Harris's use of psychiatric terminology put *I'm OK—You're OK* far above other pop-psychology books of the day, its title became a catch phrase of the self-approving 1970s. Indeed, the volume was a publishing phenomenon in the 1970s. In 1971 it ranked as the fourth best-selling nonfiction book in the country, and it remained the second or third bestseller in that category for each of the next three years with a total of at least 15 million copies in print. In addition to popularizing the basic tenets of transactional analysis among the public, *I'm OK—You're OK* became an accepted psychiatric methodology, with scholarly works continuing to refine and expand its basic principles. In the 1990s transactional analysis was the basis for another major bestseller, James Redfield's *The Celestine Prophecy.*

In the twenty years of its existence, an estimated 700,000 people enjoyed or endured the est experience. Through a carefully managed public image that retained the mystique of est's concepts, Werner Erhard became one of the most celebrated figures of the 1970s. After a slew of lawsuits exposed Erhard's questionable financial dealings and his domineering personality, however, est's appeal declined in the 1980s. The program changed its name to the Forum in 1985, but the attempt to revamp est into a more results-oriented program failed to match its former success. With his reputation effectively shattered by a devastating *60 Minutes* profile in 1991, which included allegations of molestation and tax evasion, Erhard sold the Forum to a group led by his brother and left the country. Est's successor, the Landmark Education Corporation, marketed its seminars as less confrontational than Erhard's previous offerings. With the demand for business-oriented, self-help programs surging in the 1990s, its leadership and personal growth programs expanded to eleven countries, with revenues reaching $48 million in 1997.

Primary Source

I'm OK—You're OK: A Practical Guide to Transactional Analysis [excerpt]

SYNOPSIS: In one of the most popular nonfiction books of the 1970s, psychiatrist Thomas A. Harris explains that the personality is comprised of three basic archetypes, the parent, child, and adult. These archetypes interact to produce one of four positions that explain how an individual interacts (or "transacts") with others. Through an understanding of transactional analysis, Harris guides the reader to realize the value in reaching the fourth stage, "I'm OK—You're OK," in which the adult archetype prevails.

The Four Life Positions

Transactional Analysis constructs the following classification of the four possible life positions held with respect to oneself and others:

1. I'M NOT OK—YOU'RE OK
2. I'M NOT OK—YOU'RE NOT OK
3. I'M OK—YOU'RE NOT OK
4. I'M OK—YOU'RE OK

Before I elaborate each position I wish to state a few general observations about positions. I believe that by the end of the second year of life, or sometime during the third year, the child has decided on one of the first three positions. The I'M NOT OK—YOU'RE OK is the first tentative decision based on the experiences of the first year of life. By the end of the second year it is either confirmed and settled or it gives way to Position 2 or 3: I'M NOT OK—YOU'RE NOT OK or I'M OK—YOU'RE NOT OK. Once finalized, the child stays in his chosen position and

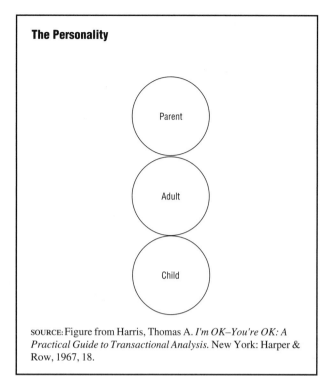

The Personality

SOURCE: Figure from Harris, Thomas A. *I'm OK–You're OK: A Practical Guide to Transactional Analysis.* New York: Harper & Row, 1967, 18.

it governs everything he does. It stays with him the rest of his life, unless he later consciously changes it to the fourth position. People do not shift back and forth. The decision as to the first three positions is based totally on stroking and nonstroking. The first three are nonverbal decisions. They are conclusions, not explanations. Yet they are more than conditioned responses. They are what Piaget calls intellectual elaborations in the construction of causality. In other words, they are a product of Adult data processing in the very little person. . . .

I'm OK—You're OK

There is a fourth position, wherein lies our hope. It is the I'M OK—YOU'RE OK position. There is a qualitative difference between the first three positions and the fourth position. The first three are unconscious, having been made early in life. I'm not ok—you're ok came first and persists for most people throughout life. For certain extremely unfortunate children this position was changed to positions two and three. By the third year of life one of these positions is fixed in every person. The decision as to position is perhaps one of the first functions of the infant's Adult in the attempt to make sense out of life, so that a measure of predictability may be applied to the confusion of stimuli and feelings. These positions are arrived at on the basis of data from the Parent and Child. They are based on emotion or impressions without the benefit of external, modifying data.

The fourth position, I'M OK—YOU'RE OK, because it is a conscious and verbal decision, can include not only an infinitely greater amount of information about the individual and others, but also the incorporation of not-yet-experienced possibilities which exist in the abstractions of philosophy and religion. *The first three positions are based on feelings. The fourth is based on thought, faith, and the wager of action.* The first three have to do with *why.* The fourth has to do with *why not?* Our understanding of OK is not bound to our own personal experiences, because we can transcend them into an abstraction of ultimate purpose for all men.

We do not drift into a new position. It is a decision we make. In this respect it is like a conversion experience. We cannot decide on the fourth position without a great deal more information than most persons have available to them about the circumstances surrounding the original positions decided on so early in life. Fortunate are the children who are helped early in life to find they are OK by repeated exposure to situations in which they can prove, to themselves, their own worth and the worth of others.

Primary Source

The Book of est [excerpt]

SYNOPSIS: Although est trainers insisted that the only way to understand the program was to take the seminar, a number of books were published at the height of the est craze in 1976 to give everyone a sampling of its methods. *The Book of est,* written with Erhard's approval and input, took readers through the entire training seminar over two weekends. This passage highlights the theatrical staging and confrontational techniques that est used to instigate personal breakthroughs.

est, the Erhard Seminars Training, is currently the fastest-growing and most important, original, and controversial "enlightenment" program in the United States. The *est* Standard Training consists of two long weekend sessions lasting over sixty hours, during which 250 people are shouted at, ordered around, insulted, lectured, and introduced to various "processes" (exercises in observation during altered states of consciousness). As a result they come to share intimate experiences, discover hidden aspects of themselves, and are eventually led, miraculously enough, to the experience of "getting it": seeing at last what life really is and being able to let it work.

Since its creation in 1971, *est* has expanded with explosive force, almost doubling its number of graduates each year. By the fall of 1976 demand for the training has so outstripped *est*'s ability to supply it that thousands of people who have signed up for the training are sometimes having to wait months to receive it. Already over 100,000 people have graduated from the two-week training. These include hundreds of psychologists and psychotherapists and numerous "name" personalities—John Denver, Peter Max, Valerie Harper, Cloris Leachman, Yoko Ono, Roy Scheider, Jerry Rubin—many of whom have become enthusiastic supporters of the program.

est makes use of the best techniques of many different traditional religious and psychotherapeutic disciplines. Its purpose is to bring people over two weekends to a unique experience that transforms their lives. Many graduates find that their "problems" tend to evaporate as they begin to take total responsibility for all they experience; their goals in life are clarified, their concentration is sharpened, and for the first time, it often seems, their lives begin to work.

After taking the *est* training myself for the first time, I realized that it is indeed an extraordinary training, one which, in a short time, has remarkably powerful effects on people's lives. It clearly deserved a book, but certainly not the normal expository work such a subject usually receives. Although I have done graduate work in psychology, worked for several years in mental hospitals, read widely in Western psychologies and Eastern religions for over a decade, and have a PhD from Columbia University, I felt that a scholarly or academic book about *est,* while interesting, would be counterproductive. "Understanding" and "beliefs," I had effectively learned from both Zen and *est,* are barriers to liberation. "Knowledge" about *est* would in many cases prove to be a barrier to people's choosing to *experience* the *est* training.

For *est* to work, the training must be experienced. One can, of course, come to believe one understands *est,* or to see *est*'s relation to gestalt therapy or scientology. One can learn facts about *est*: number of graduates, methods used, programs offered. This book will offer some such facts. But understanding and information have nothing to do with the essence of *est.* One can read *about* the training, just as one can read about LSD, but one shouldn't then expect to have a dramatic awakening.

The problem is that *est* is not a religion, not a therapy, not an academic course, and not a belief system. It might best be described, if it can be described at all, as theater—as living theater, participatory theater, encounter theater. Once we begin to see *est* in these terms, much that fails to fit the scheme of therapy or religion or science begins to make sense. . . .

If the training can best be described as participatory theater, it can also best be presented to a reading audience as drama. A book that summarizes the *est* training by describing its "philosophy" and analyzing what some people call its "therapy" may perpetuate precisely the way of life that *est* itself attempts to explode: namely, the adherence to the mind's belief systems. "In life, understanding is the booby prize" is a frequently heard *est* aphorism. Experiencing the training itself is the *only* way to get what the training offers, but the closest approximation to the training is a dramatization. . . .

■ ■ ■

"All right, then," says Michael a bit later to Elaine, who is seated on a chair beside him on the platform before the other trainees. "What I want you to do, Elaine, is to pretend I have here in my two hands two ice-cream cones, one chocolate, one vanilla. I want you to choose one or the other, chocolate or vanilla. Which do you choose?"

Elaine, smiling with her hands folded on her lap in front of her, replies, "Vanilla."

"Fine," says Michael. "Why did you choose vanilla?"

"I'm in the mood for vanilla."

"No," says Michael. "Here are two cones, one vanilla, one chocolate. Choose one."

"Okay," says Elaine, her smile a little nervous. "I choose vanilla."

"Fine. Why did you choose vanilla?"

"I chose vanilla because I like vanilla better than chocolate."

"No," says Michael. "Here are two ice-cream cones. Which do you choose?"

Elaine frowns. "I choose chocolate," she says.

"Good. Why do you choose chocolate?"

"I figured I'm not getting anyplace with vanilla, I'll try chocolate."

"No," says Michael firmly. "Look, here are two ice-cream cones, one vanilla and one chocolate. Choose one."

Werner Erhard, 1976. Erhard founded Erhard Seminar Training (est) in 1971. The seminars were usually a two-day, all-day affair for which participants paid several hundred dollars to attend.
© BETTMAN/CORBIS. REPRODUCED BY PERMISSION.

Elaine stares at Michael, at his two fists holding the imaginary cones, and then out at the audience.

"Well . . . but I *like* vanilla best!" she blurts out.

"Choose one, Elaine."

"VANILLA!"

"Great. Why did you choose vanilla?"

"Because I *like* vanilla."

"No," says Michael firmly. "That's reasonableness. Here's a chocolate cone. Here's vanilla. Choose one."

Elaine looks flushed and irritated, and she sits frozen for several seconds.

"I . . . choose . . . chocolate . . . ," she says carefully.

"Good. *Why* did you choose chocolate?"

"I choose chocolate . . . because . . . I feel like eating chocolate."

"No, that's reasonableness. Here are two cones, vanilla and chocolate. Choose one."

Elaine is now clearly vexed. Many in the audience feel they know the response Michael is seeking and are squirming with impatience at Elaine's failure to come up with it. Elaine is now staring at the back of the room.

"Vanilla . . . ," she says without much enthusiasm.

"Fine. *Why* did you choose vanilla?"

"I . . . chose . . . vanilla . . . because . . . I like vanilla ice cream better than any oth—"

"No! That's reasona—"

"BUT I LIKE VANILLA BETTER!"

"That's great, Elaine," says Michael. "I get that. You like vanilla ice cream better than chocolate ice cream. Right?"

"YES!"

"Fine. Here are two cones, one chocolate, one vanilla. Choose one."

"VANILLA!"

"That's great, Elaine. Now listen carefully, why did you choose vanilla?"

"I chose vanilla because I chose it!"

(Laughter and applause)

"Good. Why did you choose to come up on the stage for this demonstration?"

Elaine, looking pleased that she's escaped her torment, says, "Damned if I know."

"Why did you choose to volunteer for the demonstration?"

"Because I wanted to get as much as possible out of the training . . ."

"No!" says Michael. "That's reasonableness, consideration, that's making yourself the *effect* of something. *Why* did you choose to volunteer for—"

"Because I DID!"

"Because you did what?" asks Michael.

"I chose to volunteer because I chose to volunteer!"

(Applause and laughter)

"That's very good," says Michael. "Now, Elaine, you can either stay on the platform or return to your seat with the other trainees. Choose one."

Elaine smiles.

"I choose to sit," she says, standing and moving off the platform.

"HOLD IT!" shouts Michael. "That's fine. *Why* do you choose to sit?"

Elaine stares back at him for five, ten seconds.

"It's quite simple," she says after a while and now smiling fully. "I choose to sit because . . . *I choose to sit.*"

As Elaine proceeds to sit, the trainees applaud. Michael stands up and paces off to his right.

"Okay, more *est* nonsense. Anyone want to question or comment? Yes. Jack?"

"Now I know what Don was trying to tell me last weekend. I told him I was taking *est* because some friends had recommended it and he kept insisting that *I choose* to be here. At the time I pretended I understood. Now I *get* it."

"Thank you, Hank. Betsy?"

(Applause)

"Well, I *don't* get it. Elaine prefers vanilla to chocolate. Isn't that *why* she chooses vanilla?"

"It's why she chooses vanilla in the world of effect, effect, effect, in the world of unreality—code word reality—but it's *not* why people choose things in *reality,* in the realm of self-responsibility, in the realm of cause, cause, cause. In *that* realm, we *choose* things because we *choose* them."

"It seems to me a kind of trivial distinction to make," says Betsy.

"I'm afraid if the distinction between reality and unreality still seems trivial to you, Betsy, you may encounter some problems. Look. Most people say, 'I got mad because my friend lost my twenty dollars,' or, 'I ate vanilla ice cream because my palate always prefers vanilla.' They experience their friend or their body as cause and themselves as effect. It's a sure way to keep your life not working. In *est* we are cause in the matter. Our palate prefers vanilla, loves vanilla, but *we choose* . . . either vanilla or chocolate; we choose what we choose, but we don't experience ourselves as simply the effect of our bodies."

"But I thought you said we were nothing but machines."

"I said *that?*" says Michael, making an expression of mock surprise. "Oh yes, I said that. And I said you were all machines because you *are* machines, and now that you get it you're *choosing* your machineness and acting as cause rather than at effect."

"Then we *do* have free will after all?" asks Betsy.

"We haven't mentioned 'will' or 'free' or 'free will' once in the training and we're not going to start now. 'Free will' is a concept and can only lead to trouble. Just *choose*, Betsy, *choose* what you get, choose what you choose, and take responsibility for what happens."

"Well, for myself, I think I'd always eat what I like. I'd probably have a thousand vanilla cones."

"That's great. If you got a vanilla cone would you choose a vanilla cone?"

"Of course."

"And if they only had chocolate cones and you got a chocolate cone, would you choose chocolate?"

Betsy stares up at Michael.

"Oh!" she says abruptly. "Now I get it," and she begins laughing.

"Why are you laughing?" Michael asks.

"I'm laughing," Betsy answers, smiling happily, "because I choose to laugh . . ."

Further Resources

BOOKS

Bry, Adelaide. *est: Sixty Hours That Transform Your Life.* New York: Harper & Row, 1976.

Frederick, Carl. *est: Playing the Game the New Way.* New York: Delacorte Press, 1974.

Hargrove, Robert. *est: Making Life Work.* New York: Delacorte Press, 1976.

Harris, Amy Bjork, and Thomas A. Harris. *Staying OK.* New York: Harper & Row, 1985.

Pressman, Steven. *Outrageous Betrayal: The Dark Journey of Werner Erhard from est to Exile.* New York: St. Martin's Press, 1993.

PERIODICALS

Faltermayer, Charlotte. "The Best of est?: Werner Erhard's Legacy Lives on in a Kinder, Gentler, and Lucrative Version of His Self-Help Seminars." *Time,* March 16, 1998, 52.

WEBSITES

"The International Transactional Analysis Association." Available online at http://www.itaa-net.org (accessed March 24, 2003).

"Transactional Analysis Journal Internet." Available online at http://www.tajnet.org/ (accessed March 24, 2003).

"United States of America Transactional Analysis Association." Available online at http://www.usataa.org/ (accessed March 24, 2003).

AUDIO AND VISUAL MEDIA

Meet Your Parent, Adult, Child. Phoenix Films and Video, 1975.

Go Ask Alice
Diary

By: Anonymous [Beatrice Sparks]

Date: 1971

Source: Anonymous [Beatrice Sparks]. *Go Ask Alice.* New York: Avon, 1971, 32–36, 38, 54–57, 89, 152–153.

About the Author: Beatrice Sparks (1918–), who published *Go Ask Alice* anonymously, worked in drug treatment programs for teenagers in the 1960s in Southern California. After moving to Utah, she remained involved with the issue of teen drug use and appeared regularly as a public speaker on the subject. Following the success of *Go Ask Alice,* Sparks wrote and published several other "real life" diaries for the young-adult market, including books on AIDS, suicide, and the occult. ∎

Introduction

The use of illegal drugs skyrocketed in the 1960s, for a number of reasons. Advances in international transportation and travel explained part of the increased supply of drugs, many of which came from Asia and Latin America. In addition, some of the half-million American soldiers who served in Vietnam were introduced to heroin during their tour of duty and brought their drug habits back home. Demographic changes also contributed to the upswing in drug use. As baby boomers hit their teenage years, some used drugs as part of their rebellion against authority. By the end of the 1960s, many young people even viewed drug use as a rite of passage. Some took drugs to express their independence or creativity, and others did it simply to be fashionable. With few drug treatment programs in place at the beginning of the decade, however, there were few places to seek help once drug use turned into addiction. Between 1960 and 1967, juvenile arrests for narcotics use or possession increased by 800 percent.

Beatrice Sparks, a Utah-based writer who had worked as a drug counselor in Southern California, was a popular lecturer on the topic of drug use by young people. As she later recalled, after one of her talks she met a young woman, Alice, who wanted to talk with her about her own struggle to overcome drug use. Sparks and the teenager struck up a friendship, and Alice later gave Sparks her diary, compiled in books and on scraps of paper, which detailed her years of drug use. After Alice died of an overdose, Sparks decided to turn her diary into a book in order to educate other young people about the dangers of drug abuse. With the help of Art Linkletter—whose daughter, Diane, died in 1969 after she fell out a window while on LSD—Sparks found a publisher and *Go Ask Alice* appeared in bookstores in 1971.

President Nixon and his chief anti-drug law enforcement officials review a chart showing an increase in the number of arrests for drug violations from 1969 to 1972. As reported drug use steadily climbed, one of Nixon's initiatives while in office was a "war on drugs." © BETTMANN/CORBIS. REPRODUCED BY PERMISSION.

Significance

Publicized as the diary of a real teenager, *Go Ask Alice* was a publishing phenomenon. By the end of the 1970s, more than four million copies had been sold through forty-three printings in sixteen languages. The reviews for the book were overwhelmingly positive. Critics praised the book's ability to convey the mindset of a teenager with low self-esteem who is slowly pulled into a life of drug abuse, though some reviewers were concerned that the book's descriptions of Alice's drug trips might glamorize drug use. It was not until several years after the book's publication that questions about its authenticity were aired by reviewers. By that time, Sparks had gone on to write several other "diaries" on social problems for young adults. The true identity of "Alice" has never been revealed. Sparks claimed that she wanted to protect the privacy of Alice's family; her critics questioned whether Alice ever really existed.

The popularity of *Go Ask Alice* and its antidrug message corresponded with the federal government's first major, coordinated effort to stem the use of illegal drugs. After taking office in 1969, President Richard M. Nixon announced a "war on drugs" that focused on diminishing the supply of drugs from international sources while educating Americans on the dangers of drug use so that

there would be less demand for the substances. The Controlled Substances Act of 1970 codified the government's approach to the war on drugs. It divided drugs of abuse into five categories, and the penalties for possessing or using these drugs corresponded with how dangerous they were considered. Despite these efforts, rates of drug use continued to climb in the 1970s. According to the government's 1972 National Household Survey on Drug Abuse, 7 percent of twelve- to seventeen-year-olds and 27.8 percent of eighteen- to twenty-five-year-olds had used marijuana or hashish in the month before the survey. By 1979, the rates had climbed to 16.7 and 35.4 percent, respectively. For the older group, cocaine use increased from 3.1 percent in 1974 to 9.3 percent in 1979.

Primary Source

Go Ask Alice [excerpt]

SYNOPSIS: Although Alice's first drug experience takes place without her consent, she enjoys the LSD trip and the new circle of friends it gives her. Within ten days of using illegal drugs for the first time, she starts shooting speed and soon progresses to using marijuana and other drugs. Alice is eventually institutionalized for her drug use, and though she makes one final attempt to get off drugs, she later dies of an overdose.

July 10

Dear Diary,

I don't know whether I should be ashamed or elated. I only know that last night I had the most incredible experience of my life. It sounds morbid when I put it in words, but actually it was tremendous and wonderful and miraculous.

The kids at Jill's were so friendly and relaxed and at ease that I immediately felt at home with them. They accepted me like I had always been one of their crowd and everyone seemed happy and unhurried. I loved the atmosphere. It was great, great, great. Anyway, a little while after we got there Jill and one of the boys brought out a tray of coke and all the kids immediately sprawled out on the floor on cushions or curled up together on the sofa and chairs.

Jill winked at me and said, "Tonight we're playing 'Button, Button, Who's Got the Button?' You know, the game we used to play when we were kids." Bill Thompson, who was stretched out next to me, laughed, "Only it's just too bad that now somebody has to baby-sit."

I looked up at him and smiled. I didn't want to appear too stupid.

Everyone sipped their drinks slowly, and everyone seemed to be watching everyone else. I kept my eyes on Jill supposing that anything she did I should do.

Suddenly I began to feel something strange inside myself like a storm. I remember that two or three records had played since we had had the drinks, and now everyone was beginning to look at me. The palms of my hands were sweating and I could feel droplets of moisture on my scalp at the back of my neck. The room seemed unusually quiet, and as Jill got up to close the window shades completely I thought, "They're trying to poison me! Why, why would they try to poison me?"

My whole body was tense at every muscle and a feeling of weird apprehension swept over me, strangled me, suffocated me. When I opened my eyes, I realized that it was just Bill who had put his arm around my shoulder. "Lucky you," he was saying in a slow-motioned record on the wrong speed voice, "But don't worry, I'll baby-sit you. This will be a good trip. Come on, relax, enjoy it, enjoy it." He caressed my face and neck tenderly, and said, "Honestly, I won't let anything bad happen to you." Suddenly he seemed to be repeating himself over and over like a slow-motioned echo chamber. I

started laughing, wildly, hysterically. It struck me as the funniest, most absurd thing I had ever heard. Then I noticed the strange shifting patterns on the ceiling. Bill pulled me down and my head rested in his lap as I watched the pattern change to swirling colors, great fields of reds, blues and yellows. I tried to share the beauty with the others, but my words came out soggy, wet and dripping or tasting of color. I pulled myself up and began walking, feeling a slight chill which crept inside as well as outside my body. I wanted to tell Bill, but all I could do was laugh. . . .

After what seemed eternities I began to come down and the party started breaking up. I sort of asked Jill what happened and she said that 10 out of the 14 bottles of coke had LSD in them and, "button, button," no one knew just who would wind up with them. Wow, am I glad I was one of the lucky ones. . . .

July 13

Dear Diary,

For two days now I've tried to convince myself that using LSD makes me a "dope addict" and all the other low-class, unclean, despicable things I've heard about kids that use LSD and all the other drugs; but I'm so, so, so, so, so curious, I simply can't wait to try pot, only once, I promise! I simply have to see if it's everything that it's cracked up not to be! All the things I've heard about LSD were obviously written by uninformed, ignorant people like my parents who obviously don't know what they're talking about; maybe pot is the same. Anyway Jill called this morning, and she's going to her friend's for the weekend and she'll call me the first thing Monday. . . .

July 20

Dear close, warm, intimate friend, Diary,

What a fantastic, unbelievable, expanding, thrilling week I've had. It's been like, wow—the greatest thing that has ever happened. Remember I told you I had a date with Bill? Well he introduced me to torpedos on Friday and Speed on Sunday. They are both like riding shooting stars through the Milky Way, only a million, trillion times better. The Speed was a little scary at first because Bill had to inject it right into my arm. I remembered how much I hated shots when I was in the hospital, but this is different, now I can't wait, I positively can't wait to try it again. No wonder it's called Speed! I could hardly control myself, in fact I couldn't have if I had wanted to, and I didn't want to. I danced like I had never dreamed possible for introverted, mousy little me. I felt great, free, abandoned, a different, improved, perfected specimen of a different, improved, perfected species. It was wild! It was beautiful! It really was. . . .

September 26

Last night was the night, friend! I finally smoked pot and it was even greater than I expected! Last night after work, Chris fixed me up with a college friend of hers who knew I'd been on acid, etc., but who wanted to turn me on to hash.

He told me not to expect to feel like I felt with liquor and I told him I'd never had more than champagne at birthday parties and leftovers from cocktail parties. We all got hilarious over that and Ted, Chris' date, said that lots of kids never try booze, not only because it's their parents' thing, but because it's a lot harder to get than pot. Ted said that when he first started experimenting he found he could steal a lot of money from his parents and they would never miss it, but let him take one swig out of any of their booze bottles and it was as though they had it measured to the ounce.

Then Richie showed me how to smoke. And I've never even had a cigarette! He gave me a small orientation lecture, like I should listen for small things I wouldn't ordinarily hear and just relax. At first I took too deep a drag and almost choked to death, so Richie told me to suck in open-mouthed gulps to mix as much air in as possible. But that didn't work too well either and after a while Ted gave up and brought out a hookah pipe. It seemed funny and exotic but at first I couldn't get any smoke and I felt cheated because the other three were obviously stoned. But finally it started to work, just when I thought it never would, and I really began to feel happy and free as a bright canary chirping through the open, endless heavens. And I was so relaxed! I don't think I've been that relaxed in my whole entire life! It was really beautiful. Later Rich brought a sheepskin rug out of his room and we began walking through the thickness of it and there was a sensation in my feet that was totally indescribable, a softness that enveloped my complete body, and quite suddenly I could hear the strange almost silent sound of the long silky hairs rubbing against each other and against my feet. It was a sound unsimilar to any I have ever heard, and I remember trying desperately to give a dissertation upon the phenomena of each individual hair having perfect pitch within itself. But of course I couldn't; it was too perfect. . . .

P.S. Richie gave me some joints to smoke when I'm alone and I want to be in heaven. Isn't that nice, nice, nice! . . .

January 24

Oh damn, damn, damn, it's happened again. I don't know whether to scream with glory or cover myself with ashes and sackcloth, whatever that means. Anyone who says pot and acid are not addicting is a damn, stupid, raving idiot, unenlightened fool! I've been on them since July 10, and when I've been off I've been scared to death to even think of anything that even looks or seems like dope. All the time pretending to myself that I could take it or leave it!

All the dumb, idiot kids who think they are only chipping are in reality just existing from one experience to the other. After you've had it, there isn't even life without drugs. It's a prodding, colorless, dissonant bare existence. It stinks. And I'm glad I'm back. Glad! Glad! Glad! I've never had it better than I had it last night. Each new time is the best time and Chris feels the same way. Last night when she called and asked me to come over, I knew something terrible had happened. She sounded like she didn't know what to do. But when I got there and smelled that incredible smell, I just sat down on the floor of her room with her and cried and smoked. It was beautiful and wonderful and we'd been without it for so long. I'll never be able to express how really great it is. . . .

July 22

I could tell Mom had been crying when she came to see me today, so I tried to be very strong and put on a really happy face. It's a good thing I did because they are sending me to an insane asylum, a loony bin, a crazy house, freak wharf, where I can wander around with the other idiots and lunatics. I am so scared I cannot even take a full breath. Daddy tried to explain it all very professionally but it was obvious that he had been completely unhinged by the whole thing. But not as much as I am. No one could be.

He said that when my case was taken before the juvenile judge, Jan and Marcie both testified that I had been trying for weeks to sell them LSD and marijuana and that around school I was a known user and pusher.

Circumstances really were quite against me. I have a drug record and Daddy said that when Mrs. Larsen's neighbor heard me screaming, she and the gardener came over to see what was happening and thinking I had gone insane they locked me in a small closet, ran to check the baby who had apparently also been awakened by my screams, and called the police. By the time they got there I had injured myself severely and was trying to scratch the rough plaster off the walls to get out and had beaten my head against the door until I had a brain concussion and a fractured skull.

Now they are going to send me to the Boobie Hatch which is probably where I belong. Daddy says I probably won't be there long and he will immediately start proceedings to have me released and put into the hands of a good psychiatrist.

Dad and Mom keep calling the place where I'm going a youth center, but they aren't fooling anybody. They aren't even fooling themselves. They are sending me to an insane asylum! And I don't understand how can that be. How is it possible? Other people have bad trips and they don't get sent to an insane asylum. They tell me my worms aren't real and yet they're sending me to a place that's worse than all the coffins and the worms put together. I don't understand why this is happening to me. I think I have fallen off the face of the earth and that I will never stop falling. Oh, please, please don't let them take me. Don't let them put me away with insane people. I'm afraid of them. Please let me go home to my own room and go to sleep. Please God.

Further Resources

BOOKS

Baum, Dan. *Smoke and Mirrors: The War on Drugs and the Politics of Failure.* Boston: Little, Brown, 1996.

Gottfried, Ted. *Should Drugs Be Legalized?* Brookfield, Conn.: Twenty-first Century, 2000.

Jonnes, Jill. *Hep-Cats, Narcs, and Pipe Dreams: A History of America's Romance With Illegal Drugs.* New York: Scribner's, 1996.

Levine, Herbert M. *American Issues Debated: The Drug Problem.* Austin, Tex.: Raintree Steck-Vaughan, 1998.

Sharp, Elaine B. *The Dilemma of Drug Policy in the United States.* New York: HarperCollins, 1994.

PERIODICALS

Adams, Lauren. "*Go Ask Alice*: A Second Look." *Horn Book Magazine,* 74, no. 5, September–October 1998, 587–592.

Nilsen, Alleen Pace. "The House That Alice Built: An Interview With the Author Who Brought You *Go Ask Alice.*" *School Library Journal,* 262, no. 2, October 1979, 109–112.

WEBSITES

National Institute on Drug Abuse. Available online at http://www.nida.nih.gov (accessed February 13, 2003).

AUDIO AND VISUAL MEDIA

Go Ask Alice. Directed by John Korty. Golden Age Video. Videocassette, 1973.

"Sisterhood"
Essay

By: Gloria Steinem

Date: 1972

Source: Gloria Steinem. "Sisterhood." *Ms.,* 1972. Reprinted in *Outrageous Acts and Everyday Rebellions.* New York: Holt, Rinehart and Winston, 1983, 112–113, 116–118.

About the Author: Gloria Steinem (1934–) was born in Toledo, Ohio. She graduated magna cum laude with a degree in government from Smith College in 1956. After attending an abortion-rights rally in 1969, Steinem embraced a feminist perspective in her life and work. A co-founder of the National Women's Political Caucus (NWPC) in 1971, Steinem also founded *Ms.* magazine in 1971. The author of several best-selling books, Steinem remains a leading advocate of women's causes. She married David Bale, a South African-born entrepreneur and political activist, in 2000. ∎

Introduction

As the modern women's movement gathered momentum in the wake of Betty Friedan's 1963 book *The Feminine Mystique,* feminism produced some fundamental changes in American society. Many Americans began to question the common assumptions about a woman's place in society, which traditionally had been defined through her identity as a wife and mother. Others demanded reforms in the educational system to end bias against female students, who were often denied access—formally or informally—to professional programs. In the work place as well, critics noted that women almost always were paid far less than men, even when they performed the same work.

Journalist Gloria Steinem, who enjoyed a successful career in the 1960s as a writer for magazines such as *Esquire* and *New York,* seemed to be the prototypical "Single Girl" of Helen Gurley Brown's advice books and columns in *Cosmopolitan* magazine, to which Steinem also contributed. She even gained a measure of celebrity as the author of the 1963 exposé "A Bunny's Tale," written for *Show* magazine after a two-week undercover stint at the New York City Playboy Club. Although the article demonstrated a certain feminist perspective, Steinem did not identify with the women's movement throughout most of the decade.

Steinem's feminist awakening occurred in 1969. A political liberal, Steinem joined the founding staff of *New York* that year as the author of "The City Politic" column. For one of her assignments she attended a meeting of the feminist group Redstockings to rally support for legalizing abortion. Impressed by the women's commitment to political change, Steinem began writing with a more pronounced feminist tone. With extensive media coverage—usually focusing on her good looks, wit, and lifestyle—Steinem became one of the best-known feminists in America by 1971. Although she refused to be drawn into the ideological differences that split the feminist movement in the early 1970s, Steinem's own visibility earned her criticism from some feminists who argued that no individual should be singled out, however unwillingly, as the "leader" of the women's movement.

Significance

Steinem's best known contribution to the feminist movement in the 1970s came with the publication of *Ms.* magazine. With the support of *New York* publisher Clay S. Felker, Steinem and Pat Carbine published the inaugural issue as a supplement in *New York* in December 1971. The following month the first stand-alone issue of *Ms.* was an instant success that sold out its first run of 300,000 copies in just over a week. As a monthly magazine with Steinem as its editor, *Ms.* claimed a subscriber base of half a million readers by the mid-1970s.

The success of *Ms.* and Steinem's regular appearances as a lecturer and talk show guest throughout the 1970s confirmed her status as America's best-known feminist. Although she came under her fair share of attacks by conservative commentators, not to mention other feminists, Steinem's accessibility and good humor helped to alleviate criticism of feminists in general as strident or out of touch with the average person. Steinem also helped to restore a sense of unity to the women's movement, which had witnessed ideological and personal battles based on generational, class, race, and sexual orientation lines.

By the end of the decade, the women's movement had made substantial progress on many of the issues for which it had advocated—access to family planning and safe, legal abortions, parity in educational opportunities, and recognition of gender stereotyping in the media. Other goals remained more elusive. Despite efforts to ratify the Equal Rights Amendment—the proposed Constitutional amendment to outlaw gender discrimination—the period of ratification ended without success in 1982. The movement made only partial progress in fighting for equal economic opportunity in the 1970s: although the segregation of jobs by gender eased by nine percent during the 1970s, the gap between men's and women's paychecks, which stood at sixty-four cents for women for every dollar a man earned in 1955, remained at sixty-four cents in 1986.

Primary Source

"Sisterhood" [excerpt]

SYNOPSIS: In this piece, first published in *Ms.* magazine in 1972, Steinem traces her own development as a feminist and its implications. Touching upon

race, class, and gender in her analysis, Steinem presents her awakening as the beginning of a personal and social transformation. Envisioning feminism as a force for social justice, Steinem hopes for "a society in which, at a minimum, no one is born into a second-class role because of visible difference, because of race or of sex."

A very, very long time ago (about three or four years), I took a certain secure and righteous pleasure in saying the things that women are supposed to say. I remember with pain—

"My work won't interfere with marriage. After all, I can always keep my typewriter at home." Or:

"I don't want to write about women's stuff. I want to write about foreign policy." Or:

"Black families were forced into matriarchy, so I see why black women have to step back and let their men get ahead." Or:

"I know we're helping Chicano groups that are tough on women, but *that's their culture.*" Or:

"Who would want to join a women's group? I've never been a joiner, have you?" Or (when bragging):

"He says I write like a man."

I suppose it's obvious from the kinds of statements I chose that I was secretly nonconforming. I wasn't married. I was earning a living at a profession I cared about. I had basically—if quietly—opted out of the "feminine" role. But that made it all the more necessary to repeat the conventional wisdom, even to look as conventional as I could manage, if I was to avoid some of the punishments reserved by society for women who don't do as society says. I therefore learned to Uncle Tom with subtlety, logic, and humor. Sometimes, I even believed it myself.

If it weren't for the women's movement, I might still be dissembling away. But the ideas of this great sea-change in women's view of ourselves are contagious and irresistible. They hit women like a revelation, as if we had left a dark room and walked into the sun.

At first my discoveries seemed personal. In fact, they were the same ones so many millions of women have made and are continuing to make. Greatly simplified, they go like this: Women are human beings first, with minor differences from men that apply largely to the single act of reproduction. We share the dreams, capabilities, and weaknesses of all human beings, but our occasional pregnancies and other visible differences have been used—even more pervasively, if less brutally, than racial differ-

Gloria Steinem participates with other feminists at an ERA rally, Washington, D.C., 1981. Steinem also founded *Ms.* magazine and authored many articles and books as a leading advocate of women's causes. **AP/WIDE WORLD PHOTOS. REPRODUCED BY PERMISSION.**

ences have been used—to create an "inferior" group and an elaborate division of labor. The division is continued for a clear if often unconscious reason: the economic and social profit of males as a group.

Once this feminist realization dawned, I reacted in what turned out to be predictable ways. First, I was amazed at the simplicity and obviousness of a realization that made sense, at last, of my life experience. I couldn't figure out why I hadn't seen it before. Second, I realized how far that new vision of life was from the system around us, and how tough it would be to explain this feminist realization at all, much less to get people (especially, though not only, men) to accept so drastic a change. . . .

Looking back at all those male-approved things I used to say, the basic hang-up seems clear—a lack of esteem for women, whatever our race, and for myself.

This is the most tragic punishment that society inflicts on any second-class group. Ultimately the brainwashing works, and we ourselves come to believe our group is inferior. Even if we achieve a little success in the world and think of ourselves as "different," we don't want to associate with our group. We want to identify up, not down (clearly my problem in not wanting to join women's groups). We want to be the only woman in the office, or the only black family on the block, or the only Jew in the club.

The pain of looking back at wasted, imitative years is enormous. Trying to write like men. Valuing myself and other women according to the degree of our acceptance by men—socially, in politics, and in our professions. It's as painful as it is now to hear two grown-up female human beings competing with each other on the basis of their husband's status, like servants whose identity rests on the wealth or accomplishments of their employers.

And this lack of esteem that makes us put each other down is still the major enemy of sisterhood. Women who are conforming to society's expectations view the nonconformists with justifiable alarm. *Those noisy, unfeminine women,* they say to themselves. *They will only make trouble for us all.* Women who are quietly nonconforming, hoping nobody will notice, are even more alarmed because they have more to lose. And that makes sense, too.

The status quo protects itself by punishing all challengers, especially women whose rebellion strikes at the most fundamental social organization: the sex roles that convince half the population that its identity depends on being first in work or in war, and the other half that it must serve as docile, unpaid, or underpaid labor.

In fact, there seems to be no punishment inside the white male club that quite equals the ridicule and personal viciousness reserved for women who rebel. Attractive or young women who act forcefully are assumed to be either unnatural or male-controlled. If they succeed, it could only have been sexually, through men. Old women or women considered unattractive by male standards are accused of acting out of bitterness, because they could not get a man. Any woman who chooses to behave like a full human being should be warned that the armies of the status quo will treat her as something of a dirty joke. That's their natural and first weapon. She will *need* sisterhood.

All of that is meant to be a warning but not a discouragement. There are more rewards than punishments.

For myself, I can now admit anger and use it constructively, where once I would have submerged it and let it fester into guilt or collect for some destructive explosion.

I have met brave women who are exploring the outer edge of human possibility, with no history to guide them, and with a courage to make themselves vulnerable that I find moving beyond the words to express it.

I no longer think that I do not exist, which was my version of that lack of self-esteem afflicting many women. (If male standards weren't natural to me, and they were the only standards, how could I exist?) This means that I am less likely to need male values and approval and am less vulnerable to classic arguments. ("If you don't like me, you're not a real woman"—said by a man who is coming on. "If you don't like me, you can't relate to other people, you're not a real person"—said by anyone who understands blackmail as an art.)

I can sometimes deal with men as equals and therefore can afford to like them for the first time.

I have discovered politics that are not intellectual or superimposed. They are organic. I finally understand why for years I inexplicably identified with "out" groups: I belong to one, too. And I know it will take a coalition of such groups to achieve a society in which, at a minimum, no one is born into a second-class role because of visible difference, because of race or of sex.

I no longer feel strange by myself or with a group of women in public. I feel just fine.

I am continually moved to discover I have sisters.

I am beginning, just beginning, to find out who I am.

Further Resources

BOOKS

Davis, Flora. *Moving the Mountain: The Women's Movement in America.* New York: Simon & Schuster, 1991.

Echols, Alice. *Daring to Be Bad: Feminism in America, 1967–1975.* Minneapolis: University of Minnesota, 1989.

Faludi, Susan. *Backlash: The Undeclared War Against American Women.* New York: Anchor Books, 1991.

Heilbrun, Carolyn G. *The Education of a Woman: The Life of Gloria Steinem.* New York: Dial Press, 1995.

Ladensohn, Sydney Stern. *Gloria Steinem: Her Passions, Politics, and Mystique.* Seacaucus, NJ: Carol Publications, 1997.

Moving Beyond Words. New York: Simon & Schuster, 1994.

Steinem, Gloria. *Revolution from Within: A Book of Self-Esteem.* Boston: Little, Brown, 1992.

WEBSITES

"Ms. Foundation for Women." Available online at http://www.ms.foundation.org/ (accessed March 7, 2003).

"Ms. Magazine." Available online at http://www.msmagazine.com/ (accessed March 7, 2003).

"The National Organization for Women." Available online at http://www.now.org (accessed March 7, 2003).

Changing Gender Roles

"Coffee, Tea, or He"
Magazine article

By: Anonymous
Date: March 19, 1973
Source: *Newsweek,* March 19, 1973, p. 65.

"You've Come a Long Way, Baby"
Advertisement

By: Philip Morris Company
Source: Philip Morris Company. "You've Come a Long Way, Baby." Advertisement for Virginia Slims. Reprinted in The Advertising Archive, Ltd. Image Ref.: 30520065. ∎

Introduction

The changing gender roles of the 1970s resulted in part from the legal and social developments that overturned traditional gender concepts during the 1960s.

Through the early 1960s, newspaper job ads routinely divided jobs into "male" and "female" employment; the women's jobs typically paid less than the men's jobs, even if the work itself was essentially the same. As the Civil Rights movement put discrimination on the nation's legal agenda, however, many women began to call for equal rights in employment regardless of gender.

One of the key provisions of the Civil Rights Act of 1964—Title VII—prohibited employment discrimination based on race, color, religion, sex, or national origin. In the first years of the act the federal government moved quickly to enforce the law against racial discrimination in the workplace, but in 1970 the first lawsuit over gender discrimination, filed by female workers at a glass factory in Toledo, Ohio, made its way to court. Other suits soon followed and employers were forced to end discriminatory hiring and promotional practices, or face additional lawsuits.

Congress enacted another landmark piece of federal legislation in 1972, when it passed Title IX of the Educational Amendments Act. Title IX prohibited sex discrimination in educational programs by institutions that received any federal funding. After a period of confusion over how Title IX would be applied, Congress issued its Title IX regulations in 1975, which specified that the legislation applied to athletic opportunities as well as to academic programs. Although the regulations were typically not enforced regarding sports programs over the next two decades, the federal government—responding to a series of lawsuits over the application of Title IX—finally began enforcing the law in the mid-1990s. Some colleges and universities responded by closing down some of their men's athletics programs, while other institutions bolstered their athletic offerings for women.

Significance

Title VII of the Civil Rights Act of 1964 and Title IX of the Educational Amendments Act of 1972 both reflected changes in gender roles while ushering in additional changes in the way Americans dealt with issues of equality and opportunity. Both also proved controversial to many Americans. Supporters of the laws envisioned a society with less discrimination and stereotyping based on traditional gender roles. Opponents of the legislation predicted that the laws would undermine traditional social mores, weaken family life, and create psychological problems as young Americans struggled to adapt to the changes. Leading the charge against the new gender order was Phyllis Schlafly, an activist and political candidate who argued that the American family was being irreparably harmed by the changes. Although she did not overturn Title VII or Title IX, Schlafly was successful in mobilizing many Americans against the proposed Equal Rights Amendment (ERA), which would have put a gen-

der anti-discrimination clause in the U.S. Constitution. Schlafly was given most of the credit for defeating the ERA, which was not ratified by its 1982 deadline.

As the activists and social critics argued over the meaning of the changes in America's gender identities, the media reflected the debates over men's and women's roles in society. In the marketplace, items such as deodorants and shampoos that had previously been advertised to attract either men or women were now marketed as "unisex" items. Other products, such as the Virginia Slims cigarette with its references to the history of feminism and its slogan, "You've come a long way, baby," were advertised as part of the gender revolution. In music, artists such as David Bowie and David Johansen took on ambiguous gender roles and made the unisex look fashionable. Even in the corporate world, fashion emphasized a more unisex look, best exemplified by the suit coats, high-necked blouses, and toned-down accessories that John T. Molloy urged professional women to wear in his 1977 guide *Women's Dress for Success*

Primary Source

"Coffee, Tea, or He"

SYNOPSIS: This article appeared in *Newsweek* shortly after the first male flight attendants were hired under a court order to end gender discrimination on airlines. Suggesting that some passengers might be physically sickened by being served by men, the writer offers the reassurance that the new flight attendants have traditionally macho, heterosexual credentials.

"Good morning, ladies and gentlemen, and welcome aboard Continental's proud bird, our Golden Fan Jet," announced the stewardess trainee inside the mockup 707 cabin at Continental Airlines' instructional facility at Los Angeles International Airport. "I am Miss Bailey. Your hostesses in the cabin are Barbara, Jackie and . . . (pause) . . . John?" Twenty-eight-year-old trainee John Thomas dropped his demonstration oxygen mask in disgust. "They've gotta do something about that announcement," he sighed.

The kinks in the professional image are still being hammered out, but ever since a 1971 court decision overruled the "women only" requirements for stewardess applicants, the nation's airlines have been busily hiring—and training—male stewards. Pan American now flies nearly 300 male attendants, while American and United employ 200 apiece—with United fielding the only husband-and-wife team in the friendly skies. In recent years, stewards have flown aboard the international flights of American and for-

Primary Source

"You've Come a Long Way, Baby"

SYNOPSIS: In 1968 Philip Morris launched a new cigarette line, Virginia Slims, aimed at the female market. The advertising campaign highlighted times throughout history when women asserted their independence by smoking, but its tagline, "You've Come a Long Way, Baby," irked some women as being condescending and sexist. THE ADVERTISING ARCHIVE LTD./VIRGINIA SLIMS. REPRODUCED BY PERMISSION.

eign carriers in supervisory roles, but now men are gamely stowing coats and serving up meals on regular runs—and bravely swallowing hefty doses of coffee-tea-or-me teasing.

Although the sight of a man doing modified bunny dips at high altitudes may cause some passengers to reach for the airbag, the typical steward is not the sort to tolerate jibes at his manhood. Tony McMahon was the lightweight amateur boxing champion of Ireland before he joined Hughes Air West last June, while Continental's Steve Levinson previously taught physical education. For their part, some stewardesses concede that the male attendants have set a noticeable example for their own behavior. "The men don't prostitute their charm like a lot of us," United stewardess Donna Jones told Newsweek's Peter Greenberg.

Nevertheless, whether they flaunt it or not, the men must submit to the same grooming requirements as the women, suffering through a training curriculum that is still largely geared to the feminine touch. In a recent Continental class, six male students—fresh from the hair stylists—sat studying Family Circle's guide to beauty. "The only exception in our contract," quips David Jiminez of Western Airlines, "is that we don't have to carry an extra pair of pantyhose."

Single

For the moment, at least, some male stews have found advantages in their gender. "Nine times out of ten I get a single room when the crew gets a layover," boasts United's Brock Harris, who is a former administrator at an Ohio college. "And I've had more luck with women on planes than ever before." While the fun far outweighs the steward's bankbook ("A single woman can live on the $500-a-month salary, but a single man can't," claims Harris), the job also offers a lofty opportunity for advancement. "The major difference between the men and women," says Lin O'Neill, a regional manager at Western Airlines, "is that the men are more career-oriented."

Before moving on to airline desk jobs, however, male stews are learning to appreciate the occupational hazards of the job—long flights: screaming babies, jet lag and lecherous passengers. During one of Jiminez's early flights for Western, he leaned over to serve food to a passenger in the window seat—and a lady sitting on the aisle gently placed her hand on his thigh. Shocked, Jiminez hustled to the senior stew to report the incident. "The girls had watched the whole thing," he recalls, "and when I told them

A male flight attendant stands in the middle of this 1976 publicity photo from United Airlines. United Airlines began hiring large numbers of male "stewardesses" in 1972, prompting the change in job title to flight attendant. COURTESY OF UNITED AIRLINES ARCHIVES. REPRODUCED BY PERMISSION.

what happened, they simply said, 'Well, you finally got a grab—now you know what it feels like to be a stewardess.'"

Further Resources

BOOKS

Amott, Teresa, and Julia A. Mattaei. *Race, Gender, and Work: A Multicultural Economic History of Women in the United States.* Cambridge, Mass.: South End Press, 1996.

Anderson, Jami L. *Race, Gender, and Sexuality: Philosophical Issues of Identity and Justice.* Upper Saddle River, N.J.: Prentice Hall, 2002.

Kimmel, Michael S. *The Gendered Society.* New York: Oxford University Press, 2001.

Levit, Nancy. *The Gender Line: Men, Women, and the Law.* New York: New York University Press, 1998.

Molloy, John T. *Dress for Success.* New York: P.H. Wyden, 1975.

Schlafly, Phyllis. *The Power of the Positive Woman.* New Rochelle, N.Y.: Arlington House, 1977.

Tomaskovic-Devey, Donald. *Gender and Racial Inequality at Work: The Sources and Consequences of Job Segregation.* Ithaca, N.Y.: ILR Press, 1993.

Women's Dress for Success. Chicago: Follett, 1977.

WEBSITES
"The Equal Employment Opportunity Commission." Available online at http://www.eeoc.gov (accessed March 17, 2003).

AUDIO AND VISUAL MEDIA
In the Spirit of Title IX. First Run/Icarus Films, 1981.

Women in Sports: The Title IX Generation. PBS Video, 1997, VHS.

The American Indian Movement

"The American Indian Movement," "Tourist Boycott," and "March July 4 from Keystone to Mt. Rushmore"

Flyers

By: American Indian Movement

Date: 1973; 1976

Source: "The American Indian Movement," "Tourist Boycott," and "March July 4 from Keystone to Mt. Rushmore." Michigan State University Library, Urban Policy and Planning File.

About the Authors: Under the leadership of its national director, Russell Means (1939–), the American Indian Movement (AIM) used the standoff at Pine Ridge to publicize its grievances against the federal government and the elected leadership of the reservation. Criminal charges against Means and other AIM leaders at Pine Ridge were later dropped after some of the FBI's investigation techniques were discredited at trial. In the 1990s Means pursued an acting and producing career while continuing to speak out on issues of importance to Native Americans. ■

Airlift to Wounded Knee

Memoir

By: Bill Zimmerman

Date: 1976

Source: Zimmerman, Bill. *Airlift to Wounded Knee.* Chicago: Swallow Press, 1976, 175–177.

About the Author: Bill Zimmerman left a career in teaching and research to work against the United States' involvement in Vietnam and southeast Asia. After his participation in the Wounded Knee standoff, Zimmerman became the executive director of the Campaign for New Drug Policies, a group that advocated the legalization of marijuana for medical use, treatment instead of jail terms for first-time drug offenders, and other drug laws.

Wounded Knee 1973

Personal journal

By: Stanley David Lyman

Date: 1991

Source: *Wounded Knee 1973.* Lincoln, Nebraska: University of Nebraska Press, 1991, 91–92.

About the Author: Stanley Lyman (1913–1979) began working for the federal government in the War Food Administration during World War II. He joined the Bureau of Indian Affairs (BIA) in the early 1950s and became the superintendent of the Pine Ridge Indian Reservation in 1972. As a specialist in economic development, hoped to expand business opportunities at Pine Ridge. In his view, BIA officials had no choice but to deal with the recognized, elected tribal leaders during the standoff, a stance that put him at odds with the insurgents at Pine Ridge.

Introduction

The mass protests by Native Americans in the late 1960s and 1970s shared much with the Civil Rights movement of the 1960s. Like African American activists, American Indian leaders wanted to publicize their grievances against the social and economic problems they faced, particularly on the reservations where most of them lived under federal supervision. Yet the unique history of federal and Native American relations complicated the Native American rights movement, at times making it far more militant than previous civil rights protests. Such was the case at the seventy-one-day standoff at the Pine Ridge Indian Reservation in Wounded Knee, South Dakota, beginning February 27, 1973.

The siege at Wounded Knee was led by the American Indian Movement (AIM) and its national director, Russell Means. AIM was founded in 1968 in Minneapolis as a support agency for Native American migrants to urban areas. In addition to helping its members find jobs and investigating reports of police brutality, AIM adopted a far-reaching platform of self-determination. This included demands to regain lands taken over by the federal government and to implement changes in federal policies toward Native Americans. In 1969 AIM coordinated a dramatic takeover of the former federal prison at Alcatraz Island in San Francisco Bay to protest against the Bureau of Indian Affairs (BIA) and its alleged mismanagement, corruption, and lack of responsiveness to Native Americans. The takeover lasted two years before the protesters were removed. In 1972 AIM organized "The Trail of Broken Treaties," a march on Washington that culminated in a takeover of the BIA headquarters for six days. AIM was demonstrating a growing militancy, and during the takeover, they destroyed many BIA files.

In early 1973 Russell Means came to the Pine Ridge Indian Reservation to support a movement to oust the Oglala (Sioux) Tribal President, Dick Wilson, and his supporters in the tribal council. Wilson's group, many of whom had mixed-raced Sioux heritage, was accused of being too accommodating to the BIA, particularly to the detriment of full-blooded tribal members. After a referendum to impeach Wilson failed on February 24, a force of about two-hundred armed AIM members announced a takeover of Wounded Knee village on the reservation on February 27. The village held symbolic value as a site of protest, as it had witnessed a bloody confrontation between the Sioux and the U.S. Seventh Calvary in 1890. After raiding the trading post and destroying the town's museum, the insurgents took eleven hostages and held them at the Sacred Heart Catholic Church. After FBI and BIA officials set up roadblocks around the village, AIM members opened fire on the agents. Throughout the seventy-one-day siege, both sides continued to trade gunfire as negotiations dragged on.

Significance

Although AIM succeeded in drawing national attention to its agenda, its use of force—including an alleged murder of one Wilson supporter—shocked many Americans, even those who supported its cause. After the siege, Means and other AIM leaders were indicted on several criminal charges. The charges were dismissed by a federal judge who found that the FBI had engaged in misconduct during its investigation, making a fair trial impossible. Means emerged from the trials as the most visible Native-American activist of the era, with AIM as the movement's leading civil-rights organization.

Despite the controversy over the siege at Wounded Knee, AIM was undeniably successful in publicizing its platform of self-determination for Native Americans. Although most reservations still endured poverty and social problems throughout the decade, several self-help and federally sponsored economic development programs were inaugurated. Most importantly, the Indian Self-Determination Act of 1974 gave tribes control of federal and educational funds disbursed to the reservations. Some federal lands were also returned to Native American tribes in the 1970s; in the years that followed, multimillion-dollar cash grants were authorized as restitution to tribes that had lost their traditional tribal lands. These changes, along with the continuing presence of AIM as a national advocate for Native Americans, led to a cultural resurgence that some labeled "Red Power," a reference to the Black Power movement that reached a peak in the late 1960s. "Before AIM in 1968, culture had been weakened in most Indian communities due to U.S. policy, the American boarding schools, and all the other efforts to extinguish Indian secular and spiritual life," an AIM history announced thirty years after Wounded Knee. It also noted that "Now, many groups cannot remember a time without culture. This great revival has also helped to restore spiritual leaders and elders to their former positions of esteem for the wisdom and history they hold."

Primary Source

"The American Indian Movement"

> **SYNOPSIS:** One of AIM's primary goals in the Wounded Knee standoff was to gain national attention for its grievances against the federal government. Like the Civil Rights movement in the 1960s, AIM sponsored protest marches, boycotts, and other mass actions to rally support for its agenda, as these documents show.

1. How? When? Where? did AIM start?

The American Indian Movement was founded on July 28, 1968 in Minneapolis, Minn. to unify the more than 20 Indian organizations which were then felt to be doing little, if anything, to change life in the Indian ghetto. As it became clear that most of these organizations treated Indians paternalistically, with little incentive to manage their own affairs, AIM, first called the Concerned Indian American (CIA), redirected its attention away from the organizations and toward the Indian people as the means to Indian self-determination.

A catalyst for AIM in 1968 in the city of Minneapolis was the pervasive police harassment of Indian people. While Indians represented only 10% of the city's population, 70% of the inmates in the city jails were Indian. To divert Indians from the jails, AIM formed a ghetto patrol, equipped with two-way radios which monitored the police radios. Whenever a call came over involving Indians, AIM was there first, and for 29 successive weekends prevented any undue arrests of Indian people. The Indian population in the jails decreased by 60%. And out of the patrol evolved the federally funded Legal Rights Center, where established attorneys donated up to 80% of their time to serve poor people.

2. Who founded AIM?

The cofounders of AIM are Dennis Banks, Clyde Bellecourt and George Mitchell, Chippewas of Minnesota. Banks is from Leach Lake Reservation and Mitchell and Bellecourt are from White Earth. Banks now serves as national director, succeeding Vern Bellecourt, also of the White Earth Reservation.

How extensive an organization is AIM?

There are 79 chapters of AIM internationally, eight of which are in Canada. AIM has also developed ties with aboriginal organizations in Australia and with natives in Micronesia, and continues to grow on and off the reservation.

4. What is the structure of AIM?

Unlike other organizations and agencies dealing with Indian affairs, AIM uniquely begins with the peo-

Tourist Boycott

SEE SOUTH DAKOTA LAST!

FREE

ALL CUSTER VICTIMS

Roam free in South Dakota

Going on 200 Years of
Independence -- Washington,
Jefferson, Roosevelt, Lincoln.
It took a mountain of
granite and the
sculpturing genius of
Gutzon Borglum
to capture the
enormity of their
influence on
American History

South Dakota 1976

MT. RUSHMORE - SHRINE OF DEMOCRACY / USA BICENTENNIAL FOCAL POINT

As a Shrine to
Democracy,
it is equal to the
vision.
And there are
no admission
charges or parking
fees. It's an inheritance of all Americans.

99 Years of Western History —

Let the Free Phone Ring!

1-800-843-1930

For fast information,
call this TOLL FREE number.

THE S.D. STATE DIVISION OF TOUR-
ISM ran this ad all over the U.S.
From their ad, you wouldn't know
Wounded Knee is in S.D., though
they mention mass-murderer Gen.
Custer as an attraction. This ad
cost $$$, but they get it back--
1/3 of S.D.'s income comes from
the tourist trade. Write for
our boycott brochure--AIM, Box
3677, St. Paul, MN, 55101.

INHERITANCE OF ALL AMERICANS!?! WHAT ARE THEY THINKING OF!
Brooding down on the woman and child here is Teddy R., the
Great American Imperialist. THEIR "shrine" in OUR sacred
Paha Sapa--by the Treaty of 1868, that's our inheritance!

--And you'd THINK they'd be ashamed of it!

CALL 'EM UP AND TELL 'EM HOW YOU FEEL ABOUT THIS. THEIR PHONE
IS FREE. INDIAN PEOPLE AREN'T FREE IN SOUTH DAKOTA...........

Primary Source

"Tourist Boycott"

A 1976 AIM pamphlet urges tourists to boycott trips to South Dakota. COURTESY OF MICHIGAN STATE UNIVERSITY LIBRARIES, SPE-
CIAL COLLECTIONS.

MARCH JULY 4

from KEYSTONE to Mt RUSHMORE

South Dakota 1976
USA BICENTENNIAL

SHRINE OF "DEMOCRACY"? U.S. BICENTENNIAL

FOR 200 YEARS...

the USA has made war on our Nations. Before there was a USA, for nearly 300 years, the invaders attacked us.
1778--First U.S. Indian Treaty (with the Delawares)
1779--The "new nation" contin- ues the invaders' policies; Pres. Washington orders Gen. Sullivan to wipe out the Iroquois."Not to be merely overrun, but destroyed."
A few dates: 1713 Attack on S. Carolina Tuscarora
1814--Horseshoe Bend massacre (Creeks)
1832--Massacre of Black Hawk's Sauk Band (Illinois)
1832--Trail of Tears: Cherokee and other East Coast tribes removed to Oklahoma--3/4 die on the forced march
1862--Minnesota Santee Sioux uprising; 38 hanged
1864--Col. Chivington's Sand Creek Massacre
1868--Gen, Custer massacres Sand Creek survivors
1868--Fort Laramie Treaty
1890--Wounded Knee massacre
1973--Wesley Bad Heart Bull slain
1973--Frank Clearwater and Buddy Lamont killed at Wounded Knee
1973--Pedro Bissonette murdered

A.I.M. will sponsor a non-violent march and ceremony at the place where U.S. leaders' heads mar Paha Sapa's sacred stone. The ceremony honors our In- dian war dead and our 371 broken trea- ties, as the U.S. starts celebrating its 200th birthday. These Hills are ours by the 1868 Treaty--return Paha Sapa to the Lahkota Nation!

We also honor our people's struggles to free our Nations. Release our warriors and drop charges brought by South Dakota's system of injustice.

NATIVE AMERICAN PEOPLE'S BICENTENNIAL

For more information:

AIM National, Box 3677, St. Paul 55101 (612)227-7085

Rapid City AIM, 807 Fairview St. Rapid City (605)348-5629

AMERICAN INDIAN MOVEMENT

Primary Source

"March July 4 from Keystone to Mt. Rushmore"
Flyer for an AIM-sponsored march during the U.S.'s bicentennial celebrations. COURTESY OF MICHIGAN STATE UNIVERSITY LI-BRARIES, SPECIAL COLLECTIONS.

ple and pyramids to a national organization. It is the chapters which direct and dictate priorities to the national officers, who in turn create and guide AIM in the long-range strategy to meet those priorities. Each chapter is independent and autonomous. The current national officers are: Chairman, John Trudell; Treasurer, Larry Anderson; Secretary, Carol Stubbs; National Executive Director, Dennis Banks.

5. What are the goals of AIM?

From its beginning AIM identified three main forces destructive to the Indian people: Christianity, white oriented education and the federal government. To secure Indian self-determination and the right to be and think Indian, these forces must be eliminated from Indian life, along with the yoke of the Bureau of Indian Affairs.

6. What has been the role of AIM in protest demonstrations around the country?

AIM has played the major role in Indian demonstrations over the last five years; AIM was in evidence in more than 150 demonstrations prior to 1972 alone. Its role has been a peaceful one, to work within the system toward its goals, unless pushed by counterforces into a militant stand. Often AIM's presence is a direct response to a call from the Indian people, and AIM will shoulder the blame, deserved or not, for political actions by Indian people.

7. What is AIM's position on the traditional foundations of Indian life?

AIM is always first a spiritual movement. In the words of Kills Straight, an Oglala Sioux on the Pine Ridge

> . . . from the inside, AIM people are cleansing themselves. Many have returned to the old religions of their tribes, away from the confused notions of a society which has made them slaves of their own unguided lives. AIM is first a spiritual movement, a religious rebirth, and then a rebirth of Indian dignity. AIM succeeds because it has beliefs to act on. AIM is attempting to connect the realities of the past with the promises of tomorrow.

Primary Source

Airlift to Wounded Knee [excerpt]

SYNOPSIS: Bill Zimmerman, a veteran of many civil rights and antiwar actions, felt compelled to help the insurgents at Wounded Knee as a protest for social justice. In this excerpt he describes the events leading up to the airlift of food and supplies to the Pine Ridge Indian Reservation, which took place on April 14, 1973, about six weeks into the siege.

Airlift: Machine Guns in the Snow

Saturday, April 14, 1973

Council Bluffs, Iowa . . .

It was easy enough to distract the one man on duty. We asked for a detailed forecast and insisted on carefully checking the satellite pictures and radar screens ourselves. In the process, however, hopes for a dawn food drop were shattered. The weather could not possibly improve in time. Another plan had to be scuttled. At one point, while the weatherman looked directly at me, Billy pointed to something on the bulletin board from behind his back.

Several minutes later we had reshuffled our positions so that I could look at the bulletin board while Billy held the weatherman's eye. On it was an FAA teletype notification that the area for a five-nautical-mile radius around Wounded Knee, South Dakota, stretching from the ground to 9,000 feet above sea level, was declared a restricted zone effective two days earlier, on April 12. Permission to fly into this area had to be obtained from the U.S. Department of Justice, upon whose request the restriction was being instituted. I nodded to Billy that I had seen the notice and rejoined him just as the conversation turned to camping and fishing.

The talkative weatherman invited us into a side room for coffee. Since the little office lacked any windows facing the area where our friends were working, we happily accepted. When the weatherman heard that we were headed for the southern Rockies, he first told us that he had a son living in that area and then mentioned how many airplanes were used there to smuggle marijuana across the border from Mexico. Billy and I looked at each other struggling to contain our laughter. The weatherman thought we were dope runners! What a lucky break! With that in his mind, he would never consider the possibility that we were actually en route to Wounded Knee. And there was no reason for him to notify police as long as we were going south. For the next fifteen minutes we decried, somewhat less vehemently than the weatherman, the horrible effects marijuana had on the nation's youth.

But our decoying conversation took an ugly turn. The weatherman asked what we thought of "those goddamn Indians down on the reservation." He said they had a lot of nerve complaining about the government when "most of them live off the government" anyway. It was impossible to change the subject. We had to sit listening to how Indian women purposely had a lot of children "to get bigger welfare checks" and how Indian men "would rather get drunk than hold down a decent job." He asked what more they wanted from whites since white people like himself paid the high taxes that supported them. Coming from a big city in the East, it all sounded painfully familiar to me. Finally Larry came in to get a drink of water. It was the signal that work outside was finished and we could leave.

On the way out to the car, Billy started laughing. "You know what?" he said, slapping me on the back. "That dude would've been saying all of that shit about 'niggers' if I wasn't sittin' there beside him."

"That's right," I answered, "but wouldn't you like to see his face when he picks up the paper in a day or two and reads about the airlift to Wounded Knee. He'll be kicking himself remembering who he was talking to tonight."

Back at the motel Billy opened a bottle of fifteen-year-old bourbon, and we started passing it around. The cargo was all set to be dropped, but we were under another front that was going stationary on top of us. It was virtually certain that we could not fly visually the next morning, Sunday. We would probably still be grounded at sunset. Sunrise Monday began to look like the earliest possible drop time.

But Billy had a regular job back in Chicago. He had promised his boss that he would be there on Monday to fly a special charter. There were too many unemployed pilots hanging around Midway Airport to expect any consideration from his employer if he didn't show up on schedule. I was suddenly worried that some of the others might also have conflicts that would undermine their determination to carry out the airlift. Apprehensively, I asked Billy what he was going to do about his job, wishing we did not have to discuss it in front of everybody else. But Billy's answer was not what I expected.

"Look, man, the job is gone. I might as well do what I'm doing now and do it right. When you commit yourself to something, you're supposed to do it. Even if you decide somewhere in the middle that you don't like it, you got to do it 'cause you said you were going to do it. Like, I want to relax about time, man. I don't care any more when we do this, what day it is. Let's just take our time, relax, and do it right. This is a job that I want to see done. This is the kind of thing people would've done a few years ago for those blacks down South."

I looked up surprised. It was not the kind of thing Billy usually said. The idea that we all indefinitely postpone our other responsibilities until the airlift

Dennis Banks, co-founder of AIM, marches with protesters in Rapid City, South Dakota, in 1973. AP/WIDE WORLD PHOTOS. REPRODUCED BY PERMISSION.

was accomplished made an impact on everyone. We went around the room, one by one, agreeing "to relax about time." Jim had walked off his job the week before. John said that he would telephone his parents to call in sick for him at Sears. Strobe promised to get friends to do likewise for him. Tom, who sat watching it all, was doing his job by being there.

We still had to deal with the teletype FAA notice declaring Wounded Knee a restricted air zone. But that took only a minute. No one cared much what the U.S. government decided to call the air over the Pine Ridge Reservation. We were going in anyway. Again Billy reinforced our decision. He pulled a copy of the Federal Air Regulations out of his flight case and read us the section on restricted air space. It stated in no uncertain terms that the FAA had to give 45 days notice prior to the declaration of a new restricted zone. Billy insisted that it didn't take a lawyer to figure out that the restricted zone over Wounded Knee was illegal and that the Justice Department had simply seized the airspace from the FAA.

Primary Source

Wounded Knee 1973 [excerpt]

SYNOPSIS: Superintendent of the Pine Ridge Indian Reservation, Stanley Lyman, kept a running account of the action at Wounded Knee. During the civil war between the elected leadership of the Lakota people and the insurgents, Lyman was horrified by the level of violence that occurred. Here he describes one morning of the standoff, made memorable not only by the crossfire but by the unexpected appearance of a small airplane making a dropoff.

April 17, 1973

This morning the firing started early, about 1:30 or so in the morning. Of course it was all begun by the occupants of Wounded Knee. A few hours later, around 5:00 A.M., two light airplanes flew in and dropped supplies by parachute, in a total of seven different drops. The drops were observed quite closely through binoculars from the bunkers surrounding Wounded Knee. The material dropped consisted of long cases, cylindrical in shape. The marshals were able to identify the make of the planes making the drops—a Cessna and a Cherokee, I believe—but they couldn't catch them. The FBI helicopter, Snooper 1, did dive down into the area, but it got fired at and pulled out.

Shortly after the drops, about 5:30 in the morning, the firing began in earnest. AIM insurgents were very active outside of Wounded Knee proper, approaching several of the government bunkers and firing on them. It appeared as though they were trying to take over one of the bunkers, but perhaps this strong, aggressive action on their part was designed to cover up some other activity. With all this heavy firing it was inevitable that someone would get shot, and indeed, there were casualties. We are certain that four or five AIM individuals were wounded in this morning's action. Some of them were seen to fall, and the marshals could see them being carried from the field on litters. One man, who was hit a couple of hundred yards from a government bunker, was critically wounded. The AIM people sent out a flag of truce and said that they wanted this man evacuated. They asked for a helicopter to come into Wounded Knee and pick him up. The marshals would not consent to a helicopter landing within the Wounded Knee perimeter, so it was arranged that the man would be brought outside the perimeter by car. He was then picked up by a helicopter and taken to Pine Ridge Hospital. His wound was to the head, and he had suffered massive brain damage. He was flown immediately to Rapid City. We have as yet no identification of the man. He is apparently an Indian and had one dollar and a map of Nebraska in his pocket—nothing else, no means of identification.

It is the casualties in this whole mess that are the most regrettable. Look at the situation: AIM is up against a disciplined force, firing coolly and purposefully and only on command. The men in the government bunkers are well-trained riflemen with high-powered weapons. Under these conditions, although there is sure to be a marshal or two hurt, it is obvious that the folks taking the aggressive action within the perimeter are the ones who are going to be really hurt. That is what happened this morning.

Further Resources

BOOKS

Bordewich, Fergus M. *Killing the White Man's Indian: Reinventing Native Americans at the End of the Twentieth Century.* New York: Doubleday, 1996.

Crow Dog, Mary, with Richard Erdoes and Mary Brave Bird. *Lakota Woman.* New York: Grove Press, 1990.

Johnson, Troy R. *The Occupation of Alcatraz Island: Indian Self-Determination and the Rise of Indian Activism.* Urbana: University of Illinois Press, 1996.

Josephy, Jr., Alvin M., and Joane Nagel and Troy Johnson, eds. *Red Power: The American Indians' Fight for Freedom.* 2nd ed. Lincoln, Nebr: University of Nebraska Press, 1999.

Matthiessen, Peter. *In the Spirit of Crazy Horse.* New York: Viking Press, 1983.

McCormick, Anita L. *Native Americans and the Reservation in American History.* Springfield, N.J.: Enslow Publishers, 1996.

Means, Russell, with Marvin J. Wolf. *Where the White Men Fear to Tread: The Autobiography of Russell Means.* New York: St. Martin's Press, 1997.

Nagel, Joane. *American Indian Ethnic Renewal: Red Power and the Resurgence of Identity and Culture.* New York: Oxford University Press, 1996.

Stern, Kenneth S. *Loud Hawk: The United States Versus the American Indian Movement.* Norman: University of Oklahoma Press, 1994.

WEBSITES

"A Brief History of the American Indian Movement." Available online at http://www.aimovement.org/ggc/history.html (accessed March 7, 2003).

AUDIO AND VISUAL MEDIA

Lakota Woman: Siege at Wounded Knee. Directed by Frank Pierson. Turner Home Entertainment, Videocassette, 1994.

Fear of Flying
Novel

By: Erica Jong

Date: 1973

Source: Jong, Erica. *Fear of Flying.* New York: Plume, 1973.

About the Author: Erica (Mann) Jong (1942–) was born in New York City. Married to psychiatrist Allan Jong from 1966–1975, Jong paralleled the relationship in her first novel, *Fear of Flying,* published in 1973 to great commercial and critical acclaim. The main character of the novel, Isadora Wing, appeared in two later novels, *How to Save Your Own Life* (1977) and *Parachutes & Kisses* (1984). Jong has continued to explore issues of gender, identity, history, and mysticism in her subsequent fiction and memoirs. ■

Introduction

The "sexual revolution" of the 1960s had a direct impact on the media in the following decade, as the sexually explicit content of magazines, movies, books, and television programs became much more commonplace. In 1972 the pornographic movie *Deep Throat,* the first full-length adult film with more than a trace of a plot, made its star, Linda Lovelace, a household name. Made for a $25,000-investment put up by a New York organized crime family, *Deep Throat* grossed between $400 and $600 million. Its popularity spawned a deluge of pornographic films aimed at mainstream audiences; many social critics downplayed the obvious obscenity of the movies and instead referred to their value in sexually liberating the average American. In the 1973 case *Miller v. California,* the U.S. Supreme Court confirmed the change in social mores by announcing that works with serious literary, artistic, political, or scientific value could not be considered obscene. Although the decision allowed local officials to follow community standards in limiting access to adult-oriented materials, the ruling made pornography much more widely available in the United States.

The 1973 publication of Erica Jong's novel *Fear of Flying* demonstrated how far social attitudes had changed toward topics that would have been considered taboo just a few years earlier. Detailing the odyssey of Isadora Wing, who leaves her psychiatrist husband to embark on a series of sexual relationships, the book illuminated Wing's struggle to reconcile traditional notions of domesticity, feminity, and sexuality with her own desire for independence and creative fulfillment. Describing Wing's sexual encounters in graphic, yet nonjudgmental terms, Jong's work was condemned by some critics for its liberal use of explicit language. Others hailed the novel as one of the first pieces of feminist fiction, as it presented a woman's point of view on sexuality and relationships. The book eventually sold an estimated 12 million copies in twenty-seven languages and made Jong into a media celebrity.

Significance

The new openness in sexual expression was not confined to the worlds of pornography and literature in the 1970s. The best-selling non-fiction book in 1970 was Dr. David Reuben's *Everything You Always Wanted to Know About Sex, But Were Afraid to Ask.* In third place that year was *The Sensuous Woman,* a sex-tips book written by the anonymous author "J." In 1972 the explicit sex manual *The Joy of Sex: A Gourmet Guide to Lovemaking* became a bestseller and was one of the decade's top-selling non-fiction books with more than 8 million copies

Author Erica Jong sits in front of an airplane-shaped cake in 1977. Jong's *Fear of Flying* (1973) encountered some controversy for its explicit language and sexual encounters. However, its publication demonstrated the change in attitudes toward taboo subjects.
© BETTMANN/CORBIS. REPRODUCED BY PERMISSION.

in print. Sexually related books indeed topped the bestseller lists in most years of the early 1970s, from the anonymously penned *The Sensuous Man* (1971) to Nena and George O'Neill's *Open Marriage* (1972). Even evangelical and born-again Christians had their own sex manual, *The Total Woman,* by Marabel Morgan. It was the best-selling non-fiction book of 1974 and included advice to married, Christian women such as greeting their husbands at the front door wearing only Saran Wrap.

The champions of the new sexual openness argued that the candor in sexual matters would help both men and women to lead more fulfilling and exciting lives. Yet others viewed the continuing sexual revolution in more complicated terms. Readers of *Fear of Flying* could not have missed the ambiguities in Isadora Wing's experience: greater sexual experimentation did not, after all, necessarily lead to happiness and self-fulfillment. By the late 1970s a backlash from both religious conservatives and feminists against outright pornography had largely discredited the industry's claims of furthering a valid sexual revolution. Whereas conservative critics deemed pornography as an assault upon the American family and its traditional relationships, some feminists linked

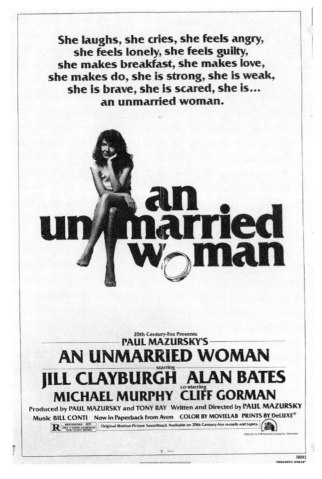

She laughs, she cries, she feels angry,
she feels lonely, she feels guilty,
she makes breakfast, she makes love,
she makes do, she is strong, she is weak,
she is brave, she is scared, she is...
an unmarried woman.

an
un
married
woman

20th Century-Fox Presents
PAUL MAZURSKY'S
AN UNMARRIED WOMAN
starring
JILL CLAYBURGH   ALAN BATES
co-starring
MICHAEL MURPHY   CLIFF GORMAN
Produced by PAUL MAZURSKY and TONY RAY   Written and Directed by PAUL MAZURSKY
Music BILL CONTI   Now in Paperback from Avon   COLOR BY MOVIELAB   PRINTS BY DeLUXE®
Original Motion Picture Soundtrack Available on 20th Century-Fox records and tapes.

Promotional poster for the movie *An Unmarried Woman,* directed by Paul
Mazursky, 1978, an example of movies that pushed the envelope in terms
of formerly taboo subject matter. **GETTY IMAGES/20TH CENTURY
FOX. REPRODUCED BY PERMISION.**

pornography with incidences of physical abuse and rape
against women. Former adult film star Linda Lovelace
bolstered the anti-pornography viewpoint when she later
revealed that she had been abused by her husband and
forced into the adult film industry.

Primary Source

Fear of Flying [excerpt]

SYNOPSIS: *Fear of Flying* follows the struggles of
Isadora Wing, the well–educated wife of a psychiatrist, as she questions the meaning of her marriage,
identity, and sexuality. Wing leaves her husband
and embarks on a quest for self-fulfillment, hoping
to restore both her creative energy and sense of independence. In the book's ambiguous ending, Wing
returns to her husband, but it is not clear that the
marriage will continue.

Growing up female in America. What a liability!
You grew up with your ears full of cosmetic ads,
love songs, advice columns, whoreoscopes, Hollywood gossip, and moral dilemmas on the level of
TV soap operas. What litanies the advertisers of
the good life chanted at you! What curious cate-
chisms!

"Be kind to your behind." "Blush like you mean
it." "Love your male in the zodiac." "The stars and
sensual you. To a man they say Cutty Sark." "A diamond is forever." "If you're concerned about douch-
ing . . ." "Length and coolness come together." "How
I solved my intimate odor problem." "Lady be cool."
"Every woman alive loves Chanel No. 5." "What
makes a shy girl get intimate?" "*Femme,* we named
it after you."

What all the ads and all the whoreoscopes
seemed to imply was that if only you were narcissistic *enough,* if only you took proper care of your
smells, your hair, your boobs, your eyelashes, your
armpits, your crotch, your stars, your scars, and
your choice of Scotch in bars—you would meet a
beautiful, powerful, potent, and rich man who
would satisfy every longing, fill every hole, make
your heart skip a beat (or stand still), make you
misty, and fly you to the moon (preferably on gos-
samer wings), where you would live totally satisfied forever.

And the crazy part of it was that even if you were
clever, even if you spent your adolescence reading
John Donne and Shaw, even if you studied history
or zoology or physics and hoped to spend your life
pursuing some difficult and challenging career—you
still had a mind full of all the soupy longings that
every high-school girl was awash in. It didn't matter,
you see, whether you had an IQ of 170 or an IQ of
70, you were brainwashed all the same. Only the
surface trappings were different. Only the *talk* was
a little more sophisticated. . . .

Five years of marriage had made me itchy for all
those things: itchy for men, and itchy for solitude.
Itchy for sex and itchy for the life of a recluse. I knew
my itches were contradictory—and that made things
even worse. I knew my itches were un-American—
and that made things *still* worse. It is heresy in America to embrace any way of life except as half of a
couple. Solitude is un-American. It may be condoned
in a man—especially if he is a "glamorous bachelor" who "dates starlets" during a brief interval between marriages. But a woman is always presumed
to be alone as a result of abandonment, not choice.
And she is treated that way: as a pariah. There is
simply no dignified way for a woman to live alone.
Oh, she can get along financially perhaps (though

not nearly as well as a man), but emotionally she is never left in peace. Her friends, her family, her fellow workers never let her forget that her husband-lessness, her childlessness—her *selfishness,* in short—is a reproach to the American way of life.

Even more to the point: the woman (unhappy though she knows her married friends to be) can never let *herself* alone. She lives as if she were constantly on the brink of some great fulfillment. As if she were waiting for Prince Charming to take her away "from all this." All what? The solitude of living inside her own soul? The certainty of being herself instead of half of something else? . . .

At times I was defiant and thought I had every right to snatch whatever pleasure was offered to me for the duration of my short time on earth. Why *shouldn't* I be happy and hedonistic? What was *wrong* with it? I knew that the women who got most out of life (and out of men) were the ones who demanded most, that if you acted as if you were valuable and desirable, men *found* you valuable and desirable, that if you refused to be a doormat, nobody could tread on you. I knew that servile women got walked on and women who acted like queens got treated that way. But no sooner had my defiant mood passed than I would be seized with desolation and despair, I would feel terrified of losing both men and being left all alone, I would feel sorry for Bennett, curse myself for my disloyalty, despise myself utterly for everything. Then I wanted to run to Bennett and plead forgiveness, throw myself at his feet, offer to bear him twelve children immediately (mainly to cement my bondage), promise to serve him like a good slave in exchange for *any* bargain as long as it included security. I would become servile, cloying, saccharinely sweet: the whole package of lies that passes in the world as femininity.

The fact was that neither one of these attitudes made any sense and I knew it. Neither dominating nor being dominated. Neither bitchiness nor servility. Both were traps. Both led nowhere except toward the loneliness both were designed to avoid. But what could I do? The more I hated myself, the more I hated myself for hating myself. It was hopeless. . . .

I must have slept. I woke up to see the sunlight streaming in through the brilliant blue of the pup tent. Adrian was still snoring. His hairy blond arm had fallen heavily across my chest and was pressing down on it, making me uncomfortably conscious of my breathing. The birds were chirping. We were in France. By some roadside. Some crossroads

in my life. What was I doing there? Why was I lying in a tent in France with a man I hardly knew? Why wasn't I home in bed with my husband? I thought of my husband with a sudden wave of tenderness. What was he doing? Did he miss me? Had he forgotten me? Had he found someone else? Some ordinary girl who didn't have to take off on adventures to prove her stamina. Some ordinary girl who was content with making breakfast and raising kiddies. Some ordinary girl of car pools and swimming pools and cesspools. Some ordinary American girl out of *Seventeen* Magazine?

I suddenly had a passion to *be* that ordinary girl. To be that good little housewife, that glorified American mother, that mascot from *Mademoiselle,* that matron from *McCall's,* that cutie from *Cosmo,* that girl with the Good Housekeeping Seal tattooed on her ass and advertising jingles programmed in her brain. *That* was the solution! To be ordinary! To be unexotic! To be content with compromise and TV dinners and "Can This Marriage Be Saved?" I had a fantasy then of myself as a happy housewife. A fantasy straight out of an adman's little brain. Me in apron and gingham shirtwaist waiting on my husband and kiddies while the omnipresent TV set sings out the virtues of the American home and the American slave-wife with her tiny befuddled brain.

Further Resources

BOOKS

Brownmiller, Susan. *Against Our Will: Men, Women, and Rape.* New York: Simon and Schuster, 1975.

Comfort, Alex. *The Joy of Sex: A Cordon Bleu Guide to Love-making.* New York: Crown, 1972.

Jong, Erica. *Fear of Fifty: A Midlife Memoir.* New York: HarperCollins, 1994.

——. *How to Save Your Own Life.* 1977; Reprint, New York: Plume 1985.

——. *Parachutes & Kisses.* 1984; Reprint, New York: New American Library, 1985.

——. *What Do Women Want?: Reflections on a Century of Change.* New York: Harper Perennial, 1999.

Klassen, Albert D. et al. *Sex and Morality in the U.S.* Middletown, Conn.: Wesleyan University Press, 1989.

Lovelace, Linda and Mike McGrady. *Out of Bondage.* Secaucus, New Jersey: L. Stuart, 1986.

Morgan, Marabel. *The Total Woman.* New York: Pocket Books, 1974.

Suleiman, Susan Rubin, ed. "(Re)writing the Body: The Politics and Poetics of Female Eroticism." In *The Female Body in Western Culture: Contemporary Perspectives.* Cambridge: Harvard University Press, 1986.

PERIODICALS

Olshan, Joseph. "Bawdy by Jong." *People,* September 12, 1994, 77.

Virshup, Amy. "For Mature Audiences Only." *New York,* July 18, 1994, 38.

The Energy Crisis Hits Home

"Cadillac Sedan deVilles Average 15.8 mpg at 55 mph in Fuel Economy Tests"

Magazine advertisement

By: General Motors Corporation

Date: 1974

Source: General Motors Corporation, GM Media Archives. "Cadillac Sedan deVilles Average 15.8 mpg at 55 mph in Fuel Economy Tests." Advertisement, 1974.

"You Save Heat and Gas by Weatherproofing Your Home"

Magazine advertisement

By: American Gas Association

Date: 1976

Source: American Gas Association. "You Save Heat and Gas by Weatherproofing Your Home." Advertisement, 1976 ■

Introduction

On October 6, 1973, Egypt and Syria launched a military offensive against Israel in a conflict that came to be known as the Yom Kippur War, after the Jewish holy day that marked the conflict's first day. After the United States came to Israel's aid, the seven Arab nations in the Organization of the Petroleum Exporting Countries (OPEC) announced an oil embargo against Israel's supporters, which included the United States, Japan, and most western European countries. The embargo, which lasted from October 1973 to March 1974, created fundamental changes in the global economy and had an immediate impact on American society as well. The most visible change was the long lines at gas pumps around the country. Only during World War II had gasoline been rationed, and gas prices had remained low by world standards since then. Suddenly, the average American had to contend with a peacetime gasoline shortage; when there was gas, its price had increased by 40 percent in just a few months. The American econ-

Drivers wait for gas at an Exxon station along Route 4 in Fort Lee, New Jersey. During the OPEC embargo, lines at gas stations were common. **AP/WIDE WORLD PHOTOS. REPRODUCED BY PERMISSION.**

omy, which had been built in large part on the availability of cheap oil, experienced a sharp recession. Along with the inflation triggered by higher energy prices, a period of "stagflation"—an economic downturn accompanied by persistent inflation and unemployment—shook the confidence of the American consumer in 1973 and 1974.

Many Americans were surprised at the country's vulnerability to faraway events such as the Yom Kippur War and the willingness of OPEC nations to use their oil reserves as leverage against American foreign policy in the Middle East. Founded in 1960, OPEC eventually had eleven member states—most of them Arab countries in the Middle East—and controlled about 40 percent of the world's oil output. Its attempt to enact an oil embargo after the Six-Day War between Israel and Arab allies Jordan, Syria, and Egypt in 1967 had ended in failure as the United States had sufficient domestic oil reserves to make up for the lost imports. Yet domestic oil producers had run out of surplus capacity after 1970, and after import quotas on foreign oil were lifted by the Nixon administration, the United States became increasingly dependent on foreign oil. In 1967, 2.2 million barrels of oil were imported each day, which represented 19 percent of American oil consumption. On the eve of the energy cri-

> # Proving ground facts reveal:
>
> # Cadillac Sedan deVilles average 15.8 mpg at 55 mph in fuel economy tests.
>
> 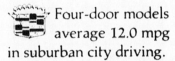 **Four-door models average 12.0 mpg in suburban city driving.**
>
> Results of recent Cadillac fuel economy tests are now official.
>
> They show that ten Cadillac Sedan deVilles, selected at random, averaged an impressive 15.8 miles per gallon at a steady speed of 55 miles per hour (maximum federal speed). In suburban city driving (average speed 24 mph with 1.6 stops per mile) the same ten new Sedan deVilles averaged 12.0 miles per gallon.
>
> For those who have always thought of Cadillac as a highly efficient automobile, it comes as no great surprise. For others who think first of Cadillac roominess and comfort as the flagship of the GM fleet, the results are most revealing.
>
> Engineers conducted the tests at our proving ground under actual driving conditions using four-door Sedan deVilles with radial tires and a standard 2.93 axle. Cars were equipped with popular options, but air conditioning was turned off. In all tests, cars carried the weight of two average-sized passengers.
>
> Of course, the mileage you get depends upon how and where you drive. But Cadillac's performance in these tests shows that you don't have to sacrifice quality, comfort or security for efficiency. Not when you consider, too, that no Cadillac made since 1971 requires premium gasoline.
>
> This kind of mileage is another example of the kind of engineering General Motors is putting into its cars.
>
> For a personal demonstration of the efficiency of the 1974 Cadillac, we invite you to visit your authorized Cadillac dealer soon.
>
> General Motors wants you to drive what you like...and like what you drive. And mileage is one more reason to like...and buy ...Cadillac.
>
> *Cadillac* The quality car that makes sense for today.
>
>

Primary Source

"Cadillac Sedan deVilles Average 15.8 mpg at 55 mph in Fuel Economy Tests"

SYNOPSIS: The energy crisis had a dramatic impact on U.S. automakers. Decades of low gas prices had encouraged Americans to buy large and powerful cars that guzzled gasoline. Fuel shortages and high prices now made fuel efficiency a key feature. This new emphasis on efficiency affected advertising efforts even for luxury products such as the full-sized Cadillac Sedan deVille. Meanwhile, the energy shortage became a boon for Japanese auto manufacturers who sold smaller, more fuel-efficient cars. GENERAL MOTORS CORP. USED WITH PERMISSION, GM MEDIA ARCHIVES. GENERAL RESEARCH DIVISION, THE NEW YORK PUBLIC LIBRARY, ASTOR, LENOX AND TILDEN FOUNDATIONS.

You save heat and save gas by weatherproofing your home.

These unretouched infra-red photographs prove it:

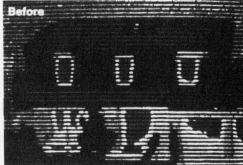

Before

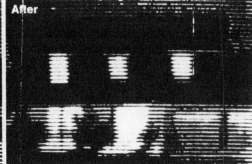

After

This infra-red photograph shows weatherproofing is needed in this home. The red areas are warm. That shows where heat is escaping and natural gas is being wasted.

This photograph was taken after insulating the attic and weatherproofing the windows, too. The red areas are now gone, showing that the heat loss has been cut dramatically.

These actual infra-red photographs prove that by weatherproofing your home, you can cut heat loss dramatically and save natural gas. Wasted gas costs you money. And even more important, America needs natural gas to keep her factories running. Millions of jobs depend on gas. Maybe yours. So make your own home weather-tight. Turn your thermostat down a few degrees, too. Do all you can to save gas. Remember, the gas you save could save a job. Use gas wisely. It's clean energy for today and tomorrow.

AGA American Gas Association

Primary Source

"You Save Heat and Gas by Weatherproofing Your Home"

SYNOPSIS: Responding to the public outrage over energy shortages and price increases after the OPEC oil embargo in 1973, energy companies used public relations to explain why energy costs had increased so rapidly. Energy trade associations began educational programs to show consumers how to conserve energy at home. "AMERICAN GAS ASSOCIATION" IS A REGISTERED TRADEMARK OF THE AMERICAN GAS ASSOCIATION USED WITH PERMISSION. © AMERICAN GAS ASSOCIATION. GENERAL RESEARCH DIVISION, THE NEW YORK PUBLIC LIBRARY, ASTOR, LENOX AND TILDEN FOUNDATIONS.

sis in late 1973, America imported six million barrels of oil a day—36 percent of its total oil consumption.

Significance

Although America's dependency on OPEC oil had been growing for several years, the immediate impact of the oil embargo took most Americans by surprise in October 1973. Fueled by inexpensive energy, the country had enjoyed almost uninterrupted economic growth since World War II. For many Americans the prosperity translated into new homes in far-flung suburbs and ever-larger automobiles to take them to work and back home again. The energy crisis thus led to a fundamental reevaluation of the typical American's lifestyle. Conservation and fuel efficiency became popular in this new era. There was also an uncertainty about the country's economic prospects and its ability to influence the foreign policies of OPEC's members. The energy crisis also contributed to a new awareness of the environmental impact of America's past energy consumption. Even as there were calls to exploit new domestic sources of energy, particularly in Prudhoe Bay, Alaska, environmental watchdogs warned that only by using energy more efficiently could the country find a long-term solution to the energy crisis.

The manufacturing sector, especially the automobile industry, was hard hit by the energy crisis. This led to predictions that America's place as the world's leading industrial nation might be endangered. The Watergate scandals, which culminated in President Nixon's resignation in August 1974, added to the public's lack of trust in the country's leaders and the nation's future. The sudden shift in international relations, brought on by the rapid rise in OPEC's influence, completed the picture of uncertainty that Americans confronted by the mid-1970s. After another price hike by OPEC near the end of the decade, energy prices rose an additional 60 percent, contributing to a 14 percent inflation rate in 1979.

Further Resources

BOOKS

Adelman, M.A. *The Economics of Petroleum Supply.* Cambridge, Mass.: The MIT Press, 1993.

———. *The Genie Out of the Bottle: World Oil since 1970.* Cambridge, Mass.: The MIT Press, 1995.

Heal, Geoffrey, and Graciela Chichilnisky. *Oil and the International Economy.* New York: Oxford University Press, 1991.

Kapstein, Ethan B. *The Insecure Alliance: Energy Crises and Western Politics since 1944.* New York: Oxford University Press, 1990.

Schneider, Steven A. *The Oil Price Revolution.* Baltimore: Johns Hopkins University Press, 1983.

Yergin, Daniel. *The Prize: The Epic Quest for Oil, Money, and Power.* New York: Simon & Schuster, 1991.

Yergin, Daniel, and Martin Hillenbrand, eds. *Global Insecurity: A Strategy for Energy and Economic Renewal.* New York: Penguin Books, 1982.

WEBSITES

"U.S. Department of Energy." Available online at http://www.energy.gov/index.html (accessed March 23, 2003).

"Organization of the Petroleum Exporting Countries." Available online at http://www.opec.org/homepage/frame.htm (accessed March 23, 2003).

Pat Loud: A Woman's Story
Memoir

By: Pat Loud; Nora Johnson

Date: 1974

Source: Loud, Pat, with Nora Johnson. *Pat Loud: A Woman's Story.* New York: Coward, McCann & Geoghegan, Inc., 1974, 15, 51–52, 121, 177–178.

About the Author: Pat (Russell) Loud (1926–), born in Oregon, married Bill Loud in 1950, and the couple had five children over the next seven years. The Louds' marriage was plagued by Bill Loud's infidelities. In 1971 the family agreed to be filmed as part of a documentary series, which aired on public television stations in 1973. In the most memorable segment, Pat Loud told her husband that she was going to seek a divorce. Pat Loud published a memoir in 1974, *Pat Loud: A Woman's Story.* ■

Introduction

The rise in divorce rates transformed American family life in the 1970s. In 1965 more than one-third of all marriages ended in divorce, but by 1979 the rate had climbed to one-half of all marriages. Where children were involved, the mother almost always retained parental custody, leading to a rise in the number of children growing up in single-parent families headed by a single woman. In 1972, 14 percent of American children lived in households headed by a single woman (a statistic that included divorced and single mothers as well as single, unmarried female relatives with custody of children); by 1980 the figure stood at 20 percent. Whereas 44.2 percent of all American households at the beginning of the 1960s typified the "nuclear family"—married couples with children—by 1980 only 30.9 percent of Americans fit into the category.

Social scientists struggled to explain the seeming disintegration of American family life. Some commentators pointed to the individualism fostered by the youth and countercultures of the 1960s, in which personal fulfillment seemed to outweigh obedience to traditional social norms. In this atmosphere, divorce became a more acceptable option for those who were unhappy in their marriages. Others blamed feminism and the women's movement for encouraging women to seek out more independence, both socially and economically. Feminists countered that the economic reality for most women in

Watching An American Family

Ten million Americans watched *An American Family* each week in increasing fascination as the Louds revealed a picture that ran counter to what everyone thought the American family was or ought to be. During the course of the twelve weekly episodes, audiences learned of Bill's philandering, saw the couple fight bitterly and eventually decide on a divorce, and watched one of the children, Lance, come to terms with being gay.

Despite its success, however, and with the exception of an anniversary program made for HBO in 1983, the Louds were forgotten and the innovative format lost its mainstream appeal until 1998, when actor Jim Carey starred in the film *The Truman Show,* in which a young insurance adjuster discovers that his entire life is a television show. The film was a popular and critical success, leading once again to commentary about the role of television on viewers' perception of reality. A few years later, a new generation of reality shows, such as *Survivor, Big Brother,* and *The Osbournes,* proved immensely popular with both network executives (the shows were relatively inexpensive to produce) and young audiences. Around this time, fifty-year-old Lance Loud asked the producers of *An American Family* to make a documentary about his struggle with drug addiction and AIDS. Lance, dying of AIDS-related diseases in a California hospice, remarked that he needed the kind of closure that only a television film about his life and death could give.

In 2003, *TV Guide* listed *An American Family* as one of the fifty greatest programs of all time.

"An American Family: Things Are Keen but Could Be Keener" [excerpt]

I felt despair and fascination watching the Loud family, and this could only have been caused by vibrations ricocheting down through my own experiences. The Louds are enough like me and mine to create havoc in my head, and I had to fight a constant strong desire to push away those Louds, dismiss them as unique, empty, shallow, unlike others, and yet on serious reflection, we can all learn from them, perhaps just enough to begin understanding that saddest of mysteries, the American family. . . .

Of course, we're all Peeping Toms, and so I suppose we should be glad that some of us are also exhibitionists. The Louds permitted the cameras into their home for no financial reward and signed all the required releases willingly. They say they thought it would be fun to be on TV. . . . I suppose they must have thought of themselves as "The Partridge Family," "My Three Sons" or "The Brady Bunch," but, unsurprisingly enough, reality turns out to bear no resemblance to a typical TV comedy. . . . What art has revealed before we now see stripped of style, language, pace, tension, and stretched into that nearly nauseous mass, reality, but nevertheless fascinating precisely because it is nearly life, not imitation.

SOURCE: Roiphe, Anne. "An American Family: Things Are Keen but Could Be Keener." *The New York Times Magazine,* February 18, 1973.

terms of wages and professional opportunities remained dismal compared to the reality of men, and that almost all women experienced declining incomes after a divorce. Indisputably, divorce became easier to obtain in the 1960s and 1970s as many states passed "no-fault" divorce laws that did not require specific grounds for separation such as adultery or physical abuse. Despite the concern over rising divorce rates, the change in divorce laws reflected the growing admission by many Americans that divorce was an acceptable choice for those who wanted to end their marriages.

Significance

For American television viewers in 1973, Pat Loud came to personify the contemporary American divorced woman. Loud and her husband, Bill, the owner of a successful engineering supplies company, allowed a public television crew to film their domestic life for a proposed documentary series in 1971. When the resulting twelve-part series, *An American Family,* aired a year-and-a-half later, the Louds endured a storm of criticism over their affluent lifestyle and seeming emotional distance from

one another. The homosexuality of their eldest son, Lance, who came out in the second segment, also shocked some viewers; for many of them, it was the first time they had seen an openly gay man in the media. The fact that he was accepted by his family and unapologetic for his sexuality added to Loud's celebrity even as he endured a homophobic reaction from some television critics and viewers.

Although Lance Loud emerged as the star of *An American Family* and turned his celebrity into a career as a punk-rock singer and journalist, Pat Loud provided the most dramatic moment of the series. She had been aware of her husband's numerous affairs throughout their marriage and although she hoped that the subject would not be brought into *An American Family,* the tensions in the Loud household forced her to make a decision. With the cameras rolling, she told her husband that she was going to seek a divorce. After the scene aired, she received criticism for doing this. She responded in her 1974 memoir, *Pat Loud: A Woman's Story.* Loud tried to draw a positive lesson from the experience: "My anger and anguish—as well as Bill's and the kids'—was *real* anguish

The PBS documentary "An American Family" first aired in 1973 and featured the Loud family. **COURTESY THIRTEEN/WNET NEW YORK. REPRODUCED BY PERMISSION.**

and anger. . . . Couldn't it be that since circumstance and fate had put me into a position to rip away the curtain of hypocrisy, that maybe, just maybe, we could help other families face their own problems more honestly?" The hostility of some of the criticism led Lance Loud to offer this opinion of *An American Family*: "Television," he said, "ate my family."

As the subjects of America's first reality television series, the Louds were the inspiration for the drama series *Family,* as well as numerous documentaries on everyday Americans that followed. The 1990s fad for reality shows, kicked off by MTV's *The Real World,* revived interest in the Louds. In 2002 the documentary *Lance Loud!: A Death in the American Family* updated the family's story as it detailed the final days of the Louds' eldest son, who was dying of Hepatitis C and AIDS-related illnesses. Lance Loud died on December 22, 2001; honoring his final request, Pat and Bill Loud reconciled more than a quarter-century after they divorced to attend Lance's funeral together.

Primary Source

Pat Loud: A Woman's Story [excerpt]

SYNOPSIS: As the subjects of one of the first documentaries on an American family, the Louds of Santa Barbara, California, encountered instant fame in 1973. With the celebrity came harsh criticism of the family; Pat Loud responded in her 1974 memoir, *Pat Loud: A Woman's Story.* Comparing the ideals of marriage that she learned as she was growing up with the realities that she encountered in her life, Loud shows how social attitudes on marriage and divorce had changed by the 1970s.

Most people become famous for a reason. They develop a vaccine, or cross the ocean on a raft, or star in a movie, or embezzle a lot of money or . . . or . . . or. But we, the Louds, Pat, Bill, and our five kids, managed to get famous without doing a thing except giving our permission for PBS to follow us around with a camera for a while—to lend our lives for seven months to the making of *An American Family.* And it seems that if you're on TV, you're famous, and free game in a weird way, no matter what you're on TV *for.* And this is what came along to save me—temporarily, anyway—from my forty-six-year-old identity crisis. . . .

Anybody who is unaware of the effect of weddings on aimless, tradeless girl graduates has missed a vast, vital portion of the lore of this land, particularly in those palmy postwar days, with returning GI's and ardent waiting girls, all clamoring to settle down in this now safe and peaceful land and

get back to the business of repopulating the earth. It really gets you where it hurts. Weddings are—or were, the world has changed under our feet—practically orgasmic experiences, particularly if you (like old Pat) had a touch of the True Church: Organs playing, tears brimming, choked-up Dads handing their little treasure over to some bloke who probably couldn't support her, triumphant Moms (that takes care of *her!*), bubbling virginal bridesmaids grabbing for the bouquet, Radiant Bride in Juliet Cap and twenty-button white kids, three hundred bucks' worth of satin and organdy, and adorable blue garter on one leg, just below the Merry Widow (see late forties' and fifties' archives), tables groaning with salad bowls, neat place settings in The Pattern (my mother had me pick mine when I was twelve), chafing dishes, damask linens, silver coffee pots, cocktail shakers, hors d'ouevre forks, initialed towels, cookbooks (mostly designated "To Be Returned").

And, oh, the reception with champagne and Mr. Music's band and the aunties in blue lace and the old boyfriends and envious girlfriends and the groom—I haven't even *mentioned* the groom—smiling bravely though exhausted from the traditional bachelors' party prowl through the cathouses the night before (did it really happen or did they just tell us it did?), trying to look happy and confident though probably terrified about the performance expected by the bride later in the evening, waiting in agony as she runs off to change into her going-away suit (a costume once worn by brides, consisting of a skirt and matching jacket) and gardenia and pumps and little overnight case packed with lacy nightie and peignoir (sic Merry Widow) and other Personals to go off to the long-reserved hotel room for the Wedding Night, where waits in ice the traditional bottle of Mumm's. God, I still sweat and rattle even to think of it all. . . .

After you've played the same old marriage game for as long as we had, with both of you hitting the same foul balls and stealing the same old bases, your tolerance for the whole performance dwindles down to nothing. All the other person has to do is look the wrong way at the wrong time and you're ready to throw down your bat and quit. I hated myself so for my part in it; I was so tired of goading and being goaded back, it was as though my whole being had been reduced to a mass of suspicion and hurting self-hatred and weary, forced participation in this lousy play that should have closed long ago. . . .

I told Bill I wanted a divorce on the series, but, as he says, I'd told him that three or four times before. He moved out, but he'd spent so much time out before that it was hardly a novelty. It was all so gradual, a creeping process that hardly seemed to be moving in any direction. Slowly his clothes disappeared from the closets. The divorce decree was as unreal as any legal document; it didn't look like it had anything to do with us. We still talked on the phone and I was understanding about money, and he was concerned about the kids and it wasn't all that terribly different. He still had his girls, the same old ones, and I didn't have any men.

I suppose I expected something external to happen and didn't realize that the only thing that was going to make me divorced was something inside me. *Me,* not Bill. Bill's whole point of view was that I was a fool to break up the marriage and I had always expected too much of marriage anyway and my views of the institution were old-fashioned and parochial and why couldn't we have that nice European marriage with each of us doing our own thing, but together, for the sake of the kids, because all the mixed-up kids *he* knew came from broken homes. So according to this theory I was the one who did it, which fitted in neatly with my belief that I'd driven him to all the other women because I simply didn't have it, whatever it took, never did and never would.

Further Resources

BOOKS

Coontz, Stephanie. *The Way We Never Were: American Families and the Nostalgia Trap.* New York: Basic Books, 1992.

Fisher, Helen E. *Anatomy of Love: The Natural History of Monogamy, Adultery, and Divorce.* New York: W.W. Norton, 1992.

Mintz, Steven, and Susan Kellogg. *Domestic Revolutions: A Social History of American Family Life.* New York: Free Press, 1988.

Riley, Glenda. *Divorce: An American Tradition.* New York: Oxford University Press, 1991.

Ruoff, Jeffrey. *An American Family: A Televised Life.* Minneapolis: University of Minnesota Press, 2001.

Skolnick, Arlene. *Embattled Paradise: The American Family in an Age of Uncertainty.* New York: Basic Books, 1991.

WEBSITES

"Lance Loud." Available online at http://www.pbs.org /lanceloud/ (accessed March 24, 2003).

"The Louds." Available online at http://www.thelouds.com (accessed March 24, 2003).

AUDIO AND VISUAL MEDIA

Lance Loud!: A Death in the American Family. Directed by Alan Raymond and Susan Raymond. Washington, D.C., WETA, Videocassette, 2002.

Aunt Erma's Cope Book: How to Get from Monday to Friday . . . In Twelve Days

Nonfiction work

By: Erma Bombeck

Date: 1979

Source: Bombeck, Erma. *Aunt Erma's Cope Book: How to Get from Monday to Friday . . . In Twelve Days.* New York: McGraw-Hill, 1979, 19–20, 31–33.

About the Author: Erma (Fiste) Bombeck (1927–1996) grew up in a working-class family in Dayton, Ohio. In 1964 she began writing a weekly humor column for a local newspaper that eventually was titled "At Wit's End" and that appeared in more than eight-hundred newspapers nationally. Bombeck also released a series of bestsellers, including *The Grass Is Always Greener Over the Septic Tank* (1976) and *If Life Is a Bowl of Cherries, What Am I Doing in the Pits?* (1978). ∎

Introduction

According to the 1970 U.S. Census, for the first time in American history more people lived in suburban areas than in cities or on farms. It was a trend that began with the post-World War II building boom, when returning veterans and their growing families took advantage of high wages, low interest rates, and a booming economy to buy their piece of the American Dream: a new home. Indeed, in the decade after World War II, ninety-seven percent of all homes built in the United States were detached, single-family dwellings; for many of the purchasers, it was the first time anyone in their family could afford to buy a home instead of renting an apartment or sharing a town house. The federal government encouraged Americans to buy their own homes by offering low-interest loans through the Veterans Administration and by investing billions of dollars in a new interstate highway system. As a result, eighty-three percent of America's population growth took place in the suburbs between 1950 and 1970. America's Cold War leaders cited the trends toward suburbanization and home ownership as proof that the country was winning the war against its communist rivals. As William J. Levitt, the man behind the country's most famous suburban development, Levittown, New York, stated in 1948, "No man who owns his own house and lot can be a Communist. He has too much to do."

Critics of suburbanization noted that the new developments took up huge amounts of land, much of it in prime agricultural areas, and made automobile ownership a necessity as most cities did not expand their mass transit operations into suburban areas. With restrictive covenants denying home ownership based on race and

Erma Bombeck, New York, November 28, 1979. Bombeck's humorous syndicated newspaper column "At Wit's End" debuted in 1964 in the *Kettering-Oakwood Times*, a paper serving the Dayton, Ohio, metropolitan area. It eventually was carried by over eight hundred newspapers nationally. **AP/WIDE WORLD PHOTOS. REPRODUCED BY PERMISSION.**

religion, suburbanization also reinforced racial segregation; even though such covenants were declared illegal by the U.S. Supreme Court in 1948, many realtors continued to practice racial segregation. Feminists noted that the suburbs alienated many women, who were now cut off from job opportunities and expected to devote themselves full-time to being wives, mothers, and homemakers. Social critics also condemned the typical suburbanite as an apolitical conformist, obsessed with status symbols and fitting in.

Significance

The life of Erma Bombeck personified America's suburban experience. After growing up in blue-collar neighborhoods in Dayton, Ohio, she moved to the Dayton suburb of Centerville after her marriage. In the 1970s she joined thousands of other Americans in the move to the sunbelt states when she relocated with her husband and three children to suburban Phoenix, Arizona. By that time Bombeck had resumed her career as a newspaper columnist, which she had put aside when her first child arrived. The subject matter of her columns was the some-

times mundane, sometimes frustrating world of the American housewife. In Bombeck's hands, however, the material was always delivered in humorous fashion and helped to undermine the stereotype of the allegedly alienated and unfulfilled middle-class, suburban housewife.

The popularity of Bombeck's work in the 1970s also showed that much of the country was relatively untouched by the massive social changes that seemed to glorify sexual exploration and self-indulgence. Her 1976 book *The Grass Is Always Greener Over the Septic Tank* ranked as one of the top-ten best-selling nonfiction works in 1976 and 1977; *If Life Is a Bowl of Cherries, What Am I Doing in the Pits?* was the top-selling nonfiction book of 1978; and *Aunt Erma's Cope Book* repeated the feat in 1979. By the end of the decade, Bombeck's "At Wit's End" column appeared three times a week in more than eight-hundred newspapers. Although some reviewers criticized her work as being lightweight and apolitical, Bombeck herself was active in the political fight to pass the Equal Rights Amendment (ERA), a proposal to add a gender anti-discrimination clause to the U.S. Constitution. Although she never injected the issue into her columns, Bombeck's endorsement led many "typical housewives" to join feminist activists in supporting the ERA.

Primary Source

Aunt Erma's Cope Book: How to Get from Monday to Friday . . . In Twelve Days [excerpt]

SYNOPSIS: Bombeck's writing reflected the struggles that many middle Americans had in adapting to the permissiveness and materialism of the 1970s. The chapter of the first excerpt, "Is There a Draft in Your Open Marriage?" is a send-up of a best-selling 1972 sex advice manual, *Open Marriage,* which encouraged married couples to take other sexual partners. The second excerpt, a critique of consumerism, comes from the chapter "Fear of Buying," a reference to the popular 1973 novel about a woman's search for self-fulfillment, *Fear of Flying.*

Is There a Draft in Your Open Marriage?

I could just see my son coming home from school one day . . . his shirt torn, blood around his mouth, sneaking to his room to avoid a confrontation.

When cornered, he'd finally admit he had a fight on the playground.

"But why?" I'd ask.

"Because Rich said . . . he accused you and Dad . . . he said you and Dad were MARRIED!"

"And what did you say?"

"I told him he was a creep. Then he said everyone in school knew it and if you weren't, then how come my last name is the same as yours? Is it true?"

When I finally nodded my head, I could see him shouting angrily, "Why can't you and Dad live together like everyone else's parents?"

I'd explain: "I'm sorry. Your father and I never wanted to embarrass you. Do you think we liked sneaking around checking into hotels *with* luggage? Wearing my wedding ring on a chain around my neck? Pinching one another in front of your friends to make them think we were not married? I'm glad the charade is over. I'm sick of going to Marriage Encounter meetings in separate cars."

When pressed as to why we did it, I'd explain we wanted to try marriage to see if it got on our nerves and if it didn't work out, we'd just quietly get a divorce and no one would get hurt that way. . . .

Fear of Buying

If commercials were supposed to make me feel good about myself, they were failing miserably. My paper towels turned to lace in my hands. My cough medicine ran out at 2 A.M., and my garbage bags broke on impact with the garbage.

It's funny I hadn't thought about it before. I was responsible for my husband's underarms being protected for twelve hours. I was responsible for making sure my children had a well-balanced breakfast. I alone was carrying the burden for my dog's shiny coat and spritzing just the right amount of lemon throughout the house so they wouldn't pucker to death. When my daughter's love life fell through it was up to me to remind her that whiter teeth would bring him back.

I was reflecting on my responsibilities when the commercial came on of the husband who came home after a twelve-hour day, beat, depressed and exhausted. He opened the door and seventy-five people jumped up and yelled, "Happy Birthday! Surprise!" The man grabbed his wife, kissed her, and said, "Honey, what a surprise."

She backed off from him like he was a three-day-old dead chicken and said, "What a breath! We'd better do something about it . . . and FAST!"

You would have thought that would have taken the hats and horns out of the occasion if anything would. Instead, we see them in the bathroom, where he is gargling his bad breath into remission. The last scene is one of pure joy. He has finally been allowed to attend his own party and she is beaming, knowing that she has once again saved her husband from himself.

Couldn't the big jerk tell if he had the breath of a camel? Did his wife have to do everything? I was interrupted by my husband, who came out of the bedroom holding a sport shirt. "Honey," he grinned good-naturedly, "I hate to tell you this, but there's a ring around my collar."

I looked up and snapped, "What a coincidence! It matches the one around your neck!"

I don't know what made me say it . . . only the resentment of being in charge of everyone's welfare, I guess.

I had been naive. I should have realized it the night I showered, put perfume behind each knee, and heard my husband snore in the darkness . . . thus capping the first PG-rated Aviance Night in the history of cosmetics.

Further Resources

BOOKS

Braden, Maria. "Erma Bombeck." In *She Said What?: Interviews with Women Newspaper Columnists.* Lexington: University of Kentucky Press, 1993, 36–46.

Colwell, Lynn Hutner. *Erma Bombeck: Writer and Humorist.* Hillside, N.J.: Enslow Publishers, 1992.

Duany, Andres, et al. *Suburban Nation: The Rise of Sprawl and the Decline of the American Dream.* New York: North Point Press, 2000.

Edwards, Susan. *Erma Bombeck: A Life in Humor.* New York: Avon Books, 1997.

Garreau, Joel. *Edge City: Life on the New Frontier.* New York: Anchor Books, 1992.

Jackson, Kenneth T. *Crabgrass Frontier: The Suburbanization of the United States.* New York: Oxford University Press, 1985.

King, Norman. *Here's Erma!: The Bombecking of America.* Aurora, Ill.: Caroline House Publishers, 1982.

Kunstler, James Howard. *The Geography of Nowhere: The Rise and Decline of America's Man-Made Landscape.* New York: Simon & Schuster, 1993.

WEBSITES

"Erma Bombeck Museum." Available online at http://www.ermamuseum.org/home.asp (accessed March 25, 2003).

May 4 Collection
Eyewitness accounts

By: Carol Mirman; Diane Williams; Art Koushel
Date: 2000; 1990; 1995
Source: Kent State University Libraries, Department of Special Collections and Archives. May 4 Collection. http://

www.library.kent.edu/exhibits/4may95/ohmirman.html; http://
speccoll.library.kent.edu/4may70/dwilliam.html; http://
speccoll.library.kent.edu/4may70/box110/110koushel.html;
website home page: http://www.library.kent.edu/exhibits
/4may95/ (accessed July 15, 2003).

About the Authors: Each of these witnesses to the disturbances at Kent State University (KSU) in May 1970 presents
a different perspective. Although she was against the war in
Vietnam, Carol Mirman, then a KSU senior, did not approve
of the riots in downtown Kent, Ohio, that led to the antiwar
rally of May 4. Diane Williams was a seventeen-year-old
Kent native who attended the antiwar rally that ended with
the National Guard opening fire on the crowd. Art Koushel
was a politically active student at KSU who later testified
at the Scranton Commission, a government inquiry into
the events. ■

Introduction

After President Richard M. Nixon's announcement
on April 30, 1970, that American troops would take part
in a military offensive into Cambodia in conjunction with
South Vietnamese troops, a new round of protests against
the Vietnam War swept across college campuses. Nixon
had been elected in 1968 in part because of his promise
to end America's involvement in the southeast Asian conflict, and his statement seemed to betray that pledge.

Kent, Ohio, was a small town located about forty
miles southeast of Cleveland. As the site of Kent State
University (KSU), the town had a large student population. After President Nixon ended draft deferments for
college students in 1969, Kent's university population
was especially disturbed by the continuation of the war.
On Friday, May 1, 1970, about five hundred people gathered on the KSU commons in the center of campus.
While they watched, a small group of students symbol-
ically buried a copy of the U.S. Constitution in protest
against the Vietnam War. Another rally, held by the
Black United Students, took place later that afternoon
and by the end of the day, students began talking about
holding another rally on Monday, May 4, at noon on the
KSU commons.

Tensions quickly escalated after the Friday rallies,
however. That evening, hundreds of students staged a
spontaneous antiwar rally on North Water Street in downtown Kent, an area filled with bars and nightclubs. After
setting a bonfire in the street, some onlookers began breaking the windows of the businesses that lined the street.
The mayor then declared a state of emergency and the police cleared the streets with tear gas and night sticks. The
following night another antiwar rally that began with a
couple of hundred students on campus quickly swelled to
as many as two thousand protesters. The crowd marched
to the ROTC building and someone set it on fire. Once
again the police dispersed the crowd with tear gas; one
student was struck with a bayonet as he fled the scene.

Although it seemed that Sunday would pass without
incident, a speech given by Governor James Rhodes in-
cited another round of protests. Rhodes, who was campaigning in a Republican Senate primary as the "law and
order" candidate, came to Kent and labeled the protesters as outside, radical agitators. Taking a hard stand
against the antiwar movement, he promised, "We are going to eradicate the problem. We're not going to treat the
symptoms." Rhodes then sent in the Ohio National Guard
to patrol the campus, and a curfew was enforced. When
some students staged a peaceful protest against the presence of the Guard and the curfew, the Guard used tear
gas on them.

As a group of about fifteen hundred people gathered
for the noontime antiwar rally on the KSU commons on
Monday, May 4, they were met by about 116 Guardsmen
armed with M-1 rifles. After General Robert Canterbury
gave an order to clear the area, the Guardsmen fired tear
gas into the crowd, which immediately dispersed. The
Guardsmen then marched into an adjacent area to continue the dispersal; after a ten-minute standoff with a
small group of students, Canterbury ordered the Guardsmen to return to the commons. As the group followed the
order, members of Troop G, who had been conferring
with one another separately from the rest of the group,
suddenly turned around and stared firing into the crowd,
most of whom had thought the confrontation was over.
Four KSU students, Allison Krause, Jeffrey Miller, Sandra Scheuer, and William Schroeder, were killed and nine
other KSU students were shot.

Significance

The events at Kent State served both as a continuation of the 1960s and as a horrific introduction to the
1970s. With America's involvement in Vietnam dragging
on, a new wave of protests engulfed college campuses.
Ten days after the Kent State shootings took place, an
antiwar and civil rights protest at Jackson State University ended with one student and a bystander being shot
and twelve others being wounded when police opened
fire on the crowd. The seeming senselessness of the
tragedies at Kent State and Jackson State also crystallized
the distrust of government officials that many Americans
had started to feel during the Vietnam War. There were
allegations of a cover up to protect the National Guardsmen from being held responsible for their actions at Kent
State, and with the intervention and support of Governor
Rhodes, none of the Guardsmen was ever convicted for
the shootings.

Despite his attempt to capitalize on the disturbances
in his Senate campaign, Governor Rhodes came under
criticism for his harsh tactics and was defeated in the May
1970 primary. He staged a political comeback in 1975
when he returned to the governor's office, but he re-

National guardsmen toss tear gas toward rioters on the campus of Kent State University, May 1970. The National Guard was called in to help control uprisings that began as student protests of the Vietnam War. AP/WIDE WORLD PHOTOS. REPRODUCED BY PERMISSION.

mained a controversial figure throughout his political career. Rhodes defended his decisions and refused to retract his remarks against the protesters as radicals, an attitude that struck many as callous. As Carol Mirman later remembered, "What I found so painful, and still find painful to this day, are the number of citizens across the board who said, 'The students should have been shot.' To understand what the difference is between exercising your right to free speech—there's a difference between free speech and burning down a building . . . It was really, really, really painful for people to say that the students should have been shot, based on misconceptions and narrow-minded views of 'love it or leave it.'"

Primary Source

May 4 Collection [excerpt]

SYNOPSIS: In all three of these excerpts, eyewitnesses describe the Kent State tragedy. Carol Mirman first describes the outbreak of rioting that occurred over the weekend prior to the antiwar rally on Monday, May 4, 1970. She also details the shootings that took the lives of four students and wounded nine others. After the shootings Mirman tried to comfort another eyewitness, Mary Ann Vecchio, the subject of a famous photo which showed her kneeling by a shooting victim with her arms outstretched. Diane Williams, a high school student living in Kent, contrasts the peaceful tone that

prevailed on Monday morning with the unexpected violence that ensued. Koushel describes the shock and sense of unreality that took hold after the National Guardsmen opened fire.

Carol Mirman

I believe that what happened on Friday night happened because it had been a very hard winter—it had really been a long, cold, dark winter—and that weekend was the first weekend of real spring that year. Consequently, people were down in the bars, down on Water Street, and out on the streets and just in kind of one of those youthful hormonal (or harmonal) party places and I was there with a girlfriend. We decided we were goin' downtown to find her a boy friend—she'd been lonely too long. So that was my motivation for being downtown that night. And we were down in one of the bars. And it got crowded and hot and we went up the street and there was a lot of people gathered around, including bikers and political people. And what I do recall—because the days are cumulative up to the shootings—is that lots of people were milling around, more and more people gathering together I think it was on Water Street. And somebody brought a barrel and started to put things in there and they lit a fire in the barrel. And more and more people gathered and some started talking about the war and people were drinking and what I do remember is some people started to block off the street. And then more and more crowds gathered. And the part that was—none of that was a big bother to me—it was all interesting. I was just kind of watching the whole show.

It became a little scarier for me when the streets were blocked off and I remember distinctly elderly couples in their cars trapped—the light had turned red, they were stopped in the traffic and they were surrounded by students. And the students started to rock the car. And they were scared. They would lock their door, they rolled up the windows and I think people were just kind of feeling their oats basically. I didn't understand it as being a political sort of issue. Although some people did mention Viet Nam and we were aware that Cambodia had been bombed. And that things had begun down at Ohio State. From my perspective it was drinkin' beer with the guys. I mean that was what it was about. Then it went from there.

It went from there. The next thing that I can recall is that people started after the blocking off and getting angry and rocking cars, then some people began running down the streets and throw rocks and break windows. At that point I left. I wasn't in favor of the war. But I didn't see that the people that had the shoe store and the butcher store had anything to do with being the cause of the war. And I went home, to the dorm.

The next day was Saturday and I thought all of the excitement was over with. But in fact that's the day that the ROTC Building was burned. But I wasn't anywhere around. . . .

So they (National Guardsman) got up and moved and, I thought retreated up the hill. I was with that group of people that followed them up the hill and said "Yeh, get off campus, get outta here, we don't want you here, get outta here" and I was makin' lots of noise. And then I heard a single shot. And there was a volley. I was very close to the Guard and the bullets whizzed past my ear. I was very much in the line of fire.

I do recall—some of these things are sort of burned into my memory. I remember thinking so clearly when that volley went by my ear "This is not what it sounds like on tv. This is not what bullets sound like on cartoons." It was a very different sound, the bullets so close to one's head, to one's ears. Very different sound. And I jumped over bodies and ran down the hill. I also recall some students saying "Walk, don't run. They're only blanks." And I remember thinking, "Huh? Why carry a weapon

if you don't have something in it that's intended to work." I'm outta here. And I did. I ran over bodies two, three deep were hittin' the ground. And so I ran down the hill to a place of safety, but by the time I was behind that yellow Volkswagen which was right near where Jeff Miller was shot, the volley had stopped. I got up when the volley had stopped to look to see what the heck had happened. And I did see Jeff Miller at that time—and—that's when the photograph of me was taken by Jeff Miller. I'd never seen blood like that. I'd never seen anything like that. It was a complete shock. I wanted to touch him. I remember wanting to hold him, but I was afraid of the blood. I did touch and hold his hand. I didn't want him to feel alone. I figured how can anybody live with this. Life is running down the sidewalk. Running. Just kept flowing. And there was nothing to be done, that I felt that I could do.

However, being the superficial young person that I was, I had a crush on someone from the Art Department, and I got up from this person and went to look for that other guy. And I didn't see him. And when I came back to the side of Jeff Miller that's when Mary Ann Vechio was there. And I didn't know who she was. I knew she was a young person and she was freaking out and I put my arms around her shoulder and—cause I had already been to the site—and I remember feeling her. She was like a block of ice. She was frozen. She was stone. She couldn't move. That picture was—in that picture sure—but what was going on in her after her arms were outstretched—cause that's when I reached her. And I don't remember, I think it was before, when I was at Jeff first that there was a guy who had a flag and he dipped the flag in the blood, and I remember feeling—and then he jumped in the blood. His feet touched the blood and the blood smashed/splashed out. He was so angry. He was waving that, you know, "Look!" It was all kind of shocking to me.

Ah, well then more people started gathering around. I didn't see anybody else shot. I didn't wander any place else. I was a touch on the frozen side. I remember feeling like I wanted to cry but I was in such shock I didn't know what to do. And then some of the National Guard came into the area, and this is all in the photographs. And I remember the Guard in that particular vicinity were as shocked as I was. I remember the looks on their faces. They didn't know what to do. And they didn't know what to say. But there were many students that had come from other areas that were gathered and they became afraid of what, of the emotion that was going on and they retreated. And more students gathered and then ambulances came and people took things away.

Diane Williams

And then Sunday, the guard was up on campus, and I had gone up and walked around with a girl friend. She was like, taking daisies and sticking them in the barrels of the guards rifles. Just trying to say, "Look, you don't need these here. This is—we're gonna have a peaceful demonstration on Monday." It was announced, and yes, there were people that came in from out of state, specifically for this demonstration. They had speeches scheduled, certain people were going to lecture. I mean, these demonstrations had taken place before on a smaller scale, but this was going to be a big one, because it was right after we'd found out the—the war had spilled over the borders into Cambodia. And everybody was really upset about it. So on Monday, when we are sitting there, waiting for the various lecturers to speak, you know, people were throwing frisbees and—and just kind of being normal college students. They weren't just sitting; but we were ordered to disperse. And we were supposed to leave. And I'm pretty sure it was Dr. Franks, comes running through the crowd, saying, "Look, they've got live guns, these are real bullets this time." Well, nobody believed him, because they had used pellet guns before, and we just kind of thought that's what they would have. Well they started with the tear gas first, and they'd throw the tear gas, and the students would pick it up and say, "OK we've had enough of this," and they'd throw it back at the guardsmen. And then, yeah, rocks and bottles started going, but, to my knowledge, I never heard a sniper. I never heard any gunfire whatsoever, until the National Guard actually opened fire. And when—when I first heard the gunshots, it's like, I real quick, ran behind this—this car, a yellow Volkswagen. And a bullet went right through the car. I mean, it went thr___ from one side of the car, right straight through the other. When I saw this—all of a sudden, this hole was like, instantly there in the side of the car, I decided it was time to leave, to get out. And I saw other, like—groups of students, where somebody had obviously been hit, but I didn't stick around to find out. I mean, I just—I left. . . .

The way it [a proposed memorial] was drawn up, it looked beautiful, it was the neatest concept. Because if you had taken all of those pieces, and were able to push them all in together, it formed a box. But the way it was, it was like a box that had ex-ploded, it was like, the perfect piece of art to depict the explosive attitude about the whole situation. It was perfect. . . . But yeah, I'm glad the memorial is going in. I think it's important for—for generation after generation to remember. I mean, there are kids on the campus right now who don't even understand the Vietnam War. They don't understand why there were demonstrations. They don't understand the heated situation of the seventies. They don't understand why there were people that were against the war, or those who were for the war. And that's an important part of history. Not just here for Kent, but for the nation, the world.

Art Koushel

When we—after the shoo—after the incident, the shootings—I was there—I wasn't in the group of people that got pushed up over the pagoda hill, I was the group of people that got pushed to the left and came around the parking lot on the back side. Because the concept, at least I believed, was to separate the group into smaller groups that actually were on the front side of Taylor Hall and the Commons hill. Well, we went to the left, instead of getting pushed up over the right side of the building, we got pushed up over the backside of the building. The actual shooting—I froze. I didn't dive for cover, or—I just stood there. It happened extremely quickly—before I realized what was going on it was over. Did not expect them to not only shoot, but never realized that they actually had loaded weapons at all. When you talk to a soldier, you debate politics, when you talk to a policeman, you move. When the police took over—afterwards, when an Ohio Highway Patrolman with a string of bullets across his chest with an automatic pump shotgun says move, you—you really don't debate politics with that individual. You really don't. But an Army person you do and I guess the expectation for—that they had guns, but they—and they had tear gas. Was the extent of what their arsenal was. So not expecting them to not only not fire, but the fact that they had live ammunition, never really crossed my mind. Never even thought about it.

Further Resources

BOOKS

Anderson, Maggie, and Alex Gildzen, eds. *A Gathering of Poets.* Kent, Ohio: Kent State University Press, 1992.

Bills, Scott L., ed. *May Fourth: Echoes Through a Decade.* Kent, Ohio: Kent State University Press, 1982.

Gordon, William. *Four Dead in Ohio: Was There a Conspiracy at Kent State?* Laguna Hills, Calif.: North Ridge, 1995.

Perlman, Sandra. *Nightwalking: Voices from Kent State.* Kent, Ohio: Franklin Mills Press, 1995.

WEBSITES

"Kent State University: Freedom of Information Act Files." Available online at http://foia.fbi.gov/kentstat.htm (accessed January 1, 2003).

"May 4, 1970." Available online at http://www.library.kent.edu /exhibits/4may95/index.html (accessed January 1, 2003).

"The May 4 Center." Available online at http://www.may4.org/ (accessed January 1, 2003).

AUDIO AND VISUAL MEDIA

Kent State: The Day the War Came Home. Landmark Films, 2000.

Seductive Poison: A Jonestown Survivor's Story of Life and Death in the Peoples Temple

Memoir

By: Deborah Layton

Date: 1998

Source: Layton, Deborah. *Seductive Poison: A Jonestown Survivor's Story of Life and Death in the Peoples Temple.* New York: Anchor Books, 1998, 66–69, 91–92, 151, 299.

About the Author: Deborah Layton (1953–) was born in Utah. She joined Jim Jones' Peoples Temple in 1971 and served as the financial secretary. She moved to the group's Jonestown compound in Guyana, but the brutal conditions prompted her to flee in May 1978. She released an affidavit describing the conditions at Jonestown to alert American officials about the abuses. Convinced that the American government was going to destroy the Peoples Temple, Jones ordered his followers to commit mass suicide on November 18, 1978. ∎

Introduction

Although thousands of Americans had experimented with collective living arrangements on communes in the 1960s as part of a stance against materialism and individualism, larger, more structured groups—typically professing a spiritual purpose—rose to prominence in the 1970s. The group attracting the largest number of adherents, the Unification Church of South Korean Presbyterian minister Sun Myung Moon, was labeled a cult by the mainstream media, who reported financial irregularities and repressive rules inside the group. Moon's followers, derisively called "Moonies," participated in mass weddings where as many as sixty-five hundred of them were joined in marriage by the reverend, even if they

had not previously met. Reverend Moon bought some respectability by purchasing the *Washington Times* newspaper and turning it into a conservative mouthpiece, yet the accusations against the Unification Church and Moon continued unabated.

Unlike many of the spiritually oriented groups that sprang up seemingly overnight in the 1970s, the Peoples Temple, a group led by the Christian Church, Disciples of Christ minister Jim Jones, had been around since the 1950s. Born in Indiana in 1931, Jones began preaching a mixture of socialism and racial equality in Indianapolis in 1954 at the Community Unity Church, later renamed the Peoples Temple Full Gospel Church. He also attracted followers by his charismatic displays of faith healing and distribution of food and clothing to the poor. Jones achieved a measure of respectability for his efforts and gained a seat on the Indianapolis Human Rights Commission in 1961. Fearing a nuclear holocaust, Jones took his family to Brazil for two years in the early 1960s; he later settled with about 145 followers in Ukiah in northern California in 1965. The Peoples Temples opened missions in San Francisco and Los Angeles by 1972, and its membership included between three and five thousand people. After eight Peoples Temple members left the organization in 1973 and aired allegations of physical and mental abuse by Jones and his lieutenants, Jones laid plans for reestablishing the Peoples Temple in the remote jungle of Guyana, near the border with Venezuela. By 1975 about fifty Peoples Temple members were at work building a compound, named Jonestown, that housed about one thousand people by early 1978.

Significance

Jones had squelched a number of critical stories in the media. An exposé in *New West,* however, as well as continuing complaints by the Committee of Concerned Relatives, a group of former members and their families, led Jones to flee to Guyana in June 1977. After financial secretary Deborah Layton fled the cult's Guyana base in May 1978 and filed an affidavit detailing the harsh mind and physical control techniques in place at Jonestown, a committee led by Congressman Leo Ryan traveled to Guyana to investigate. The group's findings were inconclusive, but as it prepared to leave, some Peoples Temple representatives attacked the party and killed Ryan and four others. Announcing that American forces were now coming to destroy Jonestown, Jones ordered a mass suicide on the evening of November 18, 1978. Most of the 914 Jonestown members who died, including Jones and his wife, Marceline, appeared to have taken lethal doses of poison willingly, but some were shot as they tried to escape.

The Jonestown tragedy was one of the darkest moments of the 1970s. From its declared origins as a utopia of socialism and racial equality, the Peoples Temple had descended into violence, fraud, and finally, mass fatalities. The incident also raised fears that other new groups with religious foundations, from the Moonies to the Hare Krishnas—followers of the eastern mystic, Swami A.C. Bhaktivedanta—were a threat to American society. Although the issue of "brainwashing" was rejected by some experts, who maintained that most of the people who joined the organizations found the experience to be positive, others found their recruiting and retention techniques to be fraudulent and coercive. As the events at Jonestown demonstrated, the continuing search for spiritual and personal fulfillment by Americans in the 1970s sometimes had a dark side.

Primary Source

Seductive Poison: A Jonestown Survivor's Story of Life and Death in the Peoples Temple [excerpt]

SYNOPSIS: Deborah Layton's loyalty to the Peoples Temple outweighed the occasional doubts she had about the group's charismatic leader, Jim Jones, and the tactics he used to keep tight control over his followers. In May 1978, six months after moving to the Peoples Temple compound in Jonestown, Guyana, Layton staged a daring escape and exposed the cult's repressive methods. Six months later, more than nine hundred Peoples Temple members perished in a mass suicide and murder spree carried out under Jim Jones's orders.

After ten minutes of singing and clapping, Jim resumed the clairvoyant segment of our service. He began to hum into the microphone. His head was down, his eyes closed, and he seemed to be concentrating on listening to an ethereal voice.

"There is someone in the room with an Aunt Dora, who is going blind. She lives in West Virginia. Please stand if you know who you are."

Mama rose up sheepishly as all eyes turned to glimpse her. She looked younger than fifty-eight, I thought.

"I have an Aunt Dove who is going blind," she said reverently.

"Ahhh." Jim raised his brows. "Through the ether plane I sometimes am unable to decipher the exact words that are being given to me."

"Yes, she is the sister of my mother-in-law."

"Sshhh," Jim hushed her. "I know. I have the powers to see and know everything." Mama stood still. "You also had an Aunt Dora in Germany who was going blind."

Jim Jones, November 18, 1978. Jones was the leader of the People's Temple cult, a religious group founded originally as a utopia of socialism and racial equality. **AP/WIDE WORLD PHOTOS. REPRODUCED BY PERMISSION.**

I watched in amazement. Karen and Paula had just come back from visiting Mama, and now Jim was doing a psychic reading on her. This was exciting!

"Lisa, you have been sad a very long time and hold yourself responsible for a tragedy you have no right to weigh yourself down with."

What tragedy, I wondered.

"In this house you will grow strong once more and proud. You've felt entrapped by the secret for too long. Step out now and come to me. You are a beautiful Jew and your children have inherited your good looks."

I was embarrassed that through my mother, I, too, was being singled out as a Jew. Was that the tragedy he had referred to? But no, in his eyes it seemed to be an honor. He often preached that Jews had suffered racism similar to that of our black brethren, and that our government was going to implement the same tactics to get rid of them that Germany had used against the Jews. Perhaps there was no need to be ashamed after all.

A vat that contained a grape-flavored drink laced with deadly cyanide sits on a sidewalk at People's Temple in Jonestown, Guyana, November 20, 1978. Over nine hundred bodies of cult members who participated in the mass suicide were found at the commune. **AP/WIDE WORLD PHOTOS. REPRODUCED BY PERMISSION.**

Later, I saw Mama at the podium, her cheeks flushed. Jim seemed to be consoling her, holding her hand, stroking it gently, both of them seemingly enchanted with one another. Watching her face, I knew Jim had made another faithful member.

Soon thereafter, Mama separated from Papa and Jim urged her to invite Annalisa. My bearded brother, Tom, and Papa were never invited. Mama missed Annalisa and begged her to give the church a chance. Annalisa came to several meetings with her two little children but I could tell she wouldn't make it. Even though Jim gave her the royal treatment, she had too many questions. She wouldn't be a good follower. . . .

It's hard to explain why I didn't realize something was seriously wrong; why I stayed deaf to the warning calls ringing in my ears. I ignored my doubts and my conscience because I believed that I could

not be wrong, not that wrong. A healer, socialist, and important civic leader could not possibly be an immoral abuser, a blackmailer, a liar. It did not occur to me that Jim could be all those things. I thought that it must be extremely painful for Father to sacrifice his own goodness for the larger cause, as he did when he committed—or ordered us to commit—reprehensible and illegal acts. I saw his moral transgressions as purely altruistic—something like the means justify the end. And who was I to criticize him? My own development, I was told (and believed), was not advanced enough to allow me to understand Father's motives and actions. I could only hope to be enlightened by imitating his example and striving to become wiser, more principled, and closer to him. . . .

For the past two years Jim had suggested that those who had defected were all in the FBI's pockets and on their payroll. The Diversions Committee had been advised to model a revenge tactic after Synanon's, to frighten traitors. Started in the late sixties by Charles Dederich, Synanon used harsh catharsis, self-denial, and physical coercion to force heroin addicts into abstinence. Jim admired their tactics. They, too, believed outsiders were no good, untrustworthy, and they had put a large rattlesnake in the mailbox of an adversarial attorney; when he reached inside it, he was bitten. Our diversion campaign was far less deadly, geared toward making the recipients miserable and helping them to question their faulty ways. Once these treasonous former members had been tracked down, Teresa and I would then take a hike through Tilden Park. Armed with plastic bags and gloves, we would harvest enough virulent red and orange leaves of poison oak to saturate a threatening letter typed on our nontraceable typewriter . . .

We know what you are up to.

The one who cares the most prays no harm will come your way.

Only you can prevent it.

The victims would never know, when they opened the envelope and pulled out the letter, that their hands would carry the toxin all over them. Father told us that the traitors deserved to have their eyes and faces severely irritated and possibly damaged. They'd be forced to wonder how this had happened to them and would later understand that "God acts in strange ways to safeguard his chosen people," as Father always said. They had been fairly warned. Or had they? I wondered. . . .

As we were systematically stripped of our previous identities, never to be allowed private possession or autonomous thought again, the lost souls watched. Later on I, too, would feel the excitement when the siren sounded to announce the new arrivals. It was a strange rush to watch these outsiders, these newcomers, pull into the camp and realize they'd been desperately wrong. We felt vindicated when we saw other new arrivals' faces fall. But after trying it once, I never wanted to make contact with new arrivals again. It was too painful to look into their faces as they searched ours, mine, for silent reassurance, for hope.

Once you were in, it didn't take long to learn the ropes: keep your head down and don't talk unless it's absolutely necessary. For each person showing weakness by speaking of his or her fears, another would become more trusted for reporting it. There were no enduring friendships—everyone soon learned that it was just too dangerous to run the risk of confrontation or public beating and not being trusted. No, it was best to write everyone off and keep to yourself, the only place one could dream, hope, and plan, and not get reported. . . .

Looking back, there are a few things I have come to learn. People do not knowingly join "cults" that will ultimately destroy and kill them. People join self-help groups, churches, political movements, college campus dinner socials, and the like, in an effort to be a part of something larger than themselves. It is mostly the innocent and naive who find themselves entrapped. In their openhearted endeavor to find meaning in their lives, they walk blindly into the promise of ultimate answers and a higher purpose. It is usually only gradually that a group turns into or reveals itself as a cult, becomes malignant, but by then it is often too late.

I hope my book will give my daughter some answers about how I got caught and how the Jonestown tragedy happened. I hope it will provide clues about the workings of a cult and shed light on the darkness of deceit. There are essential warning signs early on. Our alarm signals ought to go off as soon as someone tells us their way is the only right way.

When our own thoughts are forbidden, when our questions are not allowed and our doubts are punished, when contacts and friendships outside of the organization are censored, we are being abused for an end that never justifies its means. When our heart aches knowing we have made friendships and secret attachments that will be forever forbidden if we leave, we are in danger. When we consider staying in a group because we cannot bear the loss, disappointment, and sorrow our leaving will cause for ourselves and those we have come to love, we are in a cult.

If there is any lesson to be learned it is that an ideal can never be brought about by fear, abuse, and the threat of retribution. When family and friends are used as a weapon in order to force us to stay in an organization, something has gone terribly wrong. If I, as a young woman, had had someone explain to me what cults are and how indoctrination works, my story might not have been the same.

Further Resources

BOOKS

Chidester, David. *Salvation and Suicide: An Interpretation of Jim Jones, the Peoples Temple, and Jonestown.* Bloomington: Indiana University Press, 1988.

Edwards, Christopher. *Crazy for God.* Englewood Cliffs, N.J.: Prentice-Hall, 1979.

Hall, John R. *Gone from the Promised Land: Jonestown in American Cultural History.* New Brunswick, N.J.: Transaction Publishers, 1987.

Lane, Mark. *The Strongest Poison.* New York: Hawthorn Books, 1980.

Maaga, Mary McCormick. *Hearing the Voices of Jonestown: Putting a Human Face on an American Tragedy.* Syracuse, N.Y.: Syracuse University Press, 1998.

Reston, James. *Our Father Who Art in Hell: The Life and Death of Jim Jones.* New York: Crown, 1981.

PERIODICALS

Wright, Lawrence. "The Sons of Jim Jones." *New Yorker,* 69, no. 39, November 1993, 66–89.

WEBSITES

"Deborah Layton." Available online at http://www.deborahlayton .com/bio.html (accessed March 26, 2003).

"Father Cares: The Last of Jonestown." Available online at http://www.npr.org/programs/specials/jonestown.html (accessed March 26, 2003).

AUDIO AND VISUAL MEDIA

Guyana Tragedy: The Story of Jim Jones. Directed by William A. Graham. Konigsberg Company, 1986.

8

THE MEDIA

JOSEPH R. PHELAN

Entries are arranged in chronological order by date of primary source. For entries with one primary source, the entry title is the same as the primary source title. Entries with more than one primary source have an overall entry title, followed by the titles of the primary sources.

Important Events in Media, 1970–1979

1970

- President Richard M. Nixon signs the Failing Newspaper Act (later renamed the Newspaper Preservation Act) into law. The act, overturning a U.S. Supreme Court decision from the previous year, allows local newspapers to share production facilities provided that one of the papers is in financial trouble and that the agreement does not deter competition.

- The Harris Corporation of Cleveland introduces the first computer editing terminal for newspapers; its first customers include the Gannett group.

- The Postal Reorganization Act raises second-class rates and eliminates a relaxed scale for periodicals, resulting in the failure or size reduction of several magazines.

- *Negro Digest* is renamed *Black World.*

- An article in *Playboy* calls underground comics "obscene, anarchistic, sophomoric, subversive and apocalyptic."

- *National Lampoon* first appears.

- *Smithsonian* magazine is founded; within the decade its circulation expands from around 160,000 to nearly 2,000,000.

- On January 26, Atlanta entrepreneur Ted Turner purchases a small independent television station. WTCG (later renamed WTBS) becomes a superstation valued at more than $40 million by 1978.

- In March, the Federal Communications Commission outlaws the common ownership of radio and television stations in the same market.

- On April 1, Congress bans cigarette advertising on radio and television. The ban takes effect on January 1, 1971.

- In May, the first issue of *Essence* magazine, directed at African American women, appears on newsstands.

- In May, the Federal Communications Commission, hoping to bolster local programming on public affairs, enacts the Prime Time Access Rule, which limits prime-time programming by networks to three hours a night.

- On May 2, Mississippi educational television bans *Sesame Street* for its racial content. The State Commission for Educational TV reverses the decision on May 24.

- On September 19, *The Mary Tyler Moore Show,* a sitcom about an independent single woman, debuts on CBS.

- On September 21, *Monday Night Football* premieres on ABC.

- On October 5, National Educational Television (NET) is superseded by the Public Broadcasting System (PBS).

- On November 3, in a nationally televised speech, President Richard Nixon coins the term "Silent Majority" in asking the nation's vast number of quiet, conforming citizens for support against the antiwar demonstrations filling the streets.

1971

- CBS debuts the controversial sitcom *All in the Family,* featuring a bigoted, white, blue-collar protagonist, Archie Bunker.

- *The New York Times* acquires *Family Circle* magazine.

- In January, Marvel Comics' Captain America teams with the Falcon, an African American superhero.

- On February 20, a false alert of a nuclear attack is broadcast across the country when an operator mistakenly plays the alert tape instead of the usual emergency test tape. More than forty minutes are required to cancel the false alert.

- On April 29, the *Amsterdam News,* the African American newspaper with the largest U.S. circulation, is sold to a group of African American investors for $2 million.

- On June 6, *The Ed Sullivan Show,* which debuted on CBS as *Toast of the Town* in 1948, is canceled.

- On June 10, the Federal Trade Commission announces that it will begin requiring substantiation of all advertising claims. Auto ads will be the first to receive federal scrutiny.

- On June 13, *The New York Times* prints the first installment of the Pentagon Papers, top secret documents about America's involvement in the Vietnam War, in its newspaper. The government quickly forces a halt to the series. But on June 30, the Supreme Court reverses a lower court's order and allows the documents' publication to resume.

- On July 26, *Apollo 15* sends the first color pictures from space via television.

- On October 13, at the urging of NBC, the World Series offers its first night game so that the series can be shown during prime time.

- On October 19, *Look* magazine ceases publication after thirty-four years in business.

1972

- In *Branzburg v. Hayes* the U.S. Supreme Court rules that journalists do not have special immunity from testifying before grand juries, even if to do so threatens their relationships with their sources.

- The National Association of Broadcasters bans hosts of children's shows from making sales pitches to children on behalf of sponsors. The resulting drop in sponsorship leads to the cancellation of many local children's programs and an increased emphasis on cartoons for those that survive.

- The business magazine *Money* is founded.

- In February, the Federal Communications Commission places limits on CATV, which by this time refers more to cable than "community antenna television," in one hundred markets in America. Stations are required to offer channels for public access as well as to schools and governments.

- In Spring, the first videotape film rentals are available from Sears.
- On April 30, *Arthur Godfrey Time,* on CBS Radio for twenty-seven years, goes off the air.
- On May 1, *The Tonight Show* moves from New York to Los Angeles.
- In June, the feminist magazine *Ms.* is founded by Gloria Steinen and Letty Cottin Pogrebin.
- In August and September, one billion people watch the Olympics, held in Munich, via satellite television broadcasts.
- On November 8, HBO premieres on cable television. Its first subscribers are 365 Pennsylvanians.
- In December, *Life* magazine ceases publication after thirty-six years.

1973

- In two decisions the U.S. Supreme Court declares that broadcasters are under no obligation to sell time for editorial advertisements, provided that networks do not violate the FCC's Fairness Doctrine, which requires broadcasters to allow ample treatment of controversial topics and to provide those with opposing viewpoints the opportunity to express their ideas.
- *Playgirl* magazine is founded.
- *Evergreen Review,* an experimental literary journal begun in 1957, publishes its last issue.
- On October 15, the *Tomorrow* show, hosted by Tom Snyder, premieres on NBC.
- On October 26, NBC, acknowledging past unfairness in dealing with homosexuality on TV, agrees to seek advice from homosexuals on this issue in the future.

1974

- In January, *Happy Days* premieres on ABC.
- In March, *Nova* premieres on PBS.
- On March 4, *People,* a weekly featuring stories on "the stars, the important doers, the comers, and . . . ordinary men and women caught up in extraordinary situations," publishes its first issue. It quickly becomes one of the most successful magazines of the decade.
- On March 4, the U.S. Supreme Court rules that cable television providers do not violate U.S. copyright laws by picking up long-distance television signals and offering them to paid customers.
- On March 16, *Editor and Publisher* announces that U.S. daily newspapers increased their total circulation by six hundred thousand in 1973.
- On June 25, the Supreme Court rules that a newspaper is not required to print a political candidate's reply to an editorial that was critical of the candidate.
- In August, Marvel Comics begins *Savage Sword of Conan,* a black-and-white magazine that does not have to carry the

Comics Code Authority seal and thus can address a more adult audience.

- On August 8, a television audience of 100 million watches Richard Nixon announce his resignation as president of the United States.
- On November 30, Ridder Publications and Knight Newspapers combine to create a thirty-six-newspaper conglomerate in sixteen states.
- On December 21, *The New York Times* reports that the CIA spies on Americans and that it has files on about ten thousand citizens. CIA director William Colby admits the allegation is true.

1975

- Bert and Ernie, two of Jim Henson's muppets from PBS's *Sesame Street,* are exhibited at the Smithsonian Institution in Washington, D.C.
- Sony introduces its Betamax videocassette recorder.
- On September 1, *Gunsmoke,* which premiered in 1955, goes off the air.
- On September 25, the FCC ends the requirement that radio and TV stations must offer equal broadcast time to all candidates for a political office.
- On September 29, WGPR-TV, an African American station in Detroit, begins operations.
- On September 30, HBO becomes a national cable network via satellite.
- On October 11, *Saturday Night Live* debuts on NBC.
- In November, DC Comics and Marvel Comics publish their first joint venture, an adaptation of *The Wizard of Oz.* The following year they publish *Superman vs. the Amazing Spider-Man.*

1976

- More than one hundred children from ages four to six are asked which they prefer—"television or daddy?" Forty-five percent respond that they prefer television.
- Chicago educational station WTTW hires film critics Gene Siskel and Roger Ebert, from rival newspapers, to review new movies for a show called *Sneak Previews.*
- In January, Marvel Comics publishes the first issue of *Howard the Duck,* a satiric comic that quickly becomes a campus sensation.
- On January 5, *The Robert MacNeil Report,* an in-depth news program, appears on PBS across the country after a trial run on the East Coast beginning October 20, 1975. Later in 1976 it becomes *The MacNeil-Lehrer Report.*
- On April 22, Barbara Walters becomes the first female anchor of a network newscast.
- On July 10, Showtime debuts on cable television.
- In September, President Gerald Ford signs into law the Sunshine Act, which reduces the permissibility of most closed-door meetings in more than fifty government agencies. The act goes into effect March 12, 1977.
- On September 27, the first televised presidential debate between an incumbent and a challenger is held when President

Gerald Ford debates Jimmy Carter. An estimated ninety million viewers tune in.

• On November 3, *Good Morning America* premieres on ABC.

1977

• Warner Cable Corporation establishes QUBE, an interactive multichannel cable system, in Columbus, Ohio.

• ABC becomes the highest-rated network for the first time, thanks to popular shows such as *Charlie's Angels, Happy Days, The Six Million Dollar Man,* and the phenomenally successful miniseries *Roots.*

• National Lampoon, Inc., publishes the first issues of *Heavy Metal,* which reprints European adult comics.

• On February 7, the Federal Trade Commission prohibits television advertising for Spider-Man vitamins directly to children.

• In Spring, *Isaac Asimov's Science Fiction Magazine* appears for the first time.

• On March 5, President Jimmy Carter holds a national call-in interview show on radio.

• In April, the Christian Broadcasting Network (CBN) makes its debut.

• In September, the cable-television USA Network debuts.

• On October 10, *The Dick Cavett Show* premieres on PBS.

• On November 30, Eric Sevareid retires after thirty-eight years with CBS.

1978

• Led by Knight-Ridder and Gannett, 167 newspaper groups own more than 60 percent of the 1,753 daily newspapers published in the United States and enjoy 72 percent of newspaper circulation.

• The Library of Congress announces a future archive for radio and television to "preserve the broadcasting heritage of the American people."

• Jim Davis's comic strip "Garfield" first appears in newspapers.

• *Dallas* premieres on CBS.

• On January 1, the new Copyright Act, passed in 1976, goes into effect. New broadcast regulations allow programs to be copyrighted and for CATV systems to acquire secondary

rights for programs they receive on the air and send to subscribers.

• On March 4, the Chicago *Daily News* shuts down after fifteen Pulitzer Prizes and 103 years of publication.

• On July 3, the U.S. Supreme Court rules that the Federal Communications Commission can ban language that is not obscene by legal standards. The court thus overturns a 1977 Court of Appeals decision against the FCC's ability to censor programming in response to a 1973 complaint over a public-radio broadcast of George Carlin's comedy routine about the "seven dirty words you can never say on television."

• On September 25, a suit by *Sports Illustrated* reporter Melissa Ludtke is resolved by U.S. District Court judge Constance Baker Motley, who rules that baseball teams cannot keep a female sportswriter out of the locker room following a game.

• In October, *Omni* magazine, combining science articles with science fiction and fantasy, appears on the newsstands.

• On October 14, in a two-part special, "Rescue from Gilligan's Island," the seven characters from the 1964–1967 television show are finally rescued, only to be marooned on the same island at the end.

• In November, a giant Kermit the Frog balloon debuts in the Macy's Thanksgiving Parade in New York.

1979

• In the first network broadcast using fiber-optic technology, CBS employs a fiber-optic link of nearly six miles to connect Tampa Stadium with its downtown studio; from there an NFL game is broadcast to twenty cities.

• *Reader's Digest* announces that it will publish a condensed version of the Bible, reducing the content by 40 percent.

• In March, the U.S. House of Representatives establishes the Cable Satellite Public Affairs Network (C-SPAN) and allows television cameras into the chambers.

• In April, Nickelodeon makes its debut on cable television.

• In August, in response to a suit filed by Lone Ranger Television, Inc., the Los Angeles Superior Court forbids actor Clayton Moore to wear the Lone Ranger mask in public appearances. Moore appeals the decision, in the meantime donning large, dark sunglasses as part of his costume.

• On September 25, ABC offers the winning bid, $225 million, to broadcast the 1984 Summer Olympics. Rights for the previous games were acquired by NBC for $87 million.

address these issues, the *Times* saw the need to publish "writing on the widest possible range of subject matter and the widest possible variety of opinions." Finally the idea of a forum of diverse opinion is grounded in the Jeffersonian notion that freedom, democracy, knowledge go together. "The health of this democracy," as the *Times* article puts it, "has depended on deeper public understanding of difficult issues."

The Op-Ed Page Is Born

"Times Will Offer Daily Forum Page," "Op. Ed. Page"

Newspaper article, Statement

By: *The New York Times*

Date: July 20, 1970; September 20, 1970

Source: "Times Will Offer Daily Forum Page." *The New York Times,* July 20, 1970; "Op. Ed. Page." *The New York Times,* September 20, 1970.

About the Publication: Founded in 1850 as *The Daily Times, The New York Times* was originally a relatively obscure local paper. By the early part of the twentieth century, it had grown into a widely known, well-respected news source, and has remained such since. ∎

Introduction

Every major newspaper in the United States contains an Op-Ed section (so-called because it is opposite the editorial page) reserved for the opinions and views of people from outside the newspaper's regular pool of writers and columnists. Today, the "Op-Ed" page is taken for granted, but it has only been around since September 20, 1970, when *The New York Times* published its first Op-Ed columns. The *Times,* one of the world's leading media institutions, publishes "all the news that's fit to print," and while it presents balanced and fair-minded reporting and analysis, its editorial policy is unapologetically liberal, representing the liberal-leaning East Coast establishment. Why, then, did the *Times* decide to add this feature in 1970?

One reason would be the death of other major editorial voices, as newspapers in the New York City area such as the *Herald Tribune* and in other large metropolitan centers went out of business in the late 1960s. Another reason would be the complexity of problems Americans faced in this period: the war in Vietnam and the cold war, the draft and dissent on the home front, and the swift pace of the civil rights revolution. Just on the horizon was the sexual liberation movement and the struggle of women for full equality. To understand and

Significance

The original intention of the *Times* in establishing its daily Op-Ed forum on "the whole range of human affairs" was to welcome opinions that were in disagreement with those of the editorial page. The objective was to allow "greater opportunity for exploration of issues and presentation of new insights and new ideas by writers . . . whose views will frequently be completely divergent from our own." This in turn is based on "our belief [that] the diverse voices of our society must be given the greatest possible opportunity to be heard." Just two-and-a-half years later, Carl Gresham remarks in his *Commentary* article "The 'Times' Op-Ed Page: Both Ends Against the Middle" that the Op-Ed page had become a powerful presence in American culture.

Yet Gersham also points out evidence that during the first thirty months of op-ed pieces, the focus on current political and social issues was skewed along "radical chic" lines. This may have been inevitable, given the *Times'* original intention to find views "completely divergent" from its own. If the *Times* is the voice of the northeastern liberal establishment, then completely divergent views would be those held by the far ends, left and right, of the political spectrum. Thus, on a whole range of issues—student protest, race relations, moral responsibility, and the political health of American society—the *Times* gave a voice to the few on the side of the "apocalyptic," the radical, the alienated, and the extreme against the large moderate middle. As an example, the *Times* favored thinkers who drew a moral equivalence between the free and democratic America and the totalitarian Soviet Union, as well as those who praised the "reforms" and revolutions of Chairman Mao.

Primary Source

"Times Will Offer Daily Forum Page"

SYNOPSIS: In this article *The New York Times* announces that it will soon be creating a new "Op-Ed page." It explains that the purpose behind the new feature is to create a public forum for editorial views of people not associated with, and sometimes in opposition to, the editors of the newspaper.

A.M. Rosenthal, managing editor of *The New York Times* in 1970.
AP/WIDE WORLD PHOTOS. REPRODUCED BY PERMISSION.

Special Opinion Articles Will Supplement Columns

A daily forum providing a wide variety of views and opinions will be established on the page opposite the editorial page of The New York Times, Arthur Ochs Sulzberger, publisher of The Times, announced yesterday.

Mr. Sulzberger said the new Op-Ed page "was designed to afford a greater opportunity than has heretofore existed in The Times for American and foreign writers to put forward their ideas in the form of original signed articles on subjects covering the whole range of human affairs, but with specific attention to current political and social issues."

"Points of view in disagreement with the editorial position of The Times will be particularly welcomed," the publisher added.

The new page, conceived as part of an expanded editorial department, will be under the supervision of John B. Oakes, editor of the editorial page of The Times.

Harrison E. Salisbury, who for the last several years has served as an assistant managing editor of The Times, has been appointed editor of the Op-Ed page. The assistant editor will be Herbert Mitgang of the editorial board of The Times, who has been in charge of the weekly "Topics" column, which will be merged into the new page.

Comment From Abroad

In addition to the daily articles by non-Times writers, the page will also contain occasional material from foreign periodicals of special interest to American readers.

The five regular columnists of The Times—James B. Reston, C. L. Sulzberger, Tom Wicker, Russell Baker and Anthony Lewis—and the signed Monday column written by members of the editorial board will be moved to the Op-Ed page from their present weekday location on the editorial page.

Other Times writers will not be excluded, but the publisher emphasized: "The purpose of the Op-Ed page is not to offer our own in-house experts more space. Rather, it is a spot for the expert on the outside."

The space devoted to letters to the editor on the editorial page will be expanded, permitting. The Times to publish about twice as many letters from readers as at present. Kalman Seigel will continue as letters editor, also under the editorial department.

The obituary page of The Times, which has been opposite the editorial page for many years, will be moved to a regular position elsewhere in the daily paper.

The publisher said the changes would take place in mid-September.

Primary Source

"Op. Ed. Page"

SYNOPSIS: This brief article marks the innauguration of *The New York Times*', Op-Ed page on September 20, 1970.

As the world has grown smaller, the nation more powerful, the problems besetting man infinitely more complex, the pressures more intense, the health of this democracy has increasingly depended on deeper public understanding of difficult issues. Through the new page opposite the Editorial Page that we inaugurate today, we hope that a contribution may be made toward stimulating new thought and provoking new discussion on public problems. All of The Times's regular Editorial Page columnists will appear with their usual frequency on the new page, but they will be joined by two or more outside contributors six days a week, writing on the widest possible range of subject matter and expressing the widest possible variety of opinion.

The purpose of the Op. Ed. page is neither to reinforce nor to counterbalance The Times's own editorial position, which will continue to be presented as usual in these columns. The objective is rather to afford greater opportunity for exploration of issues and presentation of new insights and new ideas by writers and thinkers who have no institutional connection with The Times and whose views will very frequently be completely divergent from our own. In this respect, the Op. Ed. page is in fact a logical outgrowth of the "Topics" column that has appeared on this page each Saturday for the past few years.

In furtherance of our belief that the diverse voices of our society must be given the greatest possible opportunity to be heard, we are at the same time approximately doubling the weekday space devoted to letters from our readers.

The two pages together—Editorial and Op. Ed.—are designed to create an intellectual forum from which, to paraphrase Terence, nothing will be foreign that relates to man and his society.

Further Resources

BOOKS

Goulden, Joseph C. *Fit to Print: A.M. Rosenthal and his Times.* Secaucus, N.J.: L. Stuart, 1988.

Salisbury, Harrison, with David Schneiderman, ed. *The Indignant Years: Art and Articles from the Op-Ed Page of the "New York Times."* New York: Crown/Arno Press, 1973.

Salisbury, Harrison. *Without Fear or Favor: An Uncompromising Look at the "New York Times."* New York: Ballantine Books, 1981.

PERIODICALS

Brown, Clyde. "Daring to Be Heard: Advertorials by Organized Interests on the Op-Ed Page of *The New York Times,* 1985–1998." *Political Communication,* January 2001, 23, 28.

Gersham, Carl. "The 'Times' Op-Ed Page: Both Ends Against the Middle." *Commentary,* April 1973.

Rosenfeld, Stephen S. "The Op-Ed Page: A Step to a Better Democracy." *Harvard International Journal of Press/Politics* 5, no. 3, 2000, 7–11.

"A Personal Report from *Ms.*"

Magazine article

By: *Ms.* Magazine

Date: July 1972

Source: "A Personal Report from *Ms.*" *Ms.,* July 1972, 4–7.

About the Publication: *Ms.* magazine was founded in 1972 under the editorial leadership of Gloria Steinem and Robin Morgan. Since then, it has served as a vehicle for writing by, for, and about women. Since 1990, the publication has been ad free, enabling it to maintain its editorial independence. ■

Introduction

In the 1970s, women were increasingly present in the higher reaches of American education and in higher paying jobs, and they were increasingly likely to be in the market for the same goods and services as men: cars, travel, electronics, insurance, and so on. Women were also being more assertive politically and socially, with many fighting for an end to sex discrimination and the acceptance of women as equal to men in all walks of life. There was a need for a magazine that would reflect these changes in the lifestyle of American women. *Ms.* magazine was designed to fill this need. It would be a national magazine in the mould of *Time* or *Newsweek,* but it would be controlled by women and reflect the interests and values of "the New American Woman."

There were huge obstacles to be overcome if this project was to be successful. No one had attempted a magazine of this nature before, and it was difficult to find funds and staff. A small but dedicated group of founders, who believed sincerely in the project, were able to overcome these problems. They managed to secure the backing of some key individuals, such as Katherine Graham, publisher of *The Washington Post* and Clay Felker of *New York* magazine. Once the first issue was launched "on a wing and a prayer," and proved to be more successful than anyone had dared to hope, Warner Communications Inc. stepped in to provide the financial backing for *Ms.* to move forward as a major vehicle for the feminist point of view.

Significance

Ms. became a successful journalistic and business enterprise by creating a magazine that catered to the modern woman's tastes and preferences in just the right way. It was run by women, took women's concerns seriously, and treated its female audience as every bit as capable and important as men. The very title *Ms.* became a symbol of the new attitude toward women that would be required of all who would have dealings with her. Rather than the terms "Miss," or "Mrs.," with their focus on a woman's marital status, this new woman was "Ms.," a title that gives no indication of marital status, indicating its irrelevance. *Ms.* argued strenuously for the main issues it saw as vital to women in the 1970s: a woman's right to choose an abortion, equal pay for equal work, the Equal Rights Amendment to the Constitution, and women's health. Gloria Steinem became the most well known of the magazine's founders, for many putting a face on the concept or "ideal" of the modern woman.

The role of women in American society has been an issue of crucial importance and serious debate since the nation's founding. Susan B. Anthony and Elizabeth Cady Stanton stood up for women's rights as part of the temperance and antislavery movements of the nineteenth century, the suffragettes fought hard to win women the vote in the World War I period, and "Rosie the Riveter" showed what she could do in the factories during World War II. Thus, nothing was new about women playing a key role in American history. In some ways, these earlier phases reached their culmination in the women's movement in the 1960s and 1970s. At this time, the women's movement identified itself with the struggle of African Americans for civil rights, which had reached its own milestone in 1964 with the passage of civil rights legislation under the Johnson administration. In this context, the reenergizing of the women's movement seemed to form a part of a broader historical trend to extend freedom and equality to segments of society that had hitherto played a subordinate role in the politics and economy of the country.

Thirty years after it founding, *Ms.* may no longer draw the attention it did in the heady days of the 1970s, but it has continued as a successful participant in the competitive magazine wars. *Ms.,* like many other print productions in the new digital age, is online. To the issues the magazine has always supported, it has added more contemporary concerns it sees as of special interest to women, such as the fight against AIDS and smoking, voter registration, and national energy policies. Steinem continues to believe that the women's movement has many more mountains to climb and that the best is yet to come. She suggested that "the changes made by women's movements here and around the world in just a few decades" have been "wider and deeper than the Industrial Revolution." She then asks her readers to "project that same degree of transformation into the future." To think in terms of such sweeping change, she says, "is the first step toward creating it." Steinem "thought big" in the 1970s and proceeded to turn her and her colleagues' daring idea into a successful national magazine. She has continued to see the future as an open-ended adventure for women and with them, society as a whole.

Primary Source

"A Personal Report from *Ms.*"

SYNOPSIS: This article provides an overview of the creation of *Ms.*, including its initial conception and the struggles of its founders to get it up and running. It recounts the immense difficulties involved in launching a new nationwide magazine and the even greater difficulties in launching one with a special mission to give voice to a social movement.

First, there were some women writers and editors who started asking questions. Why was our work so unconnected to our lives? Why were the media, including women's magazines, so rarely or so superficially interested in the big changes happening to women? Why were we always playing the game by somebody else's (the publisher's, the advertiser's) rules?

Then, there were questions from activists; women who were trying to raise money for an information service and self-help projects, particularly for poor or isolated women, and having very little luck. Mightn't a publication—say, a newsletter—serve to link up women, and to generate income as well?

The two groups met several times early in 1971, and agreed that we all wanted a publication that was owned by and honest about women. Then we did some hard financial figuring. Newsletters that made decent profits seem confined to giving stock-market tips, or servicing big corporations. Some small but valuable ones for women were already struggling along. Besides, newsletters were a fine service for people already interested, but weren't really meant to reach out in a populist way.

So the idea of a full-fledged national magazine came up; a publication created and controlled by women that could be as serious, outrageous, satisfying, sad, funky, intimate, global, compassionate, and full of change as women's lives really are.

Of course, we knew that many national magazines were folding, or doing poorly. Rocketing production and mailing costs, plus competition from television for both advertising and subject matter, had discouraged some of the people who loved magazines most. Even those magazines still flourishing were unresponsive to the silenced majority. Women just weren't getting serious or honest coverage, and we doubted that we were the only people who felt the need for change. Besides, the Women's Movement had raised our hopes; it had given us courage.

So we had many more meetings, and we made big plans: long lists of article ideas, a mock-up of illustration and design, proposed budgets; everything. Then we spent many months making appointments, looking for backing from groups that invest in new ventures—and just as many months getting turned down. Flat.

Why? Well, we usually heard one or several reasons like these from potential investors:

. . . all around us, magazines are failing; why spend money to buck the tide?

. . . even though local or "special interest" magazines are making money (curiously, anything directed at the female 53 percent of the population is regarded as "special interest"), they are bad investments compared to, say, apartment buildings, computer hardware, and the like;

. . . the more we insisted on retaining at least 51 percent of the stock, the more everyone told us that investors don't give money without getting control; who ever heard of a national magazine controlled by its staff?

. . . setting aside some of the profits (supposing there were any) to go back to the Women's Movement is so unbusinesslike as to be downright crazy—even black magazines or other publications attached to movements haven't managed that;

. . . and, finally, the investors said, there are probably only ten or twenty thousand women in the country interested in changing women's status anyway; certainly not enough to support a nationwide magazine.

We got discouraged. Some of us thought we would either have to jettison a requirement or two, or give up. But there was support: friendly magazine people who thought we should try to find "public-spirited" money; women in advertising who were themselves trying to create ads that were a service to women; feminist speakers who had been traveling around the country and *knew* that a mass audience was there.

Most of all, there were the several women writers and editors, one businesswoman, and some all-purpose feminist volunteers who were willing to contribute their talents and time in return for very little except hope. "It's very simple," said one of the writers. "We all want to work for a magazine we read."

Then, two concrete things happened to bolster our hopes. First, Katherine Graham, one of the few women publishers in the country, was willing to pretend that a few shares of stock in a nonexistent magazine were worth buying; a fiction that allowed

Gloria Steinem stands in front of the White House with a large mock-up cover of *Ms.* magazine. **AP/WIDE WORLD PHOTOS. REPRODUCED BY PERMISSION.**

us some money for out-of-pocket expenses. . . . Second and even more unusual was an offer from Clay Felker, editor and publisher of *New York,* a weekly metropolitan magazine. He had thought up an ingenious way of helping *Ms.* produce the thing it needed most: a nationwide test; a sample issue to prove that we could create a new kind of magazine, and that women would buy it.

The plan was this. *New York* needed something special for its year-end double issue, and also wanted practice in producing national "one-shot" magazines (single issues devoted to a particular area or subject). *Ms.* needed the money and editorial freedom to produce a sample issue. Therefore, *New York* offered to bear the full risk of the $125,000 necessary to pay printers, binders, engravers, paper mills, distributors, writers, artists, and all the other elements vital to turning out 300,000 copies of our Preview Issue. (Plus supplying the great asset of *New York*'s production staff, without which the expenses would have been much higher.) In return, some of the *Ms.* articles and features would appear first as an insert in that year-end issue of *New York,* half of the newsstand profits (if any) of our own Preview Issue would go to *New York,* and so would all of the advertising proceeds. . . .

It was an odd way of introducing a magazine, but a generous and unusual offer—the first time, as far as we knew, that one magazine would give birth to another without the *quid pro quo* of editorial control, or some permanent financial interest. Clay Felker made a few gruff noises about how it was strictly a business deal. After all, didn't *New York* stand to make a profit if *Ms.* did very well? (This last was generally said in earshot of his Board of Directors, who might otherwise think he was as crazy as we were.)

Several of us were regular writers for *New York,* however, and we had a different idea. Over the years, we must have convinced him, or at least worn him down: Clay had begun to believe, like us, that something deep, irresistible, and possibly historic was happening to women.

The Preview Issue

In a small office, with four people working full time and the rest of us helping when we could get away from our jobs, the Spring Preview Issue was put together, start to finish, in two months. There were a lot of close calls and emergencies: cherished article ideas that didn't get finished on time, authors whose other commitments made them drop out at the last minute, indecision about the cover which resulted in doing four of them, and an eleventh-hour discovery that we had one week and eight pages less than we thought.

But the work got done, and the decisions got made. They happened communally. We never had time to sit down and discuss our intellectual aversion to the hierarchy of most offices, where decisions and orders float down from above. We just chose not to do anything with which one of us strongly disagreed. And we didn't expect our more

junior members to get coffee, or order lunch, or do all the typing, or hold some subordinate title. We each did as much of our own phone-answering and manuscript typing as deadlines and common sense would allow. On the masthead, we listed ourselves alphabetically, divided only by area of expertise and full-or part-time work.

Feminist philosophies often point out that a hierarchy, military or otherwise, is an imitation of patriarchy, and that there are many other ways of getting work done. We didn't approach the idea so intellectually, but we did arrive at the same conclusion from gut experience. As women, we had been on the bottom of hierarchies for too long. We knew how wasteful they really were. . . .

When the insert from our Preview Issue appeared as part of *New York* in December, the issue set a newsstand sales record; more than *New York* had ever sold. Of course, said the doomsayers, women in a metropolitan area might be interested. But would we appeal to the women of Ohio or Arizona?

When the full-length Spring Preview Issue of *Ms.* was distributed nationally in January, we packed off all available authors and staff to talk to women's groups around the country, and to appear on any radio or television shows that reached women. (Thus changing the lives of several of us, who had never spoken in public before.)

The Preview Issue was designed to stay on the newsstands for at least two months (which is why it was dated "Spring"), and we wanted to make sure women knew about it. But we got to our various assigned towns only to be met with phone calls: "Where is *Ms.?*" "We can't find a copy." "What newsstands are selling it?"

Worriedly, we called the distributor, and the truth finally dawned on us. The 300,000 copies supposed to last for at least eight weeks had virtually disappeared in eight days. *Ms. had sold out.*

We celebrated. We breathed sighs of relief. And only in that moment did we realize how worried we had been—worried that we would make the Women's Movement seem less far-reaching and strong than it was by creating a feminist magazine that did poorly; worried about *New York* Magazine's risk, and all the friends who had helped us; worried about letting down ourselves, and other women.

But the most gratifying experience was still to come. Letters came pouring into our crowded office: more than 20,000 long, literate, simple, disparate, funny, tragic and very personal letters from women all over the country, including Ohio and Arizona. They wrote about their experiences and problems. They supported or criticized, told us what they needed, what they thought should be included or excluded, and generally spoke of *Ms.* as "our" magazine. . . .

We were feeling inundated by all the mail, but didn't realize how unusual it was until we asked the editor of another women's magazine—with a circulation of 7 million, compared to our 300,000—how much editorial response each issue got. "About 2,000 letters," she said, "and a lot of them not very worthwhile. Four thousand letters of any kind would be considered quite extraordinary."

Obviously, the need for and interest in a non-establishment magazine were greater and deeper than even we had thought. More out of instinct than skill, the women of *Ms.* had tapped an emerging and deep cultural change that was happening to us, and happening to our sisters.

When all the returns were in, *New York* breathed a sigh of relief, too. Their share of the newsstand sales was $20,000. And so was ours. We felt very rich indeed, until we figured out that our check wouldn't pay even half the postage for one national mailing of a letter inviting people to subscribe. In fact, if we had paid ourselves salaries, we would have just about broken even. We were learning the terrible truth of how much it costs to start a magazine, even one that readers want. . . .

Where We Are Now . . .

After the Preview Issue, we spent another three months looking for investors who believed in the magazine, and who would therefore give us the backing we needed without taking financial and editorial control.

In spite of all the looking, we can't take credit for finding Warner Communications. They found us. We are grateful to them for exploring many kinds of new media. And we are especially impressed that they took the unusual position of becoming the major investor, but minority stockholder, in *Ms.* It's a step forward for free women, and free journalism.

We still must reach the break-even point with a third of the money, and in a third of the time, that most magazines require. (The average seems to be $3 million and three years before a national publication begins to show profit.) But, thanks to the head start from *New York* and our subscribers, plus the opportunity given us by Warner Communications, we have a fighting chance.

If we do make it, we will own ourselves. We will also be able to give a healthy percentage of our profits back to the Women's Movement; to programs and projects that can help change women's lives.

In addition to financial struggles, the past few months have been spent gathering a staff. Our full-time members now number twenty instead of four, and a few more of us are helping part-time. Soon, there will be more names added to the masthead, mostly in advertising and circulation.

At the moment, we vary in age from 17 to 45, from no college at all to a Ph.D., and from experience as the editor of one of the country's biggest magazines to experience as a taxi driver. We are white Southerners, black Midwesterners, Latin American-born New Yorkers, homesick country-lovers and urbanites who never miss fresh air. One of us, an assistant art director, is male. (Since he was already working for our woman art director, he feels right at home. And so do we.) One of us is a radical Catholic, several are Jewish, and many are garden-variety WASP. We got more or less educated at Malcolm X College, Darien High School, Vassar, Smith, the University of Delhi, Millsaps College, Columbia, Radcliffe, Willamette University, the Sorbonne, the University of Wisconsin, and VISTA. We are married, never-been-married, and divorced. Some of us have children; some don't. Some of us have turned our friends into family, and some have done just the reverse.

All together, we're not a bad composite of the changing American woman.

If you asked us our philosophy for ourselves and for the magazine, each of us would give an individual answer. But we agree on one thing. We want a world in which no one is born into a subordinate role because of visible difference, whether that difference is of race or of sex. That's an assumption we make personally and editorially, with all the social changes it implies. After that, we cherish our differences. We want *Ms.* to be a forum for many views.

Most of all, we are joyfully discovering ourselves, and a world set free from old patterns, old thoughts. We hope *Ms.* will help you—and us—to explore this new world. There are few guidelines in history, or our own past. We must learn from each other.

So keep writing. *Ms.* belongs to us all.

Further Resources

BOOKS

Carroll, Peter. *It Seemed Like Nothing Happened: The Tragedy and Promise of America in the 1970s.* New York: Holt, Rinehart and Winston, 1982.

Ehrenreich, Barbara. *The Worst Years of Our Lives: Irreverent Notes from a Decade of Greed.* New York: Random House, 1990.

Mitchell, Catherine. *Yours in Sisterhood: 'Ms.' Magazine and the Promise of Popular Feminism.* New York: Simon and Schuster, 1988.

Morgan, Robin, ed. *Sisterhood Is Powerful: An Anthology of Writings from the Women's Liberation Movement.* New York: Vintage, 1990.

Noonan, John T. *A Private Choice: Abortion in the Seventies.* New York: Free Press, 1972.

Rosenberg, Rosalind. *Divided Lives: American Women in the Twentieth Century.* New York: Hill and Wang, 1992.

Sondra, Henry, and Emily Taitz. *One Woman's Power: A Biography of Gloria Steinem.* Dillon Press, 1987.

Steinem, Gloria. *Outrageous Acts and Everyday Rebellions.* New York: Holt, Rinehart, and Winston, 1983.

"Keeping Archie Engaging and Enraging"

Newspaper article

By: John Brady

Date: February 24, 1974

Source: Brady, John. "Keeping Archie Engaging and Enraging." *The New York Times,* February 24, 1974.

About the Author: John Joseph Brady (1942–) is an American journalist. He was a partner and president of Brady and Paul Communications, a former Hearst Visiting Professor at the University of Missouri School of Journalism, and a lecturer at Boston University. He wrote a book on interviewing called *The Art of the Interview.* ■

Introduction

All in the Family premiered on CBS television on January 21, 1971. The show depicted the life of a family living in a blue-collar neighborhood in the borough of Queens in New York City. Although shows about working-class families had become rarer on television, one of the classics, *The Honeymooners,* was famous for its portrayal of a New York City bus driver, his working wife, and his best friend, a sewer worker. While the working-class characters of *All in the Family* were unusual, it was its dose of contemporary American reality that truly set it apart from other comedies, and even many dramas.

The Bunker family consisted of Archie, father and breadwinner; Edith, housewife and mother; Gloria, their college student daughter; and her husband, Mike Stivic. Together, they lived the changing face of America in the early 1970s, as viewers saw their own hopes and fears for the future portrayed each week in, for the first time,

a comedy format. Many of the era's most explosive and divisive issues, including the Vietnam War and the civil rights movement, were made the stuff of comic confrontation between right-wing bigot Archie and his liberal college student son-in-law Mike. Later, the show added another focus, the rise of the women's movement, reflected in the roles of Edith and Gloria.

Producers Norman Lear and Bud Yorkin adapted a British comedy series about a bigoted dock worker, *Till Death Us Do Part,* into a pilot called *Those Were the Days,* but ABC turned it down. CBS President Robert D. Wood, who was looking for new shows that would appeal to a more affluent, urban audience, liked the show and made a place for it. During its first few months, the show languished at the bottom of its time slot, but the critics began to take notice and word of mouth was strong. After appearing as an opening skit on the Emmy telecast, the show won three major awards, including Outstanding Comedy Series. *All in the Family* became the top-rated show in prime time and held that position for the following five seasons.

Significance

Throughout its ten-year run, *All in the Family* used humor to help its viewers confront the major controversies of its day. Archie Bunker's blatant racism was featured on virtually every episode, and many other formerly taboo or controversial subjects were dealt with on the series, including abortion, homosexuality, impotence, menopause, civil disobedience, rape, and transgender issues. Among other "firsts" on the show were the sound of a toilet flushing and a discussion of toilet paper.

The show kept its edge thanks to evolving character development and strong supporting characters, such as Edith's visiting cousin, Maude Finlay, a vehement liberal feminist played by Bea Arthur, and the Bunkers' new next-door neighbors, the upwardly mobile African American Jefferson family. Both Maude and the Jeffersons proved to be so popular that Lear created new series for them, the former centering on the burgeoning women's movement and the latter on the rise of African Americans to upper-middle-class status.

When the show became the subject of newspaper editorials and op-ed pieces, it became clear that its impact extended well beyond television. In portraying controversial topics with a humorous tone, *All in the Family* became controversial itself. There was even national debate about the use of television comedy to combat racial prejudice and social inequality. The decision by Lear to present the bigoted Archie in a sympathetic light proved especially controversial, with some critics arguing that viewers sympathetic to Archie's views would feel their prejudices were justified.

In a scene from the television show *All in the Family,* Archie Bunker, played by Carroll O'Connor, argues with the rest of his on-screen family, 1972.
© BETTMANN/CORBIS. REPRODUCED BY PERMISSION.

All in the Family had a lasting impact on television by supplanting the light, domestic plots and refined humor of previous family sitcoms with topical and controversial issues treated with realism and humor. The show also brought a more vulgar sense of comedy to television, paving the way for the crude humor of shows such as *Roseanne, Married with Children,* and *The Simpsons.*

Primary Source

"Keeping Archie Enraged and Engaging"

> **SYNOPSIS:** In this article, the two head writers for the sitcom *All in the Family* explain how they make Archie's bigotry both foolish and funny without alienating the audience.

Behind the anger of America's foremost WASP bigot, blustering Archie Bunker, are two fiftyish "total New Yorkers" who have been close friends and partners, off and on, for the past 30 years. Michael Ross and Bernie West, as the story editors for "All

in the Family," are the chief architects for the plotlines, jokes and jabs that engage and often engage millions of viewers each week.

In addition to doing their own original scripts for "All in the Family," Ross and West oversee the writing of every story idea accepted from freelance writers. Their involvement with the show is total. "Most situation comedies in Hollywood are 10-to-5 jobs for the writers," says Ross. "But on 'Family' there is a kind of community effort. Everybody stays with it until the final moment."

"We start the season a few scripts ahead, but right now the script we're writing this week will be ready for shooting next week," Ross continues. "It's hectic, but it also allows us to use a lot of topical humor."

Occasionally, *too* topical. Last summer, for instance, Ross and West wrote a "run" in which Carroll O'Connor, as Archie, calls somebody a Mick, then says, "What's wrong with that? I wouldn't mind it if somebody called me an American."

TV producer Norman Lear, creator of *All in the Family* and its spinoff *The Jeffersons.* AP/WIDE WORLD PHOTOS. REPRODUCED BY PERMISSION.

One week later, John J. Wilson, the lawyer for John Ehrlichman and H.R. Haldeman, called Senator Inouye of the Watergate Committee "that little Jap," then explained away the racial slur by saying he wouldn't mind being called "a little American." "The script was broadcast, but that run was dropped because it would have looked like we were copying Washington," recalls Ross. "It was life imitating art, and we beat life to it."

The chief joy of working on "All in the Family," according to Ross and West, is the tremendous freedom the show gives its writers. "When you hear about other shows not being able to say this or that, it's nice to be with a show where we can be as free as we are," says West. "I'm not just talking about profanity either. It's the topics, the treatments, and the latitude we have to make things as funny and as true-to-life as possible. Other shows have problems."

Actually, the show's writers are insulated from network flak by producer Norman Lear, who fights all the battles and generally has his way. "When you are number one, they're more lenient. It's a commercial enterprise, television," reflects Ross. Ross

and West do hear about hate mail, however, such as the bagfuls that arrived after an episode in which Lionel, the Bunkers' black neighbor, dated Archie's niece.

On another occasion, when Ross and West were on a California radio show, a woman phoned the station. "I love the show," she said, "but the language! Could you cut out a few of the hells and the damns?" Ross: "I sympathized with her. In terms of her upbringing, a hell and a damn are shocking things. I tried to tell her that we did not use hell or damn for the hell of it." West: "And shocked her again."

This season the language barrier for sitcoms was vaulted once again in an "All in the Family" episode called "We're Having a Heat Wave." After being provoked by son-in-law Mike's taunts about Nixon and Watergate, Archie explodes: "Goddamit, I don't want to hear any more!" When a shocked Edith chastises him, he explains that it's not a swear word, really: "God, that's your most popular word in the Bible. And dam—like you dam your rivers or something, you know. When somebody does something bad, God dams him. So there it is: Goddamit. A great word in the Bible."

"A lot of mail on that one, too," says West. The script that got the most mail of all, however, was "The Battle of the Month" last season. This episode featured Gloria, in the midst of her menstrual period, having a serious quarrel with, of all people, Edith. "People wrote in saying things like, 'How can you mention menstruation?' We never expected that, but we were inundated with letters," recalls Ross.

Archie's Goddamit, Gloria's menstrual woes and similar groundbreaking material are defended by Ross and West as being integral to particular scripts. "The thinking behind the Goddamit is that a man like Archie will occasionally, when completely infuriated, say Goddamit as we all do," says Ross. "He was really provoked. We didn't throw it into the script just for the sake of throwing it in. Nor did we do the menstrual episode for shock value. We needed Gloria irritated to the point where she would blow up at Edith. In fact, we got the idea from Sally Struthers herself. When she has her menstrual period, forget it. She can't work, she's headachy, she's irritable—we took it from her. And it worked."

The complaints that hurt Ross and West the most are the ones from special interest groups, such as the writer from Ebony magazine who said, "There is evidence that impressionable white children have picked up and are using many of the old racial slurs

which Archie has resurrected, popularized and made 'acceptable' all over again."

"I've lived in the ghettos, I was brought up in the slums," says Ross. "You cannot tell me that a black hears the words 'nigger' or 'spade' for the first time from someone who's just watched Archie Bunker. At least when Archie says it, we hit him hard for it." Adds West: "There are many instances where Lionel has told Archie off, or Mike and Gloria have put Archie down. We've done things very much pro-black."

The two Jewish writers are especially sensitive to the criticism of Rabbi Benjamin R. Epstein, national director of the Anti-Defamation League of B'nai B'rith, who has called it "regrettable that a very funny program makes light of the vicious ethnic slur and makes the bigot tolerable."

"I don't think we make the bigot or the racial epithet tolerable," says West. "We show him up for the ridiculous fellow he is. We show the epithet up for being inaccurate and ridiculous not only for the Jewish people but for any racial or ethnic group. Archie makes statements so ridiculous that nobody but a real bigot would go along with them." Adds Ross, "We write for what we think, in these miserable, rotten times, are still rational, halfway moralistic, thinking people. We'll never please everybody. Ever."

In a lighter vein, a group of nuns once wrote to the show complaining about the way Archie treats Edith. He should be nicer to her, they said. While it's debatable whether or not Archie is nicer this season, most will agree that Edith at least seems more formidable. In an episode called "The Gambler" she even slapped Archie when he lied to her about betting on a horse.

"Edith is The Innocent," says West, "but in her innocence she is knowledgeable. She is truth all the way, but when pushed far enough she says, 'Wait a minute. This is it.' We try very hard not to make her too dumb, too much of a Gracie Allen character. Edith is growing. She is not going to be a doormat."

"As we write the characters more and more, they all grow," says Ross, "Edith is tougher, Gloria is no longer the itsy-poo wife just waiting for Mike to come home from work, and Mike has learned a lot about himself, too. 'All in The Family' has reached that point in the life of a series when people say, 'Why don't you sit back and let it run?' But we are always introducing new angles, new ideas, trying to open up the characters and make them more three-dimensional."

The toughest character to open up, of course, is Archie. Ross and West acknowledge that an ongoing problem at script conferences is one of definition: Would Archie say this? Or would he say that?

A point of dispute between Carroll O'Connor and his writers is Archie's sex life. "The writers suggest that there's something wrong with Archie in a sexual way, what with the little jokes they give to Edith that have reference to his sexual inertia," says O'Connor. "But I don't believe that and I've complained about it." Observes West: "Sometimes we'll use a remark by Edith, like 'he fell asleep on the honeymoon.' But I don't think that Archie is a Don Juan in the bedroom after 25 years of marriage."

Regarding Archie's goal-line defense of the Nixon Administration, Ross says, "I think that in the back of his mind there are some suspicions, but he's gone with Nixon for so many years—as so many people in this country have—that he's going to keep right on defending him, I guess, as long as he can."

How long can a show like this go on before the material wears thin? "We are always reading the papers and looking for important subjects," says West, "but we have also found that a simple topic—like the family sitting around playing a little game of group therapy—often makes as funny and exciting a show as the big topic if we do it right. Of course, we do have a few standbys if we need them—incest, Archie's conversion to faggotry . . ."

"Don't print that," says Ross. "You won't believe the mail we'll get."

Further Resources

BOOKS

Gitlin, Todd. *Inside Prime Time.* New York: Pantheon, 1985.

Metz, Robert. *CBS: Reflections in a Bloodshot Eye.* Chicago: Playboy, 1975.

O'Neil, Thomas. *The Emmys.* New York: Penguin, 1992.

PERIODICALS

"CBS-TV's Bigot That BBC Begat Figures to Salt Up Second Season." *Variety,* July, 22, 1970.

"Family Fun." *Newsweek,* March 15, 1971.

Ferretti, Fred. "Are Racism and Bigotry Funny?" *New York Times,* January 12, 1971.

Hano, Arnold. "Can Archie Bunker Give Bigotry a Bad Name?" *The New York Times,* March 12, 1972.

Kasindorf, Martin. "Archie and Maude and Fred and Norman and Alan." *The New York Times Magazine,* June 24, 1973.

Leonard, John. "Bigotry as a Dirty Joke." *Life,* March 19, 1971.

Shayon, Robert Lewis. "Love That Hate." *Saturday Review,* March 27, 1971.

WEBSITES
All in the Family home page. Available online at http://www
.allinthefamilysit.com/ (accessed April 1, 2003).

All the President's Men
Nonfiction work

By: Bob Woodward and Carl Bernstein

Date: 1974

Source: Woodward, Bob, and Carl Bernstein. *All the President's Men.* New York: Simon and Schuster, 1974, 136–145.

About the Authors: Bob Woodward (1943–) graduated from Yale, then served for five years as a Navy communications officer during the Vietnam War (1964–1975). He joined *The Washington Post* as a reporter in 1971. He and Carl Bernstein worked together in covering the Watergate break-in and scandal in 1972–74. Their reporting and subsequent book, *All the President's Men* revealed many details about Watergate to the public for the first time and made them celebrities. Woodward went on to write many more best-selling books and was an assistant managing editor at *The Washington Post* in 2003.

Carl Bernstein (1944–) was born in Washington D.C. Bernstein joined *The Washington Post* as a full-time reporter in 1966. He and Bob Woodward covered the Watergate break-in and ensuing scandal together in 1972–74, as well as writing a book on their experience *All the President's Men.* In 1976 Bernstein left *The Washington Post,* working thereafter as a freelance reporter and for ABC. ∎

Introduction

On June 17, 1972, five men with cameras and electronic surveillance equipment were arrested late at night in the headquarters of the Democratic National Committee at the Watergate Hotel and Office Complex in Washington, D.C. Apparently a "third-rate burglary," *The Washington Post* assigned veteran crime reporter, Alfred Lewis, to the story, as well as several staff reporters, including Bob Woodward and Carl Bernstein. Woodward and Bernstein recognized early on that the break-in might have serious implications, and they continued to investigate and report on it.

Woodward and Bernstein were correct. The break-in had in fact been planned and financed by top officials at the White House and the reelection campaign of President Richard Nixon (served 1969–1974)—The Committee to Reelect the President (CRP). It would take two years of methodical investigation to prove this, however. This was due in no small part to a conspiracy by top administration officials, including Nixon himself, to cover up their role in the affair. Most of the actual investigative work into the events surrounding Watergate was done by the government itself. Many

governmental entities were eventually involved, including the police, FBI, the U.S. Attorney's Office, grand juries, and eventually U.S. House and Senate committees, the courts, and the United States Supreme Court.

Initially, however, the investigation was small and focused on the burglars themselves. The public largely ignored it. Thus the break-in had little immediate impact, and President Nixon was reelected in November 1972 by a wide margin. Woodward and Bernstein were among the few who continued to report on it and tried to keep the issue in the public eye. It was in this manner that, during the summer and fall of 1972, Woodward and Bernstein became the lead reporters for *The Washington Post's* coverage of what would become the Watergate Scandal.

Woodward and Bernstein focused on two activities during the early portions of their investigation—corroborating and publishing information leaked by government officials involved in the investigation, and discovering the activities of David Segretti, a political operative hired by White House officials to sabotage the efforts of Democrats seeking the 1972 presidential nomination. Woodward's principal source for leaked government information, "Deep Throat," remains a mysterious figure. "Deep Throat" provided corroboration for many of the Watergate stories published by *The Washington Post,* as well as suggesting that Woodward and Bernstein investigate Segretti. Although Segretti's activities ultimately proved unrelated to Watergate, the publication of the results of Woodward and Bernstein's inquiry into the "dirty tricks" done on behalf of Nixon focused public scrutiny on the Watergate scandal and added to the political pressure mounting on the administration in 1973.

Despite the efforts of Nixon and his advisors to cover-up their involvement in the Watergate break-in, the case against them slowly mounted throughout 1973 and 1974. Some of those involved in Watergate began to testify against each other, and in July 1973 it was revealed that Nixon had all conversations at the White House since 1970 on tape. These tapes could resolve who was involved in Watergate and when, and the Senate committee and special prosecutor investigating Watergate demanded they be released. Nixon fought hard to keep them secret, but the U.S. Supreme Court ruled unanimously on July 24, 1974, that he had to surrender the secret White House tapes to investigators.

With no choice but to comply, Nixon handed over the tapes. They demonstrated that virtually all of the administration's top officials, including President Nixon, conspired to cover up the administration's role in the burglary. Congress soon began procedures to impeach

Nixon, and his advisors informed him that he was sure to be removed from office as a result. Rather than face this added humiliation, Nixon resigned as president on August 8, 1974.

Significance

Woodward and Bernstein's book, *All the President's Men,* provides a detailed account of the first eleven months of *The Washington Post's* investigation and internal decisions surrounding its coverage of Watergate. The official investigation into Watergate was still in its early stages at that point. Few realized its significance. Woodward and Bernstein's reporting played an important role in revealing to the public the various illegal and unethical activities of Nixon's 1972 presidential campaign, adding to the pressure that the official government investigation was putting on Nixon's administration. *The Washington Post* won a Pulitzer Prise in 1973 for their coverage of Watergate.

Published in 1974, *All the President's Men,* was a huge commercial success and made its authors stars. A 1976 movie version was also very successful. This success and fame has contributed to the idea that Woodward and Bernstein's investigative work was what uncovered the truth about Watergate. In reality, they principally corroborated and reported on information leaked to them by people involved in the official investigation. The book itself is dedicated "To the President's other men and women—in the White House and elsewhere—who took risks to provide us with confidential information. Without them there would have been no Watergate story told by *The Washington Post.*"

While it is not true that the media investigation uncovered Watergate, the media nevertheless played an important part in the scandal. The criminal investigation into the scandal was performed largely by government entities that were focused on collecting evidence for trial, not informing the public. By corroborating leaked information, challenging the administration relentlessly for explanations, and publicizing the administration's abuses of power, Woodward, Bernstein, and the press revealed the illegal activities of Nixon and his advisors to public scrutiny.

The Washington Post's coverage of Watergate was also significant in that it helped usher in a new era of public cynicism toward government actions. This scandal, coming after years of mounting distrust of government caused by the unpopular Vietnam War (1964–75), greatly damaged the faith most Americans had previously held in their government. Americans in general, and the media in particular, would no longer accept government statements without scrutiny.

Primary Source

All the President's Men [excerpt]

SYNOPSIS: *All the President's Men* is the story of Bob Woodward and Carl Bernstein's investigation of the Watergate break-in and the scandal that resulted from it. This excerpt demonstrates how the two men and their colleagues at *The Washington Post* explored and reported on many aspects of the 1972 Republican presidential campaign's "dirty tricks," including the forged "Canuck Letter" that made Democractic presidential candidate Edmund Muskie seem like a racist.

Woodward arrived at the office four hours later and typed his notes from the meeting with Deep Throat. A carbon was in Bernstein's typewriter when he arrived half an hour later. Woodward, Bernstein, Sussman and Rosenfeld met briefly. There would be three stories: a lead by Bernstein and Woodward outlining the general program of . . . espionage and sabotage by at least 50 agents; Bernstein's story on Segretti; an account by Woodward of White House involvement in the Canuck Letter episode. . . .

As he often did when he was experiencing difficulty writing, Bernstein walked across the newsroom to the water cooler. Marilyn Berger a national-staff reporter who covers the State Department, came up to him as he scanned the bulletin board. She asked if he and Woodward knew about the Canuck Letter.

Sure, he said, they were writing it for tomorrow.

He took another sip before the peculiarity of the question struck him. Woodward had only found out about the Canuck Letter at six that morning. They were careful in the office not to talk about what they were working on. The only people Bernstein or Woodward had mentioned the letter to were Sussman, Rosenfeld, Simons, Bradlee and David Broder, the *Post*'s senior political reporter.

How did Marilyn know about it?

"Dave [Broder] hasn't told you?" she asked.

Told them what?

"That Ken Clawson wrote the Canuck Letter," Marilyn said. . . .

Berger explained that Clawson, their former colleague on the *Post,* had told her matter of factly over a drink that he had written the Canuck Letter. He had said it several times.

The coincidence seemed too much. Bernstein suspected a set-up. On the same morning they learn that the White House is responsible for the Canuck

Carl Bernstein and Bob Woodward, reporters who broke the news of the Nixon campaign's involvement in the break-in of the Watergate Hotel, 1973. AP/WIDE WORLD PHOTOS. REPRODUCED BY PERMISSION.

Letter, Marilyn Berger waltzes into the newsroom and says Ken Clawson did it?

But Berger said Clawson had told her about it more than two weeks earlier—before Bernstein had ever heard of Segretti. Besides, he thought. Clawson was just the kind who would think nothing of pulling such a trick.

. . . It was decided that Berger should try to lunch with Clawson that afternoon and see if he would repeat himself.

Meanwhile, she filed a memo describing her conversation with Clawson.

Memo from M. Berger (Eyes Only). On the evening of September 25, 1972, at approximately 8:30 P.M., Ken Clawson telephoned me at my apartment to invite me out for a drink. I said I had already eaten dinner, was very tired, but if he wanted to come over for a drink he could. I invited him because he had called twice before with the same invitation in the course of the previous weeks, and I had said "no" each time. When Ken arrived I offered him a drink. He accepted a scotch—I forget if it was with water or soda, but I know he took ice. We sat down to talk. I had Sanka. In the course of the discussion (I would say

about the first ten minutes or so) we started talking about being a reporter and being a government official. He said we reporters knew only a fraction of what goes on. I asked him if, now that he was in the White House, he would be a better reporter when he left. He said he had covered the White House before, but could *really* cover it now. He may have said something about knowing where all the bodies are buried, but I'm not absolutely sure of that.

It was then that he said, "I wrote the . . . letter." I think he said the Canuck letter, but in any case he clearly announced that he wrote that [Muskie] letter. I was so shocked I felt queasy. I asked him why. He said it was because Muskie was the candidate who would represent the strongest opposition and they wanted him out. When I said Muskie must have reacted beyond all their expectations, he indicated "yes."

. . . This is the part of the conversation that evening that dealt with the Canuck letter and related matters. Naturally we spoke about a number of other things. . . .

Clawson accepted her invitation for a one-o'clock lunch. Berger returned to the office about three and filed another memo.

Lunch at Sans Souci (he bought). I told Ken that Woodward and Bernstein were on to a big story of which the Canuck letter was a part, that they had traced it to the White House and that I had said, "That's not new, Ken said he did it." Ken looked very serious, as he had throughout the lunch. . . .

. . . Concerning the Canuck letter, he said he wished I hadn't said that to the boys. I said I didn't know that was anything new. He said that Woodward and Bernstein "can't possibly have traced it to the White House" or, "it can't possibly have been traced to the White House." On the statement to me, he said he would "deny it on a stack of Bibles over his mother's grave." He dropped it, then returned to it, asking what they had. I told him I wasn't entirely sure, but on the letter part they had traced some fellow from New England who went to Florida for the Muskie thing etc. I was very vague. He said he would deny it.

Later he returned to it and asked if I wanted to take down what he wanted to say about it or if I wanted to let them [Woodward and Bernstein] call. Then he said better let them call.

Bradlee, the other editors and Bernstein and Woodward studied Berger's memo. Clawson had not denied saying that he had written the letter. Woodward called Clawson at the White House. Now Clawson asserted that he had not admitted writing the letter in the first place and that the entire matter was a misunderstanding.

Woodward said that the editors believed Berger and that the *Post* was going to use what she had reported.

Clawson said: "That's your privilege. I just hope you include my denial. Marilyn misunderstood. She's a professional and did not deliberately do anything unprofessional. We were just shooting the breeze about the election. We were not in an interview situation." . . .

Clawson maintained that the first time he had heard of the Canuck Letter was when "I saw it on television" following Muskie's February 26 appearance. "I know nothing about it" aside from that, he insisted.

■ ■ ■

At about 6:00 P.M. the editors and Bernstein and Woodward had a final meeting with Bradlee on the stories.

"What do you have and how are you saying it?" Bradlee asked.

The reporters had abandoned the earlier plan for three stories. Instead, Woodward was writing an account of the Canuck Letter, including Clawson's alleged role, and Bernstein was writing a Segretti-espionage-sabotage story. Copies of the half-finished accounts were passed to Bradlee.

He brought his chair close to his oval table-desk, held his hand in the air to request silence and began reading. Simons was reading another set of carbons. Rosenfeld nervously swiveled his orange chair in quarter-turns. Occasionally, whispered comments went back and forth. Sussman sat quietly with his legs crossed.

"Fellas"—Bradlee broke the silence—"you've got one story here. Put it into one, fit it together. It's all part of the same thing."

He turned his chair 180 degrees to his own typewriter on the ledge behind the oval table, opened a drawer and pulled out a piece of two-ply paper.

"Never mind the first several paragraphs," Bradlee said, "you work that out." He began on a section which would deal with Clawson and the letter. He banged out two long paragraphs, then flipped the page across the table to Woodward, Bernstein, meanwhile, went to his desk and wrote:

FBI agents have established that the Watergate bugging incident stemmed from a massive campaign of political spying and sabotage conducted on behalf of President Nixon's re-election and directed by officials of the White House and the Committee for the Re-election of the President.

The activities, according to information in FBI and Department of Justice files, were aimed at all the major Democratic presidential contenders and—since 1971—represented a basic strategy of the Nixon re-election effort.

Bernstein passed the draft around, first to Woodward and then to the editors who had gathered around his desk. All agreed. Not a word was changed, unusual on such a sensitive story, especially given the number of editors involved.

Woodward added the third paragraph:

During their Watergate investigation federal agents established that hundreds of thousands of dollars in Nixon campaign contributions had been set aside to pay for an extensive undercover campaign aimed at discrediting individual Democratic presidential candidates and disrupting their campaigns.

And, from suggestions made primarily by Sussman, the fourth paragraph.

"Intelligence work" is normal during a campaign and is said to be carried out by both political parties. But federal investigators said what they uncovered being done by the Nixon forces is unprecedented in scope and intensity.

Despite lack of specific examples, the crucial fifth and sixth paragraphs related that the espionage and sabotage included:

Following members of Democratic candidates' families; assembling dossiers of their personal lives; forging letters and distributing them under the candidates' letterheads; leaking false and manufactured items to the press; throwing campaign schedules into disarray; seizing confidential campaign files and investigating the lives of dozens of Democratic campaign workers.

In addition, investigators said the activities included planting provocateurs in the ranks of organizations expected to demonstrate at the Republican and Democratic conventions; and investigating potential donors to the Nixon campaign before their contributions were solicited.

Woodward called Shumway, CRP's principal spokesman, read him the first six paragraphs and outlined the Segretti business and the allegations involving Clawson and the letter.

"Now read me that again," Shumway said, apparently stunned.

Woodward repeated.

"That's one I'll have to get back to you on," Shumway said. "Now let me get it straight. You're doing that for tomorrow? . . . This never ceases to amaze me."

Shumway called back an hour later, saying: "Now, are you ready? We've got a statement. 'The *Post* story is not only fiction but a collection of absurdities.'"

Woodward waited.

"That's it," Shumway said.

Woodward asked about specific points.

"It's no use, Robert," said Shumway. "That's all we are going to say. The entire matter is in the hands of the authorities."

To Woodward and Bernstein, the latest non-denial seemed to confirm their account.

The two lead paragraphs, with their sweeping statements about massive political espionage and sabotage directed by the White House at part of a basic re-election strategy, were essentially interpretive—and risky. No source had explicitly told the reporters that the substance represented the stated conclusions of the federal investigators. But they knew that there was information in the files of the FBI and the Justice Department to support their conclusions. . . . Specific examples of some of the tactics listed in the fifth and sixth paragraphs were lacking, but the hard evidence was in the Canuck Letter and Segretti's activities. Hopefully, the story would push the missing examples into the open.

Shumway's statement ran as the seventh paragraph, accompanied by the refusal of the White House to comment on the story. The next 10 paragraphs dealt with the Canuck Letter. They reported the Ken Clawson had told Marilyn Berger, on September 25, that he had written the letter, and recorded his denial.

The Segretti findings were not mentioned until the 18th paragraph, the point at which the story was continued in the inside of the paper.

The involvement of "at least 50 undercover Nixon operatives (who)traveled throughout the country trying to disrupt and spy on Democratic campaigns" was not mentioned until the 19th paragraph. And the remaining text of the 65 paragraph story was a narrative of Segretti's travels, job approaches, conversation with Bob Meyers and biographical details.

The four-column, two line head on the top half of page one read "FBI Finds Nixon Aides/Sabotaged Democrats."

The story went out over *The Washington Post—Los Angeles Times* News Service wire about 7:00 P.M. More than half of the 220 domestic subscribers used the story, several on page one, and non-subscriber coverage was broad. . . .

At the White House that noon, Ron Ziegler faced an increasingly skeptical press corps determined to challenge the administration's refusal to discuss Watergate substantively. During a 30-minute briefing, a clearly uncomfortable presidential press secretary declined 29 times to discuss the *Post* story. His response was that CRP and Clawson had "appropriately" responded, and that the White House had nothing further to say.

Further Resources

BOOKS

Hudson, Robert V. *Mass Media: A Chronological Encyclopedia of Television, Radio, Motion Pictures, Magazines, Newspapers, and Books in the United States.* New York: Garland, 1987.

Schudson, Michael. *Watergate in American Memory: How We Remember, Forget, and Reconstruct the Past.* New York: Basic Books, 1992.

Woodward, Bob, and Carl Bernstein. *The Final Days.* New York: Simon and Schuster, 1976.

PERIODICALS

McDaniel, Ann. "Watergate's Shadow." *Newsweek,* June 21, 1999, 38.

Neuchterlein, James. "Shadow: Five Presidents and the Legacy of Watergate." *Commentary,* September 1999, 66.

Rawson, Hugh. "The Words of Watergate." *American Heritage,* October 1997, 24.

Schwarz, Frederic D. "1974: Twenty-five Years Ago." *American Heritage,* April 1999, 130.

WEBSITES

Epstein, Edward J. "Did the Press Uncover Watergate?" Available online at: http://www.edwardjayepstein.com/archived/watergate.htm; website home page: http://www.edwardjayepstein.com/index.htm (accessed June 16, 2003).

Washington Post. "Watergate Revisited." Available online at http://www.washingtonpost.com/wp-srv/national/longterm/watergate/front.htm; website home page: http://www.washingtonpost.com/ (accessed April 27, 2003).

AUDIO AND VISUAL MEDIA

All the President's Men. Directed by Alan Paluka. Warner Home Video. Videocassette. 1976.

"'Sesame Street,' Child of the Sixties, Faces a New Era"

Newspaper article

By: Grace Hechinger

Date: January 15, 1975

Source: Hechinger, Grace. "'Sesame Street,' Child of the Sixties, Faces a New Era." *The New York Times,* January 15, 1975, 57 ff.

About the Author: Grace Hechinger (1931) is an American educator and educational consultant. With her husband, Fred M. Hechinger, she has collaborated on titles such as *Teenage Tyranny* and *Growing Up in America.* On her own, she is responsible for the acclaimed 1984 volume, *How to Raise a Street Smart Child.* Hechinger has also served as the education columnist for *Glamour* magazine. ■

Introduction

At the time of its invention and development in the 1930s, television was envisaged as an educational tool and a vehicle for the dissemination of knowledge. But the rise of commercial broadcasting in the post-World War II period, with its zany and frothy fare, seemed to give the lie to that expectation. While television became increasingly popular from the 1940s on, it was often called "the boob tube" or "the idiot box" because of the generally low intellectual quality of its programs.

With this profile, television seemed at odds with serious educational purposes by the 1960s, however much these may have been part of the original vision of the new medium. *Sesame Street,* however, came on the scene to redeem television's earlier promise, at least as far as children were concerned. This new children's program moved away from "lowest common denominator" entertainment and indicated that television could respond to society's interest in the spread of knowledge and the improvement of language skills.

The program began in 1969 and was an instant success. It had corporate sponsorship from the Ford and Carnegie Foundations, and with a high initial investment, it went on to spend an unprecedented amount of money on programming for children. The concept behind this project from the Children's Television Workshop was to use sophisticated television-style imagery and scene making as vehicles for teaching the alphabet and numbers. The show reached its young audience with an unlikely cast of characters that have since become famous, the marionette/puppets called "Muppets." These Muppets included Big Bird, Oscar the Grouch, the Cookie Monster, Bert and Ernie, and the Dracula-inspired "The Count" (who liked to count things). The show used all kinds of techniques, from catchy tunes to comedy sketches, to get across its lessons to the young television viewer. Each show was sponsored by a daily letter and number, and it would close with such words as "This program was brought to you by the letter 'P' and the number '4.'" And in a takeoff of another successful PBS program, there was "Monsterpiece Theatre" hosted by "Alistair Cookie," who was in fact the Cookie Monster putting on airs. One might also expect to see a tree or an egg as the special guest on the *Sesame Street* version of "This Is Your Life." Another segment might have roving reporter Kermit the Frog doing exclusive interviews with important figures such as Humpty Dumpty, Cinderella, or the "Old Lady who lived in a shoe." When the preschooler arrived home from kindergarten, or the elementary student came in from class, there was now something for them to watch with high production values and talented performers. The show made television an ally rather than an opponent of the school.

Significance

Sesame Street was a ground-breaking experiment, because it made use of a medium, television, that had sometimes been seen as a threat to the development of sound reading skills and good study habits and used it to inspire them instead. Commentators such as Neil

Postman have been critical of the effects of television and have pictured it as opposed to the traditional values of the "little red school house" on which he thinks all sound education and democracy must ultimately rest. *Sesame Street* showed that television is not simply an enemy to the goals of the schoolhouse, that for all its faults, television at its best could be an ally of educational development.

Despite some criticism for being too visual in its approach to entertaining the child and for getting children too used to a frenetic pace and excessive variety, the overall legacy of *Sesame Street* has been the promotion of learning and education. The show has evolved over time to introduce new themes while always stressing the importance of literacy and numeracy. But above all, it has set an example of excellence in children's programming, by showing that it can be entertaining and instructional to a considerably higher degree than was earlier thought possible. Still popular more than thirty years after its creation, the show has shown a staying power such that a generation of young adults already look back on their childhood as unimaginable without the charming and special characters of *Sesame Street*.

Primary Source

"'Sesame Street,' Child of the Sixties, Faces a New Era"

SYNOPSIS: This article presents an account of the arrival on the television screen of the children's show *Sesame Street* and its amazing success with both children and their parents. It explains how the show established itself on the PBS network at a time of heightened concern about education, especially in the inner city and among minority groups. The article outlines the unique innovations made by the show and how after *Sesame Street,* educational television for children would never be the same.

In November, 1969, an educational rocket named "Sesame Street" blasted off in a glare of publicity. Five short years later, what streaked across the television screen as an ungraded visual one-room schoolhouse, a 20th-century McGuffey's Reader, had revolutionized the attitudes of millions of children toward learning and the attitudes of countless adults on what the young were capable of learning.

Along with Head Start, a preschool program only for disadvantaged children, "Sesame Street" was the product of the hopes and fears of the "Great Society." The idea had its roots in the sixties' anxieties about poverty, racial unrest and declining reading scores of schoolchildren.

Designed by the Children's Television Workshop to teach letters and numbers to preschoolers using the techniques of commercial television, "Sesame Street" has also taught educators and parents that the medium is an irresistible presence. The program's impact has made television, at long last, a legitimate subject for academic concern and inquiry.

Not too long ago, an educator asked his five-year-old son where he had learned the alphabet. The boy answered: "From 'Sesame Street,' but my teacher thinks she's teaching me."

The precise factors of a child's learning may never be measured exactly but the clear gain of the television program has been that all those involved with young children have become conscious of the visual lesson's power. Children's television, commercial as well as educational, will never be the same. "Sesame Street" has made it impossible for television networks ever again to say that quality children's programing will not attract a mass audience.

The show appears five times weekly on the Public Broadcasting Network. It features live and animated segments, none longer than six minutes and most considerably shorter. While they seem spontaneous, each is part of a carefully formulated lesson plan. The make-believe urban street scene is inhabited by an integrated cast of real adults and children along with an assortment of muppets (a cross between a puppet and marionette created for the show).

Favorites include Oscar the Grouch, who lives in a garbage can and specializes in contrariness: "Of course I took a bath, I took it all the way to 100th Street." A 4-year-old grins and says, "I like how he's funny." There is a 7-foot-tall canary called Big Bird, who waddles around constantly making mistakes. Even a 3-year-old could sell him a bottle of sunshine. Preschoolers everywhere zip into their own kitchens bellowing "Cooooooookie," copying the Cookie Monster, their furry friend with his Ping-Pong-ball eyes.

Each hour features one or two letters and numbers as sponsors. ("This show has been brought to you by the letter A and the number 5.") To "teach" the number 5, for example, a fast-paced cartoon wallpapered with 5's will be quickly followed by a film of 5 members of the New York Knicks shooting baskets. During the show, a muppet regular—the Cookie Monster or Bert or Ernie or Grover—will "teach" by pricking five balloons.

Sesame Street attracts children from ages 2 to 11. Elementary-school youngsters use it as a "security blanket," an old friend that they can still watch and enjoy. One 8-year-old told his mother. "When I was young, I used to watch 'Sesame Street.' I saw a movie about how peanuts grow and that's how I learned. Maybe you should watch, too."

All Techniques Employed

No sophisticated film technique is left unused—quick cutting back and forth between live people and muppets as well as using them in the same sequence; zoom lens close-ups for emphasis and rapid dissolves. Catchy tunes become as familiar as nursery rhymes. Slow motion, and its opposite called pixilation, follow each other in rapid succession. Adults may complain of too much repetition, but they forget how often a child asks to have the same bedtime story read over and over.

"I doubt whether 'Sesame Street' could be created today," says Mrs. Joan Ganz Cooney, the show's originator, now the workshop president. "We were education nuts in the sixties."

Americans have always looked to education with a naive faith as a panacea for social problems. The response to the ghetto riots was to turn to education, combined with technical know-how—and money—to provide solutions. Tensions might be eased, the thinking went, if television could narrow the learning gap between the children of the affluent suburbs and the underprivileged ghettos.

"Sesame Street" was the brainchild of sophisticated observers of television and of education. TV, available to more than 95 per cent of the population, would be a testing ground for the theories of such psychological pioneers as Benjamin Bloom and Jerome Bruner, who believed that all children could learn more complex material at an earlier age than conventional educational wisdom believed, if it was properly presented.

"We believed in education then, particularly for preschoolers. It was the right time," Mrs. Cooney recalls. Her optimism was shared by the show's bluechip backers—the Ford Foundation, the Carnegie Corporation and the United States Office of Education. This was not a grass-roots response to public pressure, but a commitment of courage, confidence and cash from the top.

Audience of 9 Million

Much of the top creative talent had graduated from "Captain Kangaroo," the most prestigious, longest-running commercial children's show on the air. "Sesame Street," a brilliant exploitation of the medium's hard-sell commercial techniques, also has

Joan Ganz Cooney, creator of *Sesame Street* poses with several "cast members" including Big Bird, Oscar the Grouch, and Bert and Ernie in the 1970s. **AP/WIDE WORLD PHOTOS. REPRODUCED BY PERMISSION.**

the distinction of being the most expensive children's television show ever produced, with an initial investment of $7-million. Today it reports an audience of nine million. Indeed, the idea was so successful that the workshop created a spin-off in 1971—"The Electric Company"—to teach reading to a slightly older group between the ages of 6 and 9.

Although the initial target audience for "Sesame Street" was in urban ghettos, the show was instantly embraced by middle-class children—and their parents. After 20 years of television, there finally was a show parents could encourage their children to watch without feeling guilty about abandoning them to the electronic babysitter. "It's what we used to do for our children," a friend said, "in our better moments." There are even parents who complain that their children do not watch "Sesame Street" enough!

While there is no longer any doubt that children do learn from the program the nature of the lesson is often in the eye of the beholder. When asked what he found most interesting, a 6-year-old replied: "I didn't know hippopotamuses had belly-buttons."

After the program's first year, the superintendent in a suburban district told his kindergarten teachers that he expected at least 10 per cent of the following year's 5-year-olds to read at second-grade level. Teachers, he demanded, should put a stop to the "babyish" activities and be prepared to meet the "Sesame Street" children at their new high level.

The response of experienced classroom teachers, while often enthusiastic, is more realistic. "It's part of the children's lives now," one teacher said. "It's something they all know." Another said, "Even if the program doesn't do all the producers claim, I'd still rather have my children watch it over most of the garbage on TV."

Many parents, as they watched their youngsters learn letters with apparent ease, have pressured schools to begin formal academic work sooner. "Five years ago, nobody would have dreamed of teaching letters and numbers in kindergarten," one teacher said. "Sesame Street" has provided highly visible fuel for the age-old parental complaint, "the-teacher-doesn't-know-how-smart-Susie-is."

But some thoughtful teachers are concerned that concepts acquired via TV may be hazy. "He can count to 20, but can't bring you eight pencils," one teacher explained. Others worry that too much TV-watching leaves little time for imaginative play, that visually oriented youngsters have trouble following spoken directions, and that children have lost patience with slower-moving tasks like cutting and pasting.

A psychologist wondered whether TV "nurtures in children an expectation of the [Sesame Street] kind of pacing in the real world, where it doesn't exist." Others have expressed concern about "sensory overkill" and that too many adults on the show "act like damn fools."

Attitude Toward Learning

Even as such controversies continue, few observers would quarrel with the statement by Jerome Kagan, Harvard psychologist, that "Sesame Street" is "telling millions of people that learning itself is important and maybe the youngsters will carry this attitude toward learning with them even when the TV set is off."

Dr. Edward A. Davies, chief of pediatrics at Lenox Hill Hospital, put the matter in perspective when he said that for preschoolers the importance of watching "Sesame Street" is "not what the child learns, but whether the experience fosters a positive attitude toward learning. It matters very little at that age how many numbers or letters a child actually knows, even though these accomplishments may be a source of ego satisfaction to his parents."

Though largely unnoticed by its fans, "Sesame Street" has undergone many changes since its conception during the sixties. In the beginning it borrowed heavily from the psychedelic approach of the Beatles' "Yellow Submarine" and the slapstick incongruity of the then popular "Laugh-In." "We had to get the kids where they were," Mrs. Cooney explains. Since then, the program's creators have learned to relax. "We don't have to get everything across in one year," said Ed Palmer, the research director.

The pace has slowed down. While letters and numbers are still important, new areas have been added, such as the world of work and concern for women's rights. Recently, a show featured several segments showing a female worker on a construction site. Humor conquers social significance when a helpful muppet discovers "somebody riveted my sandwich to the girder."

Segments of the show are now in Spanish. A New York City teacher reported that her English-speaking children are delighted that they now can "talk" in Spanish.

On the curriculum side, also, goals have broadened to deal with word recognition, simple addition and subtraction and perhaps most innovative, exploration of children's emotions.

"Sesame Street" was conceived with a built-in intention to pursue program-oriented research, testing the reactions of young viewers to a wide variety of visual techniques. The workshop's "child-watching" technique—observation by trained researchers to see how children react while watching—is perhaps the ultimate in audience participation. The children actually guide the show. "We once had a muppet character named Dr. Hastings who was always falling asleep. All he did was put the children to sleep." A special "monster" segment proved "too scary" when tested, and "we had to drop it," David Connell, the producer, recalled.

The Power of Example

There is universal agreement that all children's television has improved during the last five years. That the example set by "Sesame Street" has clearly been a factor is only grudgingly acknowledged by the networks. Five years ago, Squire Rushnell, head of children's programing at ABC, which runs "Schoolhouse Rock," says he cannot imagine a network executive five years ago saying, "would you like to do grammar on Saturday mornings?" While there is more awareness, many observers believe too much of the "new" approach still seems concerned with the kind of marginal tinkering shown when a consultant penciled on a script, "Change popcorn to apples."

What is the future of "Sesame Street?"

Despite a large—and, final—grant from the Ford Foundation, the Children's Television Workshop's financial picnic is over. Already, more old segments have been brought out of "retirement" and run more frequently than the show's creators like to admit.

Indeed "Sesame Street's" first five years have proved so dynamic that there is concern whether CTW can keep its pioneering spirit of '69 alive during the depressed '70s. The big question now is whether the combination of success and a weak economy will spoil "Sesame Street," luring it into a pedagogical rut or into television's penchant for reruns.

Further Resources

BOOKS

Hechinger, Grace. *How to Raise a Street Smart Child: The Complete Parents' Guide to Safety on the Streets and at Home.* New York: Facts on File, 1984.

Hechinger, Grace, with Fred H. Hechinger. *Growing Up in America.* New York: McGraw Hill, 1975.

———. *Restoring Confidence in Public Education.* Mount Kisco, N.Y.: Seven Springs Center, 1982.

Polsky, Richard M. *Getting to Sesame Street: Origins of the Children's Television Workshop.* New York: Praeger, 1974.

Skolnick, Jerome, and Elliot Currie. *The Crisis in American Institutions,* 4th ed. Boston: Little, Brown, 1979.

"'Saturday Night' Never Plays It Safe"

Newspaper article

By: Peter Andrews

Date: February 29, 1976

Source: Andrews, Peter. "'Saturday Night' Never Plays It Safe." *The New York Times,* February 29, 1976, 1, 27.

About the Publication: Founded in 1850 as *The Daily Times, The New York Times* was originally a relatively obscure local paper. By the early part of the twentieth century, it had grown into a widely known, well-respected news source, and has remained such since. ∎

Introduction

In 1975 television producer Lorne Michaels assembled a cast of performers with experience in improvisational comedy, known as the "Not Ready For Prime Time Players," and a group of writers, many from the satirical magazine *National Lampoon.* Together they created a new program that would become a legend in American television, *Saturday Night Live.*

Debuting on October 11, 1975, from its start *Saturday Night Live* was a late-night show, running for an hour and a half, and broadcast live from NBC studios in New York every Saturday night. An irreverent and cutting brand of humor came to distinguish the program. The show featured a fast-paced mix of skits, imitations, send-ups, and spoofs with many topical references to current events and headlines.

While there had been sketch comedy on television long before *Saturday Night Live* debuted, *SNL* took far more risks than earlier shows. The show was performed in front of a live studio audience, leaving open the possibility of mistakes or badly received jokes going out to a national audience. The emphasis on being current and topical meant that ideas and concepts for each week's new show had to be worked out and made into actual performable material in a very short time. The show was produced at a frenetic pace throughout the week for the live performance on Saturday night. Rewrites and adjustments would be made right up until airtime.

The writers and performers were also committed to taking chances and pushing the boundaries of previously acceptable television humor. In 1969, *The Smothers Brothers Comedy Hour* had been canceled because of its satirical approach to political and social issues. Now, only six years later (but out of prime time) *Saturday Night Live* was openly mocking current events and public figures. A sketch making light of drug use might be followed by one of Chevy Chase's famous send-ups of President Gerald Ford as a bumbler incapable of taking three steps without falling over. In the more relaxed atmosphere of the 1970s, *Saturday Night Live* did not suffer the same fate as the Smothers Brothers. Instead, their edgy style of entertainment with its on-the-fly character appealed to a young, relatively well-educated urban audience. Such an audience accepted social and political comment as a natural element in humor. They also appreciated the appearance of popular musical acts and guest hosts.

One of *Saturday Night Live*'s most famous early creations was "The Blues Brothers" featuring John Belushi and Dan Aykroyd. Dark glasses, suits, and fedora hats would transform these two regulars on the show into the musical duo Jake and Elroy Blues, wild exponents of the hard-edged Chicago blues tradition. The point of the Blues Brothers was that the musical tastes of the 1970s had become commercial and bland and what was needed was a return to the roots of popular music, where there was real feeling and fire. (Ironically enough, Belushi and Aykroyd went on to make a Hollywood movie based on these characters, which turned out to be a box office success.) Their act was emblematic of the show's mission in reminding the audience that great comedic entertainment should be dynamic, forceful, risky, and sometimes controversial.

Significance

Since 1975 *Saturday Night Live* has become an institution on American television and in the American consciousness. Its satirical style has had enormous influence on television humor, encouraging the shows that followed it to take greater risks. Many of its cast have gone on to become major motion picture or television stars in their own right. (Tragedy has also been associated with the show, as alumni such as John Belushi, Gilda Radner, and Phil Hartmann have met untimely deaths due to drugs, cancer, and homicide respectively.) Political figures feel obliged to go on the show if invited, as it gives them a reputation for a sense of humor as well as exposure to younger voters. Former Attorney-General Janet Reno made her appearance by bursting through a wall, thus making humor out of her reputed toughness and relentlessness.

In all, *SNL* is one of the most successful programs ever to be on American television. Nearly thirty years after its debut it continued to draw an audience and to cycle new performers through its troupe. Despite its roots in the 1970s, when Vietnam, Watergate, and the energy crunch were the major issues of the decade, it has successfully adapted itself to the moods and issues of ensuing decades and has made itself a fixture on the television schedule. Saturday night would just not seem the same without the words "Live! From New York! It's Saturday Night!"

Primary Source

"'Saturday Night' Never Plays It Safe"

SYNOPSIS: In the mid-1970s, *Saturday Night Live* was an innovative development in television programming that introduced a new kind of comedy entertainment for late-night television. As a result of its success, a new generation of comedians who cut their teeth on this show would go on to be household names with careers in film and on television. This article takes a look at the show about a year after its initial broadcast. It outlines the features that made the show a new departure in the medium.

NBC's "Saturday Night" is a comedy-variety show that just begs for trouble. To begin with, it is broadcast live, which is of course risky. In addition, with its resident company of improvisational actor-writers, the Not Ready for Prime Time Players, it is unabashedly youthful, which is even riskier. Then, too, the show deals mainly in satire and social commentary, which, as everybody knows, is supposed to close on Saturday night. Furthermore, it doesn't have the backstopping of canned laughter, nor does anyone plead with its studio audience for applause to cover a bad gag. When a supposedly funny sketch falls flat on "Saturday Night," the reverberations can be heard all over the studio and, one imagines, in every Nielsen household. Finally, "Saturday Night" strives to fill a 90-minute time slot, the same as Sid Caesar's "Your Show of Shows," but with less than half the staff.

The entire show, with all its comedy and musical numbers, is pulled together in one heroic effort on Saturday afternoon a few hours before going on the air live. When the production starts to become unstitched, as it does from time to time, the situation can turn into a producers' nightmare. The day before "Saturday Night" was broadcast last week, for example, producer Lorne Michaels hastily had to order up substitute sketch material when he found himself an act short after a scheduled rock group canceled out at the last minute because one of its members had come down with the flu. On the air, a piece of business misfired when the show's guest star, Desi Arnaz, dropped a key line. Later, announcer Don Pardo read the wrong introduction to the comic news segment, Update, and even the cool Chevy Chase couldn't come up with a good cover. And then, Saturday Night's resident stuffed cow was brought on stage and an audio man threw in a loud "moo," which Michaels had expressly forbidden. Michaels, normally a particularly low-key operator as producers go, was driven into a not-too-quiet rage backstage: "We *do not* do moo-cow jokes on this show."

"Saturday Night" consists of a series of fast-paced sketches and songs, usually performed by a guest star as well as the resident company. The humor is always topical and irreverent, in some ways reminiscent of such predecessors as "That Was the

Week That Was" and "Laugh-In," although the real inspiration for the show is the magazine The National Lampoon, to which many of the show's writers contribute. The National Lampoon, of course, always offers a generous helping of obscenities, and while the TV show can't go that far, it can skirt the limits of what is traditionally considered good taste in television. Whether the jokes have to do with women taking speed to help them with their house-work or getting a laugh out of the Patty Hearst trial, someone, somewhere is bound to accuse the writers and producer of bad taste. When the comic pieces work, they crackle with a manic urgency. When they don't work, they can be pretty dreadful.

"The important thing," explained John Belushi, a burly young actor from Chicago with a face like an angry pudding, "is to take chances with your material. You can't play safe."

"Sunday," according to Michaels, "is given over almost entirely to sulking over Saturday's mistakes. But, thank God. Monday is a day of redemption. Everyone comes in brimming over with ideas."

Like almost all good comedy writers, the people on "Saturday Night" look around a troubled world and just naturally, as they say in the trade, "see things funny." Dan Ackroyd, a 23-year-old Canadian actor-writer, once worked up an elaborate routine based entirely on the freight schedules of the Penn Central Railroad. Michaels, a veteran writer for Woody Allen and Lily Tomlin, noted the extraordinary number of people in New York who talk to themselves on the street and called for a citywide program to have such people walk in pairs "so visitors would think they're talking to each other." When told someone representing The New York Times was on the set, Michael O'Donoghue, a co-founder of the National Lampoon, immediately sketched out an omnibus article for the Op Ed page.

"It's headlined 'The Aswan Dam—Hope for the Future or Usurper of the Past?'" he said, "I take all four sides of the issue and am terribly fair to everyone."

Once a guest host is signed, the writers rally round with a series of appropriate routines. When Desi Arnaz came to New York to promote his new autobiographical book, Michaels grabbed him. "The network officials thought he was a strange choice for a young hip show, but Desi was a giant when most of us were growing up, and we wanted to work with him."

In fairly short order the staff whipped up a series of skits for Desi to work with, including a take-

The original cast of "Saturday Night Live," also known as the "Not Ready for Prime-Time Players," 1977. From left to right: John Belushi, Dan Akroyd, Gilda Radner, Bill Murray, Jane Curtin, Laraine Newman, and Garrett Morris. **AP/WIDE WORLD PHOTOS. REPRODUCED BY PERMISSION.**

off on the old Desilu Productions' war horse, "The Untouchables," and a lunatic skit in which Desi played a Cuban acupuncturist who uses cigars instead of pins.

The basic sketches were approved on Wednesday and preliminary staging got underway the following afternoon. Not all straight performers are comfortable with the strongly improvisational techniques familiar to the regulars on the show, but the old pro Arnaz professed to be enchanted.

"I love it," he said. "It's just like the old days on the Lucy show. We never knew what we were going to do next there, either."

On other shows, once the script is set it is not unusual for writers to be kept away during rehearsals unless called upon by an outraged star complaining about dialogue. On "Saturday Night," the writers swarm over the set like camp followers, fixing material, offering line readings to other actors, polishing jokes and generally meddling. O'Donoghue is a self-proclaimed accomplished meddler.

"That's one of the best things about this show. No one else would put up with a writer making trouble on the set. But here I can be just as difficult as I want."

O'Donoghue was on the set to watch rehearsals of one of his sketches about a gorgeous vampire peddling her book of beauty secrets from within an open coffin—"I drink the blood of Girl Scouts and Brownies . . . and had all my bones replaced with those of cheerleaders and pom-pom girls." He was unhappy about the stage setting and decided to go out and buy a set of picture-frame props. As he was leaving, he turned to Laraine Newman, who was playing the vampire, and said, "Try saying. 'Buy *my* book or I'll steal *your* lungs.'"

Chevy Chase always waits until the last minute before completing his satiric Update news segment script. Last week, he was pleased with a bogus item announcing Muhammad Ali's forthcoming title-defense bout with Helen Hayes in the spring, but was stuck for a punch line to end an item on Richard Nixon's trip to Communist China. Finally, he hit on the happy inspiration of having the former President telling reporters at the Peking airport. "I am not a clook."

Lorne Michaels admits he sometimes wishes there was more time to put a final polish on the entire show but feels that the challenge and excitement of a late-night live performance more than compensates for the hectic preparations.

"We go on at 11:30 P.M., the best time slot in all of television," Michaels said, "and have the largest single concentration of a young urban audience. I wouldn't want to move to prime time under any circumstances."

"Where's Chevy? Where's Chevy?" shouted a production assistant a few minutes before air time.

"I think he's out in the alley shooting up. It's always good luck to shoot up before a performance," someone replied.

Since "Saturday Night" first was aired last October, Michaels has found the show has taken him over completely.

"I have no personal life at all any more. Sometimes I worry about losing touch with the real world out there. I don't know anything but this show. I've been reduced in hearing the news from Chevy's Update segment. Now, that's a frightening thought."

But more fun than hearing it from Gabe Pressman.

Further Resources

BOOKS

Hill, Doug, and Jeff Weingrad. *Saturday Night: A Backstage History of "Saturday Night Live."* New York: William Morrow, 1986.

Shales, Tom, and James Andrew Miller. *Live from New York: An Uncensored History of "Saturday Night Live."* Boston: Little, Brown, 2002.

PERIODICALS

Barol, Bill, and Jennifer Foote. "Saturday Night Lives!" *Newsweek,* November 24, 1975, 159–166.

Barbara Walters Moves to ABC

"Barbara Walters Accepts ABC's Offer"

Newspaper article

By: Robert D. McFaden
Date: April 23, 1976
Source: Robert D. McFaden. "Barbara Walters Accepts ABC's Offer." *The New York Times,* April 23, 1976.

"What Makes Barbara Walters Worth a Million?"

Interview

By: Les Brown
Date: May 2, 1976
Source: Brown, Les. "What Makes Barbara Walters Worth a Million?" *The New York Times,* May 2, 1976. ∎

Introduction

Barbara Walters worked for years behind the scenes in television as a writer, guest booker, and producer long before she was hired to work in front of the camera. In 1963, she was offered a trial opportunity to be a "Today girl," a spot typically reserved for attractive young women whose purpose was no more than to look good on camera. Her first decade with NBC's *Today* show, though, allowed her to fine-tune her talents as an interviewer and demonstrate her popularity with audiences. This popularity led to cohosting the show in 1974, making her the first ever female to cohost a network news show. She showed herself to be a savvy all-around journalist with a knack for lining up and interviewing important guests. In 1976, ABC offered her a million-dollar-a-year contract to co-anchor the *ABC Evening*

News and host four yearly specials. Walters, accepted, becoming the highest paid television news anchor in history.

ABC's offer and Walters acceptance became a major story in itself, with many in the news media weighing in about her journalistic credentials, her market value, and the purity of broadcast journalism in America. The contract stirred professional jealousy and criticism; the majority of the press questioned what they perceived as a "show-biz" tint to the sober task of news reporting. Walter Cronkite, the most trusted man in television news at the time, said: "There was a first wave of nausea, the sickening sensation that we were going under, that all of our efforts to hold network television news aloof from show business had failed." Cronkite then tempered his criticism. "Her background is not what I would call well-rounded," he said, "but who is to say that there is only one route to a career in journalism?" Executives of other networks warned that their established anchors might demand salary increases. Her male counterparts, including Cronkite, John Chancellor, and her co-anchor Harry Reasoner, were making less than half that salary.

Finally, some questioned whether the public would accept a woman news anchor. In fact, women viewers predominated in the period before prime time when the news broadcasts are presented. "My biggest fans," Walter noted, "are women and not men." ABC's private polls before they made their record offer indicated that only 13 percent of the viewing public preferred a male anchor, and they knew even a small bost in ratings caused by Walters's presence could easily increase advertising revenues far exceeding her salary.

Significance

Walters's anchoring of the *Evening News* did not yield the ratings boost that ABC had hoped for, and she was pulled from the anchor position in 1979. The fact that she had even been given the job, however, demonstrated that women were now being taken seriously by the TV news media, both within the business and as an important segment of their audience.

While Waters work as an anchor wasn't as successful as ABC had hoped, her specials and her appearances on *20/20* spotlighted her strength as an interviewer. Her first special aired on December 14, 1976, when she interviewed President and First Lady Jimmy and Rosalyn Carter and Barbara Striesand. The next year she went to Cuba to interview Fidel Castro. These intimate and insightful interviews with important political leaders and fascinating celebrities made her a household name. She exhibited a gift for asking the questions that the public most wanted answered and—despite her sometimes tart, probing interviewing techniques—she seldom seemed to

alienate the person she was interviewing. She became a regular on *20/20,* and eventually a co-host, while continuing to do many specials.

In the decades that followed, Walters became a fixture on American television and one of the best known of all television newspeople, male or female. Walters was not without critics. Some interview subjects said that her "shrill" aggressiveness and nervousness distracted them. Washington press corps members charged that she acted more as a "star" than as a reporter on presidential trips, echoing the concerns that Walters was a sign of the TV news becoming part of show business. However, her professional admirers outnumbered her detractors. As Tom Shales, television critic for *The Washington Post,* observed, many of the presumed flaws in her style of interviewing were really virtues: "She simply got more intimate than anyone else had before. She pioneered the style of getting the guest to cry. And she's genuinely nosy, which is a good thing for a journalist to be." Walters herself notes in *The New York Times* interview that her success as an interviewer is the result of women identifying with her: "Other women tell me I ask the questions they wanted to ask." Ultimately, Barbara Walters proved that women could be both popular and highly effective television journalists, thereby playing an important role in breaking the monopoly men had held on important TV news positions.

Primary Source

"Barbara Walters Accepts ABC's Offer"

> **SYNOPSIS:** This *New York Times'* article describes the events surrounding ABC's offer of a million dollars to Barbara Walters to become the first female anchorperson, and Walters decision to accept that offer.

Barbara Walters yesterday accepted an offer of $1 million a year over the next five years to become a major personality of ABC News and the co-anchor, with Harry Reasoner, of "The Evening News."

She will thus become the world's highest-paid newscaster and the first woman ever to present the evening news over a major television network.

Miss Walters, who has been co-host of the NBC "Today" show for the last two years and a writer and personality with NBC for 12 years, has a contract with NBC that runs until next September.

It was unclear yesterday whether that contract would be canceled early or allowed to run its course, but William Sheehan, the president of ABC News,

Barbara Walters announces on the *Today* show her decision to accept ABC's $1 million a year offer to anchor their "Evening News", April 23, 1976.
© BETTMANN/CORBIS. REPRODUCED BY PERMISSION.

said that ABC would put her on the air soon after any cancellation, or in the autumn, at the latest.

Broadcasting-industry sources yesterday called Miss Walters's decision to switch networks a coup for ABC. It was expected to boost the ratings for ABC, not only of the evening news program but also of the network's "Good Morning, America" show, which appears opposite "Today" on weekday mornings—because of her affiliation with the network, though she will not appear on the early program.

"The Evening News," ABC's entry in the prime-time news programming, will be expanded to 45 minutes from a half-hour when Miss Walters joins the program, broadcast sources said. Affiliated stations would expand their preceding local programs to 45 minutes, they said, creating a 90-minute evening news program.

In addition to her major spot on the evening news program, Miss Walters's contract, which is ex-pected to be signed in a few days, stipulates that she will anchor four hour-long prime-time "special" programs that will be produced each year by her own production company and paid for by ABC.

The cost of each of these programs, which confer virtual star status on the person in the anchor role, is expected to be in the $300,000 to $350,000 range. The subject matter is yet to be determined.

Miss Walters's contract also calls for her appearances from time to time as the host of the Sunday ABC News series "Issues and Answers," in which politicians and others are interviewed, and for contributions to other ABC news and documentary programs.

'Circus Atmosphere'

Both ABC and NBC had been in negotiations with Miss Walters in recent weeks and had offered her approximately the same financial terms, although the NBC offer did not include a job as co-anchor of the network's major news program, "The Nightly News" with John Chancellor.

It appeared yesterday that Miss Walters's departure from NBC might be effected on something less than amicable terms.

The first word that she was switching to ABC came about 4 P.M., in a telephone call from an NBC spokesman who, asking not to be quoted by name, said that NBC had withdrawn its contract offer, both because of the expenses of the terms and what he called the "circus atmosphere" of the negotiations over them.

"It got to the point where it was getting unseemly," said the spokesman. "There were things that one would associate with a movie queen, not a journalist, and we had second thoughts."

Miss Walters, asked about the NBC spokesman's contentions, in a telephone interview shortly afterward, expressed shock and said. "Whoever is speaking for NBC is doing them a disservice."

"They did not withdraw their offer," Miss Walters said, "I called them. They asked me to wait, but I decided not to. It would have been unfair to them. ABC has offered me an exciting prospect, a real challenge, and I made this decision to accept."

Miss Walters scoffed at the NBC spokesman's contention that a "circus atmosphere" had crept into negotiations between her representatives, the William Morris Agency, and NBC. "It was done with great dignity," she contended.

In citing the expense of contract demands by Miss Walters, the NBC spokesman said the cost of the 20 special programs over the five-year life of the contract might exceed $8 million, bringing the total cost of the contract to $13 or $14 million.

Miss Walters also scoffed at this figure, as did Mr. Sheehan, the ABC News president, who said most specials cost $200,000 to $350,000 to produce. He said a contractual limit on the production expenses for the specials would be imposed, but he said he did not know what the figure was.

The NBC spokesman, who said no formal announcement had been made because his company never announced "negative events like not signing somebody," listed a "hairdresser," "her own press agent," and "a full-time limousine at her disposal" as being among her demands.

Miss Walters said that NBC had for years provided these services to her, and she called the spokesman's remarks "absurd."

"I'm leaving with nothing but the happiest feelings," she said. "It's not a matter of whose offer was better. I'm not so concerned about money. This is a breakthrough for all of us in journalism."

One implication of the contract to be given to Miss Walters was that other big-name newscasters—Walter Cronkite on CBS. Mr. Chancellor on NBC and even Mr. Reasoner on ABC—probably will ask for more money.

Reasoner Comments

They are each believed to have salaries over $400,000, and industry sources said they might very well ask for substantial increases. Mr. Reasoner, asked about this last night, said he never discussed salaries publicly.

But during his news program, in an announcement of Miss Walters's move to ABC, he said: "Some of you may have seen speculation about this in the papers. It's had more attention than Catfish Hunter, and Barbara can't even throw left-handed. Many of the stories said that I had some reservations when the idea came up. If I did, they've been taken care of, and I welcome Barbara with no reservation."

Mr. Reasoner said that a woman co-anchor "may well be an idea whose time has come, and if it is, there's no better candidate."

As for billing on the program. Mr. Reasoner had a suggestion . . ."I suggest we just do it alphabetically by last name."

Mr. Chancellor, on his program, also took note of Miss Walters's impending switch and said: "NBC valued Barbara's service highly, but the negotiations for a renewal of her contract involved a million dollars and other privileges, and this afternoon NBC pulled out of the negotiations, leaving her a clear path to ABC. We wish her luck in her new job."

Cooperation Expected

Broadcast sources last night said that ABC had decided to expand its evening news program by 15 minutes when Miss Walters goes on the air in order to be able to sell more commercials and thus help her salary.

Affiliated stations were said to be likely to go along with the increased time, according to one ABC executive, because it also would increase their time available for commercial sales.

The ABC announcement yesterday made no mention of the program expansion, and it gave no details about her duties, salary or prerequisites.

Miss Walters, however, confirmed the major points of the contract.

The change at ABC was foreshadowed last month when people in the company said the news division was under pressure to raise the ratings of the evening news program. The pressure was strong, these sources said, because ABC was doing well in sports coverage and was showing good gains in prime-time programming.

It was concluded that the best way to improve the ratings for the evening news would be to get a co-anchor to work with Mr. Reasoner, preferably a woman, the sources said.

This view was based on a study by Magid Associates, a leading news-consulting concern, that said that the public considered the three networks to be about equal in their news-gathering abilities.

However, the study said, the difference in the popularity of newscasts rested on two factors: the appeal of the anchorman and the popularity of the local newscasts on stations carrying the network news roundups.

The study found that Mr. Cronkite on CBS was more widely liked and trusted than either Mr. Chancellor on NBC or Mr. Reasoner on ABC, and that this was why "The CBS Evening News With Walter Cronkite" remained first in the ratings.

Since 1973, the CBS evening newscast has maintained a steady average of 27 to 28 percent of the television audience. The NBC nightly news has drawn 25 to 27 percent, but the ABC newscast has declined from an average of 22 to 23 percent in 1973, to an average now of 10 to 20 percent.

Replacement a Question

The ABC coup in hiring Miss Walters was seen by industry executives as an oblique effort to improve the ratings of the ABC Entertainment production "Good Morning, America," which competes with the NBC "Today" show in the 7 to 9 A.M. weekdays' slot. Miss Walters is not slated to appear on "Good Morning, America," in any event.

Yesterday, NBC had no comment on any replacement for Miss Walters on "Today," whose co-host is Jim Hartz. "Good Morning, America" has as host David Hartman, an actor whose face became familiar to millions of television viewers as the title-role character on "Lucas Tanner," a former NBC series.

One indication that NBC had been anticipating a possible move by Miss Walters came several months ago when NBC hired Candice Bergen, the actress, photographer and writer, to make several appearances on "Today" in the role of photo-journalist She is said to have been well-received.

Miss Walters had made no secret recently of her dissatisfaction with the "Today" show's early-morning grind. She also recently decided to discontinue "Not for Women Only," because of its claims on her time, leaving the program's future in doubt.

Primary Source

"What Makes Barbara Walters Worth a Million?"

SYNOPSIS: In this interview article by Les Brown from *The New York Times,* Walters talks about the considerations that went into her controversial decision to accept ABC's offer of one million dollars a year to become the first woman co-anchor of a network news show.

Dinner was franks and beans, "the house specialty," a carryover perhaps from humbler times. But it came with candlelight and a good Bordeaux, and Barbara Walters spoke of never having to confront again her old demon, insecurity. One might have expected manic conversation from a hard-working woman who had just struck it rich, but instead she was reflective in a muted tone that seemed out of character with her aggressive, and even at times shrill, television persona.

Flowers, some beginning to droop and sere, were banked against the wall like the hangover from a wedding. It was four days after the Big Decision and the front-page press reports that Barbara would be leaving NBC after almost two decades to become the co-anchor of the ABC evening newscast with Harry Reasoner for $1 million a year. The obvious questions were how was she taking it and what makes her worth such a royal paycheck?

"The night it all happened, the flowers began to arrive and the phone never stopped ringing. My friends were so pleased for me and so warm. And yet, through it all, I wondered why I was so unhappy," Barbara said.

She told of how her friends often joke about her inability to decide upon the smallest things, whether to buy the green dress or the blue. But this was one of the biggest decisions she had ever had to make— whether to switch to ABC for a million or remain at NBC, whose counter offer had also reached a million dollars. The difference between them was the immediate chance, at ABC, of becoming an anchor-woman.

Why the sadness? Part of it was leaving old friends at NBC for a lot of strangers at the new network. As if to illustrate, she recounted her secretary's faux pas with a call from a "Mr. Goldenson."

"What is it in reference to, please?" the secretary had asked, not recognizing the name. The caller was Leonard Goldenson, chairman of the American Broadcasting Companies, Inc., Miss Walters's new employer.

"But it was not just the sadness of leaving NBC. It was all the publicity about the million dollars, a kind of publicity I've never been used to," Barbara said. "I worried all night about public reaction. Some people were going to be resentful of me because of it. But my own feeling was, why should I quarrel about getting a raise? I didn't ask for it."

She feels somewhat less concerned now about the reaction, having sampled how the news was received by some of her public. "Most people, I found, were used to the idea of basketball players getting fantastic sums for a few ball games. My driver—we all have drivers and hairdressers on the show, there's nothing special about that—told me that none of his friends found it unseemly that ABC would pay me a million a year.

"Yet, I know there are many who believe news people should be more pure than show-business people. They seem to feel that if you get a million bucks, you're a superstar. And if you're a superstar, you're show biz. And if you're show biz, you can't be pure and can't do justice to the news."

Her agent, Lee Stevens of the William Morris Agency, had put it well, she thought. Why, he observed, should a good reporter get less on television than a good comedian when news executives at the networks don't get paid less than executives in other departments of the company?

"I don't worry about being able to do the job at ABC but only whether people will accept a woman on the news at night, and whether they feel a woman can have the proper authority," she remarked. "People tend to go to male doctors. We still have to learn whether they can accept the idea of going to a female."

She continued: "I know now that I'm totally professional and good at what I do. I may not be great at ABC, but I know I won't be terrible. This is the kind of confidence that men have always known but women are only just beginning to get. If I make it, there'll be other women in these anchor jobs all over the country. This was why I wanted Sally Quinn

to succeed at CBS, but few people understood that."

Barbara reviewed the pros and cons of her heavy decision, as if making it all over again. "If I had stayed at NBC, I'd have been safe," she began. "No matter what I did—left the 'Today' show, conducted a new magazine, become eventually a co-anchor of the news—I could not be humiliated. This was home. Going to ABC is challenging, scary. Everyone is watching, looking for failure. But the offer was there, and I'm still young enough to take a chance. Finally, I knew I'd always regret it if I didn't seize the opportunity."

She paused for a cigarette. "I won't fall apart if this doesn't work. My entire life is not what I do for a living. Meanwhile, it's exciting to think about some of the things I'd like to do on the newscast."

What are some of those things? Well, that's for later, closer to the time she joins ABC—sometimes between now and when her NBC contract runs out in September.

"I can tell you this, though," she said. "For me, it's not going to be a matter of just reading the Teleprompter. I think Harry [Reasoner] and I will be balanced and will spark off good things in each other. I wouldn't have wanted this job if all it meant was reading the news.

"Look, this isn't to suggest that I want to do 'happy news' or that I would alter the integrity of the newscast, but we are beyond Watergate and Vietnam—those periods when the news was compelling and carried itself. What you find—what all the studies show—is that the three newscasts are about the same except for the appeal of the people before the cameras. As a team, Harry and I could be more interesting than the others."

Women viewers predominate before the sets in the periods before prime time when the newscasts are presented. Part of ABC's bet on Barbara is its belief that she will attract the viewers of her sex, and she appears confident of that.

"My biggest fans are women, and not men," she said. "I can tell from the mail and the people I meet that women do identify with me. I couldn't possibly have stayed on the air 12 years without being female. Other women tell me I ask the questions they wanted to ask. Quite frankly, although some people fault me for being aggressive, I can't stand not asking the questions that have to be asked."

All right, then, what makes her—of all journalists—worth a million a year? "If that's what two networks think I should get," she answered, "they'll get no argument from me. But the money was not what this was all about. It was about opportunity and challenge. I work hard and do good work, and I want to be judged by that and not by how much I earn."

The question was not for Barbara Walters herself to answer. Network television—a $2.5 billion industry in which only three companies share—operates on a grander scale than most media. It responds, too, at every level, to the basic law of show business that governs the price of things: whatever the traffic will allow. To put it simply, the traffic has allowed Barbara Walters to be traded on the talent market for $1 million a year because she possibly will boost the news ratings a notch or two. At the high stakes the networks play for, the investment of a mere million toward lifting ABC's long-static news ratings is a minor gamble, indeed. A television personality overnight can add hundreds of thousands of households to a program simply through his or her presence. The gain of a single rating point puts the newscast in 710,000 additional homes, where it may be watched by approximately 1.2 million extra people. At the rates paid for commercials on the network newscasts in today's market, the gain of a single rating point should mean a gain of at least $1 million in revenues.

Thus, if by her presence Barbara Walters should improve the ratings for the ABC Evening News by a single point, she pays back her spectacular salary. If by two points, it's a bonanza.

Further Resources

BOOKS

Barbara Walters Best Interviews. New York: Meredith Corporation, 1994.

Diamonstein, Barbaralee. *Open Secrets.* New York: Viking, 1972.

Walters, Barbara. *How to Talk with Practically Anybody About Practically Anything.* New York: Doubleday, 1970.

PERIODICALS

Interview given by Commander-in-Chief Fidel Castro to the American Journalist Barbara Walters, May 19, 1977. Oficina de Publicaciones del Consejo de Estado (Havana, Cuba), 1978.

WEBSITES

Biography.com. "Barbara Walters: A Driving Force." Available online at http://www.biography.com/tv/listings/walters_b.html; website home page: http://www.biography.com/ (accessed April 1, 2003).

"'Roots' Getting a Grip on People Everywhere"
Newspaper article

By: Charlayne Hunter-Gault

Date: January 28, 1977

Source: Hunter-Gault, Charlayne. "'Roots' Getting a Grip on People Everywhere." *The New York Times,* January 28, 1977, B1, B5.

About the Author:: Charlayne Hunter-Gault (1942–) was an American journalist born in Due West, South Carolina. She was the first black woman admitted to the University of Georgia. She graduated in 1963 with a degree in journalism. She was the creator and chief of the Harlem bureau of *The New York Times* in the late 1960s. Her career has included work with the *The New Yorker* magazine, NBC News in Washington, D.C., and PBS's *MacNeil/Lehrer NewsHour.* Hunter-Gault has also taught at the Columbia University School of Journalism. ∎

Introduction

Alex Haley (1921–1992) first learned of his African heritage from his maternal grandmother. After retiring from the Coast Guard and achieving success as an author, Haley spent twelve years traveling three continents to discover his ancestry. He traced his family tree to Kunta Kinte, a Mandingo youth sold into slavery from a small village in Gambia, West Africa. Records indicate that Kunta Kinte likely arrived at Annapolis, Maryland on a slave ship in 1767. Haley returned from Gambia on a cargo boat, sleeping on planks in the hull of the ship for ten days to gain a better understanding of Kinte's experience.

On a mission to infuse pride to African Americans—many knowing that their ancestors were enslaved but little else about them—Haley took his research into his family history and weaved in narrative fiction to create *Roots,* a powerful story of how Kinte and his descendants for seven generations maintained their strength and unconquerable spirit through all of their hardships. *Roots* was serialized in *Readers Digest* in 1974, and published in book form in 1976. It was instant success, becoming the number one bestseller in America. Readers bought over 1.6 million copies of *Roots* in its first year in print. *Roots* received a National Book Award in 1976, and Haley won a special Pulitzer Prize in 1976 for his important contribution to the literature of slavery. *Roots* would eventually be translated into thirty-seven languages.

ABC purchased the film rights to bring *Roots* to television. Deciding that the story needed to be presented over several episodes, ABC hired well-known producer, David Wolper, to create an eight-part, twelve-hour miniseries. Miniseries were then a new format for television, albeit one that proved successful the previous year when ABC aired *Rich Man, Poor Man.* Despite the wide appeal of the book, network executives were anxious about how America would respond to a story focusing on the experience of slaves. Executives decided to show the miniseries on eight consecutive evenings—reasoning that if the series failed, at least it would be over quickly. *Roots* featured an all-star cast including John Amos, Ed Asner, Maya Angelou, Chuck Connors, Louis Gossett Jr., Lorne Green, O.J. Simpson, Cicely Tyson, Leslie Uggams, and Ben Vereen. Newcomer LaVar Burton played Kunta Kinte.

Significance

The *Roots* miniseries was an enormously popular success, captivating America for eight days. An estimated 120 million people—three out of every four Americans watching television at the time—tuned in for the series' conclusion, making it the most watched program in the history of television. Discussion about the series was the leading topic of conversation throughout the country.

The phenomenal success of *Roots* led Haley to write the teleplay for a fourteen hour sequel, *Roots: The Next Generation,* starring James Earl Jones as Haley. Although not matching the audience of the first miniseries, the 1979 sequel was very successful. Both miniseries achieved further success through syndication around the world. The series produced such a profound impact on the American public that NBC aired a special commemorating the twenty-fifth anniversary of its broadcast in 2002.

Roots provided an occasion for an overdue national discussion of race and America's slavery experience. Race—whether in the context of slavery, affirmative action, integration, or the Civil Rights movement—has stirred strong emotions throughout American history. Told in a powerful fashion, the miniseries forced the American public to confront and appreciate the struggles faced by slaves. Creating compelling characters, Haley revealed the brutal reality of slavery through the experience of slaves with whom the audience identified. The moment when Kunta Kinte finally accepted his slave name, "Toby," to stop being whipped provided a poignant point of departure for constructive conversations on race across America.

Given its popularity, it is no surprise that *Roots* sparked several national trends. Prior to *Roots,* slavery was a topic rarely discussed in schools or on television except as an abstract political and economic concept. After the miniseries aired many Americans, especially African Americans, became much more interested in learning about the realities of life under slavery. Many also became more interested in exploring their "roots"—having watched Alex Haley's family history unfold in *Roots* and *Roots: The Next Generation.*

Roots also had a profound impact on television. Its success demonstrated that the American public would

LeVar Burton plays Kunta Kinte, an African enslaved and brought to America, in the television mini-series *Roots* based on the novel by Alex Haley, 1977. **AP/WIDE WORLD PHOTOS. REPRODUCED BY PERMISSION.**

watch quality programs that addressed serious issues. It also proved the viability of the miniseries format. Television was now emboldened to tackle other difficult subjects, and to try and create new miniseries events, as demonstrated by NBC's acclaimed 1978 miniseries, *The Holocaust,* a program inconceivable without the strong precedent of *Roots.* The appeal of the miniseries remains strong decades after *Roots,* and is not limited to drama. Several miniseries broadcast on PBS by Ken Burns, including *Baseball: An Illustrated History, The Civil War: An Illustrated History,* and *Jazz: A History of America's Music* achieved considerable success.

Primary Source

"'Roots' Getting a Grip on People Everywhere"

SYNOPSIS: In this article, Charlayne Hunter-Gault reports on the way the television miniseries *Roots* became a national experience as millions of Americans watched the series unfold over eight nights.

"My children and I just sat there, crying," said a black public relation director in Nashville. "We couldn't talk. We just cried."

"It has made the brutality of slavery more vivid for me than anything I've seen or read," said a black economist in Philadelphia.

"It's so powerful," said a white secretary in New York. "It's so distressful, I just feel awful, but I'm glad my children are watching."

All across the country this week, millions of people have been drawn to the unfolding drama of "Roots," the eight-part television, adaptation of the book by Alex Haley, tracing his origins back to an African village. It has produced the third largest audience in television history (only the two parts of Gone With the Wind in 1976 drew more).

Nearly 80 million people have sat before their television sets in penthouses and tenements, bars and brownstones, fraternity houses and dormitories as the saga of Kunta Kinte had flashed before them night after night since last Sunday.

Doubters and enthusiasts, whites as well as blacks, young and old, wealthy and poor had reactions they wanted to share.

Some laughed when a hungry Kunta Kinte, who was thought to have learned no English, suddenly thrust his plate toward the older slave, Fiddler, and said, "Grits, dummy."

Some cried as Kunta Kinte finally gave in to the whip's lash and accepted the slave name Toby.

And some got angry at the long, deep scars on his back in a later episode.

But however different their reactions might have been, people everywhere, even those who had not seen it, were talking about "Roots."

Doubleday reports that sales of "Roots," now in its 13th printing since publication in October, have soared even higher since the television serial went on the air. The best-selling book is Mr. Haley's narrative account of his 12-year search for his origins—a search that started with stories of family members and a handful of African words, including the name Kinte.

The search ended in Gambia, a tiny state in West Africa where, with the help of the griot—the oral historian—Mr. Haley went back in time to 1750, when Kunta Kinte, his ancestor, was born.

The story dovetailed with the one Mr. Haley had heard from his family.

The people of Gambia embraced "Meester Kinte" immediately, telling him "Through our flesh, we are you, and you are us."

After a young black writer from the West Coast watched the first two-hour episode on Sunday, he shook his head and, referring respectively to the author of the book and the director of the television adaptation, said:

"Haley, yes. [David] Wolper no."

The production, he said, was "too Hollywood," lacking in both depth and truth to the original narrative.

After Monday night's showing, which included the scene where Kunta Kinte is whipped by the white overseer to force him to give up his African ancestral name and accept the slave name Toby, the writer, smiling, said to his host:

"Haley, yes. Wolper, maybe."

A black man carrying an attache case stepped into the elevator of the predominantly white company where he worked.

"Good morning, Kunta Kinte," said a white colleague, cheerfully.

The black man lowered his head, smiled and said, "Toby."

In one middle-class white Queens household, there was a lively debate over coffee and bagels after the second installment.

"It doesn't show any good white people," said the wife. "There must have been some decent white people and it should have been more balanced."

"No, the good whites had their day with 'Gone With the Wind,'" said the husband. "Anyhow, how good could any whites look to a slave? And that's whose eyes we're seeing it through. All the white bosses must have looked pretty bad, like Nazi Party members did to Jews."

"They were terrible," shouted the 18-year-old son. "Slavery was evil and this shows how bad it was, stealing those people from their homes and carrying them far away and buying and selling them."

A group of six young black men and women gathered at a counter as the short-order cook, her jaw set firmly, commented tersely about "Roots."

"I had to cut the thing off about half way through and go to bed," she said. "It was getting to me."

"I cried like a baby," said another of the women. "I just never thought it was so bad. I never thought they could treat you so bad."

"I tell you one thing," injected a somber young man in the group, "Those white folks better not mess with me today. I just might have to stomp one."

"Don't do that," another of the group snapped. "Things ain't changed that much. And jobs don't grow on trees."

In a scene from the landmark ABC mini–series *Roots,* Kunta Kinte is born. Actresses Cicely Tyson (left) and Maya Angelou played Kinte's mother and grandmother. **AP/WIDE WORLD PHOTOS. REPRODUCED BY PERMISSION.**

It took a little while for the 4-and 5-year-olds in the kindergarten class at the Patterson School for Heritage and Education in Harlem to come alive, since most of them had stayed up way past their normal bed time to watch Roots.

"I was having a hard time getting my 4-year-old up," said one young mother, "but, at one point I said, 'Okay, Mandinka warrior. Time to go hunting in the forest.' He smiled, opened his eyes and rolled out."

"It's just incredible," Mr. Haley, the author of "Roots," said from O'Hare Airport in Chicago yesterday during a stopover between lectures. "A.B.C. has preserved the integrity of the thing as best they could. And I think they've done a fantastic job."

"A young white boy told me yesterday in Texas that his father had always hated my people, but af-ter seeing "Roots," he said, 'I watched my father cry for the first time in his life.'

"A black man saw me in the airport, and for a long time, didn't say anything. Finally, he turned to me and said, 'Look man, I just can't be cool. I've just got to say thank you.'"

Jock's, a popular Harlem bar and restaurant with a TV has been jammed all week with patrons like Ronald Guy, a lawyer, who "wanted to watch it with other people around."

Joe Kirkpatrick, the owner, said that one night viewers got so angry over the treatment of Kunte Kinte that they would not allow the juke box to be turned on even after the show had ended.

"They just wanted to talk it out," he said, "and it wasn't until they had talked and talked for a very long time that they finally remembered they were in a bar.

"That's when they started drinking up."

John Henrik Clarke, the black historian, said there were some "cultural inaccuracies" in the television series, "but those are minor."

"Overall," he said, "I think it has opened up a delicate situation that will probably cause some embarrassment on both the black and white sides. But it has paved the way for a much needed, long overdue discussion."

Further Resources

BOOKS

Barnouw, Erik. *Tube of Plenty: The Evolution of American Television,* rev. ed. New York and Oxford: Oxford University Press, 1990.

Edelstein, Andrew J., and Kevin McDonough. *The Seventies: From Hot Pants to Hot Tubs.* New York: Dutton, 1990.

MacDonald, J. Fred. *Blacks and White TV: African Americans in Television since 1948,* 2nd ed. Chicago: Nelson-Hall, 1992.

Terrace, Vincent. *Television, 1970–1980.* San Diego, Calif.: A.S. Barnes /London: Tantivy, 1981.

PERIODICALS

Baye, Betty Winston. "Alex Haley's 'Roots' Revisited." *Essence,* February 22, 1992, 88.

Podolsky, J. D. "Torn Up by the Roots." *People Weekly,* October 5, 1992, 71–72.

WEBSITES

The Kunta Kinte-Alex Haley Foundation. Available online at http://www.kintehaley.org/beginning.html (accessed June 13, 2003).

Sowell, Thomas. "Alex Haley's "Roots:" Fact or Fiction?" *Capitalism Magazine.* Available online at http://www.capmag.com/article.asp?ID=1384; website home page: http://www.capmag.com/ (accessed June 13, 2003).

"Anita Bryant's Crusade"

Editorial

By: Jean O'Leary and Bruce Voeller

Date: June 7, 1977

Source: O'Leary, Jean, and Bruce Voeller. "Anita Bryant's Crusade." *The New York Times,* June 7, 1977, 35.

About the Authors: Jean O'Leary (1948–) is a prominent lesbian activist. She entered a convent after graduating from high school in 1966, but had to leave four years later because of her romantic attraction to other women. She then became openly gay and moved to New York City. She quickly became involved in gay and lesbian social and political organizations, and was co-director of the National Gay Task Force with Bruce Voeller during the 1970s. In subsequent decades she continued her activism, becoming the first openly gay person to serve on a presidential commission, and holding important positions within the Democratic Party.

Bruce Voeller (1935–1994) was a biologist and an advocate for gay rights. He co-founded the National Gay Task Force in 1973 and was co-director of that organization with Jean O'Leary in the 1970s. Voeller coined the phrase Aquired Immune Deficiency Syndrome (AIDS) in 1981 to describe the recently discovered disorder. He studied human sexuality and methods of preventing sexually transmitted disease. Bruce Voeller died of AIDS in 1994. ■

Introduction

The gay and lesbian rights movement in the late 1970s worked for the passage of antidiscrimination legislation. But it proved difficult to organize factionalized homosexual communities around legislative issues. Gay activism was only slowly emerging outside of a few large cities. Then came Anita Bryant's "Save the Children" campaign.

Gay liberation advocates did rally in response to one particular anti–gay rights crusade. In 1978, Anita Bryant, a popular gospel singer, became the focus of national attention when she led a campaign to repeal one of the first gay rights ordinances in the United States. A year before, Dade County, Florida, which includes the city of Miami, had passed a bill that prohibited discrimination in housing, employment, and other areas on the basis of sexual orientation. Bryant insisted that there was an imminent danger that homosexuals would obtain employment as teachers in public and private schools. She encouraged local officials to put the repeal effort before voters in a special referendum. Bryant, a former Miss Oklahoma and runner-up for Miss America, relied heavily on her wholesome Christian image to claim that such a policy went against the word of God as expressed in the Bible. In her media interviews and speeches, she frequently made reference to gay people having an "abnormal" lifestyle and asserted that they would use the law to recruit and abuse children. The special referendum was put forward and pased. Within a year, Bryant's "Save Our Children" organization, other evangelical groups, and religious leaders such as the Reverend Jerry Falwell led successful efforts to repeal similar laws in Minnesota, Kansas, and Oklahoma, and they attempted to do so in Oregon and California.

Significance

Despite the initial success of Bryant's campaign, it proved hugely controversial and counterproductive, for it focused national public attention on the nature of the prejudice and discrimination faced by gay men and lesbians. Furthermore, the direct threat energized the gay community to organize. They lobbied, rallied public support, and fought back. Soon the anti-discrimination ordinance was re-enacted in Florida, and similar ordinances were passed in other areas, notably Washington, D.C. At around the same time, Harvey Milk, an openly gay San

Singer Anita Bryant, an outspoken critic of gay rights and creator of "Save Our Children," a so-called crusade to keep children safe from the supposed dangers of homosexuals, speaks at a press conference on September 1, 1978. **AP/WIDE WORLD PHOTOS. REPRODUCED BY PERMISSION.**

Francisco supervisor, and Mayor George Moscone were murdered, and the light sentence given the man convicted of both shootings galvanized gay communities. In the 1980s, gay and lesbian organizations began a strategy of visibility aided by the few entertainment and sports figures who "came out" (movie star Rock Hudson, tennis champion Martina Navratilova, and country singer K.D. Lang, for example). Gay advocates such as the Gay and Lesbian Alliance Against Defamation (GLAAD) monitored the media for tone and content. Though Bryant stirred up the media for a time, her pro-family crusade eventually backfired, signaling the end of her career as the spokeswoman for orange juice when the controversy-shy Florida Citrus Growers Association cancelled her $100,000-a-year contract. Her already declining career as an entertainer was never to recover, despite repeated attempts over the next two decades. In later years, Bryant declined to be brought into any gay-rights controversy, but she told *The Washington Post* in May 1990, "What I did, I feel today still was right."

Primary Source

"Anita Bryant's Crusade"

> **SYNOPSIS:** In this op-ed piece from *The New York Times,* the codirectors of the National Gay Task

Force argue against "Save Our Children's" campaign asking gay men and women to stay in the closet and "keep their deviant activity to themselves." The authors state that such a policy is immoral and destructive because it propagates a lie about the reality of people who are gay. The fight against the "Save Our Children" campaign was a watershed in the national gay rights movement.

Anita Bryant and her Save Our Children Inc. are doing the 20 million lesbians and gay men in America an enormous favor: They are focusing for the public the nature of the prejudice and discrimination we face.

Homosexuals, the Save Our Children folks said in a recent full-page ad in The Miami Herald, used to be stoned to death. But nowadays, they said, there's developed "an attitude of tolerance . . . based on the understanding that homosexuals will keep their deviant activity to themselves, will not flaunt their lifestyles, will not be allowed to preach their sexual standards to, or otherwise influence, impressionable young people." Anita Bryant herself said it even more clearly on a recent network television show: "We're not going after their jobs, as long as they do their jobs and do not want to come out of the closet."

What this means should be abundantly clear: Gay women and men in this country have been required to join a conspiracy to pretend we don't exist, so that other people can lie to children.

All of us millions of lesbians and gay men were once American children. And the first lie most of us were told about homosexuality is that it didn't have anything to do with anyone we knew. It certainly wasn't about anyone we loved or respected. It wasn't about Uncle Jim and that nice friend he lived with, or Great-Aunt Sally, who'd been sharing an apartment with her friend "Aunt Jennie" for the last 40 years. It certainly wasn't about any of our teachers.

If we heard words like "queer" and wanted to know what they meant, our parents told us that it wasn't something for children to talk about, but to be sure to stay away from strangers with candy, since "those people" wanted to hurt little children. So what we learned about gay people we had to find out from our friends. What they were, we discovered, were funny men who wanted to be women and talked with a lisp. Most of our friends didn't think there were any women who were "that way," but some of them suspected there were some and that they all wore leather jackets and beat up people with chains.

So we learned all these lies, like everybody else, and from them we derived the biggest lie of all about homosexuality, that it couldn't possibly have anything to do with us. Those loving feelings we had for members of our own sex were just a "childish stage" we were going through. As we grew up, we were told, we'd see that we'd be able to repress such feelings or pretend to ourselves we didn't have them. Even later, when we knew we couldn't do that, and weren't prepared to lie to ourselves, we still weren't ready to believe that we were "homosexuals." After all, we didn't want to hurt children, or brandish chains, or talk with a lisp.

It took many of us a long time to realize that these stereotypes were lies, and that there were so many healthy, happy, productive, responsible human beings in this world who had refused to deny or repress their capacity to love members of their own sex. For some of us this realization had to wait until we were well into adulthood, and we suffered because we, too, believed the lies that we were sinful, criminal, sick.

We are not the only ones who suffered. Our parents suffered from the lie that they were somehow responsible for making us "queer." Everyone who cared for us suffered, believing the lie that we were sick. And every child in America who has learned the

lies has suffered from the dehumanizing experience of learning to hate.

So we believe that Anita Bryant is correct to put the focus right where it belongs: On children. And on morality.

We believe it is immoral to lie to children. We believe it is immoral to teach them to hate people whom they choose to love. We believe it is immoral to pretend to children that they don't have a variety of loving options in their own lives, or to force them to believe that they are the only ones in the world to have loving or sexual feelings for their own sex. We think it is immoral to foster prejudice and discrimination by pretending to children that there are no real people who are gay.

Along with a great many people in the churches these days, we believe that these are where the real moral issues lie, not in the sort of selective fundamentalism that allows people like Anita Bryant to quote St. Paul's injunction against homosexuality while sensibly disobeying his rule against women's speaking in church. We choose another passage from St. Paul: "Love worketh no ill to his neighbor. Love therefore is the fulfillment of the law."

Further Resources

BOOKS

Adam, Barry D. *The Rise of a Gay and Lesbian Movement.* New York: 1995.

Bryant, Anita. *The Anita Bryant Story: The Survival of Our Nation's Families and the Threat of Militant Homosexuality.* Old Tapan, N.J.: Fleming H. Revell, 1977.

Cruikshank, Margaret. *The Gay and Lesbian Liberation Movement.* London: Routledge, 1992.

PERIODICALS

Podhorets, Norman. "How the Gay Rights Movement Won." *Commentary,* November 1996, 32.

"What Becomes a Legend Most?"

Advertisements

By: Great Lakes Mink Association

Date: 1970s

Source: Great Lakes Mink Association's "What Becomes a Legend Most?" advertising campaign, 1970–79. Reproduced from The Advertising Archive, Ltd.

About the Organization: The Great Lakes Mink Association (GLMA) was formed in 1941 by mink ranchers in the Great Lakes region to further research and to promote the ranchers'

WHAT BECOMES A LEGEND MOST?

An exquisite extra-dark
natural mink
bred only by
the Great Lakes Mink men
and designed by Geoffrey Beene
for Sakowitz.

BLACKGLAMA®

Primary Source

"What Becomes a Legend Most?" (1 OF 3)

SYNOPSIS: Scores of celebrity "legends" posed for photos wearing Blackglama furs, in the most famous fashion campaign of the seventies. Leontyne Price, the dramatic soprano of the Metropolitan Opera, appears in this 1970 ad. THE ADVERTISING ARCHIVE LTD./BLACKGLAMA. REPRODUCED BY PERMISSION.

Primary Source

"What Becomes a Legend Most?" (2 OF 3)

Broadway performer Carol Channing poses for a Blackglama "What Becomes a Legend Most?" advertisement in 1972. THE ADVERTISING ARCHIVE LTD./BLACKGLAMA. REPRODUCED BY PERMISSION.

Primary Source

"What Becomes a Legend Most?" (3 OF 3)

Actress Joan Fontaine, a movie star most famous for her 1940s roles, appears in Blackglama's "What Becomes a Legend Most?" advertising campaign in 1978. THE ADVERTISING ARCHIVE LTD./BLACKGLAMA. REPRODUCED BY PERMISSION.

interests. It merged with the Mutation Mink Breeders Association in 1986 to form the American Legend Cooperative. ■

Introduction

"What becomes a legend most?" was the question posed by one of the most famous fashion advertising campaigns of all time. Launched in 1968, the ads for Blackglama furs answered the question with glamorous black-and-white photos of stars wrapped in luxurious mink. The images were shot by Richard Avedon and, after 1972, Bill King.

The legends who posed for Blackglama were a gallery of the twentieth century's greatest female stars: Marlene Dietrich, Bette Davis, Joan Crawford, Judy Garland, Maria Callas, Diana Ross, Barbra Streisand, and Lillian Hellman, to mention a few. "There's no denying that as a group, they comprise the most illustrious list of names ever brought together for commercial purposes," wrote Peter Rogers, author of the 1979 book *The Blackglama Story.*

The Blackglama campaign was devised by the New York advertising executive Jane Trahey for the Great Lakes Mink Association (GLMA), which was facing falling sales because some thought that fur was ecologically and economically offensive. Trahey came up with the name Blackglama. It did not indicate a designer or manfacturer, but rather that a fur had been made with pelts from one of 400 GLMA ranches. (Within two years, however, furriers were stitching the name on their labels as a supposed indicator of quality.) Trahey then assembled a group of legendary women to revive the glamour of the fur coat. Peter Rogers, her partner in the campaign, defined the criteria for inclusion: "All legends share a timelessness, a glamour, an endurance that goes beyond what's currently or merely in vogue."

The majority of the "Legend" divas were in their twilight years and were no longer mainstream icons. The only movie offers Bette Davis and Joan Crawford were getting in the 1970s were for horror films. At the time of her shoot, Garland had just been fired from the set of *Valley of the Dolls.* By the late 1960s and early 1970s, "Legends" like Ethel Merman, Claudette Colbert, and Barbara Stanwyck were looking aged compared to more contemporary stars Marianne Faithful and Jane Fonda.

The photo shoots for Blackglama are themselves the stuff of legend. Dietrich showed up at her Blackglama shoot fully made up, then proceeded to teach Avedon about lighting. Peter Rogers tells of a debt-ridden Judy Garland complete with pillow fights, rows, and excessive drinking. Lillian Hellman the writer had never been a diva in the sense that the others were but was enjoying a new-found popularity with the publication of her autobiographies and the film production of *Julia.* She came to photographer Bill King's studio on an hour's notice to replace Ginger Rodgers in 1976.

Significance

"What Becomes a Legend Most?" shone in the days when celebrities rarely endorsed products and always wore fur. But by 1987, when Tommy Tune the male dancer and choreographer appeared, the campaign was losing steam, in part because wearing fur had become even more politically charged than it had been when the ad campaign started. In 1989, People for the Ethical Treatment of Animals (PETA) targeted the product by running a parody of the ad with a startled, mink-wrapped Casandra Petersen (the actress who portrays the character Elvira in horror-movie parodies) beneath the headline "what disgraces a legend most?"

Despite these problems, the campaign continued with occasional ads in the 1990s and 2000s. Jessica Tandy appeared in 1991 as the sixtieth "legend." In 2001, a new generation of supermodels took over, beginning with Linda Evangelista. Yet Edward Brennan, the head of American Legend, observed, "Let's be honest, we don't have the legends we had in the past. Our list was a very short shortlist." The original legends of the Blackglama ads were famous figures from a bygone generation. They suggested worldliness, urbanity, and sophistication, unlike, the view of some, more recent stars. Major designers continue to work with pelts.

Further Resources

BOOKS

Rogers, Peter. *The Blackglama Story.* New York: Simon and Schuster, 1979.

PERIODICALS

Rubenstein, Hal. "How They Stole the Story." *The New York Times,* October 24, 1993.

Sherwood, James. "The Making of a Legend." *Independent on Sunday,* December 2, 2001.

WEBSITES

"What Becomes a Legend Most?" http://www.blackglama.com/ (accessed June 9, 2003).

9

MEDICINE AND HEALTH

CHRISTOPHER CUMO

Entries are arranged in chronological order by date of primary source. For entries with one primary source, the entry title is the same as the primary source title. Entries with more than one primary source have an overall entry title, followed by the titles of the primary sources.

Important Events in Medicine and Health, 1970–1979

1970

- Hospital-care costs in the United States reach an average of $81 per patient per day, with average patient costs of $664.28 per stay.

- The first nerve transplant is performed.

- On January 1, only 12 percent of U.S. physicians are in group practices.

- On April 1, Congress bans cigarette ads on radio and television beginning January 1, 1971.

- On April 3, Congress passes the Occupational Safety and Health Act.

- On July 1, the most liberal abortion law in the United States takes effect in the state of New York.

- On July 23, children's advocate Robert Burnett Choats, Jr., testifies before the U.S. Senate Commerce Committee that breakfast cereals have too much sugar and too few nutrients.

- On July 27, the Food and Drug Administration (FDA) warns that birth-control pills may produce blood clots.

- On October 28, the FDA orders the makers of baby food to label the nutritional value of their products.

- On December 15, the FDA announces that, at a minimum, nearly one million cans of tuna fish have been removed from the market as a precaution because tests indicated mercury contamination.

- On December 23, the FDA announces that excessive amounts of mercury have been found in 89 percent of samples of frozen swordfish tested, and nearly all brands sold in the United States have been removed from the market.

- On December 30, Congress passes the Poison Prevention Packaging Act, requiring manufacturers of potentially dangerous products to put safety tops on their containers so children will not be able to open them.

1971

- The diamond-bladed scalpel is introduced in surgery.

- The first heart and lung transplants are performed.

- Britain's Royal College of Physicians reports that cigarette smoking has become a cause of death comparable to the great epidemic diseases of typhoid and cholera in the nineteenth century.

- In January, the human growth hormone is synthesized at the University of California at Berkeley.

- On February 18, President Richard Nixon urges Congress to loan money to Health Maintenance Organizations (HMOs) to encourage their spread.

- On March 18, soft contact lenses win FDA approval.

- In April, researchers at the Anderson Tumor Institute in Texas isolate the cold-sore herpes virus from the lymph cell-cancer known as Burkitt's lymphoma.

- On August 6, the Federal Communications Commission bans cigarette advertising on U.S. radio and television.

- On October 19, Congress limits lead content in paint to protect children from lead poisoning.

- In November, the FDA warns U.S. physicians against administering the steroid diethylstilbestrol (DES) to pregnant women because of the increased risk of vaginal cancer in their daughters.

- On December 24, President Richard Nixon signs into law the National Cancer Act, authorizing appropriations of $1.5 billion per year to combat the second leading cause of death in the U.S.

1972

- On January 10, the U.S. Surgeon General's report on smoking warns that cigarette smoke may harm nonsmokers.

- On January 21, the U.S. Department of Health and Human Services requires six cigarette companies to strengthen warning on cigarette advertisements.

- On March 10, the FDA orders the lowering of lead content in all household paints, toys, and other articles to no more than 0.5 percent after December 31, and to no more than 0.06 percent after December 31, 1973. Fifty thousand to one hundred thousand children a year require treatment for lead poisoning.

- On March 14, the U.S. Department of Agriculture reports that 1.25 million chickens were destroyed in Maine after high polychlorinated biphenyls (PCBs) were found in some of them. Contaminated feed was believed to be the source.

- On March 17, the FDA publishes limits on the use of PCBs. The chemicals were implicated in skin irritations, liver damage, and birth defects.

- On May 16, the National Academy of Sciences announces that air pollution may explain why city dwellers suffer twice the rural rate of cancer.

- On May 26, a patient undergoing a skin graft in New York City is anesthetized by acupuncture.

- On December 8, the FDA reports that antibiotic overuse results in tens of thousands of unnecessary deaths in the United States each year.

- On December 13, the FDA proposes to restrict the amounts of vitamins A and D sold in over-the-counter products. Overdoses can retard children's growth, enlarge liver and spleen, or increase calcium deposits, leading to hypertension and kidney failure.

1973

- The American Psychiatric Association removes homosexuality from its list of mental illnesses, redefining it as a "sexual orientation disturbance."

- The birth rate slips below the 2.1 child-per-woman ratio required for the natural replacement of the population and remains about 1.8 for the remainder of the decade.

- The Boston Women's Health Collective publishes *Our Bodies, Ourselves,* which becomes a popular book directed at women's health issues and needs.

- On January 8, the American Hospital Association releases a twelve-point patients' bill of rights intended to "contribute to more effective patient care and greater satisfaction for the patient, his physician, and the hospital organization."

- On January 22, the U.S. Supreme Court in *Roe* v. *Wade* guarantees women the right to an abortion during the first trimester of pregnancy.

- On March 9, scientists at the Medical College of Wisconsin report substantial concentrations of carbon monoxide in the blood of Americans living in cities, especially among cigarette smokers.

- On March 11, the FDA recalls all products containing mushrooms from a mushroom company in Ohio because of botulism in one lot of cans on retail shelves.

- In April, the Centers for Disease Control and Prevention identifies the first of the survivors of the Tuskegee Syphilis Study. Congress will pay their medical care the rest of their lives.

- On April 5, the Centers for Disease Control and Prevention report that botulism afflicted forty-seven Americans over the past two years, killing ten.

- On April 20, Nevada establishes a state-licensing system for acupuncture therapists.

- On December 29, Congress passes the HMO Act, regulating Health Maintenance Organizations.

1974

- The computerized axial tomography (CAT) scanner gains wide use.

- Dentists are warned about exposing patients to excessive radiation through too-frequent use of dental X rays.

- The Manufacturing Chemists Association releases evidence showing vinyl chloride, a plastic used in bottling, is linked to human cancer.

- U.S. insurance companies raise rates on malpractice policies, leading physicians and hospitals to raise fees.

- In February, the contamination of chicken feed by the insecticides aldrin and dieldrin force the killing of thousands of chickens in Mississippi.

- On February 6, President Richard Nixon calls national health insurance "an idea whose time has come in America."

- In June, the Heimlich maneuver is introduced as first aid for choking.

- On August 12, President Gerald Ford asks Congress to pass national health insurance.

1975

- Lyme disease is identified in Lyme, Connecticut.

- Mexican authorities spray marijuana fields with the herbicide paraquat in a $35 million U.S.-funded program to wipe out the drug.

- Versions of antibodies produced by the body are first manufactured in the laboratory.

- On January 1, only seven percent of U.S. physicians are women.

- On January 8, National Cancer Institute scientists announce the isolation of the first human cancer virus in an uncontaminated state. On March 17, physicians strike New York City hospitals, the first physician strike in the U.S.

- In May, California doctors organize a month-long strike to protest rising insurance costs and slowdowns in health care.

- On July 1, major malpractice insurance companies announce a tripling of doctors' premiums and a general cancellation of malpractice policies.

- On July 5, researchers report that infants who died from sudden infant death syndrome or crib death show an abnormally low concentration of the enzyme PEPCK.

- On August 28, the FDA proposes to eliminate polyvinyl chloride from food packaging because it may cause cancer.

- In December, a Cornell University study claims two to four million needless operations a year cause some twelve thousand deaths. One-third of all hysterectomies and tonsilectomies may be unnecessary.

1976

- Perrier water is introduced to U.S. markets and gains popularity as fitness-minded Americans switch from alcoholic beverages.

- A viral cause of multiple sclerosis is discovered.

- On January 8, the General Accounting Office of Congress reports that the Indian Health Service sterilized thousands of Native American women without their consent.

- On February 8, the National Cancer Institute finds the highest U.S. cancer rates are downwind of chemical plants along the New Jersey turnpike.

- On February 15, President Gerald Ford withdraws a plan for national health insurance, saying it would worsen inflation.

- In February, soldiers at Fort Dix, New Jersey, are the first Americans to contract swine flu.

- In March, President Gerald Ford announces a campaign to immunize all Americans against swine flu, and Congress appropriates $135 million for this campaign.

- On March 13, the New Jersey Supreme Court grants Joseph Quinlan the right to remove a respirator from Karen Ann Quinlan, his comatose daughter. She lives nine years without the respirator.

- In May, the FDA approves the use of inderal, a beta-blocker effective in treating high blood pressure.
- On June 23, the National Institutes of Health end the voluntary moratorium on recombinant DNA research but ban certain forms of genetic experimentation and regulate others.
- In July, Legionnaires' disease infects participants at an American Legion convention in Philadelphia, killing twenty-nine.
- On September 16, Congress passes the Hyde Amendment, banning federal funds for abortions "except where the life of the mother would be endangered if the fetus were brought to term."
- On November 13, Donald A. Henderson, Johns Hopkins University physician and head of the World Health Organization (WHO) campaign against smallpox, reports that Asia is free of smallpox for the first time in history.

1977

- The baby-food industry agrees to decrease salt and sugar from its products.
- Lung cancer deaths among U.S. women (14.9 per 100,000, up from 1.5 per 100,000 in 1930) surpass the number of colorectal-cancer deaths (14.3 per 100,000) and begin to approach the number of breast-cancer deaths.
- Balloon angioplasty is developed for reopening clogged arteries.
- A life-threatening viral infection—herpes encephalitis—is treated with a drug for the first time.
- In February, the FDA announces a correlation between saccharin intake and bladder cancer.
- On April 26, President Jimmy Carter's plan to contain hospital costs passes the Senate. The House of Representatives will reject the bill.
- On May 23, the first recombinant DNA product—human insulin—is produced.
- In June, the National Center for Health Statistics announces death rates caused by strokes and cardiovascular disease declined in the 1970s. Between 1969 and 1977 the death rate from heart disease declined 19.2 percent for men, 24.1 percent for women.
- On July 2, the first magnetic resonance imaging (MRI) scanner is tested.
- On August 23, the FDA approves Tagamet (cimetidine), a new ulcer-treating drug developed in Britain.
- In September, the U.S. Department of Agriculture urges meat processors to reduce the amount of nitrates in meat following reports that crisply fried bacon contains carcinogens.
- On October 26, Dr. Donald A. Henderson reports the world's last known case of smallpox in Somalia.
- On November 2, Dr. Donald Fraser, head of the Council for Disease Control, leads a team of physicians and scientists in identifying the previously unknown bacterium responsible for Legionnaires' disease.
- On November 15, U.S. manufacturers defend the addition of sugar in breakfast cereals as the only way to entice children to eat a nutritious breakfast.

1978

- On January 11, Department of Health, Education and Welfare (HEW) secretary calls cigarette smoking "slow-motion suicide."
- On January 13, the FDA requires blood intended for transfusions to be labeled by source: a paid or volunteer donor. Blood from paid donors and commercial blood banks causes hepatitis three to ten times more often than blood from volunteer donors.
- On February 17, the FDA issues the first federal mandatory safety performance standard for equipment producing ultrasonic radiation used in physical-therapy treatments.
- On April 17, Donald A. Henderson reports no new cases of smallpox.
- On May 15, the U.S. Department of Agriculture issues regulations to reduce the amount of nitrates in bacon. Sodium nitrate was found to produce lymph cancer in laboratory rats.
- On May 16, Washington University researchers report that panfrying hamburgers might increase the risk of cancer. The concern was the heat, not the meat itself.
- On June 28, the Supreme Court rules in *Regents of the University of California v. Bakke* against racial quotas to assure the entry of a minimum number of minority students each year into the University of California Davis, medical school. It orders the admission of Allan Bakke, a white male applicant denied admission despite higher grades and Medical College Aptitude Test (MCAT) scores than some minority applicants the medical school had admitted.
- On July 11, experts testify before a House subcommittee that X-raying mothers needlessly during pregnancy produces seventy children a year who could be expected to develop cancer.
- In August, a HEW study of occupational health concludes that at least 20 percent of all cancers in the United States "may be work related."

1979

- The rising cost of Medicare-funded kidney dialysis treatment raises questions about how much the U.S. can afford without slighting other health needs.
- On January 1, a record 63,800 students are enrolled in U.S. medical schools.
- On January 20, officials of the Venereal Disease Control Division of the National Center for Disease Control report that oral doses of the antibiotic tetracycline are as effective as penicillin injections in treating gonorrhea.
- On February 11, the Commerce Department reports that the output of U.S. cigarette manufacturers continues to increase despite cancer warnings.
- On March 19, the American Heart Association says moderate consumption of alcoholic beverages may protect against death from heart disease.
- On June 25, the Office of Technology Assessment, a research arm of Congress, reports that the widespread use of antibiotics in animal feeds cause the evolution of antibiotic resistant bacteria.

- On September 10, a panel of doctors and former Valium users tells a Senate Human Resources health subcommittee that the drug, the most widely prescribed tranquilizer in the United States, is potentially addictive, even in moderate doses.

- On September 14, a panel of national experts warns that women who took estrogen after menopause may have increased their risk of uterine cancer as much as 800 percent.

- In October, demonstrations by marijuana smokers in Washington, D.C., force Congress to end support for the paraquat program after the Centers for Disease Control and Prevention warns that cannabis tainted with paraquat may damage the lungs.

- On November 18, the Centers for Disease Control and Prevention reports that the incidence of gonorrhea has leveled off, but syphilis, a more serious venereal disease, is on the increase.

ing coverage to all pregnant women and infants to age one.

Significance

Johnson's withdrawal from the 1968 presidential race gave his opponents an opportunity to renew their attack against national health care, particularly since Republican Richard M. Nixon's (served 1969–1974) election as president that year signaled a return to conservatism.

In 1970, Sidney R. Garfield mounted a common attack on national health care: Medicare and Medicaid had flooded the medical system with too many patients, increasing the demand for services. Prices rose with demand, as economic theory would predict. A national health care system would exacerbate the problem by further increasing demand and prices.

Instead, Garfield wanted to preserve the system of private insurance through health maintenance organizations. He believed patients should not consult their physician as the first course of action. A less expensive option would be for a patient to visit "paramedical personnel" who would enter that patient's data into a computer. Only the truly sick would be funneled to a physician, reducing demand on them. Physicians could save additional time and expense, Garfield believed, by delegating routine care to paraprofessionals. Under a physician's guidance, paraprofessionals might even care for ill patients whose treatment involved a progression of simple treatments.

Such measures, Garfield wrote, might reduce physician workloads and presumably costs by 50 percent. His solution was a more efficient use of medical services within the private sector rather than the creation of a bloated government health care system.

Garfield thus made two assertions. First he opposed government-sponsored health care. This was the position of the American Medical Association, which since the 1940s had denounced government-sponsored coverage as socialized medicine. This attack was effective in the U.S., which had from its inception adhered to Alexander Hamilton's faith in the free market.

Second Garfield promoted what we now call Health Maintenance Organizations (HMOs) as a free-market solution to rising medical costs. That is, Garfield appealed to market forces to set the price of medical services. Congress confirmed this belief in 1973, passing the HMO Act. An HMO, so the argument runs, slows the rise of medical costs by combining consumers into large units that purchase medical services at a fixed price. An HMO is a private entity and thereby avoids the specter of socialized medicine.

"The Delivery of Medical Care"

Journal article

By: Sidney R. Garfield

Date: April 1970

Source: Garfield, Sidney R. "The Delivery of Medical Care." *Scientific American* 222, no. 4, April 1970, 15–23.

About the Author: Sidney R. Garfield, a surgeon at Contractors General Hospital in the middle of the California's Mojave Desert during the 1930s, created a health care plan in which members prepaid for access to care rather than paid a fee for each visit to a physician. In the late 1930s, he accepted an invitation from Henry Kaiser, a wealthy businessman, to help establish Kaiser Permanente, the first health maintenance organization (HMO) in the United States. ∎

Introduction

Despite his broad reforms, Franklin D. Roosevelt (served 1933–1945), president from 1933 to 1945, did not press Congress for government-sponsored medical coverage for Americans. His successor, Harry S. Truman (served 1945–1953), however, did favor it, and in the 1948 presidential campaign, both he and Progressive Party candidate Henry A. Wallace proposed government-sponsored coverage for all Americans, an idea opposed by Republican candidate Thomas Dewey. Truman won the election but could not budge Congress, where Republicans and conservative southern Democrats branded national health care as socialized medicine.

There matters rested until Lyndon Baines Johnson (served 1963–1969) became president. He had grown up in poverty and believed the federal government had an obligation to all Americans, not just the affluent. He understood that Congress would reject national health care as too sweeping and decided to proceed in increments. In 1965, he persuaded Congress to enact Medicare, extending coverage to Americans at least for those age sixty-five and over. The next year, he pushed Medicaid through Congress, guaranteeing coverage to all Americans who fell below an income threshold. In 1968, though, he failed to push through legislation guarantee-

Primary Source

"The Delivery of Medical Care" [excerpt]

SYNOPSIS: In this excerpt, Sidney R. Garfield opposes national health care on the premise that it would increase the demand and cost of care. Instead he proposed that paraprofessionals assume routine duties, saving patients the cost of visiting a physician.

The U.S. system of high-quality but expensive and poorly distributed medical care is in trouble. Dramatic advances in medical knowledge and new techniques, combined with soaring demands created by growing public awareness, by hospital and medical insurance, and by Medicare and Medicaid, are swamping the system by which medical care is delivered. As the disparity between the capabilities of medical care and its availability increases, and as costs rise beyond the ability of most Americans to pay them, pressures build up for action. High on the list of suggested remedies are national health insurance and a new medical-care delivery system.

National health insurance, an attractive idea to many Americans, can only make things worse. Medicare and Medicaid—equivalents of national health insurance for segments of our population—have largely failed because the surge of demand they created only dramatized and exacerbated the inadequacies of the existing delivery system and its painful shortages of manpower and facilities. It is folly to believe that compounding this demand by extending health insurance to the entire population will improve matters. On the contrary, it is certain that further overtaxing of our inadequate medical resources will result in serious deterioration in the quality and availability of service for the sick. If this country has learned anything from experience with Medicare and Medicaid, it is that a rational delivery system should have been prepared for projects of such scope.

The question then becomes: What are the necessary elements of a rational medical-care delivery system? Many have proposed that prepaid group practice patterned after the Kaiser-Permanente program, a private system centered on the West Coast, may be a solution. We at Kaiser-Permanente, who have had more than 30 years' experience working with health-care problems, believe that prepaid group practice is a step in the right direction but that it is far from being the entire answer. Lessons we have learned lead us to believe there is a broader solution that is applicable both to the Kaiser-Permanente

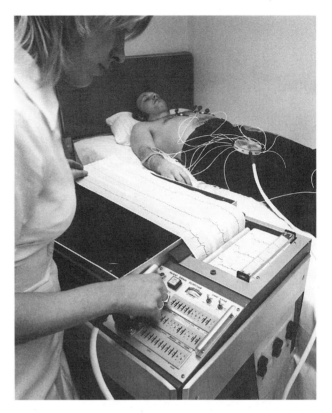

A Compu-Gram computer, developed in 1972 to measure a patient's heart rate and automatically analyze it. It was marketed as the first system in which a computer could give a doctor, even one in another city, a complete analysis of a patient's heart condition. Such tools save physicians time by relieving them of routine tasks. © BETTMANN/ CORBIS. REPRODUCED BY PERMISSION.

system and to the system of private practice that prevails today. . . .

The traditional medical-care delivery system has evolved over the years with little deliberate planning. At the end of the 19th century medical care was still relatively primitive: there was the doctor and his black bag and there were hospitals—places to die. People generally stayed away from the doctor unless they were very ill. In this century expanding medical knowledge soon became too much for any one man to master, and specialties began developing. Laboratories, X-ray facilities and hospitals became important adjuncts to the individual physician in his care of sick people. Since World War II a chain reaction of accelerated research, expanding knowledge, important discoveries and new technology has brought medical care to the level of a sophisticated discipline, offering much hope in the treatment of illness, yet requiring the precise and costly teamwork of specialists operating in expensively equipped and highly organized facilities. . . .

Throughout these years of remarkable medical achievement the delivery system has remained relatively unchanged. . . .

Let us look at another medical-care delivery system: the Kaiser-Permanente plan. . . .

Let us examine the functioning of these two systems—the traditional system and the Kaiser-Permanente one. In the language of systems analysis, the traditional medical-care system has an input (the patient), a processing unit of discrete medical resources (individual doctors and individual hospitals) and an output (one hopes the cured or improved patient). Customarily the patient decides when he needs care. This more or less educated decision by the patient creates a variable entry mix into medical care consisting of (1) the well, (2) the "worried well," (3) the "early sick" and (4) the sick. This entry mix has markedly increased in quantity and changed in character over the years as medical-care resources have grown in complexity and specialization. One constant throughout this evolution has been the point of entry into the system, which is and always has been the appointment with the doctor. Moreover, in traditional practice the patient enters with a fee.

The Kaiser-Permanente program alters the traditional medical-care delivery system in only two ways. It eliminates the fee for service, substituting prepayment, and it organizes the many units of medical-care resources into a coordinated group practice in integrated clinic and hospital facilities. We have come to realize that ironically the elimination of the fee has created a new set of problems. The lessons we have learned in seeking to solve these problems have a direct bearing on the difficulties besetting the country's faltering medical-care system. . . .

Originally designed to meet our ever increasing demand for periodic health checkups, health testing combines a detailed computerized medical history with a comprehensive panel of physiological tests administered by paramedical personnel. Tests record the function of the heart, thyroid, neuromuscular system, respiratory system, vision and hearing. Other tests record height and weight, blood pressure, a urine analysis and a series of 20 blood-chemistry measurements plus hematology. The chest and (in women) the breasts are X-ray'd. By the time the entire process is completed the computerized results generate "advice" rules that recommend further tests when needed or, depending on the urgency of any significant abnormalities an immediate or routine appointment with a physician. The entire record is stored by the computer as a health profile for future reference.

This health-testing procedure is ideally suited to be a regulator of entry into medical care. Certainly it is more sophisticated than the usual fee for service or our present first-come, first-served method. As a new entry regulator, health testing serves to separate the well from the sick and to establish entry priorities. In addition it detects symptomless and early illness, provides a preliminary survey for the doctors, aids in the diagnostic process, provides a basic health profile for future reference, saves the doctor (and patient) time and visits, saves hospital days for diagnostic work and makes possible the maximum utilization of paramedical personnel. Most important of all, it falls into place as the heart of a new and rational medical-care delivery system.

As I have indicated, much of the trouble with the existing delivery system derives from the impact of an unstructured entry mix on scarce and valuable doctor time. Health testing can effectively separate this entry mix into its basic components: the healthy, the symptomless early sick and the sick. This clear separation is the key to the rational allocation of needed medical resources to each group. With health testing as the heart of the system, the entry mix is sorted into its components, which fan out to each of three distinct divisions of service: a health-care service, a preventive-maintenance service and a sick-care service. Compare this with the existing process, where the entire heterogeneous entry mix empties into the doctor's appointment, a sick-care service. . . .

Preventive-maintenance service, like health-care service, has been submerged in sick care. Essentially it is a service for high-incidence chronic illness that requires routine treatment, monitoring and follow-up; its object is to improve the patient's condition or prevent progression of the illness, if possible, and to guard against complications. This type of care, performed by paramedical personnel reporting to the patient's doctor, can save a great deal of the doctor's time and (because it allows more frequent visits) provide closer and better surveillance.

The use of paramedical personnel with limited knowledge and limited but precise skills to relieve the physician of minor routine and repetitious tasks requires that such tasks be clearly defined and well supervised. Procedures are automatically defined and structured in the new system by the clear separation of services. Three of the four divisions of the proposed system—health-testing service, health-care service and preventive maintenance service—

are primarily areas for paramedical personnel. Supervising physicians will be involved in varying degrees least in health testing and most in preventive maintenance. This leaves sick care, with its judgments on diagnosis and treatment, clearly in the physician's realm. Even here, however, he will be aided by the three other services: in diagnosis, by health testing; in follow-up care, by preventive maintenance, in repetitive explanations and instructions to patients and relatives, by the audio-visual library of the healthcare service. We believe, incidentally, that the doctor-patient relationship, which is suffering from the pressure of crowded schedules today, would gain under this system. Giving the doctor more time for care of the sick can help to preserve the relationship at the stage where it counts most.

Implementing the new delivery system should be relatively simple in the Kaiser-Permanente program, since there are no basic conflicts. The subscribers will benefit from better and prompter service to both the well and the sick; the doctors will have more time for their sick patients and their work will be more interesting and stimulating. Although the complete system remains to be tested and evaluated at each step, our hypothesis, on the basis of our research to date, is that we can save at least 50 percent of our general practitioners', internists' and pediatricians' time. This should greatly enhance our service for the sick and improve our services for the well.

Implementing this new medical-care delivery system in the world of traditional medical practice will be more difficult, but it still makes sense. Many forward looking physicians will see in these new methods an opportunity to improve their services to patients. Most doctors these days have more work than they can handle and begrudge the time they must spend on well people. The assistance they could get from health-testing and health-care services will be welcome to many of them if such services are carefully designed and planned to help them. The sponsorship of health-testing and health-care services for private practice logically falls to the local medical societies. Some have already moved in the direction of health evaluation. A few local medical societies in northern California have for several years been operating a mobile unit evaluating the health of cannery workers. Some leaders of other medical societies have expressed interest in health testing as an entry into medical care. They realize that improvement of the delivery system is essential for the preservation of the private enterprise of medicine in this country.

The proposed delivery system may offer a solution to the hitherto insoluble problem of poverty medical care in many areas. The need is to make health services accessible to poor people. To this end neighborhood clinics are established, but staffing these clinics with physicians has proved virtually impossible. Physicians in general want to be in a stimulating medical environment; they like to associate with well-trained colleagues in good medical centers and tend to avoid isolated clinics.

In the system being proposed a central medical center, well staffed and equipped, would provide sick care. It could have four or five "outreach" neighborhood clinics, each providing the three primarily paramedical services: health testing, health care and preventive maintenance. Staffing these services with paramedical personnel should be much less difficult than staffing clinics with doctors; many of the workers could be recruited from the neighborhood itself. Such outreach clinics, coordinated with the sick-care center, could provide high-quality, personal service—better service, perhaps, than is available to the affluent today—at a cost probably lower than the cost of the inferior service poor people now receive.

The concept of medical care as a right is an excellent principle that both the public and the medical world have now accepted. Yet the words mean very little, since we have no system capable of delivering quality medical care as a right. This is hardly surprising. Picture what would happen to say, transportation service if fares were suddenly eliminated and travel became a right. What would happen to our already overtaxed airports and what chance would anyone have of getting anywhere if he really needed to? National-health insurance, if it were legislated today, would have the same effect. It would create turmoil. Even if sick care were superbly organized today, with group practice in well-integrated facilities, the change from "fee" to "free" would stagger the system.

Quality medical care as a right cannot be achieved unless we can establish need, separate the well from the sick and do that without wasting physicians' time. It follows that to make medical care a right, or national health insurance possible, it is mandatory that we first make available health testing and health-care services throughout the country. It is our conviction that these services should be provided or arranged for by the physicians themselves in order to be responsive to their needs and not just a commercial operation.

Further Resources

BOOKS

Falkson, Joseph L. *HMOs and the Politics of Health System Reform.* Chicago: American Hospital Association, 1980.

Starr, Paul. *The Social Transformation of American Medicine.* New York: Basic Books, 1982.

Vahovich, Samuel. *Profile of Medical Practice.* Chicago: American Medical Association, 1973.

PERIODICALS

"A Group-Health Plan that Has Come of Age." *U.S. News & World Report,* October 8, 1979, 79.

"Health Costs: What Limit?" *Time,* May 28, 1979, 60–68.

WEBSITES

What Is a Health Maintenance Organization? Available online at http://outreach.missouri.edu/hes/fmhlth/whatishmo.htm; website home page: http://outreach.missouri.edu (accessed February 5, 2003).

"Our Experiences with the Silastic Gel Breast Prosthesis"

Journal article

By: Thomas D. Cronin and Roger L. Greenberg

Date: July 1970

Source: Cronin, Thomas D., and Greenberg, Roger L. "Our Experiences with the Silastic Gel Breast Prosthesis."*Plastic & Reconstructive Surgery,* July 1970, 1–7.

About the Authors: Thomas D. Cronin received an M.D. from the University of Texas Medical School and specialized in plastic surgery. In 1963, he and a colleague developed a silicone gel breast implant that he used in surgery. The University of Texas Medical School endowed a chair in plastic surgery in his honor.

Roger L. Greenberg practices plastic surgery in San Francisco, California. He has been president of the California Society of Plastic Surgeons and has chaired the Department of Plastic Surgery at the California Pacific Medical Center in San Francisco. ∎

Introduction

The desire for health was not alone in energizing the fitness movement of the 1970s. People jogged, bicycled, and otherwise sweated their way to fitness because they wanted to be lean and tan. The desire to improve appearance led women to consider breast enhancement in addition to exercise and diet. Breast augmentation bore similarities to the fitness movement of which it was a part. Both stemmed at least partly from vanity. Both also drew class distinctions. The fitness movement never sunk roots in the working class. Cosmetic breast surgery like-

wise excluded the working class who could not afford surgery that insurance would not cover. Cosmetic breast surgery thus became a status symbol as much as a medical procedure.

In 1854, a French physician was the first to shape a woman's breasts through surgery. Since the 1950s, surgeons added plastic implants to breasts to firm their appearance. Thomas D. Cronin and Roger L. Greenberg characterized these implants as attractive but hard. Such hardness caused women pressure and pain, and breasts with these implants did not feel natural to the touch. In 1963, Cronin and his colleague Francis Gerow developed a gel implant that was soft to the touch while having enough firmness to shape the breast. Since then, Dow Corning Corporation in Midland, Michigan, has manufactured these implants and in 1969 introduced a new gel implant that had a thin rubber wall, that had a teardrop shape mimicking the shape of the breast, and that lacked a seam that in earlier models had been evident to the touch.

Significance

Cronin and Greenberg studied 183 women in whom surgeons had implanted a gel prothesis. The women averaged age 30.5, and 53 percent had the implant to enlarge their breasts. Another third had surgery to reduce breasts. Others had surgery to make both breasts the same size. Most of the women were married. Cronin and Greenberg recommended implants of small size because they are best in shaping breasts. Sizes range as small as 125 cubic milliliters in volume. An object of 125 milliliters fits into a human hand.

Cronin and Greenberg recommended that women avoid stretching their shoulders for two weeks after surgery to permit an implant to embed itself in the breasts. For this reason, they caution women not to swim or play tennis for six weeks following surgery. Thereafter women may resume normal activity. Cronin and Greenberg's references to sports link the fitness movement of the 1970s to cosmetic breast surgery.

In two of the 183 women, the breasts bled internally following surgery. Severe bleeding required a surgeon to remove the implants, close the wounds that had bled, and reinsert the implant if this remained the woman's desire. Others may forgo the implant after severe bleeding. As with any surgery, scars cover the wound. In this case a scar may encompass the implant, giving the breasts additional firmness. When too much scar tissue forms, surgeons remove excess tissue and give women a steroid injection to minimize new scarring.

Seven of the 183 women developed infection after surgery. Although antibiotics kill bacteria (in the case of a bacterial infection), reinfection is common enough that

Cronin and Greenberg recommended removal of implants. In five of seven cases of infection, surgeons removed the implants and reinserted them after infection had ceased.

Cronin and Greenberg judged the implants in 155 (85 percent) of the 183 women as "good or excellent" and found the surgery "a highly satisfactory procedure." By 1975, 88 percent of all breast implants in the U.S. were silicone gel. Between 1975 and 1991, 110,000 U.S. women had these implants.

Beyond these numbers the rise of breast implants as a form of cosmetic surgery during the 1970s added a dimension to medicine. By tradition medicine was an applied science that aimed to increase longevity and quality of life through preventative measures (eg. vaccines) and by fighting disease (eg. antibiotics to kill streptococcus bacteria). Cosmetic surgery, however, had neither of these objectives. Rather cosmetic surgery, in this case breast implants, aimed to increase the sexual appeal of women.

Primary Source

"Our Experiences with the Silastic Gel Breast Prothesis" [excerpt]

SYNOPSIS: Thomas D. Cronin and Roger L. Greenberg studied 183 women in whom surgeons had implanted gel protheses. Although acknowledging complications in a few cases, Cronin and Greenberg judged the implants in 155 of the 183 women as "good or excellent."

Through the ages, the contour of the female breast has been glorified in paintings and in sculpture. Admired by the opposite sex and desired by the female, the shapely feminine breast is preferred. Velpeau, in 1854, was the first to describe attempts to correct altered shapes and sizes of the breast.

During the last 15 to 20 years, many attempts have been made to augment the hypoplastic or atrophic female breast with various types of plastic sponge material. Many of these produced breasts pleasing to the eye, but all were characterized by hardness—sometimes rocklike, but always unnaturally firm. In 1963, Cronin and Gerow reported a new "natural feel" Silastic gel prosthesis. The implant has since become the most popular implantable breast prosthesis on the world market. This implant combined the flexible, inert qualities of various silicones by containing, in a contoured silicone-rubber bag, a silicone gel of weight comparable to that of mammary tissues. Silicone gel has a specific gravity of 0.98, while breast tissue has a specific grav-

ity of 0.94. The Silastic gel prosthesis has undergone continued improvement since its first introduction in 1963. Major improvements were incorporated in the latest model, which was introduced in January 1969. These consisted of the use of a much thinner and stronger wall of Silastic rubber, elimination of the seam around the base (which was sometimes palpable), and redesign of the contour to a more natural teardrop shape—simulating the normal breast contour.

The present report is based on a study of 183 consecutive cases of augmentation mammaplasty, utilizing the Silastic gel prosthesis. The average age of our patients was 30½ years. Over half (53 per cent) requested the operation because they had always had small breasts and were self-conscious about this lack of development. Nearly all of our women were married; almost a third desired augmentation because of a reduction in breast size following child-birth. Other indications for augmentation included asymmetry of the breasts and benign fibrocystic disease.

The frequently encountered problem of chronic but benign fibrocystic breast disease, of a severe degree, is a perplexing one for the physician—distressing to the patient. While simple mastectomy is a solution to this problem, it is a disfiguring procedure; patients resist accepting it and surgeons are loath to perform it. An alternate procedure, subcutaneous mastectomy, offers a welcome psychological and anatomical alternative. This procedure permits cosmetic breast restoration with a Silastic gel prosthesis.

Examination

Evaluation of the patient's height, weight, and chest contour are important considerations in choosing an implant size that will achieve a breast size proportional to her body. A careful history obtained from the patient is valuable in determining the amount of enlargement desired, and the degree of the patient's motivation for this surgery. The breasts should be carefully examined preoperatively to determine any asymmetry in size, any abnormal masses, or any other unusual findings. In questionable cases, a preoperative mammagram may be of value.

Generally, the size of the implant chosen is based on the above criteria. However, the general tendency in recent years has been to insert smaller sizes: these frequently give a more pleasing contour and a better proportioned figure for the patient. More than 60 per cent of our patients receive the small size implant.

Patients are instructed to bathe with pHisoHex or Betadine for several days prior to surgery, to minimize the possibility of infection from the skin. . . .

A light elastic adhesive dressing, giving support inferiorly and on each side, seems to be adequate. The patient is instructed to restrict motion of her shoulders for two weeks, to permit fibrous tissue to grow into the Dacron mesh and to fix the implant to the pectoral fascia. Strenuous shoulder motion, such as swimming and tennis, should be restricted for 6 weeks. A brassiere should be carefully fitted and used as soon as the bandages are removed— at about a week or 10 days. A brassiere with stiff wires or struts might cause erosion and is contraindicated.

As the prosthesis is inserted deep to the breast tissue, neither the glandular nor ductal structures are disturbed. Thus, the secretory function of the breast is not interrupted. Should the patient subsequently become pregnant, she may nurse the child— if she so desires.

Complications

Fluid Accumulation

With the older model implants, fluid accumulation was not infrequent and was sometimes excessive. The fluid was typically straw-colored and clear but initially could be blood-tinged. A small PE-240 polyethylene tube (lumen accepts a 15-gauge needle) was often inserted at the time of surgery, the end being sealed by match heat and a crushing clamp. Postoperatively, the end of the tube was cut off with a sterile scissors, drainage allowed to flow out, and then it was resealed again. This maneuver was repeated every two or three days, as necessary, until the drainage subsided; the tube was then removed.

Fluid accumulation with the new implants seems to be much less and the tubes are not used routinely now. If no drain or tube is inserted at the time of surgery, and later there is clinical evidence of fluid (postoperative distension, discomfort, or pain) the breasts may be aspirated—using a #20-gauge needle with short bevel. The needle should be inserted obliquely through the skin, at either the lower medial or lower lateral quadrant—with strict aseptic precautions. Care is taken to avoid puncturing the implant.

Hematoma

Fortunately, this occurs infrequently; in 183 cases, there were two hematomas. The chance of excessive bleeding is increased when there is tearing of the pectoral muscle fibers. If there is gross bleeding postoperatively, the patient should be returned to the operating room, the incision reopened, and the implant removed. Bleeding points can then be located and controlled, after which the implant is replaced and the wound closed.

Firmness

Firmness of the breasts after augmentation is due to the formation and subsequent contracture of a thick fibrous capsule around the implant. As in other surgical procedures, different patients exhibit varying degrees of scar formation. For those who demonstrate excessive fibrous capsule formation, it has been found effective to expose the implant through the old incision and make a circumferential incision through the fibrous capsule around its entire base. The edges of this incision may be spread widely by dissection, gaining an inch or more all around in the size of the pocket. This allows a contracted pocket to be enlarged, thus improving the contour and softness of the breast. The fibrous capsule should *not* be removed, because it is already organized and stable in size. A polyethylene tube is inserted at the time of this surgery, and its external end is sealed. A few days later, when the incision is healed, the end is cut off, any fluid is drained off, and a steroid (such as 100 mg Kenalog) is injected into each breast cavity. The idea of this is to minimize new fibrous tissue formation. The delay in injecting this preparation is for the theoretical purpose of allowing the incision to heal somewhat.

Infection

Infection tends to be a late complication; it was found in approximately 4 per cent of our patients. Sixty-five of our patients had prophylactic antibiotics, 95 had no antibiotics. There was no correlation between those patients who developed infection and those who received the antibiotics. If a patient develops an infection in the operative site, systemic antibiotics and a local drip infusion of antibiotic solution into the implant cavity have been attempted, with temporary benefit. Ultimately, however, removal of the implant has usually been necessary. The implants may be reinserted at a later date (5 cases).

Malposition

Malposition of an implant may occur occasionally. Repositioning is best accomplished during the first week, before attachment is firm—but it can be done at any time, if desired.

Palpable Edges

In the past this has been cause for an occasional complaint—due largely to a thick seam around the base of the implant. In cases with contracture of the fibrous capsule, there was occasionally some buckling of this seam or of the thick-walled implant, which could then be palpated through the breast. The new thin-walled, seamless model (now on the market) seems to have eliminated this complication. In the past, this condition was corrected by release of the fibrous capsule (as mentioned under *Firmness*). Complete replacement of the implant with the new seamless model may be a better answer.

Failure of Fixation to z Wall

Sometimes there may be a failure of scar tissue to grow into and fix the Dacron patches on the back of the prosthesis. This is usually due to excessive movement of the arms during the first two weeks—or to the accumulation of excessive fluid, which is not aspirated. Ptosis of the implant may occur. To correct this, the implant is exposed through the old scar and the fibrous capsule over the pectoralis muscle only is excised. The fibrous capsule overlying the top of the implant should *not* be removed. Before replacing the implant, the Dacron mesh is cleaned and freed of all coagulum and tissue (as far as possible) so that new in growth of fibrous tissue can occur and fix the implant to the muscle. Immobilization of the shoulder joint should then be insisted upon, for two or three weeks.

Exposure

If there is undue pressure on the implant, the tissues may melt away over it—with resulting exposure. This may be due to too small a pocket, to scar contracture, to old biopsy scars, or to striae. The risk of exposure is greatly increased with implants which follow a subcutaneous mastectomy—due to the thinness of the subcutaneous fat and skin layer which remains after removal of the parenchyma. If a thin area is noted in the overlying skin flap, particularly after a subcutaneous mastectomy, this area should be reinforced by suturing a piece of D-116 tricot Dacron mesh on the inside of the cavity under the area. If the tissues, subsequent to surgery, are noted to be thinning out, this may be combated by reopening the cavity and patching the area with the Dacron mesh or Marlex. If the implant has already become exposed and if there are sufficient tissues present, the defect may be excised and repaired. Particularly after subcutaneous mastectomy, tissues may be thin and deficient; it may be necessary to remove the implant completely in order to repair the defect. When subsequent replacement is considered several months later, the possibility of inserting the implant beneath the pectoralis major muscle should be considered, if the overlying skin flap remains thin and deficient.

Results

Postoperatively, our patients were followed closely for about 4 to 6 weeks; and then recalled 6 months to a year later. All were graded on the degree of palpability of the implant, contour, and softness of the breasts.

To achieve an excellent rating, the breast had to possess a natural softness with good contour. There could be no palpable margins. A good rating indicated slightly less softness with good contour, and a possible slightly palpable implant margin. A fair rating referred to a slightly firm breast and/or palpable margins. Of 183 augmentation mamma plastics, 155, or 85 per cent were either good or excellent results. It was gratifying to observe the satisfaction which these patients experienced, and the favorable personality changes which were often exhibited after successful mammaplasty.

Summary

Our experiences with implantation of the Silastic gel prosthesis under breasts is described. Our present operative technique is given in some detail. Possible complications are listed, with suggestions for prevention and/or treatment. Results of follow-up examinations on 183 patients are given. This type of augmentation mammaplasty is a highly satisfactory procedure.

Further Resources

BOOKS

Berger, Karen J., and John Bostwick. *What Women Want to Know about Breast Implants.* St. Louis: Quality Medical Publishers, 1995.

Guthrie, Randolph H. *The Truth about Breast Implants.* New York: John Wiley, 1994.

Johnson, Judith A. *Breast Implants: Safety and FDA Regulation.* Washington, D.C.: Library of Congress, 1992.

Middleton, Michael S., and Michael P. McNamara. *Breast Implant Imaging.* Philadelphia: Lippincott, Williams & Wilkins, 2003.

PERIODICALS

"Repeat after Us: I Love My Body!" *Glamour,* March 2003, 49.

WEBSITES

Breast Augmentation and Breast Implants Information Web. Available online at http://www.implantinfo.com (accessed February 5, 2003).

Breast Implants: An Informational Update. Available online at http://www.fda.gov/cdrh/breastimplants/indexbip.html (accessed February 5, 2003).

Frontline: Breast Implants on Trial. Available online at http://www.pbs.org/wgbh/pages/frontline/implants (accessed February 5, 2003).

Silicone Breast Implants Home Page. Available online at http://www.silicone-review.gov.uk (accessed February 5, 2003).

The National Cancer Act of 1971

Law

By: Richard Nixon

Date: December 23, 1971

Source: *The National Cancer Act of 1971.* U.S. Public Law 92–218. 97th Cong. 1st sess., December 23, 1971. Reprinted in *United States Statutes at Large.* Washington, D.C.: U.S. Government Printing Office, 1972.

About the Author: Richard Milhous Nixon (1913–1994) was born in Yorba Linda, California, and received a law degree in 1937 from Duke University. In 1946, he won election to the U.S. House of Representatives, and in 1952 he joined Dwight D. Eisenhower as candidate for vice president. He won the 1968 presidential election, but on August 8, 1974, in the wake of the Watergate scandal, he became the only U.S. president to resign. ■

Introduction

The development and widespread use of vaccines and antibiotics during the twentieth century greatly reduced the number of deaths from infectious diseases so that by the 1950s, heart disease and cancer were the leading killers of Americans. U.S. deaths from cancer grew steadily from 1900 to 1976, nearly quadrupling during these years. Modern medicine had done nothing to blunt this increase, noted a 1955 U.S. Department of Agriculture report.

The alarm over cancer grew in 1964 when the U.S. Department of Health, Education and Welfare released the surgeon general's report on smoking. The report amassed evidence from animal experiments, autopsies of bodies of those who had smoked, and comparison of death rates for smokers and nonsmokers. All evidence pointed to smoking as a cause of lung cancer, cancer of the larynx, cancer of the esophagus, and oral cancer. The report strengthened fears that cancer was ubiquitous and that smokers were living under a death sentence. Cancer also struck nonsmokers and those who had been careful about their diet and exercised regularly. Worse, by the 1950s leukemia had become the leading killer of American children. No one was immune from cancer.

Cancer inspired fright because of its remorseless progression. Too often it struck Americans in their prime, sapping them of their physical and mental powers. The disease wasted away victims, sinking them deeper into an abyss of pain. Medical treatment might slow cancer's progression, buying victims time, but in the end they died in agony. Americans during the 1970s viewed a diagnosis of cancer as a death sentence.

Richard M. Nixon inherited this crisis as president. His predecessor, Lyndon Baines Johnson, had elevated medical care and health to national issues. Under his leadership, Congress passed a flurry of legislation to extend medical benefits, school lunches, and much else to millions of Americans.

Significance

Richard Nixon, following a president who actively pressed health care legislation, also sought to better American health care. In 1971, he pledged to devote the federal government to finding a cure for cancer, a bold initiative that rivaled Johnson's proposals. Congress, acting on Nixon's promise, passed the National Cancer Act on December 23.

The act acknowledged cancer as a leading cause of death in the United States but tempered this pessimism by stating that medical and scientific research had the potential to prevent and treat cancer. The act authorized the National Institutes of Health to direct federal research into the causes and treatment of cancer and created fifteen federal research centers to combat cancer by discovering the most effective treatments.

The act followed the example of the U.S. Department of Agriculture, which, since the nineteenth-century, had established research outposts throughout the United States to breed disease-resistant crops and the like. The result was the world's most abundant food supply. The National Cancer Act applied this model of decentralized federal research to fight cancer.

The act raised expectations of a cure during the 1970s, expectations that were premature. Cancer was not a single disease, as some Americans assumed, but a complex of diseases of unknown origin. Physicians and sci-

President Richard Nixon offers up a souvenir pen after signing the National Cancer Act, Washington, D.C., December 23, 1971. The legislation launched a $1.6 billion federal program to conquer cancer. **AP/WIDE WORLD PHOTOS. REPRODUCED BY PERMISSION.**

entists wondered whether bacteria or viruses could cause some cancers. (The answer now appears to be yes.) In other instances heredity and lifestyle predisposed one to cancer. Such a complex of factors meant that medicine would need to track down cures to one cancer at a time. Medicine would need decades, not years, to advance knowledge of the causes and treatment of cancer.

Primary Source

The National Cancer Act of 1971 [excerpt]

> **SYNOPSIS:** The National Cancer Act authorized the National Institutes of Health to direct federal research into the causes and treatment of cancer and created fifteen federal research centers to combat cancer by discovering the most effective treatments of it.

An act to amend the Public Health Service Act so as to strengthen the National Cancer Institute and the National Institutes of Health in order more effectively to carry out the national effort against cancer.

Be it enacted by the Senate and House of Representatives of the United States of America in Congress assembled,

Section 1. This Act may be cited as "The National Cancer Act of 1971."

Findings and Declaration of Purpose

Sec. 2. (a) The Congress finds and declares

1. that the incidence of cancer is increasing and cancer is the disease which is the major health concern of Americans today;

2. that new scientific leads, if comprehensively and energetically exploited, may significantly advance the time when more adequate preventive and therapeutic capabilities are available to cope with cancer;

3. that cancer is a leading cause of death in the United States;

4. that the present state of our understanding of cancer is a consequence of broad advances across the full scope of the biomedical sciences;

5. that a great opportunity is offered as a result of recent advances in the knowledge of this dread disease to conduct energetically a national program against cancer;

6. that in order to provide for the most effective attack on cancer it is important to use all of the biomedical resources of the National Institutes of Health; and

7. that the programs of the research institutes which comprise the National Institutes of Health have made it possible to bring into being the most productive scientific community centered upon health and disease that the world has ever known.

(b) It is the purpose of this Act to enlarge the authorities of the National Cancer Institute and the National Institutes of Health in order to advance the national effort against cancer.

National Cancer Program

Sec. 3. (a) Part A of title IV of the Public Health Service Act is amended by adding after section 406 the following new sections: . . .

Sec. 407. (a) The Director of the National Cancer Institute shall coordinate all of the activities of the National Institutes of Health relating to cancer with the National Cancer Program.

(b) In carrying out the National Cancer Program, the Director of the National Cancer Institute shall:

1. With the advice of the National Cancer Advisory Board, plan and develop an expanded, intensified, and coordinated cancer research program encompassing the programs of the National Cancer Institute, related programs of the other research institutes, and other Federal and non-Federal programs.

2. Expeditiously utilize existing research facilities and personnel of the National Institutes of Health for accelerated exploration of opportunities in areas of special promise.

3. Encourage and coordinate cancer research by industrial concerns where such concerns evidence a particular capability for such research.

4. Collect, analyze, and disseminate all data useful in the prevention, diagnosis, and treatment of cancer, including the establishment of an international cancer research data bank to collect, catalog, store, and disseminate insofar as feasible the results of cancer research undertaken in any country for the use of any person involved in cancer research in any country.

5. Establish or support the large-scale production or distribution of specialized biological materials and other therapeutic substances for research and set standards of safety and care for persons using such materials.

6. Support research in the cancer field outside the United States by highly qualified foreign nationals which research can be expected to inure to the benefit of the American people; support collaborative research involving American and foreign participants; and support the training of American scientists abroad and foreign scientists in the United States.

7. Support appropriate manpower programs of training in fundamental sciences and clinical disciplines to provide an expanded and continuing manpower base from which to select investigators, physicians, and allied health professions personnel, for participation in clinical and basic research and treatment programs relating to cancer, including where appropriate the use of training stipends, fellowships, and career awards.

8. Call special meetings of the National Cancer Advisory Board at such times and in such places as the Director deems necessary in order to consult with, obtain advice from, or to secure the approval of projects, programs, or other actions to be undertaken without delay in order to gain maximum benefit from a new scientific or technical finding.

9. (A) Prepare and submit, directly to the President for review and transmittal to Congress, an annual budget estimate for the National Cancer Program, after reasonable opportunity for comment (but without change) by the Secretary, the Director of the National Institutes of Health, and the National Cancer Advisory Board; and (B) receive from the President and the Office of Management and Budget directly all funds appropriated by Congress for obligation and expenditure by the National Cancer Institute.

(c) (1) There is established the President's Cancer Panel (hereinafter in this section referred to as the 'Panel') which shall be composed of three persons appointed by the President, who by virtue of their training, experience, and background are exceptionally qualified to appraise the National Cancer Program. At least two of the members of the Panel shall be distinguished scientists or physicians.

(2) (A) Members of the Panel shall be appointed for three-year terms, except that (i) in the case of two of the members first appointed, one shall be ap-

pointed for a term of one year and one shall be appointed for a term of two years, as designated by the President at the time of appointment, and (ii) any member appointed to fill a vacancy occurring prior to the expiration of the term for which his predecessor was appointed shall be appointed only for the remainder of such term.

(B) The President shall designate one of the members to serve as Chairman for a term of one year.

(C) Members of the Panel shall each be entitled to receive the daily equivalent of the annual rate of basic pay in effect for grade GS-18 of the General Schedule for each day (including traveltime) during which they are engaged in the actual performance of duties vested in the Panel, and shall be allowed travel expenses (including a per diem allowance) under section 5703(b) of title 5, United States Code.

(3) The Panel shall meet at the call of the Chairman, but not less often than twelve times a year. A transcript shall be kept of the proceedings of each meeting of the Panel, and the Chairman shall make such transcript available to the public.

(4) The Panel shall monitor the development and execution of the National Cancer Program under this section, and shall report directly to the President. Any delays or blockages in rapid execution of the Program shall immediately be brought to the attention of the President. The Panel shall submit to the President periodic progress reports on the Program and annually an evaluation of the efficacy of the Program and suggestions for improvements, and shall submit such other reports as the President shall direct. At the request of the President, it shall submit for his consideration a list of names of persons for consideration for appointment as Director of the National Cancer Institute.

National Cancer Research and Demonstration Centers

Sec. 408. (a) The Director of the National Cancer Institute is authorized to provide for the establishment of fifteen new centers for clinical research, training, and demonstration of advanced diagnostic and treatment methods relating to cancer. Such centers may be supported under subsection (b) or under any other applicable provision of law.

(b) The Director of the National Cancer Institute, under policies established by the Director of the National Institutes of Health and after consultation with the National Cancer Advisory Board, is authorized to enter into cooperative agreements with public or private nonprofit agencies or institutions to pay all or part of the cost of planning, establishing, or strengthening, and providing basic operating support for existing or new centers (including, but not limited to, centers established under subsection (a)) for clinical research, training, and demonstration of advanced diagnostic and treatment methods relating to cancer. Federal payments under this subsection in support of such cooperative agreements may be used for (1) construction (notwithstanding any limitation under section 405), (2) staffing and other basic operating costs, including such patient care costs as are required for research, (3) training (including training for allied health professions personnel), and (4) demonstration purposes; but support under this subsection (other than support for construction) shall not exceed $5,000,000 per year per center. Support of a center under this section may be for a period of not to exceed three years and may be extended by the Director of the National Cancer Institute for additional periods of not more than three years each, after review of the operations of such center by an appropriate scientific review group established by the Director of the National Cancer Institute.

Further Resources

BOOKS

Professional Guide to Diseases. 6th ed. Springhouse, Pa.: Springhouse Corporation, 1998.

Rettig, Richard A. *Cancer Crusade: The Story of the National Cancer Act of 1971.* Princeton, N.J.: Princeton University Press, 1977.

PERIODICALS

Brown, H.G. "Control of Cancer: The Promise of the Future." *Seminars in Oncology Nursing,* November 2002, 305–310.

DeVita, Vincent T. "A Perspective on the War on Cancer." *The Cancer Journal,* September–October 2002, 352–357.

Dunn, F.B. "Legislators Rally for Support of Revised National Cancer Act." *Journal of the National Cancer Institute,* March 20, 2002, 410–412.

————. "National Cancer Act: Leaders Reflect on 30 Years of Progress." *Journal of the National Cancer Institute,* January 2, 2002, 8–10.

Hubbard, S.M., D.K. Mayer, and Vincent T. DeVita. "Evolution of the National Cancer Program: An American Investment for Conquering Cancer." *Seminars in Oncology Nursing,* November 2002, 252–264.

Vastag, Brian. "Samuel Broder, M.D., Reflects on the 30th Anniversary of the National Cancer Act." *Journal of the American Medical Association,* December 19, 2001, 2929–2932.

WEBSITES

Legislative History of the National Cancer Act. Available online at http://www.cancersource.com/nclac/leghistory; website home page: http://www.cancersource.com/ (accessed February 5, 2003).

National Cancer Act. Available online at http://rex.nci.nih .gov/wlcm/NCI_History/html/national_cancer_act.html; website home page: http://rex.nci.nih.gov (accessed February 5, 2003).

Health Maintenance Organization Act of 1973
Law

By: Richard Nixon

Date: December 29, 1973

Source: *Health Maintenance Organization Act of 1973.* U.S. Public Law 93–222. 93rd Cong. 1st sess. December 29, 1973. Reprinted in *United States Statutes at Large.* Washington, D.C.: U.S. Government Printing Office, 1974.

About the Author: Richard Milhous Nixon (1913–1994) was born in Yorba Linda, California, and received a law degree in 1937 from Duke University. In 1946, he won election to the U.S. House of Representatives, and in 1952 he joined Dwight D. Eisenhower as candidate for vice president. He won the 1968 presidential election but on August 8, 1974, he became the only U.S. president to resign. ∎

Introduction

Medical costs increased during the 1970s as they had in the previous decade. In 1970, Americans spent $74.9 billion for medical care, a figure that more than doubled to $212 billion in 1979. By then, medical costs totaled nearly 10 percent of gross domestic product (the total value of goods and services produced in the United States). Physician fees rose nearly 10 percent in 1977 alone, an increase 50 percent greater than the increase in prices for nonmedical goods and services. In 1974, orthopedic surgeons averaged $62,410 a year, and the next year the median salary for physicians was $47,520, more than triple the median household income of Americans. These costs led 75 percent of Americans in 1970 to fear that medical care in the United States was in crisis.

The rise in costs stemmed partly from Congress's coverage in 1965 of all Americans sixty-five and older (Medicare) and in 1966 of all Americans who fell below an income threshold (Medicaid). In 1968, President Lyndon Baines Johnson estimated that Medicare and Medicaid covered more than 25 million Americans. During the 1960s and 1970s, the aged and poor, who could not have afforded treatment without Medicare and Medicaid but who needed a disproportionate share of medical care,

flocked to physicians and hospitals. This rise in the demand for care increased its price, as economic theory would predict.

Another culprit was what one might call intensive medicine during the 1970s. Fearful of lawsuits, physicians ordered an array of tests on patients in an effort to demonstrate the thoroughness of treatment. The additional tests added cost but not quality to treatment. At the same time, patients who had doubts about the quality of their care visited specialists, who charged higher fees than did general practitioners. The consultation of specialists did not guarantee higher quality care, only higher costs.

Significance

Americans could contain medical costs in two ways. First, the nation could adopt a government-sponsored program that covered everyone. In this case, government would be the sole payer for medical services and could cap fees. Lyndon Johnson, president from 1963 to 1969, had tried to cover all Americans in increments, but it is unclear that Johnson would have favored caps on medical fees. Without national heath care, physicians could drop patients under plans that paid too little, as they did when Congress capped Medicaid payments in 1969.

The absence of government coverage for everyone left private insurers, the second option, alone in their attempt to slow the growth of medical costs. In response, they created health maintenance organizations (HMOs). President Richard M. Nixon persuaded Congress in 1973 to pass the HMO Act, which defined an HMO and its responsibilities. This excerpt states that a person or a group of people (usually employees in business, government, or nonprofits) may buy into an HMO by prepaying for coverage in fixed amounts at specified intervals. An HMO must provide coverage at a group rate that is cheaper than an individual rate. An HMO may provide levels of coverage dependent on member payments.

An HMO purchases medical coverage for its members by contracting physicians and hospitals to provide medical care at a lower rate, in the form of a salary, than they might charge in a free market. An HMO substitutes a salary for fee for service. The HMO Act mandated that HMOs set aside at least thirty days each year when new members may enroll. Once a person bought into an HMO, it cannot drop him should his health deteriorate.

By 1979 five percent (roughly 9 million) of Americans were in an HMO. By 1990 the number had increased to 36 million. In 1987 27 percent of U.S. employees participated in an employer-sponsored HMO. By 1996 the percentage reached 74.

No less important was the effect on government-sponsored health care. The Republican Party had been the opponent of government-sponsored coverage, yet in

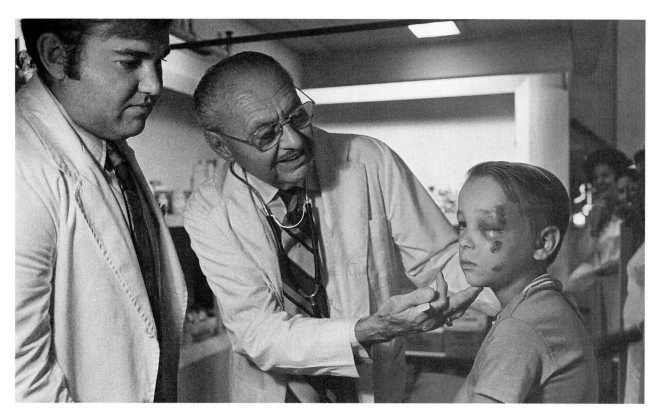

Dr. Eugene Balthazar examines eight-year-old Charles Ames, who fell from his bicycle. Congress passed the Health Maintenance Organization Act of 1973 to make medical and health care more available and affordable to the average American. © BETTMANN/CORBIS. REPRODUCED BY PERMISSION.

1973 Republican President Richard M. Nixon signaled to Congress his willingness to sign legislation that would extend government-sponsored health coverage to all Americans. With support from the liberal wing of the Democratic Party, Nixon might have achieved the goal that had eluded Democratic presidents Harry S. Truman and Lyndon Johnson. The HMO Act killed this ambition by allowing conservatives to claim that HMOs could contain health-care costs better than could government-sponsored coverage.

Primary Source

Health Maintenance Organization Act of 1973
[excerpt]

> **SYNOPSIS:** This excerpt defines an HMO and its responsibilities. It mandates that HMOs set aside at least thirty days each year when new members may enroll. Once a person buys into an HMO, it cannot drop him should his health deteriorate.

Title XIII—Health Maintenance Organizations
Requirements for Health Maintenance Organizations

Sec. 1301. (a) For purposes of this title, the term 'health maintenance organization' means a legal entity which (1) provides basic and supplemental health services to its members in the manner prescribed by subsection (b), and (2) is organized and operated in the manner prescribed by subsection (c).

(b) A health maintenance organization shall provide, without limitations as to time or cost other than those prescribed by or under this title, basic and supplemental health services to its members in the following manner:

(1) Each member is to be provided basic health services for a basic health services payment which (A) is to be paid on a periodic basis without regard to the dates health services (within the basic health services) are provided; (B) is fixed without regard to the frequency, extent, or kind of health service (within the basic health services) actually furnished; (C) is fixed under a community rating system; and (D) may be supplemented by additional nominal payments which may be required for the provision of specific services (within the basic health services), except that such payments may not be required where or in such a manner that they serve (as determined under regulations of the Secretary) as a

barrier to the delivery of health services. Such additional nominal payments shall be fixed in accordance with the regulations of the Secretary.

(2) For such payment or payments (hereinafter in this title referred to as 'supplemental health services payments') as the health maintenance organization may require in addition to the basic health services payment, the organization shall provide to each of its members each health service (A) which is included in supplemental health services (as defined in section 1302(2)), (B) for which the required health manpower are available in the area served by the organization, and (C) for the provision of which the member has contracted with the organization. Supplemental health services payments which are fixed on a prepayment basis shall be fixed under a community rating system.

(3) The services of health professionals which are provided as basic health services shall be provided through health professionals who are members of the staff of the health maintenance organization or through a medical group (or groups) or individual practice association (or associations), except that this paragraph shall not apply in the case of (A) health professionals' services which the organization determines, in conformity with regulations of the Secretary, are unusual or infrequently used, or (B) any basic health service provided a member of the health maintenance organization other than by such a health professional because it was medically necessary that the service be provided to the member before he could have it provided by such a health professional. For purposes of this paragraph, the term 'health professionals' means physicians, dentists, nurses, podiatrists, optometrists, and such other individuals engaged in the delivery of health services as the Secretary may by regulation designate.

(4) Basic health services (and supplemental health services in the case of the members who have contracted therefor) shall within the area served by the health maintenance organization be available and accessible to each of its members promptly as appropriate and in a manner which assures continuity, and when medically necessary be available and accessible twenty-four hours a day and seven days a week. A member of a health maintenance organization shall be reimbursed by the organization for his expenses in securing basic or supplemental health services other than through the organization if it was medically necessary that the services be provided before he could secure them through the organization.

(c) Each health maintenance organization shall—

(1) have a fiscally sound operation and adequate provision against the risk of insolvency which is satisfactory to the Secretary;

(2) assume full financial risk on a prospective basis for the provision of basic health services, except that a health maintenance organization may obtain insurance or make other arrangements (A) for the cost of providing to any member basic health services the aggregate value of which exceeds $5,000 in any year, (B) for the cost of basic health services provided to its members other than through the organization because medical necessity required their provision before they could be secured through the organization, and (C) for not more than 90 per centum of the amount by which its costs for any of its fiscal years exceed 115 per centum of its income for such fiscal year;

(3) enroll persons who are broadly representative of the various age, social, and income groups within the area it serves, except that in the case of a health maintenance organization which has a medically undeserved population located (in whole or in part) in the area it serves, not more than 75 per centum of the members of that organization may be enrolled from the medically undeserved population unless the area in which such population resides is also a rural area (as designated by the Secretary);

(4) have an open enrollment period of not less than thirty days at least once during each consecutive twelve-month period during which enrollment period it accepts, up to its capacity, individuals in the order in which they apply for enrollment, except that if the organization demonstrates to the satisfaction of the Secretary that—

(A) it has enrolled, or will be compelled to enroll, a disproportionate number of individuals who are likely to utilize its services more often than an actuarially determined average (as determined under regulations of the Secretary)

and enrollment during an open enrollment period of an additional number of such individuals will jeopardize its economic viability, or

(B) if it maintained an open enrollment period it would not be able to comply with the requirements of paragraph (3),

the Secretary may waive compliance by the organization with the open enrollment requirement of this paragraph for not more than three consecutive twelve-month periods and may provide additional waivers to that organization if it makes the demonstration required by subparagraph (A) or (B);

(5) not expel or refuse to re-enroll any member because of his health status or his requirements for health services;

(6) be organized in such a manner that assures that (A) at least one-third of the membership of the policymaking body of the health maintenance organization will be members of the organization, and (B) there will be equitable representation on such body of members from medically undeserved populations served by the organization;

(7) be organized in such a manner that provides meaningful procedures for hearing and resolving grievances between the health maintenance organization (including the medical group or groups and other health delivery entities providing health services for the organization) and the members of the organization;

(8) have organizational arrangements, established in accordance with regulations of the Secretary, for an ongoing quality assurance program for its health services which program (A) stresses health outcomes, and (B) provides review by physicians and other health professionals of the process followed in the provision of health services;

(9) provide medical social services for its members and encourage and actively provide for its members health education services, education in the appropriate use of health services, and education in the contribution each member can make to the maintenance of his own health;

(10) provide, or make arrangements for, continuing education for its health professional staff; and

(11) provide, in accordance with regulations of the Secretary (including safeguards concerning the confidentiality of the doctor-patient relationship), an effective procedure for developing, compiling, evaluating, and reporting to the Secretary, statistics and other information (which the Secretary shall publish and disseminate on an annual basis and which the health maintenance organization shall disclose, in a manner acceptable to the Secretary, to its members and the general public) relating to (A) the cost of its operations, (B) the patterns of utilization of its services, (C) the availability, accessibility, and acceptability of its services, (D) to the extent practical, developments in the health status of its members, and (E) such other matters as the Secretary may require.

Further Resources

BOOKS
Starr, Paul. *The Social Transformation of American Medicine.* New York: Basic Books, 1982.

Vahovich, Samuel. *Profile of Medical Practice.* Chicago: American Medical Association, 1973.

PERIODICALS
"A Group-Health Plan That Has Come of Age." *U.S. News & World Report,* October 8, 1979, 79.

"Health Costs: What Limit?" *Time,* May 28, 1979, 60–68.

WEBSITES
Health Maintenance Organization Definition. Available online at http://www.investorwords.com/cgi-bin/getword.cgi?2290; website home page: http://www.investorwords.com (accessed February 5, 2003).

What Is a Health Maintenance Organization? Available online at http://outreach.missouri.edu/hes/fmhlth/whatishmo.htm (accessed February 5, 2003).

"Aortic Regurgitation in the Tuskegee Study of Untreated Syphilis"

Journal article

By: Joseph G. Caldwell

Date: 1973

Source: Caldwell, Joseph G., et al. "Aortic Regurgitation in the Tuskegee Study of Untreated Syphilis." *Journal of Chronic Diseases* 26, 1973, 187–194.

About the Author: Joseph G. Caldwell, who worked for the Center for Disease Control in Atlanta when he and his colleagues published this article, received an MD from the University of Kentucky in 1970, specializing in endocrinology. In the early 2000s he worked in private practice as a physician. ∎

Introduction

The spirochete *Treponema pallidum* causes syphilis. (A spirochete is a class of bacteria.) The spirochete incubates in the body as long as three weeks, when it may cause lesions filled with clear fluid on genitals, the anus, fingers, lips, tongue, nipples, tonsils, and eyelids. The lesions cause no pain and disappear in three to six weeks. Their disappearance signals the end of the first stage of syphilis.

The second stage may overlap the first or may begin two to five weeks after the disappearance of the lesions. In this stage, the spirochete infects the lymph nodes and erupts in a second manifestation of lesions, which appear as a rash on the arms, palms, face, scalp, and soles of the feet. Whereas the first stage causes no pain, the second causes headache, fatigue, weight loss, nausea, vomiting, sore throat, and fever. These symptoms may disappear and recur several times during the next four years. Symptoms may disappear thereafter, without progressing to the third and final stage, as is the case for two-thirds of victims.

The other third develop the final stage, which may not arise until ten years after infection. In this stage, the spirochete causes lesions on skin, bones, the respiratory tract, stomach, or liver. In reaction, the liver may enlarge and cause pain. Victims may thereafter develop anemia. The spirochete may damage bones and organs enough to kill its victims. In 10 percent of third-stage victims, the spirochete inflames the aorta, the artery that carries blood from the heart to the body. The spirochete may also cause meningitis or infect the central nervous system. Such damage is fatal without treatment.

Significance

Because the spirochete that causes syphilis is a bacterium, antibiotics kill it. The prospect for recovery is high when physicians treat syphilis with antibiotics during the first stage of infection. Even though antibiotics kill the spirochete in all three stages, antibiotic therapy is less effective during the second and third stages because antibiotics cannot repair the spirochete's damage to the body and its organs.

Untreated syphilis is lethal. Yet U.S. Public Health Service physicians conducting the Tuskegee Study did not treat four hundred African American victims, using them instead to study the onset and progression of syphilis. The study might have escaped detection had not the *Washington Evening Star* reported the story on 25 July 1972. The next day the story made headlines in newspapers throughout the U.S. Critics of the study believed that the physicians who conducted the study had betrayed their Hippocratic oath in allowing others to die while withholding treatment. Race complicated the issue, for the physicians were white and the patients were African American, raising charges of racism.

The scandal forced the Public Health Service to end the study, but the furor did not abate. In 1973 the National Association for the Advancement of Colored People (NAACP) filed a class-action suit on behalf of survivors, winning them $9 million. Equally important, NAACP lobbying persuaded Congress to give survivors free medical care the rest of their lives. Not until 1997 did the federal government admit responsibility for the study. That year President Bill Clinton apologized to the study's survivors and their families for their suffering. By then fewer than 20 percent of the study's victims remained alive.

Primary Source

"Aortic Regurgitation in the Tuskegee Study of Untreated Syphilis" [excerpt]

SYNOPSIS: In this excerpt, lead author Joseph G. Caldwell and his colleagues report the damage third-stage syphilis causes to the aorta. Although they acknowledged that antibiotics might have helped these victims, they nonetheless withheld treatment, noting that the rarity of syphilis in the United States made victims worth medical scrutiny.

Introduction

Aortic regurgitation (AR) presenting in older patients has frequently resulted from syphilis, although the frequency of both clinical and postmortem syphilitic aortic regurgitation has been declining in the United States. A unique opportunity to follow the course of untreated syphilis and aortic valvular disease has existed in the Tuskegee Study of untreated syphilis. Initiated nearly four decades ago in Tuskegee, the county seat of Macon County, Alabama, by the U.S. Public Health Service, this study was proposed to determine the incidence of long-term complications of untreated syphilis in the Negro male.

In the 1920s, Bruusgaard had demonstrated from the Oslo Study that untreated syphilis in Caucasians was more pathogenic for men than women, as men developed life-threatening central nervous system and cardiovascular syphilis in a two to one predominance over women. Furthermore, postulates had been proposed prior to the Tuskegee Study suggesting that syphilis ran a more fatal course in Negroes. Therefore, the original Tuskegee Study subjects were 611 Negro men—410 with a previous history of syphilis and 201 age-matched controls with no clinical or serologic evidence of syphilis. At approximately 5-yr intervals, follow-up clinical and laboratory evaluations of these men have been conducted. The following is a report of the cardiovascular findings observed during the most recent 1968–1970 survey of surviving subjects.

Methods

Of the 625 original participants in this study, 127 were located and examined in the 2-yr time period (1968–1970). Four hundred and thirteen (66 per cent) of the study participants are now dead, and since many of the 68 (23 per cent) lost to followup would be nonagenarians or older, most are presumed to be dead. The large majority (84 per cent) of those recently surveyed had last been examined by study physicians as late as 1963 or

1966. However, special efforts were made to find and examine all possible patients. Seven participants who had not been located since their initial selection and examination in 1932 to 1934 were seen.

Of the 127 patients examined, 114 (90 per cent) were found in Macon County or in adjacent Russell and Bullock Counties. Other patients, however, were examined in the following cities: three each in Gary, Indiana, and Cleveland, Ohio; and one in East Chicago, Indiana; Chicago, Illinois; Lima, Ohio; Dayton, Ohio; Atlanta, Georgia; East Gadsden, Alabama; and Birmingham, Alabama. Examinations consisted of medical history and physical examination, electrocardiogram, chest X-ray in most patients, serologic tests, rarely lumbar puncture, and where appropriate, phonocardiogram and pulse pressure recordings. These procedures were generally performed in the Macon County Health Department or other local health department facilities, although by necessity, 26 examinations (20.5 per cent) were performed at the homes of the subjects. In these latter cases, chest X-rays were often not obtained. Blood specimens were tested at the Venereal Disease Research Laboratory (VDRL), National Communicable Disease Center, and results were obtained by the VDRL, Automated Reagin, Treponema Pallidum Immobilization (TPI), and Fluorescent Treponemal Antibody Absorption (FTA-ABS) Tests.

In order to further evaluate the entire study group, the records of 229 autopsied subjects were reviewed for evidence of aortitis and myocardial scarring. One hundred and sixty-six (72.5 per cent) were syphilitics and the remaining 63 (27.5 per cent) were controls. Criteria (6) of microscopic syphilitic aortitis were: (1) gross thickening of the aortic wall; (2) medial necrosis; (3) adventitial fibrosis; (4) medial scarring; (5) intramural perivascular infiltration; (6) thickened vasa vasorum; and (7) adventitial perivascular infiltration. Signs of macroscopic aortitis due to syphilis included linear striations of the thoracic aorta, subintimal pearly white scarring, diminution of elasticity of the aorta, fusiform dilatation, saccular aneurysm, and valvular changes in the cusps and commissures of the aortic valve.

Antimicrobial and antisyphilitic treatment histories were obtained from all patients during each survey throughout the years. In order to avoid bias, the previous classification, treatment status, or previous findings of any of the located subjects were not revealed to examiners until examinations were completed.

Results

Of those examined, 76 (17.4 per cent of the total syphilitics) had previous clinical, serologic, or historical evidence of syphilis. The other 51 males (27.0 per cent of the total controls) had no positive syphilitic anamnesis. The median age of the 76 patients with syphilis was 69 yr with a range of 52–91. The median age of the 51 controls was 70.5 yr with a range of 62–89. All but one of the originally untreated syphilitics seen in 1968–1970 have received therapy, although heavy metals and/or antibiotics were given for a variety of reasons by many nonstudy physicians and not necessarily in doses considered curative for syphilis.

Aggregate findings from the clinical histories, physical examinations, chest X-rays and electrocardiograms from this survey showed that there was no significant statistical difference in cardiovascular morbidity between the two groups of subjects. Syphilitics noted more orthopnea, palpitations, and chest pains than controls, and by examination, the former exhibited more clinical cardiomegaly and abnormal pulses (referring to both qualitative changes and rhythm disturbances). Syphilitics further had more tortuosity and elongation of the thoracic aorta and calcification of the ascending aorta by X-ray and more infarction patterns and conduction disturbances by electrocardiography. However, all of these slight differences showed no consistent trend of increased morbidity between the two groups. . . .

The transmission and associated clinical findings of aortic regurgitation in all four patients were consistent in all cases with syphilitic aortic regurgitation. The later realization that two of the involved patients were controls without any evidence of syphilis was totally unexpected. Ironically the subject with the most marked clinical evidence of aortic regurgitation including head nod and capillary pulsations was a control, No. 495.

Electrocardiograms demonstrated cardiac abnormalities in all but No. 603. No. 194 recordings showed development of atrial fibrillation in 1970 in addition to the previous stable findings of left ventricular hypertrophy (LVH) and anterolateral ischemia (ALI). The tracings of No. 603 showed persistent ALI changes, while the only tracing available from No. 495 showed LVH.

External pulse recordings and phonocardiograms of the four subjects with AR confirmed the auscultatory findings in all cases. During the three-month interval between examination and phonocardiogram recording for subject No. 603, the AR murmur reduced

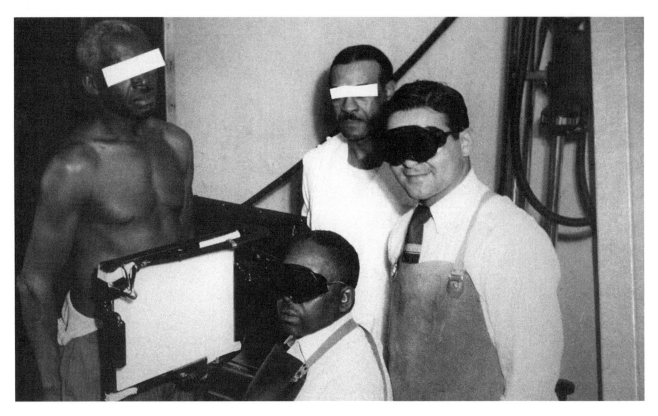

Doctors take an X-ray of a Tuskegee Syphilis Study subject. Their faces are obscured to hide their identities. Penicillin became the standard cure for this deadly disease in 1947, but for decades it was withheld from the men, all African Americans, in this experiment so scientists could continue studying the disease in them. © CORBIS SYGMA. REPRODUCED BY PERMISSION.

greatly in intensity, however, and coincided with considerable clinical deterioration with drop in blood pressure and increase of congestive heart failure.

Roentgenograms of the chest of the four subjects with AR (Fig. 1) showed no distinguishing features between the syphilitics and controls.

The most marked difference between those who had presumed syphilitic AR and the two with nonsyphilitic AR was the rapid and progressive deterioration clinically of the controls. Despite recent hospitalizations, both men had continued to have symptoms and findings of progressive cardiac decompensation. On the other hand, the chronic, indurated edema and cardiomegaly of syphilitic subject No. 194 had not changed during the last 7 yr (and possibly not for 19 yr, as the comparison of findings by different examiners with each survey is difficult). The only notable change was the development of atrial fibrillation since the 1963 examination. The other syphilitic subject with AR (No. 329) had been asymptomatic for the past 7 yr (1963–1970), although he had previous cardiopulmonary symptoms (1952 and 1958). Both syphilitic subjects had received penicillin two

decades prior, following which VDRL Test reactivity decreased in both.

Evidence of aortitis by both gross and microscopic examination according to established criteria have been demonstrated much more frequently in syphilitics than controls, 44.3 vs 14.8 per cent. Also, the incidence of a normal aortic arch pathologically has been significantly greater in control subjects, 61.1 vs 27.1 per cent ($P \leqq 0.005$). However, there was no significant difference of focal myocardial scarring or infarction demonstrated between the syphilitic and control groups, 34.3 vs 37.0 per cent with both gross and microscopic evidence and 25.0 vs 31.5 per cent with neither ($P \leqq 0.25$).

Twenty-five (33 per cent) of the 76 syphilitics who were blood tested had nonreactive results by nontreponemal testing (VDRL and Automated Reagin Tests), while all but one had reactive results by treponemal testing (FTA-ABS and TPI Tests). (That one subject, No. 480, had reactive results by TPI testing in 1952 and 1963 and non-reactive result in 1970. His FTA-ABS Test result, reactive in 1963, was also non-reactive in 1970.) None of the control patients had reactive results by either treponemal or nontreponemal testing.

Discussion

Syphilis in its early clinical stages is no longer the dread disease that it was as the Great Pox in the Middle Ages. Rupial or malignant secondary syphilis is a rare disease today. On the other hand, observations from the Oslo Study, the Yale University Studies and those previously reported from this study have shown that infections with *T. pallidum* in untreated patients could result in considerable late destructive complications and threaten life when involving the central nervous system or cardiovascular system. Reported findings from the earlier surveys of this study included the following observations: (1) The life expectancy of men found to have syphilis between the ages of 25 and 50 yr was decreased by 20 per cent. The death rate in syphilitics in this age span was 75 per cent greater than that of controls. (2) Systolic and diastolic hypertension, arteriosclerosis, and general morbidity were all more common in syphilitics than controls in all previous surveys. (3) In the first 5-yr follow-up, cardiovascular disease in men under 40 yr of age appeared in 25.3 per cent of syphilitics as opposed to only 5.7 per cent of controls. Aortitis as detected by fluoroscopy was present in 23.6 per cent of the syphilitics vs 5.0 per cent of the controls. (4) Of the 125 autopsied subjects reported in 1955, 50 (57.5 per cent) of the syphilitics had either macroscopic or microscopic evidence of aortitis (87 aortas thoroughly examined). Of those autopsied, 28 (30.4 per cent) of the 92 syphilitic patients had cardiovascular or central nervous system syphilitic lesions as their primary cause of death.

For the first time since the inception of this study, no significant disparity of cardiovascular morbidity was demonstrated between the syphilitic and control populations in 1968–1970. Thus, at this late phase in the study, the clinical manifestations of syphilis appear to have fully exerted themselves. The only remaining evidence of the increased mortality of syphilis is that revealed by the composition of the surviving study population. Seventeen per cent of the original syphilitics were seen in 1968–1970 as compared to 27 per cent of the control population.

One of the first clinical uses of penicillin was the treatment of all stages of syphilis. Despite some recent reports of persisting viable spiral forms following adequate treatment of syphilis, *T. pallidum* has remained *in vitro* as sensitive to penicillin as it was initially. For many years, benzathine penicillin has been the advised treatment for all stages of syphilis, as long lasting serum levels of penicillin are considered necessary for optimal spirochetocidal effect. Schroeter and others have recently demonstrated that short acting penicillin (procaine penicillin G), when given in sufficient doses to obtain high blood levels for gonorrhea treatment, has successfully aborted incubating disease in contacts to early syphilis. Thus, perhaps even small doses of short acting penicillins can prevent further tissue destruction of syphilis. In this age of widespread penicillin and antibiotic usage, it is seldom that a person can live 25 yr without receiving one of these effective drugs. Following the introduction of penicillin, only one of the Tuskegee syphilitics has apparently received no treatment. Thus, not only the duration of the study but also the effects of antimicrobial therapy probably accounted for the lack of morbidity in the 1968–1970 survey.

Our most unexpected observation during this survey was the detection of aortic regurgitation in two control patients clinically indistinguishable from the AR of two subjects with treated syphilis. Although one of the control patients had previously had gonorrhea (No. 603), at no time was there any clinical evidence of syphilis in either of the patients and their serum nonreactivity by varied methods of syphilis testing has persisted for many years. Although gonococcal endocarditis and subsequent AR could have occurred in subject No. 603, the long course of documented hypertension was more related temporally to the late appearance of aortic regurgitation. The cause of valvular disease in patient No. 495 is unclear. Presumably his disease could have resulted from myxomatous degeneration of the valve, bacterial endocarditis on a bicuspid aortic valve, or other undetermined causes, such as rheumatic heart disease. Our observation of clinical improvement of one patient (No. 329) with syphilitic AR plus stabilization of disease in the other (No. 194) following penicillin treatment suggests that specific antimicrobial therapy of late disease may still be beneficial. Certainly both subjects have far outlived the 3-yr longevity prognosticated for untreated patients with such disease. Although others feel differently, withholding penicillin treatment from such patients probably cannot be justified by the argument that repair of already existing destruction would be minimal compared to the risk of Jarisch-Herxheimer reactions of fever, angina, or rupture of aneurysm. The importance of such reactions in this form of late syphilis is certainly debatable. Therefore, in such cases we suggest that antibiotic therapy be recommended in addition to supportive therapeutic measures such as digitalization, diuretics, salt restriction, and other measures to counter the resulting congestive heart failure.

Barondess and Sande have observed that aortic regurgitation resulting from syphilis was associated with a significantly higher incidence of ischemic myocardial changes at autopsy when compared to that of age-matched patients with AR of rheumatic heart disease. In reviewing the autopsy records of this study, we have noted the pathologic findings of aortitis were more frequent in syphilitics as expected, but associated ischemic myocardial changes were no more frequent. Syphilitic involvement of coronary ostia, according to this study, has not resulted in increased myocardial scarring.

The cumulative decreasing incidence of aortic arch pathology with time suggests that those who had severe involvement died within the first decades of the study. In recent years, aortitis has been demonstrated infrequently in the elderly syphilitics at postmortem examination, thereby accounting for a drop in the overall incidence of such pathology from 58 to 44 per cent in the last 15 yr. These figures also approach those of the Oslo and Yale University Studies. Race, therefore, does not appear to influence the longevity of patients with untreated syphilis. In the Yale University autopsy series, the only study in which both major races of this country were compared, syphilitic lesions of all organ systems were four times more frequent in Negroes, but the risk of death due to syphilis was no greater than that for syphilitic Caucasians.

As observed previously by Rockwell, again the treponemal tests (FTA-ABS and TPI Tests) have shown enhanced confirmation of treated or untreated latent disease. However, as the course of the two patients with syphilitic AR demonstrated, the quantitative nontreponemal blood test (VDRL Test) was more valuable for following patients after treatment.

Summary

For the first time in nearly four decades, aortic regurgitation and cardiovascular morbidity occur equally in the 127 surviving syphilitic and control subjects of the long-continuing Tuskegee Study of untreated syphilis. When examined in 1968–1970, two of the living 76 syphilitics and two of 51 controls manifested findings of aortic regurgitation. All but one of the syphilitic survivors have received some amount of antiluetic therapy. Either stability or improvement of subsequent clinical courses followed therapeutic administration of penicillin to the two subjects with syphilitic aortic valvular disease. Of the subjects studied postmortem, evidence of gross and/or microscopic aortitis has continued to preponderate in the syphilitics, but the frequency of detection of focal myocardial scarring has been equal in the syphilitic and control groups at autopsy.

Further Resources

BOOKS

Gray, Fred D. *The Tuskegee Syphilis Study.* Montgomery, Ala.: Black Belt Press, 1998.

Jones, James H. *Bad Blood: The Tuskegee Syphilis Experiment.* New York: Free Press, 1981.

Professional Guide to Diseases. 6th ed. Springhouse, Pa.: Springhouse Corporation, 1998.

Reverby, Susan M. *Tuskegee's Truths: Rethinking the Tuskegee Syphilis Study.* Chapel Hill, N.C.: University of North Carolina Press, 2000.

PERIODICALS

Witchel, Alex. "Vanquishing a Troubled Legacy." *New York Times,* February 27, 2003, D1.

WEBSITES

Internet Resources on the Tuskegee Study. Available online at http://www.dc.peachnet.edu/~shale/humanities/composition /assignments/experiment/tuskegee.html (accessed February 5, 2003).

Racism and Biomedical Research: Tuskegee Syphilis Study. Available online at http://www.scils.rutgers.edu/~lyonsm /tuskegee.html (accessed February 5, 2003).

The Troubling Legacy of the Tuskegee Syphilis Study. Available online at http://hsc.virginia.edu/hs-library/historical /apology (accessed February 5, 2003).

AUDIO AND VISUAL MEDIA

The Deadly Deception. Films for the Humanities & Sciences, 1993, VHS.

Tuskegee. Films for the Humanities & Sciences, 1993, VHS.

Death: The Final Stage of Growth

Nonfiction work

By: Elisabeth Kübler-Ross

Date: 1975

Source: Kübler-Ross, Elisabeth. *Death: The Final Stage of Growth.* London: Prentice-Hall, 1975.

About the Author: Elisabeth Kübler-Ross (1926–) earned an M.D. in 1957 from the University of Switzerland and a second M.D., with a specialization in psychiatry, in 1963 from the University of Colorado. She holds both Swiss and U.S. citizenship and has written nine books on the medical, philosophical, and theological implications of death. In 1995, she suffered a series of strokes and has partially recovered. She lives in Arizona. ■

Introduction

American medicine does not dwell on death but on the conquest of disease. Medicine, one likes to believe, has put death in retreat, postponing it until one is old and has lived a full life. The story of American medicine in the twentieth century has been the acquisition of new and better antibiotics and vaccines to save lives.

The federal government shares this view that medicine earns its keep by fighting death's approach. Congress created and funded the Centers for Disease Control and Prevention and the National Institutes of Health to combat disease. In the 1970s, Congress poured money into research to cure cancer. Government-sponsored medical research extends to universities throughout the United States.

U.S. medical schools train physician-apprentices to identify and treat diseases. The hierarchy of medicine, made explicit at our medical schools, justifies itself as a rational scheme to treat diseases. The general practitioner treats routine cases, sending unusual or serious cases up the hierarchy to the proper specialist who is expert at treating a tiny subset of diseases.

Physicians leave death to theologians and novelists. One who wants insight into the meaning of death does not consult the family physician but rather reads Tolstoy or Camus or Faulkner.

Significance

Elisabeth Kübler-Ross broke from this tradition, using her skill as a psychiatrist to understand how people make sense of their own impending death. Kübler-Ross wrote about death with a candor one expects from a novelist, not a psychiatrist. The thought of death may make one a pessimist, even a nihilist. But this is untrue of Kübler-Ross. She believed death's approach provided people an opportunity to grow.

She acknowledged the variety of responses to death. Some people sink into despair, others deny death as though it cannot claim them, and yet others make it a "religious" experience, meaning that they attempt to understand its meaning, to share their understanding with intimates, and to deepen these relationships. Kübler-Ross emphasized the importance of relationships because she defined humans as social animals, a definition that harkens back to Aristotle's *Politics*. The fear of death lies in the recognition that it ends these relationships.

Dr. Elisabeth Kübler-Ross, holding two of her books, in Flossmoor, Illinois, May 25, 1975. A psychiatrist, Dr. Kübler-Ross sought to understand how people deal with dying and bereavement and wrote many books aimed at helping the public understand these experiences.
© BETTMANN/CORBIS. REPRODUCED BY PERMISSION.

The acceptance of death transforms one, wrote Kübler-Ross, as Isaiah's acceptance of his role as prophet transformed him and as Jesus' experience in the wilderness transformed him. This is not the language of medicine but of the nation's Judeo-Christian heritage. One suspects Kübler-Ross, as a psychiatrist, understood that medicine could do much good but it could not give life meaning. The search for meaning is not a medical or scientific quest. It is first an introspective quest, whether one calls it theological or philosophical, and second a communal quest when one seeks understanding and affection from others to validate life's goodness in the face of death.

What is remarkable is that the attempt to understand death is more ancient than our own species. Neanderthals began the ritual of burying their dead, sometimes with flowers, as an act of devotion and as surely an attempt to understand their own finitude before *Homo sapiens* walked the earth. Neanderthals have been extinct thirty thousand years. In their place we continue their quest to understand death.

Elisabeth Kübler-Ross' books have been translated into more than 25 languages. Her appeal, as the foregoing paragraphs suggest, was strongest among American intellectuals. As early as 1965 University of Chicago anthropologist Francis Clark Howell had called attention to the significance of Neanderthal burials, and during the 1970s his colleagues, the American anthropologists Elwyn Simons and Allan Walker, expanded Howell's insight to document the nearly universal practice of burial among both Neanderthals and Homo sapiens. (This language assumes that Neanderthal and H. sapiens were separate species. Most paleoanthropologists hold this view though the evidence is not strong enough for consensus.) Anthropologists were thus making clear during the 1970s that a preoccupation with death sank roots deep into human prehistory. Although a psychiatrist rather than an anthropologist, Kübler-Ross during the 1970s tapped into the human longing to understand death.

Primary Source

Death: The Final Stage of Growth [excerpt]

SYNOPSIS: In this excerpt, Elisabeth Kübler-Ross acknowledges the variety of responses to death. Some people sink into despair, others deny death, and yet others make it a "religious" experience by attempting to understand its meaning, to share their understanding with intimates, and to deepen these relationships.

We abhor and reject the moment when we will confront the nearness of our death. But the dying stage of our life can be experienced as the most profound growth event of our total life's experience. The shock, the pain and the anxiety are great, but if we are fortunate enough to have time to live and experience our own process, our arrival at a plateau of creative acceptance will be worth it. . . .

When the things we value most in life are destroyed, we can respond in several ways. We can live a life of depressed feelings and in extreme circumstances, give up investing in life entirely by developing a life of psychotic separation. This is the ultimate or extreme despair. The second alternative is to conceal the negative of our existence from consciousness. This is always an attempt at concealment because the defense is seldom effective for very long especially in situations of extreme stress like those involving our own death or the death of a significant other. The third alternative, I call religious. It is investing ourselves in creative and appreciative relationships with others. Becoming open to other people and remaining open to them is more easily said than done in time of crisis. It is especially difficult if we have not been in the practice of relating

that way with others. In those moments when we experience the pain of our own dying and the dying of others, we are not likely to reach out to give or receive comfort or support unless our lives have been previously open to others in situations of joy, sorrow, anger and hate. This third response, our reaching out to others, is the step leading to a growth experience for the terminally ill person.

Our struggle for growth as we approach death is "the struggle . . . for meaning and significance of our person." Being, existing at this time of crisis *"is to mean something to someone else."* As we mature as adults, the threat of losing relationships with other significant persons in our lives is greater than the fear of losing our own life. We are animals who think of ourselves through our transactions with other persons. We are basically social being fellow-persons. And we cannot break our bonds with one another without becoming of no value. Since our highest values focus on ourselves in relation to others, death means termination of transaction with others or a "failure in communion." . . .

I designed and executed a research project, hoping to gain an understanding of the religious dynamics behind the denial process and the terminally ill patient's resistance to moving through to acceptance. The most important finding for me from the study was that there was empirical support for all that we have been discussing up to now. It demonstrated that people who deny less and are more able to move through the five stages after they discover that they have a terminal illness are those people who (1) are willing to converse in depth with significant others about what their present experience is like, (2) meet others on equal terms, that is, are able to enter into real dialogue with others where both can share what is "real" with the other, and (3) accept the good with the bad. They have a framework within which the tragic and happy events of their present and past life take on meaning and give their life a sense of direction and fulfillment.

The study showed, among other things, that the process of dying is a process of re-commitment to life, coming out of a new situation. The three indicators of this re-commitment process are very much like the three attributes of the mature personality described in the writings of Gordon Allport.

The dying patient's willingness to converse in depth about his or her present awareness of memories, dreams and hopes while remaining fully cognizant of the present realities of the illness is what Allport calls "self-objectification." Allport describes self-objectivity as "the ability to objectify oneself, to be reflective and insightful about one's own life. The individual with insight sees himself as others see him, at certain moments glimpses himself in a kind of cosmic perspective." . . .

We humans are, above all, capable of experiencing great transcendence. In dealing with significant change situations in our lives, we go through a process very much like that of the dying patient, as illustrated in the diagram of the five stages.

Learning how to live life as a dying person is not unlike the re-learning necessary after a divorce or a separation from an important person. Leaving a job or receiving an important award or recognition may begin us along the same path of transcendence walked by all of us if we have the opportunity to experience our last days of life. Religious conversion, opening ourselves to radical new life directions, will also take us along the road of the five steps. Isaiah, chapter 6, of the Old Testament is a reporting of the prophet's experiencing of those same five steps, beginning with shocked denial, moving through the emotions of awe and guilt, the redemptive bargaining, the working depression as he faces the reality of the true cost of his new commitment, to the final acceptance of his prophetic task. Paul, the Apostle, has his Road to Damascus experience and the conversion experience of Jesus is described in the Gospel of Luke, beginning with his baptism and continuing through his temptation on the mountain (Luke 3:21ff).

The "five stages" are the way of optimum growth and creative living. The three modes of human commitment and human development are our guides along the journey. We *can* live life fully until we die.

Further Resources

BOOKS

Kübler-Ross, Elisabeth. *Death Is of Vital Importance: On Life, Death and Life after Death.* Barrytown, N.Y.: Station Hill Press, 1995.

———. *Living with Death and Dying.* New York: Macmillan, 1981.

———, and David Kessler. *Life Lessons: Two Experts on Death and Dying Teach Us about the Mysteries of Life and Living.* New York: Scribner, 2000.

PERIODICALS

States, Bert O. "Death as a Fictitious Event." *Hudson Review,* Autumn 2000, 423–433.

WEBSITES

"Elisabeth Kübler-Ross." *Women's International Center.* Available online at http://www.wic.org/bio/eross.htm (accessed February 5, 2003).

Elisabeth Kübler-Ross. Available online at http://www.elisabeth kublerross.com (accessed February 5, 2003).

"Malpractice: The Problem in Perspective"
Journal article

By: James M. Vaccarino

Date: August 22, 1977

Source: Vaccarino, James M. "Malpractice: The Problem in Perspective." *Journal of the American Medical Association* 238, no. 8, August 22, 1977, 861–863.

About the Author: James M. Vaccarino received a law degree from the State University of New York at Buffalo in 1957. After working in private practice, he joined the Massachusetts General Hospital as general counsel in 1972. ∎

Introduction

During the 1970s, malpractice arose as a medical and legal concern. Malpractice is an error in treating a patient that results either from the failure to implement the correct treatment or the initiation of an incorrect treatment. Malpractice is thus an error of commission or omission. In either case, the treatment or lack of it must harm a patient in a way correct treatment would have prevented. All these elements must be present for malpractice. Negligence, no matter how egregious, is not malpractice unless it harms a patient in a way correct treatment would have prevented.

Particularly damaging was the 1972 revelation that physicians at the U.S. Public Health Service had watched four hundred African Americans suffer progressive debilitation from syphilis. Many died, yet these physicians did nothing to treat them. Rather, they had used the victims as test subjects to study the onset and progression of syphilis. If physicians were capable of such intentional acts, then surely, many Americans thought, they could be guilty of the lesser sin of malpractice, which flowed from negligence rather than intent.

Significance

Increases in charges of malpractice put physicians in retreat. Indeed, an attorney, James M. Vaccarino, rather than a physician, wrote the 1977 commentary excerpted here for the *Journal of the American Medical Association.* Vaccarino defended physicians, asserting that "the vast majority of malpractice claims have no merit." Rather, malpractice claims arise from poor rapport between physician and patient, treatment that a patient judges substandard, or a bill that a patient judges too

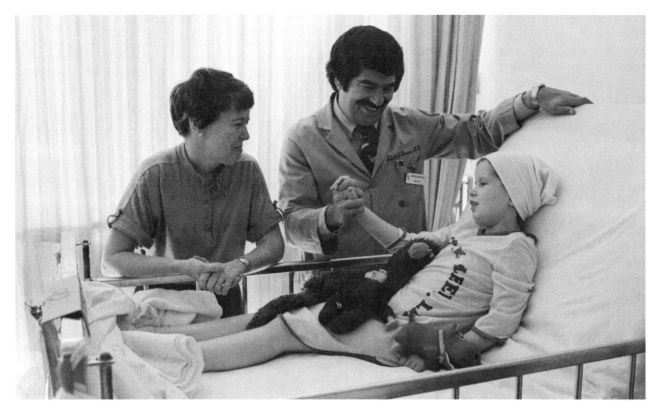

Dr. Edward Baum joins the mother of one of his patients in a bedside visit, Chicago, Illinois, August 8, 1980. At the Colorado Medical Society in 1975, James Vaccarino stressed to physicians that a good relationship with a patient is the most important factor in preventing malpractice suits. © BETTMANN/CORBIS. REPRODUCED BY PERMISSION.

large. Vaccarino cited poor rapport between physician and patient as the largest factor in "frivolous" lawsuits.

At every turn, Vaccarino denigrates patients, calling their fears "shallow" and asserting that they cannot make sense of a hospital bill, that they have illusions about the prospect for cure of a disease, and that physicians can manipulate patients' beliefs with ease. In the article, Vaccarino claims that "the vast majority" of malpractice suits are specious and that the courts reject a large percentage of malpractice claims. Moreover, he asserts that three factors lead to malpractice claims: poor rapport between physician and patient, treatment that a patient judges substandard, or a bill that a patient judges too large.

Primary Source

"Malpractice: The Problem in Perspective" [excerpt]

> **SYNOPSIS:** In this excerpt, James M. Vaccarino asserts that "the vast majority of malpractice claims have no merit." Rather, he says, malpractice claims arise from poor rapport between physician and patient, treatment that a patient judges substandard, or a bill that a patient judges too large.

Simply stated, except for diligent practice, there are no preventive measures to avoid the unpredictable act of malpractice.

In terms of protection, the only available mechanism is the purchase of liability insurance, a device that does not assure that ordinary negligence will not occur but rather affords you the luxury of taking damages from someone else's pocket when you have been negligent. Some physicians believe that practicing without insurance is an effective deterrent to suit by unscrupulous individuals, postulating that if no pot of gold exists no suit will ensue. It is curious that, in my experience, all malpractice suits are commenced without any prior knowledge of the insurance status of the physician. This information is just not readily available. Moreover, by not carrying liability insurance, you actually cheat patients who have been negligently injured out of any rightful compensation for such injuries, unless you are financially capable of remunerating them personally. Therefore, from a practical as well as a moral standpoint, it is more reasonable to carry insurance.

It is illogical to conclude that there is more malpractice in medicine today given the relative status of medical science. The quality of medical practice has never been higher; the standards have never been more strictly defined; the caliber of the individual practitioner is historically unsurpassed; the volume and intensity of review activities are unprecedented.

It is apparent, however, that the volume of malpractice suits is increasing. Hospital medical staffs are plagued by them; the courts are glutted by them; insurance companies overwhelmed by them.

The vast majority of malpractice claims have no merit. They are a product of a suit-conscious society of which we are members. The public avidly pursues these claims, spurred on by a growing recognition of their rights and capabilities of seeking reimbursement for elements of health care that they feel were poorly provided. "That they feel"— these are the key words—that subjective element of individual perception that can so easily be influenced. The problem, in great measure, results from a growing misconception by patients of what modern medicine can do, plus a lack of personal identity and rapport with the physician, owing to the increasing commercialization of medical practice. The frivolous suits are, on close inspection, easily understood and wholly preventable. More specifically, they have as their foundation any one or a combination of three factors: a poor relationship with the provider, a poor result, and a bill deemed by the patient to be excessive. Each of these factors arises from a lack of understanding and unrealistic patient expectation.

Poor Relationship

The most significant contributive factor to frivolous claims is the poor relationship with the provider. An excellent example of a failure to meet expectations is the current concept of the "physician-patient relationship." You might like to blame the media for these expectations, the impossible-to-live-up to handsome and compassionate television physician image. The fact is that a patient who goes to the hospital seeking relief is very receptive to the slightest overture of kindness or sympathy on the part of the administering physician and staff. Is that too much to expect? Kindness, consideration, and a sensitivity to the patient put the physician in a most favorable light. The patient so viewing his physician will rarely misconstrue, distrust, or fail to harmonize with the physician's actions. Human nature has evidenced time and time again that a person who is truly enamored of his physician will not breach that respect and trust.

Conversely, the abrasive, insensitive, and alienating personality breeds mistrust and lack of confidence. If magnification in the patient's mind is tenfold for a gesture of kindness, it is 100-fold for the cold attitude of a physician who does not have the time to develop a sound rapport.

As far back as 1823, the importance of a good physician-patient relationship was recognized:

> He who does not understand the art to acquire the confidence and esteem of his patient—to make himself beloved—to inspire a good opinion, will make but a sorry progress, should his knowledge be ever so profound. . . . If he can get the people . . . to say, "the doctor is a fine man"—he is safe: his skill will hardly be questioned, provided he knows how to please.
>
> (General Guide for Practicing Physicians in the Examination of the Sick, 1823)

Unfortunately, the development of a good bedside manner appears to be obsolete. Patients still hope that the medical encounter will be a personal, intimate, and somehow sanctified experience. That is not unrealistic; physicians are, in fact, dealing with the most precious possession of the patient—his body. To treat it with any less dignity than would the patient is unforgivable.

Poor Result

The second factor that more often than not finds its way into the basis of a frivolous malpractice suit is the poor result or anything that fails to meet the expectation of the patient with respect to outcome. It need not be culpable negligence such as a retained sponge, but may be only a minor stitch infection or inflammation at the operative site. It may even be as insignificant as being compelled to leave the hospital setting, because of current utilization review guidelines, in a condition the patient believes to be inappropriate.

In short, the poor result may run the gamut from hard-core negligence to the most insignificant of trivial risks ordinarily accompanying hospitalization. The patient often believes he was promised a specific result or may have imagined a more positive outcome, concluding this from the physician's explanation of the procedure or owing to the belief that medicine is a precise and sophisticated science, the practice of which is relatively risk-free. These problems often arise when the physician does not fully inform the patient or explains routine procedures superficially.

If you add a poor patient-physician relationship to a situation where an individual is unhappy with the result, then you are more apt to have a patient construe a complication as something actionable. The poor result begins to emerge as "negligence."

Hospital Costs

The third, and probably the most dominant, factor in the actual initiation of the suit is the bill. Patients may easily misunderstand current hospital costs, which are defensibly high. More often the problem arises from a mistaken belief on the part of the patient that insurance will adequately cover all hospital charges. This is just not true! There is little that can be done about the availability of insurance benefits, but to compound such an unfortunate reality with a callous collection process is unconscionable. An insensitive billing procedure often acts as the irritant compelling the patient to seek legal assistance. Dunning a patient who believes no one cared about him as a person and who suffered some complication may be the decisive factor between merely an unhappy experience and the initiation of a meritless claim.

Prevention of the Frivolous Claim

Prevention of frivolous suits is predicated on the understanding of the three precipitating causes plus the application of three basic principles.

Rapport

Probably the most elementary factor is rapport—the development of a good relationship with the patient. How much time is taken explaining things to the patients before surgery, and afterward? This element is singularly most critical. When a patient has questions about results, he needs added attention immediately. It is too easy to shrug off these questions and be "unavailable."

This is perhaps one of the most crucial phases of the claim sequence, for what is done at this time may either stop a potential claim or force the patient to see a lawyer. As the pressure for time increases on the staff, it becomes more difficult to put all the time you would like into friendly conversation with patients and their relatives about care. However, if you are arrogant, distant, not available often enough, or difficult to talk to, then the patient may begin to question clinical competence. If that happens, you are well on the way to a claim! Some

of the most clinically adept doctors who cannot develop a warm relationship with a patient get sued more often for meritless allegations than those who perhaps are not as clinically outstanding but who are kind and sympathetic. Remember that patients are usually not qualified to judge your clinical competence. They can only judge you as they see you, based on your actions as a person.

> Of the tens of thousands of malpractice actions . . . how many are directed against quacks? Disconcertingly few. What accounts for this . . . state of affairs? The reason . . . is not difficult to find. The only skill that the quack has to sell is the ability to establish the maintain rapport with another person. Medical skill is completely absent, yet, so are malpractice suits.
>
> (Journal of the American Medical Association, *Vol. 169, 2037*)

There is no merit in the position that the pressure of practice does not afford enough time to develop rapport, to waste precious minutes with patients calming their shallow fears. Rapport is not generally correlative with time. It is attitudinal. A caring glance or smile is worth an hour of conversation; a touch of hands is immeasurable!

Medical Record Documentation

Physicians cannot afford to offer less than a high standard of care. This standard of care must be shown to have been violated if a plaintiff is to prevail in an action for malpractice. The only forum for documentation of the standard of care is the medical record. It must speak for itself and accurately reflect the care the patient has received.

As a general rule, the plaintiff's attorney will examine the records prior to the commencement of the claim, and if it is clearly indicated that what the patient complains of was no more than a risk that was understandable under the circumstances, the claim may be prevented. Conversely, an absence of detail or an ambiguous entry will imply an attempt to conceal the facts.

If the physician has indeed departed from the usual course of treatment in a specific case, but justifiably so, he should note his thought process in the record. Missing a diagnosis may imply negligence to some, but a mere showing, in the record, that diligence was utilized in arriving at the diagnosis will usually rebut such a presumption.

> In the objective, interpretive, and plan sections of the progress notes, the physician has a chance to reveal exactly why he took a given

course of action, exactly what he chose to neglect, exactly what his priorities were . . . and most important, why he may have deviated from the usual criteria for the management of a specific problem. . . .

(Arch Intern Med, Vol 127: 101–105)

Alter your clinical routine only where indicated for medical reasons in the patient's best interests, not in a vain attempt to avoid malpractice. Practice good medicine, document your rationale, be sure that it can be justified as consonant with a reasonable number of your colleagues' actions for they will be your judges. Remember that the law is less concerned with rightness or wrongness than it is with justifiability. So long as medicine is the art and science of treating the ill, and no two people are alike, there must be flexibility in the application of standards. You are free to apply those standards in a diligent, reasonable, and justifiable way, but be sure you document your reasoning. Malpractice lawyers will tell you that the decision to drop or pursue a case is frequently based solely on what the medical record contains. A significant number of potential claims are eliminated in the lawyer's office based on a review of the medical record.

What should the medical record contain? A good rule of thumb is whatever you, as a new consultant, would expect to find to assure yourself of capably understanding the history and effectively commencing treatment.

Finally, it should be noted that medical records should be used for communication purposes, not, as is frequently found, to release frustration, as a forum for petty disputes, to effect change, to criticize the care of a local colleague, referring physician, or other hospital. "They should be written in a professional style, not like a diary and certainly not with subjective comments about the patient. They should not—although the temptation is great—be written with the judge, rather than the patient, in mind."

Communication

If you work in a hospital environment, sensitizing the hospital administration to potential problems is an absolute must in preventing frivolous claims. In this respect, the administrator of the hospital should have an effective reporting mechanism whereby he is constantly aware of patient "incidents" and potential claims. These may be surmised from patient letters of complaint, failure to pay bills, or an expression of discontent during hospitalization.

This requires constant communication and trust between staff and administration. Once the information has been noted, the administrator can review the circumstances and counsel the staff on how to handle the problem.

In the overall practice of medicine, keep the patient in mind, let the lawyers worry about the law, and exercise some old-fashioned common sense. I can assure you that if this advice is followed, you will realize fewer law suits but, more importantly, experience a greater level of professional satisfaction.

James M. Vaccarino, JD
The Massachusetts General Hospital
Boston

Further Resources

BOOKS

Curran, William J. *How Lawyers Handle Medical Malpractice Cases.* Rockville, Md.: National Center for Health Services, 1976.

Goldsmith, Lee S., ed. *Medical Malpractice: Guide to Medical Issues.* New York: Bender, 1985.

PERIODICALS

Treaster, Joseph B. "Malpractice Insurance: No Clear or Easy Answers." *The New York Times,* March 5, 2003, C1.

WEBSITES

Medical Malpractice. Available online at http://www.civilrights.com/medical.html; website home page http://www.civilrights.com (accessed February 5, 2003).

The Complete Book of Running

Manual, Table

By: James F. Fixx

Date: 1977

Source: Fixx, James F. *The Complete Book of Running.* New York: Random House, 1977, 39–41, 42–45.

About the Author: James F. Fixx (1932–1984) was born in New York City and graduated from Oberlin College in Ohio. During the 1960s, he began jogging to trim down his weight from 220 pounds to 159 pounds. His books on jogging made his reputation. Ironically, Fixx died of a heart attack while jogging. ∎

Introduction

Exercise, in the form of bicycling, attracted Americans of all classes around 1900. Physicians praised cycling's health benefits. Ads featured husbands and wives cycling together, emphasizing the social aspect of the sport. But after Henry Ford unveiled the Model T in 1907,

Americans had the mobility and the freedom to go wherever they pleased. The Model T transformed Americans from cyclists to drivers. The first exercise mania had spent itself.

During the 1970s, interest in exercise reemerged. Jogging, the archetypal sport of the decade, emphasized the communal spirit of cycling at the beginning of the century. As cycling had, it attracted men and women. Unlike the fitness movement at the turn of the century, though, that of the 1970s appealed primarily to the middle class, whereas the cycling craze around 1900 appealed as much to the working class as to the middle class.

During the 1970s, some 8 million Americans took up jogging. The competitive among them entered marathons, swelling the ranks of the Boston Marathon and the New York City Marathon. The Boston Marathon established a time threshold to prevent being overwhelmed by entrants. With no threshold, the New York City Marathon emerged during the 1970s as an event that drew more participants than any other sport in the United States. In the 1970s jogging came to enjoy the prestige that cycling and soccer had long enjoyed in Europe.

Significance

James F. Fixx emerged as an advocate for jogging. His *The Complete Book of Running* topped sales lists in 1977. Fixx was as uncompromising as any competitive runner, asserting jogging to be superior to other sports. He defended this view by appealing to the President's Council on Physical Fitness and Sports. The council compared eight sports, and the accompanying table summarizes the results. The council judged these sports by nine criteria, beginning with cardiorespiratory endurance and ending with sleep. Jogging had the highest rating, followed by bicycling, swimming, handball, tennis, walking, golf, and bowling.

The table merits scrutiny given that Fixx used it to justify the superiority of jogging. The table, for example, reveals that running surpassed bicycling in building muscular endurance and strength despite the fact that cycling clubs throughout the nation feature rides of 100 miles and that cycling more than jogging strengthens the quadriceps muscles. Fixx admits in this excerpt that not everyone praised jogging's health benefits, though he emphasized that its detractors had no evidence for their opposition. Instead, he drew attention to a meeting of the New York Academy of Sciences, whose participants "documented the benefits of running."

Despite Fixx's enthusiasm, the fitness movement of the 1970s had no more longevity than the bicycling craze around 1900. In 1979, nearly one-fourth of Americans said that nothing could induce them to exercise. Moreover, as a white, middle-class movement, the fitness ma-

nia of the 1970s never attracted minorities or a mass following.

Primary Source

The Complete Book of Running [excerpt]: Book

SYNOPSIS: In this excerpt, James F. Fixx defends jogging as the most healthful exercise, citing evidence in the form of a table from the President's Council on Physical Fitness and Sports and the New York Academy of Sciences.

Why Running?

There is no lack of information on what various types of physical activity do for our health. Not long ago seven exercise experts were asked by the President's Council on Physical Fitness and Sports to rank popular forms of exercise on the basis of how much they help cardiorespiratory endurance, muscular endurance, muscular strength, flexibility, balance and general well-being. Each panelist was permitted to award a given activity anything from no votes (signifying no benefit) to three (maximum benefit). Thus twenty-one is a perfect score. Their findings for selected sports are summarized in the table ["Eight Sports: How Much They Help What"]. . . .

Or consider, for the same activities, calorie costs per hour, a direct measure of intensity:

Running.	800–1,000
Bicycling (13 mph)	660
Swimming.	300–650
Handball/squash	600
Tennis	400–500
Walking briskly (4 mph)	300
Bowling.	270
Golf	250
Walking slowly (2 mph)	200

Running, it is clear, is not the only sport that improves health. Bicycling, swimming, handball and squash all confer worthwhile benefits and may seem pleasanter to some people. In *Sports in America* James A. Michener writes: "As one who has jogged many weary miles I personally agree . . . that this is one of the world's dullest pastimes." And William F. Buckley, Jr., once confessed: "All I ever managed on those few occasions when I jogged was to concentrate on what a miserable form of self-punishment jogging is."

Nonetheless, for those who like running's subtle and solitary pleasures, there is no sport like it.

Eight Sports: How Much They Help What

	Running	Bicycling	Swimming	Handball/ Squash	Tennis	Walking	Golf	Bowling
Physical Fitness								
Cardio-respiratory endurance	21	19	21	19	16	13	8	5
Muscular endurance	20	18	20	18	16	14	8	5
Muscular strength	17	16	14	15	14	11	9	5
Flexibility	9	9	15	16	14	7	8	7
Balance	17	18	12	17	16	8	8	6
General Well-Being								
Weight control	21	20	15	19	16	13	6	5
Muscle definition	14	15	14	11	13	11	6	5
Digestion	13	12	13	13	12	11	7	7
Sleep	16	15	16	12	11	14	6	6
Total	148	142	140	140	128	102	66	51

SOURCE: Table from Fix, James F. *The Complete Book of Running*. New York: Random House, 1977, 39.

Primary Source

The Complete Book of Running: Table

SYNOPSIS: This table from Fix's book compares the physical benefits of eight sports. Seven exercise experts awarded physical activities 0–3 points on how much they help aspects of peoples' physical fitness and general well-being. Twenty-one is the maximum score.

But forget the fun of it for a moment and consider only its unique contributions to physical fitness.

Chapter 1 pointed out that running can serve as an antidote to many of the hazards of twentieth-century living. Moreover, running appears to confer long-term benefits that are now only beginning to be appreciated. Nathan Pritikin, director of the Longevity Research Institute in Santa Barbara, California, told me that in checking *Who's Who in American Sports* he discovered that the average life-span of former football players is fifty-seven years, of boxers and baseball players sixty-one years, and of track competitors seventy-one years. And Dr. Paul S. Fardy, a cardiac rehabilitation specialist at St. Catherine Hospital in East Chicago, Indiana, reports that in a study of more than 500 people, the hearts of former athletes—runners prominent among them—tended to function better than the hearts of those who had never participated in athletics.

Fardy is one of a growing number of investigators who are discovering that running has distinct advantages over many other sports. In a recent article in the *American Physical Therapy Journal* he wrote: "Walking and/or jogging is the simplest and probably most popular aerobic activity." And Dr. Moe, the physician mentioned earlier, wrote in a letter to a medical magazine:

It is hard for me to see how something with such great merit can be so largely ignored by the medical profession. We profess interest in preventive medicine, and we know that arteriosclerotic diseases, especially of the coronary arteries, account for over 50% of our annual death rate. It has been shown in animal and human studies that endurance-type training increases cardiac perfusion, enhances cardiopulmonary efficiency, lowers the resting pulse, and reduces blood lipids. Why, then, is it not obvious to more of us that we need to do endurance training ourselves and teach it to our patients?

Dr. Moe is plainly, and justifiably, a frustrated man—perhaps the price of being so far ahead of his time.

Even if we grant that there are other sports that are as good for one's health as running, there remain good reasons to choose running. One is the time devoted to it. When I played tennis, I was a member of a regular foursome who played from nine to eleven every Saturday and Sunday. What with time for dressing, showering and driving to and from the courts, I was spending six hours a weekend at tennis. Furthermore, I was burning up 2,000 calories at most. Nowadays, unless I am trying to put in high mileage to get ready for a marathon, I run ten miles a day—a total, on a weekend, of about two and a half hours, and even the world's longest showers could not possibly raise it to more than three hours. Thus in half the time it used to require, I get the same 2,000 calories' worth of exercise. . . .

James F. Fixx, August 27, 1978. The author of *The Complete Book of Running,* Fixx was an advocate for jogging and running, which he argues is the best form of exercise. © BETTMANN/CORBIS. REPRODUCED BY PERMISSION.

I would be misleading you if I tried to force upon you the impression that there is nothing wrong with running. You can be forced into a ditch by a car. You can get Achilles tendinitis or a pulled muscle. . . . You can find yourself, at five o'clock on a January morning, cursing the moment you first thought of running. (Don't worry; you'll feel fine once you get moving.)

But an even more general—and more serious—charge has been made against running: that it simply isn't good for you, that the harm it does outweighs the benefits. As I write this, the most visible proponent of this view is a physician named J. E. Schmidt, who practices in Charlestown, Indiana. The March 1976 issue of *Playboy* carried an article by Schmidt entitled "Jogging Can Kill You!" (exclamation point his—or *Playboy's*). In a spirit of fair play Dr. Schmidt starts out by acknowledging that running can help your legs and heart and give you "that tanned, outdoorsy look." But his enthusiasm fades quickly. "The fact is," he writes, "that, for both men and women, running or jogging is one of the most wasteful and hazardous forms of exercise. Jogging

takes more from the body than it gives back. It exacts a price that no one can afford or should be willing to pay for leg and thigh muscles or for that specious indicator of good health—the tan." Specifically, Dr. Schmidt says jogging can loosen the linkage between the sacrum and the hipbones, cause slipped discs, contribute to varicose veins, dislodge the uterus from its "perch," produce droopy breasts and, in men, bring on inguinal hernia. Jogging, he asserts, can even harm the heart by causing it to "tug" on its blood vessels and shake crusted material loose, inducing heart attack. Furthermore, he says, jogging can cause such architectural anomalies as "dropped" stomach, loose spleen, floating kidney and fallen arches.

When Dr. Schmidt's article came out, it created quite a stir. Although no one I spoke to gave up running because of it, there was concern that beginners might be frightened away. As for me, I simply found the article puzzling. I had been a fairly close student of the medical literature on running, and I thought I had a clear sense of what the hazards were. Although the ones Dr. Schmidt cited were not among them, it was, of course, possible that I had missed something.

One day, therefore, I talked with Dr. George Sheehan about the article. Sheehan is one of the world's most widely consulted physicians concerning the effects of running on the human body, having for years combined running and medicine in such a way as to establish himself as the one man to be consulted when you've got a stubborn or baffling injury. Sheehan shrugged and told me he knew of no studies that support Schmidt's views. "He went by what I suppose we would call common sense," said Sheehan. "But when you start using common sense where the human body is concerned, you sometimes are brought up short. The body doesn't always operate the way you think it does. These indictments of jogging are done on the basis of *a priori* thinking, but that's not the way to do it. I'm suspicious when people say, 'It stands to reason.' I think the thing to do is go and find out for yourself whether something does occur."

(Sheehan, who exercises his sense of humor as assiduously as he does his body, told me he took modest revenge on Schmidt after a similar article by him appeared in a newspaper. The article, said Sheehan, was accompanied by a biographical sketch of Schmidt that mentioned his hobby was gardening. Sheehan wrote to warn Schmidt that working in a garden was a hazardous avocation. "I told him," said

Sheehan with a grin, "that he might accidentally stick a pitchfork in his foot and get lockjaw.")

Schmidt's criticisms of running nevertheless stuck in my mind, troubling me. If there were any truth in them, no matter how slight, I didn't want to be guilty of ignoring them. So I finally wrote to him, saying in part:

> Your article in the March *Playboy* has, as you no doubt know, stirred up quite a bit of interest among runners. Right now I find myself in the thick of the flurry because I am writing a book on running . . . and in one way or another I'm going to have to deal with the questions you raise.
>
> Specifically, I am puzzled by the fact that none of the physicians most closely identified with running have acknowledged the truth of very much of what you said in the *Playboy* piece, and some have said publicly that there are no studies to support any of it. . . . I would be most grateful if you could tell me your sources. . . .

Schmidt replied:

> . . . Let me say, first, that I would not be writing an article for *Playboy* in which I rehash well-known medical facts. To do that would be very boring. The understanding of the relationship between running and the traumata I described—plus a few others!—is now in its nascence, but I discovered it through fortuitous medical events more than twenty years ago.
>
> For centuries, scientists held that the earth is flat and that the sun revolves around the earth. You know of the obloquy that fell upon those who first proposed that this is not so! The physicians to whom you refer are unaware of the jogging hazards because they don't suspect jogging. The loving husband is the last to know about the faithlessness of his spouse. To suspect jogging is outré.
>
> Alas, I cannot go beyond these meager generalities, because I expect to do a book of my own on the subject, and there is where I will present the evidence.

A few months after Schmidt's piece appeared, I attended a conference, sponsored by the New York Academy of Sciences, on the physiological, medical, epidemiological and psychological effects of running. The conference brought together some seventy authorities who for four days, from early morning until far into the night, discussed the results of their studies. Most of the authorities documented the benefits of running, but four or five did mention occasional adverse effects. Schmidt's were not among them. Until convincing evidence appears, perhaps in the

book he promises us, it seems not only perfectly safe to run but a smart thing to do.

Further Resources

BOOKS
Costill, David L. *A Scientific Approach to Distance Running.* Los Altos, Calif.: Track & Field News, 1979.
Morehouse, Lawrence E., and Leonard Gross. *Total Fitness in 30 Minutes a Week.* New York: Simon and Schuster, 1975.

PERIODICALS
Clark, Matt, and Mariana Gosnell. "How It Helps—And Hurts." *Newsweek,* May 23, 1977, 82–83.

"Fitness Findings." *Reader's Digest,* June 1979, 10.

Waters, Harry F., Lisa Whitman, Ann Ray Martin, and Dewey Gram. "Keeping Fit: America Tries to Shape Up." *Newsweek,* May 23, 1977, 78–79.

Freedom to Die
Nonfiction work

By: Ruth Olive Russell
Date: 1977
Source: Russell, Ruth Olive. *Freedom to Die.* New York: Human Sciences Press, 1977, 13, 15–17, 19–20, 33–34, 283.
About the Author: Ruth Olive Russell (1897–1979) was born in Ontario, Canada, and received a Ph.D. in psychology from the University of Waterloo in Canada. She worked in private practice in Canada and the United States, developing an interest in medical ethics. ∎

Introduction

The tragedy of Karen Ann Quinlan focused attention during the 1970s on the questions of when life ends and who has the right to end life. On April 15, 1975, Quinlan slipped into a coma after consuming alcohol and tranquilizers. She stopped breathing, damaging her brain by depriving it of oxygen. Paramedics rushed her to Newton Memorial Hospital in New Jersey, where physicians feared the damage to her brain was permanent. Her parents hoped she would recover, but as the severity of damage to her brain became clear, they lost hope. Her father, Joseph Quinlan, compared her existence to that of a "vegetable." In her condition, Karen Quinlan was "not really living," said Joseph. She only remained alive, her parents believed, because a respirator kept her breathing.

Her parents could see no value in Karen's indefinite existence in a coma. Joseph Quinlan granted physicians permission to take Karen off the respirator, but they refused in the belief that he did not have legal authority to end his daughter's life. Just months earlier, the American

Medical Association had stated that only physicians could determine when someone was dead.

Joseph Quinlan sued the hospital for the right to take his daughter off the respiratory, losing in a lower court but winning in the New Jersey Supreme Court in 1976. Once off the respirator, Karen Quinlan continued to breathe, leading her physicians to continue her care. She remained in a coma until pneumonia killed her in 1985 at age thirty-one.

Significance

Joseph Quinlan had won the right to remove his daughter from a respirator in the expectation that she would die. If Joseph Quinlan had a right to end his daughter's life, did Americans have a right to decide when to end their own lives? Did physicians with patient consent have a right to decide when to end that patient's life?

Ruth Olive Russell asserted that medical technology can keep people alive long after they would rather have died, robbing them of dignity and prolonging their suffering. She attacked the idea that only God can end life, claiming that God would prefer that people act with compassion in ending life when a patient no longer wished to live and when every day brought agony without hope of recovery. She wrote that Americans in the 1970s wanted the right to choose to die with dignity. Yet U.S. law denied this right, leading her to urge legislators to pass laws granting this right while protecting patients with "carefully devised safeguards."

Russell admitted that the definition of life's end is unclear, muddying the discussion of the circumstances under which a person or a legal guardian may decide to end life. Is a person whose heart beats and whose lungs function alive even if his or her brain is dead, as was the case with Karen Quinlan? Is the cessation of consciousness sufficient to declare one dead?

Americans continue to debate these questions. Michigan physician Jack Kevorkian has helped the terminally ill end their lives, action that critics brand murder and supporters call heroism. Like the debate over abortion, the debate over euthanasia has polarized Americans to the extent that compromise is difficult. That is, the debate over euthanasia pits competing interests against one another. On the one hand proponents of euthanasia claim the right for each person to decide when his quality of life has deteriorated to a degree that permits euthanasia as an ethical alternative to remaining alive. On the other hand physicians claim an obligation to preserve life. Indeed physicians, particularly the clinicians, define their success as a function of their skill in preserving life. No consensus exists in the U.S. to balance a patient's claim to determine the circumstance and time of his death and a physician's obligation to preserve life.

Primary Source

Freedom to Die [excerpt]

SYNOPSIS: In this excerpt, Ruth Olive Russell defends the right of terminally ill Americans to choose to die rather than to live in agony and diminished capacity to function. She defended her belief as compassion toward people who suffer pointlessly.

In this century, and especially in the past decade, we have witnessed amazing changes in man's power over both birth and death. Radical changes have taken place in beliefs and practices pertaining to the beginning of life. Family planning and birth control, instead of being condemned, are now accepted as a duty and responsibility, and the battle to legalize abortion has been won in many places. It is hard to believe that it was less than 60 years ago that Margaret Sanger served a month in jail for conducting her crusade for the freedom of every woman to determine the number of children she will have. In spite of strong opposition, especially from the medical profession and organized religion, she persisted in her efforts until today birth control is accepted practice throughout much of the world. . . .

The spotlight is now being focused also on the other end of life—on man's new power over death. Due to the amazing successes of medical science and technology, physicians are now able to keep the body functioning long past its natural span, long after the mind and spirit have ceased to exist, sometimes almost indefinitely by artificial means. They can produce what some have called a living death, or, as David Hendin has said, "Dying is rendered obscene by technology."

This power has reached such a stage and keeps increasing so rapidly, that many people are now asking, what are we doing with this new power to prolong life—power undreamed of only a few years ago—and what are our moral responsibilities in regard to it? Many of the epidemics and diseases that only a few years ago killed people off in great numbers have been replaced by long chronic illnesses and degenerative diseases, and the proportion of the aged ill and defective children who survive is constantly increasing. As the end of life approaches, many patients have their lives prolonged against their wishes and against all good sense. By means of respirators, oxygen tanks, heart-lung and kidney-dialysis machines, intravenous feeding, drainage tubes, and other modern devices and medications, many are forced to live on when they want nothing so much as to die. Today there is a groundswell of indignation and revolt against many such efforts in hospitals throughout the land.

We are faced with a crucial question: Will we use our knowledge and new power intelligently, or will we let it be a force leading us blindly while we adhere to dogmas and beliefs that have no relevance for this age of biological revolution, population explosion, and spectacular medical skills? We must ask not merely what man can do but what he ought to do. It is absurd to argue that "man must not usurp God's power" and "God alone must determine when life shall begin and when it shall end;" man is already exerting very great power over both birth and death. And in any case it seems doubtful God's will would require of doctors that they persist in prolonging life as long as possible regardless of the patient's suffering and wishes or beyond the point when life has meaning to him. It is doubtful that God would disapprove of shortening life when it is done out of compassion and in accordance with the safeguards law and the medical profession could provide. It is more likely, on the contrary, that man has a moral obligation to permit avoidance of useless suffering.

A new freedom is being demanded today: the freedom to choose death. More and more people are now realizing that the right to die with dignity . . . is a basic human right that should be available to those hopelessly ill patients who request it.

Law does not now recognize this right, nor does it distinguish between a merciful act of hastening the death of a dying or hopelessly ill or incapacitated person and an act of murder; neither does it clarify when it is permissible for doctors to discontinue treatment or not initiate efforts to prolong the life of terminal patients who want to die. In order for such persons to be assured that they will be permitted and assisted in carrying out their wish to avoid futile suffering or a meaningless, degrading existence, it is necessary to develop new medical guidelines and enact legislation that will recognize the right to choose death with dignity under the protection of carefully devised safeguards. . . .

We would all agree that compulsory, or state imposed euthanasia is wrong; it is unthinkable in a free society. But it is time to give serious consideration to what might be classified as (a) *euthanasia at the request of the patient* and (b) *euthanasia at the request of the patient's legal guardian* in cases in which the patient is not of testamentary capacity. It is this writer's belief, however, that euthanasia should be permitted and administered only in ac-

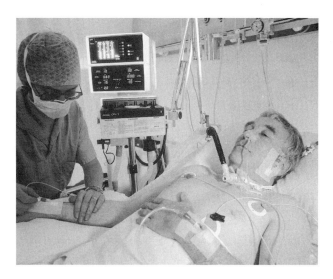

A nurse cares for a patient on life-support. During the 1970s advances in science and technology made it possible to keep even severely ill people alive almost indefinitely, but without hope of recovery, prompting questions as to when it might be best not to. **PHOTO RESEARCHERS, INC. REPRODUCED BY PERMISSION.**

cordance with the safeguards that would be specified in a good euthanasia law.

Because medical science and technology have now made it possible to prolong the life of the body almost indefinitely in many cases, the act of dying is often prolonged to horrifying lengths. It therefore seems urgent to enact appropriate legislation to protect the rights of both physicians and patients. Without it, many persons will be denied relief from suffering and the right to death with dignity and might even be denied the right to live as long as they wish. An adequate euthanasia law would doubtless provide also that a person while in good health could make an advance declaration of his wish for euthanasia in the event that he became incapacitated in the future. . . .

But there is an urgent need for society to go beyond even the questions of biological or brain death, to a recognition of psychological death—that is, death of the individual as a conscious person. Dr. W. Spann of the Institute of Legal Medicine in Helsinki is quoted by Richard Restak as saying, "It is not a question of the scientific boundary between life and death, but what is involved is a value judgment as to what is considered *human* life in its real sense. This kind of judgment is not a matter for . . . the doctor on his own authority."

It should be noted that much of this new concentration on death and dying is not necessarily directed to the subject of euthanasia, and among those who stress the importance of death with dignity, there are many for whom even the word euthanasia is anathema. These people say they merely want doctors to refrain from useless prolongation and help the patient die a "natural death" as comfortably as possible, with dignity; they condemn any action that intentionally hastens death. But to think that death will be easy and dignified if only doctors refrain from prolonging life by heroic efforts is a delusion. The fact is that many people will go on suffering in great distress and indignity unless active steps are taken to induce death. . . .

Statistics indicate that the population over 75 years of age is increasing at about two and one-half times the rate of the general population, and some scientists have predicted that the average lifespan will be increased by at least 15 years within the next couple of decades. Such facts compounded with the high survival rate of severely and permanently defective infants make it clear that there is a gradually growing number of helpless, dependent individuals, many of whom are no longer real persons able to communicate, but patients requiring medical, nursing and hospital services that are already in short supply and very expensive.

Reverence for life and freedom of choice must be the basis for any action regarding euthanasia. Society must recognize also that undesirable pressures arise when freedom and justice are denied and also when citizens are required to bear useless, unreasonable expenditures and suffering. To avoid such undesirable pressures, society must act now to permit an easy and dignified exit from life when life is no longer something to be desired. We must treat death as an inevitable part of existence to be faced realistically, not evasively; it is often man's friend.

It seems certain that it is only a matter of time until laws will be passed that will permit the administration of painless death when the only alternative is an agonizing or meaningless existence. It is a challenge to every citizen to hasten that day.

Further Resources
BOOKS
Cantor, Norman L. *Advance Directives and the Pursuit of Death with Dignity.* Bloomington: Indiana University Press, 1993.

Magnusson, Roger S. *Angels of Death: Exploring the Euthanasia Underground.* New Haven, Conn.: Yale University Press, 2002.

Willke, Jack C. *Assisted Suicide and Euthanasia: Past and Present.* Cincinnati, Ohio: Hayes, 1998.

PERIODICALS
Harris, John. "Consent and End of Life Decisions." *Journal of Medical Ethics,* February 2003, 10–16.

"Smallpox—Epitaph for a Killer?"
Magazine article

By: Donald A. Henderson
Date: December 1978
Source: Henderson, Donald A. "Smallpox—Epitaph for a Killer?" *National Geographic* 154, no. 6, December 1978, 796–805.
About the Author: Donald A. Henderson (1928–) was born in Ohio and received an M.D. from the University of Rochester in New York. In 1965, the World Health Organization appointed Henderson, then a professor at Johns Hopkins University, to direct its campaign to eradicate smallpox. In 1979, Henderson announced that the world was free of smallpox. ∎

Introduction
The virus *Poxvirus variole* causes smallpox. The virus incubates for ten to fourteen days in the body, causing chills, seizures, fever above 104 degrees Fahrenheit, vomiting, delirium, and stupor or coma. These symptoms peak on the second day and begin to subside thereafter, leading a victim to hope he has not contracted anything serious. The hope is false. Within days of feeling better, a victim will develop a sore throat, cough, and lesions on the mouth, throat, and respiratory tract. Days later, lesions erupt on the skin and fill with pus giving a victim a frightful appearance. Fever will return, and after ten days the lesions rupture, dry, and form scabs. Victims may die of internal bleeding or a secondary infection such as pneumonia. Scars disfigure the skin of people who survive infection.

The smallpox virus spreads through the air from droplets coughed up by a victim. Once airborne, the virus can infect anyone who inhales it. A person may contract smallpox by touching the lesions of an infected person or by touching any fabric that contains the virus. These factors make smallpox a highly contagious disease that spreads rapidly through a population.

In 1796 British physician Edward Jenner developed a vaccine against smallpox. The first vaccine against any disease, Jenner's smallpox vaccine is a landmark of medicine. A vaccine is a weakened or dead strain of a virus or bacterium or of a closely related virus or bacterium injected into a person whose immune system produces antibodies against it. The body thereafter stores these antibodies against future infection, conferring immunity.

Significance
Vaccination made the U.S. free from smallpox after 1949. In 1965, the World Health Organization (WHO) appointed Donald A. Henderson to direct its campaign to

A young girl displays the characteristic rash of smallpox, Hakegora, India, June 23, 1974. Over 25,000 people died of smallpox in the Indian state of Bihar in 1974. Smallpox kills roughly 30 percent of its victims, and leaves survivors scarred, and often blinded, for life. **AP/WIDE WORLD PHOTOS. REPRODUCED BY PERMISSION.**

eradicate smallpox from the rest of the world. He admitted that some physicians feared smallpox more than any other disease, and he recounted the ease with which smallpox spread, making its eradication difficult. When he took charge of the WHO campaign, a colleague told him "You don't stand a chance."

Despite this pessimism, Henderson was not disheartened. He knew smallpox can live only in humans, in contrast to the yellow-fever and malaria pathogens, which cycle in mosquitoes, hiding from detection. If physicians quickly quarantined a smallpox victim and anyone he may have been near, they can stop the virus's spread.

By 1971, Henderson had mobilized the WHO for a worldwide vaccination program. Aggressive vaccination and quarantining of victims and people near them reduced the number of countries reporting smallpox cases from seventeen in 1970 to six in 1973. All six were in Asia and Africa. In 1974, Pakistan reported its last case, and in 1975 Nepal and India followed suit. By 1976, Ethiopia remained the last country, Henderson thought, until the last case appeared in 1977 in Somalia. On April 17, 1978, he received a telegram from a colleague reporting the discovery of no new cases. Next year, the WHO declared the world free from smallpox.

Primary Source

"Smallpox—Epitaph for a Killer?" [excerpt]

SYNOPSIS: In this excerpt, Donald A. Henderson recounts his role in directing the WHO campaign to eradicate smallpox. Colleagues doubted he could succeed, but in 1977 Henderson recorded the world's last case of smallpox, and in 1979 the WHO declared the world free from smallpox.

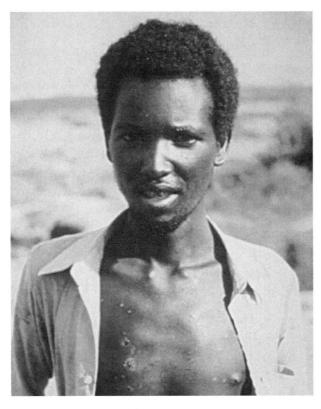

Ali Maow Maalin, of Somalia. In the 1970s the World Health Organization mounted a successful campaign to wipe out smallpox. Maalin, who died of the disease in 1977, is the last known natural victim of smallpox. © SCIENCE VU/CDC/VISUALS UNLIMITED. REPRODUCED BY PERMISSION.

April 17, 1978. The telegram from Nairobi. Kenya, lay on my desk.

"Search complete. No cases discovered. Ali Maow Maalin is world's last known smallpox case."

For ten arduous years I had directed the campaign of the World Health Organization (WHO), a campaign that had enlisted close to 700 advisers from 55 countries and upwards of 200,000 national health officers and volunteers to eradicate smallpox once and for all.

Now, it seemed, we had reached our goal: zero cases of the most devastating and feared of the great pestilences—the first disease to be eradicated by man.

I could comprehend that victory was at hand: emotionally, I was numb.

Six months earlier Maalin, a hospital cook in Merca, Somalia, had become severely ill with high fever and the typical smallpox' rash. . . . Five days later he was discovered. Somali health teams and WHO staff at once isolated him under guard and be-

gan the painstaking search to find and vaccinate 161 people who had been in contact with him. None developed smallpox.

The search spread, house by house, through the town of forty thousand, then into the surrounding Ogaden desert and across adjacent areas of Kenya. Ethiopia, and Djibouti. Thousands of people with chicken pox and other skin rashes were examined and a thousand laboratory specimens taken. None was smallpox.

Final confirmation of eradication requires at least two years of search in every infected area. Certification is thus not possible before October 1979. But on April 17 we were confident that the name Ali Maalin would be recorded as the world's last case in a chain of infection that began long before written history.

In late August, however, a mishap at a university laboratory in Birmingham, England, underscored my concern about live virus kept in laboratories. Preventive measures failed to confine the virus and a medical photographer contracted smallpox and died. Her mother also became infected.

The lesson was clear: the more labs with stocks of live virus, the greater the risk. Requests by WHO have already reduced the number of facilities using smallpox virus from at least 76 to 12 others are expected to comply.

Smallpox has been called one of the most loathsome diseases. I know that no matter how many visits I made to smallpox wards, filled with seriously ill and dying patients. I always came away shaken.

The disease is caused by a virus usually transmitted from person to person in minute droplets expelled from the mouth and nose. Someone not vaccinated or previously infected who inhales the droplets develops a high fever and aching pains after 10 to 14 days. Two to four days later a rash spreads over the body. Blisterlike vesicles fill with pus, and after another 10 to 14 days, scabs form.

In the past, 20 to 30 percent of those afflicted with the severe Asian strain died. Survivors were permanently scarred and sometimes blinded. There is no treatment.

Before vaccines, everyone was susceptible to smallpox. The disease spread in any climate, anywhere. It repeatedly altered the course of history. Brought by Cortés to the New World, it eventually killed an estimated 3.5 million Indians and contributed to the collapse of the Inca and Aztec civilizations. Decimation of North American Indians paved the way for European settlement.

In Europe the problem was no less severe. Lord Macaulay wrote of its effects in 17th-century England: "That disease . . . was then the most terrible of all the ministers of death. . . . smallpox was always present, filling the churchyards with corpses . . . and making the eyes and cheeks of the betrothed maiden objects of horror to the lover."

In 1796 English country physician Edward Jenner showed that a mild infection acquired from cows, called cowpox, gave immunity from smallpox. Material taken from a cowpox pustule could be used to protect others. Within years, cowpox vaccine was being distributed around the world. Yet, until the present century, problems in producing and preserving vaccine precluded more than partial control.

Not until the 1940's were Europe and North America rid of smallpox. In developing countries it remained epidemic, and cases were often exported into smallpox-free areas. Health officials feared it as no other disease. In all countries vaccination programs continued, and quarantine inspectors tried to enforce the international edict that all travelers be vaccinated.

In 1959 an initial attempt by WHO to eradicate smallpox was begun, but the effort failed. Most countries had too few resources, and WHO could offer little help.

I had been working on a measles-smallpox program for 18 West African nations, sponsored by the Agency for International Development and the Center for Disease Control in Atlanta. I was learning firsthand in seven-day weeks the problems of planning, logistics, and personnel. Then in May 1966 WHO was authorized to begin a global smallpox-eradication campaign.

The goal was to stamp out smallpox within ten years. As I was to learn, few believed that smallpox, or any other disease, could really be eliminated. Malaria and yellow fever eradication had failed. Reservations were understandable. Smallpox moved readily across open borders. It seemed unreasonable to expect that programs could be orchestrated in fifty affected countries, including the world's least developed, many with large, remote areas and populations that had never seen a health worker.

Shortly I was surprised by a call from WHO's director-general, who asked me to head the campaign. I was hesitant, and my doubts were confirmed by a respected colleague, who said: "If you think you have problems now in coping with bureaucracy, multiply the problems by the number of UN countries. You don't stand a chance."

Convinced that it would be a waste of time, I so informed the surgeon general of the U. S. Public Health Service, my superior then. He, in turn, informed me that I was ordered to go—for at least nine months. Reluctantly my wife and I stored our furniture and left with our children for Geneva, Switzerland, WHO headquarters. I hardly anticipated the saga ahead, or that 11 years would pass before we would see our furniture again.

Despite the enormity of the task, the nature of smallpox gave grounds for optimism. Unlike many diseases, smallpox virus has no known reservoir other than man. Transmission normally occurs from face-to-face contact, and a victim rarely infects more than five others. The disease spreads slowly and, in scarred survivors, leaves visible evidence that it was present.

To stop the spread, much less to eliminate it, we had to know where the cases were. In 1967 the reporting system was a shambles. Some countries reported irregularly; some denied they had smallpox. That year 131,000 cases were reported. We now estimate there were actually 10 to 15 million cases in 44 countries.

Survey Paints Grim Picture

We put roving teams into the field. They began to piece together a reporting network of hospitals and health centers and to discover more and more cases as they investigated outbreaks. Gradually we began to see the true size of what we had undertaken.

We had to have vaccine, 200 to 250 million doses annually, but tests showed that only 10 percent of the vaccine then in use met acceptable standards—some contained no vaccine virus whatever. Hat in hand, we went from government to government for donations. The Soviet Union, whose proposal initiated the campaign, and the United States were the principal donors, but more than forty other countries also contributed. Using their contributions and WHO funds, we established vaccine-producing laboratories, most of them in infected countries, and devised a system of quality control.

Now we needed a simple, effective, and economical way to administer vaccine in the field. We found it in a two-tined needle developed by Wyeth

Smallpox Erased in a Decade

1967

Forty-Four Countries

The assault on smallpox begins . . . although some experts are skeptical that the effort can succeed.

To mass vaccination is added the strategy of surveillance-containment—patient isolation and intense vaccination in areas of reported disease—to break the chain of human transmission.

1972

Nineteen Countries

The strategy works. Smallpox is eliminated in the Western Hemisphere and in most of Africa. A few cases imported into Europe are quickly contained but illustrate the need for total eradication.

Populations massed in Asia and dispersed on the Horn of Africa offer formidable challenges as the global campaign moves toward "target zero."

1975

Five Countries

Rewards for reporting smallpox help pinpoint outbreaks and motivate health workers and the public to aid the campaign. Vigorous containment measures then stop further spread. Though forty thousand die in Asia in 1974, the tide is turned. By 1976 Asian smallpox—the most virulent strain—has disappeared and the largest continent is rid of the disease.

1978

No Countries

Since October 1977 no cases have been reported in the field, though at least two cases resulted from an accidental exposure in August 1978 at one of the 12 labs that still retained smallpox virus, essential for medical research. To lessen the risk of such lab infections, all facilities except four—in Atlanta, London, Moscow, and Tokyo—have been asked by WHO to give up their virus stocks.

SOURCE: Henderson, Donald A. "Smallpox—Epitaph for a Killer?" *National Geographic* 154, no. 6, December 1978, 800.

vaccination, administered by 15 rapid jabs to the arm. Vaccinators could be trained in minutes, and the needles could be sterilized and reused. Virtually all the vaccinations were positive, and, most important, one vial now protected a hundred people rather than 25 by previous methods.

While we worked to assure adequate supplies of needles and vaccine—the guns and bullets of the campaign—we started programs in country after country. Most were begun by 1969 and all by 1971. Until 1967 mass vaccination had been the standard strategy, but even when 95 percent were vaccinated, the disease would sometimes continue to spread.

We added a second strategy, called surveillance-containment, by forming "fire-fighting" teams to improve reporting and discover outbreaks. The teams rushed to infected areas, isolated patients, and vaccinated entire villages. By hunting for the source of infection, they found other outbreaks and contained them—breaking, one by one the chains of transmission.

New Strategy Proves a Blessing

The experiences of Bill Foege, an AID-CDC adviser in Nigeria, showed the new approach to be far more effective than we had expected, and we gave it priority over mass vaccination. Bill arrived before most of his supplies. Losing no time, he set up a reporting network, using radios already operated by missionaries. Then he began vaccination and containment of known outbreaks. By the time supplies arrived, no smallpox could be found, yet less than half the population had been vaccinated.

By 1970 the number of countries where smallpox was endemic, or continuously present, had dropped from 33 to 17, and by 1973 to only six. But among these were India, Bangladesh, Pakistan, and Nepal—with more than 700 million people. A professor from England warned me: "Bear in mind that Asia is the ancient home of smallpox. Eradication in South America or Africa is one thing; Asia is quite impossible."

I wondered if he might not be right, but 1973 marked a turning point. All that intensely hot summer, we worked with Indian colleagues to develop new procedures, training programs, and reporting forms. The offensive began in autumn. Tens of thousands of new cases were found, but more rigorous containment slowed the spread. Guards were hired for 24-hour duty to prevent patients from leaving their homes and to vaccinate all visitors. Health workers and villagers searched for and vaccinated everyone in affected vil-

Laboratories, which generously waived its patent charges.

When the needle was dipped into vaccine, the two tines captured enough of it between them for

lages and for a five-mile radius around them. With better reporting, the number of recorded cases increased, and the newspapers proclaimed disaster.

But now, I knew, the end was in sight. Steadily we tightened the noose. In 1974 the last case occurred in Pakistan; in 1975 in Nepal and India; and on October 16, 1975. Rahima Banu, a 3-year-old Bangladesh girl, contracted the last case of the severe Asian strain of smallpox. She survived.

As 1976 began, Ethiopia alone remained infected by a far milder strain of smallpox. However, the logistics were all but insuperable. The country was torn by civil war, by famine, by heavy summer rains.

To the civil war was added a war with Somalia. Our surveillance teams were kidnapped by guerrillas and vanished for days to weeks at a time. Their helicopters were hit by rifle fire, and one was blown up by a grenade. Some staffers were wounded, and a few were killed. But a determined Ethiopian and WHO staff was not to be denied. In August 1976 the last known case occurred in a nomad encampment in the Ogaden desert.

I believed that victory finally was at hand. But at the time of the last cases in Ethiopia, smallpox was imported into previously uninfected Somalia. Tragic delays hampered our efforts. More than three thousand were stricken, but by early October 1977 only two cases remained. It was from them that Ali Maalin was infected.

Smallpox no longer afflicts humanity, and remaining virus will be confined to a few laboratories under high security.

Prudence Dictates Vaccine Storage

Routine vaccinations will be stopped everywhere, but can we abandon our first and oldest vaccine? Are we sure there is no animal reservoir? Might not old scabs be a risk? All outbreaks in smallpox-free areas have been investigated for more than a decade; all have been traced to a source in a known infected area. No "spontaneous" cases or outbreaks have ever been detected.

Finally there remains the chance that smallpox or other biological agents might be used in warfare, an unlikely possibility with smallpox since it spreads slowly and can be contained with vaccination.

As insurance, WHO and many governments are storing vaccine, which at low temperatures retains its potency for decades. The chances of another outbreak are remote, but we are ready. For the first time, children are being born in a smallpox-free world. I am confident their children and grandchildren will enjoy that freedom.

For this, the credit belongs to the tens of thousands of health workers from around the world and to the WHO staff that, again and again, devised ingenious solutions to never ending, almost impossible problems.

I remember a hot, steaming night in a small village in Bangladesh. We were a dirty, unshaven, intense group ranged around a table—several Bengalis, a Soviet, an Indonesian, two Americans, a Brazilian, and a Swiss. The debate was heated, but the differences had nothing to do with nationality. They focused entirely on the best strategy to use against our common enemy.

And against it, we—all of us everywhere—have prevailed.

Further Resources

BOOKS

Koplow, David A. *The Fight to Eradicate a Global Scourge.* Berkeley: University of California Press, 2003.

Professional Guide to Diseases. 6th ed. Springhouse, Pa.: Springhouse Corporation, 1998.

PERIODICALS

"Smallpox." *Science World,* March 7, 2003, 2.

WEBSITES

CDC Smallpox Home. Available online at http://www.bt.cdc .gov/agent/smallpox/index.asp; website home page: http:// www.bt.cdc.gov/ (accessed February 5, 2003).

HHS—Smallpox. Available online at http://www.hhs.gov/small pox (accessed February 5, 2003).

MEDLINEplus: Smallpox. Available online at http://www.nlm .nih.gov/medlineplus/smallpox.html; website home page: http://www.nlm.nih.gov/ (accessed February 5, 2003).

AUDIO AND VISUAL MEDIA

Plagued: Invisible Armies. Filmmakers Library, Videocassette, 1992.

Smallpox: What Every Clinician Should Know. Centers for Disease Control and Prevention, Videocassette, 2001.

"A M*A*S*H Note for Docs"

Speech

By: Alan Alda

Date: May 28, 1979

Source: Alda, Alan. "A M*A*S*H Note for Docs." *Time,* May 28, 1979, 68.

Alan Alda's Hawkeye Pierce character on the popular TV show
*M*A*S*H* was an Army surgeon who demonstrated a compassion and
human interest in his patients that many felt genuine doctors had come to
lack during the 1970s. © HULTON-DEUTSCH COLLECTION/CORBIS.
REPRODUCED BY PERMISSION.

About the Author: Alan Alda (1936–) was born in New
York City and began acting at age sixteen. His role as Army
surgeon Hawkeye Pierce in the television program *M*A*S*H*
made his reputation. He has been nominated for twenty-nine
Emmy Awards, winning five times. He has also won three
Directors Guild Awards, six Golden Globes, and seven People's Choice Awards. In 1994, he was inducted into the Television Hall of Fame. ∎

Introduction

The intimacy of the relationship between physician
and patient diminished, many observers believed, as
physician incomes grew, particularly during the 1960s.
From 1962 to 1969, the median salary of male physicians
and surgeons nearly doubled. By 1969, physicians earned
more than twenty-five times the income of farm laborers
and more than 50 times the income of housekeepers. No
other occupation the U.S. Commerce Department surveyed during these years provided an income that approached that of physicians.

The rise of physician income accompanied the rise
of medicine as a science that demanded an impersonal,
detached approach to treatment. The physician was a clinician who identified symptoms, matched them to an ill-

ness, and prescribed treatment. Some patients began to
feel as though they represented an aggregate of symptoms
rather than a person. Because of advances in medical technology, physicians took on an aura of infallibility.

The gap between physician and patient widened during the 1970s as physician fees leapt nearly 10 percent
in 1977 alone, an increase 50 percent greater than the increase in the price of nonmedical goods and services. In
1974, orthopedic surgeons earned $62,410, nearly five
times the median household income in the United States.
In 1975, the median salary of physicians was $47,520,
more than triple the median household income. Physicians thus became prominent members of an affluent upper middle class.

Significance

Alan Alda is recognized not only for his acting skills
but for his sensitivity and compassion. He sensed a growing rift between physicians and patients, so in a 1979 address to the graduates of Columbia University College of
Physicians and Surgeons, he challenged them to restore
an intimate connection with patients.

Alda began his speech by acknowledging that
physicians had distanced themselves from others by
possessing an expertise that no one else possessed. He
went on to challenge these graduates to do more than
amass wealth. He acknowledged their possession of specialized skills but asked them not to allow their skills
to possess them. He acknowledged their power but reminded them how quickly the mastery of power becomes the abuse of it.

Alda told the Columbia graduates that if they were
really to make a difference, they must "Put people first."
He challenged them to replace hubris with humility in
their profession. American medicine had tamed technology in its service but physicians should not allow technology to come between themselves and their patients.
Sometimes, they had to admit that a condition baffled
them and to comfort a patient in fear. In a profession that
provided high incomes, success could be measured by
other factors.

Alda challenged these graduates to define themselves
as more than physicians. He reminded them that they
would also be a spouse and parent and that relationships,
whether between mother and child, physician and nurse,
or physician and patient, meant more than status.

Primary Source

"A M*A*S*H Note for Docs"

SYNOPSIS: In this speech, Alan Alda challenged the
graduates of Columbia University College of Physicians and Surgeons to restore compassion and hu-

mility to medicine. He reminded them that people were more important than money or prestige.

Be skilled, be learned, be aware of the dignity of your calling. But please don't ever lose sight of your own simple humanity.

Unfortunately, that may not be so easy. You're entering a special place in our society. People will be awed by your expertise. You'll be placed in a position of privilege. You'll live well, people will defer to you, call you by your title, and it may be hard to remember that the word doctor is not actually your first name.

I ask of you, possess your skills, but don't be possessed by them. You are entering a very select group. You have a monopoly on medical care. Please be careful not to abuse this power that you have over the rest of us.

Put people first. And I include in that not just people, but that which exists *between* people. Let me challenge you. With all your study, you can read my X rays like a telegram. But can you read my involuntary muscles? Can you see the fear and uncertainty in my face? Will you tell me when you don't know what to do? Can you face your own fear, your own uncertainty? When in doubt, can you call in help?

Will you be the kind of doctor who cares more about the case than the person? ("Nurse, call the gastric ulcer and have him come in at three.") You'll know you're in trouble if you find yourself wishing they would mail in their liver in a plain brown envelope.

Where does money come on your list? Will it be the sole standard against which you reckon your success? Where will your family come on your list? How many days and nights, weeks and months, will you separate yourself from them, buried in your work, before you realize that you've removed yourself from an important part of your life? And if you're a male doctor, how will you relate to women? Women as patients, as nurses, as fellow doctors—and later as students?

Thank you for taking on the enormous responsibility that you have—and for having the strength to have made it to this day. I don't know how you've managed to learn it all. But there is one more thing you can learn about the body that only a non-doctor would tell you—and I hope you'll always remember this: the head bone is connected to the heart bone. Don't let them come apart.

Further Resources

BOOKS

Feldstein, Paul J. *Health Care Economics.* New York: Wiley, 1979.

Kurtz, Richard A., and H. Paul Chalfant. *The Sociology of Medicine and Illness.* Boston: Allyn and Bacon, 1984.

Starr, Paul. *The Social Transformation of American Medicine.* New York: Basic Books, 1995.

Tushnet, Leonard. *The Medicine Men: The Myth of Quality Medical Care in America Today.* New York: St. Martin's Press, 1972.

Twaddle, Andrew C., and Richard M. Kessler. *A Sociology of Health.* New York: Macmillan, 1987.

PERIODICALS

"Doctors Fees—Free from the Law of Supply and Demand." *Science,* April 7, 1978, 30.

"Health Costs: What Limit?" *Time,* May 28, 1979, 60–68.

"Keynote Address: The Australia Antigen Story"
Speech

By: Baruch S. Blumberg

Date: November 1982

Source: Blumberg, Baruch S. "Keynote Address: The Australia Antigen Story," November 1982. In *Hepatitis B: The Virus, the Disease, and the Vaccine.* New York: Plenum Press, 1984, 7, 9–11, 12–14.

About the Author: Baruch S. Blumberg (1925–) was born in New York City and received an M.D. from Columbia University and a Ph.D. in biochemistry. He won the Nobel Prize for physiology or medicine in 1976 along with Dr. D. Carleton Gajdusek for their work with infectious diseases. He has been professor of medicine and anthropology at the University of Pennsylvania and became the first scientist and first American to hold the position of Master at Balliol College at Oxford University. ■

Introduction

Hepatitis is a viral infection of which five types exist: A, B, C, D and E. One may contract Type A from contaminated food, milk, water, or seafood from contaminated water. Type B spreads through contact with infected blood, saliva, mucus, and feces, making health care professionals at risk for exposure to Type B. It also transmits through intercourse. Type C spreads through blood transfusion and accounts for 20 percent of cases. Type D, which kills most of its victims, is a complication of Type B infection. The virus causing Type D can only replicate in cells infected by Type B. Type E spreads through the same routes as Type A, though it is rarer than

A. Although Type E is uncommon in the United States, it occurs in southern and eastern Asia and in Africa.

In its early stage, the viruses that cause the five types of hepatitis cause fatigue, weakness, weight loss, depression, headache, nausea, vomiting, and impairment of taste and smell. Fever ranges from 100 to 102 degrees Fahrenheit. After five days of these symptoms, a hepatitis virus will begin to damage the liver, causing jaundice. Symptoms include abdominal pain and indigestion. Patients may recover from liver damage, though convalescence may take three months.

The U.S. Centers for Disease Control and Prevention (CDC) in Atlanta, Georgia, reported 8,310 cases of hepatitis B in America in 1970, 13,121 cases in 1975, and 19,015 in 1980. The CDC did not enumerate the number of deaths from hepatitis B in 1970 and 1975 because it lumped together deaths from all sources of hepatitis, making it impossible to extract the number from hepatitis B alone. In 1980 the CDC reported 294 deaths in the U.S. from hepatitis B.

The increase in the number of cases during these years heightened the need for a treatment against hepatitis B. This disease was not very well understood in the 1960s and 1970s, but it was thought to be caused by a virus. This meant that antibiotics could not kill it, as they are only effective against diseases caused by bacteria. What was needed to deal with hepatitis B was a vaccine. A vaccine stimulates the immune system to create and manufacture antibodies against a virus (the same is true of against a bacterium). Should that virus later enter an immunized human, their immune system is prepared to fight back. It manufactures antibodies from the template the immune system had created in response to the introduction of the attenuated or dead virus (the vaccine). These antibodies overwhelm the virus, protecting the body from damage.

Significance

In the late 1960s and early 1970s, Irving Millman developed what would become the first vaccine for hepatitis B vaccine. He first discovered that the immune system produced a protein, Au, as a marker of the virus and an antibody, anti-HB (anti-Hepatitis B), when infected by hepatitis B. The isolation of anti-HB led to its use as a vaccine. When exposed to anti-HB, the body manufactures its own anti-HBs, which it then stores as a defense against Hepatitis B. Should the virus causing hepatitis B invade an inoculated body, it would produce anti-HB to attack the virus. In 1971, Millman collaborated with Merck and Company, a pharmaceutical firm, in developing a vaccine, purified anti-HB. In 1981, the Food and Drug Administration (FDA) approved the vaccine.

The vaccine reduced the number of new cases of hepatitis B in the U.S. After peaking at 26,611 cases in 1985, the incidence of hepatitis B declined to 21,102 in 1990, to 10,805 in 1995 and to 6,495 in 2000, reported the CDC. By 2003, doctors urged all Americans to be innoculated against hepatitis B, and babies routinely received the vaccine shortly after birth.

Despite the decrease in the number of hepatitis B cases, the death rate from the disease rose during the 1980s and 1990s. In the U.S. 490 died of hepatitis B in 1985, 816 in 1990, 1,027 in 1995 and 5,357 in 2000. The rise in the number of deaths despite the vaccine stems in part from the Human Immunodeficiency Virus (HIV) which causes Acquired Immunodeficiency Syndrome (AIDS). HIV undermines the immune system, rendering it unable to manufacture antibodies against hepatitis B (or other viruses) as it would in an immunized person free from HIV. People with HIV who contract hepatitis B are 29 times more likely to die of hepatitis B than are people without HIV who contract hepatitis B according to the *Journal of Acquired Immune Deficiencies*.

The increase in the number of deaths from hepatitis B may also be related to changes in the hepatitis B virus itself. The viruses that cause influenza display the ability to make rapid changes, some combinations of which are more lethal than others. The hepatitis B virus may also be changing, and growing more lethal, complicating the development of new hepatitis B vaccines.

Primary Source

"Keynote Address: The Australia Antigen Story" [excerpt]

> **SYNOPSIS:** In this excerpt, Baruch S. Blumberg describes his work in developing a vaccine against hepatitis B, which the FDA approved in 1981.

Discovery of Australia Antigen

In 1963 a major interest in our laboratory was the study of human biochemical and immunologic variation. A fundamental question that faces the physician is that of why some people become ill and others remain healthy even though all are exposed to the same disease hazard. Clearly, some of this is a consequence of chemical and immunologic variation in humans. We started in 1965 to study variation in serum proteins using the newly introduced starch gel electrophoresis method. We soon learned from studies in British, Basque, African, Alaskan and other populations that there was indeed a considerable polymorphic variation in several serum proteins. . . . We then made the hypothesis that if some of these serum protein variants were antigenic, transfused patients might develop detectable antibodies in their serum against variants which they had not inherited or acquired. . . .

During the course of this ongoing research, a precipitin reaction dissimilar from any seen before was observed; and this reaction was between the serum from an Australian aborigine and that of a frequently transfused hemophilia patient from New York City. Figure 2 is an illustration, taken from an early publication illustrating such a precipitin reaction. (This is not the original Australia aborigine/hemophilia band, for which we do not apparently have a photograph.) What was this new phenomenon? What was the character and significance of "Australia antigen" (abbreviated Au), as we termed the protein present in the aborigine? . . .

This observation, then, generated the hypothesis that Au was associated with "viral hepatitis." For many years this clinical syndrome was assumed to be of viral etiology, but the virus itself had not been identified. We tested the association hypothesis by requesting specimens of blood from patients with the clinical diagnosis of hepatitis for our clinical colleagues. We soon were able to establish that there was a much higher frequency of Au in the hepatitis patients, both acute and chronic, than in the controls. We also completed a systematic analysis of the Down's syndrome patients with and without Au and found that the former had significantly higher levels of SGPT and other evidences of liver abnormality than the latter. With this support for the association hypothesis, we then proceeded to test the concept that Au was, or was on, the hepatitis virus. With the collaboration of our colleague Manfred Bayer of our Institute, we visualized particles with the appearance of a virus in a series of electron microscope studies; and a variety of other studies indicated that these particles, which reacted with the antibody against Au, were hepatitis viruses. We found that these particles did not have nucleic acid and it later eventuated that they were a part of the virus which consisted only of the surface antigen.

Early in 1969 it became apparent to us that a vaccine could be produced from the peripheral blood of carriers. We postulated the existence of a whole virus particle (and this was later seen and identified by Dane and his colleagues) and proposed that the particles containing only the surface antigen of the hepatitis virus (the same small particles we had originally visualized in the EM) could be used as an immunogen. Our epidemiologic observations indicated that people with anti-HBs (as the antibody against the surface was later designated) did not usually become infected with HBV. More convincing evidence came from the studies of Professor Kazuo Okochi who was then in Tokyo. He

Dr. Baruch S. Blumberg headed the research team that developed the Hepatitis B vaccine. AP/WIDE WORLD PHOTOS. REPRODUCED BY PERMISSION.

found that patients who had anti-HBs when transfused with Au (i.e. hepatitis virus) were much less likely to develop hepatitis than those who did not have antibody; that is, anti-HBs was protective. Dr. Irving Millman, who had joined our group in 1967, had, by what in retrospect was a remarkable coincidence, a considerable amount of experience in the invention of vaccines. We devised a method for separating the surface antigen particles from the postulated whole virus using centrifugation and other physical-chemical means. A United States patent for this product was applied for in 1969 and issued in 1971. In that year we began negotiations with Merck & Company whose vaccine development facilities were located near Philadelphia. After extensive trials, including those of Szmuness, Hilleman and others, the vaccine was approved by the Food and Drug Administration in 1981 and came into general use by the end of that year. . . .

Although we were convinced that this technique could be applied, it was some time (in fact, a relatively short time) before it gained general acceptance. What happened between the time we were convinced and others became convinced of its clinical application? A detailed investigation of what occurred may be useful in understanding how research results achieve general acceptance. The facts of which we are aware that appeared to have a bearing on this process will now be reviewed.

Curiously, there does not appear to have been any large amount of additional scientific data which changed convictions; rather, a series of meetings, administrative steps and certain legal procedures occurred during this interval. In June 1969 we had published a short note in the *Bulletin of Pathology* inferring that testing might be appropriate. In May 1969 Gocke and Kavey published the results of a preliminary transfusion study involving eight patients which also supported the hypothesis. On October 31 and November 1, 1969, a panel of the Committee on Plasma and Plasma Substitutes of the National Research Council met and suggested that the results of the studies on Australia antigen should be reviewed in respect to eventually developing a test for donors. They did not, however, recommend specific action for testing. It was during 1969 that we began to hear of cases of pending or actual litigation in several parts of the country which had very clear effects on the introduction of testing in hospitals and blood banks. In several cases patients who had developed post-transfusion hepatitis, or their families, had sued hospitals and blood banks claiming that they had failed to test for Australia antigen. It was our impression that these legal actions effectively focused the interest of hospital authorities on the use of the Australia antigen test.

On July 18, 1970 Paul Schmidt and his colleague from the blood bank of the National Institutes of Health published an article in the "Point of View" section of *Lancet* entitled "Hepatitis associated antigen: To test or not to test?" Using essentially the same data available to the National Research Council panel, they recommended that all blood bank laboratories equipped to do the test should do so; that is, a recommendation quite different from that of the NRC. The article contained a disclaimer from the National Institutes of Health to the effect that "This article was written by the authors in their private capacity. No official support or endorsement by the National Institutes of Health is intended or inferred." This was an unusual statement by the NIH which usually would stand by the publications of its scientific staff. Some ten days later, on July 29, 1970, a column appeared in *The New York Times* reporting on the Schmidt article and thus focused greater attention on the testing question.

The "To test or not to test" article, according to Dr. Schmidt, occasioned a reconvening of the NRC Committee on October 5, 1970. At this meeting they recommended that testing should be done, if possible. The official report was prepared rapidly and presented at the annual meeting of the American Association of Blood Banks in San Francisco on October 29, 1970, and published soon thereafter. A report was also made at that time by J. Stengle of the National Heart and Lung Institute of the NIH, that his Institute would make the test materials available to laboratories and blood banks. Hence, October 1970 may be taken as the date when many blood banks began to use the blood donor test for hepatitis B carriers. It required only 16 months between the time we became convinced of the validity of the data and many others did.

Further Resources

BOOKS

Atkinson, William. *Epidemiology and Prevention of Vaccine-Preventable Diseases.* Atlanta: Centers for Disease Control and Prevention, 2002.

Professional Guide to Diseases. 6th ed. Springhouse, Pa.: Springhouse Corporation, 1998.

Root, Richard K., ed. *Clinical Infectious Diseases.* New York: Oxford University Press, 1999.

WEBSITES

CDC—Viral Hepatitis B—Vaccine Fact Sheet. Available online at http://www.cdc.gov/ncidod/diseases/hepatitis/b/factvax.htm; website home page: http://www.cdc.gov/ (accessed February 5, 2003).

Hepatitis B. Available online at http://www.who.int/inf-fs/en/fact204.html; website home page: http://www.who.int/ (accessed February 5, 2003).

Vaccinations for Hepatitis A & B. Available online at http://www.niddk.nih.gov/health/digest/pubs/vacc4hep/vacc4hep.htm; website home page: http://www.niddk.nih.gov/ (accessed February 5, 2003).

Legionella pneumophila
Photograph

By: Photo Researchers, Inc.

Source: Dowsett, A.B. "Legionella pneumophila." Photo Researchers, Inc. Image no. 2G6682. ∎

Introduction

The bacterium *Legionella pneumophila* causes Legionnaires' disease. The bacterium spreads through the air,

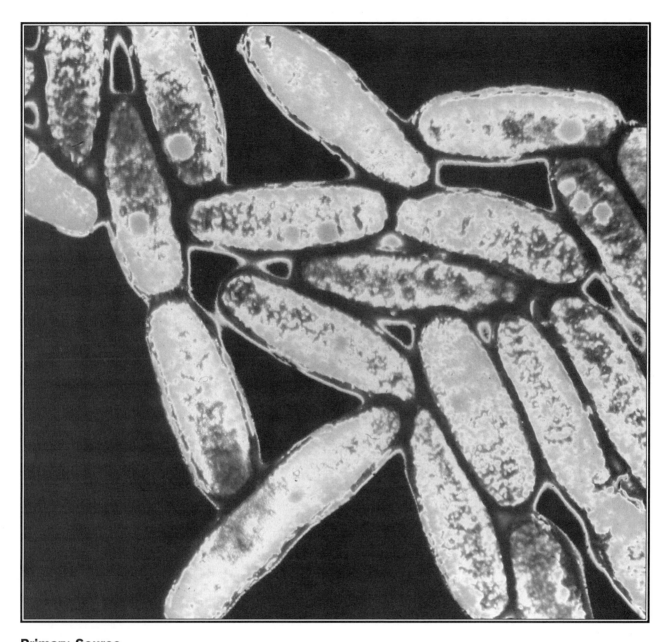

Primary Source

Legionella pneumophila

SYNOPSIS: The accompanying photo illustrates the rod-shaped bacterium that causes Legionnaires' disease, which infected 182 Americans, killing 29, in July 1976. The bacterium spread to nineteen states, killing three in Indiana in 1978, when two scientists, Charles C. Shephard and Joseph E. McDade, at the Centers for Disease Control and Prevention identified *Legionella pneumophila*. According to U.S. Department of Health and Human Services, "more than 20 species in the Legionella genus have been identified and the mystery surrounding many illnesses associated with them solved, in the grand tradition of the microbe hunters of the late 19th and early 20th centuries. Many of these modern-day microbe hunters or epidemiologists were trained in the Centers for Disease Control and Prevention's Epidemic Intelligence Service, which was established by Dr. Alexander Laugmuir in 1951." © A.B. DOWSETT/SCIENCE PHOTO LIBRARY/PHOTO RESEARCHERS, INC. REPRODUCED BY PERMISSION.

infecting people who inhale it. People in a building with the bacterium may, for example, inhale it through the air-conditioning system. The bacterium also lives in soil and can infect someone in contact with soil harboring it.

The bacterium strikes people in middle and old age. People with weak immune systems, such as those with acquired immunodeficiency syndrome (AIDS), are vulnerable to infection. Others susceptible to infection include people with diabetes and pulmonary disease, alcoholics, and smokers, who are nearly four times more likely to contract Legionnaries' disease than nonsmokers.

Upon entering the body, the bacterium incubates for two to ten days, when it causes diarrhea, weight loss, fatigue, weakness, headache, chills, and fever as high as 105 degrees Fahrenheit. A cough will accompany symptoms. As the disease intensifies, victims will cough up blood mixed with mucous. As the disease progresses, its causes nausea, vomiting, disorientation, confusion, amnesia, and chest pain. The bacterium may settle in the lungs, causing pneumonia. Other dangers include heart and respiratory failure and shock, all of which may be fatal.

Significance

Legionnaires' disease struck in July 1976. This outbreak was the first of its kind, suggesting that *Legionella pneumophila* had newly evolved. For reasons unknown, the bacterium was part of an eruption of new pathogens during the 1970s. The same year Legionnaires' disease struck, the Ebola virus killed nine of ten people it infected in Zaire. Marburg, a second new virus, and one closely related to Ebola, also emerged from Africa. The new diseases caught physicians off guard worldwide and reminded people that despite medicine's advances during the twentieth century, it had not conquered infectious diseases. Indeed medicine could hardly keep pace with the eruption of new pathogens during the 1970s.

The accompanying photo illustrates the rod-shaped bacterium *Legionella pneumophila* at high magnification. The bacterium infected 182 people at an American Legion conference (hence the name Legionnaires' disease) in Philadelphia, Pennsylvania, in July 1976, killing twenty-nine. Thereafter, Legionnaires' disease spread to nineteen states. Scientists at the Centers for Disease Control and Prevention identified the bacterium in 1978 in an Indiana hotel, where it had infected twenty-one people, killing three. The discovery that *Legionella pneu-mophila* was a bacterium made it possible for physicians to treat it with antibiotics. The most effective antibiotics were erythromycin and rifampin, which physicians prescribed in combination for maximum effect.

While the discovery and treatment of *Legionella pneumophila* was a medical triumph, it raised concerns that infectious diseases during the 1970s were reemerging as killers of millions of humans worldwide. Human immunodeficiency virus (HIV) has already killed millions since its emergence around 1980. Legionnaires' disease has the potential to kill thousands in countries with scant supplies of antibiotics. Likewise, Marburg and Ebola, viruses with no cure, could kill thousands if they erupted in a populous city. Despite the availability of vaccines and antibiotics, humans remain vulnerable to pathogens.

Further Resources

BOOKS

Bartlett, Christopher. *Legionella Infections.* London: Edward Arnold, 1986.

Berger, Melvin. *Disease Detectives.* New York: Crowell, 1978.

Jones, Gilda L., and G. Ann Hebert. *Legionnaires: The Disease, the Bacterium and Methodology.* Washington, D.C.: U.S. Government Printing Office, 1978.

Lattimer, Gary L., and Richard A. Ormsbee. *Legionnaires' Disease.* New York: M. Dekker, 1981.

PERIODICALS

Jaret, Peter. "The Disease Detectives." *National Geographic,* January 1991, 114–140.

WEBSITES

Legionnaires' Disease. Available online at http://www.niehs.nih .gov/external/faq/legion.htm (accessed February 5, 2003).

U.S. National Library of Medicine. *Images from the History of the Public Health Service: A Photographic Exhibit.* Bethesda, Md.: U.S. Department of Health and Human Services and the Public Health Service, 1994. Available online at http://www.nlm.nih.gov/exhibition/phs_history/93.html (accessed March 10, 2003).

10

RELIGION

PETER J. CAPRIOGLIO

Entries are arranged in chronological order by date of primary source. For entries with one primary source, the entry title is the same as the primary source title. Entries with more than one primary source have an overall entry title, followed by the titles of the primary sources.

Important Events in Religion, 1970–1979

1970

- On January 17, the Right Reverend John M. Burgess is installed as bishop of the Massachusetts diocese. He is the first black presiding bishop in the Episcopal church.

- On February 2, Sister Anita Caspary, president of the Immaculate Heart of Mary religious order in Los Angeles, announces that 315 of the 400 members of the order will end their religious ties and set up a lay community to continue their work.

- On February 6, the Orthodox church in the Soviet Union grants autonomy to the United States Russian Orthodox Greek Catholic church over the protests of the Ecumenical patriarch in Istanbul. The new 800,000-member, autocephalous denomination takes the name the Orthodox Church in America.

- On April 20, the General Conference of the United Methodist Church accepts a statement characterizing the war in Vietnam as a "fiasco" and urges accelerated talks to end the conflict.

- On June 16, the *New English Bible,* the work of a group of British religious and literary scholars, is published.

- On June 29, the Lutheran Church in America agrees to the ordination of women, the first Lutheran denomination to permit this.

- On July 2, the twentieth biennial meeting of the Clergy-Laity Congress of the Greek Orthodox church agrees to allow the use of the vernacular in liturgies, when approved by the local bishop.

- On September 30, the *New American Bible* is published, the first Roman Catholic translation from Hebrew and Greek texts into English.

- On October 24, the American Lutheran Church approves the ordination of women.

- On October 25, Three hundred members of the First Baptist Church of Birmingham, Alabama, including the pastor, split from the church when the congregation refuses to approve the membership of a black woman and her daughter. They organize a new congregation.

1971

- Billy Graham publishes *The Jesus Generation,* a book that celebrates the revivalist enthusiasm among young Chris-

tians. It sells two hundred thousand copies in its first two weeks.

- On February 2, to protest the system of apartheid the General Assembly of the Episcopal church petitions General Motors Corporation to end manufacturing in South Africa.

- On November 2, a synod of bishops, meeting in Vatican City, reaffirms celibacy for Roman Catholic religious orders.

- On December 21, the New York Federation of Catholic Teachers votes to end their twenty-nine-day strike against schools run by the New York archdiocese and accept the terms offered by the archdiocese. This is the first major strike against a parochial school system in the United States.

1972

- On January 27, the black and white United Methodist Church conferences in South Carolina agree to merge.

- On March 22, the Supreme Court overturns a ninety-three-year-old Massachusetts law banning the sale of birth control devices to the unmarried.

- On May 22, the General Assembly of the United Presbyterian church asks for a total, immediate withdrawal of American forces from Vietnam.

1973

- On January 8, the Society of Jesus announces that it will close two of its five training institutes because of declining applications. Woodstock College in New York and the Saint Louis School of Divinity will stop taking Jesuit students.

- On February 2, Pope Paul VI nominates the Most Reverend Luis Aponte Martinez, archbishop of Puerto Rico, to the College of Cardinals. He is the first Puerto Rican to be named cardinal.

- On April 6, Delegates of the eight Protestant denominations engaged in the Consultation on Church Union (COCU) vote to postpone indefinitely the study of plans for a merger called the Church of Christ Uniting.

1974

- On March 3, a commission of U.S. Roman Catholic and Lutheran theologians declares that the issue of papal primacy need not be an obstacle to the reconciliation of the two denominations, divided since the Reformation.

- On April 8, the Rev. C. Shelby Rooks is named the first black president of the predominantly white Chicago Theological Seminary.

- On June 16, the Rev. Dr. Lawrence Bottoms is elected as the first black moderator of the Presbyterian church (U.S.).

- On July 29, four bishops of the Episcopal church defy church law by ordaining eleven women into the priesthood.

1975

- The United Church of Christ endorses ending all discrimination "relating to sexual or affectional preference."

- In January, volume one of *The Torah: A Modern Commentary* is published by the Union of American Hebrew Congregations (Reform).

- On January 17, a joint session of the Pacific Association of Reform Rabbis and the Western States Region of the Rabbinical Assembly (Conservative) asks the government of Israel to allow Reform and Conservative rabbis to perform ceremonies for "life-cycle occasions" in the Jewish state.

- On February 12, the National Council of Catholic Bishops approves a "New American Sunday Missal."

- On September 14, Pope Paul VI canonizes Mother Elizabeth Ann Bayley Seton. She is the first saint born in the United States.

- On October 11, the Central Conference of American Rabbis (Reform) issues a new prayer book, *The Gates of Prayer: the New Union Prayer Book*. It incorporates a gender-neutral vocabulary.

1976

- On September 16, the General Convention of the Episcopal church approves the ordination of women. Six years earlier the House of Bishops of the convention had rejected a similar motion.

- On December 4, the Association of Evangelical Lutheran Churches is formed from moderates leaving the Lutheran Church-Missouri Synod.

1977

- On January 19, Pope Paul VI canonizes Bishop John N. Newman, the first American male saint.

- On October 25, the Orthodox Church in America elects its first American-born prelate, Bishop Theodosius of Baltimore.

1978

- On June 9, Spencer W. Kimball, president of the Church of Jesus Christ of Latter-day Saints (Mormons), signs a letter admitting black men to the Mormon priesthood. Women are still excluded.

- On December 7, eleven high-ranking members of the Church of Scientology are convicted for conspiring to infiltrate the Justice Department and the Internal Revenue Service in order to monitor government investigations of the church. They are given four- and five-year sentences.

1979

- On September 12, the Triennial Convention of the Episcopal church approves a new *Prayerbook* to replace the 1928 revision.

- From October 1 to October 7, Pope John Paul II visits the United States. He is the first pope to meet a U.S. president at the White House.

Walz v. Tax Commission of City of New York

Supreme Court decision

By: Warren Earl Burger

Date: May 4, 1970

Source: *Walz v. Tax Commission of City of New York.* 397 U.S. 664 (1970). Available online at http://caselaw.lp.findlaw .com/scripts/getcase.pl?navby=search&court=US&case=/us/397 /664.html; website home page: http://www.caselaw.lp.findlaw .com (accessed March 1, 2003).

About the Author: Warren Earl Burger (1907–1995), born in St. Paul, Minnesota, earned a law degree from St. Paul College of Law in 1931. After a brief stint as assistant attorney general, he served as a judge in the United States Court of Appeals from 1956 to 1969. Burger, appointed by President Nixon, served as chief justice of the Supreme Court from 1969 until 1986. Though generally conservative, he was noted for supporting civil rights and federal court system administrative reforms. ■

Introduction

Tax exemptions for religious properties have been granted since the earliest days in American history. These exemptions were traditionally applied to educational and charitable groups—provided that they were being used exclusively for educational or charitable purposes—and could be found in all town, county, state, and federal tax laws.

Historically, the United States Supreme Court, through its many decisions regarding the role of religion in society, had worked toward establishing the appropriate relationship between church and state. The court consistently ruled that the state could provide special concessions to religious groups (for example, tax exemptions) without violating the Establishment Clause of the Constitution (prohibition of the state promoting a particular church or religious group). The court clearly established that religious institutions were advantageous to the functioning of society and should be allowed to continue their efforts unimpeded by the burdens of taxation.

Most Americans took the church tax exemption for granted; it never occurred to them that the exemptions

should be challenged or changed. However, during the 1960s and 1970s, some taxpayer groups around the nation began questioning the constitutionality of this traditional tax exemption granted to churches and other religious groups. They believed that the state, by not taxing these institutions directly or indirectly, was showing favoritism to them at the expense of taxpayers. Furthermore, the taxpayers groups argued that the tax exemption was a violation of the church-state barrier; therefore, this action by the government was in violation of the Constitution.

One taxpayer lawsuit in eventually found its way to the United States Supreme Court in 1970. Frederick Walz was a New York City real estate owner who sued the city tax commission in regard to its policy of exempting religious organizations from the property tax if the property was used only for worship purposes. Walz lost his suit in the state courts, and then appealed to the Supreme Court.

Significance

In challenging this tax commission policy, Walz argued that by granting this exemption, all taxpayers were being placed in a position of being required to indirectly contribute to all religious organizations. Because these groups are not required to pay property taxes, the taxpayers have to pay more taxes to make up for the income loss to the municipality. Those taxpayers—who may not belong to any religious group—were being forced to subsidize churches, synagogues, and other houses of worship. Walz believed this was a clear violation of the Establishment Clause. Walz also argued that the property tax exemption was unfair because religious organizations were receiving local government services (for example, police and fire security) without contributing to the financial maintenance of these services. The religious groups were, in effect, living off the state, another example of the violation of the Establishment Clause. In addition, by not paying taxes, these religious groups had more money to spend in their religious programs. Walz stated the government, therefore, was indirectly providing financial support to these organizations.

Chief Justice Warren Earl Burger ruled that the tax-exempt status granted to all houses of worship was not in violation of the Constitution. He cited several reasons: Making these groups pay taxes would inhibit their efforts toward fostering the moral or mental improvement of people; taxing churches would place them in a position of supporting the government—an undesirable outcome; and granting a tax exemption does not mean the establishment, sponsorship, or support of religious institutions by the state.

The *Walz v. Tax Commission of the City of New York* decision was important because it mandated that the interaction between church and state be minimized, as much as possible, in order to satisfy the Establishment Clause. Taxing religious groups would involve more potential entanglements than not taxing them. This avoidance of any excessive entanglements between the religious and political institutions was to become part of the Lemon Test criteria later adopted in the *Lemon v. Kurtzman* decision of 1971.

Primary Source

Walz v. Tax Commission of City of New York
[excerpt]

SYNOPSIS: Frederick Walz, a real estate owner and taxpayer in New York, sued the city tax commission, challenging the property tax exemption granted to churches and other religious groups. He claimed that the exemption indirectly placed taxpayers in the position of contributing to the religious organizations. In these excerpts, the Supreme Court, in an eight to one vote, presented its reasoning in deciding that the property tax exemption granted to religious organizations was constitutional.

Mr. Chief Justice Burger delivered the opinion of the Court.

Appellant, owner of real estate in Richmond County, New York, sought an injunction in the New York courts to prevent the New York City Tax Commission from granting property tax exemptions to religious organizations for religious properties used solely for religious worship. The exemption from state taxes is authorized by . . . the New York Constitution, which provides in relevant part:

> Exemptions from taxation may be granted only by general laws. Exemptions may be altered or repealed except those exempting real or personal property used exclusively for religious, educational or charitable purposes as defined by law and owned by any corporation or association organized or conducted exclusively for one or more of such purposes and not operating for profit.

The essence of appellant's contention was that the New York City Tax Commission's grant of an exemption to church property indirectly requires the appellant to make a contribution to religious bodies and thereby violates provisions prohibiting establishment of religion under the First Amendment which under the Fourteenth Amendment is binding on the States.

Appellee's motion for summary judgment was granted and the Appellate Division of the New York Supreme Court, and the New York Court of Appeals

Warren E. Burger, Chief Justice of the Supreme Court (1969–86). Justice Burger delivered the decision in *Walz v. Tax Commission of City of New York*, in which the Supreme Court ruled that exempting religious institutions from taxes was legal. **THE LIBRARY OF CONGRESS.**

affirmed. We noted probable jurisdiction and . . . affirm. . . .

The Establishment and Free Exercise Clauses of the First Amendment are not the most precisely drawn portions of the Constitution. The sweep of the absolute prohibitions in the Religion Clauses may have been calculated; but the purpose was to state an objective not to write a statute. In attempting to articulate the scope of the two Religion Clauses, the Court's opinions reflect the limitations inherent in formulating general principles on a case-by-case basis. The considerable internal inconsistency in the opinions of the Court derives from what, in retrospect, may have been to sweeping utterances on aspects of these clauses that seemed clear in relation to the particular cases but have limited meaning as general principles. . . .

Mr. Justice Douglas, in *Zorach v. Clauson,* supra, after recalling that we 'are a religious people whose institutions presuppose a Supreme Being,' went on to say:

> We make room for as wide a variety of beliefs and creeds as the spiritual needs of man

deem necessary. . . . When the state encourages religious instruction . . . it follows the best of our traditions. For it then respects the religious nature of our people and accommodates the public service to their spiritual needs.

With all the risks inherent in programs that bring about administrative relationships between public education bodies and church-sponsored schools, we have been able to chart a course that preserved the autonomy and freedom of religious bodies while avoiding any semblance of established religion. This is a "tight rope" and one we have successfully traversed. . . .

The legislative purpose of a property tax exemption is neither the advancement nor the inhibition of religion; it is neither sponsorship nor hostility. New York, in common with the other States, has determined that certain entities that exist in a harmonious relationship to the community at large, and that foster its 'moral or mental improvement,' should not be inhibited in their activities by property taxation or the hazard of loss of those properties for nonpayment of taxes.

It has not singled out one particular church or religious group or even churches as such; rather, it has granted exemption to all houses of religious worship within a broad class of property owned by nonprofit, quasi-public corporations which include hospitals, libraries, playgrounds, scientific, professional, historical, and patriotic groups. The State has an affirmative policy that considers these groups as beneficial and stabilizing influences in community life and finds this classification useful, desirable, and in the public interest. Qualification for tax exemption is not perpetual or immutable; some tax-exempt groups lose that status when their activities take them outside the classification and new entities can come into being and qualify for exemption.

Governments have not always been tolerant of religious activity, and hostility toward religion has taken many shapes and forms-economic, political, and sometimes harshly oppressive. Grants of exemption historically reflect the concern of authors of constitutions and statutes as to the latent dangers inherent in the imposition of property taxes; exemption constitutes a reasonable and balanced attempt to guard against those dangers. . . .

Determining that the legislative purpose of tax exemption is not aimed at establishing, sponsoring, or supporting religion does not end the inquiry, however. We must also be sure that the end result—the effect—is not an excessive government entan-glement with religion. The test is inescapably one of degree. Either course, taxation of churches or exemption, occasions some degree of involvement with religion. Elimination of exemption would tend to expand the involvement of government by giving rise to tax valuation of church property, tax liens, tax foreclosures, and the direct confrontations and conflicts that follow in the train of those legal processes.

Granting tax exemptions to churches necessarily operates to afford an indirect economic benefit and also gives rise to some, but yet a lesser, involvement than taxing them. In analyzing either alternative the questions are whether the involvement is excessive, and whether it is a continuing one calling for official and continuing surveillance leading to an impermissible degree of entanglement. Obviously a direct money subsidy would be a relationship pregnant with involvement and, as with most governmental grant programs, could encompass sustained and detailed administrative relationships for enforcement of statutory or administrative standards, but that is not this case.

The hazards of churches supporting government are hardly less in their potential than the hazards of government supporting churches; each relationship carries some involvement rather than the desired insulation and separation. We cannot ignore the instances in history when church support of government led to the kind of involvement we seek to avoid.

The grant of a tax exemption is not sponsorship since the government does not transfer part of its revenue to churches but simply abstains from demanding that the church support the state. No one has ever suggested that tax exemption has converted libraries, art galleries, or hospitals into arms of the state or put employees "on the public payroll."

There is no genuine nexus between tax exemption and establishment of religion. As Mr. Justice Holmes commented in a related context "a page of history is worth of volume of logic." *New York Trust Co. v. Eisner* (1921). The exemption creates only a minimal and remote involvement between church and state and far less than taxation of churches. It restricts the fiscal relationship between church and state, and tends to complement and reinforce the desired separation insulating each from the other.

Separation in this context cannot mean absence of all contact; the complexities of modern life inevitably produce some contact and the fire and police protection received by houses of religious worship are no more than incidental benefits accorded all persons or institutions within a State's boundaries, along with many other exempt organizations. The appellant has not established even an arguable quantitative correlation between the payment of an ad valorem property tax and the receipt of these municipal benefits.

All of the 50 States provide for tax exemption of places of worship, most of them doing so by constitutional guarantees. For so long as federal income taxes have had any potential impact on churches—over 75 years—religious organizations have been expressly exempt from the tax. Such treatment is an "aid" to churches no more and no less in principle than the real estate tax exemption granted by States.

Few concepts are more deeply embedded in the fabric of our national life, beginning with pre-Revolutionary colonial times, than for the government to exercise at the very least this kind of benevolent neutrality toward churches and religious exercise generally so long as none was favored over others and none suffered interference.

It is significant that Congress, from its earliest days, has viewed the Religion Clauses of the Constitution as authorizing statutory real estate tax exemption to religious bodies. In 1802 the 7th Congress enacted a taxing statute for the County of Alexandria, adopting the 1800 Virginia statutory pattern which provided tax exemptions for churches.

As early as 1813 the 12th Congress refunded import duties paid by religious societies on the importation of religious articles. During this period the City Council of Washington, D.C., acting under congressional authority, Act of Incorporation, (May 3, 1802), enacted a series of real and personal property assessments that uniformly exempted church property. In 1870 the Congress specifically exempted all churches in the District of Columbia and appurtenant grounds and property "from any and all taxes or assessments, national, municipal, or county." Act of June 17, 1870. . . .

It is obviously correct that no one acquires a vested or protected right in violation of the Constitution by long use, even when that span of time covers our entire national existence and indeed predates it. Yet an unbroken practice of according the exemption to churches, openly and by affirmative state action, not covertly or by state inaction, is not something to be lightly cast aside. Nearly 50 years ago Mr. Justice Holmes stated: "If a thing has been practised for two hundred years by common consent, it will need a strong case for the Fourteenth

Amendment to affect it. . . ." *Jackman v. Rosenbaum Co.,* (1922). Nothing in this national attitude toward religious tolerance and two centuries of uninterrupted freedom from taxation has given the remotest sign of leading to an established church or religion and on the contrary it has operated affirmatively to help guarantee the free exercise of all forms of religious belief.

Thus, it is hardly useful to suggest that tax exemption is but the "foot in the door" or the "nose of the camel in the tent" leading to an established church. If tax exemption can be seen as this first step toward "establishment" of religion, as Mr. Justice Douglas fears, the second step has been long in coming. Any move that realistically "establishes" a church or tends to do so can be dealt with "while this Court sits."

Mr. Justice Cardozo commented in The Nature of the Judicial Process 51 (1921) on the "tendency of a principle to expand itself to the limit of its logic"; such expansion must always be contained by the historical frame of reference of the principle's purpose and there is no lack of vigilance on this score by those who fear religious entanglement in government.

The argument that making "fine distinctions" between what is and what is not absolute under the Constitution is to render us a government of men, not laws, gives too little weight to the fact that it is an essential part of adjudication to draw distinctions, including fine ones, in the process of interpreting the Constitution. We must frequently decide, for example, what are "reasonable" searches and seizures under the Fourth Amendment. Determining what acts of government tend to establish or interfere with religion falls well within what courts have long been called upon to do in sensitive areas.

It is interesting to note that while the precise question we now decide has not been directly before the Court previously, the broad question was discussed by the Court in relation to real estate taxes assessed nearly a century ago on land owned by and adjacent to a church in Washington, D.C. At that time Congress granted real estate tax exemptions to buildings devoted to art, to institutions of public charity, libraries, cemeteries, and "church buildings, and grounds actually occupied by such buildings." In denying tax exemption as to land owned by but not used for the church, but rather to produce income, the Court concluded (that the state) may tax them at a lower rate than other property. *Gibbons v. District of Columbia* (1886).

It appears that at least up to 1885 this Court, reflecting more than a century of our history and un-interrupted practice, accepted without discussion the proposition that federal or state grants of tax exemption to churches were not a violation of the Religion Clauses of the First Amendment. As to the New York statute, we now confirm that view.

Affirmed.

Further Resources

BOOKS

Brody, Evelyn, ed. *Property-Tax Exemption for Charities: Mapping the Battlefield.* Washington, D.C.: The Urban Institute Press, 2002.

Lewis, Henry Wilkins. *Property Tax Exemptions.* Chapel Hill, N.C.: Institute of Government, University of North Carolina, 1970.

WEBSITES

"Taxing Church Property: An Imminent Possibility?" Religion Online. Available online at http://www.religiononline.org /cgibin/relsearchd.dll/showarticle?item_id=1030; website home page: http://www.religiononline.org (accessed March 1, 2003).

University of Virginia, "Religious Freedom Page: *Walz v. Tax Commission of the City of New York.*" http://religiousfreedom .lib.virginia.edu/court/walz_v_taxc.html; website home page: http://religiousfreedom.lib.virginia.edu/home.html (accessed March 1, 2003).

"*Walz v. Tax Commission of the City of New York* (1970)." Agnosticism/Atheism. Available online at http://atheism .about.com/library/decisions/religion/bl_l_WalzTax Commission.htm; website home page: http://www.about.com (accessed March 1, 2003).

Islam, a Way of Life
Theological work

By: Philip Khuri Hitti

Date: 1970

Source: Hitti, Philip Khuri. *Islam, a Way of Life.* Minneapolis: University of Minnesota Press, 1970, 2–4, 8–11, 54, 55.

About the Author: Philip Khuri Hitti (1886–1978) was born in Shimlan, Lebanon. He earned his bachelor's degree from the American University of Beirut in 1908 and his doctorate from Columbia University in 1915. He taught at Columbia from 1915 to 1920, at the American University of Beirut from 1920 to 1926, and at Princeton from 1926 to 1954. He was professor emeritus at Princeton from 1954 to 1978. He authored over a dozen books on Islam and the Arab culture. ∎

Introduction

In the 1970s, Islam was the religion of only a few million adherents in the United States, even though the world's population of Muslims was approaching almost one billion. The followers of Islam in the United States were mostly composed of Black Muslims, a predominantly African American religious group called the Nation of Islam, and immigrants from east Europe and surrounding areas of the Middle East, including Arabs.

According to a study on Muslims in America by Anayat Durrani, during the early twentieth century several hundred thousand Eastern European Muslims immigrated to the United States. As of 2002, estimates of the total number of Muslims in America were roughly six million, with two thousand mosques, Islamic centers, and Islamic schools throughout the United States.

Few Christian Americans during the 1970s realized that Islam, like Judaism and Christianity, was a monotheistic religion, adhering to the doctrine that there was only one God. All three religions—Islam, Judaism, and Christianity—believed that they had a common origin in Abraham, the Biblical patriarch. Islam's followers promoted the acceptance of the doctrine of submission to God. They also believed that Muhammad was the chief and last prophet sent by God.

Prof. Philip Hitti, a leading American expert on the history of Arabs and Islam, knew of the need for his fellow citizens to have a comprehensive understanding of Islam. He realized that very few non-Muslim Americans had much knowledge of this large, growing, and influential world religion. His book, *Islam, a Way of Life,* would serve to enlighten people to the true nature of this religion.

Significance

Islam, a Way of Life is divided into three parts: Islam as a religion, Islam as a state, and Islam as a culture. To orthodox Muslims, therefore, Islam has a broad effect in their lives. Because of this threefold interrelationship, Muslims who may be racially or geographically diverse could feel bound together into a common unit, Islam.

Hitti's book was an outgrowth of a series of lectures he delivered in 1967 as a visiting professor on a Hill Foundation grant, at the Department of Middle Eastern Languages at the University of Minnesota. Those lectures as well as *Islam, a Way of Life* were the result of many years of research. His previously published books set the foundation for this classic work on Islam. In 1937, *The History of the Arabs, from the Earliest Times to the Present* was published. Because three of the world's major religions (Judaism, Christianity, and Islam) traced their origins to the ancient cultures of the Middle East, his book on the history of the Arabs was considered to be a much needed contribution to the study of monotheistic religions.

Five other books also functioned as foundation works for *Islam, a Way of Life: Origins of the Islamic*

Muslims worship at the Kaaba, in the city of Mecca, Saudi Arabia. The Kaaba is the holiest site in all of Islam, to which all Muslims must make a pilgrimage, and face when praying every day. © CORBIS/BETTMANN. REPRODUCED BY PERMISSION.

State (1916), *History of Syria, Including Lebanon and Palestine* (1951), *Islam and the West, a Historical Cultural Survey* (1962), *Arab Heritage* (1963), and *Makers of Arab History* (1968).

Hitti faced the difficult task of changing the perception of Islam in America. Since the Muslim immigrants and their descendents in the 1970s composed a fairly small percentage of the population, most non-Muslim Americans were not very aware—or understanding—of Islam. Hitti's book attempted to change all that.

After the terrorism experienced by Americans on September 11, 2001, there was an increased demand for a more thorough knowledge of Islam. People trying to attach some meaning to the tragic events of that day sought books by Prof. Philip Hitti and other experts in Islam.

Primary Source

Islam, a Way of Life [excerpt]

SYNOPSIS: The following excerpts come from two chapters. "The Prophet and the Man" centers on defining the meanings of Islam as a religion, state, and culture. In "Sufism: A Feature of Islamic Piety," Hitti relates the characteristics of Sufism, a religious group within Islam that stressed the role of mysticism.

Islam is a way of life. As such it has three main aspects: religious, political, and cultural. The three overlap and interact, sometimes imperceptibly passing from one to the other.

Islam the religion is a system of beliefs and practices initially revealed by Allah to Muhammad, enshrined in the Arabic Koran, supplemented by tradition, and modified through the ages in response to changes in time and place. It is the third and last major monotheistic religion. A historical offshoot of Judaism and Christianity, it is most closely related to them. Originally the simple, humble religion of a few unsophisticated tribes in Arabia, Islam swelled in the course of time to become the faith of some of the most cultured peoples in medieval times.

Today it has approximately four hundred and fifty million followers, who represent perhaps as many races, nationalities, and ethnic groups as any world religion. Every seventh man is a Moslem. Moslems dominate in numbers in a broad swath of land from Morocco to Pakistan and in Malaysia and Indonesia.

Islam the state is a political entity with an aggregate of institutions based on koranic law, founded by Muhammad in Medina, developed by his successors (caliphs, Ar. sing. *khalifah*) at the expense of the Persian and East Roman empires to a height unattained in medieval or ancient times, and then fragmented into splinter states in western Asia, northern Africa, and southwestern and southeastern Europe. Certain Arab and non-Arab states today style themselves Islamic.

Islam the culture is a compound of varied elements—ancient Semitic, Indo-Persian, classical Greek—synthesized under the caliphate and expressed primarily through the medium of the Arabic tongue. Unlike the other two, Islam the culture was mainly formulated by conquered peoples, Arabicized and Islamized, rather than by Arabians. It holds the distinction of having been, from the mid-eighth century to the end of the twelfth century, unmatched in its brilliancy and unsurpassed in its literary, scientific, and philosophic output.

I

It all started with one man. The name given that man by his parents remains uncertain. The one by which he is generally known, Muhammad ("highly praised"), sounds like an honorary title. Hardly anyone before him bore that name. In his youth he was known to his people as al-Amin ("the trustworthy").

The name of the city of Muhammad's birth in 570, Makkah (Mecca), has become well known thanks to the hundreds of thousands of his followers who through the ages have annually flocked to its shrine. Yathrib, the city of his burial, has been designated al-Madinah (Medina), "the city," and shares with its sister Mecca the interest of the annual pilgrims. The year of Muhammad's migration (*hijrah*, Hegira, A.D. 610) from the city of his nativity to the city of his missionary activity has become the starting date of the Moslem calendar. Hijaz, the region in which he was born, had never figured prominently on a national or an international level, but it became and has remained a holy land for a sizable segment of mankind. In fact at the time of Muhammad's birth the entire Arabian peninsula—heathen, tribal, and a desolate area on the map—was in eclipse; the limelight glittered with full brilliancy over the Byzantine area to the northwest and the Persian area to the northeast. The book for which Muhammad was responsible shares with the Bible the distinction of being one of the two most widely read books, the only two perennial best sellers.

Though some historic facts about Muhammad are known, Muhammad the man eludes us. The earliest reference to him is a seventh-century passing one in Syriac, the language used by the common people of the Fertile Crescent to the north. In Greek, the lingua franca of the Fertile Crescent, the first mention of the "ruler of the Saracens and the pseudo-prophet" occurs in a chronicle written two hundred years after his death. The earliest Arabic biography was written by one who died in Baghdad a hundred and forty years after Muhammad's death; it has survived in a recension by ibn-Hisham, who died in al-Fustat (Old Cairo) in 833. By then the historical man had become a legendary figure, an archetype of the perfect man. In all the literature about him the historical is inextricably mixed with the legendary, and the halo of sanctity around the Prophet's head is forever fixed. The admiration of his followers for their national hero, founder of their faith, initiator of their state, creator of their glory, passed from idealization to idolization. . . .

II

Islam shares with Judaism and Christianity the concept of revelation, but in a different form. The concept is prompted by man's feeling of insecurity and inability to cope with the besetting problems of life and his desire for guidance and support from a supreme source. More than inspiration in the Christian sense, as the process by which the divine mind works through human consciousness, the Moslem view of revelation *(wahy)* is tantamount to dictation. Word form and contents are God's. The process is described as "sending down," down from heaven where lay an archetype. It entails a passive recipient to whom God communicates his thought and will. When thus commissioned, the recipient is "sent forth" to announce the message. He becomes God's messenger. Accordingly Allah, on one of several occasions, commissioned Muhammad:

We have given revelation to thee just as We gave revelation to Noah and the prophets after him. We also gave revelation to Abraham, to Ishmael, to Isaac, to Jacob, to the Tribes [patriarchs descended from Jacob], to Jesus, to Job, to Jonah, to Aaron, and to Solomon; while to David We gave a Psalter [*zabur,* from Heb. *mizmor*].

(4:161–2)

There were also messengers whose stories We have told thee before, and messengers whose stories We have not told thee.

To each people God sends one messenger (10:48; 16:38; cf. 23:46). In each case the messenger is entrusted with a book, confirmatory of the preceding books. Muhammad was sent to a people lacking a book, a people to whom God had not yet sent a messenger. The Koran is revealed in Arabic, and Arabic thus became an integral part of the revelation. Arabs refer to it as "the tongue of the angels," meaning, in the opinion of one struggling to learn it, no one can master it until he dies and becomes an angel. Additionally, Arabic, the language of the Koran, served as a basis for a new nation to be created by Muhammad from motley, unruly Arabian tribes that had never united before. Thus, the founder of Islam added a new dimension to his triple contribution of religion, state, and culture.

Lo, We have made it an Arabic Koran, so that ye may understand And lo, it is in the Mother of the Book [the heavenly archetype] in Our presence, exalted, wise.

(43:2–3)

Again and again the divine nature of the Koran is emphasized and Muhammad is ordered to proclaim nothing but what is revealed (43:42). Meantime the messenger's audience is duly notified:

Thus have We sent to you a messenger from amongst yourselves to recite to you Our revelation, to purify you and to instruct you in the book and the wisdom and to teach you what ye do not know.

(2:146)

And as if eager to remove all possibility of misunderstanding, Allah adds: "And Muhammad is naught but a messenger" (3:138).

Messengership was a Christian concept that had been institutionalized for centuries. Jesus "sent forth" his twelve disciples, who became apostles, or envoys. An apostle was one sent by God. The title was later applied to other than disciples, like Paul, who carried on the message. The Koran bestows on Muhammad another title—"prophet." In several verses he is commissioned as a prophet and is so addressed by Allah:

O prophet, We have sent thee as a witness, a bringer of good tidings and a warner,
A summoner to Allah by His permission and a light-giving lamp.

(33:44–5)

In another surah the prophet is characterized as *ummi.*

Say: "O mankind, I am Allah's messenger to you all, Of Him to whom belongeth the kingdom of the heavens and of the earth.

There is no god but He,
He giveth life and causeth to die.
Believe then in Allah and in His messenger,
The *ummi* prophet, who himself believeth in Allah and His words, and follow him;
Haply so ye will be guided."

(7:157–8; cf. 7:156)

Moslem commentators are in agreement that *ummi* means "unlettered," or "illiterate." Modern scholars, however, argue that Muhammad, as one engaged in trade, could probably read and write, and that the term, judged by the context, probably means one belonging to a community without a book and therefore uninstructed in scriptures (cf. 3:19).

The Arabic word for "prophet" *(nabi)* is the same as in Aramaic and Hebrew, indicating its Semitic origin. It had a long history before its koranic use, but it does not occur in pre-Islamic literature. It figured prominently in the Old Testament story of Samuel (1 Sam. 10:5), a thousand years before Christ. Even earlier Deborah is styled a prophetess and a judge (Judg. 4:4). The Old Testament records cases of a long chain of men—all chosen and addressed by God—from Moses (Exod. 3:2 et seq.) through Samuel (1 Sam. 3:3 et seq.) and Jeremiah (Jer. 1:4–10) to Ezekiel (Ezek. 1:1 et seq.) and Zechariah (Zech. 1:7 et seq.). Sixteen books of the Old Testament were written by prophets. All prophets were illuminated expounders of revelation. To them the word of God came in a variety of ways with the command that they should proclaim it. Some were oral prophets whose discourses were never committed into writing. The concern of the early prophets with law and the rules employed in executing the law gave way in the later ones to concern with ethical monotheism and its propagation.

The prophets enumerated in the Koran are largely Old Testament characters. Among them Abraham stands out as Muhammad's favorite. Besides having one surah (14) dedicated to him, he is mentioned about seventy-five times in twenty-five different surahs. Of the New Testament characters only four are given clear mention: Zacharias, John the Baptist, Jesus, and Mary. The Koran adds Muhammad to this biblical list and thereby legitimizes his prophethood.

But while the Moslem Prophet comes chronologically at the bottom of this long and honorable list, in significance he is ranked at the top. He is the "seal [*khatam*] of the prophets" (33:40), the last to be charged by God. His dispensation sums up and supplements all preceding ones; eventually it supplants them all. The abrogation of the older revelations was necessitated by their "falsification" by Jews and Christians. Muhammad is reported to have said repeatedly "no prophet after me." Through Muhammad God sent his final word to mankind. No one can thereafter improve on it. . . .

Mysticism as a religious phenomenon is shared not only by the three Scriptured religions but by all other great religions, including Hinduism and Taoism. Every religious tradition has a mystical aspect, involving a mystery behind the veil separating the human from the superhuman, and there have always been those with the earnest desire to penetrate that veil. These individuals or groups in all religious denominations are not satisfied with the offerings of their established systems; they yearn for personal communion with God. Such daring souls venture to plunge into an uncharted sea.

Being personal, that is, subjective and emotional, mysticism varies from one religion to another, and within the same religion from one group—or even from one individual—to another. Since it is based on individual experience it is impossible to systematize. Mysticism even defies definition. Perhaps the best attempt at a definition was made by an early fifteenth-century chancellor of the University of Paris: "Mystical theology is knowledge of God by experience arrived at through the embrace of unifying love." This sets mystical theology against dogmatic theology, which is arrived at through revelation (discussed in the preceding chapter), as well as against natural theology, which is an attempt to know God through reason and intellectual processes. The Koran repeatedly admonishes true believers to recognize Allah through the evidence provided by nature. In an eloquent verse it proclaims:

Verily in the creation of the heavens and the earth,
and the alternation of night and day;
and in the ships that move through the sea with
what is useful to man,
and in the rain which Allah sendeth down from heaven,
to give life to earth that is dead
and to spread over it all kinds of animals;
and in the change of winds,
and in the clouds freely serving between heaven and
earth;
—in all these are signs for those who understand.

(2:159)

Further Resources

BOOKS

Esposito, John, ed. *The Oxford History of Islam.* New York: Oxford University Press, 1999.

Hasan, Asma Gull. *American Muslims: The New Generation.* New York: Continuum, 2002.

Smith, Jane I. *Islam in America.* New York: Columbia University Press, 1999.

PERIODICALS

Ellis, Michael W. "Islam: A Short History." *Library Journal,* 125, no. 15, Sept 15, 2000, 92.

Ghaneabassiri, Kambiz. "Islam in America." *The Journal of Religion,* 81, no. 2, April 2001, 339.

Nethe, Richard H. "The Demystification of Islam." *The Humanist,* 62, no. 6, November/December 2002, 28.

WEBSITES

"Islam and the Global Islam eCommunity." IslamiCity.com. Available online at http://www.islamicity.com/ (accessed February 26, 2003).

"Islam Page." Islamworld.net. Available online at http://www.islamworld.net/ (accessed February 26, 2003).

Northumbria University, "About Islam and Muslims." Northumbria.com. Available online at http://www.unn.ac.uk/societies/islamic/ (accessed February 26, 2003).

Lemon v. Kurtzman

Supreme Court decision

By: Warren Earl Burger

Date: June 28, 1971

Source: *Lemon v. Kurtzman.* 403 U.S. 602 (1971). Available online at http://www.findlaw.com/01topics/06constitutional/cases2.html; website home page: http://www.findlaw.com/casecode/supreme.html (accessed February 26, 2003).

About the Author: Warren Earl Burger (1907–1995) was born in St. Paul, Minnesota. He received a law degree from St. Paul College of Law in 1931, and served as assistant attorney general from 1953 to 1956. He was a judge in the United States Court of Appeals from 1956 to 1969. Appointed by President Nixon, Burger served as chief justice of the Supreme Court from 1969 to 1986. Although usually conservative, Burger was noted for backing issues on civil rights and administrative reforms of the federal court system. ■

Introduction

Historically, there have been many questions and dilemmas raised concerning the separation of church and state. The founders of the United States Constitution wished to make it very clear that there should never be a state-sponsored religion, that is, there should always be a distinct barrier between the affairs and functioning of religious groups and policies and actions by the federal as well as the state governments.

The United States Supreme Court has had the responsibility of interpreting the Constitution in such a manner as to assure that this separation between church

A nun leads a music class at Beaver Island Community School in Michigan in 1972. © JAMES L. AMOS/CORBIS. REPRODUCED BY PERMISSION.

and state would never be relaxed or discarded. One of the controversial issues that arose in the 1970s was the question of whether the state government could render public assistance in the form of financial payments made to religious-sponsored schools. More specifically, would it be constitutionally permissible for the state to help pay for the salaries of teachers who taught secular subjects, not religious ones, in private schools or religious-sponsored schools?

The groups who supported this kind of state aid to religious and private schools believed that these institutions were providing a public service to the community by educating the children in secular subjects. Because the children were attending religious and private schools, this action was saving the public schools from spending their funds on educating them. With that idea in mind, the pro-state aid groups argued that it was only fair that the state should help pay some of the salaries of the teachers in the religious and private schools. Those groups who were against any kind of state financial aid to religious and private schools believed that this type of assistance would be a violation of the Constitution's prohibition of church and state relationships.

The state of Rhode Island and the commonwealth of Pennsylvania adopted the argument of the pro-state aid groups and instituted programs that paid the salaries of teachers who taught secular subjects in private and reli-

gious schools. The anti-state aid groups filed suit in order to stop this state action, which resulted in a Supreme Court decision known as *Lemon v. Kurtzman.*

Significance

Lemon v. Kurtzman actually consisted of judgments by the United States Supreme Court on three separate cases that were decided together. The other two cases were *Earley v. DiCenso* and *Robinson v. DiCenso.* These three cases were joined together by the court because they all involved decisions concerning public assistance to private schools, some of which were religious. In each case, the teachers in question were being paid by state funds to teach secular subjects.

In *Lemon v. Kurtzman,* the appellants were Alton J. Lemon and others. David H. Kurtzman was the superintendent of public instruction of the Commonwealth of Pennsylvania. Pennsylvania's law had allowed the payment of teachers' salaries in parochial schools, and also permitted financial assistance in textbook purchases and teaching supplies. A district court upheld the Pennsylvania law as being constitutional. The United States Supreme Court reversed the judgment by the Pennsylvania District Court in *Lemon v. Kurtzman.*

In *Earley v. DiCenso,* Earley represented the Rhode Island Department of Education and DiCenso was a

Rhode Island taxpayer. In *Robinson v. DiCenso,* Robinson was the commissioner of education and DiCenso was the same taxpayer. State law had permitted partial funding of the salaries of private school teachers. A district court ruled that the Rhode Island law was unconstitutional, a decision upheld by the Supreme Court. Because of the impossibility of monitoring everything an instructor teaches, and in order to avoid this potential constitutional conflict of church and state in the future, the court decided to ban state subsidized salaries to teachers in religious schools.

Chief Justice Burger established three standards that must be employed in judging the constitutionality of legislation that involved any matters dealing with a potential relationship between church and state. The law: must have a secular legislative purpose, can neither advance nor inhibit religion, and must not foster any excessive government entanglement with religion. These standards, known as the Lemon Test, became the primary method of determining if a church-state relationship was constitutional.

Primary Source

Lemon v. Kurtzman

> **SYNOPSIS:** In these excerpts, the Supreme Court justices presents their reasoning on their decision concerning public financial assistance to private schools. The court determined that assistance of this kind was unconstitutional. Chief Justice Burger, in writing the opinion of the court, formulated the Lemon Test that would be used in future cases for analyzing statutes relating to church and state relationships.

Mr. Chief Justice Burger delivered the opinion of the Court.

These appeals raise questions as to Pennsylvania and Rhode Island statutes providing state aid to church-related elementary and secondary schools. Both statutes are challenged as violative of the Establishment and Free Exercise Clauses of the First Amendment and the Due Process Clause of the Fourteenth Amendment.

Pennsylvania has adopted a statutory program that provides financial support to nonpublic elementary and secondary schools by way of reimbursement for the cost of teachers' salaries, textbooks, and instructional materials in specified secular subjects. Rhode Island has adopted a statute under which the State pays directly to teachers in nonpublic elementary schools a supplement of 15% of their annual salary. Under each statute state aid has been given to church-related educational institutions. We hold that both statutes are unconstitutional.

The Rhode Island Statute

The Rhode Island Salary Supplement Act 1 was enacted in 1969. It rests on the legislative finding that the quality of education available in nonpublic elementary schools has been jeopardized by the rapidly rising salaries needed to attract competent and dedicated teachers. The Act authorizes state officials to supplement the salaries of teachers of secular subjects in nonpublic elementary schools by paying directly to a teacher an amount not in excess of 15% of his current annual salary. As supplemented, however, a nonpublic school teacher's salary cannot exceed the maximum paid to teachers in the State's public schools, and the recipient must be certified by the state board of education in substantially the same manner as public school teachers.

In order to be eligible for the Rhode Island salary supplement, the recipient must teach in a nonpublic school at which the average per-pupil expenditure on secular education is less than the average in the State's public schools during a specified period. Appellant State Commissioner of Education also requires eligible schools to submit financial data. If this information indicates a per-pupil expenditure in excess of the statutory limitation, the records of the school in question must be examined in order to assess how much of the expenditure is attributable to secular education and how much to religious activity.

The Act also requires that teachers eligible for salary supplements must teach only those subjects that are offered in the State's public schools. They must use "only teaching materials which are used in the public schools." Finally, any teacher applying for a salary supplement must first agree in writing "not to teach a course in religion for so long as or during such time as he or she receives any salary supplements" under the Act.

Appellees are citizens and taxpayers of Rhode Island. They brought this suit to have the Rhode Island Salary Supplement Act declared unconstitutional and its operation enjoined on the ground that it violates the Establishment and Free Exercise Clauses of the First Amendment. Appellants are state officials charged with administration of the Act, teachers eligible for salary supplements under the Act, and parents of children in church-related elementary schools whose teachers would receive state salary assistance.

A three-judge federal court was convened. . . . It found that Rhode Island's nonpublic elementary schools accommodated approximately 25% of the State's pupils. About 95% of these pupils attended schools affiliated with the Roman Catholic church. To date some 250 teachers have applied for benefits under the Act. All of them are employed by Roman Catholic schools.

The court held a hearing at which extensive evidence was introduced concerning the nature of the secular instruction offered in the Roman Catholic schools whose teachers would be eligible for salary assistance under the Act. Although the court found that concern for religious values does not necessarily affect the content of secular subjects, it also found that the parochial school system was "an integral part of the religious mission of the Catholic Church."

The District Court concluded that the Act violated the Establishment Clause, holding that it fostered "excessive entanglement" between government and religion. In addition two judges thought that the Act had the impermissible effect of giving "significant aid to a religious enterprise." We affirm.

The Pennsylvania Statute

Pennsylvania has adopted a program that has some but not all of the features of the Rhode Island program. The Pennsylvania Nonpublic Elementary and Secondary Education Act was passed in 1968 in response to a crisis that the Pennsylvania Legislature found existed in the State's nonpublic schools due to rapidly rising costs. The statute affirmatively reflects the legislative conclusion that the State's educational goals could appropriately be fulfilled by government support of "those purely secular educational objectives achieved through nonpublic education. . . ."

The statute authorizes appellee state Superintendent of Public Instruction to "purchase" specified "secular educational services" from nonpublic schools. Under the "contracts" authorized by the statute, the State directly reimburses nonpublic schools solely for their actual expenditures for teachers' salaries, textbooks, and instructional materials. A school seeking reimbursement must maintain prescribed accounting procedures that identify the "separate" cost of the "secular educational service." These accounts are subject to state audit. The funds for this program were originally derived from a new tax on horse and harness racing, but the Act is now financed by a portion of the state tax on cigarettes.

There are several significant statutory restrictions on state aid. Reimbursement is limited to courses "presented in the curricula of the public schools." It is further limited "solely" to courses in the following "secular" subjects: mathematics, modern foreign languages, physical science, and physical education. Textbooks and instructional materials included in the program must be approved by the state Superintendent of Public Instruction. Finally, the statute prohibits reimbursement for any course that contains "any subject matter expressing religious teaching, or the morals or forms of worship of any sect."

The Act went into effect on July 1, 1968, and the first reimbursement payments to schools were made on September 2, 1969. It appears that some $5 million has been expended annually under the Act. The State has now entered into contracts with some 1,181 nonpublic elementary and secondary schools with a student population of some 535,215 pupils—more than 20% of the total number of students in the State. More than 96% of these pupils attend church-related schools, and most of these schools are affiliated with the Roman Catholic church.

Appellants brought this action in the District Court to challenge the constitutionality of the Pennsylvania statute. The organizational plaintiffs-appellants are associations of persons resident in Pennsylvania declaring belief in the separation of church and state; individual plaintiffs-appellants are citizens and taxpayers of Pennsylvania. Appellant Lemon, in addition to being a citizen and a taxpayer, is a parent of a child attending public school in Pennsylvania. Lemon also alleges that he purchased a ticket at a race track and thus had paid the specific tax that supports the expenditures under the Act. Appellees are state officials who have the responsibility for administering the Act. In addition seven church-related schools are defendants-appellees.

A three-judge federal court was convened. . . . The District Court held that the individual plaintiffs-appellants had standing to challenge the Act. The organizational plaintiffs-appellants were denied standing under *Flast v. Cohen* (1968).

The court granted appellees' motion to dismiss the complaint for failure to state a claim for relief. It held that the Act violated neither the Establishment nor the Free Exercise Clause, Chief Judge Hastie dissenting. We reverse. . . .

The language of the Religion Clauses of the First Amendment is at best opaque, particularly when compared with other portions of the Amendment. Its authors did not simply prohibit the establishment of a state church or a state religion, an area history shows they regarded as very important and fraught with great dangers. Instead they commanded that there should be "no law respecting an establishment of religion." A law may be one "respecting" the forbidden objective while falling short of its total realization. A law "respecting" the proscribed result, that is, the establishment of religion, is not always easily identifiable as one violative of the Clause. A given law might not establish a state religion but nevertheless be one "respecting" that end in the sense of being a step that could lead to such establishment and hence offend the First Amendment.

In the absence of precisely stated constitutional prohibitions, we must draw lines with reference to the three main evils against which the Establishment Clause was intended to afford protection: "sponsorship, financial support, and active involvement of the sovereign in religious activity." *Walz v. Tax Commission* (1970).

Every analysis in this area must begin with consideration of the cumulative criteria developed by the Court over many years. Three such tests may be gleaned from our cases. First, the statute must have a secular legislative purpose; second, its principal or primary effect must be one that neither advances nor inhibits religion, *Board of Education v. Allen* (1968); finally, the statute must not foster "an excessive government entanglement with religion."

Inquiry into the legislative purposes of the Pennsylvania and Rhode Island statutes affords no basis for a conclusion that the legislative intent was to advance religion. On the contrary, the statutes themselves clearly state that they are intended to enhance the quality of the secular education in all schools covered by the compulsory attendance laws. There is no reason to believe the legislatures meant anything else. A State always has a legitimate concern for maintaining minimum standards in all schools it allows to operate. As in Allen, we find nothing here that undermines the stated legislative intent; it must therefore be accorded appropriate deference.

In Allen the Court acknowledged that secular and religious teachings were not necessarily so intertwined that secular textbooks furnished to students by the State were in fact instrumental in the teaching of religion. The legislatures of Rhode Island and Pennsylvania have concluded that secular and religious education are identifiable and separable. In the abstract we have no quarrel with this conclusion.

The two legislatures, however, have also recognized that church-related elementary and secondary schools have a significant religious mission and that a substantial portion of their activities is religiously oriented. They have therefore sought to create statutory restrictions designed to guarantee the separation between secular and religious educational functions and to ensure that State financial aid supports only the former. All these provisions are precautions taken in candid recognition that these programs approached, even if they did not intrude upon, the forbidden areas under the Religion Clauses. We need not decide whether these legislative precautions restrict the principal or primary effect of the programs to the point where they do not offend the Religion Clauses, for we conclude that the cumulative impact of the entire relationship arising under the statutes in each State involves excessive entanglement between government and religion. . . .

Finally, nothing we have said can be construed to disparage the role of church-related elementary and secondary schools in our national life. Their contribution has been and is enormous. Nor do we ignore their economic plight in a period of rising costs and expanding need. Taxpayers generally have been spared vast sums by the maintenance of these educational institutions by religious organizations, largely by the gifts of faithful adherents.

The merit and benefits of these schools, however, are not the issue before us in these cases. The sole question is whether state aid to these schools can be squared with the dictates of the Religion Clauses. Under our system the choice has been made that government is to be entirely excluded from the area of religious instruction and churches excluded from the affairs of government. The Constitution decrees that religion must be a private matter for the individual, the family, and the institutions of private choice, and that while some involvement and entanglement are inevitable, lines must be drawn.

The judgment of the Rhode Island District Court in No. 569 and No. 570 is affirmed. The judgment of the Pennsylvania District Court in No. 89 is reversed, and the case is remanded for further proceedings consistent with this opinion.

Mr. Justice Marshall took no part in the consideration or decision of No. 89. . . .

Mr. Justice White, concurring in the judgments in No. 153 (post, p. 672) and No. 89 and dissenting in Nos. 569 and 570. . . .

But, while the decision of the Court is legitimate, it is surely quite wrong in overturning the Pennsylvania and Rhode Island statutes on the ground that they amount to an establishment of religion forbidden by the First Amendment. . . .

It is enough for me that the States and the Federal Government are financing a separable secular function of overriding importance in order to sustain the legislation here challenged. That religion and private interests other than education may substantially benefit does not convert these laws into impermissible establishments of religion. . . .

The Court thus creates an insoluble paradox for the State and the parochial schools. The State cannot finance secular instruction if it permits religion to be taught in the same classroom; but if it exacts a promise that religion not be so taught—a promise the school and its teachers are quite willing and on this record able to give—and enforces it, it is then entangled in the "no entanglement" aspect of the Court's Establishment Clause jurisprudence. . . .

I disagree. There is no specific allegation in the complaint that sectarian teaching does or would invade secular classes supported by state funds. That the schools are operated to promote a particular religion is quite consistent with the view that secular teaching devoid of religious instruction can successfully be maintained, for good secular instruction is . . . essential to the success of the religious mission of the parochial school. I would no more here than in the Rhode Island case substitute presumption for proof that religion is or would be taught in state-financed secular courses or assume that enforcement measures would be so extensive as to border on a free exercise violation. We should not forget that the Pennsylvania statute does not compel church schools to accept state funds. I cannot hold that the First Amendment forbids an agreement between the school and the State that the state funds would be used only to teach secular subjects.

Further Resources

BOOKS

Americans United for Separation of Church and State. *The Best of Church & State, 1948–1975.* Silver Spring, Md.: Americans United for Separation of Church and State, 1975.

Berman, Harold Joseph. *Church and State.* New York: Macmillan; London: Collier Macmillan, 1987.

Woodruff, Douglas. *Church and State.* New York: Hawthorn Books, 1961.

WEBSITES

Americans United for Separation of Church and State. Available online at http://www.au.org/ (accessed February 26, 2003).

"Library: Modern Documents: Separation of Church and State." SecularWeb.com Available online at http://www.infidels.org /library/modern/church-state/index.shtml; website home page: http://www.infidels.org/index/shtml (accessed February 26, 2003).

Separation of Church and State. Available online at http://members.tripod.com/~candst/tnppage/tnpidx.htm (accessed February 26, 2003).

Wisconsin v. Yoder
Supreme Court decision

By: Warren Burger

Date: May 15, 1972

Source: *Wisconsin v. Yoder.* 406 U.S. 205 (1972). Available online at http://caselaw.lp.findlaw.com/scripts/getcase.pl?navby=search&court=US&case=/us/406/205.html; website home page: http://www.caselaw.lp.findlaw.com (accessed February 26, 2003).

About the Author: Warren Earl Burger (1907–1995), born in St. Paul, Minnesota, received his law degree in 1931 from St. Paul College of Law. He served from 1953 to 1956 as an assistant attorney general. Burger was then appointed as a judge to the United States Court of Appeals, a position he held from 1956 to 1969. Nominated by President Nixon, he served as chief justice of the Supreme Court from 1969 to 1986. Burger was noted for supporting federal court system administrative reforms and civil rights, even though he generally took conservative positions. ∎

Introduction

The Amish religion traces its roots to Anabaptist Christians, who separated from the Mennonites in Europe in the late seventeenth century. The Anabaptists were members of a religious movement in sixteenth century Europe who believed in the primacy of the Bible, in baptism as an outward sign of the believer's personal commitment and faith contract with God, in the separation of church from state, and in the separation of believers from nonbelievers.

Jakob Amman (c.1645–c.1730) was a Swiss Mennonite bishop whose followers founded the Amish community in the 1690s. Many Amish members migrated to Pennsylvania from 1730 to 1740; some of them eventually moved to Ohio, Indiana, and other states. In the twenty-first century, the descendants of the Amish immigrants reside in various rural locations, with Pennsylvania containing the highest number of communities.

The Amish are characterized by living a simple lifestyle apart from the rest of the American society. They possess a strong sense of family ties and responsibility, as well as a close affinity for members of their community. Traditionally, the Amish are pacifists and live according to a philosophy of nonviolence. Their total U.S.

An Amish boy walks horses down a country road near Lancaster, Pennsylvania, in 1977. In *Wisconsin v. Yoder* the Supreme Court decided that the state could not force Amish children to attend school, since this would interfere with the practice of the Amish religion. © RIC ERGENBRIGHT/CORBIS. REPRODUCED BY PERMISSION.

population in the year 2000 was around one hundred thousand. The United States Supreme Court, in *Wisconsin v. Yoder,* was faced with having to decide a state-church conflict. The state of Wisconsin had the responsibility of ensuring the adequate education of its children, but the religious belief of the Amish was that going to school until the eight-grade was sufficient. The basic question was: Should the state law supersede the religious rights of the Amish?

Significance

The defendants in this case were Jonas Yoder, Wallace Miller and Adin Yutzy. Yoder and Miller were members of the Old Order Amish Church and Yutzy was a member of the Conservative Amish Mennonite Church. All three respondents resided with their families in Green County, Wisconsin, and believed that their children should stay in school only through eighth grade. Wisconsin law mandated compulsory school attendance through the age of sixteen, and the state wished to compel the Amish parents to send their children to school until that age.

In October, 1968, Yoder, Miller, and Yutzy, were summoned into county court because their children,

Frieda Yoder, Barbara Miller, and Vernon Yutzy—each of school age—were not enrolled in school. The families explained their reasons for setting the eighth grade as the limit for their children's formal education: They lived in a religious community in which wisdom was expected to be gained by living at home and working on the farm, and they believed that going to high school would expose their children to temptations. Nevertheless, the court convicted the three fathers, who appealed to the circuit court and lost. They then appealed to the Wisconsin Supreme Court, who reversed the lower court decision, and declared that the Amish have a constitutional right to keep their children from enrolling in high school. The state of Wisconsin disagreed, and took the case to the United States Supreme Court. Chief Justice Warren Earl Burger upheld the Wisconsin Supreme Court, stating that the Wisconsin law violated the families' rights to the free exercise of religion.

Many religious groups supported the court's decision, believing that it decided correctly in protecting the right to believe and worship as one sees fit. Those who opposed the decision argued that it completely ignored the interests and rights of the children in regard to their education.

Primary Source

Wisconsin v. Yoder [excerpt]

SYNOPSIS: Three Amish families violated Wisconsin state law when they removed their children from school after completing just the eighth grade. They claimed their rights to freely exercise their religion were not being respected. The Supreme Court agreed with them.

Respondents, members of the Old Order Amish religion and the Conservative Amish Mennonite Church, were convicted of violating Wisconsin's compulsory school-attendance law (which requires a child's school attendance until age 16) by declining to send their children to public or private school after they had graduated from the eighth grade. The evidence showed that the Amish provide continuing informal vocational education to their children designed to prepare them for life in the rural Amish community.

The evidence also showed that respondents sincerely believed that high school attendance was contrary to the Amish religion and way of life and that they would endanger their own salvation and that of their children by complying with the law. The State Supreme Court sustained respondents' claim that application of the compulsory school-attendance law to them violated their rights under the Free Exercise Clause of the First Amendment, made applicable to the States by the Fourteenth Amendment.

Held:

1. The State's interest in universal education is not totally free from a balancing process when it impinges on other fundamental rights, such as those specifically protected by the Free Exercise Clause of the First Amendment and the traditional interest of parents with respect to the religious upbringing of their children.

2. Respondents have amply supported their claim that enforcement of the compulsory formal education requirement after the eighth grade would gravely endanger if not destroy the free exercise of their religious beliefs.

3. Aided by a history of three centuries as an identifiable religious sect and a long history as a successful and self-sufficient segment of American society, the Amish have demonstrated the sincerity of their religious beliefs, the interrelationship of belief with their mode of life, the vital role that belief and daily conduct play in the continuing survival of Old Order Amish communities, and the hazards presented by the State's enforcement of a statute generally valid as to others.

Beyond this, they have carried the difficult burden of demonstrating the adequacy of their alternative mode of continuing informal vocational education in terms of the overall interests that the State relies on in support of its program of compulsory high school education. In light of this showing, and weighing the minimal difference between what the State would require and what the Amish already accept, it was incumbent on the State to show with more particularity how its admittedly strong interest in compulsory education would be adversely affected by granting an exemption to the Amish.

4. The State's claim that it is empowered, as parens patriae, to extend the benefit of secondary education to children regardless of the wishes of their parents cannot be sustained against a free exercise claim of the nature revealed by this record, for the Amish have introduced convincing evidence that accommodating their religious objections by forgoing one or two additional years of compulsory education will not impair the physical or mental health of the child, or result in an inability to be self-supporting or to discharge the duties and responsibilities of citizenship, or in any other way materially detract from the welfare of society. . . .

Mr. Chief Justice Burger delivered the opinion of the Court.

On petition of the State of Wisconsin, we granted the writ of certiorari in this case to review a decision of the Wisconsin Supreme Court holding that respondents' convictions of violating the State's compulsory school-attendance law were invalid under the Free Exercise Clause of the First Amendment to the United States Constitution made applicable to the States by the Fourteenth Amendment. For the reasons hereafter stated we affirm the judgment of the Supreme Court of Wisconsin.

Respondents Jonas Yoder and Wallace Miller are members of the Old Order Amish religion, and respondent Adin Yutzy is a member of the Conservative Amish Mennonite Church. They and their families are residents of Green County, Wisconsin. Wisconsin's compulsory school-attendance law required them to cause their children to attend public or private school until reaching age 16 but the respondents declined to send their children, ages 14 and 15, to public school after they completed the eighth grade. The children were not enrolled in any private school, or within any recognized exception to the compulsory-attendance law, and they are conceded to be subject to the Wisconsin statute.

On complaint of the school district administrator for the public schools, respondents were charged, tried, and convicted of violating the compulsory-attendance law in Green Country Court and were fined the sum of $5 each. Respondents defended on the ground that the application of the compulsory-attendance law violated their rights under the First and Fourteenth Amendments.

The trial testimony showed that respondents believed, in accordance with the tenets of Old Order Amish communities generally, that their children's attendance at high school, public or private, was contrary to the Amish religion and way of life. They believed that by sending their children to high school, they would not only expose themselves to the danger of the censure of the church community, but, as found by the county court, also endanger their own salvation and that of their children. The State stipulated that respondents' religious beliefs were sincere.

In support of their position, respondents presented as expert witnesses scholars on religion and education whose testimony is uncontradicted. They expressed their opinions on the relationship of the Amish belief concerning school attendance to the more general tenets of their religion, and described the impact that compulsory high school attendance could have on the continued survival of Amish communities as they exist in the United States today.

The history of the Amish sect was given in some detail, beginning with the Swiss Anabaptists of the 16th century who rejected institutionalized churches and sought to return to the early, simple, Christian life de-emphasizing material success, rejecting the competitive spirit, and seeking to insulate themselves from the modern world. As a result of their common heritage, Old Order Amish communities today are characterized by a fundamental belief that salvation requires life in a church community separate and apart from the world and worldly influence. This concept of life aloof from the world and its values is central to their faith.

A related feature of Old Order Amish communities is their devotion to a life in harmony with nature and the soil, as exemplified by the simple life of the early Christian era that continued in America during much of our early national life. Amish beliefs require members of the community to make their living by farming or closely related activities. Broadly speaking, the Old Order Amish religion pervades and determines the entire mode of life of its adherents. Their conduct is regulated in great detail by the Ordnung, or rules, of the church community. Adult baptism, which occurs in late adolescence, is the time at which Amish young people voluntarily undertake heavy obligations, not unlike the Bar Mitzvah of the Jews, to abide by the rules of the church community.

Amish objection to formal education beyond the eighth grade is firmly grounded in these central religious concepts. They object to the high school, and higher education generally, because the values they teach are in marked variance with Amish values and the Amish way of life; they view secondary school education as an impermissible exposure of their children to a "worldly" influence in conflict with their beliefs. The high school tends to emphasize intellectual and scientific accomplishments, self-distinction, competitiveness, worldly success, and social life with other students. Amish society emphasizes informal learning-through-doing; a life of "goodness," rather than a life of intellect; wisdom, rather than technical knowledge; community welfare, rather than competition; and separation from, rather than integration with, contemporary worldly society.

Formal high school education beyond the eighth grade is contrary to Amish beliefs, not only because it places Amish children in an environment hostile to Amish beliefs with increasing emphasis on competition in class work and sports and with pressure to conform to the styles, manners, and ways of the peer group, but also because it takes them away from their community, physically and emotionally, during the crucial and formative adolescent period of life. During this period, the children must acquire Amish attitudes favoring manual work and self-reliance and the specific skills needed to perform the adult role of an Amish farmer or housewife. They must learn to enjoy physical labor.

Once a child has learned basic reading, writing, and elementary mathematics, these traits, skills, and attitudes admittedly fall within the category of those best learned through example and "doing" rather than in a classroom. And, at this time in life, the Amish child must also grow in his faith and his relationship to the Amish community if he is to be prepared to accept the heavy obligations imposed by adult baptism. In short, high school attendance with teachers who are not of the Amish faith—and may even be hostile to it—interposes a serious barrier to the integration of the Amish child into the Amish religious community. Dr. John Hostetler, one of the experts on Amish society, testified that the modern high school is not equipped, in curriculum or social environment, to impart the values promoted by Amish society.

The Amish do not object to elementary education through the first eight grades as a general proposition because they agree that their children must have basic skills in the "three R's" in order to read the Bible, to be good farmers and citizens, and to be able to deal with non-Amish people when necessary in the course of daily affairs. They view such a basic education as acceptable because it does not significantly expose their children to worldly values or interfere with their development in the Amish community during the crucial adolescent period. While Amish accept compulsory elementary education generally, wherever possible they have established their own elementary schools in many respects like the small local schools of the past. In the Amish belief higher learning tends to develop values they reject as influences that alienate man from God.

On the basis of such considerations, Dr. Hostetler testified that compulsory high school attendance could not only result in great psychological harm to Amish children, because of the conflicts it would produce, but would also, in his opinion, ultimately result in the destruction of the Old Order Amish church community as it exists in the United

States today. The testimony of Dr. Donald A. Erickson, an expert witness on education, also showed that the Amish succeed in preparing their high school age children to be productive members of the Amish community. He described their system of learning through doing the skills directly relevant to their adult roles in the Amish community as "ideal" and perhaps superior to ordinary high school education. The evidence also showed that the Amish have an excellent record as law-abiding and generally self-sufficient members of society.

Although the trial court in its careful findings determined that the Wisconsin compulsory school-attendance law "does interfere with the freedom of the Defendants to act in accordance with their sincere religious belief" it also concluded that the requirement of high school attendance until age 16 was a "reasonable and constitutional" exercise of governmental power, and therefore denied the motion to dismiss the charges. The Wisconsin Circuit Court affirmed the convictions. The Wisconsin Supreme Court, however, sustained respondents' claim under the Free Exercise Clause of the First Amendment and reversed the convictions. A majority of the court was of the opinion that the State had failed to make an adequate showing that its interest in "establishing and maintaining an educational system overrides the defendants' right to the free exercise of their religion." . . .

For the reasons stated we hold, with the Supreme Court of Wisconsin, that the First and Fourteenth Amendments prevent the State from compelling respondents to cause their children to attend formal high school to age 16. . . .

Nothing we hold is intended to undermine the general applicability of the State's compulsory school-attendance statutes or to limit the power of the State to promulgate reasonable standards that, while not impairing the free exercise of religion, provide for continuing agricultural vocational education under parental and church guidance by the Old Order Amish or others similarly situated. The States have had a long history of amicable and effective relationships with church-sponsored schools, and there is no basis for assuming that, in this related context, reasonable standards cannot be established concerning the content of the continuing vocational education of Amish children under parental guidance, provided always that state regulations are not inconsistent with what we have said in this opinion.

Affirmed.

Further Resources

BOOKS

Hostetler, John Andrew. *Amish Society.* Baltimore, MD.: Johns Hopkins University Press, c.1993.

Kraybill, Donald B. *On the Backroad to Heaven: Old Order Hutterites, Mennonites, Amish, and Brethren.* Baltimore, MD.: Johns Hopkins University Press, 2001.

Meyer, Carolyn. *Amish People: Plain Living in a Complex World.* New York: Atheneum, 1976.

PERIODICALS

Olson, Ray. "The Gift to be Simple: Life in Amish Country." *Booklist,* 97, no. 16, April 15, 2001, 1512.

Zvirin, Stephanie. "Life in an Amish Community." *Booklist,* 98, no. 3, October 1, 2001, 331.

WEBSITES

"The Amish: Beliefs, Practices, & Conflicts." RelgiousTolerance .org. Available online at http://www.religioustolerance.org /amish.htm (accessed February 26, 2003).

"The Amish, the Mennonites, and the Plain People." Pennsylvania Dutch Country Welcome Center, Lancaster, PA. Available online at http://www.800padutch.com/amish.shtml (accessed February 26, 2003).

"National Committee For Amish Religious Freedom." Holy Cross Lutheran Church, Livonia, Michigan. Available online at http://www.holycrosslivonia.org/amish/ (accessed February 26, 2003).

American Judaism: Adventure in Modernity

Theological work

By: Jacob Neusner

Date: 1972

Source: Neusner, Jacob. *American Judaism: Adventure in Modernity.* Englewood Cliffs, N. J.: Prentice-Hall, Inc., 1972, vii–viii, 1–3, 151–153.

About the Author: Jacob Neusner (1932–) was born in Hartford, Connecticut. He received an A.B. from Harvard in 1953, an M.H.L. from Jewish Theological Seminary of America in 1960, and a Ph.D. from Columbia in 1960. He has taught at various universities, including Columbia University, Dartmouth, and Brown. Neusner has also lectured at Yale, Notre Dame, and Oxford, among others. His hundreds of articles and books on Judaism have earned him the reputation of an expert in his field. ∎

Introduction

By the 1970s, some American Jewish families were entering into their fourth and fifth generations in the United States. These were people who descended from Jews who had immigrated to the United States between the period of 1880 and 1920. The question of the Jewish identity in America was on the minds of many Jewish scholars, rabbis, and laity.

Troublesome questions concerning the future of Judaism were being raised. Was the American Jew of the 1970s "vanishing?" Would many Jews become so assimilated into American culture that they would eventually lose their unique religious heritage and cultural identity? Would Jewish intermarriage with non-Jews, particularly Christians, mean that the faith of past generations would be abandoned? Would efforts toward modernity hurt or help Judaism as a religion and the fate of the Jewish people?

Many Jewish scholars and leaders of Jewish communities in the 1960s and 1970s had become concerned about the modern-day changes that were beginning to threaten the practice of their beloved faith. One major change was the growing numbers of Jews who were marrying non-Jews. Because of these intermarriages, some Jews began forgetting the heritage of their parents and ancestors. Another change came in the form of adopting the cultural values and practices of the majority culture while ignoring or downplaying their own unique Jewish culture.

In order to help resolve the dilemmas posed by these changes, Jacob Neusner, a notable, respected professor of religious studies and a famous Jewish scholar, wrote *American Judaism: Adventure in Modernity*. He saw the need to address these questions in a scholarly and practical manner. Certainly, Neusner felt that some of the answers to these questions would at times be speculative, but the answers had to be sought.

Significance

Jacob Neusner met the challenge of exploring contemporary American Judaism by directing his concentration on the exploration of three important areas concerning the Jewish faith and culture in the United States. First, he wanted to address the question as to what was the meaning of being Jewish in modern society. Secondly, he focused upon what was shaping the minds of Jewish Americans. The third area concentrated upon the roles of Jewish leaders and Jewish religious institutions.

Neusner pointed out that the answers to these questions were quite complicated because of the differentiations within Judaism itself. Judaism was characterized by a diversity of histories and traditions. Whether the Jewish branch that one adhered to was Orthodox, Conservative, Reform, or Reconstruction would partially determine the responses.

There was one common element, however, that bound all the branches of Judaism together: the Torah (the first five books of the Hebrew scriptures) and the Talmud (the collection of ancient Rabbinic writings). In

"What Do American Jews Believe? A Symposium," Neusner noted: "The one Torah that all of us read in synagogue and in study, the one Talmud that all of us ask to impart structure and meaning to Scripture in the here and now—these form a common inheritance."

Finding and understanding one's religious identity was of great importance, especially to members of a minority religion in a predominantly Christian society. Jacob Neusner's book helped the Jewish laity and the Jewish scholars to focus upon the question of the American Jewish identity. Neusner's book was well received by students of American Judaism because it helped provide a framework for future studies. By defining the specific aspects of Jewish life that needed to be examined, he set the foundation for further research and discourse.

Primary Source

American Judaism: Adventure in Modernity
[excerpt]

> **SYNOPSIS:** In these excerpts from the Preface, Introduction, and Epilogue from *American Judaism: Adventure in Modernity*, Jacob Neusner discussed the basic issues that needed examination in the modern Jewish identity in America. He wanted the reader to discover what was shaping the minds of Jewish-Americans, and what roles Jewish religious leaders and institutions were playing in that process.

Preface

America is the model of modernity and the American Jewish experience of modernity is in some ways paradigmatic of that of modern man. One dilemma of modernity is: What of tradition? Of the experience of the past? For the Jew it is this: How to mediate between the claims of classical Judaism, the work of ages of faith, archaic, supernatural, and sacred, and the ineluctable demands of contemporaneity, secularity, unbelief, and worldliness? What happens to religion beyond the age in which men take ritual for reality and myth for granted, thus tell *as fact* the stories meant to convey the essential structure of being in highly symbolic form and to reveal the truth of life? What happens to their imaginative life? How do they mediate between the claim of contemporaneity and the demands of their vast inheritance of institutions, rituals, myths and theologies, social and cultural patterns, derived from the archaic age? Clearly, that inheritance remains very present in the modern world. But what of that presence? Is it a wraith or an augury?

American Judaism supplies evocative materials for a case-study of the religious experience of modernity. When we ask, "What does it mean to be a Jew in contemporary America?" we seek a particular sort of religious and cultural datum, because we suppose that datum to be revealing, suggestive beyond itself. American Jews stand at the margins of society, and are therefore conscious of traits others take for granted. At the frontiers of culture, they moreover are clearly visible to others. So American Judaism may serve as a mirror of American religious life, and American Jews as a model of modernity.

Since our question is, "What happens to archaic religions in modern American civilization?" we adopt categories of inquiry into the traits of archaic religions developed by historians of religions—the modes of the sacred. American Judaism supplies important data for five of these categories: holy way—the pattern of everyday actions imposed by a religious tradition; holy man—the person set apart as a bearer of religious truth, grace, and supernatural power; holy people—the religious community as the locus at which the supernatural enters history; holy land—the place set apart for meaningful history; and holy faith—the doctrines and beliefs that explain and verify experienced reality. Other important questions raised by historians of religions elicit more interesting answers from data supplied by other religious groups in American society.

At the end we shall not evade the question of meaning: What is *religious* about contemporary religious life? Do we witness the last stages of the tradition's lingering demise, or the beginnings of a fundamentally new human creation? . . .

Introduction

What happens to religious traditions in modern times? Historians describe the development of institutions and doctrines, while sociologists uncover their social foundations. Historians of religions, however, tend to concentrate attention on archaic, or pre-modern, religious life, particularly in the Far East, Africa, South Asia, and the Middle East. They have developed questions about the nature of archaic religions and provided illuminating perspectives. Here we shall ask the questions of historians of religions about people heretofore neglected by them: religious men in modern America. The data differ from all others studied by historians of religions because they derive from a secular, modern, technologically advanced and intellectually sophisticated civilization. And that is why for the study of the history of religions, America, with the contemporary West it represents, is a new and unexplored field of inquiry.

Seattle Cantor Isaac Azose helps Robert Abolafia study for his bar mitzvah in June 1970. © **TED SPIEGEL/CORBIS. REPRODUCED BY PERMISSION.**

If we were anthropologists studying the religion of a pre-literate tribe, we should ask about the rituals and myths of that tribe, the character of its religious leadership, the social structures that embody its religious traditions, the way in which individual identity is defined. So too of America. We want to know about the religious rituals, beliefs, and stories that shape people's minds, the religious leaders and their place in those beliefs and stories, the religious institutions, the role of religion in the larger society. But with this difference: America is not tribe, but a complex and heterogeneous society. Americans are not pre-literate, but in their masses highly educated. Religiosity in skeptical, modern America is a different sort of thing from the believing in an archaic society that takes for granted the central propositions of religion, as of the broader culture, and knows nothing of doubt or unbelief.

What does it mean to be religious in America? The question is too abstract, the data insufficiently digested. Here, we focus on a small part of that question, on a group that is both well-documented and intensely self-concerned, the Jews. They form a coherent group in American society. They generally regard their group as religious, though doing so requires the revision of commonplace definitions of religion. And their intellectuals have articulately addressed themselves to what it means to be a Jew in America.

Still more interesting, the Jews came from a society that stood on the threshhold of modernity to a country that had long before become its bastion. Central and Eastern European Jewry, which supplied the vast majority of emigrants to America, had experienced no Renaissance to focus attention on man and his achievements; no Reformation to revise the traditional religion and to purify and articulate its doctrines; no Enlightenment to impose on the tradition the astringent criteria of reason and rationality; no Romantic recovery of tradition in a post-Enlightenment reaction; and no Darwinian age of Progress. The five formative centuries of Western civilization passed unnoticed, with little effect, over Central and Eastern European Jews. They came from agricultural villages to the American metropolis, from traditional patterns of human relationships to impersonal ones, from a primitive to a highly developed economic system, from a society where the stranger was an outsider to one in which all were alien to one another, from an intensely religious to a secular world. These changes produced a vast transformation of their religious life, and that is the problem of our study: What has happened to Judaism, and what does it mean to be a Jew today?

The answer to that question does not lie in the study of the history and sociology of American Jewry, or even of American Judaism. We are not going to rehearse the oft-told tales of how in 1654 a few Jewish families came to New Amsterdam, or of the three "waves" of immigration, Spanish, German, and Russian, or of the role of the Jews in fighting for America, or of the founding of various synagogues and national religious movements. Among the several good introductory studies of American Jews and Judaism, Nathan Glazer's *American Judaism* is outstanding. But all that is needed to answer our question lies in the pages of this book, though many works not quoted here deepen and broaden the inquiry. On the whole, such works concentrate on outward things: the place of Jews in American society and culture; the development of their institutions, synagogues, and community organizations; the way in which Jews became Americans. These issues dominated the interest of scholars for whom what it meant to be a Jew was generally clear and readily defined. What was problematical was the way in which Jews fit into the larger picture of American life.

Today Jews are sufficiently well integrated into that picture so that one need not wonder whether and how a well-defined foreign body is to be assimilated into a stable and equally well-defined social and cultural structure. After four generations, to be Jewish is a mode of being an American, taken for granted by Jews among other Americans, and no longer problematical. The dominant patterns and institutions of American Jewry have been established

for nearly a century. What now remains to be explored is, What do Jews now do because they are Jewish? What do they think, how do they respond, when they do as Jews, to the issues of human existence in America? What has happened to their religious tradition—the whole of it, not merely the theological surface? What of the inner life of people who superficially are the most modern of men?

Nathan Glazer observes in "The Jews":

A leading figure in Jewish community affairs relates that a Jew always eagerly asks, in any situation, "How many are Jews?" And when he gets an answer, he asks suspiciously, "How do you know?" Self-consciousness, curiosity, pride—all these are Jewish traits; caution, timidity, fear—these are Jewish traits, too.

The search for "Jewish traits" is not our task. What we want to know is much less than, "Who are the Jews?" or "What is a Jew?" We merely ask, "What is the state of 'Judaism' in contemporary America?" Defining "Judaism" as the sum of the beliefs and rites described by Jews as the way they are religious, and defining religion as the sum of beliefs and rites through which people explain and shape behavior in relationship to the supernatural or to matters of ultimate concern, we ask, "What does it mean to be a Jew, a protagonist of 'Judaism' viewed as a 'religion'?" . . .

Epilogue

What we have done is to assemble a rich array of materials without significantly contributing to the theoretical understanding of modernity or post-archaic religion. To make such a contribution, we should have had to formulate more supple, less mechanical interpretations of our central categories of inquiry. Modern and modernity, sacred, archaic, classical, secular, religious—all of these terms have been used as if I had given to them precise definitions; however, I have not. You therefore cannot be satisfied with our present interpretation of the complex materials of American Judaism, for, having presented a repertoire of data, I cannot claim to have accomplished the hermeneutical task at all, or even to have attempted it. I should argue, however, that a far wider selection of data, drawn from the religious situation of many sorts of modern men, is required for that purpose. The Jews may prove in the end merely suggestive, but by no means definitive, of the experience of modernity.

For we legitimately ask whether American Judaism, or at least its modern, non-orthodox sectors, may at all be regarded as an essentially valid datum for the study of American religions. Clearly the Jews constitute a well-demarcated ethnic community. But, among such disproportionately small numbers of Jews, is a persistent religious perspective upon themselves and upon life sufficient to characterize them all as a religious group? The process of modernization has not merely rendered their group life more complex and varied, but also seems to have obliterated from their group life the last remnants of a religious way of viewing reality. Many have lost sight of the full implications of the religious language and symbolism of the classic Judaic tradition. They scarcely make use of religious symbols to relate themselves to the conditions of their existence. Such symbols as survive scarcely relate to the conditions of group—much less individual—existence. American Jews cannot claim to apprehend the symbolic or mythic structure of traditional Judaism or of its modern developments in the way Bellah suggests: "Through religious symbols man has symbolized to himself his own identity and the order of existence in terms of which his identity makes sense." If one substitutes "Jewishness" for "religious symbols," then we have no discontinuity, for American Jews in the main do identify themselves in large measure through "being Jewish." But since the substance of "Jewishness" contains little of transcendent meaning, can it be regarded as other than of merely cultural and sociological, but not religious, interest?

Where is the human anguish, joy, tragedy, mystery, or awe in American Judaism? Where the sense of the sacred? Where the vision? Bellah cites Wilfred C. Smith: "A religious symbol is successful if men can express in terms of it the highest and deepest vision of which they are capable, and if in terms of it that vision can be nourished and can be conveyed to others within one's group." Do American Jews possess any such symbol, profess such a faith as to lead to a vision beyond the mundane data of their very worldly group life? That seems to me the central dilemma facing American Judaism: Its commitment to the rationality, respectability, and worldliness of the middle-class life to which Jews aspire, and in large part have achieved, seems to conflict with the vision contained in the holy books and deeds, indeed, with the whole symbolic structure of the Judaic inheritance. When the theologians have had their say, they still have not drawn the transcendent thorn from the rational rose—and transcendence, supernaturalism, reference to salvation and the eschaton, things not of this world—these seem the perquisites, in some form or other, of the religious quest for meaning.

Perhaps Judaism is actually disfunctional, because both its classic and its contemporary forms (and they are not so far apart) may not provide a secure, stable foundation for the collective life of the American Jews. So far as the Jews build that life solely upon this-worldly considerations, they render religious expression either irrelevant, or meretricious, or merely sentimental. But so soon as they speak of themselves in mythic language and respond to the existential challenge in accord with the Judaic response, they repudiate the worldliness, the confidence, the practicality of their present group life, for they thereby abandon their pugnacious secularity.

Which, then: ethnic group or religious community? If the former, why? If the latter, how? Individuals in the ethnic group are bound to raise religious questions, and if the answers do not come from Judaism, they will come from somewhere else—and this the ethnic group cannot endure. The religious community, however, is bound to exclude some in its commitment to a vision and symbolic structure, and the Jews have been wise in not excluding anyone born into their group, whatever his vision.

This disintegration of the archaic religious and ethnic unity of the "holy people" seems to me the most important Judaic testimony about what it means to be a modern man. But the story of the tension between the ethnic datum of Jewish group life and the religious critique and interpretation of that group life constitutes most of the history of Judaism. If so, the modern age brings new evidence of an astonishing continuity.

Further Resources

BOOKS

Bellah, Robert. *Beyond Belief.* New York: Harper and Row, 1970.

Glazer, Nathan. *American Judaism.* Chicago, Ill.: University of Chicago Press, 1989.

Glazer, Nathan, and Daniel Patrick Moynihan. "The Jews." In *Beyond the Melting Pot,* Cambridge, Mass.: MIT Press, 1964.

PERIODICALS

Orme, Marianne. "Beyond the Synagogue Gallery: Finding a Place for Women in American Judaism." *Library Journal,* 125, no. 12, July 2000, 100.

Rockaway, Robert A. "Perspectives on American Jewry." *Journal of American Ethnic History,* 17, no. 2, Winter 1998, 56.

WEBSITES

AcademicInfo.net, "American Judaism Resources- History of Jews." AcademicInfo.net. Available online at http://www .academicinfo.net/amreligjudaism.html; website home page: http://www.academicinfo.net (accessed March 1, 2003).

"American Judaism." Northwest Missouri State University. Available online at http://www.nwmissouri.edu/nwcourses

/history155/religion/midtermprojects/connieury/; website home page: http://www.nwmissouri.edu (accessed March 1, 2003).

"Can American Judaism Be Described? Or Has the Assimilation of American Jews Altered the Uniqueness of Judaism?" Northwest Missouri State University. Available online at http://www.nwmissouri.edu/nwcourses/history155/religion /papers/CONNIEURY/; website home page: http://www .nwmissouri.edu (accessed March 1, 2003).

Roe v. Wade

Supreme Court decision

By: Harry Andrew Blackmun

Date: January 22, 1973

Source: *Roe v. Wade*. 410 U.S. 113 (1973). Available online at http://caselaw.lp.findlaw.com/scripts/getcase.pl?navby=search &court=US&case=/us/410/113.html; website home page: http:// www.caselaw.lp.findlaw.com (accessed March 1, 2003).

About the Author: Harry Andrew Blackmun (1908–1999) was born in Nashville, Illinois. He graduated from Harvard in 1929 and received his law degree from that same university. From 1950 to 1959 he served as the general counsel to the Mayo Clinic. Following that position, he was appointed a federal circuit court judge. In 1970, he was installed as a Supreme Court judge, a position he held until 1994. Blackmun was noted as a strong supporter of church-state separation and civil rights. ■

Introduction

For a number of personal, social, or medical reasons, a woman faced with an unwanted pregnancy might decide to continue the pregnancy to its completion and possibly put the child up for adoption, or she might believe that an abortion was the right answer for her. If she chose the latter up until the early 1970s, her access to a safe abortion was limited by the laws of the state where she resided.

Because there was no uniformity of laws, women seeking an abortion in a state with restrictive provisions would sometimes cross state lines and have the abortion performed in a state whose laws would allow the procedure. Others resorted to having the abortion performed illegally in their home state by risky methods that often resulted in serious damage to their health, even death. Tens of thousands of women suffered severe medical trauma from these illegal operations each year.

Many religious groups across America were opposed to abortion because they believed that it was wrong to take the life of the unborn child. However, there were other groups, both religious and secular, who believed that it was up to the woman to make a choice concerning the continuation of her pregnancy. They felt that it was immoral to prevent her from making a decision concerning her own body, and that the nation's laws should be changed to allow her the right to make a choice.

In 1970, Norma N. McCorvey wished to have an abortion in Texas. She was denied that procedure because her life was not at risk, a precondition required for abortion, as mandated by Texas law. She should have the legal right to choose an abortion and joined with others in a lawsuit challenging the constitutionality of the Texas criminal abortion statute. To protect her privacy, McCorvey was referred to as Jane Roe in the trial. After going through lower courts, the case eventually reached the United States Supreme Court.

Significance

The Court held that the due process clause of the Fourteenth Amendment to the Constitution, which has been interpreted by the court as guaranteeing the right of citizens to privacy, gave a woman the right to choose an abortion. Because of that court ruling, the abortion laws in almost all of the states had to be changed.

The majority opinion of the Supreme Court, given by Justice Harry Blackmun, took the form of dividing the periods of pregnancy into three stages. The legal rules that were established by the court for abortion were: In the first three months of pregnancy, the decision for an abortion rests with the medical judgment of the pregnant woman's physician. In the fourth through sixth month of pregnancy, states may restrict—but not prohibit—abortions for the purpose of protecting a woman's health. In the seventh through ninth month of pregnancy, states may regulate or prohibit abortions to protect the life of the fetus, except in those cases when an abortion is necessary to save the mother's life.

The aftermath of *Roe v. Wade* turned out to be to one the most controversial religious issues of the 1970s and the decades that followed. Christians became divided because of this decision. The clergy of the Roman Catholic Church and many conservative Protestant denominations condemned the court's decision as being immoral, a violation of the right to life by the fetus, and diametrically opposed to God's laws. Many Orthodox Jews and Muslims also expressed opposition to abortions, and an active anti-abortion movement was born, calling for a reversal of the court's ruling.

In *Planned Parenthood v. Casey* (1992), the Supreme Court upheld the right to abortion but allowed states to impose certain restrictions. The *Roe v. Wade* ruling was upheld with minor modifications.

A billboard in western Pennsylvania advertises for an abortion clinic in distant New York City. Before *Roe v. Wade* New York was one of only a few states without tight restrictions on abortion. © BETTMANN/CORBIS. REPRODUCED BY PERMISSION.

Primary Source

Roe v. Wade [excerpt]

> **SYNOPSIS:** The United States Supreme Court held that a woman's right to an abortion fell within the constitutional right to privacy, as protected by the Fourteenth Amendment. In the following excerpts, Justice Harry Andrew Blackmun explained the court's decision on abortion. The rules concerning the permissibility of an abortion were different for each trimester of the pregnancy.

. . . State criminal abortion laws, like those involved here, that except from criminality only a life-saving procedure on the mother's behalf without regard to the stage of her pregnancy and other interests involved violate the Due Process Clause of the Fourteenth Amendment, which protects against state action the right to privacy, including a woman's qualified right to terminate her pregnancy. Though the State cannot override that right, it has legitimate interests in protecting both the pregnant woman's health and the potentiality of human life, each of which interests grows and reaches a "compelling" point at various stages of the woman's approach to term.

(a) For the stage prior to approximately the end of the first trimester, the abortion decision and its effectuation must be left to the medical judgment of the pregnant woman's attending physician.

(b) For the stage subsequent to approximately the end of the first trimester, the State, in promoting its interest in the health of the mother, may, if it chooses, regulate the abortion procedure in ways that are reasonably related to maternal health.

(c) For the stage subsequent to viability the State, in promoting its interest in the potentiality of human life, may, if it chooses, regulate, and even proscribe, abortion except where necessary, in appropriate medical judgment, for the preservation of the life or health of the mother.

The State may define the term "physician" to mean only a physician currently licensed by the State, and may proscribe any abortion by a person who is not a physician as so defined.

It is unnecessary to decide the injunctive relief issue since the Texas authorities will doubtless fully recognize the Court's ruling that the Texas criminal abortion statutes are unconstitutional. . . .

Mr. Justice Blackmun delivered the opinion of the Court.

This Texas federal appeal and its Georgia companion, *Doe v. Bolton,* . . . present constitutional challenges to state criminal abortion legislation. The Texas statutes under attack here are typical of those that have been in effect in many States for approximately a century. The Georgia statutes, in contrast, have a modern cast and are a legislative product that, to an extent at least, obviously reflects the influences of recent attitudinal change, of advancing medical knowledge and techniques, and of new thinking about an old issue.

We forthwith acknowledge our awareness of the sensitive and emotional nature of the abortion controversy, of the vigorous opposing views, even among physicians, and of the deep and seemingly absolute convictions that the subject inspires. One's philosophy, one's experiences, one's exposure to the raw edges of human existence, one's religious training, one's attitudes toward life and family and their values, and the moral standards one establishes and seeks to observe, are all likely to influence and to color one's thinking and conclusions about abortion.

In addition, population growth, pollution, poverty, and racial overtones tend to complicate and not to simplify the problem. Our task, of course, is to resolve the issue by constitutional measurement, free of emotion and of predilection. . . .

The Texas statutes that concern us here . . . make it a crime to "procure an abortion," as therein defined, or to attempt one, except with respect to "an abortion procured or attempted by medical advice for the purpose of saving the life of the mother." Similar statutes are in existence in a majority of the States. . . .

Jane Roe, a single woman who was residing in Dallas County, Texas, instituted this federal action in March 1970 against the District Attorney of the county. She sought a declaratory judgment that the Texas criminal abortion statutes were unconstitutional on their face, and an injunction restraining the defendant from enforcing the statutes.

Roe alleged that she was unmarried and pregnant; that she wished to terminate her pregnancy by an abortion "performed by a competent, licensed physician, under safe, clinical conditions"; that she was unable to get a "legal" abortion in Texas because her life did not appear to be threatened by the continuation of her pregnancy; and that she

could not afford to travel to another jurisdiction in order to secure a legal abortion under safe conditions. She claimed that the Texas statutes were unconstitutionally vague and that they abridged her right of personal privacy, protected by the First, Fourth, Fifth, Ninth, and Fourteenth Amendments. By an amendment to her complaint Roe purported to sue "on behalf of herself and all other women" similarly situated.

James Hubert Hallford, a licensed physician, sought and was granted leave to intervene in Roe's action. In his complaint he alleged that he had been arrested previously for violations of the Texas abortion statutes and that two such prosecutions were pending against him. He described conditions of patients who came to him seeking abortions, and he claimed that for many cases he, as a physician, was unable to determine whether they fell within or outside the exception . . . He alleged that, as a consequence, the statutes were vague and uncertain, in violation of the Fourteenth Amendment, and that they violated his own and his patients' rights to privacy in the doctor-patient relationship and his own right to practice medicine, rights he claimed were guaranteed by the First, Fourth, Fifth, Ninth, and Fourteenth Amendments.

John and Mary Doe, a married couple, filed a companion complaint to that of Roe. They also named the District Attorney as defendant, claimed like constitutional deprivations, and sought declaratory and injunctive relief. The Does alleged that they were a childless couple; that Mrs. Doe was suffering from a "neural-chemical" disorder; that her physician had "advised her to avoid pregnancy until such time as her condition has materially improved" (although a pregnancy at the present time would not present "a serious risk" to her life); that, pursuant to medical advice, she had discontinued use of birth control pills; and that if she should become pregnant, she would want to terminate the pregnancy by an abortion performed by a competent, licensed physician under safe, clinical conditions. By an amendment to their complaint, the Does purported to sue "on behalf of themselves and all couples similarly situated."

The two actions were consolidated and heard together by a duly convened three-judge district court. The suits thus presented the situations of the pregnant single woman, the childless couple, with the wife not pregnant, and the licensed practicing physician, all joining in the attack on the Texas criminal abortion statutes. Upon the filing of affidavits, motions were made for dismissal and for summary judgment.

The court held that Roe and members of her class, and Dr. Hallford, had standing to sue and presented justiciable controversies, but that the Does had failed to allege facts sufficient to state a present controversy and did not have standing. It concluded that, with respect to the requests for a declaratory judgment, abstention was not warranted. On the merits, the District Court held that the "fundamental right of single women and married persons to choose whether to have children is protected by the Ninth Amendment, through the Fourteenth Amendment," and that the Texas criminal abortion statutes were void on their face because they were both unconstitutionally vague and constituted an overbroad infringement of the plaintiffs' Ninth Amendment rights.

The court then held that abstention was warranted with respect to the requests for an injunction. It therefore dismissed the Does' complaint, declared the abortion statutes void, and dismissed the application for injunctive relief. . . .

To summarize and to repeat:

1. A state criminal abortion statute of the current Texas type, that excepts from criminality only a life-saving procedure on behalf of the mother, without regard to pregnancy stage and without recognition of the other interests involved, is violative of the Due Process Clause of the Fourteenth Amendment.

(a) For the stage prior to approximately the end of the first trimester, the abortion decision and its effectuation must be left to the medical judgment of the pregnant woman's attending physician.

(b) For the stage subsequent to approximately the end of the first trimester, the State, in promoting its interest in the health of the mother, may, if it chooses, regulate the abortion procedure in ways that are reasonably related to maternal health.

(c) For the stage subsequent to viability, the State in promoting its interest in the potentiality of human life may, if it chooses, regulate, and even proscribe, abortion except where it is necessary, in appropriate medical judgment, for the preservation of the life or health of the mother.

2. The State may define the term "physician," as it has been employed in the preceding paragraphs . . . of this opinion, to mean only a physician currently licensed by the State, and may proscribe any abortion by a person who is not a physician as so defined.

In *Doe v. Bolton,* . . . procedural requirements contained in one of the modern abortion statutes

are considered. That opinion and this one, of course, are to be read together.

This holding, we feel, is consistent with the relative weights of the respective interests involved, with the lessons and examples of medical and legal history, with the lenity of the common law, and with the demands of the profound problems of the present day. The decision leaves the State free to place increasing restrictions on abortion as the period of pregnancy lengthens, so long as those restrictions are tailored to the recognized state interests.

The decision vindicates the right of the physician to administer medical treatment according to his professional judgment up to the points where important state interests provide compelling justifications for intervention. Up to those points, the abortion decision in all its aspects is inherently, and primarily, a medical decision, and basic responsibility for it must rest with the physician. If an individual practitioner abuses the privilege of exercising proper medical judgment, the usual remedies, judicial and intra-professional, are available. Our conclusion . . . (is) that the Texas abortion statutes, as a unit, must fall. . . .

Although the District Court granted appellant Roe declaratory relief, it stopped short of issuing an injunction against enforcement of the Texas statutes. The Court has recognized that different considerations enter into a federal court's decision as to declaratory relief, on the one hand, and injunctive relief, on the other. *Zwickler v. Koota,* (1967); *Dombrowski v. Pfister,* (1965). We are not dealing with a statute that, on its face, appears to abridge free expression, an area of particular concern under Dombrowski and refined in *Younger v. Harris.* . . .

We find it unnecessary to decide whether the District Court erred in withholding injunctive relief, for we assume the Texas prosecutorial authorities will give full credence to this decision that the present criminal abortion statutes of that State are unconstitutional.

The judgment of the District Court as to intervenor Hallford is reversed, and Dr. Hallford's complaint in intervention is dismissed. In all other respects, the judgment of the District Court is affirmed. Costs are allowed to the appellee.

It is so ordered.

Further Resources

BOOKS

Garrow, David J. *Liberty & Sexuality: The Right to Privacy and the Making of Roe v. Wade.* New York: Macmillan, 1994.

Goldstein, Leslie Friedman. *The Constitutional Rights of Women,* revised ed. Madison, Wis.: University of Wisconsin Press, 1989.

Guitton, Stephanie, and Peter Irons, eds. *May It Please the Court: Arguments on Abortion.* New York: The New Press, 1995.

PERIODICALS

Brustman, Mary Jane. "*Roe v. Wade:* The Abortion Rights Controversy in American History." *Library Journal,* 126, no. 19, November 15, 2001, 80.

Green, Michelle. "The Woman Behind *Roe v. Wade.*" *People Weekly,* 31, no. 20, May 22, 1989, 36.

Staggenborg, Suzanne. "Doctors of Conscience: The Struggle to Provide Abortion before and after *Roe v. Wade.*" *Signs,* 23, no. 2, Winter 1998, 528.

WEBSITES

Constitutional Law. "*Roe v. Wade* in a Nutshell." Available online at http://members.aol.com/abtrbng/roeins.htm (accessed March 1, 2003).

"*Roe v. Wade.*" PBS Online NewsHour Forum. Available online at http://www.pbs.org/newshour/forum/january98/roe _1-30.html; website home page: http://www.pbs.org (accessed March 1, 2003).

"*Roe vs. Wade,* 25 Years Later." CNN.com. Available online at http://www.cnn.com/SPECIALS/1998/roe.wade/; website home page: http://www.cnn.com (accessed March 1, 2003).

"Boundary of Jewish-Christian Understanding"

Magazine article

By: Dale Stover

Date: 1974

Source: Stover, Dale. "Boundary of Jewish-Christian Understanding." *Christian Century,* June 26, 1974, 668–671. Available online at http://www.religion-online.org/cgi-bin/relsearchd .dll/showarticle?item_id=1606 (accessed February 26, 2003).

About the Author: Dale Stover received his B.A. from Washington University in St. Louis in 1957. He also earned a Bachelor of Divinity in 1961 and a Master of Sacred Theology in 1964 from Andover Newton Theological School in Newton Center, Massachusetts. In 1967, he received his Ph.D. in Religious Studies at McGill University in Montreal. He became a professor of religious studies at the University of Nebraska at Omaha in 1968. ∎

Introduction

Anti-Semitism has taken many forms in the past two thousand years: hostility, prejudice, discrimination, and segregation directed at Jews or Judaism. The German Nazis during the World War II era (1939–1945) conducted a systematic policy of genocide toward Jews, resulting in the death of at least six million people.

Anti-Semitism in the United States after the ending of Word War II took both overt and covert forms. Some Jews were denied access to certain jobs and social activities, like clubs, fraternal groups, and other associations. Restrictive real estate covenants often kept Jews out of certain neighborhoods. Many people harbored negative feelings, suspicions, and hatreds against Jews and the Jewish religion.

What was at the basic source of anti-Semitism in the United States? Could this prejudice against the Jewish religion and people ultimately be traced to the writings in the New Testament of the Christian Bible? Could some Christians rationalize their feelings by pointing out negative statements about Jews in the Bible?

Christian and Jewish theologians alike had explored these emotional and controversial questions concerning the New Testament. Scholars in both religions argued that certain writings in the Christian gospels directly and indirectly expressed anti-Jewish sentiments. Other scholars—especially Christian ones—doubted that these writings could be justifiably labeled as the source of modern anti-Semitism.

Another issue facing Christian-Jewish relations in the 1970s dealt with the question: Is anti-Semitism at the basis of criticism against the state of Israel's policies? During that time in the United States, as well as Europe, some groups began raising doubts about the validity of Israeli governmental and military policies in dealing with the Palestinians and surrounding Arab countries.

Significance

Dale Stover, a professor of religious studies, addressed these important questions in his article "Anti-Semitism: Boundary of Jewish-Christian Understanding." By validating the perspectives of both parties and offering recommendations to help mediate the debate over the source of anti-Semitism, Stover and his colleagues helped set the stage for a renewed effort of dialogue between Christians and Jews.

On the issue of anti-Semitism being at the basis of criticism against the state of Israel's policies, Stover presented the debate between Father Daniel Berrigan and Rabbi Arthur Hertzberg. Berrigan had spoken out on several occasions against the Israeli government, charging that Israel was acting in a nationalistic, exploitative, and militaristic manner against its neighbors in the Middle East. Hertzberg countercharged that Berrigan's criticism of Israel was reflective of anti-Semitic attitudes. Hertzberg equated the priest's disapproval of the Israeli state with prejudicial attacks on the religion of Judaism and the Jewish people themselves. The dispute between Father Berrigan and Rabbi Hertzberg, according to

Stover, represented a disruption of meaningful dialogue between Christianity and Judaism.

Knowing the background of these two men would help in the understanding of the issue that Stover presented in his article. Daniel Berrigan, a Roman Catholic priest, was a professor of theology at LeMoyne College in Syracuse from 1957 to 1962. He was a staunch antiwar activist during the Vietnam War (1964–1975) and is the author of more than fifty books, many of them on religion and social activism.

Rabbi Arthur Hertzberg has taught at Princeton, Rutgers, Columbia, Dartmouth, and New York University. He was a chaplain in the U.S. Air Force, and has been president of numerous Jewish organizations, including the American Jewish Policy Foundation.

In the years since Stover's article was published, efforts have been made by many Christian churches to change the anti-Semitism inherent in some of their teachings. Christians are also being encouraged to be more sensitive in their relationships with Jews and in their views toward Israel. Since the terrorist attacks of September 11, 2001, American Christians have developed a keener understanding of the terrorism that has been directed toward Israel and the Jewish people in the past decades.

Reverend Daniel Berrigan, 1972. © BETTMANN/CORBIS. REPRODUCED BY PERMISSION.\

Primary Source

"Boundary of Jewish-Christian Understanding" [excerpt]

> **SYNOPSIS:** In these excerpts, Professor Stover explores the role of the New Testament and critical attitudes concerning Israel in reference to anti-Semitism, and the failure of significant dialogue between Christians and Jews on these issues. Stover's thesis is that Jews and Christians alike should "appreciate the covenant nature of the other's faith."

"Anti-Semitism" carries a great deal of emotive force. Hitler's maniacal program of genocide, which annihilated 6 million Jews in our century, has imbued the term "anti-Semitism" with a quality of dread—dread of an incoherent and unconditional evil which is unaccountably present in human form. However, since the end of World War II and the emergence on the world's political scene of the State of Israel, "anti-Semitism" has often been used with reference to one's stance vis-à-vis this 20th century nation, and thus has acquired quite new shades of meaning.

The subtleties which register in the current use of the term are rooted in history, which gives evidence of a long series of hateful and oppressive acts against Jews. To interpret this history as "anti-Semitic" is to say that Jews were persecuted simply because they were Jews. Because Christian societies have been most notably responsible for oppression of Jews, the meaning of "anti-Semitism" is particularly connected with the way in which Jews and Christians understand one another. More specifically, it often implies an anti-Jewish bias on the part of Christians. Could it be that the current use of the term indicates the true character of relations between Jews and Christians today?. . . .

Anti-Semitism in the New Testament

The "discovery" that there is anti-Semitism in the New Testament is obviously anachronistic in several senses. For one thing, as used in that connection, "anti-Semitism" draws its meaning from an assessment of recent events; that is, the present meaning of the term is falsely applied to an ancient era. Nevertheless, the charge is widely accepted as proved. Could this be seen as an attempt on the part of Christians to cope with the frightful history of Jewish suppression in Christendom? Thus the Christian who reads in, the Gospel of John, for example, that "the Jews" are opposing Jesus winces at this imputation of guilt to a whole people. Can an interpretation be found that explains both modern anti-Semitism and the apparently anti-Semitic tenor of New Testament language?

Form-critical study of the New Testament is helpful here. Form criticism claims that the final written form of the New Testament documents was greatly influenced by the struggles the young church was undergoing. In the light of that claim, it is reasonable to attribute the New Testament's use of the phrase "the Jews" to the point of view of an era when the church was in conflict with the Jewish community, hence to conclude that the anti-Semitism in the New Testament is incidental. The anti-Semitism of subsequent centuries may be seen as related to this adventitious root. This interpretation allows us to understand the kerygma (proclamation of religious truths) and the figure of Jesus as essentially prior to and apart from anti-Semitic tradition. Indeed, it would seem that they must be so understood if we are to retain our faith, since a Christianity which is inherently anti-Semitic is abhorrent.

The trouble with this interpretation is precisely its implied admission that the New Testament is "anti-Semitic." Thanks to historical-critical research, today's Christian can look at the New Testament so dispassionately that he or she can acquiesce when it is made the dumping ground for 20th century garbage. In other words, modern anti-Semitism, even in the virulent form of Nazism, can be ultimately blamed on the New Testament writings.

But to explain anti-Semitism as both rooted in the New Testament and also as an excisable feature of it is surely to dispatch the problem of anti-Semitism too glibly. Moreover, theologically speaking, it is profoundly in error. The first century conflict between church and synagogue was hardly incidental. On the one hand, the New Testament does not represent Jesus' Jewishness as peripheral. After all, Jesus is the Messiah, the fulfiller of the Torah and the prophets, the bringer-in of the kingdom and the founder of the New Israel; and the election of the Jews is now understood in terms of the election of Jesus. On the other hand, the majority of Jews refused to accept the Christian kerygma, and in time their persistent refusal became an embarrassment to the church and an apparent refutation of the Christian claim that Jesus was the Messiah. Are not Jews and Christians perennially bound together in theological conflict by the very nature of their faith, both claiming election by the one and same God? And is it not a kind of theological self-hatred for Christians to dismiss this conflict?

Theological conflict is not necessarily tantamount to "anti-Semitism"; that is, modern anti-Jewishness. The New Testament church was not repudiating Jewishness—on the contrary! New Testament references to "the Jews" cannot be understood as a rejection of Jewishness; rather, they betoken a conflict between church and synagogue because of the church's claim of its own Jewishness. That claim would have been vindicated by the conversion of all the Jews. Hence the church could not oppose the synagogue on the grounds of the synagogue's Jewishness, but only on the grounds of its being an incomplete Jewishness.

It is clear, however, that the New Testament's so-called "anti-Semitism"—which in fact only reflects early Christian difficulties with established Judaism—was in later times used to justify real anti-Semitism. Indeed, to condone the charge of anti-Semitism in the New Testament is to follow the lead of the real anti-Semites who first proposed this line of argument. Real anti-Semitism becomes a possibility precisely when the Jewishness of Christianity is deleted. And that happens when the historical character of Christianity is ignored in favor of a rational conception of the relation of God to humankind which applies on a universal scale without regard to historical particularities. This sort of concept is likely to be based on some transcendent universal such as subjective religious experience or a categorical ethical imperative. Rationalized Christianity is especially susceptible to various kinds of anthropocentric, culture-bound claims to absoluteness. Since it is inevitably subject to some cultural or sectarian imperialism, ethics in the abstract is so far from being a guarantee against anti-Semitism as actually to be the first step toward anti-Semitism.

I suggest that when Christians charge the New Testament with anti-Semitism they have rationalized their faith and are therefore highly susceptible to anti-Semitism. It would follow that Jews have far more to fear from a rationalized Christianity than from one in conflict with Judaism over the question of Christianity's Jewishness. It might indeed be said that the so-called anti-Semitism in the New Testament is evidence of a close theological kinship between Jews and Christians which accounts for their "family quarrel" but might in the end lead them to embrace each other. . . .

Anti-Semitism in Criticism of Israel

Political critics of the State of Israel appear to fall automatically under the ban of anti-Semitism. Even Daniel Berrigan, that stalwart champion of peace, recently discovered to his surprise that his criticism of Israeli policies had deeply offended Jewish sensitivities. Arthur Hertzberg, president of the American Jewish Congress, found Berrigan's strictures so reprehensible that he called them "old-fashioned theological anti-Semitism" (*American Report,* October 29 and November 12, 1973, containing respectively Berrigan's "Responses to Settler Regimes" and Hertzberg's reply). Was this an attempt to smear Berrigan? Is the charge of anti-Semitism against political critics of Israel being employed as a coercive tactic?

A fair reading of Hertzberg's piece must lead to the conclusion that he has done his utmost to misunderstand Berrigan. He deliberately misquotes Berrigan in order to bolster his own claim that the priest favors the destruction of Israel, and he totally disregards the central questions raised by Berrigan, dismissing them as "horror stories." Nevertheless, Hertzberg has some grounds for accusing Berrigan of anti-Semitism. As the Jewish leader sees it, bias is the only possible explanation for what he considers Berrigan's perversity in posing as a "prophet" calling Israel to account. However, by citing its "Jewishness" as a ground for his criticism of Israel, Berrigan has given Hertzberg a sounder basis for the anti-Semitism charge.

The question of Israel's Jewishness is what animates both Berrigan and Hertzberg. On the one hand, Israel is a state claiming all the rights and privileges of modern nations, so that no special conditions such as exceptional ethical requirements should be placed upon it. On the other hand, Israel is essentially and above all a Jewish state, and as such claims special status.

Berrigan thinks it fair to level against Israel the same charges of nationalism, militarism and exploitation that he has already made against other countries (especially the U.S.). But at the same time he cannot resist saying that Israel is particularly guilty because as a Jewish state it should know better (than America, for instance?). As he sees it, the State of Israel can be especially castigated for moral failure. Not only has it been an errant modern state; it has sold its birthright. Consequently, in Berrigan's view, Zionism is a pseudo-Jewish nationalism engaged in "cold war" exploitation of humanity.

But Hertzberg holds that Israel should not be judged differently from other nations, and that in the exercise of nationalistic power Israel's record compares quite favorably with that of other modern states. At the same time, he claims that, whatever the remaining ambiguities concerning the conflict between Israel's rights and the rights of Palestinians, they can be morally interpreted in favor of Israel, because the State of Israel is necessary for Jewish existence. He sees Israel as fundamentally a religious community, and Zionism as a courageous affirmation of Jewish identity.

What is the meaning of this failure of dialogue between Christian and Jew? Is it not that Berrigan's pseudo-theological indictment of Israel and Hertzberg's pseudo-ethical defense of Israel reflect an identity crisis on the part of both Judaism and Christianity?

Berrigan understands his Christian faith in strictly ethical terms (though Christianity is not really a religion of ethics). On the basis of this mistake he views Jewishness as ethically normative for Christianity, and consequently charges Israel with repudiating its theological inheritance because of its moral failure. Indeed, for Berrigan the true Jew is ethically pure, a "suffering servant"; and in fact he sees himself as a true Jew in that sense, which also defines Christianity for him.

Hertzberg is especially agitated about Berrigan because the latter's ethical view of Jewishness represents the fundamental temptation for a modern Jew. The Holocaust exposed the insufficiency of interpreting Judaism as a religion of ethics. When Jews confront holocaust, they realize that there is about their existence a fearsome particularity which eludes moral categories and demands a response that is not simply ethical. Despite Hertzberg's attempted defense of Israel on ethical grounds, his real argument for Israel is "the continuity of community." In this sense, Zionism is more profoundly rooted in theological, considerations than in ethical concerns.

I suggest that Christians can repudiate anti-Semitism by (1) supporting Zionism on theological grounds and (2) criticizing it on ethical grounds. As to the first point, Christians have a positive theological investment in a Zionism which makes for a viable Jewish state. Jews are an empirical reminder of the entire human-historical dimension of the Christian faith, inasmuch as Jews are a vital sign of the Jewishness of Jesus; that is, of his historical humanity. It is precisely the historicity of Jesus which has been dangerously obscured in Christian theological history—an obscuring which coincides, with anti-Semitism. So far as present-day Jews by their existence signify for Christians the real humaness of Jesus, they are a reminder of the identification of the whole historical-human realm with the human existence of Jesus.

For Christian faith this identification embraces all humanity as such, including Jews and their Jewishness; and the redemption of man rests directly upon this identification of God with all humanity in the historical being of Jesus. Jews, therefore, serve Christians as an inescapable witness to the historical arena as the location of God's action in the world. Christian support of a positive Zionism in the form of a Jewish state means support for the historical continuation of Jewish existence and repudiation of an anti-Semitism that is willing to take advantage of Jewish powerlessness.

As to the second point, Christians will be in controversy with Israeli nationalism as with every nationalism. Christians are called to a suffering-servant role; they are to identify in non-ideological concern with all authentic human suffering in the name of Jesus the Christ. Therefore, Christians are called to oppose a Zionism which plays the cold war game along with the exploiters of the world. For example, a Christian must stand with the dispossessed Palestinians against those who dispossess them.

Daniel Berrigan is right when he scathingly denounces the ruthless side of Israeli policies, but he flirts with anti-Semitism when he comes close to begrudging Jews any entry into the sphere of nationalism. Arthur Hertzberg is right when he claims that the privilege of nationalism is proper and necessary for Jews, but he errs egregiously when he substitutes the charge of anti-Semitism for an explanation of Israeli complicity in oppressive policies. Berrigan inappropriately uses "Zionism" to denounce Israel, and Hertzberg just as inappropriately throws the term "anti-Semitism" at Berrigan. . . .

Let Christians then see Jews as a positive sign of the historical anchorage of their faith; and let Jews see Christians as nondiscriminatory critics of nationalisms, even of Israeli nationalism. Let a Berrigan realize that Hertzberg's Zionism is a simple desire for space to be human in a vital Jewish way, and let a Hertzberg understand Berrigan's outcry as a courageously impartial identification with human suffering. In sum, let Jews and Christians alike appreciate the covenant nature each of the other's faith.

Further Resources

BOOKS

Cunningham, Philip A. and Arthur F. Starr, eds. *Sharing Shalom: a Process for Local Interfaith Dialogue between Christians and Jews.* New York: Paulist Press, 1998.

Klein Halevi, Yossi. *At the Entrance to the Garden of Eden: a Jew's Search for God with Christians and Muslims in the Holy Land.* New York: W. Morrow, 2002.

Perelmuter, Gorem, ed. *Reinterpreting Revelation and Tradition: Jews and Christians in Conversation.* Franklin, Wis.: Sheed & Ward, 2000.

PERIODICALS

"Catholics Reject Efforts to Convert Jews." *The Christian Century,* 119, no. 18, August 28, 2002, 16.

Levenson, Jon D. "How Not to Conduct Jewish-Christian Dialogue." *Commentary,* 112, no. 5, December 2001, 31.

Martin, James. "Of Many Things." *America,* 186, no. 6, February 25, 2002, 2.

WEBSITES

"Ecumenical Considerations on Jewish-Christian Dialogue." World Council of Churches. Available online at http://www.wcc-coe.org/wcc/what/interreligious/j-crel-e.html; website home page: http://www.wcc-coe.org/ (accessed February 26, 2003).

"Jewish-Christian Relations." International Council of Christians and Jews. Available online at http://www.jcrelations.net/ (accessed February 26, 2003).

Levenson, Jon D. How Not to Conduct Jewish-Christian Dialogue." Originally published in *Commentary Magazine,* December, 2001. Available online at http://www.findarticles.com/cf_0/m1061/5_112/80680260/p1/article.jhtml; website home page: http://www.findarticles.com (accessed February 26, 2003).

"Will the Real Evangelical Please Stand Up?"

Magazine article

By: Lerond Curry

Date: May 26, 1976

Source: Curry, Lerond. "Will the Real Evangelical Please Stand Up?" *Christian Century,* May 26, 1976, 512–516. Available online at http://www.religion-online.org/cgi-bin/relsearchd.dll/showarticle?item_id=1822 (accessed March 1, 2003).

About the Author: Lerond Curry (1938–) was born in Bowling Green, Kentucky. After receiving his doctorate from Florida State University in 1967, he became a professor of history and religion at Western Kentucky University, a position he held until 1970, at which time he joined Averett College as a professor of religion. Curry is a noted Ecumenical Christian and wrote *Protestant-Catholic Relations in America: World War I Through Vatican II* (1972). ∎

Introduction

The term "evangelical," as used in European Christianity, referred to the followers of Protestant Reformer Martin Luther (1483–1546). In the late eighteenth and early nineteenth centuries, Methodists in England were called Evangelicals. In the United States during the 1930s and 1940s, fundamentalist Christians were also known as

Evangelicals. Several evangelists during the 1970s became familiar names to Americans because of their television programs: Billy Graham, Robert Schuller, Kathryn Kuhlman, Oral Roberts, Pat Robertson, Paul Crouch, Jim Bakker, Tammy Faye Bakker, Jerry Falwell, and Jimmy Swaggart.

The liberal Protestant tradition in America can be traced to the nineteenth and twentieth centuries. William Ellery Channing, a Congregational minister in the nineteenth century, became a Unitarian and placed a great deal of stress on moral responsibility and social causes. In the later part of the nineteenth century and the early part of the twentieth century, Reverend Walter Rauschenbusch advocated the social gospel, a belief that Christianity must be applied toward the reduction of social problems in the society. More modern liberal Christian trends can be seen in the form of the liberation theologies (political, racial, and feminist).

Some of the characteristics commonly attributed to modern-day evangelical Christians were: practicing personal witnessing of one's faith, preaching to the masses, emphasizing the conversion of non-Christians to Christianity, meeting deep spiritual needs of the individual, and adhering to traditional Biblical beliefs.

In comparison, some of the characteristics commonly attributed to modern-day liberal Christians were: preaching a people-oriented gospel in politics and religion, supporting civil rights and ecumenical movements, advocating and working toward applying the social gospel in the society, and being open to religious pluralism.

Significance

Dr. Lerond Curry examined three major questions concerning Christian evangelicals. What exactly is a Christian evangelical? What is the difference between the terms, "evangelical Christian" and religiously "liberal Christian?" Can a person be evangelical and religiously liberal at the same time?

Curry did not approve of a strict dichotomy between evangelical and liberal Christians. Many Christians embody characteristics of both models. His thesis was that being a liberal Christian and an evangelical one were not necessarily mutually exclusive.

Curry considered himself to be both a liberal and an evangelical, and hoped that Christians would stop using these labels as categorical descriptions. He pointed out that these labels were ultimately artificial and capable of building obstacles to dialogue.

There were two primary reactions to Curry's arguments for a cessation of the Christian family infighting between the evangelicals and the liberals. The first reaction came from those who agreed that the time had come for a truce between these two factions. Too much

energy was being wasted in the war of words and religious convictions between the evangelicals and the liberals. Both groups were being true to their Christian values, and neither one could be faulted for their zealousness.

The second reaction to Curry's arguments was that he was being unrealistic in his appraisal that one could be an evangelical and a follower of liberal Christianity at the same time. He was seen as oversimplifying the differences in the theology and practice of these two groups. The followers of the evangelical movements continued on their own course, as did the supporters of the liberal Christian position. Christians on both sides reacted by stating that the differences between the groups was healthy and good, because it gave people more choices in determining their own personal paths to God.

Primary Source

"Will the Real Evangelical Please Stand Up?"
[excerpt]

SYNOPSIS: Professor Lerond Curry argues that the distinctions being made between evangelical Christians and liberal Christians were creating exaggerated and artificial categories. These labels were deemed to be especially faulty when it came to applying them to individual Christians. His conclusion was that a person could be both an evangelical and religiously liberal at the same time.

Two years or so ago I picked up an issue of a widely circulated religious publication and found a statement titled "A Declaration of Evangelical Social Concern." The document put into words many of the convictions which I had been moving toward since the days when I first began to grasp the social dimensions of the gospel. I subsequently became a co-signer of the Declaration, and I am glad to have my name associated with it.

However, as I read through that magazine, many of its pages devoted to events surrounding the issuance of the Declaration, I became increasingly puzzled. For the reports of the Chicago meetings that gave birth to the document indicated that some of the original signers had in their deliberations contrasted themselves, the "evangelicals," with other church people whom they called "liberals."

Their language perplexed me. For years I had used both terms to describe myself. I grew up in a tradition which was "evangelistic," and though I now recognize the folly of reducing evangelism to acts of "personal witnessing" or of preaching to the masses, I have never lost the conviction that there is a gospel,

A billboard in South Carolina promoting National Bible Week in 1979, reads, "Welcome to the Bible, Come Inside . . . for the Good Life." Lerond Curry questioned if evangelism like this is as mutually exclusive with liberal Christianity as it is often portrayed. © FRANKEN OWEN/CORBIS. REPRODUCED BY PERMISSION.

an euangelion, and that it should be shared. Because of my commitment to this euangelion I have always thought myself to be evangelical.

A People-Oriented Gospel

I never heard the terms "liberal" and "conservative" until I was about 2 or 3 years old, but from that time I heard them used in ways which made the term "liberal" more descriptive of the convictions I was forming. As I matured, I kept hearing the term "liberal" used to describe thinking like my own—thinking which seemed to grow out of a basic concern for the gospel itself. Those whose political priorities were people-oriented rather than money-oriented or corporation-oriented were called liberal; and though I did not see politics as the salvation of the world, I felt that the gospel should have root influence in all my thinking. The Christ of the gospel was people-oriented; therefore, if to be people-oriented in politics was to be liberal, then I was happy to be called liberal. Those who supported civil rights goals were called liberal, and I felt that supporting these goals gave expression to my biblically oriented belief in the dignity and worth of all people. Those who in reli-

gious faith believed in intellectual honesty—indeed, in intellectual openness—as an expression of one's trust in God as the source of all truth were called liberal. Those who in church life believed in ecumenical Christianity because they took seriously the prayer of Jesus that his followers may be one (see John 17:11) were called liberal. If all these things meant being "liberal," then I was more than ready to embrace the term.

It continues to baffle me that "evangelical" is frequently used to suggest a spiritual virtue in contrast to "liberal" or to some other perfectly honorable word. I am not satisfied when I am told that the word liberal describes a 19th century view of humankind based on a view of Absolute Idealism. I know enough philosophy and historical theology to know when these disciplines are not the topic of discussion—and they are not in most of the places where I hear the term "evangelical" contrasted to "liberal." "Evangelical" is being used not in the sense that European Christians use it but to describe what Robert Ellwood calls a "mood or style" (*One Way: The Jesus Movement and Its Meaning* [Prentice-Hall, 1973], p. 25).

Defining the Terms

I am distressed too by the sloppy way in which so many who call themselves evangelicals throw other terms around. In otherwise sound and provocative essays and volumes the word is used in contrast to other words without any clear definitions of what the writer means. Donald Bloesch's book *The Evangelical Renaissance* is basically a courageous call for openness of attitude and spirit. Yet Bloesch tosses terms about as if his very use of them established some ecclesiastical or theological fact. For example, on page 7 he speaks of "both ecumenists and evangelicals." Are the two mutually exclusive? But on the next page he declares: "I try to speak as one who is both evangelical and ecumenical." I do too, and so I might conclude that Bloesch and I are of one mind. But in speaking of "evangelicals and liberals" he declares that "an evangelical church, unlike a liberal church, will have a passion to convert the world" (p.17). And then, as if the statement were axiomatic, he equates the terms "evangelical" and "conservative" and gives the term "liberal" another bad mark by saying, in reference to Dean Kelley's book *Why Conservative Churches Are Growing,* that "conservative churches seek to meet those deep spiritual needs while liberal churches seem to be more interested in working for social change" (p. 18). In his scheme of things it seems that one who claims to be liberal necessarily lacks a strong desire to take the gospel to the world and to meet people's "deep spiritual needs." What he has done is to set forth his own definitions and to structure his own view of the Christian world around them. But the definitions and contrasts are tenuous.

This tactic is little different from the error I once committed in a political bull session in graduate school when I said, "Conservatives do not believe in progress"—to which a friend replied, "Since you have set up your own definitions, no one can argue with you." Of course he was right. I had structured the world to suit myself, around my own emotional responses to certain terms, but this did not make what I described the real world. Similarly, the characterizations of those who claim the word "liberal" made by many who call themselves "evangelicals" are not necessarily accurate.

The Cross and the Flag (edited by Robert Clouse, Robert Linder and Richard Pierard [Creation House, 1972]) is a commendable book in its social concern and its attempt to end the marriage between some brands of popular religious thinking and right-wing ideas. Yet in discussing liberal politics one contributor asserts that "Christians must reject the liberal concept of freedom as nothing more than the absence of restraint." (Apply that view of freedom to corporations, and the concept suddenly becomes conservative!) And: "The Christian rejects the liberal concept that the human condition is fundamentally a product of the environment" (p. 87). As a political liberal I do not believe either of those "liberal" concepts. I support liberal causes and candidates because they are more often people-oriented, and to be people-oriented is to be consistent with the ethics of Jesus of Nazareth.

Evangelical One-Upmanship

But what bothers me even more than the imprecise use of other terms is the evidence of one-upmanship in the use of the term "evangelical" itself. A noticeable segment of the religious population takes this term, defines it by imposing doctrinal conclusions on what is basically an English derivative of the Greek word for "good news," and reads the rest of the religious population out of its circle of definition. In doing so the definers are really saying that "evangelical" means what they have said it means. Instead of "good theology" this is actually the fallacy of *petitio principii,* known commonly as begging the question or circular reasoning.

Just recently, in thumbing through one of America's better-known "evangelical" publications, I found a list of the nation's four-year "evangelical" colleges. What struck me was that all the schools listed seemed similarly "conservative" in the extreme. The editors admitted leaving out schools "associated with Seventh-day Adventists, non-instrumental Churches of Christ, Church of the Brethren, Lutherans, and Southern Baptists" because so many of them were so denominationally oriented (*Christianity Today,* November 7, 1975, pp. 39-41). But the list included only one United Presbyterian school, though there are probably over 20; only one Presbyterian U.S. school, when there are 17; only two American Baptist schools, though there are 22; no Disciples of Christ schools; no schools affiliated with the United Church of Christ, despite a heritage which includes the Evangelical and Reformed denomination; and no United Methodist schools, though that denomination has the rich tradition of the Evangelical United Brethren. The list is preceded by a statement that some of the colleges in omitted groups are "no longer sectarian but have become too pervaded, in our judgment, by nonevangelical views of the Bible, theology, and ethics."

In other words, the editors imply, to be "evangelical" means to agree with them. And because the word "evangelical" calls to mind the word euangelion, if one does not agree with them one is by implication not soundly committed to the gospel.

I so much as heard Harold Ockenga (now president of Gordon-Conwell Theological Seminary) say this once in a freshman assembly at a state university where I was teaching. He spoke on modern theological movements; before several hundred 18-year-olds—many of them less than six months out of small towns and rural churches, many others from no substantial religious backgrounds at all—he talked about the "liberal" and "modernistic" trends that had resulted in something that wasn't Christianity at all. He then told them, almost in passing, about "neo-orthodoxy": though it had some truth to it, it wasn't the real thing. Finally, he told them about "orthodoxy"—wherein lay the truth. Of course I had to explain his remarks to my freshman honors students later, for none of them—much less the other freshmen—had even understood what he was talking about. But though I did tell them what I thought to be the essence of Ockenga's address—that there were many theological positions but that his was the "right" one—I did not tell them that he was also a champion of political conservatism. . . .

Putting Aside the Labels

Those of us who have been excluded from the boundaries of the term "evangelical" by persons who have drawn the boundaries too narrowly must avoid reading these people out of the Kingdom. The teaching of Jesus to "love your enemies" applies to us as well. Frankly I find much to feed my spirit in writings of both the self-styled evangelicals and their critics, and for years I have remained puzzled over what many of the squabbles are really about. Both sides have resorted to knocking over straw men.

I propose that the church begin by putting aside the rampant use of labels. Whatever the shorthand labels, they quickly become flags around which people rally or barriers that divide. One "evangelical" journal to which I submitted an article pleading for attention to people instead of labels sent it back to me with the explanation that my characterization of myself as a liberal would "not be effective with our readership." This of course demonstrated the very point of my article—that all labels are ultimately artificial and capable of creating artificial barriers.

The church, if it must use labels, should use them as invitations to dialogue. I suggest the following "propositions" as a beginning: (1) The term "evangelical" refers at root to one's primary commitment. (2) If one's primary commitment is to the gospel—the euangelion—that is what is basic. (3) The gospel is the Christ Event. (4) Theological conclusions, because they vary and change in each of us, are not necessarily identical with our basic commitments. Indeed, our commitments may be the causes of some of the changes which take place. (5) We should talk to one another at the level of commitment and "judge not."

If these "propositions" are taken seriously, then the next step is to get those who think they are the evangelicals together with those whom they think are not—to talk and pray. For those of us interested in ecumenism as a theological verity, it would certainly be a necessary step. (What greater ecumenical breakthrough than an exchange of lecturers between Moody Bible Institute and the divinity school of the University of Chicago?) But more broadly it can be a revealing step. All of us might discover the following:

1. That Jesus' call is to discipleship and not to labels. That he did not say "Follow me and I will make you a conservative," or "Follow me and I will make you a liberal," or even "Follow me and I will make you an evangelical." To fishermen he said "fishers of men" and to his followers generally he simply said "followers"—disciples.

2. That Jesus had among his first disciples both Matthew the publican and Simon the zealot—an establishment conservative and a radical revolutionary—and that therefore temperament is not the mark of discipleship.

3. That the Spirit, like the wind—in both cases the pneuma—"blows where it wills"—a hint that God is not captive of theological systems nor the prior possession of certain ones.

4. That Jesus once admonished his disciples for forbidding those with another identity from casting out demons in his name and told them that "no one who does a mighty work in my name will soon after be able to speak ill of me," and that "he that is not against us is for us."

5. That, as a speaker at one ecumenical conference remarked, "brothers don't have to be twins"—but brothers should be brothers.

Further Resources

BOOKS

Ellingsen, Mark. *The Evangelical Movement: Growth, Impact, Controversy, Dialog.* Minneapolis, Minn.: Augsburg Pub. House, 1988.

June, Lee N., ed. *Evangelism & Discipleship In African-American Churches.* Grand Rapids, Mich.: Zondervan Publishing House, 1999.

Terry, John Mark. *Evangelism: a Concise History.* Nashville, Tenn.: Broadman & Holman, 1994.

PERIODICALS

George, Timothy. "If I'm an Evangelical, What Am I?" *Christianity Today,* 43, no. 9, August 9, 1999, 62.

Winner, Lauren F. "From Mass Evangelist to Soul Friend." *Christianity Today,* 44, no. 11, Oct 2, 2000, 56.

Wright, Rusty. "Downtown Evangelism Makes a Comeback." *Christianity Today,* 45, no. 1, Jan 8, 2001, 24.

WEBSITES

"Christians Online." Fish the Net- The Evangelistic Tacklebox. Available online at http://www.fishthe.net/ (accessed March 1, 2003).

"Evangelism Toolbox- Online Resources." Available online at http://www.evangelismtoolbox.com/ (accessed March 1, 2003).

"Online Web Evangelism Guide- Focus Page." Brigada Today. Available online at http://www.brigada.org/today/articles/web-evangelism.html; website home page: http://www.brigada.org (accessed March 1, 2003).

Fully Human, Fully Alive

Theological work

By: John Powell

Date: 1976

Source: Powell, John. *Fully Human, Fully Alive.* Niles, Illinois: Argus Communications, 1976, 169, 170–171, 176–178, 179–180, 181–185.

About the Author: John Joseph Powell (1925–), born in Chicago, was ordained a Roman Catholic priest. He earned degrees in theology, psychology, classics, and English. For many years, he was a professor of theology at Loyola University of Chicago, and throughout his career, he wrote several best-selling books. Among them are *Why Am I Afraid to Tell You Who I Am?* (1965), *Why Am I Afraid to Love?* (1975) and *Touched by God: My Pilgrimage of Prayer* (1996). ∎

Introduction

Religious observers have often commented that the latter half of the twentieth century could be characterized as a time when many Americans experienced a great spiritual void. Traditional religious beliefs and practices, a source of comfort to their parents and previous generations, were no longer applicable to the lives of many people.

In these people, there was a deep spiritual hunger, as expressed by searching for meaning in their lives and deeper ways of relating to God. Many people expressed a fundamental unhappiness with their day-to-day existence. There was not necessarily a lack of material items or physical wants that contributed to this discontent, but there was an emptiness within one's self. Was there any meaning to be found in living other than the daily meeting of one's physical needs and comfort?

During the 1960s and 1970s, there was much discontent in the nation that was expressed through a number of social movements. The search for racial justice, equality for women, reduction of poverty, and peace in Vietnam led to a number of protests and demonstrations, questioning the resolve of the government to deal with these issues. The unhappiness with the government was also accompanied by disenchantment with the institutions of education, the family, and religion. It seemed that almost everything was open to criticism and dissatisfaction, including religious values and practices. In order to help fill their spiritual emptiness, some people turned to destructive behaviors like drugs, alcohol, and other forms of escapism.

As a teacher and spiritual counselor, Father John Powell, a Roman Catholic priest, was exposed to people who expressed to him this basic unhappiness with their lives. Life lacked the joy that they desired and needed. Could he help them find meaning and happiness in a seemingly meaningless and unhappy world?

Significance

In trying to reach out to help these people and others suffering in the same manner, Powell wrote *Fully Human, Fully Alive.* The focus of his book was vision therapy, or the creation of a new life through the adoption of new perceptions. He believed that God intended all humans to experience happiness, and he wanted to show how this could be done.

Powell's thesis was that the process of becoming a complete fully alive human being was based upon three factors: the nature of one's intrapersonal dynamics (those qualities existing within the individual self or mind), interpersonal relationships (those qualities that mark how one deals with other people), and a frame of reference. In his previous books, he centered upon the first two. In *Fully Human, Fully Alive,* his concern shifted to the third factor: a frame of reference.

Powell defined a frame of reference as a person's basic perception or vision of reality. This perception or vision affected the way people made judgments, interpretations, and sense in the understanding of any new persons, events, and ideas that they may encounter. In order to become fully human and fully alive, one's frame of reference must include a relationship with God.

Fully Human, Fully Alive met the needs of a spiritually hungry public in the 1970s and in future decades. Powell's contribution to happiness and mental health was

John Powell's book *Fully Human, Fully Alive* promotes a combination of spiritual development and psychological conditioning as means to attain personal happiness. Here, Gerald Jampolsky, a psychiatrist who also encouraged spiritual development as a way of healing, leads a group of terminally ill children and teens in group therapy. © TED STRESHINSKY/CORBIS. REPRODUCED BY PERMISSION.

a result of his blending the concepts of personal growth, through the principles of psychology, with spiritual development, offered by religious thought. By following the steps in his vision therapy as presented in his book, people were better able to identify the unrealistic perceptions that they held. They learned how to correct these distortions and achieve a fuller sense of the joy of being a complete human being.

Primary Source

Fully Human, Fully Alive [excerpt]

> **SYNOPSIS:** Reverend Powell discussed the dynamics of the individual's perception of reality, how it affected the quality of life, and how it shaped that person's vision of life. For those seeking happiness, Powell presented his answer of vision therapy. The excerpts are taken from *Fully Human, Fully Alive,* chapter eight, "Vision Therapy and Religious Faith, An Appendix for Believers."

We need some version of reality by which we can judge the rationality of our thoughts and to which we can conform our vision or belief system. But who is to say what reality is? . . .

Psychologists are reasonable and honest in facing this problem. There are many slightly different solutions. Some suggest that we use a "universal consensus": Reality is that which most people think it is. There are others who offer the pragmatic solution of "what works" as a criterion of reality. There are still others who speak only of an "individual and personal" reality, suggesting that each person has his or her own reality. It is true, of course, that all of us perceive reality, whatever it is, in our own uniquely rational and uniquely irrational ways. . . .

Those who believe in revealed religions have a very definite criterion of reality. They are convinced that God himself has told us in his revelation some very important things about who he is, who we are, about our relationship to one another, about the purpose of life and the significance of this world. There is no logic, of course, either to prove or disprove the authenticity of this revelation of God. Ultimately, the test of faith is always religious experience, which is highly personal and individual. Most believers have at some time felt the touch of God, a conversion-to-faith experience in which they have found a new and distinct peace, power, and presence. The intuition of faith, in this moment, surpasses the reach of all natural logic and scientific knowledge.

This has certainly been my experience, as I have related it in my book, *He Touched Me.* Because of my own religious background and personal experience I have accepted the message of Jesus Christ as the master vision of reality. For me the message and person of Jesus are the source of objectification for my own vision of reality. They are the basic norm for my judgments and choices. I have chosen to live my life in the light of this revelation. I want to be God's man and to do God's work: I want to help build a world of love and a human family of mutual understanding. . . .

What is the vision of Jesus which lies under his message and manner of life? Whatever else it is, it is certainly a call to the fullness of life.

> I am come that they may have life and have it to the full.

(John 10, 10)

At the risk of seeming presumptuous, I would like now to describe some of the central features of the vision of Jesus, as I see them. I think that the message, the life, and the person of Jesus are saying to us:

1. *God is Love.* This means that all God does is love. As the sun only shines, conferring its light and warmth on those who stand ready to receive them, so God only loves, conferring his light and warmth on those who would receive them. This means that God does not have anger in him. He does not punish. When we separate ourselves from God and his love by sin, all the change takes place in us, never in him. He is unchangeably loving. Love is sharing, the sharing of one's self and one's life. God's intention in creating us in this world was to share himself and his life with us. In fathering this life in us, God calls us to be his human family, to become a community of love, each wanting and working for the true happiness of all.

2. *You are loved by God, unconditionally and as you are.* God has assured you through his prophets and through his Son that, even if a mother were to forget the child of her womb, he would never forget you. Your name is carved in the palms of his hands, inscribed indelibly in his heart. You do not have to win or earn or be worthy of his love. It is a "given." Of course, you can refuse to accept it. You can separate yourself from God's love for a while or even for an eternity. Whatever your response, all during your life and at every moment of your life he will be there offering his love to you, even at those times when you are distracted or refusing it.

Wherever you are in your development, whatever you are doing, with a strong affirmation of all your goodness and good deeds, with a gentle understanding of your weakness, God is forever loving you. You do not have to change, grow, or be good in order to be loved. Rather, you are loved so that you can change, grow, and be good. . . .

3. *The Providence of God rules the world. Jesus is the Lord of human history.* At times you may experience the feeling that everything is falling apart. You wonder: What is the world coming to? What am I coming to? How will I make ends meet? Who is going to push my wheelchair? You do not consciously define or defend the thought, but sometimes you may be tempted to imagine God with his back to the wall, furious and frustrated at the fact that everything has gotten out of hand. "King Christ, this world is aleak; and lifepreservers there are none" (e. e. cummings). In the words of St. Paul: "Jesus is the Lord!" You must remember that this world, the course of human history and human destiny are in his hands. He is in charge of this world. He alone has the game plan, total knowledge of the human situation and the power to turn things around completely. Do not try to make yourself the Messiah to all people or caretaker to the world. You are not equipped to cover so much territory or bear such a burden. . . .

4. *You are called to love: your God, your self, and your neighbor.* God, who is love, has made you in his image and likeness. Love is your calling and destiny. It is the perfection of your human nature. Love is also a gift of God, the highest gift of God's Spirit. It is necessary that you realize the importance of loving yourself. There has to be some kind of logical, if not chronological, priority to loving yourself. If you do not love yourself, you will be filled with pain, and this pain will keep all your attention riveted on yourself. Agony constricts our consciousness. If you do not love yourself, you cannot truly love either God or your neighbor. So you must learn to do the same things for yourself that you would do in loving others: You must acknowledge and affirm all that is good in you. You must gently try to understand all that is weak and limited. You must be aware of and try to fulfill your needs: physical, psychological, and spiritual. As you learn to love yourself, you must also learn to balance concern for yourself with concern for others. "Whatever you do for the least of my brothers you do for me." But remember that your success in loving will be proportionate to your openness in accepting the love and

affirmation of God. It will likewise be proportionate to the love which you have for yourself. In the end, the success of your life will be judged by how sensitively and delicately you have loved.

5. *I will be with you.* God says: I am covenanted, committed forever to love you; to do whatever is best for you. I will be kind, encouraging and enabling, but I will also be challenging. At times I will come to comfort you in your affliction. At other times I will come to afflict you in your comfort. Whatever I do, it will always be an act of love and an invitation to growth. I will be with you to illuminate your darkness, to strengthen your weakness, to fill your emptiness, to heal your brokenness, to cure your sickness, to straighten what may be bent in you, and to revive whatever good things may have died in you. Remain united to me, accept my love, enjoy the warmth of my friendship, avail yourself of my power, and you will bear much fruit. You will have life in all its fullness.

6. *Your destiny is eternal life.* God says: By all means join the dance and sing the songs of a full life. At the same time, remember that you are a pilgrim. You are on your way to an eternal home which I have prepared for you. Eternal life has already begun in you but it is not perfectly completed. There are still inevitable sufferings. But remember that the sufferings of this present stage of your life are nothing compared to the glory that you will see revealed in you someday. Eye has not ever seen, nor ear ever heard, nor has the mind of man ever imagined the joy prepared for you because you have opened yourself to the gift of my love. On your way to our eternal home, enjoy the journey. Let your happiness be double, in the joyful possession of what you have and in the eager anticipation of what will be. Say a resounding "Yes!" to life and to love at all times. Someday you will come up into my mountain, and then for you all the clocks and calendars will have finished their counting. Together with all my children, you will be mine and I will be yours forever.

This is, as I see it, the basic vision proposed in the gospels (the good news) of Christians. It offers a perspective of life and death—a vision of reality— that is reassuring and at the same time challenging. It provides a needed sense of security, but also meaning and purpose in life. It gives us a basic frame of reference to understand ourselves, our brothers and sisters in the human family, the meaning of life and the world, and God as our loving Father. For the believer it offers a vision of reality or belief system through which all the activating events of our human lives can be interpreted and evaluated. It is a reassurance of what reality is by the Maker of all that is.

This vision of religious faith remains for some people a sweet but mere construct, only a pair of lovely rose-colored glasses to tint and tone down the harsh demands of reality. Again, the decisive factor is personal religious experience, the touch of God. One must be actively engaged with and educated by the Holy Spirit, who alone can make a person a believer. Faith is not a matter of logical reasoning or a natural acquisition. It is a matter of experience. Only God's Spirit can provide the needed religious experience. Only the touch of grace can make the Christian message more than a code of conduct and comfort for pious and plastic people.

It cannot be repeated too often that a living faith is not a human skill or acquisition. We do not pick up "believing" as we would learn, for example, to play the piano. We must be touched by the Spirit of God. The difference in one who has been touched in this way is so profound that St. Paul calls this person a "new creation." Such a one is, as we say, a new person. Paul calls a life which has not been touched and transformed by the Spirit "life according to the flesh." The life of a person who has been renewed by the Spirit lives a "life according to the Spirit."

Jesus says that it is the Spirit who gives us a certain instinct or intuition that we are affirmed by God. It is through the Spirit that we know we are his beloved children. It is the Spirit who calls out of our hearts the tender and loving word: "Father!"

Further Resources

BOOKS

Powell, John Joseph. *The Christian Vision: The Truth that Sets Us.* Free Allen, Tex.: Argus Communications, 1984.

Powell, John Joseph. *The Mystery of the Church.* Milwaukee, Wis.: Bruce Publishing Co., 1967.

Powell, John Joseph. *Why Am I Afraid to Tell You Who I Am? (Insights on Self-Awareness, Personal Growth and Interpersonal Communication).* Chicago, Ill.: Argus Communications, 1969.

PERIODICALS

Andrusko, Dave. "Abortion: The Silent Holocaust." *National Right to Life News,* 25, no. 5, April 14, 1998, 18.

Graff, Ann O'Hara. "A Life-Giving Vision: How to Be a Christian in Today's World." *America,* 174, no. 16, May 11, 1996, 27.

Powell, John. "Tommy: A Story of Love and a Search for God." *Catholic Insight,* 10, no. 3, April 2002, 11.

WEBSITES

"Favorite Quotes from John Powell, S.J." AOL Hometown. Available online at http://members.aol.com/CeMesLily /quotes/favquotes.htm (accessed March 1, 2003).

Powell, John. "The 3 M's in Family." 30 Good Minutes. Available online at http://www.30goodminutes.org/csec/sermon/powell_3602.htm; website home page: http://www.30good minutes.org (accessed March 1, 2003).

"Stories from My Heart, Excerpts From A New Book By Fr. John Powell, S.J." Jesuits, Chicago Province of the Society of Jesus Available online at http://www.jesuits-chi.org/contact magazine/2002spring/stories.htm; website home page: http://www.jesuits-chi.org (accessed March 1, 2003).

The American Catholic: A Social Portrait

Nonfiction work

By: Andrew M. Greeley

Date: 1977

Source: Greeley, Andrew M. *The American Catholic: A Social Portrait*. New York: Basic Books, 1977, 9–12, 126–127.

About the Author: Andrew Moran Greeley (1928–) was born in Oak Park, Illinois. An ordained Catholic priest and distinguished sociologist, Greeley is also a prolific author, having written more than thirty novels and hundreds of scholarly and popular articles on religion, education, and various issues in sociology. Greeley is a professor of sociology, and has been awarded numerous honors for his writing and research. ∎

Introduction

Ever since the major immigration cycles of European Catholics to the United States in the early twentieth century, Roman Catholics have faced the major task of adapting to a predominantly Protestant-based culture. As the decades passed, many of these Catholic immigrants gradually became accepted as "good" Americans by Protestants and other non-Catholics, even though they retained their religious allegiance to the Roman Catholic Church. But there were still many misconceptions about who these Catholics were and what they really believed. Andrew Greeley became aware of the need to explain the Catholic experience in America and to reduce the amount of misinformation about Catholics.

One of the most prolific researchers of Roman Catholicism in America, Father Greeley embarked on several studies during the 1960s and 1970s that would ultimately provide the public with a more accurate portrait of Roman Catholics and their faith.

In *The Hesitant Pilgrim; American Catholicism After the Council* (1966), he discussed his findings of the effects of the Second Vatican Council on Catholics in the United States. In that same year, Greeley's *The Education of American Catholics* reported the evidence that American Catholics were becoming the best educated of American ethnic groups.

Can Catholic Schools Survive? was released in 1970. Greeley noted that since the very beginning, the existence of Catholic schools in America was controversial. Within the Catholic community, there were major questions being raised concerning the future of Catholic schools and whether they should even exist in American society.

In 1972, *That Most Distressful Nation: The Taming of the American Irish* was published. Greeley summarized the historical background of the Irish experience in America, with a particular emphasis on the roles of the Roman Catholic Church, the immigrant family, and the political participation of this ethnic group. He also addressed his findings on the relationships between the Irish Catholics and the African Americans.

Greeley summarized the information from these books and more in *The American Catholic: A Social Portrait*. This was the first book to consider and analyze the American Catholic experience from a sociological perspective.

Significance

The American Catholic: A Social Portrait was received as a major accomplishment in helping to reduce the misconceptions about Roman Catholics and increasing the positive perceptions by non-Catholics of the people who followed this faith. The finding that American Catholicism was not monolithic—in that most Catholics did not always "march in lockstep" with the wishes of the Pope in Rome—was especially helpful in reducing stereotypes.

Greeley noted the growing independence of American Catholics away from the authority of the pope during the 1970s. Despite the condemnation of birth control by Pope Paul VI in his "Encyclical on the Regulation of Birth" (Humanae Vitae) issued in 1968, Greeley found that a large number of Catholics, both laity and clergy, were making their own judgments about the morality of birth control. Surveys taken by other researchers on this issue during the 1980s and 1990s have confirmed his findings.

Greeley's studies also showed that the social-economic status of Roman Catholics and their educational levels were rising. This trend has continued into subsequent decades. At the beginning of the twenty-first century, American Catholics of Irish, Italian, German, Polish, and Slavic ethnic backgrounds were continuing to make gains in income and educational achievements. Catholic ethnic groups have shown that the melting pot characterization of American immigrants was a reality, and proved the validity of Greeley's thesis that these groups would succeed. Many Catholic immigrant groups from Mexico, the Caribbean, and Latin America, however, have not had the same success.

The book was praised not only by non-Catholics who wanted to better understand their Catholic neighbors, but also by Catholics themselves who learned much about

Prominent sociologist, novelist, and Catholic priest Father Andrew Greeley. AP/WIDE WORLD PHOTOS. REPRODUCED BY PERMISSION.

who they were, where they came from, and where they were going.

Primary Source

The American Catholic: A Social Portrait [excerpt]

SYNOPSIS: *The American Catholic* was the first publication of its kind in that it considered American Catholicism from a sociological perspective. In these excerpts Greeley explores the history of American attitudes toward Catholics, some misconceptions about them, and changes taking place in the American Catholic community.

Models for Viewing American Catholicism

This portrait of American Catholics is essentially a study in acculturation—in the broadest sense of the word. It is an attempt to measure how Catholic immigrants and their descendants have adjusted to a society which already had its own culture, social structure, and politics at the time the immigrants began to arrive. American Catholics are an ethnic group, in the general sense of the term, as well as being a group of ethnic groups, in the specific use of the word "ethnic" as meaning descendants of European immigrants.

The Catholic collectivity is a group which is in some respects different from the host culture. There are boundaries between Catholics and others in the United States. These boundaries are not legal, for the most part, although there are boundary-setting consequences of laws or judicial decisions. The Supreme Court decisions on Catholic schools, for example, set legal boundaries around those schools. Court decisions on "integration" (the so-called "affirmative action") in many cases discriminate against Catholics, because in many large urban centers discrimination in favor of nonwhites inevitably becomes discrimination against Catholics. However, the boundaries among religious groups in American society are cultural and social for the most part; they are implicit and unofficial.

Few subjects in American social science are more likely to stir up emotions and moral passions than ethnicity and acculturation. The pictures one carries around in one's head which deal with such subjects are not only descriptive—they are frequently prescriptive. One feels that one knows not only what has happened but that what has happened should have happened. Any attempt to question the factuality of the process is morally offensive. The moral passions which led to the restrictive immigration legislation in 1920 were based on a broad national consensus that the goal of acculturation was the assimilation of immigrant groups so that they lost their identities, and that the masses of southern and eastern European Catholic immigrants who were pouring into the society would be very difficult, if not impossible, to assimilate. The national consensus after World War I was xenophobic. (Early immigration laws required only an oath of allegiance, and the English language was not required for citizenship prior to 1907.) The strange, dark-skinned, oddly named immigrants from eastern and southern Europe were perceived as a threat to society. Their assimilation was considered a major challenge which had to be met if the society was to survive and remain healthy, and the public high school in particular was touted as the principal agent of assimilation. It was to undo all the bad habits and strange, crazy customs the children of immigrants picked up in their family environments.

The restrictive immigration legislation has been repealed, but the model of society which underlay it is still quasi official: children and grandchildren of the last waves of immigrants ought to become indistinguishable from "everybody else." A somewhat less rigid model is the "melting pot." In the "melting down" that was supposed to take place in the public cauldron, some of the characteristics of the more recent immigrant groups would be lost, others would be preserved to become part of the common heritage. Similarly, one supposes, in any effective melting pot, some of the characteristics of the host culture would be burned out, too. But the "official" assumptions of the last half century have certainly been that if anyone was going to change at all it would be the immigrants.

At a higher level of ethnic generalization, Catholicism was always viewed with dark suspicion by a sufficiently large group in the society to make it a convenient scapegoat for many social ills—both real and imagined. In the early years of the century it was the unknown dark southern and eastern European Catholics who were suspected of bringing dangerous radical ideas to the United States, and during World War I it was the largely loyal and partly Catholic German group that was thought to be treasonable. Much of the xenophobia of Attorney General A. Mitchell Palmer's crusade in the early 1920s paralleled the resurgence of anti-Catholic nativism in the post-World War I Ku Klux Klan, and both were partly manifestations of the more serious xenophobia against groups which "just happened" to be Catholic that was apparent in the report of the Dillingham commission. Paradoxically, a mere thirty years later, during the McCarthy era, the intellectual and cultural elite of America fantasized exactly the opposite position for Catholics. Instead of being the appropriate objects of the "red scare," they were among its principal advocates. Similarly, in the late 1930s and the early 1940s, when the official liberal position was interventionist, the Catholic groups were denounced for being isolationist; in the 1960s, when the "liberal" position shifted to isolationism, the Catholic ethnics were assumed to be the "middle Americans, the hardhat hawks who pushed the war in Vietnam.

For none of these "pictures" of Catholics was there any very strong empirical evidence; indeed, both the radical right of the McCarthy era and the hawks of the Vietnam war were not disproportionately Catholic. On the contrary, as we shall see in a subsequent chapter, James Wright's research shows that from the beginning Catholics were more likely than other Americans to oppose the Vietnam involvement. Still, the power of assumptions, particularly when they take the form of symbolic pictures, is such that they are not really subject to proof or disproof by empirical evidence.

Catholics in general have been viewed with suspicion since the beginning of their arrival in any num-

bers, not only by the masses but also by the cultural elites. Catholics were tolerable, perhaps, but disturbingly different. In the ideal order of things Catholics would become more like everyone else; through the passage of time and the influence of education, the differences which separated Catholics from other Americans would be melted away. Their clannishness, their divisive school system, their rigid ecclesiastical "discipline" (to use a word Justice Powell resurrected from the 1920s), their unmarried clergy, their large families, their peculiar religious practices—all of these would gradually disappear. By the beginning of this century the children of Massachusetts no longer had to go to school on Christmas day because there was no longer suspicion of this celebration as a "popish" feast; but for the first six decades of this century it was not clear that a Catholic could be elected president. Catholics, it was argued, were sufficiently different from other Americans that their "foreign allegiance" made it impossible for them to serve in the highest office in the land. When a Catholic was finally elected president, it was despite the loss of several million votes because of his religion.

Perhaps one of the major reasons for the resurgence of anti-Catholicism in the late 1960s and early 1970s in the United States was frustration over the fact that the ecumenical movement, as endorsed by the Second Vatican Council, seemed to promise the end of Catholic strangeness. But Catholics kept their schools and their "divisive" attitudes on abortion. They did not stop being "strange" as the price for ecumenical dialogue. They have not yet been assimilated.

So the Catholic collectivity is an ethnic group as well as a congeries of smaller ethnic groups. Catholics constitute a group within the larger society, and are perceived both by others and by themselves to be different to some extent. Part of the official "melting pot" model of acculturation to American society is that the differences *ought* to go away. . . .

The Change in the Church

Anyone who reads the daily newspaper is aware that there has been major change in the Catholic church as institution. In the last decade the Vatican Council was front-page headlines: the mass has been changed into English, nuns wear secular dresses, priests and nuns have resigned from their work in substantial numbers, church attendance has declined, and Catholics eat meat on Friday, practice birth control despite their church's injunction, and are getting divorces freely (if still in not quite the same number as other Americans). The "experts" who specialize in interpreting American Catholicism for non-Catholic readers have rushed to provide explanations. The old Catholic culture, we are told by such Catholic writers as Garry Wills, Wilfred Sheed, Daniel Callahan, John Cogley, and the younger Michael Novak, could not survive the twin modernizing pressures of the Second Vatican Council and the acculturation of the immigrants. Catholics have become better educated, they now think for themselves; the Vatican Council, which started out as an attempt to bring the church into the modern world gently, has ended up destroying most of the old Catholic culture. From the point of view of the non-Catholic reader, the acculturation that he has long expected has finally happened. Education and Americanization are in the process of producing a version of Catholicism which, if not altogether acceptable to the old nativist, at least is not particularly objectionable.

Change is certainly going on in the relationship between the American Catholic collectivity and the institutional church, and it is going on at a rapid rate. But the "experts" are unencumbered by data; indeed they are quite innocent of it. They have misunderstood the cause and badly described the phenomenon. Corporate Catholicism has managed to get itself into a catastrophe, but it has little to do with the Vatican Council and by no means guarantees that Catholics are "becoming just like everyone else."

Two studies of the National Opinion Research Center (NORC) in 1963 and 1974 enabled us to measure quite precisely the magnitude of change in Catholicism. In 1963, 71 percent of the Catholic respondents reported weekly mass attendance. That proportion has now fallen to 50 percent. Those going to church "practically never" or "not at all" have increased from 6 to 12 percent, and those going to confession "practically never" or "not at all" have increased from 18 to 30 percent. Visits to the church to pray at least once a week have declined from 23 to 15 percent, and daily private prayer has fallen from 72 to 60 percent. The proportion who "never pray," however, remain low at 4 percent; the proportion who pray at least once a week continue to be a quite high 82 percent.

Many of the traditional forms of religious behavior have also declined. The percentage of Catholics who attended a retreat in the last two years has fallen from 7 percent to 4 percent over the decade between the two surveys. The percentage of those who made a day of recollection has fallen from 22 percent to 9 percent, making a mission has fallen

from 34 percent to 6 percent, reading a Catholic newspaper or magazine has fallen from 61 to 56 percent, and having a religious conversation with a priest has fallen from 24 to 20 percent.

However, some of the newer forms of religious life that were infrequent a decade ago have attained a surprising popularity. Six percent have attended a charismatic or pentacostal prayer meeting during the last two years, 8 percent an informal liturgy at home, 3 percent a marriage encounter, and 20 percent report having attended a religious discussion group.

The most notable positive change is an increase in the proportion receiving weekly communion—from 13 to 26 percent. Another way of putting this is that less than one-fifth of the weekly mass attenders received communion a decade ago; now more than half of the weekly churchgoers do.

Further Resources

BOOKS

Dolan, Jay P. *The American Catholic Experience: A History from Colonial Times to the Present.* Garden City, N.Y.: Image Books, 1985.

O'Dea, Thomas F. *American Catholic Dilemma: An Inquiry Into The Intellectual Life.* New York: Sheed and Ward, 1958.

Ong, Walter J. *American Catholic Crossroads; Religious-Secular Encounters in the Modern World.* New York: The Macmillan Company, 1959.

PERIODICALS

Berg, John-Leonard. "In Search of an American Catholicism: a History of Religion and Culture in Tension." *Library Journal,* 127, no. 14, Sept 1, 2002, 182.

Greeley, Andrew M. "Psychology and American Catholicism: from Confession to Therapy." *The Journal of Religion,* 82, no. 3, July 2002, 516.

Zimdars-Swartz, Sandra L. "The Smoke of Satan: Conservative and Traditionalist Dissent in Contemporary American Catholicism." *The Journal of Religion,* October 1998, 633.

WEBSITES

"ACTS Catholic Apologetics." American Catholic Truth Society. Available online at http://www.americancatholictruthsociety .com/ (accessed February 26, 2003).

American Catholic Philosophical Association. Available online at http://www.acpa-main.org/ (accessed February 26, 2003).

"Statements and Speeches." United States Conference of Catholic Bishops. Available online at http://www.nccbuscc .org/statements/htm; website home page: http://www.nccbuscc .org/ (accessed February 26, 2003).

Turning Your Stress Into Strength

Handbook

By: Robert Harold Schuller

Date: 1978

Source: Schuller, Robert Harold. *Turning Your Stress Into Strength.* Irvine, Calif.: Harvest House, 1978, 9–13, 141–144.

About the Author: Robert Harold Schuller (1926–) was born in Alton, Iowa. He received a bachelor's degree at Hope College in 1947, a bachelor of divinity at Western Theological Seminary in 1950, and a doctor of divinity at Hope College in 1973. He was ordained by the Reformed Church in America in 1950. In 1955 he became the founder and pastor of Garden Grove Community Church in California. He is noted for his television ministry that started in 1970 and for his dozens of religious books. ■

Introduction

The time period from the end of World War II (1939–1945) through the decade of the 1970s was one of marked stress for the average American. Instead of enjoying the "peace" that followed the completion of a devastating global war, a new set of stresses began to emerge. The "cold war" between the United States and the Union of Soviet Socialist Republics involved the possibilities of a nuclear confrontation between the Western democratic countries and the Communist nations. The "hot" Korean War (1950–1953) resulted in the death of many American soldiers. The Cuban missile crisis in the early 1960s led the United States and the Soviet Union to the brink of nuclear war. The Vietnam War (1964–1975) and the antiwar movements caused additional personal and national stress.

The Civil Rights movements in the 1950s and the 1960s brought about a basic question about American values. The 1960s saw major rioting, caused by the twin conditions of poverty and racism in many cities across the nation. The 1960s and 1970s also saw "anti-establishment movements" in education, economics, family, government, and religion. Many people experiencing these stresses began to look toward the church for spiritual and psychological help, and Reverend Robert Harold Schuller thought he could help with this problem.

Schuller ministered to two different congregations: those in his home church, the Crystal Cathedral in Garden Grove, California (with a membership of about ten thousand people), and those in the television audience (numbering about three million viewers a week) through his Hour of Power programs. From both congregations, he had received questions about how to handle the multiple stresses they were facing in their daily lives.

Significance

Schuller set about the task of writing a book, *Turning Your Stress Into Strength,* that would contain helpful recommendations based upon real-life circumstances. The book contained excerpts from interviews by conducted by Pastor Schuller. The interviewees consisted of men and women from a diverse assortment of backgrounds and walks of life.

Many of these individuals had found themselves living under continually stressful, though not unusual, conditions. Reverend Schuller, through his conversation with the interviewees, developed positive and powerful spiritually based principles that could be used to conquer stress. He counseled that by reading the solutions to personal cases of stress, one might find answers to one's own problems.

The major topics of the book dealt with ways of conquering: personal tragedy, fatigue, sickness, personal failure, impossible tasks, inner self-demands, and difficult life situations. Inherent in all the recommendations for dealing with stress is first turning to God, and then the practical answers that a person needed would follow. Through faith in God, the casting out of negative thoughts, and replacing those thoughts with positive thinking, personal peace could be obtained.

Schuller's work on stress and religion reached wide reading audiences just like his Hour of Power had been reaching millions of viewers. Many considered his religious programs and his books as steady supplements to their religious lives.

Schuller's work was a valuable contribution to the mental health movement. There were some clergy and theologians, however, who did not approve of the ways Schuller was reaching his audiences. They said that he was producing a mass production type of Christianity through his television programs and many books. Other clergy and theologians, however, praised him for reaching people who would ordinarily have little to do with a local church group. These persons were being ministered to in a way that was different from the traditional Christian approaches, and there was nothing wrong with using the mass media to reach them.

Primary Source

Turning Your Stress Into Strength [excerpt]

SYNOPSIS: The excerpts come from chapter 1, "Turning Your Stress Into Strength," and chapter 9, "You Can Experience Strength and Happiness." Rev. Robert Schuller points out that even in the most stress-filled situations, God opens up opportunities for personal growth, and that prayer is the way to find out what God wants a person to do.

Turning Your Stress Into Strength

Stress can become the source of strength in your life!

You can turn the unwelcomed intrusions that threaten to destroy your life into tremendous possibilities for good!

This book will show you how.

You can conquer stress!

The place to discover a miracle in your life is at the point where you are experiencing the greatest stress. My confidence is based on this verse from the Bible:

"In my distress thou hast enlarged me"

(Psalm 4:1 KJV).

Two young boys were raised by an alcoholic father. As they became older, they separated from that broken home and each went his own way. Some years later, a psychologist was analyzing what drunkenness does to the children in a home. In his research, one of his assistants interviewed these two men. One was a clean, sharp teetotaler, the other was a hopeless drunk like his father. The researcher asked each individually why they turned out like they did. And they both gave the same identical answer: "What else could you expect when you had a father like mine?"

It's not what happens to you in life that makes the difference. It is how you react to each circumstance you encounter that determines the results! Every human being in the same situation has the possibilities of choosing how they will react—either positively or negatively.

I happen to believe in miracles. My definition of a miracle is a beautiful act of God that intervenes in a human life to do a wonderful thing. If you want to find a miracle in your life, I suggest you start by looking for a problem. Because that is the place God wants to work in your life.

But it takes two to make a miracle. God cannot use his miracle-working power in your life if you do not have the faith to let Him work.

You remember the time Jesus left a certain city without performing any great miracles. The gospel writer said, "He could do no mighty works in this city because of their unbelief." God's power can be limited by our lack of faith. God also willingly limits his own power by His own nature. He will not force us to accept His miracles. He will not treat us like robots. But in spite of these limitations, God continues to perform marvelous works in our lives.

Many of His miracles are easy to spot. For instance, several times a year ministers from around the world gather on our church campus for a special Institute for Successful Church Leadership. Early one morning during a recent Institute, one young minister was called out of the session for an emergency telephone call. He received word that his young son had fallen into a swimming pool and was being rushed to the hospital unconscious.

This young pastor from Minnesota interrupted the seminar and asked that we pray for his son as he rushed to the hospital. Later that day, I talked with his wife and found out that the boy was unconscious when they lifted him from the pool and that X-rays at the hospital indicated there was water in his lungs. Several hours later they X-rayed his lungs again and found them clear. The doctor simply said, "It's a miracle."

What a great moment we enjoyed at the close of our Institute. During our dedication service, the father, the mother and the young boy walked to the front of the church and knelt together. There wasn't a dry eye in the whole congregation.

A young family faced tremendous stress hundreds of miles from home and friends. God met them at their point of need. In the chapters that follow, you will meet friends of mine with the same testimony under a variety of circumstances—"God helped me to turn my stress into strength!" He is able and willing to help you.

But why is it so difficult to recognize God's miracles in our lives? We are just not sensitive enough to spot them. We are conditioned by negative vibrations in our impossibility-thinking society to look at problems and not at possibilities. After all, most of us read the newspaper. And what do we read? It's filled with bad news. What if someone published a daily newspaper that reported only the good things that happened? For one thing, no one would buy it. But it would be a massive paper, probably more than twelve inches thick, because there are so many beautiful things happening in so many lives each day!

"A hundred million miracles
Are happening every day,
But only he who has the faith
Will see them on life's way."

Miracles are happening all the time. If you want to spot a miracle, look for a problem, a difficulty, a mountain of stress. Because often the way God seeks to reach us is in a moment of pain. *For there is no gain without pain!* Every stress-filled situation is loaded with opportunities.

Rev. Robert Schuller inside the Crystal Cathedral in 1980. This church in Orange County, California, seats nearly 3,000 people and is constructed of over 12 thousand panes of glass. Built to house Rev. Schuller's ministry, it is a testament to the popularity of his message in the 1970s and beyond. **AP/WIDE WORLD PHOTOS. REPRODUCED BY PERMISSION**

Over the years I have discovered that trouble never leaves you where it found you. It always changes you permanently. It will either make you bitter, tough, hard, cold and angry, or it will turn you into a soft, gentle, compassionate, understanding, generous human being. The choice is yours!

If you are experiencing stress today, I predict it is the beginning of a miracle. That is why God allows us to run into stress-filled situations. Sometimes He wants to slow us down. Other times He wants to change our direction. In every situation, He wants to help us become strong! For it is not the mountain of stress that counts, it's what you do with it that matters.

You Can Experience Strength and Happiness

I want to give you a formula that will guarantee success to you in your search for strength and happiness. Every person we have met in the preceeding chapters has discovered this formula. And it is possible for you to find the strength to conquer the stress you are experiencing. Here is the key:

Discover the consciousness that God is in ultimate control of your life and that His will is unfolding as it should.

There you have it: The cure for stress! Your search is fulfilled when you develop the awareness that God is in control of your life. He has a dream for you and it is always constructive, never destructive. His plan for you is positive, which means that if you are walking close to God, you will experience strength and happiness. If you do encounter stress, you can know that it is only a phase, where God is either: (1) delaying, (2) guiding, (3) redirecting, (4) expanding your thinking, or (5) making you so humble that when joy and strength come it won't go to your head.

What can you do during times of stress? There are four words that rhyme that illustrate four simple points to help you. The words are *Pray, Obey, Pay and Stay.*

You begin with *Prayer.* "God, I want your will to be done in my life." Now some people create a lot of inner stress because they are unwilling to pray that prayer. They don't want to take this first step. They have an idea of what they want, and God is only somebody that they may want to use to get their own way. Prayer is not some device to get heaven to move to earth so that you can get what you want.

I've used this illustration before because it makes the point so clearly. If you're in a little boat approaching a sandy beach and you throw out the anchor, it digs into the sand. When you pull on the anchor rope until the boat slides onto the shore, what have you done? Have you moved the shore to the boat? Or have you moved the boat to the shore? Obviously you have pulled the boat to the shore. The purpose of prayer, likewise, is not to move God and heaven to you, but to move you closer to God so that you want what God wants.

Pray. Pray that you will be open to what God wants you to do. Pray that you will hear God speaking to you in the center of the storm of stress.

After you have prayed, then *obey* positive signals. Some people never find strength or personal happiness because frankly, they are harboring secret sins. They're not living right, they're not living clean, and they know it. Because they are not obeying God, they are not able to receive strength and power in their life. They can't hear God's messages to them because they are not within calling distance. Until you are obeying God you won't want to get close to Him, because you'll be afraid with your guilt. Take the time to search your conscience and determine to remove any secret sin that you find.

If you have prayed and are willing to obey, then determine to *pay* the price. In the Christian life there is always some sacrificing involved. Jesus Christ couldn't accomplish His task without the cross. And there will be some point where we must be willing to deny ourselves and pay the price. In order for you to find strength, you may have to pay the price of stress for a while. Be confident! God is with you!

That leads into the last point. *Stay* with God. Don't quit. What you may need is patience. Strength and happiness are just ahead. Keep trusting God. Keep believing! Never give up! *God's delays are not God's denials.* Your life is unfolding exactly as it should. How do I know that? God has promised!

"In everything you do, put God first, and he will direct you and crown your efforts with success"

(Proverbs 3:6 TLB).

"I will instruct you (says the Lord) and guide you along the best pathway for your life; I will advise you and watch your progress"

(Psalm 32:8 TLB).

"God shows how to distinguish right from wrong, how to find the right decision every time. For wisdom and truth will enter the very center of your being, filling your life with joy"

(Proverbs 2:9, 10 TLB).

"You saw me before I was born and scheduled each day of my life before I began to breathe. Every day was recorded in your Book!"

(Psalm 139:16 TLB).

"I have created you and cared for you since you were born. I will be your God through all your lifetime, yes, even when your hair is white with age. I made you and I will care for you. I will carry you along and be your Savior"

(Isaiah 46:3, 4 TLB).

The most powerful force in the world is a positive attitude in the mind of a believer who is walking close to God!

Further Resources
BOOKS

Schuller, Robert Harold. *Move Ahead with Possibility Thinking.* Garden City, N. Y.: Doubleday, 1967.

Schuller, Robert Harold. *My Journey: From an Iowa Farm to a Cathedral of Dreams.* San Francisco, Calif.: HarperSan-Francisco, 2001.

Schuller, Robert Harold. *Prayer: My Soul's Adventure with God: A Spiritual Autobiography.* New York: Doubleday, 1996.

PERIODICALS

Eisenstadt-Evans, Elizabeth. "Farm Boy Makes Good: Robert Schuller's Story is a Distillation of His Gospel." *Christianity Today,* 46, no. 9, August 5, 2002, 57.

Miller, Holly. "Living on the Edge." *Saturday Evening Post,* 273, no. 2, March 2001, 36.

"Possibility Living: Add Years to Your Life and Life to Your Years with God's Health Plan." *Publishers Weekly,* 247, no. 39, September 25, 2000, 111.

WEBSITES

"Dr. Robert Schuller." Crystal Cathedral.com. Available online at http://www.crystalcathedral.org/ (accessed March 1, 2003).

"Hour of Power." http://www.hourofpower.org/ (accessed March 1, 2003).

"Capital Punishment: The Question of Justification"

Magazine article

By: David A. Hoekema

Date: March 28, 1979

Source: Hoekema, David A. "Capital Punishment: The Question of Justification," *Christian Century*, March 28, 1979, 338. Available online at http://www.religion-online.org/cgi-bin/relsearchd.dll/showarticle?item_id=1218 (accessed March 1, 2003).

About the Author: David Andrew Hoekema (1950–) was born in Peterson, New Jersey. He earned a bachelor's degree from Calvin College in 1972 and a doctorate from Princeton University in 1981. In addition to teaching philosophy at various colleges Hoekema has written several books on Christianity. ■

Introduction

The issue of capital punishment during the 1970s received a great deal of discussion in the religious as well as the legal arenas. On June 29 1972, the United States Supreme Court ruled in *Furman v. Georgia* that the death penalty was cruel and unusual punishment since juries were found to impose it in arbitrary manners. The death penalty was found to be unconstitutional, and all existing death sentences and death penalty laws in all the states were invalidated.

During the 1970s, a rapidly rising rate of violent crime brought calls for the restoration of the death penalty in America, especially as the punishment for certain kinds of murder. Four years after the 1972 ruling, the Supreme Court revisited the issue. On July 2, 1976, in *Gregg v. Georgia,* the court ruled that under the state's new two-stage capital trial system, the death penalty was constitutional. This penalty could be restored, under certain conditions, in any state that chose to adopt it.

Within a four-year time frame, the death penalty was declared invalid and then reinstated. David Hoekema's article appeared in 1979, three years after the United States Supreme Court declared that the death penalty could be restored. After reviewing the arguments on both sides of the capital punishment issue, Hoekema concluded that a person could not morally or religiously justify that type of penalty.

Philosopher David A. Hoekema, in his article entitled "Capital Punishment: The Question of Justification," wanted his readers to examine arguments, both in the religious and moral spheres, that could be applied to a rational study on the controversial issue of capital punishment.

Significance

Hoekema's contention that capital punishment was not a reasonable or justifiable action by the government elicited mixed responses within the Christian and Jewish communities. As was expected, there was no universal agreement concerning the issue; but most of the public did favor the death penalty in cases of convicted murderers.

Several Christian groups in the late 1970s formalized their religious and moral reasons against the imposition of the death penalty. Among them were that capital punishment: violated the command by Jesus to employ the ethic of love, perpetuated the evil of retaliation, ignored the guilt that the society may have had in the causation of the crime, and prevented the possibility of any kind of rehabilitation of the criminal.

Those Jews who were opposed to capital punishment pointed out that Rabbinic interpretations from the Torah demonstrate God's aversion to the use of the ultimate penalty, death. They believed that only God has the right to take a human life.

Those Christians and Jews who were in favor of capital punishment during the 1970s used several religious and moral arguments to justify their position. Some of the arguments included that: some crimes are so violently offensive that the death penalty is the only appropriate punishment, people who deliberately and knowingly kill another human being must forfeit their right to live, and the death sentence sometimes is the only way to rid evil influences from society.

At the beginning of the twenty first century, the majority of the American public remained in favor of capital punishment in cases of murder. Gallup public opinion polls show a gradual increase in the percentage of people who favor the death penalty for a person convicted of murder. In 1969, 51 percent supported capital punishment; in 2002, that number was 72 percent.

A museum display of an electric chair used for executions in Connecticut prior to 1960. Americans found conflicting messages about the death penalty in religion during the 1970s, reflecting the unsettled opinions of the society as a whole. UPI/CORBIS-BETTMANN. REPRODUCED BY PERMISSION.

Primary Source

"Capital Punishment: The Question of Justification" [excerpt]

SYNOPSIS: These excerpts from "Capital Punishment: The Question of Justification" reflect the religious and moral arguments for and against capital punishment, as presented by David A. Hoekema, executive director of the American Philosophical Association. He concludes that the arguments against capital punishment were more morally defensible than the arguments in favor of it.

. . . [R]ecent public-opinion surveys indicate that a large number, possibly a majority, of Americans favor imposing the death penalty for some crimes. But let us ask the ethical question: Ought governments to put to death persons convicted of certain crimes?

II

First, let us look at grounds on which capital punishment is defended. Most prominent is the argument from deterrence. Capital punishment, it is asserted, is necessary to deter potential criminals.

Murderers must be executed so that the lives of potential murder victims may be spared.

Two assertions are closely linked here. First, it is said that convicted murderers must be put to death in order to protect the rest of us against those individuals who might kill others if they were at large. This argument, based not strictly on deterrence but on incapacitation of known offenders, is inconclusive, since there are other effective means of protecting the innocent against convicted murderers—for example, imprisonment of murderers for life in high-security institutions.

Second, it is said that the example of capital punishment is needed to deter those who would otherwise commit murder. Knowledge that a crime is punishable by death will give the potential criminal pause. This second argument rests on the assumption that capital punishment does in fact reduce the incidence of capital crimes—a presupposition that must be tested against the evidence. Surprisingly, none of the available empirical data shows any significant correlation between the existence or use of the death penalty and the incidence of capital crimes.

When studies have compared the homicide rates for the past 50 years in states that employ the death penalty and in adjoining states that have abolished it, the numbers have in every case been quite similar; the death penalty has had no discernible effect on homicide rates. . . .

The available evidence, then, fails to support the claim that capital punishment deters capital crime. For this reason, I think, we may set aside the deterrence argument. But there is a stronger reason for rejecting the argument—one that has to do with the way in which supporter of that argument would have us treat persons.

Those who defend capital punishment on grounds of deterrence would have us take the lives of some—persons convicted of certain crimes—because doing so will discourage crime and thus protect others. But it is a grave moral wrong to treat one person in a way justified solely by the needs of others. To inflict harm on one person in order to serve the purposes of others is to use that person in an immoral and inhumane way, treating him or her not as a person with rights and responsibilities but as a means to other ends. The most serious flaw in the deterrence argument, therefore, is that it is the wrong kind of argument. The execution of criminals cannot be justified by the good which their deaths may do the rest of us.

III

A second argument for the death penalty maintains that some crimes, chief among them murder, morally require the punishment of death. In particular, Christians frequently support capital punishment by appeal to the Mosaic code, which required the death penalty for murder. "The law of capital punishment," one writer has concluded after reviewing relevant biblical passages, "must stand as a silent but powerful witness to the sacredness of God-given life."

In the Mosaic code, it should be pointed out, there were many capital crimes besides murder. In the book of Deuteronomy, death is prescribed as the penalty for false prophecy, worship of foreign gods, kidnapping, adultery, deception by a bride concerning her virginity, and disobedience to parents. To this list the laws of the book of Exodus add witchcraft, sodomy, and striking or cursing a parent.

I doubt that there is much sentiment in favor of restoring the death penalty in the U.S. for such offenses. . . .

The retributive argument seems the strongest one in support of capital punishment. We ought to deal with convicted offenders not as we want to, but as they deserve. And I am not certain that it is wrong to argue that a person who has deliberately killed another person deserves to die.

But even if this principle is valid, should the judicial branch of our governments be empowered to determine whether individuals deserve to die? Are our procedures for making laws and for determining guilt sufficiently reliable that we may entrust our lives to them? I shall return to this important question presently. But consider the following fact: During the years from 1930 to 1962, 466 persons were put to death for the crime of rape. Of these, 399 were black. Can it seriously be maintained that our courts are administering the death penalty to all those and only to those who deserve to die?

IV

Two other arguments deserve brief mention. It has been argued that, even if the penalty of life imprisonment were acceptable on other grounds, our society could not reasonably be asked to pay the cost of maintaining convicted murderers in prisons for the remainder of their natural lives.

This argument overlooks the considerable costs of retaining the death penalty. Jury selection, conduct of the trial, and the appeals process become extremely time-consuming and elaborate when death is a possible penalty. On the other hand, prisons should not be as expensive as they are. At present those prisoners who work at all are working for absurdly low wages, frequently at menial and degrading tasks. Prisons should be reorganized to provide meaningful work for all able inmates; workers should be paid fair wages for their work and charged for their room and board. Such measures would sharply reduce the cost of prisons and make them more humane.

But these considerations—important as they are—have little relevance to the justification of capital punishment. We should not decide to kill convicted criminals only because it costs so much to keep them alive. The cost to society of imprisonment, large or small, cannot justify capital punishment.

Finally, defenders of capital punishment sometimes support their case by citing those convicted offenders—for example, Gary Gilmore—who have asked to be executed rather than imprisoned. But this argument, too, is of little relevance. If some prisoners would prefer to die rather than be imprisoned, perhaps we should oblige them by permitting them to take their own lives. But this consideration has nothing to do with the question of whether we ought to impose the punishment of death on certain offenders, most of whom would prefer to live.

V

Let us turn now to the case against the death penalty. It is sometimes argued that capital punishment is unjustified because those guilty of crimes cannot help acting as they do: the environment, possibly interacting with inherited characteristics, causes some people to commit crimes. It is not moral culpability or choice that divides law-abiding citizens from criminals—so Clarence Darrow argued eloquently—but the accident of birth or social circumstances.

If determinism of this sort were valid, not only the death penalty but all forms of punishment would be unjustified. No one who is compelled by circumstances to act deserves to be punished. But there is little reason to adopt this bleak view of human action. . . .

Second, the case against the death penalty is sometimes based on the view that the justification of punishment lies in the reform which it effects. Those who break the law, it is said, are ill, suffering either from psychological malfunction or from maladjustment to society. Our responsibility is to treat them, to cure them of their illness, so that they become able to function in socially acceptable ways. Death, obviously, cannot reform anyone.

Like the deterrence argument for capital punishment, this seems to be the wrong kind of argument. Punishment is punishment and treatment is treatment, and one must not be substituted for the other. Some persons who violate the law are, without doubt, mentally ill. It is unreasonable and inhumane to punish them for acts which they may not have realized they were doing; to put such a person to death would be an even more grievous wrong. In such cases treatment is called for.

But most persons who break the law are not mentally ill and do know what they are doing. We may not force them to undergo treatment in place of the legal penalty for their offenses. To confine them to mental institutions until those put in authority over them judge that they are cured of their criminal tendencies is far more cruel than to sentence them to a term of imprisonment. Voluntary programs of education or vocational training, which help prepare prisoners for non-criminal careers on release, should be made more widely available. But compulsory treatment for all offenders violates their integrity as persons; we need only look to the Soviet Union to see the abuses to which such a practice is liable.

VI

Let us examine a third and stronger argument, a straightforward moral assertion; the state ought not to take life unnecessarily. For many reasons—among them the example which capital punishment sets, its effect on those who must carry out death sentences and, above all, its violation of a basic moral principle—the state ought not to kill people.

The counterclaim made by defenders of capital punishment is that in certain circumstances killing people is permissible and even required, and that capital punishment is one of those cases. If a terrorist is about to throw a bomb into a crowded theater, and a police officer is certain that there is no way to stop him except to kill him, the officer should of course kill the terrorist. In some cases of grave and immediate danger, let us grant, killing is justified.

But execution bears little resemblance to such cases. It involves the planned, deliberate killing of someone in custody who is not a present threat to human life or safety. Execution is not necessary to save the lives of future victims, since there are other means to secure that end.

Is there some vitally important purpose of the state or some fundamental right of persons which cannot be secured without executing convicts? I do not believe there is. And in the absence of any such compelling reason, the moral principle that it is wrong to kill people constitutes a powerful argument against capital punishment.

VII

Of the arguments I have mentioned in favor of the death penalty, only one has considerable weight. That is the retributive argument that murder, as an extremely serious offense, requires a comparably severe punishment. Of the arguments so far examined against capital punishment, only one, the moral claim that killing is wrong, is, in my view, acceptable.

There is, however, another argument against the death penalty which I find compelling—that based on the imperfection of judicial procedure. In the case of *Furman v. Georgia,* the Supreme Court struck down existing legislation because of the arbitrariness with which some convicted offenders were executed and others spared. . . .

VIII

Even more worrisome than the discriminatory application of the death penalty is the possibility of mistaken conviction and its ghastly consequences. In a sense, any punishment wrongfully imposed is irrevocable, but none is so irrevocable as death. Although we cannot give back to a person mistakenly imprisoned the time spent or the self-respect lost, we can release and compensate him or her. But we cannot do anything for a person wrongfully executed. While we ought to minimize the opportunities for capricious or mistaken judgments throughout the legal system, we cannot hope for perfect success. There is no reason why our mistakes must be fatal.

Numerous cases of erroneous convictions in capital cases have been documented; several of those convicted were put to death before the error was discovered. However small their number, it is too large. So long as the death penalty exists, there are certain to be others, for every judicial procedure—however meticulous, however compassed about with safeguards—must be carried out by fallible human beings.

One erroneous execution is too many, because even lawful executions of the indisputably guilty serve no purpose. They are not justified by the need to protect the rest of us, since there are other means of restraining persons dangerous to society, and there is no evidence that executions deter the commission of crime. A wrongful execution is a grievous injustice that cannot be remedied after the fact. Even a legal and proper execution is a needless taking of human life. Even if one is sympathetic—as I am—to the claim that a murderer deserves to die, there are compelling reasons not to entrust the power to decide who shall die to the persons and procedures that constitute our judicial system.

Further Resources

BOOKS

Hanks, Gardner C. *Capital Punishment and the Bible.* Scottdale, Pa.: Herald Press, 2002.

Pojman, Louis P., ed. *Philosophy: The Quest for Truth.* Belmont, Calif.: Wadsworth, 1996.

Zimring, Franklin E. *Capital Punishment and the American Agenda.* Cambridge University Press, 1986.

PERIODICALS

Lamarche, Gara. "When the State Kills: Capital Punishment and the American Condition." *The American Prospect,* 12, no. 10, June 4, 2001, 40.

Langan, John. "Justice Demands It." *America,* 185, no. 7, September 17, 2001, 27.

Novak, Viveca. "The Death Penalty Under Fire." *Time,* 160, no. 15, October 7, 2002, 28.

WEBSITES

"Capital Punishment." Available online at http://members.aol.com/wardfreman/alevelre/cap.htm (accessed March 1, 2003).

"Cover Story: Capital Punishment: Retribution or Justice?" P.B.S., Religion & Ethics Newsweekly. Available online at http://www.pbs.org/wnet/religionandethics/week437/cover.html; website home page: http://www.pbs.org (accessed March 1, 2003).

"Religion and the Death Penalty." Seattle University, Lemieux Library. Available online at http://www.seattleu.edu/lemlib/web_archives/deadmanwalking/religion.htm; website home page: http://www.seattleu.edu (accessed March 1, 2003).

"Women Clergy: How Their Presence Is Changing the Church"

Magazine article

By: Nancy Hardesty, Beverly Anderson, Suzanne Hiatt, Letty Russell and Barbara Brown Zikmund

Date: 1979

Source: Symposium, "Women Clergy: How Their Presence Is Changing the Church." *Christian Century,* February 7–14, 1979, 122. Available online at http://www.religion-online.org/cgi-bin/relsearchd.dll/showarticle?item_id=1207 (accessed March 1, 2003). ■

Introduction

Prior to the 1950s, most church ministries consisted primarily of men. A few denominations allowed women ministers (for example, in 1853 the Congregationalists ordained the first woman to the ministry), but those denominations were more the exception than the rule. Between the early 1950s and the later 1970s, however, five major denominations—Baptists, Episcopalians, Lutherans, Methodists, and Presbyterians—reversed their opposition to the ordination of women and opened the doors for female clergy. This led to a dramatic increase in the enrollment of women in seminary schools—as much as 120 percent in the 1970s alone.

Even though there was a greater percentage of women in the role of church pastors in the 1970s as compared to previous decades, many of these women ministers found themselves, at times, ignored by or isolated from their male colleagues. Breaking the traditional barriers that many churches had against women ministers was a difficult task. Some found themselves open to prejudice and discrimination because of their gender. This hostility came not only from some male ministers but also from some lay members of the congregations, both male and female. Despite these obstacles, women ministers were having an impact upon the churches and slowly beginning to bring about changes.

What were some of the effects of this trend? More female role models, among students and faculty, were being made available at the seminaries and the local churches. Increased awareness of discrimination by women ministers led to a greater awareness and understanding of feminist, black, and liberation theologies. Women's insight into the Christian understanding of one's relationship to God and neighbors was opening up a national dialogue that validated perspectives that deviated from the traditional norm.

These changes, along with an increase of women in seminary enrollments, raised such questions as, Will the influx of women somehow change the clerical profession? What will happen as churches move beyond tokenism in ordaining and employing women? Do women's styles of ministry differ from traditional models? These questions were addressed in "Women Clergy: How Their Presence Is Changing the Church."

Significance

The 1979 symposium was conducted by five well respected women in the field of ministry. Their discussion of the topic was presented in terms of sexism, prejudice, fear of change, gender bias, and basic definitions of leadership and ministry.

The symposium on "Women Clergy: How Their Presence Is Changing the Church" addressed the gender situation in mainline Protestant denominations as it existed in the 1970s, and looked ahead to predict what this situation would mean in the long term. Even though the numbers of women in the Protestant clergy had been increasing since the earlier part of the decade, sizeable segments of the total Christian church in America remained reluctant to accept the ordination of women. Even in the early twenty-first century, some of the less liberal denominations have still not fully accepted the role of women ministers, and the Roman Catholic Church prohibits women from entering the priesthood.

The status of women ministers in those churches that do permit the ordination of women has improved since the 1970s. A number of studies on women clergy since the mid-1980s have shown that more of them have experienced a movement away from traditional subordinate roles, and have taken more leadership positions in the churches. But these same studies also indicated that gaining leadership positions is still more difficult for women than for men.

More recently, there has been a paradigm shift surrounding the issue of women in ministry. It is arguably noted that the battle is no longer between specific religions—Presbyterians vs. Methodists, Christians vs. Jews—but rather, between the liberal and conservative factions within each religion. Whereas the conflict once lay in figuring how to get into ministry, female clergy must now find a way to retain their positions within the church.

Primary Source

"Women Clergy: How Their Presence Is Changing the Church" [excerpt]

SYNOPSIS: In these excerpts from a symposium examining the role of women clergy and the Christian churches, five women—one layperson, one seminary student, and three ministers—from five Protestant denominations present their appraisals of how the presence of women clergy was changing the church in the 1970s and how they will change the church in the future.

Though women clergy constitute a very small minority of the ordained clergy in most denominations, current seminary enrollments—in some cases more than 40 per cent women—suggest that the next few years will see sudden and dramatic increases in the numbers of women entering parish ministries and other clergy positions.

What, we must ask, will happen as churches move beyond tokenism in ordaining and employing women? What changes are now being wrought in seminaries because of women faculty and students? What are the prospects for placement of women graduates? Will the influx of women somehow change the profession? Do women's styles of ministry and leadership differ from traditional models?

To address such questions as these, we asked five knowledgeable women from as many denominations to share their perspectives on the present reality and future prospects of women in the ordained ministry. Suzanne Watt was one of the first women ordained in the Episcopal Church. Beverly Anderson, a black seminarian, will be seeking ordination in the United Methodist Church. Nancy Hardesty, a laywoman from an evangelical tradition, and Barbara Brown Zikmund, a United Church of Christ minister, are both church historians. And theologian Letty Russell, a United Presbyterian, had extensive parish ministry experience before coming to her present seminary post. These five offer their insights on the impact women clergy are having and will have on the church.

"Women and the Seminaries" by Nancy Hardesty

The relationship of women to seminaries—initially all-male bastions for the education of the clergy, an all-male profession—seems to evolve through four stages. Movement toward the fourth stage may constitute progress.

(1) Initially a few women are grateful for the opportunity to study in seminaries. They hope to find some form of ministry on the fringes of the church to satisfy the inescapable call from God they feel in their hearts. Male students, unthreatened, are friendly and patronizing; male faculty members are solicitously paternal.

(2) As small groups of women gather in a seminary context, their consciousnesses are raised. They get in touch with the sexism of church and society and with their own anger. They form an embattled women's caucus, knowing that the skirmishes they fight in seminary are preliminary rounds for the battles they will fight for their right to full ministry in the church. Their stance evokes hostility from their male peers, resistance from the faculty. Demands are met by concessions.

(3) As more women students arrive, the fervor of women and the fever of the situation dissipate. Changes are being made; the atmosphere is different. Several women are on the faculty; a few

"feminist theology" or "women in ministry" courses are added to the curriculum. New students wonder what the problem is. Younger ones have encountered few difficulties thus far in their education or church experience. They have seen female role models in the parish, and they see themselves as being no different from their male peers. They compare notes on church politics and plan for their own parishes. Faculty and student men have learned to speak "nonsexist," and so a modicum of harmony reigns.

(4) Eventually women come to appreciate past struggles and gains while being realistic about the depths of prejudice and the difficulties remaining. Women faculty members are no longer marginal but integral to the faculty. An awareness of feminist, black and liberation theologies informs the critique of all theology and biblical hermeneutic. History courses include material about all segments of church life—clerical and lay, white and black, men and women, bishops and Sunday schools, General Conference decisions and the work of the Women's Foreign Missionary Society. Men and women choose, and the church affirms, forms of ministry for which the individuals are gifted, whether parish work or more specialized endeavors. Couples find support for flexible solutions to the complex issues raised by egalitarian marriages and family rearing. . . .

"Womanstyle: Eyes to See the Gifts in Others" by Beverly J. Anderson

A new dawning for the church is heralded by the escalation in the numbers of women entering the ordained ministry. As traditionally accepted modes of ministering are being expanded and reshaped out of women's experiences and history, what may initially appear to be radically threatening changes can be seen as signs of resurrection.

Women who have responded to God's call to the ordained ministry bring a wealth of previous experience and involvement in the local church—experience which serves to enhance their ministry with the laity in diverse ways. Many ordained women bring not only their Christian understanding of relationship to God and neighbor, but the particularized dimensions of feminist and other liberation theologies as well. The linking of these fundamental life postures prepares the way for the gifts and graces of all women, men and children to be affirmed, utilized and developed in mutual sharing in response to the gospel.

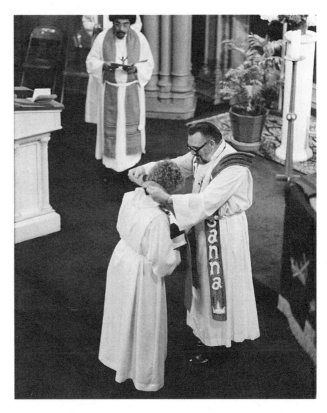

Janith M. Otte-Murphy is ordained as the first female Lutheran minister in October 1977. © **ROGER RESSMEYER/CORBIS. REPRODUCED BY PERMISSION.**

The most publicly visible changes that women bring to the ministry are in the area of leadership style. Two phrases that characterize this particular departure from tradition are "shared involvement" and "mutual pilgrimage." Because women themselves have had to struggle to arrive at ordained ministry, they often bring a heightened awareness of the dehumanizing experience of being "shut out." Women can draw on their own pilgrimage as a resource as they invite and enable others to affirm and value their own uniqueness, gifts and resources.

It is apparent, from the profile of women who attended the second Consultation of United Methodist Clergywomen in January, that the majority of women now in the ordained ministry have self-consciously dialogued with, have struggled in, and have been aided by one or another of the liberation movements, be it Third World, feminist, civil rights or human potential. As a result, women are modeling a style of leadership that acknowledges the pain of ignored talents, dual standards and narrowly defined roles. It appears then that women clergy can be more open to exploring leadership styles that are less hierarchical and more fluid than those of the majority of their male colleagues, who have been admitted to the system as a matter of fact, expectation and privilege. . . .

"Do We Have an Advocate?" by Dr. Suzanne R. Hiatt

At present there are equal numbers of black and women clergy in the Episcopal Church—slightly more than 300 of each, with an overlap of about four black women. The two groups have separate (but equal) employment problems. While there are "black" parishes looking for black rectors, there are no "woman" parishes looking for women rectors; on the other hand, the large pool of "assistant" jobs in suburban parishes is more available to women than to blacks, though it is wide open only to white males. Rectorships of large white or mixed parishes are equally closed to blacks and to women. . . .

It seems to me that the reluctance of congregations to hire an "exceptional" person such as a woman as their chief pastor is rooted in their fear of "losing face" among the parishes. That curious human dynamic, appearing here on the corporate level, needs to be recognized. It cannot simply be dealt with pastorally as that valiant UCC minister was doing; it also needs to be looked at theologically. Of course a parish wants a pastor who is immediately acceptable in the world of ecclesiastics. But doesn't the gospel have something to say for the leadership of one who is "despised and rejected of men?"

Few, if any, of the ecclesiastical authorities who help parishes decide whom to hire are strong advocates for "exceptional" people. Bishops, superintendents, synod executives all want their congregations to be contented with their clergy—a congregation "working through its grief" must be an ecclesiastic's nightmare. Yet until such men (and they are, almost without exception, men) become strong, theologically motivated advocates for the "exceptional" pastor, female and/or racial minority member, the current grim situation will not improve.

In the past when we have spoken of church leaders who were "for" the ordination of women, we meant those who were not opposed to it. It is time that "being for" minorities began to mean active advocacy—insisting that parishes interview women and blacks and actively promoting the candidacy of specific female and black persons for specific positions. Women and blacks do not "win" acceptance simply by doing excellent work and thereby converting the skeptical. Congregations will not "hear about" our talent and clamor for our ministries. We need spe-

cial help from our brother clergy, and congregations need special help in dealing with the good news "exceptional" people can bring them. . . .

"Clerical Ministry as a Female Profession" by Dr. Letty M. Russell

Along with the general ferment and change affecting social roles in all of society today, we find that the roles of women and men in ministry are also changing. Some of these changes are already happening as women enter the clerical ministry in increasing numbers. With more clergy couples looking for part-time or shared positions, there is an increased demand for the revision of ecclesiastical policies so that part-time and team ministries are possible. With women choosing ministry as a second career and entering seminaries in midlife, there is a growing recognition that both men and women frequently change their professions today. This realization in turn puts pressure on church bodies to recognize ministries of shorter duration, and to make it possible for persons to leave as well as to enter professional ministry without stigma or loss of pension.

Despite considerable resistance from the theological and ecclesiastical status quo, seminaries are responding to financial pressures and developing a variety of educational models. So that a wider group of persons may be reached, education is sometimes related to actual life experience and offered as a continuing process available to those who are also working. Women and Third World groups are especially interested in ways of pursuing theological education while continuing their ministries at home, in the church or in society. All groups are interested in the prestige of an added degree, and many younger students are beginning their careers with joint professional degrees in theology and another discipline—education, law, medicine, social work, etc.

Women are entering seminaries in greater numbers while the number of men does not increase as rapidly. From 1972 to 1977 the enrollment of women increased 118.9 per cent and that of men only 20.2 per cent ("Women Ministers in 1977: A Report," by C. H. Jacquet [National Council of Churches, 1978], p. 13). The entrance of large numbers of women into ordained ministry may cause it to become a "female profession" like nursing or primary school teaching. Sexism causes work done by women to be devalued in society; when large numbers of them enter a field, the men tend to leave; prestige and salaries drop. If this prejudice continues, it may cause ordained ministry, which is already associated with the private sphere and with feminine cultural characteristics of being loving and kind, to become not only "feminized" but also "female." This development might, however, have a side benefit: an ever-increasing erosion of clergy status would diminish the line of separation between clergy and laity. . . .

"Upsetting the Assumptions" by Rev. Barbara Brown Zikmund

I view the increased numbers of women enrolling in theological education and seeking ecclesiastical vocations as a blessing. Although the trends are unclear, these women are raising some basic theological questions about the authority, scope, style and nature of religious leadership and Christian ministry.

First, women are challenging traditional sources of religious authority. Because classic interpretations of Scripture and church history have not accepted many forms of female leadership, the very presence of woman leaders emphasizes the tension between Scripture/tradition and religious knowledge which comes directly from the Holy Spirit. This is not a new development in the history of the church. It was always true that women were able to command religious authority when there was popular confidence in the power of the Holy Spirit (e.g., medieval mystics). Whenever women have moved into visible church leadership, the relative importance of Scripture and tradition has been reduced and the legitimacy of personal religious experience has been enhanced.

In today's world, where religious institutions and leaders often seem paralyzed by canon and custom, this development has important ramifications. Although there is not a direct correlation between the women's movement and the charismatic renewal, both developments challenge traditional sources of religious authority and open up possibilities for new forms of leadership.

Second, women are expanding the understanding of religious life. Within church history Christians have often been preoccupied with an artificial dualism between body and spirit. Religious matters were frequently viewed as "things of the spirit." Only holy men and women, untainted by carnal lust and living celibate lives, could be religious leaders. Eventually only a male priest was allowed to supervise the spiritual journey of the Christian soul. Within this tradition women were generally associated with nonspiritual things. Women's bodies reminded men of sex and sin. Women were seen as unfit spiritual guides.

The movement of women into religious leadership fundamentally challenges the latent body-spirit dualism within Christianity. When women become religious leaders, they affirm the incarnational message of the gospel in a very direct manner. They proclaim, by who they are, that the church is concerned not simply with "spiritual things" but with all of life. They suggest forms of church leadership which take seriously the spiritual, intellectual, emotional, psychological and physical dimensions of the Christian life.

Third, women are changing the style of religious leadership. Historically women have been denied direct opportunities for leadership in the church. Women's gifts have been lost behind the scenes, or made auxiliary to male leadership. Women have carved out arenas of service considered unworthy by men. Within the separate spheres of "women's work," women have exercised leadership in their own ways.

Further Resources

BOOKS
Hamilton, Michael P. and Nancy S. Montgomery, eds. *The Ordination of Women—Pro and Con.* New York: Morehouse-Barlow Co., 1975.

Jewett, Paul King. *The Ordination of Women: An Essay on the Office of Christian Ministry.* Grand Rapids, Mich.: Eerdmans, 1980.

Lehman, Edward C. *Women Clergy: Breaking through Gender Barriers.* New Brunswick and U.S.A.: Transaction Books, 1985.

PERIODICALS
"Southern Baptist Convention's North American Mission Board Has Decided to Stop Endorsing Ordained Women Chaplains." *The Christian Century,* 119, no. 5, February 27, 2002, 19.

Troxell, Barbara. "Clergy Women: An Uphill Calling." *The Christian Century,* 117, no. 4, February 2, 2000, 140.

"Vatican: Stop Courses Preparing Women to Be Deacons." *America,* 185, no. 9, October 1, 2001, 5.

WEBSITES
"Together on Holy Ground: Ordination of Women—Still an Issue for Some." World Council of Churches. Available online at http://www.wcc-coe.org/wcc/assembly/pr-ord.html; website home page: http://www.wcc-coe.org (accessed March 1, 2003).

"A Voice for Women in the Roman Catholic Church." Women's Ordination Conference. Available online at http://www.womensordination.org/ (accessed March 1, 2003).

"Women as Clergy: Priests, Pastors, Ministers, Rabbis." ReligiousTolerance.org. Available online at www.religioustolerance.org/femclrgy.htm; website home page: http://www.religioustolerance.org (accessed March 1, 2003).

Brothers and Sisters to Us
Letter

By: United States Conference of Catholic Bishops

Date: 1979

Source: Office for Social Justice, Archdiocese of St. Paul & Minneapolis, "Catholic Social Teaching: *Brothers and Sisters to Us,* U.S. Catholic Bishops Pastoral Letter on Racism, 1979." Available online at http://www.osjspm.org/cst/racism .htm (accessed February 26, 2003).

About the Organization: Existing as an official assembly of the hierarchy of clergy, the United States Conference of Catholic Bishops has several functions; some of them are guiding church activities, administering charitable work, aiding education, and caring for immigrants. Tracing its beginnings to 1917, the organization of bishops has its headquarters in Washington, D.C., with two other offices: the Office of Migration and Refugee Services in Miami and the Office of Film and Broadcasting in New York City. ∎

Introduction

From the time when America was nothing more than thirteen colonies, justification for the enslavement of African slaves has been bolstered by white religious groups. The Christian churches—predominantly Protestant—during that time period often looked toward the Bible and other religious sources to justify the treatment of the enslaved. Some of these churches preached that not only was the slave an inferior human being, but also that the souls of the slaves were not as worthy, in the eyes of God, as those of the master white race.

Even after slavery was ended in the United States by the Thirteenth Amendment in 1865, many white churches continued to support racial prejudice and ignore the plight of the African American freed slaves. Even the passage of numerous Civil Rights Acts in the 1960s didn't change much in the way of racism, especially in the South. Protestant as well as Roman Catholic churches continued to support racist policies either by their actions or their inaction.

The institution of religion, upon self-examination by the hierarchy of the Roman Catholic Church in America, was found to be lacking in its attempts to combat racism and may have been, through acts of omission and commission, a contributor to that social problem. For example, by omission: very few African Americans were Catholics; and by commission: the church was slow in backing racial justice movements.

In 1979, the United States Conference of Catholic Bishops decided to take this issue on with its full ecclesiastical authority by issuing a pastoral letter on racism. One of the major reasons for the existence of the conference of Bishops was "to promote the greater good which the church offers humankind, especially through forms and programs of the apostolate fittingly adapted to the circumstances of time and place."

Significance

In this pastoral letter, the bishops issued a religious declaration to the church faithful. This declaration was meant to be not just another statement on the immorality of racism, but a call to action for Catholic laity and clergy to publicly reject the sin of racism and actively work toward its eradication.

The bishops offered several recommendations for the individual Catholic that would help reduce the presence of racism in American society. Among them were: a personal change of heart by those who harbored racist feelings; influencing the attitudes of others by openly rejecting racial stereotypes, slurs, and jokes; and participating in political efforts that would help bring justice to the victims of racism. Other recommendations to reduce racism were aimed at the structure of the church itself.

The pastoral letter was both welcomed and criticized by supporters of civil rights. Those who supported the document saw it as a strongly worded moral decree that would motivate Catholics to examine their own racial attitudes and promote their involvement in bringing about social change and justice for the nonwhite population. Those who were critical of the pastoral letter believed that the bishops had not gone far enough. In 1989, the United States Bishops' Committee on Black Catholics issued a statement that "the promulgation of the pastoral on racism was soon forgotten by all but a few. . . . The pastoral on racism had made little or no impact on the majority of Catholics in the United States. . . ."

At a church conference on racism held in Chicago, Illinois and reported in *Commonweal,* Feb 25, 1994, Bishop Joseph Francis was saddened that the 1979 pastoral letter was not more well known. The follow-through for the promotion of the document's contents had not been sufficient, and the call to action fell into the shadows of yesteryear.

Primary Source

Brothers and Sisters to Us [excerpt]

> **SYNOPSIS:** In these excerpts from a pastoral letter on racism, the United States Conference of Catholic Bishops issued an official statement that racism was a sin against God as well as humanity. It called upon Catholics to take action to eradicate this social ill.

Racism is an evil which endures in our society and in our Church. Despite apparent advances and even significant changes in the last two decades, the reality of racism remains. In large part it is only external appearances which have changed.

In 1958 we spoke out against the blatant forms of racism that divided people through discriminatory laws and enforced segregation. We pointed out the moral evil that denied human persons their dignity as children of God and their God-given rights. A decade later in a second pastoral letter we again underscored the continuing scandal of racism called for decisive action to eradicate it from our society.

We recognize and applaud the readiness of many Americans to make new strides forward in reducing and eliminating prejudice against minorities. We are convinced that the majority of Americans realize that racial discrimination is both unjust and unworthy of this nation.

We do not deny that changes have been made, that laws have been passed, that policies have been implemented. We do not deny that the ugly external features of racism which marred our society have in part been eliminated. But neither can it be denied that too often what has happened has only a covering over, not a fundamental change. Today the sense of urgency has yielded to an apparent acceptance of the status quo. The climate of crisis engendered by demonstrations, protest, and confrontation has given way to a mood of indifference; and other issues occupy our attention.

In response to this mood, we wish to call attention to the persistent presence of racism and in particular to the relationship between racial and economic justice. Racism and economic oppression are distinct but interrelated forces which dehumanize our society. Movement toward authentic justice demands a simultaneous attack on both evils. Our economic structures are undergoing fundamental changes which threaten to intensify social inequalities in our nation. We are entering an era characterized by limited resources, restricted job markets and dwindling revenues. In this atmosphere, the poor and racial minorities are being asked to bear the heaviest burden of the new economic pressures.

This new economic crisis reveals an unresolved racism that permeates our society's structures and resides in the hearts of many among the majority. Because it is less blatant, this subtle form of racism is in some respects even more dangerous—harder to combat and easier to ignore. Major segments of the population are being pushed to the margins of society in our nation. As economic pressures tighten, those people who are often black, Hispanic, Native American and Asian—and always poor—slip further

In May 1973, former Congresswoman Louise Hicks (lower right) joined a large gathering of demonstrators protesting the busing of school children in Boston. Busing was used in an effort to racially integrate the city's public schools, especially between the predominately Irish Catholic South Boston and the mostly African American Roxbury districts.
© BETTMANN/CORBIS. REPRODUCED BY PERMISSION.

into the unending cycle of poverty, deprivation, ignorance, disease, and crime. Racial identity is for them an iron curtain barring the way to a decent life and livelihood. The economic pressures exacerbate racism, particularly where poor white people are competing with minorities for limited job opportunities. The Church must not be unmindful of these economic pressures. We must be sensitive to the unfortunate and unnecessary racial tension that results from this kind of economic need.

Mindful of its duty to be the advocate for whose who hunger and thirst for justice's sake, the Church cannot remain silent about the racial injustices in society and its own structures. Our concern over racism follows, as well, from our strong commitment to evangelization. Pope John Paul II has defined evangelization as bringing consciences, both individual and social, into conformity with the Gospel. We would betray commitment to evangelize ourselves and our society were we not to strongly voice our condemnation of attitudes and practices so contrary to the Gospel. Therefore, as the bishops of the

United States, we once again address our pastoral reflections on racism to our brothers and sisters of all races.

We do this, conscious of the fact that racism is only one form of discrimination that infects our society. The United States of America rests on a constitutional heritage that recognizes the equality, dignity, and inalienable rights of all its citizens. Every form of discrimination against individuals and groups—whether because of race, ethnicity, religion, gender, economic status, or national or cultural origin—is a serious injustice which has severely weakened our social fabric. We wish to draw attention here to the particular form of discrimination that is based on race.

The Sin of Racism

Racism is a sin; a sin that divides the human family, blots out the image of God among specific members of that family, and violates the fundamental human dignity of those called to be children of the same Father. Racism is the sin that says some human beings are inherently superior and others essentially inferior because of races. It is the sin that makes racial characteristics the determining factor for the exercise of human rights. It mocks the words of Jesus: "Treat others the way you have them treat you." Indeed, racism is more than a disregard for the words of Jesus; it is a denial of the truth of the dignity of each human being revealed by the mystery of the Incarnation.

In order to find the strength to overcome the evil of racism, we must look to Christ. In Christ Jesus "there does not exist among you Jew or Greek, slave or freedom, male or female. All are one in Christ Jesus." As Pope John Paul II has said so clearly, "Our spirit is set in one direction, the only direction for our intellect, will and heart is toward Christ, the Redeemer of [humanity.]" It is in Christ, then, that the Church finds the central cause for its commitment to justice, and to the struggle for the human right and dignity of all persons.

When we give in to our fears of the other because he or she is of a race different from ourselves, when we prejudge the motives of others precisely because they are of a different color, when we stereotype or ridicule the other because of racial characteristics and heritage, we fail to heed the command of the Prophet Amos: "Seek good and not evil, that you may live; then truly will the Lord . . . be with you as you claim! . . . Then let justice surge like water, and goodness like an unfailing stream."

Today in our country men, women, and children are being denied opportunities for full participation and advancement in our society because of their race. The educational, legal, and financial systems, along with other structures and sectors of our society, impede people's progress and narrow their access because they are black, Hispanic, Native American or Asian.

The structures of our society are subtly racist, for these structures reflect the values which society upholds. They are geared to the success of the majority and the failure of the minority. Members of both groups give unwitting approval by accepting things as they are. Perhaps no single individual is to blame. The sinfulness is often anonymous but nonetheless real. The sin is social in nature in that each of us, in varying degrees, is responsible. All of us in some measure are accomplices. As our recent pastoral letter on moral values states: "The absence of personal fault for an evil does not absolve one of all responsibility. We must seek to resist and undo injustices we have not ceased, lest we become bystanders who tacitly endorse evil and so share in guilt in it."

Racism Is a Fact

Because the Courts have eliminated statutory racial discrimination and Congress has enacted civil rights legislation, and because some minority people have achieved some measure of success, many people believe that racism is no longer a problem in American life. The continuing existence of racism becomes apparent, however, when we look beneath the surface of our national life: as, for example, in the case of unemployment figures. In the second quarter of 1979, 4.9% of white Americans were unemployed; but for blacks the figure was 11.6%; for Hispanics, 8.3%; and for Native Americans on reservations, as high as 40%. The situation is even more disturbing when one realizes that 35% of black youth, 19.1% of Hispanic youth, and an estimated 60% of Native American youth are unemployed. Quite simply, this means that an alarming proportion of tomorrow's adults are cut off from gainful employment—an essential prerequisite of responsible adulthood. These same youths presently suffer the crippling effects of a segregated educational system which in many cases fails to enlighten the mind and free the spirit, which too often inculcates a conviction of inferiority and which frequently graduates persons who are ill prepared and inadequately trained. In addition, racism raises its ugly head in the violence that frequently surrounds attempts to achieve racial balance in education and housing.

With respect to family life, we recognize that decades of denied access to opportunities have been for minority families a crushing burden. Racial discrimination has only exacerbated the harmful relationship between poverty and family instability.

Racism is only too apparent in housing patterns in our major cities and suburbs. Witness the deterioration of inner cities and the segregation of many suburban areas by means of unjust practices of social steering and blockbusting. Witness also the high proportion of Hispanics, blacks, and Indians on welfare and the fact that the median income of nonwhite families is only 63% of the average white family income. Moreover, the gap between the rich and the poor is widening, not decreasing.

Racism is apparent when we note that the population is our prisons consists disproportionately of minorities; that violent crime is the daily companion of a life of poverty and deprivation; and that the victims of such crimes are also disproportionately nonwhite and poor. Racism is also apparent in the attitudes and behavior of some law enforcement officials and in the unequal availability of legal assistance.

Finally, racism is sometimes apparent in the growing sentiment that too much is being given to racial minorities by way of affirmative action programs or allocations to redress long-standing imbalances in minority representation and government-funded programs for the disadvantaged. At times, protestations claiming that all persons should be treated equally reflect the desire to maintain a status quo that favors one race and social group at the expense of the poor and the nonwhite.

Racism obscures the evils of the past and denies the burdens that history has placed upon the shoulders of our black, Hispanic, Native American, and Asian brothers and sisters. An honest look at the past makes plain the need for restitution wherever possible—makes evident the justice of restoration and redistribution.

A Look at the Past

Racism has been part of the social fabric of America since its European colonization. Whether it be the tragic past of the Native Americans, the Mexicans, the Puerto Ricans, or the blacks, the story is one of slavery, peonage, economic exploration, brutal repression, and cultural neglect. All have suffered indignity; most have been uprooted, defrauded or dispossessed of their lands; and none have escaped one or another form of collective degradation by a powerful majority. Our history is littered with the debris of broken promises and treaties, as well as lynchings and massacres that almost destroyed the Indians, humiliated the Hispanics, and crushed the blacks.

But despite this tragic history, the racial minorities of our country have survived and increased. Each racial group has sunk its roots deep in the soil of our culture, thus helping to give to the United States its unique character and its diverse coloration. The contribution of each racial minority is distinctive and rich; each is a source of internal strength for our nation. The history of all gives a witness to a truth absorbed by now into the collective consciousness of Americans: their struggle has been a pledge of liberty and a challenge to future greatness.

Racism Today

Crude and blatant expression of racist sentiment, though they occasionally exist, are today considered bad form. Yet racism itself persists in convert ways. Under the guise of other motives, it is manifest in the tendency to stereotype and marginalize whole segments of the population whose presence perceived as a threat. It is manifest also in the indifference that replaces open hatred. The minority poor are seen as the dross of a post-industrial society—without skills, without motivation, without incentive. They are expendable. Many times the new face of racism is the computer print-out, the graph of profits and lossses, the pink slip, the nameless statistic. Today's racism flourishes in the triumph of private concern over public responsibility, individual success over social commitment, and personal fulfillment over authentic compassion. Then too, we recognize that racism also exists in the attitude and behavior of some who are themselves members of minority groups. Christian ideals of justice must be brought to bear in both the private and the public sector in order that covert racism be eliminated wherever it exists.

The new forms of racism must be brought face-to-face with the figure of Christ. It is Christ's word that is the judgment on this world; it is Christ's cross that is the measure of our response; and it is Christ's face that is the composite of all persons but in a most significant way of today's poor, today's marginal people, today's minorities.

Further Resources

BOOKS

Harris, Leonard, ed. *Racism.* Amherst, N.Y.: Humanity Books, 1999.

Kelsey, George D. *Racism and the Christian Understanding Of Man.* New York: Scribner, 1965.

Mich, Marvin L. Krier. *Catholic Social Teaching And Movements.* Mystic, Conn.: Twenty-Third Publications, 1998.

PERIODICALS

"One Cheer for the Racism Conference." *America,* 185, no. 11, Oct 15, 2001, 3.

"Vatican at U.N. Conference on Racism." *America,* 185, no. 6, Sept 10, 2001, 4.

WEBSITES

"The Catholic Church and Racism." St. Martin Catholic Books and Gifts. http://www.saintmartingifts.com/race.htm (accessed February 26, 2003).

"The Church and Racism: Towards a More Fraternal Society." St. Joseph Catholic Church in Milton. Available online at http://www.stjo-milton.org/current/racism1.htm; website home page: http://www.stjomilton.org (accessed February 26, 2003).

"Theology Library, Racial Justice." Spring Hill College. Available online at http://www.shc.edu/theolibrary/race.htm (accessed February 26, 2003).

11

Science and Technology

CHRISTOPHER CUMO

Entries are arranged in chronological order by date of primary source. For entries with one primary source, the entry title is the same as the primary source title. Entries with more than one primary source have an overall entry title, followed by the titles of the primary sources.

Important Events in Science and Technology, 1970–1979

1970

- In January, molecular biologist Hamilton O. Smith isolates the first enzyme that cuts a sequence of nucleotide bases from a strand of deoxyribonucleic acid (DNA).

- On January 21, the Boeing 747, the first jumbo jet, is put into commercial service.

- In March, International Business Machines (IBM) introduces the floppy disk for storing computer data.

- On April 3, President Richard M. Nixon signs the Water Quality Improvement Act to reduce water pollution.

- On April 11, the National Aeronautics and Space Administration (NASA) launches *Apollo 13*. Two days later an oxygen leak and fire disable the spacecraft, and the astronauts barely make it home.

- On April 22, people in countries throughout the world celebrate the first Earth Day.

- In August, large reflecting telescopes are completed at Kitt Peak, Arizona, and Mauna Kea, Hawaii.

- On December 11, U.S. agronomist Norman Borlaug becomes the first scientist to receive the Nobel Peace Prize.

- On December 31, President Richard Nixon signs the National Air Quality Control Act, with the goal of reducing automobile pollution 90 percent by 1975.

1971

- People can for the first time dial directly by telephone between parts of the United States and Europe.

- On January 31, NASA launches *Apollo 14*. It returns to earth on February 9 with 98 pounds of Moon rocks.

- On February 9, an earthquake with a magnitude of 6.5 on the Richter scale hits San Fernando, California, killing sixty-two people.

- In February, Intel introduces the first computer chip (microprocessor).

- In March, molecular biologists Daniel Nathans and Hamilton Smith isolate additional restriction enzymes.

- On April 9, the Indiana legislature restricts the amount of phosphates in laundry detergents. Phosphates, when they accumulate in lakes and streams, are toxic to fish.

- On May 8, NASA launches the Mars probe *Mariner 8*. It suffers engine failure, falls back to Earth, and crashes north of Puerto Rico.

- On May 17, the U.S. Justice Department requires Florida Power and Light to clean water its pumps into Biscayne Bay to protect fish and other aquatic life.

- On May 30, NASA launches the second Mars probe, *Mariner 9*. On November 13, it begins to orbit Mars, sending back pictures of astonishing clarity.

- On July 26, NASA launches *Apollo 15*. The mission includes a ride around the Moon's surface in the Lunar Rover.

- In October, Texas Instruments introduces the first pocket calculator, weighing 2.5 pounds and costing $150.

- On November 13, the U.S. Justice Department fines Anaconda Wire & Cable $200,000 for polluting the Hudson River, endangering fish and other aquatic life.

1972

- In March, the California State Board of Education requires public schools to teach creationism alongside evolution in biology classes.

- On March 9, the U.S. House of Representatives votes to ban the killing of whales and other marine mammals in U.S. waters to protect them from extinction. On July 26, the U.S. Senate passes a 15-year ban on killing marine mammals.

- On March 22, NASA launches the *Pioneer 10* space probe to explore the outer planets. On June 13, 1983, it becomes the first man-made object to leave the solar system.

- On April 16, NASA launches *Apollo 16*, which will make the fifth Moon landing.

- On May 7, the particle accelerator at Fermi National Accelerator Laboratory in Batavia, Illinois, begins operation.

- On June 14, the Environmental Protection Agency (EPA), following warnings that the insecticide DDT hinders the reproduction of birds and may be toxic to humans, announces a ban on most uses of it, to begin December 31.

- In August, Niles Eldredge, curator of invertebrates at the American Museum of Natural History in New York City, and Harvard University biologist and geologist Stephen Jay Gould propose the theory of punctuated equilibria. Whereas British naturalist Charles Darwin had believed evolution to be gradual, Eldredge and Gould countered that it occurs in bursts of rapid change followed by long periods of statis.

- On August 2, the U.S. Department of Agriculture bans growth hormones in cattle feed, effective January 1, 1973.

- On October 2, the U.S. Atomic Energy Commission orders Consolidated Edison in New York to clean pollution at its Indian Point plant on the Hudson River.

- On October 22, the American Association for the Advancement of Science (AAAS) issues a resolution condemning the decision of the California Board of Education to mandate the teaching of creationism in public-school biology classes.

- On December 7, NASA launches *Apollo 17,* the last manned lunar landing.

1973

- Scientists express concern to the public that genetic engineering might produce new and dangerous microorganisms.
- On January 4, Congress approves Western Union's proposal to build a communications-satellite system.
- In February, astronomer Carl Sagan asserts that life had once and may still exist elsewhere in the universe.
- On March 30, Congress limits industrial emissions of asbestos, mercury and beryllium.
- On April 5, NASA launches *Pioneer 11,* which becomes the first man-made object to fly by Saturn in 1979.
- On May 25, NASA launches the first Skylab. A three-man crew conducts experiments for twenty-eight days in this space station orbiting Earth.
- In June, U.S. Department of Agriculture scientists grow a calf from a frozen embryo, proving that freezing an embryo does not kill it.
- On July 29, NASA launches the second Skylab mission, which lasts fifty-nine days.
- On October 22, Stanford University molecular biologist Stanley Cohen inserts a sequence of nucleotide bases into a bacterium, producing the world's first genetically-engineered organism.
- On November 3, NASA launches the *Mariner 10* probe to collect data from Mercury.
- On November 16, NASA launches the third Skylab. The crew gathers medical information during the eighty-four-day flight.

1974

- Scientists warn that chlorofluorocarbons used as propellants in aerosol sprays may be eroding earth's ozone layer.
- The subatomic J/psi particle is first observed.
- On July 18, scientists at the Asilomar conference call for a moratorium on genetic engineering until they can better understand its risks.
- On September 7, astronomers identify Jupiter's thirteenth moon.
- On October 26, Congress bans the dumping of waste at sea to protect marine life.
- In November, Hewlett Packard introduces a programmable pocket calculator.
- On November 24, Donald C. Johanson, then director of the Cleveland Museum of Natural History in Ohio, discovers in Ethiopia a 40 percent complete skeleton of an Australopithecine (an early man that lived between roughly 4 and 1.5 million years ago).

1975

- The first personal computer, the Altair 8800, is introduced in kit form.

- Harvard University entomology professor Edward O. Wilson publishes *Sociobiology.* Opponents criticize Wilson for arguing that genes predispose humans to behave as they do.
- On July 15, the U.S. and the Soviet Union launch the joint *Apollo-Soyuz* space station that will orbit earth.
- In August, American physicist Steven Weinberg discovers a new subatomic particle, the tau lepton, or tauon. Weinberg believes it to be the building block of quarks, which are in turn the building blocks of protons, neutrons and electrons.
- On August 20, NASA launches *Viking 1,* which begins sending pictures from Mars in June 1976.
- On September 9, NASA launches the *Viking 2* probe, which relays data from Mars between 1976 and 1980.
- On September 16, astronomers identify Jupiter's fourteenth moon.

1976

- In March, astronomers find that Pluto's surface contains frozen methane, a gas that was common in earth's primitive atmosphere.
- On May 18, molecular biologists found Genentech, the first company devoted to creating genetically-engineered organisms, in San Francisco, California.
- In June, the French-English supersonic jet Concorde begins regular passenger service.
- On June 23, the National Institutes of Health issues guidelines prohibiting many categories of recombinant DNA experiments in an attempt to assuage public fears.
- On September 4, astronomers aboard an airborne observatory discover rings around Uranus when it passes in front of a star.
- On September 12, the *Viking 2* lander extends its arm and scoops up a sample of Martian soil, which it feeds to a miniature lander on the spacecraft.
- On September 13, the U.S. National Academy of Sciences warns that chlorofluorocarbons (CFCs), especially those in aerosol cans, are thinning the ozone layer.
- In December, Donald Johanson discovers in Ethiopia the remains of thirteen Australopithecines. Johanson dubbed them the "First Family," because he suspected that all thirteen were part of the same clan and were thus related.

1977

- In February, Apple introduces the Apple II, the first personal computer that Americans buy in large numbers.
- In May, molecular biologists list the full sequence of nucleotide bases in a virus. A virus is a strand of nucleotide bases encased in a protein coat.
- In July, Mary Leakey, wife of the late anthropologist Louis S. B. Leakey, discovers a set of Australopithecine footprints some 3.5 million years old. The tracks are of an adult and child and are in synchrony, suggesting that the two had held hands as they walked.
- In July, oceanographers discover deep-sea vents on the ocean floor near the Galapagos Islands.
- On August 20, NASA launches the space probes *Voyager 1* and *Voyager 2* toward Jupiter and the outer planets.

1978

- In January, U.S. medical personnel evacuate the inhabitants of Bikini Atoll in the Pacific after scientists confirm that earlier testing of the hydrogen bomb has made the island unsafe for habitation.

- In February, Lois Gibbs of the Love Canal Homeowners Association warns that a nearby toxic waste dump causes birth defects and other ailments in residents.

- On March 15, Congress bans the sale of CFCs as spray propellants in an effort to preserve the ozone layer from further deterioration.

- On May 3, alternative energy advocates celebrate Sun Day to publicize the need for renewable sources of energy.

- On May 20, NASA launches two *Pioneer* space probes toward Venus.

- On June 22, astronomers find a moon orbiting Pluto and name it Charon.

- In September, genetically-engineered bacteria begin to produce insulin, the first human hormone derived through recombinant DNA.

- In October, Apple releases the first personal computer with a disk drive.

- On December 8, Hamilton O. Smith receives the Nobel Prize in medicine for his discovery of the first restriction enzyme.

1979

- VisiCalc introduces a spreadsheet program for personal computers, allowing users who know nothing about programming to use a business application for computers for the first time.

- Deep seabed cores show no fossils about 65 million years ago, when a mass extinction killed the dinosaurs.

- In March, *Voyager 1* identifies a ring around Jupiter.

- On March 28, the reactor at Unit 2 of Three Mile Island nuclear power plant in Harrisburg, Pennsylvania, suffers partial meltdown.

- On May 6, sixty-five thousand demonstrators in Washington, D.C., protest nuclear energy as unsafe.

- On May 7, the National Institutes of Health relaxes its guidelines on genetic engineering.

- On May 18, geologists discover 3.5 billion-year-old traces of bacteria and algae from Western Australia. The discovery is among the earliest evidence for life on Earth.

- On July 11, Skylab falls into the atmosphere, breaking up over Australia and the Indian Ocean.

- On November 28, geologists discover amino acids in an Antarctic meteorite (believed to be uncontaminated by Earth), suggesting that life may have arisen elsewhere in our solar system.

"Pesticides and the Reproduction of Birds"

Magazine article

By: David B. Peakall

Date: April 1970

Source: Peakall, David B. "Pesticides and the Reproduction of Birds." *Scientific American,* April 1970, 72–78.

About the Author: David B. Peakall (1931–2001) was born in Purley, England, and received a Ph.D. in chemistry from the University of London in 1956. In 1960, he immigrated to the U.S., where he taught pharmacology at Upstate Medical Center in Syracuse, New York. Two years later, he became assistant professor of pharmacology at the State University of New York. In 1968, he became senior research associate at Cornell University's Laboratory of Ornithology. ∎

Introduction

In 1939, a Swiss chemical company, J.R. Geigy, developed dichlorodiphenyltrichloroethane (DDT), a new type of insecticide. Older insecticides, many of them arsenic compounds, killed insects only if the bugs ate the toxin. By contrast, DDT killed on contact—that is, insects did not need to eat DDT to die from it; they merely needed to step on a spot sprayed with it.

In 1942, Geigy gave samples of DDT to the U.S. Department of Agriculture (USDA). Working with agricultural and mechanical colleges and agricultural experiment stations, the USDA publicized DDT as a miracle insecticide. These agencies and colleges sprayed barns with DDT and invited farmers to tour them. In astonishment, farmers walked through these DDT-treated barns without seeing a single fly. Even *Better Homes and Gardens* ran articles showcasing DDT's effectiveness against insects. In the 1940s, farmers and suburbanites began using DDT with little inkling of the consequences. Chemists kept abreast of demand by developing other insecticides that killed on contact, chlordane being the most widely used after DDT. Whereas farmers spent $9.2 million on insecticides in 1939, they spent $174.6 million in 1954. Farmers at last were winning their war against insects.

But U.S. Bureau of Fisheries aquatic biologist Rachel Carson condemned the use of DDT and other toxic chemicals in her book *Silent Spring* (1962). She correctly charged these chemicals with hastening the evolution of insecticide-resistant insects. Any population of insects will have a diversity of genes that code for a diversity of traits. DDT might kill millions of cockroaches, for example, but a few, by the luck of the genetic draw, will be immune to it. They will survive exposure to DDT and pass on their immunity to their offspring. In this way, a population of cockroaches invulnerable to DDT will evolve.

Carson also charged DDT with seeping into soil and water, polluting both and killing amphibians, birds, and mammals, thus undermining the balance of nature. According to her, humans were poisoning their own ecosystem in order to win a short-term victory over insects.

Significance

David B. Peakall echoed Carson's criticisms. He documented the decline in the U.S. population of peregrines (often called duck hawks), bald eagles, ospreys, and other species of hawk, charging this decline to DDT, which diminished birds' fertility and thinned eggshells to the point where they offered no protection to the developing embryo. In 1952, Peakall noted 150 pairs of osprey nesting along the Connecticut River. By 1969, that number had plummeted to five pairs. In addition, Peakall documented high death rates for young birds, in which DDT quickly reached lethal concentrations.

Birds were not DDT's only victims. Peakall demonstrated that it could quadruple the number of tumors in the liver, lungs, and lymph nodes of animals. DDT was also proved to cause cancer in humans, who accumulated it in fat cells. These dangers led Peakall to recommend that DDT be banned.

In 1972, Congress followed this advice, banning the sale of DDT in the U.S. But Geigy could still sell it overseas, and countries in Latin America, Europe, Africa, and Asia continued to use it against mosquitoes, flies, cockroaches, and other noisome insects.

Science, rather than Congress, eventually reduced farmers' reliance on insecticides. In 1996, for example, the U.S. agrochemical and biotechnology company Monsanto developed a method of gene insertion that gave different varieties of corn resistance to the European corn borer, a corn pest since the 1920s. Farmers who planted this genetically engineered corn in areas where borers were the principal pest discovered that they did not need to spray their fields with insecticide. Genetic engineering's potential value to the agriculture industry is enormous, although concerns remain over risks to beneficial insects as well as the development of pests resistant to engineered crops.

A crushed egg in the nest of a brown pelican off the California coast. The egg had such a thin shell that the weight of the nesting parent's body destroyed it. The concentration of DDT in the eggs of the 300-pair colony reached 2,500 parts per million; no eggs hatched. From David B. Peakall's "Pesticides and the Reproduction of Birds" (1970). **COURTESY OF JOSEPH R. JEHL, JR. REPRODUCED BY PERMISSION.**

Primary Source

"Pesticides and the Reproduction of Birds"
[excerpt]

SYNOPSIS: In this excerpt, David B. Peakall charges DDT with diminishing bird populations in the U.S. and Europe. In addition, he documents its potential to cause cancer in humans and other animals.

About two decades ago . . . the peregrines in Europe and in North America suddenly suffered a crash in population. The peregrine is now rapidly vanishing in settled areas of the world, and in some places, particularly the eastern U.S., it is already extinct. . . . The abrupt population fall of the peregrine (known in the U.S. as the duck hawk) has been paralleled by sharp declines of the bald eagle, the osprey and Cooper's hawk in the U.S. and of the golden eagle and the kestrel, or sparrow hawk, in Europe. The osprey, or fish hawk, has nearly disappeared from its haunts in southern New England and on Long Island; along the Connecticut River, where 150 pairs nested in 1952, only five pairs nested in 1969.

The population declines of all these raptorial birds are traceable not to the killing of adults but to a drastic drop in reproduction. It has been found that the reproduction failures follow much the same pattern among the various species: delayed breeding or failure to lay eggs altogether, a remarkable thinning of the shells and much breakage of the eggs that are laid, eating of broken eggs by the parents, failure to produce more eggs after earlier clutches were lost, and high mortality of the embryos and among fledglings.

Examination of the geographic patterns suggests a cause for the birds' reproductive failure. The regions of population decline coincide with areas where persistent pesticides—the chlorinated hydrocarbons such as DDT and dieldrin—are widely applied. Attrition of the predatory birds has been most severe in the eastern U.S. and in western Europe, where these pesticides first came into heavy use two decades ago. Analysis confirmed the suspicions about the pesticides: the birds were found to contain high levels of the chlorinated hydrocarbons. In areas such as northern Canada, Alaska and Spain, where the use of these chemicals has been comparatively light, the peregrine populations have remained normal or nearly normal. Recent studies show, however, that even in the relatively isolated North American arctic region the peregrines now have fairly high levels of chlorinated hydrocarbons and their populations apparently are beginning to decline.

The birds of prey are particularly vulnerable to the effects of a persistent pesticide such as DDT because they are the top of a food chain. As George M. Woodwell of the Brookhaven National Laboratory has shown, DDT accumulates to an increasingly high concentration in passing up a chain from predator to predator, and at the top of the chain it may be concentrated a thousandfold or more over the content in the original source. . . . The predatory birds, as carnivores, feed on birds that have fed in turn on insects and plants. Hence the birds of prey accumulate a higher dose of the persistent pesticides and are more likely to suffer the toxic effects than other birds. . . .

The recent finding by investigators at the National Cancer Institute that a dose of 46 milligrams of DDT per kilogram of body weight can produce a fourfold increase in tumors of the liver, lungs and lymphoid organs of animals indicates that DDT should be banned for that reason alone. Human cancer victims have been found to have two to two and a half times more DDT in their fat than occurs in the normal population. Investigators in the U.S.S.R. recently reported that DDD, another metabolite of DDT, reduces the islets of Langerhans, the site of insulin synthesis.

The peregrine population crash has prompted two international conferences of concerned investigators, in 1965 and again in 1969. It is encouraging to note that in Britain, where severe restrictions were imposed in 1964 on the use of chlorinated hydrocarbon pesticides, the peregrine population has increased in the past two years. The Canadian government recently announced licensing restrictions that are expected to reduce the use of these pesticides by 90 percent, and many states in the U.S. are also instituting or considering such restrictions. Environmental problems do not respect political boundaries, and in the long run it will do little good if restrictions on the use of these hazardous toxins are applied only to certain regions or parts of the globe.

The long-term effects of the chlorinated hydrocarbons in the environment on human beings are admittedly much more difficult to detect or assess than the spectacular effects that have been seen in the predatory birds. Still, the story told by the birds is alarming enough. It seems obvious that agents capable of causing profound metabolic changes in such small doses should not be broadcast through the ecosystem on a billion-pound scale.

Further Resources

BOOKS

Brown, Michael H. *Laying Waste: The Poisoning of America by Toxic Chemicals.* New York: Pantheon, 1979.

Carson, Rachel. *Silent Spring.* Boston: Houghton Mifflin, 1962.

Janick, Jules, et al. *Plant Agriculture.* San Francisco: W.H. Freeman, 1970.

Perkins, John. *Insects, Experts and the Insecticide Crisis: The Quest for New Pest Management Strategies.* New York: Plenum, 1982.

Shemilt, Lawrence W., ed. *Chemistry and World Food Supplies: The New Frontier.* New York: Pergamon, 1983.

PERIODICALS

Beckman, Tom J. "Farm Pesticides in Midwest Streams." *Ohio Farmer,* February 18, 1992, 78–79.

Finch, Robert H. "Agriculture's Role and Responsibility in Environmental Quality." *National Association of State Universities and Land Grant Colleges,* 1970, 90–94.

Gillis, Justin. "In Key Test, U.S. Allows Sale of Genetically Engineered Corn." *The Washington Post,* February 26, 2003, A01.

Wallace, Mike. "Leaning Toward the Public Sector." *Agrochemical Age,* November 1990, 12, 21–22.

WEBSITES

"The Case for DDT." *Science News* 158, no. 1, July 1, 2000. Available online at http://www.sciencenews.org/20000701/bob8.asp; website home page: http://www.sciencenews.org (accessed March 7, 2003).

"DDT: A Banned Insecticide." University of Oxford, Department of Chemistry. Available online at http://www.chem.ox.ac.uk/mom/ddt/ddt.html; website home page: http://www.chem.ox.ac.uk (accessed March 8, 2003).

"The Green Revolution, Peace, and Humanity"

Lecture

By: Norman E. Borlaug

Date: December 11, 1970

Source: Borlaug, Norman E. "The Green Revolution, Peace, and Humanity." Nobel lecture, December 11, 1970. Published in *Les Prix Nobel.* Stockholm: Almqvist & Wiksell International, 1970. Reproduced in the Nobel e-Museum. Available online at http://www.nobel.se/peace/laureates/1970/borlaug-lecture.html; website homepage: http://www.nobel.se (accessed September 27, 2002).

About the Author: Norman Ernest Borlaug (1914–) was born in Cresco, Iowa, and received a Ph.D. in plant pathology from the University of Minnesota in 1942. In 1944, he became a geneticist and plant pathologist at the Cooperative Wheat Research and Production Program in Mexico. There, he bred disease-resistant, high-yielding grains, including dwarf wheat capable of being cultivated worldwide. ∎

Introduction

Thomas Jefferson and Benjamin Franklin, two of America's leading eighteenth-century scientists and statesmen, believed that science could radically improve Americans' lives. Its greatest value, they felt, would be in teaching farmers how to produce larger harvests, thereby bringing Americans cheap, abundant food. The two men's conviction inspired George Washington to ask Congress to create and fund a national institute that would train farmers in the latest science of food production. Congress finally responded in 1862, creating and funding the U.S. Department of Agriculture (USDA). In 1887, Congress established agricultural and mechanical colleges and agricultural experiment stations.

Scientists at these institutions sought to breed crops with high yields and resistance to insects and diseases. In particular, they focused on breeding different varieties of wheat with these qualities. This focus made sense, since wheat was a staple product in the United States, Canada, Europe, Asia, and Africa.

But there were problems. In fertile soil with plentiful rain, wheat grows taller, going to the straw rather than yielding more grain. In addition, the long, thin stem of such wheat made the plant susceptible to toppling over in heavy wind or rain. For a new wheat to have worldwide importance, it had to have a short, stout stem that would keep it from toppling. Also, a short plant would produce grain instead of straw and be more efficient in yielding that grain than traditional varieties of wheat.

Significance

Agronomists (scientists who deal with field crops and soil management) struggled to achieve this combination of high yield and pest/disease resistance. Norman Borlaug eventually succeeded, breeding a form of dwarf wheat with such qualities. Other scientists used Borlaug's variety to breed Indian and Pakistani derivatives. In the 1969–1970 season, Pakistani farmers planted 55 percent of their wheat acreage to Borlaug's variety or its derivatives, while Indian farmers planted 35 percent of their wheat acreage to them.

Borlaug ushered in the "Green Revolution," the worldwide increase in crop yields—especially wheat, rice, and corn—due to the breeding of high-yield varieties of crops with insect- and disease-resistant types. These new varieties fed billions of people worldwide. They also greatly reduced the number of famines in Africa and Asia, continents where famine had long been a scourge. For his work, in 1970 Borlaug became the only American scientist to win a Nobel Peace Prize. The Nobel committee judged him to "have conferred the greatest benefit on mankind."

But Borlaug did not rest on his laurels. He challenged scientists to do even more: to concentrate on research rather than engross themselves with ministerial duties at the USDA, agricultural and mechanical colleges, and agricultural experiment stations, all of which had grown large and difficult to govern. At large institutions, Borlaug knew, scientists could easily lose sight of the fact that they served farmers, not politicians. Science, he believed, demanded a selfless devotion to duty.

The ideal of serving the farmer went to the heart of Jefferson and Franklin's vision of science. This vision motivated scientists to take positions at the USDA rather than higher-paying jobs at biotechnology or agrochemical firms. Thanks to Borlaug and scientists like him, this idealism transformed agricultural practices in the rest of the globe, leading to a greater abundance of vital crops.

Primary Source

"The Green Revolution, Peace, and Humanity" [excerpt]

SYNOPSIS: In this excerpt from his December 11, 1970, Nobel lecture, Borlaug credits several scientific disciplines for the Green Revolution. Although agronomists like himself bred high-yielding crops, it was chemists, he maintained, who developed fertilizers that pushed these crops to even higher yields, and agricultural engineers, who helped farmers move from inefficient manual labor to tractors and combines.

Norman E. Borlaug won the Nobel Prize in medicine in 1970 for developing tough, high-yield wheat that could be grown in a variety of climates, helping alleviate hunger worldwide. **AP/WIDE WORLD PHOTOS. REPRODUCED BY PERMISSION.**

The green revolution in India and Pakistan, which is still largely the result of the breakthrough in wheat production, is neither a stroke of luck nor an accident of nature. Its success is based on sound research, the importance of which is not self-evident at first glance. For, behind the scenes, halfway around the world in Mexico, were two decades of aggressive research on wheat that not only enabled Mexico to become self-sufficient with respect to wheat production but also paved the way to rapid increase in its production in other countries. It was in Mexico that the high-yielding Mexican dwarf varieties were designed, bred, and developed. There, also, was developed the new production technology which permits these varieties, when properly cultivated, to express their high genetic grain-yield potential—in general, double or triple that of the best yielders among older, tall-strawed varieties.

There are no miracles in agricultural production. Nor is there such a thing as a miracle variety of wheat, rice, or maize which can serve as an elixir to cure all ills of a stagnant, traditional agriculture. Nevertheless, it is the Mexican dwarf varieties, and their more recent Indian and Pakistani derivatives, that have been the principle catalyst in triggering off the green revolution. It is the usual breadth of adaption combined with high genetic yield potential, short straw, a strong responsiveness and high efficiency in the use of fertilizers, and a broad spectrum of disease resistance that has made the Mexican dwarf varieties the powerful catalyst that they have become in launching the green revolution. They have caught the farmers' fancy, and during the 1969–1970 crop season, fifty-five percent of the fourteen million hectares in India were sown to Mexican varieties; it involved the transfer from Mexico to Pakistan and India of a whole new production technology that enables these varieties to attain their high-yield potential. Perhaps seventy-five percent of the results of research done in Mexico in developing the package of recommended cultural practices, including fertilizer recommendations, were directly applicable in Pakistan and India. As concerns the remaining twenty-five percent, the excellent adaptive research done in India and Pakistan by the Indian and Pakistani scientists while the imported seed was being multiplied, provided the necessary information for modifying the Mexican procedures to suit Pakistani and Indian conditions more precisely. . . .

If the high-yielding dwarf wheat and rice varieties are the catalysts that have ignited the green revolution, then chemical fertilizer is the fuel that has powered its forward thrust. The responsiveness of the high-yielding varieties has greatly increased fertilizer consumption. The new varieties not only respond to much heavier dosages of fertilizer than the old ones but are also much more efficient in its use. The old tall-strawed varieties would produce only ten kilos of additional grain for each kilo of nitrogen applied. Consumption of nitrogen fertilizer in India has increased from fifty-eight thousand metric tons of nutrients in 1950–1951 to 538 thousand and 1.2 million metric tons in 1964–1965 and 1969–1970 crop cycles, respectively; and about sixty percent of this amount was produced domestically. Phosphate consumption is approximately half that of nitrogen. A large part of the fertilizer currently being used is for wheat. The targeted consumption and domestic production needs of nitrogen for 1973–1974 are three million and two and a half million metric tons, respectively, a fantastic threefold increase in consumption and a fivefold increase in production. These fertilizer targets must be attained if the targeted production of 129 million metric tons of cereal is to be realized.

Mechanization of agriculture is rapidly following the breakthrough in wheat production. Prior to the first big wheat crop in 1968, unsold tractors accumulated at the two factories then in production; at present, prospective purchasers must make written application for them and wait one or two years for delivery. Although five factories, with an output of eighteen thousand units per year, are now producing tractors, thirty-five thousand units were imported in 1969–1970.

Contrary to a widespread and erroneous opinion, the original dwarf wheat imported from Mexico definitely carried a wider spectrum of disease resistance than the local Indian types that they replaced. But the newer Indian varieties are even better in resistance and of a different genetic type than the original introductions. This greater diversity reduces the danger from disease epidemics but cannot completely eliminate the dangers of disease epidemics, as has become vividly evident from the unexpected and destructive epidemic of southern leaf blight of maize over vast areas of the U.S.A. during the summer of 1970. The only protection against such epidemics, in all countries, is through resistant varieties developed by an intelligent, persistent, and diversified breeding program, such as that being currently carried on in India, coupled with a broad disease-surveillance system and a sound plant pathology program to support the breeding program. From such a program a constant flow of new high-yielding disease-resistant varieties can be developed to checkmate any important changes in pathogens. The Indian program is also developing competence in research of biochemical, industrial, and nutritional properties of wheat. . . .

The quality of scientific leadership is certainly a vital factor in the success of any production campaign. It is deplorable but true that many agricultural scientists in some advanced countries have renounced their allegiance to agriculture for the reasons of expediency and presumed prestige. And some institutions have furnished them a curtain behind which to hide. Some educational and research institutions have even restricted the amount of basic research that can be done under the aegis of its agricultural departments, however basic these researches may be to progress in increasing and insuring food production. Let the individuals live with their own motivations; let them serve science and themselves if they wish. But the institutions have the moral obligation to serve agriculture and society also; and to discharge that obligation honorably, they must try to help educate scientists and scientific leaders whose primary motivation is to serve humanity. . . .

In my dream I see green, vigorous, high-yielding fields of wheat, rice, maize, sorghums, and millets, which are obtaining, free of expense, 100 kilograms of nitrogen per hectare from nodule-forming, nitrogen-fixing bacteria. These mutant strains of *Rhizobium cerealis* were developed in 1990 by a massive mutation breeding program with strains of *Rhizobium* sp. obtained from roots of legumes and other nodule-bearing plants. This scientific discovery has revolutionized agricultural production for hundreds of millions of humble farmers throughout the world; for they now receive much of the needed fertilizer for their crops directly from these little wondrous microbes that are taking nitrogen from the air and fixing it without cost in the roots of the cereals, from which it is transformed into grain.

Further Resources

BOOKS

Chandler, Robert F. "Dwarf Rice—A Giant in Tropical Asia." In *Yearbook of Agriculture, 1968.* Washington, D.C.: GPO, 252–255.

Glaeser, Bernhard, ed. *The Green Revolution Revisited: Critique and Alternatives.* Boston: Allen & Unwin, 1987.

Manning, Richard. *Food's Frontier: The Next Green Revolution.* New York: North Point, 2000.

Perkins, John H. *Geopolitics and the Green Revolution: Wheat, Genes, and the Cold War.* New York: Oxford, 1997.

Reitz, Louis P. "Short Wheats Stand Tall." In *Yearbook of Agriculture, 1968.* Washington, D.C.: GPO, 236–239.

Wolf, Edward C. *Beyond the Green Revolution: New Approaches for Third World Agriculture.* Washington, D.C.: Worldwatch Institute, 1986.

WEBSITES

The Norman Borlaug Heritage Foundation. Available online at http://www.normanborlaug.org (accessed March 5, 2003).

"Norman Ernest Borlaug—Biography." Nobel e-Museum. Available online at http://www.nobel.se/peace/laureates /1970/borlaug-bio.html; website home page: http://www .nobel.se (accessed March 5, 2003).

"Punctuated Equilibria: An Alternative to Phyletic Gradualism"

Essay

Stephen Jay Gould. In 1972, with his colleague Niles Eldredge, Gould postulated that evolution occurs in isolated bursts, contradicting Charles Darwin, who thought it happened gradually. **AP/WIDE WORLD PHOTOS. REPRODUCED BY PERMISSION.**

By: Niles Eldredge and Stephen Jay Gould

Date: 1972

Source: Eldredge, Niles, and Stephen Jay Gould. "Punctuated Equilibria: An Alternative to Phyletic Gradualism." Chapter 5 in *Models in Paleobiology.* Thomas J.M. Schopf, ed. San Francisco: Freeman, Cooper & Company, 1972, 83–84, 96–97.

About the Author: Niles Eldredge (1943–) was born in Brooklyn, New York, and received a Ph.D. in geology from Columbia University in 1969. From 1969 to 1974, he was assistant curator of invertebrates at the American Museum of Natural History in New York City. He was promoted to associate curator in 1974 and curator in 1979. He has taught as an adjunct at City University of New York and Columbia University.

Stephen Jay Gould (1941–2002) was born in New York City and received a Ph.D. from Columbia University in 1967. That year he joined the faculty at Harvard University, rising to become a professor of biology, geology and history of science. His books and articles found an audience among both scholars and the wider public. ∎

Introduction

British naturalist Charles Darwin announced his theory of evolution by natural selection in *On the Origin of Species* (1859). He asserted that some offspring in each generation will not survive to sexual maturity and that organisms in each generation have a diversity of traits. Other than identical twins, no two humans resemble each other in every detail. Rather, humans differ in eye color, skin color, hair color and texture, height, weight, and innumerable other features. Those organisms with traits best suited to their environments have the best chance of surviving to sexual maturity. Bats with acute hearing will have a better chance of surviving in dark caves than bats with poor hearing, and they will pass on this trait to their offspring. In this way, nature selects for survival those organisms best adapted to their environments and, over many generations, matches a species (all plants and animals that can interbreed to produce fertile offspring) to its living conditions.

Darwin accepted the commonly held geology beliefs of his day. Darwin presupposed that the environment remains constant for long durations and that changes through natural selection occur only gradually. If this is true, and if evolution matches a species to its environment through natural selection, evolution must be a slow process involving millions of years. Under Darwin's theory, the evolution of birds from reptiles must have taken countless generations, with each generation differing only in minute detail from its parents.

The problem with Darwin's theory was that the geological record showed no sign of gradual evolution. Species appeared in fossils suddenly and fully formed, remained unchanged during their tenure on earth, and went extinct as quickly as they had arisen. An outstanding example was the sudden appearance of marine invertebrates—complex organisms—as the oldest form of multicellular life discovered on earth. Life, in all its diversity and complexity, apparently arose abruptly at the base of the Cambrian era, 670 million years ago. According to the geological record, evolution must occur rapidly, not gradually as Darwin had supposed.

Significance

Well into the twentieth century, evolutionary biologists had trouble reconciling Darwin's gradualism with a geological record that implied rapid evolution and extinction. In a revision of Darwinism (gradual evolution by natural selection), Niles Eldredge and Stephen Jay Gould announced in 1972 their theory of punctuated equilibria. They affirmed the validity of the geological record; species evolve abruptly, remain unchanged during their tenure on earth, and become extinct as rapidly as they had appeared. Eldredge and Gould argued that evolution occurs within tiny, isolated populations that are small enough for favorable mutations (the addition, deletion, or chemical change in one or more genes) to spread through all members of a population. Such populations are too small to leave traces in the geological record, as fossilization is such a rare occurrence; the possibility that a member of a relatively very small population will fossilize approaches zero. Once a series of favorable mutations spreads throughout a population, transforming it into a new species, that species will increase rapidly in numbers given its increased compatibility with the environment. With large populations, the odds of leaving traces in the fossil record increase dramatically. That only large populations, rather than small, intermediary links between the two species, leave fossils explains the geological record evidencing only fully-formed species.

Eldredge and Gould noted that large populations no longer evolve, as mutations cannot spread to all of its members. Humans, with a population of more than six billion, are an example of a large population that is no longer evolving. Our anatomy has not changed in more than 100,000 years. Large populations remain essentially unchanged until they become extinct. The sudden disappearance of dinosaurs 65 million years ago is an example of extinction's rapidity. According to the new theory, evolution is not gradual, as Darwin had supposed, but occurs in bursts followed by long periods of stasis. Eldredge and Gould, in describing evolution as a rapid occurrence, redefined evolution in a manner consistent with the geological record.

Primary Source

"Punctuated Equilibria: An Alternative to Phyletic Gradualism" [excerpt]

SYNOPSIS: In this excerpt, Niles Eldredge and Stephen Jay Gould argue for the validity of the geological record in which species appear suddenly, live unchanged for millennia, and go extinct as abruptly as they appeared. This evidence implies that evolution occurs rapidly, not gradually as Charles Darwin had supposed.

In this paper we shall argue:

1. The expectations of theory color perception to such a degree that new notions seldom arise from facts collected under the influence of old pictures of the world. New pictures must cast their influence before facts can be seen in different perspective.

2. Paleontology's view of speciation has been dominated by the picture of "phyletic gradualism." It holds that new species arise from the slow and steady transformation of entire populations. Under its influence, we seek unbroken fossil series linking two forms by insensible gradation as the only complete mirror of Darwinian processes: we ascribe all breaks to imperfections in the record.

3. The theory of allopatric (or geographic) speciation suggests a different interpretation of paleontological data. If new species arise very rapidly in small, peripherally isolated local populations, then the great expectation of insensibly graded fossil sequences is a chimera. A new species does not evolve in the area of its ancestors; it does not arise from the slow transformation of all its forbears. Many breaks in the fossil record are real.

4. The history of life is more adequately represented by a picture of "punctuated equilibria" than by the notion of phyletic gradualism. The history of evolution is not one of stately unfolding, but a story of homeostatic equilibria, disturbed only "rarely" (i.e., rather often in the fullness of time) by rapid and episodic events of speciation. . . .

In summary, we contrast the tenets and predictions of allopatric speciation with the corresponding statements of phyletic gradualism previously given:

1. New species arise by the splitting of lineages.

2. New species develop rapidly.

Key Terms

PHYLETIC GRADUALISM: Organisms, however one groups them, evolve slowly according to Charles Darwin. Gould and Eldredge consider the case of grouping organisms by phylum, the largest grouping of organisms below the kingdom. The phylum chordata, for example, includes all organisms with at minimum a notochord and in full development a central nervous system. Because the species Homo sapiens satisfies this criterion it is in the phylum chordata. Phyletic gradualism implies that the environment is so stable that large suits of species hold constant over long durations of time.

HOMEOSTATIC EQUILIBRIA: As implied in the previous definition, the environment is so stable that large suits of species tend toward homeostasis, that is toward a constancy in which species become locked in an interdependent web of relationships. Because species are in interdependent relationships, rapid environmental change will cause extinction of large numbers of species and the consequent rapid evolution of those populations that escape extinction.

ALLOPATRIC SPECIATION: The rise of new species is an allopatric (a geographic) phenomenon. Large populations exist in the area (the geographic region) most conducive to their survival, otherwise many would die. I caution the reader against assuming that the species chose this area. The matching of species to an area is nothing more than the result of natural selection, a process in which choice plays no role with the exception of the hominid clade. Fossil evidence demonstrates that during their 3 million year existence, Australopithecines, a genus of hominid, never left Africa. Africa thus set the geographic boundaries in which Australopithecines existed. The boundaries of a geographic region can sustain only tiny populations because the boundaries are by definition not well suited for survival of a species. When these tiny populations separate from the parent population they become, again by definition, a distinct reproductive group. In such a small group mutations, provided they confer a survival advantage, spread quickly through the group, giving rise to a new species.

PRECAMBRIAN METAZOANS: Metazoans are a class of multi-cellular organisms. Multi-cellular organisms arose some 670 million years ago at the base of the Cambrian Epoch. Geologists classify all time before this event as Precambrian. Except for a single example, the life that existed during the Precambrian Era was single-celled bacteria and algae. The single case of Precambrian metazoans is an odd collection of marine invertebrates, fossilized in a small number of ancient rocks in Australia. These metazoans appear to have gone extinct and therefore to have contributed nothing to the subsequent origin of multi-cellular life at the base of the Cambrian Epoch.

LIPALIAN INTERVAL: The Lipalian interval spans the period from 800 to 670 million years ago. During this interval, as noted in the previous definition, a single collection of marine invertebrates, fossilized in a small number of ancient rocks in Australia, arose. These metazoans appear to have gone extinct and therefore to have contributed nothing to the subsequent origin of multi-cellular life at the base of the Cambrian Epoch.

PHANEROZOIC RECORD: The Phanerozoic record comprises the Paleozoic, Mesozoic and Cenozoic Eras. That is, the Phaneozoic record is the history of life since the base of the Cambrian Epoch 670 million years ago when multi-cellular life arose. The Phanerozoic record is the history of multi-cellular life and of single-celled life, for even today bacteria and algae remain the most numerous organisms on earth.

---

3. A small sub-population of the ancestral form gives rise to the new species.

4. The new species originates in a very small part of the ancestral species' geographic extent—in an isolated area at the periphery of the range.

These four statements again entail two important consequences:

1. In any *local* section containing the ancestral species, the fossil record for the descendant's origin should consist of a sharp morphological break between the two forms. This break marks the migration of the descendant, from the peripherally isolated area in which it developed, into its ancestral range. Morphological change in the ancestor, even if directional in time, should bear no relationship to the descendant's morphology (which arose in response to local conditions in its isolated area). Since speciation occurs rapidly in small populations occupying small areas far from the center of ancestral abundance, we will rarely discover the actual event in the fossil record.

2. Many breaks in the fossil record are real: they express the way in which evolution occurs, not the fragments of an imperfect record. The sharp break in a local column accurately records what happened in that area through time. Acceptance of this point would release us from a self-imposed status of infe-

riority among the evolutionary sciences. The paleontologist's gut-reaction is to view almost any anomaly as an artifact imposed by our institutional millstone—an imperfect fossil record. But just as we now tend to view the rarity of Precambrian metazoans as a true reflection of life's history rather than a testimony to the ravages of metamorphism or the lacunae of Lipalian intervals, so also might we reassess the smaller breaks that permeate our Phanerozoic record. We suspect that this record is much better (or at least much richer in optimal cases) than tradition dictates.

Further Resources

BOOKS

Eldredge, Niles. *Life Pulse: Episodes from the Story of the Fossil Record.* New York: Facts on File Publications, 1987.

———. *Time Frames.* New York: Simon & Schuster, 1985.

Gould, Stephen Jay. *Ever Since Darwin: Reflections in Natural History.* New York: W.W. Norton, 1977.

———. *The Panda's Thumb: More Reflections in Natural History.* New York: W.W. Norton, 1980.

———. *The Structure of Evolutionary Theory.* Cambridge, Mass.: Harvard University Press, 2002.

PERIODICALS

Gould, Stephen Jay, and Eldredge, Niles. "Punctuated Equilibria: The Tempo and Mode of Evolution Reconsidered." *Paleobiology* 3, 1977, 115–51.

WEBSITES

Punctuated Equilibria. Available online at http://www.talkorigins.org/faqs/punc-eq.html; website home page: http://www.talkorigins.org (accessed June 112003).

Punctuated Equilibrium. Available online at http://pespmc1.vub.ac.be/PUNCTUEQ.html; website home page: http://pespmc1.vub.ac.be (accessed June 112003).

Punctuated Equilibrium at Twenty: A Paleontological Perspective. Available online at http://www.skeptic.com/01.3.prothero-punc-eq.html; website home page: http://skeptic.com (accessed March 8, 2003).

Speciation by Punctuated Equilibrium. Available online at http://www.cs.colorado.edu/~lindsay/creation/punk_eek.html; website home page: http://www.cs.colorado.edu (accessed June 11, 2003).

"Extraterrestrial Life"

Essay

By: Carl Sagan, Francis Crick, and L.M. Murkhin

Date: 1973

Source: Sagan, Carl, Francis Crick, and L.M. Murkhin. "Extraterrestrial Life." In *Communication with Extraterrestrial Intelligence (CETI).* Carl Sagan, ed. Cambridge, Mass.: MIT Press, 1973, 54–57.

About the Author: Carl Edward Sagan (1934–1996) was born in Brooklyn, New York, and received a Ph.D. in astronomy from the University of Chicago in 1960. He taught at the University of California-Berkeley and Harvard University. In 1968 he joined the staff of Cornell University. Sagan is best known for his efforts to make science understandable for the general public. He authored over a dozen books, including the Pulitzer Prize winning *The Dragons of Eden* (1978). Sagan was also a television personality, appearing frequently on *The Tonight Show* and hosting a popular TV special *Cosmos.* ■

Introduction

Scientists long have debated whether life exists elsewhere in the universe. In 1903, Alfred Russell Wallace, British naturalist and co-discoverer of the theory of evolution by natural selection, asserted that the complexity of even the simplest bacterium, and the fine-tuning of earth's chemical and physical conditions, make the origin of life so improbable that it can only have arisen once.

American astronomer Percival Lowell disagreed. In 1894, he built the Lowell Observatory at Flagstaff, Arizona. Through its telescope, he scanned Mars' surface, identifying what he believed to be a network of canals. Lowell concluded that only intelligent beings could have built them, proving that Mars had once harbored life, and, perhaps, still did.

The extent to which Americans believed that Mars harbored life became evident in 1938, when Orson Wells broadcast on radio a hoax of an invasion of earth by Martians. In response, police rushed to the radio station, and people fled their homes in panic.

If life were to exist elsewhere in the universe, scientists should be able to detect it. In the 1960s, American astronomer Frank Drake created Project Ozma—named for a princess in L. Frank Baum's *The Wizard of Oz*—to search the universe for signs of life. The National Academy of Sciences funded the project, in which Drake sent radio messages to and listened for others from elsewhere in the universe. Yet, he could not scan the entire universe, only the stars closest to earth. From his headquarters at the National Radio Astronomy Observatory in Deer Creek Valley, West Virginia, Drake searched six hours a day, seven days a week. He focused on two stars about eleven light years away, hoping that they might have planets with life. Despite his efforts, Drake discovered no trace of extraterrestrial life.

Significance

In September 1971, Carl Sagan convened an international conference of scientists that included Frank

Drake and Nobel laureate and co-discoverer of DNA's structure Francis Crick to discuss whether life existed elsewhere in the universe. Sagan believed it did, basing his belief on the probability that the chemical composition of the primitive earth existed on innumerable planets. Jupiter's chemistry was similar to that of the primitive earth, said Sagan. He cited American chemist Stanley L. Miller's 1953 experiment that produced amino acids from a laboratory simulation of the primitive earth's atmosphere. Amino acids are the building blocks of proteins and, ultimately, of nucleotide bases. These in turn are the building blocks of DNA, a self-replicating molecule. This was likely the first life form.

Moreover, Sagan remarked that life had arisen "only a few hundred million years or less" after earth's formation. Such a rapid evolution of life suggested to him that, under the right conditions, life's origin must be inevitable. Sagan believed that life must have arisen on innumerable planets with a chemistry similar to primitive earth's.

Despite Sagan's optimism, the debate remains contentious. Many scientists have argued that if extraterrestrial life were as common as Sagan believes, then we would have found evidence of it by now. They point out that the earth is not a particularly old planet, so if life is common then it would have formed on older planets millions, if not billions, of years ago. Some of this life would presumably have been intelligent, and engaged in activities, such as radio broadcasting or even interstellar travel, that could be detected here on earth as unnatural. Since no such evidence of intelligent life has been found, it must be extremely rare, if not unique to humankind.

Other scientists, notably the late Harvard University biologist Stephen Jay Gould, sided with Sagan. Primitive earth's chemistry is not unique. As such chemistry exists elsewhere, probability favors life's origin on other planets. This does not mean that once life began, it would have evolved to intelligent beings comparable to humans. But the hope that it had done so led American astronomers to establish the Search for Extraterrestrial Intelligence (SETI), a 1980s project similar to Ozma. After a century of debate, the question of whether life exists elsewhere remains unresolved.

Primary Source

"Extraterrestrial Life" [excerpt]

SYNOPSIS: In this excerpt Sagan, Crick, and Murkhin write of their belief that life exists elsewhere in the universe because primitive earth's chemistry, out of which life arose, exists on other planets. Life's rapid origin on earth implies that once a planet has a suitable chemistry, the rise of life is inevitable.

Astonomer and author Carl Sagan argued that it is reasonable to suppose that life exists elsewhere in the universe and that we may one day be able to communicate with it. HULTON ARCHIVE/GETTY IMAGES. REPRODUCED BY PERMISSION.

The number of molecules actually used in biological systems is remarkably smaller than the number of possible organic molecules. There are billions of possible organic compounds. Less than 1500 of these are employed on Earth, and these 1500 are based upon 50 simpler building blocks. Of these building blocks, the most important are the amino acids, the building blocks of proteins, and the sugars and bases, the building blocks of nucleic acids. How can we understand the prebiological production of such molecules?

Suppose we were to imagine that they are made from the present environment; we could take a mixture of the gases in the present atmosphere of the earth, supply them with energy, perhaps an electrical discharge or ultraviolet light, and see what molecules we make. Under these conditions we make smog—ozone, oxides of nitrogen, and so on, and not what we are interested in making.

Suppose, then, we recall that the oxygen in the earth's atmosphere is produced by green plant photosynthesis; there could not have been green plants before the origin of life, so we now take the same gases without oxygen; that is, water, carbon dioxide, and nitrogen, and again supply that mixture with energy. At this point we make molecules like formaldehyde, not exactly where we want to go but on the way; because sugars are the polymers of aldehydes. The change that we have made is toward less oxidizing, more reducing conditions. Biochemicals have much more hydrogen, relatively, than the earth's atmosphere today.

At this point, we recall that the universe is composed primarily of hydrogen. The most abundant atoms in the universe are hydrogen, helium, carbon, nitrogen, oxygen, and neon. Since there is an excess of hydrogen, in cool bodies the molecules expected are the fully saturated hydrides of these atoms. Thus hydrogen will be present as the molecule (H_2), helium as helium, carbon as methane (CH_4), nitrogen as ammonia (NH_3), oxygen as water (OH_2), and neon as neon. It is, therefore, reasonable to assume that the early atmosphere of the earth had a composition of these molecules.

The theory of planetary exospheres clearly shows that hydrogen is able to escape from the earth, at present exosphere temperatures, in very substantial quantities over geological time, whereas atoms heavier than helium cannot escape at all. On the other hand, planets such as Jupiter have such large masses and such low exosphere temperatures that even hydrogen could not escape over geological time. It is therefore very comforting to find that the atmospheric composition of Jupiter is very likely just this mixture of H_2, He, NH_3, CH_4, Ne, and OH_2, but with water at such a depth that we do not see it spectroscopically because of its low vapor pressure at low temperatures.

With this encouragement we can then do the experiment one more time and mix together a mixture of methane, ammonia, and water, supply it with energy and see what molecules are constructed. The first such experiment was performed almost twenty years ago by Stanley Miller who found that amino acids were produced. Since then, a wide variety of such experiments have been performed, for example, in the laboratory of Professor Orgel and in our laboratory at Cornell, and what we find is that not only are amino acids made in high yield but also the nucleotide bases and sugars, and indeed all of the small fundamental building blocks of biochemistry.

To give one example of the yields of molecules which are implied in such experiments, we have done a set of experiments in which mixtures of these gases plus small amounts of H_2S, hydrogen sulfide, are irradiated with long wavelength ultraviolet light. H_2S is the photon acceptor. We produce amino acids with a quantum yield $\sim 10^{-5}$. We know what the ultraviolet photon flux of the primitive sun was from models of solar evolution, and so we can calculate how much amino acids were produced by solar ultraviolet radiation over, let us say, the first billion years of Earth history. If we were to assume, for purposes of calculation, that there was no destruction of amino acids (certainly not a correct assumption), then over the first billion years something like 200 kilograms of amino acids per square centimeter of the Earth's surface would have been synthesized. That is more than the amount of carbon available. If one puts in appropriate destruction rates of amino acids from the thermal degradation of such molecules, then one gets a yield which, if mixed in the present oceans of the earth, would give a few percent solution of amino acids.

Physics and chemistry are so constructed that very large quantities of the correct organic compounds—the ones that make us up—are produced under very general primitive planetary conditions. There is nothing in these experiments special to the earth, either in composition or in energy source. In fact, we have done experiments simulating the present atmosphere of Jupiter comprising the same gases under somewhat different conditions, and to no one's surprise we can still make lots of amino acids. Similar remarks apply to sugars and bases. In the early histories of planets throughout the Galaxy there must be efficient production of all these molecules. Precisely the molecules we need are made under the most general primitive planetary conditions.

This experimental result inclines some of us to think that the probability of the origin of life is rather high, although understanding the production of the building blocks of proteins and nucleic acids is not nearly the same as understanding the origin of life. . . .

The paleontological record has now been extended very far into the past; we now know of fossil microorganisms that are at least 3.2 billion years old. These are blue-green algae and bacteria, or at least have been identified as such by competent paleobotanists. These are very complex organisms, if one examines the microstructure and functions of the contemporary varieties. Also, the fossils that have been found to date are very likely not the oldest which will ever be found. Accordingly, the time between the origin of the first organisms, which must be much simpler than bacteria or algae, and the time of the origin of the earth, is not very long—only a few hundred million years or less. This, to me, speaks rather persuasively for a rapid origin of life on the primitive earth. Since we know of no special conditions on the primitive earth which could not be repeated on millions of other planets throughout the Galaxy, I have the sense, the feeling, that the origin of life is a very likely event. This is, of course, not a statistical probability in the sense of counting cases, but instead is a subjective probability. . . .

Further Resources

BOOKS

Dyson, Freeman. *Infinite in All Directions.* New York: Harper & Row, 1988.

Gould, Stephen Jay. *The Flamingo's Smile: Reflections in Natural History.* New York: W.W. Norton, 1985.

Sagan, Carl. *Carl Sagan's Cosmic Connection: An Extraterrestrial Perspective.* New York: Cambridge University Press, 2000.

PERIODICALS

Tipler, Frank J. "Extraterrestrial Intelligent Beings Do Not Exist." *Physics Today,* April 9, 1981, 70–71.

———. "We Are Alone in Our Galaxy." *New Scientist,* October 7, 1982, 33–35.

WEBSITES

"The Search for Extraterrestrial Intelligence (SETI) in the Optical Spectrum." The Columbus Optical SETI Observatory. Available online at http://www.coseti.org (accessed June 11, 2003).

Harvard SETI Home Page. Available at http://seti.harvard .edu/seti; website home page: http://seti.harvard.edu (accessed June 11, 2003).

Invitation to ETI. Available online at http://members.aol.com /WelcomeETI; website home page: http://members.aol.com (accessed June 11, 2003).

McDonough, Thomas R. "Two Decades of SETI." The Planetary Society. Available online at http://planetary.org /UPDATES/seti/seti-history.html; website home page: http://planetary.org (accessed June 11, 2003).

The Search for Extraterrestrial Intelligence at U.C. Berkeley. Available online at http://seti.ssl.berkeley.edu (accessed June 11, 2003).

SETI @ Home: The Search for Extraterrestrial Intelligence. Available online at http://setiathome.ssi.berkeley.edu (accessed March 8, 2003).

Scientific Creationism

Nonfiction work

By: Henry M. Morris

Date: 1974

Source: Morris, Henry M., ed. *Scientific Creationism.* San Diego, Calif.: CLP Publishers, 1974, 8–10.

About the Author: Henry M. Morris (1918–) was born in Houston, Texas, and received a Ph.D. in hydraulic engineering from the University of Minnesota in 1950. Between 1957 and 1970, he chaired the department of civil engineering at Virginia Polytechnic Institute. He founded, in 1961, the Institute for Creation Research, an organization that denies evolution in favor of a literal reading of *Genesis,* and he served as its director. ■

Introduction

Evolution has long dismayed religious leaders, for evolution claims that all life, including human life, traces its origin to bacterium nearly four billion years ago. Where in this long trek from bacterium to human did humans receive an immortal soul? Was it necessary to suppose God created life and played a role in its evolution? And, if so, what was this role? If humans had evolved from primitive life, how had God created them "in his image," as the Bible asserts?

Evolution's implications disturbed religious leaders, who attacked French naturalist Jean Baptiste Lamarck for proposing evolution in 1809 and the British amateur scientist Robert Chambers for proposing it in 1844. British naturalist Charles Darwin wanted no part of a religious controversy. Although he had conceived the theory of evolution by natural selection as early as 1838, he was wary of publishing it. In 1858, he received a manuscript from British naturalist Alfred Russell Wallace outlining the same theory. Darwin realized that he would need to publish in order to preserve his claim of priority. In 1859, he published *On the Origin of Species,* which created the uproar he feared. Religious leaders attacked his ideas as atheistic materialism. Yet by century's end, European clerics either made their peace with Darwinism or ignored it. Only in the United States did religious opposition to evolution remain vigorous into the twentieth century.

In the United States, creationists insisted on a literal reading of the *Genesis* creation account, an account they believed refuted Darwin's theory. The initial wave of intolerance crested in the 1920s. Texas governor Miriam Ferguson pledged not "to let that kind of rot go into Texas schoolbooks." In 1925, the Tennessee legislature banned the teaching of evolution in public schools. With support from the American Civil Liberties Union, Tennessee biology teacher John Scopes defied the law. Attorney Clarence Darrow and Baltimore journalist Henry L.

Many Americans reject the theory that mankind evolved from primates in favor of the story of man's creation found in the Bible. The boy in this Al Kaufman cartoon has a less serious complaint: "You call that progress? We descend from monkeys and lose the best part!" **THE LIBRARY OF CONGRESS.**

Mencken used the subsequent trial to expose creationists' intolerance and ignorance of science.

Significance

Creationists needed a new strategy. If they could not ban the teaching of evolution in public schools, they needed a way to bring creationism into the classroom by labeling it as a scientific theory. In 1972, the California State Board of Education mandated the teaching of creationism alongside evolution in public schools. Other states followed suit.

The arguments in favor of teaching creationism in the schools are presented in Henry Morris's *Scientific Creationism* (1974). This book asserted that either of two theories could account for the origin and diversity of life. In the first, life evolved to its current diversity. In the other, God created life in its diversity. Morris believed that science could not determine which theory was true,

for neither theory had a monopoly on the evidence. Public schools should expose students to both theories and allow them to decide what to believe. By claiming the need for balanced treatment and students' freedom of choice, Morris and other creationists sought to require the teaching of creationism in public schools.

This strategy worked for fifteen years but met with widespread protests from scientists. Legal action was taken to force creationism off the curriculum. At an Arkansas trial, Harvard University biologist Stephen Jay Gould led a group of prominent scientists and philosophers of science to discredit the teaching of creationism as science.

Particularly effective was philosopher of science Michael Ruse's distinction between science and religion. Ruse focused on the doctrine of falsification. For an assertion to be good science one must be able to test it in a way that has the possibility of disproving (falsifying) it. The assertion that the current diversity of life has evolved from microbes meets this criterion, for if it were wrong then scientists could demonstrate this, by amassing fossil and genetic evidence to disprove the assertion. Some scientists have tried to do so but failed, as the evidence does seem to support the theory of evolution.

The doctrines of religion, however, cannot meet the test of falsification. One cannot, for example, devise any test that is capable of disproving the assertion "God exists." Because this is so, the assertion "God exists" cannot claim scientific accuracy. Rather, it exists in a realm apart from science, namely religion. Religion demands faith because it cannot claim evidence in its defense. This does not make it wrong, but it does make it unscientific.

A state court enjoined the Arkansas statute, and in 1987 the U.S. Supreme Court struck down Louisiana's law that mandated equal time for creationism in the classroom. The courts sided with science. As science, evolutionary biology belonged in the curricula of public schools. As religion, creationism was outside the bounds of public education, forbidden by the "separation of church and state" interpretation of the Constitution's ban on the official establishment of religion. The controversy persisted into the twenty-first century, however, as the concept of intelligent design—a scientific theory that intelligent causes are responsible for the origin of the universe and of life and its diversity—arose to take the place of strict creationism.

Primary Source

Scientific Creationism [excerpt]

> **SYNOPSIS:** In this excerpt, Henry Morris asserts that science cannot determine whether life had evolved or God had created it. Both positions are thus legitimate and deserve inclusion in public schools. Students would then benefit from hearing both arguments and having the freedom to determine what to believe.

The Two Models of Origins

It is, as shown in the previous section, impossible to demonstrate scientifically which of the two concepts of origins is really true. Although many people teach evolution as though it were a proven fact of science, it is obvious that this is false teaching. There are literally thousands of scientists and other educated intellectuals today who reject evolution, and this would certainly not be the case if evolution were as obvious as many scientists say it is.

The same is true of creation, of course. Although many believe special creation to be an absolute fact of history, they must believe this for theological, rather than scientific reasons. Neither

evolution nor creation can be either confirmed or falsified scientifically.

Furthermore, it is clear that neither evolution nor creation is, in the proper sense, either a scientific theory or a scientific hypothesis. Though people might speak of the "theory of evolution" or of the "theory of creation," such terminology is imprecise. This is because neither can be *tested*. A valid scientific hypothesis must be capable of being formulated experimentally, such that the experimental results either confirm or reject its validity.

As noted in the statement by Ehrlich and Birch cited previously, however, there is no conceivable way to do this. Ideally, we might like to set up an experiment, the results of which would demonstrate either evolution or creation to have been true. But there is no one test, nor any series of tests, which can do this scientifically.

All of these strictures do not mean, however, that we cannot discuss this question scientifically and objectively. Indeed, it is extremely important that we do so, if we are really to understand this vital question of origins and to arrive at a satisfactory basis for the faith we must ultimately exercise in one or the other.

A more proper approach is to think in terms of two scientific models, the *evolution model* and the *creation model*. A "model" is a conceptual framework, an orderly system of thought, within which one tries to correlate observable data, and even to predict data. When alternative models exist, they can be compared as to their respective capacities for correlating such data. When, as in this case, neither can be proved, the decision between the two cannot be solely objective. Normally, in such a case, the model which correlates the greater number of data, with the smallest number of unresolved contradictory data, would be accepted as the more probably correct model.

When particular facts do show up which seem to contradict the predictions of the model, it may still be possible to assimilate the data by a slight modification of the original model. As a matter of fact, in the case of the evolution model, as Ehrlich and Birch said: "Every conceivable observation can be fitted into it."

The same generalization, of course, is true of the creation model. There is no observational fact imaginable which cannot, one way or another, be made to fit the creation model. The only way to decide objectively between them, therefore, is to note

"AAAS Resolution: Creationism and California Public Schools"

[In this resolution, the American Association for the Advancement of Science (AAAS) challenges the California State Board of Education's 1972 decision to include the teaching of creationism in public schools.]

Whereas the new *Science Framework for California Public Schools* prepared by the California State Advisory Committee on Science Education has been revised by the California State Board of Education to include the theory of creation as an alternative to evolutionary theory in discussions of the origins of life, and

Whereas the theory of creation is neither scientifically grounded nor capable of performing the roles required of scientific theories, and

Whereas the requirement that it be included in textbooks as an alternative to evolutionary theory represents a constraint upon the freedom of the science teacher in the classroom, and

Whereas its inclusion also represents dictation by a lay body of what shall be considered within the corpus of a science,

Therefore we, the members of the Board of Directors of the American Association for the Advancement of Science, present at the quarterly meeting of October 1972, strongly urge that the California State Board of Education not include reference to the theory of creation in the new *Science Framework for California Public Schools* and that it adopt the original version prepared by the California State Advisory Committee on Science Education. [*Adopted by the AAAS Board of Directors, October 22, 1972.*]

SOURCE: American Association for the Advancement of Science. "AAAS Resolution: Creationism and California Public Schools." October 22, 1972. Available online at http://archives.aaas.org/docs /resolutions.php?doc_id=293; website home page: http://www.aaas.org (accessed June 26, 2003).

Since the rest of this book is devoted primarily to a comparison of these two models, it is important that everyone using it, both teachers and students, clearly understand the formulation of the two models and their implications.

Further Resources

BOOKS

Hanson, Robert W., ed. *Science and Creation: Geological, Theological, and Educational Perspectives.* New York: Macmillan, 1986.

Kitcher, Philip. *Abusing Science: The Case against Creationism.* Cambridge, Massachusetts: MIT Press, 1982.

Larson, Edward J. *Trial and Error: The American Controversy over Creation and Evolution.* New York: Oxford University Press, 1985.

Whitcomb, John C., and Henry M. Morris. *The Genesis Flood: The Biblical Record and Its Scientific Implications.* Philadelphia: Presbyterian and Reformed Publishing, 1961.

Zetterberg, J. Peter, ed. *Evolution versus Creationism: The Public Education Controversy.* Phoenix: Oryx Press, 1977.

PERIODICALS

Callaghan, Catherine A. "Evolution and Creationist Arguments." *American Biology Teacher,* 1980, 422–27.

Cavanaugh, Michael A. "Scientific Creationism and Rationality." *Nature,* 1985, 185–89.

Gatewood, Willard B. "From Scopes to Creation Science: The Decline and Revival of the Evolution Controversy." *South Atlantic Quarterly,* 1984, 363–383.

Gould, Stephen Jay. "The Verdict on Creationism." *The New York Times Magazine,* July 19, 1987, 32–33.

Nelkin, Dorothy. "The Science-Textbook Controversies." *Scientific American,* April 1976, 33–39.

Numbers, Ronald L. "Creationism in 20th-Century America." *Science,* 1986, 538–44.

Scott, Eugenie C., and Henry P. Cole. "The Elusive Scientific Basis of Creation Science." *Quarterly Review of Biology,* 1985, 21–30.

WEBSITES

Institute for Creation Research. Available online at http://www .icr.org (accessed March 8, 2003).

which model fits the facts and predictions with the smallest number of these secondary assumptions.

Creationists are convinced that, when this procedure is carefully followed, the creation model will always fit the facts as well as or better than will the evolution model. Evolutionists may, of course, believe otherwise. In either case, it is important that everyone have the facts at hand with which to consider *both* models, rather than one only. The latter is brainwashing, not brain-using!

Sociobiology: The New Synthesis
Monograph

By: Edward O. Wilson

Date: 1975

Source: Wilson, Edward O. *Sociobiology: The New Synthesis.* Cambridge, Mass.: Belknap Press/Harvard University Press, 1975, 254–255.

About the Author: Edward Osborn Wilson (1929–) was born in Birmingham, Alabama, and received a Ph.D. in entomology from Harvard University in 1955. An authority on ants, he has published articles and books on their behavior. He became professor at Harvard in 1956 and published *Sociobiology* in 1975, arguing that genes predispose humans to behave within a narrow range of options. In 1990, he shared Sweden's prestigious Crafoord Prize with Stanford University biologist Paul Ehrlich. ∎

Introduction

In the early 20th century, American psychologists John B. Watson and B.F. Skinner founded behaviorism. They sought to measure and record behavior as a scientist gathers data from an experiment. They observed that animals, including humans, modified their behavior in response to their environment. One's surroundings shaped behavior and, ultimately, the person. Children could rise to their potential in an environment of parental love, stimulating books and toys, and proper nutrition or descend into criminality in an environment of abuse and neglect.

Hard-line hereditarians stood against the environmentalists. In 1900, the rediscovery of Austrian monk Gregor Mendel's paper on pea hybridization launched the science of genetics. Mendel believed that particles (genes) coded for traits and were passed unaltered from generation to generation. Scientists understood that these genes coded for innumerable traits. In humans, they determine skin color, eye color, hair color and texture, the length and width of the nose, the thickness of lips and much else. American geneticists Charles B. Davenport and Harry H. Laughlin took this understanding to the extreme and claimed that genes directed every facet of a person. They posited that genes determined not only physical attributes but also intelligence and behavior. Poets and criminals were born, not constructed by their environments.

Significance

In the debate over environment and heredity—sometimes called nature versus nurture—Edward O. Wilson sided with heredity. In *Sociobiology* (1975), he argued that behavior was under genetic control. The fact that humans and apes were aggressive under a variety of circumstances suggested to Wilson that humans and apes must share genes that are ubiquitous in both. These genes predispose them to be aggressive toward others. Wilson did not believe that genes dictated behavior. Rather, genes channel behavior into a small number of potential outlets, giving a person only a narrow range of actions in any circumstance. "A much more likely circumstance for any given aggressive species," said Wilson, "and one that I suspect is true for man, is that the aggressive responses vary according to the situation in a genetically-programmed manner." This is the sort of genetic programming that leads a child, for example, to vent aggression in the form of a tantrum.

Sociobiology reinvigorated the debate about how much of human behavior is under conscious control and how much results from a genetic program—much the way software programs a computer. Wilson's subtlety lay in an ability to argue for genetic predisposition without robbing humans of some freedom to direct their actions.

Yet, even this went too far for some biologists. Stephen Jay Gould argued for "biological potentiality" rather than "biological determinism," of which he accused Wilson. Gould believed that humans' large brains gave them the flexibility to meet any circumstance with a wide range of behaviors. Behavior was under genetic control only to the extent that genes code for large brains in humans. Once the human brain began functioning, nearly any behavior was possible.

As Wilson and Gould demonstrate, the debate between environment and heredity remains unresolved. Science cannot provide an unequivocal answer at this time.

Primary Source

Sociobiology: The New Synthesis [excerpt]

> **SYNOPSIS:** In this excerpt, Edward O. Wilson argues that the ubiquity of aggression in humans and apes suggests that both share genes that predispose them to be aggressive.

Human Aggression

Is aggression in man adaptive? From the biologist's point of view it certainly seems to be. It is hard to believe that any characteristic so widespread and easily invoked in a species as aggressive behavior is in man could be neutral or negative in its effects on individual survival and reproduction. To be sure, overt aggressiveness is not a trait in all or even a majority of human cultures. But in order to be adaptive it is enough that aggressive patterns be evoked only under certain conditions of stress such as those that might arise during food shortages and periodic high population densities. It also does not matter whether the aggression is wholly innate or is acquired part or wholly by learning. We are now sophisticated enough to know that the capacity to learn certain behaviors is itself a genetically controlled and therefore evolved trait.

Such an interpretation, which follows from our information on patterned aggression in other animal species, is at the same time very far removed from the sanguinary view of innate aggressiveness which

Edward O. Wilson lectures on insects at Woods Hole, Mass., 1974. In 1975 Wilson's *Sociobiology* created controversy by arguing that human social and anti-social behavior was determined in large part by genetics. **AP/WIDE WORLD PHOTOS. REPRODUCED BY PERMISSION.**

was expressed by Raymond Dart (1953) and had so much influence on subsequent authors:

> The blood-bespattered, slaughter-gutted archives of human history from the earliest Egyptian and Sumerian records to the most recent atrocities of the Second World War accord with early universal cannibalism, with animal and human sacrificial practices or their substitutes in formalized religions and with the worldwide scalping, head-hunting, body-mutilating and necrophiliac practices of mankind in proclaiming this common blood lust differentiator, this mark of Cain that separates man dietetically from his anthropoidal relatives and allies him rather with the deadliest of Carnivora.

This is very dubious anthropology, ethology, and genetics. It is equally wrong, however, to accept cheerfully the extreme opposite view, espoused by many anthropologists and psychologists (for example, Montagu, 1968) that aggressiveness is only a neurosis brought out by abnormal circumstances and hence, by implication, nonadaptive for the individual. When T. W. Adorno, for example, demonstrated (in *The Authoritarian Personality*) that bullies tend to come from families in which the fa-

ther was a tyrant and the mother a submerged personality, he identified only one of the environmental factors affecting expression of certain human genes. Adorno's finding says nothing about the adaptiveness of the trait. Bullying behavior, together with other forms of aggressive response to stress and unusual social environments, may well be adaptive—that is, programmed to increase the survival and reproductive performance of individuals thrown into stressful situations. A revealing parallel can be seen in the behavior of rhesus monkeys. Individuals reared in isolation display uncontrolled aggressiveness leading frequently to injury. Surely this manifestation is neurosis and nonadaptive for the individuals whose behavioral development has been thus misdirected. But it does not lessen the importance of the well-known fact that aggression is a way of life and an important stabilizing device in free-ranging rhesus societies.

This brings us to the subject of the crowding syndrome and social pathology. Leyhausen (1965) has graphically described what happens to the behavior of cats when they are subjected to unnatural crowding: "The more crowded the cage is, the less relative hierarchy there is. Eventually a despot emerges, 'pariahs' appear, driven to frenzy and all kinds of neurotic behaviour by continuous and pitiless attack by all others; the community turns into a spiteful mob. They all seldom relax, they never look at ease, and there is a continuous hissing, growling, and even fighting. Play stops altogether and locomotion and exercises are reduced to a minimum." Still more bizarre effects were observed by Calhoun (1962) in his experimentally overcrowded laboratory populations of Norway rats. In addition to the hypertensive behavior seen in Leyhausen's cats, some of the rats displayed hypersexuality and homosexuality and engaged in cannibalism. Nest construction was commonly atypical and nonfunctional, and infant mortality among the more disturbed mothers ran as high as 96 percent.

Such behavior is obviously abnormal. It has its close parallels in certain of the more dreadful aspects of human behavior. There are some clear similarities, for example, between the social life of Calhoun's rats and that of people in concentration and prisoner-of-war camps, dramatized so remorselessly, for example, in the novels *Andersonville* and *King Rat.* We must not be misled, however, into thinking that because aggression is twisted into bizarre forms under conditions of abnormally high density, it is therefore nonadaptive. A much more likely circumstance for any given aggressive species, and one that I suspect is true for man, is that the aggressive responses vary according to the situation in a genetically programmed manner. It is the total *pattern* of responses that is adaptive and has been selected for in the course of evolution.

The lesson for man is that personal happiness has very little to do with all this. It is possible to be unhappy and very adaptive. If we wish to reduce our own aggressive behavior, and lower our catecholamine and corticosteroid titers to levels that make us all happier, we should design our population densities and social systems in such a way as to make aggression inappropriate in most conceivable daily circumstances and, hence, less adaptive.

Further Resources

BOOKS

Goldsmith, Timothy H. *The Biological Roots of Human Nature.* New York: Oxford University Press, 1991.

Gould, Stephen Jay. *Ever Since Darwin: Reflections in Natural History.* New York: W.W. Norton, 1977.

Lorenz, Konrad. *On Aggression.* London, England: Methuen, 1966.

Pope, Geoffrey Grant. *The Biological Bases of Human Behavior.* Boston: Allyn and Bacon, 2000.

Science for the People. *Biology as Destiny: Scientific Fact or Social Bias?* Cambridge, Mass.: Science for the People, 1984.

Segerstrale, Ullica. *Defenders of the Truth: The Sociobiology Debate.* Oxford: Oxford University Press, 2000.

Walsh, Anthony. *Biosociology: An Emerging Paradigm.* Westport, Conn.: Praeger, 1995.

PERIODICALS

Wilson, Edward O. "Human Decency is Animal." *The New York Times Magazine,* October 12, 1975, 14–19.

WEBSITES

Boeree, C. George. Sociobiology. Available at http://www.ship.edu/~cgboeree/sociobiology.html; website home page: http://www.ship.edu/~cgboeree (accessed June 12, 2003).

Kardas, Edward P. "Sociobiology." Available online at http://peace.saumag.edu/faculty/kardas/Courses/GPWeiten/C1Intro/Sociobiology.html; website home page: http://peace.saumag.edu/faculty/kardas (accessed June 12, 2003).

Sociobiology. Available at http://www.psych.nwu.edu/~sengupta/sociob.html; website home page: http://www.psych.nwu.edu/~sengupta (accessed June 12, 2003).

"Haplodiploidy and the Evolution of the Social Insects"

Journal article

By: Robert L. Trivers and Hope Hare

Date: January 23, 1976

Source: Trivers, Robert L., and Hope Hare. "Haplodiploidy and the Evolution of the Social Insects." *Science* 191, no. 4224, January 23, 1976, 250, 261.

About the Authors: Robert L. Trivers (1943–) was born in Washington, D.C., and received a Ph.D. in anthropology from Harvard University in 1965. He is professor of anthropology and biological sciences at Rutgers University in New Brunswick, New Jersey. His research focuses on social evolution and natural selection.

Hope Hare (1951–) was born in Boston, Massachusetts, and received an M.S. in genetics from Yale University in 1974. Since then, she has been a research assistant at Harvard University's Museum of Comparative Zoology. ∎

Introduction

In 1866, Gregor Mendel announced that particles (genes) code for traits in pea plants and, by implication, all life. These particles pass unaltered from generation to generation. In humans, genes code for skin color, eye color, hair color and texture, the shape and length of the nose, the thickness of lips, and much else. Between 1909 and 1927, Columbia University embryologist Thomas Hunt Morgan and his team of researchers demonstrated that genes are found in a line on chromosomes—the linear units within the nucleus of each cell that contain the genes and are passed from generation to generation by gametes. Genes and chromosomes are analogous to a package of roll candy, with each candy analogous to a gene and the package to a chromosome.

Organisms are either diploid or haploid. A diploid contains two sets of chromosomes, one inherited from the father and the other from the mother. Humans are diploid organisms. Humans receive twenty-three chromosomes from their fathers and twenty-three from their mothers for a full complement of forty-six chromosomes. In diploid organisms, chromosomes from the father pair with those from the mother. Thus humans have twenty-three pairs of chromosomes. Haploid organisms, on the other hand, contain only a single set of chromosomes, inherited from their mothers. Fathers contribute no chromosomes. An unfertilized bee egg will develop into a haploid bee. Haploid bees are male, and diploid bees are female. Male bees have half the chromosomes of female bees.

By studying social insects, including bees, Robert Trivers and Hope Hare concluded that genetics programmed the insects to care more for siblings with whom they shared more genes. © BRIAN S. TURNER; FRANK LANE PICTURE AGENCY/CORBIS. REPRODUCED BY PERMISSION.

Significance

Robert L. Trivers and Hope Hare demonstrated that female worker bees spend 300 percent more time and effort feeding sisters rather than brothers, and they correlated this finding to the fact that the females are three times more related to their sisters. A female worker bee receives half of her chromosomes (and, thus, half her genes) from her mother, the queen, and the other half from her father, a drone. She shares all her paternal chromosomes with every sister, because a drone has only a single set of chromosomes to pass to offspring. On average, she shares half her maternal chromosomes with every sister, because there is a 50 percent chance that she and a sister will inherit the same chromosomes from the queen. Consider a simple example: A queen has two chromosomes because she is diploid, A and B, but can pass only one to each of two offspring. If offspring one receives chromosome A, there is a 50 percent chance that offspring two also will receive chromosome A. The average between 100 percent (the certainty that all sisters share the same paternal chromosomes) and 50 percent (the likelihood that 2 sisters will receive the same maternal chromosomes) is 75 percent. Every worker bee thus shares, on average, 75 percent of her chromosomes with every sister. On the other hand, each drone (male) has only a single set of chromosomes inherited from the queen. The probability that a male can share paternal chromosomes with a sister is zero, because a male inherits no paternal chromosomes. The probability that a male and a sister share the same maternal chromosomes is one-half, as demonstrated above. The average between zero and half is 25 percent. A male drone shares, on average, 25 percent of its chromosomes with every brother. Thus, a worker bee is three times more related to a sister than to a brother.

Remarkably, the genes in each worker apparently program it to spend 300 percent more time and effort feeding sisters than brothers, ensuring their own survival in three of every four cases. The genes act independently of the bee in which they exist; evolution acts to preserve genes rather than organisms. The traditional Darwinian explanation was that evolution could only act on an organism in its totality of traits. Trivers and Hare exposed this explanation as too simple to explain the behavior of bees. Their work raises the possibility that animals, including humans, are little more than receptacles for genes. Animals perish, but genes live on in succeeding generations. Genes, therefore, attain a kind of immortality that transcends the animal in which they temporarily reside.

Primary Source

"Haplodiploidy and the Evolution of the Social Insects" [excerpt]

> **SYNOPSIS:** In this excerpt, Robert Trivers and Hope Hare demonstrate that female worker bees instinctively spend thrice the time and effort feeding sisters than brothers because they share, on average, three times more genes with sisters than brothers. Genes act to preserve themselves through this instinct.

Capitalizing on the Asymmetrical Degrees of Relatedness

In haplodiploid species, a female is symmetrically related to her own offspring (by sex of offspring) but asymmetrically related to her siblings, while a male is symmetrically related to his siblings but asymmetrically related to his own offspring. It is the male parent and the female offspring who can exploit the asymmetrical r's [degrees of relatedness] (for personal gain in inclusive fitness); but there is not much scope for such behavior in males . . . , while the females can exploit the r's by investing resources disproportionately in sisters compared to brothers or by investing in sisters and sons (or sisters and nephews) instead of sons and daughters.

1) Skewing the colony's investment toward reproductive females and away from males

Imagine a solitary, outbred species in which a newly adult female can choose between working to rear her own offspring and working to rear her mother's (but not both). Assuming that such a female is equally efficient at the two kinds of work, she will enjoy an increase in inclusive fitness by raising siblings in place of offspring as long as she invests more in her sisters than in her brothers—thereby trading, so to speak, r's of 1/4 for r's of 3/4. For example, by working only on sisters instead of offspring, her initial gain in inclusive fitness would be 50 percent per unit invested. Were this altruism to spread such that all reproductives each generation are reared by their sisters, in a ratio controlled by the sisters, we expect three times as much to be invested in females as in males, for at this ratio of investment (1:3) the expected RS [reproductive success] of a male is three times that of a female, per unit investment, exactly canceling out the workers' greater relatedness to their sisters. Were the mother to control the ratio of investment, it would equilibrate at 1:1, so that in eusocial species in which all reproductives are produced by the queen but reared by their sisters, strong mother-daughter conflict is expected regarding the ratio of investment, and a measurement of the ratio of investment is a measure of the relative power of the two parties. . . .

Summary

Hamilton was apparently the first to appreciate that the synthesis of Mendelian genetics with Darwin's theory of natural selection had profound implications for social theory. In particular, insofar as almost all social behavior is either selfish or altruistic (or has such effects), genetical reasoning suggests that an individual's social behavior should be adjusted to his or her degree of relatedness, r, to all individuals affected by the behavior. We call this theory kinship theory.

The social insects provide a critical test of Hamilton's kinship theory. When such theory is combined with the sex ratio theory of Fisher, a body of consistent predictions emerges regarding the haplodiploid Hymenoptera. The evolution of female workers helping their mother reproduce is more likely in the Hymenoptera than in diploid groups, provided that such workers lay some of the male-producing eggs or bias the ratio of investment toward reproductive females. Once eusocial colonies appear, certain biases by sex in these colonies are expected to evolve. In general, but especially in eusocial ants, the ratio of investment should be biased in favor of females, and in ants it is expected to equilibrate at 1:3 (male to female). We present evidence from 20 species that the ratio of investment in monogynous ants is, indeed, about 1:3, and we subject this discovery to a series of tests. As expected, the slave-making ants produce a ratio of investment of 1:1, polygynous ants produce many more males than expected on the basis of relative dry weight alone, solitary bees and wasps produce a ratio of investment near 1:1 (and no greater than 1:2), and the social bumblebees produce ratios of investment between 1:1 and 1:3. In addition, sex ratios in monogynous ants and in trap-nested wasps are, as predicted by Fisher, inversely related to the relative cost in these species of producing a male instead of a female. Taken together, these data provide quantitative evidence in support of kinship theory, sex ratio theory, the assumption that the offspring is capable of acting counter to its parents' best interests, and the supposition that haplodiploidy has played a unique role in the evolution of the social insects.

Finally, we outline a theory for the evolution of worker-queen conflict, a theory which explains the queen's advantage in competition over male-producing workers and the workers' advantage regarding the ratio of investment. The theory uses the asymmetries of haplodiploidy to explain how the evolved outcome of parent-offspring conflict in the social Hymenoptera is expected to be a function of certain social and life history parameters.

Further Resources

BOOKS

Allen, Garland E. *Life Science in the Twentieth Century.* New York: John Wiley & Sons, 1975.

Fisher, R.A. *The Genetical Theory of Natural Selection.* Oxford: Clarendon Press, 1930.

Garber, Edward, ed. *Genetic Perspectives in Biology and Medicine.* Chicago: University of Chicago Press, 1985.

Gould, Stephen Jay. *Ever Since Darwin: Reflections in Natural History.* New York: W.W. Norton, 1977.

Magner, Lois. *A History of the Life Sciences.* New York: Dekker, 1979.

Mayr, Ernest. *The Growth of Biological Thought: Diversity, Evolution, and Inheritance.* Cambridge, Mass.: Harvard University Press, 1982.

Portugal, Franklin H., and Jack S. Cohen. *A Century of DNA.* Cambridge, Mass.: MIT Press, 1977.

Ruse, Michael. *The Philosophy of Biology.* London: Hutchinson, 1973.

PERIODICALS

Hamilton, William D. "The Genetical Theory of Social Behavior." *Journal of Theoretical Biology,* 1964, 1–52.

Schaffner, Kenneth F. "Theories and Explanations in Biology." *Journal of the History of Biology,* 1969, 19–33.

WEBSITES

Irwin, Rebecca. Kin Selection and the Evolution of Altruism. Available online at http://www.utm.edu/~rirwin/391KinSel.htm; website home page: http://www.utm.edu (accessed June 12, 2003).

Kin Selection. Available online at http://www.taumoda.com/web/PD/library/kin.html; website home page: http://www.taumoda.com/web/index.html (accessed June 12, 2003).

"Ethiopia Yields First 'Family' of Early Man"

Magazine article

By: Donald C. Johanson

Date: December 1976

Source: Johanson, Donald C. "Ethiopia Yields First 'Family' of Early Man." *National Geographic* 150, December 1976, 791–793.

About the Author: Donald C. Johanson (1943–) was born in Chicago, Illinois, and received a Ph.D. in anthropology from the University of Chicago in 1974. That year, he became curator at the Cleveland Museum of Natural History in Ohio.

Johanson rose to world fame by his discovery of Lucy, a 40 percent complete skeleton of an Australopithecine female. In 1981, he founded the Institute of Human Origins at Berkeley, California. ∎

Introduction

British naturalist Charles Darwin announced in *On the Origin of Species* (1859) that all life, including humans, evolved from primitive ancestors. Three years earlier, a teacher in Germany, Carl Fuhlrott, identified a partial skeleton from the Neander Valley (hence the name "Neanderthal Man") as the remains of a robustly-built early man. Additional Neanderthal discoveries followed, and in 1897 Dutch physician Eugene Dubois found the partial cranium and femur of a more primitive early man, *Homo erectus* (upright man) in Indonesia.

Especially important was British anatomist Raymond Dart's find of a toddler's skull in South Africa in 1924. He recognized it as the remains of a biped having a chimpanzee-sized brain. Here was the earliest human ancestor, *Australopithecus africanus* (southern ape from Africa), discovered in Africa, the continent Darwin predicted as the birthplace of humanity. This discovery drew Scottish physician Robert Broom in the 1930s to South Africa, where he found additional *Australopithecus* remains, including a partial pelvis and spine that proved *Australopithecus* walked upright, as Dart surmised. In that decade, British anthropologists Louis and Mary Leakey began searching Olduvai Gorge in eastern Africa for traces of early man. In 1959, Mary discovered a nearly-complete adult *Australopithecus* skull, a find that propelled the Leakeys to worldwide fame. At 1.75 million years old, it was the most ancient discovery of human remains. Although paleoanthropologists had found complete Neanderthal skeletons, no one previously had found more than fragments of the men who predated Neanderthal.

Significance

In 1974, Donald Johanson electrified the world with his discovery of a 40 percent complete *Australopithecus* skeleton. In this article, he described the fortuitous discovery. Glancing over his shoulder, his eye by chance noticed the outline of an arm bone. His graduate student dismissed it as the bone of a monkey, but Johanson intuited that it was from an early man. Surveying the terrain, Johanson spotted skull fragments, then a lower jaw, leg bones, more arm bones, ribs, vertebrae and a partial pelvis. Johanson rushed back to camp with a few fragments. Later in camp, while his colleagues were listening to Beatles' songs, Johanson christened the find "Lucy," after "Lucy in the Sky with Diamonds." Once he and Kent State University anthropologist C. Owen Lovejoy reconstructed the skeleton, filling in missing bones by matching them to the actual skeleton, both came

Dr. Donald Johanson clears dirt from a horse fossil found in Ethiopia, 1974. During this same Ethiopian expedition Johanson discovered "Lucy," the fossilized remains of a human ancestor (*Australopithecus afarensis*) over three million years old. © **1976 DAVID L. BRILL. REPRODUCED BY PERMISSION.**

to the conclusion that Lucy had been a woman because of the width of her pelvis. Johanson dated Lucy at over 3 million years old, nearly doubling the age of Mary Leakey's *Australopithecus* and making Lucy the oldest *Australopithecus* discovered to that date.

Lucy was the strongest evidence to that date that man's ancestors walked upright long before they evolved a large brain, for Lucy had a brain little larger than a chimpanzee's. In fact, Lovejoy judged her to have been a more efficient biped than modern humans. The discoverers also believed she demonstrated, at more than three million years old, that man's ancestors walked upright soon after diverging from African apes, chimpanzee and gorilla, five million years ago. Bipedalism, not brainpower, was the signature trait of being human. Indeed, recent discoveries in Africa suggest that man's ancestors walked upright more than four million years before they evolved a brain of modern volume, about 1250 cubic milliliters.

Primary Source

"Ethiopia Yields First 'Family' of Early Man" [excerpt]

> **SYNOPSIS:** In this excerpt, Donald C. Johanson described his discovery of Lucy, a 40 percent com-

plete skeleton of an Australopithecine woman. When he glanced over his shoulder, his eye happened to notice the outline of an arm bone. Surveying the terrain, he spotted skull fragments, a lower jaw, leg bones, more arm bones, ribs, vertebrae, and a partial pelvis.

It was November 24, 1974, and the sun stood scorchingly overhead. Our Land-Rover wallowed through a maze of ravines and gullies. Finally, where the track dead-ended at a sandy hill, I said to graduate student Tom Gray, "This is the place."

I had intended to devote this Sunday morning to bringing my field notes up-to-date. But Tom had persuaded me to help him relocate a spot where we had collected fossil animal bones the year before. We spent some time surveying, gathered up what bones we found, and started back toward the Land-Rover. As we walked, I glanced over my shoulder—and there on the ground I saw a fragment of an arm bone.

"Look at that, right there," I said to Tom.

"An arm bone of a monkey?" Tom guessed.

My pulse was quickening. Although the bone was very small, it lacked the characteristic bony flange of the comparable anatomical portion of a monkey. Suddenly I found myself saying, "It's hominid!"

Something else caught my eye. "Do you suppose it belongs with those skull fragments next to your hand?" Startled, Tom sent his glance after mine. It was high noon that memorable day when the realization struck us both that we might have found a skeleton. An extraordinary skeleton.

We looked up the slope. There, incredibly, lay a multitude of bone fragments—a nearly complete lower jaw, a thigh bone, arm bones, ribs, vertebrae, and more! The searing heat was forgotten. Tom and I yelled, hugged each other, and danced, mad as any Englishmen in the midday sun.

We were working with surface materials three million years old. We knew that a skeleton of that antiquity, whether of the genus *Homo* or—as it later turned out—another genus of hominids, would be one of the most meaningful finds in the history of man's search for the rootstock of his species.

The ride back to camp seemed endless. Roaring into camp, with dust billowing behind the Land-Rover and the horn honking, we could see people in the dining tent.

"We found it, we found it!" I shouted. "You won't believe it! A hominid skeleton just lying there, waiting to be collected."

We had brought back some fragments, and everyone crowded around to have a look. Lunch was forgotten.

That evening the camp bubbled with excitement. We cooled beer in the Awash River, and a special goat barbecue was laid on.

For the rest of that 1974 expedition, our major effort was screening and collecting all the bone fragments at the spot that we called Afar Locality 288. Taken together, the recovered parts made up nearly 40 percent of a single skeleton. The form of the pelvis identified it as a female. She was small of stature—the short leg bones suggested a height of three and a half to four feet. She had cut her wisdom teeth, so she was grown when she died.

Later geological study confirmed that the sediments from which the skeleton emerged dated from about three million years ago.

Surely such a noble little fossil lady deserved a name. As we sat around one evening listening to Beatles' songs, someone said, "Why don't we call her Lucy? You know, after 'Lucy in the Sky With Diamonds.'" So she became Lucy. But she is also known as Denkenesh, an Ethiopian name meaning "You are wonderful"—well deserved, since her discovery marked a milestone in the study of mankind's prehistory.

Further Resources

BOOKS

Bowler, Peter J. *Theories of Human Evolution.* Baltimore: Johns Hopkins University Press, 1986.

Dobzhansky, Theodosius. *Mankind Evolving.* New Haven, Conn.: Yale University Press, 1962.

Gould, Stephen Jay. *Ever Since Darwin: Reflections in Natural History.* New York: W.W. Norton, 1977.

Johanson, Donald C., and Edey Maitland. *Lucy: The Beginning of Humankind.* New York: Simon & Schuster, 1981.

Leakey, Richard E., and Roger Lewin. *Origins: What New Discoveries Reveal about the Emergence of Our Species and Its Possible Future.* New York: Dutton, 1977.

Lewin, Roger. *In the Age of Mankind: A Smithsonian Book of Human Evolution.* Washington, D.C.: Smithsonian Books, 1988.

———. *Principles of Human Evolution: A Core Textbook.* Malden, Mass.: Blackwell Science, 1998.

Tanner, Nancy M. *On Becoming Human.* New York: Cambridge University Press, 1981.

PERIODICALS

Hausler, Martin, and Peter Schmid, "Comparison of the Pelvis of Sts 14 and AL 288-1: Implications for Birth and Sexual Dimorphism in Australopithecines." *Journal of Human Evolution* 29, 1995, 363-383.

Landau, Misia. "Human Evolution as Narrative." *American Scientist,* 1984, 262–68.

Lovejoy, C. Owen. "Evolution of Human Walking." *Scientific American,* November 1988, 118–25.

———. "The Origin of Man." *Science,* January 23, 1981, 341–50.

Stern, Jack T. Jr., and Randall L. Susman, "The Locomotor Anatomy of *Australopithecus afarensis*," *Journal of Physical Anthropology* 60, 1983, 279-317.

Tague, Robert G., and C. Owen Lovejoy. "The Obstetric Pelvis of AL 288-1 (Lucy)." *Journal of Human Evolution,* May 1986, 237–55.

Weaver, Kenneth F., et al. "The Search for Early Man." *National Geographic,* November 1985, 560–629.

WEBSITES

Finding Lucy. Available online at http://www.pbs.org/wgbh /evolution/library/07/1/l_071_01.html; website home page: http://www.pbs.org (accessed June 12, 2003).

The Human Origins Program: In Search of What Makes Us Human. Available online at http://www.mnh.si.edu/anthro /humanorigins; website home page: http://www.mnh.si.edu (accessed June 12, 2003).

"Lucy in the Earth." Human Evolution. Available at http:// www.pbs.org/wgbh/aso/tryit/evolution/lucy.html; website home page: http://www.pbs.org (accessed June 12, 2003).

Walker, Phillip L., and Edward H. Hagen. Human Evolution: The Fossil Evidence in 3D. Available online at http://www.anth.ucsb.edu/projects/human; website home page: http://www.anth.uscb.edu (accessed June 12, 2003).

Energy: The Solar Prospect

Paper

By: Denis Hayes

Date: March 1977

Source: Hayes, Denis. *Energy: The Solar Prospect.* Worldwatch Paper 11. [Washington]: Worldwatch Institute, 1977, 21–23.

About the Author: Denis Allen Hayes (1944–) was born in Wisconsin Rapids, Wisconsin, and graduated from Stanford University Law School in 1985. In 1969, he founded Environmental Action Inc. in Washington, D.C. He was a visiting scholar at the Smithsonian Institution in Washington, D.C., in 1971 and 1972. In 1974 and 1975, he was director of the Illinois State Energy Office in Springfield. He was a senior researcher at Worldwatch Institute in Washington, D.C., from 1975 to 1979. ∎

Introduction

Since the nineteenth century, Americans have depended on fossil fuels for energy. Petroleum refined into gasoline made possible the widespread use of the automobile in the early twentieth century, and the burning of coal and natural gas generated electricity.

Alternatives existed, but they supplied only a fraction of domestic needs. In 1882, a Wisconsin utility built the first hydroelectric plant in the United States. In a hydroelectric plant, falling water rushes through a turbine, spinning it to generate electricity. Another alternative is nuclear power. In 1954, a Pennsylvania utility built the first U.S. nuclear plant, which began generating electricity three years later. Nuclear power generates electricity in a manner similar to the burning of coal and natural gas. The burning of these fossil fuels boils water, whose steam spins a turbine. In a nuclear power plant, neutrons (particles in the nucleus of an atom) are fired at uranium atoms, causing them to split. The energy released boils water and causes a turbine to spin.

Alternative sources of energy captured Americans' attention in 1973, when Arab nations in the Organization of Petroleum Exporting Countries (OPEC) cartel stopped shipping oil to the United States to protest the United States' support of Israel in the Yom Kippur War. The shock of rising gasoline prices convinced Americans that they needed alternatives to fossil fuels.

Significance

Solar energy emerged as a promising alternative. Each day, the sun floods the earth with 10,000 to 15,000 times more energy than humans use worldwide in the form of fossil fuels, hydroelectric power, and nuclear power combined. If science and technology could harness a fraction of this energy, Americans would no longer need to rely on fossil fuels to generate electricity and to heat their homes and businesses. Denis Hayes described two methods of generating electricity from sunlight. In one, the "power tower" mirrors concentrate sunlight on a tower of water, boiling it to generate steam, thereby spinning a turbine. In the second, the "solar farm" mirrors concentrate sunlight on pipes, heating the gases within them. The hot gases boil water, generating steam to spin a turbine.

A third alternative, which Hayes omits, is the photovoltaic cell (PV cell) in which sunlight strikes a solar panel. Electrons in the panel capture the sun's energy, giving them the energy to flow through metals. The flow of electrons is, by definition, an electric current.

In 1974, the promise of solar energy led the U.S. Department of Energy (DOE) to begin spending $400 million a year on developing ways to generate electricity from sunlight. Prior to 1974, the DOE had never spent more than $1 million a year on solar energy. Optimists predicted that within a few years, solar power would replace fossil fuels in generating electricity in the United States.

Yet this has not happened. The decline of oil prices in the 1980s returned Americans to their reliance on fossil fuels. In response to the decline in interest in solar energy, Congress slashed federal support for research. In 1981, Congress spent $160 million on solar energy research. By 1989, federal funding fell to less than $30 million.

Solar energy nevertheless holds promise. The first PV cell in 1954 converted only 4 percent of sunlight into electricity. Fifty years later it could convert 33 percent of sunlight into electricity. U.S. energy companies Amoco and Enron believe they have the technology to build PV cells that can generate 100 megawatts of electricity, enough to power 100,000 homes at a cost of 5.5 cents a kilowatt-hour—just under the 5.8 cents needed to convert fossil fuels into electricity. Solar energy remains an alternative to the burning of fossil fuels.

Primary Source

Energy: The Solar Prospect [excerpt]

> **SYNOPSIS:** In this excerpt, Denis Hayes describes two methods of generating electricity from sunlight. In one, mirrors concentrate sunlight on a tower of water, boiling it to generate steam that spins a turbine.

Solar panels collect sunlight, Los Angeles area, California, 1977. Interest in using the energy from sunlight to generate electricity rose during the 1970s, in response to the high price of oil. © JAMES L. AMOS/CORBIS. REPRODUCED BY PERMISSION.

In the other, mirrors concentrate sunlight on pipes, heating the gases within them. The hot gases boil water, again generating steam that spins a turbine.

Electricity from the Sun

It was long believed that nuclear power would replace the fossil fuels. Because nuclear power is best utilized in centralized electrical power plants, virtually all energy projections therefore show electricity fulfilling a growing fraction of all projected energy demands. Some solar proponents advocate large centralized solar power plants as direct replacements for nuclear power plants to meet this demand. However, solar technologies can provide energy of any quality, and remarkably little of the world's work requires electricity. A sensible energy strategy demands more than the simple-minded substitution of sunlight for uranium.

Electricity now comprises less than 20 percent of energy use in virtually all countries. If energy sources were carefully matched with energy uses, it is difficult to imagine a future society that would need more than one-tenth of its energy budget as electricity—the highest quality and most expensive form of energy. Today, only 11 percent of U.S. energy is

used as electricity, and much of this need could be met with other energy sources. To fill genuine needs for electricity, the most attractive technology in many parts of the world will be direct solar conversion.

Two types of large, land-based solar thermal power plants are receiving widespread attention. The "power tower" is currently attracting the most money and minds, although a rival concept—the "solar farm"—is also being investigated. The power tower relies upon a large field of mirrors to focus sunlight on a boiler located on a high structure—"the tower." The mirrors are adjusted to follow the sun across the sky, always maintaining an angle that reflects sunlight back to the boiler. The boiler, in turn, produces high pressure steam to run a turbine to generate electricity. The French, who successfully fed electricity into their national grid from a small tower prototype in January of 1977, plan to have a 10-megawatt unit operating by 1981 and have been aggressively trying to interest the desert nations of the Middle East in this effort. The United States is now testing a small prototype involving a 40-acre mirror field and a 200-watt tower in New Mexico, and it plans to put a 10-megawatt power plant into operation by 1980 at Barstow, California.

An electric utility in New Mexico plans to combine three 430-foot power towers that generate a total of 50 megawatts with an existing gas-fired power plant at Albuquerque. The proposed complex would utilize the existing generators, turbines, condensers, switchyard, etc. The resulting hybrid, which would cost $60 million and cover 170 acres, would have no heat storage capacity; it would simply heat its boilers with gas when the sun failed to shine. A survey by the utility identified 600 existing power plants in the American Southwest (with about 40,000 megawatts of electrical generating capacity) that could be retrofitted with solar power towers.

The "solar farm" concept would employ rows of parabolic reflectors to direct concentrated sunlight onto pipes containing molten salts or hot gases. Special heat exchangers would transfer the 600 degrees C heat from the pipes to storage tanks, filled with melted metal, from whence it could be drawn to generate high pressure steam to run a turbine.

Both the solar farm and the power tower approaches require direct sunlight because their concentrating mirrors cannot use diffuse light. Both will also probably be feasible only in semi-arid regions with few cloudy days and little pollution. One objection raised to such facilities is that they would despoil large tracts of pristine desert. However, proponents point out that the area needed to produce 1,000 megawatts of solar electricity is less than the amount of land that would have to be strip-mined to provide fuel for a similar sized coal plant during its 30-year lifetime and that the solar plant's land could be used forever. In fact, according to Aden and Marjorie Meinel, a 1,000-megawatt solar farm on the Arizona desert would require no more land than must, for safety reasons, be deeded for a nuclear reactor of the same capacity.

Large, centralized solar electric plants consume no finite fuels, produce no nuclear explosives, and hold no ecological punches. With development, such plants should also be economically competitive with fossil-fueled, fission, and fusion power plants. However, they produce only electricity and they are subject to all the problems inherent in centralized high technologies. To the extent that energy needs can be met with lower quality sources or decentralized equipment, the centralized options should be avoided.

Further Resources
BOOKS

Dvorkin, David. *At Home with Solar Energy: A Consumer's Guide.* Nashville, Tenn.: T. Nelson, 1979.

Franta, Gregory E., and Kenneth R. Olson, eds. *Solar Architecture.* Ann Arbor, Mich.: Ann Arbor Science Publishers, 1978.

Gunn, Anita. *A Citizen's Handbook on Solar Energy.* Washington, D.C.: Public Interest Research Group, 1976.

Halacy, Daniel S. *The Coming of Age of Solar Energy.* New York: Harper & Row, 1973.

Hayes, Denis. *Blueprint for a Solar America.* Washington, D.C.: Solar Lobby, 1979.

———. *Rays of Hope: The Transition to a Post-Petroleum World.* New York: Norton, 1977.

Meinel, Aden B., and Marjorie P. Meinel. *Applied Solar Energy: An Introduction.* Reading, Mass.: Addison-Wesley, 1976.

Weinberg, Alvin Martin. *Can the Sun Replace Uranium?* Oakridge, Tenn.: Institute for Energy Analysts, 1977.

PERIODICALS
Ewing, Rex A. "Freedom with the Sun & Wind." *Mother Earth News,* October/November 2002, 128–29.

Patton, Phil. "A Role for Solar, But It's a Cameo." *The New York Times,* September 13, 2002, F9.

WEBSITES
The American Solar Energy Society. Available online at http://www.ases.org (accessed June 12, 2003).

Renewable Energy Technologies–Solar. U.S. Department of Energy. Office of Energy Efficiency and Renewable Energy. Available online at http://www.eren.doe.gov/RE/solar.html; website home page: http://eren.doe.gov (accessed June 12, 2003).

Solar Energy and Energy Efficiency Information. Available online at http://www.epsea.org (accessed March 10, 2003).

Solar Energy Industries Association. Available online at http://www.seia.org (accessed June 12, 2003).

"Microelectronics and the Personal Computer"
Magazine article

By: Alan C. Kay

Date: September 1977

Source: Kay, Alan C. "Microelectronics and the Personal Computer." *Scientific American,* September 1977, 231, 242–244.

About the Author: Alan C. Kay (1941–) was born in Springfield, Massachusetts, and received a Ph.D. in computer science from the University of Utah in 1969. In 1970, he became professor at Stanford University's Artificial Intelligence Laboratory. Two years later, he joined the Xerox Palo Alto Research Center in California. In 1984, he became research fellow at Apple Computer. ■

Richard Connor plays a game on a personal computer at The Computer Store, Los Angeles, September 22, 1977. With technology rapidly reducing both the size and cost of computers, Alan C. Kay predicted that by 1987 many people would own a notebook-size computer. AP/WIDE WORLD PHOTOS. REPRODUCED BY PERMISSION.

Introduction

The first computers were large and massive, in part because their circuitry contained vacuum tubes, large partly or wholly evacuated cylinders through which an electric charge passed. Computers of such size could not fit on a desk and were not portable. Scientists needed to reduce their size, mass, and cost before Americans could buy computers for their own use, called personal computers (PCs).

The first step toward miniaturization was the invention of the transistor, in 1947, by Bell Telephone Laboratories physicists John Bardeen, Walter H. Brattain, and William B. Shockley. This invention won all three 1956 Nobel Prizes in physics. The transistor was smaller and lighter than the vacuum tube and, for this reason, began replacing it in appliances including computers in the 1950s. In 1971, Intel scientist Theodore Hoff invented the microchip that contained transistors, diodes, and resistors. The microchip had greater memory and could process information faster than a single transistor. The first integrated circuit contained ten components on a silicon chip of three square millimeters. Within a few years, scientists could fit thousands of transistors on a chip, increasing a computer's speed and memory by orders of magnitude.

A computer the size of a modest television had become feasible, and in 1974 the American company MITS marketed the first PC, the Altair, which used Intel chips. Three years later, American entrepreneurs Steven P. Jobs and Stephen G. Wozniak founded Apple Computer and introduced the Apple II, a PC they mass produced at low cost—just as Henry Ford had mass produced the Model T earlier in the century. In 1977, U.S. companies Radio Shack and Commodore Business Machines introduced their own PCs.

Significance

Alan C. Kay predicted that the continued miniaturization, decreased cost, and increased speed and memory would make PCs ubiquitous in the United States within a decade. The computer represented a new medium for processing information, for its users could interact with a PC that responded to queries as television and radio could not. The chief drawback of computers, Kay believed, was that they required users to have some knowledge of programming. If computers were to become ubiquitous, scientists would need to develop software that novices could operate with ease. Well before other social commentators, Kay understood that computers might create a digital divide, with affluent, well-educated

Americans using computers in greater numbers than impoverished, poorly educated Americans.

The computer industry grew as Kay had foreseen. In 1981, IBM unveiled the IBM PC, a computer that was only slightly faster than its competitors but which had ten times their memory. The next year, the IBM PC ran a spreadsheet developed by the American company Lotus Development Corporation. IBM's introduction of the Intel 8088 chip and the Microsoft operating system established the company as the world's leading computer manufacturer.

In 1983, Apple introduced a PC with a mouse with which one could select icons from a variety of options. In 1986 and 1987, Compaq Computer Corporation introduced PCs with still greater speed and memory. PCs of the late 1970s had 64 kilobytes of memory (64,000 characters); by the early 1990s they had some 100 megabytes (100 million characters).

The PC's potential to link people became clear with the rise of the Internet, which the U.S. Defense Department had created in 1969 as an electronic network for the exchange of information via electronic mail (e-mail). Academics quickly came to use it, and the National Science Foundation financed its growth. In 1989, Tim Berners-Lee, a computer scientist at CERN, a scientific organization in Geneva, Switzerland, pioneered the World Wide Web (WWW), an information retrieval system. By the mid-1990s, millions of users worldwide linked to the WWW through their PCs.

Primary Source

"Microelectronics and the Personal Computer" [excerpt]

> **SYNOPSIS:** In this excerpt, Alan C. Kay predicts that continued miniaturization, decreased cost, and increased speed and memory would make PCs ubiquitous within a decade. Yet Kay worried that the PC might create a digital divide, with affluent, well-educated Americans using PCs in greater numbers than impoverished, poorly educated Americans.

The future increase in capacity and decrease in cost of microelectronic devices will not only give rise to compact and powerful hardware but also bring qualitative changes in the way human beings and computers interact. In the 1980's both adults and children will be able to have as a personal possession a computer about the size of a large notebook with the power to handle virtually all their information-related needs. Computing and storage capacity will be many times that of current microcomputers: tens of millions of basic operations per second will

manipulate the equivalent of several thousand printed pages of information.

The personal computer can be regarded as the newest example of human mediums of communication. Various means of storing, retrieving and manipulating information have been in existence since human beings began to talk. External mediums serve to capture internal thoughts for communication and, through feedback processes, to form the paths that thinking follows. Although digital computers were originally designed to do arithmetic operations, their ability to simulate the details of any descriptive model means that the computer, viewed as a medium, can simulate any other medium if the methods of simulation are sufficiently well described. Moreover, unlike conventional mediums, which are passive in the sense that marks on paper, paint on canvas and television images do not change in response to the viewer's wishes, the computer medium is active: it can respond to queries and experiments and can even engage the user in a two-way conversation.

The evolution of the personal computer has followed a path similar to that of the printed book, but in 40 years rather than 600. Like the handmade books of the Middle Ages, the massive computers built in the two decades before 1960 were scarce, expensive and available to only a few. Just as the invention of printing led to the community use of books chained in a library, the introduction of computer time-sharing in the 1960's partitioned the capacity of expensive computers in order to lower their access cost and allow community use. And just as the Industrial Revolution made possible the personal book by providing inexpensive paper and mechanized printing and binding, the microelectronic revolution of the 1970's will bring about the personal computer of the 1980's, with sufficient storage and speed to support high-level computer languages and interactive graphic displays.

Ideally the personal computer will be designed in such a way that people of all ages and walks of life can mold and channel its power to their own needs. Architects should be able to simulate three-dimensional space in order to reflect on and modify their current designs. Physicians should be able to store and organize a large quantity of information about their patients, enabling them to perceive significant relations that would otherwise be imperceptible. Composers should be able to hear a composition as they are composing it, notably if it is too complex for them to play. Businessmen should have an active briefcase that contains a working simulation of their company. Educators should be able to implement their own version of a Socratic dialogue with dynamic simulation and graphic animation. Homemakers should be able to store and manipulate records, accounts, budgets, recipes and reminders. Children should have an active learning tool that gives them ready access to large stores of knowledge in ways that are not possible with mediums such as books.

How can communication with computers be enriched to meet the diverse needs of individuals? If the computer is to be truly "personal," adult and child users must be able to get it to perform useful activities without resorting to the services of an expert. Simple tasks must be simple, and complex ones must be possible. Although a personal computer will be supplied with already created simulations, such as a general text editor, the wide range of backgrounds and ages of its potential users will make any direct anticipation of their needs very difficult. Thus the central problem of personal computing is that nonexperts will almost certainly have to do some programming if their personal computer is to be of more than transitory help. . . .

How will personal computers affect society? The interaction of society and a new medium of communication and self-expression can be disturbing even when most of the society's members learn to use the medium routinely. The social and personal effects of the new medium are subtle and not easy for the society and the individual to perceive. To use writing as a metaphor, there are three reactions to the introduction of a new medium: illiteracy, literacy and artistic creation. After reading material became available the illiterate were those who were left behind by the new medium. It was inevitable that a few creative individuals would use the written word to express inner thoughts and ideas. The most profound changes were brought about in the literate. They did not necessarily become better people or better members of society, but they came to view the world in a way quite different from the way they had viewed it before, with consequences that were difficult to predict or control.

We may expect that the changes resulting from computer literacy will be as far-reaching as those that came from literacy in reading and writing, but for most people the changes will be subtle and not necessarily in the direction of their idealized expectations. For example, we should not predict or expect that the personal computer will foster a new revolution in education just because it could. Every new communication medium of this century—the telephone, the motion picture, radio and television—has elicited similar predictions that did not come to pass. Millions of uneducated people in the world have ready access to the accumulated culture of the centuries in public libraries, but they do not avail themselves of it. Once an individual or a society decides that education is essential, however, the book, and now the personal computer, can be among the society's main vehicles for the transmission of knowledge.

The social impact of simulation—the central property of computing—must also be considered. First, as with language, the computer user has a strong motivation to emphasize the similarity between simulation and experience and to ignore the great distances that symbols interpose between models and the real world. Feelings of power and a narcissistic fascination with the image of oneself reflected back from the machine are common. Additional tendencies are to employ the computer trivially (simulating what paper, paints and file cabinets can do), as a crutch (using the computer to remember things that we can perfectly well remember ourselves) or as an excuse (blaming the computer for human failings). More serious is the human propensity to place faith in and assign higher powers to an agency that is not completely understood. The fact that many organizations actually base their decisions on—worse, take their decisions from—computer models is profoundly disturbing given the current state of the computer art. Similar feelings about the written word persist to this day: if something is "in black and white," it must somehow be true.

Further Resources

BOOKS

Berners-Lee, Tim. *Weaving the Web.* San Francisco: HarperSanFrancisco, 1999.

Freiberger, Paul, and Michael Swaine. *Fire in the Valley: The Making of the Personal Computer.* Berkeley, Calif.: Osborne/McGraw-Hill, 1984.

Gates, Bill. *The Road Ahead.* New York: Penguin Books, 1995.

Yourdon, Edward. *Nations at Risk: The Impact of the Computer Revolution.* New York: Yourdon, 1986.

PERIODICALS

Peled, Abraham. "The Next Computer Revolution." *Scientific American,* October 1987, 57–64.

Smarte, Gene, and Andrew Reinhardt. "1975-1990: 15 Years of Bits, Bytes, and Other Great Moments."*Byte,* September 1990, 369–400.

Thompson, Tom. "The Macintosh at 10."*Byte,* February 1994, 47–54.

WEBSITES

Knight, Dan. "Personal Computer History." Low End PC. Available online at http://lowendpc.com/history/index.shtml; website home page: http://lowendpc.com (accessed June 12, 2003)

Polsson, Ken. Chronology of Personal Computers. Available online at http://www.islandnet.com/~kpolsson/comphist; website home page: http://www.islandnet.com/~kpolsson (accessed June 12, 2003).

Pop Quiz: What Was the First Personal Computer? Available online at http://www.blinkenlights.com/pc.shtml; website home page: http://www.blinkenlights.com (accessed June 27, 2003)

Veit, Stan. PC–History. Available online at http://www.pc-history.org (accessed June 12, 2003).

"The Surface of Mars"

Magazine article

By: Raymond E. Arvidson, Alan B. Binder, and Kenneth L. Jones

Date: March 1978

Source: Arvidson, Raymond E., Alan B. Binder, and Kenneth L. Jones. "The Surface of Mars." *Scientific American,* March 1978, 76, 81–83.

About the Authors: Raymond Ernest Arvidson (1948–) was born in Brooklyn, New York, and received a Ph.D. in geology from Brown University in 1974. Between 1974 and 1984, he taught at Brown University. In 1984, he became professor of earth and planetary science at Washington University in St. Louis, being promoted to department chair in 1991.

Alan B. Binder (1939–) was born in San Diego, California, and received a Ph.D. in geology from the University of Arizona. He is a research scientist at the University of Kiel in Germany, where he specializes in examining lunar rock.

Kenneth Lester Jones (1905–) was born in Keweenaw Bay, Michigan, and received a Ph.D. in botany from the University of Michigan in 1933. Between 1929 and 1937, he was an instructor at the University of Michigan, being promoted to assistant professor in 1937 and to department chair in 1950. Since 1977, he has been emeritus professor of biological sciences at the University of Michigan. ∎

Introduction

The planet Mars derives its name from the Roman god of war. Such a name was an honor, coming from a people who steeped themselves in the craft of warfare and whose armies welded the Mediterranean basin into an empire. Like other ancients, the Romans had a weakness for supposing that the motion of Mars and the other planets determined the course of events on Earth. This superstition survived the empire's collapse, and only the rise of science in the sixteenth century began to substitute rationality for superstition.

By the eighteenth century, European scientists had founded astronomy as a science, and in 1894 American astronomer Percival Lowell established the Lowell Observatory at Flagstaff, Arizona. Through its telescope, he scanned Mars' surface, convinced that it contained a network of canals. Lowell concluded that intelligent beings had built them, evidence Mars once harbored life and perhaps still did.

The possibility that the United States might explore Mars at close range flowed from the space race. In answer to the Soviet launch of *Sputnik* in 1957, Congress created the National Aeronautics and Space Administration (NASA) the next year to recapture U.S. leadership in space. In 1961, President John F. Kennedy (served 1961–1963) challenged Congress and the American people to land a man on the moon before decade's end. Congress responded with record appropriations to NASA, enabling it to dispatch two rockets to Mars in 1964, while setting its sights on the moon. Technical problems scuttled *Mariner III*, the first mission to Mars, but *Mariner IV* came within 6,000 miles of Mars in July 1965, photographing its surface that was cratered, much like the moon's. In 1969, NASA launched *Mariner VI* and *Mariner VII* for Mars.

Significance

NASA crowned these ventures by launching two Viking rockets in 1975. Each carried a landing craft with cameras and a small, automated laboratory. The *Viking II* cameras relayed photos of Mars to earth until 1980. The lab collected soil samples that revealed no trace of life, though they strengthened evidence from *Mariner IX* that Mars had active volcanoes and liquid water early in its history. Photographs revealed that even the most ancient geological features remained sharply defined, evidence that, aside from windstorms, nothing has eroded the surface. The Viking probes revealed that Mars' poles may contain frozen water. Arvidson, Binder, and Jones even suspected that Mars' atmosphere once held clouds from which rain fell, the runoff of which etched tiny channels on the planet's surface. Mars' crust also contained water which was once liquid, they believed.

Early in its history, Mars, with its atmosphere, liquid water, and geological activity, may have harbored microbial life, though scientists continue to debate the issue. In 1996, NASA held a news conference in which its scientists announced the discovery of organic molecules in a Martian meteorite. Organic compounds may mean that microbes once inhabited Mars. Electron microscopes revealed wormlike etchings that may be fossilized Martian microbes. Yet, other scientists asserted that lunar rocks had similar etchings without the moon having ever harbored life. Moreover, critics charged that the Martian meteorite had formed at temperatures too high to sustain life.

The success of the Viking probes led NASA to send *Pathfinder* and its land rover, *Sojourner,* to Mars. *Pathfinder* landed on Mars on July 4, 1997, and *Sojourner* trekked across the surface to collect soil and rocks. In three months, *Pathfinder* relayed some 16,000 photos back to earth. In 2001 *Odyssey* was put in orbit around the planet, and in June 2003 NASA launched the first of two surface rovers, *Spirit* and *Opportunity,* scheduled to land in early 2004. NASA plans additional probes of Mars in 2005.

Primary Source

"The Surface of Mars" [excerpt]

> **SYNOPSIS:** In this excerpt, Raymond Arvidson, Alan Binder, and Kenneth Jones interpret evidence from the Viking probes to mean that Mars once had active volcanoes and liquid water. These two conditions, along with Mars' thin atmosphere, make it possible that the planet once harbored life. Yet little chance exists that Mars has life today. Photos from the Viking probes reveal a desolate surface with no trace of life.

The two Viking landers have now been on the surface of Mars for nearly a full Martian year; the two Viking orbiters have been circling and photographing the planet for slightly longer. Ever since the landers touched down in the summer of 1976 they have been gathering data on the characteristics of the Martian atmosphere, rocks and soil. Meanwhile the orbiters have been monitoring the water-vapor content of the atmosphere, mapping the temperature of the surface and photographing the surface with unprecedented resolution and clarity.

Together the photographs made and analytical experiments done by the four spacecraft reveal that Mars is a planet with an even more complex history than had been suspected. They have provided evidence that even the most ancient cratered terrain has been modified by volcanic activity, that early in the planet's history flowing water was a significant agent in shaping its features and that since then surface material has been extensively redistributed by high-velocity winds. Surprisingly, the surface has been little eroded by such aeolian activity. In appearance the surface of Mars is more like rocky volcanic deserts on the earth than it is like the highly cratered surface of the moon, yet Mars, once visualized as being largely a world of gently rolling dunes, seems to possess little sand. The Viking mission has also provided evidence that has both strengthened and altered hypotheses concerning the early

Martian atmosphere and climate proposed after the *Mariner 9* mission of 1971 and 1972. . . .

The Viking Orbiter Observations

The Viking orbiters, which began their coverage of Mars early in the summer of 1976, photographed the planet with much greater clarity than *Mariner 9* did. The difference was due largely to the fact that *Mariner 9* approached Mars when the planet was still enveloped in a dust storm. Moreover, after the storm enough dust remained suspended in the atmosphere to significantly obscure the surface of Mars for several terrestrial months. The Viking orbiters began making images of Mars when the atmosphere was relatively free of dust. Moreover, although the Viking orbiter cameras were Vidicon systems similar to those carried on *Mariner 9,* they had considerably better resolution.

The Viking orbiter photographs show that much of the surface of Mars retains crisp topographic detail: lava flows, wrinkle ridges and crater ejecta stand out in sharp relief. In addition the photographs show numerous lava flows in even the most primitive cratered terrain. From these last features Michael H. Carr of the U.S. Geological Survey and his colleagues suggest that early in Mars's history even much of the ancient cratered terrain in the southern hemisphere was flooded with lava. Such volcanic leveling would explain why the highly cratered terrain on Mars is relatively smooth compared with the mountainous highlands of the moon.

The fact that the most ancient features on Mars are still sharply defined also indicates that during the planet's history there has been relatively little breakdown of rock and redistribution of debris. The only clear evidence for wind erosion on a large scale is found in regions composed of older sedimentary deposits, such as those near the poles. It is likely that the polar deposits are only partly consolidated and are therefore easily eroded by the wind.

The Viking orbiters have shown that the northern plains at high latitudes are more than simple mantles of debris. They are a complex of lava flows and deposits of windblown dust that have themselves been partially stripped by the wind. Closer to the north pole the orbiter cameras found large fields of dunes girdling the residual ice cap; the dunes seem to be composed of particles the size of grains of sand. Sand-sized particles, which on Mars probably range from 1 millimeter to several millimeters, are too large and heavy to remain suspended in the rarefied atmosphere and be carried away, but they

A photo of the Arandis crater on Mars, taken by *Viking Orbiter I* on July 26, 1977. The pattern of debris around this crater suggests that water ice beneath the planet's surface was vaporized by the heat of the meteorite impact that formed the crater. **LUNAR AND PLANETARY INSTITUTE. REPRODUCED BY PERMISSION.**

are sufficiently small and light to be rolled and lifted for short distances by the wind. Dust particles, however, which on Mars are smaller than about 1 millimeter, are sufficiently small and light to be carried away in suspension.

The bulk of both the debris on the northern plains and the dunes closer to the poles apparently consists of material eroded from the polar deposits themselves. When the deposits were stripped by the wind, the embedded dust was carried away and any sand lagged behind and accumulated in dunes close to the poles. A puzzle here is that although the polar deposits contain dust, they seem to be yielding both dust and sand. The answer may be that the sand-sized particles are actually dust-sized particles that have been cemented together by oxides, salts or perhaps even ice.

Interpretation of the data from the radiometers on the Viking orbiters by Hugh H. Kieffer of the University of California at Los Angeles and his associates showed that during the summer in the northern hemisphere of Mars the temperature over the residual north-polar ice cap was some 205 degrees Kelvin (68 degrees below zero Celsius). This result was striking. Since the atmospheric pressure at the surface of Mars is only about six millibars, the temperature would have to be less than 148 degrees K. to maintain a permanent cap of carbon dioxide ice. Even if the ice in the ice cap were a clathrate compound in which carbon dioxide ice was caged inside water ice, it could not exist at a temperature higher than about 155 degrees K. The only condensate that can remain stable at 205 degrees K. is water ice.

Further support for the view that the residual polar cap consists only of water ice comes from an analysis of data from the Viking orbiter spectrometers made by Crofton B. Farmer and his associates at the Jet Propulsion Laboratory. They find that during the summer at northern latitudes the amount of water vapor in the atmosphere is such that the temperatures must be higher than 200 degrees K.

Observations of the residual south-polar cap during the summer in the southern hemisphere are difficult to interpret because of the effect of a global dust cloud that may have modulated atmospheric temperatures. The residual southern ice cap is probably water ice too, although measurements of its temperature are ambiguous, and there is a slim chance that its major constituent is carbon dioxide ice.

Since it seems that there is water ice at both poles, hypotheses involving water as an active agent in Mars's past have gained measurably more acceptance. Moreover, the Viking orbiter photographs have revealed that the channels on Mars are even more abundant than was indicated by the *Mariner 9* photographs and that the channels extend to smaller sizes and form a much more integrated drainage system than had been previously perceived. The runoff of rain from an ancient dense atmosphere may have carved some of the treelike networks of channels. Other channels may have been formed when underground ice was melted by heat released in volcanic activity. Then the channels would have been created when the ice melted, the ground above it slumped and the water flowed away. In this case the formation of the channels would seem to be directly linked to the thermal history of the planet.

Intriguing evidence for the presence of water ice in the crust and regolith of Mars has also been obtained from examining pictures of the peculiar terraces, ramparts and lobes characteristic of the ejecta of many of the large craters. On the moon the ejecta from impact craters appear to have been blocks of material that were hurled outward by the original impact and fell back to the surface, excavating myriads of secondary impact craters. On Mars the ejecta deposits surround the impact craters almost like a solidified flow. The probable explanation is that the heat of the impact melted and vaporized water ice trapped in the crust, and the liquid water and steam transported the ejecta away from the crater in a coherent, ground-hugging flow of debris. In some photographs one can even see where the flow was diverted around obstacles in its path.

Although water is now being recognized as an important agent in Mars's past, the discovery that the polar regions are probably dominated by water ice instead of carbon dioxide ice places severe constraints on the intensity of past climatic fluctuations. If a water-ice cap on Mars received more sunlight, it would begin to evaporate, subliming directly from the solid ice to a vapor. In order for the vapor pressure of water on Mars to reach the pressure required for liquid water to exist the temperature would have to be raised by at least 70 degrees K. Such a dramatic rise in temperature would be most unlikely to occur even if the luminosity of the sun varied by the maximum amount allowed by theory or if the inclination of the planet's axis periodically changed to the maximum extent. Indeed, the fact that the most ancient surfaces of Mars are so well preserved is consistent with the hypothesis that the atmospheric conditions on Mars have not fluctuated greatly over most of the planet's history. It seems likely that the bulk of the polar deposits formed very early and have since been eroded by the wind. The exact time they formed and the reason for their formation, along with the history of any early, dense atmosphere that may have been supported by greenhouse effects, however, remain a mystery.

Further Resources

BOOKS

Asimov, Isaac. *Mars: Our Mysterious Neighbor.* Milwaukee, Wisc.: G. Stevens Publishers, 1988.

Glasston, Samuel. *The Book of Mars.* Washington, D.C.: NASA, 1968.

Goldsmith, Donald. *The Hunt for Life on Mars.* New York: Dutton, 1997.

Hoyt, William Groves. *Lowell and Mars.* Tucson: University of Arizona Press, 1976.

Landau, Elaine. *Mars.* New York: F. Watts, 1991.

Moore, Patrick. *Guide to Mars.* London: Lutterworth Press, 1977.

PERIODICALS

Carr, Michael H. "The Volcanoes of Mars." *Scientific American,* January 1976, 32–43.

James, J. N. "The Voyages of *Mariner IV*." *Scientific American,* March 1966, 42–52.

WEBSITES

Mars Pathfinder Science Results. Available online at http://science.ksc.nasa.gov/mars/science/geology.html; website home page: http://science.ksc.nasa.gov (accessed March 10, 2003).

AUDIO AND VISUAL MEDIA

The Fourth Planet. Cleveland, Ohio: NASA Lewis Research Center, 1983, VHS.

Science Policy Implications of DNA Recombinant Molecule Research

Report

By: U.S. House Committee on Science and Technology. Subcommittee on Science, Research and Technology

Date: March 1978

Source: U.S. House Committee on Science and Technology. Subcommittee on Science, Research and Technology. *Science Policy Implications of DNA Recombinant Molecule Research.* 95th Cong., 2d sess., 1978. Committee Print 10. 15–17.

About the Organization: Congress created the Committee on Science and Technology for the U.S. House of Representatives, in 1958, as the Select Committee on Astronautics and Space Exploration. In 1974, Congress changed the name to the Committee on Science and Technology, giving it jurisdiction over scientific research and development, energy, and environmental, atmospheric, and civil aviation research and development. ∎

Introduction

In 1866, Austrian monk Gregor Mendel announced that particles (genes) code for traits in pea plants and, by implication, all life. These are passed unaltered from generation to generation. Scientists paid scant attention to his work until 1900, when three scientists rediscovered his paper on pea hybridization. Early in the twentieth century, they understood that genes code for traits through a chemical pathway, implying that genes must be molecules.

The molecular structure of genes remained a mystery until the American chemist James D. Watson and his British colleague, Francis Crick, discovered its shape, resembling a spiral staircase, in 1953. A gene was simply a strand of a fixed length of deoxyribonucleic acid (DNA), which looked like a ladder twisted into a spiral. The rungs of the ladder were formed by four nucleotide bases; adenine, guanine, thymine, and cytosine. Adenine always bonded with thymine and cytosine with guanine. One rung of a ladder might be the pair adenine and thymine, and the next rung might be the pair cytosine and guanine. Given half a ladder as the sequence adenine, guanine, thymine, cytosine, and cytosine, its corresponding bases on the ladder's other half must be thymine, cytosine, adenine, guanine, and guanine. The sequence of nucleotide bases told a cell what proteins to manufacture and how to join them into larger molecules. DNA programmed a cell as software programs a computer.

Significance

With this knowledge emerged the possibility that scientists might be able to extract parts of a genetic program (a sequence of nucleotide bases) to learn how the program worked and, perhaps, to transfer it into another cell. One might thereby genetically engineer an organism with strands of foreign DNA.

During the 1970s, this possibility became reality, according to a 1978 report of the U.S. House Committee on Science and Technology. Molecular biologists discovered and catalogued a series of enzymes. These acted as a knife, slicing strands of DNA from their origin and freeing them for insertion into the DNA of other cells. Each enzyme snipped off a unique sequence of nucleotide bases. For example, enzyme A might cut out the sequence adenine, guanine, guanine, adenine, cytosine, and thymine, and only that sequence. Enzyme B might cleave only the sequence guanine, cytosine, thymine, thymine, and adenine. Scientists could then insert these sequences into other cells, a technique called "gene splicing."

This technique gave scientists the power to transfer strands of DNA across a given species (all plants and animals that can interbreed to produce fertile offspring). One scientist testified before a 1978 U.S. House Committee on Science and Technology that scientists could transfer a strand of DNA from a fish to a bacterium. The bacterium would then reproduce by cell division, multiplying itself and the fish DNA.

Other possibilities arose in the 1980s. During the decade, scientists at the National Institute of Allergy and Infectious Diseases inserted the DNA strands of the Human Immunodeficiency Virus (HIV) into mouse embryos to study the progress of the disease. Critics worried that an infected mouse might escape the lab, breed with other mice, and spread the virus. The National Institutes of Health responded by quarantining this work in an stainless-steel receptacle surrounded by a moat of bleach, all enclosed in a secure facility.

Of greater promise, in 1996, the agrochemical and biotechnology company Monsanto inserted genes that code for resistance to the European corn borer, a corn pest, into a variety of corn. This saved farmers the expense of spraying their fields with insecticide. Yet critics labeled the corn "Frankenfood" and raised concerns regarding risks to beneficial insects and the possibility that pests would develop resistance to the new corn's properties. Media coverage of their demonstrations led Monsanto to withdraw the corn, prompting scientists to wonder whether the American public would accept any genetically engineered food or medicine.

Primary Source

Science Policy Implications of DNA Recombinant Molecule Research [excerpt]

SYNOPSIS: In this excerpt, scientists describe before the U.S. House Committee on Science and

Chemical Formula of a Single Chain of Deoxyribonucleic Acid

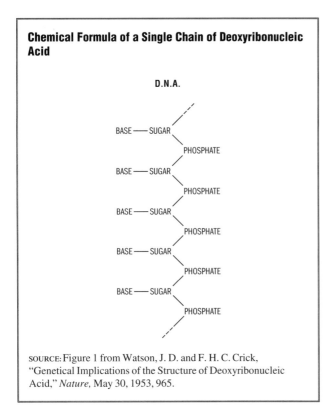

SOURCE: Figure 1 from Watson, J. D. and F. H. C. Crick, "Genetical Implications of the Structure of Deoxyribonucleic Acid," *Nature,* May 30, 1953, 965.

Technology the technique of gene splicing—the extraction of a strand of DNA from one cell and its insertion into another cell. With this technique, scientists could transfer genes across species.

I. The Biology of DNA Recombinant Molecule Research

A. Introduction

About five years ago, investigators in the field of cell biology discovered and made available for laboratory research a series of enzymes which permit the researcher to cut with precision the molecule containing the hereditary units which control the reproduction and functioning of a cell. This molecule, known as deoxyribonucleic acid or DNA, long a subject of intense study, now is chemically accessible for detailed examination. The enzymes permit the investigator to cut the molecule at precise locations, and to insert into the molecule new bits of DNA from any other organism. These newly formed DNA molecules, called recombinant DNA molecules, can then be reinserted into a host cell and will multiply as the host cell (or cloning cell) divides in its normal reproductive processes. The most frequently used cloning cell has been a special variant of a bacterium common in the human intestine known as *Escherichia coli* although other host cells are available. This ability to transfer, with precision, small units of DNA from one species to another, is one of the most exciting scientific developments in this century, for it offers the potential for identifying many aspects of the DNA regulatory mechanisms for which knowledge was not readily available by more traditional techniques in biochemistry and genetics.

Origin of the Technique

Chairman Thornton pointed out in his opening statement that the work which established the basic molecular structure of the hereditary units of the cell opened the door to this vast new field of research. The molecular definition of the basic structure of DNA in 1953 led to the accelerating accumulation of knowledge, including the appearance of the DNA recombinant molecule research technique, which in turn is leading toward the capability to manipulate the very fundamental biological controls of life. These new developments have produced an unexpected and almost unparalleled public interest in biomedical research. This interest has been expressed both in support of and opposition to the continuation of this line of investigation. This public involvement has induced an intense interest in the evaluation of science policies for basic research including not only the justifications for public funding for such research but also an examination of the long-term moral, legal, and ethical implications of basic research which offers the potential for eventual direct and precise control and possible intervention in the hereditary characteristics of man. In the first series of hearings on the science policy implications of the DNA recombinant molecule research issue, the Subcommittee asked selected witnesses to provide background information on the biology of this technique.

B. Basic Biology of the DNA Recombinant Molecule Technique

Dr. Singer

As pointed out by Maxine Singer, Laboratory of Biochemistry, National Cancer Institute, all cellular or cell-like structures which are propagated, or which induce propagation, such as viruses, contain the chemical information which that cell needs to carry out its various functions (unless of course it is defective). In addition to providing this information in a precise biochemical form, the cell must also possess the ability to turn on and off various segments of this information in response to appropriate stimuli, either internal or external to the information center of the cell. Within the last several decades, this information center has been subjected to intense study in an attempt to describe its structure in precise biochemical terms. This has been accomplished and the molecule is now known as deoxyribonucleic acid or DNA. A great deal is known about this molecule and the way that it is duplicated and how information flows from this structure to regulate the activities of the cell. However, there is still a great deal more that is unknown such as the operational controls or "on-off switches" and the change in control systems which produce genetic errors. It is the need to characterize the nature of genes, and to obtain more precise data about the unknown regulators and duplication processes which is producing the pressure to develop and use the best techniques available for the study of DNA. DNA recombinant molecule research has evolved as the latest and potentially best technique now available for use in the research laboratory.

The DNA recombinant molecule technique was described by Dr. Singer. She demonstrated with a simple model the processes involved in the cutting of segments from the circular DNA (or plasmid) of a bacterium. This process involves the extraction and isolation of the DNA molecules (in her example of bacterial plasmids) using a number of sophisticated laboratory techniques. The special enzymes are used to split the molecule at precise locations and then using other techniques, the molecule can be rejoined in a similarly precise fashion. If a separate fragment of DNA is cut, from a fish for example, it is possible to add this unit of fish DNA into the piece of cut bacterial DNA. When the bacterial DNA is rejoined it will be a "recombinant molecule" of bacterial DNA containing the fish DNA. When this recombinant DNA is processed back into a bacterial cell it will be reproduced in a normal fashion except that the "recombinant molecule," which is the term used to describe the modified plasmid, now will also replicate the fish segment of DNA within the bacterial cell. Thus, the scientist in the laboratory can reproduce in a few hours, because of the rapid multiplication time of bacterial cells, a large quantity of the portion of fish DNA which was added to the bacterial DNA. This portion of new DNA can then be isolated in pure form in large quantities for further study.

An essential factor of DNA recombinant work is the survival and replication of the laboratory constructed recombinant molecule when it is reintroduced back into a cell system. For the purpose of the Federal guidelines which are now in effect to regulate, DNA recombinant molecule research is defined as:

> molecules that consist of different segments of DNA which have been joined together in cell-free systems, and which have the capacity to infect and replicate in some host cell, either autonomously or as an integrated part of the host's genome.

The discoveries which were crucial to the recombinant molecule technique were the identification of the very special enzymes which permit the "cutting" of the molecules and the development of techniques to collect the small recombinant molecules and reintroduce them into a living cell so that they will replicate.

Further Resources

BOOKS

Cavalieri, Liebe F. *The Double-Edged Helix: Genetic Engineering in the Real World.* New York: Praeger, 1981.

Glover, David M. *Gene Cloning: The Mechanics of DNA Manipulation.* New York: Chapman and Hall, 1984.

Lampton, Christopher. *DNA and the Creation of New Life.* New York: Arco Publishers, 1983.

Lappe, Marc. *Broken Code: The Exploitation of DNA.* San Francisco: Sierra Club Books, 1984.

Messel, Harry, ed. *The Biological Manipulation of Life.* Elmsford, N.Y.: Pergamon Press, 1981.

Williamson, Robert, ed. *Genetic Engineering.* New York: Academic Press, 1981.

PERIODICALS

"Field-Test Rules Proposed for Transgenetic Crops." *Chemical & Engineering News,* August 12, 2002, 21.

Perpich, Joseph G. "The Recombinant-DNA Debate and Bioterrorism." *Chronicle of Higher Education,* March 15, 2002, B20.

"Superfood or Double Trouble?" *Scholastic Choices,* February 2002, 15–18.

WEBSITES

The Nobel Prize in Physiology or Medicine 1978. Available online at http://www.nobel.se/medicine/laureates/1978 /presentation-speech.html; website home page: http:// www.nobel.se (accessed March 10, 2003).

Smith, Hamilton O. *Nucleotide Sequence Specificity of Restriction Endoculeases.* Available online at http://www .nobel.se/medicine/laureates/1978/smith-lecture.html; website home page: http://nobel.se (accessed March 10, 2003).

AUDIO AND VISUAL MEDIA

Cutting and Splicing DNA. Princeton, N.J.: Films for the Humanities & Sciences, 1990, VHS.

Laying Waste: The Poisoning of America by Toxic Chemicals

Nonfiction work

By: Michael H. Brown

Date: 1979

Source: Brown, Michael H. *Laying Waste: The Poisoning of America by Toxic Chemicals.* New York: Pantheon Books, 1979, 4–7.

About the Author: Michael Harold Brown was born in Niagara Falls, New York, in 1952 and received a B.A. from Fordham University in 1974. Between 1977 and 1979, he wrote for the *Niagara Gazette,* leaving in 1979 to become an independent writer. He received four Pulitzer Prize nominations in journalism for his reporting of the effect of toxic waste at Love Canal in Niagara Falls. In 1979, the Environmental Protection Agency honored him for his coverage of Love Canal. ∎

Introduction

Love Canal is perhaps a misnomer, for it never was a canal but rather an unfinished portion of the Erie Canal. The city of Niagara Falls, New York, unable to use Love Canal for transit, instead made it a cesspool, dumping refuse in it as early as 1920. The fact that the city owned Love Canal, that it had designated the site a landfill, and that environmental laws were lax combined to allow the city to dump what it wished into the canal. Amid the Great Depression, the city gained revenues in 1933 by leasing to the U.S. Army the right to dump waste into Love Canal. Among other toxins, the Army dumped the byproducts of its chemical weapons program. One should keep in mind that Love Canal was full of water. Solid waste sank to the bottom, and liquid waste spread through the water, contaminating all of Love Canal.

In 1942 the city sold Love Canal to the Hooker Chemical Company of New York. Between 1942 and 1954 Hooker dumped more than 400 types of chemicals into Love Canal, making it the third agency to pollute Love Canal. Saturated with chemicals, the canal caught fire several times during these years.

Despite Love Canal's hazards, residents behaved as though nothing was amiss. Children swam in parts of it they thought uncontaminated, and real estate developers responded to the post–World War II (1939–1945) baby boom by building houses near Love Canal. The increase in population forced the city's public schools to expand to accommodate more students. In 1952 school officials offered to buy Love Canal from Hooker, fill it with earth, and build a new elementary school. Hooker hesitated for fear of exposing itself to a lawsuit should anyone at the school fall ill, but pressure from city and school officials led Hooker to donate Love Canal to the school board in 1954. In return, the school board assumed legal responsibility for Love Canal. Hooker took a $2.3 million tax deduction for its donation of Love Canal, the district built its school, and the city built a playground on land the school did not need. More houses were built in the area as well.

Significance

In his book, Michael H. Brown, a Niagara Falls resident and a reporter, describes the decades of human tragedy attributable to the chemicals buried at Love Canal. Plants and buildings were damaged by chemicals. Many people became ill, and some died from unusual diseases and disorders often associated with chemical exposure. Babies were born with a variety of birth defects.

By 1977, chemicals had seeped into streams and sewer lines and had spread through soil. Dirt in the city playground was caustic enough to burn skin. People became ill from eating their home-grown tomatoes. Fearful of negative press, city officials first tried to minimize the extent to which it, the U.S. Army, and Hooker had polluted Love Canal and tried to keep state and federal agencies from conducting independent investigations. This position became untenable in 1978, when the New York State Health Commission declared Love Canal "a great and imminent peril to the health of the public" and asked the U.S. Environmental Protection Agency (EPA) to investigate Love Canal. It quickly concluded that the former canal contained hundreds of dangerous chemicals.

Some residents fled the neighborhood, and in 1980 the state agreed to buy the homes in the neighborhood in order to compensate residents for the depressed real estate values. Yet the city has found it easier to right economic wrongs than medical ones. Because the chemicals concentrated in the liver and kidneys, residents suffered diseases of these organs. Chemicals were strong enough to damage even human chromosomes, which each cell protects by a mechanism whose complexity molecular biologists are only beginning to understand. Chromosomal damage included the deletion of genes and, in other cases, the duplication of them. Particularly serious was damage to regulatory genes: those genes that switch other genes on and off. The distortion in the timing of regulatory genes that shut off genes that code for the production of teeth may account for the fact, as Brown noted, that Karen Schroeder's baby developed two rather than one set of teeth. Another possibility is that the baby had two rather than one set of genes to code for the production of teeth, hence the double row of teeth. Scientists are unlikely ever to know the extent of chromosomal damage.

The tragedy at Love Canal heightened Americans' awareness of the dangers of industrial waste. People became much more concerned with what might be buried on or around their property, demanding to know the history of any newly developed land before moving there and reacting strongly to any signs of chemical contamination. Rules regarding the proper disposal of toxic waste and the responsibility of polluters for cleaning up contaminated sites were strengthened.

In 1998, much of the area around Love Canal was declared safe by the EPA. The region, renamed Black Creek Village, was reopened to the public, and homes once abandoned were sold at discounted prices. The canal itself remains contaminated. Encased in a plastic liner, clay, and topsoil, it is also fenced off as permanently off-limits.

Primary Source

Laying Waste: The Poisoning of America by Toxic Chemicals [excerpt]

> In this excerpt, Michael H. Brown charges the Hooker Chemical Company with dumping 21,000 tons of chemicals into Love Canal since the 1940s. He documented that these chemicals killed trees, caused women to have miscarriages and deformed children, and afflicted residents with cancer.

The Legacy of the Hooker Chemical Company

A major proportion of those who live in the city of Niagara Falls work in chemical plants, the largest owned by the Hooker Chemical Company. Timothy Schroeder did not. He was a cement technician by trade, dealing with the factories only if they needed a pathway poured or a small foundation set. Tim and his wife, Karen, lived on 99th Street in a ranch-style home with a brick and wood exterior. They had saved all they could to redecorate the inside and to make additions, such as a cement patio covered with an extended roof. One of the Schroeders' most cherished possessions was a fiberglass pool, built into the ground and enclosed by a redwood fence. Though it had taxed their resources, the yard complemented a house that was among the most elegant in a residential zone where most of the homes were small frame buildings, prefabricated and slapped together *en masse*. It was a quiet area, once almost rural in character, and located in the city's extreme southeast corner. The Schroeders had lived in the house only since 1970, but Karen was a lifelong resident of the general neighborhood. Her parents lived three doors down from them, six miles from the row of factories that stood shoulder to shoulder along the Upper Niagara.

Karen Schroeder looked out from a back window one October morning in 1974 and noted with distress that the pool had suddenly risen two feet above the ground. She called Tim to tell him about it. Karen then had no way of knowing that the problem far ex-

Warning sign in the Love Canal neighborhood of Niagara Falls, N.Y., 1978. Industrial waste buried in the neighborhood led to ecological damage, birth defects for those who lived there, and eventually the evacuation of the neighborhood. **AP/WIDE WORLD PHOTOS. REPRODUCED BY PERMISSION.**

ceeded a simple property loss—that in fact it was the first sign of a great tragedy.

Accurately enough, Mrs. Schroeder figured that the cause of the uplift was the unusual groundwater flow of the area. Twenty-one years before, an abandoned hydroelectric canal directly behind their house had been backfilled with industrial rubble. The underground breaches created by this disturbance, aided by the marshy nature of the region's surficial layer, had collected large volumes of rainfall, and this water had undermined the backyard. The Schroeders allowed the pool to remain in its precarious position until the next summer and then pulled it from the ground, intending to replace it with a cement one. Immediately, the gaping hole filled with what Karen called "chemical water," rancid liquids of yellow and orchid and blue. These same chemicals, mixed with the groundwater, had flooded the entire yard; they attacked the redwood posts with such a caustic bite that one day the fence simply collapsed. When the groundwater receded in dry weather, it left the gardens and shrubs withered and scorched, as if by a brush fire.

Environmental Activist Lois Gibbs

In 1978 Lois Gibbs was a housewife with two sick children when she read about the toxic waste that had been dumped on the site where her family and hundreds of other Love Canal residents lived. After being dismissed by local officials, she did her own investigating about the physical ailments that area residents had suffered, an effort that eventually led state and federal agencies to order an evacuation and cleanup of the area. In an interview for a 2002 episode of the PBS program *P.O.V* (*Point of View*) Gibbs spoke of her campaign to close the elementary school and playground on Love Canal:

> Going door to door was probably the most frightening thing I did. I believed that when I knocked on the door, everybody was going to tell me that I was crazy, that I was in fact a hysterical housewife, a hysterical mom and that people were just going to dismiss me. It took a lot of courage to begin to go door to door, because it was like these people are going to think that I am nuts. But then when I actually went door to door and actually got up enough courage to do that, people were incredibly receptive and people would tell me stories that were very similar to my story, in the sense that their children were sick, their husband was sick, their wife was sick; they had different colored chemicals coming into their basement. In fact, it became a problem because people had so much to share that it was taking forever to go around and get the petitions signed which is what I started with, to close the school.

SOURCE: Gibbs, Lois M. Point of View: Fenceline: Get Involved. Available online at http://www.pbs.org/pov/pov2002/fenceline/getinvolved_article01.html (accessed March 26, 2003).

How the chemicals had got there was no mystery: they came from the former canal. Beginning in the late 1930s or the early 1940s, the Hooker Company, whose many processes included the manufacture of pesticides, plasticizers, and caustic soda, had used the canal as a dump for at least 20,000 tons of waste residues—"still-bottoms" in the language of the trade. The chemical garbage was brought to the excavation in 55-gallon metal barrels stacked on a small dump truck and was unloaded into what, up to that time, had been a fishing and swimming hole in the summer and an ice-skating rink during the city's long, hard winter months.

When the hazardous dumping first began, much of the surrounding terrain was meadowlands and orchards, but there was also a small cluster of homes on the immediate periphery, only thirty feet from the ditch. Those who lived there remembered the deep holes being filled with what appeared to be oil and gray mud by laborers who rushed to borrow their garden hoses for a dousing of water if they came in contact with the scalding sludge they were dumping. Children enjoyed playing among the intriguing, unguarded debris. They would pick up chunks of phosphorus and heave them against cement. Upon impact the "fire rocks," as they were called, would brilliantly explode, sending off a trail of white sparks. Fires and explosions erupted spontaneously when the weather was especially hot. Odors similar to those of the industrial districts wafted into the adjacent windows, accompanied by gusts of fly ash. On a humid moonlit night, residents would look toward the canal and see, in the haze above the soil, a greenish luminescence.

Karen's parents had been the first to experience problems with seepage from the canal. In 1959, her mother, Aileen Voorhees, noticed a strange black sludge bleeding through the basement walls. For the next twenty years, she and her husband, Edwin, tried various methods of halting the irritating intrusion, coating the cinder-block walls with sealants and even constructing a gutter along them to intercept the inflow. Nothing could stop a smell like that of a chemical plant from permeating the entire household, and neighborhood calls to the city for help were unavailing. One day, when Edwin punched a hole in the wall to see what was happening, quantities of black liquid poured out. The cinder blocks were full of the stuff.

Although later it was to be determined that they were in imminent danger, the Voorhees treated the problem at first as a mere nuisance. That it involved chemicals, industrial chemicals, was not particularly significant to them. All their life, all of everyone's life in the city, malodorous fumes had been a normal ingredient of the surrounding air.

More ominous than the Voorhees basement seepage was an event that occurred in the Schroeder family at 11:12 P.M. on November 21, 1968. Karen gave birth to her third child, a seven-pound girl named Sheri. But no sense of elation filled the delivery room, for the baby was born with a heart that beat irregularly and had a hole in it, bone blockages of the nose and partial deafness, deformed external ears, and a cleft palate. By the age of two, it became obvious that the child was mentally retarded. When her teeth came in, there was a double row of them at the bottom. She also developed an enlarged liver.

The Schroeders looked upon these health problems, as well as certain illnesses among their other children, as acts of capricious genes, a vicious quirk of nature. Like Aileen and Edwin Voorhees, they were mainly aware that the chemicals were devaluing their property. The crab-apple tree and evergreens in the back were dead, and even the oak in the front of the house was sick; one year, the leaves fell off on Father's Day.

Resources

BOOKS

Fowlkes, Martha R., and Patricia Y. Miller. *Love Canal: The Social Construction of Disaster*. Washington, D.C.: Federal Emergency Management Agency, 1982.

Gibbs, Lois Marie. *Love Canal: My Story*. Albany, N.Y.: State University of New York Press, 1982.

Mazur, Allan A. *A Hazardous Inquiry: The Rashomon Effect at Love Canal*. Cambridge, Mass.: Harvard University Press, 1998.

Shaw, L. Gardner, and Lester W. Milbrath. *Citizen Participation in Government Decision Making: The Toxic Waste Threat at Love Canal, Niagara Falls, New York*. Albany, N.Y.: State University of New York Press, 1983.

Zuesse, Eric. *Love Canal: The Truth Seeps Out*. Santa Barbara, Calif.: Reason Enterprises, 1981.

PERIODICALS

McNeil, Donald. "Upstate Waste Site May Endanger Lives." *New York Times*. August 2, 1978, 1.

WEBSITES

ATOMCC Science News. *Love Canal, USA*. Available online at http://www.globalserve.net/~spinc/atomcc/lovecana.html; website home page http://www.globalserve.net (accessed March 10, 2003).

Love Canal @ 20. Available online at http://ublib.buffalo.edu /libraries/units/sel/exhibits/lovecanal.html; website home page http://ublib.buffalo.edu (accessed March 10, 2003).

Love Canal Collection. Available online at http://ublib.buffalo .edu/libraries/projects/lovecanal; website home page http:// ublib.buffalo.edu (accessed March 10, 2003)

Love Canal History. Available online at http://www .globalserve.net/~spinc/atomcc/lovecana.html; website home page http:// www.globalserve.net (accessed March 10, 2003).

AUDIO AND VISUAL MEDIA

Handle with Care. Oley, Pa.: Bullfrog Films, 1992.

A Love Canal Family. University Park, Pa.: Penn State Audiovisual Services, 1980.

Investigation into the March 28, 1979, Three Mile Island Accident

Report

By: Office of Inspection and Enforcement, U.S. Nuclear Regulatory Commission

Date: 1979

Source: Office of Inspection and Enforcement, U.S. Nuclear Regulatory Commission. *Investigation into the March 28, 1979, Three Mile Island Accident*. Washington, D.C.: GPO, 1979.

About the Organization: In 1974, Congress created the U.S. Nuclear Regulatory Commission to oversee the safety of U.S. nuclear power plants. It licenses the construction of new plants and oversees the use, processing and disposal of nuclear waste. Commissioners serve by presidential appointment. ∎

Introduction

In 1831, British physicist Michael Faraday discovered that he could generate an electric current by spinning a coil of copper wire between the north and south poles of a magnet. Utilities could generate electricity on a large scale by spinning a turbine, the equivalent of spinning a coil of copper wire between a magnet's poles.

Until 1955, U.S. utilities generated electricity in two ways. First, they burned the fossil fuels coal and natural gas to boil water. The steam from the boiling water would rush through a turbine, spinning it to generate electricity. Second, they built hydroelectric plants—the first in Wisconsin in 1882—in which falling water spun a turbine to generate electricity. Of the two methods, hydroelectric power is cheaper and does not pollute the environment, although hydroelectric plants along the Columbia River in the Pacific Northwest have disrupted salmon migration to spawning grounds. Neither method of generating electricity comes without cost.

During the 1950s, U.S. utilities began to tap the energy in uranium atoms for electricity. The United States' detonation of three atomic bombs in 1945, one in a test in the New Mexico desert and the other two on Japanese cities, demonstrated the tremendous energy locked inside uranium atoms. Americans could reap this energy in peace, as well as war, by building nuclear power plants. Neutrons (particles in the nucleus of an atom) are fired at uranium atoms, causing them to split and release energy to boil water. As with fossil fuels, the steam from boiling water spins a turbine to generate electricity.

In 1954, Pennsylvania utility Duquesne Light built the first U.S. nuclear power plant in Shippingport, Pennsylvania. The next year, the Idaho National Energy Laboratory generated the first electricity from nuclear power,

The cooling towers at the Three Mile Island nuclear power plant rise above the surrounding area near Harrisburg, Pennsylvania, March 28, 1979. They are shut down because of the malfunction that occurred there that day, one which resulted in radioactive gas escaping into the atmosphere. © BETTMANN/CORBIS. REPRODUCED BY PERMISSION.

supplying it to residents and businesses in Arco, Idaho. In 1957, the Shippingport Nuclear Power Plant began generating electricity to residents and businesses in Pittsburgh. By 1979, U.S. utilities had built 70 nuclear power plants.

Significance

That year disaster threatened the Three Mile Island nuclear power plant near Harrisburg, Pennsylvania. Because nuclear power plants generate tremendous heat, they require an influx of water to cool them. On March 28, 1979, the plant's cooling system failed. Technicians misdiagnosed the problem and shut off water to the reactor, exacerbating the danger of overheating. Temperatures surpassed 5,000 degrees Fahrenheit, and the containment dome, filled with radiation, began to leak radiation into the atmosphere. Two days later, with the crisis over, officials belatedly evacuated pregnant women and children.

The U.S. Nuclear Regulatory Commission investigated the accident. In its report, the commission blamed no one for the accident, though it admitted, "radioactive gas leaks caused very high concentrations of airborne radioactivity." Nevertheless, the report noted that much of the radiation remained within the plant; little leaked outside, although the leakage exceeded federal limits.

The commission may have adopted a cautious tone in this report for fear of alarming the public. Yet an April 1979 Gallup poll found that 66 percent of respondents believed nuclear power to be unsafe. Activist Ralph Nader now found audiences willing to accept his assertions that nuclear power plants were inherently flawed.

Despite the incident, the nuclear power industry proved resilient. In 1983, nuclear power generated more electricity than did the burning of natural gas. The next year, it surpassed hydroelectric power as the second-leading source of electricity after burning coal. In 1986, the Perry Nuclear Power Plant in Ohio became the 100th plant in the United States. In 1986, nuclear power generated 19 percent of electricity in the U.S. The 1980s witnessed the construction of 46 new plants, and by 1993, the U.S. had 109 nuclear power plants.

Primary Source

Investigation into the March 28, 1979 Three Mile Island Accident [excerpt]

> **SYNOPSIS:** In this excerpt, the U.S. Nuclear Regulatory Commission blames no one for the accident at Three Mile Island, though it admits, "very high concentrations" of radiation accumulated in the plant, some of which leaked into the atmosphere.

Summary of Radiological Aspects

Health physics operations at TMI Unit 2 were routine prior to 0400 hrs March 28, 1979. . . .

At 0400 hrs, the Unit 2 turbine and reactor tripped. At 0411 hrs, there was a reactor building sump high water level alarm. By 0415 hrs, the reactor coolant pressure had dropped from 2435 psig at the time of the reactor trip to approximately 1275 psig. This pressure was below the setpoint for emergency core cooling system initiation (1600 psig). At 0415 hrs, there was a pressure rise of 1.4 psig inside the reactor building. A site emergency should have been declared, based on these indications and criteria in the Site Emergency Plan. However, because the drop in reactor pressure was believed to be under control, and the reactor building pressure increase was considered to be slight, and because there was no evidence of a release of radioactivity from the station, an emergency was not declared. Subsequently, there were several radiation monitor alarms indicative of an emergency situation, but no emergency was declared.

At 0622 hrs the first radiation monitor response to cladding failure occurred. Radiation levels continued to increase and a site emergency was declared at 0655 hrs based on these alarms.

The emergency organization was promptly activated following the declaration of a Site Emergency. The Station Manager arrived in the Unit 2 control room at 0705 hrs and relieved the Shift Supervisor as Emergency Director. Initially, the emergency organization approximated the planned organization described in the TMI Emergency Plan. An exception was that Repair Parties were assembled and controlled by both the Emergency Control Center (ECC) in the Unit 2 control room and the Emergency Control Station (ECS) in the Unit 1 health physics/chemistry lab area. According to Emergency Plan Implementing Procedures, the Repair Party was to assemble only at the ECS, under the direction of the Supervisor of Maintenance, and coordinated through the Supervisor of Radiation Protection.

Offsite consequences were assessed by performing dose rate calculations. Because of errors in these calculations, the dose rates initially predicted (10 and 40 rem/hr at Goldsboro) were higher than actual dose rates. Radiation measurements by survey teams revealed actual doses were low (less than 0.001 rem/hr at Goldsboro). Offsite agencies and support groups were notified of the Site Emergency by telephone. At 0724 hrs, a General Emergency was declared based on radiation levels inside the reactor building. Again, offsite agencies and groups were phoned.

Following the turbine trip, about 8000 gallons of reactor coolant were pumped from the reactor building sump to the auxiliary building sump tank. This transfer was terminated at 0438 hrs and was not resumed. The auxiliary building sump tank overflowed to the auxiliary building sump, causing water containing a relatively low concentration of radioactivity to back up through floor drains onto the fuel handling building and auxiliary building floors. Following fuel damage, the concentration of radioactivity in the reactor coolant increased by several orders of magnitude. A flow of this highly contaminated reactor coolant was maintained through the makeup and purification system for several days following the accident. This flow was the principal pathway by which radioactivity was transferred from the damaged reactor core to the auxiliary and fuel handling buildings, and ultimately to the environment.

Gases evolving from reactor coolant in the makeup and purification system were collected in the waste gas system. Small leaks in these systems were of little radiological significance during normal operation. However, following fuel damage, radioactive gas leaks caused very high concentrations of airborne radioactivity inside the auxiliary and fuel handling buildings and resulted in much higher than normal environmental releases via ventilation exhausts from these buildings. Radiation levels in the vicinity of some makeup and purification system components exceeded the limits of the licensee's measurement capability (i.e., greater than 1000 R/hr). High radiation levels inside the Unit 2 auxiliary building caused full scale readings on several station effluent monitors. A full scale reading for the plant vent gas monitor is equal to 2.8 E-2 μ;Ci/cc of xenon-133. The particulate and iodine monitors were off-scale due to interference from the large amounts of radioactive noble gases.

Further Resources

BOOKS

Cantelon, Philip L., and Robert C. Williams. *Crisis Contained: The Department of Energy at Three Mile Island.* Washington, D.C.: U.S. Department of Energy, 1980.

Del Tredici, Robert. *The People of Three Mile Island.* San Francisco: Sierra Club Books, 1980.

Shrivastava, Prakash K. *Known Effects of Low-Level Radiation Exposure: Health Implications of the Three Mile Island Accident.* Bethesda, Md.: Department of Health, Education, and Welfare, 1980.

Stephens, Mark. *Three Mile Island: The Hour-by-Hour Account of What Really Happened.* New York: Random House, 1980.

PERIODICALS

Adkins, Sean. "Three Mile Island Power Plant Security Plan Covers Many Bases." *York Daily Record,* September 11, 2002, 4.

Sherzer, Michael. "Three Mile Island, Pa.-Area Residents Receive Anti-Radiation Pills." *The Patriot-News,* August 16, 2002, 2.

WEBSITES

Johnson, Scott. "Inside Three Mile Island: Minute By Minute." Available online at http://kd4dcy.net/tmi; website home page: http://kd4dcy.net (accessed June 13, 2003).

Meltdown at Three Mile Island. The American Experience. Available online at http://www.pbs.org/wgbh/amex/three; website home page: http://www.pbs.org (accessed June 13, 2003).

Three Mile Island Alert. Available online at http://www.tmia.com (accessed June 13, 2003).

"Three Mile Island: The Judge's Ruling." Frontline. Available online at http://www.pbs.org/wgbh/pages/frontline/shows/reaction/readings/tmi.html; website home page: http://www.pbs.org (accessed June 13, 2003).

AUDIO AND VISUAL MEDIA

Meltdown. Princeton, N.J.: Films for the Humanities & Sciences, 1997, VHS.

Meltdown at Three Mile Island. Alexandria. Va.: PBS Home Video, 1999, VHS.

12

Sports

WILLIAM J. THOMPSON

Entries are arranged in chronological order by date of primary source. For entries with one primary source, the entry title is the same as the primary source title. Entries with more than one primary source have an overall entry title, followed by the titles of the primary sources.

Important Events in Sports, 1970–1979

1970

- On January 11, Billy Casper wins the Los Angeles Open golf tournament and becomes the second pro golfer (Arnold Palmer was the first) to earn $1 million in his career. By the end of the season Jack Nicklaus would surpass his earnings total.

- On January 11, in an upset the Kansas City Chiefs win the Super Bowl over the Minnesota Vikings, 23-7.

- On January 26, National Football League (NFL) commissioner Pete Rozelle announces a four-year, $142 million contract with the three major television networks to broadcast professional football games.

- On February 16, Joe Frazier wins the undisputed world heavyweight boxing championship, knocking out Jimmy Ellis in the fifth round.

- On February 19, Detroit Tigers pitcher Denny McLain receives the first of his two suspensions from baseball, this one for consorting with gamblers. He is suspended again on September 9 for carrying a gun.

- On March 4, Pete Maravich of Louisiana State University is named NCAA player of the year.

- On March 21, UCLA defeats Jacksonville University 80-69 to win its fourth straight NCAA basketball championship.

- In April, the American League (AL) baseball team the Seattle Pilots moves to Milwaukee and becomes the Brewers.

- On April 13, Billy Casper wins the Masters golf tournament in Augusta, Georgia.

- On May 8, the New York Knicks defeat the Los Angeles Lakers four games to three to win their first NBA championship.

- On May 10, the Boston Bruins win the Stanley Cup over the St. Louis Blues in four games, ending the first NHL playoff since 1918 that included no Canadian teams.

- On May 31, Al Unser wins the Indianapolis 500 with an average speed of 155.749 MPH and a purse of $271,697.

- On July 5, Donna Caponi wins the U.S. Women's Open golf title for the second consecutive year.

- On July 16, the opening game is played at Three Rivers Stadium, the new home of the Pittsburgh Pirates baseball team; the Pirates lose to the Cincinnati Reds, 3-2.

- On August 3, NFL players end a four-day strike for increased pension benefits.

- On August 12, in a case brought by Philadelphia Phillies outfielder Curt Flood, federal court judge Ben Cooper rules that a 1922 Supreme Court decision finding that organized baseball does not violate antitrust laws is still binding. The Major League Baseball Players Association announces that it will take the case to the Supreme Court.

- On August 16, Dave Stockton wins the Professional Golfers Association (PGA) championship.

- On August 31, the United States wins the Davis Cup, defeating West Germany, 5-0.

- On September 7, thirty-nine-year-old jockey Willie Shoemaker sets a new world record with 6,033 wins.

- On October 15, the Baltimore Orioles win the World Series in five games over the Cincinnati Reds.

- On October 26, Muhammad Ali knocks out Jerry Quarry in three rounds in his first fight since his license to box was revoked in 1967.

1971

- On January 1, the University of Nebraska finishes an unbeaten season and earns the Associated Press's (AP) vote as best collegiate football team of the year by winning the Orange Bowl 17-12 over Louisiana State University.

- On January 17, the Baltimore Colts defeat the Dallas Cowboys 16-13 in Super Bowl V.

- On February 9, Satchell Paige, who spent twenty-two years in the Negro Leagues, is elected to the Baseball Hall of Fame.

- On February 28, Jack Nicklaus becomes the first golfer to win the PGA championship twice.

- On March 8, Joe Frazier wins a fifteen-round unanimous decision over Muhammad Ali to retain the world heavyweight boxing championship. Each boxer is guaranteed $2.5 million.

- On March 27, UCLA wins its seventh NCAA basketball title in eight years, defeating Villanova University, 68-62.

- On April 11, Charles Coody wins the Masters golf tournament.

- On April 27, professional baseball player Curt Flood, who tested baseball's reserve clause, announces his retirement.

- On April 30, the Milwaukee Bucks win the NBA championship in four games over the Baltimore Bullets.

- On May 1, Cannonero II is the fourth field horse in history to win the Kentucky Derby.

- On May 7, the American Basketball Association (ABA) and the National Basketball League (NBL) seek congressional approval to merge.

- On May 16, Marty Liquori, world-record holder in the mile, meets Jim Ryun, former world-record holder in several distance events, in the "Dream Mile" at the King Games in Philadelphia. Liquori won in three minutes fifty-six seconds; Ryun was one stride back.

- On May 18, the Montreal Canadiens defeat the Chicago Blackhawks four games to three in the Stanley Cup hockey championship.

- On May 30, Willie Mays scores his National League record 1,950th run.

- On June 21, Lee Trevino defeats Jack Nicklaus in the U.S. Open golf championship.

- On June 24, the National Basketball Association commissioner announces that the league will no longer require four years of college for eligibility to play in the NBA.

- On June 28, the United States Supreme Court rules that the Justice Department erred in denying Muhammad Ali an exemption from the draft as a conscientious objector.

- On July 10, Lee Trevino wins the British Open golf tournament. He is the fourth golfer in history to win the U.S. Open and the British Open in the same year. (Bobby Jones in 1930, Gene Sarazen in 1932, and Ben Hogan in 1953 are the others.)

- On July 25, Arnold Palmer wins the $250,000 Westchester Classic golf tournament, his third win of the year.

- On July 31, Vince Lombardi and Jim Brown are among inductees in the Pro Football Hall of Fame.

- On August 26, the New York Giants football team relocates from New York to New Jersey, where they play at the seventy-five-thousand-seat Meadowlands Stadium.

- On August 29, Hank Aaron becomes the first National League baseball player to drive in one hundred runs in eleven straight seasons.

- On September 9, all-time professional hockey scoring leader Gordie Howe retires from the Detroit Red Wings, ending a twenty-five-year career.

- On September 15, Billie Jean King and Stan Smith win the U.S. Open tennis singles championships.

- On October 17, the Pittsburgh Pirates win the World Series in seven games over the Baltimore Orioles.

- On October 30, Cornell University football running back Ed Marinaro sets an NCAA record of 4,132 career yards after gaining 272 yards against Columbia University.

- On November 9, the NHL announces new franchises in Atlanta and Los Angeles.

- On November 14, golfers Jack Nicklaus and Lee Trevino team to win the World Cup for the United States.

- On December 6, winning the Disney World golf tournament, Jack Nicklaus brings his season's earnings to a record $244,490.

1972

- On January 1, the University of Nebraska football team clinches a national championship after winning its twenty-third consecutive game, defeating the University of Alabama in the Orange Bowl, 38-6.

- On January 16, the Dallas Cowboys win the Super Bowl, defeating the Miami Dolphins, 24-3.

- On January 19, golfer Lee Trevino, winner of six tournaments in 1971, is named male athlete of the year by the Associated Press.

- On January 30, Wilt Chamberlain, center for the Los Angeles Lakers, sets a career record for rebounds with 21,734.

- On February 3, the Winter Olympics open in Sapporo, Japan.

- On February 10, Ann Henning sets an Olympic record, winning the gold medal in the women's 500-meter speed skating.

- On February 11, Barbara Cochran wins the only U.S. gold medal in skiing, the women's special slalom.

- On February 23, the Villanova University basketball team is stripped of its second place finish in the 1971 basketball championship by the NCAA after it is learned that the team's All-American guard, Howard Porter, had signed a professional contract in 1970. Similar action is taken against Western Kentucky two weeks later when it is learned that its center, Jim McDaniels, had also signed a pro contract in 1970.

- On March 6, Jack Nicklaus becomes golf's career-earnings leader after winning the Doral Open, bringing his earnings to $1,427,200.

- On March 25, UCLA wins its sixth consecutive NCAA championship basketball title with an 81-76 win over Florida State University.

- On April 13, the thirteen-day-old professional baseball strike ends when the players and owners agree on a settlement which adds five hundred thousand dollars to the players' pension fund.

- On May 7, the Los Angeles Lakers win the NBA championship over the New York Knicks in five games.

- On May 11, the Boston Bruins win the Stanley Cup championship over the New York Rangers in six games.

- On May 27, Mark Donahue wins the Indianapolis 500.

- On June 13, Bobby Byrne testifies before a congressional committee that he had drugged hundreds of racehorses in attempts to fix races.

- On June 19, the United States Supreme Court reaffirms the exemption of professional baseball from anti-trust laws.

- On July 2, Susie Maxwell Berning wins the U.S. Women's Open golf championship.

- On July 7, Billie Jean King wins the Wimbledon women's tennis championship.

- On July 9, Stan Smith wins the Wimbledon men's tennis championship.

- On July 13, owners of the Baltimore Colts and Los Angeles Raiders trade entire teams with one another. The players on both teams remain the same, only team ownership changes.

- On August 6, U.S. Olympic trials in Chicago conclude. During the meet American swimmers break eleven world records.

- On August 22, the XX Olympic Games open in Munich.

- On September 4, swimmer Mark Spitz wins his seventh gold medal, one for each event in which he competed.

- On September 5, the Olympic Games are suspended for two days after Arab terrorists kill two Israeli athletes and kidnap nine others.

- On September 10, the Olympic Games close. The U.S. team wins thirty-three gold medals among its ninety-four total, second only to the Soviet Union, with ninety-nine medals, including fifty gold.

- On September 18, Art Williams is the first black umpire in major-league baseball.

- On October 15, Stan Smith leads the United States tennis team to its fifth consecutive Davis Cup championship.

- On October 22, the Oakland Athletics win the World Series over the Cincinnati Reds in seven games.

1973

- On January 1, the University of Southern California football team beats Ohio State in the Rose Bowl 45-23 to earn the designation as the top team in the nation.

- On January 14, the Miami Dolphins win the Super Bowl over the Washington Redskins and are the first professional football team to complete a season undefeated.

- On January 22, George Foreman knocks out Joe Frazier in the second round to become the new world heavyweight boxing champion.

- On February 18, Richard Petty wins the Daytona 500 stock-car race with an average speed of 157.2 mph.

- On February 25, baseball owners and players reach a three-year agreement to submit salary disputes to binding arbitration.

- On March 4, eighteen-year-old Chris Evert wins her first professional tennis title, in the S&H Green Stamp tournament.

- On March 5, NBA players sign a three-year collective bargaining agreement that stipulates a twenty-thousand-dollar minimum salary for the 1973–1974 season.

- On March 31, Ken Norton defeats Muhammad Ali in a twelve-round split decision.

- On April 22, Chris Evert wins the Saint Petersburg Open tennis tournament, her fifth straight professional win.

- On May 5, Secretariat wins the Kentucky Derby.

- On May 10, the New York Knicks defeat the Los Angeles Lakers four games to one to win the NBA championship.

- On May 10, the Montreal Canadiens defeat the Chicago Blackhawks four games to two to win the Stanley Cup hockey championship.

- On May 19, Secretariat wins the Preakness.

- On May 30, Gordon Johncock wins the Indianapolis 500.

- On June 9, Secretariat wins the Belmont Stakes and is the first horse since 1948 to win horse racing's Triple Crown.

- On June 18, forty-five-year-old Gordie Howe signs a four-year, $1 million contract with the Houston Aeros in the World Hockey Association.

- On July 7, Billie Jean King defeats Chris Evert in an all-American final in the Wimbledon women's singles tennis championship.

- On July 15, Nolan Ryan pitches his second no-hitter of the year, becoming the first professional pitcher in twenty-one years to do so.

- On July 24, Los Angeles Rams star receiver Lance Rentzel is suspended from professional football for possession of marijuana.

- On August 1, the New York Nets of the ABA pay $4 million for the contract of Julius Erving.

- On August 12, Jack Nicklaus wins the PGA tournament by four strokes.

- On August 19, Chris Evert wins the U.S. Clay Court tennis championship.

- On September 2, Detroit Tigers manager Billy Martin is suspended by the American League, then fired, for instructing his pitchers to throw illegal spitballs.

- On September 20, Billie Jean King defeats Bobby Riggs in a highly publicized tennis match billed as the "Battle of the Sexes."

- On September 26, Wilt Chamberlain signs a $1.8 million contract to serve as player-coach for the San Diego Conquistadors in the ABA.

- On October 21, the Oakland Athletics win the World Series in seven games over the New York Mets.

- On October 28, Secretariat runs, and wins the Canadian International Championship, the last race of his career.

- On December 11, Houston Astros baseball star Cesar Cedeno is jailed in the Dominican Republic for involuntary manslaughter.

- On December 16, after a two-hundred-yard day against the New York Jets, Buffalo Bills running back O. J. Simpson becomes the first player to gain over two thousand yards in one season.

- On December 31, Notre Dame defeats the University of Alabama football team 24-23 in the Sugar Bowl and is named national champion.

1974

- On January 13, the Miami Dolphins win the Super Bowl for the second year in a row, defeating the Minnesota Vikings, 24-7.

- On January 28, Muhammad Ali beats Joe Frazier in a unanimous twelve-round decision.

- On January 30, the ABA files a $600 million antitrust suit against the NBA.

- On February 17, Richard Petty wins his fifth Daytona 500 stock-car race.

- On March 24, North Carolina State University wins the NCAA basketball championship over Marquette University, 76-64.

- On April 8, Hank Aaron of the Atlanta Braves hits his 715th career home run, breaking Babe Ruth's record.

- On April 25, the NFL announces major rule changes, including a sudden-death play-off to settle ties and moving the goal posts from the goal line to the back line.

- On May 3, UCLA basketball star center Bill Walton signs a five-year, $2.5 million contract with the Portland Trailblazers.

- On May 12, the Boston Celtics win the NBA championship in seven games over the Milwaukee Bucks.

- On May 19, the Philadelphia Flyers win the Stanley Cup hockey championship in six games over the Boston Bruins.
- On May 26, Johnny Rutherford wins the Indianapolis 500.
- On June 12, Little League Baseball announces that girls will be allowed to play on teams.
- On June 30, Tom Watson wins his first professional golf tournament, the forty-thousand-dollar Western Open.
- On July 1, NFL players begin a seven-week strike for free-agency rights.
- On July 18, St. Louis Cardinals pitcher Bob Gibson strikes out his three-thousandth batter, a National League record.
- On August 12, California Angels pitcher Nolan Ryan strikes out nineteen Boston Red Sox players in nine innings, a major-league record.
- On September 10, St. Louis Cardinals Lou Brock steals his 105th base, setting a major-league baseball record. Brock steals ten more bases before the season ends.
- On September 16, world light heavyweight boxing champion Bob Foster retires, having defended his championship fourteen times.
- On September 29, California Angels pitcher Nolan Ryan pitches his third no-hitter, defeating the Minnesota Twins.
- On October 1, all-time scoring leader Wilt Chamberlain announces his retirement from professional basketball.
- On October 3, Frank Robinson is named manager of the Cleveland Indians and becomes the first black manager in major-league baseball.
- On October 17, the Oakland Athletics win their third World Series in a row, defeating the Los Angeles Dodgers in five games.
- On October 30, Muhammad Ali knocks out George Foreman in the eighth round to regain the world heavyweight boxing championship.
- On November 27, New York Yankees owner George Steinbrenner is banned from baseball for two years after he is found guilty of making illegal campaign contributions to Richard Nixon and others.
- In December, Ara Parseghian announces his retirement as football coach at Notre Dame University.
- On December 20, a federal court judge rules that the NFL contract and reserve system is illegal.

1975

- On January 1, the University of Southern California defeats Ohio State in the Rose Bowl 18-17 to earn a contested designation as the nation's best college football team.
- On January 12, the Pittsburgh Steelers win the Super Bowl, defeating the Minnesota Vikings, 16-6.
- On February 8, Bill Russell is elected to the Basketball Hall of Fame.
- On February 16, Jimmy Connors is the first player to win three straight national indoor tennis tournaments.
- On March 31, UCLA defeats the University of Kentucky 92-85 to win the NCAA basketball championship. Having coached his team to national championships in ten of the past twelve seasons, John Wooden retires as coach.

- On April 5, Chris Evert wins the forty-thousand-dollar Virginia Slims tennis tournament, claiming the largest purse ever offered for a women's tennis match.
- On April 13, Jack Nicklaus wins the forty-thousand-dollar Masters golf tournament.
- On April 26, Jimmy Connors wins five hundred thousand dollars in a tennis challenge match against Australian John Newcomb.
- On April 30, former chairman of the Democratic National Committee and Postmaster General Lawrence O'Brien is named commissioner of the NBA.
- On May 1, in a game against the Detroit Tigers, Hank Aaron of the Milwaukee Brewers breaks Babe Ruth's record of 2,209 RBIs.
- On May 25, the Golden State Warriors win the NBA championship in four games over the Washington Bullets.
- On May 25, Bobby Unser wins the Indianapolis 500 when a storm causes flooding, ending the race after 435 miles.
- On May 31, the Philadelphia 76ers sign high-school basketball player Daryl Dawkins to a $1 million contract; Dawkins is the first high-school player to be signed by an NBA team.
- On June 1, California Angels pitcher Nolan Ryan matches Sandy Koufax's record of four no-hitters in a career with a win against the Baltimore Orioles.
- On June 3, the New York Cosmos professional soccer team signs Pele to a three-year, $7 million contract, making him the highest-paid athlete in the world.
- On June 14, Chris Evert wins the French Open tennis tournament singles championship for the second year in a row.
- On July 5, Arthur Ashe defeats Jimmy Connors to win the Wimbledon men's singles championship.
- On July 7, the unbeaten filly Ruffian breaks down at Belmont Park during a match race with Foolish Pleasure and is destroyed.
- On August 10, Jack Nicklaus wins his fourth PGA Championship.
- On September 6, Chris Evert wins the U.S. Open women's tennis championship.
- On October 22, the Cincinnati Reds win the World Series over the Boston Red Sox in seven games.
- On November 6, Detroit Red Wing Dan Maloney is charged with assault for behavior during a hockey game with the Toronto Maple Leafs.
- On December 2, Ohio State running back Archie Griffin is the first football player ever to win the Heisman Trophy twice. He ends his college career with a record 5,177 yards rushing.
- On December 10, a syndicate headed by Bill Veeck buys the Chicago White Sox baseball team for $9.75 million.

1976

- On January 18, the Pittsburgh Steelers defeat the Dallas Cowboys 21-17 to win the Super Bowl.
- On February 4, the Winter Olympics open in Innsbruck, Austria.

- On February 15, the Winter Olympics end. Speed skaters Peter Mueller and Sheila Young and figure skater Dorothy Hamill win the only gold medals among the ten total medals won by Americans.

- On March 29, Indiana University defeats the University of Michigan 86-68 to complete the season unbeaten and win the NCAA basketball championship.

- On April 11, Ray Floyd wins the Masters golf tournament by eight strokes with a record-equaling 271 total score.

- On May 16, the Montreal Canadiens beat the Philadelphia Flyers in four games to win the Stanley Cup hockey championship.

- On May 30, Johnny Rutherford wins the Indianapolis 500 for the second time in three years. The race was stopped after 102 laps (355 miles) due to heavy rain.

- On June 6, the Boston Celtics with their thirteenth NBA championship, defeating the Phoenix Suns in six games.

- On June 17, the NBA accepts four of the six teams in the ABA in a merger recommended by a federal judge to settle antitrust litigation.

- On July 17, the Summer Olympics open in Montreal.

- On August 1, the XXI Olympiad ends. The United States is third in medals after the Soviet Union and East Germany, winning thirty-four gold among its ninety-four total medals.

- On August 27, Dr. Renee Richards, a transsexual, is barred from competition in the U.S. Open tennis tournament.

- On September 11, Chris Evert wins the U.S. Open women's tennis singles championship, her second Grand Slam championship win of the year.

- On September 12, Jimmy Connors defeats Bjorn Borg to win the U.S. Open men's tennis singles.

- On October 16, Ove Johansson of Abilene Christian College kicks a sixty-nine-yard field goal, the longest ever in competition, including professional football.

- On October 21, the Cincinnati Reds defeat the New York Yankees in four games to win the World Series.

1977

- On January 1, the University of Pittsburgh defeats the University of Georgia in the Sugar Bowl 27-3 and is subsequently named the national champion college football team by the Associated Press.

- On January 9, the Oakland Raiders defeat the Minnesota Vikings 32-14 in Super Bowl XI.

- On March 27, Chris Evert wins her fourth Virginia Slims tennis tournament.

- On March 28, Marquette University defeats the University of North Carolina 67-59 to win the NCAA basketball championship.

- On April 10, Tom Watson wins the Masters golf tournament.

- On April 25, the fifteen-day strike by NBA referees ends.

- On May 14, the Montreal Canadiens win the Stanley Cup hockey championship in four games over the Boston Bruins.

- On May 23, forty-nine-year-old Gordie Howe and his two sons sign a multimillion-dollar contract with the World Hockey Association New England Whalers.

- On May 29, A. J. Foyt wins his record fourth Indianapolis 500.

- On June 5, the Portland Trail Blazers beat the Philadelphia 76ers in six games to win the NBA championship.

- On June 11, Seattle Slew wins the Belmont Stakes and the Triple Crown. He is the tenth Triple Crown winner and the first undefeated winner.

- On August 14, Lanny Wadkins wins the PGA tournament.

- On August 29, Lou Brock of the St. Louis Cardinals breaks the stolen-bases record previously held by Ty Cobb.

- On September 7, fourteen-year-old Tracy Austin, the youngest player ever to advance to the quarterfinals of the U.S. Open tennis tournament, is defeated.

- On September 10, Chris Evert wins her third straight U.S. Open women's tennis championship.

- On September 29, an estimated seventy million television viewers, the largest audience in history for a boxing match, watch Muhammad Ali win a unanimous decision over Earnie Shavers.

- On October 18, the New York Yankees win the World Series, defeating the Los Angeles Dodgers in six games.

- On December 7, Gordie Howe scores his one thousandth career hockey goal, setting a record.

- On December 10, seventeen-year-old jockey Steve Cauthen earns $6 million in horse racing purses during the year, a record.

1978

- On January 2, Notre Dame, with quarterback Joe Montana, defeats the previously unbeaten University of Texas 38-10 in the Cotton Bowl and is subsequently named national collegiate football champion.

- On January 15, the Dallas Cowboys defeat the Denver Broncos 27-10 in Super Bowl XII.

- On January 24, Joe Namath retires as a professional football player.

- On February 15, Leon Spinks wins a split decision against Muhammad Ali to become world heavyweight champion of the world.

- On March 27, the University of Kentucky wins the NCAA basketball championship, defeating Duke University 94-88.

- On May 6, Affirmed, ridden by eighteen-year-old Steve Cauthen, wins the Kentucky Derby.

- On May 20, Affirmed, with Cauthen up, wins the Preakness.

- On May 25, the Montreal Canadiens win the Stanley Cup hockey championship over the Boston Bruins in six games.

- On May 28, Al Unser wins the Indianapolis 500.

- On May 29, John McEnroe of Stanford University wins the NCAA men's singles tennis championship.

- On June 7, the Washington Bullets win the NBA championship in seven games over the Seattle Supersonics.

- On June 10, Affirmed, with Cauthen as jockey, wins the Belmont Stakes and becomes the eleventh racehorse to win the Triple Crown.

- On June 18, first-year professional golfer Nancy Lopez breaks the Ladies Professional Golfers Association (LPGA) record for consecutive wins and accumulates record earnings for a rookie of $153,336.

- On July 15, Jack Nicklaus wins his third British Open golf tournament.

- On September 10, Chris Evert and Jimmy Connors win singles championships at the U.S. Open tennis tournament.

- On September 15, Muhammad Ali becomes the first man ever to win the heavyweight boxing championship three times, defeating Leon Spinks in a fifteen-round decision. Reportedly the televised fight is viewed in more homes than any sporting event ever before.

- On October 17, the New York Yankees win the World Series in six games over the Los Angeles Dodgers.

- On December 5, Pete Rose, a free agent in the professional baseball draft, signs a $3.2 million contract with the Philadelphia Phillies, making him baseball's highest-paid player.

- On December 29, Clemson University defeats Ohio State 17-15 in the Gator Bowl. Ohio State coach Woody Hayes is fired after punching a Clemson player on the sideline after the player had intercepted an Ohio State pass.

1979

- On January 1, the University of Alabama defeats Penn State in the Sugar Bowl 14-7 and is named collegiate football champion by the Associated Press.

- On January 21, the Pittsburgh Steelers defeated the Dallas Cowboys 35-31 to win their third Super Bowl in a row, a record.

- On March 22, the NHL and the World Hockey League merge.

- On March 26, Michigan State University, led by Ervin "Magic" Johnson, wins the NCAA basketball championship over Larry Bird's Indiana State University, 75-64.

- On May 18, professional baseball umpires settle a three-month strike.

- On May 21, the Montreal Canadiens win the Stanley Cup hockey championship over the New York Rangers in five games.

- On May 27, Rick Mears, in his second season of major track racing, wins the Indianapolis 500.

- On June 1, the Seattle Supersonics win the NBA championship in five games over the Washington Bullets.

- On September 9, Tracy Austin, age sixteen, and John McEnroe win the singles championships at the U.S. Open tennis tournament. Austin is the youngest women's champion in the history of the tournament.

- On October 17, the Pittsburgh Pirates win the World Series over the Baltimore Orioles in four games.

- On November 19, pitcher Nolan Ryan signs a $4.5 million four-year contract with the Houston Astros.

- On November 30, Sugar Ray Leonard wins the World Boxing Council welterweight championship in a fifteen-round TKO over Wilfredo Benitez.

Curt Flood and the Reserve Clause

The Way It Is

Autobiography

By: Curt Flood, with Richard Carter

Date: 1971

Source: Flood, Curt, with Richard Carter. *The Way It Is.* New York: Trident Press, 1971, 14–16, 184, 185–186, 188, 189–191, 192–193.

About the Author: Curt Flood (1938–1997) was born in Houston, Texas. After high school, Flood signed as an outfielder with the Cincinnati Reds before being traded to the St. Louis Cardinals in 1958. Flood spent twelve seasons with Cardinals, winning seven gold gloves, and helping St. Louis to three World Series championships. Flood was traded to Philadelphia Phillies after the 1969 season. Refusing to report, Flood sued baseball for his freedom from the reserve clause. While his case was on appeal, Flood played two months with the Washington Senators before quitting. In retirement, Flood was a portrait painter, broadcaster, and community recreation official.

"Curt Flood's Thirteenth Amendment"

Newspaper article

By: Red Smith

Date: 1969

Source: Smith, Red. "Curt Flood's Thirteenth Amendment." 1969. Reprinted in *The Red Smith Reader.* Dave Anderson, ed. New York: Vintage Books, 1983, 126–128.

About the Author: Red Smith (1905–1982) was born in Green Bay, Wisconsin. After graduating from Notre Dame in 1927, Smith was a reporter for the *Milwaukee Sentinel,* as well as copy editor and sportswriter for the *St. Louis Star-Times.* In 1936, Smith moved to the *Philadelphia Record,* then the *New York Herald-Tribune* nine years later, becoming one of America's most respected sportswriters. After the *Herald-Tribune* folded in 1967, Smith wrote in syndication until joining the *The New York Times* in 1971, remaining there until his death. Smith authored several collections of his columns, and won numerous honors, including the Pulitzer Prize in 1976.

Flood v. Kuhn

Supreme Court decision

By: Justice Harry A. Blackmun

Date: 1972

Source: *Flood v. Kuhn.* 407 U.S. 258 (1972). 32 L.Ed.2d 728, 92 S.Ct. 2099, 2099–2100, 2112–2113.

About the Author: Harry A. Blackmun (1908–1999) served as a justice on the United States Supreme Court from 1970 to 1994. A lifelong Republican, Blackmun was appointed to the U.S. Federal Court of Appeals in 1959 by President Dwight D. Eisenhower (served 1953–1961). Appointed to the Supreme Court by President Richard Nixon (served 1969–1974), Blackmun is most famous for writing the controlling opinion in *Roe v. Wade,* the Supreme Court decision that legalized abortion in the United States. ■

Introduction

For nearly a century, the reserve clause in a baseball player's contract kept team owners in control of the game. First adopted in the 1880s, the reserve clause bound a player to a team until he was sold, traded, or released. Started as a way to prevent players from "jumping" from team to team, the system became a way of reducing the players to, as some observed, "high-price peonage." In 1922, the reserve clause was further strengthened when the U.S. Supreme Court ruled that baseball was not subject to antitrust business regulation; in other words, the sport was granted a legal monopoly. For the next fifty years, the reserve clause remained constant in baseball and was rarely challenged. That, however, would change through the actions of one player.

In 1969, Curt Flood had been a major leaguer for twelve seasons. Originally signed by the Cincinnati Reds, he felt misused when he was traded without his consent to the St. Louis Cardinals in 1958, and Flood resolved not to allow it to happen again. With St. Louis, Flood won seven gold gloves as one of baseball's best center fielders, and helped the Cardinals to three World Series, including two championships. He lived in St. Louis and became a portrait painter. After a disappointing 1969 season, the Cardinals made several trades, including dealing Flood to the Philadelphia Phillies. Flood, aware of the Phillies' reputation and the city's as racist, refused to accept the trade. After unsuccessfully seeking commissioner Bowie Kuhn's permission to become a free agent, Flood decided to take baseball to court, even at the price of losing a year or more of his career.

Flood's decision was backed by Marvin Miller, executive director of the Players Association, who asked former U.S. Supreme Court justice and United Nations Ambassador, Arthur Goldberg, to represent the ballplayer in legal action. Flood's trial, tried in U.S. District Court in New York City, began in May 1970 and lasted ten weeks—filling two thousand pages of testimony. While the commissioner and management testified for baseball, Jackie Robinson and Bill Veeck were among those who stood with Flood. The District Court ruled against Flood, and his attorneys appealed first to the Second Circuit Court of Appeals, and ultimately to the Supreme Court.

Flood sat out the 1970 season, but signed with the Washington Senators in 1971; after two months and playing poorly, he suddenly quit and left for the island of Minorca. On June 19, 1972, two years after Flood's original case against baseball was filed, the Supreme Court, in a 5-3 decision, written by Justice Harry Blackmun (a noted baseball fan), ruled that baseball continued to be exempt from antitrust laws.

Significance

The Court said less about the reserve clause than about a reluctance to overturn prior Supreme Court decisions establishing an "anomaly" or "aberration" that exempted baseball from antitrust laws. Justice William O. Douglas, dissenting along with Thurgood Marshall and William Brennan, believed that antitrust laws were as important to baseball players as to any other "class of workers."

Curt Flood had lost his two-year struggle against the reserve clause, but the battle was not over. In 1975, pitchers Andy Messersmith and Dave McNally tested the reserve clause. The standard player contract bound them for one year. But would a player become a free agent if he did not sign a contract while playing for his team that year? Baseball said no, and Messersmith and McNally appealed their case to an arbitrator, Peter Seitz. Seitz ruled the players free agents, ushering in a new era for the sport.

New rules were established with the coming of free agency, including players becoming eligible as free agents after several seasons in baseball. With the exception of Reggie Jackson and a few other players, most free agents in 1976—the first year without the reserve clause—were either past their prime or flops. Over the years, the owners learned to choose players better and spread their money wisely, while free agents became savvier with whom they were negotiating. Today, players can make one or even two hundred million dollars in long-term contracts, exercising the freedom to choose their employers.

But it took a single player like Curt Flood, who essentially gave up his career, to stand up against the reserve clause. As the Players Association statement said at the time of Flood's death—at fifty-nine, of complications from throat cancer—"Every major league baseball player owes Curt Flood a debt of gratitude that can never be repaid. With the odds overwhelmingly against him, he was willing to take a stand for what he knew was right."

Primary Source

The Way It Is [excerpt]

SYNOPSIS: Curt Flood, baseball player, in a memoir, describes his feelings when the St. Louis Cardinals traded him to the Philadelphia Phillies. Flood explains why he refused to report to the Phillies and the details surrounding his challenge of the reserve clause in court.

I was on the St. Louis Cardinals for twelve years. With the exception of one or two outstanding pitchers and home-run hitters (I was neither), I became the most highly paid performer in the history of the team. In October 1969, five months before the day on which these reminiscences begin, the Cardinals traded me and some other players to Philadelphia.

Player trades are commonplace. The unusual aspect of this one was that I refused to accept it. It violated the logic and integrity of my existence. I was not a consignment of goods. I was a man, the rightful proprietor of my own person and my own talents.

A salesman reluctant to transfer from one office to another may choose to seek employment on the sales force of a different firm. A plumber can reject the dictates of his boss without relinquishing his right to plumb elsewhere. At the expiration of one contract, an actor shops among producers for the best arrangement he can find. But the baseball monopoly offers no such option to the athlete. If he elects not to work for the corporation that "owns" his services, baseball forbids him to ply his trade at all. In the hierarchy of living things, he ranks with poultry.

The Philadelphia Phillies offered me $100,000 to play center field for them during the 1970 season. I did not earn that much from the struggling Curt Flood Photo Studios, or from painting portraits. One of the leading wags in the baseball establishment remarked that, unless Curt Flood were another Rembrandt, he'd show up in time to play for the Phillies and collect his pay. Members of that establishment, including its wags, were entirely incapable of understanding that a basic principle of human life was involved. More to the point, they recognized no principle so basic that it could not be nullified by payment of a few extra dollars.

I sued. The distinguished Mr. Justice Arthur J. Goldberg went to Federal Court in my behalf and challenged the right of entrepreneurs to use me for barter, like a chattel. Baseball had been sued on similar grounds in the past, but never by an Arthur Goldberg and never by a player with my credentials, my resources or my particular brand of rage. . . .

I think I had known it for months without admitting it to myself. Now I said to me, "Brother Flood, you are going to be traded. You have had it."

To which I answered, "They would not dare!"

"Wanna bet?" I replied.

On October 8, I was sitting in my apartment, waiting for my nervous system to come down to earth. The season was over. I had finished with a batting average of .285, which was below my usual standard. On the other hand, only nineteen full-time players in the league had managed higher averages. I had hit safely 173 times—eleventh in the league. If only nine more batted balls had dropped in, I'd have hit .300. Reveries of a baseball player. No wonder so many of us drink during the off-season. No wonder so many of us drink all year round. . . .

The telephone sounded.

"Hello, Curt?"

"Yes."

"Jim Toomey, Curt."

A chill entered my belly. Toomey was assistant to Bing Devine in the front office.

"Curt, you've been traded to Philadelphia."

Silence.

"You, McCarver, Hoerner and Byron Browne. For Richie Allen, Cookie Rojas and Jerry Johnson."

Silence.

"Good luck, Curt."

"Thanks. Thanks a lot."

Twelve years of my life. I spent the rest of the day in the chair right next to the telephone, answering none of the calls. *Twelve years of my life.*

I said to Marian, "There ain't no way I'm going to pack up and move twelve years of my life away from here. No way at all."

Let Him Go

The formality materialized the next day: A printed form on which filled-in blanks officially advised Mr. Curtis Charles Flood that his contract had been assigned to the Philadelphia Club of the National League. Signed by Vaughn P. Devine. Bing's personal bye-bye.

I was an expert on baseball's spurious paternalism. I was a connoisseur of its grossness. I had known that I was out of phase with management. I therefore had known that I might be traded. Yet now, when the industry was merely doing its thing, I took

Curt Flood loosens up during winter camp before his last season of professional baseball, St. Petersburg, Florida, November 19, 1970. Flood ended his career with the Washington Senators after only twelve full seasons. **AP/WIDE WORLD PHOTOS. REPRODUCED BY PERMISSION.**

it personally. I felt unjustly cast out. Days passed before I began to see the problem whole.

Philadelphia. The nation's northernmost southern city. Scene of Richie Allen's ordeals. Home of a ball club rivaled only by the Pirates as the least cheerful organization in the league. When the proud Cardinals were riding a chartered jet, the Phils were still lumbering through the air in propeller jobs, arriving on the Coast too late to get proper rest before submitting to murder by the Giants and Dodgers. I did not want to succeed Richie Allen in the affections of that organization, its press and its catcalling, missile-hurling audience.

"I have only two choices," I told Marian, after treating her to another outburst of my inexhaustible anger and hurt. "I can go to Philadelphia or I can quit baseball altogether. I will not go to Philadelphia." The words of a typical baseball player, prostrated by the unchallengable rules of the industry.

I telephoned Bing Devine and told him that I would retire.

"That's entirely up to you, Curt. Good luck."

Curtis Flood converses with attorney Allan H. Zerman (left), St. Louis, March 6, 1970. In a move that eventually forced him to early retirement, Flood challenged baseball's reserve clause, arguing that players should be able to become free agents. He took the case all the way to the Supreme Court. © BETTMANN/CORBIS. REPRODUCED BY PERMISSION.

I told the reporters that I would retire. Nobody believed me. Traded players are forever threatening to pack it in. Few can afford to. . . .

John Quinn, general manager of the Phillies, had been trying to reach me. He was in St. Louis on business.

"Mr. Quinn, you're wasting your time. I've made my decision."

"Can't you spare a few minutes for a chat?"

I met him at a hotel and was impressed. He was warm and understanding. He told me that the Philadelphia operation was being overhauled. Good new players were coming. A new ball park was in construction. Money was there for me. I agreed to see him again. I no longer was bothered about Philadelphia, as such. I was thinking more clearly. The problem was no particular city but was the reserve clause, which afflicted all players equally no matter where.

I dropped in on Allan H. Zerman, a young lawyer who counseled the operators of the photography business that bore my name. I liked him. He was the only man who had ever refused to take free World Series tickets from me. He had helped my brother Carl. I told him my story in fairly clear perspective. I no longer was bleeding. The issue was not me alone but the reserve system. Like thousands of players before me, I had been caught in its machinery. Before being ground to bits, I'd get out.

"St. Louis is my home," I said. "I'm known and liked here. I have business possibilities here. What the hell is there for me in Philadelphia? Screw 'em. I'm quitting."

"There's one other alternative," said Zerman.

"Are you talking about suing baseball?"

"Have you considered the idea?" he parried.

It had been germinating in me for weeks. Sooner or later, someone would challenge baseball's right to treat human beings like used cars. If this lawyer had not ruled out the possibility of a suit, why should I?

I telephoned Marvin Miller for an appointment and flew to New York to pick his brains.

"I want to sue baseball on constitutional grounds," I told him. His eyebrows rose. "I want to give the courts a chance to outlaw the reserve system. I want to go out like a man instead of disappearing like a bottle cap."

Marvin looked at me hard.

"How much thought have you given this?"

"Plenty. I should be able to negotiate for myself in an open market and see just how much money this little body is worth. I shouldn't be confronted with an either-or proposition like the one now facing me. Somebody needs to go up against the system. I'm ready."

"A lawsuit might take two or three years," said Marvin. "It would cost a fortune. And you could lose, you know. Others have."

"I could also win."

Marvin wouldn't let me off the hook.

"If you have any idea about becoming the first black manager, you can forget it after suing. You can also forget jobs as a coach or scout."

"I never had a chance anyway."

"Your present salary is around ninety thousand, right? You're only thirty-one. Think of the money you'd lose by staying out of the game during the next two or three seasons."

"You're not telling me anything I don't know."

"Is there anything in your personal life that they could smear you with? They would."

"You haven't begun to scare me yet. Let's sue."

He took a deep breath.

"Not yet, please," he insisted. "I won't raise a finger to help you until I'm sure that you've given enough thought to all the possibilities. Go back to St. Louis and think. When you're done thinking, start all over again. Don't commit yourself to this until you have covered every detail and are sure that the positive outweighs the negative. Please."

I promised. . . .

I would not settle out of court for any amount, unless the bargain included employer-employee relations of a kind acceptable to me and the Major League Baseball Players Association. I had little money, but I was fortified by what I am not ashamed to call spiritual resources. . . . Win or lose, the baseball industry would never be the same. I would leave my mark.

Primary Source

"Curt Flood's Thirteenth Amendment"

SYNOPSIS: Sportswriter Red Smith, in a syndicated column, expresses his view of Curt Flood's impending suit against major league baseball, including criticism of commissioner Bowie Kuhn.

Curt Flood was nineteen years old and had made one hit in the major leagues (a home run) when his telephone rang on December 5 of 1957. The call was from the Cincinnati Reds advising him that he had been traded to the St. Louis Cardinals.

"I knew ballplayers got traded like horses," he said years later, "but I can't tell you how I felt when it happened to me. I was only nineteen, but I made up my mind then it wouldn't ever happen again."

It happened again last October. The Cardinals traded Flood to Philadelphia. "Maybe I won't go," Curt said. Baseball men laughed. Curt makes something like $90,000 a year playing center field, and less than that painting portraits in his studio in Clayton, Missouri. "Unless he's better than Rembrandt," one baseball man said, "he'll play."

It was beautiful comment, superlatively typical of the executive mind, a pluperfect example of baseball's reaction to unrest down in the slave cabins.

"You mean," baseball demands incredulously, "that at these prices they want human rights, too?"

Curtis Charles Flood is a man of character and self-respect. Being black, he is more sensitive than most white players about the institution of slavery as it exists in professional baseball. After the trade he went abroad, and when he returned his mind was made up. He confided his decision to the twenty-four club representatives in the Major League Players Association at their convention in San Juan, Puerto Rico.

He told them it was high time somebody in baseball made a stand for human freedom. He said he was determined to make the stand and he asked their support. The players questioned him closely to make sure this was not merely a ploy to squeeze money out of the Phillies. Then, convinced, they voted unanimously to back him up.

Realizing that if Flood lost his case through poor handling they would all be losers, the players arranged—through their executive director, Marvin Miller—to retain Arthur J. Goldberg, former Secretary of Labor, former Justice of the Supreme Court, former United States ambassador to the United Nations, and the country's most distinguished authority on labor-management relations.

Baseball's so-called reserve clause, which binds the player to his employer through his professional life, had been under fire before. Never has it been attacked by a team like this.

The system is in deep trouble, and yesterday's action by the baseball commissioner, Bowie Kuhn, did nothing to help it out. Because the news was out that Flood was going to take baseball to court, Kuhn released to the press the following correspondence:

"Dear Mr. Kuhn," Flood wrote on December 24, 1969, "after twelve years in the major leagues I do not feel that I am a piece of property to be bought and sold irrespective of my wishes. I believe that any system that produces that result violates my basic rights as a citizen and is inconsistent with the laws of the United States and of the several states.

"It is my desire to play baseball in 1970, and I am capable of playing. I have received a contract offer from the Philadelphia club, but I believe that I have the right to consider offers from other clubs before making any decisions. I, therefore, request that you make known to all the major league clubs my feelings in this matter, and advise them of my availability for the 1970 season."

Kuhn replied:

Dear Curt: This will acknowledge your letter of December 24, 1969, which I found on returning to my office yesterday.

I certainly agree with you that you, as a human being, are not a piece of property to be bought and sold. That is fundamental in our society and I think obvious. However, I cannot see its application to the situation at hand.

You have entered into a current playing contract with the St. Louis club which has the same assignment provisions as those in your annual major league contracts since 1956. Your present playing contract has been assigned in accordance with its provisions by the St. Louis club to the Philadelphia club. The provisions of the playing contract have been negotiated over the years between the clubs and the players, most recently when the present basic agreement was negotiated two years ago between the clubs and the Players Association.

If you have any specific objections to the propriety of the assignment I would appreciate your specifying the objections. Under the circumstances, and pending any further information from you, I do not see what action I can take, and cannot comply with your request contained in the second paragraph of your letter.

I am pleased to see your statement that you desire to play baseball in 1970. I take it this puts to rest any thought, as reported earlier in the press, that you were considering retirement.

Thus the commissioner restates baseball's labor policy: "Run along, sonny, you bother me."

Primary Source

Flood v. Kuhn [excerpt]

> **SYNOPSIS:** The following excerpt is from the U.S. Supreme Court decision in *Flood v. Kuhn,* in which Curt Flood sued baseball for his right to play for the team of his choice rather than be subject to the reserve clause. The case was argued on March 20, 1972, and decided on June 19, 1972.

Mr. Justice White joined in the judgment of the Court, and in all but Part I of the Court's opinion.

The Chief Justice filed a concurring opinion.

Mr. Justice Douglas and Mr. Justice Marshall filed dissenting opinions, in which Mr. Justice Brennan joined.

Mr. Justice Powell took no part in consideration or decision of the case. . . .

1. Professional baseball is a business and it is engaged in interstate commerce.

2. With its reserve system enjoying exemption from the federal antitrust laws, baseball is, in a very distinct sense, an exception and an anomaly. *Federal Baseball* and *Toolson* have become an aberration confined to baseball.

3. Even though others might regard this as "unrealistic, inconsistent, or illogical," see *Radovich,* 352 U.S., at 452, 77 S.Ct., at 394, the aberration is an established one, and one that has been recognized not only in *Federal Baseball* and *Toolson,* but in *Shubert, International Boxing,* and *Radovich,* as well, a total of five consecutive cases in this Court. It is an aberration that has been with us now for half a century, one heretofore deemed fully entitled to the benefit of *stare decisis,* and one that has survived the Court's expanding concept of interstate commerce. It rests on a recognition and an acceptance of baseball's unique characteristics and needs.

4. Other professional sports operating interstate—football, boxing, basketball, and, presumably, hockey and golf—are not so exempt.

5. The advent of radio and television, with their consequent increased coverage and additional revenues, has not occasioned an overruling of *Federal Baseball* and *Toolson.*

6. The Court has emphasized that since 1922 baseball, with full and continuing congressional awareness, has been allowed to develop and to expand unhindered by federal legislative action. Remedial legislation has been introduced repeatedly in Congress but none has ever been enacted. The Court, accordingly, has concluded that Congress as yet has had no intention to subject baseball's reserve system to the reach of the antitrust statues. This, obviously, has been deemed to be something other than mere congressional silence and passivity. Cf. *Boys Markets, Inc. v. Retail Clerk's Union,* 398 U.S. 235, 241–242, 90 S.Ct. 1583, 1587–1588, 26 L.Ed.2d 199 (1970).

7. The Court has expressed concern about the confusion and the retroactivity problems that inevitably would result with a judicial overturning of *Federal Baseball.* It has voiced a prefer-

ence that if any change is to be made, it come by legislative action that, by its nature, is only prospective in operation.

8. The Court noted in *Radovich,* 352 U.S., at 452, 77 S.Ct., at 394, that the slate with respect to baseball is not clean. Indeed, it has not been clean for half a century.

This emphasis and this concern are still with us. We continue to be loath, 50 years after *Federal Baseball* and almost two decades after *Toolson,* to overturn those cases judicially when Congress, by its positive inaction, has allowed those decisions to stand for so long and, far beyond mere inference and implication, has clearly evinced a desire not to disapprove them legislatively.

Accordingly, we adhere once again to *Federal Baseball* and *Toolson* and to their application to professional baseball. We adhere also to *International Boxing* and *Radovich* and to their respective applications to professional boxing and professional football. If there is any inconsistency or illogic in all this, it is an inconsistency and illogic of long standing that is to be remedied by the Congress and not by this Court. If we were to act otherwise, we would be withdrawing from the conclusion as to congressional intent made in *Toolson* and from the concerns as to retrospectivity therein expressed. Under these circumstances, there is merit in consistency even though some might claim that beneath that consistency is a layer of inconsistency.

The petitioner's argument as to the application of state antitrust laws deserves a word. Judge Cooper rejected the state law claims because state antitrust regulation would conflict with federal policy and because national "uniformity [is required] in any regulation of baseball and its reserve system." 316 F.Supp., at 280. The Court of Appeals, in affirming, stated, "[A]s the burden on interstate commerce outweighs the states' interests in regulating baseball's reserve system, the Commerce Clause precludes the application here of state antitrust law." 443 F.2d, at 268. As applied to organized baseball, and in the light of this Court's observations and holdings in *Federal Baseball,* in *Toolson,* in *Shubert,* in *International Boxing,* and in *Radovich,* and despite baseball's allegedly inconsistent position taken in the past with respect to the application of state law these statements adequately dispose of the state law claims.

The conclusion we have reached makes it unnecessary for us to consider the respondents' additional argument that the reserve system is a mandatory subject of collective bargaining and that federal labor policy therefore exempts the reserve system from the operation of federal antitrust laws.

We repeat for this case what was said in *Toolson:*

> Without re-examination of the underlying issues, the [judgment] below [is] affirmed on the authority of *Federal Baseball Club of Baltimore v. National League of Professional Baseball Clubs, supra,* so far as that decision determines that Congress had no intention of including the business of baseball within the scope of the federal antitrust laws. 346 U.S., at 357, 74 S.Ct., at 79.

And what the Court said in *Federal Baseball* in 1922 and what it said in *Toolson* in 1953, we say again here in 1972: the remedy, if any is indicated, is for congressional, and not judicial, action.

The judgment of the Court of Appeals is affirmed.

Judgment affirmed.

Further Resources

BOOKS

Harrison, Maureen, and Steve Gilbert, eds. *Landmark Decisions of the United States Supreme Court, Volume V.* San Diego: Excellent Books, 1995.

Lowenfish, Lee, and Tony Lupien. *The Imperfect Diamond: The Story of Baseball's Reserve System and the Men Who Fought to Change It.* New York: Stein and Day, 1980.

Miller, Marvin. *A Whole Different Ballgame.* New York: Simon and Schuster, 1992.

PERIODICALS

Durso, Joseph. "Curt Flood is Dead at 59; Outfielder Defied Baseball." *The New York Times,* January 19, 1997.

Koppett, Leonard. "Baseball's Exempt Status Upheld by Supreme Court." *The New York Times,* June 20, 1972.

Ball Four
Memoir

By: Jim Bouton

Date: 1970

Source: Bouton, Jim. *Ball Four: My Life and Hard Times Throwing the Knuckleball in the Big Leagues.* Leonard Shecter, ed. Cleveland, Ohio: The World Publishing Company, 1970, 29–31, 89–90, 238.

About the Author: Jim Bouton (1939–) was born in Newark, New Jersey. After attending Western Michigan University, Bouton signed with the New York Yankees. After winning twenty-one games in 1963 and eighteen the following season (plus two World Series victories), Bouton hurt his arm, and by 1967 was demoted to the minor leagues. In 1969, Bouton pitched for the expansion Seattle Pilots, before being traded to the Houston Astros. He retired in 1970. In 1978, Bouton came back and pitched a season for the Atlanta Braves. Since then, Bouton has been involved in various baseball-related enterprises.

Introduction

In the early 1960s, Jim Bouton was one of baseball's most promising young pitchers. Signed out of Western Michigan University by the New York Yankees, Bouton made the major leagues in 1962, and within a year had made an impact. Bouton won twenty-one games against seven losses in 1963, and the next season he went 18-13 and won two World Series games in the Yankees' seven-game loss to the St. Louis Cardinals. Although bookish and college educated, Bouton fit into an aging Yankee team that still had Yogi Berra (who became the manager in 1964), Mickey Mantle, Whitey Ford, and Roger Maris.

Bouton hurt his arm in 1965, as he went just 4-15 on the year; meanwhile, the Yankees collapsed, experiencing their first losing season in forty years. Things got worse for the team and Bouton in 1966, as the Yankees finished last in the American League, and he went 3-8. In 1967 and 1968, Bouton spent most of both seasons in the minors, winning only two major league games. Meanwhile, in hopes of returning to the big leagues, Bouton learned techniques of pitching the knuckleball, with the help of former major league pitcher Johnny Sain.

In 1969, major league baseball expanded by four teams including the Seattle Pilots. The Pilots acquired Bouton's contract, and he hoped for a new beginning. Making the big league squad, Bouton pitched fifty-seven games in relief, compiling a 2-1 record. More than halfway through the season, Bouton was traded to the Houston Astros, who were contending for the National League West title. In Houston, he would go 0-2 in sixteen games. Throughout the season, Bouton kept a journal of his various on- and off-field activities, as well as those of his Seattle and Houston teammates, with the intention of publishing it afterward. Some players suspected Bouton of being up to no good when seeing him scribble comments in the dugout or clubhouse. A few years earlier, Jim Brosnan, another relief pitcher, wrote *The Long Season,* his account of the 1959 baseball season, which was considered candid for its time. Bouton's book, however, promised to be different.

Significance

Bouton published his book, *Ball Four: My Life and Hard Times Throwing the Knuckleball in the Big Leagues,*

in 1970, with editorial assistance from anti-establishment sportswriter Leonard Shecter. In the spring and summer of 1970, while Bouton was pitching for the Astros, major newspapers and publications began reviewing *Ball Four.* Meanwhile, players, managers, and owners were criticizing the book and its account of ballplayer voyeurism (and naming Mantle as a frequent participant), use of pep pills, or "greenies," management greed and cheapness, and subtle racism. In May 1970, baseball commissioner Bowie Kuhn summoned Bouton to his New York office, in effect to ask the pitcher to refute what he wrote. Bouton met with the commissioner, accompanied by Players Association head Marvin Miller, and he told reporters afterward that he defended everything in the book.

As *Ball Four* became a best seller, Bouton's pitching career was ending. After a sub-par 1970 season, he decided to retire. Returning to New York, Bouton became a television sportscaster and wrote another book, *I'm Glad You Didn't Take It Personally,* which recounted reaction to *Ball Four,* including his meeting with Commissioner Kuhn. The New York Yankees, Bouton's first major league team, declared him a persona non grata and would not invite him back for Old Timers Day until 1998—by then Mantle and Maris, two targets in *Ball Four,* were dead. In 1978, Bouton, nearing forty, attempted a comeback with the Atlanta Braves. Used primarily in relief, Bouton compiled a 1-3 record before retiring again, with a career record of 62-63. Since then, Bouton has written articles and lectured widely. He also invented and runs a business that markets Big League Chew—bubble gum packaged in a chewing tobacco–like pouch.

Today, over thirty years after it was first published, *Ball Four* seems tame compared to the "tell-all" sports memoirs of recent times—and their escapades with alcohol, drugs, women, and criminal behavior. But Bouton's account of life in the season of a ballplayer opened the once sanctified world of the clubhouse and revealed a place that in many ways mirrored the rest of society.

Primary Source

Ball Four [excerpt]

SYNOPSIS: Jim Bouton, Seattle Pilots and Houston Astros pitcher, in a diary of the 1969 season in *Ball Four,* shows the inside view of a baseball team, describing activities of ballplayers (some notable, such as Mickey Mantle) unknown to the public.

March 4

Mickey Mantle announced his retirement the other day and I got to thinking about the mixed feelings I've always had about him. On the one hand I

Team photo of the 1969–1970 Seattle Pilots from Jim Bouton's book, *Ball Four Plus Ball Five*. Bouton is the third from the left in the middle row.
REPRINTED FROM JIM BOUTON, *BALL FOUR PLUS BALL FIVE*. STEINER AND DAY/PUBLISHERS, 1981.

really liked his sense of humor and his boyishness, the way he'd spend all that time in the clubhouse making up involved games of chance and the pools he got up on golf matches and the Derby and things like that.

I once invested a dollar when Mantle raffled off a ham. I won, only there was no ham. That was one of the hazards of entering a game of chance, Mickey explained.

I got back by entering a fishing tournament he organized and winning the weight division with a ten-pounder I'd purchased in a store the day before. Two years later Mantle was still wondering why I'd only caught that one big fish and why all the other fish that were caught were green and lively while mine was gray and just lay there, staring.

I also remember the time I won my first major-league game. It was a shutout against the Washington Senators in which I walked seven guys and gave up seven hits and had to pitch from a stretch position all game. They were hitting line drives all over the place and Hector (What a Pair of Hands) Lopez bailed me out with about four leaping catches in left field. When the game was over I walked back

into the clubhouse and there was a path of white towels from the door to my locker, and all the guys were standing there, and just as I opened the door Mickey was putting the last towel down in place. I'll never forget him for that.

And I won't forget the time—1962, I guess it was—in Kansas City. I was sitting alone in a restaurant, eating, when Mickey and Whitey Ford came in and Mickey invited me to eat with them and picked up the tab and it made me feel good all over and like a big shot besides.

On the other hand there were all those times when he'd push little kids aside when they wanted his autograph, and the times when he was snotty to reporters, just about making them crawl and beg for a minute of his time. I've seen him close a bus window on kids trying to get his autograph. And I hated that *look* of his, when he'd get angry at somebody and cut him down with a glare. Bill Gilbert of *Sports Illustrated* once described that look as flickering across his face "like the nictitating membrane in the eye of a bird." And I don't like the Mantle that refused to sign baseballs in the clubhouse before the games. Everybody else had to sign, but Little Pete

"Young Ideas" [excerpt]

[Dick Young, *New York Daily News'* syndicated columnist, denounces *Ball Four,* and also Bouton personally for writing a tattletale book in revealing the less-than-exemplary behavior of baseball players.]

I feel sorry for Jim Bouton. He is a social leper. He didn't catch it, he developed it. . . . People like this, embittered people, sit down in their time of deepest rejection and write. They write, oh, hell, everybody stinks, everybody but me, and it makes them feel much better. . . .

Jim Bouton ridicules Sal Maglie, deplores the fact that Mickey Mantle drank liquor instead of going to bed to kill the ache in his knee, brags that he refuses to take greenies to pep him up before a game like some other pitchers do. This tells you something about Jim Bouton:

I was creamed. Five runs were scored off me before I was mercifully taken out of the game with two out in the fourth. . . . I blocked it all almost as quickly as I could shower, dress and join my family in the stands. That's the easiest way for me to forget. Some guys drink. I talk about the kids needing new shoes.

A man who worries about the little kiddies not having new shoes if he doesn't get the knuckleball over, must be a bit tense out there on the mound, and a man who worries about the kiddies needing new shoes when he was making $22,000 for six months work is perhaps a bit of a put-on.

That tells you something about Jim Bouton. I don't recommend it, but perhaps he should take an unwinding drink or two. It probably never occurred to Jim Bouton that a tee-totaling Mickey Mantle might have batted .220, lifetime, beating out ground balls. When Don Larsen was the biggest thing in baseball, somebody said just imagine how great he would be if he didn't drink so much, and Casey Stengel said, "I don't know. My guys who drink chocolate malteds aren't winning any games." . . .

There are some beautiful passages in "Ball Four." The book could have made it without the petty jealousy that seeps through, and the unwise criticism of his bosses.

Jim Bouton is a marginal talent, at best. And this book will hasten his end.

SOURCE: Young, Dick. "Young Ideas." *New York Daily News,* May 28, 1970.

---

forged Mantle's signature. So there are thousands of baseballs around the country that have been signed not by Mickey Mantle, but by Pete Previte.

Like everybody else on the club I ached with Mantle when he had one of his numerous and extremely painful injuries. I often wondered, though, if he might have healed quicker if he'd been sleeping more and loosening up with the boys at the bar less. I guess we'll never know.

What we do know, though, is that the face he showed in the clubhouse, as opposed to the one he reserved for the outside world, was often one of great merriment.

I remember one time he'd been injured and didn't expect to play, and I guess he got himself smashed. The next day he looked hung over out of his mind and was sent up to pinch-hit. He could hardly see. So he staggered up to the plate and hit a tremendous drive to left field for a home run. When he came back into the dugout everybody shook his hand and leaped all over him, and all the time he was getting a standing ovation from the crowd. He squinted out at the stands and said, "Those people don't know how tough that really was."

Another thing about Mantle. He was a pretty good practical joker. One time he and Ford told Pepitone and Linz that they'd finally arrived, they were ready to go out with the big boys. Mantle told them to get dressed up, tie and all—this was in Detroit—and meet them in a place called The Flame. Mickey gave them the address and said to be sure to ask for Mickey Mantle's table.

Pepitone and Linz were like a couple of kids at Christmas. They couldn't stop talking about what a great time they were going to have with Mickey Mantle and Whitey Ford. They got all fancied up, hopped into a cab and told the driver to take them to The Flame. After about a half-hour the cab pulled up in front of a place that was in the heart of the slum section, a hole in the wall with a broken plate-glass window in front and a little broken-down sign over the door: THE FLAME. No Mantle. No Ford. No table. . . .

March 30

Holtville

Now about Roger Maris. Roger fought a lot with the people in the stands, especially in Detroit, where he used to give them the finger. He and the fans would get to calling each other names and then Maris would roll out his heavy artillery.

"Yeah? How much money are *you* making?"

Roger was making $70,000 a year.

After a while every time Maris got into an argument the guys in the dugout would say, "C'mon Rodg, hit him with your wallet." . . .

And a final word about my favorite baseball writer, Jim Ogle, of the Newhouse papers. Ogle was a Yankee fan and he reacted to players purely on how much they were helping the Yankees to win. Charm, personality, intelligence—nothing counted. Only winning. Ogle didn't have even the pretense of objectivity. He was the only writer in the pressbox who would take the seventh-inning stretch in the Yankee half.

Once at a winter press conference, when the Yankees were announcing the signing of three or four guys, Stan Isaacs, who writes a really good column for *Newsday,* on Long Island, passed a note to Houk. It said: "Has Ogle signed his contract yet?"

Isaacs may not have known how ironic he was being. In fact Ogle's ambition was to work for the Yankees. But they would never give him a job.

Not that this prevented him from doing little jobs for them. Like when I was sent down he was on television with Yankee broadcasters and said that it wasn't so much that I was pitching poorly, but because of the kind of person I was. He said that none of the players liked me and there were some terrible things about me he couldn't even talk about. This left it up to the public imagination. What was I? Rapist, murderer, dope peddler? Jim Ogle wouldn't say.

Further Resources

BOOKS

Bouton, Jim. *Ball Four: The Final Pitch.* Champaign, Ill.: Sports Publishing, 2000.

———. *I'm Glad You Didn't Take It Personally.* New York: Morrow, 1971.

PERIODICALS

Angell, Roger. "Books: Scribe." *The New Yorker,* July 25, 1970, 79–80.

Halberstam, David. "American Notes: Baseball and the National Mythology." *Harper's,* September 1970.

Lehmann-Haupt, Christopher. "Not All Peanuts and Cracker Jack, Exactly." *The New York Times,* June 19, 1970.

WEBSITES

Jim Bouton Offical Website. Available online at http://www.jimbouton.com (accessed April 23, 2003).

Baseball Reference.com. Available online at http://www.baseball-reference.com (accessed April 23, 2003).

Bobby Orr

Bobby Orr: My Game
Autobiography

By: Bobby Orr, with Mark Mulvoy
Date: 1974
Source: Orr, Bobby, with Mark Mulvoy. *Bobby Orr: My Game.* Boston: Little, Brown, 1974, 40–44, 56–58.
About the Author: Bobby Orr (1948–) was born in Parry Sound, Ontario, Canada. Discovered at twelve as a hockey phenom, Orr signed a junior amateur contract. The Boston Bruins signed Orr to a professional contract in 1966, and he was named Rookie of the Year at eighteen. Orr won the Norris Trophy as best defenseman eight consecutive seasons, and led the Boston Bruins to Stanley Cup championships in 1970 and 1972. Orr's career was shortened by several knee operations, and he retired after twelve National Hockey League (NHL) seasons. In retirement, Orr has been a commercial spokesman and is a player agent.

"Sportsman of the Year: Bobby Orr"
Magazine article

By: Jack Olsen
Date: December 21, 1970
Source: Olsen, Jack. "Sportsman of the Year: Bobby Orr." *Sports Illustrated,* December 21, 1970, 36, 39, 42.
About the Author: Jack Olsen (1925–2002) was born in Indianapolis, Indiana. Olsen worked as a journalist for various newspapers, and a correspondent for *Time,* before becoming a freelance writer and author in the early 1960's. He wrote over thirty books, some on sports, and many on crime and criminal behavior. ■

Introduction

In the 1960s in ice hockey, two defensemen, who rarely scored, patrolled the blue line between center ice and the goal crease. Defensemen were defenders, keeping the puck out of their own zone, clearing the corners, protecting the goalie, and passing the puck up ice to the forwards. Only on the power play did the defenseman venture into the offensive end of the rink. All this was the case until Bobby Orr entered the NHL.

Bobby Orr began skating at age four, started playing hockey in kindergarten, and by twelve had attracted scouts from the NHL's Boston Bruins, who signed him to a junior amateur contract. In junior hockey, Orr averaged thirty-four goals a season—extraordinary for a defenseman. In 1966, the Bruins believed Orr was ready to jump to the NHL and signed the eighteen-year-old to the largest rookie contract ever. Boston needed someone to change their fortunes, as they had finished last in the league five of the previous six years.

That season Orr scored thirteen goals, had twenty-eight assists, and was named Rookie of the Year. That year he also suffered the first of several knee injuries that ultimately shortened his career. The next season, he played in only forty-six of seventy-four regular season games, but he still won the Norris Trophy for the first of eight consecutive years as the league's best defenseman—and he was named a first team all-star. In 1968–1969, Orr scored twenty-one goals and forty-three assists for sixty-four points, establishing a new record for defensemen. In 1969–1970, Orr's statistics were amazing: thirty-three goals, eighty-seven assists for 120 points—only the third player to score over one hundred points in a season. With that total he became the first defenseman ever to lead the league in scoring. The Bruins also won their first Stanley Cup in nearly forty years, with Orr scoring the winning goal in overtime. The moment was captured in a famous photograph, with Orr seemingly flying in the air after the shot (he was actually tripped in front of the net).

At the still young age of twenty-two, Orr was arguably the NHL's best player. Between 1969 and 1975, he averaged thirty goals and 122 points a season; Orr's 1971 season was statistically his best, as he scored thirty-seven goals and 102 assists. The 102 assists were the most by any player in NHL history. The 1971–1972 season saw him win the Art Ross Trophy as the league's most valuable player for the third consecutive year. That same year, Orr led the Bruins to another Stanley Cup championship.

Significance

By 1974, five knee operations had taken their toll on Bobby Orr. In 1974–1975, Orr somehow played in all eighty regular season games, scoring forty-six goals and eighty-nine assists for 135 points. But Orr would play only thirty-six more NHL games. He signed a five-year, three-million-dollar contract with the Chicago Blackhawks in 1976. Orr played in twenty games for the Blackhawks in 1976–1977, missed the entire 1977–1978 season with his sixth knee operation, and six games to start the 1978–1979 year, before retiring at thirty.

Even with his career cut short, Orr's record was impressive. In his twelve seasons, Orr tallied 270 goals and 645 assists for 915 points in only 657 games. Orr's amazing offensive output for a defenseman never compromised his skill on the blue line. Orr was an excellent penalty killer, who often after getting the puck would skate round and round, refusing to surrender it. As one observer said, Orr "was a one-man penalty killing unit." He also was unafraid to mix it up with other players, as he averaged 101 penalty minutes a season. But it was his rushing up the ice with the puck that struck fear into the hearts of Bruins opponents. As one goalie recalled, all he could do "when I saw Orr coming down on me . . . was to say a little prayer, if I had time."

When Orr retired in 1978, the Hockey Hall of Fame suspended its three year waiting period and inducted him the next year—at thirty-one, the youngest player ever enshrined. A later generation of players have emulated his style, but few hockey players have combined his finesse, skill, toughness, and, with his bad knees, physical courage. As his teammate Phil Esposito said of Orr, he "changed the face of hockey all by himself."

Primary Source

Bobby Orr: My Game [excerpt]

SYNOPSIS: Bobby Orr, Boston Bruins hockey player, gives a perspective on how he prepares for a game, including practicing and assessing the opponent, as well as evaluating the status of his often injured knees.

Let me make one thing perfectly clear right here. Hockey is just a game. It is not a science or something that only a computer can play. No robots, please. Ted Williams claims that hitting a round baseball with a round bat is the single most difficult thing to do in sport. Wilt Chamberlain probably thinks that shooting free throws from the foul line is twice as difficult as hitting a baseball. And I'm certain that George Blanda believes kicking field goals with eleven monsters charging toward you is much tougher than shooting free throws. Then again, I've never read or heard any athlete in any sport say that some other game is physically or mentally tougher than his. That is only natural.

Me? I can't imagine a sport any tougher than hockey. . . .

Hockey simply is a game of instinct and mistakes. When I am on the ice, I look for openings. That's what the game is all about. I see an opening on the ice—maybe one of my teammates has skated into the clear or maybe I know I can beat a particular defenseman because he has turned the wrong way, things like that—and I instantly react to it. Maybe I react to openings quicker than other players, I don't know for sure. When I see something that looks open to me, I go. See you later! Believe me, nothing I do on the ice is the result of any grand master plan. I never stand behind my net with the puck and decide that I'm going to skate down the right wing, cut through center at the red line, stop at the far blue line, and fire a slap shot two inches off the ice and one inch inside the near post. I simply stand behind my net and head wherever my instinct tells me to go. In football you hear a lot of television talk to the effect that "his primary receiver was covered, so he went to his secondary receiver and completed the pass." In hockey there is no one primary receiver on the ice; there are four primary receivers—all the other players on your team. I play defense by instinct, too. I see some player coming toward me, then I react instinctively. He has the puck, so what I do depends on what he does. I would look pretty foolish if I committed myself to, say, taking the puck carrier to the boards when he already had committed himself to going inside of me. I never decide—in fact, I can't decide—upon my course of defensive action until the confrontation is live, staring me in the face. Then I react.

I know that all may sound pretty farfetched, but it's true. Many times after a game I sit in the dressing room and ask myself why I did certain things that night on the ice. As a rule, I cannot even answer my own questions. I remember one night I watched a video-taped replay of the game we had just played, and I really could not believe I had done some of the things that the tape showed I had done in living color. On this one play I tried to crash between two defensemen in an attempt to get in alone on the goaltender. I never made it—I was dumped to the ice—and as I looked at the tape I thought how dumb I must have been even to try such a stupid play. Then the more I thought about it, the more I realized it wasn't such a stupid play after all. The cameras filming the game provided only a side view of the action, while down on the ice all the action was squarely ahead of me. In other words, what I saw on the ice, the cameras did not see from the press box, and what the cameras saw, I didn't see. As I remembered the play, one of the defenseman had made a move that indicated he planned to play me to go wide on him. Seeing this, I reacted by going to the inside where the *opening* should have been. He faked me out, though, and when he came back inside himself, I was in trouble. Win some, lose some.

At times it's impossible for me to explain what I do on the ice, and why I do it. I remember another game when I suddenly did something I had never done before. I had the puck in the other team's end of the ice, and there were two players checking me pretty closely. The next thing I knew, there I was all alone in front of the goaltender. I honestly did not know what I had done to get there; in fact, I was so surprised to find myself in that unguarded position that I missed the net completely with my shot. After

the game I watched the video tape and discovered that I had sneaked past the defensemen by making a sudden counter-clockwise circle on the ice. Well, the next day I was back on the ice at the Boston Garden to take some pictures for a promotional booklet, and the photographer asked me to "do that thing you did last night when you spun around like a top." I spent the next twenty minutes trying to re-create that move, but I just couldn't do it. So how did I do it during the game? Instinct. Reflexes. I never planned to do that move, and I certainly never consciously tried to do it. It just happened, that's all I can say.

I trust my instinct. When it tells me to take a chance and make a certain play, I never worry too much about the possible repercussions if the play does not work for some reason. I may be a defenseman, but I never take a defensive attitude into a game. As I learned when I was back in Parry Sound, hockey is one sport that tolerates mistakes. Hockey, remember, has that great equalizer—the goaltender—waiting back there to cover up a great majority of the mistakes that the forwards and defensemen make during a game. And, of course, sometimes the *mistakes* you make really aren't mistakes after all. . . .

My Knees

Despite what you may have read, I do not live with an ice pack wrapped around my left knee. For one thing, I won't stand still long enough to let someone wrap such a thing around my knee. For another, I simply refuse to play hockey with any type of ice pack, harness brace, or anything else on my knee. Phil Esposito wears a brace on his knee, and he claims it does not bother him during the games. Maybe I should wear a brace, too, but I like to feel nice and loose on the ice—and I know that a brace would restrict my movements.

To set the record straight, here's a summary of my knee troubles. I hurt my right knee first. In the summer of 1967 I went to Winnipeg to play a charity exhibition game. Late in the game Bobby Leiter, one of my teammates on the Bruins at the time, and I broke down the ice on a two-on-one. I had the puck, and when I dropped it over to Bobby, the lone defenseman checked me into the goal post. Before I could recover from that check, Leiter accidentally crashed into me—and I stretched the ligaments in my right knee. The doctors immediately covered my right leg with a cast, and later they determined that I would not need an operation. Still, I missed a lot of games early in the 1967–68 season while recovering from

Bobby Orr takes a shot in a game at the Boston Garden, November, 1973. In Orr's ten seasons with the Bruins he set many records for defensemen and helped Boston win two Stanley Cups. © BETTMANN/CORBIS. REPRODUCED BY PERMISSION.

the injury. Since then, I have not had any troubles with my right knee.

I wish I could say the same thing for my left knee. I have already had three operations on that one, and I don't want a fourth operation under any conditions. My troubles all started one night during the 1967–68 season when Marcel Pronovost, a very good defenseman then playing for the Toronto Maple Leafs, caught me with a solid check as I tried to sneak past him along the boards in the Boston Garden. Ligaments. Operation Number 1. Then, late the following season, I damaged the ligaments again when my skate got caught in a rut in the ice at the Forum in Los Angeles. I played the rest of the schedule and through the play-offs, but I went under the knife during the summer. Operation Number 2. Except for the usual soreness and stiffness, I had no trouble with the left knee for the next three years. But in March of 1972, a few days before the start of the play-offs, I got hit hard—and clean—in a game against the Red Wings in Detroit—and the ligaments came undone again. The knee was terribly sore throughout the play-offs and kept swelling up. One game I had to leave our bench halfway through a period for a quick ice-pack treatment. In June of 1972

Dr. Carter Rowe of Boston cut the knee open and tightened up the ligaments. At the same time he cleaned up the insides of the knee and smoothed out the rough surfaces around the cartilage area. Operation Number 3. Some people think that bone rubs against bone in that left knee, but they're all wrong. Dr. Rowe told me there is some lubrication in there that makes the joints slide smoothly. I know that if I had not let Dr. Rowe open the knee that third time I would not be playing today. I played for a long time when the knee was sore, and it was close to unbearable. I could not play the game the way I wanted—the way I always had. In fact, I could hardly play at all. I had to have that operation. It was my only hope.

I never worried too much after my first two knee operations, but I was pretty scared after that third operation in 1972. Hockey is my life, you know, and you can't survive for long with a bad knee. When Dr. Rowe cut my knee that June, I was certain it would be strong enough for me to play at least some of the games in the Canada-Russia hockey series in September. However, when I joined Team Canada at its practice camp in Toronto it was obvious that my knee was not ready. I'd skate during practice, then afterward the knee would swell up. A couple of times some doctors in Toronto had to drain fluid from the knee. I was worried, so I called Dr. Rowe in Boston. He said not to worry, that it would get better in time. . . . I rejoined the Bruins for a game against the New York Islanders and happened to score a goal on my first shift on the ice. I didn't miss another game the rest of that season.

Have my knees slowed me down? Yes. I definitely don't think I skate now like I used to skate, but, believe me, I'm very happy to be skating at all. People always ask me why I continue to take chances on the ice, considering the condition of my knees. I don't know why, to tell the truth. It's the way I have always played the game, the only way I know how to play the game. When I have the puck and I'm moving up the ice, I don't think about my injuries. The only thing in my mind is the goalie at the other end of the ice. You can't be gun-shy and still survive in hockey.

Primary Source

"Sportsman of the Year: Bobby Orr" [excerpt]

SYNOPSIS: Jack Olsen, in *Sports Illustrated,* writes a profile of Boston Bruins hockey great Bobby Orr as the magazine's "Sportsman of the Year" for all-around athletic achievement.

Only 22, he set entire new standards of hockey excellence. While leading his team to a championship and emerging as an alltime star, he ushered a growing sport into the '70s with a flash of flying ice.

When Robert Gordon Orr comes walking out of the Boston Bruins' dressing room in his halfway mod attire and head-down shy manner, you would be excused for thinking that he is the water boy or perhaps an assistant bookkeeper learning the trade of attendance-padding. He is a mere 5′ 11′, 185 pounds, with blue-gray eyes and a thick shock of hair that is browner than blond and blonder than brown and flops down over his forehead, producing a little-boy-lost effect that is deadly to the female. His legs are muscular, but not much more than Carol Channing's. His arms are of normal length and look strong, but not strikingly so. His hands remind one of an e. e. cummings line: "nobody, not even the rain, has such small hands." His shoulders are squared, but not with the slablike precision of Bobby Hull's. His overall physique is adequate but not impressive; he will never gain employment as a male model or appear covered with salad oil in today's

Bruins defenseman Bobby Orr poses with the Hart and Norris Trophies, Boston, May 8, 1970. Orr was named the NHL's top defenseman and most valuable player after already winning the Art Ross Trophy as the league's top scorer; he was the first defenseman ever to win the scoring crown. © BETTMANN/CORBIS. REPRODUCED BY PERMISSION.

versions of *Sunshine and Health.*

At 22, Orr . . . is beginning to show the indelible facial evidences of his occupation: the thick tissue over the eye sockets, the spidery scars from interrupted pucks and sticks, the drooping lip and asymmetric nose from medical insult and injury. After five years in the bullpits of the National Hockey League, Orr does not yet resemble Marlon Brando in *On the Waterfront* ("Cholly, Cholly, I cudda been a contenduh!"), but he is en route. His nose has been fractured three or four times and he has taken 50 or so stitches, mostly in the face. His strong, sturdy jaw remains intact, but from the way he plays hockey one can easily foresee the day when he will be wired up and sipping tomato juice through a straw. Then the devastation will be complete, as it has been complete with almost all the great defensemen of the National Hockey League.

"Look at him," says Orr's crony and roommate, Assistant Trainer John (Frosty) Forristall. "He's the key to everything—to the Boston Bruins, to the National Hockey League, to the whole game of hockey. And he skates like he's afraid he'll be sent back to the minors. He takes chances like a rookie." . . .

To students of Bobby Orr, the spectacular has become routine, and the routine has become unacceptable. One of a defenseman's primary jobs is to get the puck out of his own end and down the ice, and some players carry out this task with all the grace and ease of a starving man eating a pomegranate through a screen door. Orr does it routinely. "As soon as Bobby gets the puck on his stick," says Tom Johnson, "you *know* it's coming out. People take it for granted. They forget that this isn't automatic. At least it never used to be.

When the Bruins are on offense Orr takes up the traditional defenseman's stance, guarding the point, but it by no means is certain that he will remain there. "If he has the puck at the point and somebody takes a run at him," says a teammate, "that's the end. He'll give them that one-two-circle dance of his, that ballerina twirl, and he's moving in on the net at top speed. No other defenseman would dare do this, because meanwhile he's leaving the whole wing wide open. But I've never seen him get caught." . . .

"Bobby Orr is a whole 'nother ball game, a whole new breed of superstar," says a National Hockey League official. "He brings a new image to the game. He's modest, he's restrained, he's understated. He's the exact opposite of a Joe Namath. Namath reached millionaire status as a kind of mixed-up anti-hero, but Orr will reach it as a hero in the classic sense. The ones who cultivate the image of the big bad athlete, boozing or chasing broads or blowing their cool, they're the vanishing breed: the Namaths, the Denny McLains. The Bobby Orrs are the incoming breed, and we better be thankful they are around."

"It's very nice of people to say that I have a special role," says Bobby Orr, "but all I can do about it is go out there and play the very best I can. I can't let it bug me. We have 18 guys and they all play to win. The Bruins, they're team guys."

Further Resources

BOOKS

Fischler, Stan. *Bobby Orr and the Big Bad Bruins.* New York: Dodd, Mead, 1969.

McInnis, Craig, ed. *Remembering Bobby Orr: A Celebration.* Buffalo, N.Y.: General Distribution Systems, 1999.

WEBSITES

BostonBruins.com. Available online at http://www.bostonbruins.com (accessed April 23, 2003).

"Bobby Orr." Hockey Hall of Fame. Available online at http://www.legendsofhockey.net:8080/LegendsOfHockey/jsp/LegendsMember.jsp?type=Player=P197902&list=By Name#photo; website home page: http://www.hhof.com (accessed April 23, 2003).

"Ego"

Magazine article

By: Norman Mailer

Date: March 19, 1971

Source: Mailer, Norman. "Ego." *Life* 70, March 19, 1971, 30, 32–36.

About the Author: Norman Mailer (1923–) was born in Long Branch, New Jersey. After graduating from Harvard and military service in World War II (1939–1945), Mailer began writing, publishing his first book, *The Naked and the Dead*, a best selling novel in 1948. Mailer has written over thirty books, including novels, plays, political commentary, and essay collections, as well as numerous magazine articles. He won the Pulitzer Prize in 1969 and 1979. ■

Introduction

Muhammad Ali's conviction for draft evasion in 1967, and the subsequent stripping of his heavyweight championship title, created an opening for several challengers. Emerging from the group of fighters was Joe Frazier. Frazier was born in South Carolina and moved to Philadelphia, where he took up boxing. After winning the heavyweight boxing gold medal at the 1964 Tokyo Olympics, Frazier turned professional the next year—capturing the vacant New York heavyweight championship with an eleventh round knockout of Buster Mathis in 1968, followed by the world crown in 1970.

In late 1970, while Ali's appeal was being decided by the U.S. Supreme Court and after his boxing license was restored, he and Frazier signed for $2.5 million each to fight for the heavyweight crown at Madison Square Garden in New York on March 8, 1971. In the months leading up to the fight, publicity reached a feverish pitch, and soon the bout was billed as the "fight of the century." The fighters verbally attacked each other. Ali described himself as "pretty," calling Frazier "ugly," a "gorilla," and the "white man's fighter." A divided country itself lined up behind each fighter, as those against the Vietnam War (1964–1975) were for Ali, while "Middle America" backed Frazier.

On March 8, 1971, a crowd of 20,455, including Frank Sinatra and other celebrities, gathered at Madison Square Garden. In the opening rounds, Ali, talking and taunting Frazier, took blows from "Smokin' Joe's" patented left hook and seemed unaffected. Soon, however, the years away from the ring and the pounds added to his physique began to show on Ali as Frazier dominated the middle rounds, bloodying the ex-champ's nose in the fifth round. Ali's sixth round victory prediction came and went as Frazier continued his relentless punching.

By the ninth and tenth rounds, inspired by pro-Ali chants from the crowd, the former champion seemed to gain a second wind. But Ali slipped to the canvas and Frazier landed a left hook sending him into the ropes during round eleven. From rounds twelve through fourteen, Frazier continued jabbing, although both fighters moved around each other cautiously. Finally, in the fifteenth and final round, Frazier came out strong and uncorked a left hook, which dropped Ali to the canvas—only the third time in his career he had been knocked down. When the bell rang, ending the fight, both boxers retreated to their corners, utterly exhausted. Then the decision was rendered: a unanimous victory for Frazier. Referee Arthur Mercante and two ring judges scored the fight for the reigning heavyweight champion. After boasting so much before the fight and taunting Frazier during, Ali was quiet afterward, as his swollen jaw sent him to the hospital.

Significance

Frazier's victory over Ali was seen as disappointing to many African Americans, while large numbers of whites, upset over Ali's draft stance, were delighted by the decision. Frazier defended his title twice before losing to George Foreman in January 1973. Ali wanted a rematch with Frazier, and in January 1974, he got revenge with a twelve round decision. Nine months later, Ali won back the heavyweight crown when he knocked out Foreman in Kinshasa, Zaire.

After three title defenses, Ali met Frazier for the third time, the rubber match of their epic series. Billed as the "Thrilla' In Manila," Ali again took the verbal offense, at one point holding up a toy gorilla to represent Frazier. In a fight described by observers as the most brutal they had ever seen, the two fighters, their dislike, even hatred of one another, showed in the relentless pounding that both gave and each took. The battle lasted for fourteen rounds, until Ali emerged with a technical knockout of Frazier.

Frazier retired from boxing after a knockout loss to Foreman in mid-1976, with a career record of thirty-two wins (sixteen by knockout) and four defeats (two each to Ali and Foreman). Ali lost his title in February, 1978, to Leon Spinks, then regained it for the third time seven months later. Ali retired in 1979, but attempted comebacks in 1980 and 1981, resulting in humiliating defeats. The effects of years in the ring became apparent thereafter, as Ali developed a form of Parkinson's disease. For years, Ali has resided on a Michigan farm and makes many public appearances, undaunted by his physical af-

fliction. Frazier has been involved in various activities, including an unsuccessful career as a nightclub singer. Frazier saw his son, Marvis, become a heavyweight fighter of note in the 1980s, while still harboring lingering resentment at Ali for all the name-calling.

Primary Source

"Ego" [excerpt]

SYNOPSIS: Award-winning novelist and essayist Norman Mailer covered the first Ali-Frazier fight for *Life* magazine, and this article is his first-hand account of the bout, called by many the "fight of the century."

What kills us about a.k.a. Cassius Clay is that the disagreement is inside us. He is *fascinating*—attraction and repulsion must be in the same package. So, he is obsessive. The more we don't want to think about him, the more we are obliged to. There is a reason for it. He is America's Greatest Ego. He is also, as I am going to try to show, the swiftest embodiment of human intelligence we have had yet, he is the very spirit of the 20th Century, he is the prince of mass man and the media. . . .

The referee gave his instructions. The bell rang. The first 15 seconds of a fight can be the fight. It is equivalent to the first kiss in a love affair. The fighters each missed the other. Ali blocked Frazier's first punches easily, but Ali then missed Frazier's head. That head was bobbing as fast as a third fist. Frazier would come rushing in, head moving like a fist, fists bobbing too, his head working above and below his forearm, he was trying to get through Ali's jab, get through fast and sear Ali early with the terror of a long fight and punches harder than he had ever taken to the stomach, and Ali in turn, backing up, and throwing fast punches, aimed just a trifle, and was therefore a trifle too slow, but it was obvious Ali was trying to shiver Frazier's synapses from the start, set waves of depression stirring which would reach his heart in later rounds and make him slow, deaden nerve, deaden nerve went Ali's jab flicking a snake tongue, whooeet! whoo-eet! but Frazier's head was bobbing too fast, he was moving faster than he had ever moved before in that bobbing nonstop never-a-backward step of his, slogging and bouncing forward, that huge left hook flaunting the air with the confidence it was enough of a club to split a tree, and Ali, having missed his jabs, stepped nimbly inside the hook and wrestled Frazier in the clinch. Ali looked stronger here. So by the first 45 seconds of the fight, they had each surprised the

Joe Frazier connects with a left hook on Muhammad Ali during the fifteenth round, Madison Square Garden, New York, March 8, 1971. Frazier won the fifteen-round heavyweight title fight in a unanimous decision. **AP/WIDE WORLD PHOTOS. REPRODUCED BY PERMISSION.**

other profoundly. Frazier was fast enough to slip through Ali's punches, and Ali was strong enough to handle him in the clinches. A pattern had begun. Because Ali was missing often, Frazier was in under his shots like a police dog's muzzle on your arm, Ali could not slide from side to side, he was boxed in, then obliged to go backward, and would end on the ropes again and again with Frazier belaboring him. Yet Frazier could not reach him. . . .

The first round set a pattern for the fight. Ali won it and would win the next. His jab was landing from time to time and rights and lefts of no great consequence. Frazier was hardly reaching him at all. Yet it looked like Frazier had established that he was fast enough to get in on Ali and so drive him to the ropes and to the corners, and that spoke of a fight which would be determined by the man in better condition, in better physical condition rather than in better psychic condition, the kind of fight Ali could hardly want for his strength was in his pauses, his nature passed along the curve of every dialec-

tic, he liked, in short, to fight in flurries, and then move out, move away, assess, take his time, fight again. Frazier would not let him. Frazier moved in with the snarl of a wolf, his teeth seemed to show through his mouthpiece, he made Ali work. Ali won the first two rounds but it was obvious he could not continue to win if he had to work all the way. And in the third round Frazier began to get to him, caught Ali with a powerful blow to the face at the bell. That was the first moment where it was clear to all that Frazier had won a round. Then he won the next. Ali looked tired and a little depressed. He was moving less and less and calling upon a skill not seen since the fight with Chuvalo when he had showed his old ability, worked on all those years ago with Shotgun Sheldon, to lie on the ropes and take a beating to the stomach. He had exhausted Chuvalo by welcoming attacks on the stomach but Frazier was too incommensurable a force to allow such total attack. So Ali lay on the ropes and wrestled him off, and moved his arms and waist, blocking punches, slipping punches, countering with punches—it began to look as if the fight would be written on the ropes, but Ali was getting very tired. At the beginning of the fifth round, he got up slowly from his stool, very slowly. Frazier was beginning to feel that the fight was his. He moved in on Ali jeering, his hands at his side in mimicry of Ali, a street fighter mocking his opponent, and Ali tapped him with long light jabs to which Frazier stuck out his mouthpiece, a jeer of derision as if to suggest that the mouthpiece was all Ali would reach all night.

■ ■ ■

As the fight moved through the fifth, the sixth and the seventh, then into the eighth, it was obvious that Ali was into the longest night of his career, and yet with that skill, that research into the pits of every miserable contingency in boxing, he came up with odd somnambulistic variations, holding Frazier off, riding around Frazier with his arm about his neck, almost entreating Frazier with his arms extended, and Frazier leaning on him, each of them slowed to a pit-a-pat of light punches back and forth until one of them was goaded up from exhaustion to whip and stick, then hook and hammer and into the belly and out, and out of the clinch and both looking exhausted, and then Frazier, mouth bared again like a wolf, going in and Ali waltzing him, tying him, tapping him lightly as if he were a speed bag, just little flicks, until Frazier, like an exhausted horse finally feeling the crop, would push up into a trot and try to run up the hill. It was indeed as if they were both running up a hill. As if Frazier's offensive was so great and so great was Ali's defense that the fight could only be decided by who could take the steepest pitch of the hill. So Frazier, driving, driving, trying to drive the heart out of Ali, put the pitch of that hill up and up until they were ascending an unendurable slope. And moved like somnambulists slowly working and rubbing one another, almost embracing, next to locked in the slow moves of lovers after the act until, reaching into the stores of energy reaching them from cells never before so used, one man or the other would work up a contractive spasm of skills and throw punches at the other in the straining slow-motion hypnosis of a deepening act. And so the first eight rounds went by. The two judges scored six for Frazier, two for Ali. The referee had it even. Some of the Press had Ali ahead—it was not easy to score. For if it were an alley fight, Frazier would win. Clay was by now hardly more than the heavy bag to Frazier. Frazier was dealing with a man, not a demon. He was not respectful of that man. But still! It was

Ali who was landing the majority of punches. They were light, they were usually weary, but some had snap, some were quick, he was landing two punches to Frazier's one. Yet Frazier's were hardest. And Ali often looked as tender as if he were making love. It was as if he could now feel the whole absence of that real second fight with Liston, that fight for which he had trained so long and so hard, the fight which might have rolled over his laurels from the greatest artist of pugilism to the greatest brawler of them all—maybe he had been prepared on that night to beat Liston at his own, be more of a slugger, more of a man crude to crude than Liston. Yes, Ali had never been a street fighter and never a whorehouse knock-it-down stud, no, it was more as if a man with the exquisite reflexes of Nureyev had learned to throw a knockout punch with either hand and so had become champion of the world without knowing if he was the man of all men or the most delicate of the delicate with special privilege endowed by God. Now with Frazier, he was in a sweat bath (a mud-pile, a knee, elbow, and death-thumping chute of a pit) having in this late year the fight he had sorely needed for his true greatness as a fighter six and seven years ago, and so whether ahead, behind or even, terror sat in the rooting instinct of all those who were for Ali for it was obviously Frazier's fight to win, and what if Ali, weaknesses of character now flickering to the surface in a hundred little moves, should enter the vale of prizefighting's deepest humiliation, should fall out half conscious on the floor and not want to get up. What a death to his followers.

The ninth began. Frazier mounted his largest body attack of the night. It was preparations-for-Liston-with-Shotgun-Sheldon, it was the virtuosity of the gym all over again, and Ali, like a catcher handling a fast-ball pitcher, took Frazier's punches, one steamer, another steamer, wing! went a screamer, a steamer, warded them, blocked them, slithered them, winced from them, absorbed them, took them in and blew them out and came off the ropes and was Ali the Magnificent for the next minute and thirty seconds. The fight turned. The troops of Ali's second corps of energy had arrived, the energy for which he had been waiting long agonizing heart-sore vomit-mean rounds. Now he jabbed Frazier, he snake-licked his face with jabs faster than he had thrown before, he anticipated each attempt of Frazier at counterattack and threw it back, he danced on his toes for the first time in rounds, he popped in rights, he hurt him with hooks, it was his biggest round of the night, it was the best round yet of the fight, and

Frazier full of energy and hordes of sudden punishment was beginning to move into that odd petulant concentration on other rituals besides the punches, tappings of the gloves, stares of the eye, that species of mouthpiece-chewing which is the prelude to fun-strut in the knees, then Queer Street, then waggle on out, drop like a steer.

It looked like Ali had turned the fight, looked more like the same in the 10th, now reporters were writing another story in their mind where Ali was not the magical untried Prince who had come apart under the first real pressure of his life but was rather the greatest Heavyweight Champion of all time for he had weathered the purgatory of Joe Frazier.

But in the 11th, that story also broke. Frazier caught him, caught him again and again, and Ali was near to knocked out and swayed and slid on Queer Street himself, then spent the rest of the 11th and the longest round of the 12th working another bottom of Hell, holding off Frazier who came on and on, sobbing, wild, a wild honor of a beast, man of will reduced to the common denominator of the will of all of us back in that land of the animal where the idea of man as a tool-wielding beast was first conceived. Frazier looked to get Ali forever in the 11th and the 12th, and Ali, his legs slapped and slashed on the thighs between each round by Angelo Dundee, came out for the 13th and incredibly was dancing. Everybody's story switched again. For if Ali won this round, the 14th and the 15th, who could know if he could not win the fight? . . . He won the first half of the 13th, then spent the second half on the ropes with Frazier. They were now like crazy death-march-maddened mateys coming up the hill and on to home, and yet Ali won the 14th, Ali looked good, he came out dancing for the 15th, while Frazier, his own armies of energy finally caught up, his courage ready to spit into the eye of any devil black or white who would steal the work of his life, had equal madness to steal the bolt from Ali. So Frazier reached out to snatch the magic punch from the air, the punch with which Ali topped Bonavena, and found it and thunked Ali a hell and hit Ali a heaven of a shot which dumped Muhammad into 50,000 newspaper photographs—Ali on the floor! Great Ali on the floor was out there flat singing to the sirens in the mistiest fogs of Queer Street (same look of death and widowhood on his far-gone face as one had seen in the fifth blind round with Liston) yet Ali got up, Ali came sliding through the last two minutes and thirty-five seconds of this heathen holocaust in some last exercise of the will, some iron fundament of the ego

not to be knocked out, and it was then as if the spirit of Harlem finally spoke and came to rescue and the ghosts of the dead in Vietnam, something held him up before arm-weary triumphant near-crazy Frazier who had just hit him the hardest punch ever thrown in his life and they went down to the last few seconds of a great fight, Ali still standing and Frazier had won.

Further Resources

BOOKS

Ali, Muhammad. *The Greatest: My Own Story.* New York: Random House, 1975.

Frazier, Joe. *Smokin' Joe.* New York: Macmillan, 1996.

Hauser, Thomas. *Muhammad Ali: His Life and Times.* New York: Simon and Schuster, 1991.

PERIODICALS

Anderson, Dave. "Frazier Outpoints Ali and Keeps Title." *The New York Times,* March 9, 1971.

Daley, Arthur. "Epic Worth the Price." *The New York Times,* March 9, 1971.

WEBSITES

"Joe Frazier." International Boxing Hall of Fame. Available online at http://www.ibhof.com/frazier.htm; website home page: http://www.ibhof.com (accessed April 23, 2003).

"Muhammad Ali." International Boxing Hall of Fame. Available online at http://www.ibhof.com/ali.htm; website home page: http://www.ibhof.com (accessed April 23, 2003).

Munich Olympics

My Wide World
Autobiography

By: Jim McKay

Date: 1973

Source: McKay, Jim. *My Wide World.* New York: Macmillan, 1973, 200–203, 208, 211–214, 216–219, 221, 224–227.

About the Author: Jim McKay (1921–) was born James McManus in Philadelphia, Pennsylvania. After college and military service in World War II (1939–1945), McManus joined the *Baltimore Evening Sun* as a reporter, and a year later for the newspaper's TV station. Beginning in 1950 and over the next decade, McManus, given the professional name McKay, worked as a sportscaster and television show host for CBS. In 1961, ABC hired McKay to host the new *Wide World of Sports* program. Over the next three decades, McKay broadcast nearly every important ABC sporting event, including five Olympics. In retirement, McKay resides on a horse farm in Maryland.

"The Show Goes On"

Newspaper article

By: Red Smith

Date: September 6, 1972

Source: Smith, Red. "The Show Goes On." *The New York Times,* September 6, 1972.

About the Author: Red Smith (1905–1982) was born in Green Bay, Wisconsin. After graduating from Notre Dame in 1927, Smith was a reporter for the *Milwaukee Sentinel,* and copy editor and sportswriter for the *St. Louis Star-Times.* In 1936, Smith moved to the *Philadelphia Record,* then the *New York Herald-Tribune* nine years later, becoming one of America's most respected sportswriters. After the *Herald-Tribune* folded in 1967, Smith wrote in syndication until joining *The New York Times* in 1971, remaining there until his death. Smith authored several collections of his columns, and won numerous honors, including the Pulitzer Prize in 1976. ∎

Introduction

When the Olympic Games were celebrated in ancient Greece, all hostilities came to a halt to celebrate athletic achievement. The 1972 Games in Munich, West Germany, were supposed to be no different. The West German government was determined to avoid any repeat of the 1936 Olympics, used by Hitler to advance his Nazi ideology. The police dressed in colorful athletic uniforms without weapons. Arriving in Munich, the Israeli team was small in number, primarily weightlifters and wrestlers, with little chance of winning any medals. As a remembrance of the Holocaust, the delegation visited the Dachau concentration camp site outside the city. For the West Germans, everything was working splendidly.

Early in the morning of September 5, 1972, Arab commandos, dressed as athletes, climbed a fence around the Olympic Village, picked up a cache of weapons, and proceeded to 31 Connollystrasse, Israeli team quarters. Encountering a coach, Moshe Weinberg, the terrorists shot him as he tried to prevent them from breaking a door down. The gunmen entered a group of rooms, shot another man and took nine Israeli athletes and coaches as hostages; one team member was David Berger, an Ohio native. The terrorists demanded the release of over two hundred Palestinians held in Israeli jails. The hours passed, through several deadlines, but no more killing occurred (two already were dead). Negotiations were underway between the terrorists and the West German government. The irony was clear to everyone; Jews had again been murdered on German soil.

On television, ABC's sports production team, headed by Roone Arledge, praised for its coverage of the Olympics, quickly shifted their resources to news coverage after the hostage crisis began—providing dramatic camera shots of the negotiations going on outside the Israeli team quarters with the terrorist in a white fedora.

Sportscaster Jim McKay, slated for a day off during the Games, was pressed into anchoring duties throughout the day, keeping Americans and others around the world informed about developments in the Olympic Village. ABC's coverage of the dramatic events of the day would earn Arledge and McKay Emmy Awards.

As evening came, the Arabs demanded buses to take the hostages to helicopters. They would fly to a nearby air base, where a passenger jet waited to take the terrorists and their hostages to a Middle East location. Finally, seventeen hours after the Israeli team headquarters were invaded, the nine hostages and their captors boarded buses under the Village for a short trip. The two helicopters took off for Furstenfeldbruck Air Base, about fifteen miles away. After arriving at the air base, West German sharpshooters at the airport began a gun battle with the terrorists. At one point, a grenade was tossed into one helicopter, killing those hostages. Another terrorist sprayed the other chopper with machine gun fire, killing the remaining Israelis. In the end, four Arabs and a policeman were also killed in the ill-conceived rescue attempt.

Meanwhile, word that the hostages were alive and had been rescued mistakenly reached Munich and was transmitted around the world, first reported by McKay on ABC. Soon, however, optimism turned to uncertainty, as reports of the hostage rescue appeared premature. At last, word came that nobody wanted to hear. Jim McKay, in one of television history's most unforgettable moments—voice calm, belying emotion—informed viewers that the nine Israeli athletes were dead. "They're all gone," he said.

Significance

The hostage drama stopped Olympic competition during the afternoon of September 5, but a surreal atmosphere prevailed in the Village: some practicing for their events, others taking in the sun. Meanwhile, just yards away in Building 31, one athlete killed, another lay dead, while their comrades were bound hand and foot, held by machine gun–toting terrorists. Before word came of the deaths of the remaining nine athletes, International Olympic Committee president Avery Brundage announced that a memorial service would be held at the Olympic Stadium the next morning. Bewildered athletes attended the service, where they heard Brundage emphatically declare, "The Games must go on," a decision that provoked much controversy.

The Israeli government retaliated by bombing selected Palestinian targets, and over the next few years, hunting down and killing all but one of the surviving terrorists involved in the Olympic operation. Security at the Olympics would never be the same as an increased presence was always in force. Even then, there was no guarantee of safety, as a woman died in a terrorist bombing in 1996 at Atlanta. For many, the tragic events of September 5, 1972, were a prelude to later and deadlier terrorist acts, culminating in the September 11, 2001 attacks on the United States.

Primary Source

My Wide World [excerpt]

SYNOPSIS: Jim McKay, ABC television sportscaster, recalls the events of September 5, 1972, at the Olympic Games in Munich, when he anchored the all-day coverage of the hostage drama of the Israeli athletes ultimately murdered by their captors.

Eleven Are Dead—Tragedy at the Games

Munich—Wednesday, September 6 (5:00 A.M.)

Henry Meyer called early in the morning, somewhere around eight o'clock. I had asked him to pick us up around noon, so the call confused both Margaret and me, half asleep, vaguely annoyed at the interruption of our one sleep-in morning of the games.

"What is it, Henry?" Margaret said. "I'm sorry, but I don't quite understand. Here, perhaps you'd better speak to Jim."

"Jim," he said. "It's Henry. Something fantastic has happened. The Arabs have invaded the Israeli team quarters in the village. They're holding the Israeli Olympic team as hostages and there's a report that they have already killed one man. They asked me to call you and ask you to stand by, because they are going to need you today."

I walked to the window and opened the draperies. It was another beautiful, just slightly hazy day. Straight ahead in the distance was the familiar sight of the Olympic Stadium on the left, huddled under the outspread umbrella of the roof, and the Olympic Village on the right, white, angular buildings reflecting the early morning sun. . . .

The only people outdoors there were a half-dozen little girls in summer dresses riding their bikes through the grass. Automobile traffic was normally heavy for the beginning of the Munich morning rush hour. In short, there was nothing at all out of the ordinary.

Then a car moved into the circle, the word "Polizei" on its side, its two-note siren (BAA-baa, BAA-baa) blaring urgently. The car threaded its way skillfully through the traffic and accelerated out the Mittlerer Ring, across John F. Kennedy Bridge, toward the Olympic grounds.

There were a few seconds more of normal traffic sounds, then another police car appeared. This one, blocked by a large trailer truck, bumped off the road onto the grass of the traffic circle, then wheeled back onto the roadway. There was no question there. This policeman was in a hurry, and he, too, was headed toward the Olympic Village.

Margaret was standing beside me.

"I guess it must be true," she said. "Imagine. It's an irony of history. Those are Germans going to the rescue of Jews."

It was the first of many ironies that struck us during the course of that day. . . .

As the questions came to my mind, the relaxation was tempered by anxiety. After the ice-cold shower, I pulled on a pair of yellow cotton bathing trunks and went out to the pool. My thought was to take a couple of laps, which is all I can manage, then wait for the call from Roone.

Instead, I reached for the telephone in back of the bar at the side of the pool and called associate producer Geoff Mason out at the ABC headquarters. It wasn't conscious reversal of plan, just the kind of thing you do when you see a phone and have a question in the front of your mind that needs answering.

As with Henry Meyer's original call, I think I remember Geoff's words almost exactly. It is part of that permanent photo-engraving process that the mind possesses, whereby certain moments of your life are retained, like how you heard about Pearl Harbor, or President Kennedy's death.

"Jesus, I'm glad you called," he said. "I've just started trying to reach you. The thing is terrible. One man is dead, they think they've killed another, and now they are threatening to kill one athlete every hour until their demands are met. We're going on the air live to the States at one o'clock (just one hour away) and Roone wants you to anchor the show. . . .

First reports said that the Arabs wanted several hundred political prisoners freed by Israel or they would execute one team member every hour. Then the reports said that there was a noon deadline for execution of all the hostages. Noon passed and a new deadline was fixed—1700 Munich time, five o'clock in the afternoon, or noon New York time. . . .

In the moment before we went on the air, we were not aware, of course, that we would finally leave the studio almost fifteen hours later, after one of the most emotionally draining days of our lives.

Our basic coverage team was in place. In the control room, Roone Arledge would run the show, give the orders, feed me information and suggestions, and occasionally, just try to encourage me. Chuck Howard stood behind Roone. Behind him, at the table on the higher level, were Geoff Mason and Marvin Bader, both on walkie-talkies to our people around the Olympic grounds and the village. . . .

It would be impossible and tedious to detail everything we did and said after Roone cued me to talk on our first live transmission, but certain sights and thoughts do float to the surface of my mind.

I am sure I will never forget the heads of the terrorists, popping out of windows and doors regularly like some sort of dreadful puppet show, turning from side to side, alertly spotting their adversaries; the man in the mask, the man in the white hat. . . .

The border guards, in uniform, with submachine guns in their hands, were unloading from the trucks. The incongruity that linked sport with terror, though, was the sight of other border guards, holding guns but dressed in athletic sweat suits of red and blue, disguises for a planned assault on the terrorists. Uniform of the day—sweat suits and submachine guns.

I remember going to the offices of Israeli television after our first transmission, looking for their producer-reporter, who had been inside the village and was now semi-official spokesman for the team. It was not a pleasant walk to the office. I expected to find women weeping and men cursing.

What I found was different. The Israelis seemed less *surprised* by the tragedy than anyone else I had seen. As they moved quietly and competently about the offices, there was great sadness and bitterness in their eyes, but I also sensed a determination and a preparedness; not resignation, but an acceptance of reality. . . .

Aside from a camera on top of the television tower, which had been commandeered and was being directed by the Munich police, our lone live camera, on a sidewalk just outside the village fence, peering some seventy-five yards away at the Israeli apartments and the terrorist lookouts, was the world's window on the incredible afternoon. . . .

What had been important and exciting yesterday, seemed almost blasphemy today. Why were the games still going on? The question was being asked all over Munich, and in time it was announced that they would stop, temporarily, but not until this afternoon's competitions were completed. We wondered if Avery Brundage and the other IOC members could have listened to Tuvia Sokolsky and still permitted "Olympics as usual."

Another announcement came. There would be a memorial service in the Olympic Stadium at 10:00 tomorrow morning for the slain Moshe Weinberg and the other man presumed dead inside the suite of rooms.

The hours from four to six in the afternoon grew increasingly tense. The deadline was five o'clock, the terrorists had said, and shortly after four, it appeared that an assault would be made, an attempt to free the prisoners by force. . . .

The news came that the helicopters had gone to an air base at Fürstenfeldbruck.

Then, a report that we could scarcely believe moved on the wire service ticker. It said that all of the terrorists had been killed at the airport, and all of the hostages had been saved. . . .

Chris and I summed up the events of the long day, including the sports events which had taken place before the Olympics were halted. There was no word as to whether, or when, the games would be resumed.

On a commercial break, I went into the control room and found out that a press conference was scheduled soon at the press center. We had no camera there, but Marvin Bader had gone over with a walkie-talkie. If there was any word before we had to leave the air, Roone told me, he would give it to me instantly in the earpiece. Everyone's mood was even darker than it had been hours earlier. You had to feel that something was wrong.

Shortly before we were scheduled to go off the air, at 2:30 A.M. Munich time, Roone said,

"This is important, Jim. Tell the stations that we will take a 33-second station break, then come back and wait for the announcement from the press conference of what happened to the hostages."

I did. . . .

At 2:23, the meeting broke up. Marvin went to Otto Kentsch, assistant to Klein. Kentsch and Bader, a German and a Jew, had become good friends during the several years of preparation for the games. . . .

Geoff was still calling in the walkie-talkie when Marvin asked Kentsch, earnestly, looking straight into his eyes, "Otto, what the hell happened out there?"

Members of the Olympic teams sit on chairs on the field during a memorial ceremony for the eleven slain Israeli team members, Munich Olympic Stadium, Germany, September 6, 1972. Arab terrorists disguised as athletes snuck into the Olympic Village the day before and killed eleven Israelis in what was dubbed "The Munich Massacre." **AP/WIDE WORLD PHOTOS. REPRODUCED BY PERMISSION.**

Kentsch looked deeply said. His eyes were watery.

"I can't tell you, Marvin," he said.

Marvin pulled him aside from the group that was about to begin the press conference. He explained that we were about to go off the air, that he knew Kentsch couldn't make the official statement, but that we had to have some idea, something to base our summary on.

The two men continued to stare into each other's eyes.

Then Kentsch said, "They're all dead, Marvin."

"What are you talking about? All the hostages?"

"Yes, Marvin, all the hostages." . . .

After the station break, Roone filled me in. I said on the air that we had reason to believe the news would be very bad. We did not say categorically that they were all dead, because this was privileged information from Otto to Marvin and it was not official. It seemed that the official word would be given by the interior minister any minute, because the conference was under way. After all, the family of David Berger, for example, was probably watching in Ohio, waiting to hear if he was alive or dead. We had to be as cautious of Kentsch's report as we had been of the earlier cruelly erroneous bulletin. . . .

We talked and waited. The interior minister was describing all of the day's events chronologically, instead of telling immediately what had happened to the hostages.

At one point, Roone said that we now had a radio line out of the press conference. We did, and we put it on the air. First, we heard a long passage of the interior minister talking in German. Then, as the English translation began, the voices of two German commentators came in and drowned it out. Naturally, they were beginning to discuss on German radio the remarks that they already understood. The radio line, then, was useless.

The tension was as thick as I have ever felt in a studio. My recollection of what we talked about is dim at this moment. But I remember Roone telling me that it was official, that they were all dead, and I remember summarizing the day's events.

I remember saying, "This morning at ten o'clock, in a little more than six and a half hours, the athletes and the people of Munich will gather in the great Olympic Stadium for a memorial service. They will pay tribute to the slain Israelis, then try to find some hope and solace for themselves and for this poor old world."

I finished with the three words that, I thought, summarized everything that had happened, everything that had been said in the twenty-three hours since the assassins scaled the fence of the village.

"They're all gone," I said.

Margaret had half-awakened when I turned the key in the lock of room 1810.

"What happened, Jim?" she asked. "Someone said they were all saved."

"They're all dead, Margaret," I answered.

Now I stand in the dark getting undressed, clad at the moment, ridiculously, in my bathing trunks, which I had put on to take that swim almost twenty hours ago.

The wonderful games of the Twentieth Olympiad lie in ruins after the events of yesterday and early this morning. The people of the nations gathered here have retired to their beds in deep despair. The city is silent. The cheering has stopped.

Primary Source

"The Show Goes On"

SYNOPSIS: *New York Times* columnist Red Smith criticizes the International Olympic Committee and Avery Brundage for their seemingly cavalier attitude about the tragedy that had occurred at the Olympics.

Munich, West Germany, Sept. 5—Olympic Village was under siege. Two men lay murdered and nine others were held at gunpoint in imminent peril of their lives. Still the games went on. Canoeists paddled through their races. Fencers thrust and parried in make-believe duels. Boxers scuffled. Basketball players scampered across the floor like happy children. Walled off in their dream world, appallingly unaware of the realities of life and death, the aging playground directors who conduct this quadrennial muscle dance ruled that a little blood must not be permitted to interrupt play.

It was 4:30 A.M. when Palestinian terrorists invaded the housing complex where athletes from 121 nations live and shot their way into the Israeli quarters.

National flags fly at half-staff around the Olympic torch, Munich, Germany, September 6, 1972. A day earlier, Arab terrorists killed eleven Israeli athletes before being captured or killed themselves by police. **AP/WIDE WORLD PHOTOS. REPRODUCED BY PERMISSION.**

More than five hours later, word came down from Avery Brundage, retiring president of the International Olympic Committee, that sport would proceed as scheduled. Canoe racing had already begun. Wrestling started an hour later. Before long, competition was being held in 11 of the 22 sports on the Olympic calendar.

Not until 4 P.M. did some belated sense of decency dictate suspension of the obscene activity, and even then exception was made for games already in progress. They went on and on while hasty plans were laid for a memorial service tomorrow. Later word came that the nine hostages had also been murdered.

No Pros Need Apply

The men who run the Olympics are not evil men. Their shocking lack of awareness can't be due to callousness. It has to be stupidity.

Four years ago in Mexico City when American sprinters stood on the victory stand with fists uplifted in symbolic protest against injustice to blacks, the brass of the United States Olympic committee couldn't distinguish between politics and human rights. Declaring that the athletes had violated the Olympic spirit by injecting "partisan politics" into the festival, the waxworks lifted the young men's credentials and ordered them out of Mexico, blowing up a simple, silent gesture into an international incident.

When African nations and other blacks threatened to boycott the current Games if the white supremacist government of Rhodesia were represented here, Brundage thundered that the action was politically motivated, although it was only through a transparent political expedient that Rhodesia had been invited in the first place. Rhodesia and Brundage were voted down not on moral grounds but to avoid having an all-white carnival.

On past performances, it must be assumed that in Avery's view Arab-Israeli warfare, hijacking, kidnapping and killing all constitute partisan politics not to be tolerated in the Olympics.

"And anyway," went the bitter joke today, "these are professional killers; Avery doesn't recognize them."

Too Big for the Britches?

The fact is, these global clambakes have come to have an irresistible attraction as forums for ideological, social or racial expression. For this reason, they may have out-grown their britches. Perhaps in the future it will be advisable to substitute separate world championships in swimming, track and field and so on, which could be conducted in a less hysterical climate.

In the past, athletes from totalitarian countries have seized upon the Olympics as an opportunity to defect. During the Pan-American Games last summer in Cali, Colombia, a number of Cubans defected and a trainer jumped, fell or was pushed to his death from the roof of the Cuban team's dormitory.

Never, of course, has there been anything like today's terror. Once those gunmen climbed the wire fence around Olympic Village and shot Moshe Weinberg, the Israeli wrestling coach, all the fun and games lost meaning. Mark Spitz and his seven gold medals seemed curiously unimportant.

Further Resources

BOOKS

McKay, Jim. *The Real McKay: My Wide World of Sports.* New York: Dutton, 1998.

Sugar, Bert Randolph. *The Thrill of Victory: The Inside Story of ABC Sports.* New York: Hawthorn, 1978.

PERIODICALS

Binder, David. "9 Israelis on Olympic Team Killed With 4 Arab Captors." *The New York Times,* September 6, 1972, 1.

"A Little Greedy, and Exactly Right"

Newspaper article

By: Red Smith

Date: June 11, 1973

Source: Smith, Red. "A Little Greedy, and Exactly Right." *The New York Times,* June 11, 1973.

About the Author: Red Smith (1905–1982) was born in Green Bay, Wisconsin. After graduating from Notre Dame in 1927, Smith was a reporter for the *Milwaukee Sentinel,* and copyeditor and sportswriter for the *St. Louis Star-Times.* In 1936, Smith moved to the *Philadelphia Record,* then the *New York Herald-Tribune* nine years later, becoming one of America's most respected sportswriters. After the *Herald-Tribune* folded in 1967, Smith wrote in syndication until joining *The New York Times* in 1971, remaining there until his death. Smith authored several collections of his columns, and won numerous honors, including the Pulitzer Prize in 1976. ■

Introduction

By the early 1970s, a quarter century had passed since Citation had won horse racing's Triple Crown (Kentucky Derby, Preakness, Belmont Stakes). In the ensuing years, none of the great thoroughbreds had won the Triple Crown. But nobody had seen true greatness in horseracing until the arrival of Secretariat.

Secretariat was born March 29, 1970, at Meadow Stable in Doswell, Virginia, son of 1957 Preakness winner Bold Ruler. A beautiful colt with shiny copper coat with a white stripe running from his forehead to the tip of his nose, Secretariat developed a barrel chest and an enormous stride. Secretariat lost his first race as a two-year-old in July 1972 at Aqueduct Racetrack in New York; after that race, Ron Turcotte took over the reigns as Secretariat's jockey. Winning his remaining eight races that year, Secretariat was named Horse of the Year.

As a three-year-old in 1973, Secretariat burst onto the national stage as no horse had done before. After winning his first two starts, Secretariat finished third in the Wood Memorial—causing some concern, particularly with the Kentucky Derby looming in two weeks. On May 5, in the Kentucky Derby at Churchill Downs, Secretariat started slowly from gate ten, near the back at the one-quarter mark. He moved to the middle of the pack halfway through the race. But into the stretch, Secretariat's trademark stride was evident as he bolted into the lead. Secretariat won by two-and-one-half lengths, setting a new Kentucky Derby time record in the process. Two weeks later, at the Preakness in Baltimore, Secretariat moved to the front quickly, and on the final clubhouse turn, again accelerated his powerful stride, running to a three-and-a-half-length victory, just missing the track record.

In the weeks leading up to the Belmont Stakes, Secretariat was featured on the cover of *Time* magazine and other national publications. With his shiny copper coat, engaging personality, and tremendous power as a thoroughbred, Secretariat even succeeded in knocking the widening Watergate scandal off the front page for a short time. The red horse with the blue and white blinders seemed to typify an American hero.

The running of the Belmont Stakes on June 8, 1973, completed Secretariat's quest for the Triple Crown, propelling him into American horse racing and sports history. Emerging fast from the starting gate, Secretariat was ahead by seven lengths at the halfway mark, then by almost twenty heading down the home stretch. The distance became so great near the finish line that Turcotte looked back to his left to see the competition trailing far behind. Secretariat finished an amazing thirty-one lengths in front, establishing a new race time record. Finally, after a quarter century, there was a Triple Crown winner again.

Significance

Secretariat's Triple Crown victory, as spectacular as it was, began a decade of racing achievement. In 1977, Seattle Slew won the Triple Crown, followed a year later by Affirmed—three horses winning the big prize in six years. Secretariat would race six more times, four with Turcotte as jockey, finishing first on four occasions, and concluding his brilliant career victorious at the Canadian International on October 28, 1973. Then "Big Red II," as Secretariat was nicknamed (named for the original Big Red, Man O' War) was retired to stud. In twenty races, Secretariat had won sixteen and placed second three times, earning $1,316,808 in purse money.

In retirement, Secretariat sired many thoroughbreds, but was unfairly regarded as a disappointment for not siring offspring with talent equal to his own. As the years passed by, Secretariat's popularity endured—he received dozens of birthday cards and letters each year from fans. At Claiborne Farms in Kentucky where he was stabled, Secretariat was a shameless ham and mischievous "practical joker" with admiring human visitors, who traveled long distances to see him.

In 1989, Secretariat began suffering from laminitis, a painful and degenerative disease of the hoof's inner tissues. Finally, after surgery was considered but ultimately ruled out, Secretariat was euthanized on October 4, at age nineteen. After a necropsy, it was revealed that the secret behind Secretariat's power as a racer was his heart—twice the average size, not abnormally shaped, but simply larger. Big heart or not, Secretariat was one of the all-time great champions of American sport. As an admiring fan said sadly the day after his death, "he wasn't a horse; he was Secretariat."

Primary Source

"A Little Greedy, and Exactly Right"

SYNOPSIS: Here Red Smith, writing for *The New York Times,* gives a firsthand account of Secretariat and his significance to the sport of horseracing.

The thing to remember is that the horse that finished last had broken the Kentucky Derby record. If there were no colt named Secretariat, then Sham would have gone into the Belmont Stakes Saturday honored as the finest 3-year-old in America, an eight-length winner of the Kentucky Derby where he went the mile and a quarter faster than any winner in 98 years and an eight-length winner of the Preakness. There is, however, a colt named Secretariat. In the Derby he overtook Sham and beat him by two and a half lengths. In the Preakness he held Sham off by two and a half lengths. This time he and Sham dueled for the lead, and he beat Sham by more than a 16th of a mile. There is no better way to measure the class of the gorgeous red colt that owns the Triple Crown. Turning into the homestretch at Belmont Park, Ron Turcotte glanced back under an arm to find his pursuit. He saw nothing, and while he peeked, his mount took off.

Secretariat had already run a mile in one minute, 34⅕ seconds. Up to three weeks ago, no horse in Belmont history had run a mile in less than 1:34⅖. He had run a mile and a quarter in 1:59, two-fifths of a second faster than the Derby record he had set five weeks earlier. Now he went after the Belmont record of 2:26⅗ for a mile and a half, which was also an American record when Gallant Man established it 16 years ago.

With no pursuit to urge him on, without a tap from Turcotte's whip, he smashed the track record by two and three-fifth seconds, cracked the American record by two and a fifth, and if Turcotte had asked him he could have broken the world record. If he had been running against Gallant Man, the fastest Belmont winner in 104 years, he would have won by 13 lengths. Unless the competition spurred him to greater speed.

Secretariat's Career Racing Record

ch. c. 1970, by Bold Ruler (nasrullah)-Somethingroyal, by Princequillo
Own.-Meadow Stable
Br.-Meadow Stud Inc (Va)
Tr.-L. Laurin

Lifetime record: 21 16 3 1 $1,316,808

Date-Track	Cond/Dist	Times	Race	PP	St	¼	½	¾/Str	Fin	Jockey	Wt	Med	Odds	SR	Finish (top three)	Comment
28Oct73-8WO	fm 1⅝①	:47² 1:37³ 2:41⁴↑	Can Int'l-G2	12	2	2¹¹/₂	1¹²	1¹²	1⁶¹/₂	Maple E	117	b	*.20	96-04	Secretariat117⁶¹/₂BigSpruce126¹¹/₂Goldendon117³/₄	Ridden out 12
8Oct73-7Bel	fm1¹/₂①	:47 1:11³2:00 2:24⁴³↑	Man o'War-G1	3	1	1³	1¹¹/₂	1⁵	1⁵	Turcotte R	121	b	*.50	103-01	Secretariat121⁵Tentam126⁷¹/₂BigSpruce126¹/₂	Ridden out 7
29Sep73-7Bel	sly 1¹/₂	:50 1:13²2:01⁴ 2:25⁴³↑	Woodward-G1	5	2	2¹/₂	1ʰᵈ	2¹¹/₂	2⁴¹/₂	Turcotte R	119	b	*.30	86-15	ProveOut126⁴¹/₂Secretariat119¹¹Cougarll126¹/₂	Best of rest 5
15Sep73-Bel	fst 1¹/₈	:45³ 1:09¹ 1:33 1:45²³	Marl Cup Inv'l H 250k	7	5	5¹¹/₄	3¹/₂	1²	1³¹/₂	Turcotte R	124	b	*.40e	104-07	Secretariat124³¹/₂Riva Ridge127²Cougar II126⁶¹/₂	Ridden out 7
4Aug73-7Sar	fst 1¹/₈	:47⁴ 1:11 1:36 1:49¹³↑	Whitney H-G2	3	4	3¹	2¹/₂	2¹	2ⁿᵈ	Turcotte R	119	b	*.10	94-15	Onion119¹Secretariat119¹/₂Rule by Reason119²	Weakened 5
30Jun73-8AP	fst 1¹/₈	:48¹:11¹ 1:35 1:47	Invitational 125k	4	1	1³	1²	1⁶	1⁹	Turcotte R	126	b	*.05	99-17	Secretariat 126⁹My Gallant120ⁿᵏOur Native 120¹⁷	Easily 4
9Jun73-8Bel	fst 1¹/₂	:46¹ 1:09⁴ 1:59 2:24	Belmont-G1	1	1ʰᵈ	1²⁰	1²⁸	1³¹	1³¹	Turcotte R	126	b	*.10	113-05	Secretariat 126³¹TwiceaPrince126¹/₂My Glint126¹³	Ridden out 5
19May73-8Pim	fst 1³/₁₆	:48¹:11¹:35³ 1:54²	Preakness-G1	3	4	1¹/₂	1²¹/₂	1²¹/₂	1²	Turcotte R	126	b	*.30	98-13	Secretariat 126²Sham126⁸Our Native126¹	Handily 6
5May73-9CD	fst 1¹/₄	:47² 1:11⁴ 1:36¹ 1:59²	Ky Derby-G1	10	11	6⁹¹/₂	2¹/₂	1¹/₂	1¹/₂	Turcotte R	126	b	*1.50e	103-10	Secretariat 126²¹/₂Sham126⁸Our Native 126¹/₂	Handily 13
21Apr73-7Aqu	fst 1¹/₈	:48¹ 1:12¹ 1:36⁴ 1:49⁴	Wood Memorial-G1	6	7	6⁶	5⁵¹/₂	4⁵¹/₂	3⁴	Turcotte R	126	b	*.30e	83-17	Angle Light126ⁿᵈSham126⁴Secretariat126¹/₂	Wide,hung 8
7Apr73-7Aqu	fst 1	:23¹ :45¹ 1:08³ 1:33²	Gotham-G2	3	3	3¹ʰᵈ	1²	1²	1³	Turcotte R	126	b	*.10	100-08	Secretariat126³Champagne Charl117¹⁰Flush117²¹/₂	Ridden out 6
17Mar73-7Aqu	slv 7f	:22¹ :44⁴ 1:10 1:23¹	Bay Shore-G3	4	5	5⁶	5³	1ʰᵈ	1⁴¹/₂	Turcotte R	126	b	*.20	85-17	Secretariat126⁴¹/₂Champgn Chrl118²¹/₂Impcunous126ᴹᴰ	Mild drive 6
18Nov72-8GS	fst 11/16	:24¹ :47² 1:12 1:44²	Garden State 298k	6	6	4⁶¹/₄	3³	1¹¹/₂	1³¹/₂	Turcotte R	122	b	*.10e	83-23	Secretariat122³¹/₂Angle Light122¹/₂Step Nicely122³/₄	Handily 6
28Oct72-7Lrl	sly1¹/₁₆	:22⁴ :45⁴ 1:11² 1:42⁴	Lrl Futurity 133k	5	6	5¹⁰	5³	1⁵	1⁸	Turcotte R	122	b	*.10e	99-14	Secretariat122⁸Stop the MusicAngle Light122¹	Easily 6
14Oct72-7Bel	fst 1	:22⁴ :45¹ 1:09⁴ 1:35	Champagne 146k	4	11	9⁸¹/₂	5³¹/₂	1¹/₂	1²	Turcotte R	122	b	*.70e	97-12	ⒹSecretariat122²StoptheMusic122²StepNicly122¹¹/₂	Bore in 12
															Disqualified and placed second	
16Sep72-Bel	fst 6¹/₂f	:22³ :45³ 1:10 1:16²	Futurity 144K	4	5	6⁵¹/₂	5³¹/₂	1²	1¹³/₄	Turcotte R	122	b	*.20	98-09	Secretariat122¹³/₄Stop the Music122⁵SwiftCourr122²¹/₂	Handily 7
26Aug72-7Sar	fst 6¹/₂f	:22⁴ :46³ 1:09⁴ 1:16¹	Hopeful 86k	8	8	9⁶¹/₂	1ʰᵈ	1⁴	1⁵	Turcotte R	121	b	*.30	97-12	Secretariat121⁵FlighttoGlory121ⁿᵏStopthMusc121²	Handily 9
16Aug72-7Sar	fst 6f	:22⁴ :46¹ 1:10	Sanford 27k	2	5	5⁴	4¹	1¹/₂	1³	Turcotte R	121	b	1.50	96-14	Secretariat121³Lnd'sChf121⁶NorthstrDncr121³¹/₂	Ridden out 5
31Jly72-4Sar	fst 6f	:23¹ :46² 1:10⁴	Alw 9000	4	7	7³³/₄	3¹/₂	1ʰᵈ	1¹¹/₂	Turcotte R	118	b	*.40	92-13	Secretariat118¹¹/₂Russ Miron118⁷Joe Iz118²¹/₂	Ridden out 7
15Jly72-4Aqu	fst 6f	:22¹ :45² 1:10³	©Md Sp Wt	8	11	6⁶¹/₂	4³	1¹/₂	1⁶	Feliciano P5	113	b	*1.30	90-14	Secretariat113⁶Master Achiever118³/₄Be on It118⁴	Handily 11
4Jly72-2Aqu	fst 5¹/₂f	:22² :46¹ :58⁴ 1:05	©Md Sp Wt	2	11	10⁷	10⁸³/₄	7⁵¹/₂	4¹¹/₄	Feliciano P5	113	b	*3.10	87-11	Herbull118ⁿᵒMaster Achiever118¹Fleet 'n Royal118ᴺᴼ	Handily 11

Daily Racing Form time 1:53 2/5

Impeded,rallied

12

SOURCE: *Career Racing Record*. Available online at http://www.secretariat.com/past_performance.htm; website home page: http://www.secretariat.com (accessed April 9, 2003).

Secretariat works out with jockey Ron Turcotte, Belmont Park, Elmont, N.Y., March 14, 1973. In 1973 Secretariat rejuvinated horse racing by breaking several track records on his way to the Triple Crown. **AP/WIDE WORLD PHOTOS. REPRODUCED BY PERMISSION.**

Hard Times in Baltimore

"It seems a little greedy to win by 31 lengths," said Mrs. John Tweedy, the owner, and then repeated the rider's story of how he saw the fractional times blinking on the tote board, realized there was a record in the making, and went after it in the final 16th.

It is hard to imagine what a 31-length margin looks like, because you never see one, but Secretariat lacked eight panels of fence—80 feet—of beating Twice a Prince by a 16th of a mile. This was the classic case of "Eclipse first, the rest nowhere."

The colt was entitled to his margin and his record. At the Derby he drew a record crowd that broke all Churchill Downs betting records and he set a track record. He set attendance and betting records at the Preakness and may have broken the stakes record, but if he did discrepancies in the clocking denied him that credit. Last Saturday belonged to him.

Indeed, Belmont was kinder to the Meadow Stable than Pimlico had been, in more ways than one. On Preakness day, while the Tweedy party lunched in the Pimlico Hotel near the track, a parking lot attendant smashed up their car. They walked to the clubhouse gate, found they hadn't brought credentials, and paid their way in. While the horses were being saddled in the infield, somebody in the crowd accidentally pressed a lighted cigarette against Mrs. Tweedy's arm. On his way back to his seat, John Tweedy had his pocket picked.

"Boy," he said after that race, "we needed to win this one today, just to get even."

Belmont Was Warmer

At Belmont there were the few scattered boos that most odds-on favorites receive here, but the prevailing attitude was close to idolatry. Well, perhaps that isn't the best word because it suggests a cathedral restraint. Idols are remotely chilly. This congregation was warm. Horse players passing the Tweedy box raised friendly voices:

"Mrs. Tweedy, good luck."

"Thank you."

The voices followed her to the paddock where her colt was cheered all around the walking ring. They followed as she returned to the clubhouse.

"Mrs. Tweedy, good luck."

"Thank you."

Secretariat was cheered in the post parade, cheered as he entered the gate, and when he caught and passed Sham on the backstretch the exultant thunders raised gooseflesh. At the finish the crowd surged toward the winner's circle, fists brandished high. After 25 years, America's racing fans had a sovereign to wear the Triple Crown.

Parallels are striking between this one and his predecessor, Citation. Both colts raced nine times as 2-year-olds and finished first eight times. At 3, each lost once en route to the Derby, Preakness and Belmont. Both made each event in the Triple Crown easier than the last. After the Belmont, Citation won his next 10 starts for a streak of 16 straight. Secretariat's stud duties won't permit that. Love will rear its pretty, tousled head.

Further Resources

BOOKS

Nack, William. *Secretariat: The Making of a Champion.* Cambridge, Mass.: DeCapo Press, 2002.

Woolfe, Raymond G. *Secretariat.* Radnor, Pa.: Chilton Books, 1974.

PERIODICALS

Crist, Steven. "Secretariat, Racing Legend and Fan Favorite, Is Dead." *The New York Times,* October 5, 1989.

WEBSITES

The Official Secretariat website. Available online at http://www .secretariat.com (accessed April 24, 2003).

Hank Aaron Sets New Home Run Record

I Had a Hammer: The Hank Aaron Story
Autobiography

By: Henry Aaron, with Lonnie Wheeler

Date: 1991

Source: Aaron, Henry, with Lonnie Wheeler. *I Had a Hammer: The Hank Aaron Story.* New York: HarperCollins, 1991, 235–236, 238, 242–243, 266–272.

About the Author: Henry Aaron (1934–) was born in Mobile, Alabama. After high school, Aaron played with the Negro League Indianapolis Clowns, before signing with the Boston Braves in 1952. Aaron spent twenty-one seasons in Milwaukee and Atlanta, leading the Braves to World Series appearances in 1957 and 1958, and a championship in 1957.

After breaking Babe Ruth's home run record, Aaron spent his final two seasons with the Milwaukee Brewers, retiring in 1976 with twelve major league records—including most career home runs with 755. After retirement, Aaron became director of player development for the Braves, and has been involved in other baseball-related activities.

Interview by Phil Pepe
Interview

By: Al Downing

Date: 1993

Source: Downing, Al. Interview by Phil Pepe. In *Talkin' Baseball: An Oral History of Baseball in the 1970s.* New York: Ballantine Books, 1993, 149–152, 154–156.

About the Author: Alphonso Erwin Downing (1941–) was born on June 28 in Trenton, New Jersey. Called by some "the black Sandy Koufax," Downing entered the major leagues with much hype. He never lived up to that billing, partly because of control problems and inconsistency and later because of arm miseries, though he did have four stellar seasons. He pitched for the New York Yankees (1961–1969), both Oakland and Minnesota in 1970, then finished his career with the Los Angeles Dodgers (1971–1977).

"The Sound of 715"
Newspaper article

By: Dave Anderson

Date: April 9, 1974

Source: Anderson, Dave. "The Sound of 715." *The New York Times,* April 9, 1974.

About the Author: Dave Anderson (1929–) was born in Troy, New York. After graduating from Holy Cross in 1951, Anderson wrote sports for the *Brooklyn Eagle* until 1955, then for the *New York Journal-American* until 1966, when he joined *The New York Times,* becoming a columnist in 1971. Author of twenty-one books and dozens of magazine articles, Anderson won the Pulitzer Prize in 1981. ∎

Introduction

When Babe Ruth retired in 1935, few believed his record 714 career home runs would ever be broken. Over the years, 714 was challenged, but not broken. A number of players had hit over five hundred home runs, but until Henry Aaron challenged in the early 1970s, nobody had approach Ruth's remarkable record.

Henry Aaron began his major league career with the Milwaukee Braves in 1954. During the 1960s, Aaron gradually moved up the all-time home run list, hitting his five hundredth in July 1968. Once Aaron hit his six hundredth in April 1971, the eyes of baseball turned to the Atlanta Braves outfielder. From that point forward, the only question remaining was *when* Aaron would break the Ruth mark. Aaron finished the 1972 season with 673

Hank Aaron eyes the flight of his 715th career home run, Atlanta, April 8, 1974. The homer, given up by L.A. Dodger southpaw Al Downing, broke Babe Ruth's career home run record. **AP/WIDE WORLD PHOTOS. REPRODUCED BY PERMISSION.**

home runs, just forty-one short of Ruth. His twenty-seventh home run of 1973 was his seven hundredth. On September 29, 1973, Aaron hit his 713th home run off Houston Astros pitcher Jerry Reuss, but Aaron failed to homer in the season's final game.

The pressure built up on Aaron in the off-season, as he began receiving more mail, some complimentary, but mostly hate letters—primarily because Aaron, an African American was about to break a white man's home run record. Before spring training, the Braves owner suggested that since the team opened in Cincinnati, Aaron should sit those games out, and go for the record before the home crowd in Atlanta. Baseball commissioner, Bowie Kuhn, quickly rejected the idea as detrimental to the game, and all but ordered Aaron to play in Cincinnati. The 1974 season opened April 4 in Cincinnati, and opposing Aaron would be Reds pitcher Jack Billingham. The drama of 714 ended on the first pitch in his opening at bat, as Aaron connected on a Billingham pitch for a home run over the left field wall. Hitting no more homers in Cincinnati, Aaron and the Braves returned home to Atlanta.

The night of April 8, 1974, Atlanta-Fulton County Stadium had a festive atmosphere. The crowd of 53,775 was the largest crowd in Atlanta's baseball history—in attendence were Georgia governor Jimmy Carter, and entertainers Sammy Davis Jr. and Pearl Bailey. Commissioner Kuhn was not in attendance, due to a "previous commitment"; the crowd booed his emissary, former player Monte Irvin. The opponent was the Los Angeles Dodgers, and the starting pitcher was veteran left-hander, Al Downing. Aaron's first time up, leading off the second inning, he walked and later scored on a double. The run broke the National League record held by Willie Mays. Aaron came up again in the fourth inning with the Dodgers ahead 3-1, with one man on base. Downing's first pitch was inside for a ball. The next pitch, Aaron swung and connected, sending the ball toward the left field fence. Bill Buckner, the Dodgers left fielder, started climbing the fence, but to no avail. The ball was over the fence, the 715th home run of Aaron's illustrious career.

Significance

The home run ball traveled over the fence and into the Brave's bullpen, landing in the glove of Braves relief pitcher Tom House after traveling 385 feet. As Aaron was rounding the bases, two fans, both white, came out of the stands and ran alongside, patting him on the back. An impromptu ceremony was held at home plate, and House ran in from the bullpen with the ball. The game was delayed for over ten minutes, while family and teammates surrounded Aaron. Later in the game, Aaron received a call from President Richard Nixon (served 1969–1974).

After finishing the 1974 season with the Braves, Aaron signed with the Milwaukee Brewers, playing the final two seasons in the city where he began his big league career. When Aaron retired after the 1976 season, he had hit 755 home runs in twenty-three years. He also set other major league records in several categories, including most games played, most at bats, most extra base hits, and most runs batted in.

While a number of players have broken Ruth's single-season home run mark, Aaron's career record of 755 was not approached in the following thirty years. Aaron broke what was perhaps baseball's most hallowed record, Babe Ruth's career home run total of 714—despite a year of intense scrutiny, the glare of the media, and antagonism of many so-called fans. The volume of hate mail wore on Aaron and left him understandably bitter about the entire quest for the home run record. Aaron's achievement, however, was testament to his longevity and his skill on the field, a fitting record for an incredibly talented baseball player.

Primary Source

I Had a Hammer: The Hank Aaron Story [excerpt]

SYNOPSIS: In his autobiography, Atlanta Braves outfielder Henry Aaron recounts the evening of April 8, 1974, when he broke Babe Ruth's home run mark. Aaron also provides samples and comments on the hate mail sent to him on approaching and breaking the record.

As the hate mail piled up, I became more and more intent on breaking the record and shoving it in the ugly faces of those bigots. I'm sure it made me a better hitter. But it also made my life very, very difficult. . . . All over the league, I had to register at our hotels under fictitious names. I would reserve one room in my name, where the operator could put calls through and let them ring, and another in a name like Diefendorfer, where I actually stayed. The problem was that sometimes my children couldn't get through, and that worried me because they weren't safe. . . .

Dear Hank Aaron,

Retire or die! The Atlanta Braves will be moving around the country and I'll move with them. You'll be in Montreal June 5–7. Will you die there? You'll be in Shea Stadium July 6–8, and in Philly July 9th to 11th. Then again you'll be

in Montreal and St. Louis in August. You will die in one of those games. I'll shoot you in one of them. Will I sneak a rifle into the upper deck or a .45 in the bleachers? I don't know yet. But you know you will die unless you retire! . . .

Dear Mr. Aaron,

I am twelve years old, and I wanted to tell you that I have read many articles about the prejudice against you. I really think it's bad. I don't care what color you are. You could be green and it wouldn't matter. These nuts that keep comparing you in every way to Ruth are dumb. Maybe he's better. Maybe you are. How can you compare two people 30 or 40 years apart? You can't really. So many things are different. It's just some people can't stand to see someone a bit different from them ruin something someone else more like them set. I've never read where you said you're better than Ruth. That's because you never said it! What do those fans want you to do? Just quit hitting? . . .

At the end of the year, the U.S. Postal Service calculated my mail at 930,000 letters and gave me a little plaque for receiving the most of any non-politician in the country. Dinah Shore was second with 60,000. . . .

. . . I never got into the arguments over Ruth versus me, or Ruth's time versus my time, because I knew that nothing would ever be solved. If people want to hear me say that Babe Ruth was the greatest home run hitter, fine, Babe Ruth was the greatest home run hitter. . . .

I was in a foul mood when we got back to Atlanta, but Atlanta was in a good mood. The annual Dogwood Festival was going on, and the Braves had planned a big Hank Aaron Night for the home opener on Monday. There were almost 54,000 people at the ballpark that night—still the biggest crowd in team history. Bob Hope, the Braves' publicity man, had been working on the special night since the year before, not knowing that I would be tied with Ruth at the time. . . . It seemed like the only people not there were the President of the United States and the commissioner of baseball. Nixon had a pretty good excuse—Congress was on his back to produce the Watergate tapes—but I couldn't say the same for Bowie Kuhn. He was in Cleveland speaking to the Wahoo Club. Kuhn sent Monte Irvin to stand in for him, and the Atlanta fans just about booed poor Monte out of the park. . . . Whatever his reason for not being there, I think it was terribly inadequate. I took it personally, and, even though Kuhn and I have met and talked about it since then, I still do. . . .

My father threw out the first ball, and then we took the field against the Dodgers. Their pitcher was Al Downing, a veteran lefthander whom I respected. . . . I had to be patient and pick my spot. It didn't come in the second inning, when Downing walked me before I could take the bat off my shoulder. I scored when Dusty Baker doubled and Bill Buckner mishandled the ball in left field. Nobody seemed to care too much, but my run broke Willie Mays's National League record for runs scored—Willie had retired at the end of the 1973 season—and put me third all-time behind Ty Cobb and Ruth.

I came up again in the fourth, with two outs and Darrell Evans on first base. The Dodgers were ahead 3-1, and I knew that Downing was not going to walk me and put the tying run on base. He was going to challenge me with everything he had—which was what it was going to take for me to hit my 715th home run.

Downing's first pitch was a change of pace that went into the dirt. The umpire, Satch Davidson, threw it out, and the first-base umpire, Frank Pulli, tossed Downing another one of the specially marked infrared balls. Downing rubbed it up and then threw his slider low and down the middle, which was not where he wanted it but which was fine with me. I hit it squarely, although not well enough that I knew it was gone. The ball shot out on a line over the shortstop, Bill Russell, who bent his knees as if he were going to jump up and catch it.

. . . But the ball kept going. It surprised him, and it surprised me. I'm still not sure I hit that ball hard enough for it to go out. I don't know—maybe I did but I was so keyed up that I couldn't feel it. Anyway, something carried the ball into the bullpen, and about the time I got to first base I realized that I was the all-time home run king of baseball. Steve Garvey, the Dodgers' first baseman, shook my hand as I passed first, and Davey Lopes, the second baseman, stuck out his hand at second. I'm not sure if I ever shook with Lopes, though, because about that time a couple of college kids appeared out of nowhere and started running alongside me and pounding me on the back. I guess I was aware of them, because the clips show that I sort of nudged them away with my elbow, but I honestly don't remember them being there. I was in my own little world at the time. It was like I was running in a bubble and I could see all these people jumping up and down and waving their arms in slow motion. I remember that every base seemed crowded, like there were all these people I had to get through to make

Hank Aaron laughs during a press conference following the game in which he hit his record 715th home run, Atlanta, April 8, 1974. It was not all laughs, however: Aaron received not only praise but much criticism and hate mail for breaking Ruth's record. **AP/WIDE WORLD PHOTOS. REPRODUCED BY PERMISSION.**

it to home plate. I just couldn't wait to get there. I was told I had a big smile on my face as I came around third. I purposely never smiled as I ran the bases after a home run, but I suppose I couldn't help it that time. . . .

As I ran in toward home, Ralph Garr grabbed my leg and tried to plant it on the plate, screaming, "Touch it, Supe! Just touch it!" As soon as I did, Ralph and Darrell and Eddie and everybody mobbed me. Somehow, my mother managed to make it through and put a bear hug on me. Good Lord, I didn't know Mama was that strong; I thought she was going to squeeze the life out of me. . . . Then they stopped the game for a little ceremony, and I stepped up to the microphone and said exactly what I felt: "Thank God it's over."

We had a little party at the house that night, mostly family and close friends. Billye and I were alone for a little while before everybody arrived, and while she was in the bedroom getting ready, I went off downstairs to be by myself for a few minutes. When I was alone and the door was shut, I got down on my knees and closed my eyes and thanked God for pulling me through. At that moment, I knew what the past twenty-five years of my life had been all about. I had done something that nobody else in the world had ever done, and with it came a feeling that nobody else has ever had—not exactly, anyway. I didn't feel a wild sense of joy. I didn't feel like celebrating. But I probably felt closer to God at that moment than at any other in my life. I felt a deep sense of gratitude and a wonderful surge of liberation all at the same time. I also felt a stream of tears running down my face. . . .

Primary Source

Interview by Phil Pepe

SYNOPSIS: Phil Pepe, sportswriter and author, in a collection of oral histories, interviewed Al Downing, the Los Angeles Dodgers pitcher who gave up Aaron's 715th home run.

I knew Hank was going for the record, and I knew I would have to pitch to him. I always had good luck against him, keeping him in the ballpark. He was a tough out for me, but his hits were mostly singles and doubles. I think he had hit only two home runs off me. By comparison, Willie Mays hit many more homers off me than Hank.

My thinking was that I didn't want to face Hank with anybody on base, and my approach to pitching to him was to try to keep the ball down and away and if he tried to pull it, he might hit the ball to the right side or to the shortstop. The first time he came up, I walked him. The crowd booed.

The next time he came up, in the fourth inning, there was a man on base, so I was trying to get him to hit into a double play by throwing him fastballs down and away. The first pitch was a ball, low, and the crowd started booing. Now I'm thinking I have to get the ball up. Steve Yeager, my catcher, gave me the target low and away, and I threw the ball right at Yeager's right knee. It was a little bit up, higher than I wanted it, and I didn't have the velocity I once had.

People who saw the pitch on television replays say it was right over the plate, but it wasn't. It was down and away, although not down far enough, and Hank just dived into the ball, which made it look like it was right over the plate. He still had pretty good bat speed, even at forty years old, and he reached down and hit a line drive over the fence in left center. The place went crazy. . . .

I wasn't devastated by Aaron's home run. The one I gave up to Ken Boyer [a grand slam in Game 4 of the 1964 World Series] was much more devastating. Aaron's came in the first week of the season and it was early in the game and it made the score 3-3, so it didn't have a great impact on our ball club. The way I felt is that it was a great tribute to him. To me, you just learn to put those things behind you. Now it's a tie score and you just go from there. . . .

People remember me for giving up the record home run. They ask me to sign pictures and other things that Hank also has signed. I've done a couple of card shows with Hank and a luncheon, but not a lot. A few years ago, he opened a restaurant, and he sent me some baseballs and asked me to sign them for him. He's always been a gracious guy. He's done some favors for me. I consider him a friend.

Primary Source

"The Sound of 715" [excerpt]

SYNOPSIS: Dave Anderson, sports columnist for *The New York Times,* provides a firsthand account of Aaron's 715th home run, with a mention of the commissioner's absence from the game and the Cincinnati controversy.

Atlanta, April 8—In the decades to come, the memory of the scene might blur. But the memory of the sound will remain with everyone who was here. Not the sound of the cheers, or the sound of Henry Aaron saying. "I'm thankful to God it's all over," but the sound of Henry Aaron's bat when it hit the baseball tonight. The sound that's baseball's version of a thunderclap, the sound of a home run, in his case the sound of the 715th home run. The sound momentarily was the only sound in the expectant silence of 53,775 customers at Atlanta Stadium and then, as the sound faded, the ball soared high and deep toward the left-center-field fence. And over it. On the infield basepaths, Henry Aaron was trotting now, trotting past Babe Ruth into history in his 21st season.

The Missing Commissioner

. . . Quietly, he has resented Kuhn's attitude toward him, whether real or imagined. It began when Kuhn ignored his 700th home run last season and it simmered when Kuhn ordered Eddie Mathews to use him in the starting line-up in Cincinnati yesterday after the Braves' manager had planned to preserve him for the Atlanta audience. Kuhn was correct in that ultimatum, because the Braves were defying the integrity of baseball.

But the commissioner was wrong tonight in not being here. He had stood up gallantly, but suddenly he had sat down again. Henry Aaron should have ordered the commissioner to be here.

"I thought the line-up card was taken out of Eddie Matthew's hand," the man with 715 home runs said. "I believe I should've been given the privilege of deciding for myself."

It's unfortunate that controversy somewhat clouded Henry Aaron's moment. It's also untypical. Of all our superstars, Henry Aaron has been perhaps the most uncontroversial. But time will blow those clouds away. Soon only his home runs will be important, not where he hit them, not where the commissioner was. His eventual total of home runs will be his monument, although they represent only a portion of his stature as a hitter.

Convincing the Skeptics

With a normally productive season, in what he insists will be his last, Henry Aaron probably will hold six major-league career records for home runs, runs batted in, total bases, extra base hits, games and times at bat. Ty Cobb will retain the records for hits, runs, batting average and stolen bases. Babe Ruth will hold the records for slugging average and walks. Through the years. Cobb and the Babe were the ultimate in hitting, but now they must move over.

"With a good year," Henry Aaron has said, "I'll hold six records, Cobb will hold four and Ruth two."

Perhaps that will convince the skeptics who minimize his accomplishments as a hitter. Some of the skeptics are traditionalists, some are racists. Statistically, their argument is that Henry Aaron needed 2,896 more times at bat than Babe Ruth in order to break the home-run record. Those skeptics ignore Henry Aaron's durability and consistency, attributes as important as Babe Ruth's charisma. And when his 715th home run soared over the fence tonight, Henry Aaron never lost his dignity, his essence as a person.

"You don't know what a weight it was off my shoulders," he said later, "a tremendous weight."

Now the weight will be transferred to the hitter who someday challenges Henry Aaron, if that hitter appears.

Further Resources

BOOKS
Baldwin, Stanley. *Bad Henry.* Radnor, Pa.: Chilton, 1974.

Bisher, Furman. *Aaron.* New York: Crowell, 1974.

PERIODICALS
Durso, Joseph. "Aaron Hits 715, Passes Babe Ruth." *The New York Times,* April 9, 1974.

WEBSITES
National Baseball Hall of Fame and Museum. "Henry Aaron." Available online at http://www.baseballhalloffame.org /hofers_and_honorees/hofer_bios/aaron_hank.htm; website home page: http://www.baseballhalloffame.org (accessed April 24, 2003).

Paul "Bear" Bryant

Bear: The Hard Life and Good Times of Alabama's Coach Bryant
Autobiography

By: Paul W. Bryant and John Underwood
Date: 1974
Source: Bryant, Paul W., and John Underwood. *Bear: The Hard Life and Good Times of Alabama's Coach Bryant.* Boston: Little, Brown, 1974, 199–200, 202–205, 207.
About the Author: Paul W. "Bear" Bryant (1919–1983) was born in Kingsland, Arkansas. He coached football at the University of Alabama from 1936 to 1940, and again from 1958 to 1983. In between his tenures there, he coached at Vanderbilt University (1940–1941), the University of Maryland (1945–1946), the University of Kentucky (1946–1953), and Texas A&M (1954–1958). He led Alabama to twenty-five winning seasons, twenty-four bowl games, and six national championships. At the time of his death he had won more games (323) than any other coach in college football history.

"The Bear's Superstudents: Trials and Triumphs"
Magazine article

By: Joe Namath, and Ken Stabler
Date: September 29, 1980
Source: "The Bear's Superstudents: Trials and Triumphs." *Time,* September 29, 1980, 74.
About the Authors: Joe Namath (1943–) was born in Beaver Falls, Pennsylvania. After playing quarterback at the University of Alabama, he signed a $400,000 contract with the New York Jets of the American Football League. In 1968, he led the Jets to the AFL title and an upset of the Baltimore Colts in Super Bowl III. Plagued by injuries, Namath retired after twelve seasons in 1977. Since retirement, Namath has been an actor, broadcaster, and businessman.

Paul "Bear" Bryant

Kenny "Snake" Stabler (1945–) was an All-American for Paul Bryant at the University of Alabama from 1965 to 1967. He was drafted by the NFL's Oakland Raiders where he played under coach John Madden. In his ten years with the Raiders, the left-handed quarterback was named to the Pro Bowl five times (1973 to 1977). He passed for more than two hundred yards thirty-six times in league play, and in 1977 he led the Raiders to a Super Bowl victory over Minnesota. While a Raider he set a record of 143 consecutive passing attempts without an interception, and completed 1,182 passes for a Raider record. Stabler was enshrined into the Bay Area Sports Hall of Fame in 2000. ■

Introduction

College football coaches seem to be larger-than-life figures, becoming the public "face" of a university in ways that most tenured professors could not. For example, Knute Rockne is still identified with Notre Dame, Eddie Robinson with Grambling, Woody Hayes with Ohio State, and, more recently, Joe Paterno with Penn State. But perhaps no coach's image extended beyond his university to a state, and even a region, as did Alabama's Paul "Bear" Bryant.

Paul Bryant, an Arkansas native, got the nickname "Bear" after wrestling a bear for money as a youngster. After college at Alabama, where he played end on the 1935 Rose Bowl champions, Bryant was an assistant coach and World War II (1939–1945) naval officer, before becoming the head coach at Maryland in 1945.

In 1958, Bryant returned to his alma mater, Alabama, beginning a twenty-five year career that established his legend. Beginning in 1959, Alabama went to twenty-four consecutive bowl games under Bryant. In the early 1960s, Bryant survived accusations of fixing games by the Saturday Evening Post, even winning a lawsuit against the magazine. He won his first national championship in 1961, then followed with back-to-back titles in 1964 and 1965.

The late 1960s were unsuccessful, by Bryant and Alabama standards, as the team went eight seasons without a national title. The persisting segregation of the Alabama football program became clear when his friend, coach John McKay, and the University of Southern California, a team with talented African American players, came to Birmingham and beat the Crimson Tide decisively in 1970. The next season, Bryant had the first black players on his squad. Why Bryant chose then, and not five or ten years earlier, to integrate his team will always be a question of speculation. Eddie Robinson, however, credits Bryant for hastening the integration of football squads at Southern universities.

Bryant's adopting the "wishbone" offense (which emphasized the running game), relaxing rules on dress and grooming, along with his integration of black players, helped change the fortunes of the Alabama football program. Bryant's teams were highly successful throughout the 1970s. The Crimson Tide won three national championships (1973, 1978, 1979) and had four unbeaten teams (1971, 1973, 1974, 1979), compiling a record of 116-15 between 1971 and 1981. As the 1970s progressed, Bryant closed in on the all-time record for coaching victories held by Amos Alonzo Stagg with 314 wins. On November 28, 1981, Bryant passed Stagg's record. The next season, Bryant announced his retirement from coaching, and he won his last game, the Liberty Bowl, in December 1982.

Significance

Earlier in his career, Bear Bryant's reputation was as a demanding taskmaster, even to the point of taking his first Texas A&M squad to a "boot camp" in arid west Texas—where many players quit under brutal conditions. Over the years, Bryant became a venerable and revered figure, pacing the sidelines in his hounds tooth check hat, with his deep, accented voice, a familiar figure on Saturday college football telecasts. Bryant still wielded authority later in his career, however, as he climbed up his coaching tower at Alabama to watch practice carefully and point out mistakes in a booming voice through a megaphone.

Over forty of Bryant's former players became head coaches in either college or professional football. He coached some of the best players of the post-war era, including George Blanda, John David Crow (his only Heisman Trophy winner), Jack Pardee, Lee Roy Jordan, Joe Namath, Ken Stabler, and Ozzie Newsome. In Alabama, Bryant, the Arkansas native, was asked more than once to run for office as governor or a U.S. senator. Quoted as saying that he would die if he were not coaching, Bryant suffered a fatal heart attack thirty-seven days after retiring as coach of the Crimson Tide. His final coaching record was 323-85-17. Bryant's success as a coach could be summed up by a rival, who once said, "Bryant could take his'n and beat your'n and take your'n and beat his'n."

Primary Source

Bear: The Hard Life and Good Times of Alabama's Coach Bryant [excerpt]

SYNOPSIS: Alabama head football coach Paul "Bear" Bryant recalls having Joe Namath on his team, the process of recruiting his first African American player for the Crimson Tide, and how he addressed the issue of integration on his football team in the 1970s.

But I guarantee you I never had a gut check over a boy like I had with Joe Namath. Joe was the best athlete I have ever seen. He is blessed with that rare quickness—hands, feet, everything—and he's quick and tough mentally, too. . . .

. . . Nothing came easier for him than football. He could sit down and listen to some football concept for the first time, and snap, snap, he'd have a mental picture of every phase of it.

I don't classify quarterbacks as players. I think of them as coaches on the field. But Joe had more natural playing ability than anybody. Just gifted. . . .

I hadn't seen him play until he came to us, but when he walked onto that field I knew we had something special. He had that air about him. He could do it all. He could run, he could play defense. Had he chosen, he could have been a great baseball or basketball player, or a golfer. He could pick up a golf club right now and shoot par. Just an extraordinary athlete. . . .

Well, we were coming down to the end of the 1963 season. We had a game with Miami, then Mississippi in the Sugar Bowl, both on national television, and it was right about the time of President Kennedy's assassination. We had taken two weeks off. If it had happened during that period I wouldn't have done anything. We were off and players weren't bound to the training rules.

I got word that Joe and his friends had been down at some woman's store, having a party, breaking training. The woman had told a couple of my coaches about it. This was on Monday, and we were supposed to practice that night. I had planned to fly to Tennessee afterward to see a prospect. . . .

I told him what I had heard, and I said, "Joe, you know I'm going to get the truth, and I don't think you would lie to me."

He admitted it. I didn't know for months that other players were involved. They let him take the rap alone. I told him to go see Coach Bailey, who would give him a place to stay, because I was suspending him from the team.

He said, "How many days?"

I said for the year, or forever, or until he proved something to me.

I said, "I'll help you go somewhere else if you want to, or get in the Canadian league, or if you have enough in you to stay in school and prove to me this was just a bad mistake, I'll let you back on the team next spring."

I went back and called the coaches together and told them my decision and asked if they had an opinion. . . .

Finally I called them back in, and called Joe in, and I said, "Joe, everybody in the room except one pleaded for you.

"But black is black and white's white. I'd give my right arm if I didn't have to do it, but if I didn't I'd ruin you and ruin the team, too, eventually."

I said, "You're suspended, and I don't give a damn what anybody in here says. You're not going to play. The university could change this decision if they wanted to, or I could. But if they change it or I change it I'll resign."

And—I'll never forget it—he said, "Aw, no, Coach, I don't want you to do that." The only thing he asked me to do was to tell his mother before it hit the papers.

I called the squad together and told them. . . .

We lifted Joe's suspension in the spring, and when he came back he just took charge. I could tell he still had misgivings about me, though. Whenever they wanted pictures made he'd kind of shy away. But it didn't affect his play one iota.

We won another National Championship that year, sweeping ten in a row, and of course that was the year Sonny Werblin and Weeb Ewbank came to Miami for our Orange Bowl game with Texas and made Joe a rich man. . . .

They made the announcement right after the Texas game in the Orange Bowl dressing room. Joe would get $40,000 cash, and $400,000 parceled out so the taxes wouldn't kill him, and a couple of automobiles. It was by far the richest contract in pro football history. Knowledgeable people also say it was the deal that made the American Football League.

Well, that was the good part. The bad part was that Texas beat us 21-17. Joe had been hurt earlier in the season against North Carolina State, a knee injury that has plagued him ever since, but he came off the bench and almost pulled it out. We were behind 21-7 at one point. Just before the game ended Joe got us to the Texas goal, and on a fourth-down quarterback keep he came that close to winning it. Tommy Nobis met him head on. Our guys thought he scored. . . .

And I'll never forget the last game of his senior year, in the dressing room after we'd beaten Auburn. We were the only two still in there. And he said something that made me about as proud as I've ever been.

He said, "I want to look you in the eye"—that's one of my pet expressions—"I want to look you right in the eye and tell you you were right, and I want to thank you."

Alabama coach Paul "Bear" Bryant waits for the start of the Sugar Bowl, New Orleans, January 1, 1973. Bryant coached the Crimson Tide from 1958 to 1982, a period in which the Tide won more games than any other team in the nation. AP/WIDE WORLD PHOTOS. REPRODUCED BY PERMISSION.

I wouldn't take a jillion for that. . . .

■ ■ ■

For years, because we didn't have black players or play against teams that had black players, we were criticized around the country for having an "insulated schedule." One that on the surface appeared weaker than others. I would debate that anytime, but there is no need now because the problem has long been solved. . . .

When you've been raised around blacks, and had them as close friends, and even had a few fistfights with them as I did, you sure should have no trouble accepting integration. I don't say I agree with everything Martin Luther King said, but I saw the wisdom in most of it. . . .

We were in a damned-if-you-do, damned-if-you-don't situation. Our SEC opponents were as tough as any in the country, no matter what color the players were, but when we looked around for a team to play outside the conference it had to be from the South. I would have much preferred to play Michi-

gan State or Illinois or somebody, because we'd have beaten them, too, and it would have been easier getting our boys ready to play. Southern Mississippi was as good as Illinois, but our guys wouldn't have gotten excited over the match. And you'd have to give the Southern Mississippi players a saliva test, they'd be so eager to get at us. . . .

So for years I had to hold off trying to recruit blacks. We finally had some in school, and I said if they were eligible they were welcome to try out. There were a few I recommended to other schools, but the time wasn't ripe. I had one high school coach see me about his boy's chances at Alabama, and I said he'd be welcomed and treated fairly, but if it were me I'd send him someplace else, because we were still two or three years away.

I said I wasn't worried a bit about our players, but we had to play two games in Mississippi, and for that and other reasons it might be too tough on the kid. I wanted him to be treated and to act like any other Alabama player. And I damn sure wouldn't stand for him showing up with a bunch of photographers and some big-talking civil rights leader trying to get publicity.

Two or three years later we recruited Wilbur Jackson down in Ozark, Alabama. His daddy was a railroad man, at the same job thirty-five years, and Richard Williamson of our staff went down to offer Wilbur a scholarship. He invited Wilbur up to see the campus, and when he came in I laid it on the line.

I said, "Wilbur, this is all new to me. You got to have problems. Our white ones have 'em. I can't tell you you won't, or what they'll be. But before you go to anybody else with them, you come to me." From that day on I never had to raise my voice at Wilbur. Not in four years. . . .

I really can't tell you how many blacks we have now, but they're my boys and I love every one of them. I've had no problems, and, to my knowledge, neither have they. The great majority have been good players, and the whites on the team have bent over backwards to get them accepted. Which may be a mistake because it's not natural that way. . . .

When USC came in here and beat us so bad in the opening game in 1970, Jerry Claiborne made the remark that their big black fullback, Sam Cunningham, did more for integration in the South in sixty minutes than Martin Luther King did in twenty years. Sam gained about 230 yards and scored three touchdowns that night and like to have killed us all.

I think you have to have good athletes to win, and when the blacks are good they should be playing. I would rather have them for me than against me. If Willie Shelby and Wilbur Jackson and Woodrow Lowe and Mike Washington were playing for somebody else they'd be worrying us to death, and that's just naming four. Or Calvin Culliver. He's going to be an All-America fullback, and I want him on my side. . . .

Do I treat them alike? No. You can't. When I was a young coach I used to say that. "Treat everybody alike." That's bull. Treat everybody *fairly.*

Everybody is different. If you treat them all alike you won't reach them. Be fair with all of them and you have a chance. One you pat on the back and he'll jump out the window for you. Another you kick in the tail. A third you yell at and squeeze a little. But be fair. And that's what I am. . . .

Sylvester Croom was a good center for us last year. His daddy is a preacher, one of the three top black leaders in Tuscaloosa, and a warm personal friend of mine. He's one of my advisers on local affairs, and I go to him when I need answers.

Sylvester made a statement after the season that made me feel we had to be on the right track.

He was quoted as saying, "The blacks on this team love the white guys as much as they do the black guys."

Don't you think that made me proud?

Primary Source

"The Bear's Superstudents: Trials and Triumphs"

In this sidebar article from *Time* magazine, Joe Namath and Ken Stabler discuss what it was like to play quarterback for Paul "Bear" Bryant at the University of Alabama.

Namath: "Never Beaten"

Joe Willie Namath was the starting quarterback for Alabama from 1962 through 1964. In January of 1965 he became the first big bonus baby of the pro football bidding wars when he signed with the New York Jets of the A.F.L. His $420,000 salary and his love of the bright lights brought him fame as Broadway Joe, worker of the miracle victory over the Baltimore Colts in the 1969 Super Bowl. Namath reminisces about Bryant:

I was a late signee. The team was already practicing, and he was up in the tower. He calls me up and points out over the field and is talking to me, but I didn't understand a word he was saying. He's

pointing down at players, saying, "That ole stud." I didn't know what the word meant, but he was trying to relate to a young kid. Stud. That was the only word he said that I understood my first three weeks there.

He was a stern disciplinarian. If you cut classes, for example, you had to take study hall in his office at 4 a.m. You had to be there waiting for him when he got to work. Nobody wanted to do that. He was frightening. He was the boss, the main man, the leader. You looked forward to getting away from him. Every time I got called to the coach's office, it was, "Oh, damn, what did I do? I didn't do anything, did I?" And then he'd just want to say goodbye before I went home for Easter.

Coach Bryant rarely touts his own team. The growth of his players is his main concern. The most important thing, he says, is their convincing themselves that they're getting better. He wanted to show what he expected of us so we'd all be confident in one another. That really helped me in the pros. Understanding people and having them understand him are very important to him. If he doesn't understand something, he asks. He wants everybody to do the same. He teaches an individual to take a certain pride in himself, and that takes discipline.

He taught you the difference between losing and getting beaten. Sometimes you can't do anything about losing. Sometimes the guy on the other side of the line is just better than you. But getting beaten is ugly. It's humiliation. At Alabama, we did lose some. But we never got beaten.

Stabler: "Needed Guidance"

From 1965 to 1967, lefthanded Kenny Stabler quarterbacked the Tide. Picked by the Oakland Raiders in 1968, he was their starting quarterback from 1973 through 1979, leading the team to a Super Bowl title in 1977. Traded to Houston last spring, he now finds himself working under Bum Phillips, a former Bryant assistant. Like Namath, Stabler was once thrown off the 'Bama team and reinstated after serving his penance. Stabler recalls:

I'm not your basic conformist, and he was tough on me for my own good. I don't know where I'd be if it wasn't for Coach Bryant. I needed guidance.

At the end of my junior year, I had a knee injury and had been kept out of spring practice. I got frustrated, started running around and chasing ladies. One thing led to another, and I ended up in Foley, my home town. He sent me a telegram that said: "You have been indefinitely suspended. Signed, Coach Paul W. Bryant."

I enrolled in summer school, and every week I had to report to him. It was one of the hardest things I've ever had to do. I'd go in and see him. He looks like he weighs about 500 lbs. sitting across that desk. He never said anything until the end of the summer. Then he looked at me and said, "You don't deserve to be on this football team." I didn't say anything at first. But I'm kind of stubborn, like him. Finally I said, "Well, I'm coming out there anyway." One of the assistant coaches told me later that that sold him on me. Then I went out and bought a case of beer and drove back to Foley, throwing the empties at every stop sign. I was happy.

I cussed him a thousand times in practice. Not to his face; I'm not crazy. I smoke cigarettes, but never in front of him. Figure that one out. If he ever called me up on a Monday and said he needed help, I'd be on the first plane to Birmingham. Sunday would be tough because I am Houston's quarterback. But you know, I think I'd get on the plane. That would never happen, though, because of the kind of man he is. He wouldn't call me on a Sunday no matter how much he needed me. He'd wait until Monday.

Further Resources

BOOKS

Dunavant, Keith. *Coach: The Life of Paul "Bear" Bryant.* New York: Simon and Schuster, 1996.

Herskowitz, Mickey. *The Legend of Bear Bryant.* New York: McGraw-Hill, 1987.

Peterson, John A., and Bill Cromartie. *Bear Bryant: Countdown to Glory.* New York: Leisure Press, 1983.

PERIODICALS

Underwood, John. "New Tricks For an Old Bear." *Sports Illustrated,* September 11, 1972.

WEBSITES

College Football Hall of Fame. Available online at http://www.collegefootball.org (accessed April 23, 2003).

Paul W. Bryant Museum. Available online at http://www.museums.ua.edu/bryant; website home page: http://www.museums.ua.edu (accessed April 23, 2003).

Billie Jean

Autobiography

By: Billie Jean King, with Kim Chapin

Date: 1974

Source: King, Billie Jean, with Kim Chapin. *Billie Jean.* New York: Harper & Row, 1974, 164, 165, 168, 169, 177–186.

About the Author: Billie Jean King (1943–) was born in Long Beach, California. At seventeen, King won her first tennis title, in doubles, at Wimbledon in 1960. Over the next twenty years, King won nearly every major tennis championship, including twenty titles at Wimbledon, and thirty United States Open titles. A tireless promoter of tennis and outspoken advocate of women's sports, King was the first female to coach male professional athletes in the United States. She has written five books on tennis techniques and two memoirs. ■

Introduction

Prior to the late 1960s, women's tennis received neither the media attention nor anywhere near the prize money of men professionals. As the women's movement impacted much of American society, sports were also affected—and the acknowledged champion of feminism in sport was tennis's Billie Jean King. King was the dominant women's player in the world during the 1960s and 1970s, winning over fifty major championships. As the first president of the Women's Tennis Association (WTA), King played a strong part in improving conditions for female players.

In 1973, fifty-five-year-old former Wimbledon champion Bobby Riggs, a believer in male superiority on the tennis court, challenged the top female players to matches. In May 1973, Riggs defeated Margaret Court of Australia, the second-ranked player in the world, 6-2, 6-1; and after that match Riggs challenged the top player, Billie Jean King. After some reluctance and knowing what pressure would be on her, King accepted Riggs's offer. The two would play a winner-take-all, $100,000 match on September 20, 1973, at the Houston Astrodome. In the weeks leading up to the event, King kept away from the media hype, concentrating on training; meanwhile, the flamboyant Riggs reveled in the glare of publicity, granting interview after interview, trying to convince all comers that he would beat Billie Jean.

On the evening of September 20, 1973, a crowd of 30,472, one of the largest crowds to witness a tennis event, filled the Astrodome—many paying one hundred dollars a ticket. The atmosphere was not that of a genteel tennis match. Broadcasting the event on ABC television was Howard Cosell (then the most famous broadcaster in sports), dressed in tuxedo, but whose credentials to announce tennis seemed dubious at best. When the two competitors came into the arena, the circus atmosphere reached its height. King was carried in a "Cleopatra style" gold litter, held by four muscular track and field athletes from nearby Rice University; while Riggs was wheeled into the stadium on a rickshaw pulled by six female models in tight-fitting red and gold outfits.

Right from the start of the match, King established her dominance. Prevailing in the first set 6-4, King won twenty-six of her thirty-four points on outright winners (Riggs never touching the ball with his racket). King won the first set when Riggs double-faulted. Although Riggs broke King's serve in set two, King came back with a vengeance—eventually winning 6-3. Early in the third set, Riggs, who seemed to sense the difficulty of beating King from the opening game, labored, even waddling across the court to hit the ball. With King leading 4-2 in the third set, Riggs took an injury break for hand cramps, gulping pills and drinking water. Once play resumed, the match was, for all intent and purposes, over. When King won match point, she jumped, threw her racket in the air, and ran to the net to greet the dejected and tired Riggs. The "Battle of the Sexes" was over, King winning in straight sets 6-4, 6-3, 6-3.

Significance

The King-Riggs match was, first of all, an entertainment event, with little to do with tennis other than the game on the court. Curry Kirkpatrick of *Sports Illustrated* wrote that the match had "all the conflicting overtones of a political convention, championship prizefight, rock festival, tent revival, town meeting, Super Bowl, and sick joke." King was awarded a trophy and received a check for the $100,000.

Despite the hype, Billie Jean King did not treat the match against Riggs as a joke. Believing that she had an obligation to women athletes in all sports, King was determined to perform her best. While Riggs again faded into obscurity, remembered for the 1973 match at his death at seventy-seven in 1995, King remained a prominent player and tennis spokeswoman. In 1974 she founded a magazine, *Women Sports,* and remained a competitive player into the 1980s, winning her way to the Wimbledon singles semi-finals in 1982 at age thirty-eight before losing to her longtime rival, Chris Evert. The year after she defeated Riggs, King became player-coach of the Philadelphia Freedoms of World Team Tennis, the first female coach of male professional athletes.

Since her retirement from active competition in the 1980s, King has remained at the forefront of the women's tennis and feminist movement generally, even as many her tennis records have fallen. Billie Jean King, the fireman's kid from the public courts of Long Beach, established her place as one of tennis's greatest players, and the foremost champion of female athletic equality in the late twentieth century.

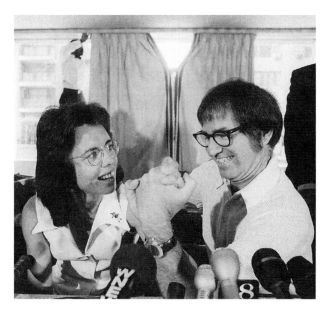

Billie Jean King arm wrestles Bobby Riggs at a press conference, New York, July 12, 1973. The conference was to promote their upcoming tennis match dubbed the "Battle of the Sexes." Riggs boasted that no woman could beat a man, saying, "Women should keep their biscuits in the oven and their buns in bed." © BETTMANN/CORBIS. REPRODUCED BY PERMISSION.

Primary Source

Billie Jean [excerpt]

> **SYNOPSIS:** Billie Jean King, women's tennis player, recounts the preparation, the hype, and the match against Bobby Riggs in the Houston Astrodome, billed as the "Battle of the Sexes."

I've Come a Long Way, Bobby: The Riggs Match

On May 13, 1973—Mother's Day—We just got the last part of a sports report: "Bobby Riggs beat Margaret Court today, 6-2, 6-1." What can I say? I went bananas. None of us could believe it. No way. Right then and there I said, "That's it. I've got to play him." The moment I heard those scores, *6-2, 6-1,* I knew I *had* to play Bobby Riggs. The door had been opened and things were out of my control. It was only a matter of time and place and money.

Until 1971 I'd never met Bobby Riggs or even seen him play, but everybody in tennis knew his record and reputation. Bobby never had a power game, but he was one of the best ball-control artists of all time and won Wimbledon once, in 1939, and Forest Hills twice, 1939 and 1941. He lost a lot of good years to World War II, turned professional, and like all professionals in those days, dropped out of sight. Riggs was a hustler from the beginning. . . .

Riggs's people got in touch with my people again almost immediately after the Court match and in late

June, just before Wimbledon, we signed to play. We announced the match on July 11, and from that moment on, right up until the time we stepped on the court in the middle of the Houston Astrodome on the night of September 20, life was one big circus. . . .

I'd begun preparing for Riggs seriously the day after I lost that TV match to Evert. At Hilton Head I got into a routine I always try to use when I'm playing night tennis. I forced myself to stay up late and sleep in until ten or eleven in the morning so that when the match came around my body would really be used to that time schedule, to having its high point from seven to ten o'clock at night, when I really feel the best. It seems like a small thing, but when I want to get psyched up I spend a lot of time on the details, to make sure everything's perfect.

I did a lot of lifting weights for my legs and knees. I did a lot of that and it really helped. My legs were so strong the night of the match I couldn't believe it. I took good care of myself and got a lot of rest. And I got my head together. . . .

That was going to be my alternate strategy—the base-line game. I wanted to be able to mix it up— go in some, stay back a little—but what I wanted to do especially at the start was to go in and put away some volleys because I thought that would break Bobby down faster psychologically. I practiced a lot of volleying and a lot of lateral movement and up-and-back movement. I felt pretty sure he didn't realize how quick I was or how good a volley I had. He knew, of course, I had a good volley—for a girl. But I thought my volley was strong in anybody's department, men's or women's, and I was counting on him underestimating me in that respect. . . .

I didn't practice my service very much because I'd already decided I wouldn't serve very hard to him. He's at his best when he can counterpunch against his opponent's power, and so I'd decided not to give him any power at all. I did practice changing my service all the time, going from a hard, flat serve to a slice serve to a topspin to a twist. . . .

Finally, I worked on keeping my shots to his backhand side—his weak side—then hitting very sharply to his forehand. Again, the idea was to confuse him, run him around the court, keep him from getting control. . . .

The days went quickly, and then it was Thursday. . . .

About four in the afternoon, I went over to the Astrodome with Dick and Marilyn. It was only the second time I'd actually been on the field, and it's really important for me to get the feel of a place, the atmosphere—like I do at Wimbledon every year—by just walking around and absorbing the sense of where I am. . . .

After I finished hitting, I had a shower and changed clothes, then had a real training-table prematch meal of Gatorade and candy. By then the people were starting to come in, the band was playing, the lights were turned on bright for the television cameras—and the pressure of the whole thing finally got to me. It hit me in a very strange way. I had my usual pre-match tension, of course, but, beyond that, in the hour or so before the match I felt more utterly alone than I ever had in my life. I just got totally wrapped up in my own thoughts. I remembered all the hassles and the headaches of the early years of the Slims tour, and I thought about how far we'd come in such a short time. It really came home to me—hard—that if I lost to Riggs much of what we'd won for ourselves might go right out the window. I'd sensed it before, but now I knew this match was one of the big three in my life—the others were against Maria Bueno in the 1966 Wimbledon finals and against Chris Evert at Forest Hills in 1971—in each case where a defeat would just about erase everything that I'd done before. Everybody else in Houston was having a ball, but that hour before Bobby and I actually stepped on the court was probably the most agonizing one of my life. . . .

Then the extravaganza began. Bobby was wheeled out in that ridiculous rickshaw, and I was carried onto the court in one of those throne-like litters, a little item I'd checked out carefully beforehand. I'm terrified of heights, and wobbling around four feet off the ground is just about my limit. Then Bobby presented me with a gigantic Sugar Daddy— about the size of a tennis racket—and I reciprocated by giving him Larimore Hustle, a little Male Chauvinist Piglet brought in for the occasion. (Bobby's middle name is Larimore.) . . .

When we walked on the court to warm up, I couldn't believe the crowd. The Astrodome wasn't sold out, but I'll guarantee you nobody else could have gotten in and had a good seat for a tennis match. Now it really was like a circus, or a baseball game, or maybe even a heavyweight title fight. Balloons, bands, noise, the works. People were shouting, "Right on, Billie Jean," or, "Go, Bobby," from the moment we entered and even well into the match. I loved it. Just the way a tennis crowd ought to be, everywhere. No indifference. I doubt if there was a neutral person in the whole Astrodome.

But once the match started, everything was straight. No gamesmanship, no hustle, no nothing except tennis. At the rules meeting the day before, when we'd decided on things like the special ten-minute injury time out, I'd been emphatic about that. I told Bobby, "I don't care what you do before we walk on the court, but once that match starts you don't walk over to my table, you don't talk to me, you don't touch me. . . ."

I didn't want there to be any doubts at all about the match. It had to be on the level, and it was. When we were warming up, he called me over for a chat and I waved him away. I knew that if the match started turning in my favor he'd try anything, and I wanted to shut him off before he could begin.

Just before the match began I told myself, "Okay, this is it. Take each point by itself and don't rush things." Geez, just thinking of that moment months later I still get nervous and start to sweat.

I served first and won the first game of the match, and I knew right away this wasn't going to be a repeat of the Margaret Court thing. I also couldn't believe how slow he was. I thought he was faking it. He had to be. At the change after the first game I asked Dennis, "He's putting me on, right?"

Dennis assured me I was seeing the real thing, but I think Riggs did coast the first three or four games, though, trying to figure me out and at the same time not give away all of his wonderful secrets.

He broke my service in the fifth game when I missed a backhand volley by two inches, and took a 3-2 lead. I thought the next game was the most crucial of the match. If he held he'd be up 4-2 and I'd have to win three of the next four games to get back even and deuce the set at 5-all. If I broke back right away it would help my confidence and also let him know he was in for a real fight. Up to that point I'd been trying to make my shots too good, but I realized I just didn't have to go for the lines every time. He was slow, he couldn't hit with a lot of pace, and I could take the net any time I wanted. I just didn't need to make that good a shot. And so I calmed down, broke his service immediately to even the first set at 3-3—and then really got into it.

I was kind of shocked because I thought he would be a lot better than he was. He didn't have a big service, and his spins—"The ones that always get the girls"—weren't that great either. And I was absolutely right about him not realizing how quick I was at the net or how well I could volley. Five of the first six times he tried to pass me off his backhand side I

Billie Jean King reaches for a low volley in her "Battle of the Sexes" winner-take-all match against Bobby Riggs, Houston, Texas, September 20, 1973. King won the match in straight sets. © **BETTMANN/CORBIS. REPRODUCED BY PERMISSION.**

just ran the ball down and—bam—volleyed away a winner. Near the end of the first set there was a great point where he hit wide and deep to my forehand, then wide and deep to my backhand. I ran 'em both down, and on the second shot I flopped up a baseline lob and got right back into the point. He didn't believe I could run down those kinds of shots.

I concentrated hard on winning that first set and when I did—on a double fault by Bobby—I knew he was in big trouble. That meant he'd have to play at least four tough sets to win the match, probably more hard competitive tennis than he'd played in years. I felt I was in pretty good shape, and that things were going my way. . . .

About midway through the second set, I knew that the match was mine if I could just keep up the pace. But I didn't let up because I'd gotten into trouble too many times before thinking I had a match won before it was over.

Everything that I thought would work before the match did work. I played conservatively those last two sets and always waited for the right shot before I came in. I thought he'd be running everything down and keep throwing up lobs the whole time, but he just didn't do it. His backhand never got any better, I missed just one overhead the entire three sets, and at the end I was playing with complete confidence.

On match point I threw my racket in the air and just when I looked down I saw him finish his jump over the net. He came over to congratulate me, and then he was really nice. He said, "You're too good," and that was it.

Up to that point I'd really had mixed feelings about Riggs. I always liked him personally but I had also resented a lot of the statements he had made, if only in jest, before the match. When it was over, though, I kind of felt sorry for him, and I put my arm around him. . . .

As far as the importance of the match, it proved just two things. First, that a woman *can* beat a man. Second, that tennis can be a big-time sport, and will, once it gets into the hands of the people who know how to promote it.

My personal opinion of Riggs? Well—now, after the match, I feel he's a very nice guy, actually a kind person who loves the spotlight and loves to hustle. And I wish him well. There was some talk of a rematch, but I can say without any hesitation that I'll never play him again. It was a one-shot deal and I think I proved my point.

6-4, 6-3, 6-3.

Further Resources

BOOKS
King, Billie Jean, with Frank Deford. *Billie Jean.* New York: Viking, 1982.

PERIODICALS
Amdur, Neil. "Mrs. King Defeats Riggs, 6-4, 6-3, 6-3, Amid Circus Atmosphere." *The New York Times,* September 21, 1973.

Kirkpatrick, Curry. "There She Is, Ms. America." *Sports Illustrated,* October 1, 1973.

WEBSITES
"Billy Jean King." ITA Women's Tennis Hall of Fame. Available online at http://www.wm.edu/tenniscenter/king.html; website home page: http://www.wm.edu/tenniscenter (accessed April 24, 2003).

Collins, Bud. "Billy Jean King." International Tennis Hall of Fame. Available online at http://www.tennisfame.com/enshrinees/billiejean_king.html; website home page: http://www.tennisfame.com (accessed April 24, 2003).

———. "Bobby Riggs" International Tennis Hall of Fame. Available online at http://www.tennisfame.com/enshrinees/bobby_riggs.html; website home page: http://www.tennisfame.com (accessed April 24, 2003).

Arthur Ashe and Jimmy Connors

"Catching Connors in the Stretch"
Magazine article

By: Arthur Ashe
Date: 1975
Source: Ashe, Arthur. "Catching Connors in the Stretch." *Sports Illustrated,* July 21, 1975, 20–21.
About the Author: Arthur Ashe (1943–1993) was born in Richmond, Virginia. Ashe graduated from UCLA and won the U.S. Open as an amateur in 1968. Turning professional in 1969, Ashe won fifty-one tournaments, including the 1970 Australian Open and Wimbledon in 1975. Ashe also played for and captained the U.S. Davis Cup team. Retiring from competition after a 1979 heart attack, Ashe contracted AIDS from a blood transfusion in 1983. In his last years, Ashe was a human rights activist and author.

"Tennis in Cold Blood"
Newspaper article

By: Dave Anderson
Date: July 6, 1975
Source: Anderson, Dave. "Tennis in Cold Blood." *The New York Times,* July 6, 1975.
About the Author: Dave Anderson (1929–) was born in Troy, New York. After graduating from Holy Cross in 1951, Anderson wrote sports for the *Brooklyn Eagle* until 1955, then for the *New York Journal-American* until 1966, when he joined *The New York Times,* becoming a columnist in 1971. Author of twenty-one books and dozens of magazine articles, Anderson won the Pulitzer Prize in 1981. ■

Introduction

The emergence of professional men's tennis as a big money sport in the late 1960s and early 1970s saw the decline of the gentleman player who exhibited class and self-control on the court, and the rise of younger, brash and often boorish competitors. Arthur Ashe, the greatest African American tennis player, typified the former, while Jimmy Connors, and then in his early twenties, represented the latter. Ashe had grown up in segregated Virginia, been a collegiate champion at UCLA, and won the U.S. Open as an amateur. After turning professional, he was a leader on the men's tour. Connors, a tennis prodigy, was coached by his mother and Pancho Segura, was also a college champion at UCLA, and turned professional at age twenty, having an immediate impact on the sport. In 1974, Connors won three of tennis's four Grand Slam events: the Australian Open, Wimbledon, and the U.S. Open. He was denied entry in the French Open because of a contract dispute, thus preventing a chance for Connors to win the Grand Slam.

Ashe and Connors were not friends, and the clash of personalities reached a breaking point in the weeks before Wimbledon in 1975. Ashe criticized Connors for refusing to play Davis Cup. Connors, who filed suit against the Association of Tennis Professionals (ATP) (Ashe was president), sued Ashe personally for five million dollars in a libel action over the Davis Cup remarks. As the tournament began, Connors, ranked number one in the world, was expected to coast to a repeat victory. At thirty-two, time was running out for Ashe to win Wimbledon. With little surprise, Connors advanced to the men's singles final, where, in somewhat of a surprise, he would face Ashe.

The Wimbledon final was played July 5, 1975. Cocky and confident at the start, Connors won the first game. But in the next twenty minutes, Ashe buried him with six straight game wins—without losing a break point—and emerged victorious in the first set 6-1. In the second set, Ashe moved out to a 3-0 lead, his demeanor calm. Connors, frustrated, heard a voice from the crowd yell, "come on Connors!" to which he replied, "I'm trying to for crissakes." After Connors won a game, Ashe continued his domination, winning the second set, also 6-1.

Ashe's tactics were, in his words later, to "throw junk" at Connors, not to try to overpower him—together with solid serving and confident volleying at the net. In the third set, Connors, on the ropes, fought back—staving off two break points and winning 7-5; afterward, he pumped his fist in the air. In the fourth set, Connors started fast, taking the lead 3-0, but Ashe fought back to tie the set, then went ahead. In the final game, with Ashe at first down 15-40, he forced Connors to backhand a volley wide, then served an ace, hit another winner, and finally hit another smash serve that Connors returned feebly into the net for the match.

Significance

Ashe had done it—having never beaten Connors before—the older player had won, at thirty-two, at Wimbledon, the world's most prestigious tennis tournament. In victory, Ashe uncharacteristically raised a fist into the air, went to the net, and looked at Connors directly while the defeated ex-champion (eyes averted from Ashe) shook hands with the winner. Ashe had become the first

African American male to win at Wimbledon (Althea Gibson had won women's titles in 1957 and 1958).

The Wimbledon victory was the zenith of Ashe's career. He continued to be a competitive player until his 1979 heart attack. He continued as a tennis official, captaining Davis Cup from 1981 to 1985, locking horns with another brash, talented tennis professional: John McEnroe. Connors would remain among tennis's elite players in the late 1970s and early 1980s, winning the U.S. Open four times. The one-time "bad boy " of tennis matured, became a crowd favorite, and reached the semi-finals of the U.S. Open at thirty-eight to the delight of his fans.

Unbeknownst to the public, Ashe contracted HIV in 1983 from a blood transfusion when undergoing another heart operation, and he nearly died in 1988. In 1992, Ashe was publicly forced to admit his having AIDS, bringing an outpouring of support. His death in 1993 created an even greater expression of world-wide grief, as Ashe was remembered for his grace and skill on the tennis court, his ardent human rights activism, and most of all, courage in fighting and facing his final illness.

Primary Source

"Catching Connors in the Stretch" [excerpt]

SYNOPSIS: In an article for *Sports Illustrated*, Arthur Ashe gives a first-person account of his upset victory at Wimbledon over Jimmy Connors, the defending champion and the world's top player in 1974.

Understand at the outset that it was not foremost a matter of beating Jimmy Connors. The primary thing is that I won Wimbledon. I beat Jimmy Connors and I beat Tony Roche, Bjorn Borg, Graham Stilwell, Brian Gottfried, Jan Kamiwazumi and Bob Hewitt. There were 128 guys at the start and one all alone at the end. They can give away a billion dollars in one of those "Challenge Matches," and it will never measure up to the value of a great tournament, especially Wimbledon. Winning the big ones is the only way you move up the rungs. . . .

I believed that I would win. I don't mean that I thought I would win. I *understood* that I would win. I was an 11-2 underdog, but by my logic I should have been the favorite. I first got the feeling that I was destined to take the title the week before when I was playing Gottfried. I was very scared of that match, but when we got in there, Brian couldn't do anything right and I couldn't do anything wrong. The draw was opening up just right for me, my schedule was good, they gave me good courts and everything was falling into place. We have an expression among

Arthur Ashe and Jimmy Connors shake hands, Wimbledon, England, July 5, 1975. Ashe defeated fellow American Connors for the men's singles title, 6-1, 6-1, 5-7, 6-4. © BETTMANN/CORBIS. REPRODUCED BY PERMISSION.

the players: "going through the zone." It comes from the old *Twilight Zone* TV show and, roughly translated, it means playing out of sight, out of this world. The trouble is, most times when you go through the zone it is in Fort Worth or Bologna, and who knows? It suddenly occurred to me that I had picked the Wimbledon weeks to go through the zone.

I was totally relaxed in the finals, never nervous for a moment. Of course, I am known for wearing a mask on the court, a poker face, but those who know me well have told me they could discern something beyond the usual unemotional coolness. They saw a serenity, a peace—and that is exactly the way it was out there.

When Connors broke me twice to win the third set and when he kept winging in the fourth, playing like a demon, do you know what went through my mind? It was a detached observation that it was about time he got hot. It was almost comforting because it violated my sense of the normal that I could beat him easily in three sets. So it was no problem to come on again.

Part of my confidence was that, strategically, I knew very well how to go about beating Connors. And the few heretics in tennis who agreed with me

all arrived independently at the same conclusions. One of these was Dennis Ralston. And what a wonderful "just desert" this is: Jimmy Connors would not play for the U.S. Davis Cup team with Ralston as captain. Dennis made two calls from California instructing me on how to beat Connors. As we tried to tell Jimmy, Dennis Ralston is a very good captain.

All of us agreed that I must not slug with Connors. That's what Roscoe Tanner did in the semis, and he turned Connors into a riptide. Roscoe had beaten Connors a couple weeks before, at Nottingham, by outhitting Jimmy, so he tried the same game at Wimbledon. But Connors was just getting used to the grass at Nottingham. Besides, they use a Dunlop ball there and a Slazenger at Wimbledon. The Dunlop is much heavier while the Slazenger will sail. So, if you hit Slazenger bullets at Connors he'll spit them back at you. Everybody always makes a big fuss about the different court surfaces in tennis, but the balls can be just as different, the adapting just as crucial.

Nonetheless, as good as Connors' ground strokes are—and this is a guy who routed Ken Rosewall from the baseline—he is better at returning serve than during the rest of the point. Remember, in their "Challenge," Connors pinned Newcombe to the baseline with his return of serve, and I thought that impossible. The oldtimers tell me that Don Budge could do that to the best people with his backhand, but Jimmy can do it from both sides. I got cocky at one point in the third set when I was rolling and up 40-15, and slugged a cannonball with all my might, perfectly, just in the corner. I never even saw it come back past me. So, you must sacrifice power in order to get a high percentage of first serves in. Don't give Connors a chance on your second serve. Moreover, as Ralston suggested, I sliced him wide to his two-handed backhand in the deuce court. . . .

. . . I lobbed better against Connors than I ever have in my life. As I say, I was in the zone.

And in a curious way Connors improved the weakest part of my game, which is my forehand volley. It tends to get wobbly when I try to do things with it, but Jimmy hits the ball so hard that all you have to do is hold your racket out there and bounce his shot back.

So that is how you beat Jimmy Connors. And, of course, it also helped that he choked. Everybody blanches at that word, but choking is really an everyday thing. I choke sometimes. We all choke. Jimmy just picked the finals of Wimbledon to choke. In the beginning of the match, when things were on the line, he kept hitting balls into the net. If you're making mistakes by swinging away and hitting long, that's one thing, but when a slugger like Connors is hitting Slazengers way short into the net, that tells you something else. When he was far behind, the pressure lifted (it's always easier to serve at love—40 than at 30-40); that's when he got loose and played well. Then, as soon as he started to get back in the match, he began hitting short again.

It had been my plan to get ahead at all costs. I practiced later than usual before the match, and then took a brisk massage, so that I was actually sweating when I took the court. I'd never been ahead of Jimmy before, and while we know that he can lay it on, play his very best from in front, we don't know much about how he reacts when he's behind. . . .

Before our match, in the little waiting room off Centre Court, Jimmy and I chatted alone for a minute or two. Small talk between pals. He sued me for $5 million a few weeks ago. Last year at Wimbledon he sued my friends Donald Dell and Jack Kramer, who are, like myself, officials of the Association of Tennis Professionals.

Despite the fact that he keeps suing people, I still rather like the kid. . . .

It seems to me that his manager, Bill Riordan, is the guy pulling the strings. But Riordan is also—let us face it—the man who has made Jimmy Connors a million dollars. In many professional respects Riordan has handled Connors beautifully, for example, letting him play only with the stacked deck on his own tour while the other good players beat each other's brains out in World Championship Tennis. You can't get beat if you don't put yourself on the line, and Riordan doesn't let Connors regularly expose himself. But at big tournaments Jimmy is primed and eager. Jack Kramer, hardly a Riordan supporter, is always telling us, "You guys play too much." He is right.

But Connors has paid a dear price for letting Bill Riordan maneuver him. In effect Connors has traded in his soul. He is nearly friendless among the players. He offends the public with vulgarity and foul language. His admirers compare him to Muhammad Ali, but Ali was never so insensitive—or so short-sighted—as to insult the paying public. Somehow I feel that Jimmy set out to fill some role that had been created for him, but that along the way he forgot where the acting took over from reality. He has fulfilled the image and made a villain of himself, and that is a sad thing for a 22-year-old boy to be. Worse, he seems to revel in it.

I've given up trying to get him to join the ATP. I only hope now that he and Riordan and Jimmy's mother will stop refusing to play for Davis Cup captains and will play for the country. I think that one move would do wonders in restoring some popularity to Connors, and I believe it would be a good experience for him as well. *Then* maybe he could play another "Challenge Match" for CBS.

It's funny how these things tend to work out. All of a sudden, the guy Jimmy Connors is suing is the only opponent he's got.

Primary Source

"Tennis in Cold Blood" [excerpt]

SYNOPSIS: Dave Anderson of *The New York Times* describes Ashe's victory over Connors at Wimbledon and its significance.

Wimbledon, England, July 5—Everything here is proper, if not genteel. At the nearby Southfields stop on the London underground, the sign reminds, "Alight Here for Wimbledon." Roses bloom on the balconies of mod apartments and in the gardens of old gingerbread homes along the narrow leafy streets. Among the flowers outside the historic center-court enclosure are porticos where strawberries and ream, champagne and bonbons are sold. Wimbledon is tennis. And tennis propriety. Not even Alfred Hitchcock would use Wimbledon as the backdrop for a murder. Unthinkable. But today Arthur Ashe stabbed Jimmy Connors in four sets and in cold blood for the men's singles championship. The traditionalists cheered.

Seldom, if ever, has there been a tennis match with such silent passion. Two weeks ago Connors announced a $5-million libel suit against Ashe for having criticized Connors's refusal to join the United States Davis Cup team. Connors previously had filed three other suits for a total of $20 million against the Association of Tennis Professionals, of which Ashe is the president.

Throughout the tournament, as Ashe advanced inexorably on a collision course with Connors, who won the title last year, each publicly minimized the significance of the lawsuits. Neither was thinking about it. Or so they said. But if that were true, they were the only ones who weren't. And when they walked onto the grass court that is more brown than green, Arthur Ashe was wearing a blue warm-up jacket with "USA" in red on the chest. Just in case Jimmy Connors had forgotten about the Davis Cup controversy.

Connors, in contrast, wore a green, red and white sweater designed by Sergio Tacchini, once a leading Italian player.

The Contrasts

The other contrasts were obvious. Arthur Ashe—cool, 32 years old next week, with a reputation of never having fulfilled his potential because of his laconic style, Jimmy Connors—fiery, only 22 years old, with a reputation as a spoiled brat and a cinch for the undisputed world's No. 1 ranking. In the William Hill betting tent next to the champagne bar, Connors was a 3-to-20 favorite, Ashe a 23-to-5 underdog. Connors was a 9-to-10 choice to win in straight sets; Ashe was 40 to 1 to win in straight sets, 16 to 1 to win in four sets. . . .

Almost immediately, the third game of the first set, Ashe broke Connors's serve on the discreet jurisprudence of George Armstrong, the umpire. Connors's shot clearly floated beyond the baseline, but the linesman indicated the ball was good. Ashe stared as the 14,000 devotees groaned in disbelief. Armstrong turned to the linesman. Moments later

Armstrong announced, "The linesman has deferred his call, the ball was out, game to Ashe," and across the net Connors reacted typically. He thrust a finger toward the gray sky.

Ashe whipped through the first set 6-1, and took a 3-0 lead in the second set.

Moments later, as Connors failed to chase down an angled cross-court volley, a voice from underneath the black tar roof of the green wooden stadium broke the silence.

"C'mon, Connors," the voice yelled loudly.

"I'm trying, for crissake," he replied.

Connors indeed was trying. With each serve, he was grunting like Joe Frazier throwing a left hook. And after losing nine consecutive games, he finally held his serve in that fourth game. But that would be his only winning game in the 6-1 second set. He hadn't lost a set in his six previous matches and now he had lost two sets. He was grunting and hunching his shoulders and shaking his hair and slapping himself on the right thigh. And in the third set, he broke Ashe's serve in the final game to win, 7-5.

Connors even took a 3-0 lead in the fourth set, but Ashe, performing with a poised purpose, lost only one more game for the 6-4 set that completed his emotional triumph.

On winning, Ashe turned to where Dell and his other friends were sitting and held up a clenched fist. He and Connors quickly shook hands at the net but then they avoided each other during the presentation ceremony.

"He didn't say anything," Ashe was saying now, "and I didn't say anything."

As outwardly cool as ever, Ashe was wearing his blue jacket with "USA" on it in the interview room. When he was asked if this was his most memorable triumph, he shook his head.

"No, winning the Davis Cup in '68 would be first," he said. "And winning Forest Hills in '68 was second until this one."

Every so often, Ashe would stab Connors subtly. It was as if he were using an icicle so that no murder weapon would exist, such as when he was asked if he was surprised at his easy victory.

"If you're a good player," he said softly, "and you find yourself winning easily, you're not surprised."

When he was asked about Connors's performance, Ashe mentioned how the dethroned champion had put about 70 per cent of his errors "into the middle of the net, he hardly ever put the ball beyond the baseline—that's a sign of choking." But he remained in character, taking his triumph with the ultimate in cool.

"Are you happy, Arthur?" wondered Dell with a smile.

"Yeah," said the first black man to win Wimbledon.

Moments later, after Ashe had departed, Connors appeared in his Italian sweater. He was polite, saying that he had lost to a "better Arthur Ashe," but he also stayed in character, making it clear that he felt he was still the superior player.

"Any guy has to play out of his mind to beat me," Connors said. "I'm not going to lose the match. Got to beat me. And he beat me today." He paused. "Today."

Asked about Ashe's reference to his choking, Connors snapped, "I don't choke, my friend, I've been playing too long to choke." He talked about his independence in the Davis Cup and the A.T.P. situation, recalling how when he was growing up, "I listened to my parents but if I didn't agree, I wouldn't do it." And then he was asked jokingly if he were going to the Wimbledon Ball tonight.

"If I can have the first dance."

"With Arthur?" somebody suggested.

Jimmy Connors scowled. But somewhere Arthur Ashe was smiling. In cold blood.

Further Resources

BOOKS

Ashe, Arthur. *Days of Grace: A Memoir.* New York: Knopf, 1993.

———. *Off the Court.* New York: New American Library, 1981.

PERIODICALS

Tupper, Fred. "Ashe Tops Connors for Crown at Wimbledon." *The New York Times,* July 6, 1975.

WEBSITES

Collins, Bud. "Arthur Ashe." International Tennis Hall of Fame. Available online at http://www.tennisfame.com/enshrinees /arthur_ashe.html; website home page: http://www.tennis fame.com (accessed April 24, 2003).

Larry Bird and Earvin "Magic" Johnson

Drive: The Story of My Life
Autobiography

By: Larry Bird, with Bob Ryan

Date: 1989

Source: Bird, Larry, with Bob Ryan. *Drive: The Story of My Life.* New York: Doubleday, 1989, 56–58.

About the Author: Larry Bird (1956–) was born in West Baden, Indiana. After briefly attending Indiana University, Bird transferred to Indiana State University, where he was a two-time All-American basketball player. After leading Indiana State to the NCAA championship game in 1979, Bird signed with the Boston Celtics of the NBA, who selected him in a supplemental draft a year earlier. In his thirteen-season career (1979–1992) with the Celtics, Bird lead Boston to three NBA championships, won three Most Valuable Player awards, and scored 21,791 career points. After retirement, Bird coached the Indiana Pacers for three seasons. Bird was enshrined in Basketball's Hall of Fame in 1998.

My Life
Autobiography

By: Earvin "Magic" Johnson, with William Novak

Date: 1992

Source: Johnson, Earvin, with William Novak. *My Life.* New York: Random House, 1992, 81–84.

About the Author: Earvin "Magic" Johnson (1959–) was born in Lansing, Michigan. After starring at Michigan State, where he led the team to the 1979 NCAA championship, Johnson was drafted by the Los Angeles Lakers. In his thirteen-season career (1979–1991, 1995–1996) with the Lakers, Johnson led Los Angeles to five NBA championships and won three Most Valuable Player awards. He also holds the league's career record for assists. In retirement, Johnson is a vice president of the Lakers, and a businessman. Johnson was enshrined in Basketball's Hall of Fame in 2002. Larry Bird, his longtime rival, introduced him.

"Johnson: Magical by Nature"
Newspaper article

By: Malcolm Moran

Date: March 26, 1979

Source: Moran, Malcolm. "Johnson: Magical by Nature." *The New York Times,* March 26, 1979.

"Herb Shriner With a Jumper"
Newspaper article

By: Dave Anderson

Date: March 26, 1979

Source: Anderson, Dave. "Herb Shriner With a Jumper." *The New York Times,* March 26, 1979.

About the Author: Dave Anderson (1929–) was born in Troy, New York. After graduating from Holy Cross in 1951, Anderson was a sports reporter for various newspapers until he joined *The New York Times,* where he became a columnist in 1971. Author of twenty-one books and dozens of magazine articles, Anderson won the Pulitzer Prize in 1981. ■

Introduction

Prior to 1979, basketball's greatest individual rivalry took place during the 1960s between NBA star centers Wilt Chamberlain and Bill Russell. They never, however, played against each other in college. The 1979 NCAA championship game saw the beginning of another individual basketball rivalry for all-time—between Larry Bird of Indiana State and the Boston Celtics, and Earvin "Magic" Johnson of Michigan State and the Los Angeles Lakers.

Bird and Johnson grew up several hundred miles apart; Bird in French Lick, Indiana, and Johnson in Lansing, Michigan. After spending only a month at Indiana University, transferring and then working for the town of French Lick, Bird entered Indiana State University. At ISU, Bird led his team to the National Invitational Tournament (NIT) as a junior, and he averaged nearly thirty points a game his first two seasons. Johnson led his high school team to the state championship, and then attended Michigan State University—leading the Spartans to the NCAA regional finals as a freshman before losing to undefeated and eventual champion University of Kentucky. In the 1979 NCAA Tournament, Bird's Indiana State team continued its undefeated season into the Final Four, then the championship game with a close victory over DePaul, giving ISU a 33-0 record. Johnson and Michigan State won the Big Ten conference after an early season funk, and had an easier time getting to the title game with a thirty-four-point victory over Pennsylvania.

As the championship game on March 26, 1979, in Salt Lake City shaped up, Michigan State, with Johnson and talented teammates Greg Kelser and Jay Vincent, looked stronger on paper than Indiana State, which, despite its undefeated record, was primarily a one-man team in Bird. From the opening tip-off, Michigan State blanketed Bird defensively, forcing him to take bad shots or pass off to teammates. Bird only connected on four of eleven first half shots. But the close guarding of Bird by the Spartans caused foul trouble for several Michigan State players, including Johnson, who was forced to sit during part of the first half with three personals. At halftime, Bird and Indiana State trailed 37-28.

In the second half, Bird missed his first two shots, and Michigan State quickly took advantage, jumping to a 44-28 lead—a deficit which already seemed too great for Indiana State. Johnson, who played with three fouls throughout the second half, was scoring, passing the ball off to teammates, and lending his infectious enthusiasm to the Michigan State effort. A big reason for Indiana State's failure to rally was their foul shooting, as the Sycamores were only ten of twenty-two from the free throw line. By midway in the second half, the game's result seemed in little doubt. Michigan State had been ahead since taking a 9-8 lead early in the game. From there, Michigan State coasted to an easy 75-64 victory for the NCAA championship.

Significance

Johnson led Michigan State with twenty-four points, while Bird was held to nineteen points, hitting only seven of twenty-one shots from the floor. Bird was named the College Player of the Year, averaging thirty points and seventeen rebounds per game; Johnson was also a first-team All-American selection. Both men were assured wealthy futures in the NBA. The entrance of Bird and Johnson into the NBA would revitalize a league that had lost some of its luster since the days of Chamberlain and Russell. Although drafted by the Boston Celtics in 1978, Bird chose to play his senior season before becoming a professional. Bird led Boston to the playoffs his first season, and the NBA title the next. Johnson, meanwhile, decided to leave college after his sophomore season, and was drafted by the Los Angeles Lakers. He made an immediate impact, as "Magic" led the team to the NBA championship in his rookie year.

Bird and Johnson would face off against one another in the NBA finals several times. In 1984, the Celtics defeated the Lakers, as Bird won playoff MVP. The next season, the Lakers and Johnson got revenge; the two met again in 1987, with Magic and Los Angeles again victorious. In 1992, the long-time rivals were finally teammates in the twilight of their careers, as Bird and Johnson played for the United States on the Olympic "Dream Team," the first time professionals were permitted to play Olympic basketball.

Over the years, both men became not only intense rivals with great respect for each other's abilities on the basketball court, but friends away from the game. They provided an interesting contrast, the outgoing Johnson and the reserved Bird. When Johnson revealed that he had the HIV virus, one of the first people he spoke to was Bird, and both players attended the other one's retirement ceremony. Larry Bird and Earvin Johnson's mutual respect for their abilities as basketball players, and their friendship is unique in sports—all of which began at the 1979 NCAA basketball championship.

Primary Source

Drive: The Story of My Life [excerpt]

SYNOPSIS: Indiana State University and later Boston Celtics star basketball player Larry Bird recalls his first meeting against Earvin "Magic" Johnson in the 1979 NCAA championship.

So now it was Michigan State and Magic Johnson against Indiana State and Larry Bird for the national championship.

The press attention was enormous. The idea of the two of us playing for the NCAA title had captured everyone's imagination. I was pretty excited because I was looking forward to playing against Magic myself.

We had played together on that All-Star team coached by Joe B. Hall and one thing we had agreed on right away was that we both should have been playing. In practice, we had played together on a second unit that was beating the first team. I loved playing on the court with Magic.

Coach Hall got mad at us one day. We were playing our game when he said, "How can we work on this stuff if you guys are throwing these crazy passes and taking these stupid shots?" We said, "Coach, those shots are going *in.*" I couldn't understand it. He was getting angry with *us* because we were embarrassing his first team.

Before our senior year, I watched Michigan State play against the Russians on TV. The Russians had beaten Kentucky, Indiana and Notre Dame. We only beat them by four or five. I'm always curious about anything connected with the Soviet Union and I was interested to see if Michigan State had improved. Well, Magic's team beat them.

Magic was just killing them with his rebounding and his coast-to-coast stuff. I said, "Right there, boys, you are looking at the team that's going to win the NCAA championship this year. Boy, they're good."

The buildup for the game was crazy. The semifinals were on Saturday afternoon and the championship game was on Monday night, so there were two full days for the press and the fans to get ready.

You couldn't concentrate because there were just too many people milling around. You'd go to practice and everybody would be at practice. You'd go to the hotel and they'd be at the hotel. Security was nonexistent. We went there hoping to have a good time and to win. It was impossible to have a good time. We would have been much better off it

we had gotten away from the center of everything. We went about it the wrong way.

We thought it was just another game and that we would win. Everything had gone our way all year. We won every close game. We really didn't fear Michigan State. We were actually *too* cocky.

We didn't go in with a good game plan. First, we were going to put Carl Nicks, who was about six-two, on Magic, who was six-nine. At the last minute, we changed to Miley. It didn't make much difference because we didn't have *anybody* who could handle him. Magic was just too good on the break.

We thought we had proved that we could beat every kind of defense, but we had never seen anything like that zone of theirs. I couldn't do anything at all against it. I couldn't get the ball and make moves anywhere on the floor. They did a really good job on me.

In addition to all this, we weren't making our free throws. I went five for eight. We could have been right there at the end if we had made some foul shots, but we didn't do that either.

They just had too much firepower for us. We played a bad game, but they were better. I think if we played them ten times, we might have beaten them twice.

People always want to know if I was having problems with my thumb that day. I can honestly say I wasn't. I can't use that excuse. It was a little tender and sore, but when you're playing in a championship game the pain just goes away—unless you jam it or something.

When the game was over, I couldn't believe it. Not that we had lost—I could see who had the better team—but because it was all over. It took me a while to realize that was the last game I would ever play with this team. I said, "I can't believe it. All I've gone through the last five years . . . this has been the greatest time of my life and now it's over."

We were very proud of ourselves. We had done everything we wanted to do, but we came up short.

Primary Source

My Life [excerpt]

SYNOPSIS: Earvin "Magic" Johnson, Michigan State University and later Los Angeles Lakers star basketball player, recalls his first meeting against Larry Bird in the 1979 NCAA championship.

By the second half, our fans were looking ahead to Monday's game against Indiana State. "We want the Bird," they chanted. "We want the Bird!"

Larry Bird and Magic Johnson pose at a press conference, Salt Lake City, March 25, 1979. The two young superstars faced each other in the NCAA championship, but the game was only the beginning of Bird's and Johnson's rivalry. © BETTMANN/CORBIS. REPRODUCED BY PERMISSION.

Indiana State's fans, who were waiting for their team to play DePaul, responded with: "You'll get the Bird! You'll get the Bird!"

When our game was over, we went into the stands to watch Indiana State and DePaul. It looked like a great game, but it was impossible to concentrate because the crowd wouldn't leave us alone. Everybody wanted autographs, and all the Michigan State fans wanted to congratulate us. We needed a good look at our next opponent, whoever it would be, so we got out of there fast and ran back to the hotel to watch the rest of the game on television.

DePaul had knocked off UCLA to get to the Final Four, and they had a hot freshman named Mark Aguirre. They were good, but we were all pulling for Indiana State. Since they were unbeaten that season, we wanted to be the team that finally stopped them.

I had another goal: I wanted to be the guy who stopped Larry Bird.

Although Bird and I were the two best-known college players in the country, our two teams had never played each other. In fact, it wasn't until that Saturday against DePaul that I saw him play. But believe me, once was enough. It wasn't just that he went 16 for 19 against DePaul, with 35 points, 16 rebounds, and nine assists. What impressed me even more was the way he refused to let his team lose. As my teammates and I watched his incredible performance, we all wondered the same thing: How on earth are we going to shut this guy down on Monday night?

"Okay," Jud told us when we got to practice on Sunday. "You've seen what Larry Bird can do. Today you're going to practice against him."

Earlier that morning, he had asked me to play on our second team during practice. "Gentlemen," Jud said, pointing to me, "meet Larry Bird. Double-team him as soon as he puts the ball on the floor. When he gets the ball, cut off all the passing lanes. Whatever you do, don't leave him open."

I had seen the real thing only once, but that morning I did the greatest Larry Bird imitation you ever saw. I made impossible passes. I knocked down shots from all over the court. I was tossing them in from twenty-five, even thirty feet out, hitting nothing but net. Our guys were playing me like Earvin Johnson, leaving me open because I didn't have that kind of range. But Bird could hit the long ones, and that day I *was* Bird.

I must have hit eight or nine in a row from out there. Jud was boiling mad. "Goddamn it!" he said. "That's Larry Bird. Get *on* him!" He was really cursing that morning, and my teammates were pissed. They couldn't believe what I was doing, and neither could I. I was laughing, and talking trash, too, although at the time I didn't even know that Bird did that. "Don't you know who I *am?*" I said. "I'm Larry Bird. Try and stop me."

I had the time of my life at that practice. Bird had the green light to do anything he wanted, so I did, too. And for that one morning, just about everything I tried was working. When the practice was over, one thing was clear: No matter how good the real Larry Bird was, he couldn't be any better than the imitation we had just seen. . . .

"Earvin, how about you? Do you think you're better than Bird?"

"I watched Larry Bird yesterday against DePaul, and he was incredible. He's older, he's more mature than I am, and at this stage he's probably a better player."

Yes, I was being diplomatic. But it was also the truth.

The championship game against Indiana State was almost an anti-climax. There were no locker-room speeches and no theatrics. This was business, pure and simple. We had a plan, and now it was time to execute it. But I still remember every shot from that game, every move.

Although we had only one day to prepare for Bird, Jud had figured out a way to contain him. Instead of playing our normal zone defense, we put a man on Bird wherever he was. Every time he got the ball, we shaded a second defender toward him. When he put it on the floor, we double-teamed him. We kept tabs on him the whole game, almost like police cars chasing down a criminal: "Okay, I've got him now. Jay, he's coming over to you."

Bird had never seen anything like it, and there wasn't much he could do. You could see how frustrated he was, how he kept calling to his teammates to get him the ball. But even when he had it, he just wasn't the same player we had seen on Saturday. He ended up shooting only 7 for 21 against us, and his teammates couldn't make up the difference.

At the half we were up by 10. Five minutes later we were ahead by 16. But with Greg on the bench with four fouls, Indiana State started to come back. With ten minutes left to play, they had closed to within six.

Now the pressure was enormous. Every moment was intense, and every play huge. Every move you made, you knew the entire country was watching. Later, we were told that this was the most widely watched game in the history of college basketball.

When Greg came back, we were able to increase our lead. And well before the game was over, we knew we had it won. It ended perfectly, with a full-court pass from me to Greg. Slam dunk! We won it, 75-64.

While we were celebrating and cutting down the net, I looked over at the Indiana State bench. I'll never forget what I saw. While half the arena was screaming with joy, Larry Bird was sitting there with his face buried in a towel. He was obviously crying, and my heart went out to him. As happy as I was, I knew that if things had gone just a little differently, *I* would have been the one sitting there with his face in a towel. I take losses the same way.

As I turned back to join the celebration, I knew in my gut that this wasn't the end of the story.

Somewhere, somehow, Larry Bird and I would be seeing each other again.

Primary Source

"Johnson: Magical by Nature"

In this article written in *The New York Times,* Malcolm Moran highlights the talent that has made Earvin "Magic" Johnson a phenom at Michigan State University—his uncanny ability to pass. He also reveals that this aspect of his game gives Johnson the most pleasure in playing.

Salt Lake City, March 25—Earvin Magic Johnson.

It is as if the name appeared just that way on the birth certificate, almost 20 years ago, like John Cameron Swayze, or Norman Vincent Peale. That is the way he is introduced by Jud Heathcote, the basketball coach at Michigan State University, and it is the way Johnson signs autographs when other students ask for them in class. "I have to," he said. "That's a request." You can call him Magic, and you can call him Earvin. You don't have to call him Johnson.

He has been Magic for several years, going back to the days at Everett High School in Lansing, where hundreds of people once welcomed him at the airport, some of them carrying signs that pleaded for him to go to Michigan State. Terry Donnelly was already a starting guard at Michigan State when Johnson was a senior at Everett, and Donnelly knew all about him. He had heard the stories and he had seen him play. And yet, Donnelly really didn't know much at all.

"It didn't really hit me until I got in the backcourt with him, on the first day of practice," Donnelly said. "You're running down the floor and you're open and most people can't get the ball to you through two or three people, and all of a sudden the ball's in your hands and you've got a layup."

Before last season, when Johnson enrolled at Michigan State, the basketball team finished more than two games above .500 in just one of the previous 10 seasons. Last season, the Spartans were 25-5, and reached the Mideast regional championship game, where they lost to Kentucky, the eventual national champion. This season, the Spartans (25-6) are one game away, the championship game tomorrow night against Indiana State.

Quick, Startling Passes

Johnson's passes are so quick, and sometimes so startling, that they have been known to loosen teeth and make mouths bleed. "I didn't mean it," he said. He handles the ball well enough to be a point guard, yet at 6 feet 8 inches and 207 pounds, he is bigger than some college centers and able to force smaller guards close to the basket. Nine times this season, including the victory over Pennsylvania in the semifinals of the National Collegiate Athletic Association tournament, Johnson has led the Spartans, or tied for the lead, in rebounds. He has averaged 16.5 points and 7.2 rebounds this season, second in both categories to Greg Kelser. Those numbers, he says, are not important to him.

"I'll take zero," he said, "as long as I get the assists."

Numbers are just numbers. "When you can make a pass that leads to a basket," Heathcote said, "where a receiver has to do nothing other than put it in the basket, the pass is more important than the basket. Earvin has proved that."

Even more than the numbers or the concept, his personality has made him magic. He was the leader as a freshman, setting up his team, shouting instructions, leading celebrations. "He gets the team going," Donnelly said. "He's got a personality that's like Muhammad Ali. It's classy, not conceited or anything. He would be running down the floor, and he's telling jokes. He's always smiling, always laughing. Never a frown on his face. Everyone likes a guy like that."

"We needed something like this," said Kelser, a senior. "I don't think it took any adjustment, because he was the new guy. He was so far advanced than any freshman in the country. We understood this. We needed it."

Loves to Talk

It is difficult to tell what Johnson enjoys more—watching Kelser leap for a perfect lob pass, inches from the rim, and jam it through, or talking about it later.

"I'm lovin' it," Johnson said. "Every minute of it. It's exciting. I'm really having a good time. I'm having a ball. It's like a kid going to a birthday party. Being in the Final Four, to get all the attention, to have your name in all the newspapers in the country. You gotta love it. All the parents from California to Germany know about it."

He smiles when he thinks about each question. He tugs on the tiny hairs on his chin, and his big, brown eyes look up, and then he'll talk about his dream last night, or the mind games he played as a child. He would go to the Main Street playground by himself, and go up and down the court, playing an imaginary game. He was always the Philadelphia 76ers, and he was always playing the Knicks, his brother's team. "I loved Philadelphia, see, and I always made sure they won the game," he said. "I'd make sure I missed a last-second shot and then Wilt Chamberlain would come down and dunk it. Except I'd lay it up."

He will smile even at the questions that are becoming annoying—the comparisons of his personality with Larry Bird's, which he thinks are unfair, and the criticism of his shooting, which he says is incorrect. He is a 45 percent shooter. It is merely good, the only unspectacular part of his game, and so it stands out. "People say, 'You can't shoot,'" he said. "I don't even care about that, as long as we win. I know deep inside myself I can shoot."

The most annoying question is whether or not this will be his last game at Michigan State, whether or not he will become a professional. "How could I think about it when I have a chance for the national championship?" he said. "That's what everyone's been asking me. Pro, pro, pro, pro. What about pro? Maybe after Monday night."

Primary Source

"Herb Shriner With a Jumper"

> Here, Dave Anderson profiles young superstar Larry Bird. This article and the previous one by Moran ran side-by-side in *The New York Times* the day prior to the NCAA championship game between Bird's Sycamores and Johnson's Spartans.

In the morning yesterday, Larry Bird was supposed to appear at a brunch honoring him as the college basketball player of the year. But when the Indiana State coach, Bill Hodges, woke him up at 9 o'clock, he said, "Coach, I'm dead—can I stay in bed?" The coach agreed. Bill Hodges likes to say that his primary contribution to the Sycamores this season has been "not messing up Larry Bird." And with Indiana State hoping to complete a 34-0 won-lost record tomorrow night against Michigan State in the National Collegiate Athletic Association championship game, the coach was not about to mess up Larry Bird's sack time. Larry Bird scored 35 points against De Paul in Saturday's 76-74 victory. If the

Indiana State's Larry Bird, guarded by Michigan State's Jay Vincent and Earvin "Magic" Johnson, looks for help during the NCAA championship game, Salt Lake City, March 27, 1979. Michigan State won the NCAA crown with a 75-64 victory. **AP/WIDE WORLD PHOTOS. REPRODUCED BY PERMISSION.**

6-foot-9-inch forward wanted to stay in bed until half-time tonight, Bill Hodges would have shrugged and considered it in the best interests of the team.

But by noon, Larry Bird was up and about and strolling into the Salt Lake Hilton for a tournament news conference. Just his appearance was news.

Throughout the season, Larry Bird had fulfilled his virtual vow of silence. He had talked on TV a few times, he had traveled to New York last week to receive an award. "And when you receive an award," Bill Hodges had told him, "you talk." And after Saturday's game, he had answered a few questions about it. But mostly, he had been the Silent Sycamore, a country bumpkin who apparently didn't know what to say.

And when he arrived for the news conference, Larry Bird was dressed for the occasion—a sleepy look, a blue warmup jacket over a white T-shirt, jeans and sneakers.

■ ■ ■

But from the beginning, it was apparent that Larry Bird was willing to answer questions. And slowly he created a new image of himself, the image of a hayseed with humor, a Herb Shriner with a jump shot. That was apparent when he was asked what he remembered about playing with Earvin (Magic) Johnson of Michigan State in a series of all-star games a year ago.

"Yeah," he said with a straight face, "Earvin passed the ball to me."

"How did you develop your style as both a shooter and a passer?"

"In high school I was a guard my sophomore year, I was little then. I had to get the ball in to the big guys. I found out that a two-foot shot by the basket is better than a 14-foot shot any day."

"How's your thumb?"

"Broke," he said of the hairline fracture of his left thumb. "It's still tender, but the doctor told me to go ahead and play."

"People who have seen you play in person for the first time think you're better than when they saw you on television."

"Yeah, they know what they're talking about."

"You seem to have a great feeling for passing."

"My feeling about passing is that it don't matter who's doing the scoring as long as it's us. I just think when a man is open, he should get the ball whether it's 30 feet out on the wing or underneath.

We had guys last year who didn't care about passing. They thought scoring was more important, but passing is more important."

■ ■ ■

"Earvin Johnson gives the impression he's having fun during a game, but you don't."

"He's probably laughing at the opponents," Larry Bird said. "But you can't have fun when the game's tied with two seconds to go and they got the ball. If you got a 1-point lead, it's different, but I got to do what I do. I can't be laughing out there. Earvin's different. I just hope he's not laughing at me."

"Ray Meyer [the De Paul coach] said you must have given some of your teammates bloody noses with your passes. Have you?"

"No, but I knocked a few out," he said. "I've bounced 'em off their legs or their knees on their heads. But no bloody noses."

"Ray Meyer also said your hands were as big as toilet seats."

"I heard him," he said, smiling. "But it's a shame I have a broken thumb. I don't usually have 11 turnovers in a game like I did yesterday."

"For somebody who has avoided interviews, you seem to be enjoying yourself."

"That's wrong," he replied with another smile. "Where all this started out was my first year I had all the pressure. My first year all they wanted to do was talk to me. That's the way it should be. But we got seven guys who play. They deserve to be talked to, too. It got so it was taking up two or three hours a day so I decided not to do interviews. If all of you were paying me, I'd enjoy it but I know that's coming. I don't mind interviews. I can handle any situation if it's all about me but I don't like it when I'm asked about my family."

Larry Bird is divorced, with a child; his father was a suicide, his mother works in a French Lick, Ind., restaurant.

"But what changed your mind," he was asked, "about doing this interview after you have avoided them throughout the season?"

"Everybody wants publicity," Larry Bird said, "I just thought the other guys on the team weren't getting it but now they are, so it's time to come back. We didn't expect to be here."

"You didn't expect to be here?"

"Did you," Larry Bird said with a smile, "expect us to be here?"

Further Resources

BOOKS

Corn, Frederick L. *Basketball's Magnificent Bird: The Larry Bird Story.* New York: Random House, 1982.

Haskins, James. *Magic: A Biography of Earvin Johnson.* Hillsdale, N.J.: 1982.

PERIODICALS

Moran, Malcolm. "Spartans Use No Cues To Silence Larry Bird." *The New York Times,* March 27, 1979.

White, Gordon S., Jr. "Michigan State Defeats Indiana State for NCAA Title." *The New York Times,* March 27, 1979.

WEBSITES

Naismith Memorial Basketball Hall of Fame. "Earvin 'Magic' Johnson." Available online at http://www.hoophall.com/hall offamers/johnson_magic.htm; website home page: http://www.hoophall.com (accessed April 24, 2003).

———. "Larry Bird." Available online at http://www.hoop hall.com/halloffamers/bird.htm; website home page: http://www.hoophall.com (accessed April 24, 2003).

The Oakland A's

Reggie: The Autobiography

Autobiography

By: Reggie Jackson, with Mike Lupica
Date: 1984
Source: Jackson, Reggie, with Mike Lupica. *Reggie: The Autobiography.* New York: Villard Books, 1984, 66–67, 70–71, 77–78.
About the Author: Reggie Jackson (1946–) was born in Wyncote, Pennsylvania. Attending Arizona State on a football scholarship, Jackson turned to baseball and was drafted by the Kansas City Athletics. By 1969, Jackson was a star player, hitting forty-seven home runs. After leading the Oakland A's to three consecutive World Series, Jackson was traded to the Baltimore Orioles in 1976; he signed with the New York Yankees as a free agent a year later. In five seasons with the Yankees, Jackson won two more World Series, hitting three homers in game six in 1977. After spending several seasons with the California Angels and Athletics again, Jackson retired in 1987, and has been a broadcaster, businessman, and consultant to the Yankees. Jackson was inducted into Baseball's Hall of Fame in 1993 in his first year of eligibility.

No More Mr. Nice Guy: A Life of Hardball

Autobiography

By: Dick Williams, and Bill Plaschke
Date: 1990

Source: Williams, Dick, and Bill Plaschke. *No More Mr. Nice Guy: A Life of Hardball.* San Diego: Harcourt Brace Jovanovich, 1990, 124–125, 129.
About the Author: Dick Williams (1929–) was born in St. Louis, Missouri. Signed by the Brooklyn Dodgers in 1947, Williams played fourteen seasons in the majors with six teams as an infielder. Williams managed the Boston Red Sox to the World Series as a rookie pilot in 1967, then won two championships with the Oakland A's in 1972 and 1973. Williams later managed the California Angels, Montreal Expos, San Diego Padres (with one World Series appearance), and Seattle Mariners—finishing with a career record of 1,571 wins and 1,451 losses. ■

Introduction

In early 1960, the Kansas City Athletics were purchased by Chicago insurance executive Charles O. Finley, who had a long-time interest in owning a baseball club. Through the 1960s, Finley established himself as baseball's most controversial owner. He bought a mule, who became the team mascot, naming it "Charlie O." Finley had a mechanical rabbit that popped up behind home plate to provide the umpire with a fresh supply of balls, and he selected green and gold uniforms with white shoes—making the team resemble a softball squad. Finley ran the team on a shoestring budget and staff, and hired and fired managers nearly every season.

Several things occurred late in the 1960s and early 1970s that helped Finley and the A's become a successful franchise. Finley moved the team to Oakland in 1968, which made him money (but not great attendance), signed a number of talented prospects, including future Hall of Famers Jim "Catfish" Hunter and Reggie Jackson, and hired former Boston Red Sox manager, Dick Williams, in 1971. Finley had numerous ideas about what baseball could do to help its slipping popularity, including the designated hitter and night World Series games, both of which were adopted—as well as proposals for the designated runner and orange-colored baseballs, which were not.

In 1971, led by Hunter, Jackson, and rookie pitcher Vida Blue, and managed by Williams, the A's won the West Division title. It was the franchise's first title in forty years, but they lost in the playoffs to the Baltimore Orioles. But Finley's groundwork had been laid and was ready for fruition. In 1972, Oakland won the West, defeated the Detroit Tigers, and then played the Cincinnati Reds in the World Series. Minus Jackson, who was injured, the A's got a lift from reserve catcher, Gene Tenace, who hit three home runs as Oakland won the Series in seven games, their first championship since 1930.

The next year, 1973, the A's repeated as division champions, beat the Orioles in the playoffs, and faced the New York Mets in the World Series, upset winners over the Cincinnati Reds in the National League playoffs.

Surviving a strong Mets effort and Finley's attempt to "fire" infielder Mike Andrews for making two errors in a game, Oakland, led by Jackson, won their second consecutive World Series, again in seven games. After three years managing for Finley, Williams resigned and was replaced by Alvin Dark, a former A's pilot. In 1974, the A's again won the West, defeated Baltimore again, and advanced to the World Series against the Los Angeles Dodgers. This time, with a balanced team effort, a hallmark of Finley's A's, even when the club members fought the owner and each other, the World Series was no contest, with Oakland winning their third straight championship in five games.

Significance

The championship run of the Oakland A's ended in 1975, and the team's fortunes fell after that. Finley lost pitcher "Catfish" Hunter after the 1974 season to the Yankees because of a contract technicality, and the A's lost the American League playoffs to the Boston Red Sox in 1975. With the coming of free agency in 1976, Finley tried to profit from the new economics, first by trading Jackson to Baltimore, and then attempting to sell several players including Blue for over a million dollars—deals that commissioner Bowie Kuhn nullified. After 1976, the A's became a bad team with poor attendance, even losing 109 games in 1979. After a brief resurgence under longtime Yankee Billy Martin as manager, Finley sold the team in 1981 and left baseball—returning to his insurance business until his death in 1996.

Since the Oakland "dynasty" of 1972 to 1974, only the New York Yankees of the 1990s have won three consecutive World Series championships. But the A's are the only baseball team besides the Yankees to win three consecutive world titles. In their era, the A's might not have had the overall hitting power or pitching prowess of the Cincinnati Reds or Baltimore Orioles, but there was one difference which separated the green and gold, white-shoed, and bearded and mustached players of the Oakland A's: they won the World Series titles.

Primary Source

Reggie: The Autobiography [excerpt]

SYNOPSIS: Former Oakland A's outfielder Reggie Jackson looks back at his teammates and what made them win three straight championships, and recalls his boss, controversial owner, Charles O. Finley.

Mr. Charles O. Finley

I played eight years in Oakland for an owner named Charlie Finley. If they ever have a Tough SOB Wing in the Hall of Fame, he will be the very first person in it. However, I have to say I kinda liked Charlie Finley. We fought all the time, like a contentious father and a headstrong son. . . .

. . . Charlie always had his shirtsleeves rolled up. And I must admit, he did have a creative baseball mind.

Night All-Star games? Charlie's idea. Night World Series games? Charlie's idea. Colored uniforms? Charlie. Players with mustaches and beards? Charlie was the first to say it was just fine. He was the first man to groom minor league pitching prospects as relievers; he did that with Rollie Fingers. . . .

Lord, the man was cheap, though.

In all the years I was with the A's, he always had this skeletal administrative staff of eight or nine people working in Oakland. They were the detail people who just kept things going while Charlie handled personnel from his Chicago office. He was the chairman, the president, the GM, the scout and the ticket manager. Not a nickel was spent that he didn't know about. . . .

There were a couple of seasons we started without a radio or television contract.

Carpet on the floor in the clubhouse? What was that? I never saw carpeting on the floor of the home clubhouse until I got to New York.

You couldn't get autographed baseballs from Charlie to give away or take home with you. You had to steal them.

You got two caps to wear all season long. Two dozen bats to use the whole season. . . .

There were no new uniforms from one season to the next. I remember starting 1975 with 1972 pants. And a jersey from 1974.

That was the season after we'd won our third World Series in a row. . . .

There was no question that Charlie wanted to be the star in Oakland, even after he'd put together this magnificent baseball machine piece by piece. He didn't care whether the team got promoted; he was popping off and promoting himself. Television contracts? Radio contracts? They were afterthoughts with him. He always wanted it to be Charles O. Finley and his Oakland A's. . . .

But he knew his baseball. Oh, yes, he did. No matter what the contract problems were, he was always figuring out ways to make us better. He had this innate sense about people and chemistry and the kind of nucleus he needed to have a winner. He

Oakland Athletics' owner Charlie O. Finley hugs Reggie Jackson, left, and Dick Green after the A's won the A.L. Championship, Oakland, October 11, 1973. **AP/WIDE WORLD PHOTOS. REPRODUCED BY PERMISSION.**

did a lot of things, Charlie did, but he never messed with the nucleus.

He had Jackson and Bando and Rudi. He had Gene Tenace and Dave Duncan, then Ray Fosse, as his catchers. He had Campaneris and Dick Green in the middle, and then when Green retired he went out and got Phil Garner. There was Rick Monday in center; then Charlie saw the need for another left-hander so he traded Monday for Kenny Holtzman and Bill North. Holtzman gave the starting pitching depth and balance, and North took over in center. Then Angel Mangual played center. He'd go out and get a Mike Epstein or a Don Mincher to play first. Balance, Charlie always understood balance. However, his first slip-up caused his eventual downfall. . . .

Charlie was always tinkering to make us a little better. Help the nucleus. Keep the balance just right. He was always poking around the waiver wire in all his years in Oakland, looking for that one extra pinch-hitter who might make a difference. A Rico Carty. A Felipe Alou. A Matty Alou. A Manny Sanguillen. A Billy Williams. . . .

The managers would change—Hank Bauer, Mc-Namara, Dick Williams, Alvin Dark—but Charlie kept the whole thing going, until free agency mugged him and he couldn't compete anymore, at least not the way he had. We had the hitting in the middle. We had speed up top in Campy and North. There was always enough catching and plenty of defense. The starting rotation was a dream. The right-handers were Cat and Blue Moon Odom; the lefties were Holtzman and Vida Blue. Paul Lindblad was our left-handed reliever, then Charlie added Darold Knowles. Rollie was the stud.

Yeah, we were Charlie Finley's Oakland A's. Gold socks and high stirrups and white pants. Gold shirts sometimes, green shirts sometimes, white shirts on Sunday. Kicked ass and took names. . . .

But How We Played the Game . . .

If there had never been free agency, if Peter Seitz hadn't made his ruling for McNally and Messersmith, if Charlie hadn't lost Cat because of a contract technicality, if Jackson had played his whole career in Oakland, and Bando and Rudi and Campaneris and Fingers, too, there is no doubt in my mind that the Oakland A's would have won eight or nine World Series in the 1970s, maybe even into the '80s. We were that good. When we left, most of us were still

Dick Williams smiles during spring training, Mesa, Arizona, March 1972. Williams was manager of the Oakland A's under owner Charles Finley from 1971 to 1973, winning two World Series championships. © BETTMANN/CORBIS. REPRODUCED BY PERMISSION.

in our prime. We were talented and mean and hungry, and we might just have turned out to be the greatest team of all time.

As it was, when you talk about the great teams, we certainly have to be among them. . . .

The eight years in Oakland were the best baseball years of my life, despite the difficulties with Charlie, despite the fights, despite the fact that I was learning to cope with celebrity the same as everyone else. It was like we were safe in Oakland. It wasn't New York. It wasn't Los Angeles. The spotlight wasn't the same until we got to the World Series, and then we handled it because we were just so . . . damn . . . good. . . .

There was always something inevitable about the A's, from the time we came together and saw day in and day out what we could all do on a ballfield. There was always the sense that Sal was in charge, but Dick Williams, who came along in 1971 and managed us to the first two world championships in '72 and '73, was the right drill sergeant for us at the right time. He might have made us jell a little sooner than we would have without him. . . .

He was the master of the game of fundamentals, and he was as big a reason as any why fundamentals became our badge of armor. Hit the cutoff man. Get the bunts down. Make every relay perfect. Do not—*do not*—screw up a relay. And do not miss a sign. . . .

By 1974, we were in our heyday, smack in the middle of it, a truly *great* professional baseball team. We could do no wrong. We played the game and won at will. In the fourth game of the playoffs that year, we got one hit and beat the Orioles anyway. I doubled off the left-center-field wall in the eighth that day to knock in Bando, and we won 1-0. That was the only hit we got, but we got thirteen walks that day, and we won. . . .

Primary Source

No More Mr. Nice Guy: A Life of Hardball [excerpt]

Former Oakland A's manager Dick Williams recalls working for Charles O. Finley, and looks back at how good his ball club was in the championship seasons of 1972 and 1973.

Only one thing helped me stomach that first A's uniform: my players looked great in it. But even in less stylish uniforms these guys would have been a beautiful sight. Already in place, waiting for me like an uncashed paycheck, were Bert Campaneris, Sal Bando, Reggie Jackson, Joe Rudi, Catfish Hunter, Blue Moon Odom, Vida Blue, and Rollie Fingers. Compared to what I'd walked into when I took over Boston, this was paradise. People talk about how I helped build the Oakland A's. I tell them: Hell no. From the moment I laid eyes on the A's I realized I'd be nothing more than a caretaker. Not that such a job is especially easy. Just ask the caretaker at your local zoo.

The clubhouse had three leaders: Reggie, Bando, and Catfish. Reggie was the guy with the lungs, the vocal one. His constant talking gave his teammates something to both laugh at and rally behind, and the best thing about it was that it was an act. . . . And right away, believe it or not, he liked me.

Bando was the quiet leader, the leader by example. Particularly the example of having cocktails with me to discuss the game. He's the only player I've ever socialized with. I'd invite him to my hotel suite after games or during an off-day, and we'd just talk baseball. The rest of the team saw this and figured I must be all right. And from those first moments Bando became my clubhouse emissary.

The third leader was Catfish Hunter, who led with a different sort of form, the practical joke. Although he and his wife, Helen, later became great friends with Norma and me, he had an early problem with me by trying to establish his turf too soon. I'll let players lead themselves, particularly veterans like Catfish, as long as they first recognize and respect the ultimate authority. Me. . . .

But how Charlie tried. The thing I first learned about managing under him [Finley]—the thing all his managers learned—is that he loved the phone. He'd call me once a day, often at home, just to chat about the team. Maybe he'd suggest a change in the batting order or in the pitching rotation. They were innocent calls from a guy who wanted to make things better. But the calls were always there, every day, and I thought I'd become used to them until a fateful July 1, a rare off-day before my A's took on the California Angels at Anaheim Stadium, when I drove the family from Oakland to Anaheim to visit Disneyland. Appropriately, this is where I first learned how Mickey Mouse Charlie's style could be. We arrived in Anaheim about 3 P.M., checked into a hotel, and went to Disneyland, staying there until after midnight and returning to the hotel around 1 A.M. When I stopped by the front desk, my heart dropped. The receptionist's face was as shiny pink as the stack of messages in his hand. The stack must have been six inches high. "Mr. Williams," he said, handing me the stack, "a Mr. Finley has been calling." Sorting the slips out, I learned that Charlie had begun calling the hotel just after I arrived at 3 P.M. and had called continuously until 12:30 A.M., upon which he left the message "I will call tomorrow at 6:30 A.M." And damned if he didn't. . . .

But aside from such things as Charlie's phone calls, Charlie's stadium, Charlie's advice, Charlie's treatment of fans and players, Charlie's style, Charlie's lack of style—aside from all this, playing with the A's was easy.

Further Resources

BOOKS

Libby, Bill. *Charlie O. and the Angry A's.* Garden City, N.Y.: Doubleday, 1975.

Markusen, Bruce. *Baseball's Last Dynasty: Charlie Finley's Oakland A's.* Indianapolis: Masters Press, 1998.

Michaelson, Herb. *Charlie O.* New York: Bobbs-Merrill, 1975.

PERIODICALS

Anderson, Dave. "Appreciating the A's." *The New York Times,* October 20, 1974.

Koppett, Leonard. "Charles O. Finley, Baseball Team Owner Who Challenged Traditions, Dies at 77." *The New York Times,* February 20, 1996.

WEBSITES

Baseball Reference.com. Available online at http://www.baseball-reference.com (accessed April 24, 2003).

National Baseball Hall of Fame and Museum. "Jim 'Catfish' Hunter." Available online at http://www.baseballhalloffame .org/hofers_and_honorees/hofer_bios/Hunter_Catfish.htm; website home page: http://www.baseballhalloffame.org (accessed April 24, 2003).

———. "Reggie Jackson." Available online at http://www .baseballhalloffame.org/hofers_and_honorees/hofer_bios/jack son_reggie.htm; website home page: http://www.baseball halloffame.org (accessed April 24, 2003).

———. "Rollie Fingers." Available online at http://www.base ballhalloffame.org/hofers_and_honorees/hofer_bios/Fingers_ Rollie.htm; website home page: http://www.baseballhallof fame.org (accessed April 24, 2003).

Olympic Gold: A Runner's Life and Times

Autobiography

By: Frank Shorter, with Marc Bloom

Date: 1984

Source: Shorter, Frank, with Marc Bloom. *Olympic Gold: A Runner's Life and Times.* Boston: Houghton Mifflin, 1984, 74–87.

About the Author: Frank Shorter (1947–) was born in Munich, Germany, and graduated from Yale University in 1969. Beginning competitive running in prep school and in college, Shorter was NCAA champion at the three- and six-mile distances. Moving into marathon running, Shorter won the Olympic gold medal in 1972, the silver medal in 1976, and was considered the world's best long-distance runner in the 1970s. Over the years, Shorter has practiced law, owned a chain of athletic clothing stores, and been a sports commentator. Shorter was inducted into the U.S. Olympic Hall of Fame in 1984, and he was inducted into the U.S. Track and Field Hall of Fame in 1989. ■

Introduction

In 1908, American Johnny Hayes was declared the winner of the Olympic marathon when an Italian runner, the first to reach the finish line, was helped across while staggering, and therefore disqualified. Over the next sixty-four years, no American marathoner won the Olympic event. In 1972, the United States had a strong contingent in the marathon. Frank Shorter, born in Munich, Yale graduate and law student, was considered one of the favorites. Shorter had been an NCAA track champion in college, and after taking up the marathon had won a number of races, including the Pan-American Games in 1971. The other U.S. runners were Kenny Moore of Oregon, and Shorter's friend and Florida Track Club teammate, Jack Bacheler. The Americans, however, faced formidable opposition from the Europeans and especially Ethiopia, whose runners had won the previous three Olympic marathons.

The marathon, held on September 10, the last day of the Games, began and ended at the Olympic Stadium, with runners racing through the streets of Munich in-between. When the race began and the runners left the stadium, Shorter was nearly knocked out of contention by a bus carrying photographers. Shorter hoped that his training regimen of 150 to two hundred miles a week would help him against his main rivals, especially Mamo Walde of Ethiopia, the defending marathon champion. At the ten-mile mark, Shorter took the lead, sensing that the pace was too slow, favoring a runner with a strong finishing kick, like Walde.

As the race proceeded, Shorter, a five-foot ten-inch, 130-pound runner, slowly increased his lead. Finally, as the Olympic Stadium came into view, Shorter glanced back and saw nobody—and the marathoner's rush came upon him, sensing victory. In the stadium, shortly before Shorter's arrival, a mysterious runner wearing number seventy-two emerged from the tunnel and began running around the track; the crowd, sensing he was a prankster, began jeering. When Shorter came through the tunnel, expecting cheers from the crowd, he heard rather a mixture of boos and applause. On ABC-TV, novelist and Yale professor Erich Segal, a marathon commentator, yelled from the booth, "Frank, he's a fake." Shorter looked a bit confused, never seeing the imposter, and completed his final lap—crossing the finish line first in just over two hours with a final time of 2:12:19.7 (the bogus runner ran back through the tunnel without crossing the finish line). Two-and-a-half minutes later, Belgium's Karl Lismont crossed the finish line for the silver, and Walde came in third, just a half minute in front of Moore. To complete a successful American effort, Bacheler finished ninth, placing three U.S. runners in the top ten.

Significance

Frank Shorter's triumph in the 1972 Olympic marathon was the first for the United States in sixty-four years, and the last in the thirty years since then. Shorter established himself as the best marathoner in the world, as he continued to win races or at least finish in the top ten through the 1970s. He won the Sullivan Award as the nation's top amateur athlete in 1972. At the Montreal Olympics in 1976, Shorter, one of the favorites, took an early lead. But it started to rain, and as Shorter later acknowledged, running on wet pavement is a weakness for him. Soon, a non-descript runner, East Germany's Waldemar Cierpinski, passed Shorter and emerged the

marathon winner, with the American getting the silver medal.

Shorter's running career was cut short by several injuries—in particular, a broken foot in the late 1970s. While no longer a champion marathoner by the 1980s, Shorter continued competing. In addition, he founded a chain of running attire stores because of his dissatisfaction with athletic apparel, and has been a television sports commentator and an activist against illegal substances used by runners.

But Frank Shorter's greatest contribution to American sports is that he made running long-distances respectable and even fashionable. After 1972, the number of Americans running marathons, the number of races held, and books published—in particular those by running "guru" James Fixx—increased dramatically. Older races, such as the Boston Marathon, and newer events, such as the New York City Marathon, attracted more media attention and greater number of participants. The running "craze" sparked by Shorter's marathon victory in 1972 led to an expanded culture of fitness in America over the last quarter of the twentieth century.

Primary Source

Olympic Gold: A Runner's Life and Times [excerpt]

> **SYNOPSIS:** Frank Shorter, marathoner and 1972 Olympic champion, retraces the race, describing how he felt during the event, his running strategy, and what the victory meant to the popularity of running.

I spent the morning of the marathon in thought, waiting. There's a certain abstraction to the Olympics, as though they are more of an idea than a thing, and it was comforting to know that at last the day had arrived when I would be running the marathon. Earlier in the week, after the murders, there'd been talk about canceling the rest of the Games. I was against it. The primary motive of the terrorists was to disrupt and possibly halt the competition. To shut down the Games would have been a submission to them. . . .

Mentally, I reviewed the course. I'd trained over parts of it during the week and felt that if someone managed to enter the English Garden, 18 miles out, with a lead, he would likely win. The 4 miles through the park were of gravel, and the path curved like the S-turns on mountain roads. With difficult footing and places to "hide," it would serve as a buffer zone. A lead could be protected there.

Historically, the marathon has had a strategic pattern. For the first two-thirds of the race, you bide your time. Then someone would pick up the race to try to pull away and go on to win. This time I was not going to let that happen because the wait-and-kick tactic did not play to my strength. I decided that I would try to be the first man to make a break, and that it would be made well before the English Garden. . . .

We ran the first half-mile in the stadium, then up a slight incline through the tunnel and turned right, toward the Olympic Village. Up near the front, I felt comfortable and took it as a sign that things might go well. Quite often I can tell in the first quarter-mile of a race whether or not I'll have a good day. This day felt good. I've learned I can't talk myself into this feeling. It's either there or it isn't. . . .

. . . I felt fine when we reached the first checkpoint, at 5 kilometers (3.1 miles), in 15:51. I wasn't wearing a watch and paid no attention to the split times. I felt it would do me no good to learn whether I was running slowly or over my head. In no way, for me, was this a race for time. It was a race against other people: I had to react to them (and they to me). And to the distance: With each passing 5-kilometer point, I would tell myself, "Okay, only thirty-seven . . . or thirty-two . . . or twenty-two kilometers to go." This is the way I run the marathon: I think of the 5-kilometer segments as "laps." . . .

Our pace had grown faster. I felt it, and as we came to the 10-kilometer mark inside Nymphenburg, a large park, 50 yards separated the leaders, Clayton and Hill, from me. I'd allowed myself the luxury of trailing, and a number of men had drifted ahead of me. Seppo Nikkari of Finland and forty-year-old Jack Foster of New Zealand were third and fourth. Usami was next. I was back enough to control the urge to be aggressive, yet close enough to see to it that no one would get away from me. . . .

The pace grew faster still as we neared 15 kilometers, a little over 9 miles. We ran down the side of a canal in front of the Nymphenburg Castle, crossed the canal, and went back on the other side of it, in the direction, briefly, from which we'd come. When we made the turn to go up the back side of the canal, a short distance before the 15-kilometer point, the pace suddenly and inexplicably slowed. Clayton was leading, and when the pace changed, those of us running close by gazed around for an instant, waiting for something to happen. I found myself moving up on Clayton and realized that if I didn't purposely slow down I was going to have the lead.

Frank Shorter crosses the finish line at Munich Olympic Stadium, September 10, 1972. Shorter won the gold medal in the Olympic Marathon for the United States. AP/WIDE WORLD PHOTOS. REPRODUCED BY PERMISSION.

I told myself, "Okay, you've got this momentum. Let it carry you."

And I pulled ahead. So fast was my move that by the 15-kilometer marker I already had a 5-second lead. I'd committed myself. This was it—the break. I told myself to get as far ahead as I could because if I got far enough ahead, I honestly thought no one would catch me. I'm not sure anyone but me considered my move a break at the time; a 5- or 10-second lead is not unusual in a marathon and certainly not much with 16 or 17 miles to go. That the break came fairly early helped me to make the most of my front-running strategy because the opposition, assuming I'd fall back before too long, was content to let me take on the pressures of the lead and risk blowing the whole thing.

I pressed on. Once you make that kind of commitment in a marathon, you have to carry that intensity, the mental intensity, to the end. Otherwise, the break is useless. . . .

The course weaved, and I tried to lose myself around the blind corners. Out of sight, out of mind. Psychologically, it's very tough on the people behind you. I played the turns. When I sensed I was hidden, I pressed a little harder to be farther ahead when I reappeared. If I could get away, I hoped, the others would start running for second.

I drew farther ahead, the press bus my only companion. By 20 kilometers, I later learned, I had a 31-second lead. I felt right, in control, and was running to get to the English Garden. . . .

It was all working. I reached the English Garden and had just the lead I wanted. Three times during the race I was told what my lead was, and this time, the first time, was most important. A journalist on the press bus who spoke English called out that I had a minute. It was a tremendous boost for me. Sixty seconds. I started figuring: Since there were 8 miles to go, they'd have to run roughly 8 seconds per mile faster than me to catch up. If I continued at a 5:05 pace, they'd have to run 4:57; if I ran 5:08, they'd have to run 5 flat. I knew it would be very difficult for anyone to run 5-minute miles at that point, given the winding nature of the path through the Garden. What's more, the footing was rough on the gravel surface, which had inspired quite a debate before the Games as to its appropriateness for an Olympic marathon course. I didn't care. If it was a disadvantage, it would be so for all of us. . . .

"If I don't die badly," I said to myself, "I'm going to win." I could suffer a little and still win. I could relax a little and still win. Whether I would soon suffer or relax was hard to say, but I did not see peril before me. The rest, to be sure, would not come easy, but in one sense the hardest part was over.

If there is a peak experience to be found in running, I came upon mine in the English Garden. More satisfying than victory itself is the anticipation of it. Not of the glory or reward, but simply the feeling of . . . doing it. To run with a kind of hypnotic rhythm, to be ahead and confident of winning while in a state of physical intensity at that level of competition, is the most satisfying feeling I've ever had.

Leaving the cover of the English Garden and heading back toward the stadium for the final 4½ miles, I felt my spirits start to sag. A fatigue had settled in. My hard running in the middle of the race, sometimes at better than 4:40 per mile, was coming back on me, and I knew it. Bad patches, the English call them. You feel bad all over, helpless, as though under a spell. . . .

I talked myself through it. "Okay, you're past the twenty-mile point. Everybody feels bad; everybody slows down. Just maintain your momentum." Though I slowed only a few seconds per mile, I felt as though I were running much slower, and I had to convince myself that I wasn't. As tired as I was, nothing *hurt.*

It was no small comfort to learn, at this point, that my lead had grown to a minute and a half. Get me to the stadium, I thought. Just get me to the stadium. . . . With the lead I had, I knew I could run a 7-minute mile at the end and still win. Thinking like that pushed me on.

In the shadows of the stadium, I hit the ramp that would take me into the tunnel that led to the track, and I knew I had it won. But I couldn't dwell on that. My attention was diverted to the huge roar that had erupted inside the stadium. I knew the high jump was scheduled for the afternoon. Had the winning jump just been made? Was that roar for a new world record? I wondered for a moment who might have done it.

Inside the tunnel, which muffles the outside noise, I braced myself. "Okay, here it comes. The roar that greets an Olympic marathon champion running into the stadium." And I got onto the track and it was silent.

I made the right turn for the lap-and-change to the finish. Someone waving an American flag yelled, "Don't worry, Frank, we love you," and I thought, Why should I worry, I'm winning. Still, it felt good to hear some acknowledgment. With about 200 meters to go, I glanced across the infield and saw some confusion at the finish. It didn't hold my interest. Suddenly it dawned on me that I'd actually done it. As I crossed the finish line, I felt a great sense of relief.

I felt awful. I felt wonderful. I was swaying: spent and achy, then flushed with joy. I knew I'd run 2:12:20, my best by 3 minutes, but that had nothing to do with it. It had not even occurred to me to try and speed up at the end for the Olympic record, the 2:12:12 by Abebe Bikila of Ethiopia, set in 1964. The race had been won outside the stadium.

I jogged a victory lap. I heard whistling, the European equivalent of booing, and thought, I know I'm an American, but give me a break. I knew nothing. At the finish again, I felt awkward. No one told me what to do. . . .

On my way, someone called, "What do you think of the guy who came in ahead of you?"

"What guy?" I said to myself. Then it hit me; it all fell into place.

An imposter. A perfectly absurd ending to an absurdly imperfect Olympics. I considered it a quirk of fate. He stole my entrance, all right, but that really didn't matter much. These Olympics were so battered by the bizarre and the tragic that I couldn't get worked up over an imposter. . . .

. . . The man who presented me with my medal was none other than Avery Brundage, the president of the International Olympic Committee. An American, Brundage was a 1912 Olympian and a staunch defender of the amateur ideals. In later years, considering my role in the changing lot of the "amateur" athlete, it seemed ironic that it was Brundage who'd handed me the medal. . . .

Further Resources

BOOKS

Martin, David, and Roger Gynn. *The Marathon Footrace: Performers and Performances.* Springfield, Ill.: Thomas, 1979.

PERIODICALS

Amdur, Neil. "U.S. Wins First Marathon Since 1908." *The New York Times.* September 11, 1972.

"A Distant Marathoner: Frank Shorter." *The New York Times,* September 11, 1972.

WEBSITES

Frank Shorter. Available online at http://www.runfrankshorter .com (accessed April 24, 2003)

A Steeler Odyssey
Memoir

By: Andy Russell

Date: 1998

Source: Russell, Andy. *A Steeler Odyssey.* Champaign, Ill.: Sports Publishing, 1998. Excerpt reprinted as "Joe Greene." In *The Steelers Reader.* Randy Roberts, and David Welky, eds. Pittsburgh: The University of Pittsburgh Press, 2001, 189–192, 195–198.

About the Author: Andy Russell (1941–) was born in Detroit, Michigan. After college at the University of Missouri, Russell played as a rookie starting linebacker for the Pittsburgh Steelers in 1963 before serving two years in the Army. In 1966, Russell returned to the Steelers to play eleven more seasons, retiring in 1976. Russell played in seven Pro Bowls and on two Super Bowl-winning Steelers teams. In retirement, Russell has been in business and banking. ∎

Introduction

For most of its first thirty-five years of existence in the NFL, the Pittsburgh Steelers was a mediocre or sorry football team, which had never won even a divisional title. Coaches and players had come and gone; some, like quarterback Johnny Unitas, became legends elsewhere. In 1969, the Steelers management made two decisions which changed its history: it hired Chuck Noll, a Baltimore Colts defensive assistant as head coach, and drafted defensive lineman "Mean" Joe Greene of North Texas State in the first round. The belief was that Noll, as coach, would change the losing attitude of the Steelers, while Greene would anchor the defense, which eventually became famous as the "Steel Curtain" during the 1970s.

After Noll's first team went 1-13, the Steelers gradually became better each year, drafting outstanding players such as quarterback Terry Bradshaw, and running back Franco Harris. The patience in rebuilding paid off in 1972 with Pittsburgh's first-ever division title and playoff victory—over the Oakland Raiders, on one of the most unusual plays in NFL history. The winning touchdown was a last-second deflected pass caught out of the air inches from the ground by Harris, who scored. The play has become known as the "Immaculate Reception."

In 1974, the Steelers drafted wide receivers Lynn Swann and John Stallworth, and linebacker Jack Lambert. The Steelers made the playoffs, and upset the favored Raiders in the AFC title game to advance to Super Bowl IX in New Orleans. There, against the veteran Minnesota Vikings, the young and somewhat brash Steelers dominated defensively for a 16-6 victory. After forty-two seasons, the Steelers finally had an NFL championship. The next season, 1975, the Steelers dominated their division, and advanced through the playoffs to Super Bowl X in Miami against the Dallas Cowboys. With Swann making several unbelievable catches, the Steelers held on to win 21-17 for consecutive Super Bowl wins.

The next two seasons the Steelers made the playoffs, but did not advance to the Super Bowl. In 1978, the Steelers won the AFC crown and advanced to Super Bowl XIII in Miami against the Cowboys. In one of the most exciting Super Bowls, Bradshaw threw for 318 yards as the Steelers won 35-31. The next year, the Steelers were beginning to show signs of age, but did advance to Super Bowl XIV in Pasadena, California, against the underdog Los Angeles Rams, whose record on the year was a mediocre 9-7. Down 19-17 after three quarters, Bradshaw and Stallworth combined to pull out the game 31-19, as the Steelers won their fourth Super Bowl in six years.

Significance

Beginning in 1980, after the Pittsburgh Steelers missed the playoffs for the first time in nine years, many of the great players from the championship years of the

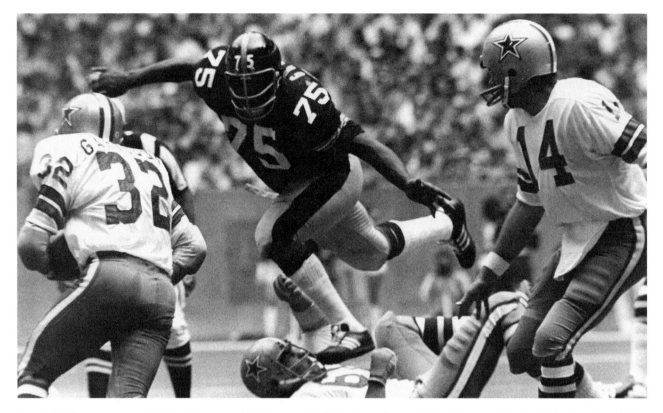

"Mean" Joe Greene steps on Blaine Nye (61) to get to Walt Garrison (32), Irving, Texas, October 8, 1972. Greene, a nine-time Pro Bowler, played left tackle for the Pittsburgh Steelers from 1969 to 1981 as part of the "Steel Curtain" defense that led Pittsburgh to four Super Bowl championships. **AP/WIDE WORLD PHOTOS. REPRODUCED BY PERMISSION.**

1970s began to retire. In 1991, Chuck Noll decided to step down after twenty-three seasons as Steelers head coach. As of 2003, there are nine Steelers players from the championship teams in the Pro Football Hall of Fame, plus Noll who was inducted as a coach, as well as team executives Art Rooney, the founder, and his son Dan Rooney.

The Pittsburgh Steelers of the 1970s, with eight consecutive playoff appearances (1972–1979) and four Super Bowl championships (1974, 1975, 1978, 1979), can claim to be one of the greatest teams in NFL history, perhaps on the same level as Vince Lombardi's Green Bay Packers teams of the 1960s. The Steelers were a dominating group that combined a strong, punishing defense, with an offense that emphasized the running game in the first two championship seasons, and a wide-open passing attack later in the decade. With the coming of free agency to football, the Steelers may be the last true dynasty in the history of the sport, built through the college draft, and kept together as a unit for a decade—they won all four Super Bowls with essentially the same players. The Pittsburgh Steelers, laughingstocks of pro football in 1969, were, by the end of the 1970s, one of sports's greatest teams.

Primary Source

A Steeler Odyssey [excerpt]

Former Pittsburgh Steelers linebacker Andy Russell recalls the dominating and forceful personality of "Mean" Joe Greene, which was evident from the time he was a rookie through the Super Bowl years.

In my opinion, Joe Greene was unquestionably the NFL's best player in the seventies. No player had a greater impact or did more for his team. But when he came to the Steelers in 1969, as our number-one draft choice from a small school, North Texas State, we veterans, having seen many highly touted draft choices come and go, were skeptical but hopeful he'd be the savior we needed. We'd wait and see.

Joe was supposed to be an impact player, a franchise player, someone who could single-handedly change the course of a game. . . .

His first full-speed "live" drill was to participate in what's known as an "Oklahoma Drill," where the defender lines head up on an offensive player, tries to defeat his block, release and make the tackle. It's normally more difficult for the defender because the offensive player has some advantages: he knows the snap count; he often has the strength and weight of the running back to help him, making it two against one; and a stalemate is usually a win for the offensive player (because despite stopping the offensive lineman's forward movement the defender still can't release quickly enough to make the tackle).

All eyes were on the number-one draft choice when he lined up against Ray Mansfield, the team's most wily old veteran offensive lineman, whose knowledge of technique and tricks was unparalleled. As Ray came off the ball, positioning himself between the hole and the new rookie, an extraordinary thing happened. Greene stopped Ray's forward momentum with only his left arm and threw him aside as though Ray were a puppy attacking a grizzly bear. He then proceeded to crush the ball carrier with his right shoulder. For a moment everyone was too stunned to speak but then the coaches began shouting encouragement and patting Joe on the back. Joe seemed oblivious to their encouragement, apparently needing no one's praise to validate himself.

Joe's next turn was against Bruce Van Dyke, a future Pro Bowler, and one of the best offensive linemen to ever play for the Steelers. Joe swatted him away like a lumberjack dealing with a bothersome mosquito. We veterans knew right then that the Steeler drafters had finally brought home a winner— this young man was going to be a force. . . .

Once, during his rookie year, when he was particularly frustrated late in the fourth quarter of a humiliating defeat at the hands of the Vikings in Minnesota, Joe lost his temper and was penalized for his rough play. As he came off the field, two respected Viking veterans, Carl Eller and Alan Page, huge defensive line stars whose bench was on the same side of the field as ours, made the mistake of berating our furious rookie. Without responding to their taunts, Joe, in a total rage, went directly to the trainer's tool box and pulled out the first tool he could find—a pair of nasty looking scissors. With weapon in hand, spinning toward his hecklers, looking totally insane, he charged toward the Viking bench, making wide swipes of the scissors in the general direction of Eller and Page. We were all so stunned that none of us moved.

Eller and Page, convinced they were dealing with a madman, both turned and sprinted toward the railing into the stands, perhaps hoping that their fans could protect them. I'm sure that Joe had no intention of actually hurting anyone. It was the ultimate

---

Looking Deep [excerpt]

The Pittsburgh Steelers of the '70s were a rare collection of men. We had great pride, reveled in the "nasty" image, and never failed to remind our opponents that we were tough guys from Steeltown. Once we got a taste of the pie, we wanted it all. It's difficult to stay on top, as NFL teams discovered in the '80s. But the Steelers' hunger pangs were boundless and that's why we won four championships in six short years. . . .

In my travels around the country, I sense it's beginning to dawn on pro football fans just how remarkable the Steelers' accomplishments really were. When they are reminded that we won four titles in six years, sometimes it completely blows them away. Only now, nearly a decade later, are people beginning to realize just how dominant we were.

One of the reasons for our dominance was Joe Greene, the cornerstone of the Pittsburgh dynasty.

Joe Greene . . . came to my rescue when I was a rookie. I was scared to death and needed somebody to reassure me of my place on this Steeler team, because it was going to be a bumpy ride. Joe must have seen something in me, because he showed his faith by saying: "Hey, man, you're going to be all right. You are our leader, the man we are going to win it with. Don't worry about what all those stupid assholes say. You are going to take us all the way. You are going to lead us. I just want you to know that." Joe warned all the reporters to get off my back the first few years and for a while they did. He always defended me for some reason. . . .

Joe Greene has a loving, sensitive spirit that I appreciated in a special way. When I needed support, Joe gave it to me. And I will never forget that. People often want to know: was Joe Greene really that good? He was the very foundation of the Steelers' success. You build teams with defense, and Joe Greene was the bedrock of the Steel Curtain.

SOURCE: Bradshaw, Terry, with Buddy Martin. Looking Deep. Chicago: Contemporary Books, 1989.

---

bluff, an act. Had Eller and Page stood their ground I'm sure that Joe would have dropped the scissors but his whole life experience told him they would turn and run.

He apparently wanted our opponents to know that he would not tolerate any insults. They would learn to respect him and his team. Despite losing by 38 points, I got on the bus to the airport after the game, thinking

Pittsburgh Steeler quarterback Terry Bradshaw looks for an open receiver against the Dallas Cowboys in Super Bowl XIII, Miami, January 21, 1979. Bradshaw was the Steelers' quarterback from 1970 to 1983 and led the team during its glory years. **AP/WIDE WORLD PHOTOS. REPRODUCED BY PERMISSION.**

"Man, this guy is something—he will absolutely not accept that we are losers." Many years later, in our first Super Bowl, those same Vikings would learn big time that they had taunted the wrong man.

Later that year, we played in Chicago against the Bears who were also struggling, despite having a couple of real superstars, Dick Butkus and Gale Sayers. Our defense was playing reasonably well but our offense was being destroyed by Butkus, who was having an All-World day, frequently sacking our quarterback, Terry Hanratty, stopping our ball carriers behind the line of scrimmage, causing and recovering fumbles, and knocking down passes.

It was one of the most impressive performances I had ever seen—Butkus was single-handedly humiliating our offense, making plays all over the field. It was an unbelievable defensive tour de force.

At one point Butkus even put himself on the kickoff team wanting to humble us even further. But this time he went too far, crushing Joe's pal, L. C. Greenwood, a blocker on the kickoff receiving team, right in front of our bench.

Seeing his friend writhing in pain was too much for Joe. He charged Butkus, from not ten feet away, and grabbed him by the shoulder pads, pulling his face up towards his own—they were face mask to face mask, Joe's 6'4", 295 lbs versus Butkus 6'3", 255 lbs. Since the face masks were apparently preventing the level of intimacy Joe wanted in this private, little conversation (only in front of the entire stadium) he tore off his own helmet and drew it back as though he intended to use it as a club to bash Butkus. I could hear Joe mumbling something and just knew it was highly insulting. Joe was clearly challenging Butkus to a fight, wanting badly to provoke him into a one-on-one confrontation and destroy the one man who was embarrassing our team.

I could see Butkus' eyes blink in disbelief. It was as though he was asking himself, "Do I die now or do I die later?" With that decision made, Butkus turned and ran back to his side of the field. None of us could believe it. Joe had just backed down the baddest man in the league. . . .

In 1974, our first Super Bowl year, frustrated by his inability to cause the kind of havoc he wanted, he developed a totally unique positioning technique that caused our opponents real problems. Instead of lining head up across from the guard he would jump in the gap between guard and center at the last second before the ball was snapped. Lining up nearly offsides, with his shoulders instead of being parallel to the ground tilted almost vertically to the ground, he would penetrate across the line of scrimmage, making it virtually impossible to block him. He experimented with it in practice during the year but, despite our offense's inability to block him, the coaches remained skeptical and refused to let him execute it during the season. Finally, Joe was allowed to try this unique new positioning in our first playoff game against O. J. and the Bills. It quickly became clear that his new technique destroyed many of the plays Buffalo wanted to run and we won easily, with O. J. getting only 48 yards on the ground.

The following week against Oakland in the AFC Championship game, the Raiders, a strong rushing team, were only able to generate a total of 29 yards on the ground. In the Super Bowl, Minnesota managed a total of 17 yards. All three of these teams based their offense around their strong running games.

The Vikings made the big mistake of running at Joe, the old Lombardi theory of running at the opponent's strength. Joe was finally doing what he had always wanted to do—dictating the action, forcing the opponent to react to him, making things happen. . . .

Over those years, Joe's personality changed from the wild, uncontrollable rookie to a more responsible, less explosive, almost fatherly figure. Once, later in his career, sitting next to me on the team bus, he asked, in total seriousness, "Captain, why do you suppose they call me 'Mean Joe Greene?'"

Without hesitation I replied, only half serious, "Because you're mean! You've got a real ugly streak, Joe, and you've got to try and control it."

He stared ominously at me for a long time, probably trying to decide if he should show me how really ugly he could be but then he smiled and said, "That's not true—I'm just misunderstood."

Later, of course, he would do the Coca-Cola TV ads winning the heart of America by throwing his jersey to the little kid. Actually, Joe was always nice to children. When leaving the stadium he would always be surrounded by youngsters asking for his autograph. Hating autographs, Joe would say, "I don't give autographs but why don't you kids get on the bus and talk to me." He would then sit, as we waited for the last stragglers from the locker room to board, and talk patiently with these kids, answering their questions and showing interest in their lives and aspirations.

The year after I retired, Joe was made the team Captain for the last exhibition game in Kansas City. Acting as the color man for the TV broadcast back to Pittsburgh, I had noted that Joe, playing with a back injury, was called for a roughing penalty late in the game, keeping the Chief's final, winning drive alive.

Afterwards, noticing Joe sitting dejectedly in the locker room, knowing how much he hated to make mistakes, I approached him, patted him on the back and said, "Joe, don't worry about it—it's just an exhibition game. It's not that important." But it was to Joe.

Shaking his head, with his eyes showing the emotional turmoil he was feeling, he said, "I'm not sure I want to be the Captain. It isn't me—it might get in the way of my natural instincts. I don't want to be worrying about how things look to the rest of the team—got to be my own man."

Realizing that he was totally conflicted and upset, I said, "You're right, Joe, just be yourself. You are a very special person. You don't need to change—do it your way. Your contribution to the team is far more important than being the Captain. You are the person everyone relies on to get the job done."

Joe, nodding his head in agreement, said, "Yep, I don't want to be acting like some gentleman, sportsman out there—it just wouldn't feel right."

With that he got up and limped into the training room. Watching him go, I realized that unless his back got better, that his best games were probably behind him. Unfortunately, it didn't and they were, but he did learn to control that temper and, unquestionably, became a very important leader in that locker room.

The young guys looked up to him and he set the tone. He would help the team win two more Super Bowls and be elected to the Hall of Fame. He was the best ever. Joe Greene was truly the player whose refusal to give in to defeat, unwillingness to accept anything but a total commitment to excellence and brilliant individual performances started and finished the Steelers' long journey, first to respectability, then to competitiveness and finally all the way to Super Bowl glory.

Further Resources

BOOKS

Blount, Roy, Jr. *About Three Bricks Shy of a Load.* Boston: Little, Brown, 1974.

PERIODICALS

Zimmerman, Paul. "They Were Just Too Much." *Sports Illustrated,* January 28, 1980.

WEBSITES

Pro Football Hall of Fame. Available online at http://www.pro footballhof.com (accessed April 24, 2003).

Steelers.com. Available online at http://www.steelers.com (accessed April 24, 2003).

GENERAL RESOURCES

General

Blum, John Morton. *Years of Discord: American Politics and Society, 1961–1974.* New York: Norton, 1991.

Campling, Elizabeth. *The 1970s.* London: Batsford, 1989.

Carroll, Peter N. *It Seemed Like Nothing Happened: The Tragedy and Promise of America in the 1970s.* New York: Holt, Rinehart & Winston, 1982.

Champlin, Charles. *Hollywood's Revolutionary Decade: Charles Champlin Reviews of the Movies of the 1970s* Santa Barbara, Calif.: John Daniel, 1998.

Cook, David A. *Lost Illusions: American Cinema in the Shadow of Watergate and Vietnam, 1970–1979.* New York: Scribner, 2000.

Duden, Jane. *The 1970s.* New York: Crestwood House, 1989.

Ehrenreich, Barbara, et al. *Remaking Love: The Feminization of Sex.* New York: Anchor/Doubleday, 1987.

Feinstein, Stephen. *The 1970s From Watergate to Disco.* Berkeley Heights, N.J.: Enslow, 2000.

Hargreaves, Robert. *Superpower: A Portrait of America in the 1970s.* New York: St. Martin's Press, 1973.

Harrison, Maureen, and Steve Gilbert. *Abortion Decisions in the United States Supreme Court: The 1970s.* Beverley Hills: Excellent, 1993.

Healey, Tim. *The 1970s.* New York: F. Watts, 1989.

Herald, Jacqueline. *Fashions of a Decade: The 1970s.* New York: Facts on File, 1992.

Hills, Ken. *Take Ten Years: The 1970s.* Austin, Tex.: Raintree Steck-Vaughn, 1992.

Kapsa, Michael J. *Labor Strife and the Economy in the 1970s: A Decade of Discord.* New York: Garland, 1998.

McQuaid, Kim. *The Anxious Years: America in the Vietnam-Watergate Era.* New York: Basic Books, 1989.

Muir, John Kenneth. *Horror Films of the 1970s.* Jefferson, N.C.: McFarland, 2002.

Olsen, James Stuart. *Historical Dictionary of the 1970s.* Westport, Conn.: Greenwood Press, 1999.

Peacock, John. *The 1970s.* New York: Thames and Hudson, 1997.

Robinson, Jerry. *The 1970s: The Best Political Cartoons of the Decade.* New York: McGraw-Hill, 1981.

Schmidt, Mark Ray. *The 1970s.* San Diego: Greenhaven Press, 2000.

Skolnik, Arlene S. *Embattled Paradise: The American Family in an Age of Uncertainty.* New York: Basic, 1991.

Szulc, Tad. *Innocents At Home: America in the 1970s.* New York: Viking, 1974.

Wandersee, Winifred D. *On the Move: American Women in the 1970s.* Boston: Twayne, 1988.

The Arts

Ashton, Dore. *American Art Since 1945.* New York: Oxford University Press, 1982.

Beardsley, John, and Jane Livingston. *Hispanic Art in the United States.* New York: Abbeville Press, 1987.

Bell, Bernard. *The Afro-American Novel and Its Tradition.* Amherst: University of Massachusetts Press, 1987.

Berkowitz, Gerald M. *New Broadways: Theater Across America 1950–1980.* Totowa, N.J.: Rowman & Littlefield, 1982.

Boyle, Donald. *Blacks in American Films and Television: An Encyclopedia.* New York: Garland, 1988.

Bronson, Fred. *The Billboard Book of Number One Hits*. New York: Billboard Publications, 1988.

Burbank, Richard. *Twentieth Century Music: Orchestral, Chamber, Operatic & Dance Music 1900–1980*. New York: Facts On File, 1984.

Chinay, Helen Krich, and Linda Walsh Jenkins. *Women in American Theater*. New York: Crown, 1981.

Christgau, Robert. *Grown Up All Wrong: 75 Great Rock and Pop Artists From Vaudeville to Techno*. Cambridge, Mass.: Harvard University Press, 1998.

Clarke, Mary, and Clement Crisp. *The History of Dance*. New York: Crown, 1981.

Craven, Wayne. *American Art: History and Culture*. New York: Harry N. Abrams, Inc., 1994.

Daval, Jean-Luc. *Photography: History of an Art*. New York: Rizzoli International Publications, 1982.

Goodman, Fred. *The Mansion on the Hill: Dylan, Young, Giffen, Springsteen and the Head-on Collision of Rock and Commerce*. New York: Random House, 1997.

Gordy, Berry. *To Be Loved: The Music, the Magic, the Memories of Motown*. New York: Warner Books, 1994.

Green, Stanley. *Broadway Musicals: Show by Show*. Milwaukee: Hal Leonard Books, 1985.

Guernsey, Otis L., Jr. *Broadway: Song and Story*. New York: Dodd, Mead, 1985.

Hall, Charles. *A Twentieth Century Musical Chronicle: Events 1900–1988*. New York: Greenwood Press, 1989.

Halliwell, Leslie. *The Filmgoer's Companion*. New York: Scribners, 1980.

Haskell, Molly. *From Reverence to Rape: The Treatment of Women in the Movies*. Chicago: University of Chicago Press, 1987.

Hill, Errol, ed. *The Theater of Black Americans*. New York: Applause Theater, 1980.

Hoffman, Ted, ed. *Famous American Plays of the 1970s*. New York: Dell, 1981.

Hughes, Robert. *American Visions: The Epic History of Art in America*. New York: Alfred A. Knopf, 1997.

Kael, Pauline. *When the Lights Go Down*. New York: Holt, Rinehart & Winston, 1980.

Karl, Frederick R. *American Fictions 1940–1980: A Comprehensive History and Critical Evaluation*. New York: Harper & Row, 1983.

Kingsbury, Paul, and Alan Axelrod, eds. *Country: The Music and the Musicians*. New York: Abbeville Press, 1988.

Klein, Leonard S., ed. *Latin American Literature in the 20th Century: A Guide*. New York: Ungar, 1986.

Kolker, Robert Phillip. *A Cinema of Loneliness: Penn, Kubrick, Coppola, Scorsese, Altman*. New York: Oxford University Press, 1980.

Long, Richard A., and Eugenia W. Colliers, eds. *Afro-American Writing: An Anthology of Prose and Poetry*. University Park: Pennsylvania State University Press, 1985.

Lucie-Smith, Edward. *Race, Sex, and Gender in Contemporary Art*. New York: Abrams, 1989.

Miller, Jim, ed. *The Rolling Stone Illustrated History of Rock and Roll*. New York: Knopf, 1980.

Mordden, Ethan. *The American Theatre*. New York: Oxford University Press, 1981.

Nite, Norm N. *Rock On Almanac: The First Four Decades of Rock 'n' Roll*. New York: Harper & Row, 1989.

Phillips, Lisa. *The American Century: Art and Culture 1950–2000*. New York: W.W. Norton & Co., 1999.

Rainwater, Catherine, and William J. Scheik, eds. *Contemporary American Women Writers: Narrative Strategies*. Lexington: University Press of Kentucky, 1985.

Raven, Arlene. *Crossing Over: Feminism and Art of Social Concern*. Ann Arbor, Mich.: UMI Research Press, 1988.

Rozelle, Robert V., Alvia Wardlaw, and Maureen A. McKenna, eds. *Black Art: The African Impulse in African-American Art*. New York: Abrams, 1989.

Selz, Peter. *Art in Our Times: A Pictorial History 1890–1980*. New York: Abrams, 1981.

Szatmary, David P. *Rockin' in Time: A Social History of Rock and Roll*. Englewood Cliffs, N.J.: Prentice-Hall, 1987.

Thomson, David. *Overexposures: The Crisis in American Filmmaking*. New York: Morrow, 1981.

Whitburn, Joel. *The Billboard Book of Top 40 Hits*. New York: Billboard Publications, 1985.

Business and the Economy

Auletta, Ken. *Greed and Glory on Wall Street*. New York: Warner Books, 1987.

Balser, Diane. *Sisterhood and Solidarity: Feminism and Labor in Modern Times*. Boston: South End Press, 1987.

Bell, Daniel. *The Coming of Post-Industrial Society*. New York: Basic Books, 1973.

Bensman, David, and Roberta Lynch. *Rusted Dreams: Hard Times in a Steel Community*. Berkeley: University of California Press, 1988.

Bluestone, Barry, and Bennett Harrison. *The Deindustrialization of America: Plant Closings, Community Abandonment, and the Dismantling of Basic Industries*. New York: Basic Books, 1982.

Blumberg, Paul. *Inequality in an Age of Decline*. New York: Oxford University Press, 1981.

Brooks, John. *The Autobiography of American Business*. Garden City, N.Y.: Doubleday, 1974.

Bryant, Keith L., Jr. *Encyclopedia of American Business History and Biography: Railroads in the Age of Regulation, 1900–1980*. Columbia, S.C.: Bruccoli Clark Layman/New York: Facts On File, 1988.

Bryant, Keith L., Jr., and Henry C. Dethloff. *A History of American Business*. Englewood Cliffs, N.J.: Prentice-Hall, 1983.

Carroll, Peter. *It Seemed Like Nothing Happened: The Tragedy and Promise of America in the 1970s*. New York: Holt, Rinehart and Winston, 1982.

Dobson, John M. *A History of American Enterprise*. Englewood Cliffs, N.J.: Prentice-Hall, 1988.

Gorey, Hays. *Nader and the Power of Everyman.* New York: Grosset & Dunlap, 1975.

Green, James R. *The World of the Worker: Labor in Twentieth-Century America.* New York: Hill & Wang, 1980.

Kelley, Donald R., ed. *The Energy Crisis: An International Perspective.* New York: Praeger, 1977.

Leary, William M., ed. *Encyclopedia of American Business History and Biography: The Airline Industry.* Columbia, S.C.: Bruccoli Clark Layman / New York: Facts On File, 1992.

Lovins, Amory B., and L. Hunter Lovins. *Brittle Power: Energy Strategy for National Security.* Andover, Mass.: Brick House, 1982.

May, George S., ed. *Encyclopedia of American Business History and Biography: The Automobile Industry, 1920–1980.* Columbia, S.C.: Bruccoli Clark Layman / New York: Facts On File, 1989.

Patterson, James T. *America's Struggle Against Poverty, 1900–1980.* Cambridge, Mass: Harvard University Press, 1986.

Porter, Glenn, ed. *Encyclopedia of American Economic History: Studies of the Principal Movements and Ideas,* 3 vols. New York: Scribners, 1980.

Pusateri, Joseph C. *A History of American Business.* Arlington Heights, Ill.: Harlan Davidson, 1984.

Ratner, Sidney, James H. Soltow, and Richard Sylla. *The Evolution of the American Economy.* New York: Basic Books, 1979.

Robinson, Archie. *George Meany and His Times: A Biography.* New York: Simon & Schuster, 1981.

Robinson, Graham. *Pictorial History of the Automobile.* New York: W.H. Smith, 1987.

Scheer, Robert. *America After Nixon: The Age of Multinationals.* New York: McGraw-Hill, 1974.

Schumacher, E.F. *Small Is Beautiful.* New York: Harper & Row, 1973.

Schweikart, Larry E., ed. *Encyclopedia of American Business History and Biography: Banking and Finance, 1913–1989.* Columbia, S.C.: Bruccoli Clark Layman/New York: Facts On File, 1990.

Seely, Bruce, ed. *Encyclopedia of American Business History and Biography: Iron and Steel in the Twentieth Century.* Columbia, S.C.: Bruccoli Clark Layman/New York: Facts On File, 1993.

Szulc, Tad. *The Energy Crisis.* New York: Watts, 1978.

Whiteside, Thomas. *The Investigation of Ralph Nader: General Motors vs. One Determined Man.* New York: Arbor House, 1972.

Yergin, Daniel. *The Prize: The Epic Quest for Oil, Money, and Power.* New York: Simon & Schuster, 1991.

Zieger, Robert. *American Workers, American Unions, 1920–1985.* Baltimore: Johns Hopkins University Press, 1986.

Websites

"After 20 Years, New Yorkers Recall Night the Lights Went Out." CNN.com. Available online at http://www.cnn.com /US/9707/12/blackout (accessed April 22, 2003).

"The Arab Oil Embargo of 1973–74." Buy and Hold. Available online at http://www.buyandhold.com/bh/en/education /history/2002/arab.html (accessed April 22, 2003).

"Background on Proposition 13." Howard Jarvis Taxpayers Association. Available online at http://www.hjta.org/prop13 .htm (accessed April 22, 2003).

Consolidated Rail Corporation (CONRAIL). Available online at http://www.conrail.com (accessed April 22, 2003).

DeLong, Brad. "The Inflation of the 1970s." Brad Delong's Website. Available online at http://econ161.berkeley.edu /Econ_Articles/theinflationofthes.html (accessed April 22, 2003).

"Environment: Here Comes the Sun—Whatever Happened to Solar Energy?" Third World Traveler. Available online at http://www.thirdworldtraveler.com/Environment/HereComes Sun.html (accessed April 22, 2003).

"The Trans Alaska Pipeline System (TAPS)." U.S. Bureau of Land Management. Available online at http://wwwndo .ak.blm.gov/dalton/pipe1.htm (accessed April 22, 2003).

U.S. Department of Energy. Available online at http://www .energy.gov (accessed April 22, 2003).

"WIN (Whip Inflation Now)." Baldwin Management. Available online at http://www.baldwinim.com/publish/commentary /q100commentary.asp (accessed April 22, 2003).

Education

Ambert, Alba N. *Bilingual Education: A Sourcebook.* New York: Garland, 1985.

Ben-David, J. *American Higher Education.* New York: McGraw-Hill, 1972.

Berube, Maurice R. *American School Reform: Progressive, Equality, and Excellence Movements, 1883–1993.* Westport, Conn: Praeger, 1994.

Cohen, Sol, ed. *Education in the U.S.: A Documentary History.* Los Angeles: UCLA Press, 1974.

Gold, Milton J., ed. *In Praise of Diversity: A Resource Book for Multicultural Education.* Washington, D.C.: Association of Teacher Educators, 1977.

Graham, Hugh Davis. *The Uncertain Triumph: Federal Education Policy in the Kennedy and Johnson Years.* Chapel Hill: University of North Carolina Press, 1984.

Hudgins, Harry C., Jr, and Richard S. Vacca. *Law and Education: Contemporary Issues and Court Decisions.* Charlottesville, Va.: Michie, 1979.

Klotman, Phyllis, ed. *Humanities Through the Black Experience.* Dubuque, Iowa: Kendall-Hunt, 1977.

Knapp, Herbert. *One Potato, Two Potato . . . The Secret Education of American Children.* New York: Norton, 1976.

Kozol, Jonathan. *Illiterate America.* Garden City, N.Y.: Anchor/Doubleday, 1985.

———. *Savage Inequalities: Children in America's Schools.* New York: Crown, 1991.

Marshner, Connaught Coyne. *Blackboard Tyranny.* New Rochelle, N.Y.: Arlington House, 1978.

McNally, D.W. *Piaget, Education and Teaching.* Sussex, U.K.: Harvester Press, 1973.

Nelkin, Dorothy. *The Creation Controversy: Science or Scripture in the Schools.* New York: Norton, 1982.

———. *Science Textbook Controversies and the Politics of Equal Time.* Cambridge, Mass: MIT Press, 1977.

Nelson, Jack, and Kenneth Carlson. *Radical Ideas and the Schools.* New York: Holt, Rinehart & Winston, 1972.

Packard, Vance. *The People Shapers.* Boston: Little, Brown, 1977.

Postman, Neil, and Charles Weingartner. *The School Book.* New York: Delacorte, 1973.

Pride, Richard A. *The Political Use of Racial Narratives: School Desegregation in Mobile, Alabama, 1954–1997.* Urbana, Ill.: University of Illinois Press, 2002.

Seller, Maxine Schwartz, ed. *Women Educators in the United States, 1820–1993: A Bio-Bibliographical Sourcebook.* Westport, Conn.: Greenwood Press, 1994.

Shane, Harold G. *Curriculum Change toward the 21st Century.* Washington, D.C.: National Education Association, 1977.

Shor, Ira. *Culture Wars: School and Society in the Conservative Restoration, 1969–1984.* Boston: Routledge & Kegan Paul, 1986.

Turow, Joseph. *Entertainment, Education, and the Hard Sell: Three Decades of Network Children's Television.* New York: Praeger, 1981.

Van Scotter, Richard. *Public Schooling in America.* Santa Barbara, Calif.: ABC-CLIO, 1991.

Velente, William D. *Law in the Schools.* Columbus, Ohio: Charles E. Merrill, 1980.

Wolcott, Harry. *Teachers Versus Technocrats.* Eugene: University of Oregon Center for Educational Policy and Management, 1977.

Websites

"1976: Arvo Juola Raises Concerns Over Grade Inflation in Higher Education." History of Education. Available online at http://fcis.oise.utoronto.ca/daniel_schugurensky/assignment1/1976juola.html (accessed April 22, 2003).

"AAAS Resolution: Creationism and California Public Schools." American Association for the Advancement of Science. Available online at http://archives.aaas.org/docs/resolutions.php?doc_id=293 (accessed April 22, 2003).

"Creation Science and the Local School District—Impact No. 67: January 1979." Institute for Creation Research. Available online at http://www.icr.org/pubs/imp/imp-067.htm (accessed April 22, 2003).

Department of Special Collections & Archives, Kent State University. Available online at http://www.library.kent.edu/exhibits/4may95 (accessed April 22, 2003).

"Regents of the Univ. of Cal. V. Bakke, 438 U.S. 265 (1978) (USSC+)." Legal Information Institute, Cornell Law School. Available online at http://www2.law.cornell.edu/cgi-bin/foliocgi.exe/historic/query=[group+438+u!2Es!2E+2 (accessed April 22, 2003).

"Resolution for Balanced Presentation of Evolution and Scientific Creationism—Impact No. 71: May 1979." Institute for Creation Research. Available online at http://www.icr.org/pubs/imp/imp-071.htm (accessed April 22, 2003).

"Rural Development Act of 1972." Cooperative State Research, Education, and Extension Service. Available online at http://www.reeusda.gov/1700/legis/ruraldev.htm (accessed April 22, 2003).

"Title IX: A Brief History." Education Development Center. Available online at http://www.edc.org/WomensEquity/pdffiles/t9digest.pdf (accessed April 22, 2003).

"U.S. Supreme Court: San Antonio School District v. Rodriguez, 411 U.S. 1 (1973)." FindLaw. Available online at http://caselaw.lp.findlaw.com/cgi-bin/getcase.pl?court=US&vol=411&invol=1 (accessed April 22, 2003).

"Wisconsin v. Yoder et al." University of Missouri–Kansas City School of Law. Available online at http://www.law.umkc.edu/faculty/projects/ftrials/conlaw/yoder.html (accessed April 22, 2003).

Fashion and Design

Batterberry, Michael. *Mirror, Mirror: A Social History of Fashion.* New York: Holt, Rinehart & Winston, 1977.

Brown, Curtis F. *Star-Spangled Kitsch.* New York: Universe Books, 1975.

Browne, Ray, and Marshal Fishwick, eds. *Icons of America.* New York: Popular Press, 1978.

Chenoune, Farid. *A History of Men's Fashion.* Paris: Flammarion, 1993.

The Encyclopedia of Fashion. New York: Abrams, 1986.

Gilmour, Sarah. *20th Century Fashion: The 70s Punk, Glam Rockers & New Romantics.* Milwaukee: Gareth Stevens Publishing, 2000.

Gold, Annalee. *90 Years of Fashion.* New York: Fairchild Fashion Group, 1991.

Goldberg, Paul. *On the Rise: Architecture and Design in a Postmodern Age.* New York: Penguin, 1983.

Herald, Jacqueline. *Fashions of a Decade: The 1970s.* New York and Oxford: Facts On File, 1992.

Howell, Georgina. *In Vogue: Six Decades of Fashion.* London: Allen Lane, 1975.

Hunt, William Dudley, Jr. *Encyclopedia of American Architecture.* New York: McGraw-Hill, 1980.

Kultermann, Udo. *Architecture in the 20th Century.* New York: Reinhold, 1993.

Maddex, Diane, ed. *Master Builders: A Guide to Famous American Architects.* Washington, D.C.: Preservation Press, 1985.

Milbank, Caroline Rennolds. *Couture: The Great Designers.* New York: Stewart, Tabori & Chang, 1985.

Mulvagh, Jane. *"Vogue" History of 20th Century Fashion.* New York: Viking, 1988.

Peacock, John. *20th Century Fashion: The Complete Sourcebook.* New York: Thames & Hudson, 1993.

Reid, Aileen. *I.M. Pei.* New York: Crescent Books, 1995.

Stegemeyer, Anne. *Who's Who in Fashion.* New York: Fairchild, 1988.

Whiton, Sherrill. *Interior Design and Decoration,* 4th ed. New York: Lippincott, 1973.

Wilson, Elizabeth. *Adorned in Dreams: Fashion and Modernity.* Berkeley: University of California Press, 1987.

Wolfe, Tom. *From Bauhaus to Our House.* New York: Farrar, Straus & Giroux, 1981.

Yarwood, Doreen. *Fashion in the Western World: 1500–1990.* New York: Drama, 1992.

Government and Politics

Ambrose, Stephen. *Nixon,* 3 vols. New York: Simon & Schuster, 1987–1991.

Anson, Robert Sam. *McGovern: A Biography.* New York: Holt, Rinehart, and Winston, 1972.

Bernstein, Carl, and Bob Woodward. *All the President's Men.* New York: Simon & Schuster, 1974.

Brodie, Fawn M. *Richard Nixon: The Shaping of His Character.* New York: Norton, 1981.

Cannon, James. *Time and Chance: Gerald Ford's Appointment With History.* New York: HarperCollins, 1994.

Damore, Leo. *Senatorial Privilege: The Chappaquiddick Cover-up.* New York: Regnery, 1988.

Evans, Rowland, and Robert Novak. *Nixon in the White House.* New York: Random House, 1971.

Furgurson, Ernest B. *Hard Right: The Rise of Jesse Helms.* New York: Norton, 1986.

Germond, Jack, and Jules Witcover. *Blue Smoke and Mirrors: How Reagan Won and Carter Lost the Election of 1980.* New York: Viking, 1981.

Gibson, James William. *The Perfect War: The War We Couldn't Lose and How We Did.* New York: Vintage, 1986.

Glad, Betty. *Jimmy Carter: In Search of the Great White House.* New York: Norton, 1980.

Greene, John Robert. *The Presidency of Gerald R. Ford.* Lawrence: University of Kansas Press, 1995.

Hoff, Joan. *Nixon Reconsidered.* New York: Basic Books, 1994.

Issacson, Walter. *Kissinger.* New York: Simon & Schuster, 1992.

Jordan, Hamilton. *Crisis: The Last Year of the Carter Presidency.* New York: Putnam, 1922.

Johnson, Haynes. *In the Absence of Power: Governing America.* New York: Viking, 1980.

Johnson, Loch K. *A Season of Inquiry: The Senate Intelligence Investigation.* Lexington: University Press of Kentucky, 1985.

Karnow, Stanley. *Vietnam: A History.* New York: Viking, 1984.

Kutler, Stanley. *The Wars of Watergate.* New York: Knopf, 1990.

Lukas, J. Anthony. *Common Ground: A Turbulent Decade in the Lives of Three American Families.* New York: Knopf, 1986.

———. *Nightmare: The Underside of the Nixon Years.* New York: Viking, 1976.

Moss, George Donelson. *Vietnam: An American Ordeal.* Englewood Cliffs, N.J.: Prentice-Hall, 1994.

Rusher, William A. *The Rise of the Right.* New York: Morrow, 1984.

Schudson, Michael. *Watergate in American Memory.* New York: Basic Books, 1992.

Shabecoff, Philip. *A Fierce Green Fire: The American Environmental Movement.* New York: Hill and Wang, 1993.

Sheehan, Neil. *A Bright Shining Lie: John Paul Vann and America in Vietnam.* New York: Random House, 1988.

Sick, Gary. *October Surprise: American Hostages in Iran and the Election of Ronald Reagan.* New York: Random House, 1991.

Szulc, Tad. *The Illusion of Peace: Foreign Policy in the Nixon Years.* New York: Viking, 1978.

White, Theodore. *The Making of the President, 1972.* New York: Atheneum, 1972.

Young, Marilyn B. *The Vietnam Wars, 1945–1990.* New York: Harper, 1991.

Law and Justice

Abraham, Henry J. *Justices, Presidents, and Senators: A History of the U.S. Supreme Court Appointments From Washington to Clinton.* New York: Rowman & Littlefield, 1999.

Bilton, Michael. *Four Hours in My Lai.* New York: Viking, 1992.

Chafe, William Henry, ed. *Remembering Jim Crow: African Americans Tell About Life in the Segregated South.* New York: New Press, 2001.

Clayborne, Carson, and Martin Luther King Jr. *In Struggle: SNCC and the Black Awakening of the 1960s.* Boston: Harvard University Press, 1995.

Foner, Philip, Martin Luther King Jr., and Julian Bond. *The Black Panthers Speak.* Cambridge, Mass.: Da Capo Press, 1995.

Franklin, John Hope, and Alfred A. Moss Jr. *From Slavery to Freedom: A History of African Americans.* New York: Knopf, 2000.

Hall, Kermit L., ed. *The Oxford Companion to the Supreme Court.* New York: Oxford University Press, 1992.

Harrison, Maureen, and Steve Gilbert, eds. *Landmark Decisions of the United States Supreme Court II.* Beverly Hills: Excellent Books, 1992.

Horwitz, Morton J. *The Warren Court and the Pursuit of Justice.* New York: Hill and Wang, 1999.

Hull, N.E.H., and Peter Charles Hoffer. *Roe V. Wade: The Abortion Rights Controversy in American History (Landmark Law Cases and American Society).* Lawrence, Kans.: University Press of Kansas, 2001.

Kelly, Alfred H., Winfred A. Harbison, and Herman Belz. *The American Constitution: Its Origins and Development–Vol. II,* 7th ed. New York: Norton, 1991.

Mikula, Mark F., and Mpho Mabunda L., eds. *Great American Court Cases.* Farmington Hills, Mich.: Gale Group, 2000.

Olson, Keith W. *Watergate: The Presidential Scandal That Shook America.* Lawrence, Kans.: University Press of Kansas, 2003.

Palmer, Kris E., ed. *Constitutional Amendments: 1789 to the Present.* Farmington Hills, Mich.: Gale Group, 2000.

West's Encyclopedia of American Law, 2d ed. 12 vols. St. Paul, Minn.: West Publishing Co., 1998.

Websites

The Charles Manson Trial. Available online at http://www .law.umkc.edu/faculty/projects/ftrials/manson/manson.html; website home page: http://www.law.umkc.edu/faculty/projects /ftrials/ftrials.htm (accessed April 20, 2003).

The My Lai Cases. Available online at http://www.law.umkc.edu /faculty/projects/ftrials/mylai/mylai.htm; website home page: http://www.law.umkc.edu/faculty/projects/ftrials/ftrials.htm (accessed April 20, 2003).

The Oyez Project of Northwestern University, a U.S. Supreme Court Multimedia Database. Available online at http:// www.oyez.com (accessed April 20, 2003).

The Presidents of the United States. Available online at http:// www.whitehouse.gov/history/presidents/; website home page: http://www.whitehouse.gov (accessed April 20, 2003).

U.S. Supreme Court Opinions. Available online at http:// www.findlaw.com/casecode/supreme.html; website home page: http://www.findlaw.com (accessed March 16, 2003).

Lifestyles and Social Trends

100 Years of the Automobile. Los Angeles: Petersen, 1985.

Bailey, Beth L. *From Front Porch to Back Seat: Courtship in Twentieth-Century America.* Baltimore: Johns Hopkins University Press, 1988.

Barone, Michael. *Our Country: The Shaping of America From Roosevelt to Reagan.* New York: Free Press, 1990.

Barker, Eileen. *The Making of a Moonie: Choice or Brainwashing?* New York: Oxford University Press, 1984.

Berger, Bennett M. *The Survival of a Counterculture.* Berkeley & Los Angeles: University of California Press, 1981.

Bird, Caroline. *The Two-Paycheck Marriage: How Women At Work Are Changing Life in America.* New York: Rawson, Wade Publishers, 1979.

Borstelmann, Thomas. *The Cold War and the Color Line: American Race Relations in the Global Arena.* Cambridge, Mass.: Harvard University Press, 2001.

Burns, James MacGregor. *The Crosswinds of Freedom.* New York: Knopf, 1989.

Casale, Anthony M., and Philip Lerman. *Where Have All the Flowers Gone?: The Fall and Rise of the Woodstock Generation.* Kansas City: Andrews and McMeel, 1989.

Clecak, Peter. *America's Quest for the Ideal Self: Dissent and Fulfillment in the 60s and 70s.* New York: Oxford University Press, 1983.

Echols, Alice. *Shaky Ground: The '60s and Its Aftershocks.* New York: Columbia University Press, 2002.

Edelstein, Andrew J., and Kevin McDonough. *The Seventies: From Hot Pants to Hot Tubs.* New York: Dutton, 1990.

Ehrenreich, Barbara. *The Worst Years of Our Lives: Irreverent Notes From a Decade of Greed.* New York: Holt, Rinehart & Winston, 1982.

Freeman, Jo, ed. *Social Movements of the Sixties and Seventies.* New York: Longman, 1983.

Frum, David. *How We Got Here: The 70's, The Decade That Brought You Modern Life (For Better or Worse).* New York: Basic Books, 2000.

Gitter, Michael, and Sylvie Anapol. *Do You Remember? The Book That Takes You Back.* San Francisco: Chronicle Books, 1996.

Gregory, Ross. *Cold War America, 1946 to 1990.* New York: Facts on File, 2003.

Gross, Michael. *My Generation: Fifty Years of Sex, Drugs, Rock, Revolution, Glamour, Greed, Valor, Faith, and Silicon Chips.* New York: Cliff Street Books, 2000.

Hoff-Wilson, Joan. *Rights of Passage: The Past and Future of the ERA.* Bloomington: Indiana University Press, 1986.

Issel, William. *Social Change in the United States, 1945–1983.* New York: Macmillan, 1985.

Jackson, Kenneth T. *The Crabgrass Frontier: The Suburbanization of the United States.* New York: Oxford University Press, 1985.

Janeway, Elizabeth. *Cross Sections From a Decade of Change.* New York: Morrow, 1982.

Jones, Landon Y. *Great Expectations: America and the Baby Boom Generation.* New York: Coward, McCann & Geoghegan, 1980.

Kennedy, Pagan. *Platforms: A Microwaved Cultural Chronicle of the 1970s.* New York: St. Martin's Press, 1994.

Knobler, Peter, and Greg Mitchell, eds. *Very Seventies: A Cultural History of the 1970s, From the Pages of Crawdaddy.* New York: Simon & Schuster, 1995.

Kowinski, William. *The Malling of America: An Inside Look at the Great Consumer Paradise.* New York: Morrow, 1985.

Leuchtenburg, William E. *A Troubled Feast: American Society Since 1945.* Boston: Little, Brown, 1983.

Long, Mark. *The World of CB Radio.* Summertown, Tenn.: Book Publishing, 1987.

Maltby, Richard. *Passing Parade: A History of Popular Culture in the Twentieth Century.* New York: Oxford University Press, 1989.

Mansbridge, Jane J. *Why We Lost the ERA.* Chicago: University of Chicago Press, 1986.

Marty, Myron A. *Daily Life in the United States, 1960–1990: Decades of Discord.* Westport, Conn.: Greenwood Press, 1997.

Meltzer, Milton, ed. *The American Promise: Voices of a Changing Nation, 1945–Present.* New York: Bantam Books, 1990.

Moore, Joan, and Harry Pachon. *Hispanics in the United States.* Englewood Cliffs, N.J.: Prentice-Hall, 1985.

Powers, Ann. *Weird Like Us: My Bohemian America.* New York: Simon & Schuster, 2000.

Rosenberg, Rosalind. *Divided Lives: American Women in the Twentieth Century.* New York: Hill & Wang, 1992.

Sale, Kirkpatrick. *The Green Revolution: The American Environmental Movement, 1962–1992.* New York: Hill & Wang, 1993.

Skolnik, Peter L. *Fads: America's Crazes, Fevers, and Fancies From the 1890s to the 1970s.* New York: Crowell, 1978.

Stein, Arthur. *Seeds of the Seventies: Values, Work, Commitment in Post-Vietnam America.* Hanover, N.H.: University Press of New England, 1985.

Waldrep, Shelton. *The Seventies: The Age of Glitter in Popular Culture.* New York: Routledge, 2000.

Weitzman, Lenore J. *The Divorce Revolution.* New York: Free Press, 1985.

Wolfe, Tom. *The Purple Decades: A Reader.* New York: Farrar, Straus & Giroux, 1982.

Wright, Lawrence. *In the New World: Growing Up With America, 1960–1984.* New York: Knopf, 1988.

Websites

"1970s Popular Culture." Available online at http://www.authentichistory.com/audio/1970s/1970s_popculture_01.html (accessed April 25, 2003).

"American Cultural History, 1970–1979." Available online at http://kclibrary.nhmccd.edu/decade70.html (accessed April 25, 2003).

"Baby Boomer Headquarters: The Seventies Section." Available online at http://www.bbhq.com/seventez.htm (accessed April 25, 2003).

"The Chronology of the Equal Rights Amendment, 1923–1996." Available online at http://www.now.org/issues/economic/cea/history.html (accessed April 25, 2003).

"Flashback to the Seventies." Available online at http://www.chem.ucla.edu/wong/flashback.html (accessed April 25, 2003).

"Meltdown at Three Mile Island." Available online at http://www.pbs.org/wgbh/amex/three/index.html (accessed April 25, 2003).

"The Seventies Nostalgia Site." Available online at http://www.inthe70s.com/index.shtml (accessed April 25, 2003).

"Super70s Culture." Available online at http://Super70s.com/Super70s/Culture (accessed April 25, 2003).

"U.S. and World News Events." Available online at http://Super70s.com/Super70s/News (accessed April 25, 2003).

The Media

Altschuler, Glenn C., and David I. Grossvogel. *Changing Channels: America in TV Guide.* Urbana: University of Illinois Press, 1992.

Barnouw, Erik. *Tube of Plenty: The Evolution of American Television,* 2d ed. New York: Oxford University Press, 1990.

Benton, Mike. *The Comic Book in America: An Illustrated History.* Dallas: Taylor, 1989.

Castleman, Harry, and Walter J. Podrazik. *Watching TV: Four Decades of American Television.* New York: McGraw-Hill, 1982.

Cohen, Marcia. *The Sisterhood: The True Story of the Women Who Changed the World.* New York: Simon & Schuster, 1988.

Collins, Jim, ed. *High-Pop: Making Culture into Popular Entertainment.* Malden, Mass.: Blackwell Publishers, 2002.

Douglas, Susan J. *Listening In: Radio and the American Imagination, From Amos 'n' Andy and Edward R. Murrow to Wolfman Jack and Howard Stern.* New York: Times Books, 1999.

Draper, Robert. *Rolling Stone Magazine: The Uncensored History.* New York: Doubleday, 1990.

Erickson, Hal. *Syndicated Television: The First Forty Years, 1947–1987.* Jefferson, N.C.: McFarland, 1989.

Greenfield, Jeff. *Television: The First Fifty Years.* New York: Crescent Books, 1981.

Janello, Amy, and Brennon Jones. *The American Magazine.* New York: Abrams, 1991.

Jones, Gerard. *Honey, I'm Home: Sitcoms, Selling the American Dream.* New York: Grove Weidenfeld, 1992.

Landy, Elliott. *Woodstock Vision: The Spirit of a Generation.* New York: Continuum, 1994.

MacDonald, J. Fred. *One Nation Under Television: The Rise and Decline of Network TV.* New York: Pantheon Books, 1990.

Steinem, Gloria. *Outrageous Acts and Everyday Rebellion.* New York: Holt, Rinehart & Winston, 1983.

Terrace, Vincent. *The Complete Encyclopedia of Television Programs: 1947–1979,* second edition. New York: Barnes, 1980.

Trow, George W.S. *My Pilgrim's Progress: Media Studies, 1950–1998.* New York: Pantheon Books, 1999.

Websites

"1970s News." Authentic History Center. Available online at http://www.authentichistory.com/audio/1970s/1970s_news_01.html; website homepage: www.authentichistory.com (accessed April 25, 2003).

"Comic Books: Experimenting With History." Authentic History Center. Available online at http://www.authentichistory.com/images/1970s/Comics/1970s_comics_01.html; website homepage: http://www.authentichistory.com (accessed April 25, 2003).

"One Nation, Indivisible." Library of Congress. Available online at http://lcweb.loc.gov/rr/print/swann/herblock/one.html; website homepage: http://www.loc.gov (accessed April 25, 2003).

"Super70s Television." Super70s.com. Available online at http://Super70s.com/Super70s/TV; website homepage: http://Super70s.com (accessed April 25, 2003).

The Wolfman Jack Online Museum. Available online at http://www.wolfmanjack.org (accessed April 25, 2003).

Medicine and Health

Anderson, James Lee. *The West Point Fitness and Diet Book.* New York: Rawson, 1977.

Babbie, Earl R. *Science and Morality in Medicine: A Survey of Medical Educators.* Berkeley: University of California Press, 1970.

Barr, Samuel J., and Dan Abelow. *A Woman's Choice.* New York: Rawson, 1977.

Bender, Arnold E. *A Dictionary of Food and Nutrition.* NewYork: Oxford University Press, 1995.

Berger, Melvin. *Disease Detectives.* New York: Crowell, 1978.

Boston Women's Health Collective. *Our Bodies, Ourselves.* New York: Simon & Schuster, 1973.

Brody, Baruch. *Abortion and the Sanctity of Human Life: A Philosophical View.* Cambridge, Mass.: MIT Press, 1975.

Brown, E. Richard. *Rockefeller Medicine Men: Medicine and Capitalism in America.* Berkeley: University of California Press, 1979.

Burt, John J. *Personal Health Behavior in Today's Society.* Philadelphia: W.B. Saunders, 1972.

Callahan, Daniel. *Abortion: Law, Choice and Morality.* New York: Macmillan, 1970.

The Cambridge World History of Human Disease. New York: Cambridge University Press, 1993.

Carlson, Rick J. *The End of Medicine.* New York: Wiley, 1975.

Cartwright, Frederic Fox. *Disease and History.* New York: Crowell, 1972.

Cassedy, James H. *Medicine in America: A Short History.* Baltimore: Johns Hopkins University Press, 1991.

Close, William T. *Ebola: A Documentary Novel of the First Explosion in Zaire by a Doctor Who Was There.* New York: Ivy Books, 1995.

Cockerham, William C. *Medical Sociology.* Englewood Cliffs, N.J.: Prentice-Hall, 1989.

Colen, B.D. *Karen Ann Quinlan: Dying in the Age of Eternal Life.* New York: Nash, 1976.

Companion Encyclopedia of the History of Medicine. London: Routledge, 1993.

Dolan, John Patrick. *Health and Society: A Documentary History of Medicine.* New York: Seabury, 1978.

Duke, Martin. *The Development of Medical Techniques and Treatments: From Leeches to Heart Surgery.* Madison, Conn.: International Universities Press, 1991.

Emmens, Carol. *The Abortion Controversy.* New York: Messner, 1987.

Feldstein, Paul J. *Health Care Economics.* New York: John Wiley & Sons, 1979.

Freeman, H., S. Levine, and L. Reeder, eds. *Handbook of Medical Sociology.* Englewood Cliffs, N.J.: Prentice-Hall, 1972.

Gill, Derek. *Quest: The Life of Elisabeth Kübler-Ross.* New York: Harper & Row, 1980.

Jarcho, Saul, and Gene Brown, eds. *Medicine and Health Care.* New York: New York Times/Arno, 1977.

Jones, James H. *Bad Blood.* New York: Free Press, 1981.

Kurtz, Richard A., and H. Paul Chalfant. *The Sociology of Medicine and Illness.* Boston: Allyn & Bacon, 1984.

Lyons, Albert S. *Medicine: An Illustrated History.* New York: Abrams, 1978.

Mayer, Jean. *Health.* New York: Van Nostrand, 1974.

Nolen, William A. *A Surgeon's World.* New York: Random House, 1972.

Nuland, Sherwin B. *Doctors: The Biography of Medicine.* New York: Knopf, 1988.

Professional Guide to Diseases, 6th ed. Springhouse, Pa.: Springhouse, 1998.

Reiser, Stanley Joel. *Medicine and the Reign of Technology.* New York: Cambridge University Press, 1978.

Rettig, Richard A. *Cancer Crusade: The Story of the National Cancer Act of 1971.* Princeton, N.J.: Princeton University Press, 1977.

Reverby, Susan M. *Tuskegee's Truths: Rethinking the Tuskegee Syphilis Study.* Chapel Hill: University of North Carolina Press, 2000.

Rubin, Jeffrey. *Economics, Mental Health, and the Law.* Lexington, Mass.: D.C. Heath, 1978.

Sass, Lauren R. *Abortion: Freedom of Choice and Right to Life.* New York: Facts On File, 1978.

Starr, Paul. *The Social Transformation of American Medicine.* New York: Basic Books, 1982.

Stevens, Rosemary. *American Medicine and the Public Interest.* New Haven, Conn.: Yale University Press, 1971.

Twaddle, Andrew C., and Richard M. Hessler. *A Sociology of Health.* New York: Macmillan, 1987.

Valenstein, Elliot S. *Great and Desperate Cures.* New York: Basic, 1986.

Websites

"Ebola Haemorrhagic Fever." World Health Organization. Available online at http://www.who.int/inf-fs/en/fact103.html; website home page: http://www.who.int (accessed July 18, 2003).

Elisabeth Kubler-Ross home page. Available online at http://www.elisabethkublerross.com (accessed July 18, 2003).

"Euthanasia and Physician Assisted Suicide: All Sides." ReligiousTolerance.org. Available online at http://www.religioustolerance.org/euthanas.htm; website home page: http://www.religioustolerance.org (accessed July 18, 2003).

"Images From the History of the Public Health Service." National Library of Medicine. Available online at http://www.nlm.nih.gov/exhibition/phs_history/contents.html (accessed July 18, 2003).

"Medicine and Madison Avenue—Timeline." Rare Book, Manuscript, and Special Collections Library, Duke University. Available online at http://scriptorium.lib.duke.edu/mma/timeline.html; website home page: http://scriptorium.lib.duke.edu (accessed July 18, 2003).

"National Cancer Policy: Legislative History." CancerSource.com. Available online at http://www.cancersource.com/nclac/leghistory.htm; website home page: http://www.cancersource.com (accessed July 18, 2003).

"Regents of the Univ. of Cal. V. Bakke, 438 U.S. 265 (1978)." Legal Information Institute, Cornell Law School. Available online at http://www2.law.cornell.edu/cgi-bin/foliocgi.exe /historic/query=bakke/doc/{ @74385 }?; website home page: http://www2.law.cornell.edu (accessed July 18, 2003).

"Roe v. Wade." Touro College Law Center. Available online at http://www.tourolaw.edu/patch/Roe; website home page: http://www.tourolaw.edu (accessed July 18, 2003).

"Surgeon General's Reports on Smoking and Health, 1964–2001." Government Publications Library, University of Minnesota. Available online at http://govpubs.lib.umn.edu /guides/surgeongeneral.phtml; website home page: http:// govpubs.lib.umn.edu (accessed July 18, 2003).

"The Tuskegee Syphilis Study." School of Communication, Information, and Library Studies, Rutgers University. Available online at http://www.scils.rutgers.edu/~lyonsm/tuskegee .html; website home page: http://www.scils.rutgers.edu (accessed July 18, 2003).

"United States Cancer Mortality, 1900–1992." HealthSentinel.com. Available online at http://www.healthsentinel .com/Vaccines; website home page: http://www.healthsentinel .com (accessed July 18, 2003).

"What Is a Health Maintenance Organization?" University of Missouri Outreach & Extension. Available online at http:// outreach.missouri.edu/hes/fmhlth/whatishmo.htm; website home page: http://outreach.missouri.edu (accessed July 18, 2003).

Religion

Allen, Steve. *Beloved Son: A Story of the Jesus Cults.* Indianapolis: Bobbs-Merrill, 1982.

Ammerman, Nancy T. *Bible Believers: Fundamentalists in the Modern World.* New Brunswick, N.J.: Rutgers University Press, 1987.

Banki, Judith Hershcopf. *Christian Responses to the Yom Kippur War: Implications for Christian-Jewish Relation.* New York: Jewish Committee, n.d.

Beckwith, Bernham P. *The Decline of U.S. Religious Faith, 1912–1984.* Palo Alto, Calif.: B.P. Beckwith, 1985.

Bellah, Robert N., and Frederick E. Greenspahn, eds. *Uncivil Religion: Irreligious Hostility in America.* New York: Crossroads, 1987.

Boyer, Paul. *When Time Shall Be No More: Prophesy Belief in Modern American Culture.* Cambridge, Mass.: Belknap Press, 1992.

Bromley, David G., and Anson D. Shupe Jr. *"Moonies" in America: Cult, Church, and Crusade.* Beverly Hills.: Sage Publications, 1979.

Brown, Charles C. *Niebuhr and His Age: Reinhold Niebuhr's Prophetic Role in the Twentieth Century.* Philadelphia: Trinity Press International, 1992.

Carroll, Jackson W. *Beyond Establishment: Protestant Identity in a Post-Protestant Age.* Louisville, Ky.: Westminster/John Knox, 1993.

Cox, Harvey. *Turning East: The Promise and Peril of the New Orientalism.* New York: Simon & Schuster, 1977.

Dolan, Jay P. *The American Catholic Experience.* Garden City, N.Y.: Doubleday, 1985.

Eighmy, John L. *Churches in Cultural Captivity: A History of the Social Attitudes of Southern Baptists.* Knoxville: University of Tennessee Press, 1987.

Ellwood, Robert S. *The Sixties Spiritual Awakening: American Religion Moving From Modern to Post Modern.* New Brunswick, N.J.: Rutgers University Press, 1994.

Fackre, Gabriel J. *The Religious Right and Christian Faith.* Grand Rapids, Mich.: Eerdmans, 1982.

Field-Bibb, Jacqueline S. *Women Toward Priesthood: Ministerial Politics and Feminist Praxis.* New York: Cambridge University Press, 1991.

Flowers, Ronald B. *Religion in Strange Times: The 1960s and 1970s.* Macon, Ga.: Mercer University Press, 1984.

Frady, Marshall. *Billy Graham: A Parable of American Righteousness.* Boston: Little, Brown, 1979.

Friedman, Robert I. *The False Prophet: Rabbi Meir Kahane, From FBI Informant to Knesset Member.* Brooklyn: Lawrence Hill, 1990.

Galanter, Marc. *Cults: Faith, Healing, and Coercion.* New York: Oxford University Press, 1989.

Garrow, David J. *Liberty and Sexuality: The Right to Privacy and the Making of Roe v. Wade.* New York: Macmillan, 1994.

Gilkey, Langdon B. *Catholicism Confronts Modernism: A Protestant View.* New York: Seabury, 1975.

Ginsburg, Faye D. *Contested Lives: The Abortion Debate in an American Community.* Berkeley: University of California Press, 1989.

Hall, John R. *Gone From the Promised Land: Jonestown in American Cultural History.* New Brunswick, N.J.: Transaction, 1987.

Hall, Mitchell K. *Because of Their Faith: CALCAV and Religious Opposition to the Vietnam War.* New York: Columbia University Press, 1990.

Harrell, David Edwin, Jr. *Oral Roberts: An American Life.* Bloomington: Indiana University Press, 1985.

Horsfield, Peter G. *Religious Television: The American Experience.* New York: Longman, 1984.

House, Ernest R. *Jesse Jackson and the Politics of Charisma: The Rise and Fall of the PUSH/Excel Program.* Boulder & London: Westview Press, 1988.

Hunter, James Davison. *American Evangelicalism: Conservative Religion and the Quandary of Modernity.* New Brunswick, N.J.: Rutgers University Press, 1983.

Jelen, Ted G., and Marthe A. Chandler, eds. *Abortion Politics in the United States and Canada.* Westport, Conn.: Praeger, 1994.

Jones, Donald G., and Russell E. Richey, eds. *American Civil Religion.* San Francisco: Mellen Research University Press, 1990.

Klineman, George, and Sherman Butler. *The Cult That Died: The Tragedy of Jim Jones and the Peoples Temple.* New York: Putnam, 1980.

Liebman, Robert C., and Robert Wuthnow, eds. *The New Christian Right: Mobilization and Legitimation.* New York: Aldine, 1983.

Martin, William C. *A Prophet With Honor: The Billy Graham Story.* New York: Morrow, 1991.

Marty, Martin. *Pilgrims in Their Own Land: 500 Years of Religion in America.* Boston: Houghton Mifflin, 1984.

Martz, Larry, and Ginny Carroll. *Ministry of Greed: The Inside Story of the Televangelists and Their Holy War.* New York: Weidenfeld & Nicolson, 1988.

McKeegan, Michele. *Abortion Politics: Mutiny in the Ranks of the Right.* New York: Free Press, 1992.

Peck, Janice. *The Gods of Televangelism.* Cresskill, N.J.: Hampton Press, 1993.

Pollock, John. *Billy Graham: Evangelist to the World.* San Francisco: Harper & Row, 1979.

Quebedeaux, Richard. *I Found It: The Story of Bill Bright and the Campus Crusade.* San Francisco: Harper & Row, 1979.

———. *The Worldly Evangelicals.* San Francisco: Harper & Row, 1978.

Rader, Stanley R. *Against the Gates of Hell.* New York: Everest House, 1980.

Richardson, James T., Joel Best, and David G. Bromley, eds. *The Satanism Scare.* New York: Aldine de Gruyter, 1991.

Rowley, Peter. *New Gods in America.* New York: McKay, 1971.

Schwerin, Jules Victor. *Go Tell It On the Mountain: Mahalia Jackson, Queen of Gospel.* New York: Oxford University Press, 1992.

Shafer, Ingrid H. *Eros and the Womanliness of God: Andrew Greeley's Romance of Renewal.* Chicago: Loyola University Press, 1991.

Shapiro, Edward S. *A Time for Healing: American Jewry since 1945.* Baltimore: Johns Hopkins University Press, 1992.

Shepard, Charles E. *Forgiven: The Rise and Fall of Jim Bakker and the PTL Ministry.* New York: Atlantic Monthly Press, 1989.

Shupe, Anson, and William A. Stacey. *Born Again Politics and the Moral Majority: What Social Surveys Really Show.* New York: Edwin Mellen Press, 1982.

Smidt, Corwin E. *Contemporary Evangelical Political Involvement: An Analysis and Assessment.* Lanham, Md.: University Press of America, 1989.

Staggenborg, Suzanne. *The Pro-Choice Movement: Organization and Activism in the Abortion Conflict.* New York: Oxford University Press, 1991.

Voskuil, Dennis N. *Mountains into Gold Mines: Robert Schuller and the Gospel of Success.* Grand Rapids, Mich.: Eerdmans, 1983.

Wangerin, Ruth. *The Children of God: A Make-Believe Revolution?* Westport, Conn.: Bergin & Garvey, 1994.

Wills, Garry. *Under God: Religion and American Politics.* New York: Simon & Schuster, 1990.

Zaretsky, Irving I., and Mark P. Leone, eds. *Religious Movements in Contemporary America.* Princeton, N.J.: Princeton University Press, 1974.

Science and Technology

Abshire, Gary M., ed. *The Impact of Computers on Society and Ethics: A Bibliography.* Morristown, N.J.: Creative Computing, 1980.

Awbrey, Frank, and William Thwaites, eds. *Evolutionists Confront Creationists.* San Francisco: California Academy of Sciences, 1984.

Bains, William. *Genetic Engineering for Almost Everybody.* New York: Pelican, 1987.

Belzer, Jack, Albert G. Holzman, and Allen Kent, eds. *Encyclopedia of Computer Science and Technology,* 16 vols. New York: Marcel Dekker, 1975–1981.

Brown, Michael. *Laying Waste: The Poisoning of America by Toxic Chemicals.* New York: Pocket Books, 1981.

Collins, Michael. *Liftoff: The Story of America's Adventure in Space.* New York: Grove, 1988.

Haraway, Donna. *Primate Visions: Gender, Race, and Nature in the World of Modern Science.* New York: Routledge, 1989.

Haugelan, J. *Artificial Intelligence: The Very Idea.* Cambridge, Mass.: MIT Press, 1985.

Hellemans, Alexander, and Bryan Bunch. *The Timetable of Science.* New York: Simon & Schuster, 1988.

Irving, Clive. *Wide-Body: The Triumph of the 747.* New York: Morrow, 1993.

Johnson, Donald C., and Maitland A. Edey. *Lucy: The Beginnings of Humankind.* New York: Simon & Schuster, 1981.

Kaplan, Fred. *The Wizards of Armageddon.* New York: Simon & Schuster, 1983.

Kirkup, Gill, and Laurie Smith Keller. *Inventing Women: Science, Technology, and Gender.* Cambridge, Mass.: Polity Press, 1992.

Leakey, Mary. *Disclosing the Past.* New York: Doubleday, 1984.

McGraw-Hill Encyclopedia of Science and Technology, 9th ed., 14 vols. New York: McGraw-Hill, 1993.

Metropolis, N., ed. *A History of Computing in the Twentieth Century.* New York: Academic Press, 1980.

Montgomery, Sy. *Walking With the Great Apes: Jane Goodall, Dian Fossey, Biruté Galdikas.* Boston: Houghton Mifflin, 1991.

Nelkin, Dorothy. *Science Textbook Controversies and the Politics of Equal Time.* Cambridge, Mass.: MIT Press, 1977.

Numbers, Ron. *The Creationists: The Evolution of Scientific Creationism.* New York: Knopf, 1992.

Patton, Phil. *Made in the USA: The Secret Histories of Things That Made America.* New York: Simon & Schuster, 1988.

Popper, Karl. *Realism and the Aim of Science.* Totowa, N.J.: Rowman and Littlefield, 1983.

Pursell, Carroll W., ed. *Technology in America: A History of Individuals and Ideas,* 2d ed. Cambridge, Mass.: MIT Press, 1990.

Reader, John. *Missing Links: The Hunt for Earliest Man.* New York: Penguin, 1988.

Rifkin, Jeremy, and Nicanor Perlas. *Algeny.* New York: Penguin, 1983.

Schichtle, Cass. *The National Space Program From the Fifties to the Eighties.* Washington, D.C.: Government Printing Office, 1983.

Science & Technology Desk Reference. Detroit: Gale, 1993.

Stephens, Mark. *Three Mile Island: The Hour-by-Hour Account of What Really Happened.* New York: Random House, 1980.

Traweek, Sharon. *Beamtimes and Lifetimes: The World of High Energy Physicists.* Cambridge, Mass.: Harvard University Press, 1988.

Watson, James, and John Tooze. *The DNA Story: A Documentary History of Gene Cloning.* San Francisco: W.H. Freeman, 1981.

Wilcox, Fred. *Waiting for an Army to Die: The Tragedy of Agent Orange.* New York: Random House, 1983.

Websites

Borlaug, Norman E. "The Green Revolution, Peace, and Humanity." Nobel e-Museum. Available online at http://www.nobel.se/peace/laureates/1970/borlaug-lecture.html; website home page: http://www.nobel.se (accessed July 21, 2003).

Institute for Creation Research. Available online at http://www.icr.org (accessed July 21, 2003).

"Lucy in the Earth." A Science Odyssey. Available online at http://www.pbs.org/wgbh/aso/tryit/evolution/lucy.html; website home page: http://www.pbs.org/wgbh/aso (accessed July 21, 2003).

Smith, Hamilton O. "Nucleotide Sequence Specificity of Restriction Endoculeases." Nobel e-Museum. Available online at http://www.nobel.se/medicine/laureates/1978/smith-lecture.html; website home page: http://www.nobel.se (accessed July 21, 2003).

"Sociobiology." Department of Psychology, Northwestern University. Available online at http://www.psych.nwu.edu/~sengupta/sociob.html; website home page: http://www.psych.nwu.edu (accessed July 21, 2003).

Solar Energy Industries Association (SEIA). Available online at http://www.seia.org (accessed July 21, 2003).

"Speciation by Punctuated Equilibrium." Department of Computer Science, University of Colorado at Boulder. Available online at http://www.cs.colorado.edu/~lindsay/creation/punk_eek.html; website home page: http://www.cs.colorado.edu (accessed July 21, 2003).

"Three Mile Island: The Judge's Ruling." Frontline. Available online at http://www.pbs.org/wgbh/pages/frontline/shows/reaction/readings/tmi.html; website home page: http://www.pbs.org/wgbh/pages/frontline (accessed July 21, 2003).

Sports

Aaron, Hank, and Lonnie Wheeler. *If I Had a Hammer: The Hank Aaron Story.* New York: HarperCollins, 1991.

Berger, Phil. *Forever Showtime: The Checkered Life of Pistol Pete Maravich.* Dallas: Taylor Press, 1999.

Blue, Vida, and Bill Libby. *Vida: His Own Story.* Englewood Cliffs, N.J.: Prentice-Hall, 1972.

Bouton, Jim, and Leonard Shecter. *Ball Four: My Life and Hard Times Throwing the Knuckleball in the Big Leagues.* New York: World Publishers, 1970.

Casper, Billy, and Al Barkow. *The Good Sense of Golf.* Englewood Cliffs, N.J.: Prentice-Hall, 1980.

Cohen, Joel. *Oscar Robertson.* New York: Rosen Central, 2002.

Corcoran, Mike. *Duel in the Sun: Tom Watson and Jack Nicklaus in the Battle of Turnberry.* New York: Simon & Schuster, 2002.

Evert, Chris, and Neil Amdur. *Chrissie: My Story.* New York: Simon & Schuster, 1982.

Feinstein, John. *The Punch: One Night Two Lives, and the Fight that Changed Basketball Forever.* Boston: Little, Brown, 2002.

Fitzpatrick, Frank. *And the Walls Came Tumbling Down: Kentucky, Western Texas, and the Game that Changed American Sports.* New York: Simon & Schuster, 1999.

Frankl, Ron. *Wilt Chamberlain.* New York: Chelsea House, 1995.

Frazier, Walt, and Neil Offen. *Walt Frazier and One Magic Season and a Basketball Life.* New York: Times Books, 1988.

Gibson, Bob, and Lonnie Wheeler. *Stranger to the Game.* New York: Viking, 1994.

Greise, Bob, and Brian Griese. *Undefeated: How Father and Son Triumphed Over Unbelievable Odds Both On and Off the Field.* Nashville,Tenn.: T. Nelson Publishers, 2000.

King, Billie Jean, and Kim Chapin. *Billie Jean.* New York: Harper & Row, 1974.

Klobucher, Jim, and Fran Tarkenton. *Tarkenton.* New York: Harper & Row, 1976.

Lipsyte, Robert. *Free to Be Muhammad Ali.* New York: Harper & Row, 1978.

MacSkimming, Roy. *Gordie: A Hockey Legend: An Unauthorized Biography of Gordie Howe.* Vancouver: Greystone, 1994.

McLain, Denny, and Mike Nahrstedt. *Strike Out: The Story of Denny McLain.* St. Louis, Mo.: Sporting News, 1988.

Nelson, George. *Elevating the Game: Black Men and Basketball.* New York: HarperCollings, 1992.

Nicklaus, Jack, and Ken Bowden. *Jack Nicklaus: My Story.* New York: Simon & Schuster, 1997.

Palmer, Arnold, and James Dodson. *A Golfer's Life.* New York: Ballantine, 1999.

Reeve, Simon. *One Day in September: The Full Story of the 1972 Munich Olympics Massacre and the Israeli Revenge Operation "Wrath of God."* New York: Arcade, 2000.

Ryan, Nolan, and Jerry B. Jenkins. *Miracle Man: Nolan Ryan, the Autobiography.* New York: World Publishing, 1992.

Thomas, Ron. *They Cleared the Lane: The NBA's Black Pioneers.* Lincoln: University of Nebraska Press, 2002.

Trevino, Lee, and Sam Blair. *They Call Me Super Mex.* New York: Random House, 1982.

Yastrzemski, Carl, and Gerald Eskenazi. *Yaz: Baseball, the Wall, and Me.* New York: Doubleday, 1990.

PRIMARY SOURCE TYPE INDEX

Primary source authors appear in parentheses. Page numbers in italics indicate images, and those followed by the letter t *indicate tables.*

Primary source authors appear in parentheses. Page numbers in italics indicate images, and those followed by the letter *t* indicate tables.

Primary source authors appear in parentheses. Page numbers in italics indicate images, and those followed by the letter *t* indicate tables.

Primary source authors appear in parentheses. Page numbers in italics indicate images, and those followed by the letter *t* indicate tables.

GENERAL INDEX

Page numbers in bold indicate primary sources; page numbers in italic indicate images; page numbers in bold italic indicate primary source images; page numbers followed by the letter t *indicate tables. Primary sources are indexed under the entry name with the author's name in parentheses. Primary sources are also indexed by title. All primary sources can be identified by bold page locators.*

A

AAAS (American Association for the Advancement of Science), 580

"AAAS Resolution: Creationism and California Public Schools," 580

Aaron, Henry, 646–651, *647*
  autobiography, **648–650**

Abortion, 340–344, 522–526, *523*

Acquired Immunodeficiency Syndrome (AIDS), 492, 495

Actors, 27–28, 34–37

Addiction (to drugs), 361–365

Adolescence, 38–41, 110–115, *113*, 362

Advertising, 180–182, 184–185, 202–203

Affirmative action programs, 321, 330, *330*

AFL-CIO, 73–76
  journal article, **74–76**

African Americans
  busing, 140–144, 288–292
  Catholic Church, 556–560
  colleges, 169–171
  dance, 51–54, *53*
  education, 171–173, 329–334
  history, 132–136
  language, 172
  literature, 9–12, 54–55
  medical experimentation, 465–470, *468*

school integration, 140–144, 288–292, *290*
  special education programs, 171–173
  television, 412, 434–438
  theatre, 51–54
  upward mobility, 412
  women and children, 9–12
  See also affirmative action programs

AFSCME (American Federation of State, County, and Municipal Employees), 80

AFT (American Federation of Teachers), 80, 83

Aggression, 581–583

Agnew, Spiro T., 219, 220–221

Agricultural engineering, 569–570

Agricultural technology, 568–571

Agronomy, 568–571

AIDS (Acquired Immunodeficiency Syndrome), 492, 495

Ailey, Alvin, 51–53, *52*

AIM (American Indian Movement), 372–378

Airlift to Wounded Knee (Zimmerman), **376–377**

Alcatraz Island, 372

Alda, Alan, 489–491, *490*
  speech, **490–491**

Ali, Muhammad, 632–636, *634*

All in the Family (television program), 412–415

All the President's Men, 416–421
  nonfiction work (Woodward, Bernstein), **417–420**

All the President's Men (movie), 246

Allah, 505, 507, 508

Allen, Woody, 199
  movie still, *200*

Altair (computer), 592

Altman, Robert, 43–48, *45*
  interview, **44–48**

"The Alvin Ailey American Dance Theater: Twenty Years Later," 51–54
  magazine article (Philp), **52–54**

AMA (American Medical Association), 454

AMC (American Motor Corporation), 182–183, *183*

American Association for the Advancement of Science (AAAS), 580

The American Catholic: A Social Portrait, 539–542
  nonfiction work (Greeley), **540–542**

American dance, 51–54

An American Family (television program), 386–389, *387*

American Federation of State, County, and Municipal Employees (AFCSME), 80

American Federation of Teachers (AFT), 80, 83

Page numbers in bold indicate primary sources; page numbers in italic indicate images; page numbers in bold italic indicate primary source images; page numbers followed by the letter *t* indicate tables.

Page numbers in bold indicate primary sources; page numbers in italic indicate images; page numbers in bold italic indicate primary source images; page numbers followed by the letter *t* indicate tables.

Page numbers in bold indicate primary sources; page numbers in italic indicate images; page numbers in bold italic indicate primary source images; page numbers followed by the letter *t* indicate tables.

Page numbers in bold indicate primary sources; page numbers in italic indicate images;
page numbers in bold italic indicate primary source images; page numbers followed by the letter *t* indicate tables.

Page numbers in bold indicate primary sources; page numbers in italic indicate images;
page numbers in bold italic indicate primary source images; page numbers followed by the letter *t* indicate tables.

Page numbers in bold indicate primary sources; page numbers in italic indicate images; page numbers in bold italic indicate primary source images; page numbers followed by the letter *t* indicate tables.

Page numbers in bold indicate primary sources; page numbers in italic indicate images;
page numbers in bold italic indicate primary source images; page numbers followed by the letter *t* indicate tables.

Page numbers in bold indicate primary sources; page numbers in italic indicate images;
page numbers in bold italic indicate primary source images; page numbers followed by the letter *t* indicate tables.

Page numbers in bold indicate primary sources; page numbers in italic indicate images;
page numbers in bold italic indicate primary source images; page numbers followed by the letter *t* indicate tables.

Page numbers in bold indicate primary sources; page numbers in italic indicate images; page numbers in bold italic indicate primary source images; page numbers followed by the letter *t* indicate tables.

Page numbers in bold indicate primary sources; page numbers in italic indicate images;
page numbers in bold italic indicate primary source images; page numbers followed by the letter *t* indicate tables.

Page numbers in bold indicate primary sources; page numbers in italic indicate images;
page numbers in bold italic indicate primary source images; page numbers followed by the letter *t* indicate tables.

Page numbers in bold indicate primary sources; page numbers in italic indicate images; page numbers in bold italic indicate primary source images; page numbers followed by the letter *t* indicate tables.

Page numbers in bold indicate primary sources; page numbers in italic indicate images; page numbers in bold italic indicate primary source images; page numbers followed by the letter *t* indicate tables.